THE AMERICAN JOURNEY

A History of the United States

VOLUME II

Second Edition

DAVID GOLDFIELD

CARL ABBOTT

VIRGINIA DEJOHN ANDERSON

JO ANN E. ARGERSINGER

PETER H. ARGERSINGER

WILLIAM L. BARNEY

ROBERT M. WEIR

Prentice Hall

Upper Saddle River, New Jersey 07458

Library of Congress Cataloging-in-Publication Data

The American journey : a history of the United States / David
  Goldfield . . . [et al.]. — 2nd ed.
     p. cm
  "Combined volume."
  Includes bibliographical references and index.
  ISBN 0-13-088243-7
  1. United States—History.   I. Goldfield, David R.,
E178.1.A4925 2001
973—dc21   00-025810

Use the Internet and eliminate mail time and postage costs
http://cip.loc. gov/cip

FOR OUR STUDENTS, WHO HELPED US WRITE THIS BOOK.

Editorial director: Charlyce Jones Owen
Senior acquisitions editor: Charles Cavaliere
Editor-in-chief, development: Susanna Lesan
Development editor: David Chodoff
AVP, director of production and manufacturing:
  Barbara Kittle
Project manager: Harriet Tellem
Prepress and manufacturing manager: Nick Sklitsis
Prepress and manufacturing buyer: Lynn Pearlman
Creative design director: Leslie Osher
Asst. creative design director: Carole Anson
Art director, interior, and cover designer: Kenny Beck

Cover art: Nicola Victor Ziroli (1908–70), "Bridges in
  Winter," 1934 (Chicago). National Museum of
  American Art, Smithsonian Institution, Washington
  DC, U.S.A./Art Resource, NY.
Photo research: Francelle Carapetyan
Manager of production services: Guy Ruggiero
Cartographers: Carto-Graphics with shaded relief
  from Mountain High Maps®, Digital Wisdom, Inc.
Map and art coordinator: Mirella Signoretto
Copy editor: Margaret Pinette
Interior image specialist: Beth Boyd
Mgr., rights & permissions: Kay Dellosa
Image permission coordinator: Michelina Viscusi

This book was set in 10/12 New Baskerville Roman by
TSI Graphics and was printed and bound by Von Hoffman Press, Inc.
The cover was printed by Phoenix Color Corp.

© 2001, 1998 by Prentice-Hall
A Division of Pearson Education
Upper Saddle River, New Jersey 07458

Printed in the United States of America
10 9 8 7 6 5 4 3 2

ISBN 0-13-088245-3

PEARSON EDUCATION (UK) LIMITED, *London*
PRENTICE-HALL OF AUSTRALIA PTY. LIMITED, *Sydney*
PRENTICE-HALL CANADA INC., *Toronto*
PRENTICE-HALL HISPANOAMERICANA, S.A., *Mexico*
PRENTICE-HALL OF INDIA PRIVATE LIMITED, *New Delhi*
PRENTICE-HALL OF JAPAN, INC., *Tokyo*
PEARSON EDUCATION PTE. LTD., *Singapore*
EDITORA PRENTICE-HALL DO BRASIL, LTDA., *Rio de Janeiro*

BRIEF CONTENTS

CONTENTS

18

19

20

INDUSTRY, IMMIGRANTS, AND CITIES, 1870–1900   577

21

TRANSFORMING THE WEST, 1865–1890   613

22

POLITICS AND GOVERNMENT, 1877–1900 641

23

THE PROGRESSIVE ERA, 1900–1917   669

24
CREATING AN EMPIRE, 1865–1917   703

25
AMERICA AND THE GREAT WAR, 1914–1920   731

26

Toward a Modern America: The 1920s   759

27

The Great Depression and the New Deal, 1929–1939   789

28

29

30

THE CONFIDENT YEARS, 1953–1964   881

31

SHAKEN TO THE ROOTS, 1965–1980   913

32

SHAPING A NEW AMERICA, SINCE 1965   943

33

SEARCHING FOR STABILITY IN A CHANGING WORLD, SINCE 1980   975

American Views

AMERICA'S JOURNEY
FROM THEN TO NOW

MAPS

FIGURES AND TABLES

OVERVIEW TABLES

PREFACE

The journey that led us to *The American Journey* began in the classroom with our students. We wrote this book for them and we kept their needs foremost as we set about preparing this second edition.

Over the years we have subjected our students to many American history books—including the first edition of this one—and they have let us know what they liked and disliked, what they found difficult and what they grasped easily, what they skipped and what they devoured. Most important, they have told us what connects history to their own experience and brings it alive.

Our goal is to make American history accessible to students. The key to that goal—the core of the book—is a strong clear narrative. American history is a compelling story and we seek to tell it in an engaging, forthright way. But we also provide students with an abundance of tools—including outlines, key topics lists, chronologies, overview tables, highlighted key terms, review questions, and hundreds of maps, graphs, and illustrations—to help them absorb that story and put it in context. We introduce them to the concerns of the participants in history with primary source documents. And, in a new feature called "America's Journey: From Then to Now," we connect events and issues from the past to the concerns of the present.

But if we wrote this book to appeal to our students, we also wrote it to engage their minds. We wanted to avoid academic trendiness, particularly the restricting categories that have divided the discipline of history over the last twenty years or so. We believe that the distinctions involved in the debates about multiculturalism and identity, between social and political history, between the history of the common people and the history of the elite, are unnecessarily confusing.

What we seek is integration—to combine political and social history, to fit the experience of particular groups into the broader perspective of the American past, to give voice to minor and major players alike because of their role in the story we have to tell.

Approach

In telling our story, we had some definite ideas about what we might include and emphasize that other texts do not—information we felt that the current and next generations of students will need to know about our past to function best in a new society.

CHRONOLOGICAL ORGANIZATION A strong chronological backbone supports the book. We have found that the jumping back and forth in time characteristic of some American history textbooks confuses students. They abhor dates but need to know the sequence of events in history. A chronological presentation is the best way to be sure they do.

GEOGRAPHICAL LITERACY We also want students to be geographically literate. We expect them not only to know what happened in American history, but where it happened as well. Physical locations and spatial relationships were often important in shaping historical events. The abundant maps in *The American Journey*—all numbered and called out in the text—are an integral part of our story.

COVERAGE OF THE SOUTH AND WEST The South and the West play significant roles in this text. American history is too often written from a Northeastern perspective, at least when it comes to discussing cities, economic development, and reform. But not only were the South and West developing in their own ways throughout American history, they were and remain important keys to the emerging character of the nation as a whole.

POINT OF VIEW *The American Journey* presents a balanced overview of the American past. But "balanced" does not mean bland. We do not shy away from definite positions on controversial issues, such as the nature of early contacts between Native Americans and Europeans, why the politidcal crisis of the 1850s ended in a bloody Civil War, and how Populism and its followers fit into the American political spectrum. If students and instructors disagree, that's great; discussion and dissent are important catalysts for understanding and learning.

RELIGION Nor do we shy away from some topics that play relatively minor roles in other texts, like religion. Historians are often uncomfortable writing about religion and tend to slight its influence. This text stresses the importance of religion in American society both as a source of strength and a reflection of some its more troubling aspects.

Historians mostly write for each other. That's too bad. We need to reach out and expand our audience. An American history text is a good place to start. Our students are not only our future historians, but more important, our future. Let their American journey begin.

Features of the Text

The American Journey includes an array of features and pedagogical tools designed to make American history accessible to students.

❖ The **Student Tool Kit** that follows this preface helps students get the most out of the text and its features. It introduces students to key conventions of historical writing and it explains how to read maps, graphs, and tables.

❖ A new feature, **America's Journey: From Then to Now**, relates important issues and events in each chapter to the issues and events of today, letting students see the relevance of history to their lives. Examples include "The American Revolution and the Teaching of American History" (Chapter 6), "From the Eaton Affair to Monicagate" (Chapter 10), "The Confederate Battle Flag" (Chapter 19), and "The Culture Wars" (Chapter 26).

❖ An **Outline** and **Key Topics** list give students a succinct overview of each chapter.

❖ Each chapter begins with an engaging **opening story** that highlights important themes.

❖ The **American Views** box in each chapter contains a relevant primary source document. Taken from letters, diaries, newspapers, government papers, and other sources, these bring the people of the past and their concerns vividly alive. An *introduction* and *prereading questions* relate the documents to the text and direct students' attention to important issues.

❖ **Overview Tables** in each chapter summarize complex issues.

❖ Chapter **chronologies** help students build a framework of key events.

❖ **Key Terms** are highlighted within each chapter and defined in an end-of-book **Glossary**.

❖ Chapter **Review Questions** help students review the material in a chapter and relate it to broader themes.

❖ A list of **Key Readings** and **Additional Sources** at the end of each chapter directs interested students to further information about the subject of the chapter.

❖ **Where To Learn More** sections describe important historical sites students can visit to gain a deeper understanding of the events discussed in the chapter.

❖ Abundant maps, charts, and graphs help students understand important events and trends. The *topographical detail* in many of the maps helps students understand the influence of geography on history.

❖ Illustrations and photographs—tied to the text with detailed captions—provide a visual dimension to history.

Supplementary Instructional Materials

The American Journey comes with an extensive package of supplementary print and multimedia materials for both instructors and students.

Print Supplements

Instructor's Resource Manual
The *Instructor's Resource Manual* contains chapter outlines, detailed chapter overviews, activities, discussion questions, readings, and information on audiovisual resources that are useful for preparing lectures and assignments.

Test Item File
The *Test Item File* includes over 1000 multiple-choice, true-false, essay, and map questions organized by chapter. A collection of blank maps can be photocopied and used for map testing or other class exercises.

Prentice Hall Custom Test
This commercial-quality computerized test management program, available for Windows and Macintosh environments, allows instructors to select items from the Test Item File and design their own exams.

Transparency Pack
This set of transparencies provides instructors with full-color acetates of all the maps, charts, and graphs in the text for use in the classroom.

Study Guide (Volumes I and II)
The *Study Guide* provides students with a brief overview of each chapter, a list of chapter objectives, study exercises, multiple-choice, short answer, and essay questions. In addition, each chapter includes two to three pages of specific map questions and exercises.

Documents in U.S. History (Volumes I and II)
This set of documents, taken from the *Retrieving the American Past* customized reader, provides five additional primary and secondary source documents—

with prereading and postreading questions—for each chapter of the textbook.

Retrieving the American Past: A Customized U.S. History Reader

This collection of documents is an on-demand history database written and developed by leading historians and educators. It offers eighty compelling modules on topics in American history, such as "Women on the Frontier," "The Salem Witchcraft Scare," "The Age of Industrial Violence," and "Native American Societies, 1870–1995." Approximately thirty-five pages in length, each module includes an introduction, several primary documents and secondary sources, follow-up questions, and recommendations for further reading. By deciding which modules to include and the order in which they will appear, instructors can compile the reader they want to use. Instructor-originated material, including other readings and exercises, can be incorporated. Contact your local Prentice Hall representative for more information about this exciting custom publishing option.

Reading Critically about History

Prepared by Rose Wassman and Lee Rinsky, DeAnza College, this brief guide provides students with helpful strategies for reading a history textbook. It is available free to students when packaged with *The American Journey.*

Understanding and Answering Essay Questions

Prepared by Mary L. Kelley, San Antonio College, this helpful guide provides analytical tools for understanding different types of essay questions and for preparing well-crafted essay answers. It is available free to students when packaged with *The American Journey.*

Themes of the Times

This special newspaper supplement is prepared jointly for students by Prentice Hall and the premier news publication, *The New York Times.* Issued twice a year, it contains recent articles pertinent to American history. These articles connect the classroom to the world. For information about a reduced-rate subscription to *The New York Times,* call toll-free: (800) 631-1222.

Multimedia Supplements

History on the Internet: A Critical Thinking Guide

This guide focuses on developing the critical thinking skills necessary to evaluate and use online sources. It provides a brief introduction to navigating the Internet with comprehensive references to History web sites. It also provides instruction on using the *Companion Website*™ available for *The American Journey.* This 96-page supplementary book is free to students with the purchase of the textbook.

Powerpoint Images CD ROM

Available in Windows and Mac formats for use with Microsoft Powerpoint™, this CD ROM provides maps, charts and graphs, summary tables, and other useful material from *The American Journey.* These resources can be used in lectures, for slide shows, printed as transparencies, or customized according to the instructor's lecture needs.

Companion Website™ and USHistory Place

Prentice Hall and Peregrine Publishers are proud to present a melding of two acclaimed interactive learning resources: Prentice Hall's **Companion Website**™ and Peregrine's **USHistory Place.**

Available at http://www.prenhall.com/goldfield, this new interactive history center provides materials to help students review chapter content and then test their knowledge of what they've read. *The American Journey Companion Website*™ offers students multiple choice, true-false, essay, identification, map labeling, and document questions based on material from the text. It also provides links to exciting World Wide Web destinations that expand on material in the text. Chat rooms and message boards allow students to share their ideas about American history with students from their own class or from colleges across the country. Additionally, students have access to numerous interactive maps and timelines, source documents, interactive exercises, and a comprehensive glossary from *USHistory Place* that have been keyed to the chapters in *The American Journey.* Entry to these resources is available through access codes that are provided free to students with the purchase of the text.

The *Faculty Module* contains materials for instructors, including a downloadable Microsoft Powerpoint™ presentation with maps, charts and graphs, summary tables, and other lecture material that can be presented as is or customized according to an instructor's specific lecture needs.

Instructor's Guide to USHistory Place

This guide provides helpful information for instructors on how to get the most out of *USHistory Place.* It includes a unique instructor's access code that provides entry to *USHistory Place* from *The American Journey Companion Website*™. For more information about these resources, contact your local Prentice Hall representative.

Course Management Systems

For instructors interested in distance learning, Prentice Hall offers fully customizable, online courses with enhanced content, web links, online testing, and many other course management features using the best available course management systems available, including *WebCT*, *Blackboard*, and *ecollege* online course architecture. Contact your local Prentice Hall representative or visit our special Demonstration Central Website at http://www.prenhall.com/demo for more information.

Acknowledgments

We would like to thank the reviewers whose thoughtful and often detailed comments helped shape this and the previous edition of *The American Journey:*

Joseph Adams, Saint Louis Community College
David Aldstadt, Houston Community College
Janet Allured, McNeese State University
Tyler Anbinder, George Washington University
Michael Batinski, Southern Illinois University
Michael Bellesiles, Emory University
Eugene Berwanger, Colorado State University
Terry Bilhartz, Sam Houston State University
Fred Blue, Youngstown State University
Eric J. Bolsteri, University of Texas at Arlington
Charles Bolton, University of Arkansas at Little Rock
James Bradford, Texas A & M University
Michael Bradley, Motlow State Community College
Henry William Brands, Texas A & M University
Neal Brooks, Essex Community College
Richard Brown, University of Connecticut
Tom Bryan, Alvin Community College
Randolph Campbell, University of North Texas
Dale Carnagey, Blinn College
E. Wayne Carp, Pacific Lutheran University
David Castle, Ohio University, Eastern Campus
Andrew Cayton, Miami University
Bill Cecil-Fronsman, Washburn University
John Chalberg, Normandale Community College
Myles Clowers, San Diego City College
David Conrad, Southern Illinois University
William Corbett, Northeastern State University
Robert Cray, Montclair State College
Richard Crepeau, University of Central Florida
Samuel Crompton, Holyoke Community College
Gilbert Cruz, Glendale Community College
Light T. Cummins, Austin College
Paul K Davis, University of Texas at San Antonio
Eugene Demody, Cerritos College
Joseph Devine, Stephen F. Austin State University
Donald Dewey, California State University
Leonard Dinnerstein, University of Arizona
Marvin Dulaney, University of Texas at Arlington

Leflett Easley, Campbell University
Iris Engstrand, University of San Diego
Robin Fabel, Auburn University
Jay Fell, University of Colorado
Nancy Gabin, Purdue University
Scott Garrett, Paducah Community College
Marilyn Geiger, Washburn University
George Gerdow, Northeastern Illinois University
Gerald Ghelfi, Rancho Santiago College
Louis Gimelli, Eastern Michigan University
James Goode, Grand Valley State University
Gregory Goodwin, Bakersfield College
Ralph Goodwin, East Texas State University
Robert Greene, Morgan State University
Mark Grimsley, Ohio State University
Ira Gruber, U.S. Military Academy
Harland Hagler, University of North Texas
Steve Haley, Shelby State Community College
Gwendolyn Hall, Rutgers University
Timothy D. Hall, Central Michigan University
David Hamilton, University of Kentucky
Joe Hapak, Moraine Valley Community College
Ronald Hatzenbuchler, Idaho State University
David G. Hogan, Heidelberg College
Alfred Hunt, SUNY Purchase
John Ingham, University of Toronto
Priscilla Jackson-Evans, Longview Community College
Donald Jacobs, Northeastern University
Frederick Jaher, University of Illinois
John Johnson, University of Northern Iowa
Wilbur Johnson, Rock Valley College
Yvonne Johnson, Central Missouri State University
Yasuhide Kawashima, University of Texas at El Paso
Joseph E. King, Texas Tech University
Gene Kirkpatrick, Tyler Junior College
Lawrence Kohl, University of Alabama at Tuscaloosa
Michael Krenn, University of Miami
Michael Krutz, Southeastern Louisiana University
Robert LaPorte, North Texas University
Armand LaPotin, SUNY Oneonta
John LaSaine, University of Georgia
Bryan LeBeau, Creighton University
Mark Leff, University of Illinois, Urbana-Champaign
Ed Lukes, Hillsborough Community College
Leo Lyman, Victor, Valley College
Ronald McArthur, Atlantic Community College
Donald McCoy, University of Kansas
David McFadden, Fairfield University
Gerald MacFarland, University of Massachusetts
Thomas McLuen, Spokane Falls Community College
Peter C. Mancell, University of Kansas
Norman Markowitz, Rutgers University
Frank Marmolejo, Irvine Valley College
James Matray, New Mexico State University
Karen Miller, Oakland University
Otis Miller, Belleville Area College
Nancy Smith Midgette, Elon College
Worth Robert Miller, Southwest Missouri State University

Timothy Morgan, Christopher Newport University
Christopher Moss, University of Texas at Arlington
Harmon Mothershead, Northwest Missouri State University
Benjamin Newcomb, Texas Technological University
Elizabeth Nybakken, Mississippi State University
Colleen O'Connor, San Diego Mesa College
Chris Padgett, Weber State University
David Parker, Kennesaw State College
Peggy Pascoe, University of Utah
Christopher Phillips, Emporia State University
Thomas L. Powers, University of South Carolina, Sumter
Kay Pulley, Trinity Valley Community College
Norman Raiford, Greenville Technical College
John Rector, Western Oregon State University
Thomas C. Reeves, University of Wisconsin, Parkside
Gary Reichard, Florida Atlantic University
Joseph Reidy, Howard University
Ronald Reitvald, California State University, Fullerton
Howard Rock, Florida International University
Hal Rothman, University of Nevada, Las Vegas
Richard Sadler, Weber State University
Henry Sage, Northern Virginia Community College, Alexandria
Bufford Satcher, University of Arkansas at Pine Bluff
Sandra Schackel, Boise State University
Michael Schaller, University of Arizona
Dale Schmitt, East Tennessee State University
Ronald Schultz, University of Wyoming
Rebecca Shoemaker, Indiana State University
Frank Siltman, U.S. Military Academy
David Sloan, University of Arkansas
J.B. Smallwood, University of North Texas
Sherry Smith, University of Texas at El Paso
Kenneth Stevens, Texas Christian University
William Stockton, Johnson County Community College
Mark Summers, University of Kentucky
William Tanner, Humbolt State University
Quintard Taylor, University of Oregon
Emily Teipe, Fullerton College
Frank Towers, Clarion University
Paula Trekel, Allegheny College
Stanley Underal, San Jose University
Andrew Wallace, Northern Arizona University
Harry Ward, University of Richmond
Ken Weatherbie, Del Mar College
Stephen Webre, Louisiana Tech University
Edward Weller, San Jacinto College, South
Michael Welsh, University of Northern Colorado
James Whittenberg, College of William and Mary
Brian Wills, Clinch Valley Community College
J. Edward Lee, Winthrop University
John Wiseman, Frostburg State University
James Woods, Georgia Southern University
Mark Wyman, Illinois State University
Neil York, Brigham Young University
William Young, Johnson County Community College
Nancy Zen, Central Oregon Community College

All of us are grateful to our families, friends, and colleagues for their support and encouragement. Jo Ann and Peter Argersinger would like in particular to thank Anna Champe, Linda Hatmaker, and John Willits; William Barney thanks Pamela Fesmire and Rosalie Radcliffe; Virginia Anderson thanks Fred Anderson, Kim Gruenwald, Ruth Helm, Eric Hinderaker, and Chidiebere Nwaubani; and David Goldfield thanks Frances Glenn and Jason Moscato. Jim Miller, Sylvia Mallory, and Sally Constable played key roles in the book's inception and initial development.

Finally, we would like to acknowledge the members of our Prentice Hall family. They are not only highly competent professionals but also pleasant people. We regard them with affection and appreciation. None of us would hesitate to work with this fine group again. We would especially like to thank David Chodoff, senior development editor, for his careful attention to detail and his insistence on clear writing; Charlyce Jones Owen, vice president and editorial director for the Humanities, who organized her team and our social functions flawlessly; Sheryl Adams, senior marketing manager, whose creative and informed marketing strategies demonstrated an appreciation for historical scholarship as well as the history textbook market; Kenny Beck and Carole Anson, art directors, and Leslie Osher, creative design director, whose creativity is evident in this book's design and layout; Harriet Tellem, senior production editor, for her efficient handling of the production process; Mirella Signoretto, line art formatter; Margaret Pinette, copy editor; Francelle Carapetyan for her photo research; Susanna Lesan, editor in chief for development, for ensuring that the book had the developmental resources it needed; Nick Sklitsis, manufacturing manager, Lynn Pearlman, manufacturing buyer, and Jan Stephan, managing editor, who kept the whole team on schedule; and Phil Miller, president of Prentice Hall's Humanities and Social Sciences division, who had the good sense to let his staff run with this book.

DG
CA
VDJA
JEA
PHA
WLB
RMW

ABOUT THE AUTHORS

David Goldfield received his Ph.D. in history from the University of Maryland. Since 1982, he has been Robert Lee Baily Professor of History at the University of North Carolina in Charlotte. He is the author or editor of twelve books on various aspects of southern and urban history. Two of his works—*Cotton Fields and Skyscrapers: Southern City and Region 1607 to 1980* (1982) and *Black, White, and Southern: Race Relations and Southern Culture, 1940 to the present* (1990)—received the Mayflower award for Nonfiction. Both books were also nominated for the Pulitzer Prize in history. When he is not writing or teaching, Goldfield applies the historical craft to history museum exhibits, federal voting rights cases, and local planning and policy issues. He is currently working on a book that asks the question: Why is the South different?

Carl Abbott is a professor of Urban Studies and planning at Portland State University. He taught previously in the history departments at the University of Denver and Old Dominion University and held visiting appointments at Mesa College in Colorado and George Washington University. He holds degrees in history from Swarthmore College and the University of Chicago. He specializes in the history of cities and the American West and serves as co-editor of the *Pacific Historical Review*. His books include *The New Urban America: Growth and Politics in Sunbelt cities* (1981, 1987), *The Metropolitan Frontier: Cities in the Modern American West* (1993), *Planning a New West: The Columbia River Gorge National Scenic Area* (1997), and *Political Terrain: Washington, D.C. from Tidewater Town to Global Metropolis* (1999).

Virginia DeJohn Anderson is Associate Professor of History at the University of Colorado at Boulder. She received her B.A. from the University of Connecticut. As the recipient of a Marshall Scholarship, she earned an M.A. degree at the University of East Anglia in Norwich, England. Returning to the United States, she received her A.M. and Ph.D. degrees from Harvard University. She is the author of *New England's Generation: The Great Migration and the Formation of Society and Culture in the Seventeenth Century* (1991) and several articles on colonial history, which have appeared in such journals as the *William and Mary Quarterly* and the *New England Quarterly*.

Jo Ann E. Argersinger received her Ph.D. from George Washington University and is Professor of History at Southern Illinois University. A recipient of fellowships from the Rockefeller Foundation and the National Endowment for the Humanities, she is a historian of social, labor, and business policy. Her publications include *Toward a New Deal in Baltimore: People and Government in the Great Depression* (1988) and *Making the Amalgamated: Gender, Ethnicity, and Class in the Baltimore Clothing Industry* (1999).

Peter H. Argersinger received his Ph.D. from the University of Wisconsin and is Professor of History at Southern Illinois University. He has won several fellowships and the Binkley-Stephenson Award from the Organization of American Historians. Among his books on American political and rural history are *Populism and Politics* (1974), *Structure, Process, and Party* (1992), and *The Limits of Agrarian Radicalism* (1995). His current research focuses on the political crisis of the 1890s.

William L. Barney is Professor of History at the University of North Carolina at Chapel Hill. A native of Pennsylvania, he received his B.A. from Cornell University and his M.A. and Ph.D. from Columbia University. He has published extensively on 19th century U.S. history and has a particular interest in the Old South and the coming of the Civil War. Among his publications are *The Road to Secession* (1972), *The Secessionist Impulse* (1974), *Flawed Victory* (1975), *The Passage of the Republic* (1987), and *Battleground for the Union* (1989). He is currently finishing an edited collection of essays on nineteenth-century America and a book on the Civil War.

Robert M. Weir is Distinguished Professor of History Emeritus at the University of South Carolina. He received his B.A. from Pennsylvania State University and his Ph.D. from Case Western Reserve University. He has taught at the University of Houston and, as a visiting professor, at the University of Southampton in the United Kingdom. His articles have won prizes from the Southeastern Society for the study of the Eighteenth Century and the *William and Mary Quarterly*. Among his publications are *Colonial South Carolina: A History, "The Last of American Freemen": Studies in the Political Culture of the Colonial and Revolutionary South,* and, most recently, a chapter on the Carolinas in the new *Oxford History of the British Empire* (1998).

STUDENT TOOL KIT

When writing history, historians use maps, tables, and graphs to help their readers understand the past. What follows is an explanation of how to use the historian's tools that are contained in this book.

Text

Whether it is a biography of George Washington, an article on the Civil War, or a survey of American history such as this one, the text is the historian's basic tool for discussing the past. Historians write about the past using narration and analysis. *Narration* is the story line of history. It describes what happened in the past, who did it, and where and when it occurred. Narration is also used to describe how people in the past lived, how they passed their daily lives and even, when the historical evidence makes it possible for us to know, what they thought, felt, feared, or desired. Using *analysis*, historians explain why they think events in the past happened the way they did and offer an explanation for the story of history. In this book, narration and analysis are interwoven in each chapter.

Study Aids

A number of features in this book are designed to aid in the study of history. Each chapter begins with *Key Topics,* a short list of the most important issues that will be covered in the chapter. A *Conclusion* at the end of each chapter puts the subject of the chapter in the broader perspective of U.S. history. Both these study aids can be used to review important concepts.

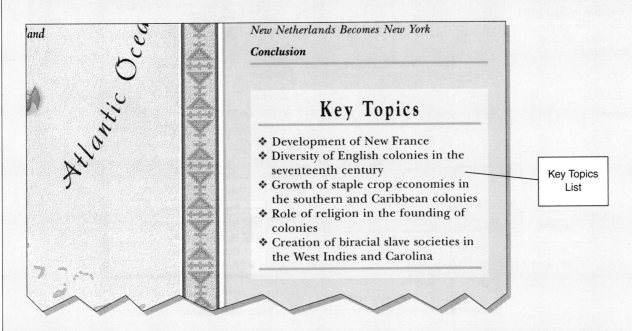

New Netherlands Becomes New York

Conclusion

Key Topics

❖ Development of New France
❖ Diversity of English colonies in the seventeenth century
❖ Growth of staple crop economies in the southern and Caribbean colonies
❖ Role of religion in the founding of colonies
❖ Creation of biracial slave societies in the West Indies and Carolina

Key Topics List

immigration to the United States from eastern and southern Europe in the late nineteenth and early twentieth centuries. Figure 3-4, for example, is a pie chart—so called because it looks like a pie cut into slices. It shows the ethnic origins of the non-Indian population of the thirteen colonies at the start of the American Revolution. Figure 4-2 is a bar graph that compares the growth in population of the four major colonial regions.

Figure 3-4   *Ethnic Distribution of Non-Indian Inhabitants of British Mainland Colonies, c. 1770*

By the third quarter of the eighteenth century, the colonial population was astonishingly diverse. Only two out of three settlers claimed British ancestry (from England, Wales, Scotland, or northern Ireland), while one out of five was African in origin.

Data Source: *Adapted from Thomas L. Purvis, "The European Ancestry of the United States Population, 1790," William and Mary Quarterly, 3d series, 41 (1984), p. 98.*

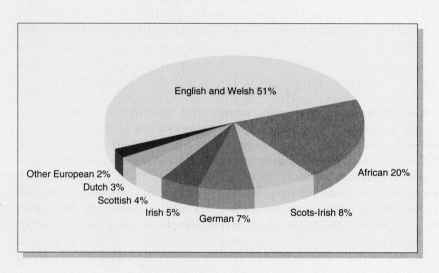

Figure 4-2   *Population Growth in British Mainland Colonies, 1700–1760*

Both natural increase and immigration contributed to a staggering rate of population growth in British North America. Some colonists predicted that Americans would soon outnumber Britain's inhabitants—a possibility that greatly concerned British officials.

Data Source: *John J. McCusker and Russell R. Menard, The Economy of British America, 1607–1789, rev. ed. (1991).*

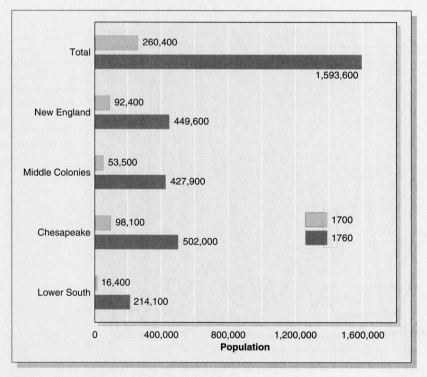

Overview Tables

The *Overview* tables in this text are a special feature designed to highlight and summarize important topics within a chapter. The Overview table shown here, for example, summarizes the purpose and significance of the major laws and constitutional amendments passed during the Reconstruction era following the Civil War.

OVERVIEW

CONSTITUTIONAL AMENDMENTS AND FEDERAL LEGISLATION OF THE RECONSTRUCTION ERA

Amendment or Legislation	Purpose	Significance
Thirteenth Amendment (passed and ratified in 1865)	Prevented southern states from reestablishing slavery after the war	Final step toward full emancipation of slaves
Freedmen's Bureau Act (1865)	Oversight of resettlement, reflief, education, and labor for former slaves	Involved the federal government directly in assisting the transition from slavery to freedom; worked fitfully to achieve this objective during its seven-year career
Southern Homestead Act (1866)	Provided blacks preferential access to public lands in five southern states	Lack of capital and poor quality of federal land thwarted the purpose of the act

Chronologies

Each chapter includes a *Chronology,* a list of the key events discussed in the chapter arranged in chronological order. The chronology for Chapter 18 lists the dates of key events during the Reconstruction era from 1865 to 1877. Chronologies provide a review of important events and their relationship to one another.

CHRONOLOGY

1863 Lincoln proposes his Ten Percent Plan.

1864 Congress proposes the Wade-Davis Bill.

1865 Sherman issues Field Order No. 15.

Freedmen's Bureau is established.

Andrew Johnson succeeds to the presidency, unveils his Reconstruction plan.

Massachusetts desegregates all public facilities.

Blacks in several southern cities organize Union Leagues.

Former Confederate states begin to pass black codes.

1866 Congress passes Southern Homestead Act, Civil Rights Act of 1866.

Ku Klux Klan is founded.

Fourteenth Amendment to the Constitution is passed (ratified in 1868).

President Johnson goes on a speaking tour.

1867 Congress passes Military Reconstruction Acts, ure of e Act.

Republican regimes topple in North Carolina and Georgia.

1871 Congress passes Ku Klux Klan Act.

1872 Freedmen's Bureau closes down.

Liberal Republicans emerge as a separate party.

Ulysses S. Grant is reelected.

1873 Severe depression begins.

Colfax Massacre occurs.

U.S. Supreme Court's decision in the *Slaughterhouse* cases weakens the intent of the Fourteenth Amendment.

Texas falls to the Democrats in the fall elections.

1874 White Leaguers attempt a coup against the Republican government of New Orleans.

Democrats win off-year elections across the South amid widespread fraud and violence.

1875 Congress passes Civil Rights Act of 1875.

1876 Supre urt's decisi *United S* v.

Primary Source Documents

Historians find most of their information in written records, original documents that have survived from the past. These include government publications, letters, diaries, newspapers—whatever people wrote or printed, including many private documents never intended for publication. Each chapter in the book contains a feature called *American Views*—a selection from a primary source document. The example shown here compares two letters by Abraham Lincoln explaining his position on slavery. Each *American Views* feature begins with a brief introduction followed by several questions—for discussion or written response—on what the document reveals about key issues and events.

Introduction

Questions

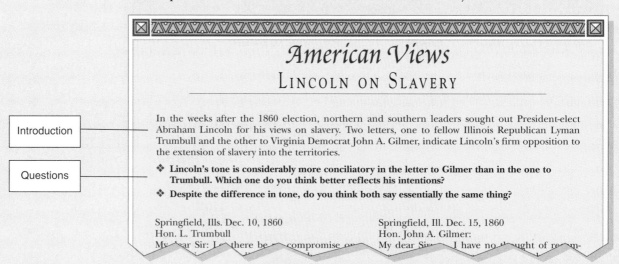

American Views
LINCOLN ON SLAVERY

In the weeks after the 1860 election, northern and southern leaders sought out President-elect Abraham Lincoln for his views on slavery. Two letters, one to fellow Illinois Republican Lyman Trumbull and the other to Virginia Democrat John A. Gilmer, indicate Lincoln's firm opposition to the extension of slavery into the territories.

❖ Lincoln's tone is considerably more conciliatory in the letter to Gilmer than in the one to Trumbull. Which one do you think better reflects his intentions?

❖ Despite the difference in tone, do you think both say essentially the same thing?

Springfield, Ills. Dec. 10, 1860
Hon. L. Trumbull
My dear Sir: Let there be no compromise on

Springfield, Ill. Dec. 15, 1860
Hon. John A. Gilmer:
My dear Sir: I have no thought of recom-

America's Journey:
From Then to Now

The feature called *America's Journey: From Then to Now* connects events and trends in the past to issues that confront Americans today, illustrating the value a historical perspective can contribute to our understanding of the world we live in. The example here, from Chapter 4, traces the vitality and diversity of religion in America today to the religious diversity of the earliest colonists.

AMERICA'S JOURNEY

FROM THEN TO NOW

The Enduring Vitality and Diversity of American Religion

In a front-page story in April 1991, *The New York Times* reported on "dozens of surprises" contained in an opinion poll on religious identification in America. The poll revealed two main features of American religious life. First, organized religion was thriving. Nine out of ten people polled identified themselves with a religious denomination. Second, the American religious scene was highly di-

had become so firmly embedded in American life that people feared the establishment of a single state church far more than the consequences of having a multiplicity of faiths within a single nation. It was this fear that inspired the First Amendment to the Constitution, with its guarantee of the "free exercise" of religion, of whatever kind, and its prohibition of any religious establish-

Recommended Readings, Additional Sources, and Where to Learn More

At the end of each chapter are two lists of books—*Recommended Readings* and *Additional Sources*—that provide greater information about the topics discussed in the chapter. The section called *Where to Learn More* lists important historical sites and museums that provide first-hand exposure to historical artifacts and settings.

Where to Learn More

❖ **Henry Ford Museum and Greenfield Village,** Dearborn, Michigan.   With 12 acres of exhibit space, the museum houses nearly 250,000 artifacts of American industry (not merely the automobile industry). The major attraction is a long-term exhibit, "Made in America: The History of the American Industrial System."

❖ **Edison National Historic Site,** West Orange, New Jersey.   The site contains the Edison archives, including photographs, sound recordings, and industrial and scientific machinery. Its twenty historic structures dating from the 1880–1887 period include Edison's home and laboratory.

❖ **Japanese American National Museum,** Los Angeles, California.   Housed in a converted Buddhist temple, this museum includes artifacts and photographs of early Japanese immigration

Glossary

Significant historical terms are called out in **heavy type** throughout the text. These are listed alphabetically and defined in a *glossary* at the end of the book.

Reconstruction,
1865–1877

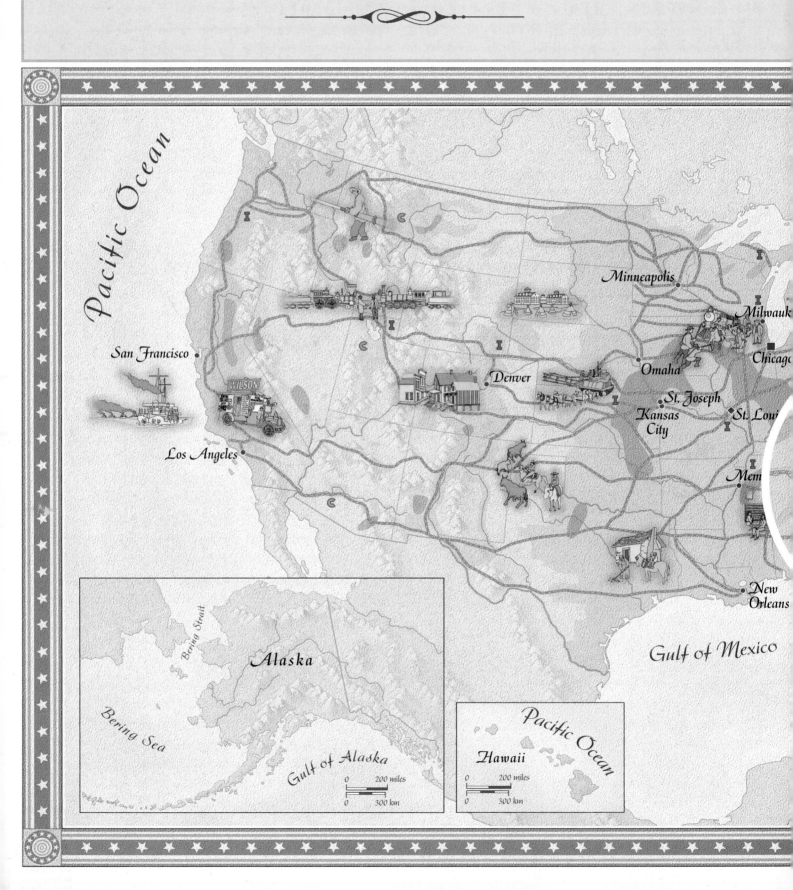

Pacific Ocean

San Francisco

Los Angeles

WILSON

Minneapolis

Milwauk

Chicago

Denver

Omaha

St. Joseph

St. Lou

Kansas
City

Mem

New
Orleans

Gulf of Mexico

Bering Strait

Alaska

Bering Sea

Gulf of Alaska

0   200 miles

0   300 km

Pacific Ocean

Hawaii

0   200 miles

0   300 km

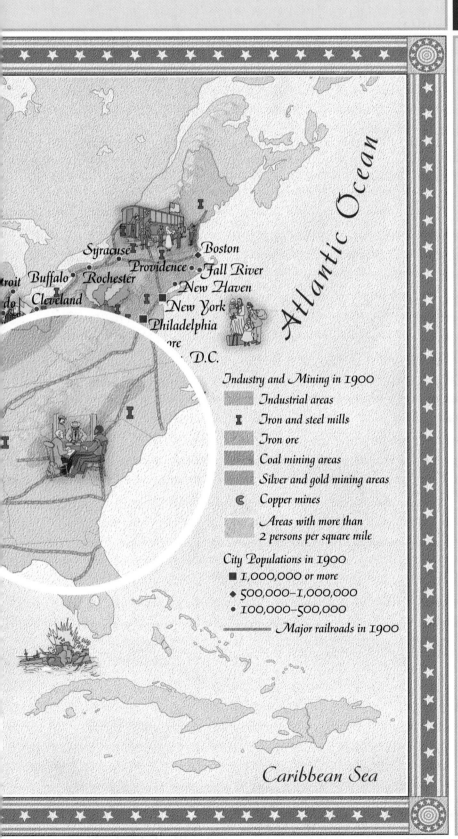

18

Chapter Outline

Key Topics

- ❖ African-American aspirations and
  southern white expectations
- ❖ Federal government plans to bring
  the South back into the Union and
  secure freedom for former slaves
- ❖ Southern Republican efforts to keep
  the allegiance of black voters and win
  white support
- ❖ Why and how Reconstruction ended

513

*A*s Union general William T. Sherman burned his way through Georgia and South Carolina in late 1864 and early 1865, slaves left their plantations to work for and follow the conquering army. In January 1865, Sherman allowed former slaves to settle on farms abandoned by their masters along the Atlantic coast. Tom Mansart, a former slave, seized this opportunity to stake out a farm near Port Royal, South Carolina. Less than a year later, the federal government returned the land to its previous owner. Mansart found work as a stevedore in nearby Charleston and joined a labor union founded by free black people before the war. By 1871, he had married and risen to prominence in his community. He was president of his eight-hundred-member union, and his backing helped elect local Republican candidates to office.

The Mansart family's good fortune declined after 1871 as first an economic depression and then racial violence stole their dream. Tom Mansart was killed at the door of his house during the election campaign of 1876, the victim of one of the white mobs roaming through South Carolina to discourage black citizens from voting. The federal troops that had been sent to Charleston to maintain an open political process instead fraternized with the city's white leaders.

Tom Mansart's story, as told by African-American leader W. E. B. Du Bois in *The Black Flame* (1957), exemplified both the promise of the **Reconstruction** era and its eventual betrayal by white people in both the North and the South. Crossing the threshold of freedom in 1865, black Southerners saw their prospects widening. Rights formerly denied them—to move, to own property, to get an education, to keep their families together, to succeed or fail in their own endeavors—were now theirs. Freedom meant more than a change in status; it marked a rebirth. But, by 1877, African Americans again faced restrictions that, though not as severe as slavery, deprived them of the promised fruits of freedom.

The position of African Americans in American society was one of the two great issues of Reconstruction. Americans of both sections disagreed about how much freedom to grant the former slaves, almost all of whom lived in the South. The other great issue was how and under what terms to readmit the former Confederate states. The Constitution was silent on the subject. As with the issue of black equality, opinions in both sections varied widely.

The formation of a national consensus on freedom and reunification began with the demands and hopes of three broad groups. One was the Republican party, which controlled the federal government and determined its policies. Most Republicans were unwilling to accept the seceding states back in the Union without an expression of loyalty and a commitment to protecting the rights of freedmen. A second group, the more than 4 million former slaves, demanded voting rights, access to education, and the opportunity to seek economic self-sufficiency. Few black Northerners yet enjoyed all these benefits, and few white Southerners could conceive of former slaves possessing them. The third group, white Southerners, hoped to restore their shattered lives, fortunes, and dignity. In their vision of a renewed South, black people remained subservient, and the federal government stopped interfering in southern affairs.

Between 1865 and 1867, under President Andrew Johnson's Reconstruction plan, white Southerners pretty much had their way with the former slaves and with their own state governments. Congressional action between 1867 and 1870 attempted to balance black rights and home rule, with mixed results. After 1870, white Southerners gradually regained control of their states and localities, often through violence and intimidation, denying black Southerners their political gains while Republicans in Washington lost interest in policing their former enemies.

By the time the last federal troops left the South in 1877, white Southerners had prevailed. The Confederate states had returned to the Union with all of their rights and many of their leaders restored. And the freed slaves remained in mostly subservient positions with few of the rights and privileges enjoyed by other Americans.

White Southerners and the Ghosts of the Confederacy, 1865

Confederate soldiers—generals and troops alike—returned to devastated homes they could scarcely recognize. General Braxton Bragg returned to his "once prosperous" Alabama home to find "all, all was lost, except my debts." Bragg and his wife found temporary shelter in a slave cabin. Yeomen farmers, the backbone of the Confederacy, found uprooted fences, farm animals dead or gone, and buildings destroyed. With no income or savings to soften their plight, they and their families wandered about in a living nightmare, seeking shelter where they could. They lived in morbid fear of vengeful former slaves or the hated Yankee soldiers wreaking more damage. "The demoralization is complete," a Georgia girl noted.

Their cause lost and their society reviled, white Southerners lived through the summer and fall of 1865 surrounded by ghosts—the ghosts of lost loved ones, joyful times, bountiful harvests, self-assurance, and slavery. Defeat shook the basic tenets of their religious beliefs. A North Carolinian cried, "Oh, our God! What sins we must have been guilty of that we should be so humiliated by Thee now!" Some praised God for delivering the South from the sin of slavery. A Virginia woman expressed thanks that "we white people are no longer permitted to go on in such wickedness, heaping up more and more wrath of God upon our devoted heads."

But many other white Southerners refused to accept their defeat as a divine judgment. Instead, they insisted, God had spared the South for a greater purpose. They came to view the war as the **Lost Cause** and interpreted it not as a lesson in humility but as an episode in the South's journey to salvation. Robert E. Lee became the patron saint of this cause, his poignant nobility a contrast to the crassness of the Yankee warlords. White Southerners would not allow the memory of the bloody struggle to die, transforming it into a symbol of courage against great odds and piety against sin. Eventually, they believed, redemption would come.

Fifteen years after the war, Mark Twain traveled the length of the East Coast. After visiting a gentlemen's club in Boston, he recalled that the conversation had covered a variety of topics, none of which included the Civil War. Northerners had relegated that conflict to history books and moved on. This was not the case in the South. There defeat and destruction demanded rationalization and remembrance. Thus Twain reported that, unlike in the

This engraving shows Southerners decorating the graves of rebel soldiers at Hollywood Memorial Cemetery in Virginia, in 1867. Northern and Southerners alike honored their war dead. But, in the South, the practice of commemorating fallen soldiers became an important element in maintaining the myth of the Lost Cause that colored white Southerners' view of the War.

North, gentlemen's talk in Atlanta inevitably wandered to the war and to heroism and sacrifice. "In the South," Twain wrote, "the war is what A.D. is elsewhere: they date from it." Such people would not accept the changes implied by defeat. They would fight to preserve as much of their past as the victors allowed.

Most white Southerners approached the great issues of freedom and reunification with unyielding views. They saw African Americans as adversaries whose attempts at self-improvement were a direct challenge to white people's beliefs in their own racial superiority. White Southerners saw outside assistance to black Southerners as another invasion. The Yankees may have destroyed their families, their farms, and their fortunes, but they would not destroy the racial order. The war may have ended slavery, but white Southerners were determined to preserve strict racial boundaries.

More than Freedom: African-American Aspirations in 1865

If black people could have peered into the minds of white Southerners, they would have been stunned. The former slaves did not initially even dream of social equality; far less did they plot the kind of vengeful murder and mayhem white people feared. They did harbor two potentially contradictory aspirations. The first was to be left alone, free of white supervision. Responding to the key question of the time,

CHRONOLOGY

1863 Lincoln proposes his Ten Percent Plan.

1864 Congress proposes the Wade-Davis Bill.

1865 Sherman issues Field Order No. 15.

Freedmen's Bureau is established.

Andrew Johnson succeeds to the presidency, unveils his Reconstruction plan.

Massachusetts desegregates all public facilities.

Black citizens in several southern cities organize Union Leagues.

Former Confederate states begin to pass black codes.

1866 Congress passes Southern Homestead Act, Civil Rights Act of 1866.

Ku Klux Klan is founded.

Fourteenth Amendment to the Constitution is passed (ratified in 1868).

President Johnson goes on a speaking tour.

1867 Congress passes Military Reconstruction Acts, Tenure of Office Act.

1868 President Johnson is impeached and tried in the Senate for defying the Tenure of Office Act.

Republican Ulysses S. Grant is elected president.

1869 Fifteenth Amendment passed (ratified 1870).

1870 Congress passes Enforcement Act.

Republican regimes topple in North Carolina and Georgia.

1871 Congress passes Ku Klux Klan Act.

1872 Freedmen's Bureau closes down.

Liberal Republicans emerge as a separate party.

Ulysses S. Grant is reelected.

1873 Severe depression begins.

Colfax Massacre occurs.

U.S. Supreme Court's decision in the *Slaughterhouse* cases weakens the intent of the Fourteenth Amendment.

Texas falls to the Democrats in the fall elections.

1874 White Leaguers attempt a coup against the Republican government of New Orleans.

Democrats win off-year elections across the South amid widespread fraud and violence.

1875 Congress passes Civil Rights Act of 1875.

1876 Supreme Court's decision in *United States* v. *Cruikshank* nullifies Enforcement Act of 1870.

Outcome of the presidential election between Republican Rutherford B. Hayes and Democrat Samuel J. Tilden is contested.

1877 Compromise of 1877 makes Hayes president and ends Reconstruction.

"What shall we do with the Negro?" former slave and abolitionist Frederick Douglass responded, "Do nothing. . . . Give him a chance to stand on his own legs! Let him alone!" But former slaves also wanted land, voting and civil rights, and education. To secure these, they needed the intervention and support of the white power structure.

In 1865, African Americans had reason to hope that their dreams of full citizenship might be realized. They enjoyed a reservoir of support for their aspirations among some Republican leaders. The views of James A. Garfield, Union veteran, U.S. congressman, and future president, were typical of these Republicans. Commenting on the ratification of the Thirteenth Amendment, Garfield asked, "What is freedom? Is it the bare privilege of not being chained? . . . If this is all, then freedom is a bitter mockery, a cruel delusion."

The first step Congress took beyond emancipation was to establish the Bureau of Refugees, Freedmen, and Abandoned Lands in March 1865. Congress envisioned the **Freedmen's Bureau**, as it came to be called, as a multipurpose agency to provide social, educational, and economic services, advice, and protection to former slaves and destitute white Southerners. The Bureau marked the federal government's first foray into social welfare legislation. Congress also authorized the bureau to rent confiscated and abandoned farmland to freedmen in forty-acre plots with an option to buy. This auspicious beginning belied the great disappointments that lay ahead.

Education

The greatest success of the Freedmen's Bureau was in education. The bureau coordinated more than fifty northern philanthropic and religious groups, which in turn established three thousand freedmen's schools in the South serving 150,000 men, women, and children.

Initially, single young women from the Northeast comprised much of the teaching force. One of them, twenty-six-year-old Martha Schofield, came to Aiken, South Carolina, from rural Pennsylvania in 1865. Like many of her colleagues, she had joined the abolitionist movement as a teenager and decided to make teaching her life's work. Her strong Quaker beliefs reflected the importance of Protestant Christianity in motivating the young missionaries. When her sponsoring agency, the Pennsylvania Freedmen's Relief Association, folded in 1871, her school closed. Undaunted, she opened another school on her own, and, despite chronic financial problems and the hostility of Aiken's white citizens, she and the school endured. (Since 1953, her school has been part of Aiken's public school system.)

By the time Schofield opened her own school in 1871, black teachers outnumbered white teachers in the "colored" schools. The financial troubles of northern missionary societies and declining interest in the freedmen's condition among white Northerners opened opportunities for black teachers. Support for them came from black churches, especially the **African Methodist Episcopal (AME) Church**.

The former slaves crowded into basements, shacks, and churches to attend school. "The children . . . hurry to school as soon as their work is over," wrote a teacher in Norfolk, Virginia, in 1867. "The plowmen hurry from the field at night to get their hour of study. Old men and women strain their dim sight with the book two and half feet distant from the eye, to catch the shape of the letter. I call this heaven-inspired interest."

At the end of the Civil War, only about 10 percent of black Southerners were literate, compared with more than 70 percent of white Southerners. Within a decade, black literacy had risen above 30 percent. Joseph Wilson, a former slave, attributed the rise to "this longing of ours for freedom of the mind as well as the body."

Some black Southerners went on to one of the thirteen colleges established by the American Missionary Association and black and white churches. Between 1860 and 1880 more than one thousand black Southerners earned college degrees at institutions still serving students today, such as Howard University in Washington, D.C., Fisk University in Nashville, Hampton Institute (now University), Tuskegee Institute, and Biddle Institute (now Johnson C. Smith University) in Charlotte.

Pursuing freedom of the mind involved challenges beyond those of learning to read and write. Many white Southerners condemned efforts at "Negro improvement." They viewed the time spent on education as wasted, forcing the former slaves to catch their lessons in bits and pieces between work, often by candlelight or on Sundays. White Southerners also harassed white female teachers, questioning their morals and threatening people who rented rooms to them. The *Atlanta Constitution,* in a vicious caricature, suggested that Harriet Beecher Stowe planned to establish a freedmen's school near Atlanta "for the benefit of mulatto children that have been born in the South since its invasion by Yankee school-marms."

After the Freedmen's Bureau folded in 1872 and

The Freedmen's Bureau, northern churches, and missionary societies established more than three thousand schools attended by some 150,000 men, women, and children in the years after the Civil War. At first, mostly young white women from the Northeast staffed these schools.

many of the northern societies that supported freedmen's education collapsed or cut back their involvement, education for black Southerners became more haphazard.

"Forty Acres and a Mule"

Although education was important to the freed slaves in their quest for civic equality, land ownership offered them the promise of economic independence. For generations, black people had worked southern farms and had received nothing for their labor. An overwhelmingly agricultural people, freedmen looked to farm ownership as a key element in their transition from slavery to freedom. "Gib us our own land and we take care of ourselves," a Charleston freedman asserted to a Northern visitor in 1865. "But without land, de ole massas can hire or starve us, as dey please."

Even before the war's end, rumors circulated through black communities in the South that the government would provide each black family with forty acres and a mule. These rumors were fueled by General William T. Sherman's **Field Order No. 15** in January 1865, which set aside a vast swath of abandoned land along the South Atlantic coast from the Charleston area to northern Florida for grants of up to forty acres. The Freedmen's Bureau likewise raised expectations when it was initially authorized to rent forty-acre plots of confiscated or abandoned land to freedmen.

By June 1865, about forty thousand former slaves had settled on "Sherman land" along the southeastern coast. In 1866, Congress passed the **Southern Homestead Act**, giving black people preferential access to public lands in five southern states. Two years later, the Republican government of South Carolina initiated a land redistribution program financed by the sale of state bonds. The state used proceeds from the bond sales to purchase farmland, which it then resold to freedmen, who paid for it with state-funded long-term low-interest loans. By the late 1870s, more than fourteen thousand African-American families had taken advantage of this program.

The highest concentration of black land ownership was in the Upper South and in areas of the Lower South with better economic conditions and less white hostility toward black people. By 1890, one out of three black farmers in the Upper South owned his land, compared to one out of five for the South as a whole. In Virginia, 43 percent of black farmers owned the land they farmed.

Land ownership did not ensure financial success. Most black-owned farms were small and on marginal land. The value of these farms in 1880 was roughly half that of white-owned farms. Black farmers also had trouble obtaining credit to purchase or expand their holdings. A lifetime of field work left some freedmen without the managerial skills to operate a farm. The hostility of white neighbors and their refusal to lend tools or animals, share work, sell land, or offer advice also played a role in thwarting black aspirations. Black farmers often had the most success when groups of families settled together, as in the farm community of Promise Land in upcountry South Carolina.

The vast majority of former slaves, however, especially those in the Lower South, never fulfilled their dreams of land ownership. Rumors to the contrary, the federal government never intended to implement a land redistribution program in the South. General Sherman viewed his field order as a temporary measure to support freedmen for the remainder of the war. President Andrew Johnson nullified the order in September 1865, returning confiscated land to its former owners. Even Republican supporters of black land ownership questioned the constitutionality of seizing privately owned real estate. Most land redistribution programs that did emerge after the war, including government-sponsored programs, required black farmers to have capital. But in the impoverished postwar economy of the South, it was difficult for them to acquire it.

Republican party rhetoric of the 1850s extolled the virtues and dignity of free labor over the degradation of slave labor. Free labor usually meant working for a wage or under some other contractual arrangement. But unlike slaves, according to the then prevailing view, free laborers could enjoy the fruits of their work and might someday become owners or entrepreneurs themselves. It was self-help, not government assistance, that guaranteed individual success. After the war, many white Northerners envisioned former slaves assuming the status of free laborers, not necessarily of independent landowners.

For most officials of the Freedmen's Bureau, who shared these views, reviving the southern economy was a higher priority than helping former slaves acquire farms. They wanted both to get the crop in the field and start the South on the road to a free labor system. They thus encouraged freedmen to work for their former masters under contract and postpone their quest for land. Bureau and military officials lectured former slaves on the virtues of staying home and working "faithfully" in the fields.

At first, agents of the Freedmen's Bureau supervised labor contracts between former slaves and masters. But after 1867, bureau surveillance declined. Agents assumed that both black laborers and white landowners had become accustomed to the mutual obligations of contracts. The bureau, however, underestimated the power of white landowners to coerce favorable terms or to ignore those they did not like. Contracts implied a mutuality that most planters could not accept in their relations with former slaves. As northern journalist Whitelaw Reid noted in 1865, planters "have no sort of conception of free labor. They do not comprehend any law for controlling laborers, save the law of force."

The former slaves had their own views of their proper place in the labor hierarchy. If they could not own land in the short term, they would strive for the best labor arrangement in the meantime. As early as 1862, slaves behind Union lines abandoned the gang system of labor, which they associated with slavery and dependence. In contracts with planters (usually their former masters) after the war, freedmen in most of the South insisted on working the land independently with their families. By contrast, freedmen in the rice districts along the South Atlantic coast retained their task system of labor, which allowed them flexibility and a degree of independence.

Throughout the South in 1865 and 1866, landlords complained of a chronic labor shortage, although few freedmen had left the region. The alleged shortage was the result of former slaves' refusal to work under conditions that resembled slavery. The withdrawal of black women from field work also contributed to the impression of a labor shortage. By staying home to care for their families, black women avoided the economic and sexual exploitation of the slavery era. They also sought to place themselves on an equal social footing with white plantation women, who likewise worked in the home and not in the fields.

Migration to Cities

While some black Southerners asserted their rights as workers on southern farms, others affirmed their freedom by moving to towns and cities. Even before the war, the city had offered slaves and free black people a measure of freedom unknown in the rural South. After the war, African Americans moved to cities to find families, seek work, escape the tedium and supervision of farm life, or simply test their right to move about.

For these same reasons, white people disapproved of black migration to the city. It reduced the labor pool for farms. It also gave black people more opportunities to associate with white people of similar social status, to compete for jobs, and to establish schools, churches, and social organizations, fueling their hopes for racial equality. White people felt confident that they could fix the freedmen's place in southern society on the farm; the city was another matter.

Between 1860 and 1870, the African-American population in every major southern city rose significantly. In Atlanta, for example, black people accounted for one in five residents in 1860 and nearly one in two by 1870.

Some freedmen came to cities initially to reunite with their families. Every city newspaper after the war carried advertisements from former slaves seeking their mates and children. In 1865, the Nashville *Colored Tennessean* carried this poignant plea: "During the year 1849, Thomas Sample carried away from this city, as his slaves, our daughter, Polly, and son. . . . We will give $100 each for them to any person who will assist them . . . to get to Nashville, or get word to us of their whereabouts."

Once in the city, freedmen had to find a home and a job. They usually settled for the cheapest accommodations in low-lying areas or on the outskirts of town where building

Milk sampling at Hampton Institute. Hampton, which opened in Virginia in 1868, was one of the first of several schools established with the help of northern philanthropic and missionary societies to allow freedmen to pursue a college education. Hampton stressed agricultural and vocational training. The military uniforms were typical for male students, black and white, at agricultural and mechanical schools.

codes did not apply. Rather than developing one large ghetto, as in many northern cities, black Southerners lived in several concentrations in and around cities.

Sometimes armed with a letter of reference from their former masters, black people went door to door to seek employment. Many found work serving white families—as guards, laundresses, maids—for very low wages. Both skilled and unskilled laborers found work rebuilding war-torn cities like Atlanta. Frederick Ayer, a Freedmen's Bureau agent in Atlanta, reported to a colleague in 1866 that "many of the whites are making most vigorous efforts to retrieve their broken fortunes and . . . rebuild their dwellings and shops. . . . This furnished employment to a large number of colored people as Masons, Carpenters, Teamsters, and Common Workmen."

Most rural black Southerners, however, arrived in cities untrained in the kinds of skills sought in an urban work force and so worked as unskilled laborers. In both Atlanta and Nashville, black people comprised more than 75 percent of the unskilled work force in 1870. Their wages were at or below subsistence level. A black laborer in Richmond admitted to a journalist in 1870 that he had difficulty making ends meet on $1.50 a day. "It's right hard," he reported. "I have to pay $15 a month rent, and only two little rooms." His family survived because his wife took in laundry while her mother watched the children. Considering the laborer's struggle, the journalist wondered, "Were not your people better off in slavery?" The man replied, "Oh, no sir! We're a heap better off now. . . . We're men now, but when our masters had us we was only change in their pockets."

Faith and Freedom

Religious faith framed and inspired the efforts of African Americans to test their freedom on the farm and in the city. White Southerners used religion to transform the Lost Cause from a shattering defeat to a premonition of a greater destiny. Black Southerners, in contrast, saw emancipation in biblical terms as the beginning of an exodus from bondage to the Promised Land.

Some black churches in the postwar South originated in the slavery era, but most split from white-dominated congregations after the war. White churchgoers deplored the expressive style of black worship, and black churchgoers were uncomfortable in congregations that treated them as inferiors. A separate church also reduced white surveillance.

The First African Baptist Church in Richmond originated in a white Baptist congregation founded before the war. An 1846 agreement allowed black worshippers to hold separate services, but only with a white minister officiating. In 1866, the white pastor resigned, noting that black worshippers "would naturally and justly prefer a minister of their own color." The white church transferred the deed to the black congregation that year, and the Reverend James Henry Holmes, a former slave, became their first black pastor. The church flourished under Holmes, paid off its debt, and by the 1870s boasted the largest black congregation in the United States.

The church became a primary focus of African-American life. It gave black people the opportunity to hone skills in self-government and administration that white-dominated society denied them. Within the supportive confines of the congregation, they could assume leadership positions, render important decisions, deal with financial matters, and engage in politics. The church also operated as an educational institution. Local governments, especially in rural areas, rarely constructed public schools for black people; churches often served that function. The desire to read the Bible inspired thousands of former slaves to attend the church school.

The church also spawned other organizations that served the black community over the next century. Burial societies, Masonic lodges, temperance groups, trade unions, and drama clubs originated in churches. By the 1870s, African Americans in Memphis had more than two hundred such organizations. They often came together to celebrate such holidays as Independence Day on July 4 and the anniversary of the Emancipation Proclamation on January 1. These commemorations antagonized white people and further divided the black and white communities.

African Americans took great pride in their churches, which became visible measures of their progress. In Charleston, the first building erected after the war was a black church. The First Colored Baptist Church in Nashville became a landmark for its imposing brick and stone façade. Black people donated a greater proportion of their earnings to their churches than white people did.

The church and the congregation were a cohesive force in black communities. They supported families under stress from discrimination and poverty. Husbands and wives joined church-affiliated societies together. Their children joined organizations such as the Young Rising Sons and Daughters of the New Testament. The church enforced family and religious values, punishing violaters guilty of such infractions as adultery. Black

The black church was the center of African-American life in the postwar urban South. Most black churches formed after the Civil War, but some, like the First African Baptist Church in Richmond, shown here in an 1874 engraving, traced their origins to before 1861.

churchwomen—both working- and middle-class—were especially prominent in the family-oriented organizations.

Most black churches looked inward to strengthen their members against the harsh realities of postwar southern society. Few ministers dared to engage in or even support protest activities. Some, especially those in the Colored Methodist Episcopal Church, counseled congregants to abide by the rules of second-class citizenship and to trust in God's will to right the wrongs of racism.

Northern-based denominations, however, notably the AME Church, were more aggressive advocates of black rights. AME ministers stressed the responsibility of individual black people to realize God's will of racial equality.

Henry McNeal Turner, probably the most influential AME minister of his day, helped expand the denomination into the South from its small primarily northern base at the end of the Civil War. The white Southern Methodist church granted the nineteen-year-old Turner a license to preach in 1853. He served as an itinerant minister for both black and white congregations during the next five years. In 1858, he joined the AME Church and moved north to lead a congregation in Baltimore. Having served as a U.S. Army chaplain, Turner moved to Georgia and evangelized former slaves who thronged to an activist church with black roots. Within five years, the AME Church had grown to 500,000 members, 80 percent of whom lived in the South. Turner entered Georgia politics

in the late 1860s and held several state elective offices. His church elevated him to bishop in 1880.

Turner's career and the efforts of former slaves in the classroom, on the farm, in cities, and in the churches reflect the enthusiasm and expectations with which black Southerners greeted freedom. But the majority of white Southerners were unwilling to see those expectations fulfilled. For this reason, African Americans could not secure the fruits of their emancipation without the support and protection of the federal government. The issue of freedom was therefore inextricably linked to the other great issue of the era, the rejoining of the Confederacy to the Union, as expressed in federal Reconstruction policy.

Federal Reconstruction, 1865–1870

When the Civil War ended in 1865, no acceptable blueprint existed for reconstituting the Union. President Lincoln believed that, at heart, a majority of white Southerners were Unionists and that they could and should undertake the task of reconstruction. He favored a conciliatory policy toward the South in order, as he put it in one of his last letters, "to restore the Union, so as to make it . . . *a Union of hearts and hands as well as of States.*" He counted on the loyalists to be fair with respect to the rights of the former slaves.

The President had outlined his policy as early as 1863 when he proposed to readmit a seceding state if 10 percent of its prewar voters took an oath of loyalty to the Union and it prohibited slavery in a new state constitution. But this Ten Percent Plan did not require states to grant equal civil and political rights to former slaves, and many Republicans in Congress thought it was not stringent enough. In 1864, a group of them responded with the **Wade-Davis Bill**, which required a majority of a state's prewar voters to pledge their loyalty to the

Union and demanded guarantees of black equality before the law. The bill was passed at the end of a congressional session, but Lincoln kept it from becoming law by refusing to sign it (an action known as a "pocket veto").

The controversy over these plans reflected two obstacles to Reconstruction that would continue to plague the ruling Republicans after the war. First, neither the Constitution nor legal precedent offered any guidance on whether the president or Congress should take the lead on Reconstruction policy. Second, there was no agreement on what that policy should be. Proposals requiring various preconditions for readmitting a state—loyalty oaths, new constitutions with certain specific provisions, guarantees of freedmen's rights—all provoked vigorous debate.

President Andrew Johnson, some conservative Republicans, and most Democrats believed that because the Constitution made no mention of secession, the southern states had been in rebellion, but had never left the Union, so there was no need for a formal process to readmit them. Moderate and radical Republicans disagreed, arguing that the defeated states had forfeited their rights. Moderates and radicals parted company, however, on the conditions necessary for readmission to the Union. The radicals wanted to treat the former Confederate states as territories—or "conquered provinces"—subject to congressional legislation. Moderates wanted to grant the seceding states more autonomy and limit federal intervention in their affairs while they satisfied the conditions of readmission. No group held a majority in Congress, and legislators sometimes changed their positions (see the overview table, "Contrasting Views of Reconstruction").

Presidential Reconstruction, 1865–1867

When the Civil War ended in April 1865, Congress was not in session and would not reconvene until December. Thus the responsibility for developing a Reconstruction policy initially fell on Andrew Johnson, who succeeded to the presidency upon Lincoln's assassination. Johnson seemed well suited to the difficult task. The new president's personal and political background was promising to his Republican colleagues. Johnson was born in humble circumstances in North Carolina in 1808. He learned the tailoring trade and struck out for Tennessee as a teenager to open a tailor shop in the eastern Tennessee town of Greenville. Gaining his education informally, he prospered modestly, purchased a few slaves, and began to pursue politics. He was elected alderman, mayor, state legislator, congressmen, governor, and then, in 1856, U.S. senator.

Johnson was the only southern senator to remain in the U.S. Senate after secession. This defiant Unionism won him acclaim in the North and credibility among Republican leaders, who welcomed him into their party. During the war, as military governor of Tennessee, he solidified his Republican credentials by advocating the abolition of slavery in Tennessee and severe punishment of Confederate leaders. His views landed him on the Republican ticket as the candidate for vice president in 1864. Indiana Republican congressman George W. Julian, who advocated harsh terms for the South and broad rights for black people, viewed Johnson's accession to the presidency in 1865 as "a godsend."

Most Northerners and many Republicans approved Johnson's Reconstruction plan when he unveiled it in May 1865. Johnson extended pardons and restored property rights, except in slaves, to Southerners who swore an oath of allegiance to the Union and the Constitution. Southerners who had held prominent positions in the Confederacy, however, and those with more than $20,000 in taxable property had to petition the president directly for a pardon. The plan had nothing to say about the voting rights and civil rights of former slaves.

Northern Democrats applauded the plan's silence on these issues and its promise of a quick restoration of the southern states to the Union. They expected the southern states to favor their party and expand its political power. Republicans, although some of them would have preferred the plan to have provided for black suffrage, approved of the restoration of property rights to white Southerners. This position was consistent with their view of former slaves as laborers, not property owners. Republicans also hoped that Johnson's conciliatory terms might attract some white Southerners to the Republican party.

White Southerners, however, were not so favorably impressed with Johnson's plan, and their response turned northern public opinion against the president. On the two great issues of freedom and reunion, white Southerners quickly demonstrated their eagerness to reverse the results of the Civil War. Although most states accepted President Johnson's modest requirements, several objected to one or more of them. Mississippi and Texas refused to ratify the Thirteenth Amendment, which abolished slavery. Alabama accepted only parts of the amendment. South Carolina declined to nullify its secession ordinance. No southern state authorized black voting. When Johnson ordered special congressional elections in the South in the fall of 1865, the

OVERVIEW

CONTRASTING VIEWS OF RECONSTRUCTION: PRESIDENT AND CONGRESS

Politician or Group	Policy on Former Slaves	Policy on Readmission of Former Confederate States
President Johnson	Opposed to black suffrage Silent on protection of black civil rights Opposed to land redistribution	Maintained that rebellious states were already readmitted Granted pardons and restoration of property to all who swore allegiance to the United States
Radical Republicans	Favored black suffrage Favored protection of black civil rights Favored land redistribution	Favored treating rebellious states as territories and establishing military districts* Favored limiting franchise to black people and loyal white people
Moderate Republicans	Favored black suffrage Favored protection of civil rights Opposed land redistribution	Favored some restrictions on white suffrage* Favored requiring states to meet various requirements before being readmitted* Split on military rule

True of most but not all members of the group.

all-white electorate returned many prominent Confederate leaders to office.

In late 1865, the newly elected southern state legislatures revised their antebellum slave codes. The updated **black codes** allowed local officials to arrest black people who could not document employment and residence or who were "disorderly" and sentence them to forced labor on farms or road crews (see "American Views: Mississippi's 1865 Black Codes"). The codes also restricted black people to certain occupations, barred them from jury duty, and forbade them to possess firearms. Apprenticeship laws permitted judges to take black children from parents who could not, in the judges' view, adequately support them. Given the widespread poverty in the South in 1865, the law could apply to almost any freed black family. Northerners looking for contrition in the South found no sign of it. Worse, President Johnson did not seem perturbed about this turn of events.

The Republican-dominated Congress reconvened in December 1865 in a belligerent mood. A few radical Republicans pushed for swift retribu-

tion. George W. Julian thundered that he would "indict, convict and hang Jefferson Davis in the name of God; as for Robert E. Lee, unmolested in Virginia, hang him too." His colleague, Benjamin F. Wade, suggested that "if the negroes by insurrection would contrive to slay one-half of the White Southerners, the remaining half would then hold them in respect and treat them with justice." Few in Congress took these statements seriously. Nonetheless, a consensus formed among radical Republicans, who comprised nearly half of the party's strength in Congress, that to gain readmission, a state would have to extend suffrage to black citizens, protect freedmen's civil rights, and have its white citizens officially acknowledge these rights. Some radicals also supported the redistribution of land to former slaves, but few pressed for social equality. They envisioned a new South of modest farms, some owned by former slaves, and a Republican party built on an alliance between black people and white loyalists.

Thaddeus Stevens of Pennsylvania led the radical forces in the House of Representatives, while abolitionist veteran Charles Sumner of Massachusetts rallied radicals in the Senate. Stevens had established himself as a partisan for black political rights in the North as early as the 1840s. As a congressman during the Civil War, he pushed Lincoln to free and arm the slaves and later to extend them the right to vote. Stevens dreamed of a South populated by white and black yeoman farmers. With no large plantations and few landless farmers, the South would become an ideal republic, a boon to the rest of the nation instead of a burden. Few shared his vision, and when he died in 1868, a reporter noted that "no man was oftener outvoted." Yet he remained the conscience of the House, a standard of idealism in an age of growing cynicism. His epitaph read in part, "The principle which I advocated through a long life, Equality of Man before his Creator."

Sumner was among the foremost abolitionist politicians before the Civil War. His combative nature won him few friends, even within his own party. As fierce as Stevens in the promotion of black civil and political rights after the war, he also believed that the Reconstruction era offered a "golden moment" to remake the South into an egalitarian region. Sumner died in 1874 as his dream was fading. The last piece of Reconstruction legislation, the Civil Rights Act of 1875, became a posthumous tribute to his uncommon ability to overcome the racial prejudices of the day with a vision of a color-blind society.

But the radicals could not unite behind a program, and it fell to their moderate colleagues to take the first step toward a Congressional Reconstruction plan. The moderates shared the radicals' desire to protect the former slaves' civil and voting rights. But they would not support land redistribution schemes or punitive measures against prominent Confederates. The moderates' first measure, passed in early 1866, extended the life of the Freedmen's Bureau and provided it with authority to punish state officials who failed to extend to black citizens the civil rights enjoyed by white citizens. But President Johnson vetoed the legislation.

Undeterred, Congress passed the **Civil Rights Act of 1866** in direct response to the black codes. The act specified the civil rights to which all U.S. citizens were entitled. In creating a category of national citizenship with rights that superseded state laws restricting them, the act changed federal–state relations (and in the process overturned the Dred Scott decision). President Johnson vetoed the act, but it became law when Congress mustered a two-thirds majority to override his veto, the first time in American history that Congress passed major legislation over a president's veto.

Andrew Johnson's position reflected both his view of government and his racial attitudes. The Republican president remained a Democrat in spirit. Republicans had expanded federal power during the Civil War. Johnson, however, like most Democrats, favored more of a balance between federal and state power. He also shared with many of his white southern neighbors a belief in black inferiority and a view that white plantation owners had conspired to limit the economic and political power of white yeomen like himself. Johnson supported abolition assuming that, once free, black people would emigrate to Africa. Given the president's views and his inflexible temperament, a clash between him and Congress became inevitable.

"Selling a Freeman to Pay His Fine at Monticello, Florida." This 1867 engraving shows how the black codes of the early Reconstruction era in the South reduced former slaves to virtually their pre–Civil War status. Scenes such as this convinced Northerners that the white South was unrepentant and prompted Congressional Republicans to devise their own Reconstruction plan.

To keep freedmen's rights safe from presidential vetoes, state legislatures, and federal courts, the Republican-dominated Congress moved to incorporate some of the provisions of the 1866 Civil Rights Act into the Constitution. The **Fourteenth Amendment**, which Congress passed in June 1866, addressed the issues of civil and voting rights. It guaranteed every citizen equality before the law. The two key sections of the amendment prohibited states from violating the civil rights of their citizens, thus outlawing the black codes, and gave states the choice of enfranchising black people or losing representation in Congress. Some radical Republicans expressed disappointment that the amendment, in a reflection of northern ambivalence, failed to give the vote to black people outright.

The amendment also disappointed advocates of woman suffrage, for the first time using the word *male* in the Constitution to define who could vote. Wendell Phillips, a prominent abolitionist, counseled them, "One question at a time. This hour belongs to the Negro." Susan B. Anthony, who had campaigned for the abolition of slavery before the war and helped mount a petition drive that collected 400,000 signatures for the Thirteenth Amendment, formed the **American Equal Rights Association** in 1866 with her colleagues to push for woman suffrage at the state level.

The Fourteenth Amendment had little immediate impact on the South. Although enforcement of black codes diminished, white violence against black people increased. In the 1870s, several decisions by the U.S. Supreme Court would weaken the amendment's provisions. Eventually, however, it would play a major role in securing the civil rights of African Americans.

President Johnson seemed to encourage white intransigence by openly denouncing the Fourteenth Amendment. In August 1866, at the start of the congressional election campaign, he undertook an unprecedented tour of key northern states to sell his message of sectional reconciliation to the public. Although listeners appreciated Johnson's desire for peace, they questioned his claims of southern white loyalty to the Union. The president's diatribes against the Republican Congress won him followers in those northern states with a reservoir of opposition to black suffrage. But the tone and manner of his campaign offended many as undignified. In the November elections, the Democrats suffered embarrassing defeats in the North as Republicans managed better than two-thirds majorities in both the House and Senate, sufficient to override presidential vetoes. Radical Republicans, joined by moderate colleagues buoyed by the election results and revolted by the president's and the South's intransigence, seized the initiative when Congress reconvened.

Congressional Reconstruction, 1867–1870

The radicals' first salvo in their attempt to take control over Reconstruction occurred with the passage over President Johnson's veto of the **Military Reconstruction Acts**. The measures, passed in March 1867, inaugurated a period known as **Congressional Reconstruction** or Radical Reconstruction. Congress divided the ex-Confederate states (except for Tennessee, the only southern state that had ratified the Fourteenth Amendment and been readmitted to the Union) into five military districts, each headed by a general (see Map 18-1). The commanders' first order of business was to conduct voter registration campaigns to enroll black people and bar white people who had held office before the Civil War and who had supported the Confederacy. The eligible voters would then elect delegates to a state convention to write a new constitution that guaranteed **universal manhood suffrage**. Once a majority of eligible voters ratified the new constitution and the Fourteenth

Map 18-1 *Congressional Reconstruction, 1865–1877*
When Congress wrested control of Reconstruction policy from President Andrew Johnson, it divided the South into the five military districts depicted here. The commanding generals for each district held the authority both to hold elections and to decide who could vote.

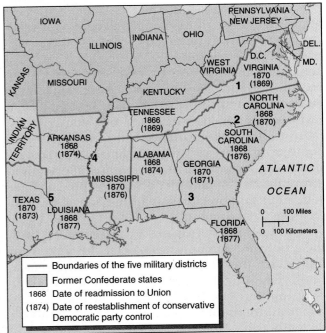

American Views
MISSISSIPPI'S 1865 BLACK CODES

White Southerners, especially landowners and business owners, feared emancipation would produce a labor crisis; freedmen, they expected, would either refuse to work or strike hard bargains with their former masters. White Southerners also recoiled from the prospect of having to treat their former slaves as full social equals. Thus beginning in late 1865, several southern states, including Mississippi, enacted laws designed to control black labor, mobility, and social status. Northerners responded to the codes as a provocation, a bold move to deny the result of the war and its consequences.

❖ **How did the black codes fit into President Andrew Johnson's Reconstruction program?**

❖ **Some Northerners charged that the black codes were a backdoor attempt at reestablishing slavery. Do you agree?**

❖ **If southern states enacted black codes to stabilize labor relations, how did the provisions below effect that objective?**

From An Act to Confer Civil Rights on Freedmen, and for other Purposes
Section 1. All freedmen, free negroes and mulattoes may sue and be sued, implead and be impleaded, in all the courts of law and equity of this State, and may acquire personal property, and choose in action, by descent or purchase, and may dispose of the same in the same manner and to the same extent that white persons may: Provided, That the provisions of this section shall not be so construed as to allow any freedman, free negro or mulatto to rent or lease any lands or tenements except in incorporated cities or towns, in which places the corporate authorities shall control the same.

Amendment, their state would be eligible for readmission to the Union.

The Reconstruction Acts fulfilled the radicals' three major objectives. First, they secured the freedmen's right to vote. Second, they made it likely that southern states would be run by Republican regimes that would enforce the new constitutions, protect former slaves' rights, and maintain the Republican majority in Congress. Finally, the acts set standards for readmission that required the South to accept the consequences of defeat: the preeminence of the federal government and the end of involuntary servitude.

To limit presidential interference with their policies, Republicans passed the **Tenure of Office Act**, prohibiting the president from removing certain officeholders without the Senate's consent. Johnson, angered at what he believed was an unconstitutional attack on presidential authority, deliberately violated the act by firing Secretary of War Edwin M. Stanton, a leading radical, in February 1868. The House responded to this defiance by approving articles of impeachment against a president for the first time in American history. After a trial, the Senate voted 35 to 19 to convict the president, one vote short of the two-thirds necessary to remove him from office. The seven Republicans who voted against their party did so not out of respect for the president but because they feared a conviction would damage the office of the presidency and violate the constitutional separation of powers. The outcome weakened the radicals and eased the way for moderate Republican Ulysses S. Grant to gain the party's nomination for president in 1868.

The Republicans viewed the 1868 presidential election as a referendum on Congressional Reconstruction. They supported black suffrage in the South but equivocated on allowing African Americans to vote in the North. Black Northerners could

Section 7. Every civil officer shall, and every person may, arrest and carry back to his or her legal employer any freedman, free negro, or mulatto who shall have quit the service of his or her employer before the expiration of his or her term of service without good cause; and said officer and person shall be entitled to receive for arresting and carrying back every deserting employee aforesaid the sum of five dollars, and ten cents per mile from the place of arrest to the place of delivery; and the same shall be paid by the employer, and held as a set off for so much against the wages of said deserting employee: Provided, that said arrested party, after being so returned, may appeal to the justice of the peace or member of the board of police of the county, who, on notice to the alleged employer, shall try summarily whether said appellant is legally employed by the alleged employer, and has good cause to quit said employer. Either party shall have the right of appeal to the county court, pending which the alleged deserter shall be remanded to the alleged employer or oth-

erwise disposed of, as shall be right and just; and the decision of the county court shall be final.

From An Act to Amend the Vagrant Laws of the State

Section 2. All freedmen, free negroes and mulattoes in this State, over the age of eighteen years, found on the second Monday in January, 1866, or thereafter, with no lawful employment or business, or found unlawful assembling themselves together, either in the day or night time, and all white persons assembling themselves with freedmen, Free negroes or mulattoes, or usually associating with freedmen, free negroes or mulattoes, on terms of equality, or living in adultery or fornication with a freed woman, freed negro or mulatto, shall be deemed vagrants, and on conviction thereof shall be fined in a sum not exceeding, in the case of a freedman, free negro or mulatto, fifty dollars, and a white man two hundred dollars, and imprisonment at the discretion of the court, the free negro not exceeding ten days, and the white man not exceeding six months.

Source: "Laws in Relation to Freedmen," 39 Congress, 2 Session, Senate Executive Document 6, Freedmen's Affairs, 182–86.

vote in only eight of the twenty-two northern states, and white Northerners had rejected equal suffrage referendums in eight of eleven states between 1865 and 1869. Republicans "waved the bloody shirt," reminding voters of Democratic disloyalty, the sacrifices of war, and the peace only Republicans could redeem. Democrats denounced Congressional Reconstruction as federal tyranny and, in openly racist appeals, warned white voters that a Republican victory would mean black rule. Grant won the election, but his margin of victory was uncomfortably narrow. Reflecting growing ambivalence in the North over issues of race and federal authority, New York's Horatio Seymour, the Democratic presidential nominee, probably carried a majority of the nation's white vote. Black voters' overwhelming support for Grant probably provided him his margin of victory.

The Republicans retained a strong majority in both houses of Congress and managed to pass another major piece of Reconstruction legislation, the

Fifteenth Amendment, in February 1869. In response to growing concerns about voter fraud and violence against freedmen, the amendment guaranteed the right of American men to vote, regardless of race. Although the amendment provided a loophole allowing states to impose restrictions on the right to vote based on literacy or property qualifications, it was nonetheless a milestone. It made the right to vote perhaps the most distinguishing characteristic of American citizenship.

The Fifteenth Amendment allowed states to keep the franchise a male prerogative, angering many in the woman suffrage movement more than had the Fourteenth Amendment. The resulting controversy severed the ties between the movement and Republican politics. Susan B. Anthony broke with her abolitionist colleagues and opposed the amendment. Fellow abolitionist and woman suffragist Elizabeth Cady Stanton charged that the amendment created an "aristocracy of sex." In an appeal brimming with ethnic

OVERVIEW

CONSTITUTIONAL AMENDMENTS AND FEDERAL LEGISLATION OF THE RECONSTRUCTION ERA

Amendment or Legislation	Purpose	Significance
Thirteenth Amendment (passed and ratified in 1865)	Prevented southern states from reestablishing slavery after the war	Final step toward full emancipation of slaves
Freedmen's Bureau Act (1865)	Oversight of resettlement, reflief, education, and labor for former slaves	Involved the federal government directly in assisting the transition from slavery to freedom; worked fitfully to achieve this objective during its seven-year career
Southern Homestead Act (1866)	Provided black people preferential access to public lands in five southern states	Lack of capital and poor quality of federal land thwarted the purpose of the act
Civil Rights Act of 1866	Defined rights of national citizenship	Marked an important change in federal–state relations, tilting balance of power to national government
Fourteenth Amendment (passed 1866; ratified 1868)	Prohibited states from violating the rights of their citizens	Strengthened the Civil Rights Act of 1866 and guaranteed all citizens equality before the law
Military Reconstruction Acts (1867)	Set new rules for the readmission of ex-Confederate states into the Union and secured black voting rights	Initiated Congressional Reconstruction
Tenure of Office Act (1867)	Required congressional approval for the removal of any official whose appointment had required Senate confirmation confirmation	A congressional challenge to the president's right to dismiss Cabinet members that led to President Andrew Johnson's impeachment trial
Fifteenth Amendment (passed 1869; ratified 1870)	Guaranteed the right of all American male citizens to vote regardless of race	The basis for black voting rights
Civil Rights Act of 1875	Prohibited racial discrimination in jury selection, public transportation, and public accommodations	Rarely enforced; Supreme Court declared it unconstitutional in 1883

and racial animosity, Stanton warned that "if you do not wish the lower orders of Chinese, African, Germans and Irish, with their low ideas of womanhood to make laws for you and your daughters . . . awake to the danger . . . and demand that woman, too, shall be represented in the government!" Such language created a major rift in the nascent women's movement. Women who supported the amendment formed the New England Woman Suffrage Association, challenging Anthony's American Equal Rights Association.

Southern Republican Governments, 1867–1870

Away from Washington, the first order of business for the former Confederacy was to draft state constitutions. The documents embodied progressive principles new to the South. They mandated the election of numerous local and state offices. Self-perpetuating local elites could no longer appoint themselves or cronies to powerful positions. The constitutions committed southern states, many for the first time, to public education. Lawmakers enacted a variety of reforms, including social welfare, penal reform, legislative reapportionment, and universal manhood suffrage.

The Republican regimes that gained control in southern states promoted vigorous state government and the protection of civil and voting rights. Three diverse Republican constituencies supported these governments. One consisted of white natives, most of them yeomen farmers. Residing mainly in the upland regions of the South and long ignored by lowland planters and merchants in state government, some had supported the Union during the war. The conflict had left many of them devastated. They struggled to keep their land and hoped for an easing of credit and for debt-stay laws to help them escape foreclosure. They wanted public schools for their children and good roads to get their crops to market. Some urban merchants and large planters also called themselves Republicans. Many were Whigs before the war, and a few had been Unionists. They were attracted to the party's emphasis on economic development, especially railroad construction, and would become prominent in Republican leadership after 1867.

Collectively, these native white Southerners were called **scalawags**, a derogatory term for an idle or mischievous person derived from Scalloway, the name of a district on Scotland's Shetland Islands known for its scraggly livestock. The term was first applied in western New York before the Civil War to an idle person and then to a mischievous one. Although their opponents may have perceived them as a unified group, scalawags held a variety of views.

Planters and merchants opposed easy debt and credit arrangements and the use of their taxes to support programs other than railroads or port improvements. Yeomen farmers desperately needed the debt and credit legislation to retain their land. And even though they supported public schools and road building—which would require increased state revenues—they opposed higher taxes.

Northern transplants, or **carpetbaggers**, as their opponents called them, constituted a second group of southern Republicans. The term also had antebellum origins, referring to a suspicious stranger. Cartoonists depicted carpetbaggers as shoddily dressed and poorly groomed, their worldly possessions in a ratty cloth satchel, slinking into a town and swindling the locals before departing with their ill-gotten gains. The reality was far different from the caricature. Thousands of Northerners came south during and after the war. Many were Union soldiers who simply enjoyed the climate and perhaps married a local woman. Most were drawn by economic opportunity. Land was cheap and the price of cotton high. Although most carpetbaggers had supported the Republican party before they moved south, few became politically active until the cotton economy nosedived in 1866. Financial concerns were not all that motivated carpetbaggers to enter politics; some hoped to aid the freedmen.

Carpetbaggers never comprised more than 2 percent of any state's population. Most white Southerners viewed them as an alien presence, instruments of a hated occupying force. They provoked resentment because they seemed to prosper while most Southerners struggled in poverty. And they further estranged themselves from their neighbors by supporting and participating in the Republican state governments that most white people despised. In Alabama, local editors organized a boycott of northern-owned shops. "STARVE THEM OUT!" they wrote. "Don't put your foot in the doors of their shops, offices, and stores. Purchase from true men and patronize those of known Southern sympathies." Because many of them tended to support extending political and civil rights to black Southerners, carpetbaggers were also often at odds with their fellow white Republicans, the scalawags.

African Americans constituted the Republican party's largest southern constituency. In three states—South Carolina, Mississippi, and Louisiana—they also constituted the majority of eligible voters. They viewed the franchise as the key to civic equality and economic opportunity and demanded an active role in party and government affairs.

Black people began to take part in southern politics even before the end of the Civil War, especially in cities occupied by Union forces. In February 1865, black people in Norfolk, Virginia, gathered to demand a say in the new government that Union supporters were forming in that portion of the state. In April, they created the Colored Monitor Union club, modeled after Republican party organizations in northern cities, called **Union Leagues**. They demanded "the right of universal suffrage" for "all loyal men, without distinction of color." Black people in other southern cities held similar meetings, seeking inclusion in the democratic process in order to protect their freedom. As a member of the Alexandria, Virginia, black Union League argued in August 1865, "The only salvation for us . . . is in the *possession of the ballot.* Give us this, and we will protect ourselves."

White Southerners viewed these developments with alarm but could not at first counter them. Despite white threats, black Southerners thronged to Union League meetings in 1867, even forging interracial alliances in states such as North Carolina and Alabama. Focusing on political education and recruitment, the leagues successfully mobilized black voters. In 1867, more than 90 percent of eligible black voters across the South turned out for elections. Black women, even though they could not vote, also played a role. During the 1868 presidential campaign, for example, black maids and cooks in the South wore buttons touting the candidacy of Republican presidential nominee Ulysses S. Grant.

Black Southerners were not content just to vote; they also demanded political office. White Republican leaders in the South often took the black vote for granted. But on several occasions after 1867, black people threatened to run independent candidates, support rival Democrats, or simply stay home unless they were represented among Republican nominees. These demands brought them some success. The number of southern black congressmen in the U.S. House of Representatives increased from two in 1869 to seven in 1873, and more than six hundred African Americans, most of them former slaves from plantation counties, were elected to southern state legislatures between 1867 and 1877.

White fears that black officeholders would enact vengeful legislation proved unfounded. African Americans generally did not promote race-specific legislation. Rather, they supported measures such as debt relief and state funding for education that benefited all poor and working-class people. Like all politicians, however, black officials in southern cities sought to enact measures beneficial to their constituents. In Atlanta, for example, black officeholders had a sidewalk laid in front of a prominent black church and diverted a road scheduled to cut through a black neighborhood. In Richmond, black people

secured an ordinance forbidding the robbing of black graves to supply medical schools with corpses. And they succeeded in having a black police commissioner appointed in Jacksonville, Florida. Gains like these underscored the advantages of suffrage for the African-American community.

During the first few years of Congressional Reconstruction, Republican governments walked a tightrope, attempting to lure moderate Democrats and unaffiliated white voters into the party without slighting the black vote. They used the lure of patronage power and the attractive salaries that accompanied public office. In 1868, for example, Louisiana's Republican governor, Henry C. Warmoth, appointed white conservatives to state and local offices, which he divided equally between ex-Confederate veterans and black people, and repealed a constitutional provision disfranchising former Confederate officials.

Republicans also gained support by expanding the role of state government to a degree unprecedented in the South. Southern Republican administrations appealed to hard-pressed upland white constituents by prohibiting foreclosure and passing stay laws that allowed farm owners extra time to repay debts. They undertook building programs that benefited both black and white citizens, erecting hospitals, schools, and orphanages. Stepping further into social policy than most northern states at the time, Republican governments in the South expanded women's property rights, enacted legislation against child abuse, and required child support from fathers of mulatto children. In South Carolina, the Republican government provided medical care for the poor; in Alabama, it provided free legal aid for needy defendants.

Despite these impressive policies, southern Republicans were unable to hold their diverse constituency together. Although the party had some success among white yeoman farmers, the liberal use of patronage to attract white conservatives failed to gain it many new adherents. At the same time, it alienated the party's core supporters, who resented seeing their former enemies rewarded with lucrative offices.

The high costs of their activist policies further undermined the Republicans by forcing them to raise state taxes. Small property holders, already reeling from declining staple prices, found the taxes especially burdensome, despite liberal stay laws. Revenues nonetheless could not keep pace with expenditures. In Mississippi—where the Republican governor built a public school system for both black and white students, founded a black university, reorganized the state judiciary, built new courthouses and two state hospitals, and pushed through legislation giving black people equal access to public facilities—the state debt soared to $1.5 million between 1869 and 1873. This was in an era when state budgets rarely exceeded $1 million.

Unprecedented expenditures and the liberal use of patronage sometimes resulted in waste and corruption. Officials charged with selecting railroad routes, appointing lesser officials, and erecting public buildings were well positioned to benefit from their power. Their high salaries offended many in an otherwise impoverished region. Problems like these were not limited to the South. They were pervasive throughout the country in the 1860s and 1870s. The perception of dishonesty was nonetheless damaging to governments struggling to build legitimacy among a skeptical white electorate.

The excesses of some state governments, high taxes, contests over patronage, and conflicts over the relative roles of white and black party members opened rifts in Republican ranks. Patronage triggered intraparty warfare. Every office secured by a Democrat created a disappointed Republican. Class tensions erupted in the party as economic development policies, favored by former Whigs, sometimes superseded relief and social service legislation supported by small farmers. The failure of Alabama Republicans to de-

"The Shackle Broken by the Genius of Freedom" is the title of this 1874 lithograph of South Carolina legislator Robert B. Elliott addressing his fellow lawmakers. Born in Boston, educated in England, Elliott served with distinction in Congress and at the state level during Reconstruction.

liver on promises of debt relief and land redistribution eroded the significant support the party had enjoyed among upcountry white voters. There were differences among black voters too. In the Lower South, divisions that had developed in the prewar era between urban, lighter-skinned free black people and darker, rural slaves persisted into the Reconstruction era. In many southern states, black clergy, because of their independence from white support and their important spiritual and educational role, became leaders. But most preached salvation in the next world rather than equality in this one, conceding more to white people than their rank-and-file constituents.

Counter-Reconstruction, 1870–1874

Republicans might have survived battles over patronage, differences over policy, and the resentment provoked by extravagant expenditures and high taxes. But they could not overcome racism. Racism killed Republican rule in the South because it deepened divisions within the party, encouraged white violence, and eroded support in the North. Southern Democrats discovered that they could use race baiting and racial violence to create solidarity among white people that overrode their economic and class differences. Unity translated into election victories.

Northerners responded to the persistent violence in the South not with outrage but with a growing sense of tedium. They came to accept the arguments of white Southerners that it was folly to allow black people to vote and hold office. Racism became respectable. Noted intellectuals and journalists espoused "scientific" theories that claimed to demonstrate the natural superiority of white people over black people. These theories influenced the **Liberal Republicans**, followers of a new political movement that splintered the Republican party, further weakening its will to pursue Reconstruction policy.

By 1874, Americans were concerned with an array of domestic problems that overshadowed Reconstruction. A serious economic depression left them more preoccupied with survival than racial justice. Corruption convinced many that politics was part of the nation's problems, not a solution to them. With the rest of the nation thus distracted and weary, white Southerners reclaimed control of the South.

The Uses of Violence

Racial violence preceded Republican rule. As African Americans moved about, attempted to vote, haggled over labor contracts, and carried arms as part of occupying Union forces, they tested the patience of white Southerners. In a racial world turned upside down from the white perspective, any black assertion of equality seemed threatening.

Cities, where black and white people competed for jobs and where black political influence was most visible, became flashpoints for interracial violence. In May 1866, the collision of two wagons in Memphis, one driven by a white carter, the other by a black carter, touched off three days of white attacks on black people and black neighborhoods. Forty-six black people and two white people died in the fray, and five black women were raped. The white mob destroyed black churches, schools, and homes.

White paramilitary groups flourished in the South during the Reconstruction era and were responsible for much of the violence directed against African Americans. Probably the best known of these groups was the **Ku Klux Klan**. Founded in Tennessee by six Confederate veterans in 1866, the Klan was initially a social club. Prominent ex-Confederates such as General John B. Gordon and General Nathan Bedford Forrest, allegedly the first Grand Wizard of the Klan, saw the political potential of the new organization. Within a year, the Klan had spread throughout the South. In 1867, when black people entered politics in large numbers, the Klan unleashed a wave of terror against them. Klan night riders in ghostlike disguises intimidated black communities. The Klan directed much of its violence toward subverting the electoral process. One historian has estimated that roughly 10 percent of all black delegates to the 1867 state constitutional conventions in the South became victims of political violence during the next decade.

Not all Klan attacks had political objectives. Klansmen struck against anyone, black or white, whom they believed had violated racial boundaries. A Georgia Klansman murdered a freedman because he could read and write. Klansmen in Florence, South Carolina, killed a black man who rented a plantation "because such a thing ought not to be." And in 1868, Klansmen murdered three southern white Republican Georgia state legislators. Membership in the Klan crossed class lines. Race became an issue on which white people, regardless of differing economic interests, could agree.

By 1868, white paramilitary organizations permeated the South. Violence was particularly severe in election years in Louisiana, which had a large and active black electorate. Before the presidential election of 1868, for example, white Louisianans killed at least seven hundred Republicans, including black leader William R. Meadows, who was dragged from his home and shot and beheaded in front of his family. As the election neared, white mobs roamed New Orleans, attacking black people and breaking up Republican rallies. The violence cut the Republican vote in the state by 50 percent from the previous spring.

The most serious example of political violence in Louisiana, if not in the entire South, occurred in Colfax in 1873 when a white Democratic mob attempted to wrest control of local government from Republicans. For three weeks, black defenders held the town against the white onslaught. When the white mob finally broke through, they massacred the remaining black defenders, including those who had surrendered and laid down their weapons.

Racial violence and the combative reaction it provoked both among black people and Republican administrations energized white voters. Democrats regained power in North Carolina, for example, after the state's Republican governor enraged white voters by calling out the militia to counter white violence during the election of 1870. That same year, the Republican regime in Georgia fell as well.

Some Republican governments countered the violence successfully for a time. Republican governor Edmund J. Davis of Texas, for example, organized a special force of two hundred state policemen to round up Klan night riders. Between 1870 and 1872, Davis's force arrested six thousand and broke the Klan in Texas. Arkansas governor Powell Clayton launched an equally successful campaign against the Klan in 1869. But other governors hesitated to enforce laws directed at the Klan, fearing that to do so would further alienate white people.

The federal government responded with a variety of legislation. One example was the Fifteenth Amendment, ratified in 1869, which guaranteed the right to vote. Another was the Enforcement Act of 1870, which authorized the federal government to appoint supervisors in states that failed to protect voting rights. When violence and intimidation persisted, Congress followed with a second, more sweeping measure, the Ku Klux Klan Act of 1871. This law permitted federal authorities, with military assistance, if necessary, to arrest and prosecute members of groups that denied a citizen's civil rights if state authorities failed to do so. The Klan Act was not successful in curbing racial violence, as the Colfax Massacre in 1873 made vividly clear. But with it, Congress, by claiming the right to override state authority to bring individuals to justice, established a new precedent in federal–state relations.

The Failure of Northern Will

The success of political violence after 1871 reflected less the inadequacy of congressional legislation than the failure of will on the part of northern Republicans to follow through on commitments to southern

Republican administrations. The erosion of northern support for Congressional Reconstruction began as early as the presidential election of 1868. Republican candidate Ulysses S. Grant's campaign theme that year was "Let Us Have Peace," a reference to the political turmoil in the South.

The commitment to voting rights for black Southerners, widespread among Republicans in 1865 and affirmed in the Fifteenth Amendment, faded as well. American politics in the 1870s seemed increasingly corrupt and irresponsible. Scandal abounded. Democratic boss William M. Tweed and his associates transformed **Tammany Hall**, a Democratic Club, into a full-fledged political machine that robbed New York City of an astounding $100 million. Federal officials allowed private individuals to manipulate the stock market for spectacular gains. Several members of Congress and President Grant's vice president exchanged government favors for railroad stock. And the president's secretary of war was caught selling contracts to firms supplying goods to Indians.

A growing number of Americans attributed the debacle to the expansion of the right to vote. Voting was a privilege to be earned, they maintained, not a basic right of citizenship. And black people, according to some Republicans, had not earned that right.

The racist assumption behind this view found growing support among intellectuals. Racism gained an aura of scientific respectability in the late nineteenth century. Science was held in high esteem at the time, helping assure public acceptance of the putatively scientific views of the racial theorists. According to those views, some peoples are inherently inferior to others, a natural state of affairs that no government interference can change.

According to white racial theorists, it was folly to grant suffrage to African Americans because an inferior race (black) could not hold power over a superior race (white). Black people, because of their race, could not understand the basic principles of democracy. Thus Missouri's Republican senator Carl Schurz looked on with equanimity as white terror toppled Republican regimes in the South in 1872. He urged his colleagues to let affairs run their course and admit that southern black voters and officeholders "were ignorant and inexperienced; that the public business was an unknown world to them, and that in spite of the best intentions they were easily misled." Allowing an unfit people to vote resulted in a "more disastrous process than rebellion," intoned *The Nation*, a leading Republican journal, in 1872. The perpetual turmoil in the South, the extravagances of some Republican southern administrations, and their persistent inability to attract sufficient numbers of white voters all reinforced the view that these governments were unnatural.

Black people were not the only targets of racial theory. Immigrants were also said to derive from inferior races. Their growing numbers coincided with the flourishing of corrupt political machines in northern cities, fueling Republican reservations about an unrestricted franchise. Like black people, immigrants were held to be incapable of understanding the American electoral process. As one Republican leader observed, "What is bad

Two Alabama Klansmen are shown here in 1868 at the height of the Ku Klux Klan's campaign of political terror. Although Congress outlawed the Klan, political terrorist groups associated with the Democratic party continued the Klan's violent legacy in the 1870s and succeeded in reestablishing white Democratic party rule in the South.

among ignorant foreigners in New York will not be good among ignorant natives in South Carolina."

Concerns about the quality of the electorate reflected the rising stakes of public office in post–Civil War America. The urban industrial economy boomed in the five years after the war. Engineers flung railroads across the continent. Steam propelled factories to unprecedented levels of productivity and ships to new speed records. Discoveries of rich natural resources such as oil and iron presaged a new age of industrial might. Republicans promoted and benefited from the boom, and it influenced their priorities. Railroad, mining, and lumber lobbyists crowded Washington and state capitals begging for financial and land subsidies and favorable legislation. In an era before conflict-of-interest laws, leading Republicans sat on the boards of railroads, land development companies, and industrial corporations. While the federal government denied land to the freedman, it doled out millions of acres to corporations. Issues of fiscal responsibility, tariffs, and hard money replaced freedom and reunion, moving the Republican party, as *The Nation* explained in 1874, "out of the region of the Civil War."

Not all Republicans approved the party's promotion of economic development. Some questioned the prudence of government intervention in the "natural" operation of the economy. The emerging scandals of the Grant administration led to calls for reform. Republican governments, North and South, were condemned for their lavish spending and high taxes.

The reform movement attracted an assortment of groups concerned about the size, activism, and expense of government. Business leaders decried the ability of wealthy lobbyists to influence economic decisions. An influential group of intellectuals and opinion makers lamented the inability of politicians to understand "natural" laws. Some reformers expressed alarm at the federal government's increasing intervention in the affairs of the states since the Civil War. And some Republicans joined the reform movement out of fear that Democrats would capitalize on the turmoil in the South and the political scandals in the North to reap huge electoral victories in 1872.

Liberal Republicans and the Election of 1872

Liberal Republicans put forward an array of suggestions to improve government and save the Republican party. They advocated civil service reform to reduce reliance on patronage and the abuses that accompanied office seeking. To limit government and reduce artificial economic stimuli, the reformers called for tariff reduction and an end to federal land grants to railroads. For the South, they recommended a general amnesty for white people and a return to "local self-government" by men of "property and enterprise."

When the Liberals failed to convince other Republicans to adopt their program, they broke with the party. Taking advantage of this split, the Democrats forged an alliance with the Liberals. Together, they nominated journalist Horace Greeley to challenge Ulysses S. Grant for the presidency in the election of 1872. Grant won resoundingly, helped by high turnout among black voters in the South. He carried all southern states except Georgia, Tennessee, and Texas. Elsewhere, Republicans again used the tactic of waving the bloody shirt to good effect. It was the Republicans, they declared, who had saved the Union, the Democrats who had almost destroyed it. Greeley had been a staunch Republican during the Civil War and had spent most of his career attacking Democrats. Republicans used his own words against him. Many Democratic voters stayed home.

The election suggested that the excesses of the Grant administration had not yet exceeded public tolerance and that the Republican experiment in the South retained some public support. But Greeley had helped the Republicans by running an inept campaign. Within a year, an economic depression, continued violence in the South, and the persistent corruption of the Grant administration would turn public opinion against the Republicans. With this shift, support for Reconstruction and black rights would also fade.

Redemption, 1874–1877

For southern Democrats, the Republican victory in 1872 underscored the importance of turning out larger numbers of white voters and restricting the black vote. They accomplished these goals over the next four years with a surge in political violence. Southern Democrats operated in the secure knowledge that federal authorities would not intervene against them. Preoccupied with corruption and economic crisis and increasingly indifferent, if not hostile, to African-American aspirations, most Americans looked the other way. The elections of 1876—on the local, state, and national levels—affirmed the triumph of white Southerners. Reconstruction did not end; it was overthrown.

In a religious metaphor that matched their view of the Civil War as a lost crusade, southern Democrats called their victory "Redemption" and depicted themselves as **Redeemers**, holy warriors who had saved the South from the hell of black Republican rule. Generations of American boys and girls would learn this interpretation of the Reconstruction era, and it would affect race relations for nearly a century.

The Democrats' Violent Resurgence

The violence between 1874 and 1876 differed in several respects from earlier attempts to restore white government by force. Attackers operated more openly and more closely identified themselves with the Democratic party. Mounted, gray-clad ex-Confederate soldiers flanked Democratic candidates at campaign rallies and "visited" black neighborhoods afterward to discourage black people from voting. With black people intimidated and white people already prepared to vote, election days were typically quiet.

Democrats swept to victory across the South in the 1874 elections. "A perfect reign of terror" redeemed Alabama for the Democrats. The successful appeal to white supremacy inspired a massive white turnout to unseat Republicans in Virginia, Florida (legislature only), and Arkansas. Texas had fallen to the Democrats in 1873. Only South Carolina, Mississippi, and Louisiana—states with large black populations—survived the debacle. But the relentless tide of terror would soon overwhelm them as well.

In Louisiana, a group of elite Democrats in New Orleans organized a military organization known as the White League in 1874 to challenge the state's Republican government. In September 1874, more than eight thousand White Leaguers staged a coup to overthrow the Republican government of New Orleans. The city's police, commanded by former Confederate general James Longstreet, and the intervention of nearby federal troops saved the government and prevented a wholesale slaughter. But the incident only inspired White Leaguers to redouble their efforts.

Few Reconstruction politicians endured greater trials than Louisiana Republican Marshall Harvey Twitchell. Born in Vermont, he led black troops during the Civil War and settled in Louisiana after the war. He married the daughter of a prominent plantation owner and launched a successful business career. But with the advent of Congressional Reconstruction, Twitchell entered politics and built a powerful Republican organization in Red River Parish. The hospitable reception he had until then enjoyed in his adopted state quickly evaporated. During the 1874 election campaign, White Leaguers murdered his brother and two brothers-in-law. Two years later, White Leaguers shot him six times in an assassination attempt. Although he lost both arms, he survived. He left Louisiana in 1877, never to return.

The Weak Federal Response

Unrest like that in Louisiana also plagued Mississippi and South Carolina. When South Carolina governor Daniel H. Chamberlain could no longer contain the violence in his state in 1876, he asked the president for help. Grant acknowledged the gravity of Chamberlain's situation but would offer him only the lame hope that South Carolinians would exercise "better judgment and cooperation" and assist the governor in bringing offenders to justice "without aid from the federal Government."

Congress responded to the violence with the **Civil Rights Act of 1875**. Introduced by Charles Sumner, the bill went through several variations. Congress finally passed a watered-down version after Sumner's death. The act prohibited discrimination against black people in public accommodations such as theaters, parks, and trains and guaranteed freedmen's rights to serve on juries. It had no provision for voting rights, which Congress presumed the Fifteenth Amendment protected. The only way to enforce the law was for individuals to bring grievances related to it before federal courts in the South.

When black people tested the law by trying to make free use of public accommodations, they were almost always turned away. Some filed suit, with disappointing results. A Texas judge fined a Galveston theater $500 for refusing to allow black people to sit wherever they wanted, but most judges either interpreted the law narrowly or declared it unconstitutional. In 1883, the U.S. Supreme Court concurred and overturned the act, declaring that only the states, not Congress, could redress "a private wrong, or a crime of the individual."

As this Thomas Nast cartoon makes clear, the paramilitary violence against black Southerners in the early 1870s threatened not only the voting rights of freedmen, but their dreams of education, prosperity, and family life as well. In this context, the slogan, "The Union As It Was" is highly ironic.

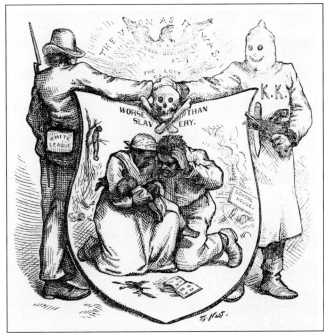

The Election of 1876 and the Compromise of 1877

Reconstruction officially ended with the presidential election of 1876 in which Democrat Samuel J. Tilden ran against Republican Rutherford B. Hayes. Republicans again waved the bloody shirt, touting their role in preserving the Union during the Civil War, but they ignored Reconstruction. The Democrats hoped that their resurgent strength in the South and a respectable showing in the North would bring them the White House. The scandals of the Grant administration, northern weariness with southern Republican governments, and the persisting economic depression worked in the Democrats' favor.

When the ballots were counted, it appeared that Tilden, a conservative New Yorker respectable enough for northern voters and Democratic enough for white southerners, had won. But despite a majority in the popular vote, disputed returns in three southern states left him with only 184 of the 185 electoral votes needed to win (see Map 18-2). The three states—Florida, South Carolina, and Louisiana—were the last in the South still to have Republican administrations.

Both camps maneuvered intensively in the months following the election to claim the disputed votes. Congress appointed a fifteen-member commission to settle the issue. Because the Republicans controlled Congress, they held a one-vote majority on the commission.

Southern Democrats wanted Tilden to win, but they wanted control of their states more. They were willing to deal. As one South Carolina newspaper editorialized in February 1877, "It matters little to us who rules in Washington, if South Carolina is allowed to have [Democratic governor Wade] Hampton and Home Rule." Hayes intended to remove federal support from the remaining southern Republican governments anyway. It thus cost him nothing to promise to do so in exchange for the contested electoral votes. Republicans also made vague promises to invest in the southern economy and support a southern transcontinental railroad, but these were secondary. What the South wanted most was to be left alone, and that is what it got. The so-called **Compromise of 1877** installed Hayes in the White House and gave Democrats control of all state governments in the South. Congress never carried through on the economic promises, and southern Democrats never pressed them to.

Southern Democrats emerged the major winners from the Compromise of 1877. President Hayes and his successors into the next century left the South alone. In practical terms, the Compromise signaled the revocation of civil rights and voting rights for black Southerners. The Fourteenth and Fifteenth Amendments would be dead letters in the South until well into the twentieth century. On the two great issues confronting the nation at the end of the Civil War, reunion and freedom, the white South had won. It reentered the Union largely on its own terms with the freedom to pursue a racial agenda consistent with its political, economic, and social interests.

The Memory of Reconstruction

Southern Democrats used the memory of Reconstruction to help maintain themselves in power. The Civil War became the glorious Lost Cause, Reconstruction the story of the Redemption against insurmountable odds from a purgatory of black rule and federal oppression. Whenever southern Democrats felt threatened over the next century, they reminded their white constituents of the sacrifices and heroism of war, the "horrors of Reconstruction," the menace of black rule, and the cruelty of Yankee occupiers. The southern view of

Map 18-2   *The Election of 1876*

The Democrat Samuel J. Tilden won a majority of the popular vote but eventually fell short of an electoral vote majority when the contested electoral votes of Florida, Louisiana, and South Carolina went to his Republican opponent, Rutherford B. Hayes. The map also indicates the Republicans' failure to build a base in the South after more than a decade of Reconstruction.

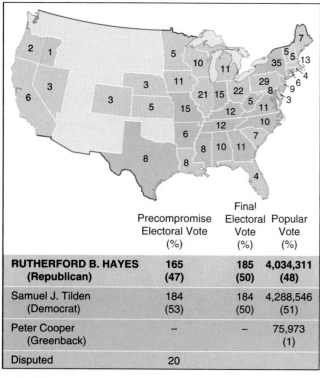

	Precompromise Electoral Vote (%)	Final Electoral Vote (%)	Popular Vote (%)
RUTHERFORD B. HAYES (Republican)	**165 (47)**	**185 (50)**	**4,034,311 (48)**
Samuel J. Tilden (Democrat)	184 (53)	184 (50)	4,288,546 (51)
Peter Cooper (Greenback)	–	–	75,973 (1)
Disputed	20		

Reconstruction permeated textbooks, films, and standard accounts of the period. By the 1920s, if not earlier, most Americans believed that the policies of Reconstruction had been misguided and had brought great suffering to the white South. The widespread acceptance of this view allowed the South to maintain its system of racial segregation and exclusion without interference from the federal government.

Not all memories of Reconstruction conformed to this thesis. In 1913, John R. Lynch, a former black Republican congressman from Mississippi, published *The Facts of Reconstruction* to "present the other side." He hoped his book would "bring to public notice those things that were commendable and meritorious, to prevent the publication of which seems to have been the primary purpose of nearly all who have thus far written upon that important subject." But most Americans ignored his book. Two decades later, a more forceful defense, W. E. B. Du Bois's *Black Reconstruction* (1935), met a similar fate. An angry Du Bois attacked the prevailing view of Reconstruction as "one of the most stupendous efforts the world ever saw to discredit human beings, an effort involving universities, history, science, social life and religion."

The Failure of Reconstruction

Most black and white people in 1877 would have agreed on one point: Reconstruction had failed. As Republican governments and black voters succumbed to the southern white reign of terror in the early 1870s, the *Atlanta Constitution* chided black people for being so presumptuous as to want to participate in the democratic process. Politics, the *Constitution* intoned, "was not intended . . . for the blacks, but for the whites. . . . This government is still a white man's government, and will remain forever such. The superior intelligence of the white race . . . will for all time secure political ascendancy." The *Constitution* excused the freedman for his delusion, blaming the "infamous carpetbagger and the radical [Republican] party."

If the demise of Reconstruction elicited a sigh of relief from most white Americans, black Southerners greeted it with frustration. Their dreams of land ownership faded as a new labor system relegated them to a lowly position in southern agriculture. Redemption reversed their economic and political gains and deprived them of most of the civil rights they had enjoyed under Congressional Reconstruction. Although they continued to vote into the 1890s, they had by 1877 lost most of the voting strength and political offices they held. Rather than becoming part of southern society, they were increasingly set apart from it, valued only for their labor.

Still, the former slaves were better off in 1877 than in 1865. They were free, however limited their freedom. Some owned land; some held jobs in cities. They raised their families in relative peace and experienced the spiritual joys of a full religious life. They socialized freely with relatives and friends, and they moved about. But by 1877, the "golden moment"—an unprecedented opportunity for the nation to live up to its ideals by extending equal rights to all its citizens, black and white alike—had passed.

Sharecropping

When they lost political power, black Southerners also lost economic independence. As the Freedmen's Bureau retreated from supervising farm labor contracts and opportunities for black people to possess their own land dried up, the bargaining power of black farm laborers decreased, and the power of white landlords increased. The faltering southern economy contributed to the loss of labor autonomy as well. Cash wages were at first high enough and rental agreements between tenant farmers and landlords at first fair enough for black farmers to be able to buy their own tools and perhaps a few extra acres. But the dramatic decline of cotton prices soon after the war reduced cash surpluses in an already cash-poor region. Unable now to purchase their own animals or tools and lacking cash to buy food and other necessities at local stores, freedmen were forced to barter their crops for credit.

The upshot was that by the late 1870s, most former slaves in the rural South had been drawn into a subservient position in a new labor system called **sharecropping** (see Maps 18-3 and 18-4). The premise of this system was relatively simple: The landlord furnished the sharecroppers a house, a plot of land to work, seed, some farm animals, and farm implements and advanced them credit at a store the landlord typically owned. In exchange, the sharecroppers promised the landlord a share of their crop, usually one-half. The croppers kept the proceeds from the sale of the other half to pay off their debts at the store and save or spend as they and their families saw fit. In theory, a sharecropper could save enough to secure economic independence.

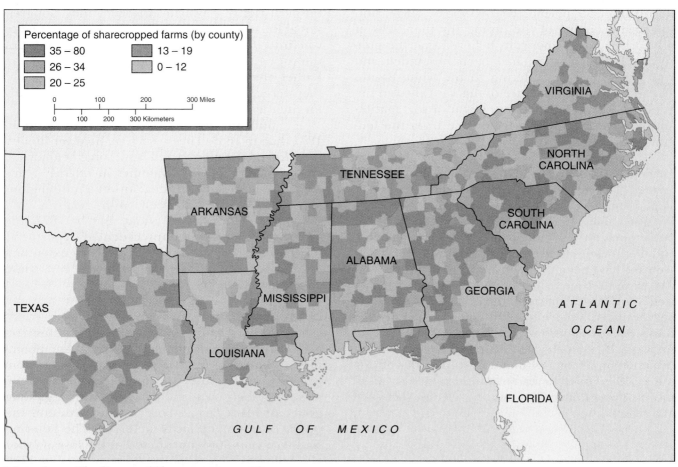

Map 18-3   *The Extent of Sharecropping, 1880*
Virtually unknown in 1865, sharecropping took hold in the South during the 1870s. Although both black and white farmers worked as sharecroppers, the labor system became most characteristic for black farmers.

But white landlords perceived black independence as both contradictory and subversive. With landlords holding the accounts at the store, black sharecroppers found that the proceeds from their share of the crop never left them very far ahead. In exchange for extending credit to sharecroppers, store owners felt justified in requiring collateral, but sharecroppers had no assets other than the cotton they grew. So southern states passed **crop lien laws**, which gave the store owner the right to the next year's crop in exchange for this year's credit. If the following year's harvest couldn't pay off the debt, the sharecropper sank deeper into dependence. Some found themselves in perpetual debt and worked as virtual slaves. They could not simply abandon their debts and go to another farm because the new landlord would check their references. Those found to have jumped their debts could end up on a prison chain gang. Not all white landlords cheated their tenants, but given the sharecroppers' innocence regarding accounting methods and crop pric-

ing, the temptation to do so was great. Thus weak cotton prices conspired with white chicanery to keep black people economically dependent.

Sharecropping represented a significant step down from tenancy. Tenants owned their own draft animals, farm implements, and seed. Once they negotiated with a land owner for a fixed rent, they kept whatever profits they earned. Eventually, they could hope to purchase some land and move into the landlord class themselves. But the continued low price of cotton made such mobility less likely during the Reconstruction era. Movement in the opposite direction was more common, especially for white people who owned small farms and could not eke out an income to at least pay taxes on loans. Landowning farmers and their families slid increasingly into tenancy and sharecropping.

Historians have often depicted the sharecropping system as a compromise between white landlord and black laborer. But compromise implies a give-and-take between relatively equal negotiators. As northern and federal support for

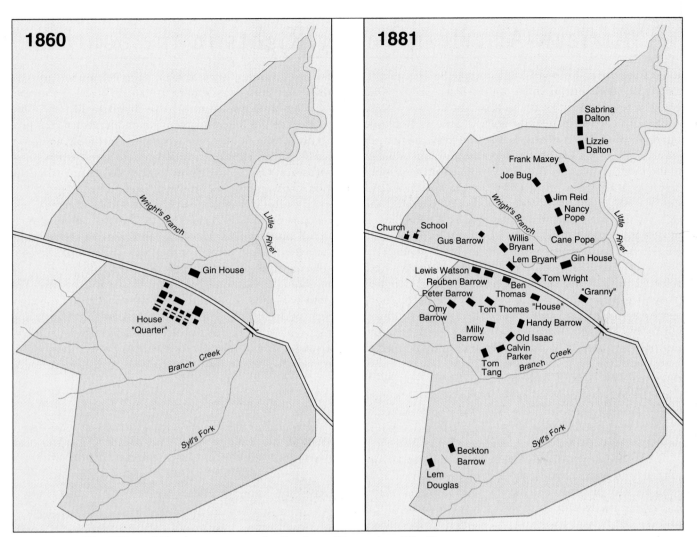

Map 18-4 *The Effect of Sharecropping on the Southern Plantation: The Barrow Plantation, Oglethorpe County, Georgia*
Sharecropping changed the landscape of the plantation South, cutting large estates into small holdings worked by sharecroppers and tenants.

Reconstruction waned after 1870 and southern Democrats regained political control, white power over black labor increased. Black people had no recourse to federal and state authorities or, increasingly, to the polls as a white reign of terror stripped them of their political rights. The prophecy of one Alabama planter in 1866 had come to pass: "The nigger is going to be made a serf, as sure as you live. It won't need any law for that. Planters will have an understanding among themselves: 'You won't hire my niggers, and I won't hire yours,' then what's left for them? They're attached to the soil, and we're as much their masters as ever."

Northern Republicans offered little opposition to southern labor practices after 1870. A resurgence of labor militancy and the emergence of a large industrial work force caused them to rethink the ideology of free labor they had espoused during the Civil War. They had trouble reconciling their notions of the dignity of independent labor with the aggressive, hostile, and increasingly foreign-born workers who now toiled in northern factories. The gap between worker and entrepreneur had widened between 1860 and 1870. Northern factory owners were now no more interested in encouraging upward mobility for their workers than southern landlords. Instead, they used the courts and state and local governments to keep workers in their place.

The only difference between northern and southern employers' outlook on labor was that Southerners exercised more control over their workers. What had been a triangular debate—among white Northerners, white Southerners, and

African-American Voting Rights in the South

Right from the end of the Civil War, white Southerners resisted African-American voting rights. Black people, with equal determination, used the franchise to assert their equal right to participate in the political process. Black voting rights proved so contentious that Congress sought to secure them with the Fourteenth and Fifteenth Amendments to the U.S. Constitution. But U.S. Supreme Court decisions in *United States* v. *Cruikshank* (1876) and in the *Civil Rights Cases* (1883) undermined federal authority to protect the rights of freedmen, including voting rights. A combination of violence, intimidation, and legislation effectively disfranchised black Southerners by the early twentieth century.

During the 1960s, a period some historians have referred to as the Second Reconstruction, Congress passed legislation designed to override state prohibitions and earlier court decisions limiting African-American voting rights. The key measure, the 1965 Voting Rights Act, not only guaranteed black Southerners (and later, other minorities) the right to register and vote but protected them from procedural subterfuges, many of which dated from the first Reconstruction era, that would dilute their votes. These protections proved necessary because of the extreme racial polarization of Southern elections: White people rarely voted for black candidates.

To ensure African-American candidates an opportunity to win elections, the federal government after 1965 insisted that states and localities establish procedures to increase the likelihood of such a result. As part of this process, the federal government also monitored state redistricting for Congressional elections, which occurs every decade in response to population shifts recorded in the national census.

By the early 1990s, states were being directed to draw districts with majority-black voting populations to ensure African-American representation in the Congress and state legislatures. The federal government cited the South's history of racial discrimination and racially polarized voting to justify these districts. But white Southerners challenged such claims, as they had more than a century earlier, and their challenges proved successful in federal court.

In 1993, the U.S. Supreme Court issued a decision in a North Carolina redistricting case, *Shaw* v. *Reno*, that struck down a majority-black Congressional district in that state. Subsequent decisions in other southern districts produced similar rulings. The general principle followed by the Court has been that if race is a key justification for drawing these districts, then they violate the Fourteenth Amendment, which, according to the Court majority, demands color-blind electoral procedures. But, as the late Supreme Court Justice William Brennan noted, "to read the Fourteenth Amendment to state an abstract principle of color-blindness is itself to be blind to history." The framers of the Reconstruction Amendments had the protection of the rights of the freedmen (including and especially voting rights) in mind when they wrote those measures. One voting rights expert has charged that the Court rulings have ushered in a "Second Redemption."

But it is also true that in 1998 black Congressional incumbents in Georgia and North Carolina, running in redrawn districts in which black voters were in the minority (and less than 40 percent at that) won reelection. These results may indicate that racially polarized voting may be diminishing in the South, although they may also reflect the power of incumbency and the weak campaigns of the challengers. In any case, the issue of African-American voting rights in the South and the degree to which the federal government may or may not intercede to protect those rights remains as much at issue as it was more than a century ago.

Casting a ballot. Black voters in Richmond vote on a state constitutional convention in 1867. A key objective of Congressional Reconstruction was to secure the voting rights of freedmen.

freedmen—had become a lopsided discourse divided along racial rather than sectional lines. In 1876, after a political campaign marked by brazen violence against Republican voters, Wade Hampton, ex-Confederate general and newly elected governor of South Carolina, provided an appropriate summary of labor perspectives in both regions. "The real North," he explained, "never liked Negroes and was not willing to attack slavery. Now that it is gone they are glad and so are we; but they no more than we want to make Negroes their equals. They want good, cheap, profitable labor and so do we."

Modest Gains and Future Victories

Black Southerners experienced some advances in the decade after the Civil War, but these owed little to Reconstruction. Black families functioned as economic and psychological buffers against unemployment and prejudice. Black churches played crucial roles in their communities. Self-help and labor organizations offered mutual friendship and financial assistance. All of these institutions existed in the slavery era, although on a smaller scale. And some of them, such as black labor groups, schools, and social welfare associations, endured because comparable white institutions excluded black people.

Black people also scored some modest economic successes during the Reconstruction era, mainly from their own pluck. In the Lower South, black per capita income increased 46 percent between 1857 and 1879, compared with a 35 percent decline in white per capita income. Sharecropping, oppressive as it was, represented an advance over forced and gang labor. Collectively, black people owned more than $68 million worth of property in 1870, a 240 percent increase over 1860, but the average worth of each was only $408. Those who had been free before the war sometimes fared worse after it, especially property-owning free black people in the Lower South. Black city dwellers, especially in the Upper South, fared somewhat better. The overwhelming majority of black people, however, were landless agricultural laborers eking out a meager income that merchants and landlords often snatched to cover debts.

The Fourteenth and Fifteenth Amendments to the Constitution are among the few bright spots in Reconstruction's otherwise dismal legacy. The Fourteenth Amendment guaranteed former slaves equality before the law; the Fifteenth Amendment protected their right to vote. Both amendments elevated the federal government over the states by protecting freedmen from state attempts to deny them their rights. But the benefits of these two landmark amendments did not accrue to African Americans until well into the twentieth century. White South-erners effectively nullified the Reconstruction amendments, and the U.S. Supreme Court virtually interpreted them, and other Reconstruction legislation, out of existence.

In the ***Slaughterhouse* cases** (1873), the Supreme Court contradicted the intent of the Fourteenth Amendment by decreeing that most citizenship rights remained under state, not federal, control. In ***United States* v. *Cruikshank*** (1876), the Court overturned the convictions of some of those responsible for the Colfax Massacre, ruling that the Enforcement Act applied only to violations of black rights by states, not individuals. Within the next two decades, the Supreme Court would uphold the legality of racial segregation and black disfranchisement, in effect declaring that the Fourteenth and Fifteenth Amendments did not apply to African Americans. The Civil War had killed secession forever, but states' rights enjoyed a remarkable revival.

As historian John Hope Franklin accurately concluded, Reconstruction "had no significant or permanent effect on the status of the black in American life. . . . [Black people] made no meaningful steps toward economic independence or even stability."

Conclusion

Formerly enslaved black Southerners had entered freedom with many hopes, among the most prominent of which was to be let alone. White Southerners, after four bloody years of unwanted attention from the federal government, also longed to be left alone. But they did not include their ex-slaves as equals in their vision of solitude. Northerners, too, began to seek escape from the issues and consequences of the war, eventually abandoning their commitment to secure civil and voting rights for black Southerners.

White Southerners robbed black Southerners of their gains and sought to reduce them again to servitude and dependence, if not to slavery. But in the processs, the majority of white Southerners lost as well. Yeoman farmers missed an opportunity to break cleanly from the Old South and establish a more equitable society. Instead, they allowed the old elites to regain power and gradually ignore their needs. They preserved the social benefit of a white skin at the cost of almost everything else. Many lost their farms and sank into tenancy, leasing land from others. Fewer had a voice in state legislatures or Congress. A new South, rid of slavery and sectional antagonism, had indeed emerged, redeemed, regenerated, and disenthralled. But the old South lingered on in the new like Spanish moss on live oaks.

As federal troops left the South to be redeployed restraining striking workers in the North and suppressing Native Americans on the Great Plains, an era of possibility for American society ended, and a new era began. "The southern question is dead," a Charleston newspaper proclaimed in 1877. "The question of labor and capital, work and wages" had moved to the forefront. The chance to redeem the sacrifice of a bloody civil war with a society that fulfilled the promise of the Declaration of Independence and the Constitution for all citizens slipped away. It would take a new generation of African Americans a long century later to revive it.

Review Questions

1. Given the devastation in the South after the Civil War and the loss of property, lives, and hope among many white Southerners, do you think they should they have supported black aspirations for civil rights, land, and suffrage? How differently would things have turned out if they had?

2. Some historians have placed a great deal of the blame for Reconstruction's failures on the backs of southern Republicans. Is this fair? Explain your response.

3. Black people did achieve some notable gains during Reconstruction, despite its overall failure. What were those gains?

Recommended Reading

W. E. B. Du Bois, *Black Reconstruction in America, 1860–1880* (1935). An early and long-ignored study by the foremost black scholar of his time that refuted the contemporary historical wisdom that Reconstruction was a horror visited on the South by an overbearing federal government and ignorant, willful black people.

Eric Foner, *Reconstruction: America's Unfinished Revolution, 1863-1877* (1988). The standard work on Reconstruction, notable for its emphasis on the experience and aspirations of black Southerners.

Gaines M. Foster, *Ghosts of the Confederacy: Defeat, the Lost Cause, and the Emergence of the New South, 1865 to 1913* (1987). A fine picture of how the memory of the Civil War affected white Southerners and their views on Reconstruction policy.

Leon Litwack, *Been in the Storm So Long: The Aftermath of Slavery* (1979). An eloquent account of the early days of freedom from the freedmen's perspective, up to 1867.

Albion W. Tourgée, *A Fool's Errand* (1879). A novel written by an Ohioan who migrated to North Carolina in 1865 to take advantage of economic opportunities in the state and eventually became involved in politics, with his frustrations with Reconstruction and his keen analysis of racism as important themes.

Additional Sources

White Southerners and the Ghosts of the Confederacy

Dan T. Carter, *When the War Was Over: The Failure of Self-Reconstruction in the South, 1865–1867* (1985).

LaWanda Cox and John Cox, *Politics, Principle, and Prejudice, 1865–1866* (1963).

Black Aspirations beyond Freedom

Ira Berlin et al., *Freedom: A Documentary History of Emancipation, 1861–1867. The Wartime Genesis of Free Labor: The Lower South* (1990).

John Blassingame, *Black New Orleans, 1860–1880* (1973).

Carol R. Bleser, *The Promised Land: The History of the South Carolina Land Commission* (1963).

Edmund L. Drago, *Black Politicians and Reconstruction in Georgia* (1982).

Michael W. Fitzgerald, *The Union League Movement in the Deep South: Politics and Agricultural Change during Reconstruction* (1989).

Herbert G. Gutman, *The Black Family in Slavery and Freedom, 1750–1925* (1976).

Gerald Jaynes, *Branches without Roots: The Genesis of the Black Working Class in the American South, 1862–1882* (1986).

Jacqueline Jones, *Labor of Love, Labor of Sorrow: Black Women, Work, and the Family from Slavery to the Present* (1985).

Peter Kolchin, *First Freedom: The Responses of Alabama's Blacks to Emancipation and Reconstruction* (1972).

Howard N. Rabinowitz, *Race Relations in the Urban South, 1865–1890* (1978).

Howard N. Rabinowitz, ed. *Southern Black Leaders of the Reconstruction Era* (1982).

Emma Lou Thornbrough, ed., *Black Reconstructionists* (1972).

Joel Williamson, *After Slavery: The Negro in South Carolina during Reconstruction, 1861–1877* (1965).

Federal Reconstruction, 1865–1870

Richard Abbott, *The Republican Party and the South, 1855–1877* (1986).

Herman Belz, *A New Birth of Freedom: The Republican Party and Freedmen's Rights, 1861–1866* (1976).

Michael Les Benedict, *A Compromise of Principle: Congressional Republicans and Reconstruction, 1863–1869* (1974).

Paul Cimbala, *Under the Guardianship of the Nation: The Freedman's Bureau and the Reconstruction of Georgia, 1865–1870* (1997).

Louis S. Gerteis, *From Contraband to Freedmen: Federal Policy toward Southern Blacks, 1861–1865* (1973).

William C. Harris, *With Charity for All: Lincoln and the Restoration of the Union* (1997).

Thomas Holt, *Black over White: Negro Political Leadership in South Carolina during Reconstruction* (1977).

William S. McFeely, *Grant: A Biography* (1981).

Carl H. Moneyhon, *Republicanism in Reconstruction Texas* (1980).

Michael Perman, *Reunion without Compromise: The South and Reconstruction, 1865–1868* (1973).

Willie Lee Rose, *Rehearsal for Reconstruction: The Port Royal Experiment* (1964).

Mark W. Summers, *Railroads, Reconstruction, and the Gospel of Prosperity: Aid under the Radical Republicans, 1865–1877* (1984).

Hans Trefousse, *The Radical Republicans: Lincoln's Vanguard for Racial Justice* (1969).

Counter-Reconstruction, 1870–1874

Richard N. Current, *Those Terrible Carpetbaggers: A Reinterpretation* (1988).

Russell Duncan, *Entrepreneur for Equality: Governor Rufus Bullock, Commerce, and Race in Post–Civil War Georgia* (1994).

Samuel C. Hyde, Jr., *Pistols and Politics: The Dilemma of Democracy in Louisiana's Florida Parishes, 1810–1899* (1996).

Michael Perman, *The Road to Redemption: Southern Politics, 1869–1879* (1984).

George C. Rable, *But There Was No Peace: The Role of Violence in the Politics of Reconstruction* (1984).

John G. Sproat, *"The Best Men": Liberal Reformers in the Gilded Age* (1968).

Allen W. Trelease, *White Terror: The Ku Klux Conspiracy and Reconstruction* (1971).

Redemption, 1874–1877

Randolph B. Campbell, *Grass-Roots Reconstruction in Texas, 1865–1880* (1997).

Laura F. Edwards, *Gendered Strife & Confusion: The Political Culture of Reconstruction* (1997).

Otto H. Olsen, ed., *Reconstruction and Redemption in the South* (1980).

Keith Ian Polakoff, *The Politics of Inertia: The Election of 1876 and the End of Reconstruction* (1973).

C. Vann Woodward, *Reunion and Reaction: The Compromise of 1877 and the End of Reconstruction* (1951).

The Failure of Reconstruction

Stephen Ward Angell, *Bishop Henry McNeal Turner and African-American Religion in the South* (1992).

John Hope Franklin, *Reconstruction after the Civil War* (1961).

James M. McPherson, *Ordeal by Fire: Reconstruction* (1982).

Roger L. Ransom and Richard Sutch, *One Kind of Freedom: The Economic Consequences of Emancipation* (1977).

James L. Roark, *Masters without Slaves: Southern Planters in the Civil War and Reconstruction* (1977).

Kenneth M. Stampp, *The Era of Reconstruction, 1865–1877* (1965).

Where to Learn More

❖ **Penn Center Historic District, St. Helena Island, South Carolina.** The Penn School was a sea-island experiment in the education of free black people established by northern missionaries Laura Towne and Ellen Murray in 1862 that they operated until their deaths in the early 1900s. The Penn School became Penn Community Services in 1948, serving as an educational institution, health clinic, and a social service agency.

❖ **Hampton University Museum, Hampton, Virginia.** Hampton University was founded by the Freedmen's Bureau in 1868 to provide "practical" training in the agricultural and mechanical fields for former slaves. In addition to a history of the institution, the museum includes one of the oldest collections of African art in the United States.

❖ **Beauvoir, Biloxi, Mississippi.** The exhibits at Beauvoir, the home of Jefferson Davis, evoke the importance of the Lost Cause for the white survivors of the Confederacy. Especially interesting is the Jefferson Davis Soldiers Home on the premises and the Confederate Veterans Cemetery. Davis spent his retirement in Beauvoir.

❖ **Levi Jordan Plantation, Brazoria County, Texas.** This site provides an excellent depiction and interpretation of the lives of sharecroppers and tenants during and immediately after the Reconstruction era. The site is especially valuable for demonstrating the transition from slavery to sharecropping.

A New South,
1877–1900

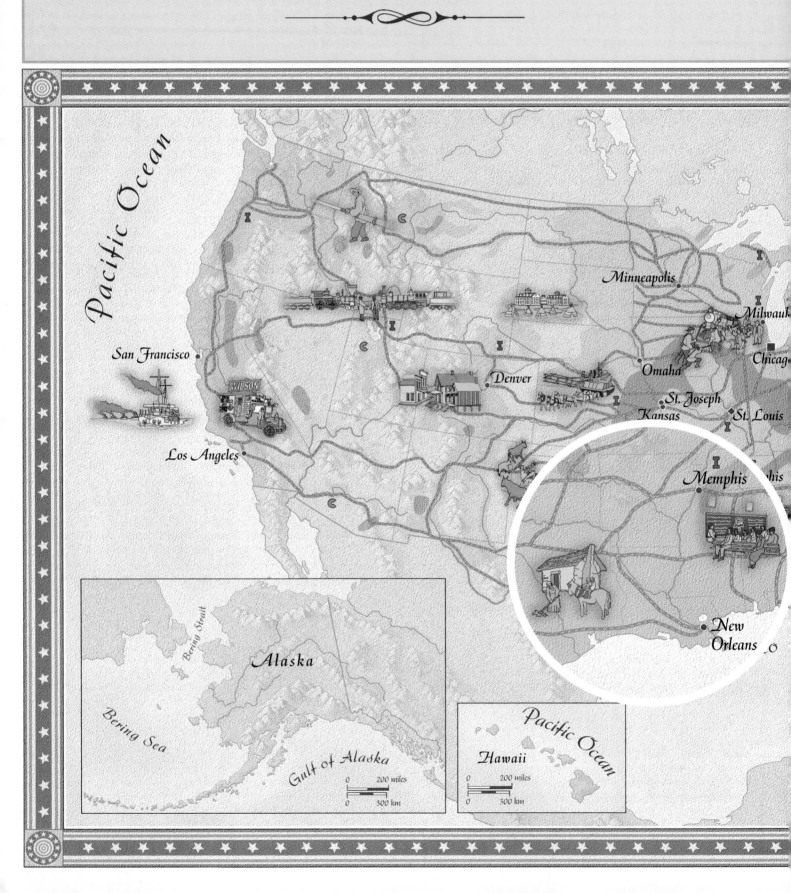

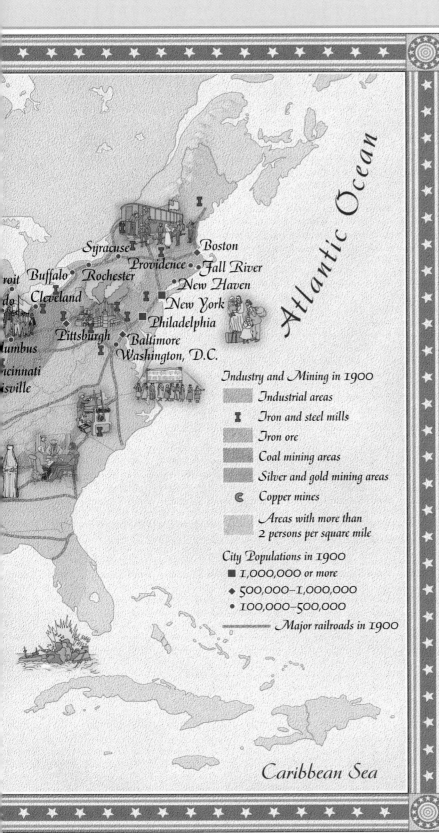

Industry and Mining in 1900

Industrial areas

Iron and steel mills

Iron ore

Coal mining areas

Silver and gold mining areas

Copper mines

Areas with more than
2 persons per square mile

City Populations in 1900

1,000,000 or more

500,000–1,000,000

100,000–500,000

Major railroads in 1900

19

Chapter Outline

Key Topics

❖ Continuity and change between the
  Old South and the New South
❖ The origins and nature of southern
  Populism
❖ Women's roles in the New South
❖ How and why segregation and disfran-
  chisement changed race relations in
  the South

*T*he members of the Holtzclaw family worked hard to supplement the meager income they earned sharecropping on an Alabama farm in the late 1870s. Little more than a decade out of slavery, they hoped to rent and eventually buy a piece of land. Ten-year-old William Holtzclaw foraged for wild nuts and fruits in the swamps around the farm. William's mother cooked for a white family. His father earned extra money hauling logs from a nearby sawmill. When the timber was all gone, he found work on a railroad that kept him away from his family three months at a time.

In 1880, the Holtzclaws bought a mule, a horse, and two oxen and rented a forty-acre farm. But then bad weather and a crippling injury suffered by the elder Holtzclaw dimmed their prospects. By 1884, they had lost their crop and farm animals to debt and were once again sharecropping.

William, a member of the first generation of black Southerners born in freedom, persevered. He graduated from Tuskegee Institute, a black college in Alabama established in 1881, and worked as a teacher and administrator of black schools. He became a prominent educator and founded a vocational college for black people in Mississippi, the Utica Normal and Industrial Institute.

In 1876, while William Holtzclaw and his family were struggling in Alabama, a fourteen-year-old white youth, William Henry Belk, went to work as a store clerk in a small North Carolina town to help support his widowed mother. Over the next twelve years, he saved $750. Borrowing an additional $500, he opened his own retail store, which he called the New York Racket Store. *Racket* in those days meant "cheap," and the word fit both his prices and his merchandise. His one-price, cash-only strategy was successful in his town of 2,500 people. By 1895, he had earned enough from his modest venture to move to Charlotte and open a department store. Charlotte had excellent railroad connections to the rest of the country, so Belk could stock his store with the latest fashions from New York City and the newest household appliances and products from the industrial centers of the Northeast and Midwest. The railroad also brought people—potential Belk customers—to Charlotte. Combining brash advertising with personal attention to customers and attractive prices, Belk prospered. He expanded, opening new stores in the Carolinas. By the early 1900s, Belk owned the largest retail chain in the South.

Both these stories—Holtzclaw's and Belk's—reflect the promise and the problems of the New South that emerged after Reconstruction. Neither would have been likely in the Old South. The experience of the Holtzclaw family shows that despite rising racial hostility in the late-nineteenth-century South, African Americans could aspire to land ownership, education, and a professional career. But it also shows the tenuous plight of southern farmers, white and black alike. And it suggests how narrowing economic opportunities and growing social and political isolation made the road to recovery harder and longer for African Americans than for white Southerners. William Belk's story shows how some Southerners, especially white Southerners, could find opportunity in the South's burgeoning urban centers. Belk and others like him took advantage of the growing transportation systems centered in the cities to translate hard work, some good ideas, and a small financial stake into good fortune.

The New South was very American in the opportunities it provided its citizens through urban and industrial growth. But it was very southern in the persistence of its rural poverty and the distinctiveness of its racial institutions.

The Newness of the New South

While southern farmers, both black and white, faced limited prospects in a stagnant agricultural economy, other Southerners were building railroads, erecting factories, and moving to towns and cities. They were doing what other Americans were doing between 1877 and 1900, only on a smaller scale and with more modest results. The factories did not dramatically alter the South's rural economy, and the towns and cities did not make it an urban region. The changes nonetheless brought political and social turmoil, emboldening black people to assert their rights, encouraging women to work outside the home and pursue public careers, and frightening some white men. By 1900, southern white leaders, urban and rural, had used the banner of white supremacy to stifle dissent. They removed African Americans from political life and constricted their social and economic role. The New South was thus like a cake with fancy new layers piled high on a very old crust. The appearance was American, but the taste was southern.

The New South's "newness" was to be found primarily in its economy. After Reconstruction, new industries absorbed tens of thousands of first-time industrial workers from impoverished rural areas. Southern cities grew faster than those in any other region of the country. A burst of railroad construction linked these cities to one another and to the rest of the country, giving them increased commercial prominence. Growing in size and taking on new functions, cities extended their influence into the countryside with newspapers, consumer products, and new values. But this urban influence had important limits. It did not bring electricity, telephones, public health services, or public schools to the rural South. It did not greatly broaden the rural economy with new jobs. And it left the countryside without the daily contact with the outside world that fostered a broader perspective.

The Democratic party dominated southern politics after 1877, significantly changing the South's political system. Through various deceits, Democrats purged most black people and some white people from the electoral process and suppressed challenges to their leadership. The result was the emergence by 1900 of the **Solid South**, a period of white Democratic party rule that lasted into the 1950s.

Although most southern women remained at home or on the farm, piecing together families shattered by war, some enjoyed new options after

By the 1890s, textile mills were a common sight in towns throughout the South. The mills provided employment for impoverished rural families, especially women and children.

1877. Middle-class women in the cities, both white and black, became increasingly active in civic work and reform. They organized clubs, preserved and promoted the memories of war, lobbied for various causes, and assumed regional leadership on a number of important issues. Tens of thousands of young white women from impoverished rural areas found work in textile mills, in city factories, or as servants. These new options posed a challenge to prevailing views about the role of women but ultimately did not change them.

The status of black Southerners changed significantly between 1877 and 1900. The members of the first generation born after Emancipation sought more than just freedom as they came of age. They also expected dignity and self-respect and the right to work, to vote, to go to school, and to travel freely. White Southerners responded with the equivalent of a second Civil War—and they won. By 1900, black Southerners found themselves more isolated from white Southerners and with less political power than at any time since 1865. Despite these setbacks, they succeeded, especially in the cities, in building a rich community life and spawning a vibrant middle class.

An Industrial and Urban South

Since the 1850s, public speakers calling for economic reform in the South had been rousing audiences with the tale of the burial of a southern

CHRONOLOGY

1872 Texas and Pacific Railway connects Dallas to eastern markets.

1880 First southern local of the Women's Christian Temperance Union is formed in Atlanta.

1881 Booker T. Washington establishes Tuskegee Institute.

1882 Agricultural Wheel is formed in Arkansas.

1883 Laura Haygood founds the home mission movement in Atlanta.

1884 James B. Duke automates his cigarette factory.

1886 Dr. John Pemberton creates Coca-Cola.

Southern railroads conform to national track gauge standards.

1887 Charles W. Macune expands the Southern Farmer's Alliance from its Texas base to the rest of the South.

1888 The Southern Farmers' Alliance initiates a successful boycott of jute manufacturers.

1890 Mississippi becomes the first state to restrict black suffrage with literacy tests.

1892 The Populist party forms.

1894 United Daughters of the Confederacy is founded.

Populist and Republican fusion candidates win control of North Carolina.

1895 Booker T. Washington delivers his "Atlanta Compromise" address.

1896 Populists endorse the Democratic presidential candidate and fade as a national force.

In *Plessy* v. *Ferguson*, the Supreme Court permits segregation by law.

1898 North Carolina Mutual Life Insurance is founded.

Democrats regain control of North Carolina.

1903 W. E. B. Du Bois publishes *The Souls of Black Folk*.

1905 James B. Duke forms the Southern Power Company.

Thomas Dixon publishes *The Clansman*.

1906 Bloody race riots break out in Atlanta.

1907 Pittsburgh-based U.S. Steel takes over Birmingham's largest steel producer.

---

compatriot. The man's headstone, his clothes, the coffin, and the gravediggers' tools all came from the North. Only the corpse and the earth of his grave were southern. The speakers urged their listeners to found industries, build railroads, and grow great cities so that the South could make its own goods and no one in the future would have to suffer the indignity of journeying to the next world accompanied by Yankee artifacts.

It is unclear whether such admonitions worked. Certainly, Southerners manufactured very little in 1877, less than 10 percent of the national total. By 1900, however, they boasted a growing iron and steel industry, textile mills that rivaled those of New England, a world-dominant tobacco industry, and a timber-processing industry that helped make the South a leading furniture-manufacturing center. A variety of regional enterprises also rose to prominence, among them the maker of what would become the world's favorite soft drink, Coca-Cola.

Birmingham, barely a scratch in the forest in 1870, exemplified one aspect of what was new about the New South. Within a decade, its iron and steel mills belched the smoke of progress across the northern Alabama hills. By 1889, Birmingham had surpassed the older southern iron center of Chattanooga, Tennessee, and was preparing to challenge Pittsburgh, the nation's preeminent steelmaking city.

The southern textile industry also experienced significant growth during the 1880s. Although the South had manufactured cotton products since the early decades of the nineteenth century, chronic shortages of labor and capital kept the industry small. In the 1870s, however, several factors drew local investors into textile enterprises. The population of the rural South was rising, but farm income was low, ensuring a steady supply of cheap labor. Cotton was plentiful and cheap. Mixing profit and southern patriotism, entrepreneurs promoted a strong textile industry as a way to make the South less dependent on northern manufactured products and capital. The entrepreneurs located their mills mostly in rural areas, not in cities. The center of the industry was in the Carolina Piedmont, a region with good railroads, plentiful labor, and cheap energy. By 1900, the South had surpassed New England to become the nation's foremost textile-manufacturing center.

The South's tobacco industry, like its textile industry, predated the Civil War. Virginia was the dominant producer, and its main product was chewing tobacco. The discovery of bright-leaf tobacco, a strain suitable for smoking in the form of cigarettes, changed Americans' tobacco habits. In 1884, James B. Duke installed the first cigarette-making machine in his Durham, North Carolina, plant. By 1900, Duke's American Tobacco Company controlled 80 percent of all tobacco manufacturing in the United States.

Although not as important as textiles or tobacco in 1900, a soft drink developed by Atlanta pharmacist Dr. John Pemberton eventually became the most renowned southern product in the world. Pemberton developed the drink—a mixture of oils, caffeine, coca leaves, and cola nuts—in his backyard in an effort to find a good-tasting cure for headaches. He called his concoction Coca-Cola. It was not an overnight success, and Pemberton, short of cash, sold the rights to it to another Atlantan, Asa Candler, in 1889. Candler tinkered with the formula to improve the taste and marketed the product heavily. By the mid-1890s, Coca-Cola enjoyed a national market. Southerners were such heavy consumers that the Georgia Baptist Association felt compelled to warn its members "the more you drink, the more you want to drink. We fear great harm will grow out of this sooner or later, to our young people in particular."

Southern railroad construction boomed in the 1880s, outpacing the rest of the nation. Overall, southern track mileage doubled between 1880 and 1890, with the greatest increases in Texas and Georgia (see Map 19-1). By 1890, nine out of ten Southerners lived in a county with a railroad running through it. In 1886, the southern railroads agreed to conform to a national standard for track width, firmly linking the region into a national transportation network and ensuring quick and direct access for southern products to the booming markets of the Northeast.

The railroads connected many formerly isolated small southern farmers to national and international agricultural markets. At the same time, it gave them access to a whole new range of products, from fertilizers to fashions. Drawn into commercial agriculture, the farmers were now subject to market fluctuations, their fortunes rising and falling with the market prices for their crops. To an extent unknown before the Civil War, the market now determined what farmers planted, how much credit they could expect, and on what terms.

The railroad also opened new areas of the South to settlement and economic development. In 1892, according to one guidebook, Florida was "in the main inaccessible to the ordinary tourist, and unopened to the average settler." But railroad construction boomed in the state in the 1890s, and by 1912, there were tourist hotels as far south as Key West. Railroads also penetrated the Appalachian Mountains, expanding markets for farmers but also opening the area to outside timber and coal-mining interests.

The railroad increased the prominence of interior cities at the expense of older cities along the southern Atlantic and Gulf Coasts. Antebellum ports such as New Orleans, Charleston, and Savannah declined as commerce rode the rails more than the water. Cities such as Dallas, Atlanta, Nashville, and Charlotte, astride great railroad trunk lines, emerged to lead southern urban growth. No fewer than five major rail lines converged on Atlanta by the 1870s. As early as 1866, it had become "the radiating point for Northern and Western trade coming Southward, and . . . the gate through which passes Southern trade and travel going northward." When the Texas and Pacific Railway linked Dallas to eastern markets in 1872, it was a small town of three thousand people. Eight years later, its population had grown to more than ten thousand, and within thirty years it had become the South's twelfth largest city. By 1920, New Orleans and Norfolk were the only coastal ports still among the ten most populous southern cities.

Railroads also spurred the growth of smaller towns that marketed and processed farm products for the surrounding countryside. A town on a rail line that invested in a cotton press and a cottonseed oil mill would become a marketing hub for the surrounding countryside within a day's wagon ride away. Local merchants would stock the latest fashions from New York, canned foods, and current issues of popular magazines such as *Atlantic* or *Harper's*. The number of towns with fewer than five thousand people doubled between 1870 and 1880 and had doubled again by 1900. During the 1880s, southern urban growth was twice the national average. By 1900, one out of six Southerners lived in an urban place.

The Limits of Industrial and Urban Growth

Rapid as it was, urban and industrial growth in the South barely kept pace with that of the booming North (see Chapter 20). Between 1860 and 1900, the South's share of the nation's manufacturing increased only marginally from 10.3 percent to 10.5 percent, and its share of the nation's capital declined slightly from 11.5 percent to 11 percent. About the same percentage of people worked in manufacturing in the southern states east of the Mississippi in 1900 as in 1850. Between 1860 and 1880, the per capita

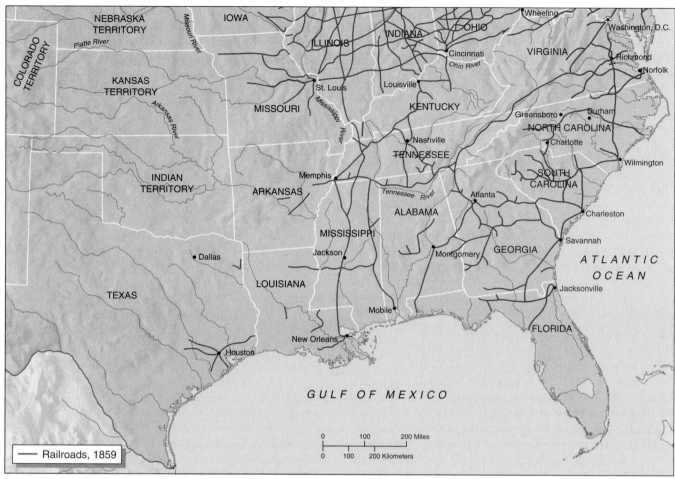

Map 19-1 *Railroads in the South, 1859 and 1899*
A postwar railroad construction boom promoted commercial agriculture and industry in the South. Unlike the railroads of the prewar South, uniform gauges and connections to major trunk lines in the North linked Southerners to the rest of the nation. Northern interests, however, owned the major southern railroads in 1899, and most of the products flowing northward were raw materials to be processed by northern industry or shipped elsewhere by northern merchants.

income of the South declined from 72 percent of the national average to 51 percent and by 1920 had recovered to only 62 percent (see Figure 19-1).

A weak agricultural economy and a high rural birthrate depressed wages in the South. Southern industrial workers earned roughly half the national average manufacturing wage during the late nineteenth century. Business leaders promoted the advantages of this cheap labor to northern investors. In 1904, a Memphis businessman boasted that his city "can save the northern manufacturer . . . who employs 400 hands, $50,000 a year on his labor bill."

Despite their attractiveness to industrialists, low wages undermined the southern economy in several ways. Poorly paid workers didn't buy much, keeping consumer demand low and limiting the market for southern manufactured goods. They also

couldn't provide the southern states with much tax revenue, restricting the states' ability to fund services like public education. Low wages meant that mostly low-skilled, labor-intensive industries flourished in the South. Well-educated workers would have been overqualified for work in such industries. They would either go north, where factories needed skilled labor to produce high-quality goods and run complicated machinery, or agitate for higher wages and better working conditions in the South. Birmingham, Alabama, for example, probably spent more on public education than any other southern city, but the skilled workers in its steel mills tended to leave as soon as they could for higher-wage opportunities in northern cities like Pittsburgh and Cleveland. As a result, investment in education lagged in the South. Per-pupil expenditure in the region was at

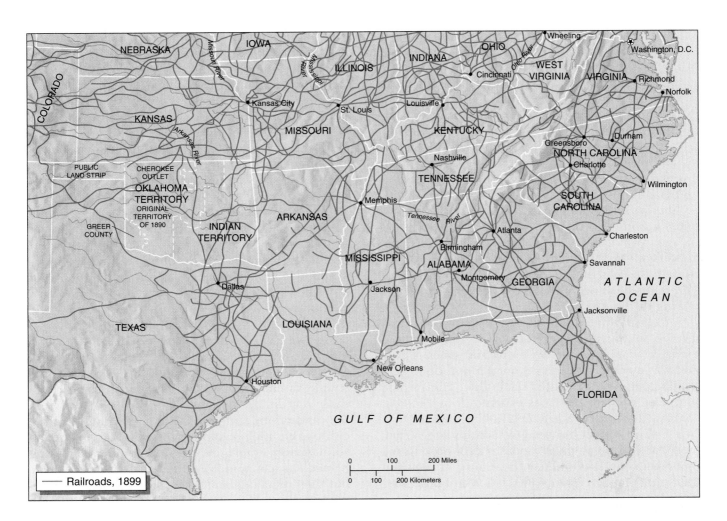

Railroads, 1899

least 50 percent below that of the rest of the nation in 1900. North Dakota, not a wealthy state, spent ten times more per pupil than North Carolina, not the poorest state in the South.

Finally, low wages kept immigrants—and the skills and energy they brought with them—out of the South. With steady work available at higher wages north of the Mason-Dixon line, only a scattering of Italian farm laborers, Chinese railroad workers, and Jewish peddlers ventured below it. Between 1860 and 1900—during one of the greatest waves of immigration the United States has yet experienced—the foreign-born population of the South actually declined from about 10 percent to less than 2 percent.

Why didn't the South do better? Why didn't it benefit more from the rapid expansion of the national economy in the last three decades of the nineteenth century? The simple answer is that despite its growing links to the national economy, the South remained a region apart.

The Civil War had wiped out the South's capital resources, leaving it in effect an economic colony of the North. Northern goods flowed into the South,

Figure 19-1   Per Capita Income in the South as a Percentage of the U.S. Average, 1860–1920
This graph illustrates the devastating effect of the Civil War on the southern economy. Southerners began a slow recovery during the 1880s that accelerated after 1900. But even as late as 1920, per capita income in the South was still lower relative to the country as a whole than it had been before the Civil War.

Data Source: Richard A. Easterlin, "Regional Economic Trends, 1840–1950," in American Economic History, ed. Seymour E. Harris (1961).

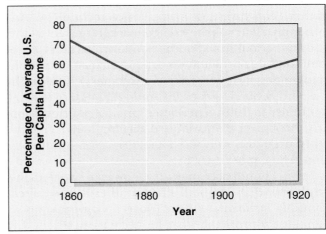

but northern capital, technology, and people did not. Northern-based national banks emerged in the wake of the Civil War to fund northern economic expansion. The South, in contrast, had few banks, and those lacked sufficient capital reserves to fuel an equivalent expansion there. In 1880, Massachusetts alone had five times as much bank capital as the entire South.

Investment in the South seemed riskier and less promising than investment in the vibrant northern economy. As a result, northern banks imposed higher interest rates and shorter terms on loans to Southerners than on loans to their northern customers. Some northern capital came south nonetheless. When southern rail lines failed during a depression in the 1870s, northern financiers purchased the companies at bargain prices. By the 1890s, northern firms owned the five major rail lines serving the South.

With limited access to other sources of capital, the South's textile industry depended on thousands of small investors in towns and cities. These investors avoided risk and shunned innovation. Most textile operations remained small-scale. The average southern firm in 1900 was capitalized at $11,000, compared with an average of $21,000 elsewhere.

The lumber industry, the South's largest, typified the shortcomings of southern economic development in the late nineteenth century. It required little capital, relied on unskilled labor, and processed its raw materials on site. After clear-cutting—felling all the trees—in one region, sawmills moved quickly to the next stand of timber, leaving behind a bare landscape, rusting machinery, and a work force no better off than before. This process—later repeated by the coal-mining industry—inflicted environmental damage on once remote areas such as Appalachia and displaced their residents.

Birmingham's iron and steel industry also suffered from financial weakness. Part of the fault lay with mill owners who relied on cheap black labor rather than investing in expensive technology. Another problem was the limited market for steel in the mostly agricultural South. Southern farmers compounded this problem with their reliance on people and mules instead of farm machinery. Pittsburgh-based U.S. Steel took over Birmingham's largest steel producer in 1907. Thereafter, pricing policies favoring Pittsburgh plants limited Birmingham's growth. Pittsburgh also won the competition for technology and skilled labor.

The tobacco industry, however, avoided the problems that plagued other southern enterprises. James B. Duke's American Tobacco Company was so immensely profitable that he became, in effect, his own bank. With more than enough capital to install the latest technology in his plants, Duke bought out his competitors. He then diversified into electric power generation, investing in an enterprise that became the Southern Power Company in 1905 (and later the Duke Power Company). He also endowed what became Duke University.

Southern industry fit into a narrow niche of late-nineteenth-century American industrialization. With an unskilled and uneducated work force, poor access to capital and technology, and a weak consumer base, the South processed raw agricultural products and produced cheap textiles, cheap lumber products, and cheap cigarettes. "Made in the South" became synonymous with bottom-of-the-line goods. When skill levels and capital resources grew after 1920, however, the quality of southern manufactured products increased.

In the North, industrialization usually occurred in an urban context and promoted rapid urban growth. This was not the case in the South. Most textile mills were typically located in the countryside, often in mill villages, where employers could easily recruit families and keep them isolated from the distractions and employment alternatives of the cities. The timber industry similarly remained a rural-based enterprise. Tobacco manufacturing helped Durham and Winston, North Carolina, grow, but they remained small compared to northern industrial cities. Duke moved his corporate headquarters to New York to be near that city's financial, advertising, and communications services.

The Impact on Southerners

If industrialization in the South was limited compared to the North, it nonetheless had an enormous impact on southern society. In the southern Piedmont, for example, textile mills erupted from the red clay and transformed a portion of the farm population into an industrial work force. Failed farmers moved to textile villages to earn a living. Entire families secured employment and often a house in exchange for their labor. Widows and single young men also moved to the mills, usually the only option outside farm work in the South. Nearly one-third of the textile mill labor force by 1900 consisted of children under the age of fourteen and women. They worked twelve hours a day, six days a week, although some firms allowed a half-day off on Saturday. They had worked long hours on the farm, too, but now they became the target of concern of middle-class urban reformers who viewed factory work as destructive of individual and family life.

Southern urban growth, which also paled in comparison with that of the North, had a similarly disproportionate impact on southern society. One observer noted the changes in a North Carolina town between 1880 and 1900. The town in 1880 presented a sorry aspect: rutted roads, a shanty for a school, a few forlorn churches, and perhaps three families of prominence. Twenty years later, another railroad, bustling commerce, and textile mills had produced a new scene: paved streets, two public schools—one for black children, one for white children—and a cosmopolitan frame of mind among its residents. "The men have a wider range of activities and the women have more clothes." Discussions changed from local gossip to "the prices of certain stocks in New York." The town now had electric lights, paved streets, and a direct train to New York. In another twenty years, the observer predicted, it will be "very like hundreds of towns in the Middle West."

In 1880, southern towns often did not differ much from the countryside in appearance, economy, religion, and outlook. Over the next twenty years, the gap between town and country widened. By 1900, a town in the New South would boast a business district and more elegant residences than before. It would have a relatively prosperous economy and more frequent contact with other parts of the country. Its influence would extend into the countryside. Mail, the telegraph, the railroad, and the newspaper brought city life to the attention of farm families. In turn, farm families visited nearby towns and cities more often. A South Carolina writer related in 1900 that "Country people who . . . went to town annually or semiannually, can now go quickly, safely, pleasantly, and cheaply several times a day." Many never returned to the farm. "Cheap coal, cheap lights, convenient water supply offer inducements; society and amusements draw the young; the chance to speculate, to make a sudden rise in fortunes, to get in the swim attracts others."

The urban South drew the region's talented and ambitious young people. White men like William Henry Belk moved to cities to open shops or take jobs as bank clerks, bookkeepers, merchants, and salesmen. White women worked as retail clerks, telephone operators, and office personnel. Black women filled the growing demand for laundresses and domestic servants. And black men also found prospects better in towns than on the farm, despite a narrow and uncertain range of occupations available to them.

The excitement that drew some Southerners to their new cities repelled others. To them, urbanization and the emphasis on wealth, new technology, and display represented a second Yankee conquest. The cities, they feared, threatened to infect the South with northern values, undermining southern grace, charm, faith, and family. Ministers warned against traffic with the urban devil, whose temptations could overcome even the most devout individual. Evangelist Sam Jones, a reformed alcoholic, chose Atlanta for his largest revivals in the 1890s, challenging its residents to keep the Sabbath holy, reject alcohol, and obey the Golden Rule.

Country people held ambivalent views of the city. Farm children looked forward to the Saturday excursion to town, when they would gaze in shop windows, watch people rushing about, wonder at the workings of electricity, and drink a "Co'Cola" at the drugstore. Their parents shared some of this excitement but experienced apprehension as well. They were disturbed by the easy blurring of class and racial distinctions in town and offended by the scorn with which town folk sometimes treated them.

White Southerners in town and country, who not long ago had lived similar lives, grew distant. Evelyn Scott recalled how rural folk looked to her when they visited her town, Clarksville, Tennessee, at the turn of the century:

> These beings [farmers and their families] I regarded as from another planet. . . . The little girls whose petticoats were never of a length with their frocks; the little boys whose misfit "store pants" were cut of material . . . uncongenial . . . to the human form; the misses in muslin dresses of [a] diluted [pink] color; . . . already-weary mothers wearing hats on which reposed entire flimsy gardens and orchards, or else pathetically alighted, stuffed birds! [They engaged] in bouts of window-shopping in which stoical hearts and vacant imaginations were replenished.

Once the backbone of the South, small landholding white farmers and their families like those Scott thought so alien had fallen on hard times. The market that lured them into commercial agriculture threatened to take away their independence. They faced the loss of their land and livelihood. Their way of life no longer served as the standard for the South. New South spokesmen promoted cities and industries and ordered farmers to get on board the train of progress before it left the station without them.

The Southern Agrarian Revolt

Even more than before the Civil War, cotton dominated southern agriculture between 1877 and 1900. And the economics of cotton brought despair to cotton farmers. Those who grew two other traditional southern cash crops—rice and tobacco—fared better. Rice and tobacco production increased, and Louisiana and Arkansas overtook South Carolina in rice production. Steady demand, however, allowed rice and tobacco growers to maintain a decent standard of living. Cotton was another matter. The size of the cotton crop continued to set annual records after 1877. Fertilizers revived supposedly exhausted soils in North and South Carolina, turning them white with cotton. The railroad opened new areas for cultivation in Mississippi and eastern Texas. But the price of cotton fell while the price of fertilizers, agricultural tools, food, and most other necessities went up (see Figure 19-2). As a result, the more cotton the farmers grew, the less money they made.

Before the Civil War, the South fed itself. After the war, with railroads providing direct access to major cotton-marketing centers, farmers cultivated more land in cotton and less in food crops. The South became an importer of food. As a common lament went in 1890, "Five-cent cotton, forty-cent meat, how in the world can a poor man eat?"

Cotton and Credit

The solution to this agrarian dilemma seemed simple: Grow less cotton. But that was not possible for several reasons. In a cash-poor economy, credit ruled. Cotton was the only commodity instantly convertible into cash and hence the only commodity accepted for credit. Food crops generated less income per acre than cotton, even in the worst years. Local merchants, themselves bound in a web of credit to merchants in larger cities, accepted cotton as collateral. As cotton prices plummeted, the merchants required their customers to grow more cotton to make up the difference. "No cotton, no credit" became a standard refrain throughout the South after 1877.

For small landowning farmers, credit proved addictive. Trapped in debt by low cotton prices and high interest rates, they lost their land in record numbers. Both black farmers, like the Holtzclaws, and white farmers were affected. But white farmers were more likely than black farmers to own their farms, and the effect on them was more dramatic. Less than one-third of white farmers in the South were tenants or sharecroppers just after the Civil War. By the 1890s, nearly half were.

Some areas did diversify. Good rail connections in Georgia, for example, made peach farming profitable for some farmers. Railroads likewise helped cattle ranching spread in Texas. But few crops or animals had the geographical range of cotton. Soil type, rainfall, animal parasites, and frost made alternatives unfeasible for many farmers. Cotton required no ma-

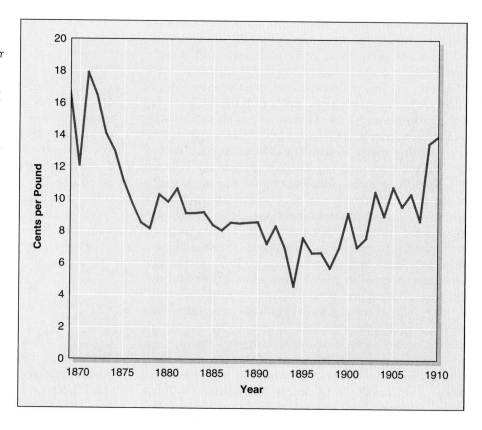

Figure 19-2 The Price of Cotton, 1869–1910

The steadily declining price of cotton after the Civil War—from 18 cents a pound to 5 cents a pound by the early 1890s—reflected extreme overproduction. Behind the numbers lay an impoverished rural South.

Data Source: U.S. Department of Commerce, Historical Statistics of the United States: Colonial Times to 1957.

chinery or irrigation system. James Barrett, a farmer outside Augusta, Georgia, said of his experiment with diversification in 1900: "I have diversified, and I have not made any money by diversification. . . . I grow green peas and everything I know of. I have raised horses, cows, and hogs, and I have diversified it for the last three years and have not been able to make a dollar."

Southern Farmers Organize, 1877–1892

As their circumstances deteriorated, southern farmers fought back. They engaged in barter when they could. They supplemented their income with occasional jobs off the farm and by selling eggs or vegetables. They lobbied for debt-stay laws and formed farmer organizations. They had lived a communal life of church, family, and kin. Now they would widen the circle of their community to include other farmers sharing their plight. These were not naive country folk—most owned their own land and participated in the market economy. They just wanted to make the market fairer, to lower interest rates and ease credit, to regulate railroad freight rates, and to keep the prices of necessities in check.

But these goals required legislation that neither the federal government nor southern state governments were inclined to support. No presidential administration between 1877 and 1900, Republican or Democrat, favored debt relief or extensive regulation of business. And the Redeemer Democrats who gained control of the southern state governments after Reconstruction represented large landowners and merchants, not poor farmers.

To strengthen their authority and suppress dissent, the Redeemer Democrats appealed to racial and regional solidarity among white Southerners. They portrayed themselves as having saved the South from the rule of black people and Republicans. Insurgent farmers who challenged this leadership risked being branded as disloyal.

The Democrats nonetheless faced opposition beginning soon after they had wrested control of southern state governments from the Republicans. In some states, like North Carolina, the Republicans retained support in mountain areas and among black people. In addition, disaffected white farmers mounted independent political campaigns against the Redeemers in several states in the late 1870s and early 1880s to demand currency reform and the easing of credit. But the Democrats, in firm control of the election machinery throughout the South, turned back these challenges. Although Independents at one point succeeded in gaining control of the Virginia legislature, their few other victories were confined to the local level. Hard-pressed farmers began to organize on a broader scale.

Southern farmers joined their colleagues nationwide to address common grievances related to pricing, credit, and tax policies. Though some of the southern farmers' problems resulted from conditions particular to the South, agricultural distress became widespread in the decades after 1870. By 1875, nearly 250,000 southern landowners had joined the National **Grange** of the Patrons of Husbandry or, more popularly, simply the Grange (see Chapter 22). The leaders of the Grange, however, were large landowners. Their interests were not the same as the small farmers who made up the organization's rank and file. The Grange leadership in the South, for example, while nominally concerned about issues of concern to small farmers, such as exploitative merchants and excessive railroad freight rates, favored policies—like fence laws to pen animals and protect crops and

The faces of this white sharecropper family in North Carolina reflect the harshness of farm life in the late nineteenth- and early twentieth-century South, a period when thousands of Southerners, white and black alike, slipped from land ownership to sharecropping.

controls on farm labor—that hurt small farmers. The rank-and-file members, in contrast, pushed a more radical agenda including establishing community stores, cotton gins, and warehouses to bypass the prevailing credit system.

Despite a few successes, the Grange failed to stem the reverses of small southern farmers. As a result, the farmers were drawn to new agricultural organizations that emerged in the 1880s promising to promote their interests more forcefully. In 1882, for example, a group of farmers in Arkansas formed an organization called the **Agricultural Wheel** that had attracted more than 500,000 southern farmers by 1887. Wheelers tried to purchase farm equipment directly from manufacturers, avoiding merchant middlemen. Unlike the Grange, they called for an array of federal programs to ease the credit and cash burdens of farmers, including a graduated income tax and the printing and distribution of more paper money.

The most potent agricultural reform organization, the **Southern Farmers' Alliance**, originated in Texas in the late 1870s. Alliance-sponsored farmers' **cooperatives** provided their members with discounts on supplies and credit. Members also benefited from marketing their cotton crops collectively. The Alliance was not the only organization to form cooperatives, but it was unique in the messianic zeal with which it promoted them. Although it endorsed some candidates for office, the Alliance was not a political party and did not challenge Democratic domination of the South.

The Alliance was still very much a Texas organization in 1887 when Charles W. Macune, a Wisconsin native, became its driving force. Macune sent a corps of speakers to create a network of southern cooperatives. Within two years, the Alliance had spread throughout the South and into the North and West. By 1890, it claimed more than a million members. With the exception of a few large landowners and some tenant farmers, almost all were small farmers who owned their own land. The success of the Alliance reflected both the desperate struggle of these small farmers to keep their land and the failure of other organizations to help them.

The Alliance operated like a religious denomination. Its leaders preached a message of salvation through cooperation to as many as twenty thousand people at huge revival-like rallies. Qualifications for membership included a belief in the divinity of Christ and the literal truth of the Bible. Alliance speakers, many of them rural ministers, often held meetings in churches. In their talks, they combined biblical nostrums with economic policy and stressed the importance of doing good as much as good farm-ing. They urged members to visit "the homes where lacerated hearts are bleeding, to assuage the suffering of a brother or a sister, bury the dead, care for the widows and educate the orphans." The Alliance lobbied state legislatures to fund rural public schools. To increase the sense of community, the Alliance sponsored picnics, baseball games, and concerts.

The Alliance became for many small farmers a surrogate government and church in a region where public officials and many mainline Protestant ministers ignored their needs. It imposed strict morality on its members, prohibiting drinking, gambling, and sexual misconduct. Alliance leaders criticized many Baptist, Methodist, and Presbyterian ministers for straying from the traditional emphasis on individual salvation and for defending a status quo that benefited large planters and towns. Cyrus Thompson, North Carolina Alliance president and a prominent Methodist, declared in 1889 that "the church today stands where it has always stood, on the side of human slavery."

Some Alliance members left their churches for new religious groups. The Holiness movement, which began in the North before the Civil War, revived among Texas farmers in the mid-1880s. Holiness disciples advocated simple dress, avoided coffee and pork, and swore off all worldly amusements. The members of the Church of God, which formed in the mountains of Tennessee and North Carolina in 1886, similarly sought to cleanse themselves of secular evils. The new churches promoted a vision of an egalitarian South. They accepted women on an equal basis and occasionally black people as well. As many as a third of Holiness preachers were women.

Women also found an active role as officers and speakers in the Alliance. As a Texas woman declared, "The Alliance has come to redeem woman from her enslaved condition. She is admitted into the organization as the equal of her brother, and the ostracism which has impeded her intellectual progress in the past is not met with."

Unlike some of the new religious movements, however, the Alliance did not accept black members. Black farmers formed the first **Colored Farmers' Alliance** in Texas in 1886. The Colored Alliance had fewer landowners and more tenants and sharecroppers in its ranks than the white organization. It concerned itself with issues relevant to this constituency, such as higher wages for cotton pickers. In 1891, the Colored Alliance attempted a regionwide strike over farm wages but was unable to enforce it in the worsening southern economy.

The white Alliance had better results with a protest over price fixing. To protect cotton shipped to market, farmers wrapped it in a burlaplike material called jute. In 1888, jute manufacturers combined to raise the price from 7 cents to as much as 14 cents a yard. The Alliance initiated a jute boycott throughout the South, telling farmers to use cotton bagging as an alternative. The protest worked, forcing the chastened jute manufacturers to offer farmers their product at a mere 5 cents per yard.

This success encouraged Macune to pursue a more ambitious project. Low cotton prices and a lack of cash kept farmers poor. To address these problems, Macune proposed his **subtreasury plan**. Alliance members were to store their crops in a subtreasury (a warehouse), keeping their cotton off the market until the price rose. In the meantime, the government would loan the farmers up to 80 percent of the value of the stored crops at a low interest rate of 2 percent per year. This arrangement would free farmers from merchants' high interest rates and crop liens.

Macune urged Alliance members to endorse political candidates who supported the subtreasury scheme. Many Democratic candidates for state legislatures throughout the South did endorse it and were elected with Alliance backing in 1890. Once in office, however, they failed to deliver.

The failure of the subtreasury plan combined with a steep drop in cotton prices after 1890 undermined the Alliance. Its cooperatives collapsed as crop liens cut down small landowners as though with scythes. A Georgia Allianceman wrote in 1891 that "Hundreds of farmers will be turned adrift, and thousands of acres of our best land allowed to grow up in weeds through lack of necessary capital to work them." Alliance membership declined by two-thirds in Georgia that year. Desperate Alliance leaders merged their organization with a new national political party in 1892, the People's or **Populist party**. Populists appropriated the Alliance program and challenged Democrats in the South and Republicans in the West. The merger reflected desperation more than calculation.

Southern Populists

Northern farmers, like their southern counterparts, faced growing financial pressure in the 1880s that by the early 1890s had led them too to join the Alliance. Just as southern farmers had turned to the Democratic party to redress their grievances, northern farmers turned to the dominant party in the northern farming states—the Republican party—to redress theirs. Like the Democrats, the Republicans failed to respond. Beginning in Kansas in 1890, disillusioned farmers formed the People's party, soon called the Populist party. The Populists held their first national nominating convention in Omaha in July 1892.

The Populists supported a wide range of reforms, many adopted from the Alliance, including the direct election of United States senators by popular vote rather than by state legislatures, an income tax, woman suffrage, government ownership of railroads, and various proposals to ease credit. As we will see in Chapter 22, the Populists stirred up national politics between 1892 and 1896. In the South, they challenged the Democratic party, sometimes courting Republicans, including black voters.

Southern populists were ambivalent about African Americans. On the one hand, black people constituted a potential voting bloc the Populists could ill afford to ignore. On the other hand, appealing to black voters would expose Populists to demagogic attacks from Democrats for undermining white supremacy, frightening away potential white backers. Populists who wanted to extend the hand of fellowship to black people risked withering fire from Democrats. The *Baton Rouge Daily Advocate*, for example, informed its readers in 1892 that the Populist party was "the most dangerous and insidious foe of white supremacy." Many southern Populists, including former members of the Alliance, supported segregation and never made the gesture of racial reconciliation.

Despite the risks, in at least two southern states, Texas and Georgia, Populists openly appealed for black votes. In Texas, black Populist John B. Rayner, the "silver-tongued orator of the colored race," spoke to racially mixed audiences around the state. The Texas Populist platform called for "equal justice and protection under the law to all citizens without reference to race, color or nationality." In Georgia, Populist leader Tom Watson supported a biracial party organization and counseled white people to accept black people as partners in their common crusade. "You are kept apart," Watson told black and white Georgians, "that you may be separately fleeced of your earnings. You are made to hate each other because upon that hatred is rested the keystone of the arch of financial despotism which enslaves you both."

Despite Rayner's and Watson's efforts, most black people remained loyal to the Republican party for its role in abolishing slavery and for the few patronage crumbs the party still threw their way. Black people also suspected Populists' motives. The party appealed mainly to small, landowning farmers, not, as most black Southerners were, propertyless tenants and sharecroppers. And even the Texas Populists, while appealing for black support, opposed black officeholding and jury service.

Unwilling or unable to mobilize black voters and unsuccessful in dislodging white voters from the

Democratic party, the Populists finished a distant third in the 1892 presidential election. In the South, their only significant inroads were in the state legislatures of Texas, Alabama, and Georgia. Even in these states, widespread voter fraud among Democrats undermined Populist strength.

Despite a deepening economic depression, the Populists had only a few additional successes in the South after 1892. Their major victory was in North Carolina in 1894. Republicans had remained a political force in the state's mountain counties and among black people in its eastern part. Adopting a fusion strategy, the Populists ran candidates on a combined ticket with Republicans. The fusion candidates captured the governorship and state legislature. Once in office, they overhauled the state electoral machinery, eased voter registration procedures, and established nonpartisan electoral panels to monitor elections. Reflecting Populist influence, they also imposed limits on interest rates, increased expenditures for education, and raised taxes on railroads.

Higher cotton prices and returning prosperity in the late 1890s, however, undermined Populist support in North Carolina, as in the rest of the South. In 1896, the Populists assisted in their own nationwide demise by merging with the Democrats for the presidential election of 1896. In 1898, Democrats surged back into office in North Carolina on the strength of a virulent white supremacy campaign and promptly undid the work of the fusionists.

Women in the New South

Just as farm women found their voices in the Alliance movement of the 1880s, a growing group of middle-class white and black urban women entered the public realm and engaged in policy issues. In the late-nineteenth-century North, women became increasingly active in reform movements, including woman suffrage, labor legislation, social welfare, and city planning. Building on their antebellum activist traditions, northern women, sometimes acting in concert with men, sought to improve the status of women in society.

Antebellum reform movements, because they included abolitionism, had made little headway in the South. As a result, southern women had a meager reform tradition to build on. The war also left them ambivalent about independence. With husbands, fathers, and brothers dead or incapacitated, many women had to care for themselves and their families in the face of defeat and deprivation. Some determined never again to depend on men. Others,

responding to the stress of running a farm or business, would have preferred less independence.

The response of southern white men to the war also complicated women's efforts to improve their status. Southern men had been shaken by defeat. They had lost the war and placed their families in peril. Many responded with alcoholism and violence. To regain their self-esteem, they recast the war as a noble crusade rather than a defeat. And they imagined southern white women as paragons of virtue and purity who required men to defend them. Demands for even small changes in traditional gender roles would threaten this image. Southern women understood this and never mounted an extensive reform campaign like their sisters in the North. Some middle-class women were openly hostile to reform, and others adopted conservative causes more inclined to reinforce the role of men in southern society than to challenge it.

Despite such limitations, middle-class southern women found opportunities to broaden their social role and enter the public sphere in the two decades after 1880. They found these opportunities primarily in the cities, where servants, stores, and schools freed them of many of the productive functions—like making clothing, cooking, and child care—that burdened their sisters in the country and kept them tied to the home.

Church Work and Preserving Memories

Southern women waded warily into the public arena, using channels men granted them as natural extensions of the home, such as church work. The movement to found **home mission societies**, for example, was led by single white women in the Methodist church. Home missions promoted industrial education among the poor and helped working-class women become self-sufficient. The home mission movement reflected an increased interest in missionary work among white southern evangelical churches. Laura Haygood, an Atlantan who had served as a missionary in China, founded a home mission in Atlanta when she returned in 1883. Lily Hammond, another Atlantan, extended the mission concept when she opened **settlement houses** in black and white city neighborhoods in Atlanta in the 1890s. Settlement houses, pioneered in New York in the 1880s, promoted middle-class values in poor neighborhoods and provided them with a permanent source of services. In the North, they were privately sponsored. In the South, they were supported by the Methodist church and known as Wesley Houses, after John Wesley, the founder of Methodism.

Religion also prompted southern white women to join the **Women's Christian Temperance**

Union (WCTU). The first southern local formed in Lucy Haygood's church in Atlanta in 1880. Temperance reform, unlike other church-inspired activities, involved women directly in public policy. Women framed temperance and the prohibition of alcohol as a family issue—alcohol ruined families, victimizing innocent women and children. WCTU members visited schools to educate children about the evils of alcohol, addressed prisoners, and blanketed men's meetings with literature. As a result, they became familiar with the South's abysmal school system and its archaic criminal justice system. They thus began advocating education and prison reform as well as legislation against alcohol.

By the 1890s, many WCTU members realized that they couldn't achieve their goals unless women had the vote. Rebecca Latimer Felton, an Atlanta suffragist and WCTU member, reflected the frustration of her generation of southern women in an address to working women in 1892:

> But some will say—you women might be quiet—you can't vote, you can't do anything! Exactly so—we have kept quiet for nearly a hundred years hoping to see relief come to the women of this country—and it hasn't come. How long must our children be slain? If a mad dog should come into my yard, and attempt to bite my child or myself—would you think me out of my place, if I killed him with a dull meat axe? . . . [You] would call that woman a brave woman . . . and yet are we to sit by while drink ruins our homes?

Despite the WCTU's roots in southern churches, the activism of its members alarmed some southern men. WCTU rhetoric implied a veiled attack on men. Felton, for example, often referred to men who drank as "beasts." And WCTU members had many other issues besides prohibition on their agenda. When the WCTU held its national convention in Atlanta in 1890, local Baptist and Methodist ministers launched a bitter attack against the organization, claiming that it drew women into activities contrary to the Scriptures and that its endorsement of woman suffrage subverted traditional family values.

Few women, however, had such radical objectives in mind. Rebecca Felton's own career highlighted the essentially conservative nature of the reform movement among middle-class women in the New South. Born in 1835 to a wealthy planter family, she attended college and married Dr. William H. Felton, a physician and minister twelve years her senior. During the Civil War and its aftermath, the Feltons eked out a modest living teaching school and working a small farm. Four

of their five children died. Seeing southern families worse off than her own, Felton threw herself into a variety of reform activities, ranging from woman suffrage to campaigns against drinking, smoking, and Coca-Cola. She fought for child care facilities, sex education, and compulsory school attendance and pushed for the admission of women to the University of Georgia. But she strongly supported textile operators over textile workers and defended white supremacy. She had no qualms about the **lynching** of black men—executing them without trial—"a thousand times a week if necessary" to preserve the purity of white women. In 1922, she became the first woman member of the U.S. Senate. By any definition, Felton was a reformer, but like most middle-class southern women, she had no interest in challenging the class and racial inequities of the New South.

The dedication of southern women to commemorating the memory of the Confederate cause also suggested the conservative nature of middle-class women's reform in the New South. Ladies' Memorial Associations formed after the war to ensure the proper burial of Confederate soldiers and suitable markings for their graves. The associations joined with men to erect monuments to Confederate leaders and, by the 1880s, to the common soldier. These activities reinforced white solidarity and constructed a common heritage for all white Southerners regardless of class or location. By the 1890s, women planned monuments in prominent civic spaces in the urban South. Their efforts sparked interest in city planning and city beautification. A new organization, the United Daughters of the Confederacy (UDC), appeared in 1894 to preserve southern history and honor its heroes. Although men formed similar associations, women remained the most active protectors of regional memory. Work for the Lost Cause reflected traditional roles, but it also offered a way for women to hone leadership and organizational skills, preparing them for less traditional public activities in the 1890s. Gertrude Thomas, for example, one of the South's leading suffragists, played an important role in the Georgia UDC.

Women's Clubs

A broader spectrum of southern middle-class women joined women's clubs than joined church-sponsored organizations or memorial associations. Most clubs began in the 1880s as literary or self-improvement societies that had little interest in reform. By 1890, most towns and cities boasted at least several women's clubs and perhaps a federated club organization. But, also by that time, some clubs and their members had begun to discuss political issues such as child labor reform, educational improvement,

FROM THEN TO NOW

The Confederate Battle Flag

Memories of the Civil War and Reconstruction formed a crucial part of southern civic and religious culture from the late nineteenth century onward. Southerners perceived themselves and the rest of the nation through the lens of the heroic Lost Cause and the alleged abuses of Reconstruction, and the symbols associated with those events took on the status of icons. During the 1890s, the memory industry that white political and religious leaders had promoted since the end of the war became institutionalized. Organizations such as the United Daughters of the Confederacy and the Sons of the Confederate Veterans strove to educate a new generation of white Southerners on the meanings of the sacrifices of the war generation, bolstering the imposition of white supremacy through racial segregation and disfranchisement.

The Confederate battle flag emerged from this process as an icon of the Lost Cause and a symbol of white supremacy. Alabama, for example, redesigned its state flag in the 1890s to resemble more closely the battle flag. Its red St. Andrews cross on a white background symbolized the blood spilled in defense of the Southern homeland and the supremacy of the white race.

Still, the Confederate battle flag itself was displayed mostly at veterans' reunions and only rarely at other public occasions—until the late 1940s, that is, when civil rights for African Americans emerged as a national issue for the first time since the Reconstruction era. In 1948, Mississippians waved the flag at Ole Miss football games for the first time. In 1956, as the civil rights struggle in the South gained momentum, the state of Georgia incorporated the battle flag into its state flag. And, in 1962, as sit-ins and Freedom Riders spread throughout the South, officials in South Carolina—claiming to be commemorating the Civil War centennial—hoisted the battle flag above the State House in Columbia.

The centennial is long-gone, but the battle flag continues to fly in Columbia and adorn the Georgia state flag. This official display has become a focus of heated controversy. Proponents argue that the battle flag represents heritage, not hate. Opponents denounce it as a symbol of white supremacy. In the mid-1990s, South Carolina's Republican Governor David Beasley, seeking to defuse the issue, proposed removing the flag from atop the Capitol and installing it at a nearby history museum. The resulting firestorm of protest from some of the Governor's white constituents forced him to reverse himself, however, and contributed to his defeat in his bid for reelection.

The flag controversy erupted again in 1999 when South Carolina's state Democratic Party chairman urged voters to return a Democratic legislature that would, once and for all, remove the flag from the State Capitol. The angry response from both Republicans and some Demo-

crats forced the new Democratic governor, who had been searching for a compromise on the issue since taking office in January 1999, to quickly distance himself from the proposal. Then, in July 1999 the National Association for the Advancement of Colored People (NAACP) announced a national boycott of South Carolina beginning in January 2000. Facing the loss of convention and tourist revenues, business groups pleaded with lawmakers to lower the flag.

When people in other parts of the country sometimes remark that white Southerners are still fighting the Civil War, it's controversies like that over the battle flag they have in mind. But the controversy is less about the past than it is about the way we use history to shape our understanding of the society we live in and our vision of its future. At issue is not just history, but *whose* history. In that sense the flag controversy, as much as it picks at wounds more than a century old, can to some extent at least generate positive dialogue. Even so, in the interests of reconciliation, it's surely time for Southerners to follow Robert E. Lee's final order to his men and "Furl the flag, boys."

The Confederate battle flag on this parade float reflects its emerging status as an icon of the Lost Cause in the late nineteenth century.

and prison reform. The Arkansas Federation of Women's Clubs launched a boycott of goods produced by "exploited" labor in 1903. The Lone Star (Texas) Federation scrutinized public hospitals, almshouses, and orphanages at the turn of the century. Its president asserted, "The Lone Star Federation stands for the highest and truest type of womanhood—that which lends her voice as well as her hand." Southern women's club members sought out their sisters in the North. As Georgia's federated club president, Mrs. A. O. Granger, wrote in 1906, "Women of intellectual keenness in the South could not be left out of the awakening of the women of the whole country to a realization of the responsibility which they properly had in the condition of their fellow-women and of the children."

This pursuit of solidarity with women in the North did not extend to the members of black women's clubs in the South. The activities of black women's clubs paralleled those of white women's clubs. Only rarely, however—as at some meetings of the Young Women's Christian Association (YWCA) or occasional meetings in support of prohibition—did black and white club members interact.

Some white clubwomen expressed sympathy for black women privately, but publicly they maintained white solidarity. Most were unwilling to sacrifice their own reform agenda to the cause of racial reconciliation. Women suffragists in the South, for example, did not make common cause with black people. On the contrary, some used racial solidarity as a weapon to promote white women's right to vote, arguing that the combined vote of white men and women would further white interests.

The primary interest of most southern white women's clubs was the plight of young white working-class and farm women. This interest reflected the growing number of such women in the work force. Single and adrift in the city, many worked for low wages, and some slipped into prostitution. The clubs sought to help them make the transition from rural to urban life or to improve their lives on the farm. To this end, they focused on child labor reform and on upgrading public education.

Settling the Race Issue

The assertiveness of a new generation of African Americans, especially those in urban areas, in the 1880s and 1890s provided the impetus and opportunity for white leaders to secure white solidarity. To counter black aspirations, white leaders enlisted the support of young white Southerners, convincing them that the struggle for white supremacy would place them beside the larger-than-life heroes of the Civil War generation. African Americans resisted the resulting efforts to deprive them of their remaining freedoms. Though some left the South, many more built new lives and communities within the restricted framework white Southerners allowed them.

The Fluidity of Southern Race Relations, 1877–1890

Race relations remained remarkably fluid in the South between the end of Reconstruction and the early 1890s. Despite the departure of federal troops and the end of Republican rule, many black people continued to vote and hold office. Some Democrats even courted the black electorate. Though segregation ruled in churches, schools, and in some organizations and public places after the Civil War, black people and white people continued to mingle, do business with each other, and often maintain cordial relations.

In 1885, T. McCants Stewart, a black journalist from New York, traveled to his native South Carolina expecting a rough reception once his train headed south from Washington, D.C. To his surprise, the conductor allowed him to remain in his seat while white riders sat on baggage or stood. He provoked little reaction among white passengers when he entered the dining car. Some of them struck up a conversation with him. Stewart, who admitted he had begun his journey with "a chip on my shoulder . . . [daring] any man to knock it off," now observed that "the whites of the South are really less afraid to [have] contact with colored people than the whites of the North." In Columbia, South Carolina, Stewart found that he could move about with no restrictions. "I can ride in first-class cars. . . . I can go into saloons and get refreshments even as in New York. I can stop in and drink a glass of soda and be more politely waited upon than in some parts of New England."

Other black people corroborated Stewart's experiences. John Gray Lucas, a native of Pine Bluff, Arkansas, attended law school in Boston. There, in an 1887 newspaper interview, Lucas noted that three of Pine Bluff's eight city councilmen and half the police force were black and that black people encountered no segregation or discrimination in public careers. Given the racial climate in Pine Bluff, Lucas wondered "why more colored young men from the North did not make Arkansas their home. It is an inviting field for them, and a grand opportunity to make something of themselves." Lucas followed his own advice and returned to Pine Bluff, where he embarked on a successful legal career in the 1890s.

During the 1880s, black people joined interracial labor unions and continued to be active in the Republican party. They engaged in business with white people. In the countryside, African Americans and white people hunted and fished together, worked side by side at sawmills, and traded with each other. Cities were segregated more by class than by race, and people of both races sometimes lived in the same neighborhoods. To be sure, black people faced discrimination in employment and voting and random retaliation for perceived violations of racial barriers. But those barriers were by no means fixed.

The White Backlash

The black generation that came of age in this environment demanded full participation in American society. As the young black editor of Nashville's *Fisk Herald* proclaimed in 1889, "We are not the Negro from whom the chains of slavery fell a quarter of a century ago. . . . We are now qualified, and being the equal of whites, should be treated as such." Charles Price, an educator from North Carolina, admonished colleagues in 1890, "If we do not possess the manhood and patriotism to stand up in the defense of . . . constitutional rights and protest long, loud and unitedly against their continual infringements, we are unworthy of heritage as American citizens and deserve to have fastened on us the wrongs of which many are disposed to complain."

For many in the generation of white Southerners who came of age in the same period, this assertiveness rankled. These young white people, raised on the myth of the Lost Cause, were continually reminded of the heroism and sacrifice of their fathers during the Civil War. Confronted with what was for many worse conditions than their families had enjoyed before the war, they resented the changed status of black people. For them, black people replaced the Yankees as the enemy; they saw it as their mission to preserve white purity and dominance. Echoing these sentiments, David Schenck, a Greensboro, North Carolina, businessman, wrote in 1890 that "the breach between the races widens as the young free negroes grow up and intrude

themselves on white society and nothing prevents the white people of the South from annihilating the negro race but the military power of the United States Government." Using the Darwinian language popular among educated white people at the time, Schenck concluded, "I pity the Negro, but the struggle is for the survival of the fittest race."

The South's deteriorating rural economy and the volatile politics of the late 1880s and early 1890s exacerbated the growing tensions between assertive black people and threatened white people. So too did the growth of industry and cities in the South. In the cities, black and white people came in close contact, competing for jobs and jostling each other for seats on streetcars and trains. Racist rhetoric and violence against black people accelerated in the 1890s.

Lynch Law

In 1892, three prominent black men, Tom Moss, Calvin McDowell, and William Stewart, opened a grocery on the south side of Memphis, an area with a large African-American population. The People's Grocery prospered while a white-owned store across the street struggled. The proprietor of the white-owned store, W. H. Barrett, was incensed. He secured an indictment against Moss, McDowell, and Stewart for maintaining a public nuisance. Outraged black community leaders called a protest meeting at the grocery during which two people made threats against Barrett. Barrett learned of the threats, noti-

Lynching became a public spectacle, a ritual designed to reinforce white supremacy. Note the matter-of-fact satisfaction of the spectators to this gruesome murder of a black man.

fied the police, and warned the gathering at the People's Grocery that white people planned to attack and destroy the store. Nine sheriff's deputies, all white, approached the store to arrest the men who had threatened Barrett. Fearing Barrett's threatened white assault, the people in the grocery fired on the deputies, unaware who they were, and wounded three. When the deputies identified themselves, thirty black people surrendered, including Moss, McDowell, and Stewart, and were imprisoned. Four days later, deputies removed the three owners from jail, took them to a deserted area, and shot them dead.

The men at the People's Grocery had violated two of the unspoken rules that white Southerners imposed on black Southerners to maintain racial barriers: They had prospered, and they had forcefully challenged white authority. During 1892, a year of political agitation and economic depression, 235 lynchings occurred in the South. White mobs lynched nearly two thousand black Southerners between 1882 and 1903. During the 1890s, lynchings occurred at the rate of 150 a year. Most lynchers were working-class whites with rural roots who were struggling in the depressed economy of the 1890s and enraged at the fluidity of urban race relations. The men who murdered Moss, McDowell, and Stewart, for example, had recently moved to Memphis from the countryside, where they had been unable to make a living farming.

The silence or tepid disapproval of white leaders condoned this orgy of violence. The substitution of lynch law for a court of law seemed a cheap price to pay for white solidarity at a time when political and economic pressures threatened entrenched white leaders. In 1893, Atlanta's Methodist bishop, Atticus G. Haygood, typically a spokesman for racial moderation, objected to the torture some white lynchers inflicted on their victims but added, "Unless assaults by Negroes on white women and little girls come to an end, there will most probably be still further displays of vengeance that will shock the world."

Haygood's comments reflect the most common justification for lynching—the presumed threat posed by black men to the sexual virtue of white women. Sexual "crimes" could include remarks, glances, and gestures. Yet only 25 percent of the lynchings that took place in the thirty years after 1890 had some alleged sexual connection. Certainly, the men of the People's Grocery had committed no sex crime. Lynchers did not carry out their grisly crimes to end a rape epidemic; they killed to keep black men in their place and to restore their own sense of manhood and honor.

Ida B. Wells, who owned a black newspaper in Memphis, used her columns to publicize the People's Grocery lynchings. The great casualty of the lynchings, she noted, was her faith that education, wealth, and upright living guaranteed black people the equality and justice they had long sought. The reverse was true. The more black people succeeded, the greater was their threat to white people. She investigated other lynchings, countering the claim that they were the result of assaults on white women. When she suggested that, on the contrary, perhaps some white women were attracted to black men, she enraged the white citizens of Memphis, who destroyed her press and office. Exiled to Chicago, Wells devoted herself to the struggle for racial justice.

Segregation by Law

Southern white lawmakers sought to cement white solidarity and ensure black subservience in the 1890s by instituting **segregation** by law and the **disfranchisement** of black voters. Racial segregation restricting black Americans to separate and rarely equal public facilities had prevailed nationwide before the Civil

Ida B. Wells, an outspoken critic of lynching, fled to Chicago following the People's Grocery lynchings in Memphis in 1892 and became a national civil rights leader.

War. After 1870, the custom spread rapidly in southern cities. In Richmond by the early 1870s, segregation laws required black people registering to vote to enter through separate doors and registrars to count their ballots separately. The city's prison and hospitals were segregated. So too were its horse-drawn railways, its schools, and most of its restaurants, hotels, and theaters.

During the same period, many northern cities and states, often in response to protests by African Americans, were ending segregation. Massachusetts, for example, passed the nation's first public accommodations law in May 1865, desegregating all public facilities. Cities such as New York, Cleveland, and Cincinnati desegregated their streetcars. Chicago, Cleveland, Milwaukee, and the entire state of Michigan desegregated their public school systems. Roughly 95 percent of the nation's black population, however, lived in the South. Integration in the North consequently required white people to give up very little to black people. And as African-American aspirations increased in the South during the 1890s as their political power waned, they became more vulnerable to segregation by law at the state level. At the same time, migration to cities, industrial development, and technologies such as railroads and elevators increased the opportunities for racial contact and muddled the rules of racial interaction.

Much of the new legislation focused on railroads, a symbol of modernity and mobility in the New South. Local laws and customs could not control racial interaction on interstate railroads. White passengers objected to black passengers' implied assertion of economic and social equality when they sat with them in dining cars and first-class compartments. Black Southerners, in contrast, viewed equal access to railroad facilities as a sign of respectability and acceptance. When southern state legislatures required railroads to provide segregated facilities, black people protested.

The railroad segregation laws required the railroads to provide "separate but equal" accommodations for black passengers. Railroads balked at the expense involved in doing so and provided black passengers with distinctly inferior facilities. Many lines refused to sell first-class tickets to black people and treated them roughly if they sat in first-class seats or tried to eat in the dining car. In 1890, Homer Plessy, a black Louisianan, refused to leave the first-class car of a railroad traveling through the state. Arrested, he filed suit, arguing that his payment of the first-class fare entitled him to sit in the same first-class accommodations as white passengers. He claimed that under his right of citizenship guaranteed by the Fourteenth Amendment, neither the state of Louisiana nor the railroad could discriminate against him on the basis of color. The Constitution, he claimed, was colorblind.

The U.S. Supreme Court ruled on the case, *Plessy v. Ferguson*, in 1896. In a seven-to-one decision, the Court held that Louisiana's railroad segregation law did not violate the Constitution as long as the railroads or the state provided equal accommodations. The decision left unclear what "equal" meant. In the Court's view, "Legislation is powerless to eradicate racial instincts," meaning that segregation of the races was natural and transcended constitutional considerations. The only justice to vote against the decision was John Marshall Harlan, a Kentuckian and former slave owner. In a stinging dissent, he predicted that the decision would result in an all-out assault on black rights. "The destinies of the two races . . . are indissolubly linked together," Harlan declared, "and the interests of both require that the common government of all shall not permit the seeds of race hate to be planted under the sanction of law."

Harlan's was a prophetic dissent. Both northern and southern states enacted new segregation laws in the wake of *Plessy v. Ferguson*. In practice, the separate facilities for black people these laws required, if provided at all, were rarely equal. A sense of futility, time, expense, and physical danger dissuaded black people from challenging the statutes. Protests in the press, appeals to white leaders, and occasional boycotts failed to stem the rising tide. By 1900, segregation by law extended to public conveyances, theaters, hotels, restaurants, parks, and schools.

The segregation statutes came to be known collectively as **Jim Crow laws**, after the blackface stage persona of Thomas Rice, a white northern minstrel show performer in the 1820s. Reflecting white stereotypes of African Americans, Rice caricatured Crow as a foolish, elderly, lame slave who spoke in an exaggerated dialect.

Economic segregation followed social segregation. Before the Civil War, black men had dominated crafts such as carpentry and masonry. By the 1890s, white men were replacing them in these trades and excluding them from new trades such as plumbing and electrical work. Trade unions, composed primarily of craft workers, began systematically to exclude African Americans. Although the steel and tobacco industries hired black workers, most other manufacturers turned them away. Confined increasingly to low or unskilled positions in

OVERVIEW

THE MARCH OF DISFRANCHISEMENT ACROSS THE SOUTH, 1889–1908

Year	State	Strategies
1889	Florida	Poll tax
1889	Tennessee	Poll tax
1890	Mississippi	Poll tax, literacy test, understanding clause
1891	Arkansas	Poll tax
1893, 1901	Alabama	Poll tax, literacy test, grandfather clause
1894, 1895	South Carolina	Poll tax, literacy test, understanding clause
1894, 1902	Virginia	Poll tax, literacy test, understanding clause
1897, 1898	Louisiana	Poll tax, literacy test, grandfather clause
1899, 1900	North Carolina	Poll tax, literacy test, grandfather clause
1902	Texas	Poll tax
1908	Georgia	Poll tax, literacy test, understanding clause, grandfather clause

railroad construction, the timber industry, and agriculture, black people underwent **deskilling**—a decline in workforce expertise—after 1890. With lower incomes from unskilled labor, they faced reduced opportunities for better housing and education.

Disfranchisement

With economic and social segregation came political isolation. The authority of post-Reconstruction Redeemer governments had rested on their ability to limit and control the black vote. Following the political instability of the late 1880s and the 1890s, however, white leaders determined to disfranchise black people altogether, thereby reinforcing white solidarity and eliminating the need to consider black interests. Obstacles loomed—the Fifteenth Amendment, which guaranteed freedmen the right to vote, and a Republican-dominated Congress—but with a national consensus emerging in support of white supremacy, they proved easy to circumvent.

Rural and urban white elites engineered the disfranchisement campaigns. Support for disfranchisement was especially strong among large landowners in the South's plantation districts, where heavy concentrations of black people threatened their political domination. Urban leaders, especially after the turmoil of the 1890s, looked on disfranchisement as a way to stabilize politics and make elections more predictable.

The movement to reduce or eliminate the black vote in the South began in the 1880s and continued through the early 1900s (see the overview table, "The March of Disfranchisement across the South, 1889–1908"). Democrats enacted a variety of measures to attain their objectives without violating the letter of the Fifteenth Amendment. They complicated the registration and voting processes. States enacted **poll taxes**, requiring citizens to pay to vote. They adopted the secret ballot, which confused and intimidated illiterate black voters accustomed to using ballots with colors to identify parties. States set literacy and educational qualifications for voting or required prospective registrants to "interpret" a section of the state constitution. To avoid disfranchising poor, illiterate white voters with these measures, states enacted **grandfather clauses** granting the vote automatically to anyone whose grandfather could have voted prior to 1867 (the year Congressional Reconstruction began). The grandfathers of

American Views

ROBERT SMALLS ARGUES AGAINST DISFRANCHISEMENT

Born in Beaufort, South Carolina, in 1839, Robert Smalls served as a slave pilot in Charleston Harbor. In 1862, he emancipated himself, with his family and friends, when he delivered a Confederate steamer, the *Planter*, to a Union fleet blockading the harbor. He entered politics in 1864 as a delegate from his state to the Republican National Convention. He helped write South Carolina's Reconstruction constitution, which, among its provisions, guaranteed the right of former slaves to vote and hold office. Smalls won election to the state house of representatives in 1869, the state senate in 1871, and the U.S. House of Representatives in 1875. With opportunities for African Americans to hold public office declining following Reconstruction, Smalls secured appointment as collector of the Port of Beaufort, a federal post he occupied until his death in 1915. In the speech excerpted here—delivered to the South Carolina Constitutional Convention of 1895—he bitterly assails the state's plan to disfranchise black voters.

❖ **From the white perspective, what is Smalls's most telling argument against the disfranchisement and the planned strategies to implement it?**

❖ **How does Smalls depict the black citizens of South Carolina?**

❖ **Why were white political leaders unmoved by Smalls's plea?**

Mr. President, this convention has been called for no other purpose than the disfranchisement of the negro. . . .

    The negroes are paying taxes in the south on $263,000,000 worth of property. In South Carolina, according to the census, the negroes pay tax on $12,500,000 worth of property. That was in 1890. You voted down without discussion . . . a proposition for a simple property and education qualification [for voting]. What do you want? . . .

most black men in the 1890s had been slaves, ineligible to vote.

    Tennessee was the first state to pass disfranchising legislation. In 1889, it required the secret ballot and a poll tax in four cities—Nashville, Memphis, Chattanooga, and Knoxville—where African Americans often held a balance of power. A year later, Mississippi amended its constitution to require voters to pass a literacy test and prove they "understood" the state constitution. The laws granted the registrar wide latitude in interpreting the accuracy of the registrant's understanding. When a journalist asked an Alabama lawmaker if Jesus Christ could pass his state's "understanding" test, the legislator replied, "That would depend entirely on which way he was going to vote."

    Lawmakers sold white citizens on franchise restrictions with the promise that they would apply only to black voters and would scarcely affect white voters. This promise proved untrue. Alarmed by the Populist uprising, Democratic leaders used disfranchisement to gut dissenting parties. During the 1880s, minority parties in the South consistently polled an average of 40 percent of the statewide vote; by the mid-1890s, that figure had diminished to 30 percent, despite the Populist insurgency. Turnout dropped even more dramatically. In Mississippi, for example, voter turnout in gubernatorial races during the 1880s averaged 51 percent; during the 1890s, it was 21 percent. Black turnout in Mississippi, which averaged 39 percent in the 1880s, plummeted to near zero in the 1890s. Over-

In behalf of the 600,000 negroes in the State and the 132,000 negro voters all that I demand is that a fair and honest election law be passed. We care not what the qualifications imposed are, all that we ask is that they be fair and honest, and honorable, and with these provisos we will stand or fall by it. You have 102,000 white men over 21 years of age, 13,000 of these cannot read nor write. You dare not disfranchise them, and you know that the man who proposes it will never be elected to another office in the State of South Carolina. . . . Fifty-eight thousand negroes cannot read nor write. This leaves a majority of 14,000 white men who can read and write over the same class of negroes in this State. We are willing to accept a scheme that provides that no man who cannot read nor write can vote, if you dare pass it. How can you expect an ordinary man to "understand and explain" any section of the Constitution, to correspond to the interpretation put upon it by the manager of election, when by a very recent decision of the supreme court, composed of the most learned men in State, two of them put one construction upon a section, and the other justice put an entirely different construction upon it. To embody such a provision in the election law would be to mean that every white man would interpret it aright and every negro would interpret it wrong. . . . Some morning you may wake up to find that the bone and sinew of your country is gone. The negro is needed in the cotton fields and in the low country rice fields, and if you impose too hard conditions upon the negro in this State there will be nothing else for him to do but to leave. What then will you do about your phosphate works? No one but a negro can work them; the mines that pay the interest on your State debt. I tell you the negro is the bone and sinew of your country and you cannot do without him. I do not believe you want to get rid of the negro, else why did you impose a high tax on immigration agents who might come here to get him to leave?

Now, Mr. President we should not talk one thing and mean another. We should not deceive ourselves. Let us make a Constitution that is fair, honest and just. Let us make a Constitution for all the people, one we will be proud of and our children will receive with delight.

Source: The Columbia State, *October 27, 1895.*

all turnout, which averaged 64 percent during the 1880s, fell to only 30 percent by 1910.

Black people protested disfranchisement vigorously. When 160 South Carolina delegates gathered to amend the state constitution in 1895, the six black delegates among them mounted a passionate but futile defense of their right to vote. Black delegate W. J. Whipper noted the irony of white people clamoring for supremacy when they already held the vast majority of the state's elected offices. He also pointed out that African Americans voted responsibly where they had a majority and frequently elected white candidates. Robert Smalls, the state's leading black politician, urged delegates not to turn their backs on the state's black population (see "American Views: Robert Smalls Argues against Disfranchisement"). Such pleas fell on deaf ears.

A National Consensus on Race

How could the South get away with it? How could Southerners openly segregate, disfranchise, and lynch African Americans without a national outcry? Apparently, the majority of Americans in the 1890s subscribed to the notion that black people were inferior to white people and deserved to be treated as second-class citizens. Contemporary depictions of black people show scarcely human stereotypes: black men with bulbous lips and bulging eyes, fat black women wearing turbans and smiling vacuously, and black children contentedly eating watermelon or romping with jungle animals. These images appeared on cereal boxes, in advertisements, in children's books, in newspaper cartoons, and as lawn ornaments. Popular theater of the day featured white men in blackface cavorting in

Racial stereotypes permeated American popular culture by the turn of the twentieth century. Images like this advertisement for Pullman railroad cars, which depicts a deferential black porter attending to white passengers, reinforced racist beliefs that black people belonged in servile roles. Immersed in such images, white people assumed they depicted the natural order of things.

ridiculous fashion and singing songs such as "All Coons Look Alike to Me" and "I Wish My Color Would Fade." Among the widely read books of the era was *The Clansman*, a glorification of the rise of the Ku Klux Klan by Thomas Dixon, a North Carolinian living in New York City and an ardent white supremacist. D. W. Griffith transformed *The Clansman* into an immensely popular motion picture epic under the title *Birth of a Nation*.

Intellectual and political opinion in the North bolstered southern policy. So-called "scientific" racism purported to establish white superiority and black inferiority on biological grounds.

Northern-born professional historians reinterpreted the Civil War and Reconstruction in the white South's favor. Historian William A. Dunning, the generation's leading authority on Reconstruction, wrote in 1901 that the North's "views as to the political capacity of the blacks had been irrational." Respected journals openly supported disfranchisement and segregation. The progressive journal *Outlook* hailed disfranchisement because it made it "impossible in the future for ignorant, shiftless, and corrupt negroes to misrepresent their race in political action." Harvard's Charles Francis Adams, Jr., chided colleagues who disregarded the "fundamental, scientific facts" he claimed demonstrated black inferiority. The *New York Times*, summarizing this national consensus in 1903, noted that "practically the whole country" supported the "southern solution" to the race issue, because "there was no other possible settlement."

These views permeated Congress, which made no effort to block the institutionalization of white supremacy in the South after 1890, and the courts, which upheld discriminatory legislation. As a delegate at the Alabama disfranchisement convention of 1901 noted, "The race problem is no longer confined to the States of the South, [and] we have the sympathy instead of the hostility of the North."

By the mid-1890s, Republicans were so entrenched in the North and West that they did not need southern votes to win presidential elections or to control Congress. Besides, business-oriented Republicans found common ground with conservative southern Democrats on fiscal policy and foreign affairs.

As the white consensus on race emerged, the status of African Americans slipped in the North as well as the South. Although no northern states threatened to deny black citizens the right to vote, they did increase segregation. The booming industries of the North generally did not hire black workers. Antidiscrimination laws on the books since the Civil War went unenforced. In 1904, 1906, and 1908, race riots erupted in Springfield, Ohio; Greensburg, Indiana; and Springfield, Illinois, matching similar disturbances in Wilmington, North Carolina, and Atlanta, Georgia.

Response of the Black Community

American democracy had, it seemed, hung out a "whites only" sign. How could African Americans respond to the growing political, social, and economic restrictions on their lives? Given white America's hostility, protest proved ineffective, even dangerous. African Americans organized more than a dozen boycotts of streetcar systems in the urban South between 1896 and 1908 in an effort to desegregate them, but not one succeeded. The Afro-American Council, formed in 1890 to protest the deteriorating conditions of black life, accomplished little and disbanded in 1908. W. E. B. Du Bois organized an annual Conference on Negro Problems at Atlanta University beginning in 1896, but it produced no effective plan of action.

A few black people chose to leave the South. In 1879, Benjamin "Pap" Singleton, a Nashville real estate agent, led several thousand black migrants to Kansas. Henry McNeal Turner of Georgia, an African Methodist Episcopal (AME) bishop, promoted migration to Liberia, but only a few hundred made the trip in the late 1870s, Turner not included, and most of those returned disappointed. Most black people who moved in the 1890s stayed within the South, settling in places like Mississippi, Louisiana, and Texas, where they could find work with timber companies or farming new lands that had opened to cotton and rice cultivation.

More commonly, black people withdrew to develop their own rich community life within the restricted confines white society permitted them. Particularly in the cities of the South, they could live relatively free of white surveillance and even white contact. In 1890, fully 70 percent of black city dwellers lived in the South; and between 1860 and 1900, the proportion of black people in the cities of the South rose from one in six to more than one in three. The institutions, businesses, and families that black people began painstakingly building during Reconstruction continued to grow, and in some cases flourish, after 1877.

By the 1880s, a new black middle class had emerged in the South. Urban-based, professional, business-oriented, and serving a primarily black clientele, its members fashioned an interconnected web of churches, fraternal and self-help organizations, families, and businesses. Black Baptists, AME, and AME Zion churches led reform efforts in the black community, seeking to eliminate drinking, prostitution, and other vices in black neighborhoods.

African-American fraternal and self-help groups, led by middle-class black people, functioned as surrogate welfare organizations for the poor. Some groups, such as the Colored Masons and the Colored Odd Fellows, paralleled white organizations. Black membership rates usually exceeded those in the white community. More than 50 percent of Nashville's black men, for example, belonged to various fraternal associations in the city. Fraternal orders also served as the seedbed for such business ventures as the North Carolina Mutual Life Insurance Company, founded in Durham in 1898. Within two decades, North Carolina Mutual became the largest black-owned business in the nation and helped transform Durham into the "capital of the black middle class." Durham's thriving black business district included several black-owned insurance firms, banks, and a textile mill. Most southern cities boasted active black business districts by the 1890s.

Nashville's J. C. Napier typified the activism of the African-American urban middle class in the New South era. He belonged to two of the city's prominent black churches, was active in Republican politics, played an important role in several temperance and fraternal societies, served as president of

The offices of the North Carolina Mutual Life Insurance Company, around 1900. Founded by John Merrick, C. C. Spaulding, and Dr. A. M. Moore (all of whom appear in this picture), this Durham-based insurance company became one of the most successful black enterprises in the country.

the local black YMCA chapter, and as an attorney helped his fellow African Americans with numerous legal matters. Before disfranchisement in the 1890s, Napier used his leverage to secure the appointment of black teachers for black schools and of black applicants to the police force and fire department.

The African-American middle class worked especially hard to improve black education (see Figure 19-3). Declining black political power encouraged white leaders to reduce funding for black public education. Black students in cities had only makeshift facilities; those in the countryside had almost no facilities. By the early 1900s, the student–teacher ratio in Nashville's segregated school system was thirty-three to one for white schools but seventy-one to one for black schools. To improve these conditions, black middle-class leaders solicited educational funds from northern philanthropic organizations.

Black women played an increasingly active and prominent role in African-American communities after 1877, especially in cities. The experience of Ida B. Wells illustrates this trend. When she moved to Memphis from Mississippi in 1884, she entered an environment that, despite her race and gender, offered her opportunities for intellectual growth and a professional career. In December 1886, for example, she attended a lecture at an interracial Knights of Labor meeting (see Chapter 20). Earlier that year, she witnessed a religious revival conducted by the nation's leading evangelist, Dwight Moody. The following year, Wells began her journalism career and soon purchased a one-third interest in a local black newspaper.

Black women's clubs evolved to address the new era in race relations. Most African-American women in southern cities worked as domestics or laundresses. Black women's clubs supported day care facilities for working mothers and settlement houses in poor black neighborhoods modeled after those in northern cities. Atlanta's Neighborhood Union, founded by Lugenia Burns Hope in 1908, provided playgrounds and a health center and secured a grant from a New York foundation to improve black education in the city. Black women's clubs also established homes for single black working women to protect them from sexual exploitation, and they worked for woman suffrage "to reckon with men who place no value on her [black woman's] virtue," as Nannie H. Burroughs of the **National Association of Colored Women** argued at the turn of the century.

Black clubwomen were aware of their leadership role in the first postemancipation generation.

Figure 19-3 Disfranchisement and Educational Spending in the South, 1890–1910
By barring black people from the political process, franchise restrictions limited their access to government services. Educational expenditures—which increased for white people but decreased for black people following disfranchisement—provide one measure of the result.

Data Source: Robert A. Margo, "Disfranchisement, School Finance, and the Economics of Segregated Schools in the United States South, 1890–1910," Ph.D. diss., Harvard University, 1982.

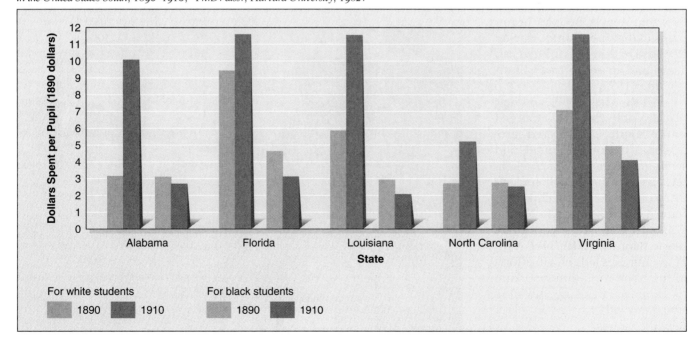

Anna J. Cooper, a Nashville clubwoman, wrote in 1892 that to be a member of this generation was "to have a heritage unique in the ages." Assertive black women did not arouse the same degree of white antagonism as assertive black men. They could operate in a broader public arena than men and speak out more forcefully. Sometimes what they spoke out about was political corruption within the black community itself. They were critical, for example, of the willingness of poor black people to accept bribes and other favors in exchange for their votes, a willingness they saw at least partially responsible for black disfranchisement.

As such views suggest, middle-class black clubwomen, like other middle-class reformers, were sometimes disdainful of the poor even as they worked to help them. Mary Church Terrell, for example, president of the National Association of Colored Women, informed her colleagues in 1900 that association-sponsored day care programs assisted their "benighted sisters in the Black Belt of Alabama . . . whose ignorance of everything that makes life sweet or worth the living, no ray of light would have penetrated but for us."

After disfranchisement, middle-class black women assumed an even more pivotal role in the black community. They often used their relations with prominent white women and organizations such as the WCTU and the Young Womens Christian Association (YWCA) to press for public commitments to improve the health and education of African Americans. Absent political pressure from black men, as well as the danger of African-American males asserting themselves in the tense racial climate after 1890, black women became critical spokespersons for their race.

The extension of black club work into rural areas of the South, where the majority of the African-American population lived, to educate families about hygiene, nutrition, and child care, anticipated similar efforts among white women after 1900. But unlike their white counterparts, these middle-class black women worked with limited resources in a context of simmering racial hostility and political and economic impotence. In response, they nurtured a self-help strategy to improve the conditions of the people they sought to help. One of the most prominent African-American leaders of the late nineteenth and early twentieth centuries, Booker T. Washington, adopted a similar approach to racial uplift.

Born a slave in Virginia in 1856, Washington and his family worked in the salt and coal mines of West Virginia after the Civil War. Ambitious and flushed with the postwar enthusiasm for advancement that gripped freedmen, he enrolled in Hampton Normal and Agricultural Institute, the premier black educational institution in the South at that time. Washington worked his way through Hampton, graduated, taught for a time, and then, in 1881, founded the **Tuskegee Institute** for black students in rural Alabama. Washington thought his students would be best served if they learned a trade and workplace discipline. By learning industrial skills, he maintained, black people could secure self-respect and economic independence. As a result, Tuskegee emphasized vocational training over the liberal arts.

Washington argued that African Americans should accommodate themselves to segregation and disfranchisement until they could prove their economic worth to American society. In exchange for this accommodation, however, white people should help provide black people with

Booker T. Washington (left) and W. E. B. Du Bois (right). The differences between these two prominent black leaders reflected in part the differences between the North and the South in the late nineteenth and early twentieth centuries. The northern-born Du Bois challenged segregation and pinned his hopes for improving the condition of African Americans on a talented elite. The southern-born Washington counseled acquiescence to segregation, maintaining that black people could ultimately gain the acceptance of white society through self-improvement and hard work.

the education and job training they would need to gain their independence. Washington articulated this position, known as the **Atlanta Compromise**, in a speech at the Atlanta Cotton States and International Exposition in 1895. Despite his conciliatory public stance, Washington secretly helped finance legal challenges to segregation and disfranchisement. The social and economic realities of the South, meanwhile, frustrated his educational mission. Increasingly, black people were shut out of the kinds of jobs for which Washington hoped to train them. Facing a depressed rural economy and growing racial violence, they had little prospect of advancement.

Another prominent African-American leader, W. E. B. Du Bois, challenged Washington's acceptance of black social inequality. Born in Massachusetts in 1868, Du Bois was the first African-American to earn a doctorate at Harvard. Du Bois promoted self-help, education, and black pride. A gifted teacher and writer, he taught at Atlanta University and wrote eighteen books on various aspects of black life in America. In *The Souls of Black Folk*, published in 1903, he described the strengths of black culture and attacked Washington's Atlanta Compromise. Du Bois was a cofounder, in 1910, of the **National Association for the Advancement of Colored People (NAACP)**, an interracial organization dedicated to restoring African-American political and social rights.

Despite their differences, which reflected their divergent backgrounds, Washington and Du Bois agreed on many issues. Both had reservations about allowing illiterate black people to vote, and both believed that black success in the South required some white assistance. As Du Bois wrote in *The Souls of Black Folk,* "Any movement for the elevation of the Southern Negro needs the cooperation, the sympathy, and the support of the best white people in order to succeed." But it became apparent to Du Bois that "the best white people" did not care to elevate black Southerners. In 1906, after a bloody race riot in Atlanta, Du Bois left the South, a decision millions of black Southerners would make over the next two decades.

A curtain had descended between black and white, North and South on the issue of race. Northerners did not care to look behind that curtain to acknowledge the injustice of southern treatment of black people. As long as it provided the raw materials for the North's new urban industrial economy and maintained the peace, the South could count on the rest of the country not to interfere in its solution to race relations. Indeed, to the extent that most white Americans concerned themselves with race, they agreed with the southern solution.

Conclusion

In many respects, the South was more like the rest of the nation in 1900 than at any other time since 1860. Southern cities hummed with activity and industries from textiles to steel dotted the southern interior. Young men and women migrated to southern cities to pursue opportunities unavailable to their parents. Advances in the production and marketing of cigarettes and soft drinks would soon make southern entrepreneurs and their products household names. Southerners ordered fashions from Sears, Roebuck catalogs and enjoyed electric lights, electric trolleys, and indoor plumbing as much as other urban Americans.

Americans idealized the South—not the urban industrial South but a mythical South of rural grace and hospitality. National magazines and publishers rushed to print stories about this land of moonlight and magnolias, offering it as a counterpoint to the crowded, immigrant-infested, factory-fouled, money-grubbing North. It was this fantasy South that white people in both the North and the South imagined as they came to a common view on race and reconciled their differences. Northern journalists offered admiring portraits of southern heroes like Robert E. Lee, of whom one declared in 1906, "the nation has a hero to place beside her greatest." The Republican-dominated Congress agreed to care for the graves of the Confederate dead and ordered the return to the South of captured Confederate flags.

White Southerners cultivated national reconciliation but remained fiercely dedicated to preserving the peculiarities of their region: a one-party political system, disfranchisement, and segregation by law. The region's urban and industrial growth, impressive from the vantage of 1865, paled before that of the North. The South remained a colonial economy characterized more by deep rural poverty than urban prosperity.

How one viewed the New South depended on one's vantage point. White Northerners accepted at face value the picture Southerners painted for them of a chastened and prosperous yet still attractive region. Middle-class white people in the urban South enjoyed the benefits of a national economy and a secure social position. Middle-class white women enjoyed increased influence in the public realm, but not to the extent of their northern sisters. And the institutionalization of white supremacy gave even poor white farmers and factory workers a place in the social hierarchy a rung or two above the bottom.

For black people, the New South proved a crueler ruse than Reconstruction. No one now stepped forward to support their cause and stem the erosion of their economic independence, political freedom, and civil rights. Yet they did not give up the American dream, nor did they give up the South for the most part. They built communities and worked as best they could to challenge restrictions on their freedom.

The New South was thus both American and southern. It shared with the rest of the country a period of rapid urban and industrial growth. But the legacy of war and slavery still lay heavily on the South, manifesting itself in rural poverty, segregation, and black disfranchisement. The burdens of this legacy would limit the attainments of both black and white Southerners for another half-century until Americans finally rejected racial inequality as an affront to their national ideals.

Review Questions

1. In what ways did the growing activism of white middle-class women, the increasing assertiveness of young urban black people, and the persistence of the agricultural depression affect the politics of the South in the late 1880s and early 1890s?

2. We associate segregation and disfranchisement with reactionary political and social views. Yet many white people who promoted both seriously believed them to be reforms. How could white people hold such a view?

3. What strategies did black Southerners employ in response to the narrowing of economic and political opportunities in the New South?

4. New South publicists promoted the South as an emerging urban and industrial region. How accurate were their assertions in 1900?

Recommended Reading

Edward L. Ayers, *The Promise of the New South: Life after Reconstruction* (1992). Illuminates how the people of the late-nineteenth-century South accommodated the conflict between the economic and cultural legacies of the slave South and the currents of modernity, such as industrialization and the creation of a national state.

Paul M. Gaston, *The New South Creed: A Study in Southern Mythmaking* (1970). Provides an important assessment of how New South booster rhetoric matched up against the economic reality; especially good at examining how New South spokesmen turned images of the Old South and other southern traditions to the ends of urban and industrial development.

Walter Hines Page, *The Rebuilding of Old Commonwealths* (1902). The classic argument for the New South from one of its most serious promoters.

Howard N. Rabinowitz, *The First New South, 1865–1920* (1992). An interpretive survey of recent research on the era that explores a continuity between the Old South and the New that may have limited the latter's potential.

Howard N. Rabinowitz, *Race Relations in the Urban South, 1865–1890* (1978). A fine survey of how African Americans built communities in the urban South despite the worsening racial situation after Reconstruction.

Joel Williamson, *The Crucible of Race: Black–White Relations in the American South since Emancipation* (1984). An innovative work that details the racial attitudes of white Southerners and reveals how elites particularly used race to further political and social objectives.

C. Vann Woodward, *Origins of the New South, 1877–1913* (1951). A classic interpretation of the New South era that stresses the discontinuities between Old South and New.

Additional Sources

The Newness of the New South

Dwight B. Billings, Jr., *Planters and the Making of a "New South"* (1979).

Orville Vernon Burton, *In My Father's House Are Many Mansions: Family and Community in Edgefield County, South Carolina* (1985).

Orville Vernon Burton and Robert C. McMath, eds., *Toward a New South?* (1982).

David L. Carlton, *Mill and Town in South Carolina, 1880–1920* (1980).

Thomas D. Clark, *Pills, Petticoats, and Plows: The Southern Country Store* (1944).

John Milton Cooper, Jr., *Walter Hines Page* (1977).

Harold E. Davis, *Henry Grady's New South: Atlanta, a Brave and Beautiful City* (1990).

Don H. Doyle, *New Men, New Cities, New South: Atlanta, Nashville, Charleston, Mobile, 1860–1910* (1990).

Robert F. Durden, *The Dukes of Durham, 1865–1929* (1975).

Ronald D. Eller, *Miners, Millhands, and Mountaineers: Industrialization of the Appalachian South, 1880–1920* (1982).

Paul D. Escott, *Many Excellent People: Power and Privilege in North Carolina, 1850–1900* (1985).

Jacqueline Dowd Hall et al., *Like a Family: The Making of a Southern Cotton Mill World* (1987).

Patrick J. Hearden, *Independence and Empire: The New South's Cotton Mill Campaign, 1865–1901* (1982).

Tony Horwitz, *Confederates in the Attic: Dispatches from the Unfinished Civil War* (1998).

Maury Klein, *The Great Richmond Terminal: A Study in Businessmen and Business Strategy* (1970).

W. David Lewis, *Sloss Furnaces and the Rise of the Birmingham District: An Industrial Epic* (1994).

Cathy McHugh, *Mill Family: The Labor System in the Southern Cotton Textile Industry, 1880–1915* (1988).

Broadus Mitchell, *The Rise of Cotton Mills in the South* (1921).

Gail W. O'Brien, *The Legal Fraternity and the Making of a New South Community, 1848–1882* (1986).

James M. Russell, *Atlanta, 1847–1890: City Building in the Old South and the New* (1988).

Laurence Shore, *Southern Capitalists: The Ideological Leadership of an Elite, 1832–1885* (1986).

John S. Spratt, *The Road to Spindletop: Economic Change in Texas, 1875–1901* (1970).

John F. Stover, *The Railroads of the South, 1865–1900* (1955).

Nannie M. Tilley, *The Bright-Tobacco Industry, 1860–1929* (1948).

Nannie M. Tilley, *The R. J. Reynolds Tobacco Company* (1985).

Gavin Wright, *Old South, New South: Revolutions in the Southern Economy since the Civil War* (1986).

The Southern Agrarian Revolt

Raymond Arsenault, *Wild Ass of the Ozarks: Jeff Davis and the Social Bases of Southern Politics, 1888–1913* (1984).

Donna Barnes, *Farmers in Rebellion: The Rise and Fall of the Southern Farmers' Alliance and People's Party in Texas* (1987).

Alwyn Barr, *Reconstruction to Reform: Texas Politics, 1876–1906* (1971).

Gregg Cantrell, *Kenneth and John B. Rayner and the Limits of Southern Dissent* (1993).

Pete Daniel, *Breaking the Land: The Transformation of Cotton, Tobacco and Rice Cultures since 1880* (1985).

Gilbert Fite, *Cotton Fields No More: Southern Agriculture, 1865–1890* (1984).

Lawrence Goodwyn, *Democratic Promise: The Populist Movement in America* (1976).

Steven Hahn, *The Roots of Southern Populism: The Transformation of the Georgia Upcountry, 1850–1890* (1983).

Michael R. Hyman, *The Anti-Redeemers: Hill-Country Political Dissenters in the Lower South from Redemption to Populism* (1990).

Albert D. Kirwan, *Revolt of the Rednecks: Mississippi Politics, 1876–1925* (1951).

Robert McMath, Jr., *The Populist Vanguard: A History of the Southern Farmers' Alliance* (1975).

Kathleen Minnix, *Laughter in the Amen Corner: The Life of Evangelist Sam Jones* (1993).

I. A. Newby, *Plain Folk in the New South: Social Change and Cultural Persistence, 1880–1915* (1989).

Ted Ownby, *Subduing Satan: Religion, Recreation, and Manhood in the Rural South, 1865–1920* (1990).

Bruce Palmer, *"Man over Money": The Southern Populist Critique of American Capitalism* (1980).

Roger Ransom and Richard Sutch, *One Kind of Freedom: The Economic Consequences of Emancipation* (1977).

Theodore Saloutos, *Farmer Movements in the South, 1865–1933* (1960).

Michael Schwartz, *Radical Politics and Social Structure: The Southern Farmers' Alliance and Cotton Tenancy, 1880–1890* (1978).

Barton C. Shaw, *The Wool-Hat Boys: A History of the Populist Party in Georgia, 1892 to 1910* (1984).

Crandall A. Shifflett, *Patronage and Poverty in the Tobacco South: Louisa County, Virginia, 1860–1900* (1982).

Peter Wallenstein, *From Slave South to New South: Public Policy in Nineteenth-Century Georgia* (1987).

Samuel L. Webb, *Two-Party Politics in the One-Party South: Alabama's Hill Country, 1874–1920* (1997).

Jonathan Wiener, *Social Origins of the New South: Alabama, 1860–1885* (1978).

Harold D. Woodman, *King Cotton and His Retainers: Financing and Marketing the Cotton Crop of the South, 1800–1925* (1968).

C. Vann Woodward, *Tom Watson: Agrarian Rebel* (1938).

Women in the New South

Virginia Bernhard et al., eds., *Southern Women: Histories and Identities* (1992).

Elizabeth York Enstam, *Women and the Creation of Urban Life: Dallas, Texas, 1843–1920* (1998).

Jean E. Friedman, *The Enclosed Garden: Women and Community in the Evangelical South, 1830–1900* (1985).

Glenda Elizabeth Gilmore, *Gender and Jim Crow: Women and Politics of White Supremacy in North Carolina, 1896–1920* (1996).

Elna C. Green, *Southern Strategies: Southern Women and the Woman Suffrage Question* (1997).

Evelyn Brooks Higginbotham, *Righteous Discontent: The Women's Movement in the Black Baptist Church, 1880–1920* (1993).

Tera W. Hunter, *To 'Joy My Freedom: Southern Black Women's Lives and Labors after the Civil War* (1997).

Katherine DuPre Lumpkin, *The Making of a Southerner* (1947).

John P. McDowell, *The Social Gospel in the South: The Woman's Home Mission Movement in the Methodist Episcopal Church, South, 1886–1939* (1982).

Anne Firor Scott, *The Southern Lady: From Pedestal to Politics, 1830–1930* (1970).

Mary Church Terrell, *A Colored Woman in a White World* (1980).

Mary Martha Thomas, *The New Woman in Alabama: Social Reforms and Suffrage, 1890–1920* (1992).

Elizabeth Hayes Turner, *Women, Culture, and Community: Religion and Reform in Galveston, 1880-1920* (1997).

Marsha Wedell, *Elite Women and the Reform Impulse in Memphis, 1875–1915* (1991).

Marjorie Spruill Wheeler, *New Women of the New South: The Leaders of the Woman Suffrage Movement in the Southern States* (1993).

Settling the Race Issue

Eric Anderson, *Race and Politics in North Carolina, 1872–1901: The Black Second* (1981).

Edward L. Ayers, *Vengeance and Justice: Crime and Punishment in the Nineteenth-Century American South* (1984).

Bess Beatty, *A Revolution Gone Backwards: The Black Response to National Politics, 1876–1896* (1987).

W. Fitzhugh Brundage, *Lynching in the New South: Georgia and Virginia, 1880–1930* (1993).

John W. Cell, *The Highest Stage of White Supremacy: The Origins of Segregation in South Africa and the American South* (1982).

Bruce Clayton, *The Savage Ideal: Intolerance and Intellectual Leadership in the South, 1890–1914* (1972).

William Cohen, *At Freedom's Edge: Black Mobility and the Southern White Quest for Racial Control, 1861–1915* (1991).

Gerald H. Gaither, *Blacks and the Populist Revolt: Ballots and Bigotry in the "New South"* (1977).

Willard B. Gatewood, Jr., *Black Americans and the White Man's Burden, 1898–1903* (1975).

Janette Thomas Greenwood, *Bittersweet Legacy: The Black and White "Better Classes" in Charlotte, 1850–1910* (1994).

Louis R. Harlan, *Booker T. Washington: The Making of a Black Leader, 1856–1901* (1972).

Stanley P. Hirshson, *Farewell to the Bloody Shirt: Northern Republicans and the Southern Negro, 1877–1893* (1962).

Gerald David Jaynes, *Branches without Roots: Genesis of the Black Working Class in the American South, 1862–1882* (1986).

Robert C. Kenzer, *Enterprising Southerners: Black Economic Success in North Carolina, 1865–1915* (1997).

J. Morgan Kousser, *The Shaping of Southern Politics: Suffrage Restriction and the Establishment of the One-Party South, 1880–1910* (1974).

Daniel Letwin, *The Challenge of Interracial Unionism: Alabama Coal Miners, 1878–1921* (1998).

Charles A. Lofgren, *The Plessy Case: A Legal-Historical Interpretation* (1987).

August Meier, *Negro Thought in America, 1880–1915: Racial Ideologies in the Age of Booker T. Washington* (1963).

H. Leon Prather, *We Have Taken a City: The Wilmington Racial Massacre and Coup of 1898* (1989).

Peter J. Rachleff, *Black Labor in the South: Richmond, Virginia, 1865–1890* (1984).

Nina Silber, *The Romance of Reunion: Northerners and the South* (1993).

George B. Tindall, *South Carolina Negroes, 1877–1900* (1952).

Stewart E. Tolnay and E. M. Beck, *A Festival of Violence: An Analysis of Southern Lynchings, 1882–1930* (1995).

Walter B. Weare, *Black Business in the New South: A Social History of the North Carolina Mutual Life Insurance Company* (1973).

C. Vann Woodward, *The Strange Career of Jim Crow* (1955).

George C. Wright, *Life behind a Veil: Blacks in Louisville, Kentucky, 1865–1930* (1985).

Where to Learn More

❖ **Museum of the New South, Charlotte, North Carolina.** The museum has exhibits on various New South themes. A permanent exhibit on the history of Charlotte and the Carolina Piedmont opens in the fall of 2001.

❖ **Atlanta History Center, Atlanta, Georgia.** The major exhibit, "Metropolitan Frontiers, 1835–2000," includes a strong segment on the New South era, including the development of separate black and white economies in Atlanta. The Herndon home, also on the grounds of the center, has an exhibit on black upper-class life in Atlanta from 1880 to 1930.

❖ **Sloss Furnaces National Historical Landmark, Birmingham, Alabama.** The site recalls the time when Birmingham challenged Pittsburgh as the nation's primary steel-producing center.

INDUSTRY, IMMIGRANTS, AND CITIES,
1870–1900

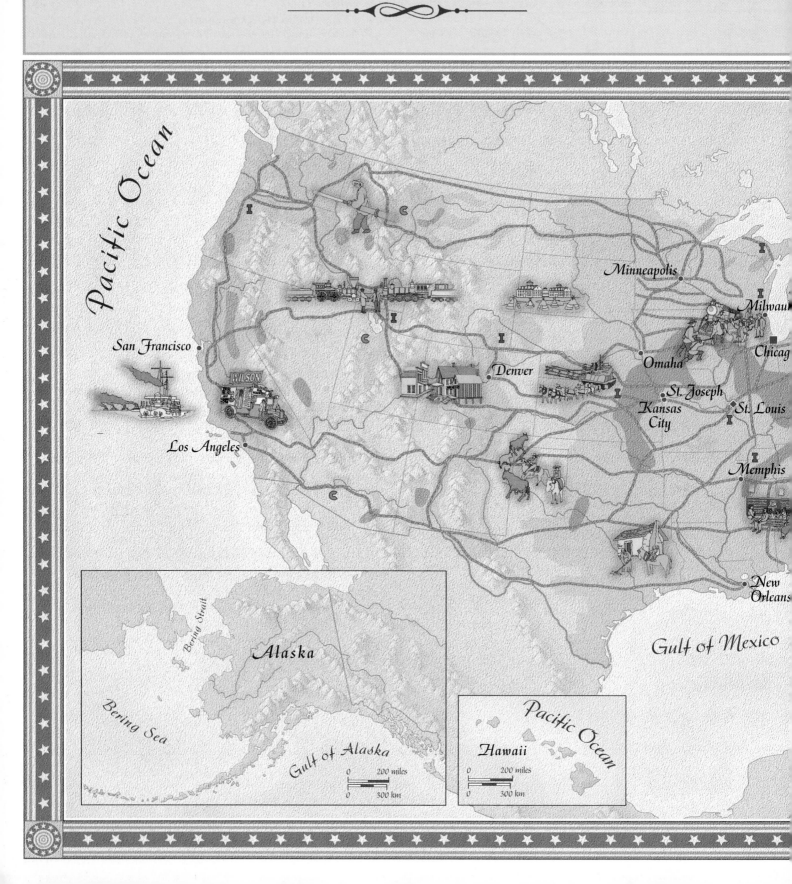

Pacific Ocean

Minneapolis

Milwau

Chicag

San Francisco

Omaha

St. Joseph

Denver

St. Louis

Kansas
City

Los Angeles

Memphis

New
Orleans

Gulf of Mexico

Bering Strait

Alaska

Bering Sea

Gulf of Alaska

0   200 miles

0   300 km

Pacific Ocean

Hawaii

0   200 miles

0   300 km

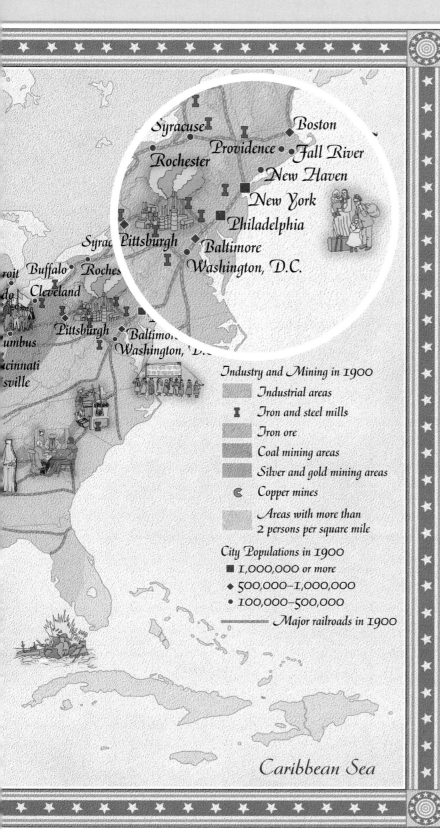

Industry and Mining in 1900

Industrial areas

⊥ Iron and steel mills

Iron ore

Coal mining areas

Silver and gold mining areas

☾ Copper mines

Areas with more than
2 persons per square mile

City Populations in 1900

■ 1,000,000 or more

◆ 500,000–1,000,000

● 100,000–500,000

—— Major railroads in 1900

Caribbean Sea

20

Chapter Outline

Key Topics

❖ The technological and organizational innovations behind the emergence of large industrial corporations

❖ Changes in the American workforce in the urban-industrial economy and the reaction of organized labor

❖ The impact of the new immigration and the start of African-American migration to the cities of the North

❖ The changing physical and social structure of the industrial city

❖ New patterns of residence and recreation in the consumer society

*P*hiladelphia, May 10, 1876: President Ulysses S. Grant and several hundred political and military dignitaries rise to their feet as the orchestra and chorale reach the climax of Handel's "Hallelujah Chorus." A huge American flag unfurls above a nearby building, and one hundred cannons roar a deafening salute to the start of America's second century.

This ceremony opened Philadelphia's Centennial Exposition, which more than 8 million people would visit over the next six months. There they witnessed the ingenuity of the world's newest industrial power. Thomas Edison explained his new automatic telegraph, and Alexander Graham Bell demonstrated his telephone to the wonder of onlookers. A giant Corliss steam engine loomed over the entrance to Machinery Hall, dwarfing the other exhibits and providing them with power. "Yes," a visitor concluded, "it is in these things of iron and steel that the national genius most freely speaks."

For many Americans, however, the fanfare of the exposition rang hollow. The country was in the midst of a depression that had begun in 1873 and would not bottom out until 1877. Tens of thousands were out of work, and countless others had lost their savings in bank failures and sour investments. With the typical daily wage a dollar, most Philadelphians could not afford the exposition's 50-cent admission price. They celebrated instead at "Centennial City," a ragtag collection of cheap bars, seedy hotels, small restaurants, and circus sideshows hurriedly constructed of wood and tin along a muddy mile-long strip across the street from the exposition's sturdy halls and manicured lawns.

This small area of Philadelphia reflected the promise and failure of late-nineteenth century America, a period often called the **Gilded Age**. The term is taken from the title of a novel by Mark Twain that satirizes the materialistic excesses of his day. It serves as a shorthand description of the shallow worship of wealth—and the veneer of respectability and prosperity covering deep economic and social divisions—that characterized the period.

Between 1870 and 1900, the country experienced a major demographic and economic transformation. Rapid industrial development changed the nature of the work force and the workplace. Large factories staffed by semiskilled laborers displaced the skilled artisans and small shops that had dominated American industry before 1870. Industrial development also accelerated urbanization. Between the Civil War and 1900, the proportion of the nation's population living in cities—swelled by migrants from the countryside and immigrants from Europe and Asia—increased from 20 to 40 percent, a rate of growth twice that of the population as a whole. During the 1880s alone, more than 5 million immigrants came to the United States, twice as many as in any previous decade.

The changes in American life were exhilarating for some, tragic for others. New opportunities opened as old opportunities disappeared. Vast new wealth was created, but poverty increased. New technologies eased life for some but left others untouched. It would be the great dilemma of early-twentieth-century America to reconcile these contradictions and satisfy the American quest for a decent life for all within the new urban industrial order.

New Industry

Between 1870 and 1900, the United States transformed itself from an agricultural nation—a nation of farmers, merchants, and artisans—into the world's foremost industrial power, producing more than one-third of the world's manufactured goods. By the early twentieth century, factory workers made up one-fourth of the work force, and agricultural workers had dropped from a half to less than a third

In this illustration celebrating the nation's centennial and the Philadelphia Centennial Exposition, a confident Uncle Sam stands astride a continent drawn together by American technology.

(see Figure 20-1). A factory with a few dozen employees would have been judged fair-sized in 1870. By the early twentieth century, many industries employed thousands of workers in a single plant. Some industries—petroleum, steel, and meatpacking, for example—had been unknown before the Civil War.

Although the size of the industrial workforce increased dramatically, the number of firms in a given industry shrank. Mergers, changes in corporate management and the organization of the workforce, and a compliant government left a few companies in control of vast segments of the American economy. Workers, reformers, and eventually government challenged this concentration of economic power.

Inventing Technology

Technology played a major role in transforming factory work and increasing the scale of production. Steam engines like the giant Corliss engine at the Centennial Exposition and, later, electricity freed manufacturers from dependence on water power. Factories no longer had to be located by rivers. They could be built anywhere accessible to the transportation system and a concentration of labor. Technology also enabled managers to substitute machines for workers, skewing the balance of power in the workplace toward employers. And it transformed city life, making available a host of new conveniences. By the early twentieth century, electric lights, appliances, ready-made clothing, and store-bought food eased middle-class life. Electric

trolleys whisked clerks, salespeople, bureaucrats, and bankers to new urban and suburban subdivisions. Electric streetlights lit up city streets at night. Amusement parks drew crowds with mechanical attractions scarcely imaginable a generation earlier. Movies entertained the masses. As historian and novelist Henry Adams put it at the turn of the century, "In the essentials of life . . . the boy of 1854 stood nearer [to] the year one than to the year 1900."

For much of the nineteenth century, the United States was dependent on the industrial nations of Europe for technological innovation. American engineers often went to England and Germany for education and training, and the textile industry, railroads, and the early steel industry benefited from German and English inventions.

In the late nineteenth century, the United States changed from a technological borrower to a technological innovator. By 1910, a million patents had been issued in the United States, 900,000 of them after 1870. Nothing represented this shift better than Thomas A. Edison's development of a practical electric lightbulb and electric generating system. Edison's invention transformed electricity into a new and versatile form of industrial energy. It also reflected a change in the relationship between science and technology. Until the late nineteenth century, advances in scientific theory usually followed technological innovation rather than the other way around. Techniques for making steel, for example, developed before scientific theories

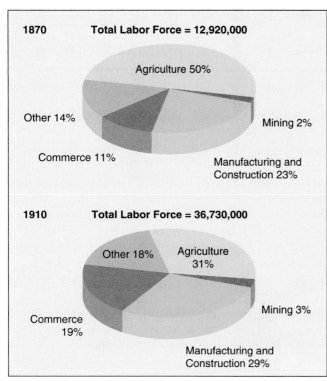

1870   **Total Labor Force = 12,920,000**

Agriculture 50%

Other 14%

Mining 2%

Commerce 11%

Manufacturing and Construction 23%

1910   **Total Labor Force = 36,730,000**

Other 18%

Agriculture 31%

Mining 3%

Commerce 19%

Manufacturing and Construction 29%

Figure 20-1   Changes in the American Labor Force, 1870–1910

The transformation of the American economy in the late nineteenth century changed the nature and type of work. By 1910 the United States was an urban, industrial nation with a matching workforce that toiled in factories and for commercial establishments (including railroads) and less frequently on farms.

emerged to explain how they worked. Textile machinery and railroad technology developed similarly. In contrast, a theoretical understanding of electricity preceded its practical use as a source of energy. Scientists had been experimenting with electricity for half a century before Edison unveiled his lightbulb in 1879. Edison's research laboratory at Menlo Park, New Jersey, also established a model for corporate-sponsored research and development that would rapidly increase the pace of technological innovation.

Edison was a problem student who had only three months of formal schooling. But he spent much of his childhood at home reading and experimenting with chemistry. In 1863, at the age of sixteen, he began working as a telegraph operator, devoting his spare time to inventing. Over the next fourteen years, he produced several practical devices, including a system for carrying multiple messages on the same telegraph wire and an improved automatic stock ticker. With the money he earned from the stock ticker, he built a factory in Newark. In 1876, he gave up the factory, established his research laboratory at Menlo Park, and turned his attention to the electric light.

Scientists had already discovered that passing an electric current through a filament in a vacuum produced light. They had not yet found a filament, however, that could last for more than a few minutes. Edison tried a variety of materials, from grass to hair from a colleague's beard, before succeeding with charred thread. In 1879, he produced a bulb that burned for an astounding forty-five hours. Then he devised a circuit that provided an even flow of current through the filament. After thrilling a crowd with the spectacle of five hundred lights ablaze on New Year's Eve in 1879, Edison went on to build a power station in New York City to serve businesses and homes by 1882. The electric age had begun.

Edison's initial success touched off a wave of research and development in Germany, Austria, Great Britain, France, and the United States. Whoever could light the world cheaply and efficiently held the key to an enormous fortune. Ultimately the prize fell not to Edison but to Elihu Thomson, a high school chemistry

A humorous view of Thomas Edison's laboratories in Menlo Park, New Jersey, around 1880. There was no joking, however, about the potential of Edison's incandescent bulb and his other practical adaptations of electricity for everyday use. Electricity would soon transform life for millions of people. Edison's methods set the precedent for corporate research and development that would accelerate the pace of new discoveries with practical applications.

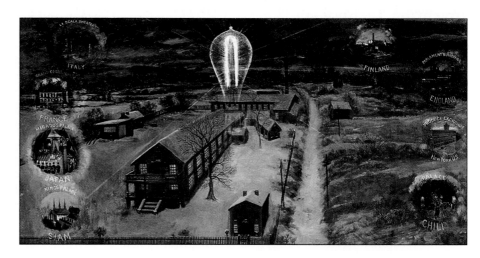

CHRONOLOGY

1869 The Knights of Labor is founded in Philadelphia.

1870 John D. Rockefeller forms the Standard Oil Company.

Congress passes the Naturalization Act barring Asians from citizenship.

1876 The Centennial Exposition opens in Philadelphia.

1877 The Great Uprising railroad strike, the first nationwide work stoppage in the United States, provokes violent clashes between workers and federal troops.

1879 Thomas Edison unveils the electric light bulb.

1880 Founding of the League of American Wheelmen in 1880 helps establish bicycling as one of urban America's favorite recreational activities.

1881 Assassination of Russian Tsar Alexander II begins a series of pogroms that triggers a wave of Russian Jewish immigration to the United States.

1882 Congress passes the Chinese Exclusion Act.

First country club in the United States founded in Brookline, Massachusetts.

1883 National League merges with the American Association and opens baseball to working-class fans.

1886 The Neighborhood Guild, the nation's first settlement house, opens in New York City.

Riot in Chicago's Haymarket Square breaks the Knights of Labor.

American Federation of Labor is formed.

1887 Anti-Catholic American Protective Association is formed.

1888 Wanamaker's department store introduces a "bargain room," and competitors follow suit.

1889 Jane Addams opens Hull House, the nation's most celebrated settlement house, in Chicago.

1890 Jacob A. Riis publishes *How the Other Half Lives.*

1891 African-American Chicago physician Daniel Hale Williams establishes Provident Hospital, the nation's first interracially staffed hospital.

1892 General Electric opens the first corporate research and development division in the United States.

Strike at Andrew Carnegie's Homestead steelworks fails.

1894 Pullman Sleeping Car Company strike fails.

Immigration Restriction League is formed.

1895 American-born Chinese in California form the Native Sons of the Golden State to counter nativism.

1897 George C. Tilyou opens Steeplechase Park on Coney Island in Brooklyn, New York.

1898 Congress passes the Erdman Act to provide for voluntary mediation of railroad labor disputes.

1901 Socialist Party of America is formed.

1905 Militant labor organization, the Industrial Workers of the World, is formed.

teacher in Philadelphia. Thomson, like Edison, enjoyed dabbling in electricity. Leaving teaching to devote himself to research full time, Thomson founded his own company and in 1883 moved to Connecticut, where he experimented with transformers and electric trolley equipment. Thomson purchased Edison's General Electric Company in 1892 and established the country's first corporate research and development division. His scientists produced what was then the most efficient lightbulb design, and by 1914, General Electric was producing 85 percent of the world's lightbulbs.

Following this precedent, other American companies established research and development laboratories. Standard Oil, U.S. Rubber, the chemical giant Du Pont, and the photographic company Kodak all became world leaders in their respective industries because of innovations their laboratories developed.

The process of invention that emerged in the United States gave the country a commanding technological lead. But the modernization of industry that made the United States the world's foremost industrial nation after 1900 reflected organizational as well as technological innovation. As industries sought efficient ways to apply technology and expand their markets within and beyond national borders, their workforces expanded, and their need for capital mounted. Coping with these changes required significant changes in corporate management.

The Corporation and Its Impact

The modern corporation provided the structural framework for the transformation of the American economy. A corporation is an association of individuals with legal rights and liabilities separate from those of its members. This form of business organization had existed since colonial times but became a significant factor in the American economy with the growth of railroad companies in the 1850s. A key feature of a corporation is the separation of ownership from management. A corporation can raise capital by selling stock—ownership shares—to people with no direct role in running it. The shareholders benefit from dividends drawn on profits and, if the corporation thrives, from the rising value of its stock.

The corporation had two major advantages over other forms of business organization that made it attractive to investors. First, unlike a partnership, which can dissolve when a partner dies, a corporation can outlive its founders. This durability permits long-term planning. Second, a corporation's officials and shareholders are not personally liable for its debts. If it goes bankrupt, they stand to lose only what they have invested in it.

As large corporations emerged in major American industries, they had a ripple effect on the economy. To build plants, merge with or acquire other companies, develop new technology, and hire workers, large corporations needed huge supplies of capital. They turned to the banks to help meet those needs, and the banks grew in response. The corporations stimulated technological change as they looked for ways to speed production, improve products, and lower costs. As they grew, they generated jobs.

Large industrial corporations also changed the nature of work. Into the late nineteenth century, well-paid skilled artisans, typically native-born, dominated the industrial workplace. Operating alone or in groups, they controlled the pace of their work, their output, and even the hiring and firing of coworkers. By the early twentieth century, control of the workplace was shifting to managers, and semi-skilled and unskilled workers were replacing skilled artisans. These new workers, often foreign-born, performed repetitive tasks for low wages.

Because corporations usually located factories in cities, they stimulated urban growth. Large industrial districts sprawled along urban rivers and near urban rail lines. There were exceptions. Southern textile manufacturers tended to locate plants in villages and small towns and on the outskirts of larger cities. A few northern entrepreneurs also constructed industrial communities outside major cities to save on land costs and ensure control over labor. George Pullman, for example, built his railway car manufacturing plant outside of Chicago in 1880. Nonetheless, by 1900, fully 90 percent of all manufacturing occurred in cities.

Two organizational strategies—vertical integration and horizontal integration—helped successful corporations reduce competition and dominate their industries. **Vertical integration** involved the consolidation of all functions related to a particular industry, from the extraction and transport of raw materials to manufacturing and finished-product distribution and sales. Vertical integration reduced a company's dependence on outside suppliers, cutting costs and delays. Geographical dispersal went hand in hand with vertical integration. Different functions—a factory and its source of raw materials, for example—were likely to be in different places, a development made possible by advances in communication like the telephone. The multiplication of functions also prompted the growth of corporate bureaucracy.

The development of the meatpacking industry provides a good example of vertical integration. Meat is perishable and cannot be transported long distances without refrigeration. To reach eastern markets, cattlemen had to ship live animals in cattle cars from western ranges to major rail centers like Chicago. Only 40 percent of a steer is edible, so shippers were paying freight charges for a lot of commercially useless weight. In addition, some animals died in transit, and many lost weight.

Gustavus Swift, a Boston native who moved to Chicago in 1875, realized that refrigerated railway cars would make it possible to ship butchered meat, eliminating the need to transport live cattle. He invented a refrigerated car but could not sell it to the major railroads because they feared losing their substantial investment in cattle cars and pens. Swift had the cars built himself and convinced a Canadian railroad with only a small stake in cattle shipping to haul them to eastern markets. He established packing houses in Omaha and Kansas City, near the largest cattle markets; built refrigerated warehouses at key distribution points; and hired a sales force to convince eastern butchers of the quality of his product. He now controlled the production, transportation, and distribution of his product, the essence of vertical integration. By 1881, he was shipping $200,000 worth of beef a week. Competitors soon followed his example.

Horizontal integration involved the merger of competitors in the same industry. John D. Rockefeller's Standard Oil Company pioneered horizontal integration in the 1880s. Born in western New York State, the son of a traveling patent medicine salesman, Rockefeller moved to Ohio at the age of 14 in 1853. Serving as family head during his father's frequent absences, Rockefeller developed a capacity for leadership, a thirst for hard work, and a devotion to the Baptist Church. He began investing in Cleveland oil refineries by his midtwenties and formed Standard Oil in 1870. Using a variety of tactics—including threats, deceit, and price wars—Rockefeller rapidly acquired most of his competitors. Supported by investment bankers like J. P. Morgan, Standard Oil controlled 90 percent of the nation's oil refining by 1890. Acquiring oil fields and pipelines as well as refineries, it achieved both vertical and horizontal integration. Rockefeller's dominant position allowed him to impose order and predictability on the industry, ensuring a continuous flow of profits. He closed inefficient refineries, opened new ones, and kept his operations up-to-date with the latest technologies.

Other entrepreneurs achieved similar dominance in other industries and amassed similarly enormous fortunes. James B. Duke, who automated cigarette manufacturing, gained control of most of the tobacco industry. Andrew Carnegie consolidated much of the U.S. steel industry within his Carnegie Steel Company (later U.S. Steel). By 1900, Carnegie's company was producing one-quarter of the country's steel.

The concentration of American industry in the hands of a few powerful corporations alarmed many Americans. Giant corporations threatened to restrict opportunities for small entrepreneurs like the shopkeepers, farmers, and artisans who abounded at midcentury. In the words of one historian, the corporations "seemed to signal the end of an open, promising America and the beginning of a closed, unhappier society." Impersonal and governed by profit, the modern corporation challenged the ideal of the self-made man and the belief that success and advancement would reward hard work. These concerns eventually prompted the federal and state governments to respond with antitrust and other regulatory laws (see Chapters 22 and 23).

Tabloid newspapers reinforced distrust of the corporations with exposés of the sharp business practices of corporate barons like Rockefeller and Carnegie and accounts of the sumptuous lifestyles of the corporate elite. Public concern notwithstanding, however, the giant corporations helped increase the efficiency of the American economy, raise the national standard of living, and transform the United States into a major world power. Corporate expansion generated jobs that attracted rural migrants and immigrants by the millions from Europe and Asia to American cities.

The Changing Nature of Work

From the perspective of the workers, immigrant and native-born alike, the growth of giant corporations was a mixed blessing. The corporations provided abundant jobs, but they firmly controlled working conditions. A Pennsylvania coal miner spoke for many of his fellows in the 1890s when he remarked:

"The working people of this country . . . find monopolies as strong as government itself. They find capital as rigid as absolute monarchy. They find their so-called independence a myth."

As late as the 1880s, shops of skilled artisans were responsible for most manufacturing in the United States. Since midcentury, however, industrialists had been introducing ways to simplify manufacturing processes so they could hire low-skilled workers. This deskilling process accelerated in the 1890s in response to new technologies, new workers, and workplace reorganization. By 1906, according to a U.S. Department of Labor report, industrial labor had been reduced to minute, low-skilled operations, making skilled artisans obsolete.

Mechanization and technological innovation did not reduce employment, although they did eliminate some jobs, most of them skilled. On the contrary, the birth of whole new industries—steel, automobiles, electrical equipment, cigarettes, food canning, and machine tools—created a huge demand for workers. Innovations in existing industries, like railroads, similarly spurred job growth. The number of people working for U.S. railroads increased from eighty thousand to more than 1 million between 1860 and 1910.

Ironically, it was a shortage of skilled workers as much as other factors that encouraged industrialists to mechanize. Unskilled workers cost less than the scarce artisans. And with massive waves of immigrants arriving from Europe and Asia between 1880 and 1920 (joined after 1910 by migrants from the American South), the supply of unskilled workers seemed limitless.

The new workers, however, shared little of the wealth generated by industrial expansion and enjoyed few of the gadgets and products generated by the new manufacturing. The eastern European immigrants who comprised three-quarters of U.S. Steel's work force during the first decade of the twentieth century received less than $12.50 a week, significantly less than the $15.00 a week a federal government survey in 1910 said an urban family needed to subsist.

Nor did large corporations put profits into improved working conditions. In 1881, on-the-job accidents maimed or killed thirty thousand railroad workers. Safety equipment existed that could have prevented many of these injuries, but the railroads refused to purchase it. At a U.S. Steel plant in Pittsburgh, injuries or death claimed one out of every four workers between 1907 and 1910. In Chicago's meat plants, injuries were commonplace. Workers grew careless from fatigue and long-term exposure to the extreme temperatures of the workplace. Meat cutters working rapidly with sharp knives often sliced fingers off their numb hands. Upton Sinclair wrote in his novel *The Jungle* (1906), a chronicle of the killing floors of meatpacking plants in Chicago, "It was to be counted as a wonder that there were not more men slaughtered than cattle."

Factory workers typically worked ten hours a day, six days a week in the 1880s. Steel workers put in twelve hours a day. Because the mills operated around the clock, once every two weeks, when the workers changed shifts, one group took a "long turn" and stayed on the job for twenty-four hours.

Long hours affected family life. By Sunday, most factory workers were too tired to do more than sit around home. During the week, they had time only to eat and sleep. As one machinist testified before a U.S. Senate investigative committee in 1883:

> They were pretty well played out when they come home, and the first thing they think of is having something to eat and sitting down, and resting, and then of striking a bed. Of course when a man is dragged out in that way he is naturally cranky, and he makes all around him cranky . . . and staring starvation in the face makes him feel sad, and the head of the house being sad, of course the whole family are the same, so the house looks like a dull prison.

Workers lived as close to the factory as possible to reduce the time and expense of getting to work. The environment around many factories, however, was almost as unwholesome as the conditions inside. A visitor to Pittsburgh in 1884 noticed "a drab twilight" hanging over the areas around the steel mills, where "gas-lights, which are left burning at mid-day, shine out of the murkiness with a dull, red-dish glare." Industrial wastes fouled streams and rivers around many plants. The factories along the Cuyahoga River in Cleveland turned that waterway into an open sewer by the turn of the century.

Big factories were not characteristic of all industries after 1900. In some, like the "needle," or garment, trade, operations remained small scale. But salaries and working conditions in these industries were, if anything, worse than in the big factories. The garment industry was dominated by small manufacturers who assembled clothing for retailers from cloth provided by textile manufacturers. The manufacturers squeezed workers into small, cramped, poorly ventilated **sweatshops**. These might be in attics or lofts or even the workers' own dwellings. Workers pieced together garments on the manufacturer's sewing machines. A government investigator

in Chicago in the 1890s described one sweatshop in a three-room tenement where the workers—a family of eight—both lived and worked: "The father, mother, two daughters, and a cousin work together making trousers at seventy-five cents a dozen pairs. . . . They work seven days a week. . . . Their destitution is very great."

Child Labor

Child labor was common in the garment trade and other industries. Shocked reformers in the 1890s told of the devastating effect of factory labor on children's lives, citing cases like that of a seven-year-old girl whose legs were paralyzed and deformed because she toiled "day after day with little legs crossed, pulling out bastings from garments."

Industries that employed many children were often dangerous, even for adults. In the gritty coal mines of Pennsylvania, breaker boys, youths who stood on ladders to pluck waste matter from coal tumbling down long chutes, breathed harmful coal dust all day. Girls under sixteen made up half the work force in the silk mills of Scranton and Wilkes-Barre, Pennsylvania. Girls with missing fingers from mill accidents were a common sight in those towns.

By 1900, Pennsylvania and a few other states had passed legislation regulating child labor, but enforcement of these laws was lax. Parents desperate for income often lied about their children's age, and authorities were often sympathetic toward mill or mine owners, who paid taxes and provided other civic benefits.

Working Women

Women accompanied children into the work force outside the home in increasing numbers after 1870. The comparatively low wages of unskilled male workers often required women family members to work as well. The head of the Massachusetts Bureau of Labor Statistics observed in 1882, "A family of workers can always live well, but the man with a family of small children to support, unless his wife works also, has a small chance of living properly." Between 1870 and 1920, the number of women and children in the workforce more than doubled.

Like child labor, the growing numbers of women in the workforce alarmed middle-class reformers. They worried about the impact on family life and on the women themselves. Working-class men were also concerned. The trend toward deskilling favored women. Employers, claiming that women worked only for supplemental money, paid them less than men. A U.S. Department of Labor commissioner asserted that women worked only for "dress or pleasure." In one

The growth of American corporate capitalism and the emergence of the United States as a major industrial power transformed the nature of work and unsettled the workforce in the late nineteenth century. As machines deskilled the workplace by taking over sophisticated tasks, laborers were left to drudge at repetitive, dead-end jobs. Wages fell as certain jobs became obsolete, and a wave of mergers reduced competition and forced layoffs. In the late twentieth century, as the country began a transition from an industrial economy to an economy based on service and information technology, many workers felt similar pressures. But capitalism, according to Nobel economist Lester Thurow, is "a process of creative destruction." Job losses and social dislocation accompanied both the industrialization of the late nineteenth century and the transition to an information economy in the late twentieth. Both also generated new wealth and created new types of work.

There are important contrasts, however, between then and now. There may be little difference in scale between the wealth of a John D. Rockefeller and the wealth of a Bill Gates, but there are significant differences in the sources of their wealth. The great moguls of industry at the turn of the twentieth century made their fortunes from natural resources such as oil and iron ore. The entrepreneurial wizards of the turn of the twenty-first century derive wealth from knowledge. Before, few Americans could command the raw materials to produce vast wealth. But now the primary resource of the economy is the mind, opening previously unimagined opportunities. One result has been to blur the line between workers, managers, and even entrepreneurs.

A second difference is the current power of the consumer. The great industries kept wages low as entrepreneurs plowed huge profits into acquiring competitors, expanding production, and building their own personal fortunes. Although a growing middle class fueled the early twentieth-century economy, its influence pales before that of today's buyers. As the wages of industrial workers improved beginning in the 1940s, the consumer base broadened, but buyers still had relatively little choice. In 1959, for example, if you wanted to purchase a car, you basically had a choice between Ford, Chrysler, and General Motors. Today, more than thirty auto makers compete for customers, dampening inflation, increasing quality, and expanding choice.

Although a global economy existed in 1900, today's version relies more on electronic mobility to shift labor and capital rapidly. Firms cast about for the best and, in some cases, the cheapest places to do business to gain a competitive edge. Why should the German car manufacturer BMW, for example, pay high wages and benefits to German workers when South Carolina workers can build their cars just as well at a lower cost?

All of these factors have made work less secure. A laborer for U.S. Steel in the early twentieth century could expect to spend his working life with that company, barring injury. And he probably could pass a job down to his son. Today, workers are likely to have several employers over time. Some work is as deadening as on the old industrial production lines, but increasingly companies are redefining work to maintain their competitive advantage in a way that offers workers new opportunities. At the Duke Energy Corporation in Charlotte, North Carolina, for example, a line technician has the authority to schedule jobs, change instructions for those jobs, and recommend and secure equipment. Some of these responsibilities were previously the province of engineers. Now, reflecting both the destructive and creative aspects of the new economy, the company needs fewer engineers. Employers today expect more flexibility and initiative from their employees, and workers have more opportunities for responsibility and advancement. But workers pay a price in diminished job security and employers in diminished worker loyalty.

Secretaries of the Metropolitan Life Insurance Company in New York City pound away on Remington typewriters. The American Industrial Revolution spawned many jobs that involved repetitive mechanical tasks, both creating and destroying employment opportunities. Before the typewriter, men dominated clerical office work.

St. Louis factory in 1896, women received $4 a week for work for which men were paid $16 a week. Women chafed under this wage system but had no recourse other than to quit. An Iowa shoe saleswoman complained in 1886, "I don't get the salary the men clerks do, although this day I am 600 sales ahead! Call this justice? But I have to grin and bear it, because I am so unfortunate as to be a woman."

Most women worked out of economic necessity. In 1900, fully 85 percent of wage-earning women were unmarried and under the age of 25. They supported siblings and contributed to their parents' income. A typical female factory worker earned $6 a week in 1900. On this wage, a married woman might help pull her family up to subsistence level. For a single woman on her own, however, it allowed little more, in writer O. Henry's words, "than marshmallows and tea." Her lodging rarely consisted of more than one room.

Working women had little opportunity for recreation or diversion. Married women could seek comfort in home and family. Cheap amusements attracted single working women. Reformer Jane Addams noted in the 1890s, "Apparently the modern city sees in these girls only two possibilities, both of them commercial: first, a chance to utilize by day their labor power in its factories and shops, and then another chance in the evening to extract from them their petty wages by pandering to their love of pleasure."

Some working-class women turned to prostitution. As with other enterprises, industrial capitalism transformed commercialized sex into big business. The consumers in this industry—mainly middle-class men—sought their pleasure in dance halls, clubs, bawdy theater reviews, and thinly veiled bordellos. The income from prostitution could exceed factory work by four or five times. "So is it any wonder," asked the Chicago Vice Commission in 1894, "that a tempted girl who receives only six dollars per week working with her hands sells her body for twenty-five dollars per week . . . ?" As much as 10 percent of New York City's female working-age population worked in the sex business in the 1890s. During depression years, the percentage was probably higher.

Despite its tacit acceptance of sexual commerce, Victorian America condemned anyone guilty of even the most trivial moral transgression to social ostracism and treated the prostitute as a social outcast. Even those who urged understanding for women who violated convention faced exclusion. Kate Chopin, a New Orleans novelist, caused a tremendous uproar in the 1890s with stories that took a compassionate view of women involved in adultery, alcoholism, and divorce. Booksellers boycotted Theodore Dreiser's 1900 novel *Sister Carrie*, whose title character lived with a succession of men, one of them married.

The mere pursuit of leisure placed working women in compromising situations. They could not afford frequent visits to amusement parks, dance halls, or theaters. Yet these were the only places where they could meet young men without supervision from their families and employers. Men often expected sexual favors in return for "treating"—paying for all the expenses on a date. Thus the pressure to conform to conventional morality conflicted with working women's desire to enjoy a break. One social reformer heard one woman commenting to a co-worker: "Don't yeh know there ain't no feller going t'spend coin on yeh for nothin'? Yeh gotta be a good Indian, Kid—as we all gotta!"

Over time, more work options opened to women, but low wages and poor working conditions persisted. Women entered the needle trades after widespread introduction of the sewing machine in the 1870s. Factories gradually replaced sweatshops in the garment industry after 1900, but working conditions improved little.

The introduction of the typewriter transformed clerical office work, dominated by men until the 1870s, into a female preserve. Women were alleged to have the greater dexterity and tolerance for repetition that the new technology required. But they earned only half the salary of the men they replaced. Middle-class parents saw office work as clean and honorable compared with factory or sales work. Consequently, clerical positions drew growing numbers of native-born women into the urban work force after 1890. A top-paid office worker in the 1890s earned as much as $900 a year. Teaching, another acceptable occupation for middle-class women, typically paid only $500 a year.

By the turn of the century, women were gaining increased access to higher education. Coeducational colleges were rare, but by 1900 there were many women-only institutions. By 1910, women comprised 40 percent of all American college students, compared to 20 percent in 1870. Despite these gains, many professions—including those of physician and attorney—remained closed to women. Men still accounted for more than 95 percent of all doctors in 1900. Women also were rarely permitted to pursue doctoral degrees.

Women college graduates mostly found employment in such "nurturing" professions as nursing, teaching, and library work. Between 1900 and 1910, the number of trained women nurses increased sevenfold. In response to the growing problems of urban society, a relatively new occupation, social work, opened to women. There were one thousand women social workers in 1890 and nearly thirty thousand by

1920. Reflecting new theories on the nurturing role of women, school boards after 1900 turned exclusively to female teachers for the elementary grades.

Despite these gains, women's work remained segregated. More than 90 percent of all wage-earning women in 1900 worked at jobs where women comprised the great majority of workers. Some reforms meant to improve working conditions for women reinforced this state of affairs. **Protective legislation** restricted women to "clean" occupations and limited their ability to compete with men in other jobs. As an economist explained in 1901, "The wage bargaining power of men is weakened by the competition of women and children, hence a law restricting the hours of women and children may also be looked upon as a law to protect men in their bargaining power."

Women also confronted negative stereotypes. Most Americans in 1900 believed a woman's proper role was to care for home and family. The single working woman faced doubts about her virtue. The system of "treating" on dates reinforced stories about loose salesgirls, flirtatious secretaries, and easy factory workers. Newspapers and magazines published exposés of working girls descending into prostitution. These images encouraged sexual harassment at work, which was rarely punished.

Working women faced a difficult dilemma. To justify their desire for education and training, they had to argue that it would enhance their roles as wives and mothers. To gain improved wages and working conditions, they increasingly supported protective legislation that restricted their opportunities in the workplace.

Responses to Poverty and Wealth

Concerns about working women merged with larger anxieties about the growing numbers of impoverished workers in the nation's cities during the 1890s and the widening gap between rich and poor. While industrial magnates flaunted their fabulous wealth, working men and women led hard lives on meager salaries and in crowded dwellings. In his exposé of poverty in New York, *How the Other Half Lives* (1890), Danish-born urban reformer Jacob Riis wrote that "the half that is on top cares little for the struggles, and less for the fate of those who are underneath so long as it is able to hold them there and keep its own seat."

The urban poor included workers as well as the unemployed, aged, widowed, and disabled. The industrial economy strained working-class family life. Workplace accidents and deaths left many families with only one parent. Infant mortality among the working poor was nearly twice the citywide norm in 1900. Epidemic diseases, especially typhoid, an illness spread by impure water, devastated crowded working-class districts. Poverty compounded itself in various ways. For example, the poor paid twice as much for coal to heat their homes as better-off people because they could only afford to buy it in small quantities.

Inadequate housing was the most visible badge of poverty. Crammed into four- to six-story buildings on tiny lots, **tenement** apartments in urban **slums** were notorious for their lack of ventilation and light. According to Jacob Riis, a typical apartment in New York's Mulberry Bend neighborhood consisted of a parlor—a combined livingroom and kitchen—and "two pitch-dark coops called bedrooms." The furniture included three beds, "if the old boxes and heaps of foul straw can be called by that name," which gave off an appalling smell. In 90-degree July heat, temperatures inside soared to 115 degrees.

Authorities did nothing to enforce laws prohibiting overcrowding for fear of leaving people homeless. The population density of New York's tenement district in 1894 was 986.4 people per acre, the highest in the world at the time. (Today, the densest areas of American cities rarely exceed 400 people per acre, and only Calcutta, India, and Lagos, Nigeria, approach the crowding of turn-of-the-century New York; today Manhattan has 84 residents per acre).

One early attempt to deal with these conditions was the settlement house. The settlement house movement, which originated in England, sought to moderate the effects of poverty through neighborhood reconstruction. New York's Neighborhood Guild, established in 1886, was the first settlement house in the country; Chicago's **Hull House**, founded in 1889 by Jane Addams, a young Rockford (Illinois) College graduate, became the most famous. Addams had visited settlement houses in England and thought the idea would work well in American cities.

The settlement house typically did not dispense charity. Rather, it provided the working poor with facilities and education to help them improve their environment and, eventually, to escape it. By 1900, there were more than one hundred settlement houses throughout the country.

Hull House, a rambling old residence in a working-class immigrant neighborhood, quickly became a neighborhood institution. On Saturday evenings, Italian immigrants and their families came to settle legal disputes. Hull House also catered to native-born Americans, who formed the Young Citizens' Club to discuss municipal issues. Addams renovated an adjacent saloon and transformed it into a gym. She began a day nursery as well. When workers at a nearby knitting factory went on strike, Addams arbitrated the conflict.

The poor seldom lived near large urban parks and could not afford to join athletic clubs.

Settlement house gyms like the one Addams built for Hull House provided them with much-needed recreational space. So too did the athletic fields and playgrounds built adjacent to public schools after 1900.

Late-nineteenth-century political ideology discouraged more comprehensive efforts to remedy urban poverty until the Progressive Era (discussed in Chapter 23). According to the **Gospel of Wealth**, a theory popular among industrialists, intellectuals, and some politicians, any intervention on behalf of the poor was of doubtful benefit. Hard work and perseverance, in this view, led to wealth. Poverty, by implication, resulted from the flawed character of the poor. Steel tycoon Andrew Carnegie sought to soften this doctrine by stressing the responsibility of the affluent to set an example for the working class and to return some of their wealth to the communities in which they lived. Carnegie accordingly endowed libraries, cultural institutions, and schools throughout the country. Beneficial as they might be, however, these philanthropic efforts scarcely addressed the causes of poverty, and few industrialists followed Carnegie's example.

Social Darwinism, a flawed attempt to apply Charles Darwin's theory of biological evolution to human society, emerged as a more common justification than the Gospel of Wealth for the growing gap between rich and poor. According to social Darwinism, the human race evolves only through competition. The fit survive, the weak perish, and humanity moves forward. Wealth reflects fitness; poverty, weakness. For governments or private agencies to interfere with this natural process is futile. Thus Columbia University president Nicholas Murray Butler, claiming that "nature's cure for most social and political diseases is better than man's," warned against charity for the poor in 1900. Standard Oil's John D. Rockefeller concurred, asserting that the survival of the fittest is "the working out of a law of nature and a law of God."

Social Darwinism provided some industrialists with an excuse to do nothing to relieve the causes of poverty. Workers, caught between harsh theory and harsher reality, began to take matters into their own hands.

Workers Organize

The growing power of industrial corporations and the declining power of workers generated social tensions reminiscent of the sectional crisis that triggered the Civil War. Wild swings in the business cycle—the fluctuation between periods of growth and contraction in the economy—aggravated these tensions. Two prolonged depressions, one beginning in 1873 and the other in 1893, threw as many as 2 million laborers out of work. Skilled workers, their security undermined by deskilling, were hit particularly hard. Their hopes of becoming managers or starting their own businesses disappearing, they saw the nation "drifting," as a carpenter put it in 1870, "to that condition of society where a few were rich, and the many very poor."

Beginning after the depression of 1873 and continuing through World War I, workers fought their loss of independence to industrial capital by organizing and striking (see the overview table, "Workers Organize"). The first episode in this conflict was the railroad strike of 1877, sometimes referred to as the **Great Uprising**. The four largest railroads, in the midst of a depression and in the wake of a series of pay cuts over the previous four years, agreed to slash wages yet again. When Baltimore & Ohio Railroad workers struck in July to protest the cut, President Rutherford B. Hayes dispatched federal troops to protect the line's property. The use of federal troops infuriated railroad workers throughout the East and Midwest, and they stopped work as well. Violence

During the Great Uprising of 1877, federal troops clashed with striking workers. Here, the Maryland militia fires at strikers in Baltimore, killing twelve. As Reconstruction ended, government attention shifted from the South to quelling labor unrest.

OVERVIEW

WORKERS ORGANIZE

Organization	History	Strategies
Knights of Labor	Founded in 1869; open to all workers; declined after 1886	Disapproved of strikes; supported a broad array of labor reforms, including cooperatives; favored political involvement
American Federation of Labor	Founded in 1886; open to craft workers only and organized by craft; hostile to blacks and women; became the major U.S. labor organization after 1880s	Opposed political involvement; supported a limited number of labor reforms; approved of strikes
Industrial Workers of the World	Founded in 1905; consisted mainly of semiskilled and unskilled immigrant workers; represented a small portion of the work force; disappeared after World War I	Highly political; supported socialist programs; approved of strikes and even violence to achieve ends

erupted in Pittsburgh when the state militia opened fire on strikers and their families, killing twenty-five, including a woman and three children. As news of the violence spread, so did the strike, as far as Galveston, Texas, and San Francisco. Over the next two weeks, police and federal troops continued to clash with strikers. By the time this first nationwide work stoppage in American history ended, more than one hundred had been killed. The wage cuts remained.

Despite its ultimate failure, the Great Uprising was notable for the way workers cooperated with one another across ethnic and, in some cases, racial lines. The experience proved important in the next major upheaval, nine years later.

The **Knights of Labor**, a union of craft workers founded in Philadelphia in 1869, grew dramatically after the Great Uprising under the leadership of Terence V. Powderly. Reflecting the views of many skilled workers, the Knights saw "an inevitable . . . conflict between the wage system of labor and [the] republican system of government." Remarkably inclusive for its time, the Knights welcomed black workers and women to its ranks. Victories in several small railroad strikes in 1884 and 1885 boosted its membership to nearly one million workers by 1886.

In that year, the Knights led a movement for an eight-hour workday. Ignoring the advice of the na-

tional leadership to avoid strikes, local chapters staged more than 1,500 strikes involving more than 340,000 workers. Workers also organized boycotts against manufacturers and ran candidates for local elections. Social reformer Henry George made a strong, though losing, effort in the New York City mayoral race, and labor candidates won several local offices in Chicago.

Employers fought back. They convinced the courts to order strikers back to work and used local authorities to arrest strikers for trespassing or obstructing traffic. In early May 1886, police killed four unarmed workers during a skirmish with strikers in Chicago. Rioting broke out when a bomb exploded at a meeting in **Haymarket Square** to protest the slayings. The bomb killed seven policemen and four strikers and left one hundred people wounded. Eight strike leaders were tried for the deaths, and despite a lack of evidence linking them to the bomb, four were executed.

The Haymarket Square incident and a series of disastrous walkouts that followed it weakened the Knights of Labor. By 1890, it had shrunk to less than 100,000 members. Thereafter, the **American Federation of Labor (AFL)**, formed in 1886, became the major organizing body for skilled workers.

The AFL was much less ambitious and less inclusive than the Knights of Labor. Led by British immigrant Samuel Gompers, it emphasized **collective** bargaining—negotiations between management and union representatives—to secure workplace concessions. The AFL also discouraged political activism. With this **business unionism**, the AFL proved more effective than the Knights of Labor at meeting the needs of skilled workers, but it left out the growing numbers of unskilled workers, black workers, and women workers to whom the Knights had given a glimmer of hope.

Rather than including all workers in one large union, the AFL organized skilled workers by craft. It then focused on a few basic workplace issues important to each craft. Workers at a given factory might be represented by five or more craft unions instead of one umbrella organization. This organizing technique assured that rank-and-file members in a union shared similar objectives. The result was greater cohesion and discipline. In 1889 and 1890, more than 60 percent of AFL-sponsored strikes were successful, a remarkable record in an era when most strikes failed. A series of work stoppages in the building trades between 1888 and 1891, for example, won an eight-hour day and a national agreement with builders.

Responding to this success, employers determined to break the power of craft unions just as they had destroyed the Knights. In 1892, Andrew Carnegie dealt the steelworkers union a major setback in the **Homestead strike**. Carnegie's manager, Henry Clay Frick, announced to workers at Carnegie's Homestead plant in Pennsylvania that he would negotiate only with workers individually and not renew the union's collective bargaining contract. Expecting a strike, Frick locked the union workers out of the plant and hired three hundred armed guards to protect the nonunion ("scab") workers he planned to hire in their place. Union workers, with the help of their families and unskilled workers, seized control of Homestead's roads and utilities. In a bloody confrontation, they drove back Frick's forces. Nine strikers and seven guards died. But Pennsylvania's governor called out the state militia to open the plant and protect the nonunion workers. After four months, the union capitulated. With this defeat skilled steelworkers lost their power on the shop floor. Eventually, mechanization cost them their jobs.

In 1894, workers suffered another setback in the **Pullman strike**, against George Pullman's Palace Sleeping Car Company. The strike began when the company cut wages for workers at its plant in the "model" suburb it built outside Chicago without a corresponding cut in the rent it charged workers for their company-owned housing. When Pullman rejected their demands, the workers appealed for support to the American Railway Union (ARU), led by Eugene V. Debs. The membership of the ARU, an independent union not affiliated with the AFL, had swelled to more

than 150,000 workers after it won a strike earlier in 1894 against the Great Northern Railroad. On behalf of the Pullman strikers, Debs ordered a boycott of any trains with Pullman cars. The result was to disrupt train travel in several parts of the country. The railroads claimed to be innocent victims of a local dispute, and with growing public support, they fired workers who refused to handle trains with Pullman cars. Debs called for all ARU members to walk off the job, crippling rail travel nationwide. When Debs refused to honor a federal court injunction against the strike, President Cleveland, at the railroads' request, ordered federal troops to enforce it. Debs was arrested, and the strike and the union were broken.

These setbacks and the depression that began in 1893 left workers and their unions facing an uncertain future. But growing public opposition to the use of troops, the high-handed tactics of industrialists, and the rising concerns of Americans about the power of big business sustained the unions. Workers would call more than 22,000 strikes over the next decade, the majority of them union-sponsored. Still, no more than 7 percent of the American work force was organized by 1900.

American Workers and Socialism

Unlike American workers, European workers formed powerful labor organizations and political parties in the late nineteenth and early twentieth centuries. These parties advocated a policy of **socialism**. They called for state ownership of industry and worker control of corporations. Socialism had some influence in the American labor movement. The Greenback-Labor Party and the Socialist Labor Party attracted some workers in the 1870s. So too did the Socialist Party of America, formed in 1901. Some European immigrants brought radical ideas with them. German socialists and anarchists (who advocated the abolition of government) played prominent roles in the Haymarket affair, for example.

Although the influence of socialist ideas in the United States grew during the Progressive Era (see Chapter 23), several factors limited socialism's appeal and that of more radical leftist movements among workers. First, American socialism was terribly fragmented. One wing supported cooperation with the Democratic party and another insisted on independent action. A third group emerged during the Progressive Era that supported the **Industrial Workers of the World (IWW)**. The IWW, founded in 1905, consisted mostly of recent immigrants espousing a fiery class-conscious program of militant action.

Second, the diversity of the American workforce limited concerted political and union activity. Semiskilled and unskilled immigrant workers formed the majority of the industrial workforce after 1900. Skilled native-born workers, their ranks diminishing, were reluctant to associate with foreigners. Ethnicity divided workers as well. Some unions, such as the Jewish- and Italian-dominated textile unions in the North, successfully organized across ethnic lines. But these were the exception.

Religious differences compounded ethnic diversity. Jewish and Catholic workers demanded a different sabbath and different holidays. Workers often mixed religious and union rituals in ways that reinforced ethnic and religious unity but inhibited worker solidarity. Jewish vestmakers quoted from the Torah to justify a strike. Slavic steelworkers in Hammond, Indiana, in 1910 voted to strike at a ceremony where "the lights of the hall were extinguished. A candle stuck into a bottle was placed on a platform along with a crucifix. One by one the men came and kissed the ivory image on the cross, kneeling before it."

Some European immigrant workers saw factory work from a short-term perspective that discouraged militancy. Their goal was to save enough money to return home to a better life.

Third, Americans prized individualism and saw it threatened by collective worker action as well as by corporate mergers. The press and political leaders discredited labor actions as evidence of foreign (and hence "un-American") political radicalism and social disorder. Middle-class reformers concerned about the increasingly chaotic and diverse urban society saw worker action increasing class, ethnic, and gender conflict. With much of public opinion and official force arrayed against radical union and political activity, many workers (especially the native-born) backed away from radical groups. In 1900, the Massachusetts Bureau of Labor Statistics reported that while most workers believed in unions "in the abstract," many considered them "simply vehicles for the fomentation of incipient riots and disorderly conduct."

Fourth, the existing political system provided some channels for the redress of labor grievances. Universal manhood suffrage preceded industrialization in the United States, unlike in most European countries. The major parties vied for workingmen's votes in the large industrial cities and sometimes championed a few of their causes in state legislatures and Congress. The Republican and Democratic parties were large and diffuse enough to appeal to the diverse working force. Big-city political machines, with thousands of patronage jobs at their disposal, lured potential third-party supporters back into major-party ranks. After labor candidates won several offices in Chicago in 1886, Chicago Democrats hired more than four hundred Knights of Labor members for various city positions. Social critic Friedrich Engels, observing

American labor from England, concluded in 1892 that "there is no place yet in America for a *third* party. . . . The divergence of interests even in the *same* class is so great . . . that wholly different groups and interests are represented in each of the two big parties."

Some states with large industrial work forces passed prolabor legislation as early as the 1880s. Massachusetts provided for arbitration of labor disputes, limits on the working hours of children and women, compensation for certain work-related accidents, and factory safety standards. New York passed similar measures during the 1880s. Southern states, with much fewer industrial workers, did not pass protective legislation until after 1900.

The federal government lagged behind the industrial states in significant prolabor legislation. Federal labor policy between 1877 and 1894 consisted primarily of mobilizing troops to put down worker uprisings. Congress appeased the fears of native-born workers about competition from Chinese immigrants with the **Chinese Exclusion Act** in 1882. Congress also established a bureau of labor in 1884,

Thomas Nast's "The Chinese Question" depicted Columbia, a common nineteenth-century symbol for American ideals, protecting a Chinese immigrant from an irate mob. Note the slogans posted behind Columbia. Nast particularly took issue with attacks on Chinese immigrants by labor unions and evangelical Protestants.

but at the outset the bureau viewed its role strictly as a compiler of statistics. After 1900, in response to the acceleration of corporate mergers and the continuation of labor unrest, states and the federal government increased surveillance over big business. Most states joined Massachusetts and New York in providing minimum protection for workers. Over the next fifteen years, additional state and federal legislation removed many important issues from labor's legislative agenda.

Fifth, the success of the AFL after 1890 kept more radical labor voices from emerging. Samuel Gompers urged his followers to reject radical programs to restructure industrial capitalism: "Whatever ideas we may have as to the future state of society . . . they must remain in the background, and we must subordinate our convictions . . . to the general good that the trades-union movement brings to the laborer." Gompers continued to stress short-term advances for workers rather than long-term solutions for the problems of urban industrial society. The AFL leadership had little interest in unifying workers across class or craft boundaries. Nor did they seek to appeal to African Americans, whom they saw as potential strikebreakers, or women, whom they saw as depressing wages and competing unfairly with men.

Perhaps another reason most American workers rejected socialism was the dramatic change in the industrial work force around 1900. As the large factories installed labor- and time-saving machinery, unskilled foreign-born labor flooded onto the shop floor. For many reasons, not least of which were the adjustments required for life in a new country, labor radicalism was not a high priority for many of the newcomers. Immigrants not only transformed the workplace, but also transformed the cities where they settled and the nation many eventually adopted. In the process, they changed themselves.

New Immigrants

The late nineteenth century was a period of unprecedented worldwide population movements. The United States was not the only New World destination for the migrants of this period. Many also found their way to Brazil, Argentina, and Canada.

Map 20-1   Patterns of Immigration, 1820–1914
The migration to the United States was part of a worldwide transfer of population that accelerated with the industrial revolution and the accompanying improvements in transportation.

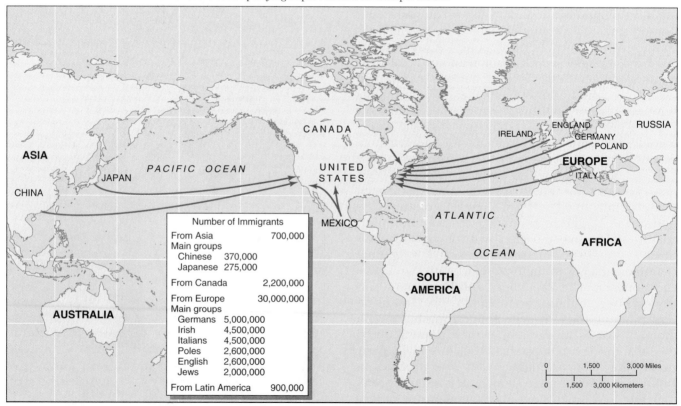

Number of Immigrants	
From Asia	700,000
Main groups	
Chinese	370,000
Japanese	275,000
From Canada	2,200,000
From Europe	30,000,000
Main groups	
Germans	5,000,000
Irish	4,500,000
Italians	4,500,000
Poles	2,600,000
English	2,600,000
Jews	2,000,000
From Latin America	900,000

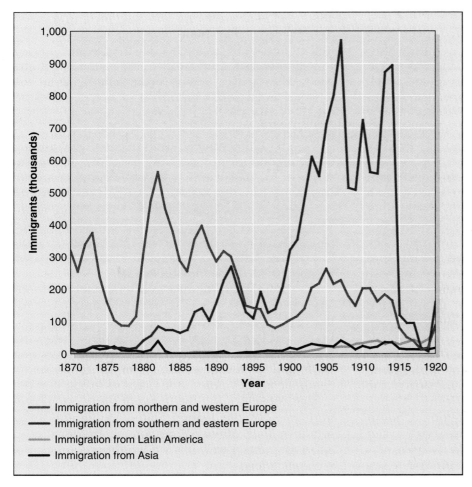

Figure 20-2   Immigration to the United States, 1870–1915
The graph illustrates the dramatic change in immigration to the United States during the late nineteenth and early twentieth centuries. As immigration from northern and western Europe slackened, the numbers of newcomers from southern and eastern Europe swelled. Latin American and Asian immigration also increased during this period.

The scale of overseas migration to the United States after 1870, however, dwarfed all that preceded it. Between 1870 and 1910, the country received more than 20 million immigrants. Before the Civil War, most immigrants came from northern Europe. Most of the new immigrants, in contrast, came from southern and eastern Europe. Swelling their ranks were migrants from Mexico and Asia, as well as internal migrants moving from the countryside to American cities (see Map 20-1 and Figure 20-2).

Old-World Backgrounds

The people of southern and eastern Europe had long been accustomed to migrating within Europe on a seasonal basis to find work to support their families. In the final quarter of the nineteenth century, however, several factors drove migrants beyond the borders of Europe and into the Western Hemisphere.

A growing rural population combined with unequal land distribution to create economic distress in late-nineteenth-century Europe. With land ownership concentrated in increasingly fewer hands, more and more people found themselves working ever-smaller plots as laborers rather than owners. In Poland, laborers accounted for 80 percent of the agricultural population in the 1860s. Similar conditions prevailed in the Mezzogiorno region of southern Italy, home of three out of four Italian emigrants to America. Declining farm commodity prices and the deterioration of the road system in southern Italy contributed to a general agricultural depression. Absentee landlords abused workers and neglected the land.

For Russian Jews, religious persecution compounded economic hardship. In tsarist Russia, Jews could not own real estate and were barred from work in farming, teaching, the civil service, and the law. Confined to designated cities, they struggled to support themselves. After the assassination of Tsar Alexander II in 1881, which some leaders falsely blamed on Jews, the government sanctioned a series of violent attacks on Jewish settlements known as **pogroms**. At the same time, the government forced Jews into fewer towns, deepening their poverty and making them easier targets for violence.

Economic hardship and religious persecution were not, of course, new to Europe. What made the late nineteenth century different was that new transportation technologies permitted people to leave. Railroad construction boomed in Europe during the 1870s and 1880s as Germany and Great Britain sought markets for their iron and steel. Steamship companies in several European countries built giant vessels to transport passengers quickly and safely across the Atlantic. The companies sent agents into Russia, Poland, Italy, and the Austro-Hungarian empire to solicit business.

Sometime during the 1880s, an agent from the Hamburg-American Line (HAPAG), a German steamship company, visited a village in the Russian Ukraine where the great grandparents of one of this book's authors lived. Shortly after his visit, they boarded a train to Austrian-occupied Poland and Hamburg. There they boarded a HAPAG steamer emblazoned with a large banner proclaiming "*Willkommen*" ("Welcome"). Just boarding that ship they felt they were entering the United States. Millions of others like them sailed on ocean liners from Germany, Italy, and Great Britain over the next thirty years.

Chinese and Japanese immigrants also came to the United States in appreciable numbers for the first time during the late nineteenth century. Most Chinese immigrants came from Canton in South China, a region of great rural poverty. They worked on railroads and in mines throughout the West and as farm laborers in California. Many eventually settled in cities such as San Francisco where they established residential enclaves referred to as Chinatowns. The Chinese population in the United States peaked at about 125,000 in 1882.

Japanese began immigrating to the United States beginning in the late 1880s, driven by a land shortage even more acute than that in Europe. The first wave came by way of Hawaii to work on farms in California, taking the place of Chinese workers who had moved to the cities. By 1900, there were some fifty thousand Japanese immigrants in the United States, nearly all on the West Coast.

Wherever they came from, most migrants saw the ocean as a two-way highway. They intended to stay only a year or two, long enough to earn money to buy land or, more likely, to enter a business back home and improve life for themselves and their families. Roughly half of all immigrants to the United States between 1880 and World War I returned to their country of origin. Some made several round trips. Jews, unwelcome in the lands they left, were the exception. No more than 10 percent of Jewish immigrants returned to Europe, and very few Jews from Russia, who accounted for almost 80 percent of Jewish immigrants after 1880, went back home.

Most newcomers were young men. (Jews again were the exception: Reflecting their intention to stay in their new home, they tended to migrate in families.) Immigrants easily found work in the nation's booming cities. The quickest way to make money was in the large urban factories with their voracious demands for unskilled labor. Except for the Japanese, few immigrants came to work on farms after 1880.

By 1900, women began to equal men among all immigrant groups as young men who decided to stay sent for their families. In a few cases, entire villages migrated, drawn by the good fortune of one or two compatriots, a process called **chain migration**. The success of Francesco Barone, a Buffalo tavern owner, convinced eight thousand residents of his former village in Sicily to migrate to that city, many arriving on tickets Barone purchased.

Immigrants tended to live in neighborhoods among people from the same homeland. Their native culture helped shape their response to their new home. For Italians from the Mezzogiorno, for example, the family was the basic institution for obtaining work and securing assistance in times of stress, death, or sickness. Family ties were so strong that voluntary associations in the towns of the Mezzogiorno were rare. In the United States, immigrants from southern Italy, almost alone among European and Asian migrants, rarely formed neighborhood or ethnic associations.

The desire of the new immigrants to retain their cultural traditions led contemporary observers to doubt their ability to assimilate into American society. Even sympathetic observers, such as social workers, marveled at the utterly foreign character of immigrant districts. In 1900, Philadelphia social worker Emily Dinwiddie visited an Italian neighborhood and described "black-eyed children, rolling and tumbling together, the gaily colored dresses of the women and the crowds of street vendors, that give the neighborhood a wholly foreign appearance."

The Neighborhood

Immigrants did not live in homogeneous communities isloated from the rest of society. Rarely did a particular ethnic group comprise more than 50 percent of a neighborhood. Chinese were the exception, but even the borders of Chinatowns usually overlapped with other neighborhoods. A particular apartment building might house families from Abruzzi in Italy, and Jews from Kiev might dominate a block of tenements in New York City's Lower East Side, but greater concentrations were rare. Even to call such districts "Jewish" or "Italian" distorts the reality. Most Italian immigrants identified not so much with

Mulberry Street, New York, 1905. The vibrant, predominantly Russian Jewish Lower East Side of New York at first reflected more the culture of the homeland than of America. Language, dress, ways of doing business, keeping house, and worshipping all followed Old-World patterns. Gradually, thanks especially to the influence of school-age children, a blend of Russian Jewish and American traditions emerged.

Italy—which had only recently been unified—as with the village of their birth. Only with time did they come to see themselves as "Italian" in the way the rest of American society saw them.

German Jews, long established in American cities, wanted little to do with their Russian coreligionists at first. Yet as the larger society conflated both groups, they began to help the newcomers assimilate into American society.

In smaller cities and in the urban South, where foreign-born populations were smaller, ethnic groups were more geographically dispersed, though occasionally they might inhabit the same neighborhood. In turn-of-the-century Memphis, for example, Irish, Italian, and Jewish immigrants lived cheek by jowl in a single immigrant district (called the "Pinch"), sharing schools and recreational space even as they led their singular institutional, religious, and family lives.

Immigrants maintained their cultural traditions through the establishment of religious and communal institutions. Charitable organizations were frequently connected to religious institutions. The church or synagogue became the focal point for immigrant neighborhood life. Much more than a place of worship, it was a school for transmitting Old World values and language to American-born children. The church or synagogue also functioned as a recreational facility and a gathering place for community leaders. In Jewish communities, associations called *landsmanshaften* arranged for burials, jobs, housing, and support for the sick, poor, and elderly.

Because religious institutions were so central to their lives, immigrant communities insisted on maintaining control over them. Polish parishioners wanted Polish priests, and Russian Jewish communities wanted Russian rabbis. The nationality of parish priests became such a heated topic for some Catholic national groups that they threatened to secede from the church, a movement the hierarchy squelched.

Religious institutions played a less formal role among Chinese and Japanese neighborhoods. For them, the family functioned as the source of religious activity and communal organization. Chinatowns were organized in clans of people with the same surname. An umbrella organization called the Chinese Consolidated Benevolent Association emerged; it functioned like the Jewish *landsmanshaften*. Perhaps most important, the association shipped the bones of deceased members back to China for burial in ancestral cemeteries. A similar association, the Japanese Association of America, governed the Japanese community in the United States. This organization was sponsored by the Japanese government, which was sensitive to mistreatment of its citizens abroad and anxious that immigrants set a good example. The Japanese Association, unlike other ethnic organizations, actively encouraged assimilation and stressed the importance of Western dress and learning English.

Ethnic newspapers, theaters, and schools supplemented associational life for immigrants. These institutions reinforced Old-World culture while informing immigrants about American ways. Thus the Jewish *Daily Forward,* first published in New York in 1897, reminded readers of the importance of keeping the Sabbath while admonishing them to adopt American customs.

The Job

If the neighborhood provided a familiar and supportive environment for the immigrant, work offered the ultimate reward for coming to America. All immigrants perceived the job as the way to independence and as a way out, either back to the Old World or into the larger American society.

Immigrants typically received their first job with the help of a countryman. Italian, Chinese, Japanese, and Mexican newcomers worked with contractors who placed them in jobs. These middlemen often provided housing, loans, and other services for recent arrivals. They exacted a fee, sometimes extortionate, for their services. In an era before employment agencies, however, they efficiently matched immigrants with jobs. Other immigrant groups, such as Poles and Russian Jews, often secured work through their ethnic associations or village or family connections. Poles in the meatpacking industries in Chicago, for example, recommended relatives to their bosses. Family members sometimes exchanged jobs with one another (see "American Views: Immigrants and Work").

The type of work available to immigrants depended on their skills, the local economy, and local discrimination. Mexican migrants to southern California, for example, concentrated in railroad construction. Mostly unskilled, they replaced Chinese laborers when the federal government excluded Chinese immigration after 1882. Mexicans built the interurban rail lines of Los Angeles in 1900 and established communities at their construction camps. Los Angeles businessmen barred Mexicans from other occupations. Similarly, Chinese immigrants were confined to work in laundries and restaurants within the boundaries of Los Angeles's Chinatown. There were no commercial laundries in China.

The Japanese who came to Los Angeles around 1900 were forced into sectors of the economy native-born white people had either shunned or failed to exploit. The Japanese turned this discrimination to their benefit when they transformed the cultivation of market garden crops into a major agricultural enterprise. By 1904, Japanese farmers owned more than fifty thousand acres in California. George Shima, who came to California from Japan in 1889 with a little capital, made himself the "Potato King" of the Sacramento Delta. By 1913, Shima owned 28,000 acres of farmland.

Other ethnic groups in other parts of the country had to conform to similar constraints. Greeks in Chicago, for example, restricted to food services, established restaurants, fruit distributorships, and ice-cream factories throughout the city.

Stereotypes also channeled immigrants' work options, sometimes benefiting one group at the expense of another. Jewish textile entrepreneurs, for example, sometimes hired only Italians because they thought them less prone to unionization than Jewish workers. Other Jewish bosses hired only Jewish workers, hoping that ethnic loyalty would overcome the lure of the unions. Pittsburgh steelmakers preferred Polish workers to the black workers who began arriving in northern cities in appreciable numbers after 1900. This began the decades-long tradition of handing down steel mill jobs through the generations in Polish families.

Jews, alone among European ethnic groups, found work almost exclusively with one another. Among the factors contributing to this pattern may have been the discrimination Jews faced in eastern Europe, the existence of an established Jewish community when they arrived, and their dominance of the needle trades. Jews comprised three-quarters of the more than half-million workers in New York City's garment industry in 1910. Jews were also heavily concentrated in the retail trade.

Like their native-born counterparts, few married immigrant women worked outside the home, but unlike the native-born, many Italian and Jewish women did piecework for the garment industry in their apartments. Unmarried Polish women often worked in factories or as domestic servants. Japanese women, married and single, worked with their families on farms. Until revolution in China in 1911 began to erode traditional gender roles, married Chinese immigrant women typically remained home.

The paramount goal for many immigrants was to work for themselves rather than someone else. Some immigrants, like George Shima, parlayed their skills and a small stake into successful businesses. Most new arrivals, however, had few skills and no resources beyond their wits with which to realize their dreams. Major banks at the time were unlikely to extend even a small business loan to a budding ethnic entrepreneur. Family members and small ethnic-based community banks provided the initial stake for most immigrant businesses. Many of these banks failed, but a few survived and prospered. For example, the Bank of Italy, established by Amadeo Pietro Giannini in San Francisco in 1904, eventually grew into the Bank of America, one of the nation's largest financial institutions today.

Immigrants could not fully control their own destinies in the United States any more than native-born Americans could. The vagaries of daily life, including death, disease, and bad luck, thwarted many immigrants' dreams. Hard work did not always ensure success. Add to these the difficulty of cultural adjustment to an unfamiliar environment, and the newcomer's confident hopes could fade quickly. Almost all immigrants, however, faced an obstacle that by its nature white native-born Americans did not. They faced it on the job, in the city at large, and even in their neighborhoods: the antiforeign prejudice of American **nativism**.

Nativism

Despite the openness of American borders in the nineteenth century and contrary to the nation's reputation as a refuge from foreign persecution and poverty, immigrants have not always received a warm reception. Ben Franklin groused about the "foreignness" of German immigrants during the colonial era. From the 1830s to 1860, nativist sentiment, directed mainly at Irish Catholic immigrants, expressed itself in occasional violence and job discrimination. Anti-immigrant sentiment gave rise to an important political party, the Know-Nothings, in the 1850s.

When immigration revived after the Civil War, so did antiforeign sentiment. But late-nineteenth-century nativism differed in two ways from its antebellum predecessor. First, the target was no longer Irish Catholics but the even more numerous Catholics and Jews of southern and eastern Europe, people whose language and usually darker complexions set them apart from the native-born majority. Second, late-nineteenth-century nativism had a pseudo-scientific underpinning. As we saw in Chapter 18, the so-called "scientific" racism of the period maintained that some people are inherently inferior to others. There was, in this view, a natural hierarchy of race. At the top, with the exception of the Irish, were northern Europeans, especially those of Anglo-Saxon descent. Following below them were French, Slavs, Poles, Italians, Jews, Asians, and Africans. Social Darwinism, which justified the class hierarchy, reinforced scientific racism.

When the "inferior" races arrived in the United States in significant numbers after 1880, nativists sounded the alarm. A prominent Columbia University professor wrote in 1887 that Hungarians and Italians were "of such a character as to endanger our civilization." Nine years later, the director of the U.S. census warned that eastern and southern Europeans were "beaten men from beaten races. They have none of the ideas and aptitudes which fit men to take up readily and easily the problem of self-care and self-government." The result of unfettered migration would be "race suicide."

The popular press translated these scientific pronouncements into blunter language. In the mid-1870s, a Chicago newspaper described recently arrived Bohemian immigrants (from the present-day Czech Republic) as "depraved beasts, harpies, decayed physically and spiritually, mentally and morally, thievish and licentious." A decade later, with eastern Europeans still pouring into Chicago, another newspaper suggested: "Let us whip these slavic wolves back to the European dens from which they issue, or in some way exterminate them." The *New York Times,* demurring from such an extreme, suggested instead some form of restriction. Referring to Russian Jewish and Italian immigrants, the *Times* concluded that Americans "pretty well agreed" that these foreigners were "of a kind which we are better without." The rhetoric of the scientific press was scarcely less extreme. *Scientific American* warned immigrants to "assimilate" quickly or "share the fate of the native Indians" and face "a quiet but sure extermination."

Such sentiments generated proposals to restrict foreign immigration. The treatment of the Chinese provided a precedent. Chinese immigrants had long worked for low wages under harsh conditions in mining and railroad construction in the West. Their different culture and their willingness to accept low wages provoked resentment among native- and European-born workers. Violence against Chinese laborers increased during the 1860s and 1870s. In 1870, the Republican-dominated Congress passed the **Naturalization Act**, which limited citizenship to "white persons and persons of African descent." The act was specifically intended to prevent Chinese from becoming citizens—a ban not lifted until 1943—but it affected other Asian groups also. The Chinese Exclusion Act of 1882, passed following another decade of anti-Chinese pressure, made the Chinese the only ethnic group in the world that could not emigrate freely to the United States. Even this drastic measure did not satisfy one Knights of Labor official, who in 1885 viewed the conflict between Chinese and native-born labor in the perspective of the 1850s sectional crisis (with a modern Darwinian twist): "This is the old irrepressible conflict between slave and white labor. God grant there may be survival of the fittest." Anti-Asian violence raced through mining communities in the West for the next two years.

Labor competition also contributed to the rise of another anti-immigrant organization. A group

American Views
IMMIGRANTS AND WORK

In 1906, a magazine called *The Independent* published a series of stories documenting immigrant work experiences, two of which are excerpted here. The first story is told by Rocco Corrersca, an Italian immigrant whose first job in the United States was as a ragpicker. The second story is told in the halting English of a young Japanese immigrant who migrated to Portland, Oregon, and worked as a domestic servant. Their jobs typified what most immigrants could expect: not glamorous, not well-paying, and probably involving hard physical labor. Although the stories are generally upbeat, they reflect some of the hardships new immigrants faced.

As Corrersca's story indicates, immigrants often received their first jobs through an agent. The agents often extracted a fee, sometimes quite high, for this service. But the system enabled employers to find staff more efficiently than they could on their own.

❖ **Did the costs of the agent system outweigh its benefits?**

❖ **Do you think it is likely that Corrersca's English was as idiomatic as it appears here? Or do you think the editors of *The Independent* corrected it for him? If so, why do you think they didn't correct it for the Japanese immigrant? Is it significant that Corrersca is named and the Japanese immigrant isn't?**

❖ **Immigrants experienced considerable job and geographical mobility. Was this good or bad?**

❖ **Were these immigrants ever exploited? What recourse did they have to counter exploitation?**

Rocco Corrersca Becomes an Entrepreneur
We came to Brooklyn, New York, to a wooden house in Adams street that was full of Italians from Naples. Bartolo had a room on the third floor and there were fifteen men in the room, all boarding with Bartolo. . . . The next morning, early, Bartolo told us to go out and pick rags and get bottles. . . . Most of the men in our room worked at digging the sewer. Bartolo got them the work and they paid him about one-quarter of their wages. Then he charged them for board and he bought the clothes for them, too. So they got little money after all. . . .

of skilled workers and small businessmen formed the **American Protective Association (APA)** in 1887 and claimed half a million members a year later. The APA sought to limit Catholic civil rights in the United States to protect the jobs of Protestant workingmen.

The **Immigration Restriction League (IRL)**, formed in 1894 in the midst of a depression, took a more modest and indirect approach. The IRL proposed to require prospective immigrants to pass a literacy test that they presumed most southern and eastern Europeans would fail. Cynically reaching out to native-born workers, the IRL vowed that its legislation would protect "the wages of our workingmen against the fatal competition of low-price labor."

The IRL ultimately failed to have its literacy requirement enacted. The return of prosperity and the growing preference of industrialists for immigrant labor put an end to calls for formal restrictions on immigration for the time being. Less than thirty years later, however, Congress would enact major restrictive legislation aimed at southern and eastern European immigrants. In the meantime, IRL propaganda encouraged northern universities to establish quotas limiting the admission of new immigrants, especially Jews.

Immigrants and their communal associations fought attempts to restrict immigration. The Japanese government even hinted at violent retaliation if Congress ever enacted restrictive legislation

We went away one day to Newark [New Jersey] and got work on the street. . . . We paid a man five dollars each for getting us the work and we were with that boss for six months. He was Irish, but a good man and he gave us our money every Saturday night. We lived much better than with Bartolo, and when the work was done we each had nearly $200 saved. Plenty of the men spoke English and they taught us, and we taught them to read and write. . . .

We went back to Brooklyn to a saloon . . . where we got a job cleaning it out and slept in a little room upstairs. There was a bootblack named Michael on the corner and when I had time I helped him and learned the business. . . . Then [Francesco and I] thought we would go into business and we got a basement and put four chairs in it. . . . Outside we had a big sign that read:

THE BEST SHINE FOR TEN CENTS

We had said that when we saved $1,000 each we would go back to Italy and buy a farm, but now that the time is coming we are so busy and making so much money that we think we will stay.

A Japanese Immigrant Becomes a Servant

The desire to see America was burning at my boyish heart. . . . My destination was Portland, Ore., where my cousin is studying. . . . I can be any use here, but become a domestic servant, as the field for Japanese very narrow and limited. . . . The place where I got work in the first time was a boarding house. My duties were to peel potatoes, wash the dishes, a few laundry work, and also I was expected to do whatever mistress, waitress and cook has told me. . . .

My real objection was that the work was indeed too hard and unpleasant for me to bear and also there were no times even to read a book. But I thought it rather impolite to say so and partly my strange pride hated to confess my weakness. . . . At the end of the second week I asked my wages, but she refused on the ground that if she does I might leave her. . . . Believing the impossibility to obtain her sanction, early in the next morning while everybody still in the bed, I hide my satchel under the bush in the back yard. . . . Leaving the note and wages behind me, I hurried back to Japanese Christian Home.

Since then I have tried a few other places with a better success at each trial and in course of time I have quite accustomed to it and gradually become indifferent as the humiliation melted down. Though I never felt proud of this vocation, in several cases I have commenced to manifest the interest of my avocation as a professor of Dust and Ashes.

Sources: The Independent, *March and May 1906.*

similar to that imposed on the Chinese. But most immigrants believed that the more "American" they became, the less prejudice they would encounter. Accordingly, leaders of immigrant groups stressed the importance of assimilation.

In 1895, a group of American-born Chinese in California formed a communal association called the Native Sons of the Golden State (a deliberate response to a nativist organization that called itself the Native Sons of the Golden West). Stressing the need to assimilate, the association's constitution declared, "It is imperative that no members shall have sectional, clannish, Tong [a secret fraternal organization] or party prejudices against each other. . . . Whoever violates this provision shall be expelled." A guidebook written at the same time for immigrant Jews recommended that they "hold fast," calling that attitude "most necessary in America. Forget your past, your customs, and your ideals. . . . A bit of advice to you: do not take a moment's rest. Run, do, work, and keep your own good in mind." Although it is doubtful whether most Jewish immigrants followed this advice whole, it nonetheless reflects the way the pressure to conform modified the cultures of all immigrant groups.

Assimilation connotes the loss of one culture in favor of another. The immigrant experience of the late nineteenth and early twentieth centuries might better be described as a process of adjustment between old ways and new. It was a dynamic process that resulted in entirely new cultural forms. It rarely followed a straight line toward or from the culture of origin. The Japanese, for example, had not gone to Los Angeles to become truck farmers, but circumstances led them to that occupation, and they used their cultural heritage of hard work, strong family ties, and sober living to make a restricted livelihood successful. Sometimes economics and the availability of alternatives resulted in modifications of traditions that nonetheless maintained their spirit. In the old country, Portuguese held *festas* every Sunday honoring a patron saint. In New England towns, they confined the tradition to their churches instead of parading through the streets. And instead of baking bread themselves, Portuguese immigrant women were happy to buy all the bread they needed from local bakers.

In a few cases, the New World offered greater opportunities to follow cultural traditions than the Old. Young women who migrated from Italy's Abruzzi region to Rochester, New York, found that it was easier to retain their Old-World moral code in late-nineteenth-century Rochester, where young men outnumbered them significantly. At the same time, the enhanced economic prospects in Rochester enabled them to marry earlier than they would have in their hometown. It also allowed these young women to work outside the home, something women rarely did in Abruzzi. Financial security allowed them to construct the nuclear household that was the cultural ideal in the old country. In a similar way, Sicilians who migrated to lower Manhattan discovered that ready access to work and relatively high geographical mobility permitted them to live near and among their extended families much more easily than in Sicily.

Despite the antagonism of native-born white people toward recent immigrants, the greatest racial divide in America remained that between black and white. Newcomers quickly caught on to this distinction and sought to assert their "whiteness" as a common bond with other European immigrant groups and a badge of acceptance into the larger society. Nativists, however, often lumped immigrants into the "black" category. The word "guinea," for example, which originally referred to African slaves, emerged as a derogatory epithet for Italians and occasionally Greeks, Jews, and Puerto Ricans. When the Louisiana legislature debated disfranchisement in 1898, a lawmaker explained that "according to the spirit of our meaning when we speak of 'white man's government,' Italians are as black as the blackest negro in existence." For immigrants, therefore, becoming "white"—distancing themselves from African-American culture and people—was often part of the process of adjusting to American life, especially as increasing numbers of black Southerners began moving to northern cities.

Roots of the Great Migration

Nearly 90 percent of African Americans still lived in the South in 1900, most in rural areas. Between 1880 and 1900, however, black families began to move into the great industrial cities of the Northeast and Midwest. They were drawn by the same economic promise that attracted overseas migrants and were pushed by growing persecution in the South. They were also responding to the appeals of black Northerners. As a leading black newspaper, the **Chicago Defender** argued in the early 1900s, "To die from the bite of frost is far more glorious than at the hands of a mob. I beg you, my brother, to leave the benighted land." Job opportunities probably outweighed all other factors in motivating what became known as the **Great Migration**. Letters to the *Defender* spoke much less of the troubled life in the South than of the promise of a new, more productive life in the North.

In most northern cities in 1900, black people typically worked as common laborers or domestic servants. They competed with immigrants for jobs, and in most cases they lost. Immigrants even claimed jobs that black workers once dominated, like barbering and service work in hotels, restaurants, and transportation. Fannie Barrier Williams, a turn-of-the-century black activist in Chicago, complained that between 1895 and 1905, "the colored people of Chicago have lost . . . nearly every occupation of which they once had almost a monopoly."

Black women had particularly few options in the northern urban labor force outside of domestic service, although they earned higher wages than they had for similar work in southern cities. The retail and clerical jobs that attracted young working-class white women remained closed to black women. Employers rejected them for any job involving direct contact with the public. As one historian concluded, advertisers and corporate executives demanded "a pleasing physical appearance (or voice)—one that conformed to a native-born white American standard of female beauty [and served] as an important consideration in hiring office receptionists, secretaries, department store clerks, and telephone operators." Addie W. Hunter, who qualified for a civil service clerical position in Boston, could not find work to match her training. She concluded in 1916, "For the way things stand at present, it is useless to have the requirements. Color . . . will always be in the way."

The lack of options black migrants confronted in the search for employment matched similar frustrations in their quest for a place to live. Even more than foreign immigrants, they were restricted to segregated urban **ghettos**. Small black ghettos existed in antebellum northern cities. In 1860, four out of every five black residents of Detroit lived in a clearly defined district, for example. After the Civil War, black ghettos emerged in southern and border cities. In Washington, D.C., black residents comprised nearly 80 percent of the population in a twenty-block area in the southwest quadrant of the city. In the 1890s, black people dominated an area east of downtown Atlanta known as "Sweet Auburn" after the avenue that cut through the neighborhood. As black migration to northern cities accelerated after 1900, the pattern of residential isolation became more pronounced. The black districts in northern cities were more diverse than those of southern cities. Migration brought rural Southerners, urban Southerners, and West Indians (especially in New York) together with the black Northerners already living there. People of all social classes lived in these districts.

The difficulties that black families faced to make ends meet paralleled in some ways those of immigrant working-class families. Restricted job options, however, limited the income of black families, even with black married women five times more likely to work than married white women. In black families, moreover, working teenage children were less likely to stay home and contribute their paychecks to the family income.

Popular culture reinforced the marginalization of African Americans. Vaudeville and minstrel shows, popular urban entertainment around 1900, featured songs belittling black people and black characters with names like "Useless Peabody" and "Moses Abraham Highbrow." Immigrants frequented these shows and absorbed the culture of racism from them. The new medium of film perpetuated the negative stereotypes.

In the North as in the South, African Americans sought to counter the hostility of the larger society by building their own community institutions. An emerging middle-class leadership—including Robert Abbott, publisher of the *Chicago Defender*—sought to develop black businesses. Despite these efforts, chronic lack of capital kept black businesses mostly small and confined to the ghetto. Immigrant groups often pooled extended family capital resources or tapped ethnic banks. With few such resources at their disposal, black businesses failed at a high rate. Most black people worked outside the ghetto for white employers. Economic marginalization often attracted unsavory businesses—dance halls, brothels, and bars—to black neighborhoods. One recently arrived migrant from the South complained that in his Cleveland neighborhood, his family was surrounded by loafers, "gamblers [and] pocket pickers; I can not raise my children here like they should be. This is one of the worst places in principle you ever looked on in your life."

An African-American religious meeting, New York City, early 1900s. Black migrants from the South found vibrant communities in northern cities typically centered around black churches and their activities. Like immigrants from Asia and Europe who sought to transplant the cultures of their homelands within urban America, black migrants reestablished southern religious and communal traditions in their new homes.

Other black institutions proved more lasting than black businesses. In Chicago in 1891, black physician Daniel Hale Williams established Provident Hospital, the nation's first interracially staffed hospital, with the financial help of wealthy white Chicagoans. Although it failed as an interracial experiment, the hospital thrived, providing an important training ground for black physicians and nurses.

The organization of black branches of the Young Men's and Young Women's Christian Association provided living accommodations, social facilities, and employment information for black young people. Many black migrants to northern cities—perhaps a majority—were single, and the Y provided them guidance and a "home." White people funded many black Y projects but did not accept black members in their chapters. By 1910, black settlement houses modeled after white versions appeared in several cities.

New Cities

Despite the hardships associated with urban life, the American city continued to act, in the words of contemporary novelist Theodore Dreiser, as a "giant magnet." Immigration from abroad and migration from American farms to the cities resulted in an urban explosion during the late nineteenth century (see Map 20-2). In 1850, six cities had a population exceeding 100,000; by 1900, thirty-eight did. In 1850, only 5 percent of the nation's population lived in cities of more than 100,000 inhabitants; by 1900, the figure was 19 percent. The nation's population tripled between 1860 and 1920, but the urban population increased ninefold. Of the 1,700 cities listed in the 1900 census, less than 2 percent even existed in 1800.

In Europe, a few principal cities like Paris and Berlin absorbed most of the urban growth dur-

Map 20-2 *The Growth of America's Cities, 1880–1900*
Several significant trends stand out on this map. First is the development of an urban-industrial core stretching from New England to the Midwest where the largest cities were located. And second is the emergence of relatively new cities in the South and West, reflecting the national dimensions of innovations in industry and transportation.

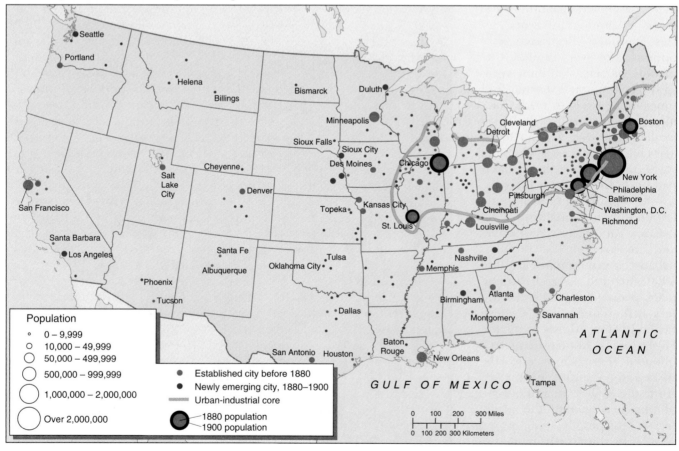

ing this period. In the United States, in contrast, growth was more evenly distributed among many cities. In 1820, about 18 percent of the urban population of the United States lived in New York, the nation's largest city; by 1890, its share had fallen to 7 percent. Put another way, many U.S. cities experienced the pains of rapid growth and industrialization in the late nineteenth century.

Despite the relative evenness of growth, a distinctive urban system had emerged by 1900, with New York and Chicago anchoring an urban-industrial core extending in a crescent from New England to the cities bordering the Great Lakes. This region included nine of the nation's ten largest cities in 1920. Western cities such as Denver, San Francisco, and Los Angeles emerged as dominant urban places in their respective regions but did not challenge the urban core for supremacy. Southern cities, limited in growth by low consumer demand, low wages, and weak capital formation, were drawn into the orbit of the urban core. Atlanta, an offspring of the railroad, prospered as the region's major way station for funneling wealth into the urban North. Dallas emerged as Atlanta's counterpart in the western South (see Chapter 19).

Urban growth highlighted the growing divisions in American society. The crush of people and the emergence of new technologies expanded the city outward and upward as urban dwellers sorted themselves by social class and ethnic group. While the new infrastructure of water and sewer systems, bridges, and trolley tracks kept steel mills busy, it also fragmented the urban population by allowing settlements well beyond existing urban boundaries. The way people satisfied their needs for food, clothing, and shelter stimulated the industrial economy while distinguishing one class from another. Although urban institutions emerged to counter these divisive trends, they could not overcome them completely.

Centers and Suburbs

The centers of the country's great cities changed in scale and function in this era, achieving a prominence they would eventually lose in the twentieth century. Downtowns expanded up and out as tall buildings arose—monuments to business and finance—creating towering urban skylines. Residential neighborhoods were pushed out, leaving the center dominated by corporate headquarters and retail and entertainment districts.

Corporate heads administered their empires from downtown, even if their factories were located on the urban periphery or in other towns and cities. Banks and insurance companies clustered in financial centers like Atlanta's Five Points district to service the corporations. Department stores and shops clustered in retail districts in strategic locations along electric trolley lines. It was to these areas that urban residents usually referred when they talked about going "downtown." In the entertainment district, electric lights lit up theaters, dance halls, and restaurants into the night.

As retail and office uses crowded out dwellings from the city center, a new phenomenon emerged: the residential neighborhood. Advances in transportation technology, first the horse-drawn railway and, by the 1890s, the electric trolley, eased commuting for office workers. Some in the growing and increasingly affluent middle class left the crowded, polluted city altogether to live in new residential suburbs. These people did not abandon the city—they still looked to it for its jobs, schools, libraries, and entertainment—but they rejected it as a place to live, leaving it to the growing ranks of working-class immigrants and African Americans. This pattern contrasted with that of Europe, where the middle class remained in the city.

The suburb emerged as the preferred place of residence for the urban middle class after 1870. As early as 1873, Chicago boasted nearly one hundred suburbs with a combined population of more than fifty thousand. Smaller cities like Cleveland, Richmond, Memphis, Omaha, and San Francisco also sprouted large suburban communities. The ideals that had promoted modest suburban growth earlier in the nineteenth century—privacy, aesthetics, and home ownership—became increasingly important for the growing numbers of middle-class families after 1880.

Consider the Russells of Short Hills, New Jersey. Short Hills lay eighteen miles by railroad from New York City. William Russell; his wife, Ella Gibson Russell; and their six children moved there from Brooklyn in the late 1880s, seeking a "pleasant, cultured people whose society we could enjoy" and a cure for Russell's rheumatism. Russell owned and managed a small metal brokerage in New York and enjoyed gardening, reading, and socializing with his new neighbors. Ella Russell cared for their six children with the help of a servant and also found time for several clubs and charities.

The design of the Russells's home reflected the principles Catharine Beecher and Harriet Beecher Stowe outlined in their suburban home Bible, *American Woman's Home* (1869). The

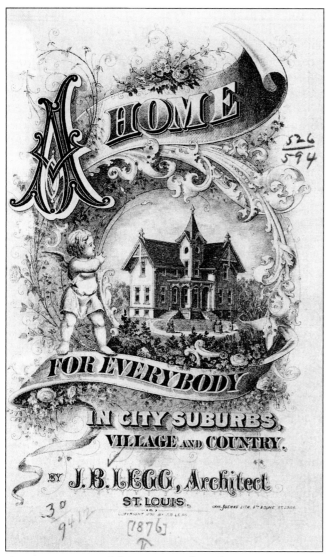

As immigrants crowded into cities and as advances in transportation technology made commuting to work feasible, more and more middle-class families abandoned the noise, bustle, and diversity of the city for dream homes in the pastoral setting of the suburbs.

kitchen, according to Beecher and Stowe, should be organized for expedience and hygiene. The home's utilities should be confined to a central core, freeing wall areas for other functions. The new technology of central heating made it unnecessary to divide a house into many small rooms, each with its own fireplace or stove. Taking advantage of this change, Beecher and Stowe recommended that a home's ground floor have fewer but larger rooms to encourage the family to pursue their individual activities in a common space. Parlors and reception rooms disappeared, along with the rigid spatial segregation of the sexes.

Such former standards as the children's wing, the male "smoking room," and the female parlor were not part of the new suburban home.

The once prevailing view that women were too frail for vigorous exercise was changing. Thus the entire Russell family was to be found enjoying the tennis, swimming, and skating facilities on the grounds of the Short Hills Athletic Club. Because the community bordered on undeveloped woodland traversed by trails, "wheel clubs" appeared in the 1880s to organize families for bicycle outings.

The emphasis on family togetherness also reflected the changing role of men in late-nineteenth-century society. Beecher and Stowe praised fathers who took active roles in child rearing and participated fully in the family's leisure activities. Women's roles also broadened, as Ella Russell's club work attested.

Suburbs differed not only from the city but also from one another. With the growth after 1890 of the electric trolley, elevated rail lines, and other relatively inexpensive forms of commuter travel, suburbs became accessible to a broader spectrum of the middle class. The social structure, architecture, and amenities of suburbs varied, depending on the rail service and distance from the city. The commuter railroad remained popular among people like the Russells who could afford the time and expense of commuting to and from the city center—a distance of fifteen miles or more. The trolley and elevated railroads generated modest middle-class urban neighborhoods and suburbs, with densities decreasing and income increasing toward the ends of the lines. But for the working class—even skilled artisans—suburban living remained out of reach.

The suburb underscored the growing fragmentation of life in and around American cities in the late nineteenth century. Residence, consumer habits, and leisure activities reflected growing social and class divisions. Yet, at the same time, the growing materialism of American society promised a common ground for its disparate ethnic, racial, and social groups.

The New Middle Class

From the colonial era, America's urban middle class had included professionals—physicians, lawyers, ministers, educators, editors—as well as merchants, shopkeepers, and skilled artisans (until they dropped from the middle class in the late nineteenth century). In the late nineteenth century, industrial technology and urban growth expanded the urban middle class to include salespeople, factory supervisors, managers, civil servants, technicians, and a broad range of "white-collar" office workers like insurance agents, bank tellers, and legal assistants. This newer middle class set national trends in residential patterns, consumption, and leisure.

The more affluent members of the new middle class, like the Russells, repaired to new subdivisions within and outside the city limits. Simple row houses sheltered the growing numbers of clerks and civil servants who remained in the city. These dwellings contrasted sharply with the crowded one- or two-room apartments that confined the working class. Rents for these apartments ran as much as $3 a week at a time when few workers made more than $9 or $10.

The new middle class transformed America into a consumer society. In earlier times, land had been a symbol of prestige. Now it was things. And the new industries obliged with a dazzling array of goods and technologies to make life easier and allow more time for family and leisure.

By 1910, the new middle class lived in all-electric homes, with indoor plumbing and appliances unavailable twenty years earlier. A typical kitchen might include a coffeepot, a hot plate, a chafing dish, and a toaster. These items eased food preparation. The modern city-dweller worked by the clock, not by the sun. Eating patterns changed: cold, packaged cereals replaced hot meats at breakfast; fast lunches of Campbell's soup—"a meal in itself"—or canned stews weaned Americans from the heavy lunch. Jell-O appeared in the 1890s, touted as America's "most quick and easy" dessert. In Nashville at the same time, Joel Cheek ground and blended coffee beans in his store for customers' convenience. He convinced the city's Maxwell House Hotel to serve his new concoction, and in 1907, when President Theodore Roosevelt visited the hotel and drained his cup, he turned to Cheek and declared that the coffee was "good to the very last drop." A slogan and Maxwell House coffee were born.

Advertising played an important role in the consumer society. Advertisers told Americans what they wanted; they created demand and developed loyalty for brand-name products. In early-twentieth-century New York, a six-story-high Heinz electric sign was a sensation, especially the forty-foot-long pickle at its top.

The middle class liked anything that saved time: trolleys, trains, electric razors, vacuum cleaners. The telephone replaced the letter for everyday communication; it was quicker and less formal. By 1900, some 1.4 million phones were in service, and many middle-class homes had one.

The new technology introduced new terms that reflected the pace of urban life: "I'll give you a buzz" or "Give me a ring."

The middle class liked its news in an easy-to-read form. Urban tabloids multiplied after 1880, led by Joseph Pulitzer's *New York World* and William Randolph Hearst's *New York Journal.* The newspapers organized the news into topical sections, used bold headlines and graphics to catch the eye, ran human interest stories to capture the imagination, inaugurated sports pages to attract male readers, and offered advice columns for women. And they opened their pages to a wide range of attractive advertising, much of it directed at women, who did about 90 percent of the shopping in American cities by 1900.

As the visual crowded out the printed in advertising, newspapers, and magazines, these materials became more accessible to a wider urban audience. Although mainly middle-class in orientation, the tabloid press drew urban society together with new features such as the comic strip, which first appeared in the 1890s, and heart-rending personal sagas drawn from real life. Immigrants who might have had difficulty reading small-type newspapers received their initiation into the mainstream of American society through the tabloids.

In a similar manner, the department store, essentially a middle-class retail establishment, became one of the city's most democratic forums and the focus of the urban downtown after 1890. Originating in the 1850s and 1860s with the construction of retail palaces such as Boston's Jordan Marsh, Philadelphia's Wanamaker & Brown, New York's Lord & Taylor, and Chicago's Marshall Field, the department store came to epitomize the bounty of the new industrial capitalism. At the time of the Philadelphia Exposition in 1876, only thirty or so department stores existed; by 1920, there were thousands. They exuded limitless abundance with their extensive inventories, items for every budget, sumptuous surroundings, and efficient, trained personnel.

At first, most department store customers were middle-class married women. Not expected to work and with disposable income and flexible schedules, these women had the means and time to wander department store aisles. The stores catered to their tastes—and the current emphasis on home and domesticity—with such items as prefabricated household furnishings, ready-made clothing, toys, and stationery.

Industry churned out uniform, high-quality products in abundance, and middle-class salaries absorbed them. Department stores maintained consumers' interest with advertising campaigns arranged around holidays such as Easter and Christmas, the seasons, and the school calendar. Each event required new clothing and accessories, and the ready-made clothing industry changed fashions accordingly.

Soon the spectacle and merchandise of the department store attracted shoppers from all social strata, not just the middle class. "The principal cause of the stores' success," one shopper explained in 1892, "is the fact that their founders have understood the necessity of offering a new democracy whose needs and habits" are satisfied "in the cheapest possible way," providing "a taste for elegance and comfort unknown to previous generations." Though many less affluent women came merely to "window-shop" (a new expression inspired by the large plate glass display windows retailers installed in their stores to attract customers), some came to buy. After 1890, department stores increasingly hired young immigrant women to cater to their growing foreign-born clientele.

The department store was the turn-of-the-century shopping mall and provided inexpensive amusement for young working-class people, especially immigrants. Mary Antin recalled how she and her teenage friends and sister would spend their Saturday nights in 1898 patrolling "a dazzlingly beautiful palace called a 'department store.'" It was there that Mary and her sister "exchanged our hateful homemade European costumes . . . for real American machine-made garments, and issued forth glorified in each other's eyes."

By 1900, department stores had added sporting goods and hardware sections and were attracting male as well as female customers from a wide social spectrum. When Wanamaker's introduced a "bargain room" in 1888, other retail stores—including Filene's famous "Automatic Bargain Basement" in Boston—followed suit.

The expanding floor space devoted to sporting goods reflected the growth of leisure in urban society. And like other aspects of that society, leisure and recreation both separated and cut across social classes. The leisure activities of the wealthy increasingly removed them from the rest of urban society. For them, the good life required such prerequisites as a mansion on Fifth Avenue, carriages and horses for transportation, a pony for the younger children, a saddle horse for the older ones, and a yacht. As sports like football became important extracurricular activites at Harvard, Yale,

and other elite universities, intercollegiate games became popular occasions for the upper class to congregate and, not incidentally, discuss business. For exercise and recreation, the elite gathered at the athletic clubs and country clubs that emerged as open spaces disappeared in the city. High fees and strict membership criteria kept these clubs exclusive. The first country club in the United States was founded in Brookline, Massachusetts, a Boston suburb, in 1882. Country clubs built golf courses for men and tennis courts primarily for women. The clubs offered a suburban retreat, away from the diverse middle- and working-class populations, where the elite could play in privacy.

Middle-class urban residents could not afford country clubs, but they rode electric trolleys to the end of the line to enjoy suburban parks and bicycle and skating clubs. Reflecting the emphasis on family togetherness in late-nineteenth-century America, both men and women participated in these sports. Bicycling in particular became immensely popular. New bikes cost at least $50, putting them beyond the reach of the working class.

If college football was the rage among the elite, baseball was the leading middle-class spectator sport. Organized baseball originated among the urban elite before the Civil War. The middle class took over the sport after the war. Baseball epitomized the nation's transition from a rural to an urban industrial society. Reflecting rural tradition, it was played on an expanse of green usually on the outskirts of the city. It was leisurely; unlike other games, it had no time limit. Reflecting industrial society, however, it had clearly defined rules and was organized into leagues. Professional leagues were profit-making enterprises, and, like other enterprises, they frequently merged. Initially, most professional baseball games were played on weekday afternoons, making it hard for working-class spectators to attend. After merging with the American Association (AA) in 1883, the National League adopted some of the AA's innovations to attract more fans, including beer sales, cheap admission, and, despite the objections of Protestant churches, Sunday games.

The tavern, or saloon, was the workingman's club. Typically an all-male preserve, the saloon provided drink, cheap food, and a place for workingmen to read a newspaper, socialize, and learn about job opportunities. Advances in refrigeration in the 1870s allowed large breweries such as Anheuser-Busch and Pabst to distribute their product nationwide. Alcoholism was a severe problem in

Eakins, Thomas. Baseball Players Practicing. 1875. Watercolor; 10⅞″ × 12⅞.″ Museum of Art, Rhode Island School of Design. Jesse Metcalf and Walter H. Kimball Funds. Photography by Cathy Carver.

Thomas Eakins created this painting of baseball players practicing in 1875. Originating as a sport of urban gentlemen, baseball eventually broadened its appeal, drawing fans from all spectrums of city life.

cities, especially, though not exclusively, among working-class men, fueling the prohibition movement of the late nineteenth century.

Amusement parks, with their mechanical wonders, were another hallmark of the industrial city. Declining trolley fares made them accessible to the working class around 1900. Unlike taverns, they provided a place for working-class men and women to meet and date.

The most renowned of these parks was Brooklyn's Coney Island. In 1897, George C. Tilyou opened Steeplechase Park on Coney Island. He brought an invention by George Washington Ferris—a giant rotating vertical wheel equipped with swinging carriages—to the park from Chicago, and the Ferris Wheel quickly became a Coney Island signature. Together with such attractions as mechanical horses and 250,000 of Thomas Edison's light bulbs, Steeplechase dazzled patrons with its technological wonders. It was quickly followed by Luna Park and Dreamland, and the Coney Island attractions became collectively known as "the poor man's paradise." Immigrant entrepreneurs, seeing a good thing, flocked to Coney Island to set up sideshows, pool halls, taverns, and restaurants. One German immigrant opened a small café serving sausages that he named "frankfurters" after his native Frankfurt. Locals called them "Coney Island hots" or "hot dogs" because they resembled the dachshund, a German-bred dog.

After 1900, the wonders of Coney Island began to lure people from all segments of an increasingly diverse city. Sightseers came from around the world. Notables such as Herman Melville, Mark Twain, and even Sigmund Freud (what did he think of Dreamland?) rubbed shoulders with factory workers, domestics, and department store clerks. In much the same manner, baseball was becoming a national pastime as games attracted a disparate crowd of people with little in common but their devotion to the home team.

Increasing materialism had revealed great fissures in American urban society by 1900. Yet places like deparment stores, baseball parks, and amusement parks provided democratic spaces for some interaction. Newspapers and schools also indirectly offered diverse groups the opportunity to share similar experiences.

Conclusion

The new industrial order, the changing nature of work, the massive migrations of populations from the countryside and abroad, and the rise of great cities changed the American landscape in the late nineteenth century. By 1900, the factory worker and the department store clerk were more representative of the new America than the farmer and small shopkeeper. Industry and technology had created thousands of new jobs, but they also eliminated the autonomy many workers had enjoyed and limited their opportunities to advance.

Immigrants thronged to the United States to realize their dreams of economic and religious freedom. They found both to varying degrees but also discovered a darker side to the promise of American life. The great cities thrilled newcomers with their possibilities and their abundance of goods and activities. But the cities also bore witness to the growing divisions in American society. As the new century dawned, the prospects for urban industrial America seemed limitless, yet the stark contrasts that had appeared so vividly inside and outside the Centennial Exposition persisted and deepened.

Still, it would be wrong to depict the nation in 1900 as merely a larger and more divided version of itself in 1876. Although sharp ethnic, racial, and class differences persisted, the nation seemed better poised to address them in 1900 than it had a quarter-century earlier. Labor unions, ethnic organizations, government legislation, and new urban institutions promised ways to remedy the worst abuses of the new urban, industrial economy.

Review Questions

1. Were there ways to achieve the benefits of industrialization without its social costs, or did the nation's political and economic systems make that impossible?

2. Given the widespread grievances among unskilled workers in the late nineteenth and early twentieth centuries, why did so few turn to socialism?

3. When historians speak of immigrant groups adjusting rather than assimilating to American society, what do they mean?

4. The growing fragmentation of urban life reflected deep divisions in modern urban industrial society. At the same time, there were forces that tended to overcome these divisions. What were these forces, and were they sufficient to bridge the divisions?

Recommended Reading

Stuart M. Blumin, *The Emergence of the Middle Class: Social Experience in the American City, 1760–1900* (1989). Analyzes the key factors in the emergence of the urban middle class, especially in the late nineteenth century, and the impact of that class on urban society and culture.

John Bodnar, *The Transplanted: A History of Immigrants in Urban America* (1985). An excellent starting point for learning about the diverse immigrant experience in the United States that is also sensitive to conditions in the countries of origin.

Roger Daniels, *Coming to America: A History of Immigration and Ethnicity in American Life* (1990). Preferred by some to Bodnar's survey. The book's great virtue is its coverage of all immigrant groups; the discussion of Asian immigrants is especially good.

Theodore Dreiser, *Sister Carrie* (1900). One of the best novels to capture life in late-nineteenth-century Chicago and New York. Few detail so clearly the moral and economic dilemmas newcomers faced in the fast-evolving American urban environment.

David Goldfield and Blaine A. Brownell, *Urban America: A History* (1990). A comprehensive overview of the development of American cities that places particular emphasis on the interaction of social, economic, and geographical forces on urban growth.

John Higham, *Strangers in the Land: Patterns of American Nativism, 1860–1925* (1965). Despite its age, serves as an excellent overview of and introduction to the subject of nativism; especially good in setting the context of nativism in American society and politics.

Raymond A. Mohl, *A New City: Urban America in the Industrial Age, 1860–1920* (1985). A fine introduction to the relationship between urbanization and industrialization.

Additional Sources

New Industry

Mark Aldrich, *Safety First: Technology, Labor, and Business in the Building of American Work Safety, 1870–1939* (1997).

Edward Bellamy, *Looking Backward* (1888).

Susan Porter Benson, *Counter Cultures: Saleswomen, Managers, and Customers in American Department Stores, 1890–1940* (1986).

Eileen Boris, *Home to Work: Motherhood and the Politics of Industrial Homework in the United States* (1994).

Stanley Buder, *Pullman: An Experiment in Industrial Order and Community Planning, 1880–1930* (1967).

W. Bernard Carlson, *Innovation as a Social Process: Elihu Thomson and the Rise of General Electric, 1870–1900* (1991).

John Cumbler, *Working-Class Community in Industrial America: Work, Leisure, and Struggle in Two Industrial Cities* (1979).

Marjorie Davies, *Woman's Place Is at the Typewriter, 1870–1930* (1982).

Allan F. Davis, *Spearheads for Reform: The Social Settlements and the Progressive Movement, 1890–1914* (1967).

Nancy Schrom Dye, *As Equals and as Sisters: Feminism, the Labor Movement, and the Women's Trade Union League of New York* (1981).

Leon Fink, *Workingmen's Democracy: The Knights of Labor and American Politics* (1982).

Timothy J. Gilfoyle, *City of Eros: New York City, Prostitution, and the Commercialization of Sex, 1790–1920* (1992).

Herbert Gutman, *Work, Culture, and Society in Industrializing America* (1976).

Tamara Hareven, *Family Time and Industrial Time: The Relationship between Family and Work in a New England Industrial Community* (1982).

William H. Harris, *The Harder We Run: Black Workers since the Civil War* (1982).

Samuel P. Hays, *The Response to Industrialism: 1885–1914* (1957).

David A. Hounshell, *From the American System to Mass Production, 1800–1932* (1984).

Nathan I. Huggins, *Protestants against Poverty: Boston's Charities, 1870–1900* (1970).

Thomas J. Jablonsky, *Pride in the Jungle: Community and Everyday Life in Back of the Yards Chicago* (1993).

David M. Katzman, *Seven Days a Week: Women and Domestic Service in Industrializing America* (1978).

Stuart Kaufman, *Samuel Gompers and the Origins of the American Federation of Labor, 1848–1896* (1973).

Alice Kessler-Harris, *Out to Work: A History of Wage-Earning Women in the United States* (1982).

James B. Lane, *Jacob A. Riis and the American City* (1974).

Bruce Laurie, *Artisans into Workers: Labor in Nineteenth Century America* (1989).

W. David Lewis, *Sloss Furnaces and the Rise of the Birmingham District: An Industrial Epic* (1994).

Walter Licht, *Getting Work: Philadelphia, 1840–1950* (1992).

David Montgomery, *The Fall of the House of Labor: The Workplace, the State, and American Labor Activism, 1865–1925* (1987).

Allan Nevins, *A Study in Power: John D. Rockefeller* (2 vols., 1953).

Dominic A. Pacyga, *Polish Immigrants and Industrial Chicago: Workers on the South Side, 1880–1922* (1991).

Harold C. Passer, *The Electrical Manufacturers, 1875–1900* (1953).

Nick Salvatore, *Eugene V. Debs, Citizen and Socialist* (1982).

Upton Sinclair, *The Jungle* (1906).

John F. Stover, *American Railroads* (1970).

Shelton Stromquist, *A Generation of Boomers: The Pattern of Railroad Labor Conflict in Nineteenth-Century America* (1987).

Leslie Woodcock Tentler, *Wage-Earning Women: Industrial Work and Family Life, 1900–1930* (1979).

Jules Tygiel, *Workingmen in San Francisco, 1880–1901* (1992).

Kim Voss, *The Making of American Exceptionalism: The Knights of Labor and Class Formation in the Nineteenth Century* (1994).

Joseph F. Wall, *Andrew Carnegie* (1970).

New Immigrants

Josef Barton, *Peasants and Strangers: Italians, Rumanians, and Slovaks in an American City, 1890–1950* (1975).

Dag Blanck, *Becoming Swedish-American: The Construction of an Ethnic Identity in the Augustana Synod, 1860–1917* (1997).

Abraham Cahan, *The Rise of David Levinsky* (1917).

Albert Camarillo, *Chicanos in a Changing Society: From Mexican Pueblos to American Barrios in Santa Barbara and Southern California, 1848–1930* (1979).

Dino Cinel, *From Italy to San Francisco: The Immigrant Experience* (1982).

Dennis Clark, *The Irish in Philadelphia: Ten Generations of Urban Experience* (1973).

Roger Daniels, *Not Like Us: Immigrants and Minorities in America, 1890–1924* (1997).

Hasia Diner, *Erin's Daughters in America* (1983).

Donna Gabaccia, *From Sicily to Elizabeth Street: Housing and Social Change among Italian Immigrants, 1880–1930* (1984).

Donna Gabaccia, *From the Other Side: Women, Gender, and Immigrant Life in the U.S., 1820–1990* (1994).

Evelyn Nakano Glenn, *Issei, Nisei, War Bride: Three Generations of Japanese American Women in Domestic Service* (1986).

Christiane Harzig, ed., *Peasant Maids – City Women: From the European Countryside to Urban America* (1997).

Irving Howe, *World of Our Fathers* (1976).

Noel Ignatiev, *How the Irish Became White* (1995).

Thomas Kessner, *The Golden Door: Italian and Jewish Immigrant Mobility in New York City, 1880–1915* (1977).

Alan M. Kraut, *The Huddled Masses: The Immigrant in American Society, 1880–1921* (1982).

Kenneth Kusmer, *A Ghetto Takes Shape: Black Cleveland, 1870–1930* (1976).

Valeria Gennaro Lerda, ed., *From "Melting Pot" to Multiculturalism: The Evolution of Ethnic Relations in the United States and Canada* (1990).

Mario Maffi, *Gateways to the Promised Land: Ethnic Cultures on New York's Lower East Side* (1995).

David C. Mauk, *The Colony that Rose from the Sea: Norwegian Maritime Migration and Community in Brooklyn, 1850–1910* (1997).

Charles J. McClain, *In Search of Equality: The Chinese Struggle against Discrimination in Nineteenth-Century America* (1994).

John Modell, *The Economics and Politics of Racial Accommodation: The Japanese of Los Angeles, 1900–1942* (1977).

Walter Nugent, *Crossings: The Great Transatlantic Migration, 1870–1914* (1992).

Janet E. Rasmussen, *New Land, New Lives: Scandinavian Immigrants to the Pacific Northwest* (1993).

David R. Roediger, *The Wages of Whiteness: Race and the Making of the American Working Class* (rev. ed. 1999).

Betty Smith, *A Tree Grows in Brooklyn* (1943).

Gerald Sorin, *A Time for Building: The Third Migration, 1880–1920*; Vol. 3 of *The Jewish People in America*, ed. Henry L. Feingold (1992).

Daniel Soyer, *Jewish Immigrant Associations and American Identity in New York, 1880–1939* (1997).

Kenneth L. Stewart and Arnoldo De Leon, *Not Room Enough: Mexicans, Anglos, and Socio-Economic Change in Texas, 1850–1900* (1993).

Rudolph J. Vecoli and Suzanne M. Sinke, eds., *A Century of European Migrations, 1830–1930* (1991).

K. Scott Wong and Sucheng Chan, eds., *Claiming America: Constructing Chinese American Identities during the Exclusion Era* (1998).

Olivier Zunz, *The Changing Face of Inequality: Urbanization, Industrialization, and Immigrants in Detroit, 1880–1920* (1982).

New Cities

Gunther Barth, *Instant Cities: Urbanization and the Rise of San Francisco and Denver* (1975).

Gunther Barth, *City People: The Rise of Modern City Culture in Nineteenth-Century America* (1982).

Catherine W. Bishir and Lawrence S. Early, eds., *Early Twentieth-Century Suburbs in North Carolina* (1986).

Daniel Bluestone, *Constructing Chicago* (1991).

Edwin G. Burrows and Mike Wallace, *Gotham: A History of New York City to 1898* (1998).

David R. Contosta, *Suburb in the City: Chestnut Hill, Philadelphia, 1850–1990* (1992).

Francis G. Couvares, *The Remaking of Pittsburgh: Class and Culture in an Industrializing City, 1877–1919* (1984).

Michael H. Ebner, *Creating Chicago's North Shore: A Suburban History* (1988).

Robert Fishman, *Bourgeois Utopias: The Rise and Fall of Suburbia* (1987).

Jessica Foy and Thomas J. Schlereth, eds., *American Home Life, 1880–1930: A Social History of Spaces and Services* (1991).

Clifton Hood, 722 Miles: *The Building of the Subways and How They Transformed New York* (1993).

Kenneth T. Jackson, *Crabgrass Frontier: The Suburbanization of the United States* (1985).

Frederic C. Jaher, *The Urban Establishment: Upper Strata in Boston, New York, Charleston, Chicago, and Los Angeles* (1982).

John F. Kasson, *Amusing the Millions: Coney Island at the Turn of the Century* (1978).

Margaret Marsh, *Suburban Lives* (1990).

Donald L. Miller, *City of the Century: The Epic of Chicago and the Making of America* (1996).

David Nasaw, *Going Out: The Rise and Fall of Public Amusements* (1993).

Kathy Peiss, *Cheap Amusements: Working Women and Leisure in Turn-of-the-Century New York* (1986).

Harold L. Platt, *The Electric City: Energy and the Growth of the Chicago Area, 1880–1930* (1991).

Roy Rosenzweig, *Eight Hours for What We Will: Workers and Leisure in an Industrial City, 1870–1920* (1983).

David Schuyler, *The New Urban Landscape: The Redefinition of City Form in Nineteenth-Century America* (1986).

Richard Sennett, *Families against the City: Middle-Class Homes of Industrial Chicago, 1872–1890* (1970).

Kathryn Kish Sklar, *Catherine Beecher: A Study of Domesticity* (1973).

William R. Taylor, *In Pursuit of Gotham: Culture and Commerce in New York* (1992).

Alexander von Hoffman, *Local Attachments: The Making of an American Urban Neighborhood, 1850–1920* (1994).

David Ward, *Cities and Immigrants: A Geography of Change in Nineteenth-Century America* (1971).

Sam Bass Warner Jr., *Streetcar Suburbs: The Process of Growth in Boston, 1870–1900* (1962).

Gwendolyn Wright, *Moralism and the Model Home: Domestic Architecture and Cultural Conflict in Chicago, 1873–1913* (1980).

Where to Learn More

❖ **Edison National Historic Site, West Orange, New Jersey.**   The site contains the Edison archives, including photographs, sound recordings, and industrial and scientific machinery. Its twenty historic structures dating from the 1880–1887 period include Edison's home and laboratory.

❖ **Japanese American National Museum, Los Angeles, California.**   Housed in a converted Buddhist temple, this museum includes artifacts and photographs of early Japanese immigration and settlement. The core exhibit is "Issei Pioneers: Japanese Immigration to Hawaii and the Mainland from 1885 to 1924."

❖ **Missouri Historical Society, St. Louis, Missouri.**   The Society displays a long-term exhibition accompanied by public programs called, "St. Louis in the Gilded Age," which focuses on the changes generated by industrialization and urban development in St. Louis from 1865 to 1900.

❖ **Senator John Heinz Pittsburgh Regional History Center, Pittsburgh, Pennsylvania.**   Through its long-term exhibition, "Points in Time: Building a Life in Western Pennsylvania, 1750-Today," the Center explores the growth of the Pittsburgh metropolitan area, especially its expansion during the great industrial boom at the turn of the twentieth century.

❖ **Angel Island State Park, San Francisco Bay.**   Angel Island served as a detention center from 1910 to 1940 for Asian immigrants who were kept there for days, months, and, in some cases, years, while immigration officials attempted to ferret out illegal entries. Exhibits depict the era through pictures and artifacts.

❖ **Strawbery Banke, Portsmouth, New Hampshire.**   This museum includes an exhibit and audiovisual presentations on the adjustment of one immigrant family to American life: "Becoming Americans: The Shapiro Story, 1898-1929," presents the story of an immigrant Jewish family in the context of immigration to the small, coastal city of Portsmouth at the turn of the twentieth century.

❖ **Statue of Liberty National Monument and Ellis Island, New York, New York.**   More than 12 million immigrants were processed at Ellis Island between 1892 and 1954. The exhibits provide a fine overview of American immigration history during this period. There is an ongoing oral history program as well.

TRANSFORMING THE WEST,
1865–1890

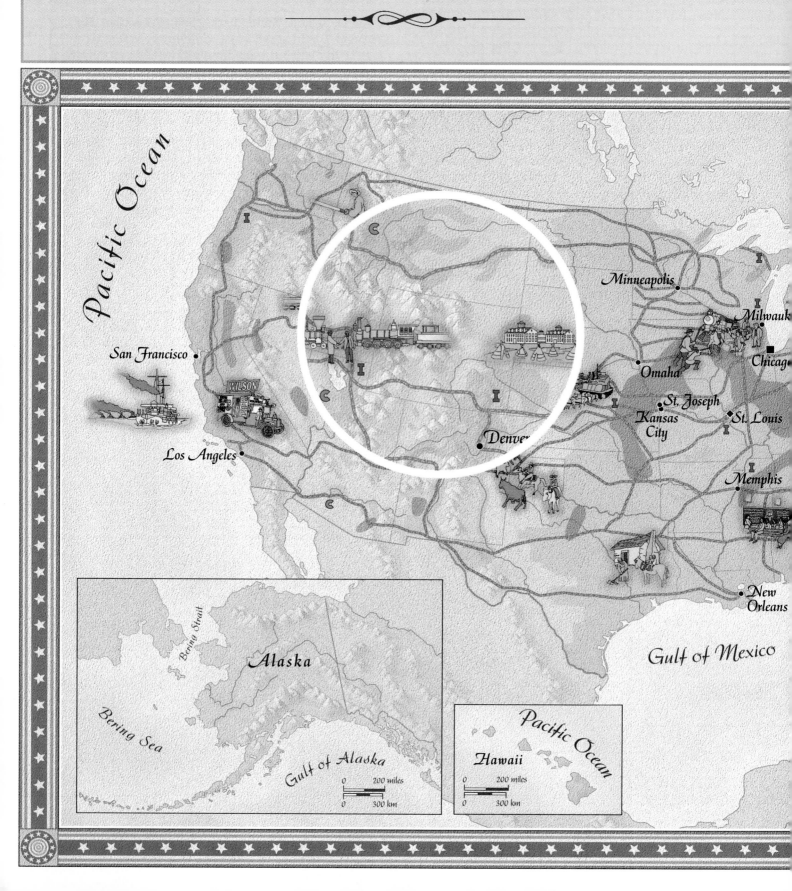

21

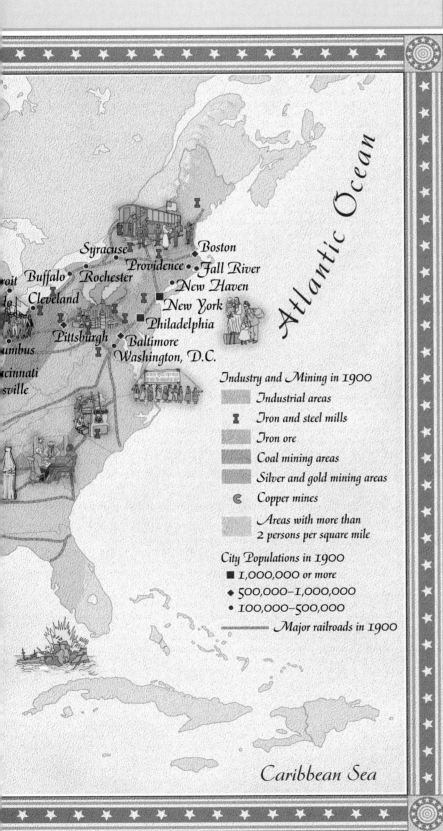

Industry and Mining in 1900

- Industrial areas
- I Iron and steel mills
- Iron ore
- Coal mining areas
- Silver and gold mining areas
- C Copper mines
- Areas with more than 2 persons per square mile

City Populations in 1900

- ■ 1,000,000 or more
- ◆ 500,000–1,000,000
- • 100,000–500,000
- —— Major railroads in 1900

Atlantic Ocean

Syracuse Boston
Providence • Fall River
Buffalo • Rochester • New Haven
Cleveland   New York
        Philadelphia
Pittsburgh   Baltimore
        Washington, D.C.

Caribbean Sea

Key Topics

- ❖ The subjugation of Native Americans in the West, their confinement to reservations, and the attempted destruction of their culture
- ❖ The integration of the West into the national economy through the construction of transcontinental railroads
- ❖ The flood of migrants to the West in the late nineteenth century seeking work as railroad workers, miners, cowboys, and farmers
- ❖ The transformation of mining, ranching, and farming in the West from individual pursuits to corporate enterprises

*T*he celebration began with a group of workers, soldiers, and railroad company officials at Promontory Point, a desolate sagebrush basin in western Utah. Chicago staged a seven-mile-long parade, Philadelphia rang the Liberty Bell, and New York held services in its greatest churches. The triumphal occasion was the completion of the nation's first transcontinental railroad, marked by the driving of a golden spike uniting the tracks of the Union Pacific and Central Pacific Railroads on May 10, 1869. The celebrations symbolized the nation's hopes, but the transcontinental railroad itself symbolized much more. It was, as the author Robert Louis Stevenson declared, "the one typical achievement of the age." It made the West as much a part of the nation as the East or the South and set a precedent for western development.

The two railroads were huge corporate enterprises, not individual efforts, and corporations would dominate western growth as much as they did eastern industrialization. But this corporate undertaking was scarcely private enterprise, for the federal government played a crucial role in railroad construction, as it did in virtually all aspects of western development. Congress had authorized the Union Pacific and Central Pacific to build the railroad link, given them the right-of-way for their tracks, and provided financial subsidies: For each mile of track laid, the companies received twenty square miles of land along the route and a loan of up to $48,000. With such backing, construction became a race between the companies to collect the largest subsidy. The Union Pacific worked westward from Omaha, Nebraska; the Central Pacific, eastward from Sacramento, California.

The separate companies that both railroads created to organize this construction siphoned money to a few major stockholders, foreshadowing the often corrupt methods by which the West would be developed. To shield these dishonest operations from government investigations, railroad officials bribed members of Congress and the Grant administration in Washington, D.C., forging yet another link between the exploitation of the West and events in the East.

The railroads' dependence on capital investment, engineering knowledge, technological innovations, and labor skills also typified western development. Their labor forces both reflected and reinforced the region's racial and ethnic diversity. Too few native-born Americans, white or black, were willing to build the roads, so the railroads looked elsewhere for workers. The Union Pacific recruited European immigrants, especially Irish; the Central Pacific hired Mexicans, Irish, and Paiute Indians, both male and female, but eventually relied on Chinese recruited in California and Asia. At the peak of construction, twelve thousand Chinese pushed the rails eastward, advancing as little as eight inches a day through the granite Sierras and as much as ten miles a day across the flat deserts of Nevada.

The railroads adopted callous and reckless construction tactics, resulting in waste, deaths, and environmental destruction. Laying track as quickly as possible to collect the subsidies awarded by the mile, each corporation built substandard railroads marked by improper grades, defective materials, dangerous curves, and flimsy bridges that might collapse under a locomotive's weight. Much of the work had to be redone almost immediately at the cost of millions of dollars. Such construction damaged the environment. Wood consumption alone was tremendous. Union Pacific tie cutters stripped the Platte Valley in Nebraska of its timber, and the Central Pacific used 64 million feet of timber just to build snowsheds. Finally, as the two corporations relentlessly drove their crews, even at night and in winter, perhaps as many as a thousand Chinese on the Central Pacific, and even more workers on the Union Pacific, died from accidents or exposure.

The construction of the transcontinental railroad was thus both a technological achievement that integrated the West into the rest of the nation and evidence that the development of the West, however fabled in folklore, was an integral part of the larger economic revolution that transformed America after the Civil War.

This contemporary engraving depicts the joining of the Central Pacific and Union Pacific railroads on May 10, 1869, at Promontory Point, Utah. Railroads transformed the American West, linking the region to outside markets, spurring rapid settlement, and threatening Indian survival.

Native Americans

The initial obstacle to exploiting the West was the people already living there, who used its resources in their own way and held different concepts of progress and civilization. For despite Easterners' image of the West as an unsettled wilderness, Native Americans had long inhabited it and had developed a variety of economies and cultures. As whites pressed westward, they attempted to subjugate the Indians, displace them from their lands, and strip them of their culture. Conquest gradually forced Indians onto desolate reservations, but efforts to destroy their beliefs and transform their way of life were less successful.

Tribes and Cultures

Throughout the West, Indians had adapted to their environment, developing subsistence economies ranging from simple gathering to complex systems of irrigated agriculture. Each activity encouraged their sensitivity to the natural world, and each had social and political implications.

In the Northwest, abundant food from rich waters and dense forests gave rise to complex and stable Indian societies. During summer fishing runs, the Tillamooks, Chinooks, and other tribes caught salmon that, after being dried in smokehouses, sustained them throughout the year. During the mild winters, they developed artistic handicrafts, elaborate social institutions, and a satisfying religious life.

At the opposite environmental extreme, the Cahuillas of the southern California desert survived only through their ability to extract food and medicines from desert plants. In the dry and barren Great Basin of Utah and Nevada, Shoshones and Paiutes ate grasshoppers and other insects to supplement their diet of rabbits, mice, and other small animals. Such harsh environments restricted the size, strength, and organizational complexity of societies. Needing to spend most of their time searching for food, these Indians lacked tribal unity. They lived in small family groups in flimsy huts rather than established villages.

In the Southwest, the Pueblos dwelled in permanent towns of adobe buildings and practiced intensive agriculture. Because tribal welfare depended on maintaining complex irrigation systems, the Zunis, Hopis, and other Pueblos emphasized community solidarity rather than individual ambition. Town living encouraged social stability and the development of complex effective governments, elaborate religious ceremonies, and creative arts. Navajos, Apaches, and other nomadic tribes in the region relied on sheepherding and hunting. They lacked the cohesion and structure of Pueblo society.

The most numerous Indian groups lived on the Great Plains. The largest of these tribes included the Lakotas or Sioux, who roamed from western Minnesota through the Dakotas; the Cheyennes and Arapahos, who controlled much of the central plains between the Platte and Arkansas

CHRONOLOGY

1858 Gold is discovered in Colorado and Nevada.

1860 Gold is discovered in Idaho.

1862 Homestead Act is passed.

Gold is discovered in Montana.

1864 Militia slaughters Cheyennes at Sand Creek, Colorado.

1867 Cattle drives make Abilene the first cow town.

1868 Fort Laramie Treaty is signed.

1869 First transcontinental railroad is completed.

1874 Gold is discovered in the Black Hills.

Turkey Red wheat is introduced to Kansas.

Barbed wire is patented.

1876 Indians devastate U.S. troops in the Battle of the Little Bighorn.

1879 "Exodusters" migrate to Kansas.

1885 Chinese massacred at Rock Springs, Wyoming.

1887 Dawes Act is passed.

1890 Government troops kill two hundred Sioux at Wounded Knee, South Dakota.

1892 Mining violence breaks out at Coeur d'Alene, Idaho.

1893 Western Federation of Miners is organized.

Rivers; and the Comanches, predominant on the southern plains. Two animals dominated the lives of these peoples: the horse, which enabled them to move freely over the plains, and the buffalo, which provided meat, hides, bones and horns for tools, and a focus for spiritual life.

Despite their diversity, all tribes emphasized community welfare over individual interest. Their economies were based on subsistence rather than profit. They tried to live in harmony with nature to ward off sickness, injury, death, or misfortune. And they were intensely religious, absorbed with the need to establish proper relations with supernatural forces that linked human beings with all other living things. The connections among these basic values appeared in the frequent religious rituals regulating hunting. The Sioux, for example, performed ceremonies in which they accorded respect to the buffalo's soul, sought its forgiveness for having to kill it, and promised not to be wasteful, so that the animals would not depart and bring starvation on the tribe. These connections also shaped Indians' attitude toward land, which they regarded—like air and water—as part of nature to be held and used communally, not as an individual's personal property from which others could be excluded.

White and Indian cultural values were incompatible. Disdaining Native Americans and their religion, white people condemned them as "savages" to be converted or exterminated. Rejecting the concept of communal property, most settlers demanded land for the exclusive use of ambitious individuals. Ignoring the need for natural harmony, they followed their own culture's goal of extracting wealth from the land for a market economy.

No one expressed these cultural differences better than the great Sioux leader Sitting Bull. Referring to the forces of the spirit world, he declared:

> It is through this mysterious power that we too have our being and we therefore yield to our neighbors, even our animal neighbors, the same right as ourselves, to inhabit this land. Yet, hear me, people. We have now to deal with another race. . . . Possession is a disease with them. These people have made many rules that the rich may break but the poor may not. . . . They claim this mother of ours, the earth, for their own and fence their neighbors away; they deface her with their buildings. . . . That nation is like a spring freshet that overruns its banks and destroys all who are in its path. We cannot dwell side by side.

Federal Indian Policy

The government had in the 1830s adopted the policy of separating whites and Indians. Eastern tribes were moved west of Missouri and resettled on land then scorned as "the Great American Desert," unsuitable for white habitation and development. This division presumed a permanent frontier with perpetual Indian ownership of western America. It collapsed in the 1840s when the United States acquired Texas, California, and Oregon, and migrants crossed Indian lands to reach the West Coast. Mormons developed a trail through Indian country in 1847 and settled on Indian lands; gold and silver discoveries beginning in 1848 prompted miners to invade Indian lands. Rather than curbing white entry into Indian country, the government built forts along the overland trails and ordered the army to punish Indians who threatened travelers.

White migration devastated the Plains Indians. Livestock destroyed timber and pastures along streams in the semiarid region; trails disrupted buffalo grazing patterns and eliminated buffalo from tribal hunting ranges. The Pawnees in particular suffered from the violation of their hunting grounds. One observer reported that "their trail could be followed by the dead bodies of those who starved to death." The Plains Indians also suffered from diseases the white migrants introduced. Smallpox, cholera, measles, whooping cough, and scarlet fever, for which Indians had no natural immunity, swept through the tribes. Smallpox killed all but thirteen Mandans out of a population of sixteen hundred. Cholera killed more than half of the Comanches and Kiowas, and most other tribes lost up to 40 percent of their population from the new diseases. Emigrants along the Platte River routes came across "villages of the dead."

By the early 1850s, white settlers sought to occupy Indian territory. Recognizing that the Great American Desert could support agriculture, they pressed on the eastern edge of the plains and demanded the removal of the Indians. Simultaneously, railroad companies developed plans to lay tracks across the plains. To promote white settlement, the federal government decided to relocate the tribes to separate and specific reserves. In exchange for accepting such restrictions, the government would provide the tribes with annual payments of livestock, clothing, and other materials. To implement this policy, the government negotiated treaties, extinguishing Indian rights to millions of acres (see Map 21-1), and ordered the army to keep Indians on their assigned reservations.

These actions alarmed Native Americans. One Cherokee complained of a government official "with a pocket full of money and his mouth full of lies. Some chiefs he will bribe, some he will flatter and some he will make drunk; and the result . . . will be called a treaty." And the treaties the army enforced were not always what the Indians, however reluctantly, had accepted. Congress, for

example, reduced by 70 percent the payments promised in the 1851 Fort Laramie Treaty. Similarly, the Comanches and Kiowas agreed in 1865 to exchange their traditional lands for new territory south of the Arkansas River, but Congress nullified the treaty provision for the new area. The commissioner of Indian affairs aptly described the Indians' lot: "By alternate persuasion and force these tribes have been removed, step by step, from mountain to valley, and from river to plain, until they have been pushed halfway across the continent. They can go no further; on the ground they now occupy the crisis must be met, and their future determined."

Warfare and Dispossession

Most smaller tribes accepted the government's conditions, but larger tribes resisted. From the 1850s to the 1880s, warfare engulfed the advancing frontier. The immediate initiative for conflict sometimes lay with Indians, especially in the form of small raids, but invading Americans bore ultimate responsibility for these wars. Even the men who led the white military assault conceded as much. General Philip Sheridan, for example, declared of the Indians: "We took away their country and their means of support, broke up their mode of living, their habits of life, introduced disease and decay among them, and it was for this and against this that they made war. Could anyone expect less?"

One notorious example of white aggression occurred in 1864 at Sand Creek, Colorado. Gold discoveries had attracted a flood of white miners and settlers onto land only recently guaranteed to the Cheyennes and Arapahos. Rather than enforcing the Indians' treaty rights, however, the government compelled the tribes to relinquish their lands, except for a small tract designated as the Sand Creek reservation. But white settlers wanted to eliminate the Indian presence altogether. John Chivington, a Methodist minister, led a militia force to the Sand Creek camp of a band of Cheyennes under Black Kettle, an advocate of peace and accommodation. An American flag flew over the Indian camp. Under Chivington's orders to "kill and scalp all, big and little," the militia attacked Black Kettle's sleeping camp without warning. With howitzers and rifles, the soldiers fired into the camp and then assaulted any survivors with swords and knives. One white trader later described the helpless Indians: "They were scalped, their brains knocked out; the [white] men used their knives, ripped open women, clubbed little children, knocked them in the head with their

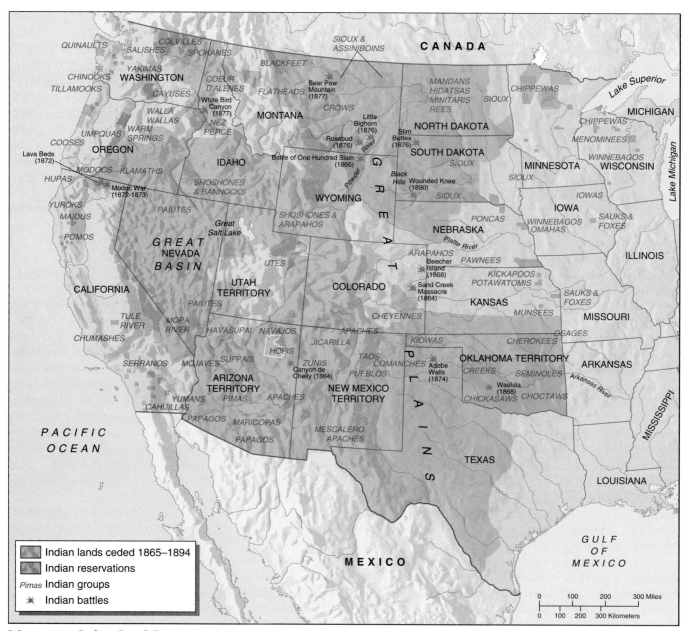

Map 21-1   Indian Land Cessions, 1860–1894
As white people pushed into the West to exploit its resources, Indians were steadily forced to cede their lands. By 1900 they held only scattered parcels, often in areas considered worthless by white people. Restricted to these reservations, tribes endured official efforts to suppress Indian customs and values.

guns, beat their brains out, mutilated their bodies in every sense of the word."

The **Sand Creek Massacre** appalled many Easterners. The Cheyennes, protested the commissioner of Indian affairs, were "butchered in cold blood by troops in the service of the United States." A congressional investigating committee denounced Chivington for "a foul and dastardly massacre which

would have disgraced the veriest savage among those who were the victims of his cruelty." Westerners, however, justified the brutality as a means to secure their own opportunities. One western newspaper demanded, "Kill all the Indians that can be killed. Complete extermination is our motto."

While assaults on smaller tribes usually "succeeded," other tribes were more formidable.

None was more powerful than the Sioux, whose military skills had been honed in conflicts with other tribes. An army offensive against the Sioux in 1866 failed completely. Entire units deserted in fear and frustration; others were crushed by the Sioux. On the Bozeman Trail, in what the Lakotas called the **Battle of One Hundred Slain**, the Sioux wiped out an army detachment led by a captain who had boasted that he would destroy the Sioux nation. General William T. Sherman, who had marched through Georgia against Confederates, knew that the odds were different in the West. Fifty Plains Indians, he declared, could "checkmate" three thousand soldiers. General Philip Sheridan calculated that the army suffered proportionately greater losses fighting Indians than either the Union or the Confederacy had suffered in the Civil War.

With the army unable to defeat the Sioux and their allies, and with many Easterners shocked by both the military's indiscriminate aggression and the expense of the fighting, the government sued for peace. Describing white actions as "uniformly unjust," a federal peace commission in 1868 negotiated the **second Treaty of Fort Laramie**, in which the United States abandoned the Bozeman Trail and other routes and military posts on Sioux territory—one of the few times Indians forced the whites to retreat. The United States also guaranteed the Sioux permanent ownership of the western half of South Dakota and the right to inhabit and hunt in the Powder River country in Wyoming and Montana, an area to be henceforth closed to all white people.

For several years, peace prevailed on the northern plains, but in 1872, the Northern Pacific Railroad began to build westward on a route that would violate Sioux territory. Rather than stopping the railroad, the government sent an army to protect the surveyors. Sherman drew up plans for the war that he expected the construction to provoke. He regarded railroad expansion as the most important factor in defeating the Indians, for it would allow troops to travel as far in a day as they could march in weeks. Other technological developments, from the telegraph to rapid-fire weapons, also undercut the skills of the Indian warrior.

The destruction of the buffalo also threatened Native Americans. From 1872 to 1874, white hunters killed 4 million buffalo. Railroad survey and construction parties disrupted grazing areas, and hunters working for the railroads killed hordes of buffalo, both to feed construction crews and to pre-

vent the animals from obstructing rail traffic. Hide hunters slaughtered even more of the beasts for their skins, leaving the bodies to rot. Reporters found vast areas covered with "decaying, putrid, stinking remains." Federal officials encouraged the buffalo's extermination because it would destroy the Indians' basis for survival.

The climactic provocation of the Sioux began in 1874 when Colonel George A. Custer led an invasion to survey the Black Hills for a military post and confirm the presence of gold. Thousands of white miners then illegally poured onto Sioux land. Ignoring Sioux demands that the government enforce the Fort Laramie treaty, the army insisted that the Indians leave their Powder River hunting grounds. When the Sioux refused, the army attacked. The Oglala Sioux under Crazy Horse repulsed one prong of this offensive at the Battle of the Rosebud in June 1876 and then joined a larger body of Sioux under Sitting Bull and their Cheyenne and Arapaho allies to overwhelm a second American column, under Custer, at the **Battle of the Little Bighorn**.

But the Indians could not follow up their dramatic victory. They had to divide their forces to find fresh grass for their horses and to hunt for their own food. Without such limitations, the U.S. Army relentlessly pursued the separate bands to exhaustion. "We have been running up and down in this country, but they follow us from one place to another," lamented Sitting Bull. He led his followers to Canada, but the other bands capitulated in

The scale of the destruction of the buffalo and its commercial organization are suggested by this photograph of a pile of buffalo skulls.

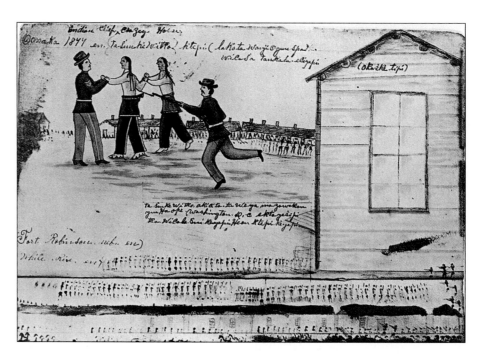

There is no photograph of Crazy Horse, but Amos Bad Heart Bull drew this pictograph of his murder at Fort Robinson, Nebraska, September 7, 1877. Bayoneted in the back, the great Sioux warrior told his followers: "It is no use to depend on me. I am going to die."

the winter of 1876–1877. In the end, the conquest of the northern plains came not through any decisive victory but through attrition and the inability of the traditional Indian economy to support resistance to the technologically and numerically superior white forces.

The defeat of the Sioux nearly completed the Indian Wars. Smaller tribes, among them the Kiowas, Modocs, and Utes, had been overrun earlier. In the Northwest, the Nez Percé resisted in 1877 when the government reneged on its agreement to protect their land. Outwitting and outfighting the larger forces of the U.S. Army over a 1,500-mile retreat toward Canada, the exhausted Nez Percé surrendered after being promised a return to their own land. But the government refused to honor that pledge, too, and imprisoned the tribe in Oklahoma, where more than a third perished within a few years.

In the Southwest, the Navajos and the Comanches were subdued, as the Sioux had been, by persistent pursuit that prevented them from obtaining food. The last to abandon resistance were the Apaches, under Geronimo. In 1886, he and thirty-six followers, facing five thousand U.S. troops, finally surrendered. Geronimo and other Apaches were sent to a military prison in Florida; the tribes were herded onto reservations. The Oglala chief Red Cloud concluded of the white invasion: "They made us many promises, more than I can remember, but they never kept but one. They promised to take our land, and they took it."

Life on the Reservation

Conquering the tribes and taking their land were only the initial objectives of government policy. The next goal was to require Indians to adopt white ways, instilled by education and religion and enforced when necessary by the military. This goal did not involve assimilation but merely "Americanization," an expression of cultural conquest.

The government received aid from many Christian denominations, which had long proposed nonviolent methods of controlling Indians. Beginning in the 1860s, they gained influence in reaction to the military's brutality. Religious groups helped staff the reservations as agents, missionaries, or civilian employees. Protestant philanthropists supervised Indian affairs and controlled several private organizations that worked to shape Indian policy, including the Indian Rights Association and the Women's National Indian Association. Reformers wanted to change Indian religious and family life, train Indian children in Protestant beliefs, and force Indians to accept private ownership and market capitalism.

Confined to reservations, Indians were a captive audience for white reformers. Furthermore, their survival depended on government rations and annual payments stipulated by treaties. Such dependence enabled government agents of the **Bureau of Indian Affairs** to control tribal life by withholding rations. The agents' power undermined tribal authority. White administrators sought to destroy traditional Indian government by prohibiting tribal councils from meeting and imprisoning tribal leaders.

White activists sought to destroy Indian religion because it was "pagan" and because it helped Indians resist assimilation. Protestant religious groups persuaded the Bureau of Indian Affairs to frame a criminal code prohibiting and penalizing tribal religious practices. Established in 1884, the code remained in effect until 1933. It was first invoked to ban the Sun Dance, the chief expression of Plains Indian religion. To enforce the ban, the government withheld rations and disrupted the religious ceremonies that transmitted traditional values. In 1890, the army even used machine guns to suppress the Ghost Dance religion, killing at least two hundred Sioux men, women, and children at **Wounded Knee**, South Dakota.

Missionaries attempted to convert Indians to Christianity but often found them reluctant to accept the creed of their conquerors. As one Crow Indian explained, "We found there were too many kinds of religion among white men for us to understand, and that scarcely any two white men agreed which was the right one to learn. This bothered us a good deal until we saw that the white man did not take his religion any more seriously than he did his laws, and that he kept both of them just . . . to use when they might do him good in his dealings with strangers. These were not our ways. We kept the laws we made and lived our religion."

The government and religious groups also used education to eliminate Indian values and traditions. They isolated Indian children from tribal influences at off-reservation boarding schools. Troops often seized Indian children for these schools, where they were confined until after adolescence. The schoolchildren were forced to speak English, attend Christian services, and profess white American values (see "American Views: Zitkala-Sa's View of Americanization").

Finally, the government and the religious reformers imposed the economic practices and values of white society on Indians. Government agents taught Indian men how to farm and distributed agricultural implements; Indian women were taught household tasks. These tactics reduced the status of Indian women, whose traditional responsibility for agriculture had guaranteed them respect and authority. Nor could men farm successfully on reservation lands, which whites had already rejected as unproductive. Kiowa chief Little Mountain suggested that if the president wanted Indians to raise corn, he should send them land fit for corn production. Whites, however, believed that the real obstacle

to economic prosperity for the Indians was their rejection of private property. The Indians' communal values, the reformers argued, inhibited the pursuit of personal success that lay at the heart of capitalism. As one Bureau of Indian Affairs official declared, Indians must be taught to be more "mercenary and ambitious to obtain riches." To force such values on Indians, Congress in 1887 passed the **Dawes Act**, which divided tribal lands among individual Indians. Western settlers who had no interest in the Indians supported the law because it provided that reservation lands not allocated to individual Indians should be sold to white settlers. Under this "reform," the amount of land held by Indians declined by more than half by 1900.

White acquisition and exploitation of Indian land seemed to be the only constant in the nation's treatment of Native Americans. Assimilation itself failed because most Indians clung to their own values and rejected as selfish, dishonorable, and obsessively materialistic those favored by whites. But if it was not yet clear what place Native Americans would have in America, it was at least clear by 1900 that they would no longer stand in the way of western development.

Exploiting the Mountains: The Mining Bonanza

Migrants to the American West exploited the region's natural resources in pursuit of wealth and success. Some were rewarded; others met tragedy and failure. In either case, the challenges they confronted and the ventures they initiated gave rise to romantic images: the West as a land of adventure, opportunity, and freedom; pioneers as self-reliant individuals. Promoters, artists, and novelists developed these images into a heroic legend that movies, television, and politicians perpetuated. All too often, however, reality differed from legend. Opportunites were frequently short-lived and rarely available to all; individualism often gave way to group, corporate, or government action; nature and technology mocked self-reliance. The appeal of the cherished images made the reality harder to bear.

In the later nineteenth century, the West experienced several stages of economic development, but all of them transformed the environment, produced economic and social conflict, and integrated

FROM THEN TO NOW
The Legacy of Indian Americanization

The assumptions, objectives, and failures of the Americanization policies of the nineteenth century continue to affect American Indians more than a century later. Although periodically modified (see Chapter 27), these policies long persisted, as did their consequences. In the 1970s official investigations reported that the continuing attempts of the Bureau of Indian Affairs to use education to force Indians into an Anglo-American mold "have been marked by near total failure, haunted by prejudice and ignorance."

Similarly, the economic problems on reservations in the nineteenth century foreshadowed conditions a century later. Today Indians rank at the bottom of almost all measures of economic well-being. Lack of economic opportunity leaves isolated reservations with unemployment rates averaging 40 percent. Off the reservation, discrimination, limited skills, and inadequate capital further restrict Indians' job prospects.

Indians also continue to suffer from poor health standards. They have the highest rates of infant mortality, pneumonia, hepatitis, tuberculosis, and suicide in the nation and a life expectancy twenty-five years less than the national average.

Indian culture, however, did not succumb to the pressure to Americanize. In the words of a Shoshone writer, "Indian history didn't end in the 1800s. Indian cultures . . . evolve, grow, and continually try to renew themselves."

In recent decades, Indian peoples have begun to reclaim their past and assert control over their future. Dramatic protests—most notably a confrontation in 1973 between Indian activists and the FBI at Wounded Knee, the site of the notorious 1890 massacre—have called attention to Indian grievances. But Indians have also moved effectively to regain control of the institutions that define their cultural identity. They have established community schools and tribal community colleges that provide a bilingual, bicultural education, seeking to preserve traditions while opening new opportunities. They have built tribal museums and visitor centers in order to shape the presentation of their histories and cultures. By the late 1990s there were more than 200 such institutions, from the Seneca-Iroquois museum in upstate New York to the Makah Tribal Museum on the Olympic peninsula.

Indians have also secured legal recognition of their right to their cultural patrimony. The Native American Graves Protection and Repatriation Act of 1990 gives Indian communities the right to reclaim, or "repatriate,"

material artifacts and skeletal remains from museums and historical societies. The Native American Religious Freedom Act of 1978 affirmed their right to practice their traditional religions and have access to sacred sites. Indian dance—once suppressed by white authorities—has revived, and the powwow has become a national Indian institution and symbol of Indian identity.

With the help of historians and lawyers, Indians are also winning enforcement of long-ignored treaty provisions guaranteeing them land ownership and water, hunting, and fishing rights. Court decisions have recognized the right of tribes to permit gambling on their reservations, and some tribes have built profitable casinos, attracting economic development that creates new job opportunities for their people and permits them to stay on their land.

Indians still confront hostility and condescension reminiscent of attitudes a century ago. A white museum official, for example—seeking to prevent the repatriation of Pawnee artifacts—claimed recently that Indians do not have a real religion. But Indians have proved resilient in preserving their cultural heritage and keeping it vibrant for future generations.

On the Pine Ridge Reservation in South Dakota, the new government boarding school, designed to isolate Indian youth from their elders and their culture, looms over the old tribal lodgings in 1891.

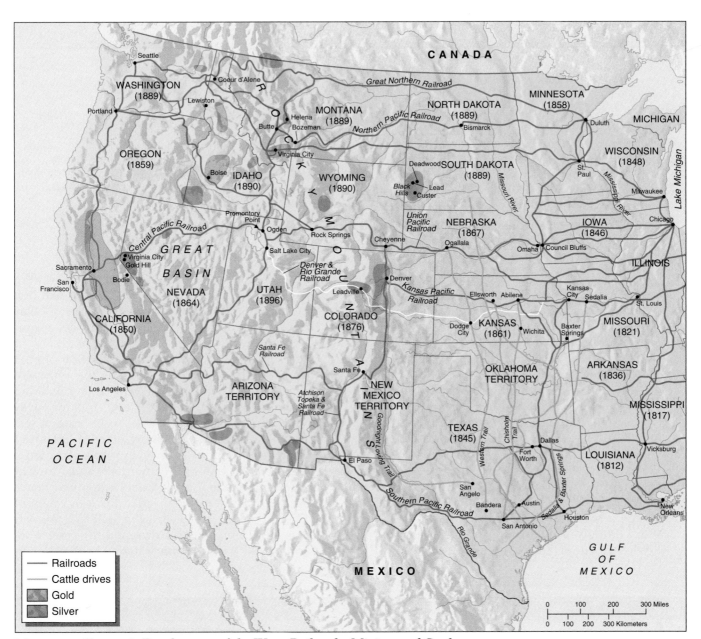

Map 21-2 *Economic Development of the West: Railroads, Mining, and Cattle, 1860–1900*
The spread of the railroad network across the West promoted economic development by providing access to outside markets for its resources. The discovery of precious metals often attracted the railroads, but stockraisers had to open cattle trails to reach the railheads.

the region into the modern national economy. The first stage of development centered on mining, which attracted swarms of eager prospectors into the mountains and deserts in search of gold and silver. They founded vital communities, stimulated the railroad construction that brought further development, and contributed to the disorderly heritage of the frontier (see Map 21-2). But few gained the wealth they had expected.

Rushes and Mining Camps

The first important gold rush in the Rocky Mountains came in Colorado in 1859. More than 100,000 prospectors crowded into Denver and the nearby mining camps. Simultaneously, the discovery of the famous Comstock Lode in Nevada produced an eastward rush of miners from California. Some seventeen thousand claims were made around Virginia City, Nevada, the main mining camp. Strikes in the

American Views
ZITKALA-SA'S VIEW OF AMERICANIZATION

Zitkala-Sa, or Red Bird, was an eight-year-old Sioux girl when she was taken from her South Dakota reservation in 1884 and placed in a midwestern missionary school, where she encountered what she called the "iron routine" of the "civilizing machine." Here she recalls her first day at the school.

❖ **What lessons were the missionaries trying to teach Zitkala-Sa by their actions?**

❖ **What lessons did Zitkala-Sa learn?**

Soon we were being drawn rapidly away by the white man's horses. When I saw the lonely figure of my mother vanish in the distance, a sense of regret settled heavily upon me. . . . I no longer felt free to be myself, or to voice my own feelings. The tears trickled down my cheeks, and I buried my face in the folds of my blanket. Now the first step, parting me from my mother, was taken, and all my belated tears availed nothing. . . . Trembling with fear and distrust of the palefaces . . . I was as frightened and bewildered as the captured young of a wild creature. . . .

[At the missionary school,] the constant clash of harsh noises, with an undercurrent of many voices murmuring an unknown tongue, made a bedlam within which I was securely tied. And though my spirit tore itself in struggling for its lost freedom, all was useless. . . .

We were placed in a line of girls who were marching into the dining room. . . . A small bell was tapped, and each of the pupils drew a chair from under the table. Supposing this act meant they were to be seated, I pulled out mine and at once slipped into it from one side. But when I turned my head, I saw that I was the only one seated, and all the rest at our table remained standing. Just as I began to rise, looking shyly around to see how chairs were to be used, a second bell was sounded. All were seated at last, and I had to crawl back into my chair again. I heard a man's voice at one end of the hall, and I looked around to see him. But all others hung their heads over their plates. As I glanced at the long chain of tables, I caught the eyes of a paleface woman upon me. Immediately I dropped my eyes, wondering why I was so keenly watched by the strange

---

northern Rockies followed in the 1860s. Boise City and Lewiston in Idaho and Helena in Montana became major mining centers, and other camps prospered briefly before fading into ghost towns. The last of the frontier gold rushes came in 1874 on the Sioux reservation in the Black Hills of South Dakota, where the roaring mining camp of Deadwood flourished. Later, other minerals shaped frontier development: silver in Nevada, silver and lead in Colorado and Idaho, silver and copper in Arizona and Montana.

Mining camps were often isolated by both distance and terrain. They frequently consisted of only flimsy shanties, saloons, crude stores, dance

halls, and brothels, all hastily built by entrepreneurs. Such towns reflected the speculative, exploitive, and transitory character of mining itself. And yet they did contribute to permanent settlement by encouraging agriculture, industry, and transportation in the surrounding areas.

The camps had an unusual social and economic structure. Their population was overwhelmingly male. In 1860, for example, about 2,300 men and only 30 women lived in the Nevada mining camps of Virginia City and Gold Hill. Women found far fewer economic opportunities than men did on the mining frontier. Several opened hotels. Those with less capital worked as seamstresses and

woman. The man ceased his mutterings, and then a third bell was tapped. Every one picked up his knife and fork and began eating. I began crying instead, for by this time I was afraid to venture anything more.

But this eating by formula was not the hardest trial in that first day. Late in the morning, my friend Judewin gave me a terrible warning. Judewin knew a few words of English; and she had overheard the paleface woman talk about cutting our long, heavy hair. Our mothers had taught us that only unskilled warriors who were captured had their hair shingled by the enemy. Among our people, short hair was worn by mourners, and shingled hair by cowards!

. . . I remember being dragged out, though I resisted by kicking and scratching wildly. In spite of myself, I was carried downstairs and tied fast in a chair. I cried aloud, shaking my head all the while until I felt the cold blades of the scissors against my neck, and heard them gnaw off one of my thick braids. Then I lost my spirit. . . . My long hair was shingled like a coward's. In my anguish I moaned for my mother, but no one came to comfort me. Not a soul reasoned quietly with me, as my own mother used to do; for now I was only one of many little animals driven by a herder. . . .

I blamed the hard-working, well-meaning, ignorant [missionary] woman who was inculcating in our hearts her superstitious ideas. Though I was sullen in all my little troubles, as soon as I felt better I was . . . again actively testing the chains which tightly bound my individuality like a mummy for burial. . . .

Many specimens of civilized peoples visited the Indian school. The city folks with canes and eyeglasses, the countrymen with sunburnt cheeks and clumsy feet, forgot their relative social ranks in an ignorant curiosity. Both sorts of these Christian palefaces were alike astounded at seeing the children of savage warriors so docile and industrious. . . .

In this fashion many [whites] have passed idly through the Indian schools during the last decade, afterward to boast of their charity to the North American Indian. But few there are who have paused to question whether real life or long-lasting death lies beneath this semblance of civilization.

Source: Zitkala-Sa, "The School Days of an Indian Girl" (1900). Reprinted in American Indian Stories (Glorieta, NM: Rio Grande Press, 1976).

cooks and took in washing. The few married women often earned more than their husbands by boarding other miners willing to pay for the trappings of family life.

But the largest source of paid employment for women was prostitution, a flourishing consequence of the gender imbalance. A few women prospered. Mary Josephine Welch, an entrepreneurial Irish immigrant, settled in Helena in 1867 and soon established the Red Light Saloon, the first of many saloons, dance halls, and brothels that she owned and operated. Most women who engaged in such activities, however, were far less successful. Many women became prostitutes because their other economic options were limited. A prostitute in Helena could earn five times more money than a saleswoman. And most prostitutes who entered brothels already suffered from economic hardship or a broken family. But prostitution usually only worsened their distress. By the 1890s, as men gained control of the vice trade from the madams, violence, suicide, alcoholism, disease, drug addiction, and poverty overcame most prostitutes. Public authorities showed little concern for the abuse and even murder of prostitutes, although they used "sporting women" to raise revenue by fining or taxing them. Condemning such moral indifference, middle-class Protestant women in Denver and other cities established "rescue homes" to protect or rehabilitate

Mary Josephine Welch adopted several names but prospered as "Chicago Joe," reigning over a red-light district that catered to miners in Helena, Montana.

prostitutes and dance-hall girls from male vice and violence. But their attempts to impose piety and purity had little success; male community leaders valued social order less than economic opportunity.

The gender imbalance in mining camps also made saloons prevalent among local businesses. An 1879 business census of Leadville, Colorado, reported 10 dry-goods stores, 4 banks, and 4 churches but 120 saloons, 19 beer halls, and 118 gambling houses. Saloons were social centers in towns where most miners lived in crowded and dirty tents and rooming houses. As Mark Twain wrote in *Roughing It* (1872), his account of Virginia City, "The cheapest and easiest way to become an influential man and be looked up to by the community at large, was to stand behind a bar, wear a cluster-diamond pin, and sell whiskey."

The male-dominated saloon society of mining camps generated social conflict. One observer of the Montana camps reported that men, "unburdened by families, drink whenever they feel like it, whenever

they have money to pay for it, and whenever there is nothing else to do. . . . Bad manners follow, profanity becomes a matter of course. . . . Excitability and nervousness brought on by rum help these tendencies along, and then to correct this state of things the pistol comes into play." A Denver editor complained of "drunken men frequently firing pistols right and left, totally indifferent as to whom or what they hit." Disputes over mining claims could become violent, adding to the disorder. The California mining town of Bodie experienced twenty-nine killings between 1877 and 1883, a homicide rate higher than that of any U.S. city a century later. But such killings occurred only within a small group of males—young, single, surly, and armed—who were known as the Badmen of Bodie. Daily life for most people was safe.

Indeed, personal and criminal violence, which remains popularly associated with the West, was less pervasive than collective violence. This, too, affected mining camps and was aggravated by their ethnic and racial diversity. Irish, Germans, English, Chinese, Australians, Italians, Slavs, and Mexicans, among others, rushed into the mining regions. In many camps, half the population was foreign-born, and another fourth consisted of first-generation Americans. Virginia City was such a mixed community that Germans, Mexicans, Chinese, French, Cornish, and Welsh each had their own churches, bands, and other social organizations and celebrated their own national holidays.

The European immigrants who sometimes encountered nativist hostility in the East experienced less animosity in the West, but nonwhite minorities often suffered. In particular, white people frequently drove Mexicans and Chinese from their claims or refused to let them work in higher-paid occupations in the mining camps. The Chinese had originally migrated to the California gold fields and thereafter spread to the new mining areas of the Rockies and the Great Basin, where they worked in mining when possible, operated laundries and restaurants, and held menial jobs like hauling water and chopping wood. In 1870, more than a quarter of Idaho's population and nearly 10 percent of Montana's was Chinese. Where they were numerous, the Chinese built their own communities and maintained their customs.

But racism and fear of economic competition sparked hostility and violence against the Chinese almost everywhere. In Colorado, town leaders boasted of having driven all Chinese out of Leadville by 1879, and white citizens destroyed Denver's Chinatown in 1880. One Chinese leader observed that if such a riot had engulfed Americans in China, 100,000 "missionaries" would have been sent to "civilize the heathen." The worst anti-Chinese violence occurred in Rock

Springs, Wyoming, in 1885 when white miners killed twenty-eight unresisting Chinese miners and drove away all seven hundred residents from the local Chinatown. Although the members of the mob were well known, the grand jury, speaking for the white majority, found no cause for legal action: "Though we have examined a large number of witnesses, no one has been able to testify to a single criminal act committed by any known white person." Such community sanction for violence against racial minorities made mob attacks one of the worst features of the mining camps.

Labor and Capital

New technology had dramatic consequences for both miners and the mining industry. Initially, mining was an individual enterprise in which miners used simple tools, such as picks and shovels, wash pans, and rockers to work shallow surface deposits known as placers. Placer mining attracted prospectors with relatively little capital or expertise, but surface deposits were quickly exhausted. More complex and expensive operations were needed to reach the precious metal buried in the earth.

Hydraulic mining, for example, required massive capital investment to build reservoirs, ditches, and troughs to power high-pressure water cannons that would pulverize hillsides and uncover the mineral deposits. California's North Bloomfield Gravel Mining Company owned hundreds of miles of ditches and used more than a million gallons of water a day to feed its huge water nozzles. Still more formidable was quartz, or lode, mining, sometimes called hard rock mining. Time, money, and technology were required to sink a shaft into the earth, timber underground chambers and tunnels, install pumps to remove underground water and hoists to lower men and lift out rock, and build stamp mills and smelters to treat the ore.

Such complex, expensive, and permanent operations necessarily came under corporate control. Often financed with eastern or British capital, the new corporations integrated the mining industry into the larger economy. Hard rock mining produced more complex ores than could be treated in remote mining towns, but, with the new railroad network, they were shipped to smelting plants as far away as Kansas City and St. Louis and then to refineries in eastern cities. Western ores thus became part of national and international business. The mining industry's increasing development of lower-grade deposits led to greater capital investment and larger operations employing more workers and machinery.

Quartz mining thus helped usher the mining frontier into a more stable period. But the new corporate mining had disturbing effects. Its impact on the environment was horrendous. Hydraulic mining washed away hillsides, depositing debris in canyons and valleys to a depth of 100 feet or more, clogging rivers and causing floods, and burying thousands of

Chinese miners in Idaho operate the destructive water cannons used in hydraulic mining. Technological changes made most miners wage workers for companies.

acres of farmland. Such damage provoked an outcry and eventually led to government regulation. Fewer Westerners worried about sterile slag heaps or toxic fumes that belched from smelters and killed the vegetation for miles. They were the signs of progress. One Montana corporate leader even praised the arsenic fumes that permeated Butte for giving women "beautiful complexions."

Corporate mining also hurt miners, transforming them into wage workers with restricted opportunities. "It is useless to say that here all have an equal chance," conceded a Colorado newspaper in 1891. Miners' status declined as new machinery like power drills reduced the need for skilled laborers and prompted employers to hire cheaper workers from eastern and southern Europe. Mining corporations, moreover, did little to protect miners' health or safety. Miners died in cave-ins, explosions, and fires or from the great heat and poisonous gases in underground mines. Others contracted silicosis, lead poisoning, or other diseases or were crippled or killed by machines. Miners called power hoists "man killers" because they frequently crushed and dismembered workers. Investigating the new machinery in 1889, the Montana inspector of mines concluded that "death lurks even in the things which are designed as benefits."

To protect themselves, miners organized unions. These functioned as benevolent societies, using members' dues to pay benefits to injured miners or their survivors. Several unions established hospitals. Union halls offered an alternative to the saloons by serving as social and educational centers. The Miners' Union Library in Virginia City was the largest library in Nevada. Unions also promoted miners' interests on the job with strikes to protest wage cuts and with mine safety campaigns. They convinced states to pass mine safety laws and, beginning in the 1880s, to appoint mine inspectors. The chief role of these state officials was, in the words of a Colorado inspector, to decide "How far should an industry be permitted to advance its material welfare at the expense of human life?"

It was the industry itself, however, that often provided the answer to that question, for mining companies frequently controlled state power and used it to crush unions. Thus in 1892, in the Coeur d'Alene district of Idaho, mining companies locked out strikers and imported a private army, which battled miners in a bloody gunfight. Management next persuaded the governor and the president to send in the state militia and the U.S. Army. State officials then suppressed the strike and the union by confining all union members and their sympathizers in stockades.

Strikes, union busting, and violence continued for years. When mining companies in Utah, Col-

orado, and Montana pursued the same aggressive tactics of lockouts and wage cuts, the local miners' unions in the West united for strength and self-protection. In 1893, they formed one of the nation's largest and most militant unions, the Western Federation of Miners.

Violence and conflict were attributable not to frontier lawlessness but to the industrialization of the mines. Earlier, when the legal system was undeveloped, disputes rarely became violent. But as the law grew stronger and the owners adopted "legalized violence" as a repressive tool, miners turned to extralegal violence. In the western mines, then, both management's tactics—blacklisting union members, locking out strikers, obtaining court injunctions against unions, and using soldiers against workers—and labor's response mirrored conditions in the industrial East. In sum, western mining, reflecting the industrialization of the national economy, had been transformed from a small-scale prospecting enterprise characterized by individual initiative and simple tools into a large-scale corporate business characterized by impersonal management, outside capital, advanced technology, and wage labor.

Exploiting the Grass: The Cattle Kingdom

The development of the range cattle industry represented a second stage of exploitation of the late-nineteenth-century West. It reflected the needs of an emerging eastern urban society, the economic possibilities of the grasslands of the Great Plains, the technology of the expanding railroad network, and the requirements of corporations and capital. It also brought "cow towns" and urban development to the West. The fabled cowboy, though essential to the story, was only a bit player.

Cattle Drives and Cow Towns

The cattle industry originated in southern Texas, where the Spanish had introduced cattle in the eighteenth century. Developed by Mexican ranchers, "Texas longhorns" proved well adapted to the plains grasslands. By the 1860s, they numbered about 5 million head. Texans attempted to market these cattle as early as the 1850s, driving some herds on dusty journeys through New Mexico and Arizona to California and others to Missouri and Illinois. These latter drives disturbed local residents, angered farmers who feared that Texas cattle diseases might infect their own livestock, and prompted quarantine laws against the herds.

Following the Civil War, however, industrial expansion in the East and Midwest enlarged the urban market for food and increased the potential value of Texas steers. The extension of the railroad network into the West, moreover, opened the possibility of tapping that market without antagonizing farmers en route. The key was to establish a shipping point on the railroads west of the settled farming regions, a step first taken in 1867 by Joseph McCoy, an Illinois cattle shipper. McCoy selected Abilene, Kansas, in his words "a very small, dead place, consisting of about one dozen log huts." But Abilene was also the western railhead of the Kansas Pacific Railroad and was ringed by lush grasslands for cattle. McCoy bought 250 acres for a stockyard and imported lumber for stock pens, loading facilities, stables, and a hotel for cowhands. Texans opened the **Chisholm Trail** through Indian Territory to drive their cattle northward to Abilene. Within three years, a million and a half cattle arrived in Abilene, divided into herds of several thousand, each directed by a dozen cowhands on a "long drive" taking two to three months.

The cattle trade attracted other entrepreneurs who created a bustling town. Bankers prospered enough to convince one reporter in 1873 that "banks are as fat a thing as gold mines." Grocers, tailors, bootmakers, laundresses, barbers, druggists, blacksmiths, lawyers, and hotelkeepers provided consumer goods and services. Entertainments mushroomed: saloons, gambling rooms, dance halls, billiard parlors, and brothels. As both railroads and settlement advanced westward, a series of other cow towns—Ellsworth, Wichita, Dodge City, Cheyenne—attracted the long drives, cattle herds, and urban development.

As with the mining camps, the cow towns' reputation for violence was exaggerated. They adopted gun control laws, prohibiting the carrying of handguns within city limits, and established police forces to maintain order. The primary duties of law officers were arresting drunks, fixing sidewalks, and collecting fines. The cow towns regulated rather than prohibited prostitution and gambling, for merchants viewed these vices as necessary to attract the cattle trade. Thus the towns taxed prostitutes and gamblers and charged high fees for liquor licenses. By collecting such "sin taxes," Wichita was able to forgo general business taxes, thereby increasing its appeal to prospective settlers.

Not all cow towns became cities like Wichita, which by 1888 boasted of "Fine Educational Institutions, Magnificent Business Blocks, Elegant Residences, and Extensive Manufacturers"; most, like Abilene, dwindled into small towns serving farm populations. But cow towns, again like mining camps, contributed to the growth of an urban frontier. Railroads often determined the location and growth of western cities, providing access to markets for local products, transporting supplies and machinery for residents, and attracting capital for commercial and industrial development. When railroads reached El Paso, Texas, for example, it became a shipping point for cattle but then built its own packing houses and opened smelters to process Arizona ores. Its Mexican workers clustered in *barrios* and developed their own religious and social organizations—just as San Francisco's Chinese did in Chinatown or European immigrants did in eastern cities. This urbanization demonstrated how western developments paralleled those in older regions. The West, in fact, had become the most urban region in the nation by 1890, with two-thirds of its population living in communities of at least 2,500 people.

Rise and Fall of Open-Range Ranching

The significance of the long drive to the cow towns faded as cattle raising expanded beyond Texas. Indian removal and extension of the railroads opened land for ranching in Kansas, Nebraska, Wyoming, Colorado, Montana, and the Dakotas. Cattle reaching Kansas were increasingly sold to stock these northern ranges rather than for shipment to the packing houses. Ranches soon spread across the Great Plains and into the Great Basin, the Southwest, and even eastern Oregon and Washington. This expansion was helped by the initially low investment that ranching required. Calves were cheap, and grass was mostly free. Ranchers did not buy, but merely used, the grazing lands of the open range, which was public land. It sufficed to acquire title to the site for a ranch house and a water source because controlling access to water in semiarid lands gave effective control of the surrounding public domain "the same as though I owned it," as one rancher explained. Ranchers thus needed to invest only in horses, primitive corrals, and bunkhouses. Their labor costs were minimal: They paid cowboys in the spring to round up new calves for branding and in the fall to herd steers to market.

By the early 1880s, the high profits from this enterprise and an expanding market for beef attracted speculative capital and reshaped the industry. Eastern and European capital flooded the West, with British investors particularly prominent. Some investors went into partnership with existing ranchers, providing capital in exchange for expertise and management. On a larger scale, British and American corporations acquired, expanded, and managed huge ranches. In 1883, the Swan Land and Cattle Company controlled a tract in Wyoming 130 miles long and 40 to 100 miles wide with more than 100,000 cattle.

Large companies soon dominated the industry, just as they had gained control of mining. They also worked together to enhance their power, especially by restricting access to the range and by intimidating small competitors. Some large companies illegally began to enclose the open range, building fences to exclude newcomers and minimize labor costs by reducing the number of cowboys needed to control the cattle. One Wyoming newspaper complained that "some morning we will wake up to find that a corporation has run a wire fence about the boundary lines of Wyoming, and all within the same have been notified to move." And a Coloradan wondered, "Will the government protect us if we poor unite and cut down their fences and let our stock have some of Uncle Sam's feed as well as them?"

The corporate cattle boom overstocked the range, and the industry collapsed in an economic and ecological disaster. Overgrazing replaced nutritious grasses with sagebrush, Russian thistle, and other plants that livestock found unpalatable. Whereas five acres of land could support a steer in 1870, ten times as much was required by the 1880s. Droughts in the mid-1880s further withered vegetation and enfeebled the animals. Millions of cattle starved or froze to death in terrible blizzards in 1886 and 1887.

These ecological and financial disasters destroyed the open-range cattle industry. The surviving ranchers reduced their operations, restricted the size of their herds, and tried to ensure adequate winter feed by growing hay. To further reduce their dependence on natural vegetation, they introduced drought-resistant sorghum and new grasses; to reduce their dependence on rainfall, they drilled wells and installed windmills to pump water.

Cowhands

One constant in the cattle industry was the cowboy, but his conditions and opportunities changed sharply over time and corresponded little to the romantic image of a dashing individual free of social constraints. Cowboys' work was hard, dirty, seasonal, tedious, sometimes dangerous, and poorly paid. Many early cowboys were white Southerners unwilling or unable to return home after the Civil War. Black cowhands made up perhaps 25 percent of the trail-herd outfits. Many others,

especially in Texas and the Southwest, were Mexicans. Indeed, Mexicans developed most of the tools, techniques, and trappings that characterized the cattle industry: from boots, chaps, and the "western" saddle to roundups and roping. Black and Mexican cowboys were often relegated to the more lowly jobs, such as wrangler, a "dust-eater" who herded horses for others to use, but most served as ordinary hands on ranch or trail. Except in the few all-black outfits, they were rarely ranch or trail bosses. Texas cowboys dominated the early years of ranching and trailing, but as the industry expanded northward, more cowboys came from rural Kansas, Nebraska, and neighboring states.

Initially, in the frontier-ranching phase dominated by the long drive, cowboys were seasonal employees who worked closely with owners. They were often the sons or neighbors of ranchers and frequently expected to become independent stock raisers themselves. They typically enjoyed the right to "maverick" cattle, or put their own brand on unmarked animals they encountered, and to "run a brand," or to own their own cattle while working for a ranch. These informal rights provided opportunities to acquire property and move up the social ladder.

As ranching changed with the appearance of large, corporate enterprises, so did the work and work relationships of cowhands. The power and status of employer and employees diverged, and the traditional rights of cowboys disappeared. Employers redefined mavericking as rustling and prohib-

Employees of the Prairie Cattle Company at the ranch headquarters in Dry Cimarron, New Mexico, in 1888. This company, a British corporation, held eight thousand square miles of land.

ited cowhands from running a brand of their own. One cowboy complained that these restrictions deprived a cowhand of his one way "to get on in the world." But that was their purpose: Cowboys were to be workers, not potential ranchers and competitors. To increase labor efficiency, some companies prohibited their cowboys from drinking, gambling, and carrying guns.

Cowboys sometimes responded to these structural transformations the same way skilled workers in the industrial East did—by forming unions and striking. Cowboy strikes broke out where corporate ranching was most advanced. The first strike occurred in Texas in 1883 when the Panhandle Stock Association, representing large operators, prohibited ranch hands from owning their own cattle and imposed a standard wage. More than three hundred cowboys struck seven large ranches for higher wages—$50 rather than $30 per month—and the right to brand mavericks for themselves and to run small herds on the public domain. Ranchers evicted the cowboys, hired scabs, and brought in the Texas Rangers for assistance. The strikers were forced to leave the region.

Other strikes also failed because corporate ranches and their stock associations had the power, and cowhands faced long odds in their efforts to organize. They were isolated across vast spaces and had little leverage in the industry. Members of the Northern New Mexico Cowboys Union, formed in 1886, recognized their weakness. After asking employers for "what we are worth after many years' experience," they conceded, "We are dependent on you."

The transformation of the western cattle industry and its integration into a national economy dominated by corporations thus made the cherished image of cowboy independence and rugged individualism more myth than reality. One visitor to America in the late 1880s commented: "Out in the fabled West, the life of the 'free' cowboy is as much that of a slave as is the life of his Eastern brother, the Massachusetts mill-hand. And the slave-owner is in both cases the same—the capitalist."

OVERVIEW
GOVERNMENT LAND POLICY

Legislation	Result
Railroad land grants (1850–1871)	Granted 181 million acres to railroads to encourage construction and development
Homestead Act (1862)	Gave 80 million acres to settlers to encourage settlement
Morrill Act (1862)	Granted 11 million acres to states to sell to fund public agricultural colleges
Other grants	Granted 129 million acres to states to sell for other educational and related purposes
Dawes Act (1887)	Allotted some reservation lands to individual Indians to promote private property and weaken tribal values among Indians and offered remaining reservation lands for sale to whites (by 1906, some 75 million acres had been acquired by whites)
Various laws	Permitted direct sales of 100 million acres by the Land Office

Exploiting the Earth: The Expansion of Agriculture

Even more than ranching and mining, agricultural growth boosted the western economy and bound it tightly to national and world markets. In this process, the government played a significant role, as did the railroads, science and technology, eastern and foreign capital, and the dreams and hard work of millions of rural settlers. The development of farming produced remarkable economic growth, but it left the dreams of many unfulfilled.

Settling the Land

Federal land grants to railroads had helped open the West to outside influences, and mining and cattle interests had also exploited public lands. To stimulate agricultural settlement, Congress passed the most famous land law, the Homestead Act of 1862 (see the overview table, "Government Land Policy"). The measure offered 160 acres of free land to anyone who

People from many countries migrated to the American West, bringing different beliefs and customs and contributing to the diversity of the region's population. Here Alsatian immigrants arrive at St. Paul, Minnesota, on their way further west.

would live on the plot and farm it for five years. The act promised opportunity and independence to ambitious farmers. The governor of Nebraska exclaimed, "What a blessing this wise and humane legislation will bring to many a poor but honest and industrious family."

Despite the apparently liberal land policy, however, prospective settlers found less land open to public entry than they expected. Federal land laws did not apply in much of California and the Southwest, where Spain and Mexico had previously transferred land to private owners, or in all of Texas. Elsewhere, the government had given away 181 million acres to railroads, transferred millions more to the states to sell for educational and other purposes (the Morrill Act provided the foundation for state agricultural colleges), and set aside millions of acres of former Indian land for sale rather than for homesteading. Moreover, other laws provided for easy transfer of public lands to cattle companies, to other corporations exploiting natural resources, and to land speculators.

Thus when settlers arrived in Kansas, Nebraska, Minnesota, and the Dakotas in the late 1860s and early 1870s, they often found most of the best land unavailable and much of the rest remote from transportation facilities and markets. Forty percent of the land in Kansas, for example, was closed to homesteading, which prompted the editor of the *Kansas Farmer* to complain that "the settlement of the state is retarded by land monopolists, corporate and individual." Although 375,000 farms were claimed by 1890 through the Homestead Act—a success by any measure—most settlers had to purchase their land.

The Homestead Act also reflected traditional eastern conceptions of the family farm, which were inappropriate in the West. A farm of 160 acres would have suited conditions in eastern Kansas or Nebraska, but farther west, larger-scale farming was necessary. And the law ignored the need for capital—for machinery, buildings, livestock, and fencing—successful farming on the Great Plains required.

Thus other forces assumed responsibility for promoting settlement. Newspaper editors trumpeted the prospects of their region. Land companies, eager to sell their speculative holdings, sent agents through the Midwest and Europe to encourage migration. Steamship companies, hoping to sell transatlantic tickets, advertised the opportunities in the American West across Europe. Religious and ethnic groups encouraged immigration. The Scandinavian Immigration Society generated both publicity and settlers for Minnesota;

Figure 21-1 The Growth of Western Farming, 1860–1900
Indian removal, railroad expansion, and liberal land policies drew farm families into the West from much of Europe as well as the East. Technological innovations like barbed wire and farm machinery soon enabled them to build farms, but economic, social, and environmental challenges remained.

Data Source: Historical Statistics of the United States (*1975*).

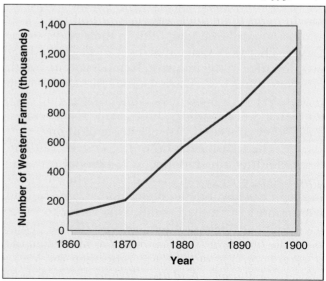

the Hebrew Emigrant Aid Society established Jewish agricultural colonies in Kansas and North Dakota. On a larger scale, the Mormons organized the Perpetual Emigrating Fund Company, which helped more than 100,000 European immigrants settle in Utah and Idaho. Their agricultural communities, relying on communal cooperation under church supervision, succeeded where individual efforts often failed in developing this region.

Most important, railroad advertising and promotional campaigns attracted people to the West. In 1882 alone, the Northern Pacific distributed more than 630,000 pieces of promotional literature in English, Swedish, Dutch, Danish, and Norwegian. "The glowing accounts of the golden west sent out by the R.R. companies," one pioneer later recalled, had convinced her that "they were doing a noble work to let poor people know there was such a grand haven they could reach." Only later did she realize the rail-

roads' selfish motive. Not only would they profit from selling their huge land reserves to settlers, but a successful agricultural economy would produce crops to be shipped east and a demand for manufactured goods to be shipped west on their lines. The railroads therefore advanced credit to prospective farmers, provided transportation assistance, and extended technical and agricultural advice.

Thus encouraged, migrants poured into the West, occupying and farming more acres between 1870 and 1900 than Americans had in the previous 250 years (see Figure 21-1). Farmers settled in every region (see Map 21-3). Many went to California, Oregon, and Washington, where American development had begun much earlier. Some journeyed into the arid Great Basin and Rocky Mountains or the Southwest, where they often acquired land at the expense of the long-established Mexican population. Most, however, streamed into the Great Plains states, from

Map 21-3 *Population Density and Agricultural Land Use in the Late Nineteenth Century*

Economic integration of the West promoted regional agricultural specialization. Stockraising and grain production dominated the more sparsely settled West, while the South grew the labor-intensive crops of cotton, tobacco, and sugar cane, and other areas concentrated on dairy products, fruit, and other crops for nearby urban markets.

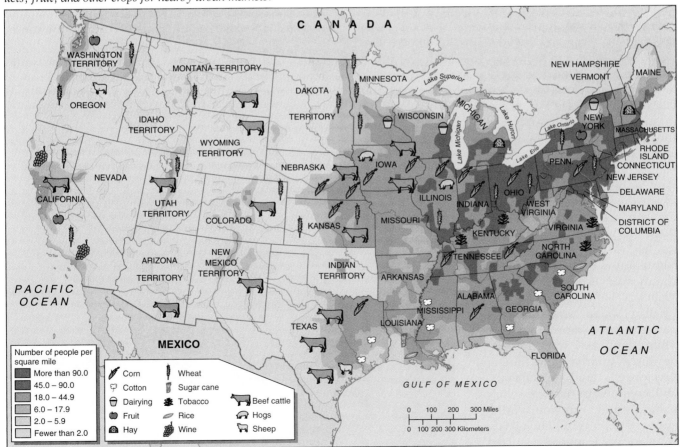

the Dakotas to Texas. Much of Oklahoma was settled in virtually a single day in 1889 when the government opened up lands previously reserved for Indians. A reporter described the wild land rush that created Oklahoma City in hours and claimed two million acres of land by nightfall: "With a shout and a yell the swift riders shot out, then followed the light buggies or wagons and last the lumbering prairie schooners and freighters' wagons, with here and there even a man on a bicycle and many too on foot—above all a great cloud of dust hovering."

So many Americans migrated west that many states east of the plains actually lost population during the 1870s. White migrants predominated in the mass migration, but African Americans initiated one of its most dramatic episodes, a millenarian folk movement they called the Exodus. Seeking to escape the misery and repression of the post-Reconstruction South, these poor "Exodusters" established several black communities in 1879 in Kansas and Nebraska on the agricultural frontier. But many of the new settlers came from Europe, sometimes in a chain migration of entire villages, bringing with them not only their own attitudes toward the land but also special crops, skills, settlement patterns, and agricultural practices. Peasants from Norway, Sweden, and Denmark flocked to Minnesota. Germans, Russians, and Irish put down roots across Texas, Kansas, Nebraska, and the Dakotas. French, Germans, and Italians developed vineyards, orchards, and nurseries in California, where laborers from Japan and Mexico arrived to work in fields and canneries. By 1890, the foreign-born population of North Dakota exceeded 40 percent, and nonnatives made up much of the population in California and other western states.

Migrants moved into the West in search of opportunity, which they sometimes seized at the expense of others already there. In the Southwest, Hispanics had long lived in village communities largely outside a commercial economy, farming small tracts of irrigated land and herding sheep on communal pastures. But as more Anglos, or white Americans, arrived as cattle raisers, railroad and mining developers, land speculators, and commercial farmers, their political and economic influence undermined traditional Hispanic society. Congress restricted the original Hispanic land grants

to only the villagers' home lots and irrigated fields, throwing open most of their common lands to newcomers. Hispanic title was confirmed to only 2 million of the 37.5 million acres at stake. Anglo ranchers and settlers manipulated the federal land system to control these lands. The notorious Santa Fe Ring, a group of lawyers and land speculators, seized millions of acres through fraud and legal chicanery.

Spanish Americans resisted these losses, in court or through violence. *Las Gorras Blancas* (the White Caps) staged night raids to cut fences erected by Anglo ranchers and farmers and to attack the property of railroads, the symbol of the encroaching new order. "Our purpose," they announced, "is to protect the rights of the people in general and especially those of the helpless classes." Such resistance, however, had little success.

As their landholdings shrank, Hispanic villagers could not maintain their pastoral economy. Few turned to homesteading, for that would require dispersed settlement and abandoning the village and its church, school, and other cultural institutions. Thus many Hispanics became seasonal wage laborers in the Anglo-dominated economy, sometimes working as stoop labor in the commercial sugar beet fields that emerged in the 1890s, sometimes working on the railroads or in the mines. Women also participated in this new labor market. Previously crucial to the subsistence village economy, they now sought wage labor as cooks and domestic servants in railroad towns and mining camps. Such seasonal labor enabled Hispanics to maintain their villages and provided sufficient income to adopt some Anglo technology, such as

Mexican Americans had to adapt to changing conditions as the Southwest was developed, but they tried to preserve much of their traditional culture. This painting by Thomas Allen depicts Mexicanos holding their market bazaar in the town plaza.

Thomas Allen, Market Plaza, 1878–1879, oil on canvas, 26 × 39¼." Witte Museum, San Antonio, Texas.

cookstoves or sewing machines. But if Hispanics retained some cultural autonomy, they had little influence over the larger processes of settlement and development that restricted their opportunities and bound them to the western and national economy.

Home on the Range

In settling the West, farmers and their families encountered many difficulties, especially on the Great Plains, where they had to adapt to a radically new environment. The scarcity of trees on the plains meant that there was little wood for housing, fuel, and fencing. Until they had reaped several harvests and could afford to import lumber, pioneer families lived in houses made of sod. Though inexpensive and sturdy, sod houses were also dark and dirty. Snakes, mice, and insects often crawled out of the walls and roofs. One Nebraska homesteader recalled that her first sight of a sod house "sickened me."

For fuel, settlers often had to rely on buffalo or cattle "chips"—dried dung—which repelled some newcomers. One farmer reported in 1879 that "it was comical to see how gingerly our wives handled these chips at first. They commenced by picking them up between two sticks, or with a poker. Soon they used a rag, and then a corner of their apron. Finally, growing hardened, a wash after handling them was sufficient. And now? Now it is out of the bread, into the chips and back again—and not even a dust of the hands!"

The scarcity of water also complicated women's domestic labor. They often transported water over long distances, pulling barrels on "water sleds" or carrying pails on neck yokes. They melted snow on the stove for wash water and used the same water over again for different chores. Where possible, they also helped dig wells by hand.

Some women farmed the land themselves. Single women could claim land under the Homestead Act, and, in some areas, women claimants made up 18 percent of the total and succeeded more frequently than men in gaining final title. At times, married women operated the family farm by themselves while their husbands worked elsewhere to earn the money needed for seeds, equipment, and building supplies. In the 1870s, one Dakota woman

recounted the demands women faced: "I had lived on a homestead long enough to learn some fundamental things: that while a woman had more independence here than in any other part of the world, she was expected to contribute as much as a man—not in the same way, it is true, but to the same degree; that people who fought the frontier had to be prepared to meet any emergency; that the person who wasn't willing to try anything once wasn't equipped to be a settler."

Isolation and loneliness troubled many early settlers on the plains. Women especially suffered because they frequently had less contact with other people than the farm men, who conducted their families' business in town and participated in such public activities as political meetings. One farm woman complained that "being cut off from everybody is almost too much for me." Luna Kellie recalled that from her Nebraska farm "there were no houses in sight and it seemed like the end of the world." The worst agony for many was the silence, unbroken by the sound of neighbors, the rush of water over rocks, or even—in the absence of trees—songbirds or rustling leaves. To break the silence, to provide some music and color, many homesteading families kept canaries among their few belongings.

Over time, conditions improved. Western settlers established churches and schools, both of which involved women in numerous social activities. They created rural social and economic organizations that

Each of the four Chrisman sisters claimed a homestead and built a sod house near Goheen, Nebraska. Farming on the Great Plains was typically a family operation, with all members of the family having important tasks.

encouraged community cooperation. Public institutions also developed to serve the rural population. Few were more important than **Rural Free Delivery**, started in 1896, which eventually brought letters, newspapers, magazines, and advertisements to farm families' doorsteps. Such changes helped incorporate Westerners into the larger society.

Farming the Land

Pioneer settlers had to make daunting adjustments to develop the agricultural potential of their new land. Advances in science, technology, and industry made such adjustments possible. The changes would not only reshape the agricultural economy but also bring their own great challenges to traditional rural values and expectations.

Fencing was an immediate problem, for crops needed to be shielded from livestock. But without timber, farmers could not build wooden fences. Barbed wire, developed in the mid-1870s, solved the problem. By 1900, farmers were importing nearly 300 million pounds of barbed wire each year from eastern and midwestern factories.

The aridity of most of the West also posed difficulties. In California, Colorado, and a few other areas, settlers used streams fed by mountain snowpacks to irrigate land. Elsewhere, enterprising farmers developed variants of the "dry farming" practices that the Mormons had introduced in Utah, attempting to maximize the limited rainfall. Some farmers built windmills to pump underground water.

Scarce rainfall also discouraged the cultivation of many of the crops that supported traditional general agriculture and encouraged farmers to specialize in a single cash crop for market. Gradually, many plains farmers turned from corn to wheat, especially the drought-resistant Turkey Red variety of hard winter wheat that German Mennonites had introduced into Kansas from Russia. Government agencies and agricultural colleges contributed to the success of such adaptations, and private engineers and inventors also fostered agricultural development. Technological advancements included grain elevators that would store grain for shipment and load it into rail cars mechanically and mills that used corrugated, chilled-iron rollers rather than millstones to process the new varieties of wheat.

Mechanization and technological innovations also made possible the large-scale farming practiced in semiarid regions. Farmers required special plows to break the tough sod, new harrows to prepare the soil for cultivation, grain drills to plant the crop, and harvesting and threshing machines to bring it in. Thanks to more and better machines, agricultural efficiency

and productivity shot up. By the 1890s, machinery permitted the farmer to produce eighteen times more wheat than hand methods had. Nearly a thousand corporations were manufacturing agricultural machinery to meet the demands of farmers, who purchased implements in steadily mounting quantities.

These developments reflected both the expansion of agriculture and its increasing dependence on the larger society. Western commercial farmers needed the high demand of eastern and midwestern cities and the expanding world market. The rail network provided essential transportation for their crops; the nation's industrial sector produced necessary agricultural machinery. Banks and loan companies extended the credit and capital that allowed farmers to take advantage of mechanization and other new advances; and many other businesses graded, stored, processed, and sold their crops. In short, because of its market orientation, mechanization, and specialization, western agriculture relied on other people or impersonal forces as it was incorporated into the national and international economy.

When conditions were favorable—good weather, good crops, and good prices—western farmers prospered. Too often, however, they faced adversity. The early years of settlement were unusually wet, but, even then, periodic droughts brought crop failures. Other natural hazards also disrupted production. Especially alarming were plagues of grasshoppers, forming what one woman called a "cloud so dense that the sun was obscured and the earth was in darkness." Grasshoppers ate crops, clothing, and bedding; they attacked sod houses and chewed woodwork and furniture. "In a few hours," one newspaper reported, "many fields that had hung thick with long ears of golden maize were stripped of their value and left only a forest of bare yellow stalks that in their nakedness mocked the tiller of the soil." Private relief organizations distributed food, clothing, and seed to farm families suffering from droughts and grasshoppers in the 1870s, and state governments and Congress appropriated public funds to combat destitution on the agricultural frontier.

In the late 1880s, drought coincided with a slump in crop prices. The large European market that had encouraged agricultural expansion in the 1870s and early 1880s contracted after 1885 when several nations erected trade barriers to U.S. commodities. More important, America's production competed with that from Argentina, Canada, Australia, and Russia, and a world surplus of grain drove prices steadily downward. The average price of wheat dropped from $1.19 a bushel in 1881 to only $0.49 in 1894; prices for other farm commodities also declined.

Squeezed between high costs for credit, transportation, and manufactured goods and falling agricultural prices, western farmers faced disaster. They responded by lashing back at their points of contact with the new system. They especially condemned the railroads, believing that the companies exploited farmers' dependence by charging excessive and discriminatory freight rates. Luna Kellie complained of the railroads, "The minute you crossed the Missouri River your fate both soul and body was in their hands. What you should eat and drink, what you should wear, everything was in their hands and they robbed us of all we produced except enough to keep body and soul together and many many times not that."

Farmers censured the grain elevators in the local buying centers. Often owned by eastern corporations, including the railroads themselves, elevators allegedly exploited their local monopoly to cheat farmers by fixing low prices or misrepresenting the quality of wheat. A Minnesota state investigation found systematic fraud by elevators, which collectively cost farmers a massive sum.

Farmers also denounced the bankers and mortgage lenders who had provided the credit for them to acquire land, equipment, and machinery. Much of the money had come from eastern investors, seeking the higher interest rates in the West. With failing crops and falling prices, however, the debt burden proved calamitous for many farmers. Beginning in 1889, many western farms were foreclosed.

Stunned and bitter, western farmers concluded that their problems arose because they had been incorporated into the new system, an integrated economy directed by forces beyond their control. And it was a system that did not work well. "There is," one of them charged, "something radically wrong in our industrial system. There is a screw loose."

Conclusion

In a few decades, millions of people had migrated westward in search of new opportunities. With determination, ingenuity, and hard work they had settled vast areas, made farms and ranches, built villages and cities, brought forth mineral wealth, and imposed their values on the land. These were remarkable achievements, though tempered by a shameful treatment of Indians and an often destructive exploitation of natural resources. But if most Westerners took pride in their accomplishments, and a few enjoyed wealth and power, many also grew discontented with the new conditions they encountered as the "Wild" West receded.

The farmers' complaints indicted the major processes by which the West was developed and exploited in the late nineteenth century. Railroad expansion, population movements, eastern investment, corporate control, technological innovations, and government policies had incorporated the region fully into the larger society. Indians experienced this incorporation most thoroughly and most tragically, losing their lands, their traditions, and often their lives; the survivors were dependent on the decisions and actions of interlopers determined to impose "Americanization," the name itself implying the imposition of national patterns. Cowboys and miners also learned that the frontier merely marked the cutting edge of eastern industrial society. Both were wage workers, often for corporations controlled by eastern capital, and if industrial technology directly affected miners more than cowhands, neither could escape integration into the national economy by managerial decisions, transportation links, and market forces. Most settlers in the West were farmers, but they too learned that their distinctive environment did not insulate them from assimilation into larger productive, financial, and marketing structures.

Western developments, in short, reflected and interacted with those of eastern industrial society. The processes of incorporation drained away Westerners' hopes along with their products, and many of the discontented would demand a serious reorganization of relationships and power. Led by angry farmers, they turned their attention to politics and government, where they encountered new obstacles and opportunities.

Review Questions

1. What factors were most influential in the subjugation of American Indians?
2. What were the major goals of federal Indian policy, and how did they change?
3. How did railroads shape the settlement and development of the West?
4. How did technological developments affect Indians, miners, and farmers in the West?
5. How did the federal government help transform the West?

Recommended Reading

Robert R. Dykstra, *The Cattle Towns* (1968). A classic analysis of town building and social conflict in

Kansas cattle towns, both fascinating and fun to read.

Gilbert C. Fite, *The Farmers' Frontier, 1865–1900* (1966). A comprehensive account of agricultural settlement in all areas of the West.

Richard E. Lingenfelter, *The Hardrock Miners: A History of the Mining Labor Movement in the American West, 1863–1893* (1974). An important analysis of the relationship between the labor movement and the industrialization of the western mines.

Rodman W. Paul, *The Far West and the Great Plains in Transition* (1988). A valuable survey of regional development that devotes particular attention to mining.

Glenda Riley, *The Female Frontier: A Comparative View of Women on the Prairie and the Plains* (1988). A useful guide to women's experiences in the West.

Robert M. Utley, *The Indian Frontier of the American West, 1846–1890* (1984). A balanced survey of United States–Indian relations in the late nineteenth century.

Philip Weeks, *Farewell, My Nation: The American Indian and the United States, 1820–1890* (1990). Modern discussions of Indian policy that provide insights into the perspectives of the Indians.

Richard White, *"It's Your Misfortune and None of My Own": A New History of the American West* (1991). An important and original analysis of the development of the West that highlights environmental, ethnic, labor, and social history.

Mark Wyman, *Hard Rock Epic: Western Miners and the Industrial Revolution, 1860–1910* (1979). Miners experiencing the dual frontiers of the West and the industrial revolution.

Additional Sources

General Studies

Leonard J. Arrington, *Great Basin Kingdom: An Economic History of the Latter-day Saints* (1958).

Anne M. Butler, *Daughters of Joy, Sisters of Misery: Prostitutes in the American West* (1985).

William Cronon, *Nature's Metropolis: Chicago and the Great West* (1991).

Robert V. Hine, *Community on the American Frontier: Separate but Not Alone* (1980).

Julie Roy Jeffrey, *Frontier Women* (1998).

Patricia Nelson Limerick, *The Legacy of Conquest* (1987).

Clyde A. Milner, Carol A. O'Connor, and Martha A. Sandweiss, eds., *The Oxford History of the American West* (1994).

Sandra L. Myres, *Westering Women and the Frontier Experience* (1982).

Peggy Pascoe, *Relations of Rescue: The Search for Female Moral Authority in the American West* (1990).

William G. Robbins, *Colony and Empire: The Capitalist Transformation of the American West* (1994).

Elliott West, *The Way to the West* (1995).

Donald Worster, *Rivers of Empire: Water, Aridity, and the Growth of the American West* (1985).

Native Americans

David W. Adams, *Education for Extinction: American Indians and the Boarding School Experience* (1995).

Henry Fritz, *The Movement for Indian Assimilation, 1860–1890* (1963).

Arrell Morgan Gibson, *The American Indian, Prehistory to the Present* (1980).

Frederick E. Hoxie, *A Final Promise: The Campaign to Assimilate the Indians, 1880–1920* (1984).

Paul Hutton, *Phil Sheridan and His Army* (1985).

Peter Iverson, *The Navajos* (1990).

Alvin M. Josephy, Jr., *The Nez Percé Indians and the Opening of the Northwest* (1965).

Robert Mardock, *The Reformers and the Indian* (1971).

Janet McDonnell, *The Dispossession of the American Indian* (1991).

Robert M. Utley, *The Lance and the Shield: The Life and Times of Sitting Bull* (1993).

Robert M. Utley, *The Last Days of the Sioux Nation* (1963).

Wilcomb E. Washburn, *The Indian in America* (1975).

David Wishart, *An Unspeakable Sadness: The Dispossession of the Nebraska Indians* (1994).

Robert Wooster, *The Military and United States Indian Policy, 1865–1903* (1988).

The Mining Bonanza

David Emmons, *The Butte Irish: Class and Ethnicity in an American Mining Town* (1989).

Rodman W. Paul, *Mining Frontiers of the Far West, 1848–1880* (1963).

Richard H. Peterson, *The Bonanza Kings: The Social Origins and Business Behavior of Western Mining Entrepreneurs* (1977).

Paula Petrik, *No Step Backward: Women and Family on the Rocky Mountain Mining Frontier, Helena, Montana* (1987).

Malcolm Rohrbough, *Aspen: The History of a Silver-Mining Town* (1986).

Duane A. Smith, *Mining America: The Industry and the Environment* (1987).

Duane A. Smith, *Rocky Mountain Mining Camps: The Urban Frontier* (1967).

Clark Spence, *British Investments and the American Mining Frontier* (1958).

Elliott West, *The Saloon on the Rocky Mountain Mining Frontier* (1979).

The Cattle Kingdom

Lewis Atherton, *The Cattle Kings* (1961).

Edward Dale, *The Range Cattle Industry* (1969).

David Dary, *Cowboy Culture* (1981).

Philip Durham and Everett L. Jones, *The Negro Cowboys* (1965).

Gene M. Gressley, *Bankers and Cattlemen* (1966).

C. Robert Haywood, *Victorian West: Class and Culture in Kansas Cattle Towns* (1991).

David E. Lopez, "Cowboy Strikes and Unions," *Labor History* (1977).

H. Craig Miner, *Wichita: The Early Years, 1865–1880* (1982).

Jimmy M. Skaggs, *The Cattle Trailing Industry* (1973).

Don D. Walker, *Clio's Cowboys* (1981).

The Expansion of Agriculture

Allan G. Bogue, *Money at Interest: The Farm Mortgage on the Middle Border* (1955).

Cletus Daniel, *Bitter Harvest: A History of California Farmworkers* (1981).

Thomas Isern, *Bull Threshers and Bindlestiffs: Harvesting and Threshing on the North American Plains* (1990).

H. Craig Miner, *West of Wichita: Settling the High Plains of Kansas, 1865–1890* (1986).

Jane Taylor Nelsen, ed., *Prairie Populist: The Memoirs of Luna Kellie* (1992).

Nell Painter, *Exodusters: Black Migration to Kansas after Reconstruction* (1976).

Donald J. Pisani, *From the Family Farm to Agribusiness: The Irrigation Crusade in California and the West* (1984).

Donald J. Pisani, *To Reclaim a Divided West: Water, Law, and Public Policy* (1992).

Fred A. Shannon, *The Farmer's Last Frontier: Agriculture, 1860–1897* (1945).

Ethnic and Cultural Frontiers

Albert Camarillo, *Chicanos in a Changing Society* (1979).

Sucheng Chan, *This Bittersweet Soil: The Chinese in California Agriculture* (1986).

Sarah Deutsch, *No Separate Refuge: Culture, Class, and Gender on an Anglo-Hispanic Frontier in the American Southwest* (1987).

Mario T. Garcia, *Desert Immigrants: The Mexicans of El Paso, 1880–1920* (1981).

Jon Gjerde, *From Peasants to Farmers: The Migration from Balestrand, Norway, to the Upper Midwest* (1985).

Frederick C. Luebke, *Ethnicity on the Great Plains* (1980).

D. Aidan McQuillan, *Prevailing over Time: Ethnic Adjustment on the Kansas Prairies, 1875–1925* (1990).

Ronald Takaki, *Strangers from a Different Shore: A History of Asian Americans* (1989).

Where to Learn More

❖ **Bodie State Historic Park, Bodie, California.** The largest authentic ghost town in the West, Bodie was an important mining center from the 1860s to the 1880s. About 170 buildings remain, including a museum with mining equipment and artifacts of everyday life.

❖ **Little Bighorn Battlefield National Monument, Crow Agency, Montana.** The site of Custer's crushing defeat includes a monument to the Seventh Cavalry atop Last Stand Hill. A new authorized Indian Memorial will include sacred texts, artifacts, and pictographs of the Plains Indians.

❖ **American Historical Society of Germans from Russia Museum, Lincoln, Nebraska.** This unique museum, consisting of a complex of restored homes, exhibitions, and archives, preserves the history and culture of Germans who emigrated to Russia and then to the American Great Plains, where they contributed importantly to the development of a multicultural society and an agricultural economy.

❖ **National Museum of the American Indian, New York, New York.** Part of the Smithsonian Institution, this museum has a collection of artifacts illustrative of more than ten thousand years of the Native American culture.

❖ **National Cowboy Hall of Fame, Oklahoma City, Oklahoma.** This large institution contains an outstanding collection of Western art, displays of cowboy and Indian artifacts, and both kitschy exhibitions of the mythic, Hollywood West and serious galleries depicting the often hard realities of the cattle industry. Its many public programs also successfully combine fun with learning.

❖ **Fort Laramie, National Historic Site, near Guernsey, Wyoming.** A fur-trading post, stop on the Oregon Trail, site of treaty negotiations with the Plains Indians, and staging area for military campaigns, Fort Laramie is now a living history museum with many original buildings.

POLITICS AND GOVERNMENT,
1877–1900

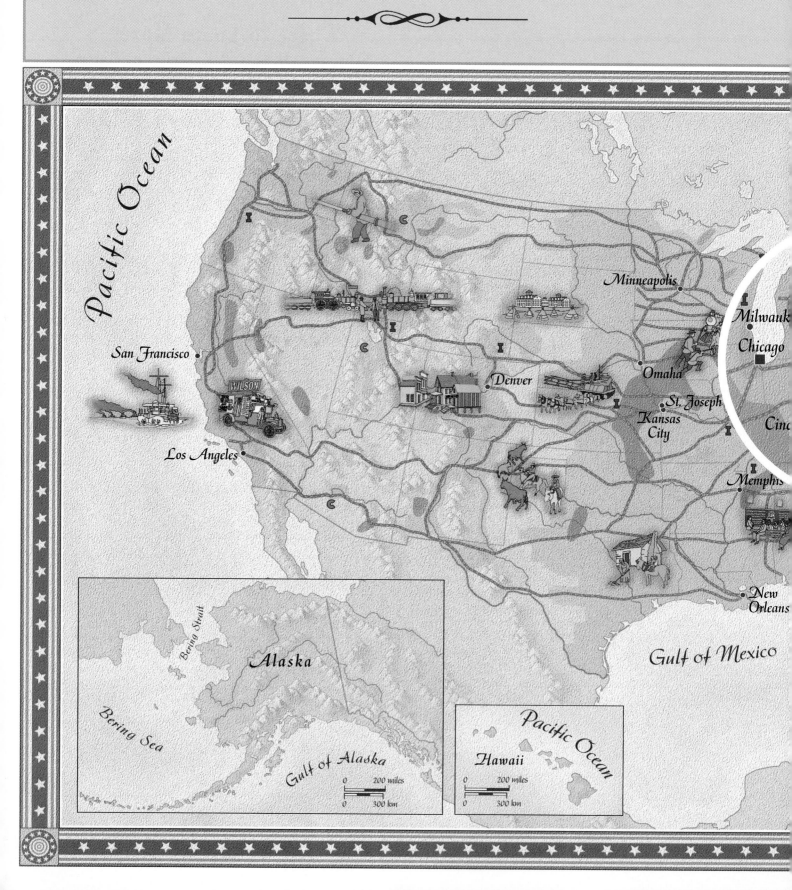

Pacific Ocean

Minneapolis

Milwauk

Chicago

San Francisco

Omaha

St. Joseph

WILSON

Denver

Cinc

Kansas
City

Los Angeles

Memphis

New
Orleans

Bering Strait

Alaska

Gulf of Mexico

Bering Sea

Gulf of Alaska

Pacific Ocean

| 0 | 200 miles |
| 0 | 300 km |

Hawaii

| 0 | 200 miles |
| 0 | 300 km |

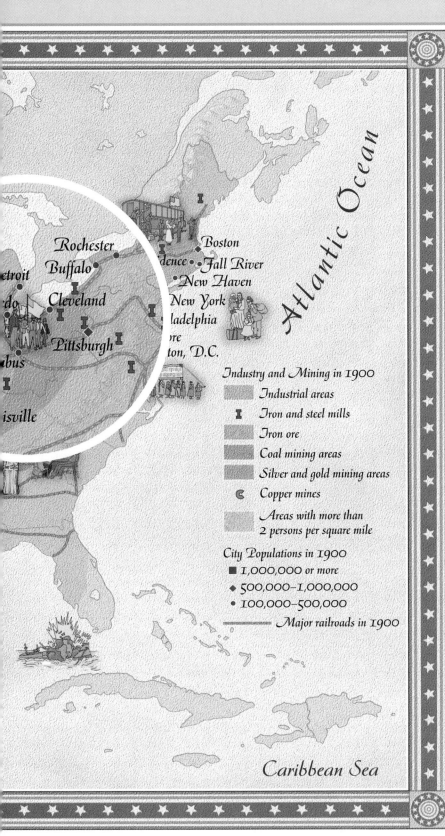

Industry and Mining in 1900

- Industrial areas
- Iron and steel mills
- Iron ore
- Coal mining areas
- Silver and gold mining areas
- Copper mines
- Areas with more than 2 persons per square mile

City Populations in 1900

- 1,000,000 or more
- 500,000–1,000,000
- 100,000–500,000
- Major railroads in 1900

22

Chapter Outline

Key Topics

❖ The exuberant partisan politics and the close balance between parties in the late nineteenth century
❖ The inability of a weak federal government to address problems of America's industrializing economy
❖ The pressure for civil service reform
❖ The tariff issue
❖ Monetary policy and the call for free silver
❖ Agricultural protest and the emergence of the Populist party
❖ The end of political stalemate after the election of 1896

*C*incinnati throbbed with excitement as the October 1884 congressional election approached. Republicans and Democrats staged mammoth campaign parades, each with more than twenty thousand torch-bearing marchers organized into uniformed companies, brigades, and divisions and accompanied by resplendent brass bands. Orators stirred the huge crowds with patriotic, religious, and cultural bombast. Partisans of the Anti-Monopoly party explained the dangers of corporate and money monopolies, but most voters ignored such complex issues amid the stirring spectacles presented by the major parties.

On October 14, in the dead of night, just hours before the polls opened, Cincinnati's police quietly entered the city's black neighborhoods. The police were a partisan force representing the Democratic-controlled city government. They arrested hundreds of African-American men and hurried them to jail. Those who promised to vote the Democratic ticket in exchange for 60 cents were escorted to the polls; those who remained steadfastly Republican were jailed until the polls closed and then released without charges. A thousand newly appointed Democratic deputies joined the police in attacking black Cincinnatians who tried to vote elsewhere in the city and arresting several hundred more Republicans at the polls.

Simultaneously, the U.S. marshal, a Republican, appointed nearly two thousand deputies, most of them paid and armed by the Lincoln Club, a Republican campaign organization. These deputies, "'roustabouts' and 'roughs,' men of no character or bad character," sought to incite violence in the city's Irish wards to keep Democratic voters from the polls. They too made mass arrests, often of Kentucky Democrats who had crossed the Ohio River to "colonize" Cincinnati's election. Several times deputies fired point-blank into Democratic crowds around the polls. Local Republican leader William Howard Taft, later a U.S. president, wrote his mother about witnessing a Democrat "shot & killed about fifteen feet from me at our polling place. . . . He drew a pistol on a Deputy Marshal but the Deputy was too quick for him." Although he considered the marshal's violence justified, Taft thought it risky for Republicans "to furnish revolvers to men who are close to or belong to the criminal class."

At the end of the day, according to the *Cincinnati Enquirer*, the "reign of terror" had left eight dead (including one federal deputy and one deputy sheriff), another two dozen with knife or bullet wounds, and "hundreds of cases of clubbing, sand-bagging, and brass-knuckle exercise." All in all, the newspaper concluded, it was a quiet election reflecting a "reasonably happy state of affairs."

As the *Enquirer* suggested, this Cincinnati election, though more riotous than some, was in many ways typical of late-nineteenth-century American politics. From the military-style campaign to the act of voting, elections were a masculine business. Marked by pageantry and hoopla, campaigns attracted mass participation but often avoided substantive policy issues. Third parties regularly challenged but rarely threatened the Democratic and Republican parties. These two major political parties shaped campaigns and controlled elections, which were usually tumultuous if not always violent. Partisan divisions overlapped with ethnic and racial divisions. The lack of a common national election day, which allowed Kentuckians to vote in Cincinnati's October election without missing their own in November, reflected localism—the belief that local concerns took precedence over national concerns. One newspaper even denied the legitimacy of federal involvement in the city's elections, declaring that federal deputies "can all be kicked and cuffed about like ordinary citizens, and will be compelled to take their chances with common people on election day."

These features of late-nineteenth-century politics would eventually be transformed in significant ways. But while they endured, they shaped not only campaigns and elections but the form and role of government as well.

The Structure and Style of Politics

Politics in the late nineteenth century was an absorbing activity. Campaigns and elections expressed social values as they determined who held the reins of government. Political parties dominated political life. They organized campaigns, controlled balloting, and held the unswerving loyalty of most of the electorate. While the major parties worked to maintain a sense of unity and tradition among their followers, third parties sought to activate those the major parties left unserved. Other Americans looked outside the electoral arena to fulfill their political goals.

Campaigns and Elections

Political campaigns and elections generated remarkable public participation and enthusiasm. They constituted a major form of entertainment at a time when recreational opportunities were limited. Campaign pageantry absorbed communities large and small. In cities and towns across the nation, thousands of men in elaborate uniforms marched in massive torch-lit parades to demonstrate partisan enthusiasm. The small town of Emporia, Kansas, once witnessed a campaign rally of twenty thousand people, several times its population. A parade of wagons stretched five miles, reported the proud local newspaper. "When the head of the procession was under the equator the tail was coming around the north pole." Political picnics and camp meetings served a comparable function in rural areas. Attending party meetings and conventions, listening to lengthy speeches appealing to group loyalties and local pride, gathering at the polls to watch the voting and the counting, celebrating victory and drowning the disappointment of defeat—all provided social enjoyment and defined popular politics.

The excitement of political contests prompted the wife of Chief Justice Morrison Waite to write longingly on election day, 1876, "I should want to vote all day." But women—though they often identified with and endorsed a political party—could not vote at all. Justice Waite himself had just a year earlier written the unanimous opinion of the Supreme Court (in *Minor* v. *Happersett*) that the Constitution did not confer suffrage on women. Men generally believed that weakness and sentimentality disqualified women from the fierce conflicts of the public realm.

Virtually all men participated in politics. In many states, even immigrants not yet citizens were eligible to vote and flocked to the polls. African Americans voted regularly in the North and irregularly in the South before being disfranchised at the end of the century. Overall, turnout was remarkably high, averaging nearly 80 percent of eligible voters in presidential elections between 1876 and 1900, a figure far greater than ever achieved thereafter (see Figure 22-1).

Political parties mobilized this huge electorate. They kept detailed records of voters, transported them to the polls, saw that they were registered where necessary, and sometimes even paid their poll

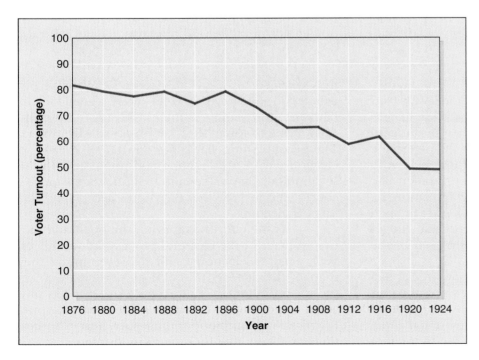

Figure 22-1 Voter Turnout in Presidential Elections, 1876–1924
The exciting partisan politics of the late nineteenth century produced very high voter turnouts, but as party competition declined and states enacted more restrictive voting regulations, popular participation in elections fell in the twentieth century.

CHRONOLOGY

1867 Patrons of Husbandry (the Grange) is founded.

1869 Massachusetts establishes the first state regulatory commission.

1873 Silver is demonetized in the "Crime of '73."

1874 Woman's Christian Temperance Union is organized.

1875 U.S. Supreme Court, in *Minor* v. *Happersett,* upholds denial of suffrage to women.

1876 Greenback party runs presidential candidate.

1877 Rutherford B. Hayes becomes president after disputed election.

Farmers' Alliance is founded.

Supreme Court, in *Munn* v. *Illinois,* upholds state regulatory authority over private property.

1878 Bland-Allison Act obliges the government to buy silver.

1880 James A. Garfield is elected president.

1881 Garfield is assassinated; Chester A. Arthur becomes president.

1883 Pendleton Civil Service Act is passed.

1884 Grover Cleveland is elected president.

1886 Supreme Court, in *Wabash* v. *Illinois,* rules that only the federal government, not the states, can regulate interstate commerce.

1887 Interstate Commerce Act is passed.

1888 Benjamin Harrison is elected president.

1890 Sherman Antitrust Act is passed.

McKinley Tariff Act is passed.

Sherman Silver Purchase Act is passed.

National American Woman Suffrage Association is organized.

Wyoming enters the Union as the first state with woman suffrage.

1892 People's party is organized.

Cleveland is elected to his second term as president.

1893 Depression begins.

Sherman Silver Purchase Act is repealed.

1894 Coxey's Army marches to Washington.

Pullman strike ends in violence.

1895 Supreme Court, in *Pollock* v. *Farmers' Loan and Trust Company,* invalidates the federal income tax.

Supreme Court, in *United States* v. *E. C. Knight Company,* limits the Sherman Antitrust law to commerce, excluding industrial monopolies.

1896 William Jennings Bryan is nominated for president by Democrats and Populists.

William McKinley is elected president.

1900 Currency Act puts U.S. currency on the gold standard.

---

taxes or naturalization fees to make them eligible. With legal regulations and public machinery for elections negligible, parties dominated the campaigns and elections. Many states did not have meaningful registration laws, making it difficult to determine voter eligibility. Kentuckians swarmed to Cincinnati's polls in 1884 because Ohio had no registration law. Until the 1890s, most states had no laws to ensure secrecy in voting, and balloting often took place in open rooms or on sidewalks. Election clerks and judges were not public officials but partisans chosen by the political parties.

Nor did public authorities issue official ballots. Instead voters used party tickets, strips of paper printed by the parties. These had only the names of the candidates of the party issuing them and often varied in size and color. The voter's use of a ballot thus revealed his party allegiance. Tickets were distributed by paid party workers known as peddlers or hawkers, who stationed themselves near the polls, each trying to force his ticket on prospective voters. These contending hawkers contributed greatly to election day chaos. Fighting and intimidation were so commonplace at the polls that one state supreme court ruled in 1887 that they were "acceptable" features of elections.

As the court recognized, the open and partisan aspects of the electoral process did not necessarily lead to election fraud, however much they shaped the nature of political participation. In these circumstances, campaigns and elections provided opportunities for men to demonstrate publicly their commitment to their party and its values, thereby reinforcing their partisan loyalties.

Partisan Politics

A remarkably close balance prevailed between the two major parties in the elections of this era. Democrats and Republicans had virtually the same level of electoral support, one reason they worked so hard to get out the vote (see Map 22-1). Control of the presidency and Congress shifted back and forth between them. Rarely did either party control both branches of government at once (see the overview table, "Party Control of the Presidency and Congress, 1877–1900"). The party balance also gave great influence to New York, New Jersey, Ohio, and Indiana, whose evenly divided voters controlled electoral votes that could swing an election either way. Both parties tended to nominate presidential and vice presidential candidates from those states to woo their voters. The parties also concentrated campaign funds and strategy on the swing states. Thus Republican presidential candidate James Garfield of Ohio commented during the election campaign in 1880: "Nothing is wanting except an immediate and liberal supply of money for campaign expenses to make Indiana certain. With a victory there, the rest is easy." Garfield narrowly carried Indiana by six thousand votes and the na-

Map 22-1   The Two-Party Stalemate of the Late Nineteenth Century

Strong parties, staunch loyalties, and an evenly divided electorate made for exciting politics but often stalemated government in the late nineteenth century. Most states voted consistently for one of the major parties, leaving the few swing states like New York and Indiana the scenes of fierce partisan battles.

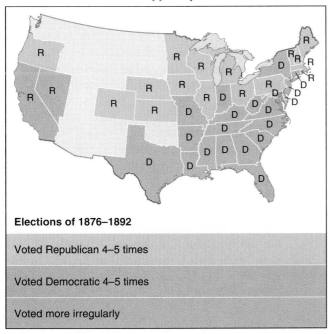

Elections of 1876–1892

Voted Republican 4–5 times

Voted Democratic 4–5 times

Voted more irregularly

tion by nine thousand out of 9.2 million cast. His victory was not the outcome of a contest over great issues but of carefully organized, tightly balanced parties mobilizing their supporters.

Interrelated regional, ethnic, religious, and local factors determined the party affiliations of most Americans. Economic issues, although important to the politics of the era, generally did not decide party ties. Farmers, for example, despite often shared economic concerns, affiliated with both major parties. Like religious belief and ethnic identity, partisan loyalty was largely a cultural trait passed from father to son, which helps explain the electoral stability of most communities.

Republicans were strongest in the North and Midwest, where they benefited from their party's role as the defender of the Union in the Civil War. But not all Northerners voted for the Grand Old Party, or GOP. The Republican party appealed primarily to old-stock Americans and other Protestants, including those of German and Scandinavian descent. African Americans, loyal to the party that had emancipated and enfranchised the slaves of the South, also supported the GOP where they could vote. Democrats were strongest in the South, where they stood as the defender of the traditions of the region's white population. But Democrats also drew support in the urban Northeast, especially from Catholics and recent immigrants.

Each major party thus consisted of a complex coalition of groups with differing traditions and interests. One observer of the Democratic party in California described it as "a sort of Democratic happy family, like we see in the prairie-dog villages, where owls, rattlesnakes, prairie dogs, and lizards all live in the same hole." This internal diversity often provoked conflict and threatened party stability. To hold its coalition together, each party identified itself with a theme that appealed broadly to all its constituents while suggesting that it was menaced by the members and objectives of the opposing party.

Republicans identified their party with nationalism and national unity and attacked the Democrats as an "alliance between the embittered South and the slums of the Northern cities." They combined a "bloody shirt" appeal to the memories of the Civil War with campaigns for immigration restriction and cultural uniformity. Seeing a threat to American society in efforts by Catholic immigrants to preserve their ethnic and cultural traditions, for example, Republican legislatures in several states in the 1880s and 1890s enacted laws regulating parochial schools, the use of foreign languages, and alcohol consumption.

OVERVIEW

PARTY CONTROL OF THE PRESIDENCY AND CONGRESS, 1877–1900

Period	Congress	House Majority Party		Senate Majority Party		Party of President	
1877–79	45th	D	153	R	39	R	Hayes
1879–81	46th	D	149	D	42	R	Hayes
1881–83	47th	D	147	R	37	R	Garfield
						R	Arthur
1883–85	48th	D	197	R	38	R	Arthur
1885–87	49th	D	183	R	43	D	Cleveland
1887–89	50th	D	169	R	39	D	Cleveland
1889–91	51st	R	166	R	39	R	B. Harrison
1891–93	52nd	D	235	R	47	R	B. Harrison
1893–95	53rd	D	218	D	44	D	Cleveland
1895–97	54th	R	244	R	43	D	Cleveland
1897–99	55th	R	204	R	47	R	McKinley
1899–1901	56th	R	185	R	53	R	McKinley

Democrats portrayed themselves as the party of limited government and "personal liberties," a theme that appealed both to the racism of white Southerners and the resentment immigrants felt about the nativist meddling the Republicans favored. The Democrats' commitment to personal liberties had limits. They supported the disfranchisement of African Americans, the exclusion of Chinese immigrants, and the dispossession of American Indians. Nevertheless, their emphasis on traditional individualism and localism proved popular.

The partisan politics of both major parties culminated in party machines, especially at the local level. Led by powerful bosses like Democrat Richard Croker of New York or Republican George Cox of Cincinnati, these machines controlled not only city politics but municipal government. Party activists used well-organized ward clubs to mobilize working-class voters, who were rewarded by municipal jobs and baskets of food or coal doled out by the machine. Such assistance was often necessary given the lack of public welfare systems, but to buy votes the machine also sold favors. Public contracts and franchises were peddled to businesses whose high bids covered kickbacks to the machine.

The partisan politics of the era left room for several third parties organized around specific issues or groups. The **Prohibition party** persistently championed the abolition of alcohol but also introduced many important reform ideas. Some farmers and workers, fed up with the major parties, formed larger but shorter-lived third parties. These parties charged that Republicans and Democrats had failed to respond to economic problems caused by industrialization or, worse still, had deliberately promoted powerful business interests at the expense of ordinary Americans. The **Greenback party** of the 1870s denounced "the infamous financial legislation which takes all from the many to enrich the few." Its policies of labor reform and currency inflation (to stimulate and democratize the economy) attracted supporters from Maine to Texas. Other significant third parties included the Anti-Monopoly party, the Union Labor party, and, most important, the **People's** or **Populist** party of the 1890s. Although third parties often won temporary success at the local or regional level, they never permanently displaced the major parties or undermined traditional voter allegiances.

Associational Politics

Associations of like-minded citizens, operating outside the electoral arena, played an increasingly important role in late-nineteenth-century politics. These organizations worked to achieve public policies beneficial to their members. Farmers organized many such groups, most notably the Patrons of Husbandry, known familiarly as the Grange (see Chapter 19). Established in 1867, with both women and men eligible for membership, the Grange had 22,000 local lodges and nearly a million members by 1875. Its campaign for public regulation of the rates charged by railroads and grain elevators helped convince midwestern

Political Parties

Few things in contemporary American politics present a sharper contrast to the nineteenth century than the role of political parties. In the late nineteenth century, parties dominated politics. They commanded the allegiance of Americans, controlled the selection of candidates, mobilized voters, shaped voting behavior, provided ballots, and ran elections. They also shaped public policies and, through patronage, staffed government positions. At the beginning of the twenty-first century, parties do virtually none of these things.

This transformation began at the end of the nineteenth century. Extreme partisanship prompted states to assert control over elections. The corruption attributed to party machines led gradually to such changes as nonpartisan municipal elections and increased public control over parties. Restrictions on campaign expenditures reduced the party hoopla that had made politics so exciting and voter turnout so high. The connection between parties and voters declined further as new voters unfamiliar with the passions and loyalties of the past joined the electorate.

The inability of the major parties to deal effectively with important national problems, so evident in the depression of the 1890s, prompted Americans to find other ways to influence public policy. Associational groups that had acted outside the partisan arena evolved into effective special-interest lobbying groups. Civil service reform, beginning with the Pendleton Act, steadily reduced party influence in government. So did the growing reliance in the twentieth century on independent regulatory commissions, rather than partisan legislative committees, to make and implement policies.

In recent decades, party decline has accelerated. The introduction and spread of primary elections have stripped parties of their control over nominations. Individual candidates have come increasingly to rely more on personal organizations than party apparatus to manage campaigns. Candidates often appeal for votes as individuals rather than as party members and communicate directly to voters through the mass media, relying less on the old door-to-door personal campaign requiring party workers. Television, in particular, with its focus on dramatic and personal sound bites, is better at promoting individual candidates than abstract entities like parties.

Campaign finance reform laws have reduced party control over the funding of campaigns. So too has the rise of political action committees (PACs) as an important source of support for candidates. PACs represent particular interests, not a collection of interests the way parties do. Candidates dependent on specific interests find it harder to make broader partisan appeals.

Polls show fewer and fewer Americans identifying with a particular party and indicate that partisanship has greatly declined as a factor in voting decisions. Americans increasingly regard parties as neither meaningful nor even useful, let alone essential to democratic government. Nearly half of the electorate favors making all elections nonpartisan or even abolishing parties. More and more people believe that interest groups better represent their political needs than parties. At the same time, fewer and fewer Americans bother to vote. Those who do are much more likely than before to split their ticket, voting for candidates of different parties for different offices. This often results in divided government—with the presidency controlled by one party and Congress by the other. The resulting stalemate increases public cynicism about parties.

Of course, parties endure and retain some importance. Election laws favor the two established parties and obstruct independent candidacies. Public funds subsidize party activities, and party coffers harvest unregulated "soft money" campaign contributions. Congress and state legislatures continue to rely on party divisions to organize their leadership and committee structures, and party discipline still influences the way legislators vote. But while such institutional factors guarantee the continued presence of a two-party system, the parties themselves no longer enjoy the influence they had in the nineteenth century.

The campaign pageantry of a Republican parade in Canton, Ohio, in 1896 illustrates the central role played by political parties in entertaining, organizing, and mobilizing voters. A century later parties have lost many of their functions and much of their popular support.

states to pass the so-called **Granger laws**. The Grange also sought reforms in the nation's financial system. Although it inspired the formation of small independent farmers' parties in the Midwest and on the Pacific coast, the Grange itself remained nonpartisan.

To the Grangers' dismay, industrialists also formed pressure groups. Organizations such as the American Iron and Steel Association and the American Protective Tariff League lobbied Congress for high tariff laws and made campaign contributions to friendly politicians of both parties. A small group of conservative reformers known derisively as **Mugwumps** (the term derives from the Algonquian word for "chief") objected to both tariffs and the government regulations farmers favored. They saw both as interfering with "natural" economic laws. They devoted most of their efforts, however, to campaigning for honest and efficient government through civil service reform. They organized the National Civil Service Reform League to publicize their plans, lobby Congress and state legislatures, and endorse sympathetic candidates. Other pressure groups focused on cultural politics. The rabidly anti-Catholic American Protective Association, for example, agitated for laws restricting immigration, taxing church property, and inspecting Catholic religious institutions.

The Grange rejected partisanship but not politics. This sympathetic cartoon shows a Granger trying to warn Americans blindly absorbed in partisan politics of the dangers of onrushing industrialization.

Women were also active in associational politics. Susan B. Anthony and others formed groups to lobby Congress and state legislatures for constitutional amendments extending the right to vote to women. The leading organizations merged in 1890 as the **National American Woman Suffrage Association**. Despite the opposition of male politicians of both major parties, suffragists had succeeded by the mid-1890s in gaining full woman suffrage in four western states—Wyoming, Colorado, Idaho, and Utah—and partial suffrage (the right to vote in school elections) in several other states, east and west.

Other women influenced public issues through social service organizations. Although the belief that women belonged in the domestic sphere kept them out of electoral politics, it furnished a basis for political action focused on welfare and moral reform. With petition campaigns, demonstrations, and lobbying, women's social service organizations sought to remedy poverty and disease, improve education and recreation, and provide day nurseries for the children of workingwomen. The Illinois Woman's Alliance, organized in 1888 by suffragists, women assemblies of the Knights of Labor, and middle-class women's clubs, investigated the conditions of women and children in workshops and factories and campaigned for protective labor legislation and compulsory school attendance laws.

Women also combined domesticity and politics in the temperance movement. Alcoholism, widespread in American society, was thought to be a major cause of crime, wife abuse, and broken homes. The temperance movement thus invoked women's presumed moral superiority to address a real problem that fell within their accepted sphere. The Woman's Christian Temperance Union (WCTU) gained a massive membership campaigning for restrictive liquor laws. Under the leadership of Frances Willard, however, it built on traditional women's concerns to develop an important critique of American society. Reversing the conventional view, Willard argued that alcohol abuse was a result, not a cause, of poverty and social disorder. Under the slogan of "Home Protection," the WCTU inserted domestic issues into the political sphere with a campaign for social and economic reforms far beyond temperance. It particularly sought to strengthen and enforce laws against rape. Willard bitterly noted that twenty states fixed the age of consent at ten and that "in Massachusetts and Vermont it is a greater crime to steal a cow" than to rape a woman. The WCTU also pushed for improved health conditions and workplace and housing reforms. It eventually

A meeting in 1880 of the National Woman Suffrage Association protested the exclusion of women from electoral politics. Susan B. Anthony noted with regret that "to all men woman suffrage is only a side issue."

supported woman suffrage as well, on the grounds that women needed the vote to fulfill their duty to protect home, family, and morality.

The Limits of Government

Despite the popular enthusiasm for partisan politics and the persistent pressure of associational politics, government in the late nineteenth century was neither active nor productive by present standards. The receding government activism of the Civil War and Reconstruction years coincided with a resurgent belief in localism and laissez-faire policies. In addition, a Congress and presidency divided between the two major parties, a small and inefficient bureaucracy, and judicial restraints joined powerful private interests to limit the size and objectives of the federal government.

The Weak Presidency

The presidency was a weak and restricted institution. The impeachment of President Johnson at the outset of Reconstruction had undermined the office. Then President Grant clearly subordinated it to the legislative branch by deferring to Congress on appointments and legislation. Other factors contributed as well. The men who filled the office between 1877 and 1897—Republicans Rutherford B. Hayes (1877–1881), James A. Garfield (1881), and Chester A. Arthur (1881–1885); Democrat Grover Cleveland (1885–1889 and 1893–1897); and Republican Benjamin Harrison (1889–1893)—were all honest and generally capable. Each had built a solid political record at the state or federal level. But they were all conservatives with a narrow view of the presidency and proposed few initiatives. The most aggressive of them, Cleveland, used his energy in a singularly negative fashion, vetoing two-thirds of all the bills Congress passed, more than all his predecessors combined. Cleveland once vetoed a relief measure for drought-stricken Texas farmers with the statement that "though the people support the Government, the Government should not support the people." This attitude limited government action.

The presidents of this era viewed their duties as chiefly administrative. They made little effort to reach out to the public or to exert legislative leadership. In 1885, Woodrow Wilson, at the time a professor of history and government, described "the business of the president" as "not much above routine" and concluded that the office might "not inconveniently" be made purely administrative, its occupant a sort of tenured civil servant. (Wilson, who helped transform the presidency into a powerful office in the twentieth century, took a very different view when he became president himself in 1913.) Benjamin Harrison devoted as many as six hours a day to dealing with office seekers, and Garfield lamented, "My day is frittered away by the personal seeking of people, when it ought to be given to the great problems which concern the whole country."

The presidency was also hampered by its limited control over bureaus and departments, which responded more directly to Congress, and by its small staff. Indeed, the president's staff consisted of no more than half a dozen secretaries, clerks, and telegraphers. As Cleveland complained, "If the President has any great policy in mind or on hand he has no one to help him work it out."

The Inefficient Congress

Congress was the foremost branch of the national government. It exercised authority over the federal budget, oversaw the cabinet, debated public issues, and controlled legislation. Its members were often state and national party leaders who were strong-willed and, as one senator conceded, "tolerated no intrusion from the President or from anybody else."

But Congress was scarcely efficient. Its chambers were noisy and chaotic, and members rarely devoted their attention to the business at hand. Instead they played cards, read newspapers, or sent a page to get fruit or tobacco from the vendors who lined the hallways of the capitol. One senator from Nevada complained in 1881 that the "confusion, noise, and interruption" in the Senate chamber disrupted his efforts to write letters. The repeated shifts in party control of Congress also impeded effective action. So too did the loss of experienced legislators to rapid turnover. In some Congresses, a majority of members were first-termers.

Procedural rules, based on precedents from a simpler time and manipulated by determined partisans, impeded congressional action. Some rules restricted the introduction of legislation; others prevented its passage. The most notorious rule required that a quorum be not only present but voting. When the House was narrowly divided along party lines, the minority could block all business simply by refusing to answer when the roll was called.

But as a nationalizing economy required more national legislation, business before Congress grew relentlessly (see Figure 22-2). The expanding scale of congressional work prompted a gradual reform of procedures and the centralization of power in the speaker of the House and the leading committees. These changes did not, however, create a coherent program for government action.

The Federal Bureaucracy and the Spoils System

Reflecting presidential weakness and congressional inefficiency, the federal bureaucracy remained small and limited in the late nineteenth century. There were little more than fifty thousand government employees in 1871, and three-fourths of them were local postmasters scattered across the nation. Only six thousand, from President Grant to janitors, worked in Washington. The number of federal employees doubled to 100,000 in 1881 and grew again to 157,000 in

1891 and 239,000 in 1901. It was still the postal service, however, that absorbed most of this increase.

The system for selecting and supervising federal officials had developed gradually in the first half of the century. Known as the spoils system, its basic principle was that victorious politicians awarded government jobs to party workers, with little regard for qualifications, and ousted the previous employees. Appointees then typically promised part of their salary and time to the political interests of their patron or party. The spoils system played a crucial role in all aspects of politics. It enabled party leaders to strengthen their organizations, reward loyal party service, and attract the political workers that parties needed to mobilize the electorate. Supporters described it as a democratic system that offered opportunities to many citizens and prevented the emergence of an entrenched bureaucracy.

Critics, however, charged that the system was riddled with corruption, abuse, and inefficiency. Rapid turnover bred instability; political favoritism bred incompetence. One secretary of the navy, appointed at the behest of Indiana's Republican machine, was said to have exclaimed during his first official inspection of a ship: "Why, the thing's hollow!" Certainly the spoils system was ineffective for filling positions that required special clerical skills, like typing, or scientific expertise like that required by the Weather Bureau (established in 1870) or the U.S. Geological Survey (established in 1879). More serious, the spoils system also absorbed the president and Congress in unproductive conflicts over patronage.

Figure 22-2 Increase in Congressional Business, 1871–1901
Industrialization, urbanization, and western expansion brought increased demands for government action, but the party stalemate, laissez-faire attitudes, and inefficient public institutions often blocked effective responses.

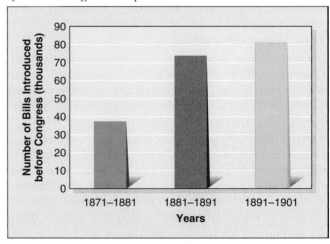

Inconsistent State Government

The public allowed state governments freer rein than the federal government. Considered closer and more responsible to the people, state governments had long exercised police power and regulatory authority. They collected taxes for education and public works, and they promoted private enterprise and public health. Still, they did little by today's standards. Few people thought it appropriate for government at any level to offer direct help to particular social groups. Some state governments contracted in the 1870s and 1880s following the wartime activism of the 1860s. Newly elected Democratic governors hewed to their party's narrow view of government, and new state constitutions restricted the scope of public authority. California's constitution of 1879, for example, limited the state government's authority so sharply that one wit even proposed abolishing the legislature, "and any person who shall be guilty of suggesting that a Legislature be held, shall be punished as a felon without the benefit of clergy."

But state governments gradually expanded their role in response to the stresses produced by industrialization. Following the lead of Massachusetts in 1869, a majority of states had by the turn of the century created commissions to investigate and regulate industry. Public intervention in other areas of the industrial economy soon followed. One observer noted in 1887 that state governments enacted many laws and established numerous state agencies in "utter disregard of the laissez-faire principle." In Minnesota, for example, the state helped farmers by establishing a dairy commission, prohibiting the manufacture or sale of margarine, creating a bureau of animal industry, and employing state veterinarians. In the lumber industry, state officials oversaw every log "floated downstream from the woods to the saw-mill." State inspectors examined Minnesota's steam boilers, oil production, and sanitary conditions. Other laws regulated railroads, telegraphs, and dangerous occupations, prohibited racial discrimination in inns, and otherwise protected the public welfare.

Not all such agencies and laws were effective, nor were all state governments as diligent as Minnesota's. Southern states especially lagged, and one Midwesterner complained that his legislature merely "meets in ignorance, sits in corruption, and dissolves in disgrace every two years." Still, the widening scope of state action represented a growing acceptance of public responsibility for social welfare and economic life and laid the foundation for more effective steps in the early twentieth century.

Public Policies and National Elections

Several great issues dominated the national political arena in the late nineteenth century, including civil service reform, tariffs, and business and financial regulation. Civil service reform attracted relatively little popular interest, but Americans argued passionately about even the smallest details of tariff, regulatory, and financial legislation. Rarely, however, did these issues clearly and consistently separate the major political parties. Instead they divided each party into factions along regional, interest, and economic lines. As a consequence, these leading issues often played only a small role in determining elections and were seldom resolved by government action.

Civil Service Reform

Reform of the spoils system emerged as a prominent issue during the Hayes administration. Reformers like the Mugwumps wanted a professional civil service based on merit and divorced from politics. They wanted officeholders to be selected on the basis of competitive written examinations and protected from removal on political grounds. They expected such a system to promote efficiency, economy, and honesty in government. But they also expected it to increase their own influence and minimize that of "mere politicians." As one Baltimore Mugwump said, civil service reform would replace ignorant and corrupt officeholders with "gentlemen . . . who need nothing and want nothing from government except the satisfaction of using their talents," or at least with "sober, industrious . . . middle-class persons who have taken over . . . the proper standards of conduct."

Not all Americans agreed with such haughty views. The *New York Sun* denounced "the proposition that men shall be appointed to office as the result of examinations in book learning and that they shall remain in office during life. . . . We don't want an aristocracy of office-holders in this country."

President Hayes favored civil service reform but did not fully renounce the spoils system. He rewarded those who had helped elect him, permitted party leaders to name or veto candidates for the cabinet, and insisted that his own appointees contribute funds to Republican election campaigns. But he rejected the claims of some machine leaders and office seekers and proposed reforms, which Congress promptly blocked. He struck a blow for change, however, when he fired Chester A. Arthur from his post as New York customs house collector after an investigation pronounced Arthur's patronage system to be

In this 1881 cartoon, the evil spirit of partisanship threatens a government clerk hesitating to kick back an assessed portion of his salary to the party in power. Civil service reformers wanted to eliminate political factors in staffing the federal bureaucracy.

"unsound in principle, dangerous in practice, . . . and calculated to encourage and perpetuate the official ignorance, inefficiency, and corruption. . . ."

The weakness of the civil service reformers was dramatically underscored in 1880 when the Republicans, to improve their chances of carrying the crucial state of New York, nominated Arthur for vice president on a ticket headed by James A. Garfield of Ohio. They won, and Garfield immediately found himself enmeshed in the demands of the unreformed spoils system. He once complained to his wife, "I had hardly arrived before the door-bell began to ring and the old stream of office-seekers began to pour in. They had scented my coming and were lying in wait for me like vultures for a wounded bison. All day long it has been a steeple chase, I fleeing and they pursuing." Within a few months of his inauguration in 1881, Garfield was assassinated by a disappointed and crazed office seeker, and Arthur became president.

Public dismay over this tragedy finally spurred changes in the spoils system. Arthur himself urged Congress to act, and in 1883, it passed the **Pendleton**

Civil Service Act. This measure prohibited federal employees from soliciting or receiving political contributions from government workers and created the Civil Service Commission to administer competitive examinations to applicants for government jobs. The act gave the commission jurisdiction over only about 10 percent of federal positions but allowed presidents to extend its authority. And subsequent presidents did so, if sometimes only to prevent their own appointees from being turned out by a succeeding administration. A professional civil service free from partisan politics gradually emerged, strengthening the executive branch's ability to handle its increasing administrative responsibilities.

The new emphasis on merit and skill rather than party ties opened new opportunities to women. Federal clerks were nearly exclusively male as late as 1862, but by the early 1890s, women held a third of the clerical positions in the executive departments in Washington. These workers constituted the nation's first substantial female clerical labor force. Their work in public life challenged the conventional belief that a woman's ability and personality limited her to the domestic sphere. To succeed, clerks had to be assertive and competent, to acquire managerial skills, and to think of their careers as permanent, not temporary. Julia Henderson described her work as an examiner of accounts in the Interior Department in 1893 as "brain work of a character that requires a knowledge not only of the rulings of this Department, but also those of the Treasury, Second Auditor, Second Comptroller, and Revised Statutes; demanding the closest and most critical attention, together with a great deal of legal and business knowledge."

The Political Life of the Tariff

Americans debated heatedly over tariff legislation throughout the late nineteenth century. This complex issue linked basic economic questions to partisan, ideological, and regional concerns. Tariffs on imported goods provided revenue for the federal government and protected American industry from European competition. They thus promoted industrial growth but often allowed favored industries to garner high profits. By the 1880s, tariffs covered four thousand items and generated more revenue than the government needed to carry on its limited operations.

Reflecting its commitment to industry, the Republican party vigorously championed protective tariffs. Party leaders also claimed that American labor benefited from tariff protection. "Reduce the tariff, and labor is the first to suffer," declared William McKinley of Ohio. Most Democrats, by contrast, favored tariff reduction, a position that reflected their

OVERVIEW

ARGUMENTS IN THE TARIFF DEBATES

Area Affected	High-Tariff Advocates	Low-Tariff Advocates
Industry	Tariffs promote industrial growth.	Tariffs inflate corporate profits.
Employment	Tariffs stimulate job growth.	Tariffs restrict competition.
Wages and prices	Tariffs permit higher wages.	Tariffs increase consumer prices.
Government	Tariffs provide government revenue.	Tariffs violate the principle of laissez-faire and produce revenues that tempt the government to activism.
Trade	Tariffs protect the domestic market.	Tariffs restrict foreign trade.

party's relatively laissez-faire outlook. They argued that lower tariffs would encourage foreign trade and, by reducing the treasury surplus, minimize the temptation for the government to pursue activist policies. They pointed out the discriminatory effects of high tariffs, which benefited some interests, like certain manufacturers, but hurt others, like some farmers, while raising the cost of living for all (see the overview table, "Arguments in the Tariff Debates").

The differences between the parties, however, were often more rhetorical than substantial. They disagreed only about how great tariffs should be and what interests they should protect. Regardless of party position, congressmen of both parties voted for tariffs that would benefit their districts. California Democrats called for protective duties on wool and raisins, products produced in California; Massachusetts Republicans, to aid their state's shoe manufacturers, supported tariffs on shoes but opposed tariffs on leather. A Democratic senator from Indiana, elected on a campaign pledge to reduce tariffs, summed up the prevailing rule succinctly: "I am a protectionist for every interest which I am sent here by my constituents to protect."

In the 1884 campaign, Republican presidential candidate James G. Blaine maintained that prosperity and high employment depended on high duties. The Democrats' platform endorsed a lowered tariff, but their candidate, New York governor Grover Cleveland, generally ignored the issue. Unable to address this and other important issues, both parties resorted to scandalmongering. The Democrats exploited Blaine's image as a beneficiary of the spoils system, which convinced the Mugwumps to

bolt to Cleveland. Republicans responded by exposing Cleveland as the father of an illegitimate child.

Cleveland continued to avoid the tariff issue for three years after his election, until the growing treasury surplus and rising popular pressure for tariff reduction prompted him to act. He devoted his entire 1887 annual message to attacking the "vicious, inequitable, and illogical" tariff, apparently making it the dominant issue of his 1888 reelection campaign. Once again, however, the distinctive political attribute of the period—intense and organized campaigning between closely balanced parties—forced both Democrats and Republicans to blur their positions. Cleveland proposed a Democratic platform that ignored his recent message and did not even use the word *tariff*. When the party convention adopted a tariff reduction plank, Cleveland complained bitterly and named high-tariff advocates to manage his campaign. "What a predicament the party is placed in," lamented one Texas Democrat, with tariff reform "for its battle cry and with a known protectionist . . . as our chairman." Cleveland won slightly more popular votes than his Republican opponent, Benjamin Harrison of Indiana, but Harrison carried the electoral college, indicating the decisive importance of strategic campaigning, local issues, and large campaign funds rather than great national issues.

The triumphant Republicans raised tariffs to unprecedented levels with the **McKinley Tariff Act** of 1890. McKinley praised the law as "protective in every paragraph and American on every page," but it provoked a popular backlash that helped return the Democrats to power. Still, the Democrats made little effort to push tariff reform. The *Atlanta Constitution* mused about such tariff politics in a bit of doggerel:

It's funny 'bout this tariff—how they've lost it or
    forgot;
They were rushing it to Congress once; their col-
    lars were so hot
They could hardly wait to fix it 'till we harvested a
    crop;
Was it such a burnin' question that they had to let
    it drop?

The Beginnings of Federal Regulation

While business leaders pressed for protective tariffs
and other public policies that promoted their interests, they otherwise used their great political influence to ensure governmental laissez-faire. Popular
pressure nonetheless compelled Congress to take
the first steps toward the regulation of business with
the passage of the **Interstate Commerce Act** in 1887
and the **Sherman Antitrust Act** in 1890.

The rapid growth of great industrial corporations and their disruptive effects on traditional practices and values profoundly alarmed the public (see
Chapter 20). Farmers condemned the power of corporations over transportation facilities and their monop-
olization of industries affecting agriculture, from those
that manufactured farm machinery to those that ran
flour mills. Small business owners suffered from the
destructive competition of corporations, workers were
exploited by their control of the labor market, and
consumers felt victimized by high prices. The result
was a growing clamor to rein the corporations in.

The first target of this concern was the nation's railroads, the preeminent symbol of big business. Both farm groups and business shippers
complained of discriminatory rates levied by railroads.
Consumers condemned the railroads' use of pooling
arrangements to suppress competition and raise rates.
The resulting pressure was responsible for the Granger
laws enacted in several midwestern states in the 1870s
to regulate railroad freight and storage rates.

At first, the Supreme Court upheld this legislation, ruling in *Munn* v. *Illinois* (1877) that state governments had the right to regulate private property
when it was "devoted to a public use." But in 1886, the
Court ruled in *Wabash, St. Louis, and Pacific Railway
Company* v. *Illinois* that only the federal government
could regulate interstate commerce. This decision effectively ended state regulation of railroads but simultaneously increased pressure for congressional action.
"Upon no public question are the people so nearly
unanimous as upon the proposition that Congress
should undertake in some way the regulation of interstate business," concluded a Senate committee. With
the support of both major parties, Congress in 1887
passed the Interstate Commerce Act.

The act prohibited rebates, discriminatory
rates, and pooling and established the **Interstate
Commerce Commission (ICC)** to investigate and
prosecute violations. The ICC was the first federal
regulatory agency. But its powers were too limited
to be effective. Senator Nelson Aldrich of Rhode Island, a leading spokesman for business interests,
described the law as an "empty menace to great interests, made to answer the clamor of the ignorant." Presidents did little to enforce it, and
railroads continued their objectionable practices.
They frustrated the commission by refusing to provide required information and endlessly appealing
its orders to a conservative judiciary. In its first fifteen years, only one court case was decided in favor
of the ICC. Not surprisingly, then, popular dissatisfaction with the railroads continued into the twentieth century. Californian Frank Norris, in his
novel *The Octopus* (1901), likened them to "a gigan-
tic parasite fattening upon the lifeblood of an entire commonwealth."

Many people saw railroad abuses as indica-
tive of the dangers of corporate power in general
and demanded a broader federal response. As with
railroad regulation, the first antitrust laws—laws intended to break up or regulate corporate monopolies—were passed by states. Exposés of the
monopolistic practices of such corporations as Standard Oil forced both major parties to endorse national antitrust legislation during the campaign of
1888. In 1890, Congress enacted the Sherman Antitrust Act with only a single vote in opposition. But
this near unanimity concealed real differences over
the desirability and purpose of the law. Although it
emphatically prohibited any combination in restraint of trade (any attempt to restrict competition), it was otherwise vaguely written and hence
weak in its ability to prevent abuses. The courts further weakened it, and presidents of both parties
made little effort to enforce it. Essentially still unfettered, large corporations remained an ominous
threat in the eyes of many Americans.

The Money Question

Persistent wrangling over questions of currency and
coinage made monetary policy the most divisive political issue in the late nineteenth century. President
Garfield suggested the complexities of this subject
when he wryly declared that a member of Congress
had been committed to an asylum after "he devoted
himself almost exclusively to the study of the currency, became fully entangled with the theories of
the subject, and became insane." Despite the sometimes arcane and difficult nature of the money ques-

tion, millions of Americans adopted positions on it and defended them with religious ferocity.

Creditors, especially bankers, as well as conservative economists and many business leaders favored limiting the money supply. They called this a **sound money** policy and insisted that it would ensure economic stability, maintain property values, and retain investor confidence. Farmers and other debtors complained that this deflationary monetary policy would exacerbate the trend toward depressed prices in the American economy. They feared it would depress already low crop prices, drive debtors further into debt, and restrict economic opportunities. They favored expanding the money supply to match the country's growing population and economy. They expected this inflationary policy to raise prices, stimulate the economy, reduce debt burdens, and increase opportunities.

The conservative leadership of both major parties supported the sound money policy, but their rank-and-file membership, especially in the West and the South, included many inflationists. As a result, the parties avoided confronting each other on the money issue.

The conflict between advocates of sound money and inflation centered on the use of paper money—"greenbacks"—and silver coinage. The greenback controversy had its roots in the Civil War. To meet its expenses during the war, the federal government issued $450 million in greenbacks—paper money backed only by the credit of the United States, not by gold or silver, the traditional basis of currency. After the war, creditors demanded that these greenbacks be withdrawn from circulation. Debtors and other Americans caught up in a postwar depression favored retaining the greenbacks and even expanding their use.

In 1875, sound money advocates in Congress enacted a deflationary law that withdrew some greenbacks from circulation and required that the remainder be convertible into gold after 1878. This action forced the money issue into electoral politics. Outraged inflationists organized the Greenback party. They charged that the major parties had "failed to take the side of the people" and instead supported the "great moneyed institutions." The Greenbackers polled more than a million votes in 1878 and elected fourteen members of Congress, nearly gaining the balance of power in the House. As the depression faded, however, so did interest in the greenback issue, and the party soon withered.

Inflationists then turned their attention to the silver issue, which would prove more enduring and disruptive. Historically, the United States had been on a bimetallic standard; that is, it used both gold and silver as the basis of its currency. But after the 1840s, the market price of silver rose above the currency value assigned to it by the government. Silver miners and owners began to sell the metal for commercial use rather than to the government for coinage, and little silver money circulated. In 1873, Congress passed a law "demonetizing" silver, making gold the only standard for American currency. Gold

"*The Bosses of the Senate*," a political cartoon of 1889, depicted the popular belief that huge corporate trusts controlled the government and corrupted public policy. This conviction helped fuel the demand for antitrust legislation but may not have been allayed by the weaknesses of the Sherman Act.

standard supporters hoped the law would promote international trade by aligning U.S. financial policy with that of Great Britain, which insisted on gold-based currency. But they also wanted to prevent new silver discoveries in the American West from expanding the money supply.

Indeed, silver production soon boomed, flooding the commercial market and dropping the value of the metal. Dismayed miners wanted the Treasury Department to purchase their surplus silver on the old terms and demanded a return to the bimetallic system. More important, the rural debtor groups seeking currency inflation joined in this demand, seeing the return to silver coinage as a means to reverse the long deflationary trend in the economy. Many passionately denounced the "Crime of '73" as a conspiracy of eastern bankers and foreign interests to control the money system to the detriment of ordinary Americans.

Again, both major parties equivocated. Eastern conservatives of both parties denounced silver; Southerners and Westerners demanded **free silver**, which meant unlimited silver coinage. One New York Democrat complained that western and southern members of his party were "mad as wild Texas steers on this silver dollar business. As we pass each other in the streets they seem to sneer, and hiss through their teeth the words 'gold bug,' and look as if they would like to spit upon [us]."

By 1878, a bipartisan coalition succeeded in passing the **Bland-Allison Act**. This compromise measure required the government to buy at least $2 million of silver a month. However, the government never exceeded the minimum, and the law had little inflationary effect. Republican President Arthur and Democratic President Cleveland recommended repealing the Bland-Allison Act, but the parties avoided the silver issue in their national platforms, fearing its divisive effect.

As hard times hit rural regions in the late 1880s, inflationists secured passage of the **Sherman Silver Purchase Act** of 1890. The Treasury now had to buy a larger volume of silver and pay for it with Treasury notes redeemable in either gold or silver. But this too produced little inflation because the government did not coin the silver it purchased, redeemed the notes only with gold, and, as western silver production increased further, had to spend less and less to buy the stipulated amount of silver. Debtors of both parties remained convinced that the government favored the "classes rather than the masses." Gold standard advocates (again of both parties) were even less happy with the law and planned to repeal it at their first opportunity. The division between them was deep and bitter.

The Crisis of the 1890s

In the 1890s, social, economic, and political pressures created a crisis for both the political system and the government. A third-party political challenge generated by agricultural discontent disrupted traditional party politics. A devastating depression spawned social misery and labor violence. Changing public attitudes led to new demands on the government and a realignment of parties and voters. These developments, in turn, set the stage for important political, economic, and social changes in the new century.

Agricultural Protest

The agricultural depression that engulfed the Great Plains and the South in the late 1880s brought misery and despair to millions of rural Americans. Falling crop prices and rising debt overwhelmed many people already exhausted from overwork and alarmed by the new corporate order. "At the age of 52 years, after a long life of toil, economy, and self-denial, I find myself and family virtual paupers," lamented one Kansan. Their farm, rather than being "a house of refuge for our declining years, by a few turns of the monopolistic crank has been rendered valueless." To a large extent, the farmers' plight stemmed from conditions beyond control, including bad weather and an international overproduction of farm products. Seeking relief, however, the farmers naturally focused on the inequities of railroad discrimination, tariff favoritism, a restrictive financial system, and apparently indifferent political parties.

Angry farmers particularly singled out the systems of money and credit that worked so completely against agricultural interests. Government rules for national banks directed credit into the urbanized North and East at the expense of the rural South and West and prohibited banks from making loans on farm property and real estate. As a result, farmers had to turn to other sources of credit and pay higher interest rates. In the West, farmers borrowed money from mortgage companies to buy land and machinery. Declining crop prices made it difficult to pay their debts and often required them to borrow more and at higher rates. In hard times, mortgage foreclosures crushed the hopes of many farmers. In the South, the credit shortage interacted with the practices of cotton marketing and retail trade to create the sharecropping system, which trapped more and more farmers, black and white, in a vicious pattern of exploitation. The government's policies of monetary deflation worsened the debt burden for all farmers.

Farmers protested other features of the nation's economic system as well. They shouldered railroad freight rates two or three times higher in the West and South than in the North and East. The near-monopolistic control of grain elevators and cotton brokerages in rural areas left farmers feeling exploited. Protective tariff rates on agricultural machinery and other manufactured goods further raised their costs. The failure of political parties and the government to devise effective regulatory and antitrust measures or to correct the inequities in the currency, credit, and tariff laws capped the farmers' anger. By the 1890s, many were convinced that the nation's great economic and political institutions were aligned against them.

In response, farmers turned to the **Farmers' Alliance**, the era's greatest popular movement of protest and reform. Originating in Texas, the Southern Farmers' Alliance spread throughout the South and across the Great Plains to the Pacific coast. By 1890, it had 1.2 million members. African-American farmers organized the Colored Farmers' Alliance. The Northwestern Farmers' Alliance spread westward and northward from Illinois to Nebraska and Minnesota. In combination, these groups constituted a massive grassroots movement committed to economic and ultimately political reform.

The Farmers' Alliance restricted its membership to men and women of the "producing class" and urged them to stand "against the encroachments of monopolies and in opposition to the growing corruption of wealth and power." At first, the Alliance attempted to establish farmers' cooperatives to market crops and purchase supplies. Although some coops worked well, most soon failed because of the opposition of established merchants and other business interests. Railroads suppressed Alliance grain elevators by refusing to handle their wheat. In Leflore County, Mississippi, when members of the Colored Farmers' Alliance shifted their trade to an Alliance store, local merchants provoked a conflict in which state troops killed twenty-five black farmers, including the local leaders of the Colored Alliance.

The Alliance also developed ingenious proposals to remedy rural credit and currency problems. In the South, the Alliance pushed the subtreasury system, which called on the government to warehouse farmers' cotton and advance them credit based on its value (see Chapter 19). In the West, the Alliance proposed a system of federal loans to farmers using land as security. This land-loan scheme, like the subtreasury system, was a political expression of greenbackism; it would have expanded the money supply while providing immediate relief for distressed farmers. These proposals were immensely popular among farmers, but the major parties and Congress rejected them. The Alliance also

took up earlier calls for free silver, government control of railroads, and banking reform, again to no avail. Denouncing the indifference of the major political parties and the institutions of government, William A. Peffer, the influential editor of the Alliance newspaper the *Kansas Farmer*, declared that the "time has come for action. The people will not consent to wait longer. . . . The future is full of retribution for delinquents."

The People's Party

In the West, discontented agrarians organized independent third parties to achieve reforms the major parties had ignored. State-level third parties appeared in the elections of 1890 under many names. All eventually adopted the labels "People's" or "Populist," which were first used by a Kansas party that formed in June 1890. The founders of the Kansas People's Party included members of the Farmers' Alliance, the Knights of Labor, the Grange, and the old Greenback party. The new party's campaign, marked by grim determination and fierce rhetoric, set the model for Populist politics and introduced many of the movement's leaders. These people, women as well as men, were earnest organizers and powerful orators. One was *Kansas Farmer* editor Peffer. Others included "Sockless Jerry" Simpson, Annie Diggs, and Mary E. Lease. When hostile business and political leaders attacked the Populist

Established interests ridiculed the Populists unmercifully. This hostile cartoon depicts the People's Party as an odd assortment of radical dissidents committed to a "Platform of Lunacy."

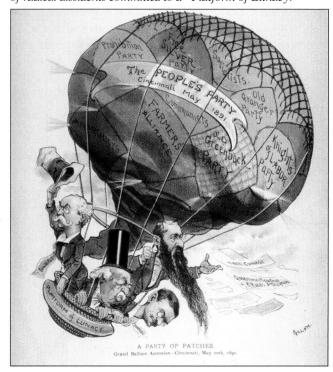

A PARTY OF PATCHES.
Grand Balloon Ascension—Cincinnati, May 20th, 1891.

plans as socialistic, Lease retorted, "You may call me an anarchist, a socialist, or a communist. I care not, but I hold to the theory that if one man has not enough to eat three times a day and another has $25,000,000, that last man has something that belongs to the first." Lease spoke as clearly against the colonial status experienced by the South and West: "The great common people of this country are slaves, and monopoly is the master. The West and South are bound and prostrate before the manufacturing East."

The Populist parties proved remarkably successful. They gained control of the legislatures of Kansas and Nebraska and won congressional elections in Kansas, Nebraska, and Minnesota. Their victories came at the expense of the Republicans, who had traditionally controlled politics in these states, and contributed to a massive defeat of the GOP in the 1890 midterm elections after the passage of the McKinley Tariff and the Sherman Silver Purchase Act. Thereafter, Populists gained further victories throughout the West. In the mountain states, where their support came more from miners than farmers, they won governorships in Colorado and Montana. On the Pacific coast, angry farmers found allies among urban workers in Seattle, Tacoma, Portland, and San Francisco, where organized labor had campaigned for reform since the 1880s. The Populists elected a governor in Washington, congressmen in California, and legislators in all three states.

Even in the Southwest, where territorial status limited political activity, Populist parties emerged. In Oklahoma, the party drew support from homesteaders and tenant farmers; in Arizona, from miners and railroad workers. In New Mexico, the Southern Alliance established itself among small stockraisers who felt threatened by corporate ranches and land companies that were exploiting the confusion of old Spanish and Mexican land grants to expand their landholdings. The fear of corporate expansion even impelled Anglo New Mexicans to cooperate with poor Hispanics for whom they had previously shown little sympathy. One Alliance paper wrote of the need to defend Hispanics from the "mighty land monopoly which is surely grinding their bones into flour that it may make its bread." In the 1890 election, Populists gained the balance of power in the New Mexico legislature.

In the South, the Alliance did not initially form third parties but instead attempted to seize control of the dominant Democratic party by forcing its candidates to pledge support to the Alliance platform. The rural southern electorate then swept these "Alliance Democrats" into office, electing four governors, several dozen members of Congress, and a majority of legislators in eight states.

With their new political power, farmers enacted reform legislation in many western states. New laws regulated banks and railroads and protected poor debtors by capping interest rates and restricting mortgage foreclosures. Others protected unions and mandated improved workplace conditions. Still others made the political system more democratic. Populists were instrumental, for example, in winning woman suffrage in Colorado and Idaho, although the united opposition of Democrats and Republicans blocked their efforts to win it in other states. In the South, the Democratic party frustrated reform, and most Alliance Democrats repudiated their Alliance pledges and remained loyal to their party and its traditional opposition to governmental activism.

Populists soon realized that successful reform would require national action. They met in Omaha, Nebraska, on July 4, 1892, to organize a national party and nominated former Greenbacker James B. Weaver for president. The party platform, known as the **Omaha Platform**, is a remarkable statement of principles. Rejecting the laissez-faire policies of the old parties, it declared: "We believe that the powers of government—in other words, of the people, should be expanded . . . to the end that oppression, injustice, and poverty shall eventually cease in the land." The platform demanded government ownership of the railroads and the telegraph and telephone systems, a national currency issued by the government rather than private banks, the subtreasury system, free and unlimited silver coinage, a graduated income tax, and the redistribution to settlers of land held by railroads and speculative corporations. Accompanying resolutions endorsed the direct popular election of senators, the secret ballot, and other electoral reforms to make government more democratic and responsive to popular wishes. When the platform was adopted, "cheers and yells," one reporter wrote, "rose like a tornado from four thousand throats and raged without cessation for 34 minutes, during which women shrieked and wept, men embraced and kissed their neighbors . . . in the ecstasy of their delirium."

The Populists left Omaha to begin an energetic campaign. Weaver toured the western states and with Mary Lease invaded the Democratic stronghold of the South where some Populists like Tom Watson of Georgia tried to mobilize black voters. Southern Democrats, however, used violence and fraud to intimidate Populist voters and cheat Populist candidates out of office. Some local Populist leaders were murdered, and Weaver was driven from the South. One Democrat confessed that Alabama's Populist gubernatorial candidate "carried the state, but was swindled out of his victory . . . with unblushing trickery and corruption." Southern Democrats also appealed effectively to white supremacy, which undermined the Populist effort to build a biracial reform coalition.

Elsewhere, too, Populists met disappointment. Midwestern farmers unfamiliar with Alliance ideas and organization ignored Populist appeals and stood by their traditional political allegiances. So did most eastern working-class voters, who learned little of the Populist program beyond its demand for inflation, which they feared would worsen their own conditions.

The Populists lost the election but showed impressive support for a new organization. They got more than a million votes (one out of every twelve cast), carried several western states, and won hundreds of state offices throughout the West and in pockets of the South like Texas and North Carolina. Populist leaders began immediately working to expand their support, to the alarm of both southern Democrats and northern Republicans.

The Challenge of the Depression

The emergence of a significant third-party movement was but one of many developments that combined by the mid-1890s to produce a national political crisis. A harsh and lengthy depression began in 1893, cruelly worsening conditions not only for farmers but for most other Americans as well. Labor unrest and violence engulfed the nation, reflecting workers' distress but frightening more comfortable Americans. The persistent failure of the major parties to respond to serious problems contributed mightily to growing popular discontent. Together these developments constituted an important challenge to America's new industrial society and its government.

Although the Populists had not triumphed in 1892, the election nonetheless reflected the nation's spreading dissatisfaction. Voters decisively rejected President Harrison and the incumbent Republicans in Congress; turning again to the other major party, they placed the Democrats in control of Congress and Grover Cleveland back in the White House. But the conservative Cleveland was almost oblivious to the mounting demand for reform. He delivered an inaugural address championing the doctrine of laissez-faire and rejecting government action to solve social or economic problems.

Cleveland's resolve was immediately tested when the economy collapsed in the spring of 1893. Railroad overexpansion, a weak banking system, tight credit, and plunging agricultural prices all contributed to the disaster. So too did a depression in Europe, which reduced American export markets and prompted British investors to sell their American investments for gold. Within a few months, hun-

dreds of banks closed, and thousands of businesses, including the nation's major railroads, went bankrupt. By winter, 20 percent of the labor force was unemployed, and the jobless scavenged for food in a country that had no public unemployment or welfare programs. "Never within memory," said one New York minister, "have so many people literally starved to death as in the past few months."

Churches, local charity societies, and labor unions tried to provide relief but were overwhelmed. Most state governments offered little relief beyond encouraging private charity to the homeless. In Kansas, however, the Populist governor insisted that traditional laissez-faire policies were inadequate: "It is the duty of government to protect the weak, because the strong are able to protect themselves." Cleveland disagreed and showed little sympathy for the struggling. The functions of the government, he said in 1893, "do not include the support of the people."

If Cleveland and Congress had no idea how the federal government might respond to the depression, some thoughtful Americans did. Jacob Coxey, a Populist businessman from Ohio, proposed a government public works program for the unemployed to be financed with paper money. This plan would improve the nation's infrastructure, create jobs for the unemployed, and provide an inflationary stimulus to counteract the depression's deflationary effects. In short, Coxey was advocating positive government action to combat the depression. Elements of his plan would be adopted for mitigating economic downturns in the twentieth century; in 1894, it was too untraditional for Congress to consider.

Coxey organized a march of the unemployed to Washington as "a petition with boots on" to support his ideas. **Coxey's Army** of the unemployed, as the excited press dubbed it, marched through the industrial towns of Ohio and Pennsylvania and into Maryland, attracting attention and support. Other armies formed in eastern cities from Boston to Baltimore and set out for the capital. Some of the largest armies organized in the western cities of Denver, San Francisco, and Seattle. Three hundred men in an army from Oakland elected as their commander Anna Smith, who promised to "land my men on the steps of the Capitol at Washington." "I am a San Francisco woman, a woman who has been brought up on this coast, and I'm not afraid of anything," Smith explained. "I have a woman's heart and a woman's sympathy, and these lead me to do what I have done for these men, even though it may not be just what a woman is expected to do."

Lewis Fry, the organizer of the Los Angeles army, declared: "If the government has a right to make us die in time of war, we have the right to demand of

Jacob Coxey's "Army" of the unemployed marches to Washington, D.C., in 1894. Many such "industrial armies" were organized during the depressed 1890s, revealing dissatisfaction with traditional politics and limited government.

her the right to live in time of peace." Fry's five hundred marchers captured a train to cross the desert regions of the Southwest and were feted and fed by townspeople from Tucson to El Paso. When the Southern Pacific uncoupled the train's locomotive and left the marchers stranded without food or water in West Texas for five days, the governor of Texas threatened to hold the railroad responsible for murder "by torture and starvation." Texas citizens quickly raised funds to speed the army on to St. Louis. From there it marched to Washington on foot.

The sympathy and assistance with which Americans greeted these industrial armies reflected more than anxiety over the depression and unemployment. As one economist noted, what distinguished the Populists and Coxeyites from earlier reformers was their appeal for federal action. Their substantial public support suggested a deep dissatisfaction with the failure of the government to respond to the country's social and economic needs.

Nonetheless, the government acted to suppress Coxey. When he reached Washington with six hundred marchers, police and soldiers arrested him and his aides, beat sympathetic bystanders in a crowd of twenty thousand, and herded the marchers into detention camps. Unlike lobbyists for business and finance, Coxey was not permitted to reach Congress to deliver his statement urging

the government to assist "the poor and oppressed."

The depression also provoked labor turmoil. There were some 1,400 industrial strikes involving nearly 700,000 workers in 1894, the largest number of strikers in any year in the nineteenth century. Cleveland had no response except to call for law and order. One result was the government's violent suppression of the Pullman strike (see Chapter 20).

In a series of decisions in 1895, the Supreme Court strengthened the bonds between business and government. First, it upheld the use of a court-ordered injunction to break the Pullman strike. As a result, injunctions became a major weapon for courts and corporations against labor unions until Congress finally limited their use in 1932. Next, in *United States* v. *E. C. Knight Company,* the Court gutted the Sherman Antitrust Act by ruling that manufacturing, as opposed to commerce, was beyond the reach of federal regulation. The Court thus allowed the American Sugar Refining Company, a trust controlling 90 percent of the nation's sugar, to retain its great power. Finally, the Court invalidated an income tax that agrarian Democrats and Populists had maneuvered through Congress. The conservative Court rejected the reform as an "assault upon capital." A dissenting judge noted that the decision gave vested interests "a power and influence" dangerous to the majority of Americans. Not until 1913, and then only with an amendment to the Constitution, would it be possible to adopt an equitable system of taxation. Surveying these developments, farmers and workers increasingly concluded that the government protected powerful interests while ignoring the plight of ordinary Americans.

Certainly the callous treatment shown workers contrasted sharply with Cleveland's concern for bankers as he managed the government's monetary policy in the depression. Cleveland blamed the economic collapse on the Sherman Silver Purchase Act, which he regarded as detrimental to business confidence and a threat to the nation's gold reserve. He persuaded Congress in 1893 to repeal the law, enraging southern and western members of his own party. These Silver Democrats condemned Cleveland for betraying the public good to "the corporate interests." (See "American Views: A Westerner Views Sound Money and American Government.")

Cleveland's policy was ineffective at ending the depression. By 1894, the Treasury had begun borrowing money from Wall Street to bolster the gold reserve. These transactions benefited a syndicate of bankers headed by J. P. Morgan. It seemed to critics that an indifferent Cleveland was helping rich bankers profit from the nation's economic agony. "A set of vampires headed by a financial trust has control of our destiny," cried one rural newspaper.

The Battle of the Standards and the Election of 1896

The government's unpopular actions, coupled with the unrelenting depression, alienated workers and farmers from the Cleveland administration and the Democratic party. In the off-year elections of 1894, the Democrats suffered the greatest loss of congressional seats in American history. Populists increased their vote by 42 percent, making especially significant gains in the South, but the real beneficiaries of the popular hatred of Cleveland and his policies were the Republicans. Denouncing Cleveland's "utter imbecility," they gained solid control of Congress as well as state governments across the North and West. All three parties began to plan for the presidential election of 1896.

As hard times persisted, the silver issue came to overshadow all others. Some Populist leaders, hoping to broaden the party's appeal, had already begun to emphasize silver rather than the more radical but divisive planks of the Omaha Platform. Weaver declared the silver issue "the line upon which the battle should be fought. It is the line of least resistance and we should hurl our forces against it at every point." Many southern and western Democrats, who had traditionally favored silver inflation, also decided to stress the issue, both to undercut the Populists and to distance themselves and their party from the despised Cleveland. In 1895, leading Democrats began using the silver issue to reorganize their party and displace Cleveland and his conservative supporters. They held rallies and conventions across the South and West, distributed silver literature, and argued that free silver would finally end the depression.

The dissension among Democrats pleased Republicans. William McKinley, governor of Ohio and author of the McKinley Tariff Act of 1890, emerged as the leader of a crowd of hopeful Republican presidential candidates. His candidacy benefited particularly from the financial backing and political management of Marcus A. Hanna, a wealthy Ohio industrialist. Hanna thought McKinley's passion for high tariffs as the key to revived prosperity would appeal to workers as well as industry and busi-

ness. As governor, McKinley had reached out to workers by supporting prolabor legislation and by avoiding the anti-Catholic positions that alienated immigrants from the Republicans. Nonetheless, he shared Hanna's conviction that government should actively promote business interests; he was not Hanna's puppet, as opponents sometimes claimed.

Republicans nominated McKinley on the first ballot at their 1896 convention. Their platform called for high tariffs but also endorsed the gold standard, placating eastern delegates but prompting several western Silver Republicans to withdraw from the party.

The Democratic convention met shortly thereafter. Embattled supporters of the gold standard soon learned that the silver crusade had made them a minority in the party. With a fervor that conservatives likened to "scenes of the French Revolution," the Silver Democrats revolutionized their party. They adopted a platform that repudiated the Cleveland administration and its policies and endorsed free silver, the income tax, and tighter regulation of trusts and

William Jennings Bryan in 1896. A powerful orator of great human sympathies, Bryan was adored by his followers as "the majestic man who was hurling defiance in the teeth of the money power." Nominated three times for the presidency by the Democrats, he was never elected.

American Views

A WESTERNER VIEWS SOUND MONEY AND AMERICAN GOVERNMENT

As a terrible depression engulfed America in 1893, Congress debated whether to repeal the Sherman Silver Purchase Act, as demanded by President Grover Cleveland. William Jennings Bryan, a young Democratic congressman from Nebraska, was a prominent opponent of repeal. In the following passages, excerpted from his congressional speeches, he eloquently outlines his views.

❖ **How does Bryan's rhetoric reflect the deep divisions over the money issue?**

❖ **What is Bryan's view of the role of government?**

❖ **In what ways might Populists find Bryan attractive?**

❖ **Can you explain why Bryan thought repeal would hurt Southerners and Westerners?**

The vote of this House on the subject under consideration may bring to the people of the West and South, to the people of the United States, and to all mankind, weal or woe beyond the power of language to describe or imagination to conceive. . . . [A vote to repeal means obeying] the dictation of the moneyed institutions of this country and those who want to appreciate the value of a dollar. . . . It means to increase by billions of dollars the debts of our people. It means a reduction in the price of our wheat and our cotton. . . .

If we who represent them consent to rob our people, the cotton-growers of the South and the wheat-growers of the West, we will be criminals whose guilt cannot be measured by words, for we will bring distress and disaster to our people. In many cases such a vote would simply be a summons to the sheriff to take possession of their property. . . .

The poor man is called a socialist if he believes that the wealth of the rich should be divided among the poor, but the rich man is called a financier if he devises a plan by which the pittance of the poor can be converted to his use. The poor man who takes property by force is called a thief, but the creditor who can by legisla-

railroads. A magnificent speech supporting this platform by William Jennings Bryan helped convince the delegates to nominate him for president. Bryan was only thirty-six years old but had already served in Congress, edited an important newspaper, and gained renown for his oratorical skills and popular sympathies.

Holding their convention last, the Populists now faced a terrible dilemma. The Democratic nomination of Bryan on a silver platform undercut their hopes of attracting into their own ranks disappointed reformers from the major parties. Bryan, moreover, had already worked closely with Nebraska Populists, who now urged the party to endorse him

rather than split the silver vote and ensure the victory of McKinley and the gold standard. Other Populists argued that fusing—joining with the Democrats—would cost the Populists their separate identity and subordinate their larger political principles to the issue of free silver. After anguished discussion, the Populists nominated Bryan for president but named a separate vice presidential candidate, Tom Watson of Georgia, in an effort to maintain their identity. They hoped the Democrats would reciprocate by replacing their nominee with Watson, but the Democrats ignored the overture. The Populists' strength was in the South and West, regions that Bryan would control anyway. They could offer him

tion make a debtor pay a dollar twice as large as he borrowed is lauded as the friend of a sound currency. The man who wants the people to destroy the Government is an anarchist, but the man who wants the Government to destroy the people is a patriot. . . .

Free government cannot long survive when the thousands enjoy the wealth of the country and the millions share its poverty in common. Even now you hear among the rich an occasionally expressed contempt for popular government, and among the poor a protest against legislation which makes them 'toil that others may reap.' I appeal to you to restore justice. . . .

Whence comes this irresistible demand for unconditional repeal? . . . Not from the workshop and the farm, not from the workingmen of this country, who create its wealth in time of peace and protect its flag in time of war, but from the middle-men, from what are termed the "business interests." . . . Go among the agricultural classes; go among the poor, whose little is as precious to them as the rich man's fortune is to him, and whose families are as dear, and you will not find the haste to destroy the issue of money or the unfriendliness to silver which is manifested in money centers.

We have come to the parting of the ways. . . . On the one side stand the corporate interests of the nation, its moneyed institutions, its aggregations of wealth and capital, imperious, arrogant, compassionless. They demand special legislation, favors, privileges, and immunities. They can subscribe magnificently to campaign funds; they can strike down opposition with their all-pervading influence, and, to those who fawn and flatter, bring ease and plenty. They demand that [Congress] . . . execute their merciless decrees.

On the other side stands the unnumbered throng. . . . Work-worn and dust-begrimed, they make their sad appeal. They hear of average wealth increased on every side and feel the inequality of its distribution. They see an overproduction of everything desired because of the underproduction of the ability to buy. They can not pay for loyalty except with their suffrages, and can only punish betrayal with their condemnation. Although the ones who most deserve the fostering care of Government, their cries for help too often beat in vain against the outer wall, while others less deserving find ready access to legislative halls. . . .

"Choose you this day whom ye will serve." What will the answer be?

Source: William Jennings Bryan, The First Battle (Chicago: W. B. Conkey Company, 1896), 77, 81, 83, 103–104, 110–114.

little help in the battle for the Midwest and East, what Bryan called "the enemy's country."

The campaign was intense and dramatic, with each side demonizing the other. Terrified by the thought of Bryan's election, eastern financial and business interests contributed millions of dollars to Hanna's campaign for McKinley. Standard Oil alone provided $250,000, about the same amount as the Democrats' total national expenses. Hanna used these funds to organize an unprecedented educational campaign, warning of economic disaster should Bryan be elected and the bimetallic standard be restored but promising that McKinley's election would finally end the depression. Republicans issued

250 million campaign documents, printed in a dozen languages. They were aided by a national press so completely sympathetic that many newspapers not only shaped their editorials but distorted their news stories to Bryan's disadvantage.

To counteract the Republicans' superior resources, the Democrats relied on Bryan's superb voice, oratorical virtuosity, and youthful energy. Bryan was the first presidential candidate to campaign systematically for election, speaking hundreds of times to millions of voters. By contrast, McKinley stayed home in Canton, Ohio, where he conducted a "front porch" campaign. Explaining his refusal to campaign outside Canton, McKinley

This Republican campaign poster of 1896 depicts William McKinley standing on sound money and promising a revival of prosperity. The depression of the 1890s shifted the electorate into the Republican column.

said, "I might just as well put up a trapeze . . . and compete with some professional athlete as go out speaking against Bryan." But Hanna brought groups of Republicans from all over the country to visit McKinley every day, and McKinley reiterated his simple promise of prosperity.

In the depression, that appeal proved enough. As the Democratic candidate, Bryan was ironically burdened with the legacy of the hated Cleveland administration. The intense campaign brought a record voter turnout. McKinley won decisively by capturing the East and Midwest as well as Oregon and California (see Map 22-2). Bryan carried the traditionally Democratic South and the mountain and plains states where Populists and silverites dominated. He failed to gain support in either the Granger states of the Midwest or the cities of

the East. His silver campaign had little appeal to industrial workers. Hanna realized that Bryan was making a mistake in subordinating other popular grievances to silver: "He's talking silver all the time, and that's where we've got him."

Bryan immediately wrote a personal account of the campaign, which he optimistically titled *The First Battle*. But Bryan and the Democrats would not win subsequent battles, at least not on the issues of the 1890s. The elections of 1894 and 1896 ended the close balance between the major parties. Cleveland's failures, coupled with an economic recovery in the wake of the election of 1896, gained the Republicans a reputation as the party of prosperity and industrial progress, firmly establishing them in power for years to come. By contrast, the Democratic party receded into an ineffectual sectional minority dominated by southern conservatives, despite Bryan's liberal views.

The People's party simply dissolved. Demoralized by fusion with the Democrats, who had earlier violently repressed them, many southern Populists dropped out of politics. The Democrats' disfranchisement laws, directed at discontented poor white Southerners as well as poor black Southerners, further undermined the Populists in the South. In the West, the silver tide of 1896 carried many Populists

Map 22-2   The Election of 1896
William Jennings Bryan carried most of the rural South and West, but his free silver campaign had little appeal to more urban and industrial regions, which swung strongly to Republican candidate William McKinley.

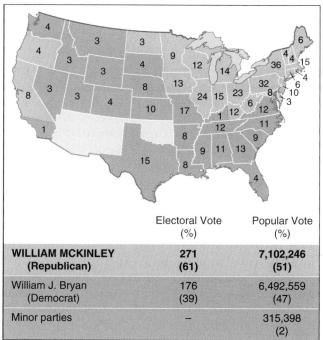

	Electoral Vote (%)	Popular Vote (%)
WILLIAM McKINLEY (Republican)	**271 (61)**	**7,102,246 (51)**
William J. Bryan (Democrat)	176 (39)	6,492,559 (47)
Minor parties	–	315,398 (2)

into office, but with their party collapsing, they had no hope of retaining office. By 1898, the Populist party had virtually disappeared. Its reform legacy, however, proved more enduring. The issues it raised would continue to shape state and national politics.

McKinley plunged into his presidency. Unlike his predecessors, he had a definite, if limited, program, consisting of tariff protection, sound money, and overseas expansion. He worked actively to see it through Congress and to shape public opinion, thereby helping establish the model of the modern presidency. He had promised prosperity, and it returned, although not because of the record high tariff his party enacted in 1897 or the Currency Act of 1900, which firmly established the gold standard. Prosperity returned instead because of reviving markets and a monetary inflation that resulted from the discovery of vast new deposits of gold in Alaska, Australia, and South Africa. The silverites had recognized that an expanding industrial economy required an expanding money supply. Ironically, the new inflation was greater than would have resulted from free silver. With the return of prosperity and the decline of social tensions, McKinley easily won reelection in 1900, defeating Bryan a second time.

Conclusion

In late-nineteenth-century America, politics and government often seemed at cross-purposes. Political contests were exciting events, absorbing public attention, attracting high voter turnout, and often raising issues of symbolic or substantive importance. Closely balanced political parties commanded the zealous support of their constituents and wielded power and influence. The institutions of government, by contrast, were limited in size, scope, and responsibility. A weakened presidency and an inefficient Congress, hampered by a restrictive judiciary, were often unable to resolve the very issues that were so dramatically raised in the political arena. The persistent disputes over tariff and monetary policy illustrate this impasse. But the issue that most reflected it was civil service reform. The patronage system provided the lifeblood of politics but also disrupted government business.

The localism, laissez-faire, and other traditional principles that shaped both politics and government were becoming increasingly inappropriate for America's industrializing society. New challenges were emerging that state and local governments could not effectively solve on their own. The national nature of the railroad network, for example, finally brought the federal government into the regulatory arena, however imperfectly, with the Interstate Commerce Act of 1887. Both the depression of the 1890s and the popular discontent articulated most clearly by the Populist rejection of laissez-faire underscored the need for change and discredited the limited government of the Cleveland administration.

By the end of the decade, the political system had changed. The Republicans had emerged as the dominant party, ending the two-party stalemate of previous decades. Campaign hoopla in local communities had given way to information-based campaigns directed by and through national organizations. A new, activist presidency was emerging. And the disruptive currency issue faded with the hard times that had brought it forth. Still greater changes were on the horizon. The depression and its terrible social and economic consequences undermined traditional ideas about the responsibilities of government and increased public support for activist policies. The stage was set for the Progressive Era.

Review Questions

1. What were the social and institutional factors that shaped the disorderly nature of elections in the late nineteenth century?

2. What social and institutional factors determined the role of government? How and why did the role of government change during this period?

3. What factors determined the party affiliation of American voters? Why did so many third parties develop during this era?

4. How might the planks of the Omaha Platform have helped solve farmers' troubles?

5. What factors shaped the conduct and outcome of the election of 1896? How did that contest differ from earlier elections?

Recommended Reading

Paul Glad, *McKinley, Bryan, and the People* (1964). An excellent brief analysis of the issues and personalities in the 1896 election.

Morton Keller, *Affairs of State: Public Life in Late Nineteenth Century America* (1977). A detailed and fascinating account of the changing dimensions of government and politics.

Robert C. McMath, Jr., *American Populism: A Social History, 1877–1898* (1993). The best modern history of Populism; balanced and readable.

Mark Summers, *The Gilded Age* (1997). A useful survey that effectively captures the complexities of the era.

R. Hal Williams, *Years of Decision: American Politics in the 1890s* (1978). A valuable synthesis of the scholarship on the political currents of the 1890s.

Additional Sources

The Structure and Style of Politics

Peter H. Argersinger, *Structure, Process, and Party* (1992).

Paula Baker, "The Domestication of Politics: Women and American Political Society, 1780–1920," *American Historical Review 89* (1984): 620–647.

Ruth Bordin, *Frances Willard: A Biography* (1986).

Rebecca Edwards, *Angels in the Machinery: Gender in American Party Politics* (1997).

Michael Goldberg, *An Army of Women: Gender and Politics in Gilded Age Kansas* (1997).

Paul Kleppner, *The Third Electoral System, 1853–1892* (1979).

Richard L. McCormick, *The Party Period and Public Policy* (1986).

Michael McGerr, *The Decline of Popular Politics: The American North, 1865–1928* (1988).

Joel H. Silbey, *The American Political Nation, 1838–1893* (1991).

The Limits of Government

Cindy Aron, *Ladies and Gentlemen of the Civil Service: Middle-Class Workers in Victorian America* (1987).

William R. Brock, *Investigation and Responsibility: Public Responsibility in the United States, 1865–1900* (1984).

Ballard C. Campbell, *Representative Democracy: Public Policy and Midwestern Legislatures in the Late Nineteenth Century* (1980).

Sidney Fine, *Laissez-Faire and the General Welfare State* (1956).

John A. Garraty, *The New Commonwealth, 1877–1890* (1968).

Ari Hoogenboom, *Rutherford B. Hayes: Warrior and President* (1996).

David Rothman, *Politics and Power: The United States Senate* (1966).

Stephen Skowronek, *Building a New American State: The Expansion of National Administrative Capacities* (1982).

Margaret S. Thompson, *The "Spider Web": Congress and Lobbying* (1985).

Leonard D. White, *The Republican Era* (1958).

Public Policies and National Elections

Ari Hoogenboom, *Outlawing the Spoils: A History of the Civil Service Movement, 1865–1883* (1961).

Robert D. Marcus, *Grand Old Party: Political Structure in the Gilded Age, 1880–1896* (1971).

H. Wayne Morgan, *From Hayes to McKinley* (1969).

Walter Nugent, *Money and American Society, 1865–1880* (1968).

Joanne Reitano, *The Tariff Question in the Gilded Age: The Great Debate of 1888* (1995).

Gretchen Ritter, *Goldbugs and Greenbacks: The Antimonopoly Tradition and the Politics of Finance* (1997).

Homer E. Socolofsky and Allan B. Spetter, *The Presidency of Benjamin Harrison* (1987).

John Sproat, *"The Best Men": Liberal Reformers in the Gilded Age* (1968).

The Crisis of the 1890s

Peter H. Argersinger, *Populism and Politics: W. A. Peffer and the People's Party* (1974).

Gene Clanton, *Populism: The Humane Preference* (1991).

Lawrence Goodwyn, *The Populist Moment* (1978).

Richard Jensen, *The Winning of the Midwest: Social and Political Conflict, 1888–1896* (1971).

J. Morgan Kousser, *The Shaping of Southern Politics* (1974).

Robert W. Larson, *Populism in the Mountain West* (1986).

Samuel McSeveney, *The Politics of Depression* (1972).

Worth Robert Miller, *Oklahoma Populism* (1987).

Jeffrey Ostler, *Prairie Populism* (1993).

Carlos A. Schwantes, *Coxey's Army: An American Odyssey* (1985).

Barton Shaw, *The Wool-Hat Boys: Georgia's Populist Party* (1984).

Richard Welch, *The Presidencies of Grover Cleveland* (1988).

C. Vann Woodward, *Tom Watson, Agrarian Rebel* (1938).

James E. Wright, *The Politics of Populism: Dissent in Colorado* (1974).

Where to Learn More

❖ **Rest Cottage, Evanston, Illinois.** Frances Willard's home, from which she directed the Woman's Christian Temperance Union, is carefully preserved as a museum. The Willard Memorial Library contains more memorabilia and papers of Willard and the WCTU.

❖ **President Benjamin Harrison Home, Indianapolis, Indiana.** President Harrison's brick Italianate mansion, completed in 1875, has been completely restored with the family's furniture and keepsakes. The former third-floor ballroom serves as a museum with exhibits of many artifacts of the Harrisons' public and private lives.

❖ **Fairview, Lincoln, Nebraska.** A National Historic Landmark, Fairview was the home of William Jennings Bryan, who described it as "the Monticello of the West." Faithfully restored to depict the Bryan family's life in the early 1900s, it includes a museum and interpretive center.

❖ **Susan B. Anthony House National Historic Landmark, Rochester, New York.** This modest house was the home of the prominent suffragist and contains Anthony's original furnishings and personal photographs.

❖ **Rutherford B. Hayes Presidential Center, Fremont, Ohio.** This complex contains President Hayes's home, office, and extensive grounds together with an excellent library and museum holding valuable collections of manuscripts, artifacts, and photographs illustrating his personal interests and political career.

❖ **James A. Garfield Home, Mentor, Ohio.** Operated by the Western Reserve Historical Society as a museum, Garfield's home is the site of his successful 1880 front-porch campaign for president.

THE PROGRESSIVE ERA, 1900–1917

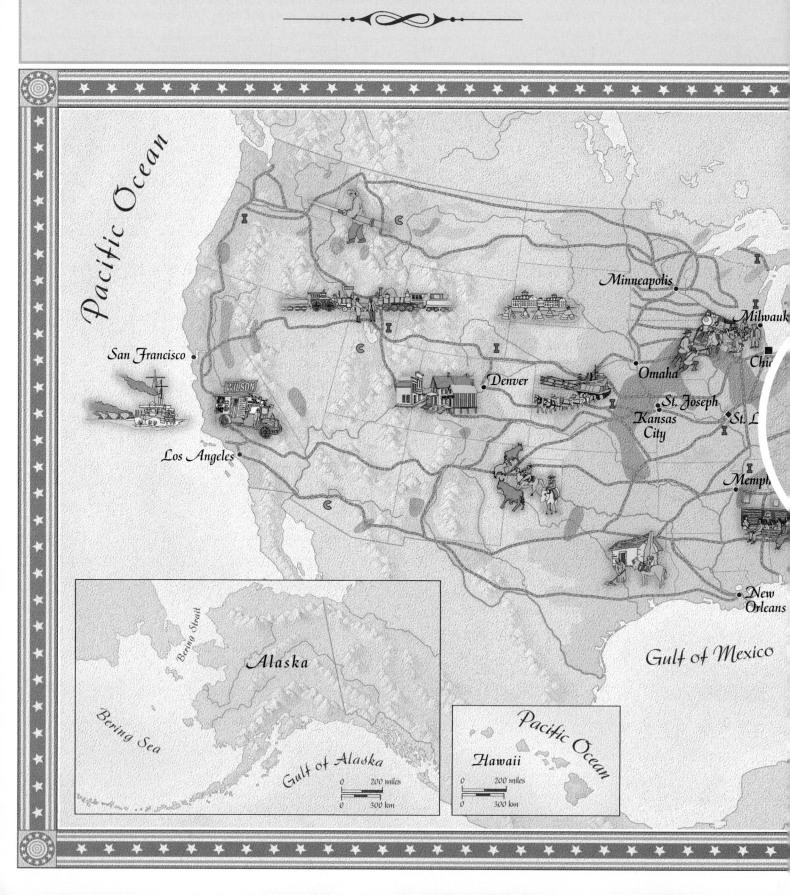

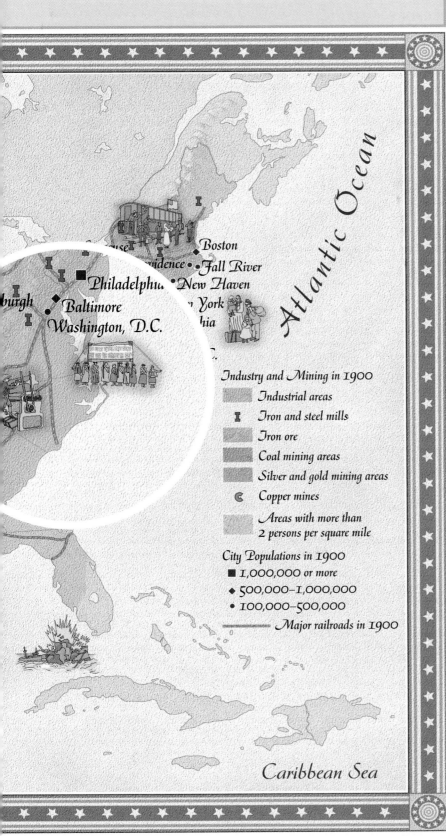

Industry and Mining in 1900

- Industrial areas
- I Iron and steel mills
- Iron ore
- Coal mining areas
- Silver and gold mining areas
- ☾ Copper mines
- Areas with more than 2 persons per square mile

City Populations in 1900
- ■ 1,000,000 or more
- ◆ 500,000–1,000,000
- • 100,000–500,000
- ——— Major railroads in 1900

Atlantic Ocean

Boston, Providence, Fall River, Philadelphia, New Haven, New York, Baltimore, Washington, D.C., Pittsburgh

Caribbean Sea

23

Chapter Outline

The Ferment of Reform
The Context of Reform
Church and Campus
Muckrakers
The Gospel of Efficiency
Labor's Demand for Rights
Extending the Woman's Sphere
Socialism/Opponents of Reform

Reforming Society
Settlement Houses and Urban Reform
Protective Legislation for Women and Children
Reshaping Public Education
Challenging Gender Restrictions
Reforming Country Life
Social Control and Moral Crusades
For Whites Only?

Reforming Politics and Government
Woman Suffrage/Electoral Reform
Municipal Reform
Progressive State Government

Roosevelt and the Progressive Presidency
TR and the Modern Presidency
Roosevelt and Labor
Managing Natural Resources
Corporate Regulation
Taft and the Insurgents

Woodrow Wilson and Progressive Reform
The Election of 1912
Implementing the New Freedom
The Expansion of Reform

Key Topics

❖ The nature of progressivism
❖ Women and progressivism
❖ Antidemocratic aspects of progressivism
❖ Strengthening of the executive under Roosevelt
❖ Climax of progressivism under Woodrow Wilson

*T*omorrow Woodrow Wilson would be inaugurated as the nation's president. But today, March 3, 1913, Washington, D.C., belonged to America's women. Women had poured into the capital from across the country. The Army of the Hudson, a group of New York women, had marched for three weeks to reach Washington. Trains carried women of all social backgrounds from every state. Illinois women captured the public's attention with their "Manless Special," a train carrying—and run by—only women.

They came to participate in a great protest parade demanding **woman suffrage**—the right of women to vote—a reform that Woodrow Wilson declined to endorse. Before half a million spectators, the women set out down Pennsylvania Avenue. Behind a banner reading "Women of the World, Unite!" rolled elaborate floats representing countries where women already had the vote. Another column of floats portrayed working women: farmers, wage earners, homemakers, government employees, and professionals, including nurses, teachers, and social workers. Large groups of women paraded with each float. Two hundred striking garment workers fresh from their picket lines in Baltimore marched with a float depicting a sweatshop. In the education division, black women in caps and gowns from Howard University walked with students from Bryn Mawr, Goucher, and other colleges. Nine-month-old Mei Ching Wu, her mother a student at George Washington University, was the parade's youngest member. Bringing up the rear were members of the National Men's League for Woman Suffrage.

Many spectators cheered, but thousands of others insulted the suffragists, broke into their ranks, attacked their floats, and blocked their passage. The embattled women fought their way "foot by foot up Pennsylvania Avenue through two walls of antagonistic humanity," reported an astonished observer. They finally gained some help when male supporters counterattacked their assailants. Even so, the parade could not be completed until troops restored order. Hundreds were hospitalized. "No inauguration has ever produced such scenes," noted one reporter, "which in many instances amounted to nothing less than riots."

This remarkable incident dramatically illustrated critical features of life in the **Progressive Era**. Important movements challenged traditional relationships and attitudes—here involving women's role in American life—and often met strong resistance. "Progressives" seeking reforms organized their supporters across lines of class, education, occupation, geography, gender, and, at times, race and ethnicity—as the variety of groups in the suffrage parade demonstrated. Rather than rely on traditional partisan politics, reformers adopted new political techniques, including lobbying and demonstrating, as nonpartisan pressure groups. Reform work begun at the local and state levels—where the suffrage movement had already met some success—inexorably moved to the national level as the federal government expanded its authority and became the focus of political interest. Finally, this suffrage demonstration revealed the exceptional diversity of the progressive movement, for the women marched, in part, against Woodrow Wilson, who had campaigned for the presidency as a progressive.

However, woman suffrage did not define progressivism. Indeed, in a sense, there was no "progressive movement," for progressivism had no unifying organization, central leadership, or consensus on objectives. Instead, it represented the coalescing of different and sometimes even contradictory movements that sought changes in the nation's social, economic, and political life. But reformers did share certain convictions. They believed that industrialization and urbanization had produced serious social disorders, from city slums to corporate abuses. They believed that new ideas and methods were required to correct these problems. In particular, they rejected the ideology of individualism in favor of broader concepts of social responsibility, and they sought to achieve social order through organization and efficiency. Finally, most progressives believed that government itself, as the organized agent of public responsibility, should address social and economic problems.

Other Americans resisted the progressives' plans. The interaction among the reformers and the conflict with their opponents made the two decades before World War I a period of remarkable ferment and excitement. The progressives' achievements, and their failures, profoundly shaped America.

The great woman suffrage parade leaves Capitol Hill and heads for the White House, March 3, 1913. Dramatic tactics and careful organizing like those that marked this parade helped secure reform in the Progressive Era.

The Ferment of Reform

The diversity of progressivism reflected the diverse impulses of reform. Reformers responded to the tensions of industrialization and urbanization by formulating programs according to their own interests and priorities. Clergy and professors provided new ideas to guide remedial action. Journalists exposed corporate excesses and government corruption and stirred public demand for reform. Business leaders sought to curtail disorder through efficiency and regulation, while industrial workers struggled to improve the horrible conditions in which they worked and lived. Women organized to protect their families and homes from new threats and even to push beyond such domestic issues. Nearly every movement for change encountered fierce opposition. But in raising new issues and proposing new ideas, progressives helped America grapple with the problems of industrial society. (See the overview table, "Major Progressive Organizations and Groups.")

The Context of Reform: Industrial and Urban Tensions

The origins of progressivism lay in the crises of the new urban-industrial order that emerged in the late nineteenth century. The severe depression and consequent mass suffering of the 1890s, the labor violence and industrial armies, the political challenges of Populism and an obviously ineffective government shattered the complacency many middle-class Americans had felt about their nation and made them aware of social and economic inequities that rural and working-class families had long recognized. Many Americans began to question the validity of social Darwinism and the laissez-faire policies that had justified unregulated industrial growth. They began to reconsider the responsibilities of government and, indeed, of themselves for social order and betterment.

By 1900, a returning prosperity had eased the threat of major social violence, but the underlying problems intensified. Big business, which had disrupted traditional economic relationships in the late nineteenth century, suddenly became bigger in a series of mergers between 1897 and 1903, resulting in huge new business combinations. The formation in 1901 of the United States Steel Corporation, the world's largest firm, symbolized this development. Such giant corporations threatened to squeeze opportunities for small firms and workers, dominate markets, and raise social tensions. They also inspired calls for public control.

Industrial growth affected factory workers most directly. Working conditions were difficult and often dangerous. Most workers still toiled nine to ten hours a day; steelworkers and textile employees usually worked twelve-hour shifts. Wages were minimal; an economist in 1905 calculated that 60 percent of all adult male breadwinners made less than a living wage. Family survival, then, often required women and children to work, often in the lowest-paid, most exploited positions. Southern cotton mills employed children as young as seven; coal mines paid twelve-year-old slate pickers thirty-nine cents for a ten-hour day. Poor ventilation, dangerous fumes, open machinery, and an absence of safety programs threatened not only workers' health but their lives as well. Such conditions were gruesomely illustrated in 1911 when a fire killed 146 workers, most of them young women, trapped inside the factory of the **Triangle Shirtwaist Company** in New York because management had locked the exits. The fire chief found "skeletons bending over sewing machines." The United States had the highest rate of industrial accidents in the world. Half a million workers were injured and thirty thousand killed at work each year. These terrible conditions cried out for reform.

Other Americans saw additional social problems in the continuing flood of immigrants who were transforming America's cities. From 1900 to 1917,

OVERVIEW

MAJOR PROGRESSIVE ORGANIZATIONS AND GROUPS

Group	Activity
Social Gospel movement	Urged churches and individuals to apply Christian ethics to social and economic problems
Muckrakers	Exposed business abuses, public corruption, and social evils through investigative journalism
Settlement House movement	Attempted through social work and public advocacy to improve living and working conditions in urban immigrant communities
National Consumers League (1898)	Monitored businesses to ensure decent working conditions and safe consumer products
Women's Trade Union League (1903)	United workingwomen and their middle-class "allies" to promote unionization and social reform
National Child Labor Committee (1904)	Campaigned against child labor
Country Life movement	Attempted to modernize rural social and economic conditions according to urban-industrial standards
National American Woman Suffrage Association	Led the movement to give women the right to vote
Municipal reformers	Sought to change the activities and structure of urban government to promote efficiency and control
Conservationists	Favored efficient management and regulation of natural resources rather than uncontrolled development or preservation

more than 14 million immigrants entered the United States, and most became urban dwellers. By 1910, immigrants and their children comprised more than 70 percent of the population of New York, Chicago, Buffalo, Milwaukee, and other cities. Most of the arrivals were so-called new immigrants from southern and eastern Europe, rather than the British, Irish, Germans, and Scandinavians who had arrived earlier. More than 3 million Italians disembarked; another 2.5 million came from the diverse nationalities of the Russian empire. Several hundred thousand Japanese also arrived, primarily in California, as did increasing numbers of Mexicans. Crowding into urban slums, immigrants overwhelmed municipal sanitation, education, and fire protection services. One Russian described his new life as "all filth and sadness."

Many native-born Americans associated the immigrants with rampant urban crime and disease and with city bosses and government corruption. Ethnic prejudices abounded. Woodrow Wilson, then president of Princeton University, declared in 1902: "The immigrant newcomers of recent years are men of the lowest class from the South of Italy, and men of the meaner sort out of Hungary and Poland, men out of the ranks where there was neither skill nor energy, nor any initiative or quick intelligence." Americans of the Old Stock often considered the predominantly Catholic and Jewish newcomers a threat to social stability and cultural identity and so demanded programs to reform either the urban environment or the immigrants themselves.

Church and Campus

Many groups, drawing from different traditions and inspirations, responded to such economic and social issues. Reform-minded Protestant ministers were es-

CHRONOLOGY

1893–1898   Depression grips the nation.

1898   South Dakota adopts initiative and referendum.

National Consumers' League is organized.

1900   Robert La Follette is elected governor of Wisconsin.

1901   United States Steel Corporation is formed, the world's largest business at the time.

President William McKinley is assassinated; Theodore Roosevelt becomes president.

Socialist Party of America is organized.

Galveston, Texas, initiates the city commission plan.

1902   Antitrust suit is filed against Northern Securities Company.

Mississippi enacts the first direct primary law.

National Reclamation Act is passed.

Roosevelt intervenes in coal strike.

1903   Women's Trade Union League is organized.

1904   National Child Labor Committee is formed.

Roosevelt is elected president.

1905   Industrial Workers of the World is organized.

1906   Hepburn Act strengthens the Interstate Commerce Commission.

Meat Inspection Act extends government regulation.

Pure Food and Drug Act is passed.

1908   *Muller* v. *Oregon* upholds maximum workday for women.

William Howard Taft is elected president.

1910   National Association for the Advancement of Colored People is organized.

Ballinger-Pinchot controversy erupts.

1912   Children's Bureau is established.

Progressive Party organizes and nominates Roosevelt.

Woodrow Wilson is elected president.

1913   Sixteenth and Seventeenth Amendments are ratified.

Underwood-Simmons Tariff Act establishes an income tax.

Federal Reserve Act creates the Federal Reserve System.

1914   Federal Trade Commission is established.

Harrison Act criminalizes narcotics.

1915   National Birth Control League is formed.

1916   Keating-Owen Act prohibits child labor.

1917   Congress enacts literacy test for immigrants.

1920   Nineteenth Amendment is ratified.

---

pecially influential, creating the **Social Gospel movement**, which sought to introduce religious ethics into industrial relations and appealed to churches to meet their social responsibilities. Washington Gladden, a Congregational minister in Columbus, Ohio, was one of the earliest Social Gospelers. Shocked in 1884 by a bloody strike crushed by wealthy members of his own congregation, Gladden began a ministry to working-class neighborhoods that most churches ignored. He endorsed unions and workers' rights and proposed replacing a cruelly competitive wage system with profit sharing.

A more profound exponent of the Social Gospel was Walter Rauschenbusch, a Baptist minister who had served impoverished immigrants in New York's slums. In his book *Christianity and the Social Crisis* (1907), he argued that Christians should support so-cial reform to alleviate poverty, slums, and labor exploitation. He attacked low wages for transforming workers "into lean, sallow, hopeless, stupid, and vicious young people, simply to enable some group of stockholders to earn 10 percent." Such ideas were popularized by Charles Sheldon, a Kansas minister whose book *In His Steps* sold 23 million copies and called on Americans to act in their daily lives as they believed Jesus Christ would in the same circumstances.

The Social Gospel was part of an emerging liberal movement in American religion. Scholars associated with this movement discredited the literal accuracy of the Bible and emphasized instead its general moral and ethical lessons. These modernists also abandoned theological dogmatism for a greater tolerance of other faiths and became more interested in social problems. To some extent, liberal Protestantism had its Jewish and Catholic counterparts. Reform Judaism renounced certain ancient religious practices and favored adapting to American life; liberal Catholics urged their church to modernize its theological and social positions, especially by showing sympathy for labor unions. But most Jewish immigrants followed Old World habits, and liberal Catholicism was checked in 1907 when Pope Pius X condemned modernism for questioning the church's authority.

Thus the Social Gospel movement flowered among certain Protestant denominations, especially Episcopalians, Congregationalists, and Methodists. It climaxed in 1908 in the formation of the Federal Council of Churches of Christ in America. The council, representing thirty-three religious groups, adopted a program that endorsed welfare and regulatory legislation to achieve social justice. By linking reform with religion (as "applied Christianity," in the words of Washington Gladden), the Social Gospel movement gave progressivism a powerful moral drive that affected much of American life.

The Social Gospel movement provided an ethical justification for government intervention to improve the social order. Scholars in the social sciences also gradually helped turn public attitudes in favor of reform by challenging the laissez-faire views of social Darwinists and traditional academics. In *Applied Sociology* (1906), Lester Ward called for social progress through rational planning and government intervention rather than through unrestrained and unpredictable competition. Economists rejected laissez-faire principles in favor of state action to accomplish social evolution. Industrialization, declared economist Richard T. Ely, "has brought to the front a vast number of social problems whose solution is impossible without the united efforts of church, state, and science."

Muckrakers

Journalists also spread reform ideas by developing a new form of investigative reporting known as **muckraking.** Technological innovations that sharply reduced production costs had recently made possible the mass circulation of magazines, and editors competed to attract an expanding urban readership. Samuel S. McClure was the first to introduce promotional gimmicks and serialized popular fiction in *McClure's Magazine;* he then sent his reporters to uncover political and corporate corruption. Sensational exposés sold magazines, and soon *Cosmopolitan, Everybody's,* and other journals began publishing investigations of business abuses, dangerous working conditions, and the miseries of slum life.

Muckraking articles aroused indignant public demands for reform. Lincoln Steffens detailed the corrupt links between "respectable" businessmen and crooked urban politicians in a series of articles called "The Shame of the Cities." Ida Tarbell revealed John D. Rockefeller's sordid construction of Standard Oil. Muckraking novels also appeared. *The Octopus* (1901), by Frank Norris, dramatized the Southern Pacific Railroad's stranglehold on California's farmers, and *The Jungle* (1906), by Upton Sinclair, exposed nauseating conditions in Chicago's meatpacking industry.

The Gospel of Efficiency

Many progressive leaders believed that efficiency and expertise could control or resolve the disorder of industrial society. President Theodore Roosevelt (1901–1909)—who called muckrakers irresponsible radicals—spoke for more moderate reformers by praising the "gospel of efficiency." Like many other progressives, he admired corporations' success in applying management techniques to guide economic growth. Drawing from science and technology as well as from the model of the corporation, many progressives attempted to manage or direct change efficiently. They used scientific methods to collect extensive data and relied on experts for analysis and recommendations. "Scientific management," a concept often used interchangeably with "sound business management," seemed the key to eliminating waste and inefficiency in government, society, and industry. Rural reformers thought that "scientific agriculture" could bring prosperity to the impoverished southern countryside; urban reformers believed that improvements in medical science and the professionalization of physicians through uniform state licensing standards could eradicate the cities' wretched health problems.

Business leaders especially advocated efficiency, order, and organization. Industrialists were drawn to the ideas of Frederick Taylor, a proponent of scientific management, for cutting factory labor costs. Taylor proposed to increase worker efficiency through imposed work routines, speedups, and mechanization. Workers, Taylor insisted, should "do what they are told promptly and without asking questions. . . . It is absolutely necessary for every man in our organization to become one of a train of gear wheels." By assigning workers simple and repetitive tasks on machines, Taylorization made their skills expendable and enabled managers to control the production, pace of work, and hiring and firing of personnel. Stripped of their influence and poorly paid, factory workers shared little of the wealth generated by industrial expansion and scientific management. When labor complained, one business leader declared that unions failed "to appreciate the progressivism of the age."

Sophisticated managers of big business combinations saw some forms of government intervention as another way to promote order and efficiency. In particular, they favored regulations that could bring about safer and more stable conditions in society and the economy. Government regulations, they reasoned, could reassure potential consumers, open markets, mandate working conditions that smaller competitors could not provide, or impose systematic procedures that competitive pressures would otherwise undercut.

Labor's Demand for Rights

Industrial workers with different objectives also hastened the ferment of reform. Workers resisted the new rules of efficiency experts and called for improved wages and working conditions and reduced work hours. They and their middle-class sympathizers sought to achieve some of these goals through state intervention, demanding laws to compensate workers injured on the job, curb child labor, and regulate the employment of women. Sometimes they succeeded. After the Triangle Shirtwaist fire, for example, urban politicians with working-class constituencies created the New York State Factory Commission and enacted dozens of laws dealing with fire hazards, machine safety, and wages and hours for women.

Workers also organized unions to improve their lot. The American Federation of Labor (AFL) claimed 4 million members by 1920. But it recruited mainly skilled workers, particularly native-born white males. New unions organized the factories and sweatshops where most immigrants and women worked. Despite strong employer resistance, the International Ladies Garment Workers Union (1900) and the Amalgamated Clothing Workers (1914) organized the garment trades, developed programs for social and economic reforms, and led their members—mostly young Jewish and Italian women—in spectacular strikes. The "Uprising of the 20,000," a 1909 strike in New York City, included months of massive rallies, determined picketing, and police repression. One observer marveled at the women strikers'

"emotional endurance, fearlessness, and entire willingness to face danger and suffering."

A still more radical union tried to organize miners, lumberjacks, and Mexican and Japanese farm workers in the West, black dockworkers in the South, and immigrant factory hands in New England. Founded in 1905, the Industrial Workers of the World (IWW), whose members were known as "**Wobblies**," used sit-down strikes, sit-ins, and mass rallies, tactics adopted by other industrial unions in the 1930s and the civil rights movement in the 1960s. "Respectable people" considered the Wobblies violent revolutionaries, but most of the violence was committed against them. Private employers and public officials used every method, legal and illegal, to destroy the Wobblies, but broader labor unrest nonetheless stimulated the reform impulse.

Extending the Woman's Sphere

Women reformers and their organizations played a key role in progressivism. Women responded not merely to the human suffering caused by industrialization and urbanization but also to related changes in their own status and role. By the early twentieth century, more women than before were working outside the home—in the factories, mills, and sweatshops of the industrial economy and as clerks in stores and offices. In 1910, more than a fourth of all workers were women, increasing numbers of them married. Their importance in the

Striking garment workers and their supporters in the 1909 "Uprising" in New York City. Working women and their allies contributed to the growing pressure for improved working conditions.

workforce and participation in unions and strikes challenged assumptions that woman's "natural" role was to be a submissive housewife. Shrinking family size, labor-saving household equipment, and changing social expectations enabled middle-class women to find more time and opportunities to pursue activities outside the home. Better educated than previous generations, they also acquired interests, information, skills, and confidence relevant to a larger public setting.

The women's clubs that had begun multiplying in the late nineteenth century became seedbeds of progressive ideas in the early twentieth century. Often founded for cultural purposes, women's clubs soon adopted programs for social reform and gave their members a route to public influence. In 1914, an officer of the General Federation of Women's Clubs proudly declared that every cause for social reform had "received a helpful hand from the clubwomen." Generally, however, the clubs focused on public issues affecting women, home, and family.

Women also joined or created other organizations that pushed beyond the limits of traditional domesticity. "Woman's place is in the home," observed one progressive, but "no longer is the home encompassed by four walls." By threatening healthy and happy homes, urban problems required that women become "social housekeepers" in the community. The National Congress of Mothers, organized in 1897, worried about crime and disease and championed kindergartens, foster-home programs, juvenile courts, and compulsory school attendance.

Still more aggressive were the National Consumers' League, formed in 1898, and the Women's Trade Union League (WTUL; 1903), both of which organized women across class lines to promote social change. Led by the crusading Florence Kelley, the National Consumers' League tried to protect both women wage earners and middle-class housewives by monitoring stores and factories to ensure decent working conditions and safe products. The WTUL united working women and their self-styled middle-class "allies" to unionize women workers and eliminate sweatshop conditions. Its greatest success came in the 1909 garment workers' strike when the allies—dubbed by one worker the "mink brigade"—assisted strikers with relief funds, bail money, food supplies, and public relations campaign. This cooperation, declared one WTUL official, demonstrated the "sisterhood of women."

Although most progressive women stressed women's special duties and responsibilities as social housekeepers, others began to demand women's equal rights. In 1914, for example, critics of New York's policy of dismissing women teachers who married formed a group called the Feminist Alliance

and demanded "the removal of all social, political, economic and other discriminations which are based upon sex, and the award of all rights and duties in all fields on the basis of individual capacity alone." With these new organizations and ideas, women gave important impetus and direction to the reform sentiments of the early twentieth century.

Socialism

The growing influence of socialist ideas also promoted the spirit of progressivism. Socialists never attracted a large following, even among workers (see Chapter 20), but their criticism of the industrial economy gained increasing attention in the early twentieth century. American socialists condemned social and economic inequities, criticized limited government, and demanded public ownership of railroads, utilities, and communications. They also campaigned for tax reforms, better housing, factory inspections, and recreational facilities for all. Muckrakers like Lincoln Steffens and Upton Sinclair were committed socialists, as were some Social Gospel ministers and labor leaders, but the most prominent socialist was Eugene Debs. In 1901, Debs helped organize the Socialist Party of America. In the next decade, the party won many local elections, especially in Wisconsin and New York, where it drew support from German and Russian immigrants, and in Oklahoma, among poor tenant farmers. Socialism was also promoted by newspapers and magazines, including the *Appeal to Reason* in Girard, Kansas, which had a circulation of 500,000 by 1906. "Socialism is coming," the *Appeal* proclaimed. "It's coming like a prairie fire and nothing can stop it."

Most progressives considered socialist ideas too drastic. Nevertheless, socialists contributed importantly to the reform ferment, not only by providing support for reform initiatives but often also by prompting progressives to push for some changes to undercut increasingly attractive radical alternatives.

Opponents of Reform

Not all Americans supported progressive reforms, and many people regarded as progressives on some issues opposed change in other areas. Social Gospeler Rauschenbusch, for instance, opposed expanding women's rights. More typically, opponents of reform held consistently traditional attitudes, like the conservatives who saw in feminism the orthodox bogies of "non-motherhood, free love, easy divorce, economic independence for all women, and other demoralizing and destructive theories."

Social Gospelers themselves faced opposition. Reacting to the rise of religious liberalism, Protestant traditionalists emphasized what they termed fundamental beliefs. Particularly strong among evangelical denominations with rural roots, these **fundamentalists** stressed personal salvation rather than social reform. "To attempt reform in the black depths of the great city," said one, "would be as useless as trying to purify the ocean by pouring into it a few gallons of spring water." Indeed, the urban and industrial crises that inspired Social Gospelers to preach reform drove many evangelical leaders to endorse social and political conservatism. The most famous evangelist, the crude but spellbinding Billy Sunday, scorned all reforms but prohibition and denounced labor unions, women's rights, and business regulation as violating traditional values. Declaring that the Christian mission was only to save individual souls, he condemned the Social Gospel as "godless social service nonsense" and attacked its advocates as "infidels and atheists."

The charismatic Eugene Debs, here speaking at Canton, Ohio, led American socialists in demanding radical economic and political changes. Debs twice received more than 900,000 votes for president.

Business interests angered by exposés of corporate abuse and corruption attacked muckrakers. To capture public opinion, business groups like the American Bankers' Association accused muckrakers of promoting socialism. Major corporations like Standard Oil created public relations bureaus to improve their image and to identify business, not its critics, with the public interest. "The voice of the public," one press agent proclaimed, was "spoken through the Chamber of Commerce." Advertising boycotts discouraged magazines from running critical stories, and credit restrictions forced some muckraking journals to suspend publication. By 1910, the heyday of muckraking was over.

Labor unions likewise encountered resistance. Led by the National Association of Manufacturers, business groups denounced unions as corrupt and radical, hired thugs to disrupt them, organized strikebreaking agencies, and used blacklists to eliminate union activists. The antiunion campaign peaked in Ludlow, Colorado, in 1914. John D. Rockefeller's Colorado Fuel and Iron Company used armed guards and the state militia to shoot and burn striking workers and their families. The courts aided employers by issuing injunctions against strikes and prohibited unions from using boycotts, one of their most effective weapons.

Progressives campaigning for government intervention and regulation also met stiff resistance. Many Americans objected to what they considered unwarranted interference in private economic matters. Their political representatives were called the "Old Guard," implying their opposition to political and economic change. The courts often supported these attitudes. In *Lochner* v. *New York* (1905), the Supreme Court overturned a maximum-hours law on the grounds that it deprived employers and employees of their "freedom of contract." Progressives constantly had to struggle with such opponents, and progressive achievements were limited by the persistence and influence of their adversaries.

Reforming Society

With their varied motives and objectives, progressives worked to transform society by improving living conditions, educational opportunities, family life, and social and industrial relations. (See the overview table, "Major Laws and Constitutional Amendments of the Progressive Era.") They sought what they called "social justice," but their plans for social reform sometimes also smacked of social control—coercive efforts to impose uniform standards on a diverse population. Organized women dominated the movement to reform society, but they

OVERVIEW

MAJOR LAWS AND CONSTITUTIONAL AMENDMENTS OF THE PROGRESSIVE ERA

Legislation	Effect
New York Tenement House Law (1901)	Established a model housing code for safety and sanitation
Newlands Act (1902)	Provided for federal irrigation projects
Hepburn Act (1906)	Strengthened authority of the Interstate Commerce Commission
Pure Food and Drug Act (1906)	Regulated the production and sale of food and drug products
Meat Inspection Act (1906)	Authorized federal inspection of meat products
Sixteenth Amendment (1913)	Authorized a federal income tax
Seventeenth Amendment (1913)	Mandated the direct popular election of senators
Underwood-Simmons Tariff Act (1913)	Lowered tariff rates and levied the first regular federal income tax
Federal Reserve Act (1913)	Established the Federal Reserve System to supervise banking and provide a national currency
Federal Trade Commission Act (1914)	Established the FTC to oversee business activities
Harrison Act (1914)	Regulated the distribution and use of narcotics
Smith-Lever Act (1914)	Institutionalized the county agent system
Keating-Owen Act (1916)	Indirectly prohibited child labor
Eighteenth Amendment (1919)	Instituted prohibition
Nineteenth Amendment (1920)	Established woman suffrage

were supported, depending on the goal, by Social Gospel ministers, social scientists, urban immigrants, labor unions, and even some conservatives eager to regulate personal behavior.

Settlement Houses and Urban Reform

The spearheads for social reform were settlement houses, community centers in urban immigrant neighborhoods. Reformers created four hundred settlement houses, largely modeled after Hull House in Chicago, founded in 1889 by Jane Addams. Settlement houses often reflected the ideals of the Social Gospel. "A simple acceptance of Christ's message and methods," wrote Addams, "is what a settlement should stand for." Yet most were secular institutions, avoiding religion to gain the trust of Catholic and Jewish immigrants.

Most settlements were led and staffed primarily by middle-class young women, seeking to alleviate poverty and do useful, professional work when most careers were closed to them. Settlement work did not immediately violate prescribed gender roles because it initially focused on the "woman's sphere": family, education, domestic skills, and cultural "uplift." Thus settlement workers organized kindergartens and nurseries; taught classes in English, cooking, and personal hygiene; held musical performances and poetry readings; and sponsored recreation.

However, settlement workers soon saw that the root problem for immigrants was widespread poverty that required more than changes in individual behavior. Unlike earlier reformers, they regarded many of the evils of poverty as products of the social environment rather than of moral weakness. Slum-dwellers, Addams sadly noted, suffered from "poisonous sewage, contaminated water, infant mortality, adulterated food, smoke-laden air, juvenile crime, and unwholesome crowding." Thus settlement workers campaigned for stricter building codes to improve slums, better urban sanitation systems to enhance public health, public parks to revive the urban environment, and laws to protect women and children.

Their crusade for housing reform demonstrated the impact that social reformers often had on urban life. His work at the University Settlement in New York City convinced Lawrence Veiller that "the improvement of the homes of the people was the starting point for everything." Organizing pressure groups to promote tenement house reform, Veiller relied on settlement workers to help investigate housing conditions, prepare public exhibits depicting rampant disease in congested slums, and agitate for improvements. Based on their findings, Veiller drafted a new housing code limiting the size of tenements and requiring toilet facilities, ventilation, and fire protection. In 1901, the New York Tenement House Law became a model for other cities. To promote uniform building codes throughout the nation, the tireless Veiller founded the National Housing Association in 1910.

Protective Legislation for Women and Children

While settlement workers initially undertook private efforts to improve society, many reformers eventually concluded that only government power could achieve social justice. They demanded that state and federal governments protect the weak or disadvantaged. As Veiller insisted, it was "unquestionably the duty of the state" to enforce justice in the face of "greed on the part of those who desire to secure for themselves an undue profit."

The maiming and killing of children in industrial accidents made it "inevitable," Addams said, "that efforts to secure a child labor law should be our first venture into the field of state legislation." The National Child Labor Committee, organized in 1904, led the campaign to curtail child labor (see Figure 23-1). Reformers documented the problem with extensive investigations and also benefited from the public outrage stirred by socialist John Spargo's muckraking book *The Bitter Cry of the Children* (1906). In 1900, most states had no minimum working age; by 1914, every state but one had such a law. Effective regulation, however, required national action, for many state laws were weak or poorly enforced (see "American Views: Mother Jones and the Meaning of Child Labor in America").

Stiff resistance came from manufacturers who used child labor, conservatives who opposed government action as an intrusion into family life, and some poor parents who needed their children's income. But finally Congress in 1912 established the **Children's Bureau** to investigate the welfare of children. Julia Lathrop, from Hull House, directed the Bureau, the first government agency headed and staffed almost entirely by women. In 1916, the Keating-Owen Act prohibited the interstate shipment of goods manufactured by children. But the law was weaker than that of many states and did not cover most child workers. Even so, the Supreme Court declared the measure unconstitutional.

Figure 23-1   *Child labor, 1870–1930.*
Nearly 2 million children worked in factories and fields in 1900, twice the number as in 1870. Progressives' efforts to curtail child labor through laws for compulsory education and a minimum working age encountered resistance, and change came slowly.
Data Source: U.S. Bureau of the Census.

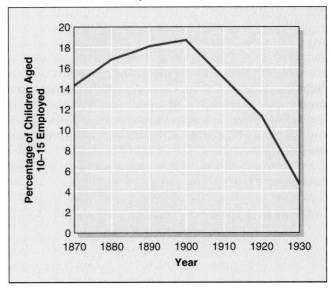

The famous photographer Lewis Hine used his camera to document child labor. The eight-year-old girl on the right in this 1911 photograph of women and children working in an Alabama canning factory had been shucking oysters for three years.

Social reformers also lobbied for laws regulating the wages, hours, and working conditions of women and succeeded in having states from New York to Oregon pass maximum-hours legislation. After the Supreme Court upheld such laws in *Muller* v. *Oregon* (1908), thirty-nine states enacted new or stronger laws on women's maximum hours between 1909 and 1917. Fewer states established minimum wages for women. In 1912, Massachusetts created a commission with the power to recommend such wages, and within a year, eight midwestern and western states authorized wage commissions to set binding rates. But few other states followed these examples.

Protective legislation for women posed a troubling issue for reformers. In California, for example, middle-class clubwomen favored protective legislation on grounds of women's presumed weakness. They wanted to preserve "California's potential motherhood." More radical progressives, as in the socialist-led Women's Trade Union League of Los Angeles, supported legislation to help secure economic independence and equality in the labor market for women, increase the economic strength of the working class, and serve as a precedent for laws improving conditions for all workers.

Progressive Era lawmakers adopted the first viewpoint. They limited protective legislation to measures reflecting the belief that women needed paternalist protection, even by excluding them from certain occupations. Laws establishing a minimum wage for women, moreover, usually set a wage level below what the wage commissions reported as subsistence rates. Protective legislation thus assured women not eco-

nomic independence but continued dependence on husbands or fathers. In practice, then, the laws reinforced women's subordinate place in the labor force.

Social justice reformers forged the beginnings of the welfare state in further legislation. Prompted by both humanitarian and paternalistic urgings, many states began in 1910 to provide "mothers' pensions" to indigent widows with dependent children. Twenty-one states, led by Wisconsin in 1911, enacted workers' compensation programs, ending the custom of holding workers themselves liable for injuries on the job.

Compared to social insurance programs in western Europe, however, these were feeble responses to the social consequences of industrialization. Attempts by various reform groups to follow up workers' compensation laws with health insurance and old-age pension programs went nowhere. Business groups and other conservative interests curbed the movement toward state responsibility for social welfare. Few more advances would come until the New Deal (1930s) and the Great Society (1960s), both heirs of progressivism in their commitment to governmental activism.

Reshaping Public Education

Concerns about child labor overlapped with increasing attention to public schools. The rapid influx of immigrants, as well as the demands of the new corporate workplace, generated interest in education not only as a means of advancement but also as a tool for assimilation and the training of future workers. Middle-class women supported public school reforms. In 1900, for example, women's clubs in North Carolina launched a program to improve school buildings, increase teachers' salaries, and broaden the curriculum. Claiming efficiency and expertise, school administrators also pushed for changes, both to upgrade their own profession and to expand their public influence. And some intellectuals predicted that schools themselves could promote social progress and reform. Philosopher John Dewey sketched his plans for such progressive education in *The School and Society* (1899).

The modern urban public school system emerged between 1880 and 1920. Compulsory school attendance laws, kindergartens, age-graded elementary schools, professional training for teachers, vocational education, parent-teacher associations, and school nurses became standard elements in American education. School reformers believed in both the educational soundness of these measures and their importance for countering slum environments. As Jacob Riis contended, the kindergartner would "rediscover . . . the natural feelings that the tenement had smothered." Others supported the kindergarten as "the earliest opportunity to catch the little Russian, the little Italian, the little German, Pole, Syrian, and the rest and begin to make good American citizens of them." Further socialization came through vocational courses intended to instill discipline in poor students and prepare them to become productive adults.

Public education in the South lagged behind the North. An educational awakening, supported by northern philanthropy and southern reformers, brought improvements after 1900. Per capita expenditures for education doubled, school terms were extended, and high schools spread across the region. But the South frittered away its limited resources on a segregated educational system that shortchanged both races. Black Southerners particularly suffered, for the new programs increased the disparity in funding for white and black schools. South Carolina spent twelve times as much per white pupil as per black pupil. Booker T. Washington complained in 1906 that the educational reforms meant "almost nothing so far as the Negro schools are concerned." As a northern critic observed, "To devise a school system which shall save the whites and not the blacks is a task of such delicacy that a few surviving reactionaries are willing to let both perish together."

Challenging Gender Restrictions

Most progressives held fairly conservative, moralistic views about sexuality and gender roles. Margaret Sanger, however, radically challenged conventional ideas of the social role of women. Despite great opposition, she initiated the modern birth control movement. A public health nurse and an IWW organizer, she soon made the struggle for reproductive rights her personal crusade. Her mother had died at forty-nine after eighteen pregnancies, and Sanger saw in New York's immigrant neighborhoods the plight of poor women worn out from repeated pregnancies or injured or dead from self-induced knitting-needle abortions. Despite federal and state laws against contraceptives, Sanger began promoting birth control as a way to avert such tragedies. In 1914, Sanger published a magazine, *Woman Rebel*, in which she argued that "a woman's body belongs to herself alone. It does not belong to the United States of America or any other government on the face of the earth." Prohibiting contraceptives meant "enforced motherhood," Sanger declared. "Women cannot be on an equal footing with men until they have full and complete control over their reproductive function."

Sanger's crusade attracted support from many women's and labor groups, but it also infuriated those who regarded birth control as a threat to the family and morality. Indicted for distributing information about contraception, Sanger fled to Europe. Other women took up the cause, forming the National Birth Control League in 1915 to campaign for the repeal of laws restricting access to contraceptive information and devices. They had little immediate success, but their cause would triumph in later generations.

Reforming Country Life

Although most progressives focused on the city, others sought to reform rural life, both to modernize its social and economic conditions and to integrate it more fully into the larger society. They worked to improve rural health and sanitation, to replace inefficient one-room schools with modern consolidated ones under professional control, and to extend new roads and communication services into the countryside. To further these goals, President Theodore Roosevelt created the Country Life Commission in 1908. The country lifers had a broad program for social and economic change, involving expanded government functions, activist government agencies staffed by experts, and the professionalization of rural social services.

Agricultural scientists, government officials, and many business interests also sought to promote efficient, scientific, and commercial agriculture. A key innovation was the county agent system: the U.S. Department of Agriculture and business groups placed an agent in each county to teach farmers new techniques and encourage changes in the rural social

American Views
MOTHER JONES AND THE MEANING OF CHILD LABOR IN AMERICA

Born in Ireland in 1830, the legendary Mother Jones (Mary Harris Jones) became one of America's greatest social activists, organizing workers, participating in strikes, and protesting social and industrial conditions from the 1870s through the 1920s. Here she recounts one of her efforts to end child labor, one of the most persistent reform goals of the Progressive Era. Using the techniques of exposure and publicity characteristic of the period and adroitly employing patriotic symbols and references, Jones skillfully raised troubling questions about the concepts of social and economic opportunity that many Americans associated with national development and identity.

❖ **How did Mother Jones direct public attention to child labor?**

❖ **How did she invoke the treasured American concept of opportunity to gain support for her goal?**

❖ **What did she argue was the relationship between child labor and the privileged status of other Americans?**

❖ **How successful was her crusade against child labor?**

In the spring of 1903 I went to Kensington, Pennsylvania, where 75,000 textile workers were on strike. Of this number at least 10,000 were little children. The workers were striking for more pay and shorter hours. Every day little children came into Union Headquarters, some with their hands off, some with the thumb missing, some with their fingers off at the knuckle. They were stooped little things, round shouldered and skinny. Many of them were not over ten years of age. . . .

We assembled a number of boys and girls one morning in Independence Park and from there we arranged to parade with banners to the court house where we would hold a meeting.

A great crowd gathered in the public square in front of the city hall. I put the little boys with their fingers off and hands crushed and maimed on a platform. I held up their mutilated hands and showed them to the crowd and made the statement that Philadelphia's mansions were built on the broken bones, the quivering hearts, and drooping heads of these children. . . .

I called upon the millionaire manufacturers to cease their moral murders, and I cried to

---

values that had spawned the Populist radicalism that most progressives decried. Farmers, it was hoped, would acquire materialistic values and learn "economy, order, . . . patriotism, and a score of other wholesome lessons," as one progressive put it in 1910. The Smith-Lever Act (1914) provided federal subsidies for county agents throughout the country. Its purpose, claimed Woodrow Wilson, was to produce "an efficient and contented population" in rural America.

Few farmers, however, welcomed these efforts. As one Illinois county agent said in 1915, "Farmers, as a whole, resent exceedingly those forces which are at work with missionary intent trying to uplift them." School consolidation meant the loss of community control of education; good roads would raise taxes and chiefly benefit urban business interests. Besides, most farmers believed that their problems stemmed not from rural life but from industrial society and its nefarious trusts, banks, and middlemen. Rural Americans did not want their lives revolutionized.

Even so, rural people were drawn into the larger urban-industrial society during the Progres-

the officials in the open windows opposite, "Some day the workers will take possession of your city hall, and when we do, no child will be sacrificed on the altar of profit."

The reporters quoted my statement that Philadelphia mansions were built on the broken bones and quivering hearts of children. The Philadelphia papers and the New York papers got into a squabble with each other over the question. The universities discussed it. Preachers began talking. That was what I wanted. Public attention on the subject of child labor.

The matter quieted down for a while and I concluded the people needed stirring up again. . . . I decided to go with the children to see President Roosevelt to ask him to have Congress pass a law prohibiting the exploitation of childhood. I thought that President Roosevelt might see these mill children and compare them with his own little ones who were spending the summer at the seashore at Oyster Bay. . . .

Everywhere we had meetings, showing up with living children, the horrors of child labor. . . . [In New Jersey] I called on the mayor of Princeton and asked for permission to speak opposite the campus of the University. I said I wanted to speak on higher education. The mayor gave me permission. A great crowd gathered, professors and students and the people; and I told them that the rich robbed these little children of any education

of the lowest order that they might send their sons and daughters to places of higher education. . . . And I showed those professors children in our army who could scarcely read or write because they were working ten hours a day in the silk mills of Pennsylvania. . . .

[In New York] I told an immense crowd of the horrors of child labor in the mills around the anthracite region and . . . I showed them Gussie Rangnew, a little girl from whom all the childhood had gone. Her face was like an old woman's. Gussie packed stockings in a factory, eleven hours a day for a few cents a day. . . . "Fifty years ago there was a cry against slavery and men gave up their lives to stop the selling of black children on the block. Today the white child is sold for two dollars a week to the manufacturers."

. . . We marched down to Oyster Bay but the president refused to see us and he would not answer my letters. But our march had done its work. We had drawn the attention of the nation to the crime of child labor. And while the strike of the textile workers in Kensington was lost and the children driven back to work, not long afterward the Pennsylvania legislature passed a child labor law that sent thousands of children home from the mills, and kept thousands of others from entering the factory until they were fourteen years of age.

Source: The Autobiography of Mother Jones, 3rd ed. (Chicago: Kerr Publishing Company, 1977).

sive Era. Government agencies, agricultural colleges, and railroads and banks steadily tied farmers to urban markets. Telephones and rural free delivery of mail lessened countryside isolation but quickened the spread of city values. Improved roads and the coming of the automobile eliminated many rural villages and linked farm families directly with towns and cities. Consolidated schools wiped out the social center of rural neighborhoods and carried children out of their communities, many never to return.

Social Control and Moral Crusades

The tendency toward social control evident in the movements to pass protective legislation and transform country life also marked other less attractive progressive efforts. These efforts, moreover, often meshed with the restrictive attitudes that conservative Americans held about race, religion, immigration, and morality. The result was widespread attempts to restrict certain groups and control behavior.

Many Americans wanted to limit immigration for racist reasons. Nativist agitation in California prompted the federal government to secure restrictions on Japanese immigration in 1907. Californians, including local progressives, also hoped to curtail the migration of Mexicans. A Stanford University researcher condemned Mexicans as an "undesirable class" compared to "the more progressive races," and in 1916 the Los Angeles County supervisors urged the federal government to deport Mexican immigrants.

Nationally, public debate focused on restricting the flow of new immigrants from southern and eastern Europe. Some labor leaders believed that immigration held down wages and impeded unionization; many sociologists thought it created serious social problems; other Americans disliked the newcomers on religious, cultural, or ethnic grounds. Many backed their prejudice with a distorted interpretation of Darwinism, labeling the Slavic and Mediterranean peoples "inferior races." As early as 1894, nativists had organized the Immigration Restriction League, which lobbied for a literacy test for admission, sure that it would "bear most heavily upon the Italians, Russians, Poles, Hungarians, Greeks, and Asiatics, and very lightly or not at all upon English-speaking immigrants or Germans, Scandinavians, and French." Congress enacted a literacy law in 1917.

Other nativists demanded the "Americanization" of immigrants already in the country. The Daughters of the American Revolution sought to inculcate loyalty, patriotism, and conservative values. Settlement workers and Social Gospelers promoted a gentler kind of Americanization by helping immigrants adapt to their new life with classes in English and home mission campaigns, but they too attempted to transfer their own values to the newcomers. The most prominent advocate of Americanization was a stereotypical progressive, Frances Kellor. She studied social work at the University of Chicago, worked in New York settlement houses, wrote a muckraking exposé of employment agencies that exploited women, and became director of the New York Bureau of Immigration. In 1915, she helped organize the National Americanization Committee and increasingly emphasized destroying immigrants' old-country ties and imposing an American culture.

Closely linked to progressives' worries about immigrants was their campaign for **prohibition**. This movement engaged many of the progressives' basic impulses. Social workers saw liquor as a cause of crime, poverty, and family violence; employers blamed it for causing industrial accidents and inefficiency; Social Gospel ministers condemned the "spirit born of hell" because it impaired moral judgment and behavior. But also important was native-born Americans' fear of new immigrants—"the

dangerous classes, who are readily dominated by the saloon." Many immigrants, in fact, viewed liquor and the neighborhood saloon as vital parts of daily life, and so prohibition became a focus of nativist hostilities, cultural conflict, and Americanization pressures. In the South, racism also figured prominently. Alexander McKelway, the southern secretary for the National Child Labor Committee, endorsed prohibition as a way to maintain social order and white supremacy. McKelway himself drank, but he helped organize the North Carolina Anti-Saloon League to deny alcohol to African Americans, whom he considered naturally "criminal and degenerate."

Protestant fundamentalists also stoutly supported prohibition, working through the Anti-Saloon League, founded in 1893. Their nativism and antiurban bias surfaced in demands for prohibition to prevent the nation's cities from lapsing into "raging mania, disorder, and anarchy." With most urban Catholics and Jews opposing prohibition—the Central Conference of American Rabbis denounced it as "born of fanaticism"—the Anti-Saloon League justified imposing its reform on city populations against their will: "Our nation can only be saved by turning the pure stream of country sentiment . . . to flush out the cesspools of cities and so save civilization from pollution."

With these varied motivations, prohibitionists campaigned for local and state laws against the manufacture and sale of alcohol. Beginning in 1907, they proved increasingly successful, especially in the South, Midwest, and Far West. By 1917, twenty-six states had prohibition laws. Congress then approved the Eighteenth Amendment, which made prohibition the law of the land by 1920.

Less controversial was the drive to control narcotics, then readily available. Patent medicines commonly contained opium, heroin, and cocaine (popularly used for hay fever), and physicians known as "dope doctors" openly dispensed drugs to paying customers. Inaccurate assumptions that addiction was spreading in "the fallen and lower classes"—and particularly among black people and immigrants—prompted calls for restrictive legislation. In 1914, Congress passed the **Harrison Act**, prohibiting the distribution and use of narcotics for other than medicinal purposes.

California provided other examples of progressives' interest in social control and moral reform. The state assembly, described by the *San Francisco Chronicle* as "a legislature of progressive cranks," prohibited gambling, cardplaying, and prizefighting. Los Angeles—influenced by the aptly named Morals Efficiency League—banned premarital sex and introduced artistic censorship. One critic in 1913 complained that the reformers' "frenzy of virtue" made "Puritanism . . . the inflexible doctrine of Los Angeles."

For Whites Only?

Racism permeated the Progressive Era. In the South, progressivism was built on black disfranchisement and segregation. Like most white Southerners, progressives believed that racial control was necessary for social order and that it enabled reformers to address other social problems. Such reformers also invoked racism to gain popular support for their objectives. In Georgia, for instance, child labor reformers warned that while white children worked in the Piedmont textile mills, black children were going to school: Child labor laws and compulsory school attendance laws were necessary to maintain white supremacy.

Governors Hoke Smith of Georgia and James Vardaman, "the White Chief," of Mississippi typified the link between racism and reform in the South. They supported progressive reforms, but they also viciously attacked black rights. Their racist demagogy incited antiblack violence throughout the South. Antiblack race riots, like that produced in Atlanta by Smith's election in 1906, and lynching—defended on the floor of the U.S. Senate by a southern progressive—were part of the system of racial control that made the era a terrible time for African Americans.

Even in the North, where relatively few black people lived, race relations deteriorated. Civil rights laws went unenforced, black customers were excluded from restaurants and hotels, and schools were segregated. A reporter in Pennsylvania found "this disposition to discriminate against Negroes has greatly increased within the past decade." Antiblack race riots exploded in New York in 1900 and in Springfield, Illinois—Lincoln's hometown—in 1908.

But although most white progressives promoted or accepted racial discrimination and most black Southerners had to adapt to it, black progressive activism was growing. Even in the South, some African Americans struggled to improve conditions. In Atlanta,

for example, black women created progressive organizations and established settlement houses, kindergartens, and day care centers. With public parks reserved for white people, the Gate City Day Nursery Association built and supervised a playground on the campus of Atlanta Baptist College. The women of the Neighborhood Union, organized in 1908, even challenged the discriminatory policies of Atlanta's board of education, demanding equal facilities and appropriations for the city's black schools. They had only limited success, but their efforts demonstrated a persisting commitment to reforming society.

In the North, African Americans more openly criticized discrimination and rejected Booker T. Washington's philosophy of accommodation. Ida Wells-Barnett, the crusading journalist who had fled the South for Chicago, became nationally prominent for her militant protests. She fought fiercely against racial injustices, especially school segregation, agitated for woman suffrage, and organized kindergartens and settlement houses for Chicago's black migrants.

Still more important was W. E. B. Du Bois, who campaigned tirelessly against all forms of racial discrimination. In 1905, Du Bois and other black activists met in Niagara Falls, Canada, to make plans to promote political and economic equality. In 1910, this **Niagara Movement** joined with a small group of white

A meeting of the Niagara Movement in Boston in 1907. W. E. B. Du Bois is seated on the left. Half of the delegates were women, indicating the important role that black women played in the struggle for racial justice.

reformers, including Jane Addams, to organize the National Association for the Advancement of Colored People. The NAACP sought to overthrow segregation and establish equal justice and educational opportunities. As its director of publicity and research, Du Bois launched the influential magazine *The Crisis* to shape public opinion. "Agitate," he counseled, "protest, reveal the truth, and refuse to be silenced." By 1918, the NAACP had 44,000 members in 165 branches. Two generations later, it would successfully challenge the racial discrimination that most early-twentieth-century white progressives either supported or tolerated.

Reforming Politics and Government

Progressives of all kinds clamored for the reform of politics and government. But their political activism was motivated by different concerns, and they sometimes pursued competing objectives. Many wanted to change procedures and institutions to promote greater democracy and responsibility. Others hoped to improve the efficiency of government, to eliminate corruption, or to increase their own influence. All justified their objectives as necessary to adapt the political system to the nation's new needs.

Woman Suffrage

One of the most important achievements of the era was woman suffrage. The movement had begun in the mid-nineteenth century, but suffragists had been frustrated by the prevailing belief that women's "proper sphere" was the home and the family. Males dominated the public sphere, including voting. Woman suffrage, particularly when championed as a step toward women's equality, seemed to challenge the natural order of society, and it generated much opposition, not only among men but among traditionalist-minded women as well. "Housewives," announced the Women's Anti-Suffrage Association of Massachusetts, "you do not need a ballot to clean out your sink spout. A handful of potash and some boiling water is quicker."

In the early twentieth century, suffragists began to outflank this opposition. Under a new generation of leaders like Carrie Chapman Catt, they adopted activist tactics, including parades, mass meetings, and "suffrage tours" by automobile. They also organized by political districts and attracted workingwomen and labor unions. By 1917, the National American Woman Suffrage Association had over 2 million members.

But some suffrage leaders shifted arguments to gain more support. They argued for woman suffrage within—not against—traditional ideas about women's role. Rather than insisting on the "justice" of woman suffrage or emphasizing equal rights, they spoke of the special moral and maternal instincts women could bring to politics if allowed to vote. The suffrage movement now appeared less a radical, disruptive force than a vehicle for extending traditional female benevolence and service to society. Many suffragists, particularly among working-class groups, remained committed to the larger possibilities they saw in suffrage, but the new image of the movement increased public support by appealing to conventional views of women. Noted one Nebraska undergraduate, women students no longer feared "antagonizing the men or losing invitations to parties by being suffragists."

Gradually, the suffrage movement began to prevail (see Map 23-1). In 1910, Washington became the first state to approve woman suffrage since the mid-1890s, followed by California in 1911 and Arizona, Kansas, and Oregon in 1912. Suffragists also mounted national action, such as the dramatic inaugural parade in March 1913 described at the beginning of this chapter. The violence surrounding that event outraged public opinion, revived interest in a federal constitutional amendment to grant women the vote, and prompted women to send petitions and organize pilgrimages to Washington from across the country. By 1919, thirty-nine states had established full or partial woman suffrage, and Congress finally approved an amendment. Ratified by the states in 1920, the **Nineteenth Amendment** marked a critical advance in political democracy.

Electoral Reform

Other electoral reforms changed the election process and the meaning of political participation. The so-called **Australian ballot** adopted by most states during the 1890s provided for secret voting, freeing voters from intimidation and making vote buying and other corruption more difficult. It also replaced the individual party tickets with an official ballot listing all candidates and distributed by public officials. The Australian ballot led to quiet, orderly elections. One Cincinnati editor, recalling the "howling mobs" and chaos at the polls in previous elections, declared: "The political bummer and thug has been relegated to the background . . . while good citizenship . . . has come to the front."

Government responsibility for the ballot soon led to public regulation of other parts of the electoral process previously controlled by parties. Be-

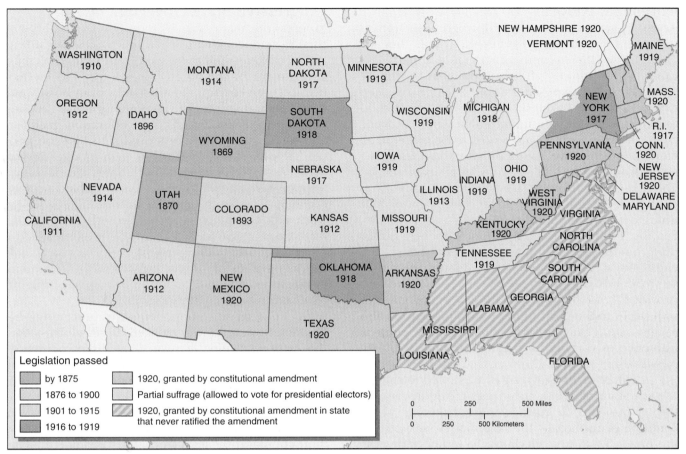

Map 23-1   Woman suffrage in the United States before the ratification of the Nineteenth Amendment.

Beginning with Wyoming in 1869, woman suffrage slowly gained acceptance in the West, but women in the South and much of the East got the ballot only when the Nineteenth Amendment was ratified in 1920.

ginning with Mississippi in 1902, nearly every state provided for direct primaries to remove nominations from the boss-ridden caucus and convention system. Many states also reformed campaign practices.

These reforms weakened the influence of political parties. Their decreasing ability to mobilize voters was reflected in a steady decline in voter participation, from 79 percent in 1896 to 49 percent in 1920. These developments had ominous implications, for parties and voting had traditionally linked ordinary Americans to their government. As parties contracted, nonpartisan organizations and pressure groups, promoting narrower objectives, gained influence. Thus the National Association of Manufacturers (1895) and the United States Chamber of Commerce (1912) lobbied for business interests; the National Farmers Union (1902) for commercial agriculture; the American Federation of Teachers (1916) for professional educators. Many of these special-interest groups represented the same middle- or upper-class interests that had led the attack on parties. Their organized lobbying would give them greater influence over government in the future and contribute to the declining popular belief in the value of voting or participation in politics.

Disfranchisement more obviously undermined American democracy. In the South, Democrats—progressive and conservative alike—eliminated not only black voters but many poor white voters from the electorate through poll taxes, literacy tests, and other restrictions. Republicans in the North adopted educational or literacy tests in ten states, enacted strict registration laws, and gradually abolished the right of aliens to vote. These restrictions reflected both the progressives' anti-immigrant prejudices and their obsessions with social control and with purifying politics and "improving" the electorate. Such electoral reforms reduced the political power of ethnic and working-class Americans, often stripping them of their political rights and means of influence.

Municipal Reform

Antiparty attitudes also affected progressives' efforts to reform municipal government, which they regarded as inefficient and corrupt, at least partly because of the power of urban political machines. Muckrakers had exposed crooked alliances between city bosses and business leaders that resulted in wasteful or inadequate municipal services. In some cities, urban reformers attempted to break these alliances and improve conditions for those suffering most from municipal misrule. For example, in Toledo, Ohio, Samuel "Golden Rule" Jones won enough working-class votes to be elected mayor four times despite the hostility of both major parties. Serving from 1897 to 1904, Jones opened public playgrounds and kindergartens, established the eight-hour day for city workers, and improved public services. Influenced by the Social Gospel, he also provided free lodging for the homeless and gave his own salary to the poor. Other reforming mayors also fought municipal corruption, limited the political influence of corporations, and championed public ownership of utilities.

More elitist progressives attempted to change the structure of urban government. Middle-class reformers worked to replace ward elections, which could be controlled by the neighborhood-based city machine, with at-large elections. To win citywide elections required greater resources and therefore helped swell middle-class influence at the expense of working-class wards. So did nonpartisan elections, which reformers introduced to weaken party loyalties.

Urban reformers developed two other structural innovations: the city commission and the city manager. Both attempted to institutionalize efficient, business-like government staffed by professional administrators. Galveston, Texas, initiated the city commission form in 1901 in response to a crisis in public services following a devastating tidal wave. Staunton, Virginia, appointed a professional city manager to run its government on a nonpartisan basis in 1908. By 1920, hundreds of cities had adopted one of the new plans.

Business groups often promoted these reforms. In Des Moines, for example, the Commercial Club dominated the movement for the city commission in 1906, and its president declared that "the professional politician must be ousted and in his place capable businessmen chosen to conduct the affairs of the city." Again, then, reform in municipal government often shifted political power from ethnic and working-class voters, represented however imperfectly by partisan elections, to smaller groups with greater resources.

Progressive State Government

Progressives also reshaped state government. Some tried to democratize the legislative process, regarding the legislature—the most important branch of state government in the nineteenth century—as ineffective and even corrupt, dominated by party bosses and corporate influences. The Missouri legislature reportedly "enacted such laws as the corporations paid for, and such others as were necessary to fool the people." Populists had first raised such charges in the 1890s and proposed novel solutions: the **initiative** and the **referendum**. The initiative enabled reformers themselves to propose legislation directly to the electorate, bypassing an unresponsive legislature; the referendum permitted voters to approve or reject legislative measures. South Dakota Populists established the first system of "direct legislation" in 1898, and progressives adopted these innovations in twenty other states between 1902 and 1915.

Conservative opponents and procedural difficulties, however, often blocked these reforms. And the reforms could be turned against progressives themselves. In the state of Washington in 1914, an initiative to establish an eight-hour workday was defeated by an electorate alarmed by conservative propaganda, and organized labor had to fight seven referendum measures, such as an antipicketing law, that conservative legislators had promoted. The head of the state federation of labor concluded that the people could be "fooled and confused" when they voted directly on legislation.

Other innovations also expanded the popular role in state government. The **Seventeenth Amendment**, ratified in 1913, provided for the election of U.S. senators directly by popular vote instead of by state legislatures. Beginning with Oregon in 1908, ten states adopted the **recall**, enabling voters to remove unsatisfactory public officials from office.

As state legislatures and party machines were curbed, dynamic governors like Robert La Follette in Wisconsin, Charles Evans Hughes in New York, and Hiram Johnson in California pushed progressive programs into law. Elected governor in 1900, "Fighting Bob" La Follette turned Wisconsin into "the laboratory of democracy." "His words bite like coals of fire," wrote one observer. "He never wearies and he will not allow his audience to weary." Overcoming fierce opposition from "stalwart" Republicans, La Follette established direct primaries, railroad regulation, the first state income tax, workers' compensation, and other important measures before being elected to the U.S. Senate in 1906.

Robert M. LaFollette was a relentless campaigner for progressive reform. Under his leadership, noted Theodore Roosevelt, Wisconsin surpassed all other states "in securing both genuine popular rule and the wise use of the collective power of the people."

La Follette also stressed efficiency and expertise. The Legislative Reference Bureau that he created was staffed by university professors to advise on public policy. He used regulatory commissions to oversee railroads, banks, and other interests. Most states followed suit, and expert commissions became an important feature of state government, gradually gaining authority at the expense of local officials. An observer in Virginia noted in 1912 that the emphasis on efficiency and expertise caused the government to "delegate all new functions, and some old ones, to state departments or commissions instead of to county officers."

"Experts" were presumed to be disinterested and therefore committed to the general welfare. In practice, however, regulators were subject to pressures from competing interest groups, and some commissions became captives of the very industries they were supposed to control. This irony was matched by the contradiction between the expansion of democracy through the initiative and referendum and the increasing reliance on nonelected professional experts to set and implement public policy. Such inconsistencies emphasize the complex mixture of ideas, objectives, and groups that were reshaping politics and government.

Theodore Roosevelt and the Progressive Presidency

When a crazed anarchist assassinated William McKinley in 1901, Theodore Roosevelt entered the White House, and the progressive movement gained its most prominent leader. Though only forty-two years old, Roosevelt had already had a remarkable career. The son of a wealthy New York family, he had been a New York legislator, U.S. civil service commissioner, and assistant secretary of the navy. After his exploits in the Spanish–American War, he was elected governor of New York in 1898 and vice president in 1900. His public life was matched by an active private life in which he both wrote works of history and obsessively pursued what he called the "strenuous life": boxing, wrestling, hunting, rowing, even ranching and chasing rustlers in Dakota Territory. His own son observed that Roosevelt "always wanted to be the bride at every wedding and the corpse at every funeral."

Roosevelt's frenetic activity, aggressive personality, and penchant for self-promotion worried some Americans. Mark Twain fretted that "Mr. Roosevelt is the Tom Sawyer of the political world of the twentieth century; always showing off; always hunting for a chance to show off; in his frenzied imagination the Great Republic is a vast Barnum circus with him for a clown and the whole world for audience." But Roosevelt's flamboyance and ambitions made him the most popular politician of the time and enabled him to dramatize the issues of progressivism and to become the first modern president.

TR and the Modern Presidency

Roosevelt rejected the limited role of Gilded Age presidents. He believed that the president could do anything to meet national needs that the Constitution did not specifically prohibit. "Under this interpretation of executive power," he later recalled, "I did and caused to be done many things not previously done. . . . I did not usurp power, but I did greatly broaden the use of executive power." Indeed, the expansion of government power and its consolidation in the executive branch were among his most significant accomplishments.

Rather than deferring to Congress, Roosevelt exerted legislative leadership. He spelled out his policy goals in more than four hundred messages to Congress, sent drafts of bills to Capitol Hill, and intervened to win passage of "his" measures. Some members of Congress resented such "executive arrogance" and "dictatorship." Roosevelt generally avoided direct challenges to the conservative Old Guard Republicans who controlled Congress, but his activities helped shift the balance of power within the national government.

Roosevelt also reorganized the executive branch. He believed in efficiency and expertise, which he attempted to institutionalize in special commissions and administrative procedures. To promote rational policymaking and public management, he staffed the expanding federal bureaucracy with able professionals. Here, too, he provoked opposition. The president, complained one Republican, was "trying to concentrate all power in Washington . . . and to govern the people by commissions and bureaus."

Finally, Roosevelt encouraged the development of a personal presidency by exploiting the public's interest in their exuberant young president. He established the first White House press room and skillfully handled the mass media. His endless and well-reported activities, from playing with his children in the White House to wrestling, hiking, and horseback-riding with various notables, made him a celebrity, "TR" or "Teddy." The publicity not only kept TR in the spotlight but also enabled him to mold public opinion.

Roosevelt and Labor

One sign of TR's vigorous new approach to the presidency was his handling of a coal strike in 1902. Members of the United Mine Workers Union walked off their jobs, demanding higher wages, an eight-hour day, and recognition of their union. The mine owners closed the mines and waited for the union to collapse. But led by John Mitchell, the strikers held their ranks. The prospect of a freezing winter frightened consumers. Management's stubborn arrogance contrasted with the workers' orderly conduct and willingness to negotiate and hardened public opinion against the owners. TR's legal advisers told him that the government had no constitutional authority to intervene.

As public pressure mounted, however, Roosevelt decided to act. He invited both the owners and the union leaders to the White House and declared that the national interest made government action necessary. Mitchell agreed to negotiate with the owners or to accept an arbitration commission ap-

pointed by the president. The owners, however, refused even to speak to the miners and demanded that Roosevelt use the army to break the union, as Cleveland had done in the Pullman strike in 1894.

Roosevelt was not a champion of labor, and he had favored shooting the Pullman strikers. But as president, he believed his role was to mediate social conflict for the public good. Furious with the owners' "arrogant stupidity" and "insulting" attitude toward the presidency, Roosevelt announced that he would use the army to seize and operate the mines, not to crush the union. Questioned about the constitutionality of such an action, Roosevelt bellowed: "To hell with the Constitution when the people want coal." Reluctantly, the owners accepted the arbitration commission they had previously rejected. The commission gave the miners a 10 percent wage increase and a nine-hour day, but not union recognition, and permitted the owners to raise coal prices by 10 percent. Roosevelt described his intervention as simply giving both labor and management a "square deal." It also set important precedents for an active government role in labor disputes and a strong president acting as a steward of the public.

Managing Natural Resources

Federal land policy had helped create farms and develop transportation, but it had also ceded to speculators and business interests much of the nation's forests, mineral deposits, waterpower sites, and grazing lands. Reckless exploitation of these resources alarmed a new generation that believed the public welfare required the **conservation** of natural resources through efficient and scientific management. Conservationists achieved early victories in the Forest Reserve Act (1891) and the Forest Management Act (1897), which authorized the federal government to withdraw timberlands from development and to regulate grazing, lumbering, and hydroelectric sites in the forests (see Map 23-2).

Roosevelt built on these beginnings and his friendship with Gifford Pinchot to make conservation a major focus of his presidency. Pinchot had been trained in French and German scientific forestry practices. Appointed in 1898 to head the new Division of Forestry (renamed the Forest Service in 1905), he brought rational management and regulation to resource development. With his advice, TR used presidential authority to triple the size of the forest reserves to 150 million acres, set aside another 80 million acres valuable for minerals and petroleum, and establish dozens of wildlife refuges. In 1908, Roosevelt held a White House conference of state and federal officials that led to the creation of

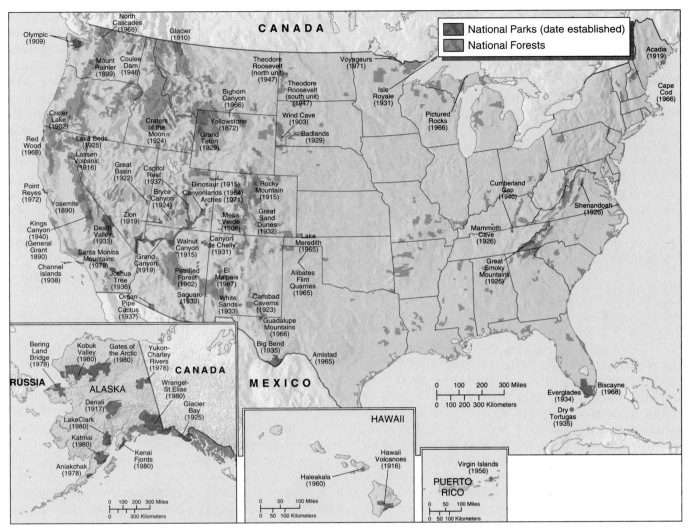

Map 23-2   The growth of National Forests and National Parks.
Rapid exploitation of the West prompted demands to preserve its spectacular scenery and protect its remaining forests. In 1872 Yellowstone became the first National Park, and the National Forest system began in the 1890s. Conservation became increasingly important during the Progressive Era but often provoked western hostility.

the National Conservation Commission, forty-one state conservation commissions, and widespread public support for the conservation movement.

Not everyone, of course, agreed with TR's conservationist policies. Some favored **preservation**, hoping to set aside land as permanent wilderness, whereas Roosevelt favored a scientific and efficient rather than uncontrolled use of resources. Pinchot declared, "Wilderness is waste." Preservationists won some victories, saving a stand of California's giant redwoods and helping create the National Park Service in 1916, but more Americans favored the utilitarian emphasis of early conservationists.

Other interests opposed conservation completely. While some of the larger timber and min-

eral companies supported conservation as a way to guarantee long-run profits, smaller western entrepreneurs cared only about quick returns. Many Westerners, moreover, resented having Easterners make key decisions about western growth and saw conservation as a perpetuation of this colonial subservience. Many ranchers refused to pay federal grazing fees. Colorado arsonists set forest fires to protest the creation of forest reserves.

But Westerners were happy to take federal money for expensive irrigation projects that private capital would not undertake. They favored the 1902 National Reclamation Act, which established what became the **Bureau of Reclamation**. Its engineers were to construct dams, reservoirs, and irrigation canals, and the government was to sell the irrigated lands in tracts no larger than 160 acres. The act helped shape the modern West. With massive dams and networks of irrigation canals, it reclaimed fertile valleys from the desert. Unfortunately, the bureau did not enforce the 160-acre limitation and thus helped create powerful corporate farms in the West.

Corporate Regulation

Nothing symbolized Roosevelt's active presidency better than his popular reputation as a "trust buster." TR took office at a time of public anxiety about corporate power, but he did not share that anxiety. On the contrary, he regarded the formation of large business combinations to be the result of a natural and beneficial process. But he understood the political implications of the public's concern. Although business leaders and Old Guard conservatives opposed any government intervention in the large trusts, Roosevelt knew better. "You have no conception of the revolt that would be caused if I did nothing," he said privately. To satisfy popular clamor, ensure social stability, and still retain the economic advantages of big modern corporations, TR proposed to "develop an orderly system, and such a system can only come through the gradually exercised right of efficient government control." Rather than invoking "the foolish antitrust law," he favored government regulation to prevent corporate abuses and defend the public interest. "Misconduct," not size, was the issue. Roosevelt preferred to use government agencies to work with corporations to avoid lawsuits. But he did sue some "bad trusts."

In 1902, the Roosevelt administration filed its most famous antitrust suit, against the Northern Securities Company, a holding company organized by J. P. Morgan to control the railroad network of the Northwest. For TR, this suit was an assertion of government power that reassured a worried public

and made corporate responsibility more likely. In 1904, the Supreme Court ordered the dissolution of the Northern Securities Company. Ultimately, Roosevelt brought forty-four antitrust suits against business combinations, but, except for a few like Standard Oil, he avoided the giant firms. Many of the cases had inconclusive outcomes, but Roosevelt was more interested in establishing a regulatory role for government than in breaking up big businesses.

Elected president in his own right in 1904 over the colorless and conservative Democratic candidate, Judge Alton B. Parker, Roosevelt responded to the growing popular demand for reform by pushing further toward a regulatory government. He proposed legislation "to work out methods of controlling

Roosevelt enjoyed this cartoon illustrating his distinction between good trusts, restrained by government regulation for the public welfare, and bad trusts. On those he put his foot down.

AMERICA'S JOURNEY

FROM THEN TO NOW

The Environmental Movement

Many of the issues that concern environmentalists today were first raised by the conservationists and preservationists of the Progressive Era. Conservationists favored the planned and regulated management of America's natural resources for the public benefit. Led by Theodore Roosevelt, they dominated the new agencies like the Forest Service that were responsible for federal lands. In contrast, preservationists—like John Muir, who founded the Sierra Club in 1892—sought to protect wilderness from any development whatsoever. Opposing both were those who championed the uncontrolled development of public lands.

Preservationists' reasons for protecting wilderness were primarily aesthetic—to preserve natural splendors intact for future generations. By the second half of the twentieth century, however, the disturbing consequences of technological change, rapid economic development, and spiraling population growth began to raise the stakes. Air pollution from smokestack industries and automobile exhaust damaged natural vegetation and caused respiratory diseases; water pollution from sewage and chemical waste spread disease; and oil spills fouled beaches and devastated marine habitats.

Public concern over these problems gave birth to the environmental movement, which drew on the legacy of both the conservation and preservation movements but had wider interests and broader support than either. Responding to the environmental movement's quickly growing strength, Congress in the 1970s passed laws to protect endangered species, reduce pollution, limit the use of pesticides, and control hazardous waste. The Environmental Protection Agency, created in 1970, subsequently became the largest federal regulatory agency.

Again, however, as during the Progressive Era, efforts to protect the environment encountered opposition from proponents of unrestricted development, especially in the West. In the Sagebrush Rebellion in the late 1970s and 1980s, some Westerners condemned "outside" federal regulation and tried to seize control of public lands for private exploitation. One oil company dismissed catastrophic oil spills as merely "Mother Earth letting some oil come out."

Three Republican presidents from the West—Californians Richard Nixon and Ronald Reagan and Texan George Bush, all closely tied to oil and real estate interests—sought in varying degrees to curtail environmental policies, agencies, and budgets and to promote development. This repudiation of Theodore Roosevelt's conservationism reflected the shift of the party's base to the sunbelt. As one Nixon adviser said, when a pipeline across the Alaskan wilderness was approved, "Conservation is not in the Republican ethic."

Ronald Reagan in particular was convinced that environmental protection fundamentally conflicted with economic growth. The business executives and corporate lawyers he appointed to key federal positions rescinded or weakened environmental regulations.

Congress, the courts, and the public, however, resisted efforts to weaken environmental policy. "Green" groups proliferated, demanding greater attention to environmental issues; some, like Greenpeace, undertook direct action to protect the environment, and even Western communities organized to oppose strip-mining, nuclear power plants, and toxic waste dumping.

Despite fluctuations, public opinion and mainstream politics now appear to favor greater environmental protection. Debate is sure to continue over the cost and effectiveness of specific policies. But as ever more challenging ecological problems arise—like ozone depletion and global warming—Americans are increasingly inclined to stand with Theodore Roosevelt and John Muir in looking to the federal government for effective action to meet them.

Theodore Roosevelt and John Muir on a 1903 camping trip in Yosemite, which became a national park largely through Muir's activism.

the big corporations without paralyzing the energies of the business community." In 1906, Congress passed the Hepburn Act, the Pure Food and Drug Act, and the Meat Inspection Act. All three were compromises between reformers seeking serious government control of the industries and political defenders and lobbyists of the industries themselves.

The Hepburn Act authorized the Interstate Commerce Commission to set maximum railroad rates and extended its jurisdiction. It was a weaker law than many progressives had wanted, but it marked the first time the federal government gained the power to set rules in a private enterprise. The two other laws aimed at consumer protection in food and drugs. In part, this legislation reflected public demand, but many business leaders also supported government regulation, convinced that it would expand their markets by certifying the quality of their products and drive their smaller competitors out of business. The laws thus did extend government supervision and regulation over business to protect the public health and safety, but they also served some corporate purposes.

Despite the compromises and weaknesses in the three laws, TR contended that they marked "a noteworthy advance in the policy of securing federal supervision and control over corporations." In 1907 and 1908, he pushed for an eight-hour workday, stock market regulation, and inheritance and income taxes. Republican conservatives in Congress blocked such reforms, and tensions increased between the progressive and conservative wings of the party. Old Guard Republicans thought Roosevelt had extended government powers dangerously, but in fact his accomplishments had been relatively modest because of his need to compromise in Congress. As La Follette noted, Roosevelt's "cannonading filled the air with noise and smoke, which confused and obscured the line of action, but, when the battle cloud drifted by and the quiet was restored, it was always a matter of surprise that so little had really been accomplished."

Taft and the Insurgents

TR handpicked his successor as president: a loyal lieutenant, William Howard Taft. Member of a prominent Ohio political family, Taft had been a federal judge, governor-general of the Philippines, and secretary of war. Later he would serve as chief justice of the United States. But if Roosevelt thought that Taft would be a successful president, continuing his policies and holding the Republican party together, he was wrong. Taft's election in 1908, over Democrat William Jennings Bryan in his third presidential campaign, led to a Republican political disaster.

Taft did preside over important progressive achievements. His administration pursued a more active and successful antitrust program than Roosevelt's. He supported the Mann-Elkins Act (1910), which extended the ICC's jurisdiction to telephone and telegraph companies. Taft set aside more public forest lands and oil reserves than Roosevelt had. He also supported a constitutional amendment authorizing an income tax, which went into effect in 1913 under the **Sixteenth Amendment**. One of the most important accomplishments of the Progressive Era, the income tax would provide the means for the government to expand its activities and responsibilities.

Nevertheless, Taft soon alienated progressives and floundered into a political morass. His problems were twofold. First, the Republicans were divided. Midwestern reform Republicans, led by La Follette, clashed with more conservative Republicans led by Senator Nelson Aldrich of Rhode Island. Second, Taft was politically inept. He was unable to mediate between these two groups, and the party split apart.

Reformers wanted to restrict the power of the speaker of the House, "Uncle Joe" Cannon, a reactionary who blocked reform. After seeming to promise support, Taft backed down when conservatives threatened to defeat important legislation. The insurgents in Congress eventually restricted the speaker's powers, but they never forgave what they saw as Taft's betrayal. The tariff also alienated progressives from Taft. He had campaigned in 1908 for a lower tariff to curb inflation, and midwestern Republicans favored tariff reduction to trim the power of big business. But when they introduced tariff reform legislation, the president failed to support them, and Aldrich's Senate committee added 847 amendments, many of which raised tariff rates. Taft justified his inaction as avoiding presidential interference with congressional business, but this excuse clashed with TR's example and the reformers' expectations. Progressives concluded that Taft had sided with the Old Guard against real change.

That perception solidified when Taft stumbled into a controversy over conservation. Gifford Pinchot had become embroiled in a complex struggle with Richard Ballinger, Taft's secretary of the interior. Ballinger, who was closely tied to western mining and lumbering interests, favored private development of public lands. When Pinchot challenged Ballinger's role in a questionable sale of public coal lands in Alaska to a J. P. Morgan syndicate, Taft upheld Ballinger and fired Pinchot. Progressives concluded that Taft had repudiated Roosevelt's conservation policies.

Progressives determined to replace Taft, whom they now saw as an obstacle to reform. In 1911, the National Progressive League organized to champion La Follette for the Republican nomination in 1912. Roosevelt rejected an appeal for support, convinced that a challenge to the incumbent president was both doomed and divisive. Besides, his own position was closer to Taft's than to what he called "the La Follette type of fool radicalism." But Taft's political blunders increasingly angered Roosevelt. Condemning Taft as "disloyal to our past friendship . . . [and] to every canon of ordinary decency," TR began to campaign for the Republican nomination himself. In thirteen state primaries, he won 278 delegates to only 46 for Taft. But most states did not then have primaries; that allowed Taft to dominate the Republican convention and win renomination. Roosevelt's forces formed a third party—the Progressive party—and nominated the former president. The Republican split almost guaranteed victory for the Democratic nominee, Woodrow Wilson.

Woodrow Wilson and Progressive Reform

The pressures for reform called forth many new leaders. The one who would preside over progressivism's culmination, and ultimately its collapse, was Woodrow Wilson. Elected president in 1912 and 1916, he mediated among differing progressive views to achieve a strong reform program, enlarge the power of the executive branch, and make the White House the center of national politics.

The Election of 1912
Despite the prominence of Roosevelt and La Follette, progressivism was not simply a Re-

publican phenomenon. In Congress, southern Democrats more consistently supported reform measures than Republicans did, and Democratic leader William Jennings Bryan surpassed Roosevelt as a persistent advocate of significant reform. As the Republicans quarreled during Taft's administration, Democrats pushed progressive remedies and achieved major victories in the state and congressional elections of 1910. To improve the party's chances in 1912, Bryan announced he would step aside. The Democratic spotlight shifted to the governor of New Jersey, Woodrow Wilson.

A portrait of Woodrow Wilson by Edward Charles Tarbell. A strong president, Wilson led Congress to enact sweeping and significant legislation.

Born in Virginia as the son and grandson of Presbyterian ministers, Wilson combined public eloquence with a cold personality; he balanced a self-righteousness that led to stubborn inflexibility with an intense ambition that permitted the most expedient compromises. Wilson first entered public life as a conservative, steeped in the limited government traditions of the South. As president of Princeton University, beginning in 1902, he became a prominent representative of middle-class respectability and conservative causes. In 1910, New Jersey's Democratic bosses selected him for governor to head off the progressives, but, once in office, Wilson championed popular reforms and immediately began to campaign as a progressive for the party's 1912 presidential nomination.

Wilson's progressivism differed from that of Roosevelt in 1912. TR emphasized a strong government to promote economic and social order. He defended big business as inevitable and healthy provided that government control ensured that it would benefit the entire nation. Roosevelt called this program the **New Nationalism**, reflecting his belief in a powerful state and a national interest. He also supported demands for social welfare, including workers' compensation and the abolition of child labor.

Wilson was horrified by Roosevelt's vision. His **New Freedom** program rejected what he called TR's "regulated monopoly." Wilson wanted "regulated competition," with the goverment's role limited to breaking up monopolies through antitrust action and preventing artificial barriers like tariffs from blocking free enterprise. Wilson opposed social welfare legislation as "paternalistic," reaching beyond the proper scope of the federal government, which he hoped to minimize. (This position, shot back the alarmed Roosevelt, meant the repeal of "every law for the promotion of social and industrial justice.")

Unable to add progressive Democrats to the Republicans who followed him into the Progressive party, TR could not win despite his personal popularity. Other reform voters embraced the Socialist candidate, Eugene V. Debs, who captured 900,000 votes—6 percent of the total. Taft played little role in the campaign. "I might as well give up as far as being a candidate," he lamented. "There are so many people in the country who don't like me."

Wilson won an easy electoral college victory, though he received only 42 percent of the popular vote and fewer popular votes than Bryan had won in any of his three campaigns (see Map 23-3). Roosevelt

came in second, Taft third. The Democrats also gained control of Congress, giving Wilson the opportunity to enact his New Freedom program.

Implementing the New Freedom

As president, Wilson built on Roosevelt's precedent to strengthen executive authority. He summoned Congress into special session in 1913 and delivered his message in person, the first president to do so since John Adams. Wilson proposed a full legislative program and worked forcefully to secure its approval. He held regular conferences with Democratic leaders and had a private telephone line installed between the Capitol and the White House to keep tabs on congressional actions. When necessary, he appealed to the public for support or doled out patronage and compromised with conservatives. With such methods and a solid Democratic majority, Wilson gained approval of important laws.

Wilson turned first to the traditional Democratic goal of reducing the high protective tariff, the symbol of special privileges for industry. "The object of the tariff duties," he announced, "must be effective competition." He forced through the **Un-**

Map 23-3   The Election of 1912.
The split within the Republican party enabled Woodrow Wilson to carry most states and become president even though he won only a minority of the popular vote.

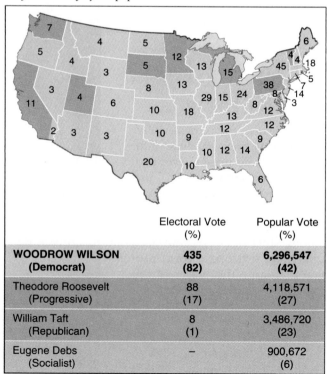

	Electoral Vote (%)	Popular Vote (%)
WOODROW WILSON (Democrat)	**435** **(82)**	**6,296,547** **(42)**
Theodore Roosevelt (Progressive)	88 (17)	4,118,571 (27)
William Taft (Republican)	8 (1)	3,486,720 (23)
Eugene Debs (Socialist)	–	900,672 (6)

derwood-Simmons Tariff Act of 1913, the first substantial reduction in duties since before the Civil War. The act also levied the first income tax under the recently ratified Sixteenth Amendment. Conservatives condemned the "revolutionary" tax, but it was designed simply to compensate for lower tariff rates. The top tax rate paid by the wealthiest was a mere 7 percent.

Wilson next reformed the nation's banking and currency system, which was inadequate for a modernizing economy. A panic in 1907 and a subsequent congressional investigation had dramatized the need for a more flexible and decentralized financial system. Wilson skillfully maneuvered a compromise measure through Congress, balancing the demands of agrarian progressives for government control with the bankers' desires for private control. The **Federal Reserve Act** of 1913 created twelve regional Federal Reserve banks that, although privately controlled, were to be supervised by the Federal Reserve Board, appointed by the president. The law also provided for a flexible national currency and improved access to credit. Serious problems remained, but the new system promoted the progressive goals of order and efficiency and fulfilled Wilson's New Freedom principle of introducing limited government regulation while preserving private business control.

Wilson's third objective was new legislation to break up monopolies. To this end, he initially supported the Clayton antitrust bill, which prohibited unfair trade practices and sharply restricted holding companies. But when business leaders and other progressives strenuously objected, Wilson reversed himself. Opting for continuous federal regulation rather than for the dissolution of trusts, Wilson endorsed the creation of the **Federal Trade Commission (FTC)** to oversee business activity and prevent illegal restrictions on competition.

The Federal Trade Commission Act of 1914 dismayed many of Wilson's early supporters because it embraced the New Nationalism's emphasis on positive regulation. Roosevelt's 1912 platform had proposed a federal trade commission; Wilson now accepted what he had earlier denounced as a partnership between trusts and the government that the trusts would dominate. Indeed, Wilson's conservative appointments to the FTC ensured that the agency would not seriously interfere with business, and by the 1920s, the FTC had become virtually a junior partner of the business community.

The fate of the Clayton antitrust bill after Wilson withdrew his support reflected his new attitude toward big business. Congressional conservatives gutted the bill with crippling amendments before permitting it to become law in 1914. As one senator complained, "When the Clayton bill was first written, it was a raging lion with a mouth full of teeth. It has degenerated to a tabby cat with soft gums, a plaintive mew, and an anemic appearance. It is a sort of legislative apology to the trusts, delivered hat in hand, and accompanied by assurances that no discourtesy is intended."

Wilson now announced that no further reforms were necessary—astonishing many progressives whose objectives had been completely ignored. Wilson refused to support woman suffrage and helped kill legislation abolishing child labor and expanding credits to farmers. Race relations provided a flagrant instance of Wilson's indifference to social justice issues. Raised in the South, he believed in segregation and backed the southern Democrats in his cabinet when they introduced formal segregation within the government itself. Government offices, shops, restrooms, and restaurants were all segregated; employees who complained were fired. Federal officials in the South discharged black employees wholesale. One Georgia official promised there would be no more government jobs for African Americans: "A Negro's place is in the cornfield."

The Expansion of Reform

Wilson had won in 1912 only because the Republicans had split. By 1916, Roosevelt had returned to the GOP, and Wilson realized that he had to attract some of TR's former followers. Wilson therefore abandoned his opposition to social and economic reforms aiding specific groups and promoted measures he had previously condemned as paternalistic and unconstitutional. But he had also grown in the White House and now recognized that some problems could be resolved only by positive federal action. "Old political formulas," he said, "do not fit the present."

To assist farmers, Wilson in 1916 convinced Congress to pass the Federal Farm Loan Act. This law, which Wilson himself had rejected twice earlier, provided farmers with federally financed, long-term agricultural credits. The Warehouse Act of 1916 improved short-term agricultural credit. The Highway Act of 1916 provided funds to construct and improve rural roads through the adoption of the "dollar-matching" principle by which the federal government would expand its power over state activities in the twentieth century.

Wilson and the Democratic Congress also reached out to labor. Wilson signed the Keating-Owen

Act prohibiting the interstate shipment of products made by child labor. In 1902, Wilson had denounced Roosevelt's intervention in the coal strike, but in 1916 he broke a labor-management impasse and averted a railroad strike by helping pass the Adamson Act establishing an eight-hour day for railway workers. Wilson also pushed the Kern-McGillicuddy Act, which achieved the progressive goal of a workers' compensation system for federal employees. Together, these laws marked an important advance toward government regulation of the labor market.

Wilson also promoted activist government when he nominated Louis Brandeis to the Supreme Court. Known as the "people's lawyer," Brandeis had successfully defended protective labor legislation before the conservative judiciary. The nomination outraged conservatives, including William Howard Taft and the American Bar Association. Brandeis was the first Jew nominated to the court, and anti-Semitism motivated some of his opponents. Wilson overcame a vicious campaign against Brandeis and secured his confirmation.

By these actions, Wilson brought progressivism to a culmination of sorts and consolidated reformers behind him for a second term. Less than a decade earlier, Wilson the private citizen had assailed government regulation and social legislation; by 1916, he had guided an unprecedented expansion of federal power. His own transformation symbolized the development of progressivism itself.

Conclusion

In the early twentieth century, progressive reformers responded to the tensions of industrial and urban development by moving to change society and government. Rejecting an earlier emphasis on individualism and laissez-faire, they organized to promote social change and an interventionist state. Programs and laws to protect women, children, and injured workers testified to their compassion; the creation of new agencies and political techniques indicated their interest in order and efficiency; campaigns to end corruption, whether perceived in urban political machines, corporate influence, drunkeness, or "inferior" immigrants, illustrated their self-assured vision of the public good.

Progressivism had its ironies and paradoxes. It called for democratic reforms—and did achieve woman suffrage, direct legislation, and popular election of senators—but helped disfranchise black Southerners and northern immigrants. It advocated social justice but often enforced social control. It de-

manded responsive government but helped create bureaucracies largely removed from popular control. It endorsed the regulation of business in the public interest but forged regulatory laws and commissions that tended to aid business. Some of these seeming contradictions reflected the persistence of traditional attitudes and the necessity to accommodate conservative opponents; others revealed the progressives' own limitations in vision, concern, or nerve.

But both the successes and the failures of progressivism revealed that the nature of politics and government had changed significantly. Americans had come to accept that government action could resolve social and economic problems, and the role and power of government expanded accordingly. The emergence of an activist presidency, capable of developing programs, mobilizing public opinion, directing Congress, and taking forceful action, epitomized this key development.

These important features would be crucial when the nation fought World War I, which brought new challenges and dangers to the United States. The Great War would expose many of the limitations of progressivism and the naiveté of the progressives' optimism.

Review Questions

1. How and why did the presidency change during the Progressive Era?

2. How did the progressive concern for efficiency affect social reform efforts, public education, government administration, and rural life?

3. How and why did the relationship between business and government change during this time?

4. Why did social reform and social control often intermingle in the Progressive Era? Can such objectives be separate?

5. What factors, old and new, stimulated the reform movements of progressivism?

6. How did the role of women change during the Progressive Era? How did that affect progressivism itself?

Recommended Reading

Jane Addams, *Twenty Years at Hull House* (1910). Jane Addams's own classic story of settlement work.

Kendrick A. Clements, *The Presidency of Woodrow Wilson* (1992). An excellent book that provides important new information on both Wilson and the presidency.

William Deverell and Tom Sitton, *California Progressivism Revisited* (1994). A valuable collection of essays that examines the complex motivations underlying progressivism in California.

Steven J. Diner, *A Very Different Age: Americans of the Progressive Era* (1998). An engaging survey of the era, stressing social history.

Lewis L. Gould, *The Presidency of Theodore Roosevelt* (1991). A balanced and comprehensive account of TR's presidency.

Arthur S. Link and Richard L. McCormick, *Progressivism* (1983). A superb brief analysis of the complexities and scholarly interpretations of progressivism.

Upton Sinclair, *The Jungle* (1906). The most famous muckraking novel.

Robert Wiebe, *The Search for Order, 1877–1920.* (1967). A masterful essay that emphasizes the organizational thrust of middle-class progressives.

Additional Sources

The Ferment of Reform

Karen Blair, *The Clubwoman as Feminist: True Womanhood Redefined, 1868–1914* (1980).

John W. Chambers, *The Tyranny of Change* (2nd ed., 1992).

Ellen Chesler, *Woman of Valor: The Life of Margaret Sanger* (1992).

Nancy Cott, *The Grounding of Modern Feminism* (1987).

Robert Crunden, *Ministers of Reform* (1982).

David B. Danbom, *"The World of Hope": Progressives and the Struggle for an Ethical Public Life* (1987).

Melvyn Dubofsky, *We Shall Be All: A History of the Industrial Workers of the World* (1969).

Susan A. Glenn, *Daughters of the Shtetl* (1990).

Eric Goldman, *Rendezvous with Destiny* (1952).

Alan Kraut, *The Huddled Masses: The Immigrant in American Society, 1880–1921* (1982).

George Marsden, *Fundamentalism and American Culture* (1980).

Henry May, *Protestant Churches and Industrial America* (1949).

Kathy Peiss, *Cheap Amusements: Working Women and Leisure in Turn-of-the-Century New York* (1986).

Nick Salvatore, *Eugene V. Debs: Citizen and Socialist* (1982).

Anne Firor Scott, *Natural Allies: Women's Associations in American History* (1991).

Elliott Shore, *Talkin' Socialism: J. A. Wayland and the Role of the Press in American Radicalism* (1988).

Margaret Spruill Wheeler, *New Women of the New South* (1993).

Reforming Society

Paul Boyer, *Urban Masses and Moral Order in America* (1978).

Mina Carson, *Settlement Folk: Social Thought and the American Settlement Movement* (1990).

Ruth H. Crocker, *Social Work and Social Order* (1992).

David Danbom, *The Resisted Revolution: Urban America and the Industrialization of Agriculture* (1979).

Allen F. Davis, *American Heroine: The Life and Legend of Jane Addams* (1973).

Allen F. Davis, *Spearheads of Reform: The Social Settlements and the Progressive Movement* (1968).

John Dittmer, *Black Georgia in the Progressive Era* (1977).

Lyle Dorsett, *Billy Sunday and the Redemption of Urban America* (1991).

Nancy S. Dye, *As Equals and as Sisters: Feminism, the Labor Movement, and the Women's Trade Union League of New York* (1980).

Noralee Frankel and Nancy S. Dye, *Gender, Class, Race, and Reform in the Progressive Era* (1991).

Louis Harlan, *Booker T. Washington: The Wizard of Tuskegee* (1983).

John Higham, *Strangers in the Land: Patterns of American Nativism* (1963).

Molly Ladd-Taylor, *Mother-Work: Women, Child Welfare, and the State, 1890-1930* (1994).

Kriste Lindenmeyer, *A Right to Childhood: The U.S. Children's Bureau and Child Welfare* (1997).

William A. Link, *The Paradox of Southern Progressivism* (1992).

Roy Lubove, *The Progressives and the Slums* (1962).

Robyn Muncy, *Creating a Female Dominion in American Reform, 1890–1935* (1991).

Daniel Nelson, *Frederick W. Taylor and the Rise of Scientific Management* (1980).

Elizabeth Anne Payne, *Reform, Labor, and Feminism: Margaret Dreier Robins and the Women's Trade Union League* (1988).

James Timberlake, *Prohibition and the Progressive Movement* (1963).

Nancy Woloch, *Women and the American Experience* (1984).

Reforming Politics and Government

John D. Buenker, *Urban Liberalism and Progressive Reform* (1973).

Ellen Carol DuBois, *Harriot Stanton Blatch and the Winning of Woman Suffrage* (1997).

Sara Hunter Graham, *Woman Suffrage and the New Democracy* (1996).

Dewey Grantham, *Southern Progressivism* (1983).

William F. Holmes, *The White Chief: James Kimble Vardaman* (1970).

Jack Temple Kirby, *Darkness at the Dawning: Race and Reform in the Progressive South* (1972).

J. Morgan Kousser, *The Shaping of Southern Politics* (1974).

Richard L. McCormick, *From Realignment to Reform: Political Change in New York State, 1893–1910* (1983).

Michael E. McGerr, *The Decline of Popular Politics* (1986).

John F. Reynolds, *Testing Democracy: Electoral Behavior and Progressive Reform in New Jersey* (1988).

Martin Schiesl, *The Politics of Efficiency: Municipal Administration and Reform in America* (1977).

David P. Thelen, *The New Citizenship: Origins of Progressivism in Wisconsin* (1972).

David P. Thelen, *Robert M. La Follette and the Insurgent Spirit* (1976).

Robert F. Wesser, *Charles Evans Hughes: Politics and Reform in New York State* (1967).

James E. Wright, *The Progressive Yankees: Republican Reformers in New Hampshire* (1987).

Theodore Roosevelt and the Progressive Presidency

John M. Blum, *The Republican Roosevelt* (1954).

David Burton, *The Learned Presidency: Theodore Roosevelt, William Howard Taft, Woodrow Wilson* (1988).

Paolo Coletta, *The Presidency of William Howard Taft* (1973).

William H. Harbaugh, *Power and Responsibility: The Life and Times of Theodore Roosevelt* (1961).

Samuel P. Hays, *Conservation and the Gospel of Efficiency: The Progressive Conservation Movement* (1962).

Morton Keller, *Regulating a New Economy* (1990).

Gabriel Kolko, *The Triumph of Conservatism* (1963).

Edmund Morris, *The Rise of Theodore Roosevelt* (1979).

George E. Mowry, *The Era of Theodore Roosevelt, 1900–1912* (1958).

Martin Sklar, *The Corporate Reconstruction of American Capitalism* (1988).

Donald Worster, *Rivers of Empire: Water, Aridity, and the Growth of the American West* (1985).

Woodrow Wilson and Progressive Reform

John M. Blum, *Woodrow Wilson and the Politics of Morality* (1956).

Kendrick A. Clements, *Woodrow Wilson* (1987).

John Milton Cooper, Jr., *The Warrior and the Priest: Woodrow Wilson and Theodore Roosevelt* (1983).

Lewis L. Gould, *Reform and Regulation: American Politics, 1900–1916* (1978).

August Hecksher, *Woodrow Wilson* (1991).

Arthur Link, *Woodrow Wilson and the Progressive Era* (1954).

James Livingston, *Origins of the Federal Reserve System* (1986).

David Sarasohn, *The Party of Reform: Democrats in the Progressive Era* (1989).

Melvin Urofsky, *Louis D. Brandeis and the Progressive Tradition* (1981).

Where to Learn More

❖ **John Muir National Historic Site, Martinez, California.** The architecture and furnishings of this seventeen-room house reflect the interests of John Muir, the writer and naturalist who founded the Sierra Club and led the preservationists in the Progressive Era.

❖ **National Museum of American History, Smithsonian Institution, Washington, D.C.** A permanent exhibition, "Parlor to Politics: Women and Reform, 1890–1925," uses design, artifacts, and recent scholarship to vividly illustrate the changing role of women in the Progressive Era. It effectively emphasizes their work in settlement houses and their growing politicization and demonstrates the importance of the work of black women's organizations.

❖ **Hull House, Chicago, Illinois.** This pioneering settlement house is now a museum on the campus of the University of Illinois, Chicago.

❖ **Lowell National Historic Park, Lowell, Massachusetts.** "The Working People," a permanent exhibition, uses artifacts and photographs to chart the activities of immigrant workers at different times in the past, particularly during the Progressive Era.

❖ **Lower East Side Tenement Museum, New York City, New York.** A six-story tenement building containing twenty-two apartments, this museum vividly illustrates the congested and unhealthy living conditions of urban immigrants from the 1870s to the early twentieth century.

❖ **Sagamore Hill, Oyster Bay, New York.** Theodore Roosevelt's home is now a National Historic Site and open to the public.

❖ **William Howard Taft National Historic Site, Cincinnati, Ohio.** Taft was born in this house, the only national Taft memorial. An informative tour focuses on Taft's public and private life.

❖ **Staunton, Virginia.** The birthplace and childhood home of Woodrow Wilson, restored with period furnishings, reveals many of the influences that shaped Wilson's career.

CREATING AN EMPIRE,
1865–1917

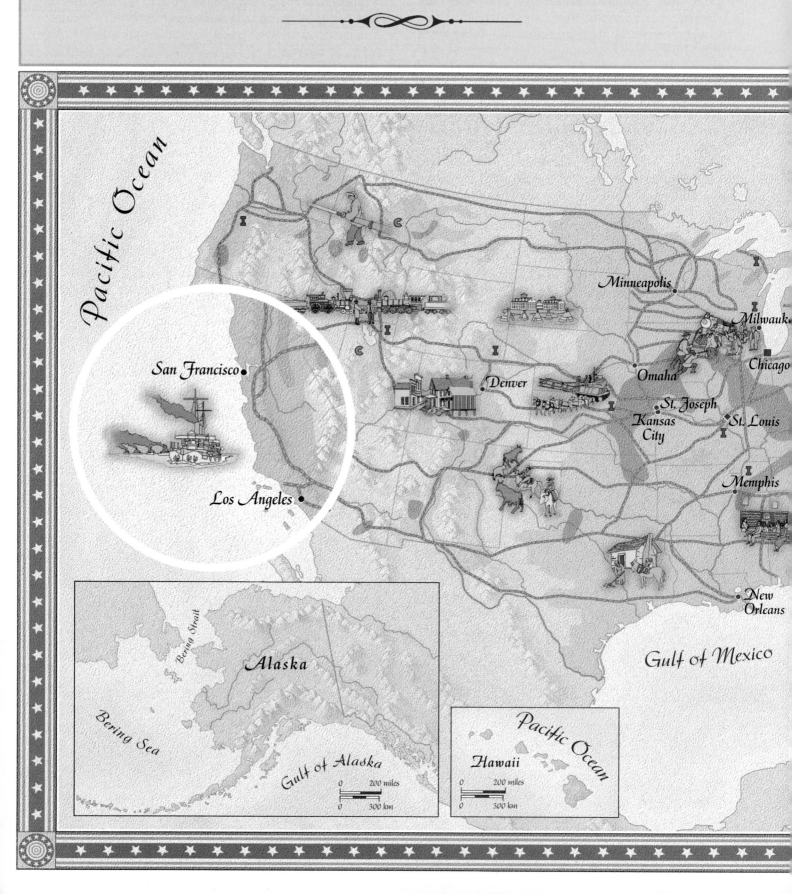

Pacific Ocean

Minneapolis

Milwauk

Chicago

Omaha

San Francisco

Denver

St. Joseph

St. Louis

Kansas
City

Los Angeles

Memphis

New
Orleans

Bering Strait

Alaska

Gulf of Mexico

Bering Sea

Gulf of Alaska

Pacific Ocean

Hawaii

0   200 miles

0   300 km

0   200 miles

0   300 km

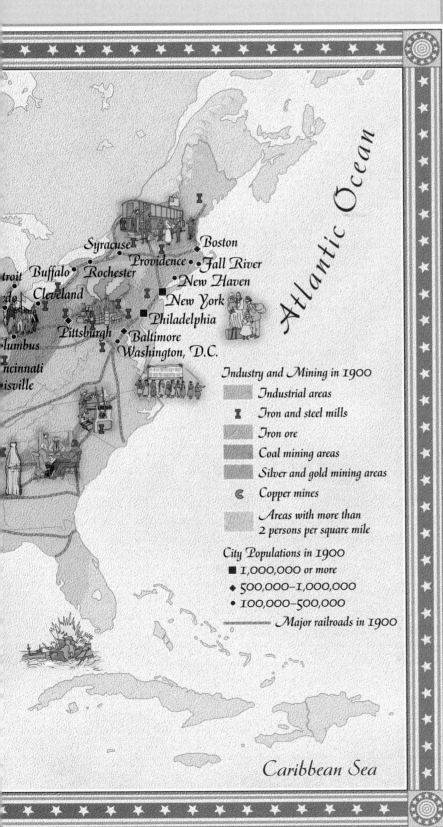

24

Key Topics

❖ Why the United States became an imperial power in the 1890s
❖ The Spanish-American War and the colonial empire the United States gained as a result
❖ U.S. involvement in Asia, and the tensions with Japan that resulted
❖ U.S. predominance in the Caribbean and Latin America

*I*n 1898, the United States became embroiled in the **Spanish-American War** over Spanish policies in Cuba. The smashing U.S. victory in that conflict triggered a nationwide debate over the terms of the peace settlement in the **Treaty of Paris**. In the U.S. Senate, which had the constitutional duty to ratify or reject the treaty, in the nation's newspapers, and in the streets and pulpits, people argued vociferously over whether the country should acquire the Spanish colony of the Philippines. Many Americans opposed expanding beyond North America; some viewed the acquisition of a colony as repudiating America's historic political principles. Republican Albert Beveridge of Indiana responded to such arguments in speeches across the nation: America's acquisition of the Philippines, he declared, was "God's great purpose made manifest in the instincts of our race, whose present phase is our personal profit, but whose far-off end is the redemption of the world and the Christianization of mankind."

In a single sentence, Beveridge had linked the ideas that coalesced in the 1890s to propel the United States to broaden its role in world affairs. Demands for economic expansion, a belief in national mission, a sense of responsibility to help others, the missionary impulses of religion, and racist convictions combined in an uneasy mixture of self-interest and idealism. Such a variety of motives—to say nothing of the positive spin that orators like Beveridge could impart to them—helped garner support for the new policies that the nation's leaders adopted, including acquisition of the Philippines.

But even Beveridge presented too simple a picture. He did not anticipate the consequences, not just for Americans but for Filipinos, Cubans, Puerto Ricans, and others who rarely perceived American motives or American actions as positively as Beveridge and other proponents of imperial expansion. Military victory in the Spanish-American War provided the United States with an extensive empire, status as a world power, and opportunities and problems that would long shape American foreign policy.

The Roots of Imperialism

The United States had a long-established tradition of expansion across the continent. Through purchase, negotiation, or conquest, the vast Louisiana Territory, Florida, Texas, New Mexico, California, and Oregon had become U.S. territory. Indeed, by the 1890s, Republican Senator Henry Cabot Lodge of Massachusetts boasted that Americans had "a record of conquest, colonization, and territorial expansion unequalled by any people in the nineteenth century." Lodge now urged the country to build an overseas empire, emulating the European model of **imperialism** based on the acquisition and exploitation of colonial possessions. Other Americans favored a less formal empire, in which U.S. interests and influence would be assured through extensive trade and investments rather than through military occupation. Still others advocated a cultural expansionism in which the nation exported its ideals and institutions. All such expansionists could draw from many sources to support their plans. Some cited political, religious, and racial ideas; some were concerned with national security and power; others pointed to economic trends at home and abroad (see the overview table, "Rationales for Imperialism").

Ideological Arguments

Scholars, authors, politicians, and religious leaders provided interlocking ideological arguments for the new imperialism. Some intellectuals, for example, invoked social Darwinism, maintaining that the United States should engage in a competitive struggle for wealth and power with other nations. "The survival of the fittest," declared one writer, was "the law of nations as well as a law of nature." As European nations expanded into Asia and Africa in the 1880s and 1890s, seeking colonies, markets, and raw materials, these advocates argued that the United States had to adopt similar policies to ensure national success.

OVERVIEW

RATIONALES FOR IMPERIALISM

Category	Beliefs
Racism and social Darwinism	Convictions that "Anglo-Saxons" were racially superior and should dominate other peoples, either to ensure national success, establish international stability, or benefit the "inferior" races by imposing American ideas and institutions on them
Righteousness	The conviction that Christianity, and a supporting American culture, should be aggressively spread among the benighted peoples of other lands
Mahanism	The conviction, following the ideas advanced by Alfred Thayer Mahan, that U.S. security required a strong navy and economic and territorial expansion
Economics	A variety of arguments holding that American prosperity depended on acquiring access to foreign markets, raw materials, and investment opportunities

Related to social Darwinism was a pervasive belief in racial inequality and, particularly, in the superiority of people of English, or Anglo-Saxon, descent. To many Americans, the industrial progress, military strength, and political development of England and the United States were proof of an Anglo-Saxon superiority that carried with it a responsibility to extend the blessings of their rule to less-able people. John Fiske, a philosopher and historian, popularized these ideas in his oft-repeated lecture "Manifest Destiny." "The work which the English race began when it colonized North America," Fiske declaimed, "is destined to go on until every land on the earth's surface that is not already the seat of an old civilization shall become English in its language, in its religion, in its political habits and traditions, and to a predominant extent in the blood of its people." As a popular expression put it, colonialism was the "white man's burden," carrying with it a duty to aid and uplift other peoples. Such attitudes led some expansionists to favor imposing American ideas and practices on other cultures, regardless of those cultures' own values and customs. The political scientist John W. Burgess, for example, concluded that Anglo-

Saxons "must have a colonial policy" and "righteously assume sovereignty" over "incompetent" or "barbaric races" in other lands.

American missionaries also promoted expansionist sentiment. Hoping to evangelize the world, American religious groups increased the number of Protestant foreign missions sixfold from 1870 to 1900. Women in particular organized foreign missionary societies and served in the missions. Missionaries publicized their activities throughout the United States, generating interest in foreign developments and support for what one writer called the "imperialism of righteousness." Abroad they pursued a religious transformation that often resembled a cultural conversion, for they promoted trade, developed business interests, and encouraged westernization through technology and education as well as religion. Sometimes, as in the Hawaiian Islands, American missionaries even promoted annexation by the United States.

Indeed, the American religious press endlessly repeated the themes of national destiny, racial superiority, and religious zeal. The Reverend J. H. Barrows in early 1898 lectured on the "Christian conquest of Asia," suggesting that American Christianity and commerce would cross the Pacific to fulfill "the manifest destiny of the Christian Republic." Missionaries also contributed to the imperial impulse by describing their work, as Barrows did, in terms of the "conquest" of "enemy" territory. Thus while missionaries were motivated by what they considered to be idealism and often brought real benefits to other lands, especially in education and health, religious sentiments reinforced the ideology of American expansion.

Strategic Concerns

Other expansionists were motivated by strategic concerns, shaped by what seemed to be the forces of history and geography. America's location in the Western Hemisphere, its coastlines on two oceans, and the ambitions and activities of other nations, particularly Germany and Britain, convinced some

An American missionary and her Chinese converts study the Bible in Manchuria in 1903 under a U.S. flag. American missionaries wanted to spread the Gospel abroad but inevitably spread American influence as well.

Americans that the United States had to develop new policies to protect and promote its national security and interests. Alfred Thayer Mahan, a naval officer and president of the Naval War College, emphasized the importance of a strong navy for national greatness in his book *The Influence of Sea Power upon History.* To complement that navy, Mahan proposed that the United States build a canal across the isthmus of Panama to link its coasts, acquire naval bases in the Caribbean and the Pacific to protect the canal, and annex Hawaii and other Pacific islands to promote trade and service the fleet. The United States must "cast aside the policy of isolation which befitted her infancy," Mahan declared, and "begin to look outward."

Mahanism found a receptive audience. President Benjamin Harrison declared in 1891 that "as to naval stations and points of influence, we must look forward to a departure from the too conservative opinions which have been held heretofore." Still more vocal advocates of Mahan's program were a group of nationalistic Republicans, predominantly from the Northeast. They included politicians like Henry Cabot Lodge and Theodore Roosevelt, journalists like Whitelaw Reid of the *New York Tribune*

and Albert Shaw of the *Review of Reviews,* and diplomats and lawyers like John Hay and Elihu Root.

Conscious of European colonialism, such men favored imperial expansion, as Shaw wrote, "for the sake of our destiny, our dignity, our influence, and our usefulness." Roosevelt promoted Mahan's ideas when he became assistant secretary of the navy in 1897, but he was even more militaristic. Praising "the most valuable of all qualities, the soldierly virtues," Roosevelt declared in 1897: "No triumph of peace is quite so great as the supreme triumphs of war." One British observer concluded on the eve of the Spanish-American War that Mahan's influence had transformed the American spirit, serving "as oil to the flame of 'colonial expansion' everywhere leaping into life" (see "American Views: An Imperialist Views the World").

Even so, Mahan was not solely responsible for the large navy policy popular among imperialists. Its origins went back to 1881, when Congress established the Naval Advisory Board, which successfully lobbied for larger naval appropriations. An extensive program to replace the navy's obsolete wooden ships with modern cruisers and battleships was well under way by 1890 when the first volume of Mahan's book appeared. The United States soon possessed the formidable navy the expansionists wanted. This larger navy, in turn, demanded strategic bases and coaling stations. One writer indicated the circular nature of this development by noting in 1893 that Manifest Destiny now meant "the acquisition of such territory, far and near," that would secure "to our navy facilities desirable for the operations of a great naval power."

Economic Designs

One reason for the widespread support for a larger navy was its use to expand and protect America's international trade. Nearly all Americans favored economic expansion through foreign trade. Such a policy promised national prosperity: larger markets for manufacturers and farmers, greater profits for

CHRONOLOGY

1861–1869	Seward serves as secretary of state.
1867	U.S. purchases Alaska from Russia.
1870	Annexation of the Dominican Republic is rejected.
1881	Naval Advisory Board is created.
1887	United States gains naval rights to Pearl Harbor.
1889	First Pan-American Conference is held.
1890	Alfred Thayer Mahan publishes *The Influence of Sea Power upon History.*
1893	Harrison signs but Cleveland rejects a treaty for the annexation of Hawaii.
1893–1897	Depression increases interest in economic expansion abroad.
1894–1895	Sino-Japanese War is fought.
1895	U.S. intervenes in Great Britain–Venezuelan boundary dispute.
	Cuban insurrection against Spain begins.
1896	William McKinley is elected president on an imperialist platform.
1898	Spanish-American War is fought.
	Hawaii is annexed.
	Anti-Imperialist League is organized.
	Treaty of Paris is signed.
1899–1902	Filipino-American War is fought.

1899	Open Door note is issued.
1901	Theodore Roosevelt becomes president.
1903	Platt Amendment restricts Cuban autonomy.
	Panama "revolution" is abetted by the United States.
1904	United States acquires the Panama Canal Zone.
	Roosevelt Corollary is announced.
1904–1905	Russo-Japanese War is fought.
1905	Treaty of Portsmouth ends the Russo-Japanese War through U.S. mediation.
1906–1909	United States occupies Cuba.
1907–1908	Gentlemen's Agreement restricts Japanese immigration.
1909	United States intervenes in Nicaragua.
1912–1933	United States occupies Nicaragua.
1914	Panama Canal opens.
1914–1917	United States intervenes in Mexico.
1915–1934	United States occupies Haiti.
1916–1924	United States occupies the Dominican Republic.
1917	Puerto Ricans are granted U.S. citizenship.
1917–1922	United States occupies Cuba.

merchants and bankers, more jobs for workers. Far fewer favored the acquisition of colonies that was characteristic of European imperialism. Commercial, as opposed to colonial, goals were the primary objective. As one diplomat declared in 1890, the nation was more interested in the "annexation of trade" than in the annexation of territory.

The United States had long aggressively fostered American trade, especially in Latin America and East Asia. As early as 1844, the United States had negotiated a trade treaty with China, and ten years later a squadron under Commodore Matthew Perry had forced the Japanese to open their ports to American products. In the late nineteenth century, the dramatic expansion of the economy caused many Americans to favor more government action to open foreign markets to American exports. Alabama Sena-

tor John Morgan had the cotton and textiles produced in the New South in mind when he warned in 1882: "Our home market is not equal to the demands of our producing and manufacturing classes and to the capital which is seeking employment. . . . We must either enlarge the field of our traffic, or stop the business of manufacturing just where it is." More ominous, a naval officer trying to open Korea to U.S. products declared in 1878, "At least one-third of our mechanical and agricultural products are now in excess of our wants, and we must *export* these products or *deport* the people who are creating them."

Exports, particularly of manufactured goods, which grew ninefold between 1865 and 1900, did increase greatly in the late nineteenth century. Still, periodic depressions fed these fears of overproduction. The massive unemployment and social unrest

American Views
AN IMPERIALIST VIEWS THE WORLD

Theodore Roosevelt, Henry Cabot Lodge, Alfred Thayer Mahan, and other influential imperialists frequently corresponded with one another, expressing their views forcefully if not always in depth. The following excerpts are from Roosevelt's private correspondence in 1897, while he was assistant secretary of the Navy and before the Spanish-American War began.

❖ **In what ways does Roosevelt reflect the influence of Mahan?**

❖ **What is Roosevelt's view of war?**

❖ **How does Roosevelt view European nations?**

❖ **How does he view the independence of other nations in the Western Hemisphere?**

I suppose that I need not tell you that as regards Hawaii I take your views absolutely, as indeed I do on foreign policy generally. If I had my way we would annex those islands tomorrow. If that is impossible I would establish a protectorate over them. I believe we should build the Nicaraguan canal at once, and in the meantime that we should build a dozen new battleships, half of them on the Pacific Coast; and these battleships should have a large coal capacity and a consequent increased radius of action. . . . I think President Cleveland's action [in rejecting the annexation of Hawaii] was a colossal

crime, and we should be guilty of aiding him after the fact if we do not reverse what he did. I earnestly hope we can make the President [McKinley] look at things our way. Last Saturday night Lodge pressed his views upon him with all his strength.

I agree with all you say as to what will be the result if we fail to take Hawaii. It will show that we either have lost, or else wholly lack, the masterful instinct which alone can make a race great. I feel so deeply about it I hardly dare express myself in full. The terrible part is to see that it is the men

---

that accompanied these economic crises also provided social and political arguments for economic relief through foreign trade.

In the depression of the 1890s, with the secretary of state seeing "symptoms of revolution" in the Pullman strike and Coxey's Army of unemployed workers (see Chapter 22), this interest in foreign trade became obsessive. More systematic government efforts to promote trade seemed necessary, a conclusion strengthened by new threats to existing American markets. In that tumultuous decade, European nations raised tariff barriers against American products, and Japan and the European imperial powers began to restrict commercial opportunities in the areas of China that they controlled. Many American leaders decided that the United States had to adopt decisive new policies or face economic catastrophe.

First Steps

Despite the growing ideological, strategic, and economic arguments for imperialism, the government only fitfully interested itself in foreign affairs before the mid-1890s. It did not pursue a policy of **isolationism** from international affairs, for the nation maintained normal diplomatic and trade ties and at times vigorously intervened in Latin America and East Asia. But in general the government deferred to the initiative of private interests, reacted haphazardly to outside events, and did little to create a professional foreign service.

Seward and Blaine

Despite this generally passive and ineffective approach, two secretaries of state, William H. Seward, secretary under Presidents Lincoln and Andrew

of education who take the lead in trying to make us prove traitors to our race.

I fully realize the importance of the Pacific coast. . . . But there are big problems in the West Indies also. Until we definitely turn Spain out of those islands (and if I had my way that would be done tomorrow), we will always be menaced by trouble there. We should acquire the Danish Islands [in the West Indies], and by turning Spain out should serve notice that no strong European power, and especially not Germany, should be allowed to gain a foothold by supplanting some weak European power. I do not fear England; Canada is a hostage for her good behavior.

I wish we had a perfectly consistent foreign policy, and that this policy was that every European power should be driven out of America, and every foot of American soil, including the nearest islands in both the Pacific and the Atlantic, should be in the hands of independent American states, and so far as possible in the possession of the United States or under its protection.

To speak with a frankness which our timid friends would call brutal, I would regard a war with Spain from two standpoints: first, the advisability on the grounds both of humanity and self-interest of interfering on behalf of the Cubans, and of taking one more step toward the complete freeing of America from European dominion; second, the benefit done our people by giving them something to think of which isn't material gain, and especially the benefit done our military forces by trying both the Navy and the Army in actual practice. I should be very sorry not to see us make the experiment of trying to land, and therefore feed and clothe, an expeditionary force [on Cuba], if only for the sake of learning from our own blunders. I should hope that the force would have some fighting to do. It would be a great lesson, and we would profit much by it.

I wish there was a chance that the [U.S. battleship] *Maine* was going to be used against some foreign power; by preference Germany—but I am not particular, and I'd take even Spain if nothing better offered.

Source: The Letters of Theodore Roosevelt *selected and edited by Elting E. Morison, Cambridge: Harvard University Press. Copyright © 1951, by the President and Fellows of Harvard College. Reprinted by permission of the publisher.*

Johnson (1861–1869), and James G. Blaine, secretary under Presidents Garfield and Harrison (1881, 1889–1892), laid the foundation for a larger and more aggressive American role in world affairs. Seward possessed an elaborate imperial vision, based on his understanding of commercial opportunities, strategic necessities, and national destiny. In his concerns for opening East Asia to American commerce and establishing American hegemony over the Caribbean, he anticipated the subsequent course of American expansion. His hopes of annexing Canada and Greenland went unfulfilled, but he did purchase Alaska from Russia in 1867, approve the navy's occupation of the Midway Islands in the Pacific, push American trade on a reluctant Japan, and repeatedly try to acquire Caribbean naval bases (see Map 24-1). But his policy of expansion, as one observer noted, "went somewhat too far and too fast for the public," and many of his plans fizzled. Congressional opposition frustrated his efforts to obtain Haiti and the Dominican Republic and to purchase the Danish West Indies; Colombia blocked his attempt to gain construction rights for a canal across the isthmus of Panama.

The Grant administration (1869–1877) haphazardly pursued some of Seward's goals, but met resistance. When Grant attempted to take over the Dominican Republic in 1870, for example, the Senate defeated the annexation treaty. Opponents of overseas expansion complained of its cost, worried about the "alien races" it would incorporate into the nation, and above all condemned it as contrary to basic American principles. Such anticolonial sentiments would weaken, however, in the next generation.

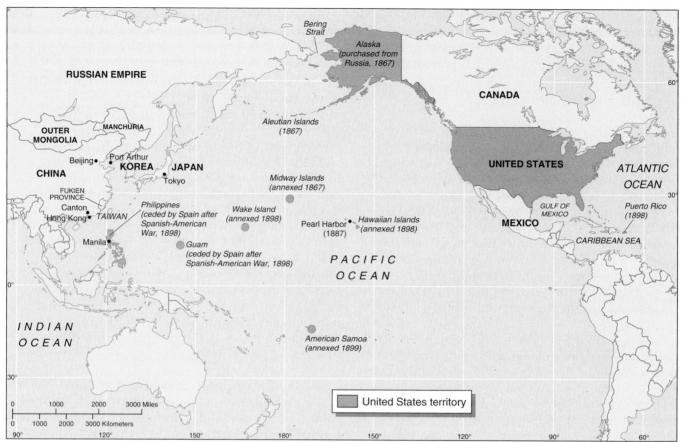

Map 24-1   United States Expansion in the Pacific, 1867-1899
Pursuing visions of a commercial empire in the Pacific, the United States steadily expanded its territorial possessions as well as its influence there in the late nineteenth century.

Blaine, though less thoughtful than Seward, was an equally vigorous, if inconsistent, advocate of expansion. He worked to extend what he called America's "commercial empire" in the Pacific. And he sought to ensure U.S. sovereignty over any canal in Panama, insisting that it be "a purely American waterway to be treated as part of our own coastline." In an effort to induce Latin American nations to import manufactured products from the United States rather than Europe, Blaine proposed a conference among the nations of the Western Hemisphere in 1881. The First International American Conference finally met in 1889. There Blaine called for the establishment of a customs union to reduce trade barriers. He expected this union to strengthen U.S. control of hemispheric markets. The Latin American nations, however, wary of economic subordination to the colossus of the north, rejected Blaine's plan. Instead, the conference established what eventually came to be known as the **Pan American Union**. Based in Washington, it helped promote hemispheric understanding and cooperation.

If U.S. officials were increasingly assertive toward Latin America and Asia, however, they remained little involved in Europe (one secretary of state declared in 1885 that he had no interest in European affairs, which he regarded "with impatience and contempt"). They were wholly indifferent to Africa, which the European powers were then carving up into colonies. In short, despite some important precedents for the future, much of American foreign policy remained undeveloped, sporadic, and impulsive.

Hawaii

Blaine regarded Hawaii as "indispensably" part of "the American system." As early as 1842, the United States had announced its opposition to European control of Hawaii, a key way station in the China trade where New England missionaries and whalers were active. Although the islands remained under native monarchs, American influence grew, particularly as other Americans arrived to establish sugar plantations and eventually dominate the economy.

Treaties in 1875 and 1887 integrated the islands into the American economy and gave the United States control over Pearl Harbor on the island of Oahu. In 1887, the United States rejected a proposal from Britain and France for a joint guarantee of Hawaii's independence and endorsed a new Hawaiian constitution that gave political power to wealthy white residents. The obvious next step was U.S. annexation, which Blaine endorsed in 1891.

A combination of factors soon impelled American planters to bid for annexation. The McKinley Tariff Act of 1890 effectively closed the U.S. market to Hawaiian sugar producers, facing them with economic ruin. At the same time, Queen Liliuokalani moved to restore native control of Hawaiian affairs. To ensure market access and protect their political authority, the American planters decided to seek annexation to the United States. In 1893, they overthrew the queen. John Stevens, the American minister, ordered U.S. Marines to help the rebels. He then declared an American protectorate over the new Hawaii government and wired Washington: "The Hawaiian pear is now fully ripe, and this is the golden hour for the United States to pluck it." A delegation from the new provisional government, containing no native Hawaiians, went to Washington to draft a treaty for annexation. President Harrison signed the pact but could not get Senate approval before the new Cleveland administration took office.

Cleveland immediately called for an investigation of the whole affair. Soon convinced that "the undoubted sentiment of the people is for the Queen, against the provisional Government, and against annexation," Cleveland apologized to the queen for the "flagrant wrong" done her by the "reprehensible conduct of the American minister and the unauthorized presence on land of a military force of the United States." But the American-dominated provisional government refused to step down, and Cleveland's rejection of annexation set off a noisy debate in the United States.

Many Republicans strongly supported annexation, which they regarded as merely part of a larger plan of expansion. One eastern Republican manufacturer called for the annexation of Hawaii as the first step toward making the Pacific "an American ocean, dominated by American commercial enterprise for all time." On the West Coast, where California business interests had close ties with the islands, the commercial and strategic value of Hawaii seemed obvious. The *San Francisco Examiner* declared, "Hoist the Stars and Stripes. It is a case of manifest destiny." Reflecting racial impe-

rialism, others argued that annexation would both fittingly reward the enterprising white residents of Hawaii and provide an opportunity to civilize native Hawaiians.

Democrats generally opposed annexation. They doubted, as Missouri Senator George Vest declared, whether the United States should desert its traditional principles and "venture upon the great colonial system of the European powers." Most Democrats believed, as another argued, that "the mission of our nation is to build up and make a greater country out of what we have, instead of annexing islands."

The Hawaiian episode of 1893 thus foreshadowed the arguments over imperialism at the end of the century and emphasized the policy differences between Democrats and the increasingly expansionist Republicans.

Chile and Venezuela

American reactions to developments in other countries in the 1890s also reflected an increasingly assertive national policy and excitable public opinion. In 1891, American sailors on shore leave in Chile became involved in a drunken brawl that left two of them dead, seventeen injured, and dozens in jail. The incident heightened the already tense relations between the United States and Chile. After supporting the unpopular (and losing) side in a recent Chilean revolution, President Harrison had warned the new leaders that "sometime it may be necessary to instruct them." Now, encouraged by a combative navy, he threatened military retaliation against Chile, provoking an outburst of bellicose nationalism in the United States. Harrison relented only when Chile apologized and paid an indemnity.

A few years later, the United States again threatened war over a minor issue but against a more formidable opponent. Though opposed to annexing Hawaii, President Cleveland adopted an increasingly aggressive policy in Latin America. In 1895, he intervened in a boundary dispute between Great Britain and Venezuela over British Guiana. Cleveland was motivated not only by the long-standing U.S. goal of challenging Britain for Latin American markets but also by ever more expansive notions of the **Monroe Doctrine** and the authority of the United States. He also seized on this foreign policy issue to divert public attention from a severe economic depression. Secretary of State Richard Olney sent Britain a blunt note (a "twenty-inch gun," Cleveland called it) demanding arbitration of the disputed territory and stoutly asserting American supremacy in the Western Hemisphere. Cleveland urged Congress to establish

As other imperial powers look on, the United States abandons its traditional principles to rush headlong into world affairs. Uncle Sam would not always find it a smooth ride.

a commission to determine the boundary and enforce its decision by war if necessary. The astonished British ambassador reported an "extraordinary state of excitement into which the Congress of the United States and the whole country were thrown by the warlike Message . . . a condition of mind which can only be described as hysterical." As war fever swept the United States, Britain agreed to arbitration, recognizing the limited nature of the issue that so convulsed Anglo-American relations.

The United States' assertion of hemispheric dominance angered Latin Americans, and their fears deepened when it decided arbitration terms with Britain without consulting Venezuela, which protested before bowing to American pressure. The United States had intervened less to protect Venezuela from the British bully than to advance its own hegemony. The further significance of the Venezuelan crisis, as Captain Mahan noted, lay in its "awakening of our countrymen to the fact that we must come out of our isolation . . . and take our share in the turmoil of the world."

But if these bold steps in Hawaii, Chile, and Venezuela indicated an increasing role for the United States in world affairs, the nation had yet to adopt a consistent policy for expanding its influence. That would happen in the next few years.

The Spanish-American War

The forces pushing the United States toward imperialism and international power came to a head in the Spanish-American War. The war had its origins in Cuba's quest for independence from the oppressive colonial control of Spain. The struggle activated Americans' long-standing interest in the island. Many sympathized with the Cuban rebels' yearning for freedom, others worried that disorder in Cuba threatened their own economic and political interests, and some thought that United States intervention would increase its influence in the Caribbean and along key Pacific routes to Asian markets. But few foresaw that the war that finally erupted in 1898 would dramatically change America's relationships with the rest of the world and give it a colonial empire.

The Cuban Revolution

In the nineteenth century, Cubans rebelled repeatedly against Spanish rule. One rebellion, the Ten Years' War from 1868 to 1878, had been brutally suppressed, but not before drawing American interest and sympathy. Cuba was the last major European colony in Latin America, with an economic potential that attracted American business interests and a strategic significance for any Central American canal. In the 1880s, Spanish control became increasingly harsh even while American investors expanded their economic influence in Cuba. Cuban discontent erupted again in 1895 when the Cuban patriot José Martí launched another revolt.

The rebellion was a classic guerrilla war in which the rebels controlled the countryside and the Spanish army the towns and cities. American economic interests were seriously affected, for both Cubans and Spaniards destroyed American property and disrupted American trade. The Cleveland administration, motivated as much by a desire to protect American property and establish a safe environment for further investments as by a concern for Cuban rights, urged Spain to adopt reforms. But the brutality with which Spain attempted to suppress the revolt promoted American sympathy for the Cuban insurgents. Determined to cut the rebels off from their peasant supporters, the Spaniards herded most civilians into "reconcentration camps," where tens of thousands died of starvation and disease.

Americans' sympathy was further aroused by the sensationalist **yellow press**. To attract readers and boost advertising revenues, the popular press of the day adopted bold headlines, fevered editorials, and real or exaggerated stories of violence, sex, and corruption. A circulation war between William Randolph Hearst's *New York Journal* and Joseph Pulitzer's *New York World* helped stimulate interest in Cuban war. "Blood on the roadsides, blood on the fields, blood on the doorsteps, blood, blood, blood! The old, the young, the weak, the crippled—all are butchered without mercy," the *World* feverishly reported of Cuba. "Is there no nation wise enough, brave enough to aid this blood-smitten land?"

The nation's religious press, partly because it reflected the prejudice many Protestants held against Catholic Spain, also advocated American intervention. One religious newspaper endorsed an American war against Spain as God's instrument for attacking "that system of iniquity, the papacy." Another promised that if war came, "every Methodist preacher will be a recruiting officer" for the American military. The *Catholic Herald* of New York sarcastically referred to the "bloodthirsty preachers" of the Protestant churches, but such preachers undeniably influenced American opinion against Spain.

As the Cuban rebellion dragged on, more and more Americans advocated intervention to stop the carnage, protect U.S. investments, or uphold various principles. Expansionists like Roosevelt and Lodge clamored for intervention, but so did their opponents. Populists, for example, sympathized with a people seeking independence from colonial rule and petitioned Congress to support the crusade for Cuban freedom; conservative Democrats hoped that the excitement of intervention and war "might do much towards directing the minds of the people from imaginary ills, the relief of which is erroneously supposed to be reached by 'Free Silver.'" In the election of 1896, both major parties endorsed Cuban independence. The Democratic platform expressed "sympathy to the people of Cuba in their heroic struggle for liberty." The Republican platform not only wished Cubans success in "their determined contest for liberty" but urged intervention on the grounds that Spain was "unable to protect the property or lives of resident American citizens."

Growing Tensions

In his 1897 inaugural address, President William McKinley outlined an expansionist program ranging from further enlargement of the navy to the annexation of Hawaii and the construction of a Central American canal in Nicaragua, but his administration soon focused on Cuba. McKinley's principal complaint was that chronic disorder in Cuba disrupted America's investments and agitated public opinion. Personally opposed to military intervention, McKinley first used diplomacy to press Spain to adopt reforms that would settle the rebellion. Following his instructions, the U.S. minister to Spain warned the Spanish government that if it did not quickly establish peace, the United States would take whatever steps it "should deem necessary to procure this result." In late 1897, Spain modified its brutal military tactics and offered limited autonomy to Cuba. But Cubans insisted on complete independence, which Spain refused to grant.

Relations between the United States and Spain deteriorated. In early 1898, the *New York Journal* published a private letter from the Spanish minister to the United States that mocked McKinley as "weak and a bidder for the admiration of the crowd." (The *Journal* called the letter "the worst insult to the United States in its history.") McKinley found more troubling the letter's intimation that Spain was not negotiating in good faith. Only days later, on February 15, 1898, the U.S. battleship *Maine* blew up in Havana harbor, killing 260 men. The Spaniards were not responsible for the tragedy, which a modern naval inquiry has attributed to an internal accident. But many Americans agreed with Theodore Roosevelt, the assistant secretary of the navy, who called it "an act of dirty treachery on the part of the Spaniards" and told McKinley that only war was "compatible with our national honor."

Popular anger was inflamed, but the sinking of the *Maine* by itself did not bring war, though it did restrict McKinley's options. Other pressures soon began to build on the president. Increasingly, business interests favored war as less disruptive than volatile peace that threatened their investments. Senator Lodge reported a consensus "that this situation must end. We cannot go on indefinitely with this strain, this suspense, and this uncertainty, this tottering upon the verge of war. It is killing to business." McKinley also feared that a moderate policy would endanger congressional candidates. Again Senator Lodge, although hesitant to suggest "war for political reasons," nevertheless advised McKinley, "If the war in Cuba drags on through the summer with nothing done, we shall go down in the greatest [election] defeat ever known."

At the end of March 1898 (when the French ambassador in Washington reported that "a sort of bellicose fury has seized the American nation"), McKinley sent Spain an ultimatum. He demanded an armistice in Cuba, an end to the reconcentration policy, and the acceptance of American arbitration, which implied Cuban independence. Desperately, Spain made concessions, abolishing reconcentration and declaring a unilateral armistice. But McKinley had already begun war preparations, withdrawing American diplomats from Cuba and Spain, ordering the navy to prepare for war, and drafting a war message for

Congress. He submitted that message on April 11, asking for authority to use force against Spain "in the name of humanity, in the name of civilization, in behalf of endangered American interests." Congress declared war on Spain on April 25, 1898.

A few national leaders welcomed the war as a step toward imperialism, but there was little popular support for such a policy. Most interventionists were not imperialists, and Congress added the **Teller Amendment** to the war resolution, disclaiming any intention of annexing Cuba and promising that Cubans would govern themselves. Congress also refused to approve either a canal bill or the annexation of Hawaii. Nevertheless, the Spanish-American War did turn the nation toward imperialism.

War and Empire

The decisive engagement of the war took place not in Cuba but in another Spanish colony, the Philippines, and it involved the favored tool of the expansionists, the new navy (see Map 24-2). In 1897, McKinley had approved plans for an attack on the Philippines in the event of war with Spain. Once war was declared, Commodore George Dewey led the U.S. Asiatic squadron into Manila Bay and destroyed the much weaker Spanish fleet on May 1, 1898. This dramatic victory galvanized expansionist sentiment in the United States. The navy had long coveted Manila Bay as a strategic harbor, but other Americans, casting an eye on commercial opportunities in China, saw a greater significance in the victory. With Dewey's triumph, exulted one expansionist, "We are taking our proper rank among the nations of the world. We are after markets, the greatest markets now existing in the world." To expand this foothold in Asia, McKinley ordered troops to the Philippines, postponing the military expedition to Cuba itself.

Dewey's victory also precipitated the annexation of Hawaii, which had seemed hopeless only weeks before. Annexationists now pointed to the is-

Map 24-2   The Spanish-American War
The United States gained quick victories in both theaters of the Spanish-American War. Its naval power proved decisive, with Commodore Dewey destroying one enemy fleet in the Philippines and a second U.S. naval force cutting off the Spanish in Cuba.

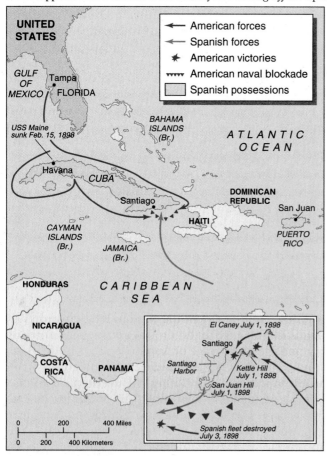

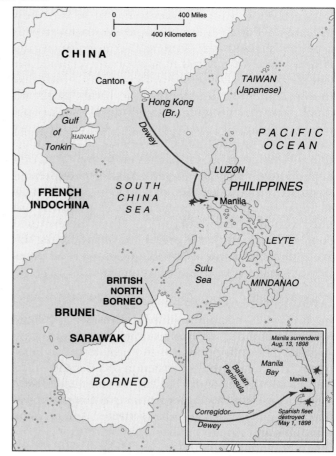

lands' strategic importance as stepping-stones to Manila. "To maintain our flag in the Philippines, we must raise our flag in Hawaii," the *New York Sun* contended. McKinley himself privately declared, "We need Hawaii just as much and a good deal more than we did California. It is Manifest Destiny." In July, Congress approved annexation, a decision welcomed by Hawaii's white minority. Natives solemnly protested this step taken "without reference to the consent of the people of the Hawaiian Islands." Filipinos would soon face the same American imperial impulse.

Military victory also came swiftly in Cuba, once the U.S. Army finally landed in late June. Victory depended largely on Spanish ineptitude, for the American army was poorly led, trained, and supplied. Troops had to fight with antiquated weapons and wear wool uniforms in the sweltering tropics. They were issued rotting and poisoned food by a corrupt and inefficient War Department. More than five thousand Americans died of diseases and accidents brought on by such mismanagement; only 379 were killed in battle. State militias supplemented the small regular army, as did volunteer units, such as the famous Rough Riders, a cavalry unit of cowboys and eastern dandies assembled by Theodore Roosevelt.

While the Rough Riders captured public attention, other units were more effective. The 10th Negro Cavalry, for example, played the crucial role in capturing San Juan Hill, a battle popularly associated with the Rough Riders. One war correspondent wrote of the black soldiers' charge: "They followed their leaders up the terrible hill from whose crest the

Fighting in Cuba in the Spanish-American War was brief but intense. This contemporary lithograph depicts the Ninth and Tenth Cavalry Regiments, African-American soldiers with white officers, charging the Spanish army at the Battle of Las Guasimos, June 24, 1898. Black soldiers composed nearly a fourth of the American army in Cuba.

desperate Spaniards poured down a deadly fire of shell and musketry. They never faltered. . . . Their aim was splendid, their coolness was superb. . . . The war had not shown greater heroism." Nevertheless, the Rough Riders gained the credit, thanks in part to Roosevelt's self-serving and well-promoted account of the conflict, which one humorist proposed retitling *Alone in Cuba.*

U.S. naval power again proved decisive. In a lopsided battle on July 3, the obsolete Spanish squadron in Cuba was destroyed, isolating the Spanish army and guaranteeing its defeat. U.S. forces then seized the nearby Spanish colony of Puerto Rico without serious opposition. Humbled, Spain signed an armistice ending the war on August 12.

Americans were delighted with their military achievements, but the *Philadelphia Inquirer* cautioned, "With peace will come new responsibilities, which must be met. We have colonies to look after and develop."

The Treaty of Paris

The armistice required Spain to accept Cuban independence, cede Puerto Rico and Guam (a Pacific island between Hawaii and the Philippines), and allow the Americans to occupy Manila pending the final disposition of the Philippines at a formal peace conference. The acquisition of Puerto Rico and Guam indicated the expansionist nature the conflict had assumed for the United States. So did the postponement of the Philippine issue. McKinley knew that delay would permit the advocates of expansion to build public support for annexation. Because the U.S. Army did not capture Manila until after the armistice had been signed, he could not claim the islands by conquest, as Spain pointed out.

McKinley defended his decision to acquire the Philippines in self-righteous imperialist rhetoric, promising to extend Christian influence and American values. But he was motivated primarily by a determination to use the islands to strengthen America's political and commercial position in East Asia. Moreover, he believed the Filipinos poorly suited to self-rule, and he feared that Germany or Japan might seize the Philippines if the United States did not. Meeting in Paris in December, American and Spanish negotiators settled the final terms for peace. Spain agreed—despite Filipino demands for independence—to cede the Philippines to the United States.

The decision to acquire the Philippines sparked a dramatic debate over the ratification of the Treaty of Paris. Imperialists invoked the familiar arguments of economic expansion, national destiny, and strategic necessity while asserting that

Americans had religious and racial responsibilities to advance civilization by uplifting backward peoples. The *United States Investor* spoke for business leaders, for example, in demanding the Philippines as "a base of operations in the East" to protect American interests in China; other economic expansionists argued that the Philippines themselves had valuable resources and were a market for American goods or warned that "our commercial rivals in the Orient" would grab the islands if the United States did not. The *Presbyterian Banner* spoke for what it termed a nearly unanimous religious press in affirming "the desirability of America's retaining the Philippines as a duty in the interest of human freedom and Christian progress." The United States, it concluded, was "morally compelled to become an Asiatic power." Conveniently ignoring that most Filipinos were Catholic, the *Baptist Union* insisted: "The conquest by force of arms must be followed up by conquest for Christ."

Opponents of the treaty raised profound questions about national goals and ideals. They included such prominent figures as the civil service reformer Carl Schurz, steel baron Andrew Carnegie, social reformer Jane Addams, labor leader Samuel Gompers, and author Mark Twain. Their organizational base was the **Anti-Imperialist League**, which campaigned against the treaty, distributing pamphlets, petitioning Congress, and holding rallies. League members' criticisms reflected a conviction that imperialism was a repudiation of America's moral and political traditions embodied in the Declaration of Independence. The acquisition of overseas colonies, they argued, conflicted with the nation's commitment to liberty and its claim to moral superiority. They regarded as loathesome and hypocritical the transformation of a war to free Cuba into a campaign for imperial conquest and subjugation.

William Jennings Bryan ridiculed the imperialists' arguments of national destiny: "When the desire to steal becomes uncontrollable in an individual he is declared to be a kleptomaniac and is sent to an asylum; when the desire to grab land becomes uncontrollable in a nation we are told that the 'currents of destiny are flowing through the hearts of men.'" Some African Americans derided the rhetoric of Anglo-Saxon superiority that underlay imperialism and even organized the Black Man's Burden Association to promote Philippine independence.

But other arguments were less high-minded. Many anti-imperialists objected to expansion on the racist grounds that Filipinos were inferior and unassimilable. Gompers feared that cheap Asian labor would undercut the wages and living standards of

Republicans countered William Jennings Bryan's attempt to make imperialism an issue in 1900 by wrapping themselves in patriotism and the American flag. "Take Your Choice," a cartoon from Judge, posed President McKinley raising Old Glory over the Philippines with a disheveled and frantic Bryan chopping down the symbol of American pride and power.

American workers. The *San Francisco Call*, representing California-Hawaiian sugar interests, also wanted no competition from the Philippines.

The debate over the treaty became bitter. Furious at the opponents of empire, Roosevelt called them "little better than traitors." Carl Schurz responded that McKinley himself had earlier termed territorial annexation through conquest "a criminal act of aggression"; the president's seizure of the Philippines, Puerto Rico, and Hawaii, said Schurz, had perverted a legitimate concern for Cuba into "a war of selfish ambition and conquest."

Finally, on February 6, 1899, the Senate narrowly ratified the treaty. All but two Republicans supported the pact; most Democrats opposed it, although several voted for the treaty after Bryan suggested that approval was necessary to end the war and detach the Philippines from Spain. Thereafter, he hoped, a congressional resolution would give the Filipinos their independence. But by a single vote, the Republicans defeated a Democratic proposal for

Philippine independence once a stable government had been established; the United States would keep the islands.

Bryan attempted to make the election of 1900 a referendum on "the paramount issue" of imperialism, promising to free the Philippines if the Democrats won. But many other issues determined the election. Some of the most ardent anti-imperialists were conservatives who remained loyal to McKinley because they could not tolerate Bryan's economic policies. Republicans also benefited from the prosperity the country experienced under McKinley after the hard 1890s, and they played on the nationalist emotions evoked by the war, especially by nominating the "hero of San Juan Hill," Theodore Roosevelt, for vice president. "If you choose to vote for America, if you choose to vote for the flag for which we fought," Roosevelt said, "then you will vote to sustain the administration of President

Roosevelt's well-advertised exploits in the Spanish-American War propelled his political career. After being elected governor of New York in 1898, he received the Republican nomination for vice president in 1900 and often seemed to overshadow President McKinley.

McKinley." Bryan lost again, as in 1896, and under Republican leadership, the United States became an imperial nation.

Imperial Ambitions: The United States and East Asia, 1899–1917

In 1899, as the United States occupied its new empire, Assistant Secretary of State John Bassett Moore observed that the nation had become "a world power. . . . Where formerly we had only commercial interests, we now have territorial and political interests as well." American policies to promote those expanded interests focused first on East Asia and Latin America, where the Spanish-American War had provided the United States with both opportunities and challenges. In Asia, the first issue concerned the fate of the Philippines, but looming beyond it were American ambitions in China, where other imperial nations had their own goals.

The Filipino-American War

Filipino nationalists, like Cuban insurgents, were already fighting Spain for their independence before the sudden American intervention. The Filipino leader, Emilio Aguinaldo, welcomed Dewey's naval victory as the sign of a de facto alliance with the United States; he then issued a declaration of independence and proclaimed the Philippine Republic. His own troops captured most of Luzon, the Philippines' major island, before the U.S. Army arrived. But the Filipinos' optimism declined as American officials acted in an increasingly imperious manner toward them, first refusing to meet with the "savages," then insisting that Filipino forces withdraw from Manila or face "forcible action," and finally dismissing the claims of Aguinaldo and "his so-called government." When the Treaty of Paris provided for U.S. ownership rather than independence, Filipinos felt betrayed. Mounting tensions erupted in a battle between American and Filipino troops outside Manila on February 4, 1899, sparking a long and brutal war.

Ultimately, the United States used nearly four times as many soldiers to suppress the Filipinos as to defeat Spain in Cuba and, in a tragic irony, employed many of the same brutal methods for which it had condemned Spain. Recognizing that "the Filipino masses are loyal to Aguinaldo and the government which he heads," U.S. military leaders adopted ever harsher measures, often directed at civilians,

who were crowded into concentration camps in which perhaps 200,000 died. Americans often made little effort to distinguish between soldiers and noncombatants, viewing all Filipinos with racial antagonism. After reporting one massacre of a thousand men, women, and children, an American soldier declared, "I am in my glory when I can sight my gun on some dark skin and pull the trigger."

Before the military imposed censorship on war news, reporters confirmed U.S. atrocities; one wrote that "American troops have been relentless, have killed to exterminate men, women, and children, prisoners and captives, active insurgents and suspected people, from lads of 10 and up." A California newspaper defended such actions with remarkable candor: "There has been too much hypocrisy about this Philippine business. . . . Let us all be frank. WE DO NOT WANT THE FILIPINOS. WE DO WANT THE PHILIPPINES. All of our troubles in this annexation matter have been caused by the presence in the Philippine Islands of the Filipinos. . . . The more of them killed the better. It seems harsh. But they must yield before the superior race."

The overt racism of the war repelled African Americans. John Mitchell, a Virginia editor, condemned all the talk of "white man's burden" as deceptive rhetoric for brutal acts that could not be "defended either in moral or international law." Mitchell argued that white Southerners needed missionary work more than freedom-loving Filipinos. "With the government acquiescing in the oppression and butchery of a dark race in this country and the enslaving and slaughtering of a dark race in the Philippines," he concluded, "we think it time to call all missionaries home and have them work on our own people."

Other Americans also denounced the war. The Anti-Imperialist League revived, citing the war as proof of the corrosive influence of imperialism on the nation's morals and principles. Professors addressed antiwar rallies on college campuses. "Alas, what a fall," one University of Michigan professor told his audience. "Within the circuit of a single year to have declined from the moral leadership of mankind into the common brigandage of the robber nations of the world." By 1902, the realities of imperial policy—including American casualties—disillusioned most who had clamored to save Cuba.

By that time, however, the American military had largely suppressed the rebellion, and the United States had established a colonial government headed by an American governor general appointed by the president. Filipino involvement in the government was limited on educational and religious grounds.

The Filipino-American War was documented extensively by photographers. "First Position Near Manila" shows soldiers of the Twentieth Kansas Infantry Regiment deployed early in what would become a lengthy and brutal war.

Compared to the Americans' brutal war policies, U. S. colonial rule was relatively benign, though paternalistic. William Howard Taft, the first governor general, launched a program that brought the islands new schools and roads, a public health system, and an economy tied closely to both the United States and a small Filipino elite. Independence would take nearly half a century.

China and the Open Door

America's determined involvement in the Philippines reflected its preoccupation with China. By the mid-1890s, other powers threatened prospects for American commercial expansion in China. Japan, after defeating China in 1895, annexed Taiwan and secured economic privileges in the mainland province of Fukien (Fujian); the major European powers then competed aggressively to claim other areas of China as their own **spheres of influence**. In Manchuria, Russia won control of Port Arthur (Lüshun) and the right

to construct a railway. Germany secured a ninety-nine year lease on another Chinese port and mining and railroad privileges on the Shandong Peninsula. The British wrung special concessions in Kowloon, opposite Hong Kong, and in other Chinese provinces, as well as a port facing the Russians in Manchuria. France gained a lease on ports and exclusive commercial privileges in southern China.

These developments alarmed the American business community. It was confident that given an equal opportunity, the United States would prevail in international trade because of its efficient production and marketing systems. But the creation of exclusive spheres of influence would limit the opportunity to compete. In early 1898, business leaders organized the Committee on American Interests in China to lobby Washington to promote American trade in the shrinking Chinese market. The committee persuaded the nation's chambers of commerce to petition the McKinley administration to act. This campaign influenced McKinley's interest in acquiring the Philippines, but the Philippines, in the words of Mark Hanna, were only a "foothold"; China was the real target. The State Department soon reported that, given overproduction for the home market, "the United States has important interests at stake in the partition of commercial facilities in regions which are likely to offer developing markets for its goods. Nowhere is this consideration of more interest than in its relation to the Chinese Empire."

In 1899, the government moved to advance those interests. Without consulting the Chinese, Secretary of State John Hay asked the imperial powers to maintain an **Open Door** for the commercial and financial activities of all nations within their Chinese spheres of influence. Privately, Hay had already approved a plan to seize a Chinese port for the United States if necessary to join in the partition of China, but equal opportunity for trade and investment would serve American interests far better. It would avoid the expense of military occupation, avert fur-

The United States usually preferred the "annexation of trade" to the annexation of territory. The Open Door policy promised to advance American commercial expansion, but Uncle Sam had to restrain other imperialists with colonial objectives.

A FAIR FIELD AND NO FAVOR.

UNCLE SAM: "I'm out for commerce, not conquest."

ther domestic criticism of U.S. imperialism, and guarantee a wider sphere for American business.

The other nations replied evasively, except for Russia, which rejected the Open Door concept. In 1900, an antiforeign Chinese nationalist movement known as the Boxers laid seige to the diplomatic quarters in Beijing. The defeat of the Boxer Rebellion by a multinational military force, to which the United States contributed troops, again raised the prospect of a division of China among colonial powers. Hay sent a second Open Door note, reaffirming "the principle of equal and impartial trade" and respect for China's territorial integrity.

Despite Hay's notes, China remained a tempting arena for imperial schemes. But the Open Door became a cardinal doctrine of American foreign policy in the twentieth century, a means by which the United States sought to dominate foreign markets. The United States promoted an informal or economic empire, as opposed to the traditional territorial colonial empire that Americans preferred to identify with European powers. Henceforth, American economic interests expected the U.S. government to oppose any developments that threatened to close other nations' economies to American penetration and to advance "private enterprise" abroad.

Rivalry with Japan and Russia

At the turn of the twentieth century, both the Japanese and the Russians were more deeply involved in East Asia than the United States was. They expressed little support for the Open Door, which they correctly saw as favoring American interests over their own. But in pursuing their ambitions in China, the two came into conflict with each other. Alarmed at the threat of Russian expansion in Manchuria and Korea, Japan in 1904 attacked the Russian fleet at Port Arthur and defeated the Russians in Manchuria.

In this Russo-Japanese war, American sympathies lay with Japan, for the Russians were attempting to close Manchuria to foreign trade. President Theodore Roosevelt privately complained that a reluctant American public opinion meant that "we cannot fight to keep Manchuria open." He thus welcomed the Japanese attack in the belief that "Japan is playing our game." But he soon feared that an overwhelming Japanese victory could threaten American interests as much as Russian expansionism did, so he skillfully mediated an end to the war. In the Treaty of Portsmouth in 1905, Japan won control of Russia's sphere of influence in Manchuria, half the Russian island of Sakhalin, and recognition of its domination of Korea.

This treaty marked Japan's emergence as a great power, but ironically, it worsened relations with the United States. Anti-American riots broke out in Tokyo. The Japanese people blamed Roosevelt for obstructing further Japanese gains and blocking a Russian indemnity that would have helped Japan pay for the war. Tensions were further aggravated by San Francisco's decision in 1906 to segregate Asian schoolchildren to avoid affecting the "youthful impressions" of white children. Japan regarded this as a racist insult, and Roosevelt worried that "the infernal fools in California" would provoke war. Finally he got the school order rescinded in exchange for his limiting Japanese immigration, which lay at the heart of California's hostility. Under the **Gentlemen's Agreement**, worked out through a series of diplomatic notes in 1907 and 1908, Japan agreed not to issue passports to workers coming to the United States, and the United States promised not to prohibit Japanese immigration overtly or completely.

To calm their mutual suspicions in East Asia, the United States and Japan adopted other agreements but failed to halt the deteriorating relationship. The Taft-Katsura Agreement (1905), the Root-Takahira Agreement (1908), and the Lansing-Ishii Agreement (1917) seemed to trade grudging American acceptance of Japan's special interests in Manchuria and control of Korea for Japanese promises to respect American rule in the Philippines and maintain the Open Door in China. But these agreements were vague, if not contradictory, and produced discord rather than harmony between the two countries.

Increasingly, Japan began to exclude American trade from its territories in East Asia and to press for further control over China. Elihu Root, Roosevelt's secretary of state, insisted that the Open Door and American access be maintained but asserted also that the United States did not want to be "a protagonist in a controversy in China with Russia and Japan or with either of them." The problem was that the United States could not sustain the Open Door without becoming a protagonist in China. This paradox, and the unwillingness to commit military force, would plague American foreign policy in Asia for decades.

Imperial Power: The United States and Latin America, 1899–1917

In Latin America, where no major powers directly challenged American objectives as Japan and Russia did in Asia, the United States was more successful in exercising imperial power (see Map 24-3). In the two decades after the Spanish-American War, the United States intervened militarily in Latin America no fewer than twenty times to promote its own strategic and economic interests (see the overview table, "U.S. Interventions in Latin America, 1891–1933"). Policymakers believed that these goals required restricting the influence of European nations in the region, building an isthmian canal under American control, and establishing the order thought necessary for American trade and investments to expand. Intervention at times achieved these goals, but it often ignored the wishes and interests of Latin Americans, provoked resistance and disorder, and created lasting ill will.

U.S. Rule in Puerto Rico

Well before 1898, expansionists like James G. Blaine had advocated acquiring Puerto Rico because of its strategic location in the Caribbean. During the Spanish-American War, Roosevelt urged Washington, "Do not make peace until we get" Puerto Rico. Military invasion and the Treaty of Paris soon brought the island under American control, with mixed consequences. A military government improved transportation and sanitation and developed public health and education. But to the dismay of Puerto Ricans, who had been promised that American rule would bestow "the advantages and blessings of enlightened civilization," their political freedoms were curtailed. "We have suffered everything. No liberty, no rights," said José Henna. "We are Mr. Nobody from Nowhere."

In 1900, the United States established a civil government, but it was under U.S. control, and popular participation was even less than under Spain. In the so-called *Insular Cases* (1901), the Supreme Court upheld Congress's authority to establish an inferior status for Puerto Rico, as an "unincorporated territory" without promise of statehood. Disappointed Puerto Ricans pressed to end this colonial status, some advocating independence, others statehood or merely greater autonomy. This division would continue throughout the twentieth century. In 1917, the United States granted citizenship and greater political rights to Puerto Ricans, but their island remained an unincorporated territory under an American governor appointed by the president.

Economic development also disappointed most islanders, for American investors quickly gained control of the best land and pursued large-scale sugar production for the U.S. market. The landless peasants struggled to survive as workers on large plantations. By 1929, the new governor—ironically, Theodore Roosevelt, Jr.—found that under the domination of American capital, "poverty was widespread

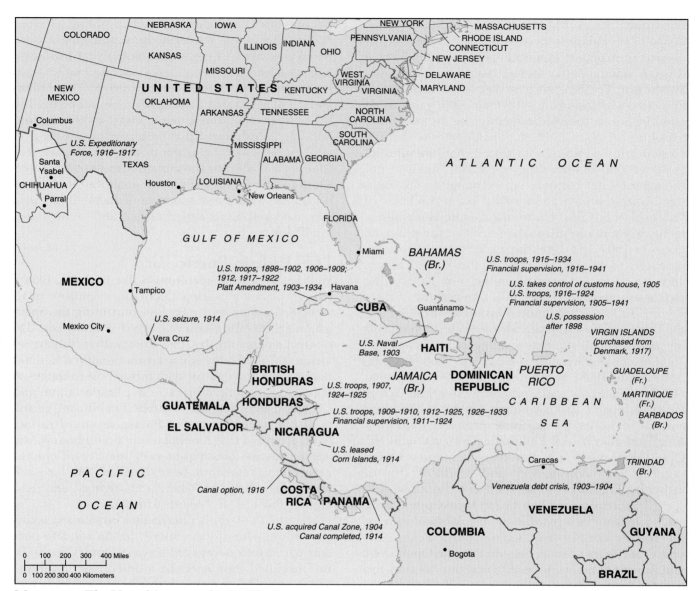

Map 24-3 **The United States in the Caribbean**
For strategic and economic reasons, the United States repeatedly intervened in the Caribbean in the first three decades of the twentieth century. Such interventions protected the U.S. claim to dominance but often provoked great hostility among Latin Americans.

and hunger, almost to the verge of starvation, common." A subsequent investigation concluded that while "the influx of capital has increased the efficiency of production and promoted general economic development," the benefits had gone largely to Americans, not to ordinary Puerto Ricans, whose conditions were "deplorable." Increasingly, they left their homes to seek work in the United States.

Cuba as a U.S. Protectorate

Despite the Teller Amendment, the Spanish-American War did not leave Cuba independent. McKinley opposed independence and distrusted the Cuban revo-

lutionaries. Many Americans considered the Cubans racial inferiors, and one U.S. general in Cuba snorted, "Why those people are no more fit for self-government than gun-powder is for hell." Accordingly, a U.S. military government was established in the island. Only in 1900, when the Democrats made an issue of imperialism, did the McKinley administration move toward permitting a Cuban government and withdrawing American troops. McKinley summoned a Cuban convention to draft a constitution under the direction of the American military governor, General Leonard Wood. Reflecting the continuing U.S. fear of Cuban autonomy, this constitution

OVERVIEW

U.S. INTERVENTIONS IN LATIN AMERICA, 1891–1933

Country	Type of Intervention	Year
Chile	Ultimatum	1891–1892
Colombia	Military intervention	1903
Cuba	Occupation	1898–1902, 1906–1909, 1912, 1917–1922
Dominican Republic	Military and administrative intervention Occupation	1905–1907 1916–1924
Haiti	Occupation	1915–1934
Mexico	Military intervention	1914, 1916–1917
Nicaragua	Occupation	1912–1925, 1927–1933
Panama	Acquisition of Canal Zone	1904
Puerto Rico	Military invasion and territorial acquisition	1898

restricted suffrage on the basis of property and education, leaving few Cubans with the right to vote.

Even so, before removing its troops, the United States wanted to ensure its control over Cuba. It therefore made U.S. withdrawal contingent on Cuba's adding to its constitution the provisions of the **Platt Amendment**, drawn up in 1901 by the U.S. secretary of war. The Platt Amendment restricted Cuba's autonomy in diplomatic relations with other countries and in internal financial policies, required Cuba to lease naval bases to the United States, and most important, authorized U.S. intervention to maintain order and preserve Cuban independence. Cubans resented this restriction on their sovereignty. As General Wood correctly observed, "There is, of course, little or no independence left Cuba under the Platt Amendment."

Cubans quickly learned that when the United States prevented Cuba from extending the same trade privileges to the British that U.S. merchants enjoyed. The Open Door would not apply in the Caribbean, which was to be an American sphere of influence. To preserve that influence, the United States sent troops into Cuba three times between 1906 and 1917 (Roosevelt admitted his recurrent itch to "wipe its people off the face of the earth"). The last occupation lasted six years. Meanwhile, American property interests in Cuba increased more than fourfold, and American exports to the island increased eightfold from 1898 to 1917.

During their occupations of Cuba, the Americans modernized its financial system, built roads and public schools, and developed a public health and sanitation program that eradicated the deadly disease of yellow fever. But most Cubans thought these material benefits did not compensate for their loss of political and economic independence. The Platt Amendment remained the basis of American policy toward Cuba until 1934.

The Panama Canal

The Spanish-American War intensified the long American interest in a canal through Central America to eliminate the lengthy and dangerous ocean route around South America. Its commercial value seemed obvious, but the war emphasized its strategic importance. McKinley declared that a canal was now "demanded by the annexation of the Hawaiian Islands and the prospective expansion of our influence and commerce in the Pacific."

Theodore Roosevelt moved quickly to implement McKinley's commitment to a canal after becoming president in 1901. He was convinced that a strong presidential role was at least as important in foreign affairs as in domestic politics. Neither Congress nor "the average American," he believed, took "the trouble to think carefully or deeply" about international affairs. Roosevelt's canal diplomacy helped establish the assertive presidency that has characterized U.S. foreign policy in the twentieth century.

First, Roosevelt persuaded Britain to renounce its treaty right to a joint role with the United States in any canal venture. Britain's willingness reflected a growing friendship between the two nations, both wary of Germany's increasing aggressiveness. Where to build the canal was a problem. Some Americans favored Nicaragua, where a sea-level canal could be built. Another possibility was through Panama, which was part of Colombia. A canal through Panama would require an elaborate system of locks. But the French-owned Panama Canal Company had been unsuccessfully trying to build a canal in Panama and was now eager to sell its rights to the project before they expired in 1904.

In 1902, Congress directed Roosevelt to purchase the French company's claims for $40 million and build the canal in Panama if Colombia ceded a strip of land across the isthmus on reasonable terms. Otherwise, Roosevelt was to negotiate with Nicaragua for the alternate route. In 1903, Roosevelt pressed Colombia to sell a canal zone to the United States for $10 million and an annual payment of $250,000. Colombia, however, rejected the proposal, fearing the loss of its sovereignty in Panama and hoping for more money. After all, when the Panama Canal Company's rights expired, Colombia could then legitimately collect the $40 million so generously offered the company.

Roosevelt was furious. After warning "those contemptible little creatures" in Colombia that they were "imperiling their own future," he began writing a message to Congress proposing military action to seize the isthmus of Panama. Instead of using direct force, however, Roosevelt worked with Philippe Bunau-Varilla, a French official of the Panama Canal Company, to exploit long-smoldering Panamanian discontent with Colombia. Roosevelt's purpose was to get the canal zone, Bunau-Varilla's to get the American money. Roosevelt ordered U.S. naval forces to Panama; from New York, Bunau-Varilla coordinated a revolt against Colombian authority directed by officials of the Panama Railroad, owned by Bunau-Varilla's canal company. The bloodless "revolution" succeeded when U.S. forces prevented Colombian troops from landing in Panama, although the United States was bound by treaty to maintain Colombian sovereignty in the region. Bunau-Varilla promptly signed a treaty accepting Roosevelt's original terms for a canal zone and making Panama a U.S. protectorate, which it remained until 1939. Panamanians themselves denounced the treaty for surrendering sovereignty in the zone to the United States, but they had to acquiesce because their independence depended on American forces. The United States took formal control of the canal zone in 1904 and completed construction of the Panama Canal in 1914.

Many Americans were appalled by what the *Chicago American* called Roosevelt's "rough-riding assault upon another republic over the shattered wreckage of international law and diplomatic usage." But others, as *Public Opinion* reported, wanted a "canal above all things" and were willing to overlook moral questions and approve the acquisition of the canal zone as simply "a business question." Roosevelt himself boasted, "I took the Canal Zone and let Congress debate," but his unnecessary and arrogant actions generated resentment among Latin Americans that rankled for decades.

The Roosevelt Corollary

To protect the security of the canal, the United States increased its authority in the Caribbean. The objective was to establish conditions there that would both eliminate any pretext for European intervention and promote American control over trade and investment. The inability of Latin American nations to pay their debts to foreign lenders raised the possibility of European intervention, as evidenced by a German and British blockade of Venezuela in 1903 to secure repayment of debts to European bankers. "If we intend to say hands off to the powers of Europe," Roosevelt concluded, "then sooner or later we must keep order ourselves."

In his 1904 annual message to Congress, Roosevelt announced a new policy, the so-called **Roosevelt Corollary** to the Monroe Doctrine. "Chronic wrongdoing," he declared, would cause the United States to exercise "an international police power" in Latin America. The Monroe Doctrine had expressed American hostility to European intervention in Latin America; the Roosevelt Corollary attempted to justify U.S. intervention and authority in the region. Roosevelt invoked his corollary immediately, imposing American management of the debts and customs duties of the Dominican Republic in 1905. Commercial rivalries and political intrigue in that poor nation had created disorder, which Roosevelt suppressed for both economic and strategic reasons. Financial insolvency was averted, popular revolution prevented, and possible European intervention forestalled.

Latin Americans vigorously resented the United States' unilateral claims to authority. By 1907, the so-called Drago Doctrine (named after Argentina's foreign minister) was incorporated into international law, prohibiting armed intervention to collect debts. Still, the United States would continue to invoke the Roosevelt Corollary to advance its interests in the hemisphere. As Secretary of State Elihu Root asserted, "The inevitable effect of our building the Canal must be to require us to police the surrounding premises." He then added, "In the nature of things, trade and control, and the obligation to keep order which go with them, must come our way."

On December 31, 1999, almost a century after the United States took control of the Panama Canal Zone, Panama reclaimed it. "The canal is ours!" proclaimed Panamanian president Mireya Moscoso, just before her country's flag was raised over the canal area, resolving, for the moment at least, a contentious and complex issue.

From the beginning, Panamanians denounced the 1903 treaty—"the treaty that no Panamanian signed"—that had given the United States a perpetual lease over a strip of land that divided their country in two. American sovereignty prevailed in the zone, and the Americans who lived there and ran the canal enjoyed a life of privilege. Panamanians were mostly excluded from the zone; those who worked there were restricted to low-paying jobs and subject to American laws and courts.

Panamanians regularly demanded an end to this "Yankee colonialism," but, for a long time, few Americans spoke up for the return of the zone. As late as 1980, one Senator defended America's continued hold on the zone by declaring, "We stole it fair and square."

But in the 1960s, the United States began to negotiate the return of the Canal Zone to Panama. It had several reasons. The canal was gradually becoming obsolete. Its machinery was aging, and it was too small to accommodate ever-larger ships. From a military standpoint, it was increasingly vulnerable to terrorism and to missile attack. It could not accommodate aircraft carriers. And in any case, its strategic importance had declined since the United States had developed a two-ocean navy. American officials concluded that the canal was no longer of such vital strategic importance that the United States needed to maintain perpetual control and exclusive jurisdiction over it. At the same time, one official noted, the canal's "potential as a source of conflict with the Panamanians had increased."

Under President Jimmy Carter, the United States negotiated two treaties with Panama in 1978. The first returned jurisdiction over the Canal Zone to Panama but left the United States responsible for operating and defending the canal until December 31, 1999. The second gave the United States the permanent right to defend the "neutrality" of the canal. Conservative Republicans worried that the treaties were giving away "our canal" and nearly blocked Senate ratification. Approval came only after the administration agreed to a condition permitting the United States to send troops into Panama after 1999 if necessary to preserve open access to the canal. Panamanians objected that this condition violated their sovereignty and contradicted other treaty provisions that prohibited American intervention in Panama's internal affairs.

The treaties, then, did not end tensions between the United States and Panama. In 1989, President George Bush sent U.S. troops to overthrow Panamanian dictator Manuel Noriega, an erratic leader with close ties to both the CIA and the international drug trade. The United Nations and the Organization of American States condemned the intervention, but the United States justified it in part as protecting "the integrity of the Panama Canal Treaties."

In the 1990s, however, Panama gradually assumed territorial and legal jurisdiction over the canal. Panamanian administrators and workers were phased in to assume responsibilities previously held by Americans, and the Panamanian government collected an ever-larger proportion of the canal's revenues. But even as Panamanians celebrated the final transfer of authority, they worried about the continuing U.S. claim to the right to keep the canal open. After all, when asked how the United States would react if Panama closed down the canal "for repairs," a top U.S. official replied, "We will move in and close down the Panamanian government for repairs."

Theodore Roosevelt at the controls of a giant steam shovel during the construction of the Panama Canal in 1906. Roosevelt's aggressive acquisition of the Canal Zone and its subsequent control by the United States angered Panamanians for nearly a century.

THE BIG STICK IN THE CARIBBEAN SEA

The Roosevelt Corollary proclaimed the intention of the United States to police Latin America. Enforcement came, as this cartoon shows, with Roosevelt and subsequent presidents sending the U.S. Navy to one Caribbean nation after another.

Dollar Diplomacy

Roosevelt's successor as president, William Howard Taft, hoped to promote U.S. interests without such combative rhetoric and naked force. He described his plan as one of "substituting dollars for bullets"—using government action to encourage private American investments in Latin America to supplant European interests, promote development and stability, and gain profits for American bankers. Under this **dollar diplomacy**, American investments in the Caribbean increased dramatically during Taft's presidency from 1909 to 1913, and the State Department helped arrange for American bankers to establish financial control over Haiti and Honduras.

But Taft did not shrink from employing military force to protect American property or to establish the conditions he thought necessary for American investments. In fact, Taft intervened more frequently than Roosevelt had, with Nicaragua a major target. In 1909, Taft sent U.S. troops there to aid a revolution fomented by an American mining corporation and to seize the Nicaraguan customs houses. Under the new government, American bankers then gained control of Nicaragua's national bank, railroad, and customs service. To protect these arrangements, U.S. troops were again dispatched in 1912. To control popular opposition to the American client government, the marines remained in Nicaragua for two decades. Military power, not the social and economic improvement promised by dollar diplomacy, kept Nicaragua's minority government stable and subordinate to the United States.

Dollar diplomacy increased American power and influence in the Caribbean and tied underdeveloped countries to the United States economically and strategically. By 1913, American investments in the region reached $1.5 billion, and Americans had captured more than 50 percent of the foreign trade of Costa Rica, Cuba, the Dominican Republic, Guatemala, Haiti, Honduras, Nicaragua, and Panama. But this policy failed to improve conditions for most Latin Americans. U.S. officials remained primarily concerned with promoting American control and extracting American profits from the region, not with the well-being of its population. One American diplomat, for instance, casually described a Guatemalan president in whose government San Francisco bankers had invested heavily under the premises of dollar diplomacy as a cruel despot who had "the good sense to be civil to our country and its citizens and to keep his cruelties . . . for home consumption." Not surprisingly, dollar diplomacy proved unpopular in Latin America.

Wilsonian Interventions

Taking office in 1913, the Democrat Woodrow Wilson repudiated the interventionist policies of his Republican predecessors. He promised that the United States would "never again seek one additional foot of territory by conquest" but would instead work to promote "human rights, national integrity, and opportunity" in Latin America. Wilson also named as his secretary of state the Democratic symbol of anti-imperialism, William Jennings Bryan. Their generous intentions were apparent when Bryan signed a treaty with Colombia apologizing for Roosevelt's seizure of the Panama Canal Zone in 1903.

Nonetheless, Wilson soon became the most interventionist president in American history, for a number of reasons. He agreed that the United States had to expand its exports and investments abroad and that U.S. dominance of the Caribbean was strategically necessary. He also shared the racist belief that Latin Americans were inferior and needed paternalistic guidance from the United States. In providing that guidance, through military force if necessary, Wilson came close to assuming that American principles and objectives were absolutes, that different cultural traditions and national aspirations were simply wrong. His self-righteousness and determination to transform other peoples' behavior led his policies to be dubbed "missionary diplomacy," but they also contained elements of Roosevelt's commitment to military force and Taft's reliance on economic power.

In 1915, Wilson ordered U.S. Marines to Haiti. They went, explained Bryan, to restore order and preserve "American interests" that were "gravely menaced." The United States saved and even enhanced those interests by establishing a protectorate over Haiti and drawing up a constitution that increased U.S. property rights and commercial privileges. The U.S. Navy selected a new Haitian president, granting him nominal authority over a client government. Real authority, however, rested with the American military, which controlled Haiti until 1934, protecting the small elite who cooperated with foreign interests and exploited their own people. As usual, American military rule improved the country's transportation, sanitation, and educational systems, but the forced-labor program that the U.S. adopted to build such public works provoked widespread resentment. In 1919, marines suppressed a revolt against American domination, killing more than three thousand Haitians.

Wilson also intervened elsewhere in the Caribbean. In 1916, when the Dominican Republic refused to cede control of its finances to U.S. bankers, Wilson ordered the marines to occupy the country. The marines ousted Dominican officials, installed a military government to rule "on behalf of the Dominican government," and ran the nation until 1924. In 1917, the United States intervened in Cuba, which remained under American control until 1922.

Wilson also involved himself in the internal affairs of Mexico. The lengthy dictatorship of Porfirio Díaz had collapsed in 1911 in revolutionary disorder. The popular leader Francisco Madero took power and promised democratic and economic reforms that alarmed both wealthy Mexicans and foreign investors, particularly Americans. In 1913, General Victoriano Huerta seized control in a brutal counterrevolution backed by the landed aristocracy and foreign interests. Most nations recognized the Huerta government, but Wilson, despite strong pressure from American investors, refused to do so. He was appalled by the violence of Huerta's power grab and was aware that opponents had organized to reestablish constitutional government.

Wilson hoped to bring the Constitutionalists to power and "to secure Mexico a better government under which all contracts and business and concessions will be safer than they have been." He authorized arms sales to their forces, led by Venustiano Carranza; pressured Britain and other nations to deprive Huerta of foreign support; and blockaded the Mexican port of Vera Cruz. In April 1914 Wilson exploited a minor incident to have the marines attack and occupy Vera Cruz. This assault damaged his image as a promoter of peace and justice, and even Carranza and the Constitutionalists denounced the American occupation as unwarranted aggression. By August, Carranza had toppled Huerta, and Wilson shifted his support to Francisco ("Pancho") Villa, who seemed more susceptible to American guidance. But Carranza's growing popular support in Mexico and Wilson's preoccupation with World War I in Europe finally led the United States to grant de facto recognition to the Carranza government in October 1915.

Villa then began terrorizing New Mexico and Texas, hoping to provoke an American intervention that would undermine Carranza. In 1916, Wilson ordered troops under General John J. Pershing to pursue Villa into Mexico, leading Carranza to fear a permanent U.S. occupation of northern Mexico. Soon the American soldiers were fighting the Mexican army rather than Villa's bandits. On the brink of full-fledged war, Wilson finally ordered U.S. troops to withdraw in January 1917 and extended full recognition to the Carranza government. Wilson lamely defended these steps as showing that the United States had no intention of imposing on Mexico "an order and government of our own choosing." That had been Wilson's original objective, however. His aggressive tactics had not merely failed but also embittered relations with Mexico.

Conclusion

By the time of Woodrow Wilson's presidency, the United States had been expanding its involvement in world affairs for half a century. Several themes had emerged from this activity: increasing American domination of the Caribbean, continuing interest in East Asia, the creation of an overseas empire, and the evolution of the United States into a major world power. Underlying these developments were an uneasy mixture of ideas and objectives. The American involvement in the world reflected a traditional, if often misguided, sense of national rectitude and mission. Generous humanitarian impulses vied with ugly racist prejudices as Americans sought both to help other peoples and to direct them toward U.S. concepts of religion, sanitation, capitalist development, and public institutions. American motives ranged from ensuring national security and competing with European colonial powers to the conviction that the United States had to expand its economic interests abroad. But if imperialism, both informal and at times colonial, brought Americans greater wealth and power, it also increased tensions in Asia and contributed to anti-American hostility and revolutionary ferment in Latin America. It also entangled the United States in the Great Power rivalries that would ultimately result in two world wars.

Review Questions

1. What factors, old and new, shaped American foreign policy in the late nineteenth century? How were they interrelated?

2. How were individual politicians and diplomats able to affect America's foreign policy? How were they constrained by government institutions, private groups, and public opinion?

3. To what extent was the United States' emergence as an imperial power a break from, as opposed to a culmination of, its earlier policies and national development?

4. How effective were U.S. interventions in Latin America? What were the objectives and consequences?

Recommended Reading

Robert L. Beisner, *From the Old Diplomacy to the New, 1865–1900*, 2d ed. (1986). An excellent analysis of historiographical issues.

Charles S. Campbell, *The Transformation of American Foreign Relations, 1865–1900* (1976). A comprehensive and cautious survey that provides many insights in U.S. foreign policy.

David F. Healy, *Drive to Hegemony: The United States in the Caribbean, 1898–1917* (1988). A valuable account that highlights a key area of American foreign policy.

Walter LaFeber, *The American Search for Opportunity, 1865–1913* (1993). A fascinating study documenting the disruptive international consequences of America's rise to world power.

Walter LaFeber, *The New Empire: An Interpretation of American Expansion, 1860–1898* (1963). An influential study that emphasizes economic factors on American foreign policy.

John L. Offner, *An Unwanted War: The Diplomacy of the United States and Spain over Cuba, 1895–1898* (1992). A revisionist account maintaining that conflict over Cuba was inevitable.

Louis A. Perez, Jr., *The War of 1898: The United States and Cuba in History and Historiography* (1998). A brief book that emphasizes how relations between Cuba and the United States shaped the war and its meaning.

David Pletcher, *The Diplomacy of Trade and Investment: American Economic Expansion in the Hemisphere, 1865–1900* (1998). Stresses the complex but inconsistent and unsystematic nature of American economic expansion.

Additional Sources

Roots of Imperialism

David L. Anderson, *Imperialism and Idealism: American Diplomats in China, 1861–1898* (1985).

Stuart Anderson, *Race and Rapprochement: Anglo-Saxonism and Anglo-American Relations, 1895–1904* (1981).

Patrick J. Hearden, *Independence and Empire: The New South's Cotton Mill Campaign, 1865–1901* (1982).

Patricia R. Hill, *The World Their Household: The American Woman's Foreign Mission Movement and Cultural Transformation, 1870–1920* (1985).

Michael H. Hunt, *Ideology and U.S. Foreign Policy* (1987).

Edmund Morris, *The Rise of Theodore Roosevelt* (1979).

Ernest Paolino, *The Foundations of the American Empire: William Henry Seward and U.S. Foreign Policy* (1973).

Milton Plesur, *America's Outward Thrust: Approaches to Foreign Affairs, 1865–1890* (1971).

David M. Pletcher, *The Awkward Years: American Foreign Relations under Garfield and Arthur* (1962).

Ronald Spector, *Admiral of the New Empire* (1974).

William Widenor, *Henry Cabot Lodge and the Search for an American Foreign Policy* (1980).

William A. Williams, *The Roots of the Modern American Empire* (1969).

The Spanish-American War

Richard Challener, *Admirals, Generals, and American Foreign Policy, 1889–1914* (1973).

Graham A. Cosmas, *An Army for Empire: The United States Army and the Spanish-American War* (1971).

John Dobson, *Reticent Expansionism: The Foreign Policy of William McKinley* (1988).

Willard B. Gatewood, Jr., *Black Americans and the White Man's Burden, 1898–1903* (1975).

Lewis L. Gould, *The Spanish-American War and President McKinley* (1982).

David F. Healy, *U.S. Expansionism: The Imperialist Urge in the 1890s* (1970).

Gerald Linderman, *The Mirror of War: American Society and the Spanish-American War* (1974).

Joyce Milton, *The Yellow Journalists* (1989).

H. Wayne Morgan, *America's Road to Empire: The War with Spain and Overseas Expansion* (1965).

Julius W. Pratt, *Expansionists of 1898* (1936).

David R. Trask, *The War with Spain in 1898* (1981).

Anti-Imperialism

Robert L. Beisner, *Twelve against Empire: The Anti-Imperialists, 1898–1900* (1968).

Thomas J. Osborne, *"Empire Can Wait": American Opposition to Hawaiian Annexation, 1893–1898* (1981).

Daniel B. Schirmer, *Republic or Empire: American Resistance to the Philippine War* (1972).

E. Berkeley Tompkins, *Anti-Imperialism in the United States: The Great Debate, 1890–1920* (1970).

Imperial Ambitions: The United States and East Asia, 1899–1917

Charles S. Campbell, *Special Business Interests and the Open Door Policy* (1951).

Warren I. Cohen, *America's Response to China* (1989).

John M. Gates, *Schoolbooks and Krags: The United States Army in the Philippines* (1973).

Michael H. Hunt, *The Making of a Special Relationship: The U.S. and China to 1914* (1983).

Akira Iriye, *Pacific Estrangement: Japanese and American Expansion, 1897–1911* (1972).

Thomas McCormick, *China Market: America's Quest for Informal Empire* (1967).

Stuart Miller, *"Benevolent Assimilation": The American Conquest of the Philippines, 1899–1903* (1982).

Paul Varg, *The Making of a Myth: The United States and China, 1897–1912* (1968).

Richard E. Welch, *Response to Imperialism: The United States and the Philippine-American War* (1979).

Imperial Power: The United States and Latin America, 1899–1917

Howard K. Beale, *Theodore Roosevelt and the Rise of America to World Power* (1956).

Jules Benjamin, *Hegemony and Development: The United States and Cuba, 1890–1934* (1977).

Bruce Calder, *The Impact of Intervention: The Dominican Republic during the U.S. Occupation of 1916 to 1924* (1984).

Raymond Carr, *Puerto Rico: A Colonial Experiment* (1984).

Arturo Morales Carrion, *Puerto Rico* (1983).

John M. Cooper, Jr., *The Warrior and the Priest: Woodrow Wilson and Theodore Roosevelt* (1983).

John Eisenhower, *The United States and the Mexican Revolution, 1913–1917* (1993).

David F. Healy, *Gunboat Diplomacy in the Wilson Era: The U.S. Navy in Haiti* (1976).

James Hitchman, *Leonard Wood and Cuban Independence, 1898–1902* (1971).

Walter LaFeber, *Inevitable Revolutions: The United States in Central America* (1993).

Walter LaFeber, *The Panama Canal* (1990).

Lester Langley, *The Banana Wars: An Inner History of the American Empire, 1900–1934* (1983).

David McCullough, *The Path between the Seas: The Creation of the Panama Canal* (1977).

Allan R. Millett, *The Politics of Intervention: The Military Occupation of Cuba, 1906–1909* (1968).

Louis A. Perez, Jr., *Cuba under the Platt Amendment, 1902–1934* (1986).

Robert E. Quirk, *An Affair of Honor: Woodrow Wilson and the Occupation of Vera Cruz* (1962).

Where to Learn More

❖ **Mission Houses, Honolulu, Hawaii.** Built between 1821 and 1841, these buildings were homes and shops of missionaries sent to Hawaii by the American Board of Commissioners for Foreign Missions. Their exhibits include furnishings and memorabilia of a group important in developing American ties with Hawaii.

❖ **Funston Memorial Home, Iola, Kansas.** Operated as a museum by the Kansas State Historical Society, this is the boyhood home of General Frederick Funston, prominent in the Spanish-American War and the Filipino-American War.

❖ **James G. Blaine House, Augusta, Maine.** The Executive Mansion of Maine's governor since 1919, this house was formerly Blaine's home and still contains his study and furnishings from the time he served as secretary of state and U.S. senator.

❖ **Rough Riders Memorial and City Museum, Las Vegas, New Mexico.** Together with the nearby Castaneda Hotel, this site provides intriguing information on Roosevelt's volunteer cavalry, recruited primarily from the Southwest.

❖ **Seward House, Auburn, New York.** The home of William H. Seward contains furniture and momentos from his career as secretary of state.

AMERICA AND THE GREAT WAR, 1914–1920

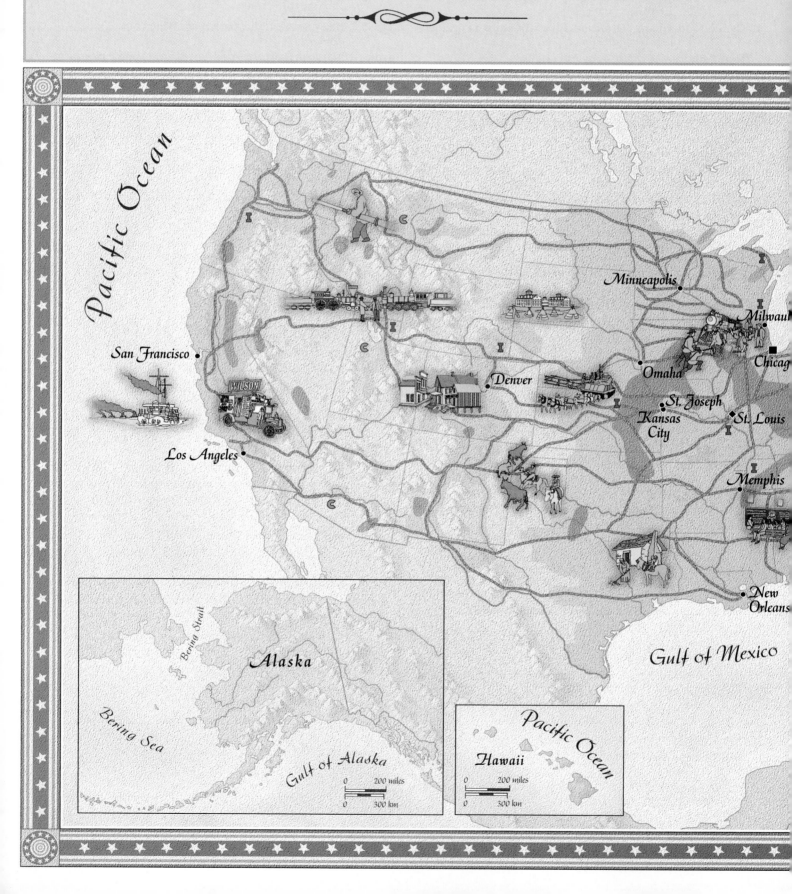

Pacific Ocean

Minneapolis

Milwau[kee]

San Francisco

Chicag[o]

Omaha

Denver

St. Joseph

St. Louis

Kansas City

Los Angeles

Memphis

WILSON

New Orleans

Gulf of Mexico

Alaska

Bering Strait

Bering Sea

Gulf of Alaska

| 0 | 200 miles |
| 0 | 300 km |

Hawaii

Pacific Ocean

| 0 | 200 miles |
| 0 | 300 km |

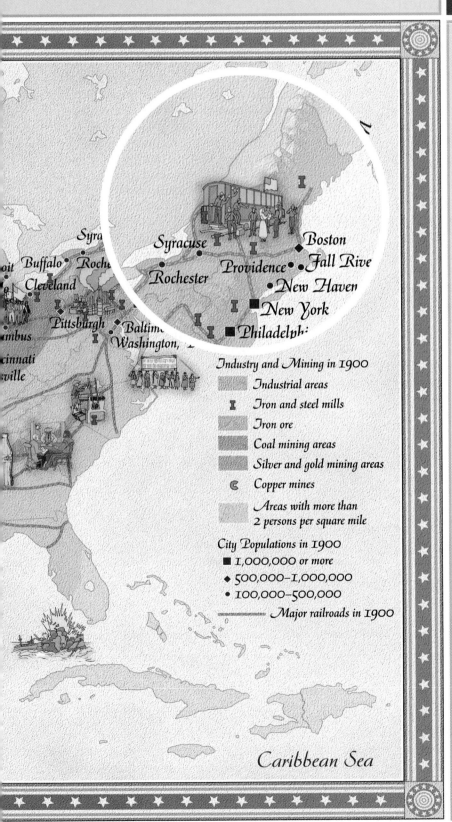

Industry and Mining in 1900

Industrial areas

I Iron and steel mills

Iron ore

Coal mining areas

Silver and gold mining areas

C Copper mines

Areas with more than
2 persons per square mile

City Populations in 1900

■ 1,000,000 or more

◆ 500,000–1,000,000

• 100,000–500,000

—— Major railroads in 1900

Caribbean Sea

Chapter Outline

Key Topics

❖ How sympathy for the Allies and outrage over German submarine warfare
undermined U.S. neutrality during
World War I
❖ Wilson's decision to join the conflict
on the side of the Allies
❖ The reorganization of the U.S. economy and the challenge to civil liberties that resulted from the war effort
❖ Wilson's influence on the Versailles
Treaty and his failure to gain its ratification in the U.S. Senate
❖ The postwar backlash

On the evening of April 2, 1917, Woodrow Wilson, escorted by cavalry, drove through a misty rain down Pennsylvania Avenue to Capitol Hill, which was eerily illuminated by searchlights. All day, the antiwar Emergency Peace Federation had lobbied Congress; Senator Henry Cabot Lodge of Massachusetts had even punched one pacifist. Now mounted police with drawn sabers held back silent crowds as the president strode into the house chamber and asked Congress to declare war on Germany, a war that many Americans opposed and that Wilson conceded would sow death, misery, and reaction among them. He threatened "the firm hand of repression" against disloyalty—obviously foreseeing battles at home as well as abroad, clashes of opinion and will scarcely hinted at by Senator Lodge's fistfight. To justify such calamities, Wilson promised that the war would make the world "safe for democracy." Waving small American flags, many members of Congress broke into cheers, and Senator Lodge congratulated Wilson. The Senate passed a resolution for war on April 4, the House on April 6.

On July 10, 1919, Wilson made the same journey down Pennsylvania Avenue to Capitol Hill. This time he rode in brilliant sunshine through cheering crowds and flag-decorated streets. He asked the Senate to ratify a peace treaty that most Americans favored and that Wilson declared would prevent future wars. But many senators received Wilson's address in silence. Several refused even to stand when he entered the chamber. Senator Lodge concealed neither his hatred of the president nor his opposition to the treaty. Apparently affected by the hostility in the room, Wilson spoke without his usual eloquence. During the fierce political struggle over the treaty that followed, the president suffered a stroke that left him crippled. The Senate ultimately rejected the treaty and Wilson's peace.

Between these two presidential appearances, Americans experienced the horrors of the Great War, confronting and overcoming challenges but also sacrificing some of their national ideals and aspirations. Both the United States' intervention in the war and its failure to secure a lasting peace were consequences of serious disagreements over national interests, errors in judgment, and the pursuit of selfish as well as lofty goals. The war declaration came after a long period in which Americans tried to balance their desires for neutrality and peace with their ambitions for wealth, their sympathies for other countries, and their perceptions of America's security and world role. Not only was the war the United States' first major military conflict on foreign soil, but it also changed American life. With economic management and social control considered essential to the war effort, government authority increased sharply. Such changes, from efficiency to Americanization, often reflected prewar progressivism, and the war years did promote reforms. But the war also diverted reform energies into new channels, subordinated generous impulses to those that were more coercive, and strengthened the conservative opposition to reform. The results were often reactionary and contributed to a postwar mood that not only curtailed further reform but also helped defeat the peace treaty.

Waging Neutrality

Few Americans were prepared for the Great War that erupted in Europe in August 1914, but fewer still foresaw that their own nation might become involved in it. With near unanimity, they supported neutrality. But American attitudes, decisions, and actions, both public and private, undercut neutrality, and the policies of governments in Berlin, London, and Washington drew the United States into the war.

The Origins of Conflict

There had been plenty of warning. Since the 1870s, the competing imperial ambitions of the European powers had led to economic rivalries, military expansion, diplomatic maneuvering, and international tensions. A complex system of alliances divided the continent into two opposing blocs. In central Europe, the expansionist Germany of Kaiser Wilhelm II allied itself with the multinational Austro-Hungarian Empire. Confronting

President Woodrow Wilson reads his war message to Congress, April 2, 1917. He predicted "many months of fiery trial and sacrifice ahead of us."

stretching across France and Belgium from the English Channel to Switzerland. Little movement occurred despite great efforts and terrible casualties from artillery, machine guns, and poison gas. The British once suffered 300,000 casualties in an offensive that gained only a few square miles before being pushed back. Machine gunners went into shock at the carnage they inflicted. In the trenches, soldiers suffered in the cold and mud, surrounded by decaying bodies and human waste, enduring lice, rats, and nightmares and dying from disease and exhaustion. The belligerents subordinated their economies, politics, and cultures to military demands. The Great War, said one German soldier, had become "the grave of nations."

them, Great Britain and France formed alliances with Tsarist Russia. A succession of crises threatened this precarious balance of power, and in May 1914 an American diplomat reported anxiously, "There is too much hatred, too many jealousies." He predicted "an awful cataclysm."

The cataclysm began a month later. On June 28, a Serbian terrorist assassinated Archduke Franz Ferdinand, the heir to the Austro-Hungarian throne, in Sarajevo. With Germany's support, Austria declared war on Serbia on July 28. Russia then mobilized its army against Austria to aid Serbia, its Slavic client state. To assist Austria, Germany declared war on Russia and then on Russia's ally France. Hoping for a quick victory, Germany struck at France through neutral Belgium; in response, Britain declared war on Germany on August 4. Soon Turkey and Bulgaria joined Germany and Austria to form the **Central Powers**. The **Allies**— Britain, France, and Russia—were joined by Italy and Japan. Britain drew on its empire for resources, using troops from India, Canada, Australia, New Zealand, and South Africa. The war had become a global conflict, waged not only in Europe but also in Africa, the Middle East, and East Asia.

Mass slaughter enveloped Europe as huge armies battled to a stalemate. The British and French faced the Germans along a line of trenches

American Attitudes

Although the United States had also competed for markets, colonies, and influence, few Americans had expected this calamity. As one North Carolina congressman said, "This dreadful conflict of the nations came to most of us as lightning out of a clear sky." Most people believed that the United States had no vital interest in the war and would not become involved. "Our isolated position and freedom from entangling alliances," noted the *Literary Digest*, "inspire our press with the cheering assurance that we are in no peril of being drawn into the European quarrel." President Wilson issued a proclamation of neutrality and urged Americans to be "neutral in fact as well as in name . . . impartial in thought as well as in action."

However, neither the American people nor their president stayed strictly neutral. German Americans often sympathized with Germany, and many Irish Americans hoped for a British defeat that would free Ireland from British rule. But most Americans sympathized with the Allies. Ethnic, cultural, and economic ties bound most Americans to the British and French. Politically, too, most Americans felt a greater affinity for the democratic Western Allies—tsarist Russia repelled them—than for Germany's more authoritarian government and society. And whereas Britain and the United States had

FROM THEN TO NOW

The United States and the Balkans

The Great War was triggered by events in the Balkans, a corner of Europe long ravaged by violent conflict rooted in ethnic and religious hostility and political rivalry. The terrorists who assassinated Archduke Ferdinand in the Bosnian city of Sarajevo were hoping to create a greater Serbia at the expense of the Austro-Hungarian Empire. Because of a web of entangling alliances, their actions drew the nations of Europe, and eventually the United States, into a cataclysmic war. At the end of the twentieth century, deadly conflict again erupted in the Balkans, producing genocidal massacres and campaigns of "ethnic cleansing"—the forced removal of peoples from their homelands. Trying to decide how to respond to the humanitarian disaster and the threat of spreading conflict, U.S. and European leaders sought lessons from the past.

The United States ignored the troubles in the Balkans before 1914 and then long remained aloof from the war. Only during the peace conference did U.S. diplomats concern themselves with the peoples and issues of the region. The peace treaty created a new nation whose name—the Kingdom of Serbs, Croats, and Slovenes—reflected its factional tensions. (In 1929 it adopted the name Yugoslavia.) President Wilson assured Americans they would not be drawn into any new conflict in the region. "If you want to put out a fire in the Balkans," he promised, "you do not send to the United States for troops."

When violence broke out in the 1990s, the United States initially pursued the same course of noninvolvement. With the Cold War over, conflict in the Balkans seemed unlikely to draw in the major nations. "This is not 1914," insisted observers in 1991. Others suggested that the religious and ethnic factionalism of the region were so historically rooted that intervention was foolish.

The Bush administration accordingly kept a low profile as Yugoslavia disintegrated into separate republics. Even after Serbia invaded Slovenia and Croatia and Serbs began ruthless ethnic cleansing in Bosnia, the United States did little beyond endorsing U.N. proposals for economic sanctions against Serbia and an arms embargo in the region. Bill Clinton criticized Bush's inaction during the 1992 presidential campaign, but once in office he at first followed a similar policy. Like Wilson, Clinton saw nothing in the Balkans worth risking American troops.

But as the violence and atrocities worsened, calls for intervention increased. Fitfully, the Clinton administration and, even more reluctantly, European nations moved to confront Serbia, strengthening sanctions, enforcing no-fly zones, and finally in 1995 bombing Bosnian Serb military forces. American-sponsored peace talks in Dayton, Ohio, supported by Russians eager for Western economic assistance, brought an uneasy peace to Bosnia and temporarily ended the fighting throughout the region. But in 1998 the focus of the conflict shifted to Kosovo, still a province of what remained of Yugoslavia. Serbian forces began a murderous ethnic cleansing campaign against Kosovo's majority population of ethnic Albanians, who were seeking greater political autonomy. The United States, if again belatedly, led NATO in a bombing campaign that forced the Serbs out of Kosovo in 1999, then contributed troops to an international peacekeeping group in the region.

In contrast to its detached role eight decades before, then, the United States, however dilatory and indecisive, led in trying to contain the violence in the 1990s. "America—and America alone—can and should make the difference for peace," Clinton declared in Wilsonian rhetoric. "The need for American leadership is stark." The lesson of World War I, he had concluded, was that European stability, including stability in the Balkans, was a vital interest of the United States.

Gavrilo Princip is arrested after the Serbian terrorist assassinated Archduke Ferdinand in 1914. The subsequent Great War of 1914–1918 was only one of many violent conflicts that engulfed the Balkans in the twentieth century and often drew in other nations, including the United States.

CHRONOLOGY

1914 World War I begins in Europe.

President Woodrow Wilson declares U.S. neutrality.

1915 Germany begins submarine warfare.

Lusitania is sunk.

Woman's Peace Party is organized.

1916 Gore-McLemore resolutions are defeated.

Sussex Pledge is issued.

Preparedness legislation is enacted.

Woodrow Wilson is reelected president.

1917 Germany resumes unrestricted submarine warfare.

The United States declares war on Germany.

Selective Service Act establishes the military draft.

Espionage Act is passed.

Committee on Public Information, War Industries Board, Food Administration, and other mobilization agencies are established.

American Expeditionary Force arrives in France.

East St. Louis race riot erupts.

Bolshevik Revolution occurs in Russia.

1918 Wilson announces his Fourteen Points.

Sedition Act is passed.

Eugene Debs is imprisoned.

The United States intervenes militarily in Russia.

Armistice ends World War I.

1919 Paris Peace Conference is held.

Steel, coal, and other strikes occur.

Red Scare breaks out.

Prohibition amendment is adopted.

Wilson suffers a massive stroke.

1920 Palmer Raids round up radicals.

League of Nations is defeated in the U.S. Senate.

Woman suffrage amendment is ratified.

U.S. troops are withdrawn from Russia.

Warren Harding is elected president.

1921 United States signs a separate peace treaty with Germany.

---

enjoyed a rapprochement since 1895, Germany had repeatedly appeared as a potential rival. Many Americans considered it a militaristic nation, particularly after it violated Belgium's neutrality.

Wilson himself admired Britain's culture and government and distrusted Germany's imperial ambitions. Like other influential Americans, Wilson believed that a German victory would threaten America's economic, political, and perhaps even strategic interests. "England is fighting our fight," he said privately. Secretary of State William Jennings Bryan was genuinely neutral, but most officials favored the Allies. Robert Lansing, counselor of the State Department; Walter Hines Page, the ambassador to England; and Colonel Edward House, Wilson's closest adviser on foreign affairs, assisted British diplomats, undercut official U.S. protests against British violations of American neutrality, and encouraged Wilson's suspicions of Germany. Early in the war, House wrote Page, "I cannot see how there can be any serious trouble between England and America, with all of us feeling as we do." House and Lansing assured the Allies privately that "we considered their cause our cause."

British propaganda bolstered American sympathies. British writers, artists, and lecturers depicted the Allies as fighting for civilization against a brutal Germany that mutilated nuns and babies. Although German troops, like most other soldiers, did commit outrages, they were not guilty of the systematic barbarity claimed by Allied propagandists. Britain, however, shaped America's view of the conflict. It cut the only German cable to the United States and censored war news to suit itself. German propaganda directed at American opinion proved so ineffectual that the German ambassador concluded it might as well be abandoned.

Sympathy for the Allies, however, did not mean that Americans favored intervention. The British ambassador complained that it was "useless" to expect any "practical" advantage from the Americans' sympathy, for they had no intention of joining the conflict. Indeed, few Americans doubted that neutrality was the appropriate course and peace the proper goal. The carnage in France solidified their convictions. Wilson was determined to pursue peace as long as his view of national interests allowed.

The Economy of War

Economic issues soon threatened American neutrality. International law permitted neutral nations to sell or ship war material to all belligerents, and, with the economy mired in a recession when the war began, many Americans looked to war orders to spur economic recovery. But the British navy prevented trade with the Central Powers. Only the Allies could buy American goods. Their orders for steel, explosives, uniforms, wheat, and other products, however, pulled the country out of the recession. One journalist rejoiced that "war, for Europe, is meaning devastation and death; for America a bumper crop of new millionaires and a hectic hastening of prosperity revival."

Other Americans worried that this one-sided war trade undermined genuine neutrality. Congress even considered embargoing munitions. But few Americans supported that idea. One financial journal declared of the Allied war trade: "We need it for the profits which it yields." Whatever its justification, however, the war trade strengthened U.S. ties with the Allies and embittered Germans. As the German ambassador noted, American industry was "actually delivering goods only to the enemies of Germany."

A second economic issue complicated matters. To finance their war purchases, the Allies borrowed from American bankers. Initially, Secretary of State Bryan persuaded Wilson to prohibit loans to the belligerents as "inconsistent with the true spirit of neutrality." But as the importance of the war orders to both the Allies and the American economy became clear, Wilson ended the ban. Secretary of the Treasury William McAdoo argued that it would be "disastrous" *not* to finance the Allies' purchases, on which "our prosperity is dependent." By April 1917, American loans to the Allies exceeded $2 billion, nearly one hundred times the amount lent to Germany. These financial ties, like the war trade they underwrote, linked the United States to the Allies and convinced Germany that American neutrality was only a formality.

The Diplomacy of Neutrality

This same imbalance characterized American diplomacy. Wilson insisted on American neutral rights but acquiesced in British violations of those rights while sternly refusing to yield on German actions. Wilson argued that while British violations of international law cost Americans property, markets, and time, German violations cost lives. As the *Boston Globe* noted, the British were "a gang of thieves" and the Germans "a gang of murderers. On the whole, we prefer the thieves, but only as the lesser of two evils."

When the war began, the United States asked belligerents to respect the 1909 **Declaration of London** on neutral rights. Germany agreed to do so; the British refused. Instead, skirting or violating established procedures, Britain instituted a blockade of Germany, mined the North Sea, and forced neutral ships into British ports to search their cargoes and confiscate material deemed useful to the German war effort. These British actions infringed U.S. trading rights. Wilson branded Britain's blockade illegal and unwarranted, but by October he had conceded many of America's neutral rights to avoid conflict with Britain. This concession reflected both Wilson's English sympathies, for he thought it unfair and unrealistic to demand that Britain abandon its most effective weapon, and the profitable war trade with the Allies. He was also convinced that the Allied cause was vital to America's interests.

The British then prohibited food and other products that Germany had imported during peacetime, thereby interfering further with neutral shipping. Even the British admitted that these steps had no legal justification, and one American official complained privately: "England is playing a . . . high game, violating international law every day." But when the Wilson administration finally protested, it undermined its own position by noting that "imperative necessity" might justify a violation of international law. This statement virtually authorized the British to violate American rights. In January 1915, Wilson yielded further by observing that "no very important questions of principle" were involved in the Anglo-American quarrels over ship seizures and that they could be resolved after the war.

This policy tied the United States to the British war effort and provoked a German response. With its army stalemated on land and its navy no match for Britain's, Germany decided in February 1915 to use its submarines against Allied shipping in a war zone around the British Isles. Neutral ships risked being sunk by mistake, partly because British ships illegally flew neutral flags. Germany maintained that Britain's blockade and the acquiescence of neutral countries in British violations of international law made submarine warfare necessary.

Submarines could not readily follow traditional rules of naval warfare. These rules had been drawn up for surface ships and required them to identify enemy merchant ships and ensure the safety of passengers before attacking. But small and fragile submarines depended on surprise attacks. They could not surface without risking disaster from the deck guns of Britain's armed merchant ships, and they were too small to rescue victims of their sinkings. Yet Wilson refused to see the "imperative necessity" in German tactics that he found in British tactics, and he warned that he would hold Germany responsible for any loss of American lives or property.

In May 1915, a German submarine sank a British passenger liner, the *Lusitania*. It had been carrying arms, and the German embassy had warned Americans against traveling on the ship, but the loss of life—1,198 people, including 128 Americans—caused Americans to condemn Germany. "To speak of technicalities and the rules of war, in the face of such wholesale murder on the high seas, is a waste of time," trumpeted one magazine. Yet only six of a thousand editors surveyed called for war, and even the combative Theodore Roosevelt estimated that 98 percent of Americans still opposed war. Wilson saw he had to "carry out the double wish of our people, to maintain a firm front in respect of what we demand of Germany and yet do nothing that might by any possibility involve us in the war."

That was difficult. Wilson demanded that Germany abandon its submarine campaign. His language was so harsh that Bryan resigned, warning that by requiring more of Germany than of Britain, the president violated neutrality and threatened to draw the nation into war. Bryan argued that "Germany has a right to prevent contraband from going to the Allies," and he protested Britain's use of American passengers as shields to protect contraband cargo. "This country cannot be neutral and unneutral at the same time," he declared. "If it is to be neutral it cannot undertake to help one side against the other." Bryan proposed prohibiting Americans from traveling on belligerent ships. His proposal gained support in the South and West, and Senator Thomas Gore of Oklahoma and Representative Jeff McLemore of Texas introduced it in congressional resolutions in February 1916.

Wilson moved to defeat the Gore-McLemore resolutions, insisting that they impinged on presidential control of foreign policy and on America's neutral rights. In truth, the resolutions abandoned no vital national interest while offering to prevent another provocative incident. Moreover, neither law nor tradition gave Americans the right to travel safely on belligerent ships. Wilson's assertion of such a right committed him to a policy that could only lead to conflict. Of the nation's "double wish," then, Wilson placed more priority on confronting what he saw as the German threat than on meeting the popular desire for peace.

Arguments over submarine warfare climaxed in April 1916. A German submarine torpedoed the French ship *Sussex*, injuring four Americans. Wilson threatened to break diplomatic relations if Germany did not abandon unrestricted submarine warfare against all merchant vessels, enemy as well as neutral. This implied war. Germany promised not to sink merchant ships without warning but made its **Sussex Pledge** contingent on the United States' requiring Britain also to adhere to "the rules of international law universally recognized before the war." Wilson's diplomatic victory, then, was hollow. Peace for America would depend on the British adopting a course they rejected. As Wilson saw it, however, "any little German lieutenant can put us into the war at any time by some calculated outrage." Wilson's diplomacy had left the nation's future at the mercy of others.

The Battle over Preparedness

The threat of war sparked a debate over military policy. Theodore Roosevelt and a handful of other politicians, mostly northeastern Republicans convinced that Allied victory was in the national interest, advocated what they called **preparedness**, a program to expand the armed forces and establish universal military training. Conservative business groups also joined the agitation. The National Security League, consisting of eastern bankers and industrialists, combined demands for preparedness with attacks on progressive reforms.

But most Americans, certain that their nation would not join the bloody madness, opposed expensive military preparations. Many supported a large peace movement. Leading feminists like Jane Addams, Charlotte Perkins Gilman, and Carrie Chapman Catt formed the Woman's Peace Party in 1915, and other organizations like the American League to Limit Armaments also campaigned against preparedness. William Jennings Bryan denounced the militarism of Roosevelt as a "philosophy [that] can rot a soul" and condemned preparedness as a program for turning the nation into "a vast armory with skull and crossbones above the door." Most opponents agreed that military spending would undermine domestic reform and raise taxes while enriching arms merchants and financiers.

Wilson also opposed preparedness initially, but he reversed his position when the submarine crisis with Germany intensified. He also began to champion military expansion lest Republicans accuse him in the 1916 election of neglecting national defense. In early 1916, he made a speaking tour to generate public support for expanding the armed forces. Continuing opposition to preparedness, especially in the South and West, forced Wilson to drop his proposal

A preparedness parade winds its way through Mobile, Alabama, on July 4, 1916. By 1916, President Wilson, invoking the spirit of patriotism, had given his support to the preparedness program of military expansion.

for a national reserve force. Nevertheless, the National Defense Act and the Naval Construction Act increased the strength of the army and authorized a naval construction plan. Draped in the flag, Wilson marched at the head of a huge preparedness parade in Washington to celebrate the military program.

The Election of 1916

Wilson's preparedness plans stripped the Republicans of one issue in 1916, and his renewed support of progressive reforms (see Chapter 23) helped hold Bryan Democrats in line. Wilson continued his balancing act in the campaign itself, at first stressing "Americanism" and preparedness but then emphasizing peace. The slogan "He Kept Us Out of War" appealed to the popular desire for peace, and the Democratic campaign became one long peace rally. Wilson disliked the peace emphasis but exploited its political appeal. He warned, "The certain prospect of the success of the Republican party is that we shall be drawn, in one form or another, into the embroilments of the European war."

The Republicans were divided. They had hoped to regain their progressive members after Roosevelt urged the Progressive party to follow him back into the GOP. But many joined the Democratic camp instead, including several Progressive party leaders who endorsed Wilson for having enacted the party's demands of 1912. Roosevelt's frenzied interventionism had also alienated many midwestern Republicans opposed to preparedness and cost him any chance of gaining the nomination for himself. Instead, the GOP nominated Charles Evans Hughes, a Supreme Court justice and former New York governor. The platform denounced Wilson's "shifty expedients" in foreign policy and promised "strict and honest neutrality." Unfortunately for Hughes, Roosevelt's attacks on Wilson for not pursuing a war policy persuaded many voters that the GOP was a war party. The link with Roosevelt also kept Hughes from exploiting qualms about Wilson's own unneutrality. "If Hughes is defeated," wrote one observer, "he has Roosevelt to thank for it."

The election was the closest in decades (see Map 25-1). When California narrowly went for Wilson, it decided the contest. The results reflected sectional differences, with the South and West voting for Wilson and most of the Northeast and Midwest for Hughes. The desire for peace, all observers concluded, had determined the election.

Descent into War

Still, Wilson knew that war loomed, and he made a last effort to avert it. In 1915 and 1916, he had tried to mediate the European conflict, using Colonel House as a secret intermediary. Now he again appealed for an end to hostilities. In January 1917, he sketched out the terms of what he called a

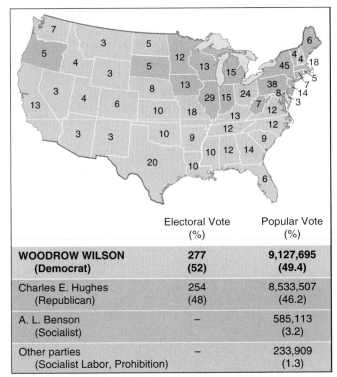

	Electoral Vote (%)	Popular Vote (%)
WOODROW WILSON (Democrat)	**277** (52)	**9,127,695** (49.4)
Charles E. Hughes (Republican)	254 (48)	8,533,507 (46.2)
A. L. Benson (Socialist)	–	585,113 (3.2)
Other parties (Socialist Labor, Prohibition)	–	233,909 (1.3)

Map 25-1   The Election of 1916
Woodrow Wilson won reelection in 1916 despite a reunified Republican party by sweeping the South and West on campaign appeals to peace and progressive reform.

"peace without victory." Anything else, he warned, would only lead to another war. The new world order should be based on national equality and **self-determination**, arms reductions, freedom of the seas, and an international organization to ensure peace. It was a distinctly American vision.

Neither the Allies nor the Central Powers were interested. Each side had sacrificed too much to settle for anything short of outright victory. Germany wanted to annex territory in eastern Europe, Belgium, and France and to take over Belgian and French colonies in Africa; Austria sought Balkan territory. The Allies wanted to destroy German military and commercial power, weaken the Austro-Hungarian empire, take Germany's colonies in Africa, and supplant Turkish influence in the Middle East. One British leader denounced Wilson as "the quintessence of a prig" for suggesting that after three years of "this terrible effort," the two sides should accept American principles rather than their own national objectives. Wilson's initiative failed.

Germany decided to resume unrestricted submarine warfare. German generals believed that even if the United States declared war, it could do little more in the short run to injure Germany than it

was already doing. German submarines, they hoped, would end the war by cutting the Allies off from U.S. supplies before the United States could send an army to Europe. On January 31, Germany announced its decision to unleash its submarines in a broad war zone.

Wilson was now virtually committed to a war many Americans opposed. He broke diplomatic relations with Germany and asked Congress to arm American merchant vessels. When the Senate refused, Wilson invoked an antipiracy law of 1819 and armed the ships anyway. Although no American ships had yet been sunk, he also ordered the naval gun crews to shoot submarines on sight. Wilson's own secretary of the navy warned that these actions violated international law and were a step toward war; Wilson called his policy "armed neutrality." Huge rallies across America demanded peace.

Yet several developments soon shifted public opinion. On March 1, Wilson released an intercepted message from the German foreign minister, Arthur Zimmermann, to the German minister in Mexico. It proposed that in the event of war between the United States and Germany, Mexico should ally itself with Germany; in exchange, Mexico would recover its "lost territory in Texas, New Mexico, and Arizona." The Zimmermann note produced a wave of hostility toward Germany and increased support for intervention in the war, especially in the Southwest, which had opposed involvement. A revolution in Russia overthrew the tsarist regime and established a provisional government. Russia was now "a fit partner" for the United States, said Wilson. When submarines sank four American freighters in mid-March, anti-German feeling broadened.

On April 2, 1917, Wilson delivered his war message, declaring that neutrality was no longer possible, given Germany's submarine "warfare against mankind." To build support for joining a war that most people had long regarded with revulsion and as alien to American interests, Wilson set forth the nation's war goals as simple and noble. The United States would not fight for conquest or domination but for "the ultimate peace of the world and for the liberation of its peoples. . . . The world must be made safe for democracy." Interventionists like Senator Lodge were delighted with the decision for war but distanced themselves from any goal other than promoting national interests. Some progressives who had opposed involvement were won over by Wilson's appeal to idealism.

But others in Congress attacked war. Senator Robert La Follette assailed Wilson's policies as unneutral. Senator George Norris of Nebraska condemned the economic motives for American belligerency, crying out, "We are going to war upon the command of gold." Ridiculing Wilson's advocacy of war as a means to promote democracy, House Democratic leader Claude Kitchin of North Carolina insisted that the American people opposed war and requested a popular referendum on the question. After vigorous debate, the Senate passed the war resolution 82 to 6 and the House 373 to 50. On April 6, 1917, the United States officially entered the Great War, what Kitchin predicted would be "one vast drama of horrors and blood, one boundless stage upon which will play all the evil spirits of earth and hell."

Waging War in America

Mobilizing for military intervention was a massive undertaking. "It is not an army that we must shape and train for war," announced President Wilson; "it is a Nation." The government reorganized the economy to emphasize centralized management, developed policies to control public opinion and suppress dissent, and transformed the role of government itself. Mobilization often built on progressives' moralism and sense of mission and their work to resolve social and economic problems by government intervention. In other respects, however, the war experience undercut progressive achievements and withered the spirits of reformers. In many different ways, people on the home front—like soldiers in Europe—would participate in the Great War; all would find their lives changed.

Managing the War Economy

Surveying the nation's economy in May 1917, Secretary of War Newton Baker echoed Wilson. War no longer involved merely soldiers and weapons, he said. "It is the conflict of smokestacks now, the combat of the driving wheel and the engine." To harness those factories and machines for the war, federal and state governments developed a complex structure of agencies and controls for every sector of the economy, from industry and agriculture to transportation and labor

OVERVIEW

MAJOR GOVERNMENT WARTIME AGENCIES

Agency	Purpose
War Industries Board	Reorganized industry to maximize wartime production
Railway Administration	Modernized and operated the nation's railroads
Food Administration	Increased agricultural production, supervised food distribution and farm labor
National War Labor Board	Resolved labor-management disputes, improved labor conditions, and recognized union rights as means to promote production and efficiency
Committee on Public Information	Managed propaganda to build public support for the war effort

(see the overview table, "Major Government Wartime Agencies"). Supervised by the Council of National Defense, these agencies shifted resources to war-related enterprise, increased production of goods and services, and improved transportation and distribution.

The most important agency was the **War Industries Board (WIB)**, established in July 1917 to set industrial priorities, coordinate military purchasing, and supervise business. Led by financier Bernard Baruch, the WIB exercised unprecedented powers over industry by setting prices, allocating scarce materials, and standardizing products and procedures to boost efficiency. The number of sizes and styles of plows was reduced by 80 percent; the number of colors of typewriter ribbon dropped from 150 to 5. The WIB even specified how many trunks traveling salesmen could carry and how many stops elevators could make. Yet Baruch was not an industrial dictator; he aimed at business–government integration. The WIB promoted major business interests, helped suspend antitrust laws, and guaranteed huge corporate profits. So many business leaders became involved in the WIB that there was a popular outcry against business infiltration of the government, and one corporate executive admitted, "We are all making more money out of this war than the average human being ought to." Some progressives began to see the dangers, and business leaders the advantages, of government economic intervention.

The **Railroad Administration** also linked business ambitions to the war economy. Under William McAdoo, it operated the nation's railroads as a unified system to move supplies and troops efficiently. Centralized management eliminated competition, permitted improvements in equipment, and brought great profits to the owners but higher prices to the general public. Progressive Republican Senator Hiram Johnson of California protested that the Railroad Administration was "outrageously generous to the railroads and shamefully unjust to the people."

Equally effective and far more popular was the **Food Administration**, headed by Herbert Hoover. Hoover had organized relief supplies for war-torn Belgium and now controlled the production and distribution of food for the United States and its allies. He persuaded millions of Americans to accept meatless and wheatless days so that the Food Administration could feed military and foreign consumers. Half a million women went door to door to secure food conservation pledges from housewives. City residents planted victory gardens in parks and vacant lots, and President Wilson even pastured sheep on the White House lawn.

Hoover also worked closely with agricultural processors and distributors, assuring profits in exchange for cooperation. Farmers profited from the war, too. To encourage production, Hoover established high prices for commodities, and agricultural income rose 30 percent. State and federal governments also provided commercial farmers with sufficient farm labor despite the military draft and competition from high-wage war industries. The Food Administration organized the Woman's Land Army to work in the fields. Most states formed units of the Boys' Working Reserve for agricultural labor. Many southern and western states required "loafers" or "slackers" to work in agriculture. Agribusinesses in the Southwest persuaded the federal government to permit them to import Mexicans to work under government supervision and be housed in special camps.

The **National War Labor Board** supervised labor relations. In exchange for labor's cooperation, this agency guaranteed the rights of unions to organize and bargain collectively. With such support, unions sharply increased their membership. The labor board also encouraged improved working conditions, higher wages, and shorter hours. War contracts stipulated an eight-hour day, and by the end of the war, nearly half

"Eat the potatoes, save the wheat; drive the Kaiser to defeat." Children in Wahoo, Nebraska, tend their victory garden. Government agencies tried to enlist everyone in the war effort.

the nation's workers had achieved the forty-eight-hour week. Wages rose, too, but often only as fast as inflation. These improvements limited labor disputes during the war, and Secretary of War Baker praised labor as "more willing to keep in step than capital." But when unions like the Industrial Workers of the World did not keep in step, the government suppressed them.

Although these and other government regulatory agencies were dismantled when the war ended, their activities reinforced many long-standing trends in the American economy, from the consolidation of business to the commercialization of agriculture and the organization of labor. They also set a precedent for governmental activism that would prove valuable during the crises of the 1930s and 1940s.

New Opportunities, Old Issues

The reorganization of the economy also had significant social consequences, especially for women and African Americans. In response to labor shortages, women took jobs previously closed to them. Besides farm work, they built airplanes, produced guns and ammunition, and manufactured tents and cartridge belts. More than 100,000 women worked in munitions plants and 40,000 in the steel industry. Women constituted 20 percent or more of all workers making electrical machinery, leather and rubber goods, and food. They operated drills and lathes, controlled cranes in steel mills, and repaired equipment in machine shops. "One of the lessons from the war," said one manufacturer, "has been to show that women can do exacting work." Harriot Stanton Blatch, a suffragist active in the Food Administration, estimated that a million women had replaced men in industry, where "their drudgery is for the first time paid for."

Many working women simply shifted to other jobs where their existing skills earned better wages and benefits. The reshuffling of jobs among white women opened new vacancies for black women in domestic, clerical, and industrial employment. As black women replaced white women in the garment and textile industries, social reformers spoke of "a new day for the colored woman worker." But such optimism was unwarranted. Racial as well as gender segregation continued to mark employment, and wartime improvements were temporary.

The war helped middle-class women reformers achieve two long-sought objectives: woman suffrage and prohibition. Women's support for the war effort prompted more Americans to support woman suffrage. Emphasizing the national cooperation needed to wage the war, one magazine noted that "arbitrarily to draw the line at voting, at a time when every man and woman must share in this effort, becomes an absurd anomaly." Even Woodrow Wilson finally endorsed the reform, terming it "vital to the winning of the war." Congress approved the suffrage amendment, which was ratified in 1920. Convinced that abstaining from alcohol would save grain and make workers and soldiers more efficient, Congress also passed the **prohibition** amendment, which was ratified in 1919.

The war also changed the lives of African Americans. The demand for industrial labor caused a huge migration of black people from the rural South, where they had had little opportunity, few rights, and no hope. In northern cities, they worked in shipyards, steel mills, and packing houses. Half a million African Americans moved north during the war, doubling and tripling the black populations of Chicago, Detroit, and other industrial cities.

Unfortunately, black people often encountered the kind of racial discrimination and violence in the North they had hoped to leave behind in the South. Fearful and resentful white people started race riots in northern cities. In East St. Louis, Illinois, where thousands of black Southerners sought defense work, a white mob in July 1917 murdered at least thirty-nine black people, sparing, as an investigating committee reported, "neither age nor sex in their blind lust for blood." Others placed the tragedy in a larger context. The *Literary Digest* noted, "Race-riots in East St. Louis afford a lurid background to our efforts to carry justice and idealism to Europe." And Wilson was told privately that the riot was "worse than anything the Germans did in Belgium."

Financing the War

To finance the war, the government borrowed money and raised taxes. Business interests favored the first course, but southern and western progressives argued that taxation was more efficient and equitable and would minimize war profiteering. Conservative and business opposition to progressive taxation prompted California Senator Johnson to note, "Our endeavours to impose heavy war profit taxes . . . have brought into sharp relief the skin-deep dollar patriotism of some of those who have been loudest in declamations on war and in their demands for blood." Nevertheless, the tax laws of 1917 and 1918 established a graduated tax structure with increased taxes on large incomes, corporate profits, and wealthy estates. Conservative opposition, however, would frustrate progressives' hopes for permanent tax reforms.

The government raised two-thirds of the war costs by borrowing. Most of the loans came from banks and wealthy investors, but the government also campaigned to sell **Liberty Bonds** to the general public. Celebrities went to schools, churches, and rallies to persuade Americans to buy bonds as their patriotic duty. "Every person who refuses to sub-

"Beat Back the Hun," a poster to induce Americans to buy Liberty Bonds, demonizes the enemy in a raw, emotional appeal. Liberty bond drives raised the immense sum of $23 billion.

scribe," Secretary of the Treasury McAdoo told a California audience, "is a friend of Germany." Using techniques of persuasion and control from advertising and mass entertainment, the Wilson administration thus enlisted the emotions of loyalty, fear, patriotism, and obedience for the war effort.

Conquering Minds

The government also tried to promote a war spirit among the American people by establishing propaganda agencies and enacting legislation to control social attitudes and behavior. This program drew from the restrictive side of progressivism: its impulses toward social control, behavior regulation, and nativism. It also reflected the interests of more conservative forces. The Wilson administration adopted this program of social mobilization because many Americans opposed the war: German Americans with ethnic ties to the Central Powers, Irish Catholics and Russian Jews who condemned the Allies for persecution and repression, Scandinavian immigrants averse to military service,

pacifists who recoiled from what Wilson himself called "the most terrible and disastrous of all wars," radicals who denounced the war as capitalist and imperialist, and many others, especially among the rural classes of the South and Midwest, who saw no reason to participate in the distant war.

To rally Americans behind the war effort, Wilson established the **Committee on Public Information (CPI)** under George Creel. Despite its title, the CPI sought to manipulate, not inform, public opinion. Creel described his goal as winning "the fight for the *minds* of men, for the 'conquest of their convictions.'" The CPI flooded the country with press releases, advertisements, cartoons, and canned editorials. An average of six pounds of government publicity went each day to every newspaper in California, for example. The CPI made newsreels and war movies to capture public attention. It scheduled 75,000 speakers, who delivered a million speeches to 400 million listeners. Its women's division targeted American women in stereotyped emotional terms. It hired artists to draw posters, professors to write pamphlets in twenty-three languages, and poets to compose war poems for children.

Other government agencies launched similar campaigns. The Woman's Committee of the Council of National Defense established the Department of Educational Propaganda and Patriotic Education. Carrie Chapman Catt dropped her peace activism to head this bureau, in the hope that the war effort would increase support for woman suffrage. The agency worked to win over women who opposed the war, particularly in the rural Midwest, West, and South. It formed women's speakers' bureaus, developed programs for community meetings at country schools, and distributed millions of pamphlets.

Government propaganda had three themes: national unity, the loathsome character of the enemy, and the war as a grand crusade for liberty and democracy. Obsessed with national unity and conformity, Creel promoted fear, hatred, and prejudice in the name of a triumphant Americanism. Germans were depicted as brutal, even subhuman, rapists and murderers. The campaign suggested that any dissent was unpatriotic, if not treasonous, and dangerous to national survival. This emphasis on unreasoning conformity helped prompt hysterical attacks on German Americans, radicals, and pacifists.

Suppressing Dissent

The Wilson administration also suppressed dissent, now officially branded disloyalty. For reasons of their own, private interests helped shape a reactionary repression that tarnished the nation's professed idealistic war goals. The campaign also established unfortunate precedents for the future.

Congress rushed to stifle antiwar sentiment. The **Espionage Act** provided heavy fines and up to twenty years in prison for obstructing the war effort, a vague phrase but one "omnipotently comprehensive," warned one Idaho senator who opposed the law. "No man can foresee what it might be in its consequences." In fact, the Espionage Act became a weapon to crush dissent and criticism. In 1918, Congress passed the still more sweeping **Sedition Act**. Based on state laws in the West designed to suppress labor radicals, the Sedition Act provided severe penalties for speaking or writing against the draft, bond sales, or war production or for criticizing government personnel or policies. Congress emphasized the law's inclusive nature by *rejecting* a proposed amendment stipulating that "nothing in this act shall be construed as limiting the liberty or impairing the right of any individual to publish or speak what is true, with good motives, and for justifiable ends." Senator Hiram Johnson lamented: "It is war. But, good God, . . . when did it become war upon the American people?"

Postmaster General Albert Burleson banned antiwar or radical newspapers and magazines from the mail, suppressing literature so indiscriminately that one observer said he "didn't know socialism from rheumatism." Even more zealous in attacking radicals and presumed subversives was the reactionary attorney general, Thomas Gregory, who made little distinction between traitors and pacifists, war critics, and radicals. Eugene Debs was sentenced to ten years in prison for a "treasonous" speech in which he declared it "extremely dangerous to exercise the right of free speech in a country fighting to make democracy safe in the world." By war's end, a third of the Socialist party's national leadership was in prison, leaving the party in shambles. Other notable radicals imprisoned included Ricardo Flores Magon, a Mexican-American labor organizer who was sentenced to twenty years for publishing antiwar material in his Los Angeles Spanish-language newspaper, *Regeneracion*.

Gregory also enlisted the help of private vigilantes, including several hundred thousand members of the reactionary **American Protective League**, which sought to purge radicals and reformers from the nation's economic and political life. They wiretapped telephones, intercepted private mail, burglarized union offices, broke up German-language newspapers, harassed immigrants, and staged mass raids, seizing thousands of people they claimed were not doing enough for the war effort. Even George Creel conceded that "at all times their patriotism was a thing of screams, violence, and extremes, and their savage intolerances had the burn of acid."

State and local authorities also sought to suppress what they saw as antiwar, radical, or pro-German activities. They established 184,000 investigating and enforcement agencies known as councils of defense or public safety committees. They encouraged Americans to spy on one another, required people to buy Liberty Bonds, and prohibited teaching German in schools or using the language in religious services and telephone conversations (see "American Views: Mobilizing America for Liberty"). Indeed, suppression of all things German reached extremes. Germanic names of towns, streets, and people were changed; sauerkraut became liberty cabbage, and the hamburger the liberty sandwich. In Tulsa, a member of the council of defense killed someone for making allegedly pro-German remarks. The council declared its approval, and community leaders applauded the killer's patriotism. A midwestern official of the Council of National Defense noted, "All over this part of the country men are being tarred and feathered and some are being lynched. . . . These cases do not get into the newspapers nor is an effort ever made to punish the individuals concerned."

Members of the business community exploited the hysteria to promote their own interests at the expense of farmers, workers, and reformers. As one Wisconsin farmer complained, businessmen "now under the guise of patriotism are trying to ram down the farmers' throats things they hardly dared before." On the Great Plains from Texas to North Dakota, the business target was the Nonpartisan League, a radical farm group demanding state control or ownership of banks, grain elevators, and flour mills. Although the League supported the war, oversubscribed bond drives, and had George Creel affirm its loyalty, conservatives depicted it as seditious to block its advocacy of political and economic reforms, including the confiscation of large fortunes to pay for the war. Minnesota's public safety commission condemned members of the Nonpartisan League as traitors and proposed a "firing squad working overtime" to deal with them. Nebraska's council of defense barred League meetings. Public officials and self-styled patriots broke up the League's meetings and whipped and jailed its leaders.

In the West, business interests targeted labor organizations, especially the Industrial Workers of the World. In Arizona, for example, the Phelps-Dodge Company broke a miners' strike in 1917 by depicting the Wobblies as bent on war-related sabotage. A vigilante mob, armed and paid by the mining company, seized twelve hundred strikers, many of them Wobblies and one-third of them Mexican Americans, and herded them into the desert without food or water. Federal investigators found no evidence of sedition among the miners and reported that the company and its thugs had been inspired not by "patriotism" but by "ordinary strike-breaking motives." Corporate management was merely "raising the false cry of 'disloyalty'" to suppress workers' complaints.

Nonetheless, the government itself assisted the business campaign. It used the army to break loggers' support for the IWW in the Pacific Northwest, and it raided IWW halls across the country in September 1917. The conviction of nearly two hundred Wobblies on charges of sedition in three mass trials in Illinois, California, and Kansas crippled the nation's largest industrial union.

In the end, the government was primarily responsible for the war hysteria, regardless of how such fears were used. It encouraged suspicion and conflict by its own inflammatory propaganda, repressive laws, and violation of basic civil rights, by supporting extremists who used the war for their own purposes, and by not opposing mob violence against German Americans. This ugly mood would infect the postwar world.

Waging War and Peace Abroad

While mobilizing the home front, the Wilson administration undertook an impressive military effort to help the Allies defeat the Central Powers. Wilson also struggled to secure international acceptance for his plans for a just and permanent peace.

The War to End All Wars

When the United States entered the war, the Allied military position was dire. The losses from three years of trench warfare had sapped military strength and civilian morale. French soldiers mutinied and refused to continue an assault that had cost 120,000 casualties in five days; the German submarine campaign was devastating the British. On the eastern front, the Russian army collapsed, and the Russian government gradually disintegrated after the overthrow of the tsarist regime.

What the Allies needed, said French Marshal Joseph Joffre in April 1917, was simple: "We want men, men, men." In May, Congress passed the **Selective Service Act**, establishing conscription. More than 24 million men eventually registered for the draft, and nearly 3 million entered the army when their numbers were drawn in a national lottery. Almost 2 million more men volunteered, as did more than ten thousand women who served in the navy. Nearly one-fifth of America's soldiers were foreign-born (Europeans spoke of the "American Foreign Legion"); 367,000 were black.

Civilians were transformed into soldiers in hastily organized training camps operated according to progressive principles. Prohibition prevailed

The United States quickly raised, trained, and transported a large military force that helped to defeat Germany in the Great War. Within it were the black troops of the Fifteenth Infantry, shown here with their white officers on board ship.

American Views
MOBILIZING AMERICA FOR LIBERTY

The war years witnessed official and popular efforts to repress dissent and diversity. Much of this repression was aimed at America's immigrant groups and sought to create national unity through coercive Americanization that trampled on the rights and values that the nation claimed to be defending. The following is an official proclamation of Governor W. L. Harding of Iowa, issued May 23, 1918.

❖ **What is the rationale for the governor's proclamation? What do you think of his interpretation of the constitutional guarantees of individual rights?**

❖ **What other "inconvenience or sacrifice" might the proclamation impose on minorities?**

❖ **How might the proclamation incite vigilantism?**

The official language of the United States and the State of Iowa is the English language. Freedom of speech is guaranteed by federal and State Constitutions, but this is not a guaranty of the right to use a language other than the language of this country—the English language. Both federal and State Constitutions also provide that "no laws shall be made respecting an establishment of religion or prohibiting the free exercise thereof." Each person is guaranteed freedom to worship God according to the dictates of his own conscience, but this guaranty does not protect him in the use of a foreign language when he can as well express his thought in English, nor entitle the person who cannot speak or understand the English language to employ a foreign language, when to do so tends in time of national peril, to create discord among neighbors and citizens, or to disturb the peace and quiet of the community.

in the camps; the poorly educated and largely working-class recruits were taught personal hygiene; worries about sin and inefficiency produced massive campaigns against venereal disease; and immigrants were taught English and American history. Some units were ethnically segregated: At Camp Gordon, Georgia, Italians and Slavs had separate units with their own officers. Racial segregation was more rigid, not only in training camps and military units but in assignments as well. The navy assigned black sailors to menial positions, and the army similarly used black soldiers primarily as gravediggers and laborers. But one black combat division was created, and four black regiments fought under French command. France decorated three of these units with its highest citations for valor. (White American officers urged the French not to praise black troops, treat black officers as equals, or permit fraternization.)

The first American troops landed in France in June 1917. This **American Expeditionary Force (AEF)** was commanded by General John J. Pershing, a career officer who had chased Pancho Villa across northern Mexico (see Chapter 24). Full-scale American intervention began in the late spring of 1918 (see Map 25-2). In June, the fresh American troops helped the French repulse a German thrust toward Paris at Château-Thierry. In July, the AEF helped defeat another German advance, at Rheims. The influx of American troops tipped the balance toward Allied victory. By July 18, the German chancellor later acknowledged, "even the most optimistic among us knew that all was lost. The history of the world was played out in three days."

Every person should appreciate and observe his duty to refrain from all acts or conversation which may excite suspicion or produce strife among the people, but in his relation to the public should so demean himself that every word and act will manifest his loyalty to his country and his solemn purpose to aid in achieving victory for our army and navy and the permanent peace of the world. . . .

The great aim and object of all should be unity of purpose and a solidarity of all the people under the flag for victory. This much we owe to ourselves, to posterity, to our country, and to the world.

Therefore, the following rules should obtain in Iowa during the war:

First. English should and must be the only medium of instruction in public, private, denominational, or other similar schools.

Second. Conversation in public places, on trains, and over the telephone should be in the English language.

Third. All public addresses should be in the English language.

Fourth. Let those who cannot speak or understand the English language conduct their religious worship in their homes.

This course carried out in the spirit of patriotism, though inconvenient to some, will not interfere with their guaranteed constitutional rights and will result in peace and tranquility at home and greatly strengthen the country in battle. The blessings of the United States are so great that any inconvenience or sacrifice should willingly be made for their perpetuity.

Therefore, by virtue of authority in me vested, I, W. L. Harding, Governor of the State of Iowa, commend the spirit of tolerance and urge that henceforth the within outlined rules be adhered to by all, that petty differences be avoided and forgotten, and that, united as one people with one purpose and one language, we fight shoulder to shoulder for the good of mankind.

Source: B. F. Shambaugh, ed., Iowa and War *(Iowa City: State Historical Society of Iowa, 1919).*

In July, Wilson also agreed to commit fifteen thousand American troops to intervene in Russia. Russia's provisional government had collapsed when the **Bolsheviks**, or communists, had seized power in November 1917. Under V. I. Lenin, the Bolsheviks had then signed an armistice with Germany in early 1918, which freed German troops for the summer offensive in France. The Allies' interventions were designed to reopen the eastern front and help overthrow the Bolshevik government. Lenin's call for the destruction of capitalism and imperialism alarmed the Allied leaders. One Wilson adviser urged the "eradication" of the Russian government. Soon American and British troops were fighting Russians in an effort to influence Russia's internal affairs. U.S. forces remained in Russia until 1920, even after

Germany had surrendered in 1918. These military interventions failed, but they did promote lasting Russian distrust of the West.

The Allies were more successful on the western front. Having stopped the German offensive in July, they launched their own advance. The decisive battle began in late September when an American army over 1 million strong attacked German trenches in the Argonne Forest. The Americans were inexperienced; some had been drafted only in July and had spent more time traveling than training. One officer worried, "With their unfamiliarity with weapons, a gun was about as much use as a broom in their hands." Nevertheless, the Americans advanced steadily, despite attacks with poison gas and heavy artillery. Lieutenant Maury Maverick (later a Texas congressman) described

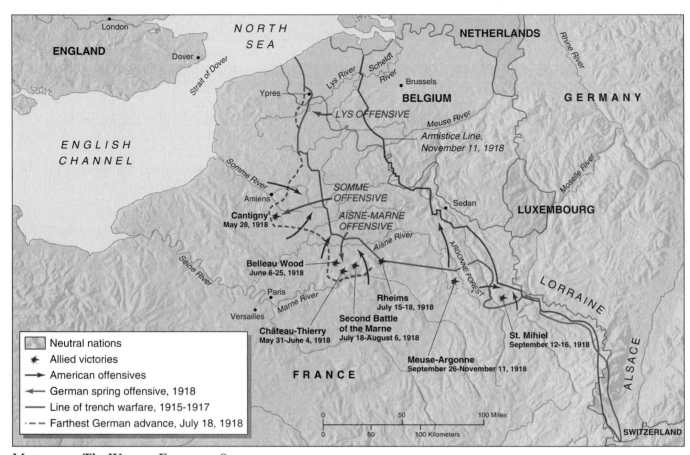

Map 25-2 The Western Front, 1918
After three years of trench warfare, the arrival of large numbers of American troops in 1918 enabled the Allies to launch an offensive that drove back the Germans and forced an armistice.

the shelling: "We were simply in a big black spot with streaks of screaming red and yellow, with roaring giants in the sky tearing and whirling and roaring." An exploding shell terrified him: "There is a great swishing scream, a smash-bang, and it seems to tear everything loose from you. The intensity of it simply enters your heart and brain, and tears every nerve to pieces."

The battle for the Argonne raged for weeks. One German general reported that his exhausted soldiers faced Americans who "were fresh, eager for fighting, and brave." But he found their sheer numbers most impressive. Eventually, this massive assault overwhelmed the Germans. Despite severe casualties, the AEF had helped the British and French defeat the enemy. With its allies surrendering, its own army in retreat, and revolution breaking out among war-weary residents in its major cities, Germany asked for peace. On November 11, 1918, an armistice ended the Great War. More than 115,000 Americans were among the 8 million soldiers and 7 million civilians dead.

The Fourteen Points

The armistice was only a step toward final peace. President Wilson had already enunciated American war objectives on January 8, 1918, in a speech outlining what became known as the Fourteen Points. In his 1917 war message, Wilson had advocated a more democratic world system, and this new speech spelled out how to achieve it. But Wilson also had a political purpose. The Bolsheviks had published the secret treaties the Allies had signed dividing up the economic and territorial spoils of war. Lenin called for an immediate peace based on the liberation of all colonies, self-determination for all peoples, and the rejection of annexations and punitive indemnities. Wilson's Fourteen Points reassured the American and Allied peoples that they were fighting for more than imperialist gains and offered an alternative to what he called Lenin's "crude formula" for peace.

Eight of Wilson's points proposed creating new nations, shifting old borders, or assuring self-determination for peoples previously subject to the Austrian, German, or Russian empires. The point about Russia would haunt Wilson after the Allied interventions there began, for it called on all nations to evacuate Russian territory and permit Russia "an unhampered and unembarrassed opportunity for the independent determination of her own political development" under "institutions of her own choosing." Another five points invoked principles to guide international relations: freedom of the seas, open diplomacy instead of secret treaties, reduction of armaments, free trade, and the fair settlement of colonial claims. Wilson's fourteenth and most important point proposed a league of nations to carry out these ideals and ensure international stability.

Wilson and the German government had these principles in mind when negotiating the armistice. The Allies, however, had never explicitly accepted the Fourteen Points, and framing a final peace treaty would be difficult. While Wilson favored a settlement that would promote international stability and economic expansion, he recognized that the Allies sought "to get everything out of Germany that they can." Indeed, after their human and economic sacrifices, Britain and France wanted tangible compensation, not pious principles.

Convinced of the righteousness of his cause, Wilson decided to attend the peace conference in Paris himself, though no president had ever gone to Europe while in office. But Wilson weakened his position before he even set sail. First, he urged voters to support Democratic candidates in the November 1918 elections to indicate approval of his peace plans. But the electorate, responding primarily to domestic problems like inflation, gave the Republicans control of both houses of Congress. This meant that any treaty would have to be approved by Senate Republicans angry that Wilson had tried to use war and peace for partisan purposes. Second, Wilson refused to consult with Senate Republicans on plans for the peace conference and failed to name important Republicans to the Paris delegation. It would be Wilson's treaty, but Republicans would feel no responsibility to approve it.

The Paris Peace Conference

The peace conference opened on January 18, 1919. Meeting at the Palace of Versailles, the delegations were dominated by the principal Allied leaders themselves: Wilson of the United States, David Lloyd George of Britain, Georges Clemenceau of France, and Vittorio Orlando of Italy. The Central Powers and Bolshevik Russia were excluded. The treaty would be one-sided except to the extent that Wilson could insist on the liberal terms of the Fourteen Points against French and British intransigence. As Clemenceau remarked, "God gave us the Ten Commandments and we broke them. Mr. Wilson has given us the Fourteen Points. We shall see."

Wilson himself had broken two of the Fourteen Points before the conference began. He had acquiesced in Britain's rejection of freedom of the seas. And he had sent U.S. troops to intervene in Russia in violation of its right to self-determination.

For months, the conference debated Wilson's other goals and the Allies' demands for compensation and security. Lloyd George later commented, with reference to the self-righteous Wilson and the assertive

The Big Four gather at the Paris Peace Conference. Vittorio Orlando of Italy, David Lloyd George of Great Britain, and Georges Clemenceau of France join Woodrow Wilson to discuss the terms of the treaty. The three Europeans had little interest in Wilson's Fourteen Points.

Clemenceau, "I think I did as well as might be expected, seated as I was between Jesus Christ and Napoleon Bonaparte." Under protest, Germany signed the **Treaty of Versailles** on June 28, 1919. Its terms were far more severe than Wilson had proposed or Germany had anticipated. Germany had to accept sole responsibility for starting the war, which all Germans bitterly resented. It was required to pay huge reparations to the Allies; to give up land to France, Poland, Belgium, and Denmark; to cede its colonies; to limit its army and navy to small self-defense forces; to destroy military bases; and to promise not to manufacture or purchase armaments.

Wilson gained some acceptance of self-determination. As the German, Austro-Hungarian, Turkish, and Russian empires had collapsed at the end of the war, nationalist groups had proclaimed their independence. On one hand, the peace settlement formally recognized these new nation-states: Poland, Finland, Estonia, Latvia, and Lithuania in eastern Europe and Austria, Hungary, Czechoslovakia, and Yugoslavia in central Europe (see Map 25-3). On the other hand, France, Italy, Romania, and Japan all annexed territory regardless of the wishes of the inhabitants. Germans were placed under Polish control in Silesia and Czech control in Bohemia. Austrians were not allowed to merge with Germany. And the conference sanctioned colonialism by establishing a trusteeship system that enabled France, Britain, and Japan to take over German colonies and Turkish territory.

Moreover, the Allied leaders endorsed the changes in eastern Europe in part because the new states there were anticommunist. Western leaders soon called these countries the **cordon sanitaire**, a barrier against Bolshevism. Indeed, the Allies at Versailles were preoccupied with Bolshevik Russia, which one of Wilson's aides called the "black cloud of the east, threatening to overwhelm and swallow up the world." Communist movements in early 1919 in Germany, Austria, and Hungary caused the Allies to fear that "the Russian idea was still rising in power," and they hoped to isolate and weaken Bolshevik Russia. Allied armies were in Russia during the peace conference, and Wilson and the other leaders agreed to provide further aid to fight the Bolsheviks. This hostility to Russia, like the punitive terms for Germany and the concessions to imperial interests, boded ill for a stable and just postwar order.

But Wilson hoped that the final section of the Versailles treaty would resolve the flaws of the agreement by establishing his great international organization to preserve peace: the **League of Nations**. The Covenant, or constitution, of the League was built into the treaty. Its crucial feature, Article Ten, bound the member nations to guarantee each other's independence, which was Wilson's concept of collective security. "At least," he told an aide, "we are saving the Covenant, and that instrument will work wonders, bring the blessing of peace, and then when the war psychosis has abated, it will not be difficult to settle all disputes that baffle us now." Sailing home, he mused: "Well, it is finished, and, as no one is satisfied, it makes me hope we have made a just peace; but it is all on the lap of the gods."

Waging Peace at Home

Wilson was determined to defeat opposition to the peace treaty. But many Americans were engaged in their own struggles with the new conditions of a nation suddenly at peace but riven by economic, social, and political conflict shaped by the war experience. Wilson's battle for the League of Nations would fail tragically. The other conflicts would rage until the election of 1920 restored a normalcy of sorts.

Battle over the League

Most Americans favored the Versailles treaty. A survey of fourteen hundred newspapers found fewer than two hundred opposed. Thirty-three governors and thirty-two state legislatures approved of the League of Nations. But when Wilson called for the Senate to accept "the moral leadership . . . and confidence of the world" by ratifying the treaty, he met resistance. Some Republicans wanted to prevent the Democrats from campaigning in 1920 as the party responsible for a victorious war and a glorious peace. But most Republican opponents of the treaty raised serious questions, often reflecting national traditions in foreign relations. Nearly all Democrats favored the treaty, but they were a minority; some Republicans had to be converted for the treaty to be approved.

Progressive Republican senators, such as Robert La Follette and Hiram Johnson, led one group of opponents. Called the **Irreconcilables**, they opposed participation in the League of Nations, which they saw as designed to perpetuate the power of imperialist countries. Article Ten, they feared, would require the United States to help suppress rebellions in Ireland against British rule or to enforce disputed European borders. Johnson declared, "I am opposed to American boys policing Europe and quelling riots in every new nation's backyard." Most of the Irreconcilables gave priority to restoring civil liberties and progressive reform at home.

A larger group of opponents had reservations about the treaty's provisions. These **Reservationists** were led by Henry Cabot Lodge, the chair of the Sen-

Map 25-3   *Europe and the Middle East after the Treaty of Versailles*
World War I and the Treaty of Versailles rearranged the borders of Europe and the Middle East.
Germany, Russia, and the Austrian and Turkish empires all lost land, and new nations were
recognized, but the principle of self-determination was only imperfectly observed.

ate Foreign Relations Committee. They regarded Article Ten as eroding congressional authority to declare war. They also fretted that the League might interfere with domestic questions, such as immigration laws. Lodge held public hearings on the treaty to rouse and focus opposition. German Americans resented the war guilt clause; Italian and Polish Americans complained that the treaty did not satisfy the territorial ambitions of Italy and Poland; Irish Americans condemned the treaty's failure to give self-determination to Ireland. Many progressives also criticized the treaty's compromises on self-determination, reparations, and colonies. Linking these failures with Wilson's domestic policies, one former supporter concluded; "The administration has become reactionary, and deserves no support from any of us."

Lodge's own opposition was shaped by both partisanship and deep personal hostility. "I never expected to hate anyone in politics with the hatred I feel toward Wilson," Lodge confessed. Wilson reciprocated, and when Lodge proposed reservations or amendments to the treaty, Wilson refused to compromise. He proposed "a direct frontal attack" on his opponents. If they wanted war, he said, he would "give them a belly full." In early September 1919, Wilson set out across the country to win popular support for the League. In three weeks, he traveled eight thousand miles and delivered thirty-seven speeches.

In poor health following a bout with influenza, he collapsed in Pueblo, Colorado. Confused and in tears, Wilson mumbled to his secretary, "I seem to have gone to pieces." Taken back to Washington, Wilson on October 2 suffered a massive stroke that paralyzed his left side and left him psychologically unstable and temporarily blind. Wilson's physician and his wife, Edith Galt Wilson, kept the nature of his illness secret from the public, Congress, and even the vice president and cabinet. Rumors circulated that Edith Wilson was running the administration, but she was not. Instead, it was immobilized.

By February 1920, Wilson had partially recovered, but he remained suspicious and quarrelsome. Bryan and other Democratic leaders urged him to accept Lodge's reservations to gain ratification of the treaty. Wilson refused. Isolated and inflexible, he ordered Democratic senators to vote with the Irreconcilables against the treaty as amended by Lodge. On March 19, 1920, the Senate killed the treaty.

Economic Readjustment and Social Conflict

The League was not the only casualty of the struggle to conclude the war. Grave problems shook the United States in 1919 and early 1920. An influenza epidemic had erupted in Europe in 1918 among the massed armies. It now hit the United States, killing perhaps 700,000 Americans, far more than had died in combat. Frightened authorities closed public facilities and banned public meetings in futile attempts to stop the contagion.

Meanwhile, the Wilson administration had no plans for an orderly reconversion of the wartime economy, and chaos ensued. The secretary of the Council of National Defense later reported with but slight exaggeration, "The magnificent war formation of American industry was dissipated in a day; the mobilization that had taken many months was succeeded by an instantaneous demobilization." The government canceled war contracts and dissolved the regulatory agencies. Noting that "the war spirit of cooperation and sacrifice" had disappeared with the

Armistice, Bernard Baruch decided to "turn industry absolutely free" and abolished the War Industries Board as of January 1, 1919. Other agencies followed in such haste that turmoil engulfed the economy.

The government also demobilized the armed forces. The army discharged 600,000 soldiers still in training camps; the navy brought AEF soldiers home from France so fast that it had to expand the troop fleet to four times its peak size during the war. With no planning or assistance, troops were hustled back into civilian life. There they competed for scarce jobs with workers recently discharged from the war industries.

As unemployment mounted, the removal of wartime price controls brought runaway inflation. The cost of food, clothing, and other necessities more than doubled over prewar rates. The return of the soldiers caused a serious housing shortage, and rents skyrocketed. Democratic leaders urged Wilson to devote less time to the League of Nations and more to the cost of living and the tensions it unleashed. Farmers also suffered from economic readjustments. Net farm income declined by 65 percent between 1919 and 1921. Farmers who had borrowed money for machinery and land to expand production for the war effort were left impoverished and embittered.

Women also lost their wartime economic advances. Returning soldiers took away their jobs. Male trade unionists insisted that women go back to being housewives. One New York union maintained that "the same patriotism which induced women to enter industry during the war should induce them to vacate their positions after the war." At times, male workers struck to force employers to fire women and barred women from unions in jobs where union membership was required for employment. Most women were willing to relinquish their jobs to veterans who had previously held them but objected to being displaced by men without experience. "During the war they called us heroines," one woman complained, "but they throw us on the scrapheap now." By 1919, half of the women newly employed in heavy industry during the war were gone; by 1920, women constituted a smaller proportion of the work force than they had in 1910.

The postwar readjustments also left African Americans disappointed. During the war, they had agreed with W. E. B. Du Bois to "forget our special grievances and close our ranks shoulder to shoulder with our own white fellow citizens." Participation in the war effort, they hoped, might be rewarded by better treatment thereafter. African Americans had contributed to the fighting and home fronts. Now, the meagerness of their reward became clear.

Housing shortages and job competition interacted with racism in 1919 to produce race riots in twenty-six towns and cities, resulting in at least 120 deaths. In Chicago, thirty-eight people were killed and more than five hundred injured in a five-day riot that began when white thugs stoned to death a black youth swimming too near "their" beach. White rioters then fired a machine gun from a truck hurtling through black neighborhoods. But black residents fought back, no longer willing, the *Chicago Defender* reported, "to move along the line of least resistance as did their sires." The new militancy reflected both their experiences in the military and in industry and their exposure to propaganda about freedom and democracy. Racial conflict was part of a postwar battle between Americans hoping to preserve the new social relations fostered by the war effort and those wanting to restore prewar patterns of power and control.

Even more pervasive discontents roiled as America adjusted to the postwar world. More than 4 million angry workers launched a wave of 3,600 strikes in 1919. They were reacting not only to the soaring cost of living, which undermined the value of their wages, but also to employers' efforts to reassert their authority and destroy the legitimacy labor had won by its participation in the war effort. The abolition of government controls on industry enabled employers not only to raise prices but also to rescind their recognition of unions and reimpose objectionable working conditions. Employers also protected their rising profits by insisting that workers' wages remain fixed. In response, strikers demanded higher wages, better conditions, and recognition of unions and the right of collective bargaining.

The greatest strike involved the American Federation of Labor's attempt to organize steelworkers, who endured dangerous conditions and twelve-hour shifts. When the steel companies refused to recognize the union or even discuss issues, 365,000 workers went out on strike in September 1919. Strikers in Pennsylvania pointed out that they had worked "cheerfully, without strikes or trouble of any kind" during the war to "make the world safe for democracy" and that they now sought "industrial democracy." Employers hired thugs to beat the strikers, used strikebreakers to take their jobs, and exploited ethnic and racial divisions among them. To undercut support for the workers, management portrayed the strikers as disruptive radicals influenced by Bolshevism. After four months, the strike failed.

Employers used the same tactic to defeat striking coal miners, whose wages had fallen behind the cost of living. Refusing to negotiate with the United Mine Workers, coal operators claimed that Russian Bolsheviks financed the strike to destroy the American economy. Attorney General Mitchell Palmer secured an injunction against the strike under the authority of wartime legislation. Because the government no longer controlled coal prices or enforced protective labor rules, miners complained bitterly that the war had ended for corporations but not for workers.

Two municipal strikes in 1919 also alarmed the public when their opponents depicted them as revolutionary attacks on the social order. In Seattle in February, the Central Labor Council called a general strike to support 35,000 shipyard workers striking for higher wages and shorter hours. When 60,000 more workers from 110 local unions also walked out, the city ground to a halt. Workers behaved peacefully and protected public health and safety by operating garbage and fire trucks and providing food, water, and electricity. Nevertheless, Seattle's mayor, business leaders, and newspapers attacked the strikers as Bolsheviks and anarchists. Threatened with military intervention, the labor council called off the strike, but not before it had caused a public backlash against unions across the nation.

In Boston, the police commissioner fired police officers for trying to organize a union to improve their inadequate pay. In response, the police went on strike. As in Seattle, Boston newspapers, politicians,

Using eight different languages, a steel company poster combines patriotic and ethnic appeals with denunciations of "alien radicals" to urge workers to abandon their 1919 strike. The strikers were seeking union recognition and an end to twelve-hour days but were forcibly suppressed.

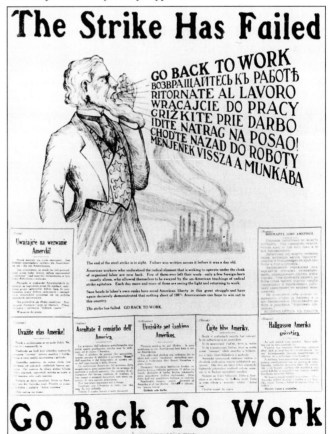

and business leaders attributed the strike to Bolshevism, although nothing indicated that the police wanted anything more than improved wages, conditions, and respect. Wilson denounced the Boston police strike as "a crime against civilization." Governor Calvin Coolidge mobilized the National Guard and gained nationwide acclaim when he stated, "There is no right to strike against the public safety by anybody, anywhere, anytime." The police were all fired; many of their replacements were war veterans.

Red Scare

The strikes contributed to an anti-Bolshevik hysteria that swept the country in 1919. This **Red Scare** reflected fears that the Bolshevik revolution in Russia might spread to the United States. Steeped in the anti-radical propaganda of the war years, many Americans were appalled by Russian Bolshevism, described by the *Saturday Evening Post* as a "compound of slaughter, confiscation, anarchy, and universal disorder." Their alarm grew in 1919 when Russia established the **Third International** to foster revolution abroad, and a few American socialists formed the American Communist Party. But the Red Scare also reflected the willingness of antiunion employers, ambitious politicians, sensational journalists, zealous veterans, and racists to exploit the panic to advance their own purposes.

Fed by misleading reports about Russian Bolshevism and its influence in the United States, the Red Scare reached panic levels by mid-1919. Bombs mailed anonymously to several prominent people on May Day seemed proof enough that a Bolshevik conspiracy threatened America. The Justice Department, Congress, and patriotic organizations like the American Legion joined with business groups to suppress radicalism, real and imagined. The government continued to enforce the repressive laws against Wobblies, socialists, and other dissenters; a Minnesota senator warned that the nation was more imperiled than during the war itself. Indeed, Wilson and Attorney General Palmer called for more stringent laws and refused to release political prisoners jailed during the war. State governments harassed and arrested hundreds.

Palmer created a new agency, headed by J. Edgar Hoover, to suppress radicals and impose conformity. Its war on radicalism became the chief focus of the Justice Department. As an ambitious and ruthless bureaucrat, Hoover had participated in the government's assault on aliens and radicals during the war. Now he collected files on labor leaders and other "radical agitators" from Senator La Follette to Jane Addams, issued misleading reports on communist influence in labor strikes and race riots, and contacted all major newspapers "to acquaint people like you with the real menace of evil-thinking, which is the foundation of the Red Movement." Indeed, the Justice Department itself promoted the Red Scare hysteria, which Palmer hoped would lead to his presidential nomination and Hoover hoped would enhance his own power and that of his bureau.

In November 1919, Palmer and Hoover began raiding groups suspected of subversion. A month later, they deported 249 alien radicals, including the anarchist Emma Goldman, to Russia. Rabid patriots endorsed such actions. One minister favored deporting radicals "in ships of stone with sails of lead, with the wrath of God for a breeze and with hell for their first port." In January 1920, Palmer and Hoover rounded up more than four thousand suspected radicals in thirty-three cities. Without warrants, they broke into union halls, club rooms, and private homes, assaulting and arresting everyone in sight. People were jailed without access to lawyers; some were beaten into signing false confessions. In Lynn, Massachusetts, thirty-nine people meeting to organize a bakery were arrested for holding a revolutionary caucus. Other arrests were just as outrageous, but the *Washington Post* clamored, "There is no time to waste on hairsplitting over infringement of liberty."

Other Americans began to recoil from the excesses and illegal acts. Assistant Secretary of Labor Louis Post stopped further deportations by demonstrating that most of the arrested were "working men of good character, who are not anarchists or revolutionists, nor politically or otherwise dangerous in any sense." They had been arrested, he said, "for nothing more dangerous than affiliating with friends of their own race, country, and language." Support for the Red Scare withered. Palmer's attempt to inflame public emotions to advance his own candidacy for the presidency backfired. When his predictions of a violent attempt to overthrow the government on May 1, 1920, came to naught, most Americans could see that no menace had ever existed. They agreed with the *Rocky Mountain News*: "We can never get to work if we keep jumping sideways in fear of the bewhiskered Bolshevik." Even one conservative Republican concluded that "too much has been said about Bolshevism in America." But if the Red Scare faded in mid-1920, the hostility to immigrants, organized labor, and dissent it reflected would endure for a decade. During the 1920s, the most acceptable forms of social change would be derived from technological and commercial innovations.

The Election of 1920

Palmer failed to win the Democratic nomination, but it would have been an empty prize anyway. The Democratic coalition that Wilson had cobbled together on the issues of progressivism and peace came apart after the war. Workers resented the administration's hostility to the postwar strikes. Ethnic groups brutalized by the Americanization of the war years blamed Wilson for the war or condemned his peace settlement. Farmers grumbled about wartime price controls and postwar falling prices. Wartime taxes and the social and economic turmoil of 1919–1920 alienated the middle class. Americans were weary of great crusades and social sacrifices; in the words of Kansas journalist William Allen White, they were "tired of issues, sick at heart of ideals, and weary of being noble." They yearned for what Republican presidential candidate Warren Harding of Ohio called "normalcy."

The Republican ticket in 1920 symbolized the reassurance of simpler times. Harding was a genial politician who in a lengthy career had devoted more time to golf and poker than to public policy. An Old Guard conservative, he had stayed with the GOP when Theodore Roosevelt led the progressives out in 1912. His running mate, Calvin Coolidge, governor of Massachusetts, owed his nomination to his handling of the Boston police strike.

Wilson called the election of 1920 "a great and solemn referendum" on the League of Nations, but such lofty appeals fell flat. Harding was ambiguous about the League, and the Democratic national platform endorsed it but expressed a willingness to accept amendments or reservations. The Democratic nominees, James Cox, former governor of Ohio, and the young Franklin D. Roosevelt, Wilson's assistant secretary of the navy, favored the League, but it was not a decisive issue in the campaign.

Harding won in a landslide reflecting the nation's dissatisfaction with Wilson and the Democratic party. "The Democrats are inconceivably unpopular," wrote Walter Lippmann, a prominent journalist. Harding received 16 million popular votes to Cox's 9 million. Running for president from his prison

In a 1920 cartoon, "A. Mitchell Palmer Out for a Stroll," the Chicago Tribune *lampooned the Attorney General for his repeated but unfounded warnings about Bolshevik threats in America. The postwar Red Scare weakened civil liberties, promoted nativist hostilities, and undermined reform.*

cell, Socialist Eugene Debs polled nearly a million votes. Not even his closest backers considered Harding qualified for the White House, but, as Lippmann said, the nation's "public spirit was exhausted" after the war years. The election of 1920 was "the final twitch" of America's "war mind."

Conclusion

The Great War disrupted the United States and much of the rest of the world. The initial American policy of neutrality yielded to sentimental and substantive links with the Allies and the pressure of German submarine warfare. Despite popular opposition, America joined the conflict when its leaders concluded that national interests demanded it. Using both military and diplomatic power, Woodrow Wilson sought to secure a more stable and prosperous world order, with an expanded role for the United States. But the Treaty of Versailles only partly fulfilled his hopes, and the Senate refused to ratify the treaty and its League of Nations. The postwar world order would be unstable and dangerous.

Participation in the war, moreover, had changed the American government, economy, and society. Some of these changes, including the centralization of the economy and an expansion of the regulatory role of the federal government, were already under way; some offered opportunities to implement progressive principles or reforms. Woman suffrage and prohibition gained decisive support because of the war spirit. But other consequences of the war betrayed both progressive impulses and the democratic principles the war was allegedly fought to promote. The suppression of civil liberties, manipulation of human emotions, repression of radicals and minorities, and exploitation of national crises by narrow interests helped disillusion the public. The repercussions of the Great War would linger for years, at home and abroad.

Review Questions

1. What were the major arguments for and against U.S. entry into the Great War? What position do you find most persuasive? Why?

2. How and why did the United States shape public opinion in World War I? What were the consequences, positive and negative, of the propaganda of the Committee on Public Information, Food Administration, and other government agencies?

3. How did other groups exploit the war crisis and the government's propaganda and repression?

4. Evaluate the role of Woodrow Wilson at the Paris Peace Conference. What obstacles did he face? How successful was he in shaping the settlement?

5. Discuss the arguments for and against American ratification of the Treaty of Versailles.

Recommended Reading

Kendrick A. Clements, *The Presidency of Woodrow Wilson* (1992). The best single volume on the Wilson presidency.

Edward M. Coffman, *The War to End All Wars* (1968). A valuable study of the U.S. military role in World War I.

Robert H. Ferrell, *Woodrow Wilson and World War I, 1917–1921* (1985). A useful synthesis that emphasizes diplomatic issues.

D. Clayton James and Anne Sharp Wells, *America and the Great War, 1914–1920* (1998). A fine, succinct synthesis of recent scholarship.

David M. Kennedy, *Over Here: The First World War and American Society* (1980). Thorough and illuminating discussion of the impact of World War I on American society.

Robert K. Murray, *The Red Scare: A Study in National Hysteria, 1919–1920* (1955). An important early study that retains much value.

Ronald Schaffer, *America in the Great War: The Rise of the War Welfare State* (1991). An effective and provocative summary that illuminates the expanding role of government.

Additional Sources

General Studies

John Whiteclay Chambers II, *The Tyranny of Change* (1992).

John M. Cooper, Jr., *Pivotal Decades: The United States, 1900–1920* (1990).

Otis L. Graham, Jr., *The Great Campaigns: Reform and War in America* (1971).

Ellis W. Hawley, *The Great War and the Search for a Modern Order* (1992).

Walter LaFeber, *The American Age* (1989).

Michael J. Lyons, *World War I: A Short History* (1994).

Neil Wynn, *From Progressivism to Prosperity: World War I and American Society* (1986).

Diplomacy of Neutrality, War, and Peace

Lloyd Ambrosius, *Woodrow Wilson and the American Diplomatic Tradition* (1987).

Thomas A. Bailey and Paul B. Ryan, *The Lusitania Disaster* (1975).

Kathleen Burk, *Britain, America, and the Sinews of War* (1985).

John Coogan, *The End of Neutrality* (1981).

John M. Cooper, Jr., *The Vanity of Power: American Isolationism and the First World War* (1969).

David S. Foglesong, *America's Secret War against Bolshevism: United States Intervention in the Russian Civil War, 1917–1920* (1995).

John A. Garraty, *Henry Cabot Lodge: A Biography* (1965).

Ross Gregory, *The Origins of American Intervention in the First World War* (1971).

Thomas J. Knock, *To End All Wars: Woodrow Wilson and the Creation of the League of Nations* (1992).

N. Gordon Levin, Jr., *Woodrow Wilson and World Politics: America's Response to War and Revolution* (1968).

Lawrence W. Levine, *Defender of the Faith: William Jennings Bryan, the Last Decade* (1965).

Arthur S. Link, *Woodrow Wilson and the Progressive Era, 1910–1917* (1954).

Ernest R. May, *The World War and American Isolation, 1914–1917* (1966).

David W. McFadden, *Alternative Paths: Soviets and Americans, 1917–1920* (1993).

Daniel M. Smith, *The Great Departure: The United States and World War I* (1965).

Ralph A. Stone, *The Irreconcilables* (1970).

Arthur Walworth, *Wilson and the Peacemakers* (1986).

The Military

Nancy Bristow, *Making Men Moral: Social Engineering During the Great War* (1996).

A. E. Barbeau and Florette Henri, *The Unknown Soldiers: Black American Troops in World War I* (1974).

John Whiteclay Chambers II, *To Raise an Army* (1987).

John Garry Clifford, *Citizen Soldiers: The Plattsburgh Training Camp Movement* (1972).

Edward M. Coffman, *The Hilt of the Sword: The Career of Peyton C. March* (1966).

Frank Freidel, *Over There: The Story of America's First Great Overseas Crusade* (1964).

Gerald W. Patton, *War and Race: The Black Officer in the American Military* (1981).

Laurence Stallings, *The Doughboys: The Story of the AEF, 1917–1918* (1963).

David Trask, *The AEF and Coalition Warmaking, 1917–1918* (1993).

Frank E. Vandiver, *Black Jack: The Life and Times of John J. Pershing* (1977).

Wartime Economy and Society

William J. Breen, *Uncle Sam at Home: Civilian Mobilization, Wartime Federalism, and the Council of National Defense, 1917–1919* (1984).

Valerie Connor *The National War Labor* (1983).

Robert D. Cuff, *The War Industries Board: Business-Government Relations during World War I* (1973).

David Danbom, *The Resisted Revolution: Urban America and the Industrialization of Agriculture* (1979).

Maurine Weiner Greenwald, *Women, War, and Work: The Impact of World War I on Women Workers in the United States* (1980).

Florette Henri, *Black Migration: The Movement North, 1900–1920* (1975).

Paul Koistinen, *Mobilizing for Modern War: The Political Economy of American Warfare, 1865–1919* (1997).

Frederick C. Luebke, *Bonds of Loyalty: German-Americans and World War I* (1974).

Elliot M. Rudwick, *Race Riot at East St. Louis, July 2, 1917* (1964).

John A. Thompson, *Reformers and War: American Progressive Publicists and the First World War* (1987).

Stephen L. Vaughn, *Holding Fast the Inner Lines: Democracy, Nationalism, and the Committee on Public Information* (1980).

Wartime Dissent and Repression

Christopher Gibbs, *The Great Silent Majority: Missouri's Resistance to World War I* (1989).

Robert Morlan, *Political Prairie Fire: The Nonpartisan League, 1915–1922* (1955).

H. C. Peterson and Gilbert Fite, *Opponents of War, 1917–1918* (1957).

William Preston, Jr., *Aliens and Dissenters: Federal Suppression of Radicals, 1903–1933* (1963).

Harry N. Scheiber, *The Wilson Administration and Civil Liberties* (1960).

James Weinstein, *The Decline of Socialism in America* (1967).

Postwar Conflict

David Brody, *Labor in Crisis: The Steel Strike of 1919* (1965).

Stanley A. Coben, *A. Mitchell Palmer, Politician* (1963).

Burl Noggle, *Into the Twenties: The United States from Armistice to Normalcy* (1974).

Athan Theoharis and John Stuart Cox, *The Boss: J. Edgar Hoover and the Great American Inquisition* (1988).

William M. Tuttle, Jr., *Race Riot: Chicago in the Red Summer of 1919* (1970).

Where to Learn More

❖ **National Infantry Museum, Fort Benning, Georgia.** This sprawling collection of weapons, uniforms, and equipment includes exhibits on World War I.

❖ **Fort George G. Meade Museum, Fort Meade, Maryland.** This museum contains unparalleled exhibits depicting U.S. military life during World War I, including artifacts, photographs, and French and American tanks designed for trench warfare.

❖ **General John J. Pershing Boyhood Home, Laclede, Missouri.** Maintained by the Missouri State Park Board, Pershing's restored nineteenth-century home exhibits some of his personal belongings and papers.

❖ **Wisconsin Veterans Museum, Madison, Wisconsin.** The most stunning museum of its size in the United States, this large building combines impressive collections of artifacts ranging from uniforms to tanks, with substantive exhibits and video programs based on remarkable historical research. It both documents and explains the participation of Wisconsin soldiers in the nation's wars, including the Spanish-American War and World War I.

TOWARD A MODERN AMERICA:
THE 1920s

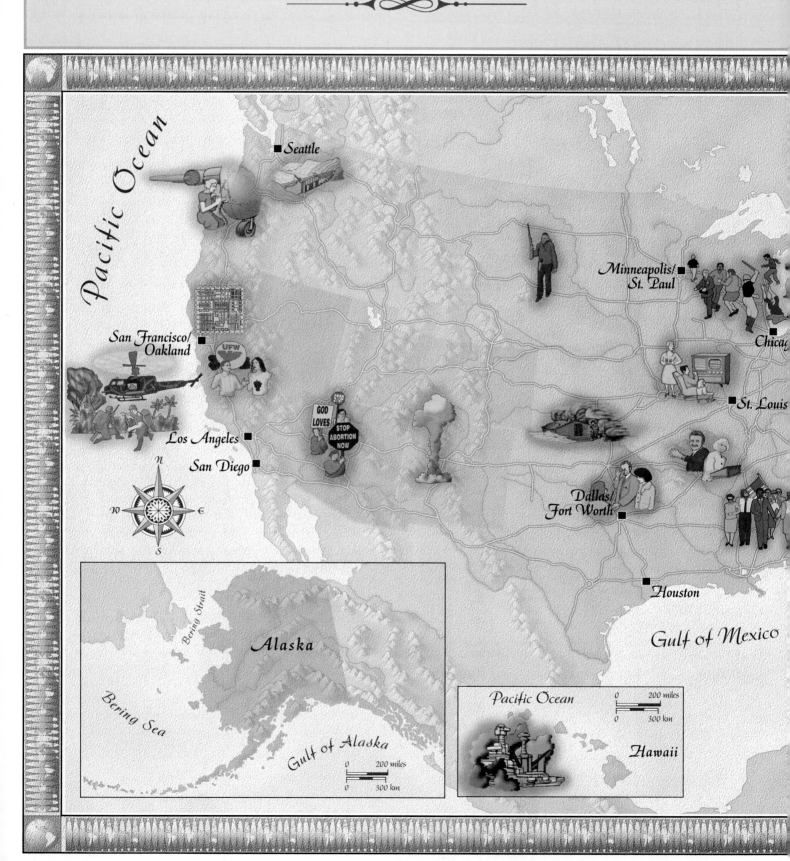

Seattle

Pacific Ocean

San Francisco/Oakland

UFW

Los Angeles

San Diego

GOD LOVES

STOP

STOP ABORTION NOW

Minneapolis/St. Paul

Chicago

St. Louis

Dallas/Fort Worth

Houston

Gulf of Mexico

Bering Strait

Alaska

Bering Sea

Gulf of Alaska

0   200 miles
0   300 km

Pacific Ocean

0   200 miles
0   300 km

Hawaii

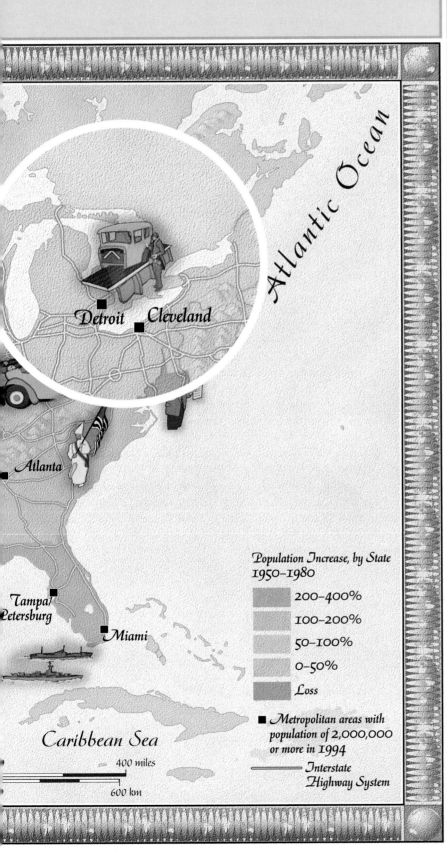

Atlantic Ocean

Detroit ■ Cleveland ■

Atlanta ■

Tampa/
Petersburg ■

■ Miami

Caribbean Sea

Population Increase, by State
1950–1980

200–400%
100–200%
50–100%
0–50%
Loss

■ Metropolitan areas with
population of 2,000,000
or more in 1994

Interstate
Highway System

400 miles

600 km

Chapter Outline

Key Topics

❖ The American economy in the 1920s
❖ The cult of business
❖ Change and social dislocation
❖ Materialism and mass culture
❖ The groups excluded from the prosperity of the 1920s

"*M*achinery," proclaimed Henry Ford, "is the new Messiah." Others in the 1920s thought Ford too deserved homage. "Just as in Rome one goes to the Vatican and endeavours to get audience of the Pope," noted one British observer, "so in Detroit one goes to the Ford Works and endeavours to see Henry Ford." Ford had introduced the moving assembly line at his automobile factory on the eve of World War I, and, by 1925, it was turning out a Model T every ten seconds. Mass production was becoming a reality; in fact, the term originated in Henry Ford's 1926 description of the system of flow production techniques popularly called "Fordism." The system symbolized the nation's booming economy: In the 1920s, Europeans used the word *Fordize* as a synonym for *Americanize.* Ford coupled machines and technology with managerial innovations. He established the "five-dollar day," twice the prevailing wage in Detroit's auto industry, and slashed the workweek from forty-eight to forty hours. These changes, Ford argued, would reduce the costs of labor turnover and boost consumer purchasing power, leading to further profits from mass production.

The assembly line, however, alienated workers. Fordism meant that skills, experience, and creativity were no longer necessary, that "upward mobility" was a meaningless phrase; all Ford wanted, said one observer, were machine tenders who "will simply do what they are told to do, over and over again from bell-time to bell-time." Even Ford conceded that the repetitive operations of the assembly line were "so monotonous that it scarcely seems possible that any man would care to continue long at the same job." Ford first tried to adapt his mostly immigrant workers to these conditions through an Americanization program. His "Education Department" taught classes in English, sobriety, obedience, and industrial efficiency to the unskilled laborers entering the factory. After the course, they participated in a symbolic pageant: They climbed into a huge "melting pot," fifteen feet across and seven feet deep. After Ford managers stirred the pot with ten-foot ladles, the workers emerged wearing new clothes and waving American flags—new Americans made for the factory. As one Ford leader said, "As we adapt the machinery in the shop to turning out the kind of automobile we have in mind, so we have constructed our educational system with a view to producing the human product in mind."

When the labor market became more favorable to management in the early 1920s, Ford abolished the Education Department and relied on discipline to control workers. To ensure efficiency, he prohibited talking, whistling, sitting, or smoking on the job. Wearing fixed expressions—"Fordization of the face"—workers could communicate only without moving their lips in the "Ford whisper." ("Ford employees are not really alive," noted one labor leader; "they are half dead.") Work under such conditions was for money, not fulfillment; workers would have to achieve personal satisfaction through consumption, not production.

Fordism, like the 1920s, had an even darker side. Henry Ford was an anti-Semite. His diatribes against Jews were reprinted by the Nazis in the 1930s. Ford also joined in the assault on labor unions that marked the 1920s. He declared that Jews organized unions to control industry. He banned unions and used spies and informants to prevent union activity, hiring an underworld thug to enforce a discipline that even involved searches of workers' homes. One observer said in 1924, "No one who works for Ford is safe from spies."

Fordism thus reflected the complexity of the 1920s. Economic growth and technological innovation were paired with social conflict as traditions were destroyed, values were displaced, and new people were incorporated into a society increasingly industrialized, urbanized, and dominated by big business. Industrial production and national wealth soared, buoyed by new techniques and markets for consumer goods. Business values pervaded society and dominated government, which promoted business interests. But not all Americans prospered. Many workers were unemployed, and the wages of still more were stagnant or falling. Farmers endured grim conditions and worse prospects. Social change brought pleasure to some and deep concern to others. City factories like the Ford Works attracted workers from the countryside, increasing urbanization; rapid suburbanization opened other horizons. Leisure activities flourished, and new mass media promoted modern ideas and stylish products. But such experiences often proved unsettling, and some Americans sought reassurance by imposing their cultural or religious values on everyone around them. The tumultuous decade thus had many unresolved issues, much like the complex personality of Henry Ford himself. And Ford so dominated the age that when college students were asked to rank the greatest people of all time, Ford came in third—behind Christ and Napoleon.

The Economy That Roared

Following a severe postwar depression in 1920 and 1921, the American economy boomed through the remainder of the decade. Gross domestic product soared nearly 40 percent; output per worker-hour, or productivity, rose 72 percent in manufacturing; average per capita income increased by a third. Although the prosperity was not evenly distributed and some sectors of the economy were deeply troubled, most Americans welcomed the industrial expansion and business principles of the "New Era."

Boom Industries

Many factors spurred the economic expansion of the 1920s. The huge wartime and postwar profits provided investment capital that enabled business to mechanize. Mass production spread quickly in American industry; machine-made standardized parts and the moving assembly line increased efficiency and production. Businesses steadily adopted the scientific management principles of Frederick W. Taylor (see Chapter 23). These highly touted systems, though often involving little more than an assembly-line "speed-up," also boosted efficiency. The nation more than doubled its capacity to generate electricity during the decade, further bolstering the economy. In factories, electric motors cut costs and improved manufacturing; in homes, electricity spurred demand for new products. Henry Ford was right: Mass production and consumption went hand in hand. Although not one in ten farm families had access to electric power, most other families did by 1929, and many bought electric sewing machines, vacuum cleaners, washing machines, and other labor-saving appliances.

Ford Motor Company's first moving assembly line in Highland Park, Michigan, in 1913. The increasing mechanization of work, linked to managerial and marketing innovations, boosted productivity in the 1920s and brought consumer goods within the reach of far more Americans than before.

CHRONOLOGY

1915 Ku Klux Klan is founded anew.

1919 Volstead Act is passed.

1920 Urban population exceeds rural population for the first time.

Warren Harding is elected president.

Prohibition takes effect.

First commercial radio show is broadcast.

Sinclair Lewis publishes *Main Street.*

1921 Sheppard-Towner Maternity and Infancy Act is passed.

Washington Naval Conference limits naval armaments.

1922 Fordney-McCumber Act raises tariff rates.

Sinclair Lewis publishes *Babbitt.*

Country Club Plaza in Kansas City opens.

1923 Harding dies; Calvin Coolidge becomes president.

1924 National Origins Act sharply curtails immigration.

Coolidge is elected president.

1925 Scopes trial is held in Dayton, Tennessee.

F. Scott Fitzgerald publishes *The Great Gatsby.*

1927 Charles A. Lindbergh flies solo across the Atlantic.

1928 Kellogg-Briand Pact is signed.

Herbert Hoover is elected president.

1929 Ernest Hemingway publishes *A Farewell to Arms.*

The automobile industry drove the economy. Its productivity increased constantly, and sales rose from about 1.9 million vehicles in 1920 to nearly 5 million by 1929, when 26 million vehicles were on the road (see Figure 26-1). The automobile industry also employed one of every fourteen manufacturing workers and stimulated other industries from steel to rubber and glass. It created a huge new market for the petroleum industry and fostered oil drilling in Oklahoma, Texas, and Louisiana. It launched new businesses, from service stations (over 120,000 by 1929) to garages. It also encouraged the construction industry, a mainstay of the 1920s economy. Large increases in road building and residential housing, prompted by growing automobile ownership and migration to cities and suburbs, provided construction jobs, markets for lumber and other building materials, and profits.

New industries also sprang up. The aviation industry grew rapidly during the 1920s, with government support.

port. The U.S. Post Office subsidized commercial air service by providing air mail contracts to private carriers. Congress then authorized commercial passenger service over the mail routes, with regular traffic opening in 1927 between Boston

Figure 26-1　Registered Motor Vehicles, 1913–1929

The rapid adoption of automobiles shaped the 1920s, stimulating demand for steel and gasoline, encouraging the use of credit, facilitating suburbanization, promoting tourism, and suggesting new cultural horizons.

Data Source:　U.S. Bureau of Public Roads.

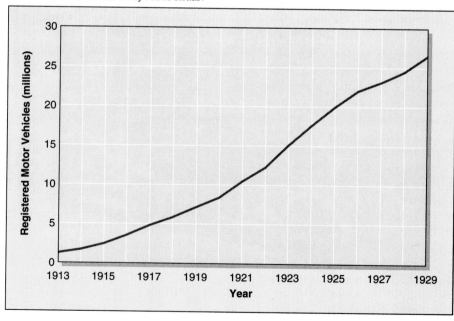

and New York. By 1930, more than one hundred airlines crisscrossed America.

The Great War also stimulated the chemicals industry. The government confiscated chemical patents from German firms that had dominated the field and transferred them to U.S. companies like Du Pont. With this advantage, Du Pont in the 1920s became one of the nation's largest industrial firms, a chemical empire producing plastics, finishes, dyes, and organic chemicals. It developed products for the commercial market: enamel for household appliances and automobile finishes, gasoline additives to eliminate engine knocks (many workers died from producing what the *New York World* called "loony gas"), rayon for women's clothing, cellophane to package consumer goods. Led by such successes, the chemicals industry became a $4 billion giant employing 300,000 workers by 1929.

The new radio and motion picture industries also flourished. Commercial broadcasting began with a single station in 1920. By 1927, there were 732 stations, and Congress created the Federal Radio Commission to prevent wave band interference. The rationale for this agency, which was reorganized as the **Federal Communications Commission (FCC)** in 1934, was that the airwaves belong to the American people and not private interests. Nevertheless, corporations quickly dominated the new industry. Westinghouse, RCA, and General Electric began opening strings of stations in the early 1920s. Large corporations also came to control radio manufacturing. Factory-made crystal radio sets became available in 1920, and some 5 million sets were sold by mid-decade, but corporate pressure and patent control eliminated more than 90 percent of the 750 manufacturers by 1927.

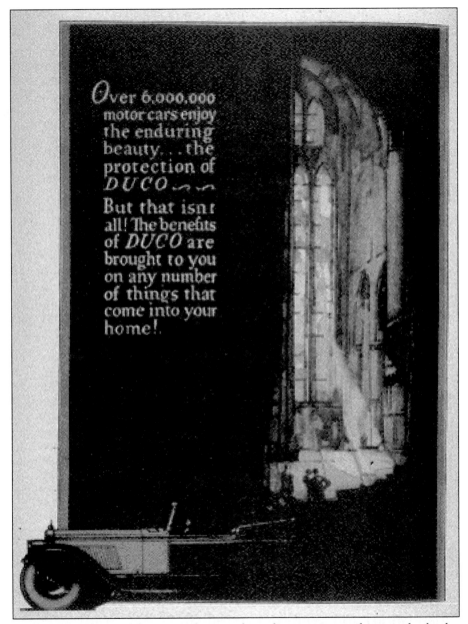

Du Pont became one of the nation's largest industrial corporations in the 1920s by developing new consumer products and marketing them aggressively. This advertisement for Duco automobile finishes blends images of a cathedral and an auto showroom, placing consumerism in a favorable light.

The motion picture industry became one of the nation's five largest businesses, with twenty thousand movie theaters selling 100 million tickets a week. Hollywood studios were huge factories, hiring directors, writers, camera crews, and actors to produce films on an assembly-line basis. While Americans watched Charlie Chaplin showcase his comedic genius in films like *The Gold Rush* (1925), corporations like Paramount were integrating production with distribution and exhibition to maximize control and profit and eliminate independent producers and theaters. The advent of talking movies later in the decade brought still greater profits and power to the major studios, which alone could afford the increased engineering and production costs.

Corporate Consolidation

A wave of corporate mergers, rivaling that at the turn of the century, swept over the 1920s economy. Great corporations swallowed up thousands of small firms. Particularly significant was the spread of oligopoly— the control of an entire industry by a few giant firms. The number of automobile manufacturers dropped from 108 to 44, but three companies—Ford, General Motors, and Chrysler—produced 83 percent of the nation's cars. Their large-scale, integrated operations eliminated competition from small firms. In the electric light and power industry, nearly four thousand local utility companies were merged into a dozen holding companies. Mergers also expanded oligopoly control over other industries. By 1929, the nation's two hundred largest corporations controlled nearly half of all nonbanking corporate wealth.

Oligopolies also dominated finance and marketing. Big banks extended their control through mergers and by opening branches. By 1929, a mere 1 percent of the nation's banks controlled half of its banking resources. In marketing, national chain stores like A&P and Woolworth's displaced local retailers. With fifteen thousand grocery stores and an elaborate distribution system, A&P could buy and sell goods for less than many corner grocers.

The corporate consolidation of the 1920s provoked little public fear or opposition. Independent retailers campaigned for local zoning regulations and laws to restrict chain stores, but Americans mostly accepted that size brought efficiency and productivity.

Open Shops and Welfare Capitalism

Business also launched a vigorous assault on labor. In 1921, the National Association of Manufacturers organized an **open shop** campaign to break union shop contracts, which required all employees to be union members. Denouncing collective bargaining as un-American, businesses described the open shop, in which union membership was not required and usually prohibited, as the "American plan." They forced workers to sign so-called **yellow-dog contracts** that bound them to reject unions to keep their jobs. Business also used boycotts to force employers into a uniform antiunion front. Bethlehem Steel, for example, refused to sell steel to companies employing union labor. Where unions existed, corporations tried to crush them, using spies or hiring strikebreakers.

Some companies advocated a paternalistic system called **welfare capitalism** as an alternative to unions. Eastman Kodak, General Motors, U.S. Steel, and other firms provided medical services, insurance programs, pension plans, and vacations for their workers and established employee social clubs and sports teams. These policies were designed to undercut labor unions and persuade workers to rely on the corporation. Home-financing plans, for instance, increased workers' dependence on the company, and stock ownership plans inculcated business values among employees. Welfare capitalism, however, covered scarcely 5 percent of the workforce and often benefited only skilled workers already tied to the company through seniority. Moreover, it was directed primarily at men. General Electric, for example, dismissed women workers when they married. Women rarely built up enough seniority to obtain vacations and pensions.

Corporations in the 1920s also promoted company unions, management-sponsored substitutes for labor unions. But company unions were usually forbidden to handle wage and hour issues. Their function was to implement company policies and undermine real unionism. General Electric's management reported that through its company union, "we have been able to educate and secure sympathy and support from a large body of employees who, under the old arrangement of bargaining with [AFL] craft unions, could not have been reached."

Partly because of these pressures, membership in labor unions fell from 5.1 million in 1920 to 3.6 million in 1929. But unions also contributed to their own decline. Conservative union leaders neglected ethnic and black workers in mass-production industries. Nor did they try to organize women, by 1930 nearly one-fourth of all workers. And they failed to respond effectively to other changes in the labor market. The growing numbers of white-collar workers regarded themselves as middle class and beyond the scope of union action.

With increasing mechanization and weak labor unions, workers suffered from job insecurity and stagnant wages. Mechanization, *Fortune* concluded, meant that "from the purely productive point of view, a part of the human race is already obsolete." Unemployment reached 12 percent in 1921 and remained a persistent concern of many working-class Americans during the decade. And despite claims to the contrary, hours were long: The average workweek in manufacturing remained over fifty hours.

The promise of business to pay high wages proved hollow. Real wages (purchasing power) did improve, but most of the improvement came before

1923 and reflected falling prices more than rising wages. After 1923, American wages stabilized. Henry Ford made no general wage hike after 1919, although his workers would have needed an increase of 65 percent to recover the buying power they had enjoyed in 1914. Indeed, in 1928, Ford lowered wage rates. U.S. Steel also reduced weekly wages, even while its profits almost doubled between 1923 and 1929. The failure to raise wages when productivity was increasing threatened the nation's long-term prosperity. In short, rising national income largely reflected salaries and dividends, not wages.

Some workers fared particularly badly. Unskilled workers—especially southern and eastern Europeans, black migrants from the rural South, and Mexican immigrants—saw their already low wages decline relative to those of skilled workers. Southern workers earned much less than Northerners, even in the same industry, and women were paid much less than men, even for the same jobs. Male furniture assemblers, for example, earned 56 cents an hour; females, only 32 cents. Overall, the gap between rich and poor widened during the decade (see Figure 26-2). By 1929, fully 71 percent of American families earned less than what the U.S. Bureau of Labor Statistics regarded as necessary for a decent living standard. The maldistribution of income meant that eventually Americans would be unable to purchase the products they made.

The expansion of consumer credit, rare before the 1920s, offered temporary relief by permitting consumers to buy goods over time. General Motors introduced consumer credit on a national basis to create a mass market for expensive automobiles. By 1927, two-thirds of automobiles were purchased on the installment plan. By 1929, providing consumer credit had become the nation's tenth-largest business. Nevertheless, installment loans did not in the long run raise the purchasing power of an income; they simply added interest charges to the price of products.

Sick Industries

Despite the general appearance of prosperity, several "sick" industries dragged on the economy. Coal mining, textile and garment manufacturing, and railroads suffered from excess capacity (too many mines and factories), shrinking demand, low returns, and management–labor conflicts. For example, U.S. coal mines had a capacity of a billion tons, but scarcely half of that was needed because of increasing use of oil, natural gas, and hydroelectricity. Using company police, strikebreakers, and injunctions, mine operators broke the United Mine Workers and slashed wages by up to a third. Unemployment in the industry approached 30 percent; by 1928, a reporter found "thousands of women and children literally starving to death" in Appalachia and the remaining miners held in "industrial slavery."

Similarly, the textile industry coped with overcapacity and declining demand by shifting operations

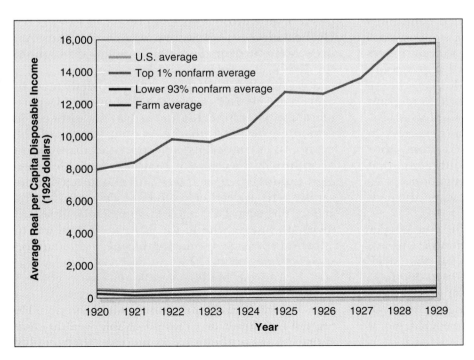

Figure 26-2   Growing Income Inequality in the 1920s
Despite the aura of prosperity in the 1920s, the vast majority of Americans received little or no increase in their real income. Farm families dragged the average down further while the wealthiest Americans doubled their own incomes.

Data Source: Charles Holt, "Who Benefited from the Prosperity of the Twenties?" Explorations in Economic History, *14 (1977)*.

from New England to the cheap-labor South, employing girls and young women for fifty-six-hour weeks at eighteen cents an hour. Textile companies, aided by local authorities, suppressed strikes in Tennessee and North Carolina. Ella May Wiggins sang of the worries in the mills:

> How it grieves the heart of a mother,
> You every one must know.
> For we can't buy for our children,
> Our wages are too low.

Wiggins was murdered by company thugs, leaving behind five small children. The textile industry, despite substandard wages and repressive policies, remained barely profitable.

American agriculture never recovered from the 1921 depression. In 1919, gross farm income amounted to 16 percent of the national income; by 1929, it had dropped to half that. Agricultural problems did not derive from inefficiency or low productivity. Mechanization (especially more tractors) and improved fertilizers and pesticides helped produce crop surpluses. But surpluses and shrinking demand forced down prices. After the war, foreign markets dried up, and domestic demand for cotton slackened. Moreover, farmers' wartime expansion left them heavily mortgaged in the 1920s. Small farmers, unable to compete with larger, better-capitalized farmers, suffered most. Many lost their land and became tenants or farm hands. By 1930, only 57 percent of American farmers owned the land they worked, the lowest percentage ever.

Racial discrimination worsened conditions for black and Hispanic tenants, sharecroppers, and farm workers. In the South, black sharecroppers trapped in grinding poverty endured segregation, disfranchisement, and violence. Mexican immigrants and Hispanic Americans labored as migrant farm workers in the Southwest and California. Exploited by a contract labor system pervasive in large-scale agriculture, they suffered from poor wages, miserable living conditions, and racism that created, in the words of one investigation, "a vicious circle" from which "few can escape through their own efforts."

By the end of the 1920s, the average per capita income for people on the nation's farms was only one-fourth that of Americans off the farm. "Widespread agricultural disaster," warned one Iowa newspaper, was producing "a highly dangerous situation." Like textile workers in New England and the Piedmont and coal miners in Appalachia, rural Americans suffered in the 1920s.

The Business of Government

The Republican surge in national politics also shaped the economy. In the 1920 election, the Republican slogan was "Less government in business, more business in government." By 1924, Calvin Coolidge, the decade's second Republican president, proclaimed, "This is a business country . . . and it wants a business government." Under such direction, the federal government advanced business interests at the expense of other objectives (see "American Views: The Cult of Business").

Republican Ascendancy

Republicans in 1920 had retained control of Congress and put Warren Harding in the White House. Harding was neither capable nor bright. One critic described a Harding speech as "an army of pompous phrases moving over the landscape in search of an idea." But he had a genial touch that contrasted favorably with Wilson. He pardoned Eugene Debs, whom Wilson had refused to release from prison, and he spoke out against racial violence. He also helped shape the modern presidency by supporting the Budget and Accounting Act of 1921, which gave the president authority over the budget and created the Budget Bureau and the General Accounting Office. Moreover, Harding recognized his own limitations and promised to appoint "the best minds" to his cabinet. Some of his appointees were highly accomplished, and two of them, Secretary of Commerce Herbert Hoover and Secretary of the Treasury Andrew Mellon, shaped economic policy throughout the 1920s.

A self-described progressive, dedicated to efficiency, Hoover made the Commerce Department the government's most dynamic office. He cemented its ties with the leading sectors of the economy, expanded its collection and distribution of industrial information, pushed to exploit foreign resources and markets, and encouraged innovation. His spreading influence led him to be called the secretary of commerce and "assistant secretary of everything else." Hoover's goal was to expand prosperity by making business efficient, responsive, and profitable.

Andrew Mellon had a narrower goal. A wealthy banker and industrialist, he pressed Congress to reduce taxes on businesses and the rich. He argued that lower taxes would enable wealthy individuals and corporations to increase their capital

One 1920s cartoon depicting a "View of Washington" showed Herbert Hoover everywhere at once. In fact, the talented and ambitious Secretary of Commerce was not a politician but a successful engineer, businessman, and administrator who symbolized to many Americans the best of the New Era.

the government to prevent the labor unions of the country from destroying the open shop."

The Republicans also curtailed government regulation. By appointing advocates of big business to the Federal Trade Commission, the Federal Reserve Board, and other regulatory agencies established earlier by the progressives, Harding made government the collaborator rather than the regulator of business. Progressive Republican Senator George Norris of Nebraska angrily asked, "If trusts, combinations, and big business are to run the government, why not permit them to do it directly rather than through this expensive machinery which was originally honestly established for the protection of the people of the country against monopoly?" Norris condemned the new appointments as nullifying "federal law by a process of boring from within" and as setting "the country back more than twenty-five years."

Finally, Harding reshaped the Supreme Court into a still more aggressive champion of business. He named the conservative William Howard Taft as chief justice and matched him with three other justices. All were, as one of them proclaimed, sympathetic to business leaders "beset and bedeviled with vexatious statutes, prying commissions, and government intermeddling of all sorts." The Court struck down much of the government economic regulation adopted during the Progressive Era, invalidated restraints on child labor and a minimum wage law for women, and approved restrictions on labor unions.

Government Corruption

The green light that Harding Republicans extended to private interests led to corruption and scandals. Harding appointed many friends and cronies who saw public service as an opportunity for graft. Attorney General Daugherty's associates in the Justice Department took bribes in exchange for pardons and government jobs. The head of the Veterans Bureau went to prison for cheating disabled veterans of $200 million. Albert Fall, the secretary of the interior, leased petroleum reserves set aside by progressive conservationists to oil companies in exchange for cash, bonds, and cattle for his New Mexico ranch. Exposed for his role in the **Teapot Dome scandal**, named after a Wyoming oil reserve, Fall became the first cabinet officer in history to go to jail. Daugherty escaped a similar fate by destroying records and invoking the Fifth Amendment.

Harding was appalled by the scandals. "My God, this is a hell of a job!" he told William Allen White. "I have no trouble with my enemies. . . . But my damned friends, . . . they're the ones that keep me walking the floor nights!" Harding died shortly thereafter, probably of a heart attack.

investments, thereby creating new jobs and general prosperity. But Mellon's hope that favoring the rich would cause prosperity to trickle down to the working and middle classes proved ill-founded. Nevertheless, despite the opposition of progressives in Congress, Mellon succeeded in lowering maximum tax rates and eliminating wartime excess-profits taxes in 1921.

The Harding administration promoted business interests in other ways, too. The tariff of 1922 raised import rates to protect industry from foreign competition. High new duties on foreign aluminum, for instance, permitted manufacturers—including Mellon's own Alcoa Aluminum—to raise prices by 40 percent. But by excluding imports, high tariffs made it difficult for European nations to earn the dollars to repay their war debts to the United States. High rates also impeded American farm exports and raised consumer prices.

The Harding administration aided the business campaign against unions. Attorney General Harry Daugherty secured an injunction against a railroad strike in 1922 and promised to "use the power of

American Views
THE CULT OF BUSINESS

During the 1920s, publicists and politicians joined manufacturers and merchants in proclaiming that business promoted not only material but also social and even spiritual well-being. In his best-seller, *The Man Nobody Knows* (1924), advertising executive Bruce Barton portrayed Jesus Christ as the founder of modern business. The following excerpt from an article by Edward E. Purinton, a popular lecturer on business values and efficiency, makes even more extensive claims for business.

❖ **How accurate are Purinton's claims of great opportunity in the corporate world of the 1920s? Of occupational mobility in the factory economy?**

❖ **What does this view of business imply about the role of government in American life?**

❖ **How do you think Protestant fundamentalists might have viewed the cult of business?**

Among the nations of the earth today America stands for one idea: *Business*. National opprobrium? National opportunity. For in this fact lies, potentially, the salvation of the world.

Through business, properly conceived, managed, and conducted, the human race is finally to be redeemed. How and why a man works foretells what he will do, think, have, give, and be. And real salvation is in doing, thinking, having, giving, and being—not in sermonizing and theorizing. . . .

What is the finest game? Business. The soundest science? Business. The truest art? Busi-

ness. The fullest education? Business. The fairest opportunity? Business. The cleanest philanthropy? Business. The sanest religion? Business.

You may not agree. That is because you judge business by the crude, mean, stupid, false imitation of business that happens to be located near you.

The finest game is business. The rewards are for everybody, and all can win. There are no favorites—Providence always crowns the career of the man who is worthy. And in this game there is no "luck"—you have the fun of taking chances but

Coolidge Prosperity

On August 3, 1923, Vice President Calvin Coolidge was sworn in as president by his father while visiting his birthplace in rural Vermont, thereby reaffirming his association with traditional values. This image reassured Americans troubled by the Harding scandals. Coolidge's calm appearance hid a furious temper and a mean spirit.

Coolidge supported business with ideological conviction. He opposed the activist presidency of the Progressive Era, cultivating instead a deliberate inactivity calculated to lower expectations of government. He endorsed Secretary of the Treasury Mellon's ongoing efforts to reverse the progressive tax policies of the Wilson years and backed Secretary of Commerce Hoover's persistent efforts on behalf of

the business community (although he privately sneered at Hoover as the "Wonder Boy").

Like Harding, Coolidge installed business supporters in the regulatory agencies. To chair the Federal Trade Commission he appointed an attorney who had condemned the agency as "an instrument of oppression and disturbance and injury instead of help to business." Under this leadership, the FTC described its new goal as "helping business to help itself"—which meant approving trade associations and agreements to suppress competition. This attitude, endorsed by the Supreme Court, aided the mergers that occurred after 1925. The *Wall Street Journal* crowed, "Never before, here or anywhere else, has a government been so completely fused with business."

the sobriety of guaranteeing certainties. The speed and size of your winnings are for you alone to determine. . . .

The soundest science is business. All investigation is reduced to action, and by action proved or disproved. The idealistic motive animates the materialistic method. . . . Capital is furnished for the researches of "pure science"; yet pure science is not regarded pure until practical. Competent scientists are suitably rewarded—as they are not in the scientific schools. . . .

The fullest education is business. A proper blend of study, work and life is essential to advancement. The whole man is educated. Human nature itself is the open book that all business men study; and the mastery of a page of this educates you more than the memorizing of a dusty tome from a library shelf. In the school of business, moreover, you teach yourself and learn most from your own mistakes. What you learn here you live out, the only real test.

The fairest opportunity is business. You can find more, better, quicker chances to get ahead in a large business house than anywhere else on earth. . . . Recognition of better work, of keener and quicker thought, of deeper and finer feeling, is gladly offered by the men higher up, with early promotion the rule for the man who justifies it. There is, and can be, no such thing as buried talent in a modern business organization. . . .

The sanest religion is business. Any relationship that forces a man to follow the Golden Rule rightfully belongs amid the ceremonials of the church. A great business enterprise includes and presupposes this relationship. I have seen more Christianity to the square inch as a regular part of the office equipment of famous corporation presidents than may ordinarily be found on Sunday in a verbalized but not vitalized church congregation. . . . You can fool your preacher with a sickly sprout or a wormy semblance of character, but you can't fool your employer. I would make every business house a consultation bureau for the guidance of the church whose members were employees of the house. . . .

The future work of the businessman is to teach the teacher, preach to the preacher, admonish the parent, advise the doctor, justify the lawyer, superintend the statesman, fructify the farmer, stabilize the banker, harness the dreamer, and reform the reformer.

Source: Edward E. Purinton, *"Big Ideas from Big Business,"* Independent, *April 16, 1921. National Weekly Corp., New York.*

And Coolidge confined the government's role to helping business. When Congress tried to raise farm prices through government intervention, Coolidge vetoed the measure as "preposterous" special-interest legislation. One economist said Coolidge's vetoes revealed "a stubborn determination to do nothing," but they revealed more. For on the same day that Coolidge vetoed assistance to farmers, he raised by 50 percent the tariff on pig iron, thereby increasing manufacturers' profits and farmers' costs for tools. Government action was acceptable for business but not for nonbusiness interests.

"Coolidge prosperity" determined the 1924 election. The Democrats, hopelessly divided, took 103 ballots to nominate the colorless, conservative Wall Street lawyer John W. Davis. His election prospects, Davis conceded, were less "than a snowball in hell." A more interesting opponent for Coolidge was Robert La Follette, nominated by discontented farm and labor organizations that formed a new Progressive party. La Follette campaigned against "the power of private monopoly over the political and economic life of the American people." The Progressive platform demanded government ownership of railroads and utilities, farm assistance, and collective bargaining. The Republicans, backed by immense contributions from business, denounced La Follette as an agent of Bolshevism. The choice, Republicans insisted, was "Coolidge or Chaos." Thus instructed, Americans chose Coolidge, though barely half the electorate bothered to vote.

The Fate of Reform

But progressive reform was not completely dead. Even Harding proposed social welfare measures, and, in the 1921 depression, he convened a conference on unemployment and helped spark voluntary relief. A small group in Congress led by La Follette and George Norris attacked Mellon's regressive tax policies and supported measures regulating agricultural processors, protecting workers' rights, and maintaining public ownership of a hydroelectric dam at Muscle Shoals, Alabama, that conservative Republicans wanted to privatize. Yet reformers' successes were few and often temporary.

The fate of women's groups illustrated the difficulties reformers faced in the 1920s. At first, the adoption of woman suffrage prompted politicians to champion women's reform issues. In 1920, both major parties endorsed many of the goals of the new **League of Women Voters**. Within a year, many states had granted women the right to serve on juries, several enacted equal pay laws, and Wisconsin adopted an equal rights law. Congress passed the **Sheppard-Towner Maternity and Infancy Act**, the first federal social welfare law, in 1921. It provided federal funds for infant and maternity care, precisely the type of protective legislation that the suffragists had described as women's special interest.

But thereafter women reformers gained little. As it became clear that women did not vote as a bloc but according to their varying social and economic backgrounds, Congress lost interest in "women's issues." In 1929, Congress killed the Sheppard-Towner Act. Nor could reformers gain ratification of a child labor amendment after the Supreme Court invalidated laws regulating child labor. Conservatives attacked women reformers as "Bolsheviks."

Disagreements among women reformers and shifting interests also limited their success. Led by the **National Woman's Party**, some feminists campaigned for an **Equal Rights Amendment**. But other reformers feared that such an amendment would nullify the progressive laws that protected working women. Reform organizations like the Consumers' League lost their energy and focus. The General Federation of Women's Clubs, always relatively conservative, promoted home economics and the use of electric appliances. Indeed, many younger women rejected the public reform focus of progressive feminists. The *Magazine of Business* even maintained that women valued the vacuum cleaner more than the vote. By 1927, the president of the Women's Trade Union League called the decade "hideous in the public life of our people and in the noisy flaunting of cheap hopes and cheaper materialism."

Cities and Suburbs

The 1920 census reported that, for the first time, more Americans lived in urban than in rural areas. The trend toward urbanization accelerated in the 1920s as millions of Americans fled the depressed countryside for the booming cities. This massive population movement interacted with technological innovations to reshape cities, build suburbs, and transform urban life (see Map 26-1).

Expanding Cities

Urbanization affected all regions of the country. In absolute terms, the older industrial cities of the Northeast and upper Midwest grew the most, attracting migrants from the rural South and distressed Appalachia. New York remained the nation's foremost metropolis. All other major cities expanded—none more spectacularly than Detroit, which grew to 1.6 million people. The "Motor City" thrived on the booming automobile industry and related industries like glass manufacturing. Old trees and wide lawns gave way to multilane highways as apartment houses and parking lots obliterated old Detroit.

Rural Southerners also headed for southern cities. In fact, the South was the nation's most rapidly urbanizing region. Migrants from the countryside poured into Atlanta, Birmingham, Memphis, and Houston. Little more than jungle before 1914, Miami became the fastest-growing city in the United States during the 1920s—"the Magic City." Not all Southerners welcomed urban growth and the values it represented. The novelist Thomas Wolfe cautioned against boosters in Asheville, North Carolina, "who shout 'Progress Progress Progress'—when what they mean is more Ford automobiles, more Rotary Clubs, more Baptist Ladies Social unions. . . . We are not necessarily four times as civilized as our grandfathers because we go four times as fast in automobiles, because our buildings are four times as tall."

In the West, Denver, Portland, and Seattle (each a regional economic hub) and several California cities grew rapidly. Los Angeles grew by 115 percent and by 1930 was the nation's fifth-largest city, with over 1.2 million people. Although it was the center of California's agricultural wealth and the motion picture industry and one of the world's busiest ports, Los Angeles was also linked to the automobile industry. The southern California oil fields and the demand for gasoline made it the nation's leading refining center.

The population surge transformed the urban landscape. As land values soared, developers built skyscrapers, giving Cleveland, Kansas City, San

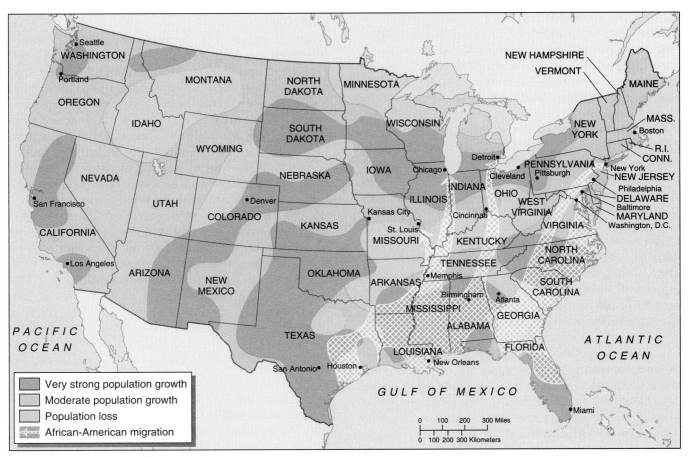

Map 26-1   *Population Shifts, 1920–1930*
Rural Americans fled to the cities during the 1920s, escaping a declining agricultural economy to search for new opportunities. African Americans in particular left the rural South for eastern and midwestern cities, but the urban population also jumped in the West and in the South itself.

Francisco, and many other cities modern skylines. By the end of the decade, American cities had nearly four hundred skyscrapers taller than twenty stories. The tallest, New York's 102-story Empire State Building, symbolized the urban boom.

The Great Black Migration

A significant feature of the rural-to-urban movement was the **Great Migration** of African Americans from the South. Like other migrants, they responded chiefly to economic factors. Southern segregation and violence made migration attractive, but job opportunities made it possible. Prosperity created jobs, and with the decline in European immigration, black workers filled the positions previously given to new immigrants. Though generally the lowest-paid and least secure jobs, they were better than share-cropping in the rural South. Black men worked as unskilled or semiskilled laborers; black women became domestics in white homes. The migrants often found adjustment to their new environment diffi-

cult. Southern rural black culture clashed with industrial work rhythms and discipline and with urban living. Still, more than a million and a half African Americans moved to northern cities in the 1920s.

There black ghettos usually developed, more because of prejudice than the wishes of the migrants. Although African Americans, like European immigrants, often wanted to live together to sustain their culture, racist restrictions meant that segregation, not congregation, most shaped their urban community. With thousands of newcomers limited to certain neighborhoods, housing shortages developed. Rapacious landlords charged ever-increasing rents for ever-declining housing. Rents doubled in New York's Harlem during the decade. In an example of the way racism exacerbated urban poverty, black workers earned less than working-class white workers but had to spend 50 percent more for housing. High rents and low wages forced black families to share inferior and unsanitary housing that threatened their health and safety. In Pittsburgh, only 20 percent of black houses had bathtubs, and only 50 percent had indoor toilets; in another city, an observer wrote that "the State would not allow cows to live in some of these apartments used by colored people." Continual migration disrupted efforts to develop a stable community; Harlem, said one social worker, was a "perpetual frontier."

However, the Great Migration also increased African Americans' racial consciousness, autonomy, and power. In 1928, for instance, black Chicagoans, using the ballot denied to African Americans in the South, elected the first black man to Congress since the turn of the century. Mutual aid societies and fraternal orders proliferated. Churches were particularly influential. A reporter in 1926 counted 140 black churches in a 150-block area of Harlem. Most of these were "storefront churches" where "cotton-field preachers" provided an emotional and fundamentalist religion familiar to migrants from the rural South.

Another organization also appealed to poor black ghetto dwellers. The **Universal Negro Improvement Association (UNIA)**, organized by Marcus Garvey, a Jamaican immigrant to New York, rejected the NAACP's goal of integration. A black nationalist espousing racial pride, Garvey exhorted black people to migrate to Africa to build a "free, redeemed, and mighty nation." In the meantime, he urged them to support black businesses. UNIA organized many enterprises, including groceries, restaurants, laundries, a printing plant, and the Black Star Steamship Line, intended as a commercial link between the United States, the West Indies, and Africa. UNIA attracted half a million members, the first black mass movement in American history. When Garvey was convicted of mail fraud and deported, however, the movement collapsed.

Racial pride also found expression in the **Harlem Renaissance**, an outpouring of literature, painting, sculpture, and music. Inspired by African-American culture and black urban life, writers and artists created works of power and poignancy. The poetry of Langston Hughes reflected the rhythm and mood of jazz and the blues. When a white patron complained that his writing was not "primitive" enough, Hughes responded, "I did not feel the rhythms of the primitive surging through me, and so I could not live and write as though I did. I was Chicago and Kansas City and Broadway and Harlem. And I was not what she wanted me to be." Other leading authors of the Harlem Renaissance who asserted their independence included Claude McKay, who wrote of the black working class in *Home to Harlem* (1928), Zora Neale Hurston, and James Weldon Johnson.

Barrios

Hispanic migrants also entered the nation's cities in the 1920s, creating their own communities, or *barrios*. Fifty thousand Puerto Ricans settled in New York, mostly in East ("Spanish") Harlem, where they found low-paying jobs. Far more migrants arrived from Mexico. Although many of them worked as migrant farm laborers, they often lived in cities in the off-season. Others permanently joined the expanding urban economy in industrial and construction jobs. The *barrios*, with their own businesses, churches, and cultural organizations, created a sense of permanency.

These communities enabled the newcomers to preserve their cultural values and build social institutions like *mutualistas* (mutual aid societies) that helped them get credit, housing, and health care. But the *barrios* also reflected the hostility that Hispanics encountered in American cities, for racism often restricted them to such districts. The number of Mexicans in Los Angeles tripled during the 1920s to nearly 100,000, but segregation confined them to East Los Angeles. Other areas of the city, like El Se-

Jessie Fauset, Langston Hughes, and Zora Neale Hurston stand at a memorial to Booker T. Washington. All authors prominent in the Harlem Renaissance, they represented a new generation of African Americans seizing what another black intellectual called their "first chances for group expression and self-determination."

gundo or Lynwood, boasted of being "restricted to the white race" and having "no Negroes or Mexicans." Los Angeles maintained separate schools for Mexicans, and a social worker reported that "America has repulsed the Mexican immigrant in every step he has taken" toward integration. As new migrants streamed in, conditions in the *barrios* deteriorated, for few cities provided adequate public services for them. Denver's *barrio* was described in 1924 as an area "both God and Denver had forgotten" with "no paving, no sidewalks, no sewers."

Some Hispanics fought discrimination. *La Orden de Hijos de America* (The Order of the Sons of America), organized in San Antonio in 1921, campaigned against inequities in schools and the jury system. In 1929, it helped launch the larger **League of United Latin American Citizens (LULAC)**, which would help advance civil rights for all Americans.

The Road to Suburbia

As fast as the cities mushroomed in the 1920s, the suburbs grew twice as fast. Park Ridge outside Chicago, Inglewood outside Los Angeles, Shaker Heights outside Cleveland, and many others expanded by 400 percent. New suburbs arose across the country. Fourteen hundred new subdivisions appeared in Los Angeles County during the 1920s; two-thirds of the new municipal incorporations in Illinois and Michigan were suburbs of Chicago, St. Louis, or Detroit. Some suburbs, such as Highland Park, where Henry Ford built his factory near Detroit, and Fairfield, Alabama, were industrial, but most were havens for the middle and upper classes.

Automobiles created the modern suburb. Nineteenth-century suburbs were small and linear, stretching along the street railway system. The new

Mexican Americans, like these farmworkers pitting apricots in Los Angeles County in 1924, often found jobs in the agribusiness enterprises of the Southwest but lived in barrios in the expanding cities of the region. More Mexicans entered the United States in the 1920s than any other group of immigrants.

developments were sprawling and dispersed, for the automobile enabled people to live in formerly remote areas. A single-family house surrounded by a lawn became the social ideal, a pastoral escape from the overcrowded and dangerous city. Many suburbs excluded African Americans, Hispanics, Jews, and working-class people. Shaker Heights, for instance, limited land sales to white buyers and required expensive building materials and professional architects. Suburbanites of more modest means found homes in places like Westwood, outside Chicago, the "World's Largest Bungalow Development."

Suburbanization and the automobile brought other changes. In 1922, J. C. Nichols opened the Country Club Plaza, the first suburban shopping center, in Kansas City; it provided free, off-street parking. Department stores and other large retailers began leaving the urban cores for the suburbs, where both parking and more affluent customers were waiting. Drive-in restaurants began with Royce Hailey's Pig Stand in Dallas in 1921. Later in the decade, the first fast-food franchise chain, White Tower, appeared, with its standardized menu and building. To serve the automobile, governments spent more on road construction and maintenance. By 1930, road construction was the largest single item in the national budget.

Mass Culture in the Jazz Age

The White Tower chain symbolized a new society and culture. Urbanization and the automobile joined with new systems of distributing, marketing, and communications to mold a mass culture of standardized experiences and interests. Not all Americans participated equally in the new culture, however, and some attacked it.

Advertising the Consumer Society

Advertising and its focus on increasing consumption shaped the new society. President Coolidge considered advertising "the most potent influence in adopting and changing the habits and modes of life, affecting what we eat, what we wear, and the work and play of the whole nation." A less complacent observer calculated that in 1925, nearly 50 percent more was spent "to educate consumers in what they may or may not want to buy" than on education from grade school through university.

Advertisers exhorted consumers via newspapers, billboards, streetcar signs, junk mail, radio, movies, and even skywriting. They sought to create a single market where everyone, regardless of region and ethnicity, consumed brand-name products. Advertisers attempted to stimulate new wants by ridiculing previous models or tastes as obsolete, acclaiming the convenience of a new brand, or linking the latest fashion with status or sex appeal. "If I wear a certain brand of underwear," observed one critic, "I have the satisfaction of knowing that my fellow-men not so fortunately clad are undoubtedly fouled swine."

The home became a focus of consumerism. Middle- and upper-class women purchased mass-produced household appliances, such as electric irons, toasters, vacuum cleaners, washing machines, and refrigerators. Working-class women bought packaged food, ready-made clothing, and other consumer goods to lighten their workload. Advertisers attempted to redefine the housewife's role as primarily that of a consumer, purchasing goods for her family. To promote sales of clothing and cosmetics, advertising depicted women as concerned with fashion, beauty, and sex appeal. It thus contributed to the declining interest in the larger social issues that the earlier women's movement had raised.

A shifting labor market also promoted mass consumption. The increasing number of white-collar workers had more time and money for leisure and consumption. Factory workers, whose jobs often provided little challenge, less satisfaction, and no prospect for advancement, found in consumption not only material rewards but, thanks to advertisers' claims, some self-respect and fulfillment as stylish and attractive people worthy of attention. Women clerical workers, the fastest-growing occupational group, found in the purchase of clothes and cosmetics a sign of social status and an antidote to workplace monotony. "People are seeking to escape from themselves," insisted a writer in *Advertising and Selling* in 1926. "They want to live in a more exciting world." Advertisers tried to portray popular fantasies rather than social realities.

Under the stimulus of advertising, consumption increasingly displaced the traditional virtues of thrift, prudence, and avoidance of debt. Installment buying became common. By 1928, fully 85 percent of furniture, 80 percent of radios, and 75 percent of washing machines were bought on credit. But with personal debt rising more than twice as fast as incomes, even aggressive advertising and the extension of credit could not indefinitely prolong the illusion of a healthy economy.

Leisure and Entertainment

During the 1920s, Americans also spent more on recreation and leisure, important features of the new mass society. Millions of people packed into movie theaters whose ornate style symbolized their social importance. In Chicago, the Uptown boasted a four thousand–seat theater, an infirmary, a nursery, and a restaurant; its turreted façade soared eight stories. Inside was a four-story lobby with twin marble staircases, crystal chandeliers, and an orchestra to entertain people waiting to enter. "It is beyond human dreams of loveliness," exclaimed one ad, "achieving that overpowering sense of tremendous size and exquisite beauty."

Movies helped spread common values and set national trends in dress, language, and behavior. Studios made films to attract the largest audiences and fit prevailing stereotypes. Cecil B. De Mille titilated audiences while reinforcing conventional standards with religious epics, like *The Ten Commandments* (1923) or *The King of Kings* (1927). Set in ancient times, such movies depicted both sinful pleasures and the eventual triumph of moral order. One Hollywood executive called for "passionate but pure" films

Advertisements for brand-name products, like this 1929 ad for Campbell's tomato soup, often tried to link simple consumption with larger issues of personal success and achievement.

The soup for men who eat to win!

MEN with the success-habit eat wisely and well, both. They enjoy Campbell's Tomato Soup regularly and they get from it a sparkle and zest, which tell in the day's work. All of the rich, tonic goodness. All of the famous tomato healthfulness. 12 cents a can.

that would give "the public all the sex it wants with compensating values for all those church and women groups."

Radio also helped mold national popular culture. The first radio network, the National Broadcasting Company (NBC), was formed in 1926. Soon it was charging $10,000 to broadcast commercials to a national market. Networks provided standardized entertainment, personalities, and news to Americans across the nation. Radio incorporated listeners into a national society. Rural residents, in particular, welcomed the "talking furniture" for giving them access to the speeches, sermons, and business information available to city-dwellers.

The phonograph, another popular source of entertainment, allowed families to listen to music of their choice in their own homes. The phonograph business boomed. Manufacturers turned out more than 2 million phonographs and 100 million records annually. Record companies promoted dance crazes, such as the Charleston, and developed regional markets for country, or "hillbilly," music in the South and West as well as a "race market" for blues and jazz among the growing urban population, black and white. The popularity of the trumpet player Louis Armstrong and other jazz greats gave the decade its nickname, the **Jazz Age**.

Jazz derived from African-American musical traditions. The Great Migration spread it from New Orleans and Kansas City to cities throughout the nation. Its improvisational and rhythmic characteristics differed sharply from older and more formal music and were often condemned by people who feared that jazz would undermine conventional restraints on behavior. One group in Cincinnati, arguing that the music would implant "jazz emotions" in babies, won an injunction against its performance near hospitals. Middle-class black Chicagoans frowned on jazz and favored "the better class of music." But conductor Leopold Stokowski defended jazz as the music of modern America: "Jazz has come to stay because it is an expression of the times, of the breathless, energetic, superactive times in which we are living; it is useless to fight against it."

Professional sports also flourished and became more commercialized. Millions of Americans, attracted by the popularity of such celebrities as Babe Ruth of the New York Yankees, crowded into baseball parks to follow major league teams. Ruth treated himself as a commercial commodity, hiring an agent, endorsing Cadillacs and alligator shoes, and defending a salary in 1932 that dwarfed that of President Hoover by declaring, "I had a better year than he did."

Large crowds turned out to watch boxers like Jack Dempsey and Gene Tunney pummel each other; those who could not get tickets listened to radio announcers describe each blow. College football attracted frenzied followers among people with no interest in higher education. Universities built huge stadiums—Ohio State's had 64,000 seats. By 1929, the Carnegie Commission noted that the commercialization of college sports "overshadowed the intellectual life for which the university is assumed to exist."

Other crazes, from flagpole sitting to miniature golf, also indicated the spread of popular culture and its emphasis on leisure. Another celebrity who captured popular fascination was the aviator Charles Lindbergh, who flew alone across the Atlantic in 1927. In the *Spirit of St. Louis*, a tiny airplane built on a shoestring budget and nearly outweighed by the massive amount of fuel it had to carry, Lindbergh fought bad weather and fatigue for thirty-four hours before landing to a hero's welcome in Paris. Named its first "Man of the Year" by *Time*, one of the new mass-circulation magazines, Lindbergh won adulation and awards from Americans who still valued the image of individualism.

The New Morality

The promotion of consumption and immediate gratification weakened traditional self-restraint and fed a desire for personal fulfillment. The failure of wartime sacrifices to achieve promised glories deepened Americans' growing disenchantment with traditional values. The social dislocations of the war years and growing urbanization accelerated moral and social change. Sexual pleasure became an increasingly open objective. Popularization of Sigmund Freud's ideas weakened prescriptions for sexual restraint; the growing availability of birth control information enabled women to enjoy sex with less fear of pregnancy; and movie stars like Clara Bow, known as "the It Girl," and Rudolph Valentino flaunted sexuality to mass audiences. Traditionalists worried as divorce rates, cigarette consumption, and hemlines went up while respect for parents, elders, and clergy went down. A sociological study of Muncie, Indiana—the nation's "Middletown"—found that "religious life as represented by the churches is less pervasive than a generation ago."

Young people seemed to embody the new morality. Rejecting conventional standards, they embraced the era's frenzied dances, bootleg liquor, smoking, more revealing clothing, and sexual experimentation. They welcomed the freedom from parental control that the automobile afforded—although the car was hardly the "house of prostitution on wheels" that one critic called it. The "flapper"—a frivolous young woman with short hair and a skimpy skirt who danced, smoked, and drank in oblivious self-absorption—was a major obsession in countless articles, bearing such titles as "These Wild Young People" and "The Uprising of the Young." Few people were more alarmed than the president of the University of Florida. "The low-cut gowns, the rolled hose and short skirts are born of the Devil," he cried, "and are carrying the present and future generations to chaos and destruction." But feminists also condemned this symbol of changing standards. "It is sickening," Charlotte Perkins Gilman wrote in 1923, "to see so many of the newly freed abusing that freedom in mere imitation of masculine vice and weakness."

But the new morality was neither as new nor as widespread as its advocates and critics believed. Signs of change had appeared before the war in the popularity of new clothing fashions, social values, and public amusements among working-class and ethnic groups. And if it now became fashionable for the middle class to adopt such attitudes and practices, most Americans still adhered to traditional beliefs and values. Legislators in Utah and Virginia, for example, proposed laws requiring hemlines within three inches of the ankle and necklines within three inches of the throat. Moreover, as Gilman's comment suggests, the new morality offered only a limited freedom. It certainly did not promote social equality for women, who remained subject to traditional double standards, with marriage and divorce laws, property rights, and employment opportunities biased against them.

The Searching Twenties

Many writers rejected what they considered the materialism, conformity, and provincialism of the emerging mass culture. Their criticism made the postwar decade one of the most creative periods in American literature. The brutality and hypocrisy of the war stimulated their disillusionment and alienation. What Gertrude Stein called the **Lost Generation** considered, in the words of F. Scott Fitzgerald, "all Gods dead, all wars fought, all faiths in man shaken." Ernest Hemingway, wounded as a Red Cross volunteer during the war, rejected idealism in his novel *A Farewell to Arms* (1929), declaring that he no longer saw any meaning in "the words *sacred, glorious,* and *sacrifice.*"

Novelists also turned their attention to American society. In *The Great Gatsby* (1925), Fitzgerald traced the self-deceptions of the wealthy. Sinclair Lewis ridiculed middle-class society and its narrow business culture in *Babbitt* (1922), whose title character provided a new word applied to the smug and shallow. In 1930, Lewis became the first American to win the Nobel Prize in literature.

Other writers condemned the mediocrity and intolerance of mass society. The critic Harold Stearns edited *Civilization in the United States* (1922), a book of essays. Its depiction of a repressive society sunk in hypocrisy, conformity, and materialism prompted his departure for Paris, where he lived, like Hemingway and Fitzgerald, as an expatriate, alienated from America. H. L. Mencken made his *American Mercury* the leading magazine of cultural dissenters. Conventional and conservative himself, Mencken heaped vitriol on the "puritans," "peasants," and "prehensile morons" he saw everywhere in American life.

When President Coolidge declined a request to exhibit American paintings in Paris by declaring that there were none, he seemed to confirm for the critics the boorishness of American society. But many of the critics were as self-absorbed as their targets. When the old progressive muckraker Upton Sinclair complained that he found nothing "constructive" in Mencken's voluminous writings, Mencken was delighted. "Uplift," he retorted, "has damn nigh ruined the country." Fitzgerald claimed to have "no interest in politics at all." Such attitudes dovetailed with the society they condemned.

Culture Wars

Despite the blossoming of mass culture and society in the 1920s, conflicts divided social groups. Some of these struggles involved reactions against the new currents in American life, including technological and scientific innovations, urban growth, and materialism. But movements to restrict immigration, enforce prohibition, prohibit the teaching of evolution, and even sustain the Ku Klux Klan did not have simple origins, motives, or consequences. The forces underlying the culture wars of the 1920s would surface repeatedly in the future (see the overview table, "Issues in the Culture Wars of the 1920s").

Nativism and Immigration Restriction

For years, many Americans, from racists to reformers, had campaigned to restrict immigration. In 1917, Congress required immigrants to pass a literacy test. But renewed immigration after the war revived the anti-immigration movement, and the propaganda of the war and Red Scare years generated public support for more restriction. Depicting immigrants as radicals, racial inferiors, religious subversives, or criminals, nativists clamored for congressional action. The Emergency Quota Act of 1921 reduced immigra-

tion by about two-thirds and established quotas for nationalities on the basis of their numbers in the United States in 1910. Restrictionists, however, demanded more stringent action, especially against the largely Catholic and Jewish immigrants from southern and eastern Europe. Coolidge himself urged that America "be kept American," by which he meant white, Anglo-Saxon, and Protestant.

Congress adopted this racist rationale in the **National Origins Act of 1924**, which proclaimed its objective to be the maintenance of the "racial preponderance" of "the basic strain of our population." This law restricted immigration quotas to 2 percent of the foreign-born population of each nationality as recorded in the 1890 census, which was taken before the mass immigration from southern and eastern Europe. Another provision, effective in 1929, restricted total annual immigration to 150,000 with quotas that nearly eliminated southern and eastern Europeans. The law also completely excluded Japanese immigrants.

Other actions targeted Japanese residents in America. California, Oregon, Washington, Arizona, and other western states prohibited them from owning or leasing land, and in 1922, the Supreme Court ruled that, as nonwhites, they could never become naturalized citizens. A Japanese newspaper in Los Angeles criticized such actions as betraying America's own ideals. Dispirited by the prejudice of the decade, Japanese residents hoped for fulfillment through their children, the *Nisei*, who were American citizens by birth.

Ironically, as a U.S. territory, the Philippines was not subject to the National Origins Act, and Filipino immigration increased ninefold during the 1920s. Most Filipino newcomers became farm laborers, especially in California, or worked in Alaskan fisheries. Similarly, because the law did not apply to immigrants from the Western Hemisphere, Mexican immigration also grew. Nativists lobbied to exclude Mexicans, but agribusiness interests in the Southwest blocked any restrictions on low-cost migrant labor.

The Ku Klux Klan

Nativism was also reflected in the popularity of the revived Ku Klux Klan, the goal of which, according to its leader, was to protect "the interest of those whose forefathers established the nation." Although founded in Georgia in 1915 and modeled on its Reconstruction predecessor, the new Klan was a national, not a southern, movement and claimed several million members by the mid-1920s. Admitting only native-born white Protestants, the Klan embodied the fears of a traditional culture threatened by social change. Ironically, its rapid spread owed

OVERVIEW

ISSUES IN THE CULTURE WARS OF THE 1920S

Issue	Proponent view	Opponent view
The new morality	Promotes greater personal freedom and opportunities for fulfillment	Promotes moral collapse
Evolutionism	A scientific advance linked to notions of progress	A threat to religious belief
Jazz	Modern and vital	Unsettling, irregular, vulgar, and primitive
Immigration	A source of national strength from ethnic and racial diversity	A threat to the status and authority of old-stock white Protestants
Great Migration	A chance for African Americans to find new economic opportunities and gain autonomy and pride	A threat to traditional white privilege, control, and status
Prohibition	Promotes social and family stability and reduces crime	Restricts personal liberty and increases crime
Fundamentalism	An admirable adherence to traditional religious faith and biblical injunctions	A superstitious creed given to intolerant interference in social and political affairs
Ku Klux Klan	An organization promoting community responsibility, patriotism, and traditional social, moral, and religious values	A group of religious and racial bigots given to violent vigilantism and fostering moral and public corruption
Mass culture	Increases popular participation in national culture; provides entertainment and relaxation	Promotes conformity, materialism, mediocrity, and spectacle
Consumerism	Promotes material progress and higher living standards	Promotes waste, sterility, and self-indulgence

much to modern business and promotional techniques as hundreds of professional recruiters raked in hefty commissions selling Klan memberships to those hoping to defend their way of life.

In part the Klan was a fraternal order, providing entertainment, assistance, and community for its members. Its picnics, parades, charity drives, and other social and family-oriented activities—perhaps a half million women joined the Women of the Ku Klux Klan—sharply distinguished the organization from both the small, secretive Klan of the nineteenth century and the still smaller, extremist Klan of the later twentieth century. Regarding themselves as reformers, Klan members supported immigration restriction and prohibition.

But the Klan also exploited racial, ethnic, and religious prejudices and campaigned against many social groups and what it called "alien creeds." It attacked African Americans in the South, Mexicans in Texas, Japanese in California, and Catholics and Jews everywhere. A twisted religious impulse ran through much of the Klan's organization and activities. It hired itinerant Protestant ministers to spread its message, erected altars and flaming crosses at its meetings, and sang Klan lyrics to the tunes of well-known hymns. One Klan leader maintained that "the Klan stood for the same things as the Church, but we did the things the Church wouldn't do." This included publishing anti-Catholic newspapers, boycotting Catholic and Jewish businesses, and lobbying

Indiana Klanswomen pose in their regalia in 1924. The Klan combined appeals to traditional family and religious values with violent attacks upon those who were not white, native-born Protestants.

for laws against parochial schools and for compulsory Bible reading in the public schools. The Klan also resorted to violence. In 1921, for example, a Methodist minister who belonged to the Klan murdered a Catholic priest on his own doorstep, and other Klansmen burned down Catholic churches. The leader of the Oregon Klan insisted that "the only way to cure a Catholic is to kill him."

To the Klan, Catholics and Jews symbolized not merely subversive religions but the ethnic diversity and swelling urban population that challenged traditional Protestant culture. To protect that culture, the Klan attempted to censor or disrupt "indecent" entertainment, assaulted those whom it accused of adultery, and terrorized doctors who performed abortions.

While the Klan's appeal seemed rooted in the declining countryside, it also attracted urban residents. Chicago had the largest Klan organization in the nation with fifty thousand members, and Houston, Dallas, Portland, Indianapolis, Denver, and the satellite communities ringing Los Angeles were also Klan strongholds. Urban Klansmen were largely lower or lower middle class, many recently arrived from the country and retaining its attitudes; others were long-term urban residents who feared being marginalized by social changes, especially by competition from immigrants and new ideas.

The Klan also ventured into politics, with some success. But eventually it encountered resistance. In the North, Catholic workers disrupted Klan parades. In the South, too, Klan excesses provoked a backlash. After the Klan in Dallas flogged sixty-eight

people in a "whipping meadow" along the Trinity River in 1922, respect turned to outrage. Newspapers demanded that the Klan disband, district attorneys began to prosecute Klan thugs, and in 1924 Klan candidates were defeated by the ticket headed by Miriam "Ma" Ferguson, whose gubernatorial campaign called for anti-Klan laws and the loss of tax exemptions for churches used for Klan meetings. Elsewhere the Klan was stung by revelations of criminal behavior and corruption by Klan leaders who had been making fortunes pocketing membership fees and selling regalia to followers. The Klan crusade to purify society had bred corruption and conflict everywhere. By 1930, the Klan had nearly collapsed.

Prohibition and Crime

Like the Klan, prohibition both reflected and provoked social tensions in the 1920s. Reformers had long believed that prohibition would improve social conditions, reduce crime and family instability, increase economic efficiency, and purify politics. They rejoiced in 1920 when the Eighteenth Amendment, prohibiting the manufacture, sale, or transportation of alcoholic beverages, took effect. Congress then passed the **Volstead Act**, which defined the forbidden liquors and established the Prohibition Bureau to enforce the law. But many social groups, especially among urban ethnic communities, opposed prohibition, and the government could not enforce the law where public opinion did not endorse it.

Evasion was easy. By permitting alcohol for medicinal, sacramental, and industrial purposes, the Volstead Act gave doctors, priests, and druggists a huge loophole through which to satisfy their friends' needs. Hearing that the use of sacramental wines increased by 800,000 gallons under prohibition, one Protestant leader complained that "not more than one-quarter of this is sacramental—the rest is sacrilegious." City-dwellers made "bathtub gin," and rural people distilled "moonshine." Scofflaws frequented the "speakeasies" that replaced saloons or bought liquor from bootleggers and rumrunners, who imported it from Canada, Cuba, or Mexico. The limited resources of the Prohibition Bureau often allowed bootleggers to operate openly. Dozens met publicly in a Seattle hotel in 1922 and adopted "fair prices" for liquor and a code of ethics "to keep liquor runners within the limits of approved business methods."

The ethics and business methods of bootleggers soon shocked Americans, however. The huge profits encouraged organized crime—which had previously concentrated on gambling and prostitution—to develop elaborate liquor distribution networks. Operating outside the law, crime "families" used violence to enforce contracts, suppress competition, and attack rivals. In Chicago, Al Capone's army of nearly a thousand gangsters killed hundreds. Using the profits from bootlegging and such new tools as the automobile and the submachine gun, organized crime corrupted city governments and police forces.

Gradually, even many "drys"—people who had initially favored prohibition—dropped their support, horrified by the boost it gave organized crime and worried about a general disrespect for law that it promoted. A 1926 poll found that four-fifths of Americans wanted to repeal or modify prohibition. Yet it remained in force because it was entangled in party politics and social conflict. Many rural, Protestant Americans saw prohibition as a symbolic cultural issue. As the comedian Will Rogers said, "Mississippi will vote dry and drink wet as long as it can stagger to the polls." Prohibition represented their ability to control the newcomers in the expanding cities. Democrats called for repeal in their 1928 and 1932 platforms, and in 1933, thirty-six states ratified an amendment repealing what Herbert Hoover had called a "noble experiment."

Old-Time Religion and the Scopes Trial

Religion provided another fulcrum for traditionalists attempting to stem cultural change. Protestant fundamentalism, which emphasized the infallibility of the Bible, including the Genesis story of Adam and Eve, emerged at the turn of the century as a conservative reaction to religious modernism and the social changes brought by the mass immigration of Catholics and Jews, the growing influence of science and technology, and the secularization of public education. But the fundamentalist crusade to reshape America became formidable only in the 1920s.

Fundamentalist groups, colleges, and publications sprang up throughout the nation, espe-

cially in the South. The anti-Catholic sentiment exploited by the Klan was but one consequence of fundamentalism's insistence on strict biblical Christianity. A second was the assault on Darwin's theory of evolution, which contradicted literal interpretations of biblical Creation. The Southern Baptist Convention condemned "every theory, evolutionary or other, which teaches that man originated or came by way of lower animal ancestry." Fundamentalist legislators tried to prevent teaching evolution in public schools in at least twenty states. In 1923, Oklahoma banned Darwinian textbooks, and Florida's legislature denounced teaching evolution as "subversive." In 1925, Tennessee forbade teaching any idea contrary to the biblical account of human origins. The governor signed it, saying that "there is a widespread belief that something is shaking the fundamentals of the country,

Prohibition was a divisive issue, involving cultural values as much as alcoholic spirits. This 1920 cartoon depicts Prohibitionists as attempting to impose their own repressive values on all Americans.

"NOW THEN, ALL TOGETHER, 'MY COUNTRY 'TIS OF THEE'"

The Culture Wars

Cultural conflict raged through American society in the 1920s as people reacted to great social changes, including new roles for women, increasing ethnic and racial diversity, rapid urbanization, and the "new morality." Nativists demanded immigration restriction; the Ku Klux Klan played on fears of racial, ethnic, and religious minorities; prohibitionists grappled with the minions of Demon Rum; and Protestant fundamentalists campaigned to prohibit the teaching of evolution in public schools.

Such conflicts are rooted in the moral systems that give people identity and purpose. As a result, the challenges of the Great Depression and World War II dampened but did not extinguish them. Beginning in the 1960s, fueled as before by challenges to traditional values and beliefs—African-American demands for civil rights, opposition to the Vietnam War, the women's rights movement and women's growing presence in the workplace, a new wave of immigration (dominated this time by Asians and Latin Americans), the gay rights movement—cultural conflict flared again and continues to burn.

In the 1920s nativists succeeded in curtailing immigration with the passage of the National Origins Act of 1924. In 1994, the people of California approved Proposition 187, which barred undocumented aliens from public schools and social services. Again, as in the 1920s, fundamentalists are mounting an attack against the teaching of evolution in public schools, sometimes seeking to persuade local school boards to give equal time to the pseudoscience of creationism. And today rap and rock 'n' roll provoke the same kind of worried condemnation that jazz provoked in the 1920s.

The central battleground of today's culture wars, however, is women's rights, and especially abortion rights. Ever since the Supreme Court ruled in *Roe* v. *Wade* in 1973 that women had a right to an abortion, opponents, primarily religious conservatives, have sought to curtail or abolish that right in the name of "family values." Antiabortion protests became increasingly violent in the 1980s and 1990s. Demonstrators have harassed women trying to enter abortion clinics, clinics have been bombed, and several abortion providers have been murdered. Although the Supreme Court has upheld *Roe* v. *Wade* and laws restraining demonstrations at abortion clinics, it has also upheld state laws imposing limits on abortion rights. Abortions have become harder to obtain in many parts of the country.

Gay rights is another new battleground in the culture wars. Religious conservatives, again in the name of "family values," have sought to counter efforts to extend civil rights protections to gays and lesbians. In 1992, for ex-

ample, Colorado approved a measure (overturned by the Supreme Court in 1996) that prohibited local governments from passing ordinances protecting gays and lesbians from discrimination.

The hostility to the Catholic Church and Catholic immigrants that had long been characteristic of American nativism has been largely absent from the current culture wars. On the contrary, conservative Catholics have joined forces with evangelical Protestants on many fronts, particularly on abortion and gay rights.

According to one popular analysis, the antagonists in today's culture wars are, on one side, those who find authority in transcendent universal sources like those that religious traditions lay claim to, and, on the other, those who find authority in society and human reason. From this perspective, perhaps the most prominent recent engagement in the culture wars was the impeachment of President Clinton. Republican leader Tom DeLay of Texas, for example, declared in 1999 that the impeachment debate was "about relativism versus absolute truth." Polls, however, showed that most Americans were more tolerant and flexible, willing to separate the president's public performance from his personal morality. With the failure to convict Clinton, one Republican lamented: "We probably have lost the culture war." But given the deeply rooted convictions that motivate it, cultural conflict is likely to remain a persistent undercurrent in American life.

The packed courtroom for the Scopes Trial in 1925 illustrates the intense interest that Americans have persistently taken in conflicts stemming from differing cultural values and ethical visions.

both in religion and in morals. It is the opinion of many that an abandonment of the old-fashioned faith and belief in the Bible is our trouble."

Social or political conservatism, however, was not an inherent part of old-time religion. The most prominent antievolution politician, William Jennings Bryan, continued to campaign for political, social, and economic reforms. Never endorsing the Klan, he served on the American Committee on the Rights of Religious Minorities and condemned anti-Semitism and anti-Catholicism. Bryan feared that Darwinism promoted political and economic conservatism. The survival of the fittest, he complained, elevated force and brutality, ignored spiritual values and democracy, and discouraged altruism and reform. How could a person fight for social justice "unless he believes in the triumph of right?"

The controversy over evolution came to a head when the **American Civil Liberties Union (ACLU)** responded to Tennessee's violation of the constitutional separation of church and state by offering to defend any teacher who tested the antievolution law. John Scopes, a high school biology teacher in Dayton, Tennessee, did so and was arrested. Scopes's trial riveted national attention after Bryan agreed to assist the prosecution and Clarence Darrow, a famous Chicago lawyer and prominent atheist, volunteered to defend Scopes.

Millions of Americans tuned their radios to hear the first trial ever broadcast. The judge, a fundamentalist, sat under a sign urging "Read Your Bible Daily." He ruled that scientists could not testify in support of evolution: Because they were not present at the Creation, their testimony would be "hearsay." But he did allow Darrow to put Bryan on the stand as an expert on the Bible. Bryan insisted on the literal truth of every story in the Bible, allowing Darrow to ridicule his ideas and force him to concede that some biblical passages had to be construed symbolically. Though the local jury took only eight minutes to convict Scopes, fundamentalists suffered public ridicule from reporters like H. L. Mencken, who sneered at the "hillbillies" and "yokels" of Dayton.

But fundamentalism was hardly destroyed, and antievolutionists continued their campaign. New organizations, such as the Bryan Bible League, lobbied for state laws and an antievolution amendment to the constitution. Three more states forbade teaching evolution, but by 1929 the movement had faltered. Even so, fundamentalism retained religious influence and would again challenge science and modernism in American life.

A New Era in the World?

Abroad, as at home, Americans in the 1920s sought peace and economic order. Rejection of the Treaty of Versailles and the League of Nations did not foreshadow isolationism. Indeed, in the 1920s, the United States became more deeply involved in international matters than ever before in peacetime. That involvement both produced important successes and sowed the seeds for serious future problems.

War Debts and Economic Expansion

The United States was the world's dominant economic power in the 1920s, changed by the Great War from a debtor to a creditor nation. The loans that the United States had made to its allies during the war troubled the nation's relations with Europe throughout the decade. American insistence on repayment angered Europeans, who saw the money as a U.S. contribution to the joint war effort against Germany. Moreover, high American tariffs blocked Europeans from exporting goods to the United States and earning dollars to repay their debts. Eventually, the United States readjusted the terms for repayment, and American bankers extended large loans to Germany, which used the money to pay reparations to Britain and France, whose governments then used the same money to repay the United States. This unstable system depended on a constant flow of money from the United States.

America's global economic role expanded in other ways as well. Exports, especially of manufactured goods, soared; by 1929, the United States was the world's largest exporter, responsible for one-sixth of all exports. American investment abroad more than doubled between 1919 and 1930. To expand their markets and avoid foreign tariffs, many U.S. companies became **multinational corporations**, establishing branches or subsidiaries abroad. Ford built assembly plants in England, Japan, Turkey, and Canada. International Telephone and Telegraph owned two dozen factories in Europe and employed more overseas workers than any other U.S. corporation.

Other companies gained control of foreign supply sources. American oil companies invested in foreign oil fields, especially in Latin America, where they controlled more than half of Venezuelan production. The United Fruit Company developed such huge operations in Central America that it often dominated national economies. In Costa Rica, the company had a larger budget than the national government.

Europeans and Latin Americans alike worried about this economic invasion; even Secretary of Commerce Hoover expressed concerns. Multinationals, he warned, might eventually take markets from American manufacturers and jobs from American workers. Business leaders, however, dismissed such reservations.

Hoover's concerns, moreover, did not prevent him from promoting economic expansion abroad. The government worked to open doors for American businesses in foreign countries, helping them secure access to trade, investment opportunities, and raw materials. Hoover's Bureau of Foreign Commerce opened fifty offices around the world to boost American business. Hoover also pressed the British to give U.S. corporations access to rubber production in the British colony of Malaya. Secretary of State Charles Evans Hughes negotiated access to Iraqi oil fields for U.S. oil companies. The government also authorized bankers and manufacturers to form combinations, exempt from antitrust laws, to exploit foreign markets.

Rejecting War

Although government officials cooperated with business leaders to promote American strategic and economic interests, they had little desire to use force in the process. Popular reaction against the Great War, strengthened by a strong peace movement, constrained policymakers. Having repudiated collective security as embodied in the League of Nations, the United States nonetheless sought to minimize international conflict and promote its national security. In particular, the State Department sought to restrict the buildup of armaments among nations.

At the invitation of President Harding, delegations from nine nations met in Washington at the Washington Naval Conference in 1921 to discuss disarmament. The conference drafted a treaty to reduce battleship tonnage and suspend the building of new ships for a decade. The terms virtually froze the existing balance of naval power, with the first rank assigned to Britain and the United States, followed by Japan and then France and Italy. Japan and the United States also agreed not to fortify their possessions in the Pacific any further and to respect the Open Door in East Asia. Public opinion welcomed the treaty; the U.S. Senate ratified it with only one dissenting vote, and the 1924 Republican platform hailed it as "the greatest peace document ever drawn."

The United States made a more dramatic gesture in 1928 when it helped draft the **Kellogg-Briand Pact**. Signed by sixty-four nations, the treaty renounced aggression and outlawed war. Without provisions for enforcement, however, it was little more than symbolic. The Senate reserved the right of self-defense, repudiated any responsibility for enforcing the treaty, and maintained U.S. claims under the Monroe Doctrine. These limitations on the treaty, Senator Hiram Johnson noted, "have made its nothingness complete."

Managing the Hemisphere

Senate insistence on the authority of the Monroe Doctrine reflected the U.S. claim to a predominant role in Latin America. The United States continued to dominate the hemisphere to promote its own interests. It exerted its influence through investments, control of the Panama Canal, invocation of the Monroe Doctrine, and, when necessary, military intervention.

In response to American public opinion, the peace movement, and Latin American nationalism, the United States did retreat from the extreme gunboat diplomacy of the Progressive Era, withdrawing troops from the Dominican Republic and Nicaragua. Secretary of State Hughes assured Latin Americans that "we covet no territory; we seek no conquest; the liberty we cherish for ourselves we desire for others; and we accept no rights for ourselves that we do not accord to others." But Haiti remained under U.S. occupation throughout the decade, American troops stayed in Cuba and Panama, and the United States directed the financial policies of other Latin American countries. Moreover, it sent the marines into Honduras in 1924 and back to Nicaragua in 1926. Such interventions could establish only temporary stability while provoking further Latin American hostility. "We are hated and despised," said one American businessman in Nicaragua. "This feeling has been created by employing American marines to hunt down and kill Nicaraguans in their own country."

Latin American resentment led to a resolution at the 1928 Inter-America Conference denying the right of any nation "to intervene in the internal affairs of another." The U.S. delegation rejected the measure, but the anger of Latin Americans prompted the State Department to draft the Clark Memorandum. This document, not published until 1930, receded from the Roosevelt Corollary and helped prepare the way for the so-called Good Neighbor Policy toward Latin America. Still, the United States retained the means, both military and economic, to dominate the hemisphere.

Herbert Hoover and the Final Triumph of the New Era

As the national economy steamed ahead in 1928, the Republicans chose as their presidential candidate Herbert Hoover, a man who symbolized the policies of prosperity and the New Era. Hoover was not a politician—he had never been elected to office—but a successful administrator who championed rational and efficient economic development. A cooperative government, he believed, should promote business interests and encourage corporations to form trade associations to assure stability and profitability. It should not regulate economic activities. Hoover's stiff managerial image was softened by his humanitarian record and his roots in rural Iowa.

The Democrats, in contrast, chose a candidate who evoked the cultural conflicts of the 1920s. Alfred E. Smith, four-term governor of New York, was a Catholic, an opponent of prohibition, and a Tammany politician tied to the immigrant constituency of New York City. He had failed to gain the presidential nomination in 1924 when the party split over prohibition and the Klan, but in 1928 he won the dubious honor of running against Hoover. His nomination plunged the nation into the cultural strife that had divided the Democrats in 1924. Rural fundamentalism, anti-Catholicism, prohibition, and nativism were crucial factors in the campaign. The fundamentalist assault was unrelenting. Billy Sunday attacked Smith and the Democrats as "the forces of hell," and a Baptist minister in Oklahoma City warned his congregation: "If you vote for Al Smith, you're voting against Christ and you'll all be damned."

But Hoover was in fact the more progressive candidate. Sympathetic to labor, sensitive to women's issues, hostile to racial segregation, and favorable to the League of Nations, Hoover had always distanced himself from what he called "the reactionary group in the Republican party." By contrast, despite supporting state welfare legislation to benefit his urban working-class constituents, Smith was essentially conservative and opposed an active government. Moreover, he was as parochial as his most rural adversaries and never attempted to reach out to them. H. L. Mencken, who voted for Smith, nevertheless said of him, "Not only is he uninterested in the great problems facing the nation, but he has never heard of them." Smith himself responded to a question about the needs of the states west of the Mississippi by asking, "What states *are* west of the Mississippi?"

Although many Americans voted against Smith because of his social background, those same characteristics attracted others. Millions of urban and ethnic voters, previously Republican or politically uninvolved, voted for Smith and laid the basis for a new Democratic coalition that would emerge in the 1930s. In 1928, however, with the nation still enjoying the economic prosperity so closely associated

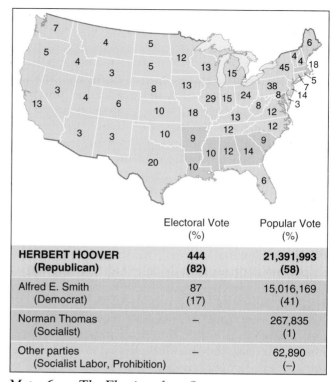

	Electoral Vote (%)	Popular Vote (%)
HERBERT HOOVER (Republican)	**444 (82)**	**21,391,993 (58)**
Alfred E. Smith (Democrat)	87 (17)	15,016,169 (41)
Norman Thomas (Socialist)	–	267,835 (1)
Other parties (Socialist Labor, Prohibition)	–	62,890 (–)

Map 26-2   The Election of 1928
The cultural conflicts of the 1920s shaped the 1928 election. Al Smith carried the largest cities, but Herbert Hoover swept most of the rest of the nation, even attracting much of the usually Democratic South.

with Hoover and the Republicans, the Democrats were routed (see Map 26-2).

In his campaign, Hoover boasted that Republican policies could bring America to "the final triumph over poverty." But 1928 would be the Republicans' final triumph for a long time. The vaunted prosperity of the 1920s was ending, and the country faced a future dark with poverty.

Conclusion

The New Era of the 1920s changed America. Technological and managerial innovations produced giant leaps in productivity, new patterns of labor, a growing concentration of corporate power, and high corporate profits. Government policies from protective tariffs and regressive taxation to a relaxation of regulatory laws reflected and reinforced the triumphs of a business elite over traditional cautions and concerns.

The decade's economic developments in turn stimulated social change, drawing millions of Americans from the countryside to the cities, creating an urban nation, and fostering a new ethic of materialism, consumerism, and leisure and a new mass culture based on the automobile, radio, the movies, and advertising. This social transformation swept up many Americans but left others unsettled by the erosion of traditional practices and values. The concerns of traditionalists found expression in campaigns for prohibition and against immigration, the revival of the Ku Klux Klan, and the rise of religious fundamentalism. Intellectuals denounced the materialism and conformity they saw in the new social order and fashioned new artistic and literary trends.

But the impact of the decade's trends was uneven. Mechanization increased the productivity of some workers but cost others their jobs; people poured into the cities while others left for the suburbs; prohibition, intended to stabilize society, instead produced conflict, crime, and corruption; government policies advanced some economic interests but injured others. Even the notion of a "mass" culture obscured the degree to which millions of Americans were left out of the New Era. With no disposable income and little access to electricity, rural Americans scarcely participated in the joys of consumerism; racial and ethnic minorities often were isolated in ghettos and *barrios*; and many workers faced declining opportunities. Most ominous was the uneven prosperity undergirding the New Era. Although living standards rose for many Americans and the rich expanded their share of national wealth, more than 40 percent of the population earned less than $1,500 a year and fell below the established poverty level. The unequal distribution of wealth and income made the economy unstable and vulnerable to a disastrous collapse.

Review Questions

1. How did the automobile industry affect the nation's economy and society in the 1920s?

2. What factors characterized the "boom industries" of the 1920s? The "sick industries"? How accurate is it to label the 1920s the "decade of prosperity"?

3. What were the underlying issues in the election of 1924? Of 1928? What role did politics play in the public life of the 1920s?

4. What were the chief points of conflict in the "culture wars" of the 1920s? What were the underlying issues in these clashes? Why were they so hard to compromise?

5. In what ways did the World War I experience shape developments in the 1920s?

6. What were the chief features of American involvement in world affairs in the 1920s? To what extent did that involvement constitute a new role for the United States?

Recommended Reading

John Braeman, Robert Bremner, and David Brody, eds., *Change and Continuity in Twentieth Century America: The 1920s* (1968). Stimulating essays that cover important features of economic, social, and political history.

Warren I. Cohen, *Empire without Tears: America's Foreign Relations, 1921–1933* (1987). A splendid brief analysis of diplomatic and economic policy.

James J. Flink, *The Car Culture* (1975). The fascinating history of the automobile and its social impact.

Ellis W. Hawley, *The Great War and the Search for a Modern Order* (1979). A valuable survey emphasizing economic and organizational changes.

Sinclair Lewis, *Babbitt* (1922). An important novel of the 1920s that ridicules the empty business values of the booster society.

Additional Sources

General Studies

John D. Hicks, *Republican Ascendancy, 1921–1933* (1960).

William Leuchtenberg, *The Perils of Prosperity* (1958).

Michael E. Parrish, *Anxious Decades: America in Prosperity and Depression, 1920–1941* (1992).

Geoffrey Perrett, *America in the Twenties* (1982).

Economic Developments

Jo Ann E. Argersinger, *Making the Amalgamated: Gender, Ethnicity, and Class in the Baltimore Clothing Industry* (1999).

Irving L. Bernstein, *The Lean Years: A History of the American Worker, 1920–1933* (1960).

James J. Flink, *The Automobile Age* (1988).

Alice Kessler-Harris, *Out to Work: A History of Wage-Earning Women* (1982).

Roland Marchand, *Advertising the American Dream* (1985).

Stephen Meyer III, *The Five Dollar Day: Labor Management and Social Control in the Ford Motor Company* (1981).

Ronald W. Schatz, *The Electrical Workers* (1983).

Susan Smulyan, *Selling Radio: The Commercialization of American Broadcasting, 1920–1934* (1994).

Susan Strasser, *Satisfaction Guaranteed: The Making of the American Mass Market* (1989).

Leslie Woodcock Tentler, *Wage-Earning Women: Industrial Work and Family Life in the United States, 1900–1930* (1979).

Robert H. Zieger, *American Workers, American Unions* (1994).

Politics and Government

David Burner, *Herbert Hoover: A Public Life* (1979).

David Burner, *The Politics of Provincialism* (1967).

Douglas B. Craig, *After Wilson: The Struggle for the Democratic Party* (1992).

Ellis W. Hawley (ed.), *Herbert Hoover as Secretary of Commerce* (1981).

Walter LaFeber, *Inevitable Revolutions: The United States in Central America* (1984).

Allan J. Lichtman, *Prejudice and the Old Politics: The Presidential Election of 1928* (1979).

Richard Lowitt, *George W. Norris: The Persistence of a Progressive* (1971).

Donald R. McCoy, *Calvin Coolidge* (1967).

Robert Murray, *The Politics of Normalcy* (1973).

Robert D. Schulzinger, *The Making of the Diplomatic Mind* (1975).

Eugene P. Trani and David L. Wilson, *The Presidency of Warren G. Harding* (1977).

Joan Hoff Wilson, *American Business and Foreign Policy, 1920–1933* (1968).

Joan Hoff Wilson, *Herbert Hoover: Forgotten Progressive* (1975).

Cities and Suburbs

Sarah Deutsch, *No Separate Refuge: Culture, Class, and Gender on an Anglo-Hispanic Frontier in the American Southwest* (1987).

Juan Garcia, *Mexicans in the Midwest, 1900-1932* (1996).

David Goldfield, *Cotton Fields and Skyscrapers* (1982).

Peter Gottlieb, *Making Their Own Way: Southern Blacks' Migration to Pittsburgh, 1916–30* (1987).

Kenneth T. Jackson, *Crabgrass Frontier: The Suburbanization of the United States* (1985).

Earl Lewis, *In Their Own Interests: Race, Class, and Power in Twentieth-Century Norfolk, Virginia* (1991).

Gilbert Osofsky, *Harlem: The Making of a Ghetto* (1968).

Ricardo Romo, *East Los Angeles: History of a Barrio* (1983).

John C. Teaford, *Cities of the Heartland* (1993).

William Worley, *J. C. Nichols and the Shaping of Kansas City* (1990).

Society and Culture

Charles C. Alexander, *The Ku Klux Klan in the Southwest* (1965).

Kathleen M. Blee, *Women and the Klan: Racism and Gender in the 1920s* (1991).

Paul Carter, *Another Part of the Twenties* (1977).

William H. Chafe, *The American Woman: Her Changing Social, Economic, and Political Roles* (1972).

Norman Clark, *Deliver Us from Evil: An Interpretation of American Prohibition* (1976).

Stanley Coben, *Rebellion against Victorianism* (1991).

Nancy F. Cott, *The Grounding of American Feminism* (1987).

Sara M. Evans, *Born for Liberty: A History of Women in America* (1989).

Stuart Ewen, *Captains of Consciousness: Advertising and the Social Roots of the Consumer Culture* (1976).

Paula Fass, *The Damned and the Beautiful: American Youth in the 1920s* (1977).

Fred Hobson, *Mencken: A Life* (1994).

Nathan Huggins, *Harlem Renaissance* (1971).

Kenneth T. Jackson, *The Ku Klux Klan in the City* (1967).

Bruce B. Lawrence, *Defenders of God: The Fundamentalist Revolt against the Modern Age* (1989).

Lawrence W. Levine, *Defender of the Faith: William Jennings Bryan, the Last Decade, 1915–1925* (1965).

David L. Lewis, *When Harlem Was in Vogue* (1981).

Nancy Maclean, *Behind the Mask of Chivalry: The Making of the Second Ku Klux Klan* (1994).

Lary May, Screening *Out the Past: The Birth of Mass Culture and the Motion Picture Industry* (1980).

Leonard Moore, *Citizen Klansmen: The Ku Klux Klan in Indiana* (1991).

Robyn Muncy, *Creating a Female Dominion in American Reform* (1991).

Kathy H. Ogren, *The Jazz Revolution* (1989).

Elizabeth A. Payne, *Reform, Labor, and Feminism: Margaret Dreier Robins and the Women's Trade Union League* (1988).

Benjamin G. Rader, *American Sports: From the Age of Folk Games to the Age of Spectators* (1983).

Robert Sklar, *Movie-Made America: A Cultural History of American Movies* (1994).

Judith Stein, *The World of Marcus Garvey* (1986).

David Wiggins, *Sport in America* (1995).

Where to Learn More

❖ **F. Scott and Zelda Fitzgerald Museum, Montgomery, Alabama.** The novelist and his wife lived a short while in this house in her hometown.

❖ **Smithsonian Institution, Washington, D.C.** "From Farm to Factory," a permanent exhibition at the National Museum of American History, splendidly portrays the human side of the Great Migration.

❖ **Herbert Hoover National Historic Site, West Branch, Iowa.** Visitors may tour Hoover's birthplace cottage, presidential library, and museum.

❖ **Henry Ford Museum and Greenfield Village, Dearborn, Michigan.** Among many fascinating exhibits, "The Automobile in American Life" particularly and superbly demonstrates the importance of the automobile in American social history.

❖ **George Norris Home, McCook, Nebraska.** This museum, operated by the Nebraska State Historical Society, is dedicated to a leading progressive Republican of the 1920s.

❖ **Warren G. Harding House, Marion, Ohio.** Harding's home from 1891 to 1921 is now a museum with period furnishings.

❖ **Rhea County Courthouse and Museum, Dayton, Tennessee.** The site of the Scopes Trial, the courtroom appears as it did in 1925; the museum contains memorabilia related to the trial.

❖ **Calvin Coolidge Homestead, Plymouth, Vermont.** Operated by the Vermont Division of Historic Sites, the homestead preserves the exact interiors and furnishings from when Coolidge took the presidential oath of office there in 1923.

THE GREAT DEPRESSION AND THE NEW DEAL, 1929–1939

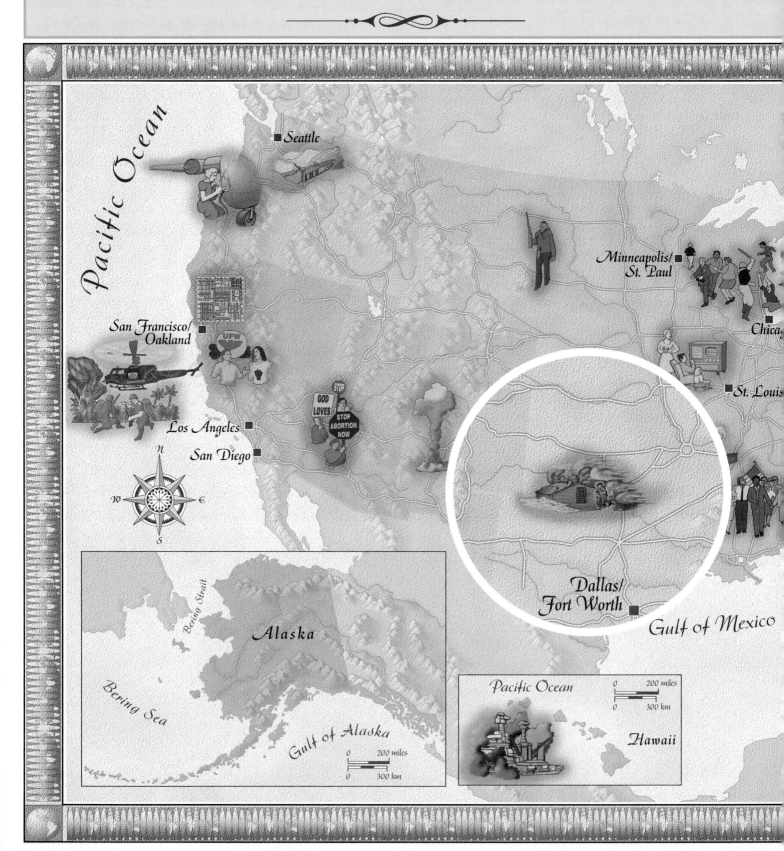

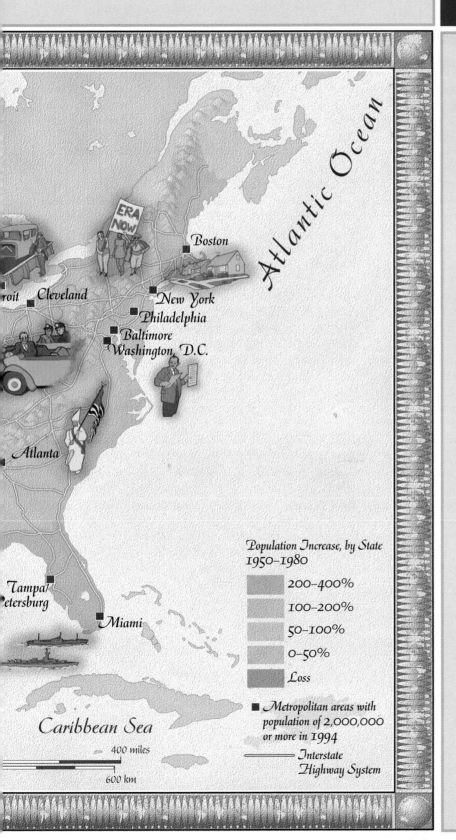

27

Key Topics

❖ The Great Depression
❖ Hoover's voluntary remedies
❖ FDR's New Deal
❖ The New Deal and organized labor, minorities, women, and farmers
❖ FDR's Democratic coalition of reformers, labor, urban ethnic groups, white Southerners, Westerners, and African Americans
❖ The faltering of the New Deal

Population Increase, by State 1950–1980

200–400%
100–200%
50–100%
0–50%
Loss

■ Metropolitan areas with population of 2,000,000 or more in 1994

── Interstate Highway System

Atlantic Ocean

Caribbean Sea

Boston
New York
Philadelphia
Baltimore
Washington, D.C.
Cleveland
roit
Atlanta
Tampa/ Petersburg
Miami

ERA NOW

400 miles
600 km

*I*n the summer of 1933, the signs were everywhere in the coal regions—on posters and billboards, in store windows: "The President wants you to join the union." In the 1920s, coal had been a sick industry, and its health had deteriorated with the onset of the **Great Depression** in 1929. Mounting unemployment and plummeting wages joined the industry's dangerous working conditions, arbitrary rules, and company domination. Membership in the United Mine Workers (UMW) had dropped from 400,000 in 1926 to barely 100,000 by 1933. Misery and hopelessness traveled in tandem. Yet now UMW officials spread the word that President Franklin Roosevelt favored the right to organize unions and bargain collectively.

The effect was electric. A UMW organizer in Pennsylvania found "a different feeling among the miners everywhere—they seem to feel that they are once more free men." In Kentucky, one organizer formed nine locals in a day, marveling that "the people have been so starved out that they are flocking into the Union by the thousands." Indeed, coal miners organized themselves spontaneously; union officials merely tried to keep up with the paperwork. The astonished governor of Pennsylvania told Roosevelt, "These people believe in you. . . . They trust you and all believe that you are working to get them recognition of the United Mine Workers of America."

The coal operators, accustomed to baronial control of the industry, vainly told their workers, "President Roosevelt is not an organizer for the United Mine Workers." But attitudes were changing. One organizer reported that whereas police had once chased union representatives out of Raton, New Mexico, "now the Mayor of the town gives us the city park for our meeting." Within two months, UMW membership numbered half a million.

Once organized, locals struck for union contracts and improved conditions. Some operators resisted, firing union leaders, recruiting strikebreakers, and employing police repression. When miners were shot, riots broke out. As one newspaper reported, "Miners' wives fought alongside their husbands, and sons joined with their fathers in battles with deputies." By September, the operators gave up, signing a contract that recognized the union, established the eight-hour day, and improved wages and working conditions. As the *New Yorker* noted, "The defeated mine-owners agreed to all the things that deputy sheriffs usually shoot people for demanding."

The union victory was not final, but these developments illustrated the forces that changed America in the 1930s. Responding to a crippling depression, the federal government—personalized by President Roosevelt—adopted an activist role in the economy and society. Its new reach seemed to extend everywhere—to the relief of those like the miners in Appalachia and the consternation of those like the coal operators. Federal activism restored hope and confidence for many Americans, often encouraging them to act for themselves.

The legislation that had spurred the miners' union drive was part of a massive and not always consistent program to promote economic recovery that in the process often promoted reform as well. The **New Deal**, as Roosevelt called his plan, achieved neither full recovery nor systematic reform, and its benefits were distributed unevenly. But it transformed American politics. The grateful union movement, for example, became an important part of Roosevelt's Democratic party. The Great Depression, Roosevelt's New Deal, and the behavior of the American people shaped the institutions and policies that would mark the nation for decades.

Hard Times in Hooverville

The prosperity of the 1920s ended in a stock market crash that revealed the flaws honeycombing the economy. As the nation slid into a catastrophic depression, factories closed, employment and incomes tumbled, and millions lost their homes, hopes, and dignity. Some protested and took direct action; others looked to the government for relief.

Crash!

The buoyant prosperity of the New Era, more apparent than real by the summer of 1929, collapsed in October when the stock market crashed. During the previous two years, the market had hit record highs, stimulated by optimism, easy credit, and speculators' manipulations. After peaking in September, it suffered several sharp checks, and on October 29, "Black Tuesday," panicked investors dumped their stocks at any price, wiping out the previous year's gains in one day. Confidence in the economy disappeared, and the slide continued for months, and then years. It hit bottom in July 1932. By then, the stock of U.S. Steel had plunged from 262 to 22, Montgomery Ward from 138 to 4. Much of the paper wealth of America had evaporated, and the nation sank into the Great Depression.

The Wall Street crash marked the beginning of the depression, but it did not cause it. The depression stemmed from weaknesses in the New Era economy. Most damaging was the unequal distribution of wealth and income. Workers' wages and farmers' incomes had fallen far behind industrial productivity and corporate profits; by 1929, the richest 0.1 percent of American families had as much total income as the bottom 42 percent (see Figure 27-1). With more than half the nation's people living at or below the subsistence level, there was not enough purchasing power to maintain the economy.

A second factor was that oligopolies dominated American industries. By 1929, the two hundred largest corporations (out of 400,000) controlled half the corporate wealth. Their power led to "administered prices," prices kept artificially high and rigid rather than determined by supply and demand. By not responding to purchasing power, this system not only helped bring on economic collapse but also dimmed prospects for recovery.

Weaknesses in specific industries had further unbalanced the economy. Agriculture suffered from overproduction, declining prices, and heavy debt; so did the coal and textile industries. These difficulties left the economy dependent on a few industries for expansion and employment; they could not carry the burden. Banking presented other problems. Poorly managed and regulated, banks had contributed to the instability of prosperity; they now threatened to spread the panic and depression.

International economic difficulties spurred the depression as well. Shut out from U.S. markets by high tariffs, Europeans had depended on American investments to manage their debts and reparation payments from the Great War. The stock market crash dried up the flow of American dollars to Europe, causing financial panics and industrial collapse and making the Great Depression global. In turn, European nations curtailed their imports of American goods and defaulted on their debts, further debilitating the U.S. economy. American exports fell by 70 percent from 1929 to

A coal miner greeting Franklin D. Roosevelt in West Virginia in 1932. Roosevelt's promise of a New Deal revived hope among millions of Americans trapped in hard times.

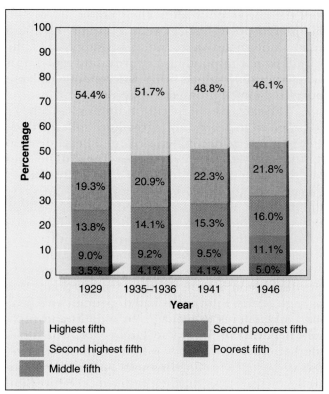

Figure 27-1 *Distribution of Income in the United States, 1929–1946*
An unequal distribution of income contributed to the Great Depression by limiting purchasing power. Only slight changes occurred until after World War II, but other factors gradually stabilized the national economy.

Data Source: U.S. Bureau of the Census.

1932. As foreign markets shrank, so did hopes for economic recovery.

Government policies also bore some responsibility for the crash and depression. Failure to enforce antitrust laws had encouraged oligopolies and high prices; failure to regulate banking or the stock market had permitted financial recklessness and irresponsible speculation. Reducing tax rates on the wealthy had also encouraged speculation and contributed to the maldistribution of income. Opposition to labor unions and collective bargaining helped keep workers' wages and purchasing power low. The absence of an effective agricultural policy and the high tariffs that inhibited foreign trade and reduced markets for agricultural products hurt farmers in the same way. In short, the same government policies that shaped the booming 1920s economy also pointed to economic disaster.

But the crash did more than expose the weaknesses of the economy. Business lost confidence and refused to make investments that might have brought recovery. Instead, banks called in loans and restricted credit, and depositors tried to withdraw their savings, which were uninsured. The demand for cash caused banks to fail, dragging the economy down further. And the Federal Reserve Board prolonged the depression by restricting the money supply.

The Depression Spreads

By early 1930, the effects of financial contraction were painfully evident. Factories shut down or cut back, and industrial production plummeted; by 1932, it was scarcely 50 percent of its 1929 level. Steel mills operated at 12 percent of capacity, auto factories at 20 percent. Unemployment skyrocketed, as an average of 100,000 workers a week were fired in the first three years after the crash. By 1932, one-fourth of the labor force was out of work (see Figure 27-2). In St. Louis, 75 percent of the workers in the building trades, a key sector of the 1920s economy, were jobless. Overall unemployment in Toledo reached 80 percent. The wages of those Americans lucky enough to work fell sharply. Personal income dropped by more than half between 1929 and 1932; by 1933, industrial workers had average weekly wages of only $16.73. Moreover, the depression began to feed on itself in a vicious circle: Shrinking wages and employment cut into purchasing power, causing business to slash production again and lay off workers, thereby further reducing purchasing power.

The depression particularly battered farmers. Commodity prices fell by 55 percent between 1929 and 1932, stifling farm income. Cotton farmers earned only 31 percent of the pittance they had received in 1929. Unable to pay their mortgages, many farm families lost their homes and fields. "We have no security left," cried one South Dakota farm woman. "Foreclosures and evictions at the point of sheriff's guns are increasing daily." The dispossessed roamed the byways, highways, and railways of a troubled country.

Urban families were also evicted when they could not pay their rent. Some moved in with relatives; others lived in **Hoovervilles**—the name reflects the bitterness directed at the president—shacks where people shivered, suffered, and starved. Oklahoma City's vast Hooverville covered a hundred square miles; one witness described its hapless residents as squatting in "old, rusted-out car bodies," orange crates, and holes in the ground.

Soup kitchens became standard features of the urban landscape, with lines of the hungry stretching for blocks. But charities and local communities could not meet the massive needs, and neither state nor federal governments had welfare or unemployment compensation programs. To survive, peo-

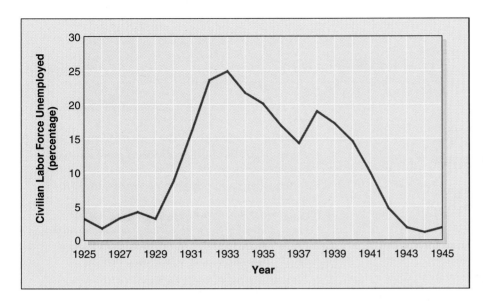

Figure 27-2   Unemployment, 1925–1945
Unemployment soared in the early 1930s, spreading distress and overwhelming charities and local relief agencies. Federal programs improved conditions, but only American entry into World War II really ended the problem.

Data Source: U.S. Bureau of the Census.

ple planted gardens in vacant lots and back alleys and tore apart empty houses or tapped gas lines for fuel. In immigrant neighborhoods, social workers found a "primitive communism" in which people shared food, clothing, and fuel in the belief that "what goes around comes around." Few Americans escaped hard times, but their experiences varied with their circumstances and expectations.

Homeless Americans gathered in squalid "Hoovervilles," like this one in Seattle, and struggled to survive.

"Women's Jobs" and "Men's Jobs"

The depression affected wage-earning women in complex ways. Although suffering 20 percent unemployment by 1932, women were less likely than men to be fired. Gender segregation had concentrated women in low-paid service, sales, and clerical jobs that shrank less than the heavy industries where men predominated. But while traditional attitudes somewhat insulated working women, they also reinforced opposition to female employment itself, especially that of married women. As one Chicago civic organization complained, "They are holding jobs that rightfully belong to the God-intended providers of the household." Nearly every state considered restricting the employment of married women, and the city council of Akron, Ohio, resolved that public agencies and private employers should stop employing wives. Three-fourths of the nation's school systems refused to hire married women as teachers, and two-thirds dismissed female teachers who married. Many private employers, especially banks and insurance companies, also fired married women.

Firing women, however, rarely produced jobs for men because few men sought positions in the fields associated

CHRONOLOGY

1929 Stock market crashes.

1932 Farmers' Holiday Association organizes rural protests in the Midwest.

Reconstruction Finance Corporation is created to assist financial institutions.

Bonus Army is routed in Washington, D.C.

Franklin D. Roosevelt is elected president.

1933 Emergency Banking Act is passed.

Agricultural Adjustment Administration (AAA) is created to regulate farm production.

National Recovery Administration (NRA) is created to promote industrial cooperation and recovery.

Federal Emergency Relief Act provides federal assistance to the unemployed.

Civilian Conservation Corps (CCC) is established to provide work relief in conservation projects.

Public Works Administration (PWA) is created to provide work relief on large public construction projects.

Civil Works Administration (CWA) provides emergency winter relief jobs.

Tennessee Valley Authority (TVA) is created to coordinate regional development.

1934 Securities and Exchange Commission (SEC) is established.

Indian Reorganization Act reforms Indian policy.

Huey Long organizes the Share-Our-Wealth Society.

Democrats win midterm elections.

1935 Supreme Court declares NRA unconstitutional.

National Labor Relations Act (Wagner Act) guarantees workers' rights to organize and bargain collectively.

Social Security Act establishes a federal social insurance system.

Banking Act strengthens the Federal Reserve.

Revenue Act establishes a more progressive tax system.

Resettlement Administration is created to aid dispossessed farmers.

Rural Electrification Administration (REA) is created to help provide electric power to rural areas.

Soil Conservation Service is established.

Emergency Relief Appropriation Act authorizes public relief projects for the unemployed.

Works Progress Administration (WPA) is created.

Huey Long is assassinated.

1936 Supreme Court declares AAA unconstitutional.

Roosevelt is reelected president.

Sit-down strikes begin.

1937 Chicago police kill workers in Memorial Day Massacre.

FDR tries but fails to expand the Supreme Court.

Farm Security Administration (FSA) is created to lend money to small farmers to buy and rehabilitate farms.

National Housing Act is passed to promote public housing projects.

"Roosevelt Recession" begins.

1938 Congress of Industrial Organizations (CIO) is founded.

Fair Labor Standards Act establishes minimum wage and maximum hours rules for labor.

Roosevelt fails to "purge" the Democratic party.

Republicans make gains in midterm elections.

---

with women. Men did displace women as teachers, social workers, and librarians, but firing women simply aggravated the suffering of families already reeling from the depression. Disapproval of female employment implied that women did not deserve equal opportunities and probably stiffened the opposition to opening "men's jobs" to women when women were desperate for work. Despite such hostility, the proportion of married women in the work force increased in the 1930s as women took jobs to help their families survive.

Families in the Depression

"I have watched fear grip the people in our neighborhood around Hull House," wrote Jane Addams as the depression deepened in 1931 and family survival itself seemed threatened. Divorce declined because it was expensive, but desertion increased, and marriages were postponed. Birthrates fell. Husbands and fathers, the traditional breadwinners, were often humiliated and despondent when laid off from work. One social worker observed in 1931: "Like searing irons, the degradation, the sheer terror and panic which loss of job brings, the deprivation and the bitterness have eaten into men's souls." Unemployed men, sociologists reported, "lost much of their sense of time and dawdled helplessly and dully about the streets," dreading to return home.

Women's responsibilities, by contrast, often grew. The number of female-headed households increased sharply. Not only did some women become wage earners, but their traditional role as homemakers also gained new significance. To make ends meet, many women sewed their own clothing and raised and canned vegetables, reversing the trend toward consumerism. Some also took on extra work at home. In San Antonio, one in every ten families had boarders, and in Alabama, housewives took in laundry at 10 cents for a week's washload.

The depression also affected children. Some parents sacrificed their own well-being to protect their children. One witness described "the uncontrolled trembling of parents who have starved themselves for weeks so that their children might not go hungry." But children felt the tension and fear, and many went without food. In New York City, 139 people, most of them children, died of starvation and malnutrition in 1933. Boys and girls stayed home from school and church because they lacked shoes or clothing; others gave up their plans for college. As hope faded, family conflicts increased. Some parents nagged their children, even considering them burdens. Many teenagers left home, either to escape parental authority or so that younger children would have more to eat. These "juvenile transients" suffered from starvation, exposure, illness, and accidents. The California Unemployment Commission concluded that the depression had left the American family "morally shattered. There is no security, no foothold, no future."

"Last Hired, First Fired"

The depression particularly harmed racial minorities. With fewer resources and opportunities, they were less able than other groups to absorb the economic pain. African Americans were caught in a double bind, reported a sociologist at Howard University in 1932: They were "the last to be hired and the first to be fired." Black unemployment rates were more than twice the white rate, reflecting increased job competition and persistent racism. Jobless white workers now sought the menial jobs traditionally reserved for black workers, such as street cleaning and domestic service. In Atlanta, white citizens paraded with banners denouncing the hiring of black workers "Until Every White Man Has a Job."

Racism also limited the assistance African Americans received. Religious and charitable organizations often refused to care for black people. Local and state governments set higher requirements for black people than for white people to receive relief and provided them with less aid. One Memphis resident saw the result of such policies: "Colored men and women with rakes, hoes, and other digging tools, with buckets and baskets, digging around in the garbage and refuse for food." By 1932, most African Americans were suffering acute privation. "At no time in the history of the Negro since slavery," reported the Urban League, "has his economic and social outlook seemed so discouraging." African Americans were "hanging on by the barest thread."

Hispanic Americans also suffered. As mostly unskilled workers, they faced increasing competition for decreasing jobs paying declining wages. They were displaced even in the California agricultural labor force, which they had dominated. By the mid-1930s, they made up only a tenth of the state's migratory labor force, which increasingly consisted of white people who had fled the South and the Great Plains. Other jobs were lost when Arizona, California, and Texas barred Mexicans from public works and highway construction jobs. Vigilantes threatened employers who hired Mexicans rather than white Americans.

Economic woes and racism drove nearly half a million Mexican immigrants and their American-born children from the United States in the 1930s. Local authorities in the Southwest urged the federal government to deport Mexicans, offered free transportation to Mexico, and adopted discriminatory policies in providing relief. By 1931, a Los Angeles official announced that tens of thousands of Mexicans "have been literally scared out of southern California." Fear of deportation kept many Mexican-American families from seeking relief or even health care in Texas.

Protest

Bewildered and discouraged, most Americans reacted to the crisis without protest. Influenced by traditional individualism, many blamed themselves for their plight. But others did act, especially to protect their families. Protests ranged from small desperate gestures like stealing food and coal to more dramatic deeds. In Louisiana, women seized a train to call attention to the needs of their families; in New Jersey, in the "bloodless battle of Pleasantville," one hundred women held the city council hostage to demand assistance.

Communists, socialists, and other radicals organized more formal protests. Communists led the jobless into "unemployment councils" that staged hunger marches, demonstrated for relief, and blocked evictions. Mothers facing eviction in Chicago told their children: "Run quick and find the Reds." Socialists built similar organizations, including Baltimore's People's Unemployment League, which had twelve thousand members. Such groups provided protection and assistance. However, local authorities often suppressed their protests. In 1932, police fired on the Detroit Unemployment Council as it marched to demand food and jobs, killing four marchers and wounding many more.

Rural protests also broke out. Again, communists organized some of them, as in Alabama, where the Croppers' and Farm Workers' Union mobilized black agricultural laborers in 1931 to demand better treatment. In the Midwest, the Farmers' Holiday Association, formed among family farmers in 1932, stopped the shipment of produce to urban markets, hoping to drive up prices. A guerrilla war broke out as farmers blocked roads and halted freight trains, dumped milk in ditches, and fought bloody battles with deputy sheriffs. Midwestern farmers also tried to prevent foreclosure of their farms. In Iowa, farmers beat sheriffs and mortgage agents and nearly lynched a lawyer conducting foreclosure proceedings; in Nebraska, a Farmers' Holiday leader warned that if the state did not halt foreclosures, "200,000 of us are coming to Lincoln and we'll tear that new State Capitol Building to pieces."

Herbert Hoover and the Depression

The Great Depression challenged the optimism, policies, and philosophy that Herbert Hoover carried into the White House in 1929. The president took unprecedented steps to resolve the crisis but shrank back from the interventionist policies activists urged. His failures, personal as well as political and economic, led to his repudiation and opened the way to a new deal.

The Limits of Voluntarism

Hoover fought economic depression more vigorously than any previous president, but he believed that voluntary, private relief was preferable to federal intervention. The role of the national government, he thought, was to advise and encourage the voluntary efforts of private organizations, individual industries, or local communities. As secretary of commerce,

Hoover had championed trade associations to achieve economic order and social progress. As president he persuaded Congress in 1929 to create the Federal Farm Board to promote voluntary agricultural cooperatives to raise farm income without government regulations. After the crash, he tried to apply this voluntarism to the depression.

Hoover first secured business leaders' pledges to maintain employment and wage levels. But most corporations soon repudiated these pledges, slashed wages, and laid off workers. An official of the Bureau of Labor Statistics complained that business leaders "are hell-bent to get wages back to the 1913 level." Hoover himself said, "You know, the only trouble with capitalism is capitalists; they're too damn greedy." Still, he rejected government action.

Hoover also depended on voluntary efforts to relieve the misery caused by massive unemployment. He created the President's Organization for Unemployment Relief to help raise private funds for voluntary relief agencies. Charities and local authorities, he believed, should help the unemployed; direct federal relief would expand government power and undermine the recipients' character. He vetoed congressional attempts to aid the unemployed. "The American way of relieving distress," said Hoover, was through "the voluntary agencies of self help in the community."

The depression rendered Hoover's beliefs meaningless. Private programs to aid the unemployed scarcely existed. Only a few unions like the Amalgamated Clothing Workers had unemployment funds, and these were soon spent. Company plans for unemployment compensation covered less than 1 percent of workers, revealing the charade of the welfare capitalism of the 1920s. Some business leaders rejected any responsibility: "Even God Almighty never promised anybody that he should not suffer from hunger," snorted the president of the Southern States Industrial Council. Private charitable groups like the Salvation Army, church associations, and ethnic societies quickly exhausted their resources. By 1931, the director of Philadelphia's Federation of Jewish Charities conceded, "Private philanthropy is no longer capable of coping with the situation." Tens of thousands of Philadelphians, he noted, had been reduced to "the status of a stray cat prowling for food. . . . What this does to the innate dignity of the human soul is not hard to guess."

Nor could local governments cope, and their efforts declined as the depression deepened. New York City provided relief payments of $2.39 a week for an entire family, and other cities much less. By

1932, more than one hundred cities made no relief appropriations at all, and the commissioner of charity in Salt Lake City reported that people were sliding toward starvation. Only eight state governments provided even token assistance. Constitutional restrictions on taxes and indebtedness stopped some from responding to the relief crisis. Others lacked the will. Texas refused to issue bonds to fund relief. (See "American Views: An Ohio Mayor on Unemployment and Relief.")

Hoover blundered not in first relying on charities and local governments for relief but in refusing to admit that they were inadequate. Even his advisers warned that voluntarism and "individual initiative" had become obsolete. Both his vision and his efforts fell short.

As the depression worsened, Hoover adopted more activist policies. He persuaded Congress to cut taxes to boost consumers' buying power, and he increased the public works budget. The Federal Farm Board lent money to cooperatives and spent millions trying to stabilize crop prices. Unable to control production, however, the board conceded failure by late 1931. More successful was the **Reconstruction Finance Corporation (RFC)**. Established in January 1932, the RFC lent federal funds to banks, insurance companies, and railroads so that their recovery could "trickle down" to ordinary Americans. Hoover still opposed direct aid to the general public, although he finally allowed the RFC to lend small amounts to state and local governments for unemployment relief.

But these programs satisfied few Americans. "While children starve," cried Pennsylvania's governor, Hoover "intends to let us have just as little relief as possible after the longest delay possible." Far more action was necessary, but Hoover remained committed to voluntarism and a balanced budget. The *New Republic* remarked in wonder: "Strangely enough, though he praises our government as representative and democratic, Mr. Hoover seems to regard most of the positive activities it might undertake as the intrusion of an alien sovereignty rather than the cooperative action of a people." Hoover's ideological limitations infuriated Americans who saw him as indifferent to their suffering and a reactionary protector of privileged business interests—an image his political opponents encouraged.

Repudiating Hoover: The 1932 Election

Hoover's treatment of the **Bonus Army** symbolized his unpopularity and set the stage for the 1932 election. In 1932, unemployed veterans of World War I gathered in Washington, demanding payment of service bonuses not due until 1945. Hoover refused to meet with them, and Congress rejected their plan. But ten thousand veterans erected a shantytown at the edge of Washington and camped in vacant public buildings. Hoover determined to evict the veterans, but General Douglas MacArthur disobeyed his cautious orders and on July 28 led cavalry, infantry, and tanks against the ragged Bonus Marchers. The troops cleared the buildings and assaulted the shantytown, dispersing the veterans and their families and setting their camp on fire.

This assault provoked widespread outrage. "What a pitiful spectacle is that of the great American Government, mightiest in the world, chasing unarmed men, women, and children with army tanks," commented the *Washington News*. The administration tried to brand the Bonus Marchers as communists and criminals, but official investigations refuted such claims. The marchers were anxious and discouraged Americans, not revolutionaries, and if any criminals were among them, noted one critic, they were proportionately fewer than in President Harding's cabinet. The incident confirmed Hoover's public image as harsh and insensitive.

In the summer of 1932, with no prospects for victory, Republicans renominated Hoover. Confident Democrats selected Governor Franklin D. Roosevelt of New York, who pledged "a new deal for the American people." A distant cousin of Theodore Roosevelt, FDR had prepared for the presidency. Born into a wealthy family in 1882, he had been educated at Harvard, trained in the law, and schooled in politics, as a state legislator, assistant secretary of the navy under Wilson, and the Democratic vice presidential nominee in 1920. In 1921, Roosevelt contracted polio, which paralyzed him from the waist down, leaving him dependent on braces or crutches. His struggle with this ordeal gave him greater maturity, compassion, and determination. His continued involvement in politics, meanwhile, owed much to his wife, Eleanor. A social reformer, she became a Democratic activist, organizing women's groups and campaigning across New York. In a remarkable political comeback, FDR was elected governor in 1928 and reelected in 1930.

The 1932 campaign gave scant indication of what Roosevelt's New Deal might involve. The Democratic platform differed little from that of the Republicans, and Roosevelt spoke in vague or general terms. He knew that the election would be a repudiation of Hoover more than an endorsement of himself. Still, observers gained clues from

American Views

AN OHIO MAYOR ON UNEMPLOYMENT AND RELIEF

Joesph Heffernan was the mayor of Youngstown, Ohio, when the nation sank into the Great Depression. Like other industrial cities, Youngstown soon confronted widespread unemployment and distress. In this document, written in 1932, Heffernan describes the obstacles he faced in responding to the suffering in Youngstown.

❖ **What would Heffernan think of President Hoover's belief that private charities and local authorities would provide unemployment relief?**

❖ **What did Heffernan see as obstacles to a public response to the depression?**

❖ **What did he fear would be the consequences of the failure to devise a rational and humane system of relief?**

[In 1930] I asked for a bond issue of $1,000,000 for unemployment relief. Many leading business men went out of their way to show their disapproval. One of them . . . said to me: "You make a bad mistake in talking about the unemployed. Don't emphasize hard times and everything will be all right." An influential newspaper chastised me for "borrowing trouble"; the depression would be over, the editor maintained, before relief would be needed. . . . The gravity of the situation was so deliberately misrepresented by the entire business community that when the bond issue finally came to a ballot, in November 1930, it was voted down.

Thus we passed into the early days of 1931—fourteen months after the first collapse—with no relief in sight except that which was provided by the orthodox charities. Not a single move had been made looking toward action by a united community.

Strange as it may seem, there was no way in which the city government could embark upon a program of its own. We had no funds available for emergency relief, and without specific authorization from the people we could not issue bonds. . . .

As time went on, business conditions showed no improvement. Every night hundreds of homeless men crowded into the municipal incinerator, where they found warmth even though they had to sleep on heaps of garbage. In January 1931, I obtained the cooperation of the City Council to con-

---

Roosevelt's record in New York, where he had created the first state system of unemployment relief and supported social welfare and conservation. More important was his outgoing personality, which radiated warmth and hope in contrast to Hoover's gloom. "If you put a rose in Hoover's hand," said one observer, "it would wilt."

FDR carried every state south and west of Pennsylvania (see Map 27-1). It was the worst rout of a Republican candidate ever (except in 1912 when the party had split). Yet Hoover would remain president for four more months, as the Constitution then required. And in those four months,

the depression worsened, with rising unemployment, collapsing farm prices, and spreading misery. When teachers in Chicago, unpaid for months, fainted in their classrooms from hunger, it symbolized the imminent collapse of the nation itself. The final blow came in February 1933 when panic struck the banking system. Nearly six thousand banks had already failed, robbing 9 million depositors of their savings. Desperate Americans rushed to withdraw their funds from the remaining banks, pushing them to the brink as well. With the federal government under Hoover immobilized, state governments shut the banks to prevent

vert an abandoned police station into a "flop house." The first night it was filled, and it has remained filled ever since. I made a point of paying frequent visits to this establishment so that I could see for myself what kind of men these down-and-outers were, and I heartily wish that those folk who have made themselves comfortable by ignoring and denying the suffering of their less fortunate neighbors could see some of the sights I saw. There were old men gnarled by heavy labor, young mechanics tasting the first bitterness of defeat, clerks and white-collar workers learning the equality of misery, derelicts who fared no worse in bad times than in good, Negroes who only a short time before had come from Southern cotton fields, now glad to find any shelter from the cold, immigrants who had been lured to Van Dyke's "land of youth and freedom"—each one a personal tragedy, and all together an overwhelming catastrophe for the nation. . . .

This descent from respectability, frequent enough in the best of times, has been hastened immeasurably by two years of business paralysis, and the people who have been affected in this manner must be numbered in millions. This is what we have accomplished with our bread lines and soup kitchens. I know, because I have seen thousands of these defeated, discouraged, hope-less men and women, cringing and fawning as they come to ask for public aid. It is a spectacle of national degeneration. That is the fundamental tragedy for America. If every mill and factory in the land should begin to hum with prosperity tomorrow morning, the destructive effect of our haphazard relief measures would not work itself out of the nation's blood until the sons of our sons had expiated the sins of our neglect.

Even now there are signs of rebellion against a system so out of joint that it can only offer charity to honest men who want to work. Sometimes it takes the form of social agitation, but again it may show itself in a revolt that is absolute and final. Such an instance was reported in a Youngstown newspaper on the day I wrote these lines:—

"FATHER OF TEN DROWNS SELF
. . . Out of work two years, Charles Wayne, aged 57, father of ten children, stood on the Spring Common bridge this morning. . . . He took off his coat, folded it carefully, and jumped into the swirling Mahoning River. Wayne was born in Youngstown and was employed by the Republic Iron and Steel Company for twenty-seven years as a hot mill worker. 'We were about to lose our home,' sobbed Mrs. Wayne. 'And the gas and electric companies had threatened to shut off the service.'"

Source: Joseph L. Heffernan, "The Hungry City: A Mayor's Experience with Unemployment," Atlantic Monthly, May 1932, pp. 538–540, 546.

their failure. By March, an eerie silence had descended on the nation. Hoover concluded, "We are at the end of our string."

Launching the New Deal

In the midst of national anxiety, Franklin D. Roosevelt pushed forward an unprecedented program to resolve the crises of a collapsing financial system, crippling unemployment, and agricultural and industrial breakdown and to promote reform. The early New Deal achieved successes and attracted support, but it also had limitations and generated criticism that suggested the need for still greater innovations.

Action Now!

On March 4, 1933, Franklin Delano Roosevelt became president and immediately reassured the American people. He insisted that "the only thing we have to fear is fear itself—nameless, unreasoning, unjustified terror, which paralyzes needed efforts to convert retreat into advance." And he promised "action, and action now!" Summoning Congress, Roosevelt pressed forward on a broad front. In the first

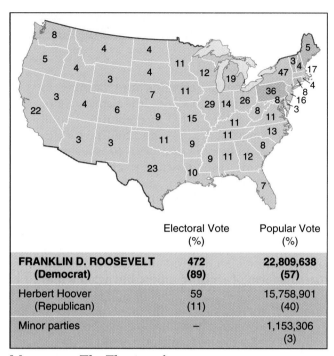

	Electoral Vote (%)	Popular Vote (%)
FRANKLIN D. ROOSEVELT (Democrat)	**472 (89)**	**22,809,638 (57)**
Herbert Hoover (Republican)	59 (11)	15,758,901 (40)
Minor parties	–	1,153,306 (3)

Map 27-1   The Election of 1932
In the midst of the Great Depression, only the most rock-ribbed Republican states failed to turn to Franklin D. Roosevelt and the Democrats for relief. The election of 1932 was a landslide.

three months of his administration, the famous Hundred Days of the New Deal, the Democratic Congress passed many important laws (see the overview table, "Major Laws of the Hundred Days").

Roosevelt's program reflected a mix of ideas, some from FDR himself, some from a diverse group of advisers, including academic experts dubbed the "brain trust," politicians, and social workers. It also incorporated principles from the progressive movement, precedents from the Great War mobilization, and even plans from the Hoover administration. Above all, the New Deal was a practical response to the depression. FDR had set its tone in his campaign when he declared, "The country needs, and, unless I mistake its temper, the country demands bold, persistent experimentation. . . . Above all, try something."

FDR first addressed the banking crisis. On March 5, he proclaimed a national bank holiday, closing all remaining banks. Congress then passed his **Emergency Banking Act**, a conservative measure that extended government assistance to sound banks and reorganized the weak ones. Prompt government action, coupled with a reassuring **fireside chat** over the radio by the president, restored popular confidence in the banks. When they reopened on March 13, deposits exceeded withdrawals. "Capitalism," said Raymond Moley of the brain trust, "was saved in

eight days." In June, Congress created the **Federal Deposit Insurance Corporation (FDIC)** to guarantee bank deposits up to $2,500.

The financial industry was also reformed. The **Glass-Steagall Act** separated investment and commercial banking to curtail risky speculation. The Securities Act reformed the sale of stocks to prevent the insider abuses that had characterized Wall Street, and in 1934 the **Securities and Exchange Commission (SEC)** was created to regulate the stock market. Two other financial measures in 1933 created the Home Owners Loan Corporation and the Farm Credit Administration, which enabled millions to refinance their mortgages.

Relief

Roosevelt also provided relief for the unemployed. The Federal Emergency Relief Administration (FERA) furnished funds to state and local agencies. Harry Hopkins, who had headed Roosevelt's relief program in New York, became its director and one of the New Deal's most important members. FERA spent over $3 billion before it ended in 1935, and by then Hopkins and FDR had developed new programs that

The first "Hundred Days" of the New Deal brought a rush of important new laws to combat the depression. This 1933 cartoon captures the popular excitement generated by Roosevelt's commitment to action and leadership of Congress.

OVERVIEW

MAJOR LAWS OF THE HUNDRED DAYS

Law	Objective
Emergency Banking Act	Stabilized the private banking system
Agricultural Adjustment Act	Established a farm recovery program based on production controls and price supports
Emergency Farm Mortgage Act	Provided for the refinancing of farm mortgages
National Industrial Recovery Act	Established a national recovery program and authorized a public works program
Federal Emergency Relief Act	Established a national system of relief
Home Owners Loan Act	Protected homeowners from mortgage foreclosure by refinancing home loans
Glass-Steagall Act	Separated commercial and investment banking and guaranteed bank deposits
Tennessee Valley Authority Act	Established the TVA and provided for the planned development of the Tennessee River Valley
Civilian Conservation Corps Act	Established the CCC to provide work relief on reforestation and conservation projects
Farm Credit Act	Expanded agricultural credits and established the Farm Credit Administration
Securities Act	Required full disclosure from stock exchanges
Wagner-Peyser Act	Created a U.S. Employment Service and encouraged states to create local public employment offices

provided work rather than just cash. Work relief, they believed, preserved both the skills and the morale of recipients. In the winter of 1933–1934, Hopkins spent nearly $1 billion to create jobs for 4 million men and women through the Civil Works Administration (CWA). The CWA hired laborers to build roads and airports, teachers to staff rural schools, and singers and artists to give public performances. The Public Works Administration (PWA) provided work relief on useful projects to stimulate the economy through public expenditures. Directed by Harold Ickes, the PWA spent billions from 1933 to 1939 to build schools, hospitals, courthouses, dams, and bridges.

One of FDR's personal ideas, the **Civilian Conservation Corps (CCC)**, combined work relief with conservation. Launched in 1933, the CCC employed 2.5 million young men to work on reforestation and flood control projects, build roads and

bridges in national forests and parks, restore Civil War battlefields, and fight forest fires. The men lived in isolated CCC camps and earned $30 a month, $25 of which had to be sent home. "I'd go anywhere," said one Baltimore applicant. "I'd go to hell if I could get work there." One of the most popular New Deal agencies, the CCC lasted till 1942.

Helping Some Farmers

Besides providing relief, the New Deal promoted economic recovery. In May 1933, Congress established the **Agricultural Adjustment Administration (AAA)** to combat the depression in agriculture caused by crop surpluses and low prices. The AAA subsidized farmers who agreed to restrict production. The objective was to boost farm prices to parity, a level that would restore farmers' purchasing power to what it had been in 1914. In the summer of 1933,

A *Civilian Conservation Corps (CCC) poster offering relief work as a "young man's opportunity." Although the CCC was a popular and effective New Deal agency, some excluded women asked where was the "she-she-she." Most New Deal programs had a gender bias against women.*

the AAA paid southern farmers to plow up 10 million acres of cotton and midwestern farmers to bury 9 million pounds of pork. Restricting production in hard times caused public outrage. "Farmers are not producing too much," said one critic. "What we have overproduction of is empty stomachs and bare backs." Secretary of Agriculture Henry Wallace defended production controls as analogous to corporations maximizing profits: "Agriculture cannot survive in a capitalistic society as a philanthropic enterprise."

Agricultural conditions improved. Farm prices rose from 52 percent of parity in 1932 to 88 percent in 1935, and gross farm income rose by 50 percent. Not until 1941, however, would income exceed the level of 1929, a poor year for farmers. Moreover, some of the decreased production and increased prices stemmed

from devastating droughts and dust storms on the Great Plains. The AAA itself harmed poor farmers while aiding larger commercial growers. As southern planters restricted their acreage, they dismissed tenants and sharecroppers, and with AAA payments, they bought new farm machinery, reducing their need for farm labor. A reporter in 1935 found thousands of sharecroppers "along the highways and byways of Dixie, . . . lonely figures without money, without homes, and without hope." Thus while big producers moved toward prosperity, many small farmers were forced into a pool of rural labor for which there was decreasing need or into the cities, where there were no jobs.

The Supreme Court declared the AAA unconstitutional in 1936, but new laws established the farm subsidy program for decades to come. Increasing mechanization and scientific agriculture kept production high and farmers dependent on government intervention.

The Flight of the Blue Eagle

The New Deal attempted to revive American industry with the **National Industrial Recovery Act (NIRA)**, which created the **National Recovery Administration (NRA)**. The NRA sought to halt the slide in prices, wages, and employment by suspending antitrust laws and authorizing industrial and trade associations to draft codes setting production quotas, price policies, wages and working conditions, and other business practices. The codes promoted the interests of business generally and big business in particular, but Section 7a of the NIRA guaranteed workers the rights to organize unions and bargain collectively, which John L. Lewis of the United Mine Workers called an Emancipation Proclamation for labor.

Hugh Johnson became director of the NRA. He persuaded business leaders to cooperate in drafting codes and the public to patronize participating companies. The NRA Blue Eagle insignia and its slogan "We Do Our Part" covered workplaces, storefronts, and billboards. Blue Eagle parades marched down the nation's main streets and climaxed in a massive demonstration in New York City.

Support for the NRA waned, however. Corporate leaders used it to advance their own goals and discriminate against small producers, consumers, and labor. Minnesota's Governor Floyd Olson condemned the dominance within the NRA of the same selfish business interests he saw as responsible for the depression: "I am not satisfied with hanging a laurel wreath on burglars, thieves, and pirates and calling them code authorities."

Businesses also violated the labor rights specified in Section 7a. Defiant employers viewed collec-

New Deal agricultural programs stabilized the farm economy, but not all farmers bene-fited. Landowners receiving AAA payments evicted these black sharecroppers huddled in a makeshift roadside camp in Missouri in 1935.

tive bargaining as infringing their authority. Employers even used violence to smother unions. The NRA did little to enforce Section 7a, and Johnson—strongly probusiness—denounced all strikes. Workers felt betrayed.

Roosevelt tried to reorganize the NRA, but it remained controversial until the Supreme Court declared it unconstitutional in 1935.

Critics Right and Left

The early New Deal had not ended the depression. Recovery was fitful and uneven; millions of Americans remained unemployed. Nevertheless, the New Deal's efforts to grapple with problems, its successes in reducing suffering and fear, and Roosevelt's own skills carried the Democratic party to victory in the 1934 elections. But New Deal policies also provoked criticism, from both those convinced that too little had been achieved and those alarmed that too much had been attempted.

Despite the early New Deal's probusiness character, conservatives complained that the expansion of government activity and its regulatory role weakened the autonomy of American business. They also condemned the efforts to aid nonbusiness groups as socialistic, particularly the "excessive" spending on unemployment relief and the "instiga-

tion" of labor organizing. By 1934, as *Time* magazine reported, "Private fulminations and public carpings against the New Deal have become almost a routine of the business day." Industrialists and bankers organized the **American Liberty League** to direct attacks on the New Deal. The league distributed over 5 million copies of two hundred different pamphlets; it also furnished editorials and news stories to newspapers. These critics attracted little popular support, however, and their selfishness antagonized Roosevelt.

More realistic criticism came from the left. In 1932, FDR had campaigned for "the forgotten man at the bottom of the economic pyramid," and some radicals argued that the early New Deal had forgotten the forgotten man. Communists and socialists focused public attention on the poor, especially in the countryside. In California, Communists organized Mexican, Filipino, and Japanese farm workers into their Cannery and Agricultural Workers Union; in Arkansas and Tennessee, socialists in 1934 helped organize sharecroppers into the Southern Tenant Farmers Union, protesting the "Raw Deal" they had received from the AAA. Both unions encountered violent reprisals. Growers killed three picketers in California's San Joaquin Valley; in Arkansas, landlords shot union organizers and led vigilante raids on sharecroppers' shacks. This terrorism, however, created sympathy for farmworkers.

Even without the involvement of socialists or communists, however, labor militancy in 1934 pressed Roosevelt. Workers acted as much against the failure of the NRA to enforce Section 7a as against recalcitrant corporations. The number of workers participating in strikes leaped from 325,000 in 1932 (about the annual average since 1925) to 1.5 million in 1934. From dockworkers in Seattle and copper miners in Butte to streetcar drivers in Milwaukee and shoemakers in Boston, workers demanded their rights. Textile workers launched the largest single strike in the nation's history, shutting down the industry in twenty states.

Rebuffing FDR's pleas for fair treatment, employers moved to crush the strikes, often using complaisant police and private strikebreakers. In Minneapolis, police shot sixty-seven teamsters, almost all in the back as they fled an ambush arranged by employers; in Toledo, company police and National Guardsmen attacked autoworkers with tear gas, bayonets, and rifle fire; in the textile strike, police killed six picketers in South Carolina, and soldiers wounded another fifty in Rhode Island. At times, the workers held their ground, and they often attracted popular support, even in general strikes that paralyzed major cities like San Francisco. But against such powerful opponents, workers needed help to achieve their rights. Harry Hopkins and other New Dealers realized that labor's demands could not be ignored.

Popular discontent was also mobilized by four prominent individuals demanding government action to assist groups neglected by the New Deal. Representative William Lemke of North Dakota, an agrarian radical leader of the Nonpartisan League, called attention to rural distress. Lemke objected to the New Deal's limited response to farmers crushed by the depression. In his own state, nearly two-thirds of the farmers had lost their land through foreclosures. The AAA's strategy of simply restricting production, he thundered, was an "insane policy in the midst of hunger, misery, want, and rags."

Labor activism and its often violent suppression influenced New Deal policy. Here striking textile workers in Georgia in 1934 have been seized by National Guard troops to be taken to internment camps.

Francis Townsend, a California physician, proposed to aid the nation's elderly, many of whom were destitute. The Townsend Plan called for a government pension to all Americans over the age of 60, provided they retire from work and spend their entire pension. This promised to extend relief to the elderly, open jobs for the unemployed, and stimulate economic recovery. Townsend attracted people who in his words "believe in the Bible, believe in God, cheer when the flag passes by, the Bible Belt solid Americans." Over five thousand Townsend Clubs lobbied for government action to help the elderly poor.

Father Charles Coughlin, a Catholic priest in the Detroit suburb of Royal Oak, threatened to mobilize another large constituency against the limitations of the early New Deal. Thirty million Americans listened eagerly to his weekly radio broadcasts mixing religion with anti-Semitism and demands for social justice and financial reform. Coughlin had condemned Hoover for assisting banks but ignoring the unemployed and initially welcomed the New Deal as "Christ's Deal." But after concluding that FDR's policies favored "the virile viciousness of business and finance," Coughlin organized the National Union for Social Justice to lobby for his goals. With support among lower-middle-class, heavily Catholic, urban ethnic groups, Coughlin posed a real challenge to Roosevelt's Democratic party.

Roosevelt found Senator Huey P. Long of Louisiana still more worrisome. Alternately charming and autocratic, Long had modernized his state with taxation and educational reforms and an extensive public works program after his election as governor in 1928. Moving to the Senate and eyeing the White House, Long proposed more comprehensive social welfare policies than the New Deal had envisaged. In 1934, he organized the Share-Our-Wealth Society. His plan to end poverty and unemployment called for confiscatory taxes on the rich to provide every family with a decent income, health coverage, education, and old-age pensions. Long's appeal was enormous. Within months, his organization claimed more than 27,000 clubs and 7 million members.

These dissident movements raised complex issues and simple fears. They built on concerns about the New Deal, both demanding government assistance and fretting about government intrusion; their programs were often ill-defined or impractical—Townsend's plan would cost more than half the national income; and some of the leaders, like Coughlin and Long, approached demagoguery. Nevertheless, their popularity warned Roosevelt that government action was needed to satisfy reform demands and assure his reelection in 1936.

Consolidating the New Deal

Responding to the persistence of the depression and political pressures, Roosevelt in 1935 undertook economic and social reforms that some observers have called the **Second New Deal**. The new measures shifted the relative weights accorded to the constant objectives of recovery, relief, and reform. Nor did FDR's interest in reform simply reflect cynical politics. He had frequently championed progressive measures in the past, and many of his advisers had deep roots in reform movements. After the 1934 elections gave the president an even more Democratic Congress, Harry Hopkins exulted: "Boys—this is our hour. We've got to get everything we want—a works program, social security, wages and hours, everything—now or never."

Lifting and Weeding

"In spite of our efforts and in spite of our talk," Roosevelt told the new Congress in 1935, "we have not weeded out the overprivileged and we have not effectively lifted up the underprivileged." To do so, he developed "must" legislation, to which his allies in Congress added. One of the new laws protected labor's rights to organize and bargain collectively. Drafted by Senator Robert Wagner of New York to replace Section 7a, it received Roosevelt's endorsement only after it was clear that both Congress and the public favored it. The **Wagner National Labor Relations Act**, dubbed "Labor's Magna Carta," guaranteed workers' rights to organize unions and forbade employers to adopt unfair labor practices, such as firing union activists or forming company unions. The law also set up the **National Labor Relations Board (NLRB)** to enforce these provisions, protect workers from coercion, and supervise union elections.

Of greater long-range importance was the **Social Security Act**. Other industrial nations had established national social insurance systems much earlier, but only the Great Depression moved the United States to accept that the federal government should protect the poor and unemployed. Even so, the law was a compromise, framed by a nonpartisan committee of business, labor, and public representatives and then weakened by congressional conservatives. It provided unemployment compensation, old-age pensions, and aid for dependent mothers and children and the blind.

The conservative nature of the law appeared in its stingy benefit payments, its lack of health insurance, and its exclusion of more than a fourth of all workers, including many in desperate need of protection, such as farm laborers and domestic servants. Moreover, unlike in other nations, the old-age pensions were financed through a regressive payroll tax on both employees and employers rather than through general tax revenues. Thus the new system was more like a compulsory insurance program. Roosevelt conceded as much but defended the taxes on workers as a tactic to protect the reform itself: "We put those payroll contributions there so as to give the contributors a legal, moral, and political right to collect their pensions and their unemployment benefits. With those taxes in there, no damn politician can ever scrap my social security program."

Roosevelt was justifiably proud. Despite its weaknesses, the Social Security Act was one of the most important laws in American history. It provided, he pointed out, "at least some measure of protection to the average citizen and to his family against the loss of a job and against poverty-ridden old age." Moreover, by establishing federal responsibility for social welfare, it inaugurated a welfare system that subsequent generations would expand.

Another reform measure, the Banking Act of 1935, increased the authority of the Federal Reserve Board over the nation's currency and credit system and decreased the power of the private bankers whose irresponsible behavior had contributed to the depression and the appeal of Father Coughlin. The Revenue Act of 1935, passed after Roosevelt assailed the "unjust concentration of wealth and economic power," provided for graduated income taxes and increased estate and corporate taxes. Opponents called it the Soak the Rich Tax, but with its many loopholes, it was scarcely that and was certainly not a redistributive measure such as Huey Long had proposed. Nevertheless, it set a precedent for progressive taxation and attracted popular support.

The Second New Deal also responded belatedly to the environmental catastrophe that had turned much of the Great Plains from Texas to the Dakotas into a "Dust Bowl" (see Map 27-2). Since World War I, farmers had stripped marginal land of its native grasses to plant wheat. When drought and high winds hit the plains in 1932, crops failed, and nothing held the soil. Dust storms blew away millions of tons of topsoil, despoiling the land and darkening the sky a thousand miles away. Families abandoned their farms in droves. Many of these poor "Okies" headed for California, their plight captured in John Steinbeck's novel, *The Grapes of Wrath* (1939).

Social Security

No politician will "ever scrap my social security program." So predicted FDR when he signed the Social Security Act in 1935. He based his confidence on the provisions in the act that linked benefits to payroll deductions. Because workers contributed to the program, they would feel a "right to collect their pensions and unemployment benefits." But Roosevelt could not have imagined just how successful the Social Security program would become. Expanded over the years since the 1930s, it now assists 44 million Americans, including the elderly, the disabled, and the survivors of contributors to the program. Certain poverty would confront half the nation's elderly without their monthly checks.

But the successful expansion of the program has also called its future into question. By 2030, the number of eligible recipients will double, but the number of employees paying Social Security taxes will increase by only 17 percent. Annual funding deficits of more than $100 billion loom ahead.

Still, as FDR predicted, no political leader dares to propose "scrapping" Social Security. Rather, proposals to solve this problem reflect conflicting views about the expansion of the federal government—and especially its efforts to promote social welfare—that began with the New Deal. No longer does the public overwhelmingly endorse federal responsibility for solving social problems as it did during the economic crisis of the 1930s. On the contrary, an increasingly intense backlash against "big government" emerged in the 1960s, ultimately finding its champion in the 1980s in Republican President Ronald Reagan, who declared, "Government is not the solution to our problems; government is the problem." Reagan's administration sought to reduce the size of government and curtail its regulatory oversight of American business. This "Reagan Revolution" appealed to those who never supported government responsibility for social welfare and to those who had lost trust in the government's ability to fulfill that role. By the 1990s, even Democratic President Bill Clinton declared an end to the era of "big government."

Support has grown for private initiatives to replace government programs, and now critics are pressing to "privatize" the Social Security system itself. They have proposed such sweeping changes as limiting benefits to contributors only and requiring contributors to invest their Social Security accounts themselves, including in the stock market. The predicted payoff would be larger earnings.

Opponents of these critics argue for reforming, not overturning, the current Social Security system. Privatization, they argue, would undermine Social Security's fundamental principle: to guarantee retirees a dependable income base. Investing retirement savings in the stock market subjects them to market volatility, which might benefit some people but could leave others with serious losses just when they were ready to retire. Privatization would also eliminate the special assistance that Social Security provides to large families, couples with one partner who has had no or limited earnings, and low-income earners.

Rather than scrap the current system, reformers propose other changes. They suggest taxing all workers for Social Security; many, especially in state and local governments, are now outside the system. Extending the age of eligibility to receive benefits, justified by the increasing life expectancy of Americans, would also bolster the Social Security funds. Another proposal would abandon the current investment strategy but have a quasi-private government entity manage the system's portfolio. Such changes would enable Social Security to continue meeting the needs of all citizens.

The current argument over Social Security echoes the disputes of the 1930s about the role and function of our government and reflects continuing differences over the degree to which the government should attempt to make American society more equitable. Finding a solution to funding Social Security in the new century will require addressing the issue of America's core values.

FDR signs the Social Security Act in 1935, establishing a program that would grow in size and importance in subsequent decades. To the left in a dark suit is Senator Robert F. Wagner; behind FDR is Secretary of Labor Frances Perkins. All three were influential in shaping an activist federal government that some Americans would later decry as unnecessary.

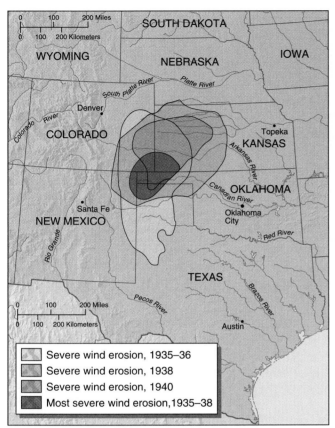

Map 27-2   The Dust Bowl
Years of overcultivation, drought, and high winds created the Dust Bowl, which most severely affected the southern Great Plains. Federal relief and conservation programs provided assistance, but many residents fled the area, often migrating to California.

In 1935, Roosevelt established the **Resettlement Administration** to focus on land reform and help poor farmers. Under Rexford Tugwell, this agency initiated soil erosion projects and attempted to resettle impoverished farmers on better land, but the problem exceeded its resources. Congress moved to save the land, if not its people, by creating the Soil Conservation Service in 1935.

Expanding Relief

If reform gained priority in the Second New Deal, relief remained critical. With millions still unemployed, Roosevelt pushed through Congress in 1935 the Emergency Relief Appropriation Act, authorizing $5 billion—at the time the largest single appropriation in history—for emergency public employment. Roosevelt created the **Works Progress Administration (WPA)** under Hopkins, who set up work relief programs to assist the unemployed and boost the economy. Before its end in 1943, the WPA gave jobs to 9 million people (more than a fifth of

the labor force) and spent nearly $12 billion. Three-fourths of its expenditures went on construction projects that could employ manual labor: the WPA built 125,000 schools, post offices, and hospitals; 8,000 parks; nearly 100,000 bridges; and enough roads and sewer systems to circle the earth thirty times. From New York City's La Guardia Airport to Atlanta's sewer system to irrigation ditches in the Far West, the WPA laid much of the nation's basic infrastructure on which it still relies.

The WPA also developed work projects for unemployed writers, artists, musicians, and actors. "Why not?" said FDR. "They are human beings. They have to live." The Federal Writers' Project put authors to work preparing state guidebooks, writing historical pamphlets, and recording the memories of ex-slaves. The Federal Art Project hired artists to teach art in night schools, prepare exhibits at museums, and paint murals on post office walls. The Federal Theatre Project organized theatrical productions and drama companies that in four years played to 30 million Americans. The Federal Music Project hired musicians to collect and perform folk songs. These WPA programs allowed people to use their talents while surviving the depression, increased popular access to cultural performances, and established a precedent for federal support of the arts. "What has happened and in such a short time is almost incredible," said one reviewer. "From a government completely apathetic to art, we suddenly have a government very art conscious."

The National Youth Administration (NYA), another WPA agency, gave part-time jobs to students, enabling 2 million high school and college students to stay in school, learn skills, and do productive work. At the University of Nebraska, NYA students built an observatory; at Duke University, law student Richard M. Nixon earned 35 cents an hour doing research in the library. Lyndon Johnson, a Texas NYA official, believed that "if the Roosevelt administration had never done another thing, it would have been justified by the work of this great institution for salvaging youth."

The Roosevelt Coalition and the Election of 1936

The 1936 election gave Americans an opportunity to judge FDR and the New Deal. Conservatives alarmed at the expansion of government, businesspeople angered by regulation and labor legislation, and well-to-do Americans furious with tax reform decried the New Deal. But they were a minority. Even the presidential candidate they supported, Republican Governor Alf Landon of Kansas, endorsed much of the New Deal, criticizing merely the inefficiency and cost of some of its programs. (Roosevelt remarked whimsically that he

On work relief with the Federal Art Project, artist Eugene Trentham painted "Baling Hay in Holt County in Early Days" on a Nebraska post office wall in 1938. Roosevelt himself appraised the work of such muralists: "Some of it good, some of it not so good, but all of it native, human, eager, and alive."

thought he could defeat himself with such a campaign.) The New Deal's earlier critics on the left had also lost most of their following. The reforms of 1935 had undercut their arguments, and the assassination of Huey Long in the same year had removed their ablest politician. They formed the Union party and nominated William Lemke for the presidency, but they were no longer a threat.

The programs and politicians of the New Deal had created an invincible coalition behind Roosevelt. Despite ambivalence about large-scale government intervention, the New Deal's agricultural programs reinforced the traditional Democratic allegiance of white Southerners while attracting many western farmers. Labor legislation clinched the active support of the nation's workers; Sidney Hillman of the Amalgamated Clothing Workers promised his union would campaign for FDR "to see to it that we hold onto the gains labor has won." Middle-class voters, whose homes had been saved and whose hopes had been raised, also joined the Roosevelt coalition.

So did urban ethnic groups, who had benefited from welfare programs and appreciated the unprecedented recognition Roosevelt's administration gave them. FDR named the first Italian American to the federal judiciary, for example, and appointed five times as many Catholics and Jews to government positions as the three Republican presidents had during the 1920s (prompting anti-Semitic critics to speak of the "Jew Deal"). African Americans voted overwhelmingly Democratic for the first time. Women, too, were an important part of the Roosevelt coalition, and Eleanor often attracted their support as much as

Franklin did. As one campaigner said to a roaring crowd in 1936, "Many women in this country when they vote for Franklin D. Roosevelt will also be thinking with a choke in the throat of Eleanor Roosevelt!"

This political realignment produced a landslide. Roosevelt polled 61 percent of the popular vote and the largest electoral vote margin ever recorded, 523 to 8. Landon even lost Kansas, his own state, and Lemke received fewer than 900,000 votes. Democrats also won huge majorities in Congress. Roosevelt's political coalition reflected a mandate for himself and the New Deal; it would enable the Democrats to dominate national elections for three decades.

The New Deal and American Life

The landslide of 1936 reflected the impact the New Deal had on Americans. Industrial workers mobilized to secure their rights, women and minorities gained increased, if still limited, opportunities to participate in American society, and Southerners and Westerners benefited from government programs they turned to their own advantage. Government programs changed daily life, and ordinary people often helped shape the new policies.

Labor on the March
The labor revival in the 1930s reflected both workers' determination and government support. Workers wanted not merely to improve their wages and benefits

but also to gain union recognition and union contracts to limit arbitrary managerial authority and achieve some control over the workplace. This larger goal provoked opposition from employers and their allies and required workers to organize, strike, and become politically active. Their achievement was remarkable.

The Second New Deal helped. By guaranteeing labor's rights to organize and bargain collectively, the Wagner Act sparked a wave of labor activism. But if the government ultimately protected union rights, the unions themselves had to form locals, recruit members, and demonstrate influence in the workplace.

At first, those tasks overwhelmed the American Federation of Labor (AFL). Its reliance on craft-based unions and reluctance to organize immigrant, black, and women workers left it unprepared for the rush of industrial workers seeking unionization. More progressive labor leaders saw that industrywide unions were more appropriate for unskilled workers in mass-production industries. Forming the Committee for Industrial Organization (CIO) within the AFL, they campaigned to unionize workers in the steel, auto, and rubber industries, all notoriously hostile to unions. AFL leaders insisted that the CIO disband and then in 1937 expelled its unions. The militants reorganized as the separate **Congress of Industrial Organizations**. (In 1955, the two groups merged as the AFL-CIO.)

The split roused the AFL to increase its own organizing activities, but it was primarily the new CIO that put labor on the march. It inspired workers previously neglected. The CIO's interracial union campaign in the Birmingham steel mills, said one organizer, was "like a second coming of Christ" for black workers, who welcomed the union as a chance for social recognition as well as economic opportunity. The CIO also employed new and aggressive tactics, particularly the sit-down strike, in which workers, rather than picketing outside the factory, simply sat inside the plant, thereby blocking both production and the use of strikebreakers. Conservatives were outraged, but Upton Sinclair said, "For seventy-five years big business has been sitting down on the American people, and now I am delighted to see the process reversed."

The CIO won major victories, despite bitter opposition from industry and its allies. The issue was not wages but labor's right to organize and bargain with management. Sit-down strikes paralyzed General Motors in 1937 after it refused to recognize the United Auto Workers. GM tried to force the strikers out of its Flint, Michigan, plants by turning off the heat, using police and tear gas, threatening strikers' families, and securing court orders to clear the plant by military force. But the governor refused to order National Guardsmen to attack, and the strikers held out, aided by the Women's Emergency Brigade, working-class women who picketed the building, heckled the police, and smuggled food to the strikers. After six weeks, GM signed a contract with the UAW. Chrysler soon followed suit. Ford refused to recognize the union until 1941, often violently disrupting organizing efforts.

Steel companies also used violence against unionization. In the **Memorial Day Massacre** in Chicago in 1937, police guarding a plant of the Republic Steel Company fired on strikers and their families, killing ten people as they tried to flee. Scores more were wounded and beaten in a police frenzy so violent that theaters refused to show a newsreel of the event. A Senate investigation found that Republic and other companies had hired private police to attack workers seeking to unionize, stockpiled weapons and tear gas, and corrupted authorities. The investigators concluded that "private corporations dominate their employees, deny them their constitutional rights, promote disorder and disharmony, and even set at naught the powers of the government itself." Federal court orders finally forced the companies to bargain collectively.

New Deal labor legislation, government investigations and court orders, and the federal refusal to use force against strikes helped the labor movement secure basic rights for American workers. Union membership leaped from under 3 million in 1932 to 9 million by 1939, and workers won higher wages, better working conditions, and more economic democracy.

Black and white laundry workers on strike in 1937. The new labor militancy helped organize workers previously neglected by unions and sometimes led to a sense of solidarity as well as better wages and working conditions.

Women and the New Deal

As federal programs proliferated in 1933, a Baltimore women's group urged the administration to "come out for a square and new deal for women." Although women did gain increased attention and influence, government and society remained largely bound by traditional values.

New Deal relief programs had a mixed impact on workingwomen. Formal government policy required "equal consideration" for women and men, but local officials so flouted this requirement that Eleanor Roosevelt urged Harry Hopkins to "impress on state administrators that the women's programs are as important as the men's. They are so apt to forget us!" Women on relief were restricted to "women's work"—more than half worked on sewing projects, regardless of their skills—and were paid scarcely half what men received. WPA training programs also reinforced traditional ideas about women's work; black women, for example, were trained to be maids, dishwashers, and cooks. Although women constituted nearly a fourth of the labor force, they obtained only 19 percent of the jobs created by the WPA, 12 percent by the FERA, and 7 percent by the CWA. The CCC excluded women altogether. Still, relief agencies provided crucial assistance to women in the depression.

Other New Deal programs also had mixed benefits for women. Despite demands by the League of Women Voters and the Women's Trade Union League for "equal pay for equal work and equal opportunity for equal ability regardless of sex," many NRA codes mandated lower wage scales for women than for men, which officials justified as reflecting "long-established customs." But by raising minimum wages, the NRA brought relatively greater improvements to women, who were concentrated in the lowest-paid occupations, than to male workers. The Social Security Act did not cover domestic servants, waitresses, and women who worked in the home but did help mothers with dependent children.

Women also gained political influence under the New Deal, although Molly Dewson, the director of the Women's Division of the Democratic party, exaggerated when she exclaimed, "The change from women's status in government before Roosevelt is unbelievable." Dewson herself exercised considerable political power and helped shape the party's campaigns. Around Dewson revolved a network of women, linked by friendships and experiences in the National Consumers' League, Women's Trade Union League, and other progressive reform organizations. Appointed to many positions in the Roosevelt administration, they helped develop and implement New Deal social legislation. Secretary of Labor Frances Perkins was the first woman cabinet member and a key member of the network; other women were in the Treasury Department, the Children's Bureau, and relief and cultural programs.

Eleanor Roosevelt was their leader. Described by a Washington reporter as "a cabinet member without portfolio," she roared across the social and political landscape of the 1930s, pushing for women's rights, demanding reforms, traveling across the country, writing newspaper columns and speaking over the radio, developing plans to help unemployed miners in West Virginia and abolish slums in Washington, and lobbying both Congress and her husband. FDR used her as his eyes and ears and sometimes his conscience. He rebuffed her critics with a jaunty, "Well, that is my wife; I can't do anything about her." Indeed, Eleanor Roosevelt had become not merely the most prominent first lady in history but a force in her own right and a symbol of the growing importance of women in public life.

Eleanor Roosevelt campaigns with FDR in Fremont, Nebraska, in 1935. A visible activist for social and economic reform, she was also politically important in building the powerful Roosevelt coalition. "Previously," said journalist Ruby Black, "a President's wife acted as if she didn't know that a political party existed."

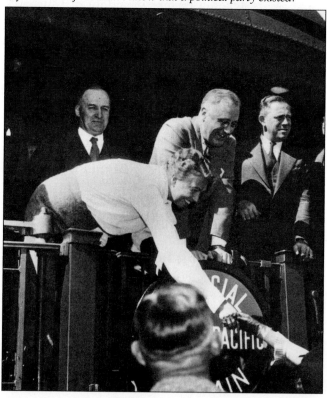

Minorities and the New Deal

Despite the move of African Americans into the Democratic party, the New Deal's record on racial issues was limited. Although Roosevelt deplored racial abuses, he never pushed for civil rights legislation, fearing to antagonize the influential Southern Democrats in Congress whose support he needed. For similar reasons, many New Deal programs discriminated against African Americans. The CCC segregated black workers; NRA codes so often specified lower wages and benefits for black workers relative to white workers or even excluded black workers from jobs that the black press claimed NRA stood for "Negro Run Around" or "Negroes Ruined Again." And racist officials discriminated in allocating federal relief. Atlanta, for instance, provided average monthly relief checks of $32.66 to white people but only $19.29 to black people.

However, disproportionately poor and unemployed, African Americans did benefit from the New Deal's welfare and economic programs. W. E. B. Du Bois asserted that "large numbers of colored people in the United States would have starved to death if it had not been for the Roosevelt policies." And key New Dealers campaigned against racial discrimination. Eleanor Roosevelt prodded FDR to appoint black officials, wrote articles supporting racial equality, and flouted segregationist laws. Attacked by white racists, she was popular in the black community. Harry Hopkins and Harold Ickes also promoted equal rights. Ickes, a former president of Chicago's NAACP chapter, insisted that African Americans receive PWA relief jobs in proportion to their share of the population and ended segregation in the Department of the Interior, prompting other cabinet secretaries to follow suit. As black votes in northern cities became important, more pragmatic New Dealers also began to pay more attention to black needs.

African Americans themselves pressed for reforms. Civil rights groups protested discriminatory policies, including the unequal wage scales in the NRA codes and the CCC's limited enrollment of black youth. African Americans demonstrated against racial discrimination in hiring and their exclusion from federally financed construction projects.

In response, FDR took more interest in black economic and social problems. He prohibited discrimination in the WPA in 1935, and the NYA adopted enlightened racial policies. Roosevelt also appointed black people to important positions, including the first black federal judge. Many of these officials began meeting regularly at the home of Mary McLeod Bethune of the National Council of Negro Women. Dubbed the Black Cabinet, they worked with civil rights organizations, fought dis-crimination in government, influenced patronage, and stimulated black interest in politics.

The New Deal improved economic and social conditions for many African Americans. Black illiteracy dropped because of federal education projects, and the number of black college students and graduates more than doubled, in part because the NYA provided student aid to black colleges. New Deal relief and public health programs reduced black infant mortality rates and raised life expectancy rates. Conditions for black people continued to lag behind those for white people, and discrimination persisted, but the black switch to the Roosevelt coalition reflected the New Deal's benefits.

Native Americans also benefited from the New Deal. The depression had imposed further misery on a group already suffering from poverty, wretched health conditions, and the nation's lowest educational level. Many New Deal programs had limited applicability to Indians, but the CCC appealed to their interests and skills. More than eighty thousand Indians received training in agriculture, forestry, and animal husbandry, along with basic academic subjects. CCC projects, together with those undertaken by the PWA and the WPA, built schools, hospitals, roads, and irrigation systems on reservations.

New Deal officials also refocused government Indian policy, which had undermined tribal authority and promoted assimilation by reducing Indian landholding and attacking Indian culture. Protests had been ignored. Appointed commissioner of Indian affairs in 1933, John Collier prohibited interference with Indian religious or cultural life, directed the Bureau of Indian Affairs to employ more Indians, and prevented Indian schools from suppressing native languages and traditions.

Collier also persuaded Congress to pass the **Indian Reorganization Act** of 1934, often called the Indians' New Deal. The act guaranteed religious freedom, reestablished tribal self-government, and halted the sale of tribal lands. It also provided funds to expand Indian landholdings, support Indian students, and establish tribal businesses. But social and economic problems persisted on the isolated reservations, and white missionaries and business interests attacked Collier's reforms as atheistic and communistic.

Hispanic Americans received less assistance from the New Deal. Its relief programs aided many Hispanics in California and the Southwest but ignored those who were not citizens. Moreover, local administrators often discriminated against Hispanics, especially by providing higher relief payments to Anglos. Finally, by excluding agricultural workers, neither the Social Security Act nor the Wagner Act gave Mexican Americans much protection or hope. Farm workers remained largely unorganized, exploited, and at the mercy of agribusinesses.

The New Deal for the South and West

The New Deal ironically offered special benefits to the South, traditionally averse to government activism, and to the West, which considered itself the land of rugged individualism.

The New Deal's agricultural program boosted farm prices and income more in the South than any other region. By controlling cotton production, it also promoted diversification; its subsidies financed mechanization. The resulting modernization helped replace an archaic sharecropping system with an emergent agribusiness. The rural poor were displaced, but the South's agricultural economy advanced.

The New Deal also improved southern cities. FERA and WPA built urban sewer systems, airports, bridges, roads, and harbor facilities. Whereas northern cities had already constructed such facilities themselves—and were still paying off their debts—the federal government largely paid for such modernization in the South, giving its cities an economic advantage.

Federal grants were supposed to be awarded to states in proportion to their own expenditures, but while southern politicians welcomed New Deal funds—"I'm gonna grab all I can for the state of Texas," said Governor Lee O'Daniel—they refused to contribute their share of the costs. Nationally, the federal proportion of FERA expenditures was 62 percent; in the South, it was usually 90 percent and never lower than 73 percent. Virginia officials refused to provide even 10 percent, declaring, "It takes people a long time to starve." Some southern cities and counties refused to contribute anything to relief, and Memphis spent less on relief—only 0.1 percent of its budget—than on maintaining public golf courses.

Federal money enabled southern communities to balance their own budgets, preach fiscal orthodoxy, and maintain traditional claims of limited government. Federal officials complained of the South's "parasitic" behavior in accepting aid but not responsibility, and even Southerners acknowledged the hypocrisy of the region's invocation of state's rights. "We recognize state boundaries when called on to give," noted the *Houston Press*, "but forget them when Uncle Sam is doing the giving."

The federal government had a particularly powerful impact on the South with the **Tennessee Valley Authority (TVA)**, launched in 1933 (see Map 27-3). Coordinating activities across seven states, the TVA built dams to control floods and generate hydroelectric power, produced fertilizer, fostered agricultural

Map 27-3 The Tennessee Valley Authority
By building dams and hydroelectric power plants, the TVA controlled flooding and soil erosion and generated electricity that did much to modernize a large region of the Upper South.

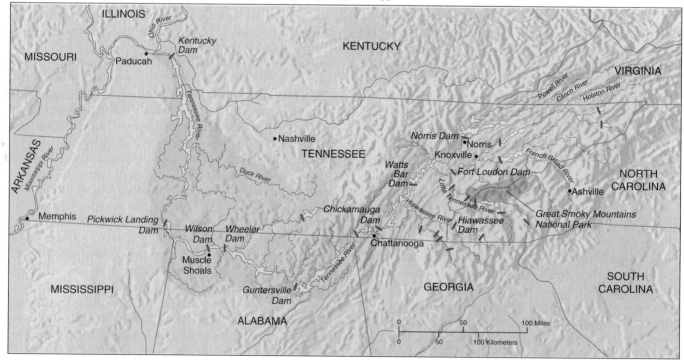

and forestry development, encouraged conservation, improved navigation, and modernized school and health systems. Private utility companies denounced the TVA as socialistic, but most Southerners supported it. Its major drawback was environmental damage that only became apparent later. Over a vast area of the South, it provided electricity for the first time.

The New Deal further expanded access to electricity by establishing the **Rural Electrification Administration (REA)** in 1935. Private companies had refused to extend power lines into the countryside because it was not profitable, consigning 90 percent of the nation's farms to drudgery and darkness. The REA revolutionized farm life by sponsoring rural nonprofit electric cooperatives. By 1941, 35 percent of American farms had electricity; by 1950, 78 percent. By providing electric power to light and heat homes and barns, pump water, and run refrigerators, washing machines, and radios, one Arkansas newspaper concluded, the REA had made "a reality" of what had been only a "utopian dream."

The New Deal also changed the West. Westerners received the most federal money per capita in welfare, relief projects, and loans. Like Southerners, they accepted federal aid and clamored for more. Utah, which received the most federal relief funds per capita, was the nation's "prize 'gimme state,'" said one FERA official. Western farmers and cattle raisers were saved by federal payments, and even refugees from the Dust Bowl depended on relief assistance and medical care in federal camps.

The Bureau of Reclamation, established in 1902, emerged as one of the most important government agencies in the West. It built huge dams to control the western river systems and promote large-scale development. The Hoover Dam on the Colorado River between Nevada and Arizona, completed in 1935; the Grand Coulee Dam on the Columbia River in Washington, finished in 1941; and other giant projects prevented flooding, produced cheap hydroelectric power, and created reservoirs and canal systems to bring water to farms and cities. By furnishing capital and expertise, the government subsidized and stimulated western economic development, particularly the growth of agribusiness.

Westerners welcomed such assistance but rarely shared the federal goals of rational resource management. Instead they often wanted to continue to exploit the land and resented federal supervision as colonial control. In practice, however, the government worked in partnership with the West's agribusinesses and timber and petroleum industries.

The New Deal and Public Activism

Despite Hoover's fear that government responsibility would discourage local initiative, the 1930s witnessed an upsurge in such activism. New Deal programs, in fact, often encouraged or empowered groups to shape public policy and social and economic behavior. Moreover, because the administration worried about centralization, some federal agencies fostered what New Dealers called "grassroots democracy." The AAA set up committees totaling more than 100,000 people to implement agricultural policy and held referendums on crop controls; local advisory committees guided the various federal arts projects; federal management of the West's public grasslands mandated cooperation with associations of livestock raisers.

At times, local administration of national programs enabled groups to exploit federal policy for their own advantage. Wealthy planters shaped AAA practices at the expense of poor tenant farmers; local control of TVA projects excluded black people. But federal programs often allowed previously unrepresented groups to contest traditionally dominant interests. By requiring that public housing projects be initiated locally, for example, New Deal programs prompted labor unions, religious and civic groups, neighborhood associations, and civil rights groups to form associations to overcome the hostility of realty agents and bankers to public housing. Often seeing greater opportunities for participation and influence in federal programs than in city and state governments, such community groups campaigned to expand federal authority. In short, depression conditions and New Deal programs actually increased citizen involvement in public affairs.

Ebbing of the New Deal

After his victory in 1936, Roosevelt committed himself to further reforms. "I see one-third of a nation ill-housed, ill-clad, ill-nourished," he declared in his second inaugural address. "The test of our progress is not whether we add more to the abundance of those who have much; it is whether we provide enough for those who have too little." But determined opponents, continuing economic problems, and the president's own misjudgments blocked his reforms and deadlocked the New Deal.

Challenging the Court

Roosevelt regarded the Supreme Court as his most dangerous opponent. During his first term, it had declared unconstitutional several important measures. FDR complained that the justices held "horse-and-buggy" ideas about government that prevented the president and Congress from responding to changes. Indeed, most of the justices were elderly conservatives appointed by Republicans and unsympathetic to an activist federal government. It seemed that the court would also strike down the Second New Deal.

Emboldened by the 1936 landslide, Roosevelt decided to restructure the federal judiciary. In early 1937, he proposed legislation authorizing the president to name a new judge for each one serving past the age of 70. Additional judges, he said, would increase judicial efficiency. But his real goal was to appoint new judges more sympathetic to the New Deal.

His court plan led to a divisive struggle. The proposal was perfectly legal: Congress had the authority, which it had used repeatedly, to change the number of judges on the Court. But Republicans and conservative Democrats attacked the plan as a scheme to "pack" the Court and subvert the separation of powers among the three branches of government. Some conservatives called the president a "dictator," but even many liberals expressed reservations about the plan or FDR's lack of candor in proposing it.

The Court itself undercut support for FDR's proposal by upholding the Social Security and Wagner Acts and minimum wage legislation. Moreover, the retirement of a conservative justice allowed Roosevelt to name a sympathetic successor. Congress rejected Roosevelt's plan.

Roosevelt's challenge to the Court hurt the New Deal. It worried the public, split the Democratic party, and revived conservatives. Opponents promptly attacked other New Deal policies, from support for unions to progressive taxation. Henceforth, a conservative coalition of Republicans and Southern Democrats in Congress blocked FDR's reforms.

More Hard Times

A sharp recession beginning in August 1937 added to Roosevelt's problems. The New Deal's deficit spending had reflected his desire to alleviate suffering, not a conviction that it would stimulate economic recovery. As the economy improved in 1936, Roosevelt decided to cut federal expenditures and balance the budget. But private investment and employment remained stagnant, and the economy plunged. A record decline in industrial production canceled the gains of the previous two years, and unemployment leaped from 7 million to 11 million within a few months. Republicans delighted in attacking the "Roosevelt recession," although it stemmed from retrenchment policies they themselves advocated.

In 1938, Roosevelt reluctantly increased spending. His decision was based on the principles of British economist John Maynard Keynes. As Marriner Eccles of the Federal Reserve Board explained, the federal government had to serve as the "compensatory agent" in the economy: It should use deficit spending to increase demand and production when private investment declined and raise taxes to pay its debt and cool the economy when business activity became excessive. New appropriations for the PWA and other government programs revived the faltering economy, but neither FDR nor Congress would spend what was necessary to end the depression. Only the vast expenditures for World War II would bring full recovery.

Political Stalemate

The recession interrupted the momentum of the New Deal and strengthened its opponents. In late 1937, their leaders in Congress issued a "conservative manifesto" decrying New Deal fiscal, labor, and regulatory policies. Holding seniority in a Congress malapportioned in their favor, they blocked most of Roosevelt's reforms. None of his "must" legislation passed a special session of Congress in December. In 1938, Congress rejected tax reforms and reduced corporate taxes.

The few measures that passed were heavily amended. The Fair Labor Standards Act established maximum hours and minimum wages for workers but authorized so many exemptions that one New Dealer asked "whether anyone is subject to this bill." The Farm Tenancy Act established the Farm Security Administration to lend money to tenant farmers and agricultural laborers to acquire their own land, but appropriations were so limited that centuries would have been required to meet the need. The National Housing Act created the United States Housing Authority to finance slum clearance and public housing projects, but its total funds were less than what was needed to demolish tenements in New York City alone.

To protect the New Deal, Roosevelt turned again to the public, with whom he remained immensely popular. In the 1938 Democratic primaries, he campaigned against the New Deal's conservative opponents. But FDR could not transfer his personal popularity to the political newcomers he supported. What his foes attacked as a "purge" failed. Roosevelt lost further political leverage when the Republicans gained seventy-five seats in the House and seven in the Senate and thirteen governorships.

The 1938 elections did not repudiate the New Deal, for the Democrats retained majorities in both houses of Congress. But the Republican revival and the survival of the conservative Southern Democrats guaranteed that the New Deal had gone as far as it ever would. With Roosevelt in the White House and his opponents controlling Congress, the New Deal ended in political stalemate.

Conclusion

The Great Depression and the New Deal mark a major divide in American history. The depression cast doubt on the traditional practices, policies, and attitudes that underlay not only the nation's economy but its social and political institutions and relationships as well. The New Deal failed to restore prosperity, but it did bring partial economic recovery. Moreover, its economic policies, from banking and securities regulation to unemployment compensation, farm price supports, and minimum wages, created barriers against another depression. The gradual adoption of compensatory spending policies also expanded the government's role in the economy. Responding to the failures of both private organizations and state and local governments, the federal government also assumed the obligation to provide social welfare. The New Deal established pensions for the elderly, aid for dependent mothers and children and the blind, public housing for the poor, and public health services. Although such programs were limited in scope and access, they helped establish a responsible government. "Better the occasional faults of a Government that lives in a spirit of charity," Roosevelt warned, "than the constant omission of a Government frozen in the ice of its own indifference."

Roosevelt also expanded the role of the presidency. As his White House took the initiative for defining public policy, drafting legislation, lobbying Congress, and communicating with the nation, it became the model for all subsequent presidents. Not only was the president's power increased, but Roosevelt made the federal government, rather than state or local governments, the focus of public interest and expectations. Under Hoover, one secretary had handled all the White House mail; under FDR, a staff of fifty was overwhelmed.

Roosevelt and the New Deal also revitalized the Democratic party, drawing minorities, industrial workers, and previously uninvolved citizens into a coalition with white Southerners. The tensions in such a coalition sometimes prevented effective public policies, but the coalition made the Democrats the dominant national party.

Political constraints explained some of the New Deal's failures. Conservative southern Democrats and northern Republicans limited its efforts to curtail racial discrimination or protect the rural and urban poor. But Roosevelt and other New Dealers were often constrained by their own vision, refusing to consider the massive deficit spending necessary to end the depression or not recognizing the need to end gender discrimination. But if the New Deal did not bring the revolution its conservative critics claimed—it did not redistribute wealth or income—it did change American life. By 1939, as international relations deteriorated, FDR was already considering a shift, as he later said, from Dr. New Deal to Dr. Win-the-War.

Review Questions

1. Why did President Hoover's emphasis on voluntarism fail to resolve the problems of the Great Depression?

2. Describe the relief programs of the New Deal. What were they designed to accomplish? What were their achievements and their limitations?

3. What were the major criticisms of the early New Deal? How accurate were those charges?

4. How did the policies of the New Deal shape the constituency and the prospects of the Democratic party in the 1930s?

5. Describe the conflict between management and labor in the 1930s. What were the major issues and motivations involved? How did the two sides differ in resources and tactics, and how and why did these factors change over time?

6. How did the role of the federal government change in the 1930s? What factors were responsible for those changes?

Recommended Reading

Paul Conkin, *The New Deal*, 3rd ed. (1992). A brief and insightful critique of FDR's programs.

Steve Fraser and Gary Gerstle, eds., *The Rise and Fall of the New Deal Order, 1930–1980* (1989). A valuable collection of essays that surveys the New Deal and explores its legacy.

Frank Freidel, *Franklin D. Roosevelt: A Rendezvous with Destiny* (1990). The best one-volume biography of FDR.

David Kennedy, *Freedom from Fear: The American People in Depression and War* (1999). The most recent and comprehensive survey of the period.

William Leuchtenburg, *Franklin D. Roosevelt and the New Deal, 1932–1940* (1963). The best single-volume study of FDR's policies during his first two terms as president.

Harvard Sitkoff, ed., *Fifty Years Later: The New Deal Evaluated* (1985). The New Deal analyzed in an excellent selection of essays.

John Steinbeck, *The Grapes of Wrath* (1939). The classic novel of Dust Bowl migrants; still makes gripping reading.

Additional Sources

Hard Times in Hooverville

Michael Bernstein, *The Great Depression* (1987).

Julia Kirk Blackwelder, *Women of the Depression: Caste and Culture in San Antonio* (1984).

William H. Chafe, *The American Woman, 1920–1970* (1972).

John Kenneth Galbraith, *The Great Crash: 1929* (1989).

John Garraty, *The Great Depression* (1986).

Robin D. G. Kelley, *Hammer and Hoe: Alabama Communists during the Great Depression* (1990).

Robert McElvaine, *The Great Depression: America, 1929–1941* (1984).

William Mullins, *The Depression and the Urban West Coast, 1929–1933* (1991).

Mark Reisler, *By the Sweat of Their Brow: Mexican Immigrant Labor in the United States* (1976).

Lois Scharf, *To Work and to Wed: Female Employment, Feminism, and the Great Depression* (1980).

John Shover, *Cornbelt Rebellion: The Farmers' Holiday Association* (1965).

Herbert Hoover and the Depression

David Burner, *Herbert Hoover: A Public Life* (1979).

Roger Daniels, *The Bonus March* (1971).

Martin L. Fausold, *The Presidency of Herbert C. Hoover* (1985).

David E. Hamilton, *From New Day to New Deal: American Farm Policy from Hoover to Roosevelt* (1991).

Donald Lisio, *The President and Protest* (1974).

Albert Romasco, *The Poverty of Abundance: Hoover, the Nation, the Depression* (1965).

Jordan A. Schwartz, *Interregnum of Despair* (1970).

Joan Hoff Wilson, *Herbert Hoover: Forgotten Progressive* (1975).

Launching the New Deal

Anthony J. Badger, *The New Deal: The Depression Years, 1933–1940* (1989).

Irving Bernstein, *Turbulent Years: A History of the American Worker, 1933–1941* (1970).

Edward C. Blackorby, *Prairie Rebel: William Lemke* (1963).

Alan Brinkley, *Voices of Protest: Huey Long, Father Coughlin, and the Great Depression* (1982).

David Conrad, *The Forgotten Farmers: The Story of the Sharecroppers in the New Deal* (1965).

Donald H. Grubbs, *Cry from the Cotton: The Southern Tenant Farmers Union and the New Deal* (1971).

Ellis Hawley, *The New Deal and the Problem of Monopoly* (1966).

William Leuchtenburg, *The FDR Years* (1995).

Leo P. Ribuffo, *The Old Christian Right: The Protestant Far Right from the Great Depression to the Cold War* (1983).

Albert Romasco, *The Politics of Recovery: Roosevelt's New Deal* (1983).

Theodore Saloutos, *The American Farmer and the New Deal* (1982).

Arthur M. Schlesinger, Jr., *The Coming of the New Deal* (1958).

T. Harry Williams, *Huey Long* (1969).

Consolidating the New Deal

John Allswang, *The New Deal and American Politics* (1978).

Kristi Andersen, *The Creation of a Democratic Majority* (1979).

Edward D. Berkowitz, *America's Welfare State* (1991).

Roger Biles, *A New Deal for the American People* (1991).

Gerald Gamm, *The Making of New Deal Democrats* (1989).

Colin Gordon, *New Deals: Business, Labor, and Politics in America* (1994).

Donald R. McCoy, *Landon of Kansas* (1966).

George McJimsey, *Harry Hopkins* (1987).

The New Deal and American Life

Jo Ann E. Argersinger, *Toward a New Deal in Baltimore: People and Government in the Great Depression* (1988).

Joseph L. Arnold, *The New Deal in the Suburbs* (1971).

John Barnard, *Walter Reuther and the Rise of the Auto Workers* (1983).

Roger Biles, *The South and the New Deal* (1994).

Lisabeth Cohen, *Making a New Deal: Industrial Workers in Chicago* (1990).

Elizabeth Faue, *Community of Suffering and Struggle: Women, Men, and the Labor Movement in Minneapolis* (1991).

Sidney Fine, *Sitdown: The General Motors Strike of 1936–1937* (1969).

Steven Fraser, *Labor Will Rule: Sidney Hillman and the Rise of American Labor* (1991).

James Gregory, *American Exodus: The Dust Bowl Migration and Okie Culture in California* (1989).

Laurence C. Kelly, *The Assault on Assimilation: John Collier and the Origins of Indian Policy Reform* (1983).

Nelson Lichtenstein, *The Most Dangerous Man in Detroit: Walter Reuther and the Fate of American Labor* (1995).

Richard Lowitt, *The New Deal and the West* (1984).

Bruce Nelson, *Workers on the Waterfront* (1988).

Harvard Sitkoff, *A New Deal for Blacks* (1978).

Douglas L. Smith, *The New Deal in the Urban South* (1988).

Catherine Stock, *Main Street in Crisis: The Great Depression and the Old Middle Class on the Northern Plains* (1992).

Graham Taylor, *The New Deal and American Indian Tribalism* (1980).

Susan Ware, *Beyond Suffrage: Women in the New Deal* (1981).

Susan Ware, *Holding Their Own: American Women in the 1930s* (1982).

Donald Worster, *Dust Bowl* (1979).

Donald Worster, *Rivers of Empire* (1985).

Robert Zieger, *The CIO, 1935–1955* (1995).

Robert Zieger, *John L. Lewis* (1988).

Ebbing of the New Deal

Alan Brinkley, *The End of Reform: New Deal Liberalism in Recession and War* (1995).

Melvyn Dubofsky, *The State and Labor in Modern America* (1994).

Mark Leff, *The Limits of Symbolic Reform: The New Deal and Taxation* (1984).

James T. Patterson, *Congressional Conservatism and the New Deal* (1967).

James T. Patterson, *The New Deal and the States* (1969).

Charles H. Trout, *Boston, the Great Depression, and the New Deal* (1977).

Where to Learn More

❖ **Center for New Deal Studies, Roosevelt University, Chicago, Illinois.**   The center contains political memorabilia, photographs, papers, and taped interviews dealing with Franklin D. Roosevelt and the New Deal; it also sponsors an annual lecture series about the Roosevelt legacy.

❖ **Herbert Hoover National Historic Site, West Branch, Iowa.**   This 186-acre site contains the birthplace cottage and grave of Herbert Hoover as well as his presidential library and museum, which contains a reconstruction of Hoover's White House office.

❖ **Labor Museum and Learning Center of Michigan, Flint, Michigan.**   Exhibits trace the history of the labor movement, including the dramatic "Sit-Down Strike" of 1936–1937.

❖ **Franklin D. Roosevelt Home and Presidential Library, Hyde Park, New York.**   The Roosevelt home, furnished with family heirlooms, and the spacious grounds, where FDR is buried, personalize the president and provide insights into his career. The nearby library has displays and exhibitions about Roosevelt's presidency, and the Eleanor Roosevelt Wing is dedicated to the career of ER.

❖ **Eleanor Roosevelt National Historic Site, Hyde Park, New York.**   These two cottages, where Eleanor Roosevelt worked and, after 1945, lived, contain her furniture and memorabilia. Visitors can also watch a film biography of ER and tour the grounds of this retreat where she entertained personal friends and world leaders.

❖ **Civilian Conservation Corps Interpretive Center, Whidbey Island, Washington.**   This stone and wood structure, built as a CCC project, now houses exhibits and artifacts illustrating the history of the CCC.

❖ **Bethune Museum and Archives National Historic Site, Washington, D.C.**   This four-story townhouse was the home of Mary McLeod Bethune, a friend of Eleanor Roosevelt and the director of the New Deal's Division of Negro Affairs, and the headquarters of the National Council of Negro Women, which Bethune founded in 1935. Exhibits feature the contributions of black activist women and activities of the civil rights movement.

WORLD WAR II,
1939–1945

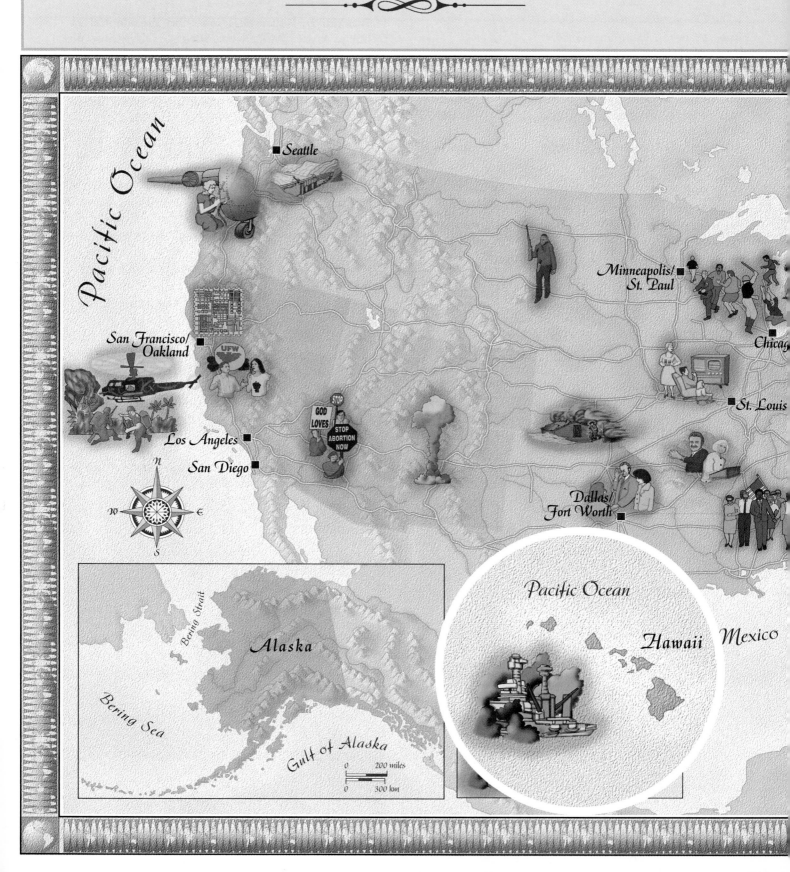

Pacific Ocean

Seattle

Minneapolis/
St. Paul

Chicago

San Francisco/
Oakland

St. Louis

Los Angeles

San Diego

Dallas/
Fort Worth

N
W   E
S

Bering Strait

Alaska

Mexico

Bering Sea

Pacific Ocean

Hawaii

Gulf of Alaska

0   200 miles

0   300 km

Atlantic Ocean

ERA NOW

Boston

troit Cleveland

New York

Philadelphia

Baltimore

Washington, D.C.

Atlanta

Tampa/
Petersburg

Miami

Population Increase, by State 1950–1980

200–400%

100–200%

50–100%

0–50%

Loss

■ *Metropolitan areas with population of 2,000,000 or more in 1994*

—— *Interstate Highway System*

Caribbean Sea

400 miles

600 km

28

Chapter Outline

Key Topics

❖ The reluctance of most Americans to get involved in World War II
❖ FDR's effort to support Britain and pressure Japan despite isolationism
❖ The nation's strategy for a two-front war against Germany and Japan
❖ The social and economic transformation of the United States by the war
❖ The beginning of the Cold War and the emergence of the United States as the richest and most powerful nation in the world

$\mathcal{L}$aura and Enrico Fermi arrived in the United States in 1939 as refugees from repression in **Fascist** Italy. In 1938, Enrico had earned a Nobel Prize in physics. By 1942, he was leading the efforts to develop an atomic bomb as the United States joined the ongoing global conflict of World War II. The next year found the Fermis, together with other atomic scientists and engineers and their families, at Los Alamos, a science city built hurriedly on a high plateau in northern New Mexico, where isolation was supposed to ensure secrecy.

The instant city was a cross between an army camp and a cheap subdivision. Big shots lived on "bathtub row," the few houses with full plumbing that were left over from a former boarding school. Most families lived in apartments awash in summer dust or winter mud. Scientists spent their days designing a bomb that would change world politics and returned to dinners cooked on wood-burning stoves. Despite the hardships, Laura Fermi and other residents remembered the sense of community. "I was in Los Alamos only a year and a half," she later wrote, "and still it seems such a big portion of my life . . . it was such intense living."

The Fermis were not the only family to give Los Alamos a multinational flavor. Britons and Canadians worked alongside U.S. scientists. So did Danes and Hungarians who had fled Nazi-dominated Europe. Workers from nearby Hispanic villages and Indian pueblos stoked the furnaces and swept the floors. Absent were scientists from the Soviet Union, which was bearing the worst of the fighting against Germany but was carefully excluded from the secret of the A-bomb.

The internationalism of Los Alamos mirrored the larger war effort. Japan's attack on Hawaii in December 1941 thrust the United States into a war that spanned the globe. U.S. allies against Japan in the Pacific and East Asia included Great Britain, Australia, and China. In Europe, its allies against Nazi Germany and Fascist Italy included Great Britain, the Soviet Union, and more than twenty other nations.

The men and women racing to perfect the atomic bomb knew that victory was far from certain. The **Axis Powers**—Germany, Italy, and Japan—had piled one conquest on another since the late 1930s, and they continued to seize new territories in 1942. Allied defeat in a few key battles could have resulted in standoff or Axis victory. Not until 1944 did American economic power allow the United States and its allies to feel confident of victory. A new weapon might end the war more quickly or make the difference between victory and defeat.

The war's domestic impacts were as profound as its international consequences. It highlighted racial inequalities, gave women new opportunities, and fostered growth in the South and West. By devastating the nation's commercial rivals, compelling workers to retrain and factories to modernize, World War II left the United States dominant in the world economy. It also increased the scope of the federal government and built an alliance among the armed forces, big business, and science that helped shape postwar America.

The Dilemmas of Neutrality

Americans in the 1930s wanted no part of another overseas war. According to a Gallup poll in 1937, 70 percent thought that the United States had made a mistake to fight in 1917. Despite two years of German victories and a decade of Japanese aggression against China, opinion polls in the fall of 1941 showed that most voters still hoped to avoid war. President Roosevelt's challenge was to lead the United States toward rearmament and support for Great Britain and China without alarming a reluctant public.

The Roots of War

The countdown to World War II started in 1931 when Japan invaded and soon conquered the northern Chinese province of Manchuria. Adding Manchuria to an empire that included Korea and Taiwan emboldened Japan's military. A full-scale invasion of China followed in 1937. Japan took many of the key cities and killed tens of thousands of civilians in the "rape of Nanking," but failed to dislodge the government of Jiang Jieshi (Chiang Kai-shek) and settled into a war of attrition.

Japan was determined to dominate Asia. Internal propaganda in the 1930s stressed the need to rebuild Japan's greatness. Japanese nationalists believed that the United States, Britain, and France after World War I had treated Japan unfairly, despite its participation against Germany. They believed that Japan should expel the French, British, Dutch, and Americans from Asia and create a **Greater East Asia Co-Prosperity Sphere** commanded by Japan.

In Germany, Adolf Hitler mixed the desire to reassert national pride and power after the defeat of World War I with an ideology of racial hatred. Coming to power by constitutional means in 1933 as the head of the **Nazi** party, Hitler quickly consolidated his grip as the German Führer, or absolute leader. Proclaiming the start of a thousand-year Reich (empire), he combined the historic German interest in eastward expansion with a long tradition of racialist thought about German superiority. In the Nazi scheme, Germany and other northern European nations ranked above the Slavs of eastern Europe. Special targets of Nazi hatred were Jews, who were prominent in German business and professional life but who soon faced persecution aimed at driving them from the country.

Germany's direct challenge to Europe began in 1936, when Hitler sent troops into the Rhineland, Germany's border region with France that had been demilitarized since 1918. The Reich absorbed German-speaking Austria in 1938. Hitler's next target was a German-speaking border district of Czechoslovakia known as the Sudetenland. As this crisis simmered in September 1938, French premier Edouard Daladier and British prime minister Neville Chamberlain flew to Munich to meet with Hitler. Chamberlain, claiming to have secured "peace in our time," agreed to German annexation of the Sudetenland in return for Hitler's pledge to make no more territorial claims. Hitler tossed aside this promise when Germany occupied the rest of Czechoslovakia six months later.

Italian aggression embroiled Africa and the Mediterranean. Benito Mussolini, Italy's leader since 1922, invaded and conquered Ethiopia in 1935–1936. To extend Italian influence in the Mediterranean, he sent arms and troops to General Francisco Franco's right-wing rebels when a civil war erupted in Spain in 1936. In the three years until Franco's victory, Spain became a bloody testing ground for new German military tactics and German and Italian ambitions against democratic Europe.

Germany and Italy formed the Rome–Berlin Axis in 1936 and the **Tripartite Pact** with Japan in 1940. Political dissidents in all three nations had already been suppressed. Mussolini boasted of burying the "putrid corpse of liberty." Politicians in Japan feared assassination if they spoke against the army, and the Thought Police intimidated the public. Hitler's Germany, however, was the most repressive. The Nazi **concentration camp** was a device for political terrorism where dissidents and "antisocials" could be separated from "pure" Germans. Hitler decreed that opponents should disappear into "night and fog." By 1939, concentration camps held 25,000 people—mostly socialists, homosexuals, and beggars—who were overworked, starved, and abused.

The raspy-voiced Adolf Hitler had a remarkable ability to stir the German people. He and his inner circle made skillful use of propaganda, exploiting German resentment over the country's defeat in World War I and, with carefully staged mass rallies such as this event in 1938, inspiring an emotional conviction of national greatness.

CHRONOLOGY

1931 Japan invades Manchuria.

1933 Hitler takes power in Germany.

1934 Nye Committee opens hearings on international arms trade.

1935 Congress passes first of three Neutrality acts.

Italy invades Ethiopia.

1936 Germany and Italy form the Rome–Berlin Axis.

Civil war erupts in Spain.

1937 Japan invades China.

1938 Germany absorbs Austria.

Munich agreement promises "peace in our time."

1939 Germany and the Soviet Union sign a nonagression pact.

Germany absorbs Czechoslovakia.

Germany invades Poland; Great Britain and France declare war on Germany.

1940 Germany conquers Denmark, Norway, Belgium, the Netherlands, and France.

Japan, Germany, and Italy sign the Tripartite Pact.

The United States begins to draft men into the armed forces.

Franklin Roosevelt wins an unprecedented third term.

1941 The United States begins a lend-lease program to make military equipment available to Great Britain and later the USSR.

The Fair Employment Practices Committee is established.

Germany invades the Soviet Union.

Roosevelt and Churchill issue the Atlantic Charter.

Japan attacks U.S. military bases in Hawaii.

1942 American forces in the Philippines surrender to Japan.

President Roosevelt authorizes the removal and internment of Japanese Americans living in four western states.

Naval battles in the Coral Sea and off the island of Midway blunt Japanese expansion.

U.S. forces land in North Africa.

Soviet forces encircle a German army at Stalingrad.

The first sustained and controlled nuclear chain reaction takes place at the University of Chicago.

1943 U.S. and British forces invade Italy, which makes terms with the Allies.

Race conflict erupts in riots in Detroit, New York, and Los Angeles.

The landing of Marines on Tarawa initiates the island-hopping strategy.

U.S. war production peaks.

Roosevelt, Churchill, and Stalin confer at Tehran.

1944 Allied forces land in Normandy.

The U.S. Navy destroys Japanese sea power in the battles of the Philippine Sea and Leyte Gulf.

The Battle of the Bulge is the last tactical setback for the Allies.

1945 Roosevelt, Stalin, and Churchill meet at Yalta to plan the postwar world.

The United States takes the Pacific islands of Iwo Jima and Okinawa.

Franklin Roosevelt dies; Harry S Truman becomes president.

Germany surrenders to the United States, Great Britain, and the USSR.

The United Nations is organized at an international meeting in San Francisco.

Japan surrenders after the detonation of atomic bombs over Hiroshima and Nagasaki.

Hitler's War in Europe

After annexing Austria and Czechoslovakia through diplomatic bullying and uncontested coups, Germany invaded Poland on September 1, 1939. Britain and France, Poland's allies, declared war on Germany but did nothing to stop the German war machine. Western journalists covering the three-week conquest of Poland coined the term *Blitzkrieg*, or "lightning war," to describe the German tactics. Armored divisions with tanks and motorized infantry punched quick holes in defensive positions and raced forward thirty or forty miles per day. Dive bombers blasted defenses. Portable radios coordinated the tanks, trucks, and motorcycles. Ground forces with horse-drawn artillery and supply wagons encircled the stunned defenders.

Hitler's greatest advantage was the ability to attack when and where he chose. From September 1939 to October 1941, Germany marched from victory to victory (see Map 28-1). Striking from a central position against scattered enemies, Hitler chose the targets and timing of each new front: east to smash Poland in September 1939; north to capture Denmark and Norway in April and May 1940; west to defeat the Netherlands, Belgium, and France in May and June 1940, an attack that Italy also joined; south into the Balkans, enlisting Hungary, Romania, and Bulgaria as allies and conquering Yugoslavia and Greece in April and May 1941. He also launched the **Battle of Britain** in the second half of 1940, sending bombers in an unsuccessful effort to pound Britain into submission.

Hitler gambled once too often in June 1941. Having failed to knock Britain out of the war, he invaded the Soviet Union (officially the Union of Soviet Socialist Republics, or USSR). The attack caught the Red Army off guard. The Nazis and Soviets had signed a nonagression pact in 1939, and the USSR had helped dismember Poland. Soviet dictator

Map 28-1 *Axis Europe, 1941, on the Eve of Hitler's Invasion of the Soviet Union*
After almost two years of war, the Axis powers controlled most of Europe from the Atlantic Ocean to the Soviet border through annexation, military conquest, and alliances. Failure to force Britain to make peace caused Hitler to look eastward in 1941 to attempt the conquest of the Soviet Union.

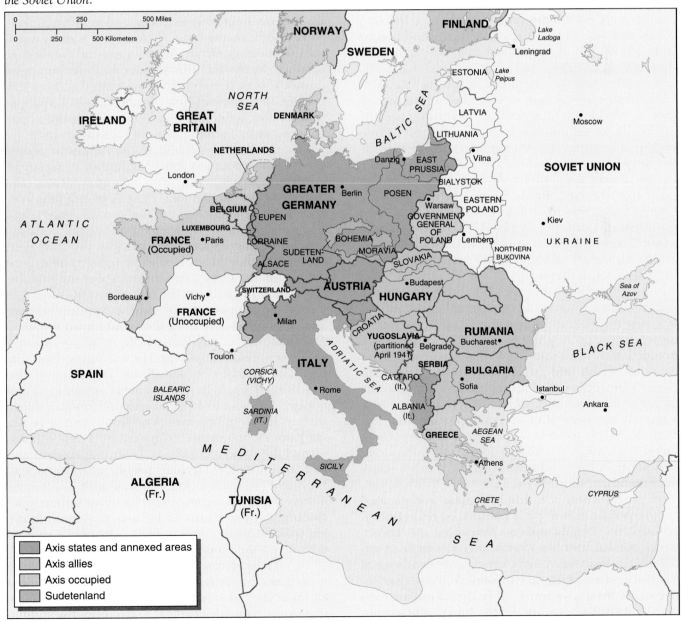

Joseph Stalin thought his border was safe. But Hitler hoped that smashing the USSR and seizing its vast resources would make Germany invincible. From June until December 1941, more than 3 million Germans, Italians, and Romanians pushed through Belorus, Ukraine, and western Russia. They encircled and captured entire Soviet armies. Before desperate Soviet counterattacks and a bitter winter stopped the German tanks, they had reached the outskirts of Moscow and expected to finish the job in the spring.

Trying to Keep Out

"We Must Keep Out!" shouted the September 7, 1939, *Chicago Daily News*. As war erupted in Europe, most Americans wanted to avoid foreign quarrels. People who opposed intervention in the European conflict were sometimes called isolationists, but they considered themselves realists. Drawing their lessons from 1914–1918, they assumed that the same situation applied in 1939.

Much of the emotional appeal of neutrality came from disillusionment with the American crusade in World War I, which had failed to make the world safe for democracy. Many opponents of intervention wanted the United States to protect its traditional spheres of interest in Latin America and the Pacific. Charles A. Lindbergh and many others argued that the best way to assure the safety of the United States was to conserve resources to defend the Western Hemisphere. Like George Washington, whose Farewell Address they quoted, they wanted to avoid becoming entangled in the perpetual quarrels of the European nations.

Congressional hearings on munitions manufacturers and financiers had strengthened antiwar leanings in 1934–1936. Senator Gerald Nye's committee investigated whether New York bankers had dragged Americans into World War I to protect their loans to Britain and France. *Fortune* magazine and *Reader's Digest* published an exposé that blamed wars on arms manufacturers. *Merchants of Death* was a bestseller on the same theme. Neutrality acts in 1935, 1936, and 1937 forbade arms sales to nations at war. Other legislation prohibited loans to nations that had not paid their debts from World War I (including France and Great Britain).

The country's ethnic variety complicated U.S. responses to European conflict. Nazi aggression ravaged the homelands of Americans of Polish, Czech, Greek, and Norwegian ancestry. In contrast, 2.7 million Irish Americans, resentful of centuries of English rule over Ireland, applauded defeats that undermined Britain's empire. More than 5 million German Americans remembered the rabid anti-German sentiment of World War I and dreaded a second fight with Germany. Many of the 4.6 million Italian Americans admired Mussolini.

Edging toward Intervention

Despite the Nazi triumphs, nonintervention had direct emotional appeal. The case for supporting beleaguered Britain and China, in contrast, rested on abstract values like the worth of free societies and free markets. Still, Roosevelt's appeals to democratic values gained support in 1939 and 1940. Nazi persecution of minorities and Japanese atrocities in China struck most Americans as worse than British or French imperialism. Radio broadcasts from England describing London under German bombing heightened the sense of imperiled freedom. The importance of open markets also bolstered interventionism. As Roosevelt pointed out, "Freedom to trade is essential to our economic life. We do not eat all the food we produce; we do not burn all the oil we can pump; we do not use all the goods we can manufacture." U.S. business leaders had little doubt that Axis victories would bring economic instability and require crushing defense budgets to protect a Fortress America.

Because 85 percent of the American people agreed that the nation should fight only if directly attacked, Roosevelt had to chip away at neutrality. The first step came in October 1939. A month-long congressional debate inspired millions of letters and telegrams in favor of keeping the arms embargo against warring nations. Nevertheless, the lawmakers reluctantly allowed arms sales to belligerent nations on a "cash-and-carry" basis. In control of the Atlantic, France and Britain were the only expected customers.

Isolationism helps explain why the United States accepted only a few thousand Jewish refugees. American law strictly limited the numbers of Europeans who could enter the United States. Unthinking anti-Semitism at the State Department also contributed to tight enforcement of immigration quotas. Bureaucrats blocked entry to "undesirables," such as left-wing opponents of Hitler, and were unsympathetic to Jewish refugees. In 1939, officials turned the passenger ship *St. Louis* away from Miami and forced its 950 German Jewish refugees back to Europe. FDR made small gestures, such as allowing fifteen thousand German and Austrian refugees, including many scientists and artists, to remain in the United States on visitor permits, but polls showed that the public supported restricted immigration.

The collapse of France in June 1940 scared Americans into rearming. A year earlier, the United States army had ranked eighteenth in the world in size—on a par with Portugal's. However, the sudden defeat of France, which had survived four years of German attacks in World War I, made the new war seem far more serious. In the summer of 1940, Congress voted to expand the army to 2 million men, build 19,000 new war planes, and add 150 ships to the navy. September brought the nation's first peacetime draft, requiring 16.5 million men between the ages of twenty-one and thirty-five to register for military service.

In the same month, the United States concluded a "destroyer deal" with Britain. The British were desperate for small, maneuverable warships to guard imports of food and war materials against German submarines. The Americans had long wanted additional air and naval bases. Roosevelt met both needs by trading fifty old destroyers for the use of bases on British territories in the Caribbean, Bermuda, and Newfoundland.

In the presidential election of 1940, however, foreign policy was secondary. Wendell Willkie, the Republican nominee, was a successful lawyer and utility executive who had fought the New Deal. He shared Roosevelt's belief in the importance of aid to Britain. The big campaign issue was therefore whether FDR's unprecedented try for a third term represented arrogance or legitimate concern for continuity in a time of peril. The voters gave Roosevelt 55 percent of their votes. The president pledged that no Americans would fight in a foreign war. But if the United States were attacked, he said privately, the war would no longer be "foreign."

The Brink of War

After the election, FDR and his advisers edged the United States toward stronger support of Britain and put pressure on Japan. In January 1941, Roosevelt proposed the "lend-lease" program, which allowed Britain to "borrow" military equipment for the duration of the war. Roosevelt compared the program to lending a garden hose to a neighbor whose house had caught fire. Senator Robert Taft of Ohio countered that it was more like lending chewing gum—you wouldn't want it back after it was used. Behind the scheme was Britain's inability to pay for American goods. "Well boys," their ambassador explained to a group of reporters, "Britain's broke."

The lend-lease proposal triggered intense political debate. The Committee to Defend America by Aiding the Allies argued the administration's position. In opposition, the **America First Committee** claimed that lend-lease would allow the president to declare anything a "defense article." Charles Lindbergh protested that the United States should not surrender weapons that it might need to defend itself. Congress finally passed the measure in March 1941, giving Great Britain an unlimited line of credit.

FDR soon began an undeclared war in the North Atlantic, instructing the navy to report sightings of German submarines to the British. In September, the U.S. destroyer *Greer* clashed with a German submarine. The encounter allowed Roosevelt to proclaim a "shoot on sight" policy for German subs and to escort British convoys to within 400 miles of Britain. In reply, German submarines torpedoed and damaged the destroyer *Kearny* on October 17 and sank the destroyer *Reuben James* with the loss of more than one hundred lives on October 30. The United States was approaching outright naval war with Germany.

The **Atlantic Charter** of August 1941 provided a political umbrella for American involvement. Meeting off Newfoundland, Roosevelt and British prime minister Winston Churchill agreed that the first priority was to defeat Germany; Japan was secondary. Echoing Woodrow Wilson, Roosevelt also insisted on a commitment to oppose territorial change by conquest, to support self-government, to promote freedom of the seas, and to create a system of economic collaboration. Churchill signed to keep Roosevelt happy, but the document papered over sharp differences in U.S. and British expectations.

Roosevelt's intent in the North Atlantic remains uncertain. Some historians think that he hoped the United States could support Britain short of war. Others believe that he accepted the inevitability of war but hesitated to outpace public opinion (the House of Representatives renewed the draft in August 1941 by just one vote). In this second interpretation, FDR wanted to eliminate Hitler without going to war if possible, with war if necessary. "I am waiting to be pushed into the situation," he told his secretary of the treasury.

That final shove came in the Pacific rather than the Atlantic. In 1940, as part of its rearmament program, the United States decided to build a "two-ocean navy." This decision antagonized Japan, prodding it into a war that most U.S. leaders hoped to postpone or avoid. Through massive investment and national sacrifice, Japan had achieved roughly 70 percent of U.S. naval strength by late 1941. However, America's buildup promised to reduce that ratio to only 30 percent by 1944. Furthermore, the United States was restricting Japan's vital imports of steel, iron ore, and aluminum. In July 1941, after Japan occupied French Indochina, Roosevelt froze Japanese assets in the United States, blocked petroleum shipments, and began to build up U.S. forces in the Philippines. The actions caused Japan's rulers to consider war against the United States while Japan still had a petroleum reserve. Both militarily and economically, it looked in Tokyo as if 1942 was their last chance for victory.

The Japanese military made its choice in September. Unless the United States and Britain ended aid to China and acquiesced in Japanese dominance of southeast Asia—impossible conditions—war preparations would be complete in October. The Japanese General Staff defined its aims as "expelling American, Dutch, and British influences from East Asia, consolidating Japan's sphere of autonomy and security, and constructing a new order in greater East Asia." War planners never seriously considered an invasion of the United States or expected a decisive victory. They hoped that attacks on American Pacific bases would shock the United States into letting Japan have its way in Asia or at least win time to create impenetrable defenses in the central Pacific.

December 7, 1941

Since 1941, Americans have questioned Roosevelt's foreign policy. If he wanted an excuse for war, was the torpedoing of the *Reuben James* not enough? If

The Japanese attack on Pearl Harbor shocked the American people. Images of burning battleships confirmed the popular image of Japan as sneaky and treacherous and stirred a desire for revenge. The attack rendered the United States incapable of resisting Japanese aggression in southeast Asia in early 1942, but it failed to achieve its goal of destroying U.S. naval power in the Pacific.

he wanted to preserve armed neutrality, why threaten Japan by moving the Pacific fleet from California to Hawaii in 1940 and sending B-17 bombers to the Philippines in 1941? It now seems that Roosevelt wanted to restrain the Japanese with bluff and intimidation so that the United States could focus on Germany. FDR also recognized the possibility of a two-front war—at least a 20 percent chance, he told military advisers in January 1941. American moves were intended to be aggressive but measured in the Atlantic, firm but defensive in the Pacific. After July, however, Washington expected a confrontation with Japan over the oil and rubber of Southeast Asia. Because the United States cracked Japanese codes, it knew by November that Japanese military action was imminent but expected the blow to come in southeast Asia.

Instead, the Japanese navy launched a surprise attack on American bases in Hawaii. The Japanese fleet sailed a four-thousand-mile loop through the empty North Pacific, avoiding merchant shipping and American patrols. Before dawn on December 7, six Japanese aircraft carriers launched 351 planes in two unopposed bombing strikes on **Pearl Harbor**.

When the smoke cleared, Americans counted their losses: eight battleships, eleven other warships, and nearly all military aircraft damaged or destroyed; and 2403 people killed. They could also count their good fortune. Dockyards, drydocks, and oil storage tanks remained intact because the Japanese admiral had refused to order a third attack. And the American carriers, at sea on patrol, were unharmed. They proved far more important than battleships.

Speaking to Congress the following day, Roosevelt proclaimed December 7, 1941, "a date which will live in infamy." He asked for—and got—a declaration of war against the Japanese. Hitler and Mussolini declared war on the United States on December 11. On January 1, 1942, the United States, Britain, the USSR, and twenty-three other nations subscribed to the principles of the Atlantic Charter and pledged not to negotiate a separate peace.

Holding the Line

When Japan was considering war with the United States and Great Britain in 1940, Admiral Isoroku Yamamoto, the chief of Japan's Combined Fleet, weighed the chances of victory: "If I am told to fight regardless of the consequences, I shall run wild for the first six months or a year, but I have utterly no confidence for the second or third year." The admiral was right. Japan's armies quickly conquered most

of southeast Asia; its navy forced the United States on the defensive in the central Pacific. As it turned out, Japan's conquests reached their limit after six months, but, in early 1942, it was far from clear that that would be so. In Europe, Allied fortunes went from bad to worse in the first half of 1942. Again, no one knew that German and Italian gains would peak at midyear. Decisive turning points did not come until November 1942, a year after the United States had entered the war.

Stopping Germany

In December 1941, the United States plunged into a truly global war that was being fought on six distinct fronts (see Map 28-2). In North Africa, the British battled Italian and German armies that were trying to seize the Suez Canal. On the **Eastern Front**, Soviet armies held defensive positions. In the North Atlantic, merchant ships dodged German submarines. In China, Japan controlled the most productive provinces but could not crush Chinese resistance, which was supported by supplies airlifted from British India. In Southeast Asia, Japanese troops attacked the Philippines, the Dutch East Indies, New Guinea, Malaya, and Burma. In the central Pacific, the Japanese fleet faced the U.S. Navy.

Despite the popular desire for revenge against Japan, the United States decided to defeat Germany first. The reasoning was simple: Germany was far stronger than Japan. Defeat of Japan would not assure the defeat of Germany, especially if it crushed the Soviet Union or starved Britain into submission. In contrast, a strategy that helped the Soviets and British survive and then destroyed German military power would doom Japan.

The strategy recognized that the Eastern Front held the key to Allied hopes. In 1941, Germany had seized control of 45 percent of the Soviet population, 47 percent of its grain production, and more than 60 percent of its coal, steel, and aluminum industries. Hitler next sought to destroy Soviet capacity to wage war. "Our aim," said Führer Directive No. 41, "is to wipe out the entire defense potential remaining to the Soviets, and to cut them off . . . from their most important centers of war industry." Hitler targeted southern Russia, an area rich in grain and oil. The German thrust was also designed to eliminate the British from the Middle East.

The scheme was easier to plot on a map than to carry out in the fields of Russia. The German offensive opened with stunning success. Every day's advance, however, stretched supply lines. Tanks ran out of fuel and spare parts. The horses that pulled German supply wagons died for lack of food.

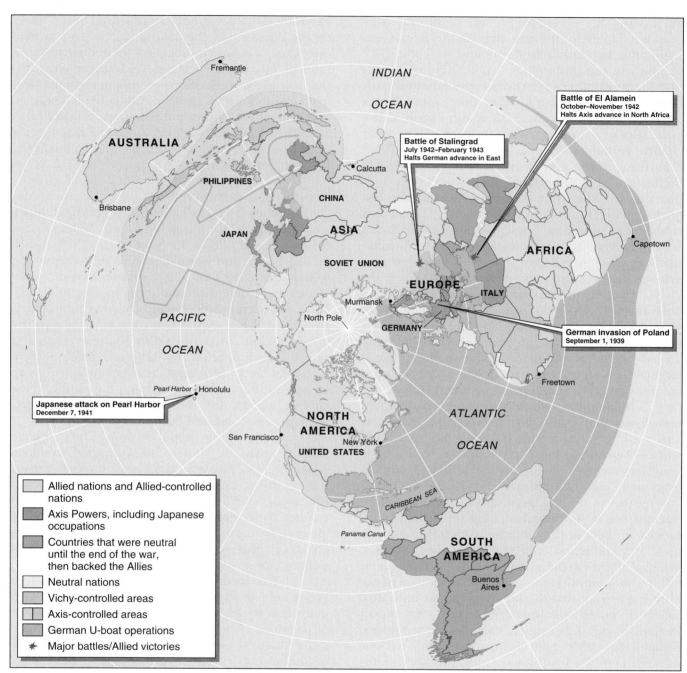

Map 28-2   A Global War

World War II was truly a global war. As this map indicates, fighting engulfed both sides of the Eurasian continent and spread deep into the Atlantic, Pacific, and Indian oceans. The United States was the only major belligerent nation that was insulated from the battle fronts by two oceans.

Disaster came at **Stalingrad** (present-day Volgograd), an industrial center on the western bank of the Volga River. The German armies had bypassed it, leaving a dangerous strongpoint on their flank that the German command decided to capture. In September and October, 1942, German, Italian, and Romanian soldiers fought their way house by house into the city. At night, the Soviets ferried their wounded across

the Volga and brought in new ammunition. For both Hitler and Stalin, the city became a test of wills that outweighed even its substantial military importance.

The Red Army delivered a counterstroke on November 18 that cut off 330,000 Axis soldiers. Airlifts kept the Germans fighting for two more months, but they surrendered in February 1943. It was the first German mass capitulation, and it came at an immense human cost to both sides. Russians call the hills around Stalingrad "white fields" because human bones still turn up after spring thaws.

The Survival of Britain

After the failure of German air attacks in 1940, the British struggled to save their empire and supply themselves with food and raw materials. In World War I, German submarines (known as U-boats, from *Unterseeboot*) had nearly isolated Great Britain. In 1940 and 1941, they tried again. From bases in France, greatly improved U-boats intercepted shipments of oil from Nigeria, beef from Argentina, minerals from Brazil, and weapons from the United States. Through the end of 1941, German "tonnage warfare" sank British, Allied, and neutral merchant vessels faster than they could be replaced.

The British fought back in what became known as the **Battle of the Atlantic**. First, they reduced their reliance on the Atlantic supply lines. Between 1939 and 1944, planning and rationing cut Britain's need for imports in half. Second, the British organized protected convoys. Merchant ships sailing alone were defenseless against submarines. Grouping the merchant ships into convoys with armed escorts "hardened" the targets and made them more difficult to find in the wide ocean. Roosevelt's destroyer deal of 1940 and U.S. naval escorts in the western Atlantic in 1941 thus contributed directly to Britain's survival.

Nevertheless, German submarines dominated the Atlantic in 1942. U-boats operated as far as the Caribbean and the Carolinas, where the dangerous Cape Hatteras forced coastal shipping out to sea. In June, U-boats sank 144 ships; drowned sailors washed up on Carolina beaches. Only the extension of the convoy system to American waters forced the subs back toward Britain. Meanwhile, allied aircraft began to track submarines with radar, spot them with searchlights as they maneuvered on the surface, and attack them with depth charges. New sonar systems allowed escort ships to measure submarines' direction, speed, and depth. By the spring of 1943, American shipyards were also launching ships faster than the Germans could sink them.

British ground fighting in 1942 centered in North Africa, where the British operated out of Egypt and the Italians and Germans from the Italian colony of Libya. By October 1942, Field Marshal Erwin Rommel's German and Italian forces were within striking distance of the Suez Canal. At **El Alamein** between October 23 and November 5, 1942, however, General Bernard Montgomery, with twice Rommel's manpower and tanks, forced the enemy to retreat and lifted the danger to the Middle East.

Retreat and Stabilization in the Pacific

Reports from east Asia in the winter of 1942 were appalling. Striking the Philippines a few hours after Hawaii, the Japanese gained another tactical surprise (see Map 28-3). They destroyed most American air power on the ground and isolated U.S. forces. Between February 27 and March 1, Japan brushed aside a combined American, British, Dutch, and Australian fleet in the Battle of the Java Sea. Earlier in February, a numerically inferior Japanese force had seized Singapore, until then considered an anchor of Allied strength.

Spring brought no better news. Japan pushed the British out of Burma. In a three-month siege, they overwhelmed Filipino and U.S. defensive positions on the Bataan peninsula outside Manila. On May 6, the last American bastion, the island fortress of Corregidor in Manila Bay, surrendered.

The first check to Japanese expansion came on May 7–8, 1942, in the **Battle of the Coral Sea**, where U.S. aircraft carriers halted a Japanese advance toward Australia. In June, the Japanese struck at the island of Midway, fifteen hundred miles northwest of Honolulu. Their goal was to destroy American carrier forces. The plan included a diversionary invasion of the Aleutian Islands (the westernmost parts of Alaska) and a main assault on Midway to draw the Americans into battle on Japanese terms. Having cracked Japanese radio codes, U.S. forces were aware of the plan and refused the bait. On the morning of June 4, the Japanese and American carrier fleets faced off across 175 miles of ocean, each sending planes to search the other out. U.S. Navy dive bombers found the Japanese fleet and sank or crippled three aircraft carriers in five minutes; another Japanese carrier sank later in the day. The Battle of Midway ended Japanese efforts to expand in the Pacific.

Mobilizing the Home Front

News of the Japanese attack on Pearl Harbor shattered a bright Sunday afternoon. Twelve-year-old Jean Bartlett's family was headed to the movies when news of the attack came over the car radio. Elliott Johnson was eating in a Chinese restaurant in Portland, Oregon, when the proprietor burst from the kitchen with a portable radio; the line was two blocks long by the time he got to the marine recruiting office. In Cincinnati, the enormously popular Andrews Sisters found that no one had shown up for their Sunday matinee concert. "Where is Pearl Harbor?" Maxine Andrews asked the theater's doorman.

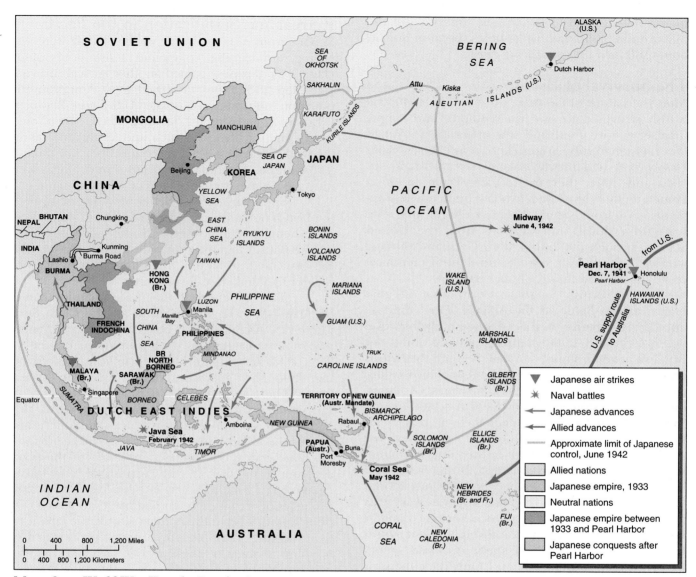

Map 28-3   *World War II in the Pacific, from Pearl Harbor to Midway*
The first six months after the Japanese attack on Pearl Harbor brought a string of Japanese victories and conquests in the Pacific, the islands southeast of Asia, and the British colonies of Malaya and Burma. Japan's advance was halted by a standoff battle in the Coral Sea, a decisive U.S. naval victory at Midway, and the length and vulnerability of Japanese supply lines to its most distant conquests.

War changed the lives of most Americans for the next four years—and for some forever. Some 350,000 woman and more than 16 million men served in the armed forces; 292,000 died in battle, 100,000 survived prisoner-of-war camps, and 671,000 returned wounded. More worked in defense industries. Youngsters saved tin foil, collected scrap metal, and followed the freedom-fighting stories of Wonder Woman in the comics. College science students might be recruited to work at scientific espionage against the Nazis. The breadth of involvement in the war effort gave Americans a common purpose that softened the divisions of region, class, and national origin while calling attention to continuing inequalities of race.

Warriors and Families

World War II required a thirtyfold expansion of the U.S. armed forces. By 1945, 8.3 million men and women were on active duty in the army and army air forces and 3.4 million in the navy and Marine Corps, totals exceeded only by the Soviet Union. The military establishment was four times larger than in World War I. Once in the military, sailors and GIs served an average of thirty-three months.

Many Americans put their lives on fast forward, as Judy Garland and Robert Walker did in the movie *The Clock* (1944). They played young people who meet in New York, fall in love, and are separated by the war in a matter of days. In real life, men and women often decided to beat the clock with instant matrimony. Couples who had postponed marriage because of the depression could afford to marry as the economy picked up. War intensified casual romances and heightened the appeal of marriage as an anchor in troubled times. Jewelers worried about running out of wedding rings. Altogether the war years brought 1.2 million "extra" marriages compared to the rate in 1920–1939.

The war's impact on families was gradual. The draft started with single men, then called up married men without children, and finally tapped fathers in 1943. Left at home were millions of "service wives," whose compensation from the government was $50 per month. Women who followed their husbands to stateside military posts and war factories often met cold welcomes from local residents. Harriet Arnow crafted a sensitive exploration of isolation from friends and family in her novel *The Dollmaker*, about a Kentucky farm woman who accompanied her husband to a Detroit war plant.

The war had mixed effects on children. Middle-class kids whose parents stayed home could treat it as an interminable scout project with salvage drives and campaigns to sell war bonds. Children in the rural Midwest picked milkweed pods to stuff life jackets; in coastal communities, they participated in blackout drills. Seattle high schools set aside one class period a day for the High School Victory Corps, training boys as messengers for air raid wardens while girls knitted sweaters and learned first aid. Between the end of school and suppertime, children listened as Captain Midnight, Jack Armstrong, and Hop Harrigan ("America's ace of the airways") fought the Nazis and Japanese on the radio.

The federal government tried to keep civilians of all ages committed to the war. It encouraged scrap drives and backyard victory gardens. The government also managed news about the fighting. Censors screened soldiers' letters. Early in the war, they blocked publication of most photographs of war casualties, although magazines such as *Life* were full of strong and haunting images. Worried about flagging commitment, censors later authorized photographs of enemy atrocities to incite the public.

Government officials had a harder time controlling Hollywood. The Office of War Information wanted propaganda in feature films, but not so heavy-handed that it drove viewers from theaters. Officials told movie directors to tone down car chases because

screeching tires implied wasted rubber. War films revealed the nation's racial attitudes, often drawing distinctions between "good" and "bad" Germans but uniformly portraying Japanese as subhuman and repulsive. The most successful films dramatized the courage of the Allies. *Mrs. Miniver* (1942) showed the British transcending class differences in their battle with the Nazis. *So Proudly We Hail* (1943) celebrated the heroism of navy nurses in the Pacific theater.

Industry Gears Up

Industry had reluctantly begun to convert from consumer goods to defense production in 1940 and 1941. Although corporations hated to give up the market for toasters and automobiles just as Americans had more money, the last passenger car for the duration of the war rolled off the assembly line in February 1942. Existing factories retooled to make war equipment, and huge new facilities turned out thousands of planes and ships. Baltimore, Atlanta, Fort Worth, Los Angeles, and Seattle became centers for aircraft production. New Orleans, Portland, and the San Francisco Bay area were shipbuilding centers. Henry J. Kaiser, who had helped build vast projects like the Grand Coulee Dam, turned out cargo ships by the thousands. One of the Kaiser shipyards built a Liberty ship (a standard-model cargo carrier) in ten and a half days.

The results of war production were staggering (see Figure 28-1). One historian estimates that 40 percent of the world's military production was coming from the United States by 1944. Equally impressive is the 30 percent increase in the productivity of U.S. workers between 1939 and 1945. Surging farm income pulled agriculture out of its long slump. The rich certainly got richer, but overall per capita income doubled, and the poorest quarter of Americans made up some of the ground lost during the Great Depression.

Behind the scenes were new federal agencies. The War Manpower Commission allocated workers among vital industries and the military. The War Production Board invested $17 billion for new factories and managed $181 billion in war supply contracts. The Office of Price Administration (OPA) fought inflation with price controls and rationing that began with tires, sugar, and coffee and eventually included meat, butter, gasoline, and shoes. "Use it up, wear it out, make it do or do without" was the OPA's slogan. Consumers used ration cards and ration stamps to obtain scarce products. By slowing price increases, the OPA helped convince Americans to buy the war bonds that financed half the war spending. Americans also felt the bite of the first payroll deductions for income taxes as the government secured a steady of flow of revenues and soaked up some of the high wages that would have pushed inflation.

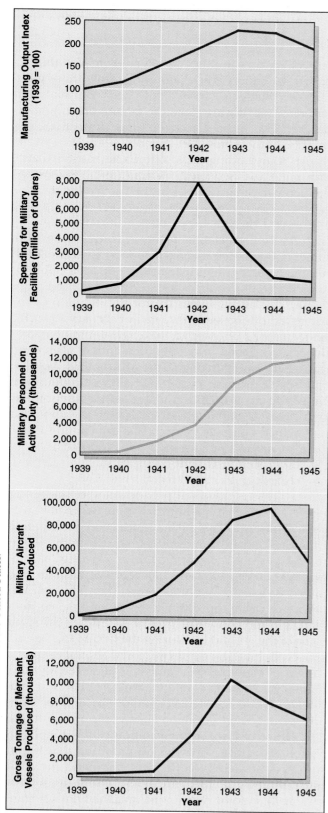

Figure 28-1 *Making War: The United States Mobilizes, 1939–45*

The U.S. economic mobilization for World War II reached its peak in 1943, the year in which the Allies prepared for the offensives against Germany and Japan that they hoped would end the war. The number of men and women in uniform continued to grow until 1945.

The Enlistment of Science

The war reached into scientific laboratories as well as shops and factories. "There wasn't a physicist able to breathe who wasn't doing war work," remembered Professor Philip Morrison. At the center of the scientific enterprise was Vannevar Bush, former dean at the Massachusetts Institute of Technology. As head of the newly established Office of Scientific Research and Development, Bush guided spending to develop new drugs, blood transfusion procedures, weapons systems, radar, sonar, and dozens of other military technologies. The scale of research and development dwarfed previous scientific work and set the pattern of massive federal support for science that continued after the war.

The biggest scientific effort was the drive to produce an atomic bomb. As early as 1939, Albert Einstein had written FDR about the possibility of such a weapon and the danger of falling behind the Germans. In late 1941, Roosevelt established what became known as the **Manhattan Project**. The work remained theoretical, however, until December 2, 1942, when scientists manipulated graphite rods inserted in a stack of uranium ingots until they were certain they could trigger and control a self-sustaining nuclear reaction. Because Enrico Fermi was in charge of the experiment, the coded message of scientific discovery recalled the voyages of Columbus—"The Italian navigator has landed in the new world."

The Manhattan Project moved from theory to practice in 1943. Physicist J. Robert Oppenheimer directed the young scientists at Los Alamos in designing a nuclear fission bomb. Engineers in other new science cities tried two approaches to producing the fissionable material. Richland, Washington, burgeoned into a sprawling metropolis that supported the creation of plutonium at the Hanford Engineer Works. Oak Ridge, Tennessee, near Knoxville, was built around gaseous diffusion plants that separated rare and vital uranium-235 from the more common uranium-238.

The Manhattan Project ushered in the age of atomic energy. Plutonium from Hanford fueled the first bomb tested at the Trinity site, 100 miles from Alamogordo, New Mexico, on July 16, 1945. The explosion astonished even the physicists; Oppenheimer quoted from Hindu scriptures as he tried to comprehend the results: "Now I am become death, destroyer of worlds."

Boom Times

The Manhattan Project was part of a regional tilt in the national economy; in effect, the war marked the takeoff of what Americans would later call the **Sunbelt** (see Map 28-4). Although most defense contracts went to established industrial states such as Michigan, New York, and Ohio, the relative impact was greatest in the South and West. Albuquerque, New Mexico, more than doubled in population during the 1940s. Wartime booms accelerated the growth of larger metropolitan areas like San Diego (up 92 percent in the decade), Phoenix (up 78 percent), Mobile (up 68 percent), and Dallas (up 54 percent).

War boom cities bustled with activity and hummed with tension. Factories operated three shifts, movies ran around the clock, and workers filled the streets after midnight. Most of the new industrial workers in 1941 and 1942 were unattached males—young men waiting for their draft call and older men separated from their families. They elbowed long-term residents in stores, snatched seats on the streetcars, and filled restaurants and theaters. Military and defense officials worried about sexually transmitted diseases and pressured cities to shut down their vice districts.

The hordes of war workers found housing scarce. Workers in Seattle's shipyards and Boeing plants scrounged for living space in offices, tents, chicken coops, and rooming houses where "hot beds" rented in shifts. When the Ford Motor Company began to build B-24 bombers at its new Willow Run plant in Michigan, the first of 42,000 workers made do with barns, garages, rented rooms, and trailers parked in thick mud. The situation was similar in small towns such as Seneca, Illinois, home to a company that normally made river barges. Between June 1942 and June 1945, it also built 157 LSTs—specialized ships to land tanks in amphibious assaults. Thousands of new workers flocked to Seneca. They lined up three deep at the bars with their Friday paychecks. Main Street clogged with cars and trucks. Residents would sometimes find a stranger rolled up in a blanket on their front porch.

Women in the War Effort

As draft calls took men off the assembly line, women changed the composition of the industrial work force. The war gave them new job opportunities that were embodied in the image of Rosie the Riveter. Women made up one-quarter of West Coast shipyard workers at the peak of employment and nearly half of Dallas

Map 28-4   *States with Population Growth of 10 Percent or More, 1940–1943*
The conversion of U.S. industry to defense production and the headlong expansion of the armed forces pulled Americans to coastal states and cities and to the South, where mild climate allowed year-round military training.

Members of Women Fliers of America examine an aircraft engine. The organization had been asked by the U.S. Army to identify women with more than 200 flying hours who might ferry planes, freeing military aviators for other duties.

and Seattle aircraft workers. Most women in the shipyards were clerks and general helpers. The acute shortage of welders and other skilled workers, however, opened thousands of journeyman positions to them as well—work that was far more lucrative than waiting tables or sewing in a clothing factory. Aircraft companies, which compounded labor shortages by stubborn "whites only" hiring, developed new power tools and production techniques to accommodate the smaller average size of women workers, increasing efficiency for everyone along the production line.

By July 1944, fully 19 million women held paid jobs, up 6 million in four years. Women's share of government jobs increased from 19 to 38 percent and their share of manufacturing jobs from 22 to 33 percent. Mirroring the sequence in which the military draft took men, employers recruited single women before turning to married women in 1943

In 1942, the federal government removed Japanese Americans from parts of four western states and interned them in isolated camps scattered through the West.

and 1944. Some women worked out of patriotism. Many others, however, needed to support their families. As one of the workers recalled of herself and a friend, "We both had to work, we both had children, so we became welders, and if I might say so, damn good ones" (see "American Views: A Woman Shipyard Worker Recalls Her Experience").

Americans did not know how to respond to the growing numbers of working women. The country needed their labor, but many worried that their employment would undermine families. The federal government assisted female entry into the labor force by funding day care programs that served 600,000 children. Employment recruitment posters showed strong, handsome women with rolled-up sleeves and wrenches in hand, but *Life* magazine reassured readers that women in factories could retain their sex appeal. Men and women commonly assumed that women would want to return to the home after victory; they were to work when the nation needed them and quit when the need was past.

The nation had the same mixed reaction to the women who joined the armed forces as army and navy nurses and as members of the WACS (Women's Army Corps), WAVES (Navy), and SPARS (Coast Guard). The armed services tried not to change established gender roles. Military officials told Congress that women in uniform could free men for combat. Most of the women hammered at typewriters, worked switchboards, inventoried supplies, and tended the ill and injured. WAC officers battled the tendency of the popular press to call females in the service "girls" rather than "women" or "soldiers" yet emphasized that military service promoted "poise and charm."

Unequal Opportunity

Not all Americans had the same chance to benefit from the economic boom. On February 19, 1942, President Roosevelt issued **Executive Order 9066**, which authorized the secretary of war to define restricted areas and remove civilian residents who were threats to national security. The targets were 110,000 Japanese Americans whom the army expelled from parts of Washington, Oregon, California, and Arizona in the spring of 1942. Those who had not moved voluntarily were sent to relocation camps in the West and Southwest. The removal satisfied anti-Japanese sentiment kindled into hatred by the war. Most evacuees left businesses and property that they were powerless to protect. Many in the camps would demonstrate their loyalty by joining the 442nd Regimental Combat Team, the most decorated American unit in the European war.

Although the U.S. Supreme Court sanctioned the removals in *Korematsu v. United States* (1944), the nation officially recognized its liability with the Japan-

ese Claims Act of 1948 and its broader moral responsibility in 1988, when Congress approved redress payments to each of the sixty thousand surviving evacuees.

The internment of West Coast Japanese contrasted with the treatment of Japanese Americans by the military government of Hawaii. Despite the greater threat that Japan posed to Hawaii than to California, local residents and officials avoided panic. Hawaii's long history as a multiethnic society made residents disinclined to look for a racial scapegoat. Less than 1 percent of Hawaii's Japanese American population of 160,000 was interned.

The experience of African Americans was also mixed, particularly in the armed forces. As it had since the Civil War, the army organized black soldiers in segregated units. Towns adjacent to army posts were sometimes open to white soldiers but off limits to blacks. At some southern bases, German prisoners of war watched movies from the first rows along with white GIs while African American soldiers watched

Dorrie Miller, a mess attendant on the battleship Arizona, *received the Navy Cross for "extraordinary courage" during the Japanese attack on Pearl Harbor. Miller helped pull the* Arizona's *captain to safety and then manned a machine gun and shot down several Japanese planes. The War Department used Miller on recruiting posters such as this, but neglected to point out that it continued to restrict black recruits mostly to kitchen and other service jobs.*

American Views
A WOMAN SHIPYARD WORKER
RECALLS HER EXPERIENCE

World War II industry gave new opportunities to millions of women. Patricia Cain Koehler later recalled her work as a teenaged electrician who helped build escort aircraft carriers in Vancouver, Washington, from 1943 to 1945.

❖ **How did Koehler's experience challenge expectations about "women's work"?**

❖ **What impression does she give about the spirit with which Americans organized to win the war?**

❖ **How did the war change the patterns of everyday life?**

We girls wore leather jackets, plaid flannel shirts, and jeans we bought in the boys department of Meier & Frank. In was 1943, we were eighteen years old, our first year of college was over. My girlfriend and her mother had moved in with my mother and me for the duration of the war. Housing was tight because of the influx of war industry workers. Our fathers were overseas.

Three local shipyards were recruiting workers from the East Coast and the South. They advertised in Portland, too: HELP WANTED: WOMEN SHIPBUILDERS. Cartoons asked, "What are you doing to help the war?" They showed women sipping tea, playing cards, and relaxing. "THIS?" And then a smiling woman worker with lunch box, her hair tied up in a scarf, a large ship in the background, "Or THIS? . . .

Together my girlfriend and I applied to be electrician helpers at the Kaiser Vancouver Shipyards. . . . Twenty thousand workers labored

from the back. Private Charles Wilson wrote President Roosevelt that Davis-Monthan Army Air Force Base in Tucson was color-coded: Barracks for African Americans were coated with black tar paper, and those for white soldiers sported white paint. Military courts were quick to judge and harsh to punish when black GIs were the accused. Despite the obstacles, all-black units such as the 761st Tank Battalion and the 99th Pursuit Squadron earned distinguished records.

African Americans also found economic advancement through war jobs. Early in the mobilization, labor leader A. Philip Randolph of the Brotherhood of Sleeping Car Porters worked with Walter White of the NAACP to plan a "Negro March on Washington" to protest racial discrimination by the federal government. To head off a major embarrassment, Roosevelt issued **Executive Order 8802** in June 1941, barring racial discrimination in defense contracts and creating the **Fair Employment Practices Committee (FEPC)**; the order coined a phrase that reverberated powerfully through the coming decades: "no discrimination on grounds of race, color, creed, or national origin."

The FEPC's small staff resolved fewer than half of the employment discrimination complaints. White resistance to black coworkers remained strong. In Mobile, New Orleans, and Jacksonville, agreements between shipyards and segregated unions blocked skilled black workers from high-wage jobs. Attempts to overturn discrimination could lead to violence. When the Alabama Dry Dock Company integrated its work force in May 1943, white workers rioted. Transportation workers in Philadelphia struck the next year to protest upgrading of jobs held by black workers. Nevertheless, African American membership in labor unions doubled, and wartime prosperity raised the average black income from 41 percent of the white average in 1939 to 61 percent by 1950.

The war was also a powerful force for the assimilation of Native Americans. Twenty-five thousand Indians served in the armed forces. Some were

around the clock to build ships—fast. At nights the yards were lit up as bright as day. . . . It was a world of strangers. . . . Coming from outside the Northwest, as most of them did, they spoke in accents we had never heard before. It became a game with us to listen and ask point of origin. Soon we could distinguish between a Brooklyn accent and one from New Jersey. . . .

The day came . . . when we graduated to journeyman-electrician at $1.20 per hour. We celebrated by applying for jobs on the hookup crews, which worked aboard ships at the outfitting dock. I was assigned to fire control. That meant guns! My leadman had never had a female working for him, and he was skeptical. Like a shadow, I followed his every move, anticipating what tool he needed next and handing it to him before he could ask. After a few days of this he relaxed and began teaching me the ropes—or, rather, the wires. . . .

We had watched some of the carriers launched, with wartime ceremony, gold braid, and ribbons. There was no glamour for us, though, as we slipped on the cluttered decks, dodged cables over our heads, and risked death crossing the tracks of the giant cranes. . . .

My first solo assignment was hooking up the forty-millimeter gun directors on the starboard side. . . . Occasionally I looked down into the swift current of the Columbia River and noticed small boats dragging for a worker who had fallen in. . . . Once when climbing down a ladder clogged with welding leads (large rubber hoses), I slammed a steel-toed boot against one of them and broke a toe. The doctor taped it to its neighbor and I went on working. On another occasion I broke my elbow in a fall, lost a day getting it set, and learned to work left-handed. . . .

Since every night we fell into bed exhausted, our hands chapped and our hair smelling of paint, there was really no time to spend our money. So we invested most of our earnings in war bonds to be cashed in for college.

Source: Patricia Cain Koehler, "Reminiscence: Pat Koehler on the Women Shipbuilders of World War II." Oregon Historical Quarterly, Fall 1990, pp. 285–291. Copyright © 1990 Oregon Historical Quarterly. Reprinted by permission.

members of radio combat-communication teams, known as "code-talkers," who transmitted vital information in Navajo and other Indian languages. Forty thousand other Native Americans moved to off-reservation jobs. The average cash income of Indian households tripled during the war. Many stayed in cities at its end. The stress of balancing tribal life and urban America is depicted in M. Scott Momaday's 1969 novel *House Made of Dawn*, which follows a World War II veteran as he moves between his home village in New Mexico and Los Angeles.

Clashing Cultures

As men and women migrated in search of work, they also crossed or collided with traditional boundaries of race and region. African-American migration out of the South accelerated in the early 1940s. Many of the migrants headed for well-established black neighborhoods in northern cities. Others created new African-American neighborhoods in western cities. White Southerners and black Northerners with different ideas of racial etiquette found themselves side by side in West Coast shipyards. In the Midwest, black migrants from the South and white migrants from Appalachia crowded into cities such as Cincinnati and Chicago, competing for the same high-wage jobs and scarce apartments.

Tensions between black and white residents exploded in at least fifty cities in 1943 alone. New York's Harlem erupted in a riot after rumors of attacks on black servicemen. In Detroit, the issue was the boundary between white and black territories. In June 1943, an argument over use of Detroit's Belle Isle Park set off three days of violence: Twenty-five black people and nine white people died in the most serious racial riot of the war.

Tensions were simultaneously rising between Mexican Americans and Anglos. In periods of labor shortage, the United States has repeatedly turned to Latin America for low-cost workers. World War II followed the pattern. In July 1942, the United States admitted hundreds of thousands of Mexican *braceros*, or temporary workers, to fill labor needs in the Southwest.

The Latino newcomers created ethnic tensions similar to those associated with the urbanization of African Americans. As the Mexican community in Los Angeles swelled to an estimated 400,000, newspapers published anti-Mexican articles. On June 6, 1943, off-duty sailors and soldiers attacked Latinos on downtown streets and invaded Mexican-American neighborhoods. The main targets were so-called *pachucos*—young Chicanos who wore flamboyant "zoot suits" with long, wide-shouldered jackets and pleated, narrow-cuffed trousers—whom the rioters considered delinquents. The "zoot suit" riots dragged on for a week of sporadic violence against black people and Filipinos as well as Latinos.

The End of the New Deal

Roosevelt's New Deal had run out of steam in 1938. The war had reinvigorated his political fortunes by focusing national energies on foreign policy, over which presidents have the greatest power. He declared that "Dr. Win the War" had replaced "Dr. New Deal." Especially after the 1942 election left Congress in the hands of Republicans and conservative southern Democrats, lawmakers followed the new tack. Conservative lawmakers ignored proposals that war emergency housing be used to improve the nation's permanent housing stock, abolished the National Resources Planning Board, curtailed rural electrification, and crippled the Farm Security Administration.

The presidential election of 1944 raised few new issues of substance. The Republicans nominated Governor Thomas Dewey of New York, who had made his reputation as a crime-fighting district attorney. The Democrats renominated Roosevelt for a fourth term. Missouri Senator Harry S Truman, a tough investigator of American military preparedness, replaced liberal New Dealer Henry Wallace as Roosevelt's running mate. The move appeased southern Democrats and moved the ticket toward the political center.

The most important issue was a fourth term for Roosevelt. Supporters argued that the nation could not afford to switch leaders in the middle of a war, but Dewey's vigor and relative youth (he was twenty years younger than FDR) pointed up the president's failing health and energy. Voters gave Roosevelt 432 electoral votes to 99, but the narrowing gap in the popular vote—54 percent for Roosevelt and 46 percent for Dewey—made the Republicans eager for 1948.

War and Peace

In January 1943, the U.S. War Department completed the world's largest office building, the Pentagon. The building housed 23,000 workers along 17.5

In the early 1940s, young Mexican-American men frequently dressed in "zoot suits" of baggy trousers, hip-length jackets with padded shoulders and wide lapels, and broad-brimmed hats. A badge of youthful defiance and ethnic identity, the style contrasted sharply with the tailored uniforms of the armed services. Zoot-suiters found themselves the targets of off-duty soldiers during the "zoot suit riots" in Los Angeles in 1943. This photo shows police arresting Mexican-American men, zoot suiters among them, in the wake of the riots.

miles of corridors. While Congress was chipping away at federal programs, the war effort was massively expanding the government presence in American life. The gray walls of the Pentagon symbolized an American government that was outgrowing its prewar roots.

Gathering Allied Strength

The unanswered military question of 1942 and 1943 was when the United States and Britain would open a second front against Germany by attacking across the English Channel. Landings in north Africa in 1942 and Italy in 1943 satisfied the British desire to secure western influence in the Mediterranean and Middle East, and they gave U.S. forces invaluable battlefield experience. But they pleased neither American policymakers nor the Soviet Union. U.S. leaders wanted to justify massive mobilization with a war-winning campaign and to strike across Europe to occupy the heart of Germany. Stalin needed a full-scale invasion of western Europe to divert German forces from the Eastern Front.

In fact, 1943 was the year in which the Allies gained the edge in quality of equipment, capacity for war production, and military sophistication. The United States poured men and equipment into Britain. The Soviets recruited, rearmed, and upgraded new armies, despite enormous losses in 1941 and 1942. They learned to outfight the Germans in tank warfare and rebuilt munitions factories beyond German reach. They also made good use of 17.5 million tons of U.S. lend-lease assistance. As Soviet soldiers reconquered western Russia and the Ukraine, they marched in 13 million pairs of American-made boots and traveled in 51,000 jeeps and 375,000 Dodge trucks. "Just imagine how we could have advanced from Stalingrad to Berlin without [lend-lease vehicles]," future Soviet Premier Nikita Khrushchev later commented.

The Allies spent 1943 hammering out war aims and strategies. Meeting in Casablanca in January 1943, Roosevelt and Churchill demanded the "unconditional surrender" of Italy, Germany, and Japan; the phrase meant no deals that kept the enemy governments or leaders in power. Ten months later, the Allied leaders huddled again. Roosevelt and Churchill met with China's Jiang in Cairo and then flew on to meet Stalin in Tehran. Jiang and Stalin could not meet directly because the USSR was neutral in the east Asian war. At Tehran, the United States and Britain promised to invade France within six months. "We leave here," said the three leaders, "friends in fact, in spirit, in purpose."

The superficial harmony barely survived the end of the war. The Soviets had shouldered the brunt of the war for nearly two and a half years, suffering millions of casualties and seeing their nation devastated. Stalin and his generals scoffed at the small scale of early U.S. efforts. Roosevelt's ideal of self-determination for all peoples seemed naive to Churchill, who wanted the major powers to carve out realistic spheres of influence in Europe. It was irrelevant to Stalin, who wanted control of eastern Europe.

Turning the Tide in Europe

The United States had entered the ground war in Europe with **Operation TORCH**. Against little opposition, British and American troops under General Dwight Eisenhower landed in French Morocco and Algeria on November 8, 1942 (see Map 28-5). These were territories that the Germans had left under a puppet French government after the French military collapsed in 1940. This Vichy government, so named after its capital city, collaborated with the Nazis. With the TORCH landings, however, Vichy officials in Africa switched sides, giving the Allies footholds in north Africa.

Despite the easy landings, German troops taught U.S. forces hard lessons in tactics and leadership. German tanks in February 1943 counterattacked U.S. divisions at **Kasserine Pass** in the Atlas Mountains of Tunisia. The battle was a tactical defeat for the untested American army, but Axis forces lacked the strength to follow it up. Allied troops forced the Axis in Africa to surrender in May. Eisenhower had already demonstrated his ability to handle the politics of military leadership, skills he perfected commanding a multinational army for the next two and a half years. He also chose the right subordinates, giving operational command to Omar Bradley and George Patton. Bradley was low-keyed and rock solid; to relax he worked algebra and calculus problems. Patton was a much flashier figure with a mighty ego and a fierce commitment to victory.

The central Mediterranean remained the focus of U.S. and British action for the next year. The British feared military disaster from a premature landing in western Europe and proposed strikes in southern Europe, which Churchill inaccurately called the "soft underbelly" of Hitler's empire. U.S. Army Chief of Staff George Marshall and President Roosevelt agreed first to the action in north Africa and then to invade Italy in 1943, in part so that U.S. troops could participate in the ground fighting in Europe. In July and August, Allied forces led by Montgomery and Patton overran Sicily. The Italian mainland proved more difficult. As Sicily fell, the Italian king and army forced Mussolini from power and began to negotiate peace with Britain

Map 28-5   World War II in Europe, 1942–1945
Nazi Germany had to defend its conquests on three fronts. Around the Mediterranean, American and British forces pushed the Germans out of Africa and Southern Italy, while guerrillas in Yugoslavia pinned down many German troops. On the Eastern Front, Soviet armies advanced hundreds of miles to drive the German army out of the Soviet Union and eastern Europe. In June 1944, U.S. and British landings opened the Western Front in northern France for a decisive strike at the heart of Germany.

and America (but not the Soviet Union). In September, the Allies announced an armistice with Italy, and Eisenhower's troops landed south of Naples. Germany responded by occupying the rest of Italy.

As American military planners had feared, the Italian campaign soaked up Allied resources. The mountainous Italian peninsula was one long series of defensive positions, and the Allies repeatedly bogged down. Week after week, the experience of GIs on the line was the same: "You wake up in the mud and your cigarettes are all wet and you have an ache in your joints and a rattle in your chest." Despite months of bitter fighting, the Allies controlled only two-thirds of Italy when the war there ended on May 1, 1945.

On the Eastern Front, the climactic battle of the German-Soviet war had erupted on July 5, 1943. The Germans sent three thousand tanks against the **Kursk Salient**, a huge wedge that the Red Army had pushed into their lines. In 1941 and 1942, such a massive attack would have forced the Soviets to retreat, but now Soviet generals had prepared a defense in depth with three thousand tanks of their own. When the attack finally stalled, it marked the last great German offensive until December 1944.

Operation OVERLORD

On **D-Day**—June 6, 1944—the western Allies landed on the coast of Normandy in northwestern France. Six divisions went ashore from hundreds of attack transports carrying four thousand landing craft.

Dozens of warships and twelve thousand aircraft provided support. One British and two American airborne divisions dropped behind German positions. When the sun set on the "longest day," the Allies had a tenuous toehold in France.

The next few weeks brought limited success. The Allies secured their beachheads and landed 500,000 men and 100,000 vehicles within two weeks. However, the German defenders kept them pinned along a narrow coastal strip. **Operation OVERLORD**, the code name for the entire campaign across northern France, met renewed success in late July and August. U.S. troops improved their fighting skills through "experience, sheer bloody experience." They finally broke through German lines around the town of St.-Lô and then drew a ring around the Germans that slowly closed on the town of Falaise. The Germans lost a quarter of a million troops.

The German command chose to regroup closer to Germany rather than fight in France. The Allies liberated Paris on August 25; Free French forces (units that had never accepted Nazi or Vichy rule) led the entry. The drive toward Germany was the largest U.S. operation of the war. The only impediments appeared to be winter weather and getting enough supplies to the rapidly advancing armies.

The story was similar on the Eastern Front, where the Soviets relentlessly battered one section of the German lines after another. By the end of 1944, the Red Army had entered the Balkans and reached central Poland. With the end in sight, the Soviets

American, British, and Canadian forces opened the long-awaited "second front" against Germany on June 6, 1944— D-Day—when tens of thousands of troops landed on the coast of Normandy in France. The landings were the largest amphibious operation ever staged. Although the Germans had expected the landings further north, their defenses pinned the Allies to a narrow beachhead for several weeks.

TABLE 28.1	MILITARY AND CIVILIAN DEATHS IN WORLD WAR II	
Nation	**Victims (millions)**
USSR	18–20
China	10–20
Germany and Austria	6
Poland	5
Japan	2.7
Yugoslavia	1.7
Romania	0.7
France	0.6
Great Britain	0.5
Hungary	0.5
Italy	0.4
Czechoslovakia	0.4
United States	0.3

had suffered nearly 20 million casualties and sustained the heaviest burden in turning back Nazi tyranny (see Table 28-1).

Victory and Tragedy in Europe

In the last months of 1944, massive air strikes finally reduced German war production. Early in the air war, flying at night, British bombers had aimed at entire cities—the smallest target they could be sure to hit. The American Eighth Air Force preferred to fly daylight raids from its bases in Britain with heavily armed B-17s ("Flying Fortresses") and B-24s ("Liberators") to destroy factories with precision bombing. On August 17, 1943, however, Germans shot down or damaged 10 percent of the bombers that attacked the aircraft factories of Regensburg and the ball-bearing factories of Schweinfurt. Air crews who were expected to fly mission after mission could count the odds, and the Americans had to seek easier targets. German war production actually increased during 1943 and much of 1944.

Gradually, however, the balance shifted. The new American P-51 escort fighter helped B-17s overfly Germany in relative safety after mid-1944. Thousand-bomber raids on railroads and oil facilities began to cripple the German economy. The raids also forced

Germany to devote 2.5 million workers to air defense and damage repair and to divert fighter planes from the front lines. Politics rather than military need governed the final great action of the European air war. British and U.S. bombers in February 1945 staged a terror raid on the nonindustrial city of Dresden, packed with refugees, filled with great art, and undefended by the Germans; a firestorm fueled by incendiary bombs and rubble from blasted buildings killed tens of thousands of civilians without military justification.

Out of the bombing raids that pitted pilots and crews against unseen enemies would come some of the most vivid efforts to relive and comprehend the experience of war. The movie *Twelve O'Clock High* (1949) focused on successive commanders of a U.S. bomber unit in Britain who became too involved with their men to function effectively. The literature of the bomber campaigns included antiwar novels like Joseph Heller's *Catch-22* (1961) and poems like Randall Jarrell's "Death of the Ball Turret Gunner":

From my mother's sleep I fell into the State,
And I hunched in its belly until my wet fur froze.
Six miles from earth, loosed from its dream of life,
I woke to black flak and the nightmare fighters.
When I died they washed me out of the turret with
a hose.*

Even as the air bombardment intensified, Hitler struck a last blow. Stripping the Eastern Front of armored units, he launched twenty-five divisions against thinly held U.S. positions in the Ardennes Forest of Belgium on December 16, 1944. He hoped to split U.S. and British forces by capturing the Belgian port of Antwerp. The attack surprised the Americans, who had treated the Ardennes as a "ghost front" where nothing was going on. Taking advantage of snow and fog that grounded Allied aircraft, the Germans drove a fifty-mile bulge into U.S. lines. Although Americans took substantial casualties, the German thrust literally ran out of gas beyond the town of Bastogne. The **Battle of the Bulge** never seriously threatened the outcome of the war, but pushing the Germans back through the snow-filled forest gave GIs a taste of the conditions that had marked the war in the Soviet Union.

The Nazi empire collapsed in the spring of 1945. American and British divisions crossed the Rhine in March and enveloped Germany's industrial

---

*"The Death of a Ball Turret Gunner" from *The Complete Poems*, by Randall Jarrell, Copyright © 1969, renewed 1997 by Mary von S. Jarrell. Reprinted by permission of Farrar, Straus, Giroux, LLC.

core. The Soviets drove through eastern Germany toward Berlin. On April 25, American and Red Army troops met on the Elbe River. Hitler committed suicide on April 30 in his concrete bunker deep under devastated Berlin, which surrendered to the Soviets on May 2. The Nazi state formally capitulated on May 8.

The defeat of Germany revealed appalling evidence of the evil at the heart of the Nazi ideology of racial superiority. After occupying Poland in 1939, Nazi officials had begun to force Jews to wear yellow six-pointed stars. Homosexuals had to wear a pink triangle. Nazis also expanded concentration camps into forced labor camps where overwork, starvation, and disease killed hundreds of thousands of Jews, Gypsies, Poles, Russians, and others the Nazis classed as subhuman. Labor conscripts from both eastern and western Europe provided forced labor in fields, factories, mines, and repair crews.

The "final solution" to what Hitler thought of as the "Jewish problem" went far beyond slave labor. The elite SS, Hitler's personal army within the Nazi party, in 1942 set out to eliminate all of Europe's Jews. The evidence of genocide—systematic racial murder—is irrefutable. At Auschwitz and Treblinka, the SS organized the efficient extermination of up to 6 million Jews and 1 million Poles, Gypsies, and others who failed to fit the Nazi vision of the German master race. Prisoners arrived by forced marches and cattle trains. Those who were not worked or starved to death were herded into gas chambers and then incinerated in huge crematoriums. Soviet troops could scarcely believe what they saw as they overran the death camps and freed the few survivors of what we now call the **Holocaust**.

The Pacific War

In the Pacific, as in Europe, the United States used 1943 to probe enemy conquests and to build better submarines, bigger aircraft carriers, and superior planes. Washington divided responsibilities in the Pacific theater. General Douglas MacArthur operated in the islands that stretched between Australia and the Philippines. Admiral Chester Nimitz commanded in the central Pacific. The Allies planned to isolate Japan from its southern conquests. The British moved from India to retake Burma. The Americans advanced along the islands of the southern Pacific to retake the Philippines. With Japan's army still tied down in China, the Americans then planned to bomb Japan into submission.

The Pacific campaigns of 1944 are often called **island hopping**. This was the American naval version of the Blitzkrieg. Planes from American carriers controlled the air, allowing the navy and land forces to isolate and capture the most strategically located Japanese-held islands while bypassing the rest. The process started in November 1943, when Marines took Tarawa (see Map 28-6). It worked to perfection with the assault on Saipan in June 1944. When the Japanese fleet challenged the attack, U.S. Navy flyers destroyed three aircraft carriers and hundreds of planes.

When Soviet troops liberated Poland and the western allies entered Germany in 1945, they found appalling evidence of the Nazi political and racial terror that had killed millions of people, including six million Jews. A handful of victims survived the death factories and concentration camps—among them these inmates of the Buchenwald concentration camp in central Germany—to bear witness to the horror.

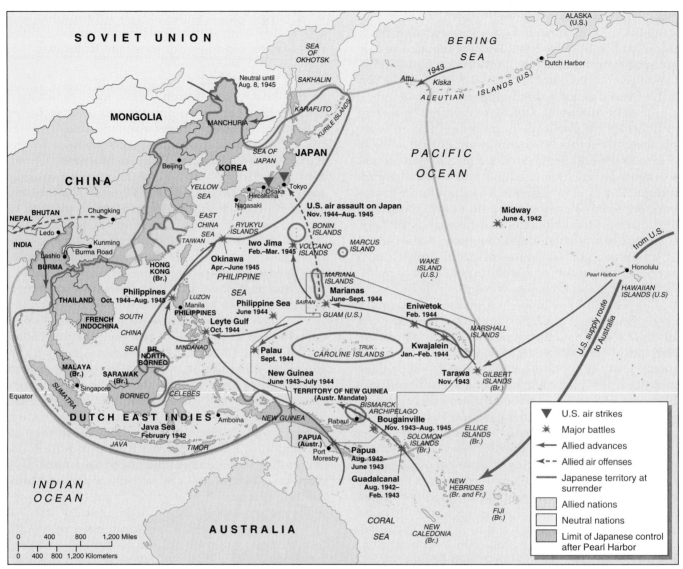

Map 28-6 *World War II in the Pacific, 1942–1945*
The Allied strategy against Japan was to cut off Japan's southern conquests by retaking the central Pacific islands, the Philippines, and Burma and then to strike at the Japanese home islands. Submarine warfare and massive air attacks from November 1944 to August 1945 crippled Japan's capacity to wage war. The detonation of atomic bombs over Hiroshima and Nagasaki then forced surrender on August 15, 1945.

Racial hatred animated both sides in the Pacific war and fueled a "war without mercy." Americans often characterized Japanese soldiers as vermin. Political cartoons showed Japanese as monkeys or rats, and some Marines had "Rodent Exterminator" stenciled on their helmets. In turn, the Japanese depicted themselves as the "leading race" with the duty to direct the rest of Asia. Chinese, Filipinos, and other conquered peoples were treated with contempt and brutality. Japanese viewed Americans as racial mongrels and called them demons. Each side expected the worst of the other and frequently lived up to expectations.

MacArthur used a version of the bypass strategy in the Solomon Islands and New Guinea, leapfrogging over Japanese strong points. The invasion of the Philippines repeated the approach by landing on Leyte, in the middle of the island chain. The Philippine campaign also destroyed the offensive capacity of the Japanese fleet. In the **Battle of Leyte Gulf**, the U.S. military sank four Japanese battleships, four carriers, and ten cruisers. The Japanese home islands were left with no defensive screen against an expected invasion.

During 1943 and 1944, the U.S. also savaged the Japanese economy. Submarines choked off food, oil, and raw materials bound for Japan and island bases. By 1945, imports to Japan were one-eighth of the 1940 level. Heavy bombing of Japan began in early 1944. Japan's dense wooden cities were more vulnerable than their German counterparts, and Japanese air defenses were much weaker. A fire-bomb raid on Tokyo on the night of March 9, 1945, killed 124,000 people and left 1 million homeless; it was perhaps the single biggest mass killing of all time. Overall, conventional bombing destroyed 42 percent of Japan's industrial capacity. By the time the United States captured the islands of Iwo Jima and Okinawa in fierce fighting (April–June 1945) and neared the Japanese home islands, Japan's position was hopeless.

Searching for Peace

At the beginning of 1945, the Allies sensed victory. Conferring from February 4 to 11 in the Ukrainian town of Yalta, Roosevelt, Stalin, and Churchill planned for the postwar world. The most important American goal was to enlist the USSR in finishing off the Pacific war. Americans hoped that a Soviet attack on Manchuria would tie down enough Japanese troops to reduce U.S. casualties in invading Japan. Stalin repeated his intent to declare war on Japan within three months of victory in Europe, in return for a free hand in Manchuria.

In Europe, the Allies had decided in 1944 to divide Germany and Austria into French, British, American, and Soviet occupation zones. The Red Army already controlled Bulgaria, Romania, and Hungary, countries that had helped the Germans; Soviet officials were installing sympathetic regimes there. Soviet armies also controlled Poland. The most that Roosevelt could coax from Stalin were vague pledges to allow participation of noncommunists in coalition governments in eastern Europe. Stalin also agreed to join a new international organization, the **United Nations**, whose foundations were laid at a conference in San Francisco in the spring of 1945.

Conservative critics later charged that the western powers "gave away" eastern Europe at the **Yalta Conference**. In fact, the Soviet Union gained little that it did not already control. In east Asia as well, the Soviets could seize the territories that the agreements granted them. Roosevelt overestimated his ability to charm Stalin, but the Yalta talks could not undo the results of four years of fighting by the Soviet Army.

On April 12, two months after Yalta, Roosevelt died of a cerebral hemorrhage. Harry Truman, the new president, was a shrewd politician, but his experience was limited; Roosevelt had not even told him about the Manhattan Project. Deeply distrustful of the Soviets, Truman first ventured into personal international diplomacy in July 1945 at a British-Soviet-American conference at Potsdam, near Berlin. Most of the sessions debated the future of Germany. The leaders endorsed the expulsion of ethnic Germans from eastern Europe and moved the borders of Poland one hundred miles west into historically German territory. Truman also made it clear that the United States expected to dominate the occupation of Japan. Its goal was to democratize the Japanese political system and reintroduce Japan into the international community—a policy that succeeded. The **Potsdam Declaration** on July 26 summarized U.S. policy and gave Japan an opening for surrender. However, the declaration failed to guarantee that Emperor Hirohito would not be tried as a war criminal. The Japanese response was so cautious that Americans read it as rejection.

Secretary of State James Byrnes now urged Truman to use the new atomic bomb, tested just weeks earlier. Japan's ferocious defense of Okinawa had confirmed American fears that the Japanese would fight to the death. Thousands of suicide missions by *kamikaze* pilots who tried to crash their planes into U.S. warships seemed additional proof of Japanese fanaticism. Prominent Americans were wondering if unconditional surrender was worth another six or nine months of bitter fighting. In contrast, using the bomb to end the conflict quickly would ensure that the United States could occupy Japan without Soviet participation, and the bomb might intimidate Stalin (see the overview table, "The Decision to Use the Atomic Bomb"). In short, a decision not to use atomic weapons was never a serious alternative in the summer of 1945.

In early August, the United States dropped two of three available nuclear bombs on Japan. On August 6 at Hiroshima the first bomb killed at least eighty thousand people and poisoned thousands more with radiation. A second bomb three days later at Nagasaki took another forty thousand lives. Japan ceased hostilities on August 14 and surrendered formally on September 2. The world has wondered ever since if the United States might have defeated Japan without resorting to atomic bombs, but recent research shows that the bombs were the shock that allowed the Emperor and peace advocates to overcome military leaders who wanted to fight to the death.

FROM THEN TO NOW

Nuclear Weapons

On May 11 and 12, 1998, India tested five nuclear weapons in its western desert. Two weeks later, Pakistan tested its own nuclear weapons. Neighbors and bitter rivals, the two became the sixth and seventh nations to publicly acknowledge the possession of a nuclear arsenal. Now the tensions between them, which had long fueled border clashes and twice erupted in open warfare, had become another factor in the delicate calculus of nuclear terror that has confronted the world since Hiroshima.

It has been a central goal of U.S. policy since 1945 to limit the number of nations with atomic weapons and place ceilings on the size of nuclear arsenals. The goal became more urgent when the Soviet Union deployed its own nuclear weapons after 1949, establishing the "balance of terror" that haunted the decades-long Cold War between the United States and the Soviet Union.

Two key steps toward reducing the nuclear threat were the Limited Test Ban Treaty of 1963—in which the United States, Britain, and the USSR outlawed atmospheric nuclear testing (see Chapter 30)—and the Nuclear Non-Proliferation Treaty, which was signed in 1968 and extended indefinitely in 1995. One hundred eighty nations have agreed not to acquire nuclear weapons, and five acknowledged nuclear powers—the United States, Russia, Britain, France, China—have agreed to eventual elimination of their own weapons.

The power of international opinion was clearly not enough to convince India and Pakistan to abandon their nuclear weapons programs, but it has been effective elsewhere in the 1990's. One justification of the Gulf War in 1991 (see Chapter 33) was to prevent Iraq from developing nuclear arms, and Iraqi interference with United Nations inspection teams triggered bombing raids on Iraq in 1998–99. The United States also orchestrated pressure on North Korea to cancel a suspected nuclear weapons program and admit international inspectors.

The 1990s saw advances in efforts to reduce the huge nuclear stockpiles of the United States and Russia. The first Strategic Arms Limitation Treaty (START I) went into effect in 1994. The United States and Russia agreed to retain a maximum of eight thousand warheads each. START II, if implemented, would cut the total to three thousand each. The breakup of the Soviet Union and the economic challenges that have confronted its constituent republics have created fears about the diversion of warheads into the hands of terrorists. The United States, however, has helped to pay for dismantling of Russian warheads and their removal from Ukraine and Kazakhstan, both formerly parts of the Soviet Union.

The frightening proliferation and growth of nuclear arsenals that began with the Manhattan Project and continued into the 1980s may be ending. The 1990s, on the contrary, may have marked the beginning of a new era of shrinking nuclear capacity, despite reversals like those in India and Pakistan. South Africa, for example, announced in 1993 that it had destroyed six warheads that it had manufactured secretly. And planned reductions in the largest nuclear arsenals offer hope that the trend will continue in the new century.

Hiroshima in the aftermath of the atomic bomb. Atomic bombs, dropped first on Hiroshima and a few days later on Nagasaki in August 1945, instantly destroyed much of both cities. Now one airplane with one bomb could wreak the kind of devastation massive fire bombing raids had inflicted on cities such as Hamburg, Dresden, and Tokyo, adding new terror to the idea of total war.

OVERVIEW

THE DECISION TO USE THE ATOMIC BOMB

Americans have long argued whether the use of atomic bombs on the Japanese cities of Hiroshima and Nagasaki was necessary to end the war. Several factors probably influenced President Truman's decision to use the new weapon.

Military necessity	Truman later argued that the use of atomic bombs was necessary to avoid an invasion of Japan that would have cost hundreds of thousand of lives. Military planners expected Japanese soldiers to put up the same kind of suicidal resistance in defense of the home islands as they had to American landings at the Philippines, Iwo Jima, and Okinawa. More recently, historians have argued that the Japanese military was near collapse and that an invasion would have met far less resistance than feared.
Atomic diplomacy	Some historians believe that Truman used atomic weapons to overawe the Soviet Union and induce it to move cautiously in expanding its influence in Europe and east Asia. Truman and his advisers were certainly aware of how the bomb might influence the Soviet leadership.
Domestic politics	President Roosevelt and his chief military advisers had spent billions on the secret atomic bomb project without the knowledge of Congress or the American public. The managers of the Manhattan Project may have believed that only proof of its military value would quiet critics and justify the huge cost.
Momentum of war	The United States and Britain had already adopted wholesale destruction of German and Japanese cities as a military tactic. Use of the atomic bomb looked like a variation on fire bombing, not the start of a new era of potential mass destruction. In this context, some historians argue, President Truman's choice was natural and expected.

Conclusion

World War II changed the lives of tens of millions of Americans. It made and unmade families. It gave millions of women new responsibilities and then sent them back to the kitchen. It put money in pockets that had been emptied by the Great Depression and turned struggling business owners into tycoons.

Most of the 16 million men and women in uniform served in support jobs that keep the war machine going. They repaired airplanes and built runways, tracked supplies, and counted coffins. Poet John Ciardi wrote out commendations for valor. Bill Mauldin drew cartoons for the Army newspaper *Stars and Stripes.*

For many readers, Mauldin's cartoon GIs, Willie and Joe, came to represent the experience of the front lines. It was loyalty to the men in their own unit that kept fighting men steady. "The only thing that kept you going was your faith in your buddies," recalled a Marine from the Pacific theater. "You couldn't let 'em down. It was stronger than flag and country."

Whether on the home front or the fighting front, Americans knew that victory was uncertain. World War II adventure movies in which Americans always win leave the impression that triumph was necessary and inevitable. In fact, victory was the hard-fought result of public leadership and military effort. Under other leaderships, the United States might have stood aside until it was too late to reverse the Axis conquest of Europe and east Asia. The collapse of the Soviet Union or failure of the North Atlantic convoy system might have made Germany unbeatable. In 1941 and 1942 in particular, Americans faced each day with fear and uncertainty.

The war unified the nation in new ways while confirming old divisions. People of all backgrounds shared a common cause. Farm boys mixed with city slickers, Northerners with Southerners. "When I woke up the first morning on the troop train in Fulton, Kentucky," recalled one Midwesterner, "I thought I was in Timbuktu." The war narrowed the distance between native-born, small-town Americans and recent European immigrants from the big cities. The chasms between Protestant, Catholic, and Jewish Americans were far narrower in 1945 than they had been in 1940.

But nothing broke the barriers that separated white and black Americans. Unequal treatment in a war for democracy outraged black soldiers, who returned to fight for civil rights. The uprooting of Japanese Americans was another reminder of racial prejudice. After the war, however, memories of the contrast between the nation's fight against Axis tyranny and the unequal treatment of American citizens fueled a gradual shift of public attitudes that climaxed in the civil rights movements of the 1950s and 1960s.

The insecurities of the war years influenced the United States for decades. A nation's current leaders are often shaped by its last war. Hitler, Mussolini, Churchill, and Truman all served in World War I and carried its memories in World War II. The lessons of World War II would similarly influence the thinking of presidents from Eisenhower in the 1950s to Bush in the 1990s. Even though the United States ended 1945 with the world's mightiest navy, biggest air force, and only atomic bomb, the instability that had followed World War I made Western leaders nervous about the shape of world politics.

One result in the postwar era was conflict between the United States and the Soviet Union, whose only common ground had been a shared enemy. After Germany's defeat, their wartime alliance gave way to hostility and confrontation in the Cold War. At home, international tensions fed pressure for social and political conformity. The desire to enjoy the fruits of victory after fifteen years of economic depression and sacrifice made the postwar generation sensitive to perceived threats to steady jobs and stable families. For the next generation, the unresolved business of World War II would haunt American life.

Review Questions

1. What motivated German, Italian, and Japanese aggression in the 1930s? How did Great Britain, the USSR, and other nations respond to the growing conflict?

2. What arguments did Americans make against involvement in the war in Europe? Why did President Roosevelt and many others believe it necessary to block German and Japanese expansion? What steps did Roosevelt take to increase U.S. involvement short of war?

3. What was the military balance in early 1942? What were the chief threats to the United States and its allies? Why did the fortunes of war turn in late 1942?

4. Assess how mobilization for World War II altered life in the United States. How did the war affect families? How did it shift the regional balance of the economy? What opportunities did it open for women?

5. Did World War II help or hinder progress toward racial equality in the United States? How did the experiences of Japanese Americans, African Americans, and Mexican Americans challenge American ideals?

6. What factors were decisive in the defeat of Germany? How important were Soviet efforts on the Eastern Front, the bomber war, and the British-American landings in France?

7. What was the U.S. strategy against Japan, and how well did it work? What lay behind President Truman's decision to use atomic bombs against Japanese cities?

Recommended Reading

Beth Bailey and David Farber, *The First Strange Place: The Alchemy of Race and Sex in World War II Hawaii* (1992). Explores the effects of the war on American ideas about the proper roles of men and women, black people, white people, and Asian Americans.

Doris Kearns Goodwin, *No Ordinary Time: Franklin and Eleanor Roosevelt, the Home Front in World War II* (1994). A prize-winning study that presents the tensions and crises of World War II through the daily lives of President Roosevelt, his wife Eleanor, and others in the White House.

John Hersey, *Hiroshima* (1946). Recounts the atomic bombing through the eyes of victims and survivors.

John Keegan, *The Second World War* (1990). A comprehensive and readable account giving a strong sense of the relative importance of the various fronts.

William L. O'Neill, *A Democracy at War: America's Fight at Home and Abroad in World War II* (1993). An insightful summary that explores the choices that the United States made in mobilizing and conducting the war.

Martin J. Sherwin, *A World Destroyed: The Atomic Bomb and the Grand Alliance* (1975). Explains why American leaders never seriously considered alternatives to the atomic bomb.

Studs Terkel, *The Good War: An Oral History of World War II* (1984). Eloquent testimony about the effects of the war on both ordinary and extraordinary Americans.

Additional Sources

The Politics of War

Wayne S. Cole, *Roosevelt and the Isolationists* (1983).

Robert Dallek, *Franklin D. Roosevelt and American Foreign Policy, 1932–1945* (1979).

Waldo Heinrichs, *Threshold of War: Franklin D. Roosevelt and American Entry into World War II* (1988).

Akira Iriye, *Power and Culture: The Japanese-American War, 1941–1945* (1981).

Warren Kimball, *The Juggler: Franklin Roosevelt as Wartime Statesman* (1991).

James Schneider, *Should America Go to War? The Debate over Foreign Policy in Chicago, 1939–1941* (1989).

Military Operations

Stephen E. Ambrose, *D-Day, June 6, 1944: The Climactic Battle of World War II* (1994).

Anthony Beevor, *Stalingrad* (1998).

John D. Chappell, *Before the Bomb: How Americans Approached the Pacific War* (1997).

John Keegan, *Six Armies in Normandy; From D-Day to the Liberation of Paris* (1982).

Samuel Eliot Morrison, *The Two-Ocean War: A Short History of the United States Navy in the Second World War* (1963).

Gordon Prange, *At Dawn We Slept: The Untold Story of Pearl Harbor* (1981).

John Ray Skates, *The Invasion of Japan: Alternative to the Bomb* (1994).

Ronald H. Spector, *Eagle against the Sun: The American War with Japan* (1985).

David Syrett, *The Defeat of the German U-Boats: The Battle of the Atlantic* (1994).

Barbara W. Tuchman, *Stillwell and the American Experience in China, 1911–1945* (1970).

Russell Weigley, *Eisenhower's Lieutenants* (1981).

H.P. Willmott, *The Great Crusade: A New Complete History of the Second World War* (1989).

The Experience of War

Craig M. Cameron, *American Samurai: Myth, Imagination, and the Conduct of Battle in the First Marine Division, 1941–1951* (1994).

Michael Doubler, *Closing with the Enemy: How GIs Fought the War in Europe, 1944–1945* (1994).

Paul Fussell, *Wartime: Understanding and Behavior in the Second World War* (1989).

Harold P. Leinbaugh and John D. Campbell, *The Men of Company K: The Autobiography of a World War II Rifle Company* (1985).

William Manchester, *Goodbye Darkness: A Memoir of the Pacific War* (1980).

Harrison Salisbury, *The 900 Days: The Siege of Leningrad* (1969).

Mobilizing the Home Front

John M. Blum, *V Was for Victory: Politics and American Culture during World War II* (1976).

Thomas Doherty, *Projections of War: Hollywood, American Culture, and World War II* (1994).

Mark Foster, *Henry J. Kaiser: Builder in the Modern American West* (1989).

Clayton Koppes and Gregory Black, *Hollywood Goes to War* (1987).

Nelson Lichtenstein, *Labor's War at Home: The CIO in World War II* (1983).

Gerald Nash, *The American West Transformed: The Impact of the Second World War* (1985).

Richard Polenberg, *War and Society: The United States, 1941–1945* (1972).

Richard Rhodes, *The Making of the Atomic Bomb* (1986).

William M. Tuttle, *Daddy's Gone to War: The Second World War in the Lives of America's Children* (1993).

Harold Vatter, *The U.S. Economy in World War II* (1985).

Women and the War Effort

Karen Anderson, *Wartime Women: Sex Roles, Family Relations, and the Status of Women during World War II* (1981).

D'Ann Campbell, *Women at War with America: Private Lives in a Patriotic Era* (1984).

Susan Hartmann, *The Home Front and Beyond: American Women in the 1940s* (1982).

Amy Kesselman, *Fleeting Opportunities: Women in Portland and Vancouver Shipyards during World War II and Reconversion* (1990).

Judy Barrett Litoff, *We're in This War Too: World War II Letters of American Women in Uniform* (1994).

Racial Attitudes and U.S. Policy

Roger Daniels, *Concentration Camps U.S.A.: Japanese Americans and World War II* (1971).

John Dower, *War without Mercy: Race and Power in the Pacific War* (1986).

Dominic J. Capeci, Jr., *Race Relations in Wartime Detroit: The Sojourner Truth Controversy of 1942* (1984).

David S. Wyman, *The Abandonment of the Jews: America and the Holocaust, 1941–1945* (1984).

Where to Learn More

❖ **USS *Arizona* Memorial and Submarine Memorial Park, Pearl Harbor, Hawaii.** The memorial commemorates the men who died in the Japanese attack of December 7, 1941, and recounts the events of the day.

❖ **Air Force Museum, Dayton, Ohio.** Visitors can walk among World War II fighter planes and bombers, including the B-29 that dropped the atomic bomb on Nagasaki, and learn about the role of aviation in the war.

❖ **Japanese-American Historical Plaza, Portland, Oregon.** The plaza uses landscaping and haiku (Japanese-style poems) to convey the meaning of internment for Japanese Americans.

❖ **Los Alamos County Historical Museum and Bradbury Science Museum, Los Alamos, New Mexico.** The museum traces the origins of atomic energy for military and civilian uses. Nearby is the Los Alamos County Historical Museum, which gives the feel of everyday life in the atomic town.

❖ **United States Holocaust Memorial Museum, Washington, D.C.** The Holocaust Museum gives visitors a deeply moving depiction of the deadly impacts of Nazi ideas in the 1930s and 1940s.

THE COLD WAR AT HOME AND ABROAD, 1946–1952

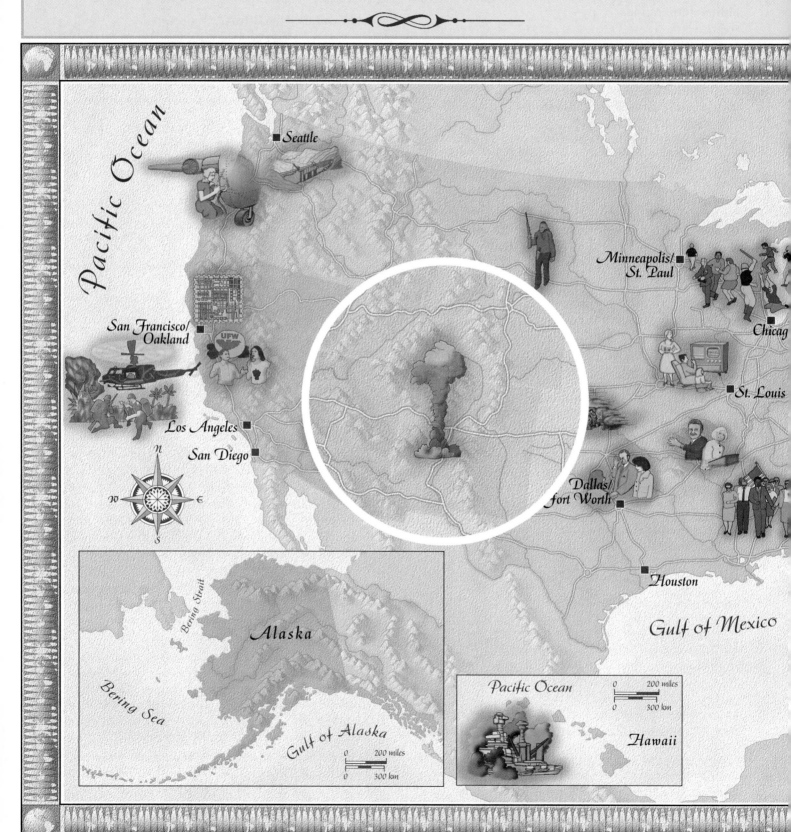

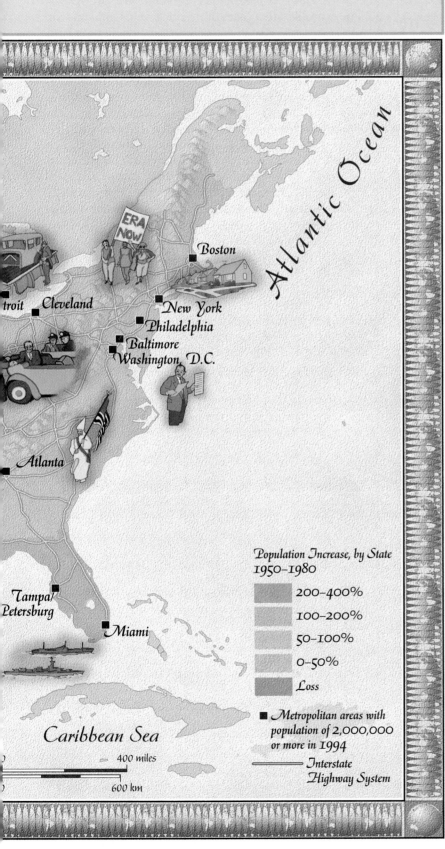

Key Topics

❖ Post-war shortages and the massive exit of women from the workforce
❖ The beginning of a twenty-five-year economic boom
❖ The beginning of the postwar civil rights movement
❖ The origins of the Cold War
❖ The reelection of Harry Truman
❖ The Korean War and the nuclear arms race
❖ McCarthy and the Second Red Scare

*I*n 1947, *The Best Years of Our Lives* swept the Academy Awards. The film won seven Oscars, including best picture, best director, and best actor. The immensely popular movie dealt with the problems of returning veterans as squarely as Hollywood could. It follows three veterans as they try to readjust to civilian life. The plot cuts between the personal problems of reconnecting with wives and sweethearts and the social challenge of finding meaningful work.

Behind the story line was nagging concern about the future. "Hard times are coming," one character predicts. The film reminded audiences of their own difficulties with postwar inflation, shortages, and strikes and their fears of another economic depression. The end, however, is upbeat. Wandering through a junkyard for discarded bombers, one of the veterans relives the nightmare of bombing runs over Germany but ends up with a job recycling the planes into building materials for new houses. After months spent in a bar trying to figure out the postwar world, he will now be able to marry his girlfriend and grab a share of the American dream.

Most Americans in 1946 wanted to follow the same script and put together the best years of their lives. After years of hardship, they defined American ideals in terms of economic opportunity and the chance to enjoy national prosperity. Even President Truman replaced the model gun on his White House desk with a model plow.

This compelling desire to enjoy the promise of American life after years of sacrifice helps explain why Americans reacted so fiercely to new challenges and threats. They watched as congressional conservatives and President Truman fought over the fate of New Deal programs. More worrisome was the confrontation with the Soviet Union that was soon being called the **Cold War**. Triggered by the Soviet Union's imposition of communist regimes throughout eastern Europe, the Cold War grew into a global contest in which the United States tried to counter Soviet influence around the world. By the time real war broke out in Korea in 1950, many Americans were venting their frustration by blaming international setbacks on internal subversion and by trying to root out suspected "reds."

The Cold War began in the late 1940s, but it would shape the United States and the world for another generation. Massive rearmament allowed U.S. presidents to act as international policemen in the name of democratic values—a vast change from earlier American foreign relations. Defense spending also reshaped American industry and helped stimulate twenty-five years of economic growth. The Cold War narrowed the range of political discussion, making many of the left-wing ideas of the 1930s taboo by the 1950s. It also made racial segregation and limits on immigration into international embarrassments and thus nudged the nation to live up to its ideals.

Launching the Great Boom

When World War II ended, Americans feared that demobilization would bring a rerun of the inflation and unemployment that had followed World War I. In the first eighteen months of peace, rising prices, labor–management strife, and shortages of everything from meat to automobiles confirmed their anxiety. In 1947 and 1948, however, an economic expansion began that lasted for a quarter century. The resulting prosperity would finance a military buildup and an activist foreign policy. It also supported continuity in domestic politics from the late 1940s to the mid-1960s.

Reconversion Chaos

Japan's sudden surrender took U.S. officials by surprise. They had planned on taking two years to phase out military spending and reintroduce veterans to the domestic economy. Now their plans were obsolete. The Pentagon, already scaling back defense spending, canceled $15 billion in war contracts in the first two days after Japanese surrender. Public pressure demanded that the military release the nation's

The Best Years of Our Lives *dealt realistically with the problems facing veterans trying to readjust to civilian life. Director William Wyler strove for a feeling of accuracy, shooting on location in Cincinnati and costuming the actors in clothing bought in local stores.*

12 million servicemen and servicewomen as rapidly as possible. GIs in Europe and the South Pacific waited impatiently for their turn on slow, crowded troop ships and calculated their order of discharge according to length of time in uniform, service overseas, combat decorations, and number of children. Even at the rate of 25,000 discharges a day, it took a year to get veterans back to the States and civilian life.

Veterans came home to shortages of food in the grocery stores and consumer goods in the department stores. High demand and short supply meant inflationary pressure, checked temporarily by continuing the Office of Price Administration until October 1946. Meanwhile, producers, consumers, and retailers scrambled to evade price restrictions and scarcities. Farmers sold meat on the black market, bypassing the big packing companies for one-on-one deals at higher prices. Automobiles were especially scarce; the number of vehicles registered in the United States had declined by 4 million during the war. For the privilege of spending a few hundred dollars on a junker, consumers sometimes had to pay used-car dealers for so-called accessories like $150 batteries and $100 lap robes.

A wave of strikes made it hard to retool factories for civilian products. Inflation squeezed factory workers, who had accepted wage controls during the war effort. Since 1941, prices had risen twice as fast as base wages. In the fall of 1945, more and more workers went on strike to redress the balance; the strikes interrupted the output of products from canned soup to copper wire. By January 1946, some 1.3 million auto, steel, electrical, and packinghouse workers were off the job. Strikes in these basic industries shut other

factories down for lack of supplies. Presidential committees finally crafted settlements that allowed steel and auto workers to make up ground lost during the war, but they also allowed corporations to pass on higher costs to consumers. One Republican senator complained of "unionists who fatten themselves at the expense of the rest of us." Bill Nation, who inspected window moldings at a GM plant in Detroit, wondered who the senator was talking about. The strike gave him an hourly raise of 18 cents, pushing his weekly income to $59. After paying for food, housing, and utilities, that left $13.44 for Bill, his wife, and five children to spend on clothes, comic books, and doctor bills.

Economic Policy

The economic turmoil of 1946 set the stage for two major—and contradictory—efforts to deal more systematically with peacetime economic readjustment. The **Employment Act of 1946** and the **Taft-Hartley Act** of 1947 represented liberal and conservative approaches to the peacetime economy.

The Employment Act was an effort by congressional liberals to ward off economic crisis by fine-tuning government taxation and spending. It started as a proposal for a full-employment bill that would have committed the federal government to ensure everyone's "right to a useful and remunerative job." Watered down in the face of business opposition, it still defined economic growth and high employment as national goals. It also established the **Council of Economic Advisers** to assist the president. Even this weak legislation, putting the federal government at the center of economic planning, would have been unthinkable a generation earlier.

In the short term, the Employment Act aimed at a problem that didn't materialize. Economists had predicted that the combination of returning veterans and workers idled by cancelled defense work would bring depression-level unemployment of 8 to 10 million. In fact, more than 2 million women provided some slack by leaving the labor force outright. Federal agencies hastened their departure by publishing pamphlets asking men the pointed question, "Do you want your wife to work after the war?" In addition, consumer spending from a savings pool of $140 billion in bank accounts and war bonds created a huge demand for workers to fill. Total employment rose rather than fell with the end of the war, and unemployment in 1946–1948 stayed below 4 percent.

From the other end of the political spectrum, the Taft-Hartley Act climaxed a ten-year effort by conservatives to reverse the gains made by organized labor in the 1930s. The act passed in 1947 because of anger about continuing strikes. For many Americans,

CHRONOLOGY

1944 Servicemen's Readjustment Act (GI Bill) is passed.

1945 United Nations is established.

1946 Employment Act creates Council of Economic Advisers.

George Kennan sends his "long telegram."

Winston Churchill delivers his "iron curtain" speech.

1947 Truman Doctrine is announced.

Truman establishes a federal employee loyalty program.

Kennan explains containment policy in an anonymous article in *Foreign Affairs*.

Marshall Plan begins providing economic aid to Europe.

HUAC holds hearings on Hollywood.

Taft-Hartley Act rolls back gains of organized labor.

National Security Act creates the National Security Council and the Central Intelligence Agency.

1948 Communists stage coup in Czechoslovakia.

Berlin airlift overcomes Soviet blockade.

Truman orders desegregation of the armed forces.

Selective Service is reestablished.

Truman wins reelection.

1949 North Atlantic Treaty Organization is formed.

Communist Chinese defeat Nationalists.

Soviet Union tests an atomic bomb.

Department of Defense is established.

1950 Senator McCarthy begins his Red hunt.

Alger Hiss is convicted of perjury.

NSC-68 is drafted and accepted as U.S. policy.

Korean War begins.

1951 Senate Internal Security Subcommittee begins hearings.

Truman relieves MacArthur of his command.

Julius and Ethel Rosenberg are convicted of conspiring to commit espionage.

Truce talks begin in Korea.

1952 United States tests the hydrogen bomb.

Eisenhower is elected president.

---

the chief culprit was John L. Lewis, head of the United Mine Workers, who had won good wages for coal miners with a militant policy that included wartime walkouts. In a country that still burned coal for most of its energy, the burly, bushy-browed, and combative Lewis was instantly recognizable—loved by his workers and hated by nearly everyone else. In April 1946, a forty-day coal strike hampered industrial production. The coal settlement was only days old when the nation faced an even more crippling walkout by railroad workers. Truman asked for the unprecedented power to draft strikers into the army; the threat led to a quick and dramatic settlement. Many middle-class Americans were convinced that organized labor needed to be curbed.

In November 1946, Republicans capitalized on the problems of reconversion chaos, labor unrest, and dissatisfaction with Truman. Their election slogan was simple: "Had enough?" The GOP won control of Congress for the first time since the election of 1928, continuing the political trend toward the right that had been apparent since 1938.

Adopted by the now firmly conservative Congress, the Taft-Hartley Act was a serious counterat-tack by big business against large unions. It outlawed several union tools as "unfair labor practices." It barred the closed shop (the requirement that all workers hired in a particular company or plant be union members) and blocked secondary boycotts (strikes against suppliers or customers of a targeted business). The federal government could postpone a strike by imposing a "cooling-off period," which gave companies time to stockpile their output. Officers of national unions had to swear they were not communists or communist sympathizers, even though corporate executives had no similar obligation. The bill passed over Truman's veto.

The GI Bill

Another landmark law for the postwar era passed Congress without controversy. The Servicemen's Readjustment Act of 1944 was designed to ease veterans back into the civilian mainstream. Popularly known as the **GI Bill of Rights**, it was one of the federal government's most successful public assistance programs. Rather than pay cash bonuses to veterans, as after previous wars, Congress tied benefits to specific public goals. The GI Bill guaranteed loans of up to $2,000 for buying a house or farm or starting a business, a substantial sum at a time when a new house cost $6,000. The program encouraged veterans to attend college with money for tuition and books plus monthly stipends.

The GI Bill democratized American higher education by making college degrees accessible to men with working-class backgrounds. It brought far more students into higher education than could otherwise have enrolled. In the peak year of 1947, veterans made up half of all college students. "We're all trying to get where we would have been if there hadn't been a war," one vet attending Indiana University told *Time* magazine. Veterans helped convert the college degree—once available primarily to the socially privileged—into a basic business and professional credential.

College life in 1946 and 1947 meant close quarters. Universities were unequipped to deal with older or married students. Prefabricated apartments from the wartime atomic energy project at Richland, Washington, were trucked to college campuses around the West to house newly enrolled veterans. Recycled Quonset huts became as much a part of campus architecture as gothic towers and ivy-covered halls. States rented surplus defense facilities for big-city extension campuses that would be easier for veterans to attend than traditional small-town universities. Many of these campuses evolved into major public universities, such as the University of Illinois at Chicago and Portland State University in Oregon.

An unfortunate side effect of the GI tide was to crowd women out of classrooms, although sixty thousand servicewomen did take advantage of educational benefits. In 1946, Cornell University made room for veterans by limiting women to 20 percent of its entering class. The University of Wisconsin closed its doors to women from out of state. Women's share of bachelor's degrees dropped from 40 percent in 1940 to 25 percent in 1950. The most common female presence on many campuses was working wives trying to make up the gap between Veterans Administration (VA) checks and the expenses of new families.

Assembly-Line Neighborhoods

Americans faced a housing shortage after the war. In 1947, fully 3 million married couples were unable to set up their own households. Most doubled up with relatives while they waited for the construction industry to respond.

Hunger for housing was fierce. Eager buyers lined up for hours and paid admission fees to tour model homes or to put their names in drawings for the opportunity to buy. When in 1946 the *Des Moines Register and Tribune* ran a fake apartment ad to check real estate industry claims that the housing crisis was over, 351 people answered it. Fifty-six of them said they lived in a hotel or rented room; sixty-eight lived with parents.

The solution started with the federal government and its VA mortgage program. By guaranteeing repayment, the VA allowed veterans to get home purchase loans from private lenders without a down payment. Neither the VA program nor the New Deal–era Federal Housing Administration (FHA) mortgage insurance program, however, could do any good unless there were houses to buy. Eyeing the mass market created by the federal programs, innovative private builders devised their own solution. In 1947, William Levitt, a New York builder who had developed defense housing projects, built two thousand rental houses for veterans on suburban Long Island. His basic house had eight hundred square feet of living space in two bedrooms, living room, kitchen, and bath, a sixty-by-one-hundred-foot lot, and an unfinished attic waiting for the weekend handyman. It gave new families a place to start. There were six thousand **Levittown** houses by the end of 1948 and more than seventeen thousand by 1951.

Other successful builders worked on the same scale. They bought hundreds of acres of land, put in utilities for the entire tract, purchased materials by the carload, and kept specialized workers busy on scores of identical houses. Floor plans were square, simple, and easy for semiskilled workers to construct. For the first time, kitchens across America were designed for preassembled cabinets and appliances in standard sizes. "On-site fabrication" was mass production without an assembly line. Work crews at the Los Angeles suburb of Lakewood started a hundred houses a day as they moved down one side of the street and back up the other, digging foundation trenches, pouring concrete, and working through the dozens of other stages of home building.

From 1946 through 1950, the federal government backed $20 billion in VA and FHA loans, approximately 40 percent of all home mortgage debt. Housing starts neared 2 million in the peak year of 1950. New subdivisions were starting places for couples in their late twenties or early thirties making up for lost time on a tight budget. By the end of the 1940s, 55 percent of American households owned their homes. The figure continued to climb until the 1980s, broadening access to the dream of financial security for many families. All during this time, the suburban population grew much faster

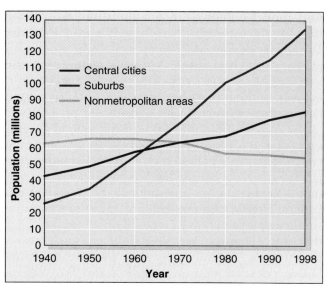

Figure 29-1   The Suburbanizing Nation
In the decades after World War II, Americans moved in un-
precedented numbers to new communities surrounding estab-
lished cities. In the early 1960s, the combined population of
suburban areas passed the populations of large central cities and
of smaller towns and rural areas.

than the population of central cities, and the population outside the growing reach of metropolitan areas actually declined (see Figure 29-1).

Unfortunately, the suburban solution to housing shortages also had costs. Vast new housing tracts tended to isolate women and children from traditional community life. They also did little to help African Americans. As the migration of black workers and their families to northern and western cities continued after the war, discrimination excluded them from new housing. As late as 1960, the 82,000 residents of Levittown had no African American neighbors; not until 1957 did a black family move into a second Levittown near Philadelphia. Federal housing agencies and private industry worsened the problem by **redlining** older neighborhoods, which involved withholding home purchase loans and insurance coverage from inner-city areas.

Public and private actions kept African Americans in deteriorating inner-city ghettos. When severe flooding in 1948 drove thousands of African Americans from leftover wartime housing in Portland, Oregon, for example, their only choice was to crowd into the city's small black neighborhood. Chicago landlords squeezed an estimated 27,000 black migrants per year into run-down buildings, subdividing larger apartments into one-room "kitchenette" units with sinks and hot plates but no private bathrooms. One tenant commented that rats came

"in teams." Families who tried to find new homes in white neighborhoods on the edge of black ghettos often met violence—rocks through windows, firebombs, angry white mobs.

Steps toward Civil Rights

The problem of securing decent housing fueled a demand for civil rights for African Americans. The wartime experience of fighting for freedom abroad while suffering discrimination at home steeled a new generation of black leaders to reduce the gap between America's ideal of equality and its performance. As had also been true after World War I, some white Americans had the opposite view, hoping to reaffirm racial segregation. A wave of racist violence surged across the South after the war; special targets were black veterans who tried to register to vote. However, many white Americans felt uneasy about the contradiction between a crusade for freedom abroad and racial discrimination at home.

In this era of rapid change and racial tension, the Truman administration recognized the importance of securing civil rights for all Americans. Caught between pressure from black leaders and the fear of alienating southern Democrats, the president in 1946 appointed the Committee on Civil Rights, whose report developed an agenda for racial justice that would take two decades to put into effect. The Justice Department began to support antisegregation lawsuits filed by the NAACP. The administration ordered federal housing agencies to modify their racially restrictive policies and prohibited racial discrimination in federal employment.

The president also ordered "equality of treatment and opportunity" in the armed services in July 1948. The army in particular dragged its feet, hoping to limit black enlistees to 10 percent of the total. Manpower needs and the record of integrated units in Korea from 1950 to 1953 persuaded the reluctant generals. Over the next generation, African Americans would find the military an important avenue for career opportunities.

Changes in national policy were important for ending racial discrimination, but far more Americans were interested in the lowering of racial barriers in professional team sports. Americans had applauded individual black champions, such as heavyweight boxer Joe Louis and sprinter Jesse Owens, but team sports required their members to travel, practice, and play together. The center of attention was Jack Roosevelt (Jackie) Robinson, a gifted African American athlete who opened the 1947 baseball season as a member of the Brooklyn Dodgers. Black baseball players had previously displayed their talents

Jackie Robinson with white teammates in the Dodger dugout at Ebbets Field, Brooklyn.

Fast-growing families also needed to stock up on household goods. Out of an average household income of roughly $4,000 in 1946 and 1947, a family of four had $300 to $400 a year for furnishings and appliances. A couple who studied *Consumer Reports* might equip their new Levittown kitchen with a Dripolator coffee maker for $2.45 and Mirro-Matic pressure cooker for $12.95. The thrifty family could get along with a Motorola table radio in brown plastic for under $30; for $100, they could have a massive radio-phonograph combination in a four-foot console—the centerpiece of a well-equipped living room before the arrival of television.

Truman, Republicans, and the Fair Deal

From new radios to new homes to new jobs, the economic gains of the postwar years propelled Americans toward the political center. After fifteen years of economic crisis and world war, they wanted to enjoy prosperity. They wanted to keep the gains of the New Deal—but without risking new experiments. William Levitt tried to humorously capture the American satisfaction with the fruits of free en-

in the Negro leagues, but Robinson broke the color line that had reserved the modern major leagues for white players. His ability to endure taunting and hostility and still excel on the ball field opened the door for other African Americans and Latinos. In the segregated society of the 1940s, Robinson also found himself a powerful symbol of racial change.

Consumer Boom and Baby Boom

The housing boom was a product of both pent-up demand and a postwar "family boom." Americans celebrated the end of the war with weddings; the marriage rate in 1946 surpassed even its wartime high. Many women who left the labor force opted for marriage, and at increasingly younger ages. By 1950, the median age at which women married would be just over 20 years—lower than at any previous time in the twentieth century. Movies in the 1930s had abounded with independent career women. By the late 1940s, Hollywood reflected new attitudes and social patterns by portraying women as helpless victims or supportive wives and publicizing hard-edged stars, such as Joan Crawford, as homebodies at heart. The United States ended the 1940s with 7 million more married couples than at the decade's start.

New marriages jump-started the "baby boom," as did already married couples who decided to catch up after postponing childbearing during the war. In the early 1940s, an average of 2.9 million children per year were born in the United States; in 1946–1950, the average was 3.6 million. Those 3.5 million "extra" babies needed diapers, swing sets, lunch boxes, bicycles, and schoolrooms (see Figure 29-2).

Figure 29-2   The Post-War Baby Boom: The U.S. Birthrate, 1930–1995

The baby boom after World War II was a product of high marriage rates and closely spaced children. The generation of Americans born between 1945 and 1960 has strongly affected American society and politics as its members have gone to school and college, entered the workforce, started their own families, and begun to plan for retirement in the twenty-first century.

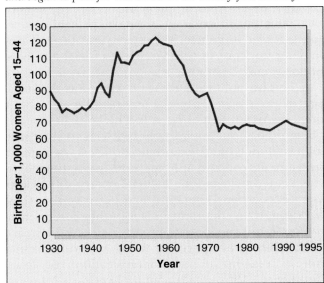

Americans were eager to enjoy the most modern appliances and houses. Manufacturers promoted streamlined kitchens to make life easier for housewives and their families.

terprise when he said in 1948 that "no man who owns his house and lot can be a Communist; he has too much to do."

Recognizing this attitude, Harry Truman and his political advisers tried to define policies acceptable to moderate Republicans as well as Democrats. This meant creating a bipartisan coalition to block Soviet influence in western Europe and defending the core of the New Deal's social and economic agenda at home.

This political package is known as the strategy of the "vital center," after the title of a 1949 book by Arthur Schlesinger, Jr. The book linked anticommunism in foreign policy with efforts to enact inclusive social and economic policies—to extend freedom abroad and at home at the same time. The vital center reflected the political reality of the Cold War years, when Democrats had to prove that they were tough on communism before they could enact domestic reforms. The approach defined the heart of the Democratic party for twenty years and found full expression in the administrations of John Kennedy (1961–1963) and Lyndon Johnson (1963–1969).

Truman's Opposition

Truman had unexpected luck in his campaign for a full term as president in 1948. Besides the Republicans, he faced new fringe parties on the far right and far left that allowed him to position himself in the moderate center. The blunt, no-nonsense Missourian entered the campaign an underdog, but, compared to his rivals, he soon looked like the country's best option for steering a steady course.

Truman's opponents represented the left-leaning American Progressive party, the **Dixiecrats** (officially the States' Rights Democrats), and the Republicans. The president also ran against the Republican-controlled "do-nothing 80th Congress," which he used as a punching bag at every opportunity. The Progressive candidate was Henry Wallace, who had been FDR's vice president from 1941 to 1945 before being dumped in favor of Truman himself; more recently, he had been Truman's secretary of commerce. The Dixiecrat, Governor Strom Thurmond of South Carolina, had bolted the Democratic party over civil rights. The most serious challenger was Republican Thomas Dewey, who had run against Roosevelt in 1944.

Wallace cast himself as the prophet for "the century of the common man." His background as a plant geneticist and farm journalist prepared him to deal with domestic policy but not world affairs. After Truman fired him from the cabinet in 1946 for advocating a conciliatory stance toward the Soviet Union, Wallace went to Europe to praise the USSR and denounced U.S. foreign policy. On his return, enthusiastic college crowds raised his sights—from "scaring the Democratic Party leftward" to running for president. Most liberal Democrats ran the other way when Wallace organized the Progressive party, leaving the Communist party to supply many of his campaign workers.

Wallace argued that the United States was forcing the Cold War on the Soviet Union and undermining American ideals by diverting attention from poverty and racism at home. He wanted to repeal the draft and destroy atomic weapons. His arguments had merit, for the United States was becoming a militarized society, but Wallace was the wrong person to change American minds. With his shy personality, disheveled appearance, and fanaticism about health food, he struck most voters as a kook rather than a statesman. Although a small core of supporters clung to his message of international reconciliation, Wallace made skepticism about the Cold War increasingly vulnerable to right-wing attack.

At the other political extreme were the Southerners who walked out when the 1948 Democratic National Convention called for full civil rights for African Americans. The raucous convention debate previewed the politics of the 1960s. Mayor Hubert Humphrey of Minneapolis challenged the Democratic party "to get out of the shadow of states' rights and walk forthrightly into the bright sunshine of human rights." His speech foreshadowed Humphrey's twenty years of liberal influence in the Democratic party, culminating in his presidential nomination in 1968.

When the angry Southerners met to nominate their own candidate, however, the South's important politicians stayed away. They had worked too long to throw away seniority and influence in Congress and the Democratic party. Major southern newspapers called the revolt futile and narrowminded. Strom Thurmond claimed that the Dixiecrats were really trying to defend Americans against government bureaucracy, not fighting to preserve racial segregation, but few listened outside the deep South.

Tom Dewey, Truman's real opponent, had a high opinion of himself. He had been an effective governor of New York and represented the moderate eastern establishment within the Republican party. Fortunately for Truman, Dewey lacked the common touch. Smooth on the outside, he alienated people who should have been his closest supporters; as one political acquaintance put it, "You have to know Dewey really well to dislike him." He was an arrogant campaigner, refusing to interrupt his morning schedule to talk to voters. He acted like a snob and dressed like the groom on a wedding cake.

Dewey was also saddled with the results of the 80th Congress (1947–1948). Truman used confrontation with Congress to rally voters who had supported the New Deal. He introduced legislation that he knew would be ignored, and he used his veto even when he knew Congress would override it. All the while he was building a list of campaign issues by demonstrating that the Republicans were obstructionists. Vote for me, Truman argued, to protect the New Deal, or vote Republican to bring back the days of Herbert Hoover. After his nomination in July 1948, Truman called Congress back into session and dared Republicans to enact all the measures for which their party claimed to stand. Congress did nothing, and Truman had more proof that the Republicans were all talk and no show.

Whistle-Stopping across America

The 1948 presidential campaign mixed old and new. For the last time, a major candidate crisscrossed the nation by rail and made hundreds of speeches from the rear platforms of trains. For the first time, national television broadcast the two party conventions, although the primitive cameras showed the handful of viewers little more than talking heads. The Repub-

lican campaign issued a printed T-shirt that read "Dew-It With Dewey"—the earliest advertising T-shirt in the collections of the Smithsonian Institution.

Truman ran on both character and issues. He was a widely read and intelligent man who cultivated the image of a backslapper. "I'll mow 'em down . . . and I'll give 'em hell," he told his vice presidential running mate. Crowds across the country greeted him with "Give 'em hell, Harry!" He covered 31,700 miles in his campaign train and gave ten speeches a day. Republicans belittled the small towns and cities he visited, calling them "whistle-stops." Democrats made the term a badge of pride for places like Laramie, Wyoming, and Pocatello, Idaho.

Truman brought the campaign home to average Americans. On the advice of political strategist Clark Clifford, he tied Dewey to inflation, housing shortages, and fears about the future of Social Security. In industrial cities, he hammered at the Taft-Hartley Act. In the West, he pointed out that Democratic administrations had built dams and helped turn natural resources into jobs. He called the Republicans the party of privilege and arrogance.

Harry Truman greets supporters and railroad workers in Pittsburgh at the start of an eighteen-state campaign tour in June 1948. Truman's grassroots campaign and down-home style helped him pull out an unexpected victory in November 1948.

The Democrats, he said, offered opportunity for farmers, factory workers, and small business owners.

Truman got a huge boost from Dewey's unwillingness to fight. Going into the fall with a huge lead in the public opinion polls, Dewey sought to avoid mistakes. He failed to counter Truman's attacks and packed his speeches with platitudes: "Our streams abound with fish." "You know that your future is still ahead of you." "Peace is a blessing that we all share." The results astounded the poll takers, who had stopped sampling opinion in mid-October—just as a swing to Truman gathered strength. Wallace and Thurmond each took just under 1.2 million votes. Dewey received nearly 22 million popular votes and 189 electoral votes, but Truman won more than 24 million popular votes and 303 electoral votes (see Map 29-1).

Truman's Fair Deal

Truman hoped to build on the gains of the New Deal. In his State of the Union address in January 1949, he called for a **Fair Deal** for all Americans. He promised to extend the New Deal and ensure "greater economic opportunity for the mass of the people." Over the next four years, however, conservative Republicans and southern Democrats forced Congress to chose carefully among Truman's proposals, accepting those that expanded existing programs but rejecting new departures.

In the Housing Act of 1949, the federal government reaffirmed its concern about families who had been priced out of the private market. Passed with the backing of conservative Senator Robert Taft—"Mr. Republican" to his admirers—the act provided money for local housing agencies to buy, clear, and resell land for housing. The intent was to clear "substandard and blighted areas" and replace them with affordable modern apartments. The program never worked as intended because of scanty appropriations and poor design of the replacement housing, but it established the goal of decent housing for all Americans.

In 1950, Congress revitalized the weak Social Security program. Benefits went up by an average of 80 percent, and 10.5 million additional people received old-age and survivors' insurance. Most of the new coverage went to rural and small-town people, thus consolidating the broad support that has made it politically difficult to change Social Security ever since, even in the face of projected shortages in the twenty-first century.

Congress rejected other Fair Deal proposals that would remain on the national agenda for decades. A plan to alter the farm subsidy system to favor small farmers rather than agribusiness went nowhere. A Senate filibuster killed a permanent Fair Employment Practices Commission to fight racial discrimination in hiring, halting progress toward civil rights. The medical establishment blocked a proposal for national health insurance as "socialistic," leaving the issue to be revisited in the 1960s (with the passage of Medicare and Medicaid) and 1990s (with Bill Clinton's proposals for health care reform). The overall message from Truman's second term was clear: Americans liked what the New Deal had given them but were hesitant about new initiatives.

Map 29-1   The Election of 1948

Harry Truman won a narrow victory in the presidential election of 1948 by holding many of the traditionally Democratic states of the South and West and winning key industrial states in the Middle West. His success depended on the coalition of rural and urban interests that Franklin Roosevelt had pulled together in the 1930s.

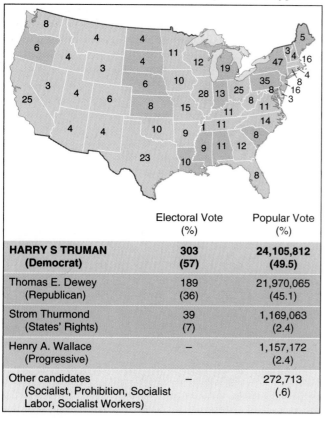

	Electoral Vote (%)	Popular Vote (%)
HARRY S TRUMAN (Democrat)	**303** **(57)**	**24,105,812** **(49.5)**
Thomas E. Dewey (Republican)	189 (36)	21,970,065 (45.1)
Strom Thurmond (States' Rights)	39 (7)	1,169,063 (2.4)
Henry A. Wallace (Progressive)	–	1,157,172 (2.4)
Other candidates (Socialist, Prohibition, Socialist Labor, Socialist Workers)	–	272,713 (.6)

Confronting the Soviet Union

In 1945, the United States and the Soviet Union were allies, victorious against Germany and planning the defeat of Japan. By 1947, they were engaged in a diplomatic and economic confrontation and soon came close to war over the city of Berlin. Business tycoon and presidential adviser Bernard Baruch characterized the conflict in April 1947 as a "cold war," and newspaper columnist Walter Lippmann quickly popularized the term.

Over the next forty years, the United States and the USSR contested for economic, political, and military influence around the globe. The heart of Soviet policy was control of eastern Europe as a buffer zone against Germany. The centerpiece of American policy was to link the United States, western Europe, and Japan into an alliance of overwhelming economic power. Both sides spent vast sums on conventional military forces and atomic weapons that held the world in a balance of terror. They also competed for political advantage in Asia and Africa as newly independent nations replaced European colonial empires. For the United States, the Cold War was simultaneously an effort to promote democracy in Europe, maintain a strategically favorable military position in relation to the USSR, and preserve its leadership of the world economy.

Each party in the Cold War thought the worst of the other. Behind the conflicts were Soviet insecurity about an aggressive West and American fear of communist expansionism. Americans and Soviets frequently interpreted each other's actions in the most threatening terms, turning miscalculations and misunderstandings into crises. A U.S. public that had suffered through nearly two decades of economic depression and war reacted to international problems with frustration and anger. The emotional burdens of the Cold War warped and narrowed a generation of American political life around the requirements of anticommunism.

The End of the Grand Alliance

The Yalta Conference of February 1945 had recognized military realities by marking out rough spheres of influence. The Soviet defeat of Germany on the Eastern Front had made the USSR the only military power in eastern Europe. The American and British attacks through Italy and France had made the Western allies dominant in western Europe and the Mediterranean. The Soviets, Americans, British, and French shared control of defeated Germany, each with its own occupation zone and its own sector of Berlin. The Western allies had the better of the bargain. Defeated Italy and Japan, whose reconstruction was firmly in Western hands, had far greater economic potential than Soviet-controlled Bulgaria, Romania, or Hungary. In addition, the British, French, and American occupation zones in western Germany had more people and industrial potential than the Russian zone in eastern Germany.

As the victorious powers tried to put their broad agreements into operation, they argued bitterly about Germany and eastern Europe. Was the Soviet Union to dominate eastern Europe, or was the region to be open to Western economic and political influence? For Poland, Truman and his advisers claimed that Yalta had assumed open elections on the American model. The Soviet Union saw Poland as the historic invasion route from the west; it claimed that Yalta had ensured that any Polish government would be friendly to Soviet interests and acted to guarantee that this would be so.

Facing Soviet intransigence over eastern Europe, Truman decided that the United States should "take the lead in running the world in the way the world ought to be run." One technique was economic pressure. The State Department "mislaid" a Soviet request for redevelopment loans. The United States and Britain objected to Soviet plans to take industrial equipment and raw materials from the western occupation zones in Germany, compensation that the Soviets thought they had been promised.

The United States also tried to involve the USSR and eastern Europe in new international organizations. The Senate approved American membership in the newly organized United Nations (UN) with only two opposing votes, a sharp contrast to its rejection of the League of Nations in 1920. The Washington-based **International Monetary Fund (IMF)** and the **World Bank** were designed to revive international trade. The IMF stabilized national currencies against the short-term pressures of international trade. The World Bank drew on the resources of member nations to make economic development loans to governments for such projects as new dams or agricultural modernization. These organizations ensured that a reviving world economy would revolve around the industrial and technological power of the United States.

In 1946, the United States also presented a plan in the United Nations to control atomic energy. Bernard Baruch suggested that an international agency should oversee all uranium production and research on atomic explosives. The Baruch plan emphasized enforcement and inspections that would have opened the Soviet nuclear effort to American interference, an unacceptable prospect for a nation trying to catch up with the United States by building its own atomic bombs. On-site inspection would remain a problem in arms control negotiations for the next half-century.

While UN delegates debated the future of atomic energy, American leaders were becoming convinced of Soviet aggressiveness. In February

1946, George Kennan, a senior American diplomat in Moscow, sent a "long telegram" to the State Department. He depicted a USSR driven by expansionist communist ideology. The Soviets, he argued, would constantly probe for weaknesses in the capitalist world. The best response was firm resistance to protect the western heartlands.

The British encouraged the same tough stand. Lacking the strength to shape Europe on its own, Great Britain repeatedly nudged the United States to block Soviet influence. Speaking at Westminster College in Missouri in March 1946, Winston Churchill warned that the USSR had dropped an "iron curtain" across the middle of Europe and urged a firm Western response.

Churchill's speech matched the mood in official Washington. Truman's foreign policy advisers shared the belief in an aggressive Soviet Union, and the president himself saw the world as a series of either-or choices. Administration leaders did not fear an immediate Soviet military threat to the United States itself, for they knew that World War II had exhausted the USSR. But they also knew that the Soviets were strong enough to brush aside the U.S. occupation forces in Germany. Added to military apprehension were worries about political and economic competition. Communist parties in war-ravaged Europe and Japan were exploiting discontent. In Asia and Africa, the allegiance of nationalists who were fighting for independence from France, Great Britain, and the Netherlands remained in doubt. America's leaders worried that much of the Eastern Hemisphere might fall under Soviet control and turn its back on North America.

Were Truman and his advisers right about Soviet intentions? The evidence is mixed. In their determination to avoid another Munich, Truman and the "wise men" who made up his foreign policy circle ignored examples of Soviet caution and conciliation. The Soviets withdrew troops from Manchuria in northern China and acquiesced in America's control of defeated Japan. They allowed a neutral but democratic government in Finland and technically free elections in Hungary and Czechoslovakia (although it was clear that communists would do well there). They demobilized much of their huge army and reduced their forces in eastern Europe while expecting a falling out between capitalist Britain and the United States.

However, the Soviet regime also did more than enough to justify American fears. The USSR could not resist interfering in the Middle East. It pressured Turkey to give it partial control of the exit from the Black Sea. It retained troops in northern Iran until warned out by the United States. The Soviets were ruthless in support of communist control in Bulgaria, Romania, and Poland. U.S. policymakers read these Soviet actions as a rerun of Nazi aggression and determined not to let a new totalitarian threat undermine Western power.

The Truman Doctrine and the Marshall Plan

Whatever restraint the USSR showed was too late or too little. Early in 1947, Truman and his advisers decided on decisive action. The British could no longer afford to back the Greek government that was fighting communist rebels, and U.S. officials feared that a communist takeover in Greece would threaten the stability of Italy, France, and the Middle East. Truman coupled his case for intervention in Greece with an appeal for aid to Turkey, which lived under the shadow of the USSR. On March 12, he told Congress that the United States faced a "fateful hour." Taking the advice of Senator Arthur Vandenberg to "scare the hell out of the country," he said that only the appropriation of $400 million to fight communism in Greece and Turkey could secure the free world. Congress agreed, and the United States became the dominant power in the eastern Mediterranean.

Framing the specific request was a sweeping declaration that became known as the **Truman Doctrine**. The president pledged to use U.S. economic power to help free nations everywhere resist internal subversion or aggression. "It must be the policy of the United States," he said, "to support free peoples who are resisting attempted subjugation by armed minorities or by outside pressures. . . . I believe that our help should be primarily through economic and financial aid, which is essential to economic stability and orderly political processes."

Meanwhile, Europe was sliding toward chaos. Germany was close to famine after the bitter winter of 1946–1947. Western European nations were bankrupt and unable to import raw materials for their factories. Overstressed medical systems could no longer control diseases such as tuberculosis. Communist parties had gained in Italy, France, and Germany. Winston Churchill, again sounding the alarm, described Europe as "a rubble-heap, a charnel house, a breeding ground of pestilence and hate."

The U.S. government responded with unprecedented economic aid. Secretary of State George C. Marshall announced the European Recovery Plan on June 5, 1947. What the press quickly dubbed the **Marshall Plan** committed the United States to help rebuild Europe. The United States invited Soviet and eastern European participation, but under terms that would have reduced Moscow's control over its satellite economies. The Soviets refused, fearing that the United States wanted to undermine its influence, instead organizing their eastern European satellites in their own association for Mutual Economic Assistance, or **Comecon**, in 1949. In western Europe, the Marshall Plan was a success. Aid totaled $13.5 billion over four years. It met many of Europe's economic needs and quieted class conflict. Unlike the heavy-handed Soviet role in eastern Europe, the Marshall Plan expanded American influence through cooperative efforts. Because Europeans spent much of the aid on U.S. goods and machinery and because economic recovery promised markets for U.S. products, business and labor both supported it. In effect, the Marshall Plan created an "empire by invitation" in which Americans and Europeans jointly planned European recovery.

U.S. policy in Japan followed the pattern set in Europe. As supreme commander of the Allied Powers, General Douglas MacArthur acted as Japan's postwar dictator. He tried to change the values of the old war-prone Japan through social reform, democratization, and demilitarization. At the end of 1947, however, the United States decided that democracy and pacifism could go too far. Policymakers were fearful of economic collapse and political chaos, just as in Europe. The "reverse course" in occupation policy aimed to make Japan an economic magnet for other nations in East Asia, pulling them toward the American orbit and away from the Soviet Union. MacArthur reluctantly accepted the new policy of "economic crank-up" by preserving Japan's corporate giants and encouraging American investment. At American insistence, the new Japan accepted American bases and created its own "self-defense force" (with no capacity for overseas aggression).

George Kennan summed up the new American policies in the magazine *Foreign Affairs* in July 1947. Writing anonymously as "X," Kennan argued that the Soviet leaders were committed to a long-term strategy of expanding communism. The proper posture of the United States, he said, should be an equally patient commitment to "firm and vigilant containment of Russian expansive tendencies." Kennan warned that the emerging Cold War would be a long conflict with no quick fixes.

Soviet Reactions

The bold American moves in the first half of 1947 put the USSR on the defensive. In response, Soviet leaders orchestrated strenuous opposition to the Marshall Plan by French and Italian communists. East of the iron curtain, Hungarian communists expelled noncommunists from a coalition government. Bulgarian communists shot opposition leaders. Ro-

mania, Bulgaria, and Hungary signed defense pacts with the Soviet Union.

In early 1948, the Soviets targeted Czechoslovakia. For three years, a neutral coalition government there on the model of Finland had balanced trade with the West with a foreign policy friendly to the USSR. In February 1948, while Russian forces assembled on the Czech borders, local communists pushed aside Czechoslovakia's democratic leadership and turned the nation into a dictatorship and Soviet satellite within a week.

The climax of the Soviet reaction came in divided Berlin, located 110 miles inside the Soviet Union's East German occupation zone. On June 24, 1948, Soviet troops blockaded surface traffic into Berlin, cutting off the U.S., British, and French sectors. The immediate Soviet aim was to block Western plans to merge their three occupation zones into an independent federal republic (West Germany). Rather than abandon 2.5 million Berliners or shoot their way through, the Western nations responded to the **Berlin blockade** by airlifting supplies to the city. Planes landed every two minutes at Berlin's Tempelhof Airport. Stalin decided not to intercept the flights. After eleven months, the Soviets abandoned the blockade, making the Berlin airlift a triumph of American resolve.

Berlin in 1948 was still a devastated city of gutted buildings and heaps of rubble. When the Soviet Union shut off ground access to Berlin's British, French, and American occupation zones, the city also became a symbol of the West's Cold War resolve. Allied aircraft lifted in food, fuel, and other essentials for West Berliners for nearly a year until the Soviets ended the blockade.

American Rearmament

The coup in Czechoslovakia and the Berlin blockade shocked American leaders and backfired on the Soviets. The economic assistance strategy of 1947 now looked inadequate. Congress responded in 1948 by reinstating the military draft and increasing defense spending. Much of the money bought new war planes, as thrifty congressmen decided that air power was the easiest way for the United States to project its military power abroad.

The United States had already begun to modernize and centralize its national security apparatus, creating the institutions that would run foreign policy in the second half of the century. The National Security Act of July 1947 created the **Central Intelligence Agency (CIA)** and the **National Security Council (NSC)**. The CIA handled intelligence gathering and covert operations. The NSC assembled top diplomatic and military advisers in one committee. In 1949, legislation also created the Department of Defense to oversee the army, navy, and air force (independent from the army since 1947). The new post of chairman of the Joint Chiefs of Staff was supposed to coordinate the rival branches of the military.

In April 1949, ten European nations, the United States, and Canada signed the North Atlantic Treaty as a mutual defense pact. American commitments to the **North Atlantic Treaty Organization (NATO)** included military aid and the deployment of U.S. troops in western Europe. As Republican Senator Robert Taft warned in the ratification debate, NATO was the sort of "entangling alliance" that the United States had avoided for 160 years. It was also the insurance policy that western Europeans required if they were to accept the dangers as well as the benefits of a revived Germany, which was economically and militarily necessary for a strong Europe. In short, NATO was a sort of marriage contract between Europe and the previously standoffish United States. After 1955, its counterpart would be the **Warsaw Pact** for mutual defense among the USSR and its European satellites (see Map 29-2).

Two years later, the United States signed similar but less comprehensive agreements in the western Pacific: the ANZUS Pact with Australia and New Zealand and a new treaty with the Philippines. The alliances reassured Pacific allies who were nervously watching the United States negotiate a unilateral peace treaty with Japan (ignoring the Soviet Union). The United States overcame opposition from nations that Japan had attacked in World War II by promising to assist their defense and maintaining military bases in Japan. Taken together, peacetime rearmament and mutual defense pacts amounted to a revolution in American foreign policy.

Cold War and Hot War

The first phase of the Cold War reached a crisis in the autumn of 1949. The two previous years had seen an uneasy equilibrium in which American success in southern and western Europe and the standoff over Berlin (the blockade ended in May 1949) balanced the consolidation of Soviet power in eastern Europe. Now, suddenly, two key events seemed to tilt the world balance against the United States and its allies. In September, Truman announced that the Soviet Union had tested its own atomic bomb. A month later, the Chinese communists under Mao Zedong (Mao Tse-tung) took power in China. The following summer, civil war in Korea sucked the United States into a fierce war with communist North Korea and China. While Americans studied maps that showed communism spreading across Europe and Asia, their government accelerated a forty-year arms race with the Soviet Union.

The Nuclear Shadow

Experts in Washington had known that the Soviets were working on an A-bomb, but the news dismayed the average citizen. As newspapers and magazines scared their readers with artists' renditions of the effects of an atomic bomb on New York or Chicago, the shock tilted U.S. nuclear policy toward military uses. In 1946, advocates of civilian control had won a small victory when Congress gave control of atomic energy to the new **Atomic Energy Commission (AEC)**. The AEC tried to balance research on atomic power with continued testing of new weapons. Now Truman told the AEC to double the output of fissionable uranium and plutonium for "conventional" nuclear weapons.

A more momentous decision soon followed. Truman decided in January 1950 to authorize work on the "super" bomb—the thermonuclear fusion weapon that would become the hydrogen bomb (H-bomb). The debate over the "super" pitted a cautious scientific advisory committee and J. Robert Oppenheimer against powerful political figures and a handful of scientists who believed correctly that the Soviets were already at work on a similar weapon. As would be true in future nuclear defense debates, the underlying question was how much capacity for nuclear destruction was enough.

Nuclear weapons proliferated in the early 1950s. The United States exploded the first hydro-

Map 29-2 Cold War in Europe
In the late 1940s and 1950s, the Cold War split Europe into rigidly divided western and eastern blocs. Members of NATO allied with the United States to oppose Soviet expansion. The Soviet Union directed the military and foreign policies of members of the Warsaw Pact.

gen bomb in the South Pacific in November 1952. Releasing one hundred times the energy of the Hiroshima bomb, the detonation tore a mile-long chasm in the ocean floor. Great Britain became the third nuclear power in the same year. The Soviet Union tested its own hydrogen bomb only nine months after the U.S. test. Americans who remembered the attack on Pearl Harbor now worried that the Soviets might send fleets of bombers over the Arctic to surprise U.S. military forces and smash its cities into radioactive powder.

The nuclear arms race and the gnawing fear of nuclear war multiplied the apprehensions of the Cold War. Under the guidance of the Federal Civil

Defense Administration, Americans learned that they should always keep a battery-powered radio and tune to 640 or 1240 on the AM dial for emergency information when they heard air raid sirens. Schoolchildren learned to hide under their desks when they saw the blinding flash of a nuclear detonation. Popular literature in the 1950s was filled with stories in which nuclear war destroyed civilization and left a handful of survivors to pick through the rubble.

More insidiously, nuclear weapons development generated new environmental and health problems. Soldiers were exposed to post-test radiation with minimal protection. Nuclear tests in the South Pacific dusted fishing boats with radioactivity

AMERICA'S JOURNEY
FROM THEN TO NOW
NATO

The North Atlantic Treaty Organization (NATO) celebrated its fiftieth anniversary at a meeting of heads of state in Washington in April 1999. Four thousand miles away, British and American warplanes under NATO command were bombing Yugoslav army units in the province of Kosovo, trying to prevent the wholesale expulsion of the province's 2 million ethnic Albanians (out of a total population of 2.2 million). A few weeks later, in June 1999, NATO ground forces entered Kosovo to maintain order in place of withdrawing Yugoslav troops. The NATO peacekeeping contingents came from Britain, France, Germany, Italy, the Netherlands, and the United States.

The seventy-eight-day air war and the occupation of Kosovo by fifty thousand NATO troops were dramatic evidence of the transformation of NATO after the end of the Cold War.

In 1949, the new North Atlantic Treaty Organization had three purposes. The first was to unite noncommunist nations of western Europe in an alliance against the Soviet Union. The second was to formally commit the United States and Canada to the defense of western Europe, a commitment that involved placing substantial U.S. military forces in Europe. The third was to establish a framework that would make the rearmament of West Germany acceptable to other European nations. For the next forty years—until the collapse of eastern European communism—NATO coordinated western European defense planning and remained a foundation stone of U.S. foreign policy.

The new NATO is a product of the new Europe of the 1990s. A key step was expansion into the former Soviet sphere in eastern Europe. At the anniversary summit in 1999, NATO formally admitted Poland, Hungary, and the Czech Republic. Over the objections of Russia, the action erased the last vestige of the buffer of satellite nations that the USSR had created after World War II.

The other fundamental change was a redefinition of NATO's purpose from defense against outside invasion to peacekeeping within Europe. The focus in the later 1990s was southeastern Europe. In the 1990s, Yugoslavia fragmented into five independent nations (the name Yugoslavia was retained by the predominantly Serbian nation with its capital at Belgrade). Bitter civil war erupted in Bosnia in middecade. Christian Serbs engaged in massacres and deportations of Muslim Bosnians with the goal of creating "ethnically clean" Serbian districts. Too late to stop most bloodshed, NATO eventually intervened in 1995. U.S. and European troops arrived to enforce a shaky peace accord and division of the territory into Serb and Bosnian sectors.

After this tentative first step, NATO in 1999 found it easier to agree on intervention in Kosovo. Here too, the issue was ethnic cleansing. A militant independence movement among ethnic Albanians led to Yougoslav reprisals and another civil war. NATO air strikes against Yugoslav forces in Kosovo began in March 1999 and eventually totaled more that thirty thousand sorties. In order to satisfy Russia, the peacekeeping force that entered Kosovo in June was technically a U.S. operation. But it was a reinvented NATO that negotiated with Yugoslavia. Insisting on "essential NATO participation in peacekeeping," the alliance defined a new role for itself as Europe's own police force.

The United States has maintained a naval presence in the Mediterranean Sea since World War II and the era of the Cold War. Shown here in June 1998, the assault carrier USS Wasp and its warplanes are engaged in a show of force by NATO along the borders of Yugoslavia with the goal of changing its government's policies toward non-Serb minorities.

and forced islanders to abandon contaminated homes. Las Vegas promoted tests in southern Nevada as tourist attractions, but radioactive fallout contaminated large sections of the West and increased cancer rates among "downwinders" in Utah. Weapons production and atomic experiments contaminated vast tracts in Nevada, Washington, and Colorado and left huge environmental costs for later generations (see Map 29-3).

The Cold War in Asia

Communist victory in China's civil war was as predictable as the Soviet nuclear bomb but no less controversial. American military and diplomatic missions in the late 1940s pointed out that the collapse of Jiang Jieshi's Nationalist regime was nearly inevitable, given its corruption and narrow support. Nevertheless, Americans looked for a scapegoat when Jiang's anticommunist government and fragments of the Nationalist army fled to the island of Taiwan off China's southern coast.

Advocates for Jiang, mostly conservative Republicans from the Midwest and West, were certain that Truman's administration had done too little. "China asked for a sword," complained one senator, "and we gave her a dull paring knife." Critics looked for scapegoats. Foreign service officers who had honestly analyzed the weakness of the Nationalists were accused of communist sympathies and hounded from their jobs. The results were tragedy for those unfairly branded as traitors and damage to the State Department—a weakness that would haunt the United States as it became entangled in southeast Asia in the 1950s and 1960s.

Mao's victory expanded a deep fissure between "Europe first" and "Asia first" approaches to American foreign policy. Both during and after World War II, the United States had made Europe its first priority. Strong voices, however, had persistently argued that America's future lay with China, Japan, and the Pacific nations. Influential senators claimed that the "loss of China" was the disastrous result of putting the needs of England and France above the long-term interests of the United States.

NSC-68 and Aggressive Containment

The turmoil of 1949 led to a comprehensive statement of American strategic goals. In April 1950, the State Department prepared a sweeping report known as **National Security Council Paper 68 (NSC-68)**. The document described a world divided between the forces of "slavery" and "freedom" and assumed that the Soviet Union was actively aggressive, motivated by greed for territory and a "fanatic faith" in communism. To defend civilization itself, said the experts, the United States should use as much force as needed to resist communist expansion anywhere and everywhere.

The authors of NSC-68 thought in terms of military solutions. Truman and his advisers in 1947 and 1948 had hoped to contain the Soviets by diplomacy and by integrating the economies of Europe and Japan with that of the United States. Now that the Soviets had the atomic bomb, however, the American atomic shield might be neutralized. Instead, NSC-68 argued that the United States needed to press friendly nations to rearm and to make its former enemies into military allies. It also argued that

Map 29-3   *The Landscape of Nuclear Weapons*
The development and production of nuclear weapons concentrated in the West and South. The World War II sites of Hanford, Los Alamos, and Oak Ridge remained active after the war. Workers at Savannah River, Rocky Flats, and Pantex produced nuclear materials. Scientists and engineers at Lawrence-Livermore and Sandia laboratories designed and assembled weapons that were tested at the Nevada Proving Grounds. Prospectors with Geiger counters swarmed over the canyons of southwestern Colorado and southeastern Utah in a uranium mining rush in the early 1950s.

the nation needed expensive conventional forces to defend Europe on the ground and to react to crises as a "world policeman." NSC-68 thus advocated nearly open-ended increases in the defense budget (which in fact tripled between 1950 and 1954).

NSC-68 summed up what many people already believed. Although it was not a public document, its portrait of implacable communist expansion would have made sense to most Americans; it certainly did to Harry Truman. The outbreak of war in Korea at the end of June 1950 seemed to confirm that communism was a military threat. The thinking behind the report led the United States to approach the Cold War as a military competition and to view political changes in Africa and Asia as parts of a Soviet plan. The need for a flexible military response became the centerpiece of an American policy of active intervention that led eventually to the jungles of Vietnam in the 1960s. And the report's implied strategy of bankrupting the communists through competitive defense spending helped destroy the Soviet Union at the end of the 1980s.

War in Korea, 1950–1953

The success of Mao and the Chinese communists forced the Truman administration to define national interests in east Asia and the western Pacific. The most important U.S. interest was Japan, still an industrial power despite its devastating defeat. The United States had denied the Soviet Union any part in the occupation of Japan in 1945 and had shaped a more democratic nation that would be a strong and friendly trading partner. Protected by American armed forces, Japan would be part of a crescent of offshore strong points that included Alaska, the Philippines, Australia, and New Zealand.

Two questions remained at the start of 1950 (and were still troublesome at the turn of the century). One was the future of Taiwan and the remnants of Jiang's regime. Some American policymakers wanted to defend Jiang against the communists. Others assumed that his tattered forces would collapse and allow Mao to complete the communist takeover of Chinese territory. The other question was Korea, whose own civil war would soon bring the world to the brink of World War III.

The Korean peninsula is the closest point on the Asian mainland to Japan. With three powerful neighbors—China, Russia, and Japan—Korea had always had to fight for its independence. From 1910 to 1945, it had been an oppressed colony of the Japanese empire. As World War II ended, Soviet troops moved down the peninsula from the north and American forces landed in the south, creating a situ-

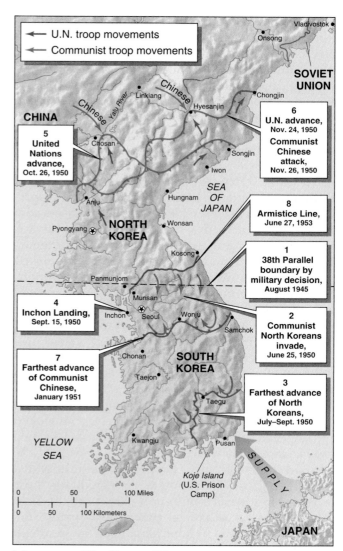

Map 29-4   The Korean War
After rapid reversals of fortune in 1950 and early 1951, the war in Korea settled into stalemate. Most Americans agreed with the need to contain communist expansion but found it deeply frustrating to fight for limited objectives rather than total victory.

ation similar to that in Germany. The 38th parallel, which Russians and Americans set as the dividing line between their zones of occupation, became a de facto border. The United States in 1948 recognized an independent South Korea, with its capital at Seoul, under a conservative government led by Syngman Rhee. Rhee's support came from large landowners and a police force trained by the Japanese before 1945. The Soviets recognized a separate North Korea, whose leader, Kim Il Sung, advocated radical social and political change. Both leaders saw the 38th parallel as a temporary barrier and hoped to unify all Koreans under their own rule. Each crushed political dissent and tried to undermine the other with economic pressure and commando raids.

As early as 1947, the United States had decided that Korea itself was not essential to American military strategy. Planners assumed that U.S. air power in Japan could neutralize unfriendly forces on the Korean peninsula. But Korea remained politically important as the only point of direct confrontation with the Soviet Union in Asia. In January 1950, Secretary of State Dean Acheson carefully excluded Korea from the primary "defensive perimeter" of the United States but kept open the possibility of international guarantees for Korean security.

On June 25, 1950, North Korea, helped by Soviet equipment and Chinese training, attacked South Korea, starting the **Korean War**, which lasted until 1953 (see Map 29-4). Truman and Acheson believed that Moscow lay behind the invasion. They worried that the attack was a ploy to suck America's limited military resources into Asia before a bigger war came in Europe or the Middle East. Republicans blamed Acheson's speech for inviting an invasion, but the war was really an intensification of an ongoing civil war that Stalin was willing to exploit. In fact, Kim originated the invasion plan and spent a year persuading Stalin to agree to it. Stalin hoped that the conquest of South Korea would force Japan to sign a favorable treaty with the USSR.

The explosion of a hot war after five years of world tension seemed to American leaders to demand a military response. As the South Korean army collapsed, Truman committed American ground troops from Japan on June 30. The United States also had the good fortune of securing an endorsement from the United Nations. Because the USSR was boycotting the UN (hoping to force the seating of Mao's People's Republic of China in place of Jiang's government), it could not use its veto when the Security Council asked UN members to help South Korea. The Korean conflict remained officially a United Nations action, although U.S. Generals Douglas MacArthur, Matthew Ridgway, and Mark Clark ran the show as the successive heads of the UN command.

The Politics of War

Fortunes in the first year of the Korean conflict seesawed three times. The first U.S. combat troops were outnumbered, outgunned, and poorly trained. They could not stop the North Koreans. By early August, the Americans clung to a narrow toehold around the port of Pusan on the tip of the Korean peninsula. As reinforcements arrived from the United States, however, MacArthur transformed the war with a daring amphibious counterattack at Inchon, 150 miles behind North Korean lines. The North Korean army was already overextended and exhausted. It collapsed and fled north.

United Nations forces in Korea fought the weather as well as communist North Koreans and Chinese. Baking summer heat alternated with fierce winters. Snow and cold were a major help to the Chinese when they surprised United States troops in November 1950 and drove the American forces southward.

The temptation to push across the 38th parallel and unify the peninsula under Syngman Rhee was irresistible. MacArthur and Washington officials disregarded warnings by China that it would enter the war if the United States tried to reunite Korea by force. U.S. and South Korean troops rolled north, drawing closer and closer to the boundary between North Korea and China.

Chinese forces attacked MacArthur's command in late October but then disappeared. MacArthur dismissed the attacks as a token gesture. In fact they were a final warning. On November 26, the Chinese struck the overextended American columns. They had massed 300,000 troops without detection by American aviation. Their assault drove the UN forces into a two-month retreat that again abandoned Seoul.

Despite his glaring mistake, MacArthur remained in command until he publicly contradicted national policy. In March 1951, with the UN forces again pushing north, Truman prepared to offer a cease-fire that would have preserved the separate nations of South and North Korea. MacArthur tried to preempt the president by demanding that China admit defeat or suffer the consequences. He then published a direct attack on the administration's policy of limiting the Asian war to ensure the security of Europe.

President Truman had no choice. To protect civilian control of the armed forces, he relieved MacArthur of his commands on April 11, 1951. The general returned to parades and a hero's welcome when he addressed a joint session of Congress. He quoted a line from an old barracks song: "Old soldiers never die; they just fade away." The song was soon heard on the radio, but Truman remained in charge of the war.

In Korea itself, U.S. and South Korean forces stabilized a strong defensive line that cut diagonally across the 38th parallel. Here the conflict settled into trench warfare. UN and communist armies faced each other across steep bare hills that choked in clouds of summer dust and froze in winter. For two years, boredom alternated with fierce inch-by-inch battles for territory with names like Heartbreak Ridge and Pork Chop Hill. The war's only glamour was in the air, where the arrival of new F-86 Saberjets in 1952 allowed American pilots to clear the skies of Chinese aviators in Russian-made MIG 15s.

Stabilization of the Korean front ushered in two years of truce negotiations beginning in July 1951, for none of the key actors wanted a wider war. The Chinese were careful to keep their war planes north of the ground combat zone. The Russians had stayed out of the war. The United States learned a painful lesson in 1950 and was willing to accept a divided Korea.

Negotiations stalled over thousands of Chinese prisoners of war who might not want to return to China. The political decision to turn free choice for POWs into a symbol of resistance to communism left Truman's administration bogged down in a grinding war. Nearly half of the 140,000 U.S. casualties came after the truce talks started. The war was a decisive factor behind the Republican victory in the November 1952 elections and dragged on until June 1953, when an armistice returned the peninsula roughly to its prewar political division.

The blindly ambitious attack into North Korea was one of the great failures of intelligence and strategic leadership in American military history. Nearly everyone in Washington shared the blame for letting the excitement of battlefield victories obscure limited war aims. Civilian leaders couldn't resist the desire to roll back communism. Truman hoped for a striking victory before the 1950 congressional elections. The Joint Chiefs of Staff failed to question a general with MacArthur's heroic reputation. MacArthur himself allowed ambition and wishful thinking to jeopardize his army.

The war in Korea was a preview of Vietnam fifteen years later. American leaders propped up an undemocratic regime to defend democracy. Both North Koreans and South Koreans engaged in savage political reprisals as the battlefront shifted back and forth. American soldiers found it hard distinguish between allied and enemy Koreans. American emphasis on the massive application of firepower led U.S. forces to demolish entire villages to kill single snipers. The air force tried to break North Korean resistance by pouring bombs on cities, power stations, factories, and dams; General Curtis Le May estimated that the bombings killed a million Koreans.

The Korean War had global consequences. It helped to legitimize the United Nations. In Washington, it confirmed the ideas behind NSC-68, with its call for the United States to expand its military and to lead an anticommunist alliance. Two days after the North Korean invasion, President Truman ordered the Seventh Fleet to protect the Nationalist Chinese on Taiwan, a decision that guaranteed twenty years of hostility between the United States and the People's Republic of China. In the same month, the United States began to aid France's struggle to retain control over its southeast Asian colony of Indochina, which included Laos, Cambodia, and Vietnam.

In Europe, the United States pushed to rearm West Germany as part of a militarized NATO and sent

American Views
INTEGRATING THE ARMY IN KOREA

Racial integration of the armed forces became official policy in 1948, but President Truman's directive was not fully implemented until during and after the war in Korea. Two veterans of that war—white G.I. Harry Summers and black officer Beverly Scott—recall some of the steps toward integration.

❖ **What do these recollections say about the pervasiveness of racism in midcentury American life?**

❖ **How has the experience of minority soldiers changed from the 1950s to the 1990s?**

Harry Summers: When they first started talking about integration, white soldiers were aghast. They would say, How can you integrate the army? How do you know when you go to the mess hall that you won't get a plate or a knife or a spoon that was used by a Negro? Or when you go to the supply room and draw sheets, you might get a sheet that a Negro had slept on. . . .

I remember a night when our rifle company was scheduled to get some replacements. I was in a three-man foxhole with one other guy, and they dropped this new replacement off at our foxhole. The other guy I was in the foxhole with was under a poncho, making coffee. It was bitterly cold. And pitch dark. He got the coffee made, and he gave me a drink, and he took a drink, and then he offered some to this new replacement, who we literally couldn't see, it was that dark. And the guy said, "No, I don't want any."

"What the hell are you talking about, you don't want any? You got to be freezing to death. Here, take a drink of coffee."

"Well," he said, "you can't tell it now, but I'm black. And tomorrow morning when you find out I was drinking out of the same cup you were using, you ain't gonna be too happy."

Me and this other guy kind of looked at each other. "You silly son of a bitch," we told him, "here, take the goddam coffee."

Beverly Scott: The 24th Regiment was the only all-black regiment in the division, and as a black officer in an all-black regiment commanded by whites I was always super sensitive about standing my ground. Being a man. Being honest with my soldiers. . . .

Most of the white officers were good. Taken in the context of the times, they were probably better than the average white guy in civilian life. But there was still that patronizing expectation of failure. White officers came to the 24th Regiment knowing or suspecting or having been told that this was an inferior regiment.

[In September 1951, members of the regiment were integrated into other units.] I was transferred to the 14th [Regiment] and right away I experienced some problems. People in the 14th didn't want anybody from the 24th. I was a technically qualified communications officer, which the 14th said they needed very badly, but when I got there, suddenly they didn't need any commo officers.

Then their executive officer said, "We got a rifle platoon for you. Think you can handle a rifle platoon?"

What the hell do you mean, can I handle a rifle platoon? I was also trained as an infantry officer. He knew that. I was a first lieutenant, been in the army six years . . . If I had been coming in as a white first lieutenant the question never would have been asked.

Source: Rudy Tomedi, No Bugles, No Drums: An Oral History of the Korean War (NY: John Wiley & Sons 1993).

troops to Europe as a permanent defense force. It increased military aid to European governments and secured a unified command for the national forces allocated for NATO. The unified command made West German rearmament acceptable to France and the smaller nations of western Europe. Rearmament also stimulated German economic recovery and bound West Germany to the political and economic institutions of the North Atlantic nations. In 1952, the European Coal and Steel Community marked an important step toward economic cooperation that would evolve into the European Union by the end of the century. Dwight Eisenhower, who had led the Western allies in the invasion of France and Germany, became the new NATO commander in April 1951; his appointment symbolized the American commitment to western Europe.

The Second Red Scare

The Korean War reinforced the second Red Scare, an assault on civil liberties that stretched from the mid-1940s to the mid-1950s and dwarfed the Red Scare of 1919–1920. The Cold War fanned fears of communist subversion on American soil. Legitimate concerns about espionage mixed with suspicions that communist sympathizers in high places were helping Stalin and Mao. The scare was also a weapon that the conservative wing of the Republican party used against men and women who had built Roosevelt's New Deal (see the overview table, "The Second Red Scare").

Efforts to root out suspected subversives operated on three tracks. National and state governments established loyalty programs to identify and fire suspect employees. The courts punished members of suspect organizations. Congressional and state legislative investigations followed the whims of committee chairs. Anticommunist crusaders often relied on dubious evidence and eagerly believed the worst. They also threatened basic civil liberties.

The Communist Party and the Loyalty Program

The Communist party in the United States was in rapid decline after World War II. Many intellectuals had left the party over the Nazi–Soviet Pact in 1939. The wartime glow of military alliance with the Soviet Union helped the party recover to perhaps eighty thousand members—still fewer than one in every fifteen hundred Americans—but the postwar years brought a series of failures. In 1946, Walter Reuther defeated a Communist for the presidency of the huge

United Auto Workers union, and other CIO unions froze Communists out of leadership positions. Communist support for Henry Wallace reduced the party's influence and separated it from the increasingly conservative mainstream of American politics.

Nevertheless, Republicans used **Red-baiting** as a campaign technique in 1944 and 1946, setting the stage for a national loyalty program. In 1944 they tried to frighten voters about "commydemocrats" by linking FDR, CIO labor unions, and communism. Democrats slung their own mud by trying to convince voters that Hitler preferred the Republicans. Two years later, Republican campaigners told the public that the basic choice was "between Communism and Republicanism." Starting a thirty-year political career, a young Navy veteran named Richard Nixon won a southern California congressional seat by hammering on his opponent's connections to supposedly "Communist-dominated" organizations.

President Truman responded to the Republican landslide with the **Executive Order 9835** in March 1947, initiating a loyalty program for federal employees. Truman may have been trying to head off more drastic action by Congress. Nevertheless, Order 9835 was a blunt instrument. It authorized the attorney general to prepare a list of "totalitarian, Fascist, Communist, or subversive" organizations and made membership or even "sympathetic association" with such groups grounds for dismissal. The loyalty program applied to approximately 8 million Americans working for the federal government or defense contractors; similar state laws affected another 5 million.

Loyalty was a moving target. The attorney general's list grew in fits and starts with often arbitrary additions. Many accusations were just malicious gossip, but allegations stayed in a worker's file even if refuted. Appointment to a new job in the federal government triggered a new investigation in which officials might paw through the same old material. Many New Dealers and people associated with presumably liberal East Coast institutions were targets. An Interior Department official boasted that he had been especially effective in squeezing out graduates of Harvard and Columbia.

Federal employees worked under a cloud of fear. Would the cooperative store they had once patronized or the protest group they'd joined in college suddenly appear on the attorney general's list? Would someone complain that they had disloyal books on their shelves? Loyalty boards asked about religion, racial equality, and a taste for foreign films; they also tried to identify homosexuals, who were thought to be targets for blackmail by foreign agents. The loyalty program resulted in 1,210 firings and

OVERVIEW

THE SECOND RED SCARE

Type of Anticommunist Effort	Key Tools	Results
Employee loyalty programs	U.S. attorney general's list of subversive organizations	Thousands of federal and state workers fired, careers damaged
Congressional investigations	HUAC McCarren Committee Army-McCarthy hearings	Employee blacklists, harassment of writers and intellectuals
Criminal prosecutions	Trials for espionage and conspiracy to advocate violent overthrow of the U.S. government	Convictions of Communist party leaders (1949), Rosenbergs (1951)

6,000 resignations under Truman and comparable numbers during Dwight Eisenhower's first term from 1953 to 1956.

Naming Names to Congress

Congress was even busier than the executive branch. The congressional hunt for subversives had its roots in 1938, when Congressman Martin Dies, a Texas Democrat, created the Special Committee on Un-American Activities. Originally intended to ferret out pro-Fascists, the Dies Committee evolved into the permanent **House Committee on Un-American Activities (HUAC)** in 1945. It investigated "un-American propaganda" that attacked constitutional government.

One of HUAC's juiciest targets was Hollywood. In the last years before television, the movie industry stood at the height of its capacity to influence public opinion. In 1946, Americans bought an average of 90 million tickets every week. But Hollywood's reputation for loose morals, foreign-born directors, Jewish producers, and left-leaning writers aroused the suspicions of many congressmen. HUAC sought to make sure that no un-American messages were being peddled through America's most popular entertainment.

When the hearings opened in October 1947, studio executives, such as Jack Warner of Warner Brothers and Louis B. Mayer of MGM, assured HUAC of their anticommunism. So did popular actors Gary Cooper and Ronald Reagan. In contrast, eight screenwriters and two directors—the Hollywood Ten—refused to discuss their past political associations, citing the free speech protections of the First Amendment to the Constitution.

HUAC countered with citations for contempt of Congress. The First Amendment defense failed when it reached the Supreme Court, and the Ten went to jail in 1950.

HUAC changed the politics of Hollywood. Before 1947, it had been fashionable to lean toward the left; even *The Best Years of Our Lives* contained criticism of American society. After the hearings, it was imperative to tilt the other way. Humphrey Bogart apologized for being a "dope" about politics. The government refused to let British-born Charlie Chaplin reenter the United States in 1952 because of his left-wing views. Other actors, writers, and directors found themselves on the Hollywood blacklist, banned from jobs where they might insert communist propaganda into American movies.

At the start of 1951, the new Senate Internal Security Subcommittee joined the sometimes bumbling HUAC. The **McCarran Committee**, named for the Nevada senator who chaired it, targeted diplomats, labor union leaders, professors, and school-teachers. Both committees turned their investigations into rituals. The real point was not to force personal confessions from witnesses but to badger them into identifying friends and associates who might have been involved in suspect activities.

The only sure way to avoid "naming names" was to respond to every question by citing the Fifth Amendment to the Constitution, which protects Americans from testifying against themselves. When the states adopted the Fifth Amendment in 1791, they wanted to protect citizens against false confessions coerced by intimidation and torture. The ordeal triggered by a congressional subpoena was certainly intimidating. Many Americans assumed that citing the amendment was a sure sign of guilt, not a matter of principle, and talked about Fifth Amendment communists. "Taking the Fifth" couldn't protect jobs and reputations.

State legislatures imitated Congress by searching for "Reducators" among college faculty in such states as Oklahoma, Washington, and California. College presidents frequently fired faculty who took the Fifth Amendment. Harvard apparently used its influence to stay out of the newspapers, cutting a deal in which the FBI fed it information about suspect faculty, whom the university quietly fired. More common was the experience of the economics professor fired from the University of Kansas City after testimony before the McCarran Committee. He found it hard to keep any job once his name had been in the papers. A local dairy fired him because it thought its customers might be uneasy having a radical handle their milk bottles.

The moral dilemma posed by the investigations was revisited in 1954's Oscar-winning movie *On the Waterfront*. The director, Elia Kazan, and the scriptwriter, Budd Schulberg, had both named names. They used the movie as a parable to justify their actions. The film's hero, played by Marlon Brando, agonizes about informing against corrupt officials in a dockworkers union. He finally speaks out at the urging of an activist priest. Most Americans called before HUAC and the McCarran Committee thought that Kazan and Schulberg had missed the point, for witnesses were usually being asked about previous political affiliations and beliefs, not current criminal activity.

Subversion Trials

In 1948, the Justice Department indicted the leaders of the American Communist party under the Alien Registration Act of 1940. Eleven men and women were convicted in 1949 of conspiring to advocate the violent overthrow of the United States government through their speech and publications. Some of the testimony came from Herbert Philbrick, an advertising manager and FBI informer who had posed as a party member. Philbrick parlayed his appearance into a bestseller titled *I Led Three Lives* and then into a popular television series on which the FBI foiled communist spies every Friday night.

The case of Alger Hiss soon followed. In 1948, former Communist Whittaker Chambers named Hiss as a Communist with whom he had asso-

ciated in the 1930s. Hiss, who had held important posts in the State Department, first denied knowing Chambers but then admitted to having known him under another name. He continued to deny any involvement with Communists and sued Chambers for slander. As proof, Chambers gave Congressman Richard Nixon microfilms that he had hidden inside a pumpkin on his Maryland farm. Tests seemed to show that the "pumpkin papers" were State Department documents that had been copied on a typewriter that Hiss had once owned. With the new evidence, the Justice Department indicted Hiss for perjury—lying under oath. A first perjury trial ended in deadlock, but a second jury convicted Hiss in January 1950.

Hiss was more important as a symbol than as a possible spy. For more than forty years, the essence of his case was a matter of faith, not facts. Even his enemies agreed that any documents he might have stolen were of limited importance. What was important, they said, was the sort of disloyalty and "weak thinking" that Hiss represented. Moreover, his smugness as a member of the East Coast establishment enraged them. To his opponents, Hiss stood for every wrong turn that the nation had taken since 1932. In contrast, his supporters found a virtue in every trait that his enemies hated, from his refined taste to his education at Johns Hopkins University and Harvard Law School. Many supporters believed that he had been framed. Both sides claimed support from Soviet records that became public in the 1990s.

The case of Julius and Ethel Rosenberg represented a similar test of belief. In 1950, the British arrested nuclear physicist Klaus Fuchs, who confessed to passing atomic secrets to the Soviets when he worked at Los Alamos in 1944 and 1945. The "Fuchs spy ring" soon implicated the Rosenbergs, New York radicals of strong beliefs but limited sophistication. Convicted in 1951 of the vague charge of conspiring to commit espionage, they were sent to the electric chair in 1953 after refusing to buy a reprieve by naming other spies.

As with Alger Hiss, the government had a plausible but not airtight case. After their trial, the Rosenbergs became a cause for international protest. Their small children became pawns and trophies in political demonstrations, an experience recaptured in E. L. Doctorow's novel *The Book of Daniel* (1971). There is no doubt that Julius Rosenberg was a convinced Communist, and he was likely a minor figure in an atomic spy net, but Ethel Rosenberg was charged to pressure her husband into confessing.

Richard Nixon (right) and the chief investigator for the House Committee on Un-American Activities inspect microfilm of the "pumpkin papers." Hidden inside a pumpkin on the Maryland farm of committee informant Whittaker Chambers, the papers helped convict Alger Hiss of perjury. Nixon's role in pursuing Hiss launched a political career that took him to the White House.

Senator McCarthy on Stage

The best-remembered participant in the second Red Scare was Senator Joseph McCarthy of Wisconsin. Crude, sly, and ambitious, McCarthy had ridden to victory in the Republican landslide of 1946. His campaign slogan—"Congress needs a tail gunner"—claimed a far braver war record than he had earned. He burst into national prominence on February 9, 1950. In a rambling speech in Wheeling, West Virginia, he latched on to the issue of communist subversion. Although no transcript of the speech survives, he supposedly stated: "I have here in my hand a list of 205 that were known to the Secretary of State as being members of the Communist Party and who, nevertheless, are still working and shaping the policy of the State Department." In the following days, the 205 Communists changed quickly to 57, to 81, to 10, to 116. McCarthy's rise to fame climaxed with an incoherent six-hour speech to the Senate. He tried to document the charges by mixing previously exposed spies with people who no longer worked for the government or who had never worked for it. Over the next several years, his speeches were moving targets full of multiple untruths. He threw out so many accusations, true or false, that the facts could never catch up.

The Senate disregarded McCarthy, but the public heard only the accusations, not the lack of evidence. Senators treated McCarthy as a crude outsider in their exclusive club, but voters in 1950 turned against his most prominent opponents. Liberal politicians ran for cover; conservatives were happy for McCarthy to attract media attention away from HUAC and the McCarran Committee. In 1951, McCarthy even called George Marshall, now serving as secretary of defense, an agent of communism. The idea was ludicrous. Marshall was one of the most upright Americans of his generation, the architect of victory in World War II and a key contributor to the stabilization of Europe. Nevertheless, McCarthy was so popular that the Republicans featured him at their 1952 convention. That fall, the Republicans' presidential candidate, Dwight Eisenhower, appeared on the same campaign platform with McCarthy and conspicuously failed to defend George Marshall—who was chiefly responsible for Eisenhower's fast-track career.

McCarthy's personal crudeness made him a media star but eventually undermined him. Given control of the Senate Committee on Government Operations in 1953, he investigated dozens of agencies from the Government Printing Office to the Army Signal Corps. Early in 1954, he began to harass the U.S. Army about the promotion of an army dentist with a supposedly subversive background. The confrontation turned into two months of televised hearings that revealed the emptiness of the charges.

Hank Walker, *Life Time Magazine.*

Senator Joe McCarthy shown here with his aide Roy Cohn, used press releases and congressional committee hearings to attack suspected communists. By 1954 he was reaching to more and more extreme accusations to keep his name before the public.

The cameras also put McCarthy's style on trial. "Have you no decency?" asked the army's lawyer Joseph Welch at one point.

The end came quickly. McCarthy's "favorable" rating in the polls plummeted. The comic strip *Pogo* began to feature a foolishly menacing figure with McCarthy's face named Simple J. Malarkey. The U.S. Senate finally voted 67 to 22 in December 1954 to condemn McCarthy for conduct "unbecoming a Member of the Senate." Until his death from alcoholism in 1957, he was an increasingly isolated figure, repudiated by the Senate and ignored by the media who had built him up.

Understanding McCarthyism

The antisubversive campaign that everyone now called **McCarthyism**, however, died a slower death. Legislation, such as the Internal Security Act (1950) and the Immigration and Nationality Act (1952), remained as tools of political repression. HUAC continued to mount investigations as late as the 1960s.

Fear of communist subversion reached deep into American society. In the early 1950s, Cincinnati's National League baseball team was phasing in a new double-play duo of second baseman Johnny Temple and shortstop Roy McMillan. The team was also trying out a new name, for it was important not to let the national game be tainted by communism. Harking back to its origins as the Red Stockings, the team was now the "Redlegs," not the "Reds." The brief revision of baseball history was one example of how the fear of communists spread from Washington through the grassroots. Cities and states required loyalty oaths from their employees; Ohio even required oaths from recipients of unemployment compensation.

In retrospect, at least four factors made Americans afraid of communist subversion. One was a legitimate but exaggerated concern about atomic spies. A second was an undercurrent of anti-Semitism and nativism, for many labor organizers and Communist party members (like the Rosenbergs) had Jewish and eastern European backgrounds. Third was southern and western resentment of the nation's Ivy League elite. Most general, finally, was a widespread fear that the world was spinning out of control. Many people sought easy explanations for global tensions. It was basically reassuring if Soviet and Chinese communist successes were the result of American traitors rather than communist strengths.

Partisan politics mobilized the fears and resentments into a political force. From 1946 through 1952, the conservative wing of the Republican party used the Red Scare to attack New Dealers and liberal Democrats. HUAC, the McCarran Committee, and McCarthy were all tools for bringing down the men and women who had been moving the United States toward a more active government at home and abroad. The Republican elite used McCarthy until they won control of the presidency and Congress in 1952 and then abandoned him.

The broader goal of the second Red Scare was conformity of thought. Many of the professors and bureaucrats targeted for investigation had indeed been Communists or interested in communism, usually in the 1930s and early 1940s. Most saw it as a way to increase social justice, and they sometimes excused the failures of communism in the Soviet Union. Unlike the handful of real spies, however, they were targeted not for actions but for ideas. The investigations and loyalty programs were efforts to ensure that Americans kept any left-wing ideas to themselves.

Conclusion

In the face of confrontation over Berlin, fighting in Korea, and growing numbers of nuclear weapons, the Cold War stayed cool because each side achieved its essential goals. The Soviet Union controlled eastern Europe, while the United States built increasingly strong ties with the NATO nations and Japan. Though the result was a stalemate that would last through the 1980s, it nevertheless absorbed huge shares of Soviet and American resources and conditioned the thinking of an entire generation.

The shift from prewar isolationism to postwar internationalism was one of the most important changes in the nation's history. To many of its advocates, internationalism represented a commitment to spread political democracy to other nations. As the 1950s and 1960s would show, the results often contradicted the ideal when the United States forcibly imposed its will on other peoples. Even as the results overseas fell short of the ideal, however, the new internationalism highlighted and helped change domestic racial attitudes.

The Truman years brought increasing stability. The economic chaos of 1946 faded quickly. By identifying liberalism at home with anticommunism abroad, Truman's efforts to define a vital center helped protect the New Deal. Americans in the early 1950s could be confident that New Deal and Fair Deal programs to expand economic opportunity and increase economic security were permanent, if incomplete, setting the stage for new social activism in the 1960s. If the Republicans had won in 1948, they might have dismantled the New Deal. By 1952, both presidential candidates affirmed the consensus that placed economic opportunity at the center of the national agenda. The suburban housing boom seemed to turn the dream of prosperity into reality for millions of families.

Despite the turmoil and injustice of the second Red Scare and deep worries about nuclear war, the United States emerged from the Truman years remarkably prosperous. It was also more secure from international threats than many nervous Americans appreciated. The years from 1946 to 1952 set the themes for a generation that believed that the United States could do whatever it set its mind to: end poverty, land an astronaut on the moon, thwart communist revolutions in other countries. There was a direct line from Harry Truman's 1947 declaration that the United States would defend freedom around the world to John Kennedy's 1961 promise that the nation would bear any burden necessary to protect free nations from communism. As the world moved slowly toward greater stability in the 1950s, Americans were ready for a decade of confidence.

Review Questions

1. What were the key differences between Harry Truman and congressional Republicans about the legacy of the New Deal? Why did regulating labor unions become a central domestic issue in the late 1940s? Why did Truman manage to win the presidential election of 1948 despite starting as an underdog?

2. How did the postwar years expand opportunity for veterans and members of the working class? How did they limit opportunities for women? How did they begin to challenge racial inequities in American society? How did the postwar readjustment create a suburban society?

3. What foreign policy priorities did the United States set after 1945? To what extent did the United States achieve its most basic objectives? How did mutual mistrust fuel the origins and deepen the Cold War?

4. How did the Cold War change character in 1949 and 1950? What were key actions by the Soviet Union and China, and how did the United States respond? What was the effect of the chaotic fighting in Korea on U.S. domestic politics and diplomacy?

5. What factors motivated an increasingly frantic fear of domestic subversion in the late 1940s and early 1950s? Who were the key actors in the second Red Scare? What was its long-term impact on American society?

Recommended Reading

Paul Boyer, *By the Bomb's Early Light: American Thought and Culture at the Dawn of the Atomic Age* (1985). Examines the mixture of hopes and fears with which Americans greeted the arrival of the atomic age, giving detailed attention to popular culture as well as national policy.

Joseph C. Goulden, *The Best Years, 1945–1950* (1976). A very readable portrayal of the ways in which Americans adjusted to the postwar years, drawing heavily on contemporary magazine accounts.

Melvyn Leffler, *A Preponderance of Power: National Security, the Truman Administration, and the Cold War* (1992). Provides a balanced interpretation of responsibility for the Cold War in a detailed but readable account of American policy.

Samuel Lubell, *The Future of American Politics* (1952). An incisive analysis of the social forces that shaped the American political scene in the 1940s, giving insights that are still telling after more than four decades.

David McCullough, *Truman* (1992). A readable and sympathetic biography of the thirty-third president.

Victor Navasky, *Naming Names* (1980). The impact of HUAC on Hollywood and the entertainment industry, told by a strong opponent of the Committee.

Arnold Rampersad, *Jackie Robinson* (1997). Presents Jackie Robinson as a pioneer of racial integration on and off the ball field.

Additional Sources

Foreign and Military Policy

John L. Gaddis, *The United States and the Cold War* (1992).

Greg Herken, *The Winning Weapon: The Atomic Bomb in the Cold War, 1945–1950* (1980).

Michael Hogan, *Cross of Iron: Harry S. Truman and the Origins of the National Security State, 1945-54* (1998).

Michael Hogan, *The Marshall Plan* (1987).

Walter Le Feber, *America, Russia, and the Cold War* (1985).

Ernest R. May, ed., *American Cold War Strategy: Interpreting NSC-68* (1993).

Thomas G. Paterson, *On Every Front: The Making of the Cold War* (1979).

Richard Rhodes, *Dark Sun: The Making of the Hydrogen Bomb* (1995).

Michael Schaller, *The American Occupation of Japan* (1985).

Herbert F. York, *The Advisors: Oppenheimer, Teller and the Super* (1976).

Vladislav Zubok and Constantine Pleshkanov, *Inside the Kremlin's Cold War: From Stalin to Khrushchev* (1996).

Korean War

Bruce Cumings, *The Origins of the Korean War* (1981, 1990).

Rosemary Foot, *The Wrong War: American Policy and the Dimensions of the Korean Conflict, 1950–1953* (1985).

D. Clayton James, *Refighting the Last War: Command and Crisis in Korea, 1950–1953* (1992).

Burton I. Kaufman, *The Korean War: Challenges in Crisis, Credibility, and Command* (1986).

William Stueck, *The Korean War: An International History* (1995).

Society and Politics at Home

Steven Gillon, *Politics and Vision: The ADA and American Liberalism* (1987).

Eric F. Goldman, *The Crucial Decade and After: America, 1945–1960* (1960.

Alonzo Hamby, *A Man of the People: A Life of Harry Truman* (1995).

Barbara M. Kelly, *Expanding the American Dream: Building and Rebuilding Levittown* (1993).

Donald R. McCoy and Richard Ruetten, *Quest and Response: Minority Rights and the Truman Administration* (1973).

James Patterson, *Mr. Republican: A Biography of Robert A. Taft* (1972).

Graham White and John Maze, *Henry A. Wallace: His Search for a New World Order* (1995).

Gwendolyn Wright, *Building the Dream: A Social History of Housing in America* (1981).

Red Scare

David Caute, *The Great Fear* (1978).

Richard Fried, *Nightmare in Red: The McCarthy Era in Perspective* (1990).

Robert Griffith, *The Politics of Fear: Joseph R. McCarthy and the Senate* (1970).

Stanley Kutler, *The American Inquisition* (1982).

Michael Paul Rogin, *The Intellectuals and McCarthy: The Radical Spectre* (1967).

Ellen Schrecker, *No Ivory Tower: McCarthyism and the Universities* (1986).

Athan Theoharis and John Stuart Cox, *The Boss: J. Edgar Hoover and the Great American Inquisition* (1988).

Where to Learn More

❖ **Harry S Truman National Historic Site, Library and Museum, Independence, Missouri.** The museum has exhibits and materials on Truman's political career and American history during his administration. Also in Independence is the Harry S Truman Courtroom and Office, with exhibits focusing on his early career.

❖ **General Douglas MacArthur Memorial, Norfolk, Virginia.** The MacArthur Memorial in downtown Norfolk commemorates the career of a key figure in the shaping of the postwar world.

❖ **United Nations Headquarters, New York, New York.** A tour of the United Nations complex in New York is a reminder of the new organizations for international cooperation and coordination that emerged from World War II.

THE CONFIDENT YEARS,
1953–1964

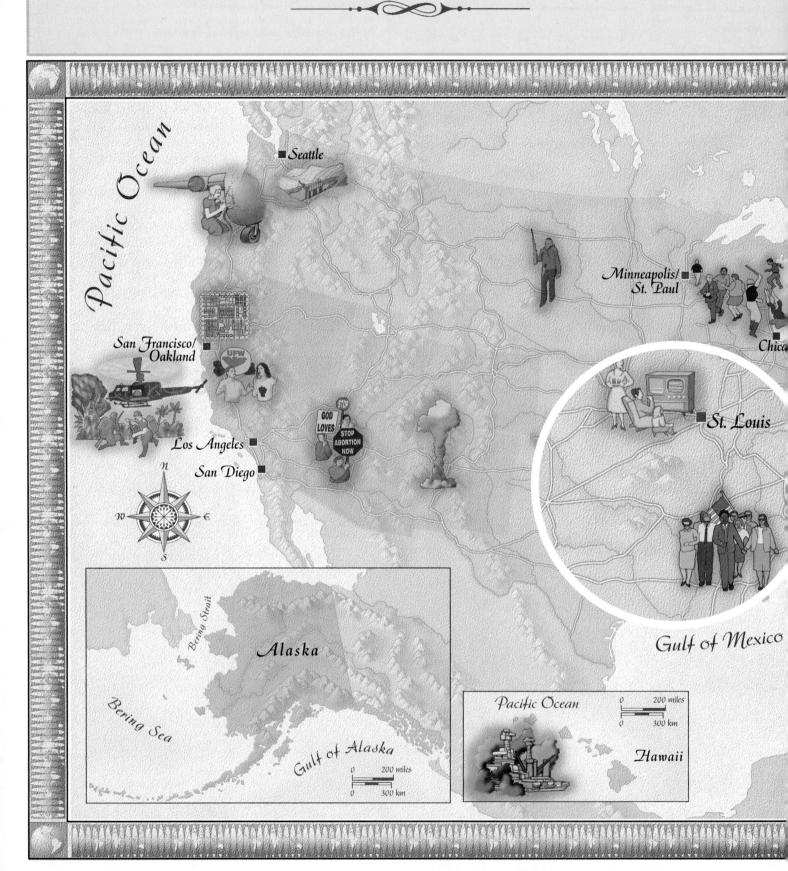

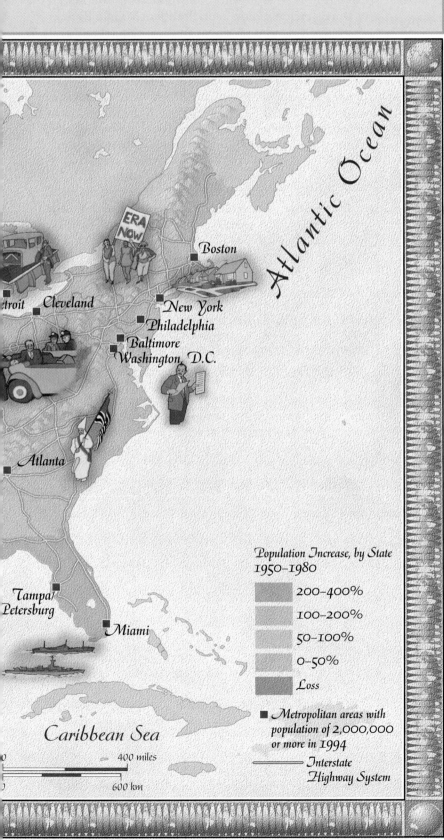

Population Increase, by State
1950–1980

200–400%

100–200%

50–100%

0–50%

Loss

■ Metropolitan areas with
population of 2,000,000
or more in 1994

——— Interstate
Highway System

400 miles

600 km

30

Chapter Outline

Key Topics

❖ Affluence and conformity in the mid-
  dle class during the 1950s
❖ The Cold War confrontation with the
  USSR during the Eisenhower and
  Kennedy administrations
❖ The struggle for African-American
  civil rights
❖ Lyndon Johnson and the Great Society

The United States gained a new hero on April 12, 1955, when Dr. Jonas Salk announced an effective vaccine for polio. In the confident mid-1950s, the polio vaccine seemed another proof of American ability to improve the world.

Poliomyelitis, or infantile paralysis, can paralyze the legs or kill by short-circuiting muscles in the throat and chest. Before 1900, infants had often encountered the polio virus in their first months and developed lifelong immunity. In the twentieth century, cleaner houses and streets delayed contact with polio until preschool years or later, when the disease could be devastating. The virus sometimes struck adults—it cost Franklin Roosevelt the use of his legs when he was in his thirties—but most victims were children.

Fear of polio haunted American families. The disease killed fewer people than heart disease or cancer, but it seemed grossly unfair. Most Americans knew at least one child who hobbled through life on crutches and metal leg braces. Hospitals filled with new cases every summer—58,000 in 1952 alone. Many children clung to life inside iron lungs, metal cylinders that pumped air in and out of a hole in the throat.

Polio season peaked in July and August. Worried parents kept their children out of movie theaters and swimming pools, but the disease struck even the most careful families. "Polio?" one girl remembered from the 1950s. "That was the big fear when I was young. . . . I remember going to Dallas and seeing television for the first time. . . . Every day they would report 'another so many polio cases today.'"

Salk's announcement was welcome news. Hundreds of thousands of children had participated in vaccine field trials, and millions of Americans had funded the research with contributions to the March of Dimes. A generation later, President Ronald Reagan would list the polio vaccine with the steam engine and silicon chip as one of the great modern discoveries.

Salk's triumph affirmed American faith in the future. The prosperous years from 1953 to 1964 spread the economic promise of the 1940s across American society. Young couples could afford large families and new houses. Labor unions grew conservative because cooperation with big business offered immediate gains for their members. Corporations used scientific research to craft new products for eager customers.

The Cold War consensus that paired strength at home with strength abroad guided U.S. foreign policy. Few leaders questioned the rightness or necessity of fighting the Cold War—or America's ultimate triumph. The consensus gave U.S. policy an overarching goal of containment but also narrowed its options by casting every issue in terms of U.S.–Soviet rivalry. When events challenged U.S. preeminence, as when the USSR launched the first artificial space satellite in 1957, the response was shock followed by redoubled efforts to regain what Americans considered their rightful world leadership.

But agreement at the top did not always bring harmony. Social dissenters argued that the United States was misusing its wealth. They criticized fifties society for ignoring the talents of women and leaving millions of Americans in poverty. Critics also spoke for a civil rights movement that sprang from deep roots in southern black communities and demanded equal access to opportunity for all Americans.

A Decade of Affluence

Americans in the 1950s believed in the basic strength of the United States. Television's *General Electric Theater* was third in the ratings in 1956–1957. Every week, its host, Ronald Reagan, a popular Hollywood lead from the late 1930s, stated, "At General Electric, progress is our most important product." It made sense to his viewers. Large, technologically sophisticated corporations were introducing new marvels: Orlon sweaters and Saran Wrap, long-playing records and Polaroid cameras. As long as the United States defended free enterprise, Reagan told audiences on national speaking tours, the sky was the limit.

Many Americans valued economic policy and family life for their contributions to the anticommunist crusade. Social and intellectual confor-

Newsweek

Special 8-PAGE Project } **Suburbia-Exurbia-Urbia**
Newsweek's Editors Explore NEW AMERICA

APRIL 1, 1957 **25c**

SUBURBIA 800 N.→

3 RD 1000 W. → ST.

WHO CORNERED DAVE BECK?
The Story of the Young Crusader and the Jailbird
(NATIONAL AFFAIRS)

In 1957 Newsweek ran a special story on the American move to the suburbs, the dominant population movement of the decade. The cover showed new cars (with tail fins and two-tone paint jobs) and older houses that mark this neighborhood as upper middle class. Most new suburbs offered far more modest housing.

What's Good for General Motors

Dwight Eisenhower presided over the prosperity of the 1950s. Both Democrats and Republicans had courted him as a presidential candidate in 1948. Four years later, he picked the Republicans and easily defeated Democrat Adlai Stevenson, the moderately liberal governor of Illinois. Stevenson was a thoughtful politician, a witty campaigner, and a favorite in academic circles. He also carried Truman's negative legacy of domestic policy confrontation, the hated war in Korea, and the "loss" of China, and he had no chance of winning.

Over the next eight years, Eisenhower claimed the political middle for Republicans. Publicists tried a variety of labels for his domestic views: "progressive moderation," "**New Republicanism**," "dynamic conservatism." Satisfied with postwar America, Eisenhower accepted much of the New Deal but saw little need for further reform. In a 1959 poll, liberals considered him a fellow liberal and conservatives thought him a conservative.

Eisenhower's first secretary of defense, "Engine Charlie" Wilson, had headed General Motors. At his Senate confirmation hearing, he proclaimed, "For years, I thought what was good for the country was good for General Motors and vice versa." Wilson's statement captured a central theme of the 1950s. Not since the 1920s had Americans been so excited about the benefits of big business. When *Fortune* magazine began in 1957 to publish an annual list of the 500 largest American corporations, it tapped a national fascination with America's productive capacity.

The economy in the 1950s gave Americans much to like. Between 1950 and 1964, output grew by a solid 3.2 percent per year. Automobile production, on which dozens of other industries depended,

mity assured a united front. Congress established Loyalty Day in 1955. National leaders argued that strong families were bulwarks against communism and that churchgoing inoculated people against subversive ideas. Under the lingering cloud of McCarthyism, the range of political ideas that influenced government policy was narrower than in the 1930s and 1940s. Nevertheless, disaffected critics began to voice the discontents that exploded in the 1960s and 1970s.

CHRONOLOGY

1953 CIA-backed coup returns the Shah to power in Iran.

USSR detonates hydrogen bomb.

1954 Vietnamese defeat the French.

Geneva conference divides Vietnam.

United States and allies form SEATO.

Supreme Court decides *Brown* v. *Board of Education of Topeka*.

CIA overthrows the government of Guatemala.

China provokes a crisis over Quemoy and Matsu.

1955 Salk polio vaccine is announced.

Black citizens boycott Montgomery, Alabama, bus system.

USSR forms the Warsaw Pact.

AFL and CIO merge.

1956 Interstate Highway Act is passed.

Soviets repress Hungarian revolt.

Israel, France, and Britain invade Egypt.

1957 U.S. Army maintains law and order in Little Rock.

Soviet Union launches Sputnik.

1958 U.S. and USSR voluntarily suspend nuclear tests.

1959 Fidel Castro takes power in Cuba.

Nikita Khrushchev visits the United States.

1960 U-2 shot down over Russia.

Sit-in movement begins in Greensboro, North Carolina.

1961 Bay of Pigs invasion fails.

Kennedy establishes the Peace Corps.

Vienna summit fails.

Freedom rides are held in the Deep South.

Berlin crisis leads to construction of the Berlin Wall.

1962 John Glenn orbits the earth.

Cuban missile crisis brings the world to the brink.

Michael Harrington publishes *The Other America*.

1963 Civil rights demonstrations rend Birmingham.

Civil rights activists march in Washington.

Betty Friedan publishes *The Feminine Mystique*.

Limited Test Ban Treaty is signed.

Ngo Dinh Diem is assassinated in South Vietnam.

President Kennedy is assassinated.

1964 Civil Rights Act is passed.

Freedom Summer is organized in Mississippi.

Office of Economic Opportunity is created.

Gulf of Tonkin Resolution is passed.

Wilderness Act launches the modern environmental movement.

1965 Medical Care Act establishes Medicare and Medicaid.

Elementary and Secondary Education Act extends direct federal aid to local schools.

Selma-Montgomery march climaxes era of nonviolent civil rights demonstrations.

Voting Rights Act suspends literacy tests.

---

neared 8 million vehicles per year in the mid-1950s; less than 1 percent of new car sales were imports.

American workers in the 1950s had more disposable income than ever before. Their productivity, or output per worker, increased steadily. Average wages rose faster than consumer prices in nine of eleven years between 1953 and 1964. Rising productivity made it easy for corporations to share gains with large labor unions. The steel and auto industries gave their workers a middle-class way of life. In turn, labor leaders lost interest in radical changes in American society. In 1955, the older and politically more conservative American Federation of Labor absorbed the younger Congress of Industrial Organizations. The new AFL-CIO positioned itself as a partner in prosperity and foe of communism at home and abroad.

For members of minority groups with regular industrial and government jobs, the fifties were also economically rewarding. Industrial cities offered them factory jobs at wages that could support a family. Black people worked through the Urban League, the National Association of Colored Women, and other race-oriented groups to secure fair employment laws and jobs with large corporations. Many Puerto Rican migrants to New York found steady work in the Brooklyn Navy Yard. Mexican-American families in San Antonio benefited from maintenance jobs at the city's military bases. Steady employment allowed black people and Latinos to build strong community institutions and vibrant neighborhood business districts.

However, there were never enough family-wage jobs for all of the African-American and Latino workers who continued to move to northern and western cities. Many Mexican Americans were still migrant farm laborers and workers in nonunionized sweatshops. Minority workers were usually the first to suffer from the erosion of industrial jobs that began in the 1960s.

Native Americans faced equally daunting prospects. To cut costs and accelerate assimilation, Congress pushed the policy of termination between 1954 and 1962. The government sold tribal land and assets, distributed the proceeds among tribal members, and terminated its treaty relationship with the tribe. Termination gave thousands of Indians one-time cash payments but cut them adrift from the security of tribal organizations. The Bureau of Indian Affairs also encouraged Indians to move to large cities, but jobs were often unavailable. The new urban populations would nourish growing militancy among Native Americans in the 1960s and 1970s.

Reshaping Urban America

If Eisenhower's administration opted for the status quo on many issues, it nevertheless reshaped American cities around an agenda of economic development. In 1954, Congress transformed the public housing program into urban renewal. Cities used federal funds to replace low-rent businesses and run-down housing on the fringes of their downtowns with new hospitals, civic centers, sports arenas, office towers, and luxury apartments. Urban renewal temporarily revitalized older cities in the Northeast and Midwest that were already feeling the competition of the fast-growing South and West. *Fortune* in 1956 concluded that some of the largest cities were the best run—Cincinnati, New York, Philadelphia, Detroit, Milwaukee.

Only a decade later, the same cities would top the list of urban crisis spots, in part because of accumulating social costs from urban renewal. The bulldozers often leveled minority neighborhoods in the name of downtown expansion. Los Angeles demolished the seedy Victorian mansions of Bunker Hill, just northwest of downtown, for a music center and bank towers. A mile to the north was Chavez Ravine, whose Mexican-American population lived in substandard housing but maintained a lively community. When conservative opposition blocked plans for public housing, the residents were evicted, and Dodger Stadium was built. Here as elsewhere, urban showplaces rose at the expense of minority groups.

The Eisenhower administration also revolutionized American transportation. By the early 1950s, Americans were fed up with roads designed for Model A Fords: They wanted to enjoy their new V-8 engines. The solution was the **Federal Highway Act of 1956**, creating a national system of Interstate and Defense Highways. The legislation wrapped a program to build 41,000 miles of freeways in the language of the Cold War. The roads would be wide and strong enough for trucks hauling military hardware; they were also supposed to make it easy to evacuate cities in case of a Soviet attack.

Although the first interstate opened in Kansas in 1956, most of the mileage came in use in the 1960s and 1970s. Interstates halved the time of city-to-city travel. They were good for General Motors, the steel industry, and the concrete industry, requiring the construction equivalent of sixty Panama Canals. The highways promoted long-distance trucking at the expense of railroads. They also wiped out hundreds of homes per mile when they plunged through large cities. As with urban renewal, the bulldozers most often plowed through African-American or Latino neighborhoods, where land was cheap and white politicians could ignore protests. Some cities, such as Miami, used the highways as barricades between white and black neighborhoods.

Interstates accelerated suburbanization. The beltways or perimeter highways that began to ring most large cities made it easier and more profitable to develop new subdivisions and factory sites than to reinvest in city centers. Federal grants for sewers and other basic facilities further cut suburban costs. Continuing the pattern of the late 1940s, suburban growth added a million new single-family houses per year.

Comfort on Credit

Prosperity transformed spending habits. The 1930s had taught Americans to avoid debt. The 1950s taught them to buy on credit. Families financed their new houses with 90 percent FHA mortgages and 100 percent VA mortgages. They filled the rooms by signing installment contracts at furniture and appliance stores and charging the drapes and carpeting on department store credit cards. The value of consumer debt, excluding home mortgages, tripled from 1952 to 1964.

New forms of marketing facilitated credit-based consumerism. The first large-scale suburban shopping center was Northgate in Seattle, which assembled all the pieces of the full-grown mall—small stores facing an interior corridor between anchor department stores and surrounded by parking. By the end of the decade, developers were building malls with 1 million square feet of shopping floor. At the start of the 1970s, the universal credit card (Visa, MasterCard) made shopping even easier.

Surrounding the new malls were the servants and symbols of America's car culture. Where cities of the early twentieth century had been built around the public transportation of streetcars and subways, the 1950s depended on private automobiles. Interstate highways sucked retail business from small-town main streets to interchanges on the edge of town. Nationally franchised motels and fast-food restaurants sprang up along suburban shopping strips, pioneered by Holiday Inn (1952) and McDonald's (nationally franchised in 1955). Many Americans identified consumption with the process of driving rather than the place of the old downtown.

More extreme than the mall were entirely new environments for high-intensity consumption and entertainment that appeared in the Southwest. Mobster Bugsy Siegel transformed Las Vegas with the Flamingo Hotel in 1947. Other hotel-casinos soon turned Vegas into a middle-class adult fantasyland. Disneyland was Las Vegas for the whole family, a walk-through fantasy designed to outperform widescreen movies as a "real" experience. Opening in Orange County, California, in 1955, Disneyland was safe and artificial—a never-ending state fair without the smells and dust.

The New Fifties Family

Family life in the Eisenhower years departed from historic patterns. Prosperity allowed children to finish school and young adults to marry right after high school. Young women faced strong social pressure to pursue husbands rather than careers; women went to college, people said, to get the "Mrs." degree rather than the B.A. In a decade when the popular press worried about "latent homosexuality," single men were also suspect. The proportion of single adults reached its twentieth-century low in 1960. At all social levels, young people married quickly and had an average of three children spaced closely together, adding to the number of baby boomers whose needs would influence American society for the rest of the century. Family activities replaced the street corner for kids and the neighborhood tavern for men. Strong families, said experts, defended against communism by teaching American values.

Television was made to order for the family-centered fifties. By 1960, fully 87 percent of households had sets (see Figure 30-1). Popular entertainment earlier had been a community activity; people saw movies as part of a group, cheered baseball teams as part of a crowd. TV was watched in the privacy of the home.

Situation comedies were the most successful programs. Viewers liked continuing characters who resolved everyday problems in half an hour. A few shows dealt with characters outside the middle-class mainstream, but most successful shows depicted the ideal of family togetherness. Lucille Ball and Desi Arnaz in *I Love Lucy* (1951–1955) started a family and left New York for suburbia. The families on *The Adventures of Ozzie and Harriet* (1952–1966), *Father Knows Best* (1954–1962), and *Leave It to Beaver* (1957–1962) were white, polite, and happy. The Nelsons, Andersons, and Cleavers bore northern Euro-

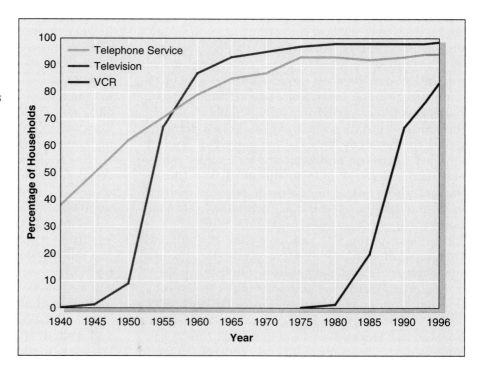

Figure 30-1   Households with Telephones, Televisions, and VCRs
American life in the twentieth century was transformed by a sequence of electronic consumer goods, from telephones to laptop computers. Entertainment items (televisions and videocassette recorders) spread even more rapidly among consumers than did the home telephone.

Data Source: Statistical Abstract of the United States.

Television sets were major pieces of living room furniture in the 1950s. This 1951 Motorola ad from Woman's Home Companion *emphasizes television as a source of family togetherness, a popular theme in the 1950s.*

pean names and lived in single-family houses with friendly neighbors. Thousands of school-aged baby boomers wondered why their families didn't have similar good times.

Television programming helped limit women's roles by power of example. Women in the fifties gave up some of their earlier educational gains. Their share of new college degrees and professional jobs fell. Despite millions of new electric appliances, the time spent on housework increased. Magazines proclaimed that proper families maintained distinct roles for dad and mom, who was urged to find fulfillment in a well-scrubbed house and children. Television actresses assured readers that they were housewives first and career women second.

In fact, far from allowing women to stay home as housewives, family prosperity in the 1950s often depended on their earnings. The number of employed women reached new highs. By 1960, nearly 35 percent of all women held jobs, including 7.5 million mothers with children under 17 (see Figure 30-2).

Teenagers in the 1950s joined adults as consumers of movies, clothes, and automobiles. Advertisers tapped and expanded the growing youth market by promoting a distinct "youth culture," an idea that became omnipresent in the 1960s and 1970s. While psychologists pontificated on the special problems of adolescence, many cities matched their high schools to the social status of their students: college-prep curricula for middle-class neighborhoods, vocational and technical schools for future factory workers, and separate schools or tracks for African Americans and Latinos. "Maturity" in middle-class high schools meant self-confidence and leadership; at vocational schools, it meant neatness and respect for authority. In effect, the schools trained some children to be doctors and officers and others to be mechanics and enlisted men.

All teenagers shared rock-and-roll, a new music of the mid-1950s that adapted black urban rhythm-and-blues for a white mass market. Rock music drew vitality from poor white Southerners (Buddy Holly, Elvis Presley), Hispanics (Richie

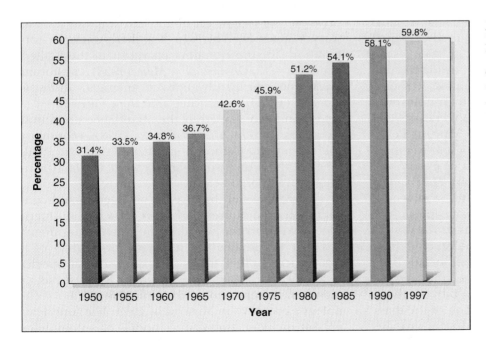

Figure 30-2 **Working Women as a Percentage of All Women, 1950–1997** *The proportion of American women who are part of the labor force (working or looking for work) has increased steadily since 1950, with the fastest increase between 1965 and 1985.*

Valens), and, in the 1960s, the British working class (the Beatles). Record producers played up the association between rock music and youthful rebellion. The 1955 movie *Blackboard Jungle* depicted juvenile delinquency to the music of Bill Haley's "Rock Around the Clock." Elvis Presley's meteoric career, launched in 1956 with "Heartbreak Hotel," depended both on his skill at blending country music with rhythm-and-blues and the sexual suggestiveness of his stage act.

Portable phonographs and 45-rpm records made rock-and-roll portable, letting kids listen in their own rooms. Car radios and transistor radios (first marketed around 1956) let disc jockeys reach teenagers outside the home. The result was separate music for young listeners and separate advertising for teenage consumers, the roots of the teenage mall culture of the next generation.

Turning to Religion

Leaders from Dwight Eisenhower to FBI Director J. Edgar Hoover advocated churchgoing as an antidote for communism. Regular church attendance grew from 48 percent of the population in 1940 to 63 percent in 1960. Moviegoers flocked to biblical epics: *The Robe* (1953), *The Ten Commandments* (1956), *Ben-Hur* (1959). *Newsweek* talked about the "vast resurgence of Protestantism," and *Time* claimed that "everybody knows that church life is booming in the U.S."

The situation was more complex. Growing church membership looked impressive at first, but the total barely kept pace with population. In some ways, the so-called return to religion was new. Congress created new connections between religion and government when it added "under God" to the Pledge of Allegiance in 1954 and required currency to bear the phrase "In God We Trust" in 1955.

Radio and television preachers added a new dimension to religious life. Bishop Fulton J. Sheen brought vigorous anticommunism and Catholic doctrine to millions of TV viewers who would never have entered a Catholic church. Norman Vincent Peale blended popular psychology with Protestantism, presenting Jesus Christ as "the greatest expert on human nature who ever lived." His book *The Power of Positive Thinking* (1952) told readers to "stop worrying and start living" and sold millions of copies.

Another strand in the religious revival was revitalized evangelical and fundamentalist churches. During the 1950s, the theologically and socially conservative Southern Baptists became the largest Protestant denomination. Evangelist Billy Graham continued the grand American tradition of the mass revival meeting. In auditoriums and stadiums, he preached personal salvation in words that everyone could understand. Graham was a pioneer in the resurgence of evangelical Christianity that stressed an individual approach to belief and social issues. "Before we can solve the economic, philosophical, and political problems in the world," he said, "pride, greed, lust, and sin are going to have to be erased."

African-American churches were community institutions as well as religious organizations. With limited options for enjoying their success, the black middle class joined prestigious churches. Black congregations in northern cities swelled in the postwar years and often supported extensive social service programs. In southern cities, churches were centers for community pride and training grounds for the emerging civil rights movement.

Boundaries between many Protestant denominations blurred as church leaders emphasized national unity, paving the way for the ecumenical movement and denominational mergers. Supreme Court decisions sowed the seeds for later political activism among evangelical Christians. In *Engel* v. *Vitale* (1962), the Court said that public schools could not require children to start the school day with group prayer. *Abington Township* v. *Schempp* (1963) prohibited devotional Bible reading in the schools. Such decisions alarmed many evangelicals; within two decades, school prayer would be a central issue in national politics.

The Gospel of Prosperity

Writers and intellectuals often marveled at the prosperity of Eisenhower's America. For scholars and journalists who had grown up during the Great Depression, the lack of economic hardship was the big story. William H. Whyte, Jr., searched American corporations for the changing character of the United States in *The Organization Man* (1956). Historian David Potter brilliantly analyzed Americans in *People of Plenty* (1954), contending that their national character had been shaped by the abundance of natural resources. In *The Affluent Society* (1958), economist John Kenneth Galbraith predicted that the challenge of the future would be to ensure the fair distribution of national wealth.

At times in these years, production and consumption even outweighed democracy in the American message to the world. Officially, the argument was that abundance was a natural by-product of a free society. In fact, it was easy to present prosperity as a goal in itself, as Vice President Richard Nixon did when he represented the United States at a technology exposition in Moscow in 1959. The American exhibit included twenty-one models of automobiles

The United States exhibit at a technology exposition in Moscow in 1959 displayed a wide range of American consumer goods, from soft drink dispensers to sewing machines. It included a complete six-room ranch house with an up-to-date kitchen where, in a famous encounter dubbed the "kitchen debate," Richard Nixon and Soviet Communist party chairman Nikita Khrushchev disputed the merits of capitalism and communism.

and a complete six-room ranch house. In its "miracle kitchen," Nixon engaged Soviet Communist party chairman Nikita Khrushchev in a carefully planned "kitchen debate." The vice president claimed that the "most important thing" for Americans was "the right to choose": "We have so many different manufacturers and many different kinds of washing machines so that the housewives have a choice."

Khrushchev heard a similar message when he visited the United States in September 1959. He went to a farm in Coon Rapids, Iowa, a machine shop in Pittsburgh, and Hollywood movie studios. Although Khrushchev never believed that ordinary workers had miracle kitchens, he returned to Moscow knowing that America meant "business."

The Underside of Affluence

The most basic criticism of the ideology of prosperity was the simplest—that affluence concealed vast inequalities. Michael Harrington had worked among the poor before writing *The Other America* (1962). He reminded Americans about the "underdeveloped nation" of 40 to 50 million poor people who had missed the last two decades of prosperity. The poor were walled off in urban and rural backwaters. They were old people living on stale bread in bug-infested hotels. They were white families in the valleys of Appalachia, African Americans in city ghettos who could not find decent jobs, and Hispanic migrant workers whose children went for months without a glass of milk.

If Harrington found problems at the bottom of U.S. society, C. Wright Mills found dangers in the way that the Cold War distorted American society at the top. *The Power Elite* (1956) described an interlocking alliance of big government, big business, and the military. The losers in a permanent war economy, said Mills, were economic and political democracy. His ideas would reverberate in the 1960s during the Vietnam War.

Other critics targeted the alienating effects of consumerism and the conformity of homogeneous suburbs. Sociologist David Riesman saw suburbia as the home of "other-directed" individuals who lacked inner convictions. Although the antisuburban rhetoric was based on intellectual snobbery rather than research, it represented significant dissent from the praise of affluence.

There was far greater substance to increasing dissatisfaction among women, who faced conflicting images of the perfect woman in the media. On one side was the comforting icon of Betty Crocker, the fictional spokeswoman for General Mills who made housework and cooking look easy. On the other side were sultry sexpots, such as Marilyn Monroe and the centerfold women of *Playboy* magazine, which first appeared in 1953. Women wondered how to be both Betty and Marilyn.

In 1963, Betty Friedan's book *The Feminine Mystique* recognized that thousands of middle-class housewives were seething behind their picture windows. It followed numerous articles in *McCall's, Redbook,* and the *Ladies' Home Journal* about the unhappiness of college-educated women who were expected to find total satisfaction in kids and cooking.

Friedan repackaged the message of the women's magazines along with results of a survey of her Smith College classmates who were then entering their forties. What Friedan called "the problem that has no name" was a sense of personal emptiness. "I got up one morning," remembered Geraldine Bean, "and I got my kids off to school. I went in to comb my hair and wash my face, and I stood in front of the bathroom mirror crying . . . because at eight-thirty in the morning I had my children off to school. I had my housework done. There was absolutely nothing for me to do the rest of the day." She went on to earn a Ph.D. and win election to the board of regents of the University of Colorado.

Eventually, the critical analysis of Harrington, Mills, and Friedan would fuel radical politics; in the short run, it inspired radical art. New York and San Francisco had long sheltered cultural rebels who liked to confront the assumptions of mainstream Americans. The artsy bohemians of New York's Greenwich Village used Pop Art to satirize consumer culture. The **Beats** came together in San Francisco, where poets, artists, and musicians drifted in and out of the City Lights bookstore. They attracted national attention in 1955 when Allen Ginsberg first chanted his poem "Howl," with its blistering attack on stifling materialism.

Facing Off with the Soviet Union

Americans got a reassuring new face in the White House in 1953, but not new policies toward the world. As had been true since 1946, the nation's leaders weighed every foreign policy decision for its effect on the Cold War. The United States pushed ahead in an arms race with the Soviet Union, stood guard on the borders of China and the Soviet empire, and judged political changes in Latin America, Africa, and Asia for their effect on the global balance of power.

U.S. and Soviet actions created a bipolar world that mimicked the effects of a magnet on a scattering of iron filings. The two poles of a magnet draw some filings into tightly packed clusters, pull others into looser alignments pointing toward one pole or the other, and leave a few in the middle unaffected. In the later 1950s and early 1960s, the United States and the USSR were the magnetic poles. Members of NATO, the Warsaw Pact, and other formal alliances made up the tight clusters. The **third world** of officially uncommitted nations felt the influence of both blocs, sometimes aligning with one or the other and sometimes struggling to remain neutral.

Why We Liked Ike

In the late twentieth century, few leaders were able to master both domestic policy and foreign affairs. Some presidents, such as Lyndon Johnson, have been more adept at social problems than diplomacy. In contrast, Richard Nixon and George Bush were more interested in the world outside the United States.

Dwight Eisenhower was one of these "foreign policy presidents." As a general, he had understood that military power should serve political ends. He had helped hold together the alliance that defeated Nazi Germany and built NATO into an effective force in 1951–1952. He then sought the Republican nomination, he said, to ensure that the United States kept its international commitments. He sealed his victory in 1952 by emphasizing foreign policy expertise, telling a campaign audience that "to bring the Korean war to an early and honorable end . . . requires a personal trip to Korea. I shall make that trip . . . I shall go to Korea."

What makes Eisenhower's administration hard to appreciate is that many of its accomplishments were things that didn't happen. Eisenhower refused to dismantle the social programs of the New Deal. He exerted American political and military power around the globe but avoided war. Preferring to work behind the scenes, he knew how to delegate authority and keep disagreements private.

In his "hidden-hand" presidency, Eisenhower sometimes masked his intelligence. It helped his political agenda if Americans thought of him as a smiling grandfather. The "Ike" who gave rambling, incoherent answers at White House press conferences knew exactly what he was doing—controlling information and keeping the opposition guessing. When his press secretary advised him to duck questions at one press conference, Ike replied, "Don't worry, I'll just confuse them." He was easily reelected in 1956, when Americans saw no reason to abandon competent leadership.

A Balance of Terror

The backdrop for U.S. foreign policy was the growing capacity for mutual nuclear annihilation. The rivalry between the United States and the USSR was therefore carried out within a framework of deterrence, the knowledge that each side could launch a devastating nuclear attack. The old balance of power had become a balance of terror.

The Eisenhower administration's doctrine of massive retaliation took advantage of America's superior technology while economizing on military spending. Eisenhower and his advisers worried that matching the land armies of China and the Soviet Union would inflate the role of the federal government in American society (see Figure 30-3). Eisen-

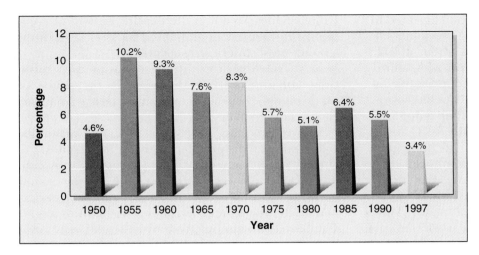

Figure 30-3   Defense Spending as a Percentage of Gross Domestic Product, 1950–1997
Defense spending has been an important force for economic development and innovation. The impact of the defense budget in the domestic economy was greatest in the mid-1950s at the height of the Cold War. Lesser peaks came during the Vietnam War in the late 1960s and the Reagan administration defense buildup in the early 1980s.

Data Source: Statistical Abstract of the United States.

hower compared uncontrolled military spending to crucifying humankind on a "cross of iron." "Every gun that is fired," he warned, "every warship launched, every rocket fired signifies . . . a theft from those who hunger and are not fed, those who are cold and not clothed." The administration concentrated military spending where the nation already had the greatest advantage—on atomic weapons. In response to any serious attack, the United States would direct maximum force against the homeland of the aggressor.

The massive retaliation doctrine treated nuclear weapons as ordinary or even respectable. It put European and American cities on the frontline in the defense of Germany, for it meant that the United

States would react to a Soviet conventional attack on NATO by dropping nuclear bombs on the Soviet Union, which would presumably retaliate in kind. The National Security Council in 1953 made reliance on "massive retaliatory damage" by nuclear weapons official policy.

The doctrine grew even more fearful as the Soviet Union developed its own hydrogen bombs. The chairman of the Atomic Energy Commission terrified the American people by mentioning casually that the Soviets could now obliterate New York City. Dozens of nuclear weapons tests in the late 1950s made the atomic threat immediate. So did signs for air raid shelters posted on downtown buildings and air raid drills

Schoolchildren in the 1950s regularly practiced taking cover in case of atomic attack. If there was warning, they were to file into interior hallways, crouch against the walls, and cover their heads with their jackets as protection from flying glass. If they saw the blinding flash of an atomic explosion without warning, they were to "duck and cover" under their school desks.

in schools. Radioactivity carried by fallout appeared in milk supplies in the form of the isotope strontium 90.

The USSR added to worries about atomic war by launching the world's first artificial satellite. On the first Sunday of October 1957, Americans discovered that Sputnik—Russian for "satellite"—was orbiting the earth. The Soviets soon lifted a dog into orbit while U.S. rockets fizzled on the pad. Soviet propagandists claimed that their technological "first" showed the superiority of communism, and Americans wondered if the United States had lost its edge. Schools beefed up science courses and began to introduce the "new math," Congress passed the National Defense Education Act to expand college and postgraduate education, and the new **National Aeronautics and Space Administration (NASA)** took over the satellite program in 1958.

The crisis was more apparent than real. Eisenhower had rejected using available military rockets for the U.S. space program in favor of developing new launch vehicles, and he overlooked the symbolic impact of Sputnik. He thus built himself into a political box, for the combination of Soviet rocketry and nuclear capacity created alarm about a missile gap. The USSR was said to be building hundreds of intercontinental ballistic missiles (ICBMs) to overwhelm American air defenses designed to intercept piloted bombers. By the early 1960s, critics charged, a do-nothing administration would have put the United States in peril. Although there was no such gap, Eisenhower was unwilling to reveal secret information that might have allayed public anxiety.

Containment in Action

Someone who heard only the campaign speeches in 1952 might have expected sharp foreign policy changes under Eisenhower, but there was more continuity than change. John Foster Dulles, Eisenhower's secretary of state, had attacked the Democrats as defeatists and appeasers. He demanded that the United States liberate eastern Europe from Soviet control and encourage Jiang Jieshi to attack communist China. Warlike language continued after the election. In 1956, Dulles proudly claimed that tough-minded diplomacy had repeatedly brought the United States to the verge of war: "We walked to the brink and looked it in the face. We took strong action." Critics protested that such "brinkmanship" endangered the entire world.

In fact, Eisenhower viewed the Cold War in the same terms as Truman. Caution replaced campaign rhetoric about "rolling back" communism. Around the periphery of the communist nations, from eastern Asia to the Middle East to Europe, the

United States accepted the existing sphere of communist influence but attempted to block its growth, a policy most Americans accepted.

The American worldview assumed both the right and the need to intervene in the affairs of other nations, especially in Latin America, Asia, and Africa. Policymakers saw these nations as markets for U.S. products and sources of vital raw materials. When political disturbances arose in these states, the United States blamed Soviet meddling to justify U.S. intervention. If communism could not be rolled back in eastern Europe, the CIA could still undermine anti-American governments in the third world. The Soviets themselves took advantage of local revolutions even when they did not instigate them; they thus confirmed Washington's belief that the developing world was a gameboard on which the superpowers carried on their rivalry by proxy.

Twice during Eisenhower's first term, the CIA subverted democratically elected governments that seemed to threaten U.S. interests. In Iran, which had nationalized British and U.S. oil companies in an effort to break the hold of western corporations, the CIA in 1953 backed a coup that toppled the government and helped the young Shah, or monarch, gain control. The Shah then cooperated with the United States until his overthrow in 1979. In Guatemala, the leftist government was upsetting the United Fruit Company. When the Guatemalans accepted weapons from the communist bloc in 1954, the CIA imposed a regime friendly to U.S. business (see Map 30-1).

For most Americans in 1953, democracy in Iran was far less important than ending the war in Korea and stabilizing relations with China. Eisenhower declined to escalate the Korean War by blockading China and sending more U.S. ground forces. Instead he shifted atomic bombs to Okinawa, only four hundred miles from China. The nuclear threat, along with the continued cost of the war on both sides, brought the Chinese to a truce that left Korea divided into two nations.

The next year, China began to shell the small islands of Quemoy and Matsu, from which the Nationalist Chinese on Taiwan were launching commando raids on the mainland. Again Secretary Dulles rattled the atomic saber, and China stopped the attacks. Evidence now suggests that Washington misread the situation. Mao's "theatrical" shelling was a political statement, not a prelude to military assault. Stepping to the "brink of war" did not deter Chinese aggression, because China never planned to attack.

In Vietnam, on China's southern border, France was fighting to maintain its colonial rule

FROM THEN TO NOW

Space Exploration and Science

In December 1998, astronauts joined the first two segments of the International Space Station. Scheduled for completion in 2003, the station is projected to cost $10 billion dollars. Japan, Brazil, Canada, and European nations, as well as the United States, are contributing to its construction. With an operating crew of seven, the orbiting laboratory will allow long-running scientific experiments in six pressurized modules and dozens of external payload sites.

The International Space Station represents a basic transformation of the American space effort from adventure to science. In 1961, President Kennedy committed the United States to be the first nation to send a human being to the moon and to do it by 1970. Cold War rivalry with the Soviet Union motivated this ambitious decision. The USSR had alarmed the United States by its early successes in space. It was the first nation to launch an artificial satellite, and it sent cosmonaut Yuri Gagarin into orbit around the earth ten months before the United States matched the feat and sent astronaut John Glenn into orbit.

Most Americans and most politicians who promoted the space program understood it as a new phase in the history of human exploration and saw the astronauts as modern-day pioneers. Thus when Neil Armstrong set foot on the lunar surface in 1969, he was seen to be following the tradition of Francis Drake, Meriwether Lewis, Charles Lindbergh, and the polar explorers of the twentieth century.

In the decades since Armstrong's famous "giant leap for mankind," the national attitude toward space has changed. From Velcro to satellite communication, many by-products of the space race have become parts of everyday life. Our lives would be far different without government and commercial satellites. Remote sensing helps geologists locate potential petroleum deposits, geographers map the destruction of rain forest, and military specialists pinpoint bombing targets in Iraq and Kosovo. Without the satellite technology developed under the pressure of the Cold War, there would be no global positioning systems for ships, no overhead pictures of storm fronts and hurricanes on The Weather Channel.

But as the world has grown increasingly accustomed to the benefits of space-centered technology, space exploration has shifted away from a focus on manned to unmanned voyages. Despite the expectations of science fiction, the landings on the moon were not followed by efforts to send humans to other planets. Instead, we have sent payloads of instruments to bring back scientific data and often stunning pictures of the surface of Venus, the moons of Jupiter, and the rings of Saturn. We have visited the surface of Mars through the lenses and sensors of special landing craft. The International Space Station is a long way from both the race to the moon and the Starship *Enterprise*, but its model of scientific cooperation may be at least a small step toward the United Federation of Planets.

Astronaut Buzz Aldrin, one of three crewmwn for Apollo 11, was the second human to walk on the moon in July 1969. In the 1980s and 1990s, space exploration shifted from manned flights to remotely controlled landers and remotely monitored instruments.

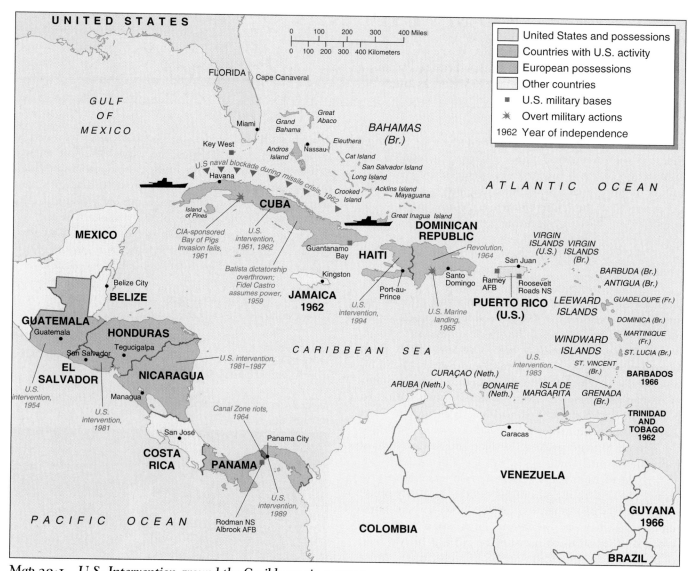

Map 30-1   U.S. Intervention around the Caribbean since 1954
The United States has long kept a careful eye on the politics of neighboring nations to its south.
In the second half of the twentieth century, the United States frequently used military assistance
or force to influence or intervene in Caribbean and Central American nations. The most common purpose has been to counter or undermine left-leaning governments; some interventions, as
in Haiti, have been intended to stabilize democratic regimes.

against rebels who combined communist ideology
with fervor for national independence under the
leadership of Ho Chi Minh. The United States
picked up three-quarters of the costs, but the French
military position collapsed in 1954 after Vietnamese
forces overran the French stronghold at Dien Bien
Phu. The French had had enough, and Eisenhower
was unwilling to join another Asian war. A Geneva
peace conference in 1954 "temporarily" divided Vietnam into a communist north and a noncommunist
south and scheduled elections for a single Vietnamese government.

The United States then replaced France as
the supporter of pro-Western Vietnamese in the
south. Washington's client was Ngo Dinh Diem, an
anticommunist from South Vietnam's Roman
Catholic elite. U.S. officials encouraged Diem to put
off the elections and backed his efforts to construct
an authoritarian South Vietnam. Ho meanwhile consolidated the northern half as a communist state that
claimed to be the legitimate government for all Vietnam. The United States further reinforced containment in Asia by bringing Thailand, the Philippines,
Pakistan, Australia, New Zealand, Britain, and

France together in the **Southeast Asia Treaty Organization (SEATO)** in 1954 (see Map 30-2).

Halfway around the world, there was a new crisis when three American friends—France, Britain, and Israel—ganged up on Egypt. France was angry at Egyptian support for revolutionaries in French Algeria. Britain was even angrier at Egypt's nationalization of the British-dominated Suez Canal. And Israel wanted to weaken its most powerful Arab enemy. On October 29, 1956, Israel attacked Egypt. A week later, British and French forces attempted to seize the canal. The United States forced a quick cease-fire, partly to maintain its standing with oil-producing Arab nations. The war left Britain and France dependent on American oil that Eisenhower would not provide until they left Egypt.

In Europe, Eisenhower accepted the status quo because conflicts there could result in nuclear war. In 1956, challenges to communist rule arose in East Germany, Poland, and Hungary and threatened to break up the Soviet empire. The Soviets replaced liberal communists in East Germany and Poland with hard-liners. In Hungary, however, open warfare broke out. Hungarian freedom fighters in Budapest used rocks and firebombs against Soviet tanks for several days, while pleading in vain for Western aid. NATO would not risk war with the USSR. Tens of thousands of Hungarians died, and 200,000 fled when the Soviets crushed the resistance.

Global Standoff

The Soviet Union, China, and the United States and its allies were all groping in the dark as they maneuvered for influence in the 1950s and 1960s. In one international crisis after another, each player misinterpreted the other's motivations and diplomatic signals. As documents from both sides of the Cold War become available, historians have realized what

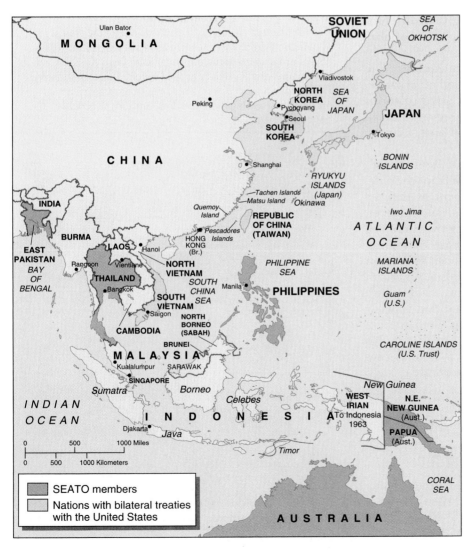

Map 30-2   SEATO and Other East Asian Countries with Ties to the United States
In East Asia and the western Pacific, the United States in the 1950s constructed a series of alliances to resist Soviet and Chinese communist influence.

dangerously different meanings the two sides gave to confrontations between 1953 and 1964.

A good example was the U-2 affair of 1960, which derailed progress toward nuclear disarmament. The Kremlin was deeply worried that West Germany and China might acquire nuclear bombs. Washington wanted to reduce military budgets and nuclear fallout. Both countries voluntarily suspended nuclear tests in 1958 and prepared for a June 1960 summit meeting in Paris, where Eisenhower intended to negotiate a test ban treaty.

But on May 1, 1960, Soviet air defenses shot down an American U-2 spy plane over the heart of Russia and captured the pilot, Francis Gary Powers. Designed to soar above the range of Soviet antiaircraft missiles, U-2s had assured American officials that there was no missile gap.

When Moscow trumpeted the news of the downing, Eisenhower took personal responsibility in hopes that Khrushchev would accept the U-2 as an unpleasant reality of international espionage. Unfortunately, the planes meant something very different to the Soviets, touching their festering sense of inferiority. They had stopped protesting the flights in 1957 because complaints were demeaning. The Americans thought that silence signaled acceptance. Khrushchev had staked his future on good relations with the United States; when Eisenhower refused to apologize in Paris, Khrushchev stalked out. Disarmament was set back for years.

The most important aspect of Eisenhower's foreign policy was continuity. Despite militant rhetoric, the administration pursued containment as defined under Truman. The Cold War consensus, however, prevented the United States from seeing the nations of the developing world on their own terms. By viewing every independence movement and social revolution as part of the competition with communism, American leaders created unnecessary problems. In the end, Eisenhower left troublesome and unresolved issues—upheaval in Latin America, civil war in Vietnam, tension in Germany, a nuclear arms race—for his successor, John Kennedy, who wanted to confront international communism even more vigorously.

John F. Kennedy and the Cold War

John Kennedy was a man of contradictions. Many Americans recall his presidency (1961–1963) as a golden age, but we are more taken by his memory than we were by Kennedy himself. A Democrat, he presided over policies whose direction was set under Eisenhower. Despite stirring rhetoric about leading the nation toward a **New Frontier** of scientific and social progress, he recorded his greatest failures and successes in the continuing Cold War.

The Kennedy Mystique

Kennedy won the presidency over Richard Nixon in a cliffhanging election that was more about personality and style than substance (see Map 30-3). Both candidates were determined not to yield another inch to communism. The charming and eloquent Kennedy narrowly skirted scandal in his personal life. Well publicized as a hero from World War II, he tempered ruthless ambition with respect for public service. His forthright campaigning allayed voter concern about his Roman Catholicism. Nixon had wider experience and was a shrewd tactician, but he was also self-righteous and awkward. Eisenhower had

Map 30-3   The Election of 1960
The presidential election of 1960 was one of the closest in American history. John Kennedy's victory depended on his appeal in northern industrial states with large Roman Catholic populations and his ability to hold much of the traditionally Democratic South. Texas, the home state of his vice-presidential running mate Lyndon Johnson, was vital to the success of the ticket.

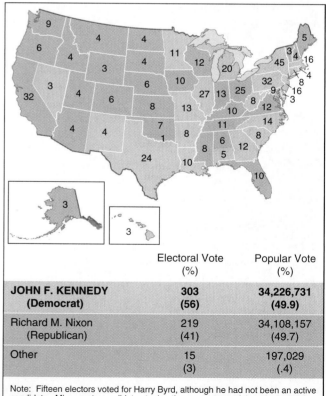

	Electoral Vote (%)	Popular Vote (%)
JOHN F. KENNEDY (Democrat)	**303** **(56)**	**34,226,731** **(49.9)**
Richard M. Nixon (Republican)	219 (41)	34,108,157 (49.7)
Other	15 (3)	197,029 (.4)

Note: Fifteen electors voted for Harry Byrd, although he had not been an active candidate. Minor party candidates took a tiny percentage of the popular vote.

wanted to drop Nixon as vice president in 1956 and gave him only lukewarm support in 1960—when a reporter asked Eisenhower to cite important decisions to which Nixon had contributed, Ike replied, "Give me a week and I might think of one."

Television was crucial to the outcome. The campaign featured the first televised presidential debates. In the first session, Nixon actually gave better replies, but his nervousness and a bad makeup job turned off millions of viewers who admired Kennedy's energy. Nixon never overcame the setback. Kennedy's televised inauguration was the perfect setting for his impassioned plea for national unity: "My fellow Americans," he challenged, "ask not what your country can do for you—ask what you can do for your country."

Kennedy brought dash to the White House. His beautiful and refined wife, Jackie, made sure to seat artists and writers next to diplomats and businessmen at White House dinners. Kennedy's staff and large family played touch football, not golf. No president had shown such verve since Teddy Roosevelt. People began to talk about Kennedy's "charisma," his ability to lead by sheer force of personality.

Behind the glamorous façade, Kennedy remained a puzzle. One day he could propose the Peace Corps, which gave thousands of idealistic young Americans a chance to help developing nations; another day he could approve plots to assassinate Fidel Castro. Visitors who expected a shallow glad-hander were astonished to meet a sharp, hardworking man who was eager to learn about the world. One savvy diplomat commented, "I have never heard of a president who wanted to know so much."

Kennedy's Mistakes

Kennedy and Khrushchev perpetuated similar problems. Talking tough to satisfy more militant countrymen, they pushed each other into corners, continuing the problems of mutual misunderstanding that had marked the 1950s. When Khrushchev promised in January 1961 to support "wars of national liberation," he was really fending off Chinese criticism. But Kennedy overreacted in his first State of the Union address by asking for more military spending.

Three months later, Kennedy fed Soviet fears of American aggressiveness by sponsoring an invasion of Cuba. At the start of 1959, Fidel Castro had toppled corrupt dictator Fulgencio Batista, who had made Havana infamous for Mafia-run gambling and prostitution. Castro then nationalized American investments, and thousands of Cubans fled to the United States. When fourteen hundred anti-Castro Cubans landed at Cuba's **Bay of Pigs** on April 17, 1961, they were following a plan from the Eisenhower administration. The CIA had trained and armed the invaders and convinced Kennedy that the landing would trigger spontaneous uprisings. But when Kennedy refused to commit American armed forces to support them, Cuban forces captured the attackers.

Kennedy followed the Bay of Pigs debacle with a hasty and ill-prepared summit meeting with Khrushchev in Vienna in June, where Khrushchev saw no need to bargain and subjected him to intimidating tirades. The meeting left the Soviets with the impression that the president was weak and dangerously erratic.

To exploit Kennedy's perceived vulnerability, the USSR renewed tension over Berlin, deep within East Germany. The divided city served as an escape route from communism for hundreds of thousands of East Germans. Khrushchev now threatened to transfer the Soviet sector in Berlin to East Germany, which had no treaty obligations to France, Britain, or the United States. If the West had to deal directly with East Germany for access to Berlin, it would have to recognize a permanently divided Germany. Kennedy sounded the alarm; he doubled draft calls, called up reservists, and warned families to build fallout shelters. Boise, Idaho, families paid $100 for a share in a community shelter with its own power plant and hospital. Outside New York, Art Carlson and his son Claude put up a prefabricated steel shelter in four hours; Sears planned to sell the same model for $700.

Rather than confront the United States directly, however, the Soviets and East Germans on August 13, 1961, built a wall around the western sectors of Berlin while leaving the access route to West Germany open. The **Berlin Wall** thus isolated East Germany without challenging the Western allies in West Berlin itself. In private, Kennedy accepted the wall as a clever way to stabilize a dangerous situation: "A wall," he said, "is a hell of a lot better than a war." Tensions remained high for months as the two sides tested each other's resolve. Berlin remained a point of East-West tension until East German communism collapsed in 1989 and Berliners tore down the hated wall.

Another indirect consequence of the Vienna summit was growing American involvement in South Vietnam. Kennedy saw South Vietnam as a promising arena for containment. The anticommunist Diem controlled the cities with the help of a large army and a Vietnamese elite that had worked with the French. In the countryside, communist insurgents known as the **Viet Cong** were gaining strength. The United States stepped up its supply of weapons and sent advisers, including members of one of

Kennedy's military innovations, the Army Special Forces Group (Green Berets).

U.S. aid did not work. Despite overoptimistic reports and the help of sixteen thousand American troops, Diem's government by 1963 was losing the loyalty—"hearts and minds"—of many South Vietnamese. North Vietnamese support for the Viet Cong canceled the effect of U.S. assistance. Diem courted a second civil war by violently crushing opposition from Vietnamese Buddhists. Kennedy's administration tacitly approved a coup on November 1 that killed Diem and his brother and installed an ineffective military junta.

Missile Crisis:
A Line Drawn in the Waves

The escalating tensions of 1961 in Southeast Asia, the Caribbean, and Germany were a prelude to the crisis that came closest to triggering a nuclear war. In the summer of 1962, congressional Republicans had hounded Kennedy about the Soviet military presence in Cuba. On October 15, reconnaissance photos revealed Soviets at work on launching sites from which nuclear missiles could hit the United States. Top officials spent five exhausting and increasingly desperate days sorting through the options. Doing nothing was never considered: The missiles would be political disaster and a threat to national security. Full-scale invasion of Cuba was infeasible on short notice, and "surgical" air strikes were technically impossible. Either sort of military operation would kill hundreds of Soviet personal and force Moscow to react. Secretary of Defense Robert McNamara suggested demanding removal of the missiles and declaring a naval "quarantine" against the arrival of further offensive weapons. A blockade would buy time for diplomacy.

Kennedy imposed the blockade in a terrifying speech on Monday, October 22. He emphasized the "deceptive" deployment of the Russian missiles and raised the specter of nuclear war. Americans would have been even more afraid had they known that some of the missiles were operational and that Soviets in Cuba were authorized to use them in self-defense. While Khrushchev hesitated, Soviet ships circled outside the quarantine line. On Friday, Khrushchev offered to withdraw the missiles in return for an American pledge not to invade Cuba. On Saturday, a second communication raised a new complaint about American missiles on the territory of NATO allies. The letter was the result of pressure by Kremlin hard-liners and Khrushchev's own wavering. Kennedy decided to accept the first letter and ignore the second. The United States pledged not to invade Cuba and secretly promised to remove obsolete Jupiter missiles from Turkey. Khrushchev accepted these terms on Sunday, October 28.

Why did Khrushchev risk the Cuban gamble? One reason was to protect Castro as a symbol of Soviet commitment to anti-Western regimes in the developing world. Americans hated the Castro government out of proportion to its geopolitical importance, but they rightly feared that Cuba would try to export revolution throughout Latin America. Kennedy had tried to preempt Castroism in 1961 by launching the **Alliance for Progress**, an economic development program for Latin America that tied aid to social reform. However, the United States had also orchestrated the Bay of Pigs invasion and funded a CIA campaign to sabotage Cuba and assassinate its leaders. High American officials were not contemplating a full-scale invasion, but Castro and Khrushchev had reason to fear the worst.

Khrushchev also hoped to redress the strategic balance. As Kennedy discovered on taking office, the United States actually led the world in the deployment of strategic missiles. Intermediate-range rockets gave the USSR a nuclear club over western Europe, but in October 1962, the USSR had fewer than fifty ICBMs to aim at the United States and China. The United States was creating a defensive triad of a thousand land-based Minuteman missiles, five hundred long-range bombers, and six hundred Polaris missiles on nuclear submarines targeted on the USSR. The strategic imbalance had sustained NATO during the Berlin confrontation, but forty launchers in Cuba with two warheads each would have doubled the Soviet capacity to strike at the United States.

Soviet missiles in Cuba thus flouted the Monroe Doctrine and posed a real military threat. Kennedy and Khrushchev had also backed each other into untenable positions. In September, Kennedy had warned that the United States could not tolerate Soviet offensive weapons in Cuba, never dreaming that they were already there. Had Khrushchev acted openly (as the United States had done in siting missiles in Turkey), the United States would have been hard pressed to object under international law. By acting in secret and breaking previous promises, the Soviets outsmarted themselves. When the missiles were discovered, Kennedy had to act.

In the end, both sides were cautious. Khrushchev backed down rather than fight. Kennedy fended off hawkish advisers who wanted to destroy Castro. The world had trembled, but neither nation wanted war over "the missiles of October."

After the missile crisis showed his toughness, Kennedy had enough political maneuvering room to respond to pressure from liberal Democrats and groups like Women Strike for Peace and the Committee for a Sane Nuclear Policy by giving priority to disarmament. In July 1963, the United States, Britain, and the USSR signed the **Limited Test Ban Treaty**, which outlawed nuclear testing in the atmosphere, in outer space, and under water, and invited other nations to join in. A more comprehensive treaty was impossible because the Soviet Union refused the on-site inspections the United States deemed necessary to distinguish underground tests from earthquakes. France and China, the other nuclear powers, refused to sign, and the treaty did not halt weapons development, but it was the most positive achievement of Kennedy's foreign policy.

Righteousness Like a Mighty Stream: The Struggle for Civil Rights

Supreme Court decisions are based on abstract principles, but they involve real people. One was Linda Brown of Topeka, Kansas, a third-grader whose parents were fed up with sending her past an all-white public school to attend an all-black school a mile away. The Browns volunteered to help the NAACP challenge Topeka's school segregation by trying to enroll Linda in their neighborhood school, beginning a legal case that reached the Supreme Court. Three years later, on May 17, 1954, the Court decided **Brown v. *Board of Education of Topeka***, opening a new civil rights era. The justices reversed the 1896 case of *Plessy* v. *Ferguson* by ruling that sending black children to "separate but equal" schools denied them equal treatment under the Constitution. Linda's mother heard about the decision on the radio while she was ironing and told her daughter when she got home from school; when Linda's father heard the news, his eyes filled with tears, and he said, "Thanks be to God."

The Brown decision made the growing effort to secure equal legal treatment for African Americans an inescapable challenge to American society. The first phase of the civil rights struggle built from the Supreme Court's decision in 1954 to a vast gathering at the Lincoln Memorial in 1963. In between, African Americans chipped away at the racial segregation of schools, universities, and public facilities with marches, boycotts, sit-ins, and lawsuits, forcing segregated communities to choose between integra-

tion and violent defiance. In the two years following the 1963 March on Washington, the federal government passed landmark legislation.

Getting to the Supreme Court

The Brown decision climaxed a twenty-five-year campaign to reenlist the federal courts on the side of equal rights (see the Overview table, "Civil Rights in the South: The Struggle for Racial Equality"). The work began in the 1930s when Charles Hamilton Houston, dean of Howard University's law school, trained a corps of civil rights lawyers. Working on behalf of the NAACP, he hoped to erode *Plessy* by suits focused on interstate travel and professional graduate schools (the least defensible segregated institutions, because states seldom provided alternatives). In 1938, Houston's student Thurgood Marshall, a future Supreme Court justice, took over the NAACP job. He and other NAACP lawyers such as Constance Baker Motley risked personal danger crisscrossing the South to file civil rights lawsuits wherever a local case emerged. In 1949, Motley was the first black lawyer to argue a case in a Mississippi courtroom since Reconstruction.

The Brown case combined lawsuits from Delaware, Virginia, South Carolina, the District of Columbia, and Kansas. In each instance, students and families braved community pressure to demand equal access to a basic public service. Chief Justice Earl Warren brought a divided Court to unanimous agreement. Viewing public education as central for the equal opportunity that lay at the heart of American values, the Court weighed the consequences of segregated school systems and concluded that separate meant unequal. The reasoning fit the temper of a nation that was proud of making prosperity accessible to all.

Brown also built on efforts by Mexican Americans in the Southwest to assert their rights of citizenship. After World War II, Latino organizations such as the League of United Latin American Citizens battled job discrimination and ethnic segregation. In 1946, the federal courts had prohibited segregation of Mexican-American children in California schools. Eight years later, the Supreme Court forbade Texas from excluding Mexican Americans from juries. These cases provided precedents for civil rights arguments.

Deliberate Speed

Racial segregation by law was largely a southern problem, the legacy of Jim Crow laws from early in the century. The civil rights movement therefore first focused on the South and allowed Americans elsewhere to think of racial injustice as a regional issue.

OVERVIEW

CIVIL RIGHTS IN THE SOUTH: THE STRUGGLE FOR RACIAL EQUALITY

Area of Concern	Key Actions	Results
Public school integration	Federal court cases	*Brown* v. *Board of Education of Topeka* (1954) Enforcement by presidential action, Little Rock (1957) Follow-up court decisions, including mandatory busing programs
Equal access to public facilities	Montgomery bus boycott (1955) Lunch counter sit-ins (1960) Freedom rides (1961) Birmingham demonstrations (1963) March on Washington (1963)	Civil Rights Act of 1964
Equitable voter registration	Voter registration drives, including Mississippi Summer Project (1964) Demonstrations and marches, including Selma to Montgomery march (1965)	Voting Rights Act of 1965

Southern responses to Brown emphasized regional differences. Few southern communities desegregated schools voluntarily, for to do so undermined the entrenched principle of a dual society. Their reluctance was bolstered in 1955 when the Supreme Court allowed segregated states to carry out the 1954 decision "with all deliberate speed" rather than immediately. The following year, 101 southern congressmen and senators issued the **Southern Manifesto**, which asserted that the Court decision was unconstitutional. President Eisenhower privately deplored the desegregation decision, which violated his sense of states' rights and upset Republican attempts to gain southern votes; he called both those who resisted the decision and those who wanted to enforce it "extremists."

Eisenhower's distaste for racial integration left the Justice Department on the sidelines. Courageous parents and students had to knock on schoolhouse doors, often carrying court orders. Responses varied: School districts in border states, such as Maryland, Kentucky, and Oklahoma, desegregated

relatively peacefully; farther south, African-American children often met taunts and violence.

The first crisis came in Little Rock, Arkansas, in September 1957. The city school board admitted nine African Americans to Central High, only to be upstaged by Governor Orval Faubus. Claiming to fear violence, he surrounded Central with the National Guard and turned the new students away. Meanwhile, segregrationists stirred up white fears. Under intense national pressure, Faubus withdrew the Guard, and a howling crowd surrounded the school. When the black students entered anyway, the mob threatened to storm the building. The police had to sneak the students out after two hours. Fuming at the governor's defiance of federal authority, which bordered on insurrection, Eisenhower reluctantly nationalized the National Guard and sent in the 101st Airborne Division to keep order. Eight of the students endured a year of harassment in the hallways of Central.

Change came slowly to state universities. Border states desegregated colleges and professional schools with few incidents. Again, the story was differ-

Elizabeth Eckford, one of the first black students to attend Central High in Little Rock, Arkansas, in 1957, enters the school amid taunts from white students and bystanders.

ent in the lower South. In 1956, the University of Alabama admitted Autherine Lucy under court order but then expelled her before she could attend class. In September 1962, James Meredith tried to enter the University of Mississippi, igniting a riot that the state refused to control. President Kennedy sent in the army. A year later, Governor George Wallace of Alabama grabbed headlines by "standing in the schoolhouse door" to prevent integration of the University of Alabama, gaining a national prominence that culminated in a third-party candidacy for president in 1968.

The breakthrough in school integration did not come until the end of the 1960s, when the courts rejected further delays, and federal authorities threatened to cut off education funds. As late as 1968, only 6 percent of African-American children in the South attended integrated schools. By 1973, the figure was 90 percent. Attention thereafter shifted to northern communities, whose schools were segregated not by law but by the divisions between white and black neighborhoods and between white suburbs and multiracial central cities, a situation known as de facto segregation.

Public Accommodations

The civil rights movement also sought to integrate public accommodations. Most southern states separated the races in bus terminals and movie theaters. They required black riders to take rear seats on buses. They labeled separate restrooms and drinking fountains for "colored" users. Hotels denied rooms to black people, and restaurants refused them service.

The struggle to end segregated facilities started in Montgomery, Alabama. On December 1, 1955, Rosa Parks, a seamstress who worked at a downtown department store, refused to give up her bus seat to a white passenger and was arrested. Parks acted spontaneously, but she was part of a network of civil rights activists who wanted to challenge segregated buses and was the secretary of the Montgomery NAACP. As news of her action spread, the community institutions that enriched southern black life went into action. The Women's Political Council, a group of college-trained black women, initiated a mass boycott of the privately owned bus company. Martin Luther King, Jr., a twenty-six-year-old pastor, led the boycott. He galvanized a mass meeting with a speech that quoted the biblical prophet Amos: "We are determined here in Montgomery to work and fight until justice runs down like water, and righteousness like a mighty stream."

Montgomery's African Americans organized their boycott in the face of white outrage. A car pool substituted for the buses despite police harassment. As the boycott survived months of pressure, the national media began to pay attention. After nearly a year, the Supreme Court agreed that the bus segregation law was unconstitutional.

Victory in Montgomery depended on the steadfastness of African-American involvement. Leaders included Ralph Abernathy, other black preachers, and faculty from Alabama State College. Participants cut across the class lines that had divided black Southerners. Success also revealed the discrepancy between white attitudes in the Deep South and national opinion. For white Southerners, segregation was a local concern best defined as a legal or constitutional matter. For other Americans, it was increasingly an issue of the South's deviation from national moral norms.

The Montgomery boycott won a local victory and made King famous, but it did not propel a wave of immediate change. King formed the **Southern Christian Leadership Conference (SCLC)** and sparred with the NAACP about community-based versus court-based civil rights tactics, but four African-American college students in Greensboro, North Carolina, started the next phase of the struggle. On February 1, 1960, they sat down at the segregated lunch counter in Woolworth's, waiting through the day without being served. Their patient courage brought more demonstrators; within two days, eighty-five students packed the store. Nonviolent sit-ins spread throughout the South.

The sit-ins had both immediate and long-range effects. In comparatively sophisticated border cities like Nashville, Tennessee, sit-ins integrated lunch counters. Elsewhere they precipitated white violence and mass arrests. Like soldiers on a battlefield, nervous participants in sit-ins and demonstrations drew strength from one another. "If you don't have courage," said one young woman in Albany, Georgia, "you can borrow it." King welcomed nonviolent confrontation. SCLC leader Ella Baker helped the students form a new organization, the **Student Nonviolent Coordinating Committee (SNCC).** (See "American Views: Nonviolent Action for Civil Rights: Mississippi 1961.")

The year 1961 brought "freedom rides" to test the segregation of interstate bus terminals. The

Students from North Carolina A&T, an all-black college, began the lunch counter sit-in movement in February 1960. Here four of the students sit patiently in the Greensboro Woolworth's without being served. Participants wore their best clothes and suffered politely through days of verbal and sometimes physical abuse.

American Views

NONVIOLENT ACTION FOR
CIVIL RIGHTS: MISSISSIPPI 1961

As sit-ins and other nonviolent civil rights protests spread across the South, Burgland High School, in McComb, Mississippi, expelled two students after they tried to integrate the local Greyhound bus station. Many fellow students boycotted the school in sympathy, attending "Nonviolent High," classes taught by workers from the Student Nonviolent Coordinating Committee. One of these students was Suzette Miller, who explained her motivations in a class assignment.

❖ **What does the episode suggest about the local roots of the civil rights movement?**
❖ **What does the statement show about the role of religion in American reform efforts?**

Suzette Miller
Subject: English
Instructor: C. McDew

Why I walked out of Burgland High School:

I am Suzette Miller, a student of the present Freshman class. I don't have much to lose, but I do have a lot to gain. That is my equal rights.

Brenda Travis is a female that made a protest in McComb Bus Station. She was also a student at Burgland Hi, but is now an ex-student.

I was in the walk out because I am A student at Burgland just like Brenda. Because she wasn't allowed back in school I don't feel that I should allow myself to go back.

I walked out and to be readmitted I have to sign a paper saying that if I walk out any more I will be expelled, and if I didn't sign the paper asking for readmittance back in school.

Now I am expelled for the remainder of the school year. But I will keep protesting until the battle is won.

I am now a student of The Nonviolent High School. In my heart I believe where there is a will there is a way.

Now is the time to put God first and to let him lead us.

Our white brothers and sisters think that we want war. War is not needed now in Mississippi. If we ever needed any thing we need God. He is the way and the light.

If we would stop and think we could see what we need and what we are doing to try to get it.

We as a race come face to face with our enemies kind and willing to have them as brothers and sisters. We would have better families, homes, churches, towns, and states.

May God forever bless us all over land and country. "Oh God show us the right way."

Source: Staughton Lynd, Nonviolence in America: A Documentary History *(Bobbs-Merrill, 1966).*

idea came from James Farmer of the **Congress of Racial Equality (CORE)**, who copied a little-remembered 1947 Journey of Reconciliation that had tested the integration of interstate trains. Two buses carrying black and white passengers met only minor problems in Virginia, the Carolinas, and Georgia, but Alabamians burned one of the buses and attacked the riders in Birmingham, where they beat demonstrators senseless and clubbed a Justice Department observer. The governor and police refused to protect the freedom riders. The riders traveled into Mississippi under National Guard protection but were arrested at the Jackson bus terminal. Despite Attorney General Robert Kennedy's call for a cooling-off period, freedom rides continued through the summer. The rides proved that African Americans were in charge of their own civil rights revolution.

March on Washington, 1963

John Kennedy was a tepid supporter of the civil rights movement and entered office with no civil rights agenda. He appointed segregationist judges to mollify southern congressmen and would have preferred that African Americans stop disturbing the fragile Democratic party coalition. As Eisenhower did at Little Rock, Kennedy intervened at the University of Mississippi in 1962 because of a state challenge to federal authority, not to further racial justice.

In the face of slow federal response, the SCLC concentrated for 1963 on rigidly segregated Birmingham. April began with sit-ins and marches that aimed to integrate lunch counters, restrooms, and stores and secure open hiring for some clerical jobs. Birmingham's commissioner of public safety, Bull Connor, used fire hoses to blast demonstrators against buildings and roll children down the streets. When demonstrators fought back, his men chased them with dogs. Continued marches brought the arrest of hundreds of children. King's own "Letter from Birmingham City Jail" stated the case for protest: "We have not made a single gain in civil rights without determined legal and nonviolent pressure. . . . Freedom is never voluntarily given by the oppressor; it must be demanded by the oppressed."

The Birmingham demonstrations were inconclusive. White leaders accepted minimal demands on May 10 but delayed enforcing them. Antiblack violence continued, including a bomb that killed four children in a Birmingham church. Meanwhile, the events in Alabama had forced President Kennedy to board the freedom train with an eloquent June 11 speech and to send a civil rights bill to Congress. "Are we to say . . . that this is the land of the free, except for Negroes, that we have no second-class citizens, except Negroes . . . ? Now the time has come for the nation to fulfill its promise."

On August 28, 1963, a rally in Washington transformed African-American civil rights into a national cause. A quarter of a million people, black and white, marched to the Lincoln Memorial. The day gave Martin Luther King, Jr., a national pulpit. His call for progress toward Christian and American goals had immense appeal. Television cut away from afternoon programs for his "I Have a Dream" speech.

The March on Washington demonstrated the mass appeal of civil rights and its identification with national values. It also papered over growing tensions within the civil rights movement. John Lewis of SNCC wanted to challenge Kennedy for doing "too little, too late" but dropped the criticism under intense pressure. He was the only speaker at the march to talk about "black people" rather than "Negroes," an indication of growing militancy that split the civil rights effort in the mid-sixties and moved younger African Americans, as well as Latinos and Native Americans, to emphasize their own distinct identities within American society.

"Let Us Continue"

The two years that followed King's speech mingled despair and accomplishment. The optimism of the March on Washington shattered with the assassination of John Kennedy in November 1963. In 1964 and 1965, however, President Lyndon Johnson pushed through Kennedy's legislative agenda and much more. Federal legislation brought victory to the first phase of the civil rights revolution, launched the **War on Poverty**, expanded health insurance and aid to education, and opened an era of environmental protection, government activism unmatched since the 1930s.

Dallas, 1963

In November 1963, President Kennedy visited Texas to patch up feuds among Texas Democrats. On November 22, the president's motorcade took him near the Texas School Book Depository building in Dallas, where Lee Harvey Oswald had stationed himself at a window on the sixth floor. When Kennedy's open car swung into the sights of his rifle, Oswald fired three shots that wounded Texas Governor John Connally and killed the president. As doctors vainly treated the president in a hospital emergency room, Dallas police arrested Oswald. Vice President Lyndon Johnson took the oath of office as president on Air Force One while the blood-spattered Jacqueline

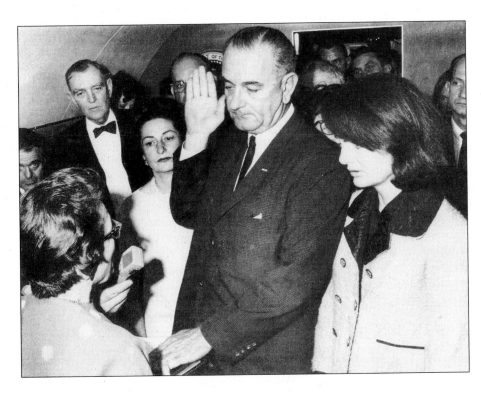

After the assassination of John Kennedy in Dallas, Lyndon Johnson, with Jackie Kennedy looking on, took the oath of office as president aboard Air Force One at Love Field in Dallas.

Kennedy looked on. Two days later, as Oswald was being led to a courtroom, Texas nightclub owner Jack Ruby killed Oswald with a handgun, in full view of TV cameras.

Lee Oswald was a twenty-four-year old misfit. He had served in the Marines and worked maintaining U-2 spy planes before defecting to the Soviet Union, which he found to be less than a workers' paradise. He returned to the United States after three years with a Russian wife and a fervent commitment to Fidel Castro's Cuban revolution. It was later learned that he had tried to shoot a right-wing general in 1963. He visited the Soviet and Cuban embassies in Mexico City in September trying to drum up a job, but neither country thought him worth hiring.

Some Americans believe there is more to the story. Why? One possibility is the expectation that important events should have great causes. Oswald seems too insignificant to be responsible on his own for the murder of a charismatic president. The sketchy job done by the Warren Commission, appointed to investigate the assassination, also bred doubts in some minds. The commission hurried to complete its work before the 1964 election. It also sought to assure Americans that Kennedy had not been killed as part of a communist plot. The Warren Commission calmed fears in the short run but left loose ends that have fueled conspiracy theories.

All of the theories remain unproved. Until they are, logic holds that the simplest explanation for cutting through a mass of information is usually the best. Oswald was a social misfit with a grievance against American society. Ruby was an impulsive man who told his brother on his deathbed that he thought he was doing the country a favor. Like presidents Garfield and McKinley before him, Kennedy died at the hands of one unbalanced man acting alone.

War on Poverty

Five days after the assassination, Lyndon Johnson claimed Kennedy's progressive aura for his new administration. "Let us continue," he told the nation, promising to implement Kennedy's policies. In fact, Johnson was vastly different from Kennedy. He was a professional politician who had reached the top through Texas politics and congressional infighting. As Senate majority leader during the 1950s, he had built a web of political obligations and friendships. Johnson's presence on the ticket in 1960 had helped elect Kennedy by attracting southern voters, but the Kennedy entourage loathed him. He lacked Kennedy's polish and easy relations with the eastern elite. He knew little about foreign affairs but was deeply committed to social equity. He had entered public life with the New Deal in the 1930s and believed in its principles. Johnson, not Kennedy, was the true heir of Franklin Roosevelt.

Johnson inherited a domestic agenda that the Kennedy administration had defined but not enacted. Kennedy's New Frontier had met the same fate as Truman's Fair Deal. Initiatives in education, medical insurance, tax reform, and urban affairs had stalled or been gutted by conservatives in Congress.

Kennedy's farthest-reaching initiative was rooted in the acknowledgment that poverty was a persistent American problem. Michael Harrington's study *The Other America* became an unexpected bestseller. As poverty captured public attention, Kennedy's economic advisers devised a community action program that emphasized education and job training, a national service corps, and a youth conservation corps. They prepared a package of proposals to submit to Congress in 1964 that downplayed the option of large-scale income transfers as politically unpopular. Instead, they focused on social programs to alter behaviors that were thought to be passed from generation to generation, thus following the American tendency to attribute poverty to the failings of the poor themselves.

Johnson made Kennedy's antipoverty package his own. Adopting Cold War rhetoric, he declared "unconditional war on poverty." The core of Johnson's program was the **Office of Economic Opportunity (OEO)**. Established under the direction of Kennedy's brother-in-law R. Sargent Shriver in 1964, the OEO operated the **Job Corps** for school dropouts, the Neighborhood Youth Corps for unemployed teenagers, the **Head Start** program to prepare poor children for school, and **VISTA** (Volunteers in Service to America), a domestic Peace Corps. OEO's biggest effort went to Community Action Agencies. By 1968, more than five hundred such agencies provided health and educational services. Despite flaws, the War on Poverty improved life for millions of Americans.

Civil Rights, 1964–1965

Johnson's passionate commitment to economic betterment accompanied a commitment to civil rights. In Johnson's view, segregation not only deprived African Americans of access to opportunity but also distracted white Southerners from their own poverty and underdevelopment. As he complained in a speech in New Orleans, southern leaders ignored the region's economic needs in favor of racial rabble-rousing.

One solution was the **Civil Rights Act of 1964**, which Kennedy had introduced but Johnson got enacted. The law prohibited segregation in public accommodations, such as hotels, restaurants, gas stations, theaters, and parks, and outlawed employment discrimination on federally assisted projects. It also created the **Equal Employment Opportunity Commission (EEOC)** and included gender in list of categories protected against discrimination, a provision whose consequences were scarcely suspected in 1964.

Even as Congress was debating the 1964 law, **Freedom Summer** moved political power to the top of the civil rights agenda. Organized by SNCC, the Mississippi Summer Freedom Project was a voter registration drive that sent white and black volunteers to the small towns and back roads of Mississippi. The target was a political system that used rigged literacy tests and intimidation to keep black Southerners from voting. In Mississippi in 1964, only 7 percent of eligible black citizens were registered voters. Local black activists had laid the groundwork for a registration effort with years of courageous effort through the NAACP and voter leagues. Now an increasingly militant SNCC took the lead. The explicit goal was to increase the number of African-American voters. The tacit intention was to attract national attention by putting middle-class white college students in the line of fire. Freedom Summer gained sixteen hundred new voters and taught two thousand children in SNCC-run Freedom Schools at the cost of beatings, bombings, church arson, and the murder of three project workers.

Another outgrowth of the SNCC effort was the Mississippi Freedom Democratic Party (MFDP), a biracial coalition that bypassed Mississippi's all-white Democratic party, followed state party rules, and sent its own delegates to the 1964 Democratic convention. To preserve party harmony, President Johnson refused to expel the "regular" Mississippi Democrats and offered instead to seat two MFDP delegates and enforce party rules for 1968. The MFDP walked out, seething with anger. Fannie Lou Hamer, a MFDP delegate who had already suffered in the struggle for voting rights, remembered, "We learned the hard way that even though we had all the law and all the righteousness on our side—that white man is not going to give up his power to us. We have to build our own power."

Freedom Summer and political realities both focused national attention on voter registration. Lyndon Johnson and Martin Luther King, Jr., agreed on the need for federal voting legislation when King visited the president in December 1964 after winning the Nobel Peace Prize. For King, power at the ballot box would help black Southerners take control of their own communities. For Johnson, voting reform would fulfill the promise of American democracy. It would also benefit the Democratic party by replacing with black voters the white Southerners who were drifting toward anti-integration Republicans.

The target for King and the SCLC was Dallas County, Alabama, where only 2 percent of eligible black residents were registered, compared with 70 percent of white residents. Peaceful demonstrations started in January 1965. By early February, jails in the county seat of Selma held 2,600 black people whose offense was marching to the courthouse to demand the vote. The campaign climaxed with a march from Selma to the state capital of Montgomery. SNCC leader John Lewis remembered, "I don't know what we expected. I think maybe we thought we'd be arrested and jailed, or maybe they wouldn't do anything to us. I had a little knapsack on my shoulder with an apple, a toothbrush, toothpaste, and two books in it: a history of America and a book by [Christian theologian] Thomas Merton."

On Sunday, March 7, five hundred marchers crossed the bridge over the Alabama River to meet a sea of state troopers. The troopers gave them two minutes to disperse and then attacked on foot and

After being attacked and dispersed by Alabama state police as they attempted a fifty-three mile march from Selma to Montgomery, Alabama, civil rights demonstrators regrouped. Under the glare of national press coverage, Alabama authorities let the march proceed. Here the leaders—including Martin Luther King, Jr., Coretta Scott King, Hosea Williams, Bayard Rustin, and Ralph Bunche—enter Montgomery.

horseback "as if they were mowing a big field." The attack drove the demonstrators back in bloody confusion while television cameras rolled.

As violence continued, Johnson addressed a joint session of Congress to demand a voting rights law: "Our mission is at once the oldest and the most basic of this country: to right wrong, to do justice, to serve man." He ended with the refrain of the civil rights movement: "We shall overcome."

Johnson signed the **Voting Rights Act** on August 6, 1965. The law outlawed literacy tests and provided for federal voting registrars in states where registration or turnout in 1964 was less than 50 percent of eligible population. It applied initially in seven southern states. Black registration in these states jumped from 27 percent to 55 percent within the first year. In 1975, Congress extended coverage to Hispanic voters in the Southwest. By the end of 1992, Virginia had elected a black governor and nearly every southern state had elected black Representatives to Congress. Less obvious but just as revolutionary were the thousands of black and Latino candidates who won local offices and the new moderation of white leaders who had to satisfy black voters.

War, Peace, and the Landslide of 1964

Lyndon Johnson was the peace candidate in 1964. Johnson had maintained Kennedy's commitment to South Vietnam. On the advice of Kennedy holdovers like Defense Secretary Robert McNamara, he stepped up commando raids and naval shelling of North Vietnam on the assumption that North Vietnam controlled the Viet Cong. On August 2, North Vietnamese torpedo boats attacked the U.S. destroyer *Maddox* in the Gulf of Tonkin while it was eavesdropping on North Vietnamese military signals. Two days later, the *Maddox* and the *C. Turner Joy* reported another torpedo attack (probably false sonar readings). Johnson ordered a bombing raid in reprisal and asked Congress to authorize "all necessary measures" to protect American forces and stop further aggression. Congress passed the **Gulf of Tonkin Resolution** with only two nay votes, effectively authorizing the president to wage undeclared war.

Johnson's militancy paled beside that of his Republican opponent. Senator Barry Goldwater of Arizona represented the new right wing of the Republican party, which was drawing strength from the South and West. A department store heir, Goldwater wanted minimal government interference in free enterprise. As a former Air Force pilot, he also wanted aggressive confrontation with communism. Campaign literature accurately described him as "a choice, not an echo." He declared that "extremism in the defense of liberty is no vice," raising visions of vigilantes and mobs. Goldwater's campaign made Johnson look moderate. Johnson pledged not "to send American boys nine or ten thousand miles from home to do what Asian boys ought to be doing for themselves" while Goldwater proposed an all-out war.

The election was a landslide. Johnson's 61 percent of the popular vote was the greatest margin ever recorded in a presidential election. Democrats racked up two-to-one majorities in Congress. For the first time in decades, liberal Democrats could enact their domestic program without begging votes from conservative Southerners or Republicans, and Johnson could achieve his goal of a **Great Society** based on freedom and opportunity for all.

The result in 1965 was a series of measures that Johnson rushed through Congress before his political standing began to erode and Vietnam distracted national attention. The **National Endowment for the Humanities**, **National Endowment for the Arts**, and highway beautification were part of the Great Society for the middle class. The Wilderness Act (1964), an early success of the modern environmental movement, preserved 9.1 million acres from all development.

More central to Johnson's vision of the Great Society were efforts to increase opportunity for all Americans, a goal that stirred the president deeply. As he told a July 1965 news conference, "When I was young, poverty was so common that we didn't know it had a name. An education was something that you had to fight for. . . . It is now my opportunity to help every child get an education, to help every Negro and every American citizen have an equal opportunity, to have every family get a decent home, and to help bring healing to the sick and dignity to the old." The Elementary and Secondary Education Act was the first general federal aid program for public schools, allocating $1.3 billion for textbooks and special education. The Higher Education Act funded low-interest student loans and university research facilities. The Medical Care Act created federally funded health insurance for the elderly (**Medicare**) and helped states offer medical care to the poor (**Medicaid**). The Appalachian Regional Development Act funded economic development in the depressed mountain counties of twelve states from Georgia to New York and proved a long-run success.

It is sometimes said that the United States declared war on poverty and lost. In fact, the nation came closer in to winning the war on poverty than the war in Vietnam. New or expanded social insurance and income support programs, such as Medicare, Medicaid, Social Security, and food stamps, cut the

Figure 30-4   Poverty Rate, 1960–1997
With the improvement of federal health insurance, assistance for the elderly, and antipoverty programs, the proportion of Americans living in poverty dropped dramatically in the later 1960s. It began to inch upward again in the 1980s when the priorities of the federal government shifted.
Data Source: Statistical Abstract of the United States.

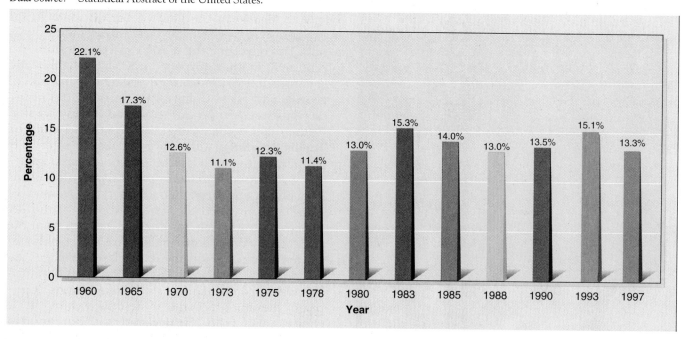

proportion of poor people from 22 percent of the American population in 1960 to 13 percent in 1970 (see Figure 30-4). Infant mortality dropped by a third because of improved nutrition and better access to health care for mothers and children. Taken together, the political results of the 1964 landslide moved the United States far toward Lyndon Johnson's vision of an end to poverty and racial injustice.

Conclusion

The era commonly remembered as "the fifties" stretched from 1953 to 1964. Consistent goals guided American foreign policy through the entire period, including vigilant anticommunism and the confidence to intervene in trouble spots around the globe. At home, the Supreme Court's *Brown* decision introduced a decadelong civil rights revolution. However, many patterns of personal behavior and social relations remained unchanged. Women faced similar expectations from the early fifties to the early sixties. Churches showed more continuity than change.

In retrospect, it is remarkable how widely and deeply the Cold War shaped U.S. society. Fundamental social institutions, such as marriage and religion, got extra credit for their contributions to anticommunism. The nation's long tradition of home-grown radicalism was virtually silent in the face of the Cold War consensus. Even economically meritorious programs like more money for science and better roads went down more easily if linked to national defense.

But the consistency and stability of the fifties were fragile. The larger world was too complex to fit forever within the narrow framework of bipolar conflict. American society was too disparate and dynamic for Cold War conformity. In the later 1960s and the 1970s, contradictions burst through the surface of the American consensus. Foreign competitors, resource scarcities, and environmental damage diminished economic abundance and sapped national confidence. Nations from Vietnam to Iran refused to cooperate with American plans for the world. Corrupt politicians threatened the constitutional order.

Under these pressures, the national consensus splintered after 1964. Some members of minority groups turned their back on integration. Some younger Americans dropped out of mainstream society to join the aptly named counterculture. Others sought the security of religious commitment and community. Perhaps most divisively, "hawks" battled "doves" over Vietnam. If civil rights and Cold War

had been the defining issues for "the fifties," Vietnam would define "the sixties," which stretched from 1965 to 1974.

Review Questions

1. What were the sources of prosperity in the 1950s and 1960s? How did prosperity shape cities, family life, and religion? What opportunities did it create for women and for young people? How did it affect the American role in the world? Why did an affluent nation still need a war on poverty in the 1960s?

2. What assumptions about the Soviet Union shaped U.S. foreign policy? What assumptions about the United States shaped Soviet policy? What did American leaders think was at stake in Vietnam, Berlin, and Cuba?

3. Who initiated and led the African-American struggle for civil rights? What role did the federal government play? What were the goals of the civil rights movement? Where did it succeed, and in what ways did it fall short?

4. How did the growth of nuclear arsenals affect international relations? How did the nuclear shadow affect American politics and society?

5. In what new directions did Lyndon Johnson take the United States? Were there differences in the goals of the New Frontier and the Great Society?

Recommended Reading

Michael Beschloss, *May-Day: Eisenhower, Khrushchev, and the U-2 Affair* (1986). The drama and confusion of the U-2 affair used to interpret the meaning of the Cold War for the United States and the Soviet Union.

William Graebner, *Coming of Age in Buffalo* (1990). In words and pictures, places the complexity of teenage life in the 1950s within the American patterns of class and race.

David Halberstam, *The Fifties* (1993). Provides a readable and detailed account of political and social change.

Michael Harrington, *The Other America* (1962). Published early in the Kennedy years, an impassioned study that reminded Americans of continuing economic inequality and helped launch the War on Poverty.

Gerald Posner, *Case Closed* (1993). As close as we are likely to get to a definitive analysis of John

Kennedy's death; convincingly refutes the most popular conspiracy theories.

Theodore White, *The Making of the President, 1960* (1961). A vivid account of the issues and personalities of the 1960 campaign.

Juan Williams, *Eyes on the Prize: America's Civil Rights Years, 1954–1965* (1988). A graphic and fast-moving account of the civil rights movement, written in conjunction with a PBS television series.

Tom Wolfe, *The Right Stuff* (1979). An irreverent account of the early years of the U.S. space program that captures the atmosphere of the 1950s and early 1960s.

Additional Sources

The Eisenhower Presidency

Stephen E. Ambrose, *Ike's Spies: Eisenhower and the Espionage Establishment* (1981).

H. W. Brands, *Cold Warriors: Eisenhower's Generation and American Foreign Policy* (1988).

Robert Divine, *Eisenhower and the Cold War* (1981).

Fred Greenstein, *The Hidden-Hand Presidency: Eisenhower as Leader* (1982).

Walter Hixson, *Parting the Curtain: Propaganda, Culture and the Cold War* (1997).

Richard Immerman, *The CIA in Guatemala: The Foreign Policy of Intervention* (1982).

Chester Pach, *The Presidency of Dwight David Eisenhower* (1991).

Science, Politics, and Society

Barbara Clowse, *Brainpower for the Cold War: The Sputnik Crisis and the National Defense Education Act* (1981).

Robert Divine, *The Sputnik Challenge* (1993).

Robert Kleidman, *Organizing for Peace: Neutrality, the Test Ban, and the Freeze* (1993).

Walter McDougall, *The Heavens and the Earth: A Political History of the Space Age* (1985).

Jane Smith, *Patenting the Sun* (1990).

M. Costandina Titus, *Bombs in the Backyard: Atomic Testing and American Politics* (1986).

Allan Winkler, *Life under a Cloud: American Anxiety about the Atom* (1993).

The Politics of Growth

Carl Abbott, *The New Urban America: Growth and Politics in Sunbelt Cities* (1986).

Elizabeth Fones-Wolf, *Selling Free Enterprise: The Business Assault in Labor and Liberalism, 1945–1960* (1994).

Kenneth Jackson, *The Crabgrass Frontier* (1985).

Kim McQuaid, *Uneasy Partners: Big Business in American Politics, 1945–1990* (1993).

William L. O'Neill, *American High: The Years of Confidence, 1945–1960* (1986).

Mark Rose, *Interstate: Express Highway Politics* (1990).

Jon Teaford, *The Rough Road to Renaissance: Urban Revitalization in America* (1990).

Family Life and Culture

Glenn Altschuler and David Grossvogel, *Changing Channels: America in TV Guide* (1992).

Wini Breines, *Young, White and Miserable: Growing Up Female in the 1950s* (1992).

Daniel Horowitz, *Vance Packard and American Social Criticism* (1994).

Eugenia Kaledin, *Mothers and More: American Women in the 1950s* (1984).

Elaine Tyler May, *Homeward Bound: American Families in the Cold War Era* (1988).

Leila Rupp and Verta Taylor, *Survival in the Doldrums: The American Women's Rights Movement, 1945 to the 1960s* (1987).

William Whyte, *The Organization Man* (1956).

The Early 1960s

Michael Beschloss, *The Crisis Years: Kennedy and Khrushchev, 1960–1963* (1991).

David Burner, *John F. Kennedy and a New Generation* (1988).

James Giglio, *The Presidency of John F. Kennedy* (1991).

Robert Alan Goldberg, *Barry Goldwater* (1995).

Elizabeth Cobbs Hoffman, *All You Need Is Love: The Peace Corps and the Spirit of the 1960s* (1998).

Doris Kearns, *Lyndon Johnson and the American Dream* (1976).

Edward Moise, *Tonkin Gulf and the Escalation of the Vietnam War* (1996).

James T. Patterson, *America's Struggle against Poverty, 1900–1985* (1986).

Mark Stern, *Calculating Visions: Kennedy, Johnson, and Civil Rights* (1992).

Peter Wyden, *Bay of Pigs: The Untold Story* (1979).

Struggles for Equal Rights

Rudolfo Acuña, *Occupied America: A History of Chicanos* (1988).

Taylor Branch, *Parting the Waters: America in the King Years, 1954–1963* (1988).

Eric Burner, *And Gently He Shall Lead Them: Robert Parris Moses and Civil Rights in Mississippii*(1994).

Claybourne Carson, *In Struggle: SNCC and the Black Awakening of the 1960s* (1981).

William Chafe, *Civilities and Civil Rights: Greensboro, North Carolina, and the Black Struggle* (1980).

John Dittmer, *Local People: A History of the Mississippi Movement* (1994).

John Egerton, *Speak Now against the Day: The Generation before the Civil Rights Movement in the South* (1994).

David Garrow, *Bearing the Cross: Martin Luther King Jr. and the Southern Christian Leadership Conference* (1986).

Roger Goldman and David Gallen, *Thurgood Marshall: Justice for All* (1993).

David Halberstam, *The Children* (1998).

Elizabeth Huckaby, *Crisis at Central High: Little Rock, 1957–1958* (1980).

Richard Kluger, *Simple Justice: The History of* Brown *v.* Board of Education (1976).

Charles Marsh, *God's Long Summer: Stories of Faith and Civil Rights* (1998).

Kay Mills, *This Little Light of Mine: The Life of Fannie Lou Hamer* (1993).

Charles Payne, *I've Got the Light of Freedom: The Organizing Tradition and the Mississippi Freedom Struggle* (1995).

Harvard Sitkoff, *The Struggle for Black Equality; 1954–1992* (1992).

Where to Learn More

❖ **National Air and Space Museum, Washington, D.C.**   Part of the Smithsonian Institution's complex of museums in Washington, the Air and Space Museum is the richest source for artifacts and discussion of the American space program.

❖ **Kansas Cosmosphere, Hutchinson, Kansas.** This is a rich collection of artifacts and equipment from the American space program.

❖ **Sixth Floor Museum, Dallas, Texas.**   Occupying the sixth floor of the former Texas School Book Depository building, exhibits examine the life, death, and legacy of John F. Kennedy.

❖ **Birmingham Civil Rights Institute, Birmingham, Alabama.**   This museum and archive deal with the background of southern racial segregation, civil rights activism, and the 1963 demonstrations in Birmingham.

❖ **Martin Luther King, Jr., National Historic Site, Atlanta, Georgia.**   The birthplace and grave of Reverend King are the nucleus of a park set in the historic black neighborhood of Auburn.

❖ **National Civil Rights Museum, Memphis, Tennessee.**   Located in the Lorraine Motel, where Martin Luther King, Jr., was killed, the museum traces the participants, background, and effects of key events in the civil rights movement.

❖ **National Afro-American Museum and Cultural Center, Wilberforce, Ohio.**   The exhibit, "From Victory to Freedom: Afro-American Life in the Fifties," looks at home, family, music, and religion as well as politics and civil rights.

❖ **New Museum at the John F. Kennedy Library, Boston, Massachusetts.**   Exhibits offer a sympathetic view of Kennedy's life and achievements.

SHAKEN TO THE ROOTS,
1965–1980

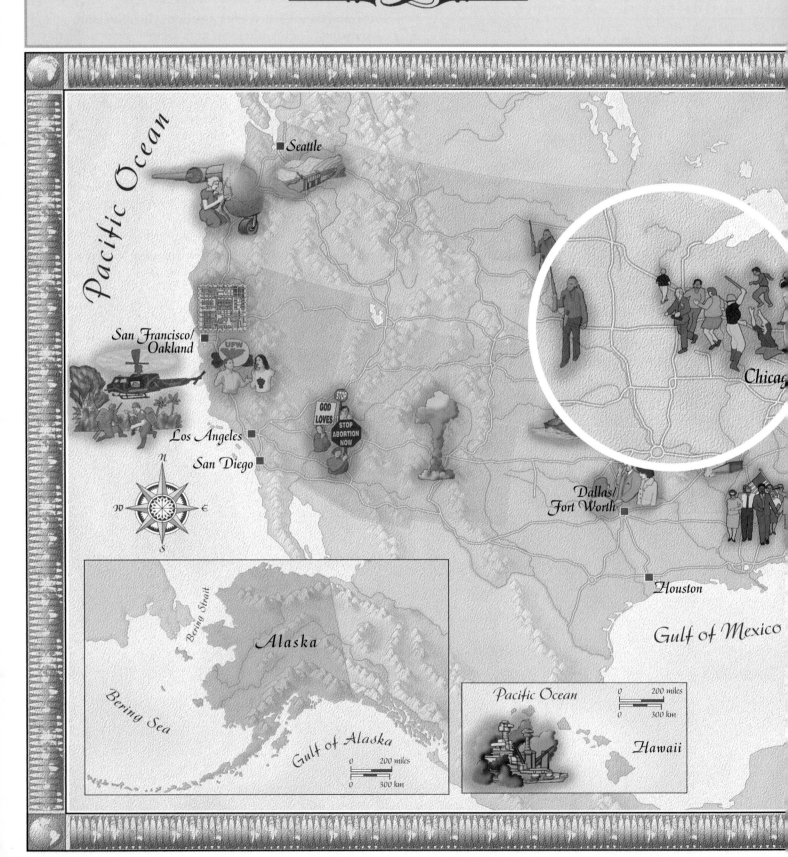

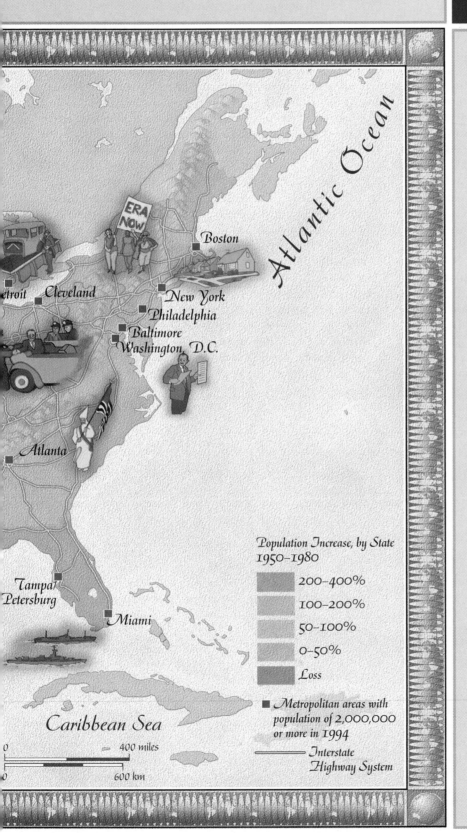

31

Key Topics

❖ Vietnam, civil rights, and the unraveling of the national consensus
❖ The escalating war in Vietnam and the growing opposition it provoked
❖ The unraveling of the New Deal coalition
❖ Nixon and the Watergate scandal
❖ The growing militance of the struggle for civil rights among African Americans, Hispanic Americans, and Native Americans

Map Legend

Population Increase, by State
1950–1980

200–400%
100–200%
50–100%
0–50%
Loss

■ Metropolitan areas with population of 2,000,000 or more in 1994

Interstate Highway System

Atlantic Ocean

Boston
New York
Philadelphia
Baltimore
Washington, D.C.
Cleveland
Detroit
Atlanta
Tampa/St. Petersburg
Miami

Caribbean Sea

400 miles
600 km

ERA NOW

𝒫LEIKU IS A TOWN 240 MILES NORTH OF SAIGON (NOW HO CHI MINH CITY). IN 1965, PLEIKU WAS THE SITE OF A SOUTH VIETNAMESE ARMY HEADQUARTERS AND AMERICAN MILITARY BASE. AT 2 A.M. ON FEBRUARY 7, THE VIET CONG ATTACKED THE U.S. base with mortars and grenades, killing eight Americans, wounding a hundred, and destroying ten planes and helicopters. National security advisor McGeorge Bundy, in Saigon on a fact-finding visit; Ambassador Maxwell Taylor; and military commander General William Westmoreland quickly recommended a retaliatory air strike against North Vietnam. President Johnson concurred, and navy bombers roared off aircraft carriers in Operation FLAMING DART. A month later, Johnson ordered a full-scale air offensive code-named ROLLING THUNDER.

The attack at Pleiku triggered plans that were waiting to be put into effect. The official reason for the bombing was to pressure North Vietnam to negotiate an end to the war. As the South Vietnamese government lost control of the countryside, air strikes on North Vietnam looked like an easy way to shore up South Vietnamese morale. In the back of President Johnson's mind were the need to prove his toughness and the mistaken assumption that China was aggressively backing North Vietnam.

The air strikes pushed the United States over the line from propping up the South Vietnamese government to leading the war effort. A president who desperately wanted a way out of southeast Asia kept adding American forces. Eventually, the war in Vietnam would distract the United States from the goals of the Great Society and drive Johnson from office. It hovered like a shadow over the next two presidents, set back progress toward global stability, and divided the American people.

The war eroded the nation's confidence. Most Americans had agreed about the goals of the Cold War, the benefits of economic growth, and the value of equal opportunity. Stalemate in Vietnam, an oil supply crisis, and political changes in other nations outside the framework of the Cold War challenged U.S. influence in the world. Frustrated with slow progress toward racial equality, many minority Americans advocated separation rather than integration. Political scandals, summarized in three syllables as "Watergate," undercut faith in government. Fifteen years of turmoil forced a grudging recognition of limits to American military power, economic capacity, governmental prerogatives, and even the ideal of a single American dream.

The End of Consensus

Nineteen sixty-five was a confusing year. In Washington, it brought triumphal progress for the goals of the Great Society with such measures as the Voting Rights Act and Medicare. Elsewhere, however, things began to go wrong. The Viet Cong gained strength in the villages of Vietnam. African Americans rioted in Los Angeles. Well-educated and articulate young people left their button-down shirts or high heels in the closet and pursued goals outside the mainstream. The cumulative effect was to unravel the national consensus of the 1950s and early 1960s.

Deeper into Vietnam

Lyndon Johnson faced limited options in Vietnam (see Map 31-1). The pervasive American determination to contain communism and Kennedy's commitments there hemmed Johnson in. Advisers persuaded him that controlled military escalation—a middle course between withdrawal and all-out war—could secure Vietnam. They failed to understand the extent of popular opposition to the official government in Saigon and the willingness of North Vietnam to sacrifice to achieve national unity.

ROLLING THUNDER put the United States on the up escalator to war. Because an air campaign required ground troops to protect bases in South Viet-

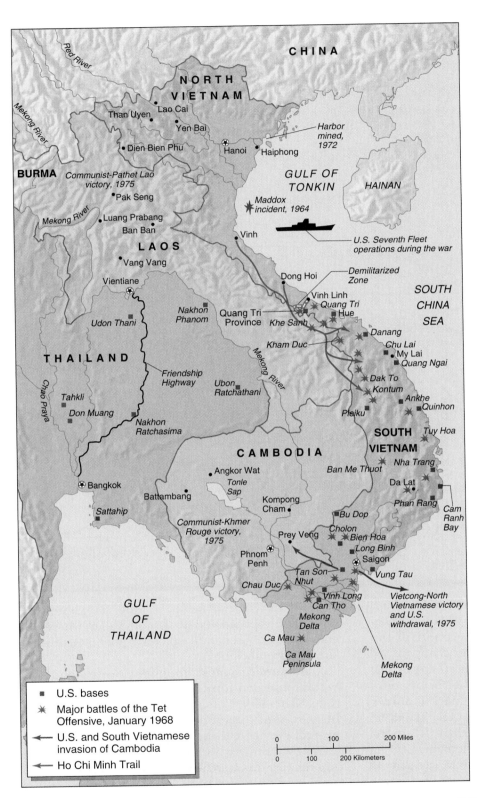

Map 31-1   The War in Vietnam
The United States attacked North Vietnam with air strikes but confined large-scale ground operations to South Vietnam and Cambodia. In South Vietnam, U.S. forces faced both North Vietnamese army units and Viet Cong rebels, all of whom received supplies by way of the so-called "Ho Chi Minh Trail," named for the leader of North Vietnam. The coordinated attacks on cities and towns throughout South Vietnam during the Tet Offensive in 1968 surprised the United States.

nam, Marines landed on March 8. Over the next four months, General Westmoreland wore away Johnson's desire to contain American involvement. More bombs, a pause, an offer of massive U.S. aid—nothing brought North Vietnam to the negotiating table. Meanwhile, defeat loomed. Johnson dribbled in new forces and expanded their mission from base security to combat. On July 28, he finally gave Westmoreland doubled draft calls and an increase in U.S. combat troops from 75,000 to 275,000 by 1966 (see Figure 31-1).

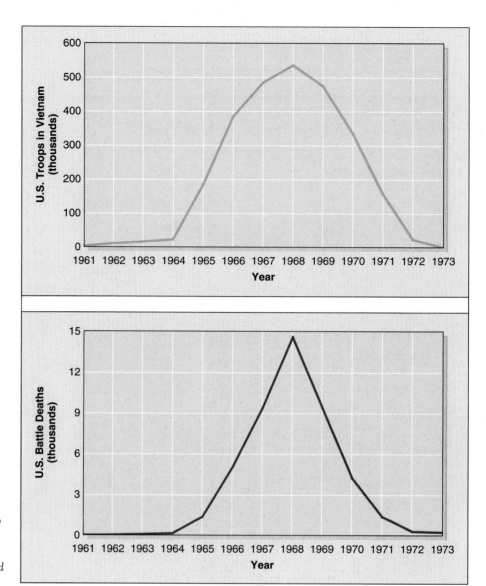

Figure 31-1 The United States in Vietnam

American involvement in Vietnam grew slowly in the Kennedy administration from 1961 to 1963, expanded rapidly under Lyndon Johnson from 1964 to 1968, and fell just as rapidly under Richard Nixon from 1969 to 1973. The "Nixon Doctrine" tried to substitute American weapons and equipment for American military personnel but failed to prevent North Vietnamese victory in 1975 after United States withdrawal.

Data Source: Statistical Abstract of the United States.

Johnson's decision turned a South Vietnamese war into an American war. Secretary of Defense McNamara was clear about the change: "We have relied on South Vietnam to carry the brunt. Now we would be responsible for a satisfactory military outcome." At the end of 1967, American forces in South Vietnam totaled 485,000; they reached their maximum of 543,000 in August 1969. In all, more than 2 million Americans served in Vietnam.

The U.S. strategy on the ground was **search and destroy**. As conceived by Westmoreland, it used sophisticated surveillance and heavily armed patrols to locate enemy detachments, which could then be destroyed by air strikes, artillery, and reinforcements carried in by helicopter. The approach made sense when the opposition consisted of North Vietnamese troops and large Viet Cong units. It worked well in

the sparsely populated Ia Drang Valley where the First Air Cavalry chewed up North Vietnamese regulars in November 1965.

However, most opponents were not North Vietnamese divisions but South Vietnamese guerrillas. The Viet Cong avoided "set-piece" battles. Instead, they forced the United States to make repeated sweeps through farms and villages. The enemy were difficult for Americans to recognize among farmers and workers, making South Vietnamese society itself the target. The American penchant for massive firepower killed thousands of Vietnamese and made millions refugees. Because the South Vietnamese government was unable to secure areas after American sweeps, the Viet Cong often reappeared after the Americans had crashed through a district.

CHRONOLOGY

1962 Rachel Carson publishes *Silent Spring.*

Port Huron Statement launches Students for a Democratic Society.

1965 Congress approves Wilderness Act.

Malcolm X is assassinated.

Residents of Watts neighborhood in Los Angeles riot.

1967 African Americans riot in Detroit and Newark.

1968 Viet Cong launches Tet Offensive.

James Earl Ray kills Martin Luther King, Jr.

Lyndon Johnson declines to run for reelection.

SDS disrupts Columbia University.

Sirhan Sirhan kills Robert Kennedy.

Peace talks start between the United States and North Vietnam.

Police riot against antiwar protesters during the Democratic National Convention in Chicago.

Richard Nixon is elected president.

1969 Neil Armstrong walks on the moon.

1970 United States invades Cambodia.

Earth Day is celebrated.

National Guard units kill students at Kent State and Jackson State Universities.

Environmental Protection Agency is created.

1971 *New York Times* publishes the secret "Pentagon Papers."

President Nixon freezes wages and prices.

"Plumbers" unit is established in the White House.

1972 Nixon visits China.

United States and Soviet Union adopt SALT I.

Operatives for Nixon's reelection campaign break into Democratic headquarters in the Watergate complex in Washington, D.C.

1973 Paris accords end direct U.S. involvement in South Vietnamese war.

United States moves to all-volunteer armed forces.

Watergate burglars are convicted.

Senate Watergate hearings reveal the existence of taped White House conversations.

Spiro Agnew resigns as vice president, is replaced by Gerald Ford.

Arab states impose an oil embargo after the third Arab-Israeli War.

1974 Nixon resigns as president, is succeeded by Gerald Ford.

1975 Communists triumph in South Vietnam.

United States, USSR, and European nations sign the Helsinki Accords.

1976 Jimmy Carter defeats Gerald Ford for the presidency.

1978 Carter brings the leaders of Egypt and Israel to Camp David for peace talks.

1979 SALT II agreement is signed but not ratified.

OPEC raises oil prices.

Three Mile Island nuclear plant comes close to disaster.

Iranian militants take U.S. embassy hostages.

1980 Iranian hostage rescue fails.

Soviet troops enter Afghanistan.

Ronald Reagan defeats Jimmy Carter for the presidency.

The American air war also had limited results. Pilots dropped tons of bombs on the "Ho Chi Minh Trail," a network of supply routes from North Vietnam to South Vietnam through the mountains of neighboring Laos. Despite the bombing, thousands of workers converted rough paths into roads that were repaired as soon as they were damaged. Air assault on North Vietnam itself remained "diplomatic," intended to force North Vietnam to stop intervening in the South Vietnamese civil war. Because Ho Chi Minh considered North and South to be one country, the American goal was unacceptable. Attacking North Vietnam's poorly developed economy, the United

States soon ran out of targets. The CIA estimated that it cost nearly $10 to inflict every $1 of damage.

At home, protest against the war mounted (see "American Views: An Antiwar Protester Describes the Generation Gap"). A March 24, 1965, "teach-in" at the University of Michigan—a night-long sequence of speeches and seminars—signaled the disaffection. In the 1950s, dissenters on the left had been too intimidated by McCarthyism to protest overcommitment to the Cold War. Now a coalition of experienced antiwar workers and new college activists openly challenged the Cold Warriors. The first national antiwar march took place in Washington on

Antiwar protests were simultaneously symbolic and disruptive. Some activists dumped jars of animal blood over draft board records. Others tried to block munitions trains. In October 1967, 100,000 people marched on the Pentagon and surrounded it with the light of burning draft cards. Some in front stuck flowers in the rifle barrels of the soldiers ringing the building; others kicked and spat. The troops and police cleared the grounds with tear gas and clubs.

April 17. Twenty-five thousand people picketed the White House, assembled at the Washington Monument for speeches by Senator Ernest Gruening of Alaska (one of the two dissenting votes on the Gulf of Tonkin Resolution) and African-American leaders, and walked up the Mall to the Capitol.

Over the next two years, antiwar activity changed to direct confrontations. Much of the anger was directed at the military draft administered by the **Selective Service System**. In theory, the Selective Service picked the young men who could best serve the nation as soldiers and deferred induction of those with vital skills. In fact, deferral criteria helped make Vietnam a working-class war. Full-time college enrollment was good for a deferment; so was graduate school until 1967. Draftees and enlistees tended to be small-town and working-class youth who had few opportunities outside the military. They were also young. The average GI in World War II had been in his midtwenties; the typical soldier in Vietnam was 19 or 20. Women who served as military nurses tended to come from the same backgrounds, where patriotism was unquestioned.

The black community supplied more than its share of combat soldiers. In 1965, when African Americans made up 11 percent of the nation's population, 24 percent of the soldiers who died in Vietnam were black. This disparity forced the Defense Department to revise its combat assignments. Martin Luther King, Jr., joined the protest in 1967. King called the war a moral disaster whose costs weighed most heavily on the poor and a new form of colonialism that was destroying Vietnamese society.

New Left and Community Activism

The antiwar movement was part of a growing grassroots activism that took much of its tone from the university-based **Students for a Democratic Society (SDS)**. The group was important for its ideas, not its size. Its **Port Huron Statement**, largely written by Tom Hayden and adopted in 1962, called for grassroots action and "participatory democracy." Building on ideas of 1950s dissenters such as C. Wright Mills, SDS tried to harness youthful disillusionment about consumerism, racism, and imperialism. It wanted to counter the trends that seemed to be turning Americans into tiny cogs in the machinery of big government, corporations, and universities. An example was its Economic Research and Action Project in which students moved to poor neighborhoods in cities such as Newark and tried to help residents protest inequitable living conditions. SDS thought of itself as a "New Left" that was free from doctrinal squabbles that hampered the old left of the 1930s and 1940s.

Many of the original SDS leaders were also participants in the civil rights movement. The same was true of Mario Savio, founder of the **Free Speech Movement (FSM)** at the University of California at Berkeley. Savio hoped to build a multi-issue "community of protest" around the idea of "a free university in a free society." FSM protests climaxed with a December sit-in that led to 773 arrests and stirred protest on other campuses.

What SDS wanted to do with its grassroots organizing resembled the federal community action programs associated with the war on poverty. The

Model Cities Program (1966) invited residents of poor neighborhoods to write their own plans for improving local housing, education, health services, and job opportunities. Model Cities assemblies challenged the racial bias in programs like urban renewal and helped train community leaders.

In the 1970s and 1980s, when SDS was long gone and Model Cities was fading, the lessons of grassroots reform would still be visible in alternative organizations and political movements that strengthened democracy from the bottom up. Activists staffed food cooperatives, free clinics, women's health groups, and drug counseling centers across the country. Community-based organization was a key element in self-help efforts by African Americans, Asian Americans, and Latinos. Neighborhood associations and community development corporations that provided affordable housing and jobs extended the "backyard revolution" into the 1980s and beyond. Social conservatives, such as antiabortionists, used the same techniques on behalf of their own agendas.

Youth Culture and Counterculture

The popular context for the serious work of the New Left was the growing youth culture and **counterculture**. Millions of young people in the second half of the 1960s expressed their alienation from American society by sampling drugs or chasing the rainbow of a youth culture. Some just smoked marijuana, grew long hair, and listened to psychedelic rock. Others plunged into ways of life that scorned their middle-class backgrounds. The middle-aged and middle-class ignored the differences and dubbed the rebellious young **hippies**.

The youth culture took advantage of the affluence of the 1950s. It was consumerism in a tie-dyed T-shirt. A high point was the 1969 Woodstock rock festival in New York State, a weekend of "sex, drugs, and rock-and-roll" for 400,000 young people. But Woodstock was an excursion, not a life-altering commitment. Members of the **Woodstock Generation** were consumers in a distinct market niche, dressing but not living like social reformers or revolutionaries. The musical *Hair* (1968) and the film *Easy Rider* (1969) harnessed their social ferment for the box office as mass culture absorbed the youth culture.

Within the youth culture was a smaller and more intense counterculture that added Eastern religion, social radicalism, and evangelistic belief in the drug LSD. Harvard professor Timothy Leary and writer Aldous Huxley claimed that hallucinogenic or psychedelic drugs, such as mescaline and LSD, would swing open the "doors of perception." Rock lyrics began to reflect the drug culture in 1966 and 1967, and young people talked about Leary's advice to "tune in, turn on, and drop out."

The mecca of the dropouts was San Francisco's Haight-Ashbury district. In the early 1960s, its cheap apartments had housed African Americans, beatniks, and homosexuals. Its radical atmosphere attracted a sudden influx of students and college dropouts in 1966. In 1967's "Summer of Love," the Haight was home to perhaps seven thousand permanent hippies and seventy thousand short-time visitors.

Writer Ken Kesey and the self-defined Merry Pranksters toured the country in a brightly painted bus, parked here in San Francisco's Golden Gate Park. They sometimes threw open parties where they served punch laced with psychedelic drugs in the hope of inciting radical social change.

American Views
AN ANTIWAR PROTESTER
DESCRIBES THE GENERATION GAP

Robert S. McNamara was one of the architects of the war in Vietnam as secretary of defense for John Kennedy and Lyndon Johnson from 1961 to 1968. Like thousands of other parents, including many Washington officials, McNamara found opposition to the war within his own family. Here his son, Craig McNamara, describes his actions as an antiwar demonstrator and his decision to drop out of mainstream society (he eventually became a farmer in northern California). In 1995, Robert McNamara revealed that he had serious but silent doubts about the wisdom of the war long before he left the Defense Department.

❖ **What do Craig McNamara's recollections tell us about the "generation gap" of the 1960s?**

❖ **What do they suggest about the connection between political dissent and decisions to drop out of mainstream culture?**

You know, things were so split in the Sixties. You were either for the war or against it, and I was definitely against it. My father knew where I stood, but we didn't discuss it. . . . It just wasn't possible during those years for us to talk about the issues of the war. . . .

Not long after I got to Stanford, I began taking part in antiwar demonstrations. . . . I participated in a major event at the San Francisco airport. A group of students had got together to read a list of the California men who had been killed in Vietnam. We just stood in one of the main terminal

---

"If you're going to San Francisco," said one song, "be sure to wear some flowers in your hair." Drugs and violence soon took over the streets, psychedelic businesses closed, and a respectable middle class bought the cheap real estate. Meanwhile, hippie districts sprang up around university campuses across the country.

The cultural rebels of the late 1950s and early 1960s had been trying to combine personal freedom with new social arrangements. Many hippies were more interested in altering their minds with drugs than with politics or poetry. Serious exploration of societal alternatives was left for a minority who devoted themselves to the political work of the New Left, communal living, women's liberation, gay liberation, and other movements.

Racial Rioting

In contrast to the youth culture, African Americans and Hispanics who rioted in city streets weren't dabbling; they were in deadly earnest. Prominent black writers, such as James Baldwin in *The Fire Next Time*

(1963), had warned of mounting anger. Suddenly the fires were real. Riots in Rochester, Harlem, and Brooklyn in July 1964 opened four years of racial violence. Before they subsided, the riots scarred most big cities and killed two hundred people, most of them African Americans.

The explosion of the Watts neighborhood in Los Angeles fixed the danger of racial unrest in the public mind. Trouble started on August 11, 1965, when a white highway patrol officer arrested a young African American for drunken driving. Loud complaints drew a crowd, and the arrival of Los Angeles police turned the bystanders into an angry mob that attacked passing cars. Rioting, looting, and arson spread through Watts for two days until the National Guard cordoned off the trouble spots and occupied the neighborhood on August 14 and 15.

The outburst frightened white Americans. In most previous race riots, white people had used violence to keep black people "in their place." In Watts, black people were the instigators. The primary tar-

buildings on a marble floor, with thirty-foot ceilings above and all the traffic of people going back and forth. It became very clear to us immediately that we were antagonizing a lot of people. . . . It was amazing to realize how threatening one person reading a list of the war dead in Vietnam could be to other people. And it was a tremendous list. . . . Each of us would read for two or three hours at a time, and then the next person would take over.

I remember a variety of men coming up to me at various times during those hours, men in their mid-fifties saying, "You son of a bitch!" or "We're going to kick your knees in!" or "You haven't been there. What do you know?" I just remember taking a deep breath and keeping on reading and feeling sad, tremendously sad. . . . I think that is the feeling that we probably all share now about Vietnam: what sadness, what tremendous sadness.

[After being physically disqualified from military service], I left for South America. Two friends and I went on motorcycles down to Texas with our shoulder-length hair and ponytails and leather pants. Nobody stopped us. We just kept going until we got into Mexico, and started the long journey to the south. When we got to Bogotá [Colombia], my two friends decided they'd gone far enough. They were going to stay, and I was on my own. I decided to send my motorcycle home. To me it represented imperialism. I set out myself, into the unknown, and traveled for the next few months on trucks, buses, trains, hitchhiking. . . .

While I was in Santiago [Chile], my father came down to a big United Nations conference on trade. He was head of the World Bank at that time. I was staying probably a mile away from where he was, but we didn't see each other. I think it was probably a decision on both our parts, that we were in different worlds and those worlds couldn't seem to come together.

Source: Joan Morrison and Robert K. Morrison, From Camelot to Kent State: The Sixties Experience in the Words of Those Who Lived It. *Copyright © 1987 by Joan Morrison and Robert K. Morrison. Reprinted by permission of Times Books, a Division of Random House, Inc.*

gets were the police and ghetto businesses that had reputations for exploiting their customers. The National Advisory Commission on Civil Disorders concluded in 1968 that most property damage was the "result of deliberate attacks on white-owned businesses characterized in the Negro community as unfair or disrespectful." In short, the riots were protests about the problems of ghetto life.

After Watts, Americans expected "long hot summers" and got them. Scores of cities suffered riots in 1966, including a riot by Puerto Ricans in Chicago that protested the same problems black people faced. The following year, the worst violence was in Newark, New Jersey, and in Detroit, where forty-three deaths and blocks of blazing buildings stunned television viewers.

Rioting in the midsixties followed a consistent scenario. A routine police action would spark rumors or draw a crowd. It might be a raid on an illegal bar, intervention in a fight, or the shooting of a crime suspect. Angry onlookers would turn into rioters when they saw that the police could not disperse crowds, enforce curfews, or even protect themselves. After the police withdrew, looting might turn into a serious assault on property. Disorder would continue until the National Guard or the army scared the crowds off the streets. Many deaths came in the last days when heavily armed and fearful soldiers fired on nonexistent snipers and killed bystanders.

Few politicians wanted to admit that African Americans and Hispanics had serious grievances. Their impulse was to blame riffraff and outside agitators—"lawbreakers and mad dogs," to quote California Governor Ronald Reagan. This theory was wrong. Almost all participants were neighborhood residents. Except that they were younger, they were representative of the African-American population, and their violence came from the frustration of rising expectations. Despite the political gains of the civil rights movement, unemployment remained high, and the police still treated all African Americans as potential criminals. The urban riots were political actions to force the problems of African-Americans onto the national agenda. "What are these people rioting about?" asked one resident. "They want recognition, and the only way they're going to get it is to riot."

Minority Separatism

Minority separatism tapped the same anger that fueled the urban riots. Separatists challenged the central goal of the civil rights movement, which sought full participation in American life. The phrase "**Black Power**" summed up the new alternative. The term came from frustrated SNCC leader Stokely Carmichael in 1966: "We've been saying freedom for six years—and we ain't got nothing. What we're going to start saying now is 'Black Power'!"

Black power translated many ways—control of one's own community through the voting machine, celebration of African-American heritage, creation of a parallel society that shunned white institutions. At the personal level, it was a synonym for black pride. It propelled the successful political campaigns of Richard Hatcher in Gary, Indiana, and Carl Stokes in Cleveland, the first African Americans elected mayors of large northern cities.

Black Power also meant increased interest in the **Nation of Islam**, or Black Muslims. Organized in 1931 by Elijah Muhammad, the Black Muslims combined a version of Islam with radical separatism. They called for self-discipline, support of black institutions and businesses, and total rejection of white America. The Nation of Islam appealed to black people who saw no future in integration. It was strongest in northern cities, such as Chicago, where it offered an alternative to the life of the ghetto streets.

In the early 1960s, Malcolm X emerged as a leading Black Muslim. Growing up as Malcolm Little, he was a streetwise criminal until he converted to the Nation of Islam in prison. After his release, Malcolm preached that black people should stop letting white people set the terms by which they judged their appearance, communities, and accomplishments. He emphasized the African cultural heritage and economic self-help and proclaimed himself an extremist for black rights. In the last year of his life, however, he returned from a pilgrimage to Mecca willing to temper his rejection of white society. Rivals within the movement assassinated him in February 1965, but his ideas lived on in *The Autobiography of Malcolm X*.

The **Black Panthers** pursued similar goals. Bobby Seale and Huey Newton grew up in the Oakland, California, area and met as college students. They saw African-American ghettos as internal colonies in need of self-determination. They created the Panthers in 1966, began to carry firearms, and recruited Eldridge Cleaver as chief publicist.

The Panthers asserted their equality. They shadowed police patrols to prevent mistreatment of African Americans and carried weapons into the California State Legislature in May 1967 to protest gun control. As Seale recalled, the goal was "to read a message to the world" and use the press to "blast it across the country." The Panthers also promoted community-based self-help efforts, such as a free breakfast program and medical clinics, and ran political candidates. In contrast to the rioters in Watts, the Panthers had a political program, if not the ability to carry it through. The movement was shaken when Newton was convicted of manslaughter for killing a police officer, Cleaver fled to Algeria, and an unjustified police raid killed Chicago Panther leader Fred Hampton. Panther chapters imploded when they attracted thugs and shakedown artists as well as visionaries. Nevertheless, the Panthers survived as a political party into the 1970s. Former Panther Bobby Rush entered Congress in 1992.

Latinos in the Southwest developed a similar "brown power" movement in the late 1960s. Led by Reies López Tijerina, Hispanics in rural New Mexico demanded the return of lands that had been lost to Anglo Americans despite the guarantees of the Treaty of Guadalupe Hidalgo in 1848. Tijerina's "Letter from the Santa Fe Jail" denounced the "rich people from outside the state with their summer homes and ranches" and "all those who have robbed the people of their land and culture for 120 years." Mexican Americans in the 1970s organized for political power in southern Texas communities where they were a majority. In Denver, Rodolfo Gonzales established the Crusade for Justice. His "Plan for the *Barrio*" emphasized Hispanic cultural traditions, community control of schools, and economic development. Best known among the Latino activists was César Chávez, who organized the multiracial United Farm Workers in California (see Chapter 32).

Latino political activism had strong appeal for young people. Ten thousand young Chicanos stormed out of Los Angeles high schools in March 1968 to protest poor education and racist teachers. Some students organized as Brown Berets to demand more relevant education and fairer police treatment. Many rejected assimilation in favor of community self-determination and began to talk about *la Raza* ("the people"), whose language and heritage descended from centuries of Mexican history. *Chicano* itself was a slang term with insulting overtones that was now adopted as a badge of pride and cultural identity.

The Black Panthers hoped to gain political power and to provide social services in black ghettos. Police repression and arrests of Panther leaders diverted much of their energy to raising money to pay legal costs.

Native Americans fought both for equal access to American society and to preserve cultural traditions through tribal institutions. Congress in 1968 restored the authority of tribal laws on reservations. A few years later, it granted native Alaskans 40 million acres to settle claims for their ancestral lands. Legally sophisticated tribes sued for compensation and enforcement of treaty provisions, such as fishing rights in the Pacific Northwest. Larger tribes established their own colleges, such as Navajo Community College (1969) and Oglala Lakota College (1971). Navajo Community College, said its catalog, "exists to fulfill many needs of the Navajo people. . . . It provides a place where Navajo history and culture can be studied and learned; it provides training in the skills necessary for many jobs on the reservation which today are held by non-Navajos."

A second development was new media-oriented protest. Chippewas in Minneapolis created the **American Indian Movement (AIM)** in 1968 to increase economic opportunity and stop police mistreatment. AIM dramatized the needs of Native Americans by seizing the abandoned Alcatraz Island as a cultural and educational center (1969–1971) and leading the cross-country Broken Treaties Caravan, which occupied the Bureau of Indian Affairs in Washington (1972).

In the early 1970s, AIM allied with Sioux traditionalists on the Pine Ridge Reservation in South Dakota against the tribe's elected government. In 1973, they took over the village of Wounded Knee, where the U.S. Army in 1890 had massacred three hundred Indians. They held out for seventy days before leaving peacefully. Although AIM itself soon collapsed, Native Americans continued to assert their distinctiveness within American society.

The slogans of Black Power, Brown Power, and Red Power spanned goals that ran from civil rights to cultural pride to revolutionary separatism. They were all efforts by minorities to define themselves through their own heritage and backgrounds, not simply by looking in the mirror of white society. They thus questioned the American assumption that everyone wanted to be part of the same homogeneous society.

The American Indian Movement (AIM) drew its strength from young Indians in the cities. In 1972 AIM led a march of Indians along the "Trail of Broken Treaties" to Washington, D.C., where members occupied the offices of the Bureau of Indian Affairs. The occupation ended after a week but succeeded in publicizing Native American grievances.

The Year
of the Gun, 1968

Some years are turning points that force society to reconsider its basic assumptions. In 1914, the violence of World War I undermined Europe's belief in progress. In 1933, Americans had to rethink the role of government. In 1968, mainstream Americans turned against the war in Vietnam, student protest and youth counterculture turned ugly, and political consensus shattered.

The Tet Offensive

The longer the Vietnam War continued and the less interest that China or the Soviet Union showed in it, the less valid the conflict seemed to the American people. It looked more and more like a war for pride, not national security.

The Viet Cong's Tet Offensive on January 30, 1968, undermined that pride. At the end of 1967, U.S. officials were over-confidently predicting victory. They also fell for a North Vietnamese feint by committing U.S. forces to the defense of Khe Sanh, a strongpoint near the North–South border. The defense was a tactical success for the United States but thinned its forces elsewhere in South Vietnam. Then, at the beginning of Tet, the Vietnamese New Year, the Viet Cong attacked thirty-six of forty-four provincial capitals, the historic city of Hue, and the capital, Saigon. They hit the U.S. embassy and reached the runways of Tan Son Nhut air base. If the United States was winning, the Tet offensive should not have been possible.

As a military effort, the attacks failed. U.S. and South Vietnamese troops repulsed the attacks and cleared the cities. But the offensive was a psychological blow that convinced the American public that the war was quicksand.

Television coverage of the Tet battles made the bad publicity worse. During World War II, officials had censored pictures from the front. Images from Vietnam went direct to the evening news; it was a "living room war." At least until Tet, the commentary from network news anchors had supported the American effort, but the pictures undermined civilian morale. Viewers could hear cigarette lighters clicking open to set villages in flames. A handful of images stayed in people's memories—a Buddhist monk burning himself to death in protest; a child with flesh peeled off by napalm; a South Vietnamese official executing a captive on the streets of Saigon.

In the wake of the Tet crisis, General Westmoreland's request for 200,000 more troops forced a political and military reevaluation. Clark Clifford, a dedicated Cold Warrior, was the new secretary of defense. Now he had second thoughts. Twenty "wise men"—the big names of the Cold War—told the president that the war was unwinnable on terms acceptable to America's allies and to many Americans. By devouring resources and souring relations with other nations, it endangered rather than enhanced American security. Most scholars have agreed with this assessment. The best option, the wise men told LBJ, was disengagement. "He could hardly believe his ears," Clifford remembered.

LBJ's Exit

The president was already in political trouble. After other prominent Democrats held back, Minnesota's liberal Senator Eugene McCarthy had decided to challenge Johnson in the presidential primaries. Because he controlled the party organizations in two-

GIs evacuate a wounded comrade from fighting near the border between Vietnam and Cambodia.

thirds of the states, Johnson didn't need the primary states for renomination and ignored the first primary in New Hampshire. Enthusiastic college students staffed McCarthy's campaign. McCarthy won a startling 42 percent of the popular vote and twenty of twenty-four delegates in the March 16 election. The vote was a protest against Johnson's Vietnam policy rather than a clear mandate for peace. As an unknown, McCarthy attracted voters who wanted the United States out of Vietnam and those who wanted all-out victory. Nevertheless, the vote proved that the political middle ground would no longer hold.

By showing Johnson's vulnerability, New Hampshire also drew Robert Kennedy into the race. Younger brother of the former president, Kennedy inspired both fervent loyalty and strong distaste. In the 1950s, he had worked for Senator Joe McCarthy and had been a reluctant supporter of civil rights during his brother's administration. He was arrogant and abrasive but also bright and flexible. More than other mainstream politicians of the 1960s, he touched the hearts of Hispanic and African-American voters as well as the white working class. He had left his position as attorney general to win election to the Senate from New York in 1964. Now he put the Kennedy mystique on the line against a man whom he despised.

Facing political challenges and an unraveling war, on March 31, 1968, Johnson announced a halt to most bombing of North Vietnam, opening the door for negotiations. He then astounded the country by withdrawing from the presidential race. It was a statesmanlike act by a man who had been consumed by a war he didn't want, had never understood, and couldn't end. As he told an aide, the war made him feel like a hitchhiker in a hailstorm: "I can't run, I can't hide, and I can't make it stop." Hoping to save his domestic program, he served out his term with few friends and little credit for his accomplishments.

Red Spring

In the months that followed the Tet crisis, much of the industrial world was in ferment. Grassroots rebellion shook the Soviet grip on eastern Europe. University students in Poland protested the stifling of political discussion. Alexander Dubček, the new leader of the Czech Communist party, brought together students and the middle class around reforms that caused people to talk about "Prague Spring"—a blossoming of democracy inside the iron curtain. In August, the Soviets sent in their tanks to crush the reforms and bring Czechoslovakia back into line.

Western Europe was also in turmoil. Students rioted in Italy and Berlin. Workers and students protested against the Franco regime in Spain. In Paris, student demonstrations against the Vietnam War turned into attacks on the university system and the French government. One slogan proclaimed: "Professors, you are past it, and so is your culture." Students fought police in the Paris streets in the first days of May. Radical industrial workers called a general strike. The government nearly toppled.

Students at Columbia University in New York echoed Europe with their own rebellion. Columbia's African-American students and its SDS chapter had several grievances. One was the university's cooperation with the Pentagon-funded Institute for Defense Analysis. Another was its plan to build a gymnasium on park land that might better serve the residents of Harlem. Some students wanted changes in university policy, others a confrontation that would recruit new radicals. They occupied five university buildings, including the library and the president's office, for a week in April until police evicted them. A student strike and additional violence lasted until June. The "battle of Morningside Heights" (the location of Columbia) was tame when compared to the events in Warsaw or Paris, but it gave Americans a glimpse of the gap that divided radicalized students from national institutions.

Violence and Politics

Red Spring in France, Prague Spring in Czechoslovakia, and turmoil in New York were background for the violent disruption of American politics through assassination and riot. On April 4, 1968, ex-convict James Earl Ray shot and killed Martin Luther King, Jr., as he stood on the balcony of a Memphis motel. King's death was the product of pure racial hatred, and it triggered a climactic round of violence in black ghettos. Fires devastated the West Side of Chicago and downtown Washington, D.C. The army guarded the steps of the Capitol, ready to protect Congress from its fellow citizens.

The shock of King's death was still fresh when another political assassination stunned the nation. On June 5, Robert Kennedy won California's primary election. He was still behind Vice President Hubert Humphrey in the delegate count but coming on strong. As Kennedy walked out of the ballroom at his headquarters in the Ambassador Hotel in Los Angeles, a Jordanian immigrant named Sirhan Sirhan put a bullet in his brain. Sirhan may have wanted revenge for America's tilt toward Israel in that country's victorious Six-Day War with Egypt and Jordan in 1967.

Kennedy's death ensured the Democratic nomination for Humphrey, a liberal who had loyally supported Johnson's war policy. After his nomination, Humphrey faced Republican Richard Nixon and Independent George Wallace. Nixon positioned himself as the candidate of the political middle. Wallace appealed to white Southerners and working-class Northerners who feared black militancy and hated "the ivory-tower folks with pointed heads."

Both got great help from the Democratic Convention, held in Chicago on August 26–29. While Democrats feuded among themselves, Chicago Mayor Richard Daley and his police department monitored antiwar protesters. The National Mobilization Committee to End the War in Vietnam drew on the New Left and on older peace activists—sober and committed people who had fought against nuclear weapons in the 1950s and the Vietnam War throughout the 1960s. They wanted to embarrass the Johnson-Humphrey administration by marching to the convention hall on nomination night. Mixed in were the **Yippies**. The term supposedly stood for Youth International Party, but the idea of "hippies making yippie!" came first and the word later. The Yippies planned to attract young people to Chicago with a promise of street theater, media events, and confrontation that would puncture the pretensions of the power structure. To the extent they had a program, it was to use youth culture to attract converts to radical politics.

The volatile mix was ready for a spark. On August 28, the same night that Democratic delegates were nominating Humphrey, tensions exploded in a police riot. Protesters and Yippies had congregated in Grant Park, across Michigan Avenue from downtown hotels. Undisciplined police waded into the crowds with clubs and tear gas. Young people fought back with rocks and bottles. Television caught the hours of violence that ended when the National Guard separated police from demonstrators. On the convention floor, Senator Abraham Ribicoff of Connecticut decried "Gestapo tactics" on the streets of Chicago. Mayor Daley shouted back obscenities. For Humphrey, the convention was a catastrophe, alienating liberal Democrats and associating Democrats with disorder in the public mind.

The election was closer than Humphrey had any right to hope (see Map 31-2). Many Americans who liked Wallace's message were unwilling to vote for a radical third party. Nixon appealed to the white middle class and claimed he had a secret plan to end the war. Humphrey picked up strength in October after he separated himself from Johnson's war policy. Election day gave Wallace 13.5 percent of the popular vote, Humphrey 42.7 percent of the popular vote and 191 electoral votes, and Nixon 43.4 percent of the popular vote and 301 electoral votes.

The Wallace candidacy was a glimpse of the future. The national media saw Wallace in terms of bigotry and backlash against civil rights, getting only part of the story. Many of Wallace's northern backers were unhappy with both parties. Liberal on economic issues but conservative on family and social issues, many of these working-class voters evolved into "Reagan Democrats" by the 1980s. In the South, Wallace was a way station for conservative voters who would eventually transfer their allegiance from the Democratic to the Republican party.

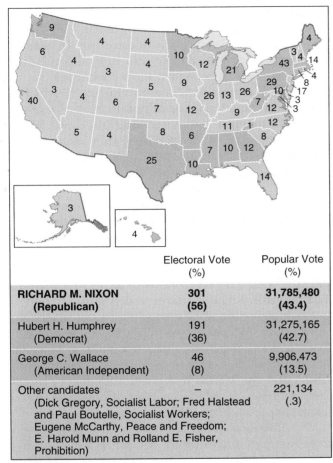

	Electoral Vote (%)	Popular Vote (%)
RICHARD M. NIXON **(Republican)**	**301** **(56)**	**31,785,480** **(43.4)**
Hubert H. Humphrey (Democrat)	191 (36)	31,275,165 (42.7)
George C. Wallace (American Independent)	46 (8)	9,906,473 (13.5)
Other candidates (Dick Gregory, Socialist Labor; Fred Halstead and Paul Boutelle, Socialist Workers; Eugene McCarthy, Peace and Freedom; E. Harold Munn and Rolland E. Fisher, Prohibition)	–	221,134 (.3)

Map 31-2   The Election of 1968
Richard Nixon won the presidency with the help of American Independent party candidate George Wallace. Wallace won several southern states, offering an alternative to white Southerners unhappy with the Democratic party but not yet prepared to vote Republican. He also drew northern working class votes away from Hubert Humphrey and helped Nixon take several midwestern states.

Nixon and Watergate

The new president was an unlikely politician, ill-at-ease in public and consumed by a sense of inferiority. A product of small-town California, he felt rejected by the eastern elite. After losing a 1962 race for governor of California, he announced that he was quitting politics and that the press would no longer have Dick Nixon "to kick around." In 1968, he skillfully sold a "new Nixon" to the media. Seven years later, the press was his undoing as it uncovered the Watergate scandal.

Nixon's painful public presence and dishonesty have tended to obscure his administration's accomplishments. He reduced tensions in the Cold War. He reluctantly upgraded civil rights enforcement, set goals for minority hiring by federal contractors, and presided over impressive environmental legislation.

Getting Out of Vietnam, 1969–1973

After 1968, things got worse in southeast Asia before they got better. Nixon had no secret plan to end the war. Protests culminated in 1969 with the Vietnam Moratorium on October 15, when 2 million protesters joined rallies across the country. Disaffection also mounted in Vietnam. Nurses found their idealism strained as they treated young men maimed in thousands of nasty skirmishes in the jungles and mountains. Racial tensions sapped morale on the front lines. Troops lost discipline, took drugs, and hunkered down waiting for their tours of duty to end. Soldiers "fragged" (killed) their own gung-ho or racist officers, and the high command had to adapt its code of justice to keep an army on the job.

Nixon and Vice President Spiro Agnew responded by trying to isolate the antiwar opposition, but Nixon also reduced the role of U.S. ground forces. He claimed that his policies represented "the great silent majority of my fellow Americans." Agnew blamed bad morale on journalists and intellectuals—on "nattering nabobs of negativism" and "an effete corps of impudent snobs." The administration arranged for a "spontaneous" attack by construction workers on antiwar protesters in New York. The hard-hat counterattack was a cynically manipulated symbol, but Nixon and Agnew tapped genuine anger about failure in Asia and rapid change in American society.

The New Left had already split into factions. Many activists continued to focus on peace work, draft resistance, and other efforts to link radical and liberal agendas. About a hundred angry SDS members, however, declared themselves the **Weather Underground** in 1969, taking their name from a Bob Dylan lyric ("You don't need a weatherman to know which way the blows"). They tried to disrupt Chicago and Washington with window-smashing "days of rage." Three Weatherpeople blew themselves up with a homemade bomb in New York in 1970. Others robbed a Boston bank to get money for the revolution. Still others bombed a University of Wisconsin building and killed a student.

Nixon's secretary of defense, Melvin Laird, responded to the antiwar sentiment with "Vietnamization," withdrawing U.S. troops as fast as possible without undermining the South Vietnamese government. In July 1969, the president announced the "Nixon Doctrine." The United States would help other countries fight their wars with weapons and money but not soldiers. The policy substituted machines for men. Americans rearmed and expanded the South Vietnamese army and surreptiously bombed communist bases in neutral Cambodia.

The secret war against Cambodia culminated on April 30, 1970, with an invasion. Americans who had hoped that the war was fading away were outraged. Students shut down hundreds of colleges. At Kent State University in Ohio, the National Guard was called in to maintain order. Taunts, tossed bottles, and the recent record of violence put them on edge. On May 4, one unit unexpectedly fired on a group of nonthreatening students and killed four of them. At Jackson State University in Mississippi, two unsuspecting students were killed when troops fired on their dormitory.

The Cambodian "incursion" extended the military stalemate in Vietnam to United States policy. Beginning in December 1969, a new lottery system for determining the order of draft calls by birth date let two-thirds of young men know they would not be drafted. In December 1970, Congress repealed the Gulf of Tonkin Resolution and prohibited use of U.S. ground troops outside South Vietnam. Cambodia, however, was already devastated. The U.S. invasion had destabilized its government and opened the way for the bloodthirsty Khmer Rouge, who killed millions of Cambodians in the name of working-class revolution. Vietnamization continued; only ninety thousand U.S. ground troops were still in Vietman by early 1972. A final air offensive in December smashed Hanoi into rubble and helped force four and a half years of peace talks to a conclusion.

The cease-fire began on January 27, 1973. It confirmed American withdrawal from Vietnam. North Vietnamese and Viet Cong forces would remain in control of the territory they occupied in South Vietnam, but they were not to be reinforced or substantially reequipped. The United States promised not to increase its military aid to South Vietnam. There were no solid guarantees for the South Vietnamese government. Immediately after coming to terms with North Vietnam, Nixon suspended the draft in favor of an all-volunteer military.

Nixon and the Wider World

To his credit, Richard Nixon took American foreign policy in new directions even while he was struggling to escape from Vietnam and Cambodia. Like Dwight Eisenhower before him, Nixon's reputation as an anticommunist allowed him to improve relations with China and the USSR. Indeed, he hoped to distract the American people from frustration in southeast Asia with accomplishments elsewhere.

Nixon's first foreign policy success was a gift from Kennedy and Johnson. NASA had been working

The shootings at Kent State University in May 1970 reflected the deep divisions in American society created by the Vietnam War, including those between antiwar college students and young people serving in the armed forces.

since 1961 to meet Kennedy's goal of an American on the moon before the end of the decade. The trial runs were Apollo 8, which sent American astronauts in orbit around the moon on Christmas Eve of 1968, and Apollo 10 in May 1969. The following summer, a Saturn V booster lifted the Apollo 11 crew of Edwin Aldrin, Neil Armstrong, and Michael Collins toward the untouched world. On July 20, the lunar lander Eagle detached from the command module circling the moon and landed on the level plain known as the Sea of Tranquillity. Six hours later, Armstrong was the first human to walk on the moon. Astronauts made five more trips to the moon between 1969 and 1972 and restored American prestige as the world's technological leader.

Back on earth, Nixon and Henry Kissinger, his national security adviser (and later secretary of state), shared what they considered a realistic view of foreign affairs. For both men, foreign policy was not about crusades or moral stands. It was about the balance of world economic and military power and securing the most advantageous agreements, alliances, and military positions. In particular, they hoped to trade improved relations with China and the USSR for help in settling the Vietnam War.

Since 1950, the United States had acted as if China didn't exist, refusing economic relations and insisting that the Nationalist regime on Taiwan was the legitimate Chinese government. But China was increasingly isolated within the communist world. In 1969, it almost went to war with the USSR. Nixon was eager to take advantage of Chinese–Soviet tension. Secret talks led to an easing of the American trade embargo in April 1971 and a tour of China by a U.S. table tennis team. Kissinger then arranged for Nixon's startling visit to Mao Zedong in Beijing in February 1972.

Playing the "China card" helped improve relations with the Soviet Union. The Soviets needed increased trade with the United States and a counterweight to China, the United States was looking for help in getting out of Vietnam, and both countries wanted to limit nuclear armaments. In 1969, the Senate came within one vote of stopping the development of defensive antiballistic missiles (ABMs). Opponents feared that strong antimissile defenses would encourage the idea that a nation could launch a first strike and survive the retaliation. Nixon treated the ABM program as a bargaining chip. Protracted negotiations led to arms agreements known as **SALT**—the Strategic Arms Limitation Treaty—that Nixon signed in Moscow in May 1972. The agreements blocked creation of extensive ABM systems but failed to limit bombers, cruise mis-

siles, or multiple independently targeted warheads on single missiles.

Diplomats used the French word **détente** to describe the new U.S. relations with China and the Soviet Union. *Détente* means an easing of tensions, not friendship or alliance. It facilitated travel between the United States and China. It allowed U.S. farmers to sell wheat to the Soviets. More broadly, *détente* implied that the United States and China recognized mutual interests in Asia and that the United States acknowledged the Soviet Union as an equal in world affairs. *Détente* made the world safer.

Courting Middle America

Nixon designed domestic policy to help him win re-election. His goal was to solidify his "Middle American" support; the strategy targeted the suburbs and the South. Political writers Richard Scammon and Ben Wattenberg warned the Democrats that blue-collar voters were ready to defect to law-and-order Republicans.

The Nixon White House preferred to ignore troubled big cities. Spokesmen announced that the "urban crisis" was over and then dismantled the urban initiatives of Johnson's Great Society, even though programs like Model Cities had never been given enough money to work. Instead, Nixon tilted federal assistance to the suburbs. The centerpiece of his **New Federalism** was General Revenue Sharing (1972). By 1980, it had transferred more than $18 billion from the federal treasury to the states and more than $36 billion to local governments. Revenue sharing was a suburban aid program. Its "no-strings" grants supplemented the general funds of every full-service government, whether a city of 2 million or a suburban town of five hundred.

Nixon pursued the southern strategy through the symbolism of Supreme Court nominations. His first nominees were Clement Haynsworth of Florida and G. Harrold Carswell of Alabama. Although the Senate rejected both as unqualified, the nominations nonetheless gave Nixon a reputation as a champion of the white South. He hoped to move cautiously in enforcing school desegregation, but a task force led by Secretary of Labor George Shultz crafted an approach that allowed substantial desegregation. In this instance, as elsewhere with his domestic policies, Nixon was inflammatory in speeches but moderate in action, increasing the funding of federal civil rights agencies.

More troublesome was inflation, one of Lyndon Johnson's unpleasant legacies (see Figure 31-2). The cost of living began to outpace wages in the late 1960s. Economists saw the situation as a classic

Affirmative Action

In 1996, California voters approved a ballot measure to eliminate state-sponsored affirmative action. One effect was to prohibit state-funded colleges and universities from using race or ethnicity as a factor in deciding which applicants to admit. In the same year, the Supreme Court let stand a lower court ruling that had forbidden the University of Texas to consider race in admission decisions. The number of black freshmen in the University Texas at Austin dropped by half in 1997, and the number of black and Hispanic students entering its law school dropped by two-thirds. At the law school of the University of California at Berkeley, where the number of entering black students dropped from twenty to one.

These events were part of a widespread reaction in the 1990s against policies that emerged in the 1960s as part of an effort to redress inequalities that handicapped minorities in American society. An executive order by Johnson required businesses that received federal contracts to "take affirmative action to ensure that applicants are employed, and that employees are treated during employment without regard for their race, creed, color, or national origin." By the 1970s, many states and cities had adopted similar policies and had extended affirmative action to women as well as minorities. Colleges and universities adopted affirmative action policies for faculty recruitment and admissions.

As affirmative action spread, it evolved from an effort to prevent discrimination to an active ("affirmative") effort to increase diversity in schools and the workplace. Government agencies began to set aside a certain small percentage of contracts for woman-owned or minority-owned firms. Cities actively worked to hire more minority police officers and firefighters. Colleges made special efforts to attract minority students.

In the late 1970s, however, affirmative action began to face court challenges. In a landmark case, Allan Bakke, an unsuccessful applicant to the medical school of the University of California at Davis, claimed the university had improperly set aside places in its entering class for minority students, thereby engaging in reverse discrimination against white applicants. In a narrow decision, the U.S. Supreme Court in 1978 ordered Bakke admitted because the only basis for his rejection had been race. At the same time, the Court stated that college and universities could legally base admissions decisions on race and ethnicity among other factors.

Since *Bakke*, affirmative action has come under increasing scrutiny and attack. The Supreme Court has narrowed the scope of affirmative action, and states like California and Texas have acted to curtail their affirmative action programs. The problem is that the goal of diversity seems to conflict with the fundamental American value of individual opportunity. Americans reject the idea that past injustice and unequal opportunity can justify special consideration for all members of a group. Instead they believe that individual merit should be the sole basis for getting into school or getting a job. Many minority group members worry that affirmative action undermines their own success by suggesting that it resulted from preferential treatment rather than merit.

Yet the concerns that affirmative action has addressed since its inception are still valid. The nation surely benefits when members of minority groups are able to build successful businesses. A city with large minority populations benefits when members of those groups are serving on its police force and working in its classrooms. Students benefit when they interact with people of diverse backgrounds and opinions in the course of their studies. As a result, affirmative action programs are likely to endure, if in a substantially limited form, into the twenty-first century.

Students demonstrate while University of California Regents consider affirmative action programs in 1995.

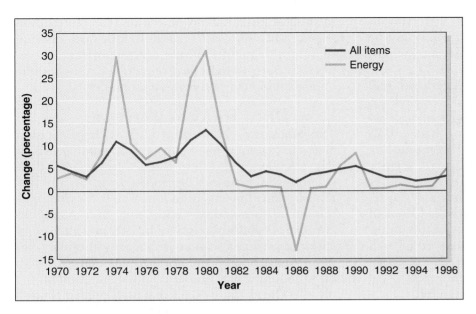

Figure 31-2 **Changes in the Consumer Price Index and Energy Prices**
From 1974 to 1982, price inflation was one of the nation's most serious problems. Spikes in energy prices in 1974 and 1979 were one cause. Another was the effort to fight a war in southeast Asia without raising taxes to offset federal defense spending. Inflation eroded the value of savings and hurt people on fixed incomes, such as the elderly.
Data Source: U.S. Bureau of Labor Statistics.

example of "demand-pull" inflation in which too many dollars from government and consumers were chasing too few goods and services. One of the causes was LBJ's decision to fight in Vietnam without tax increases until 1968. An income tax cut in 1969, supported by both parties, made the situation worse. Inflation eroded the value of savings and pensions. It also made U.S. goods too expensive for foreign buyers and generated a trade deficit.

In August 1971, Nixon detached the dollar from the gold standard. The Treasury would no longer sell gold at $35 an ounce, a practice that had made the dollar the anchor around which other currencies fluctuated. The dollar could now float in value relative to other currencies, making U.S. exports more competitive. Nixon took the action without consulting America's allies, even though it triggered drastic readjustments of international markets. It was an example of the political expediency behind his economic policy.

After the 1972 election, inflation came roaring back in the form of "cost-push" inflation in which a price increase for one key product raises the cost of producing other items. The main cause was sharp increases in the cost of energy, an input to every product and service. Angry at American support for Israel in the Arab-Israeli War of October 1973, Arab nations imposed an embargo on oil exports that lasted from October 1973 to March 1974. Gasoline and heating oil became scarce and expensive. Long lines at gas pumps and hurried rationing systems panicked auto-dependent Americans. The shortages eased when the embargo ended, but the **Organization of Petroleum Exporting Countries (OPEC)** had

challenged the ability of the industrial nations to dictate world economic policy.

Rising energy prices forced Americans to switch off unused lights, turn down thermostats, and put on sweaters. Consumers compared the efficiency ratings of appliances and the gas mileage of cars. Congress required states to enforce a highway speed limit of 55 miles per hour to get federal highway funds. Congress also enacted the first fuel economy standards for automobiles. The fuel efficiency of the average new car doubled from 14 miles per gallon in 1973 to 28 miles per gallon by the late 1980s, and more efficient imports captured a third of the U.S. car market by 1980.

While Nixon searched for short-term political advantage, the underlying problems of the American economy went untreated. After thirty years at the top, the United States could no longer dominate the world economy by itself. Germany and Japan now had economies as modern as that of the United States. Declining rates of saving and investment in industrial capacity seemed to put the United States in danger of following the British road to economic obsolescence and second-level status. Indeed, a new term entered the popular vocabulary in 1971. **Stagflation** was the painful combination of inflation, high unemployment, and flat economic growth that matched no one's economic theory but everyone's daily experience.

Americans as Environmentalists

In the turbulent 1970s, Americans found one issue they could agree on. In the 1970s, resource conservation grew into a multifaceted environmental movement. Environmentalism dealt with serious problems. It was broad enough for both scientific experts and activists, for both Republican Richard Nixon and Democrat Jimmy Carter.

After the booming 1950s, Americans had started to pay attention to "pollution," a catchall for the damage that advanced technologies and industrial production did to natural systems. Rachel Carson's *Silent Spring* in 1962 pushed pollution onto the national agenda. Carson, a well-regarded science writer, described the side effects of DDT and other pesticides on animal life. In her imagined future, spring was silent because all the birds had died of pesticide poisoning. Other side effects of the industrial economy made headlines. An offshore oil well polluted the beaches of Santa Barbara, California, in 1969. Fire danced across the Cuyahoga River in Cleveland when industrial discharges ignited.

Environmentalism gained strength among Americans in 1970. On April 22, students and teachers from ten thousand schools as well as 20 million other people took part in Earth Day, an occasion first conceived by Wisconsin Senator Gaylord Nelson. Earth Day gained a grassroots following in towns and cities across the country. New York closed Fifth Avenue to automobiles for the day. Companies touted their environmental credentials.

The American establishment had been looking for a safe and respectable crusade to divert the idealism and discontent of the 1960s. Now the mainstream media discovered the ravaged planet. So did a politically savvy president. An expedient proenvironmental stance might attract some of the antiwar constituency. Nixon had already signed the National Environmental Policy Act on January 1, 1970, and later in the year created the **Environmental Protection Agency (EPA)** to enforce environmental laws. The rest of the Nixon years brought legislation on clean air, clear water, pesticides, hazardous chemicals, and endangered species (see the overview table, "The Environmental Decades") that made environmental management and protection part of governmental routine.

As Americans became more aware of human-caused environmental hazards, they realized that low-income and minority communities had more than their share of problems. Residents near the Love Canal in Buffalo discovered in 1978 that an entire neighborhood was built on land contaminated by decades of chemical dumping. Activists sought to understand the health effects and force compensation, paving the way for the **Superfund** cleanup legislation.

In other areas of industrial contamination, such as the Louisiana petrochemical belt along the Mississippi River, African Americans often lived downstream and downwind. Landfills and waste disposal sites were frequently located near minority neighborhoods. Efforts to fight environmental racism became important in many minority communities.

From Dirty Tricks to Watergate

The **Watergate** crisis pivoted on Richard Nixon's character. Despite his solid political standing, Nixon saw enemies everywhere and overestimated their strength. Subordinates learned during his first administration that the president would condone dishonest actions—"dirty tricks"—if they stood to improve his political position. In 1972 and 1973, dirty tricks grew from a scandal into a constitutional crisis when Nixon abused the power of his office to cover up wrongdoing and hinder criminal investigations.

The chain of events that undermined Nixon's presidency started with the **Pentagon Papers**. In his last

The first Earth Day in 1970 tapped growing concern about the environment. It helped turn the technical field of pollution control into the broad-based environmental movement.

OVERVIEW

THE ENVIRONMENTAL DECADES

Administration	Focus of Concern	Legislation
Johnson	Wilderness and wildlife	Wilderness Act (1964) National Wildlife Refuge System (1966) Wild and Scenic Rivers Act (1968)
Nixon	Pollution control and endangered environments	National Environmental Policy Act (1969) Environmental Protection Agency (1970) Clean Air Act (1970) Occupational Safety and Health Act (1970) Water Pollution Control Act (1972) Pesticide Control Act (1972) Coastal Zone Management Act (1972) Endangered Species Act (1973)
Ford	Energy and hazardous materials	Toxic Substances Control Act (1976) Resource Conservation and Recovery Act (1976)
Carter	Energy and hazardous materials	Energy Policy and Conservation Act (1978) Comprehensive Emergency Response, Compensation, and Liability Act (Superfund) (1980)

year as secretary of defense, Robert McNamara had commissioned a report on America's road to Vietnam. The documents showed that the country's leaders had planned to expand the war even while they claimed to be looking for a way out. In June 1971, one of the contributors to the report, Daniel Ellsberg, leaked it to the *New York Times*. Its publication infuriated Nixon.

In response, the White House compiled a list of journalists and politicians who opposed Nixon. As White House staffer John Dean put it, the president's men could then "use the available federal machinery [Internal Revenue Service, FBI] to screw our political enemies." Nixon set up a special investigations unit in the White House. Former CIA employees E. Howard Hunt and G. Gordon Liddy became the chief "plumbers," as the group was known because its job was to prevent leaks of information. The plumbers contributed to an atmosphere of lawlessness in the White House. They cooked up schemes to embarrass political opponents and ransacked the office of Ellsberg's psychiatrist.

Early in 1972, Hunt went to work for CREEP—the Committee to Re-Elect the President—

while Liddy took another position on the presidential staff. CREEP had already raised millions from corporations and was hatching plans to undermine Democrats with rumors and pranks. Then, on June 17, 1972, five inept burglars hired with CREEP funds were caught breaking into the Democratic National Committee office in Washington's Watergate apartment building. The people involved knew that an investigation would lead directly to CREEP and then to the White House. Nixon felt too insecure to ride out what would probably have been a small scandal. Instead, he initiated a coverup. On June 23, he ordered his assistant H. R. Haldeman to warn the FBI off the case with the excuse that national security was involved. Nixon compounded this obstruction of justice by arranging a $400,000 bribe to keep the burglars quiet.

The coverup worked in the short run. As midlevel officials from the Justice Department pursued their investigation, the public lost interest in what looked more like slapstick than a serious crime. Nixon's opponent in the 1972 election was South Dakota Senator George McGovern, an impassioned opponent of the Vietnam War. McGovern was honest, intelligent, and well to the left on issues like the defense budget and legalization of marijuana. He did not appeal to the white Southerners and blue-collar Northerners whom Nixon and Agnew were luring from the Democrats. An assassination attempt that took George Wallace out of national politics also helped Nixon win in a landslide.

The coverup began to come apart with the trial of the Watergate burglars in January 1973. Federal Judge John Sirica used the threat of heavy sentences to pressure one burglar into a statement that implied that higher-ups had been involved. Meanwhile, the *Washington Post* was linking Nixon's people to dirty tricks and illegal campaign contributions. The White House scrambled to find a defensible story. John Dean, who coordinated much of the effort, reported to Nixon in March that the scandal and coverup had become a "cancer on the presidency." Nixon was aware of many of the actions that his subordinates had undertaken. He now began to coach people on what they should tell investigators, claimed his staff had lied to him, and tried to set up Dean to take the fall.

In the late spring and early summer, attention shifted to the televised hearings of the Senate's Select Committee on Presidential Campaign Activities. Its chair was Sam Ervin of North Carolina, whose down-home style masked a clever mind. A parade of White House and party officials described their own pieces in the affair, often accusing each other and revealing the plumbers and the enemies list. The real questions, it became obvious, were what

the president knew and when he knew it. It seemed to be John Dean's word against Richard Nixon's.

A bombshell turned the scandal into a constitutional crisis. A midlevel staffer told the committee that Nixon made tape recordings of his White House conversations. Both the Senate and the Watergate special prosecutor, Archibald Cox, subpoenaed the tapes. Nixon refused to give them up, citing executive privilege and the separation of powers. In late October, after he failed to cut a satisfactory deal, he fired his attorney general and the special prosecutor. This "Saturday night massacre" caused a storm of protest, and many Americans thought that it proved that Nixon had something to hide. In April 1974, he finally issued edited transcripts of the tapes, with foul language deleted and key passages missing; he claimed that his secretary had accidentally erased crucial material. Finally, on July 24, 1974, the U.S. Supreme Court ruled unanimously that Nixon had to deliver sixty-four tapes to the new special prosecutor.

Congress was now moving to impeach the president. On July 27, the House Judiciary Committee took up the specific charges. Republicans joined Democrats in voting three articles of impeachment: for hindering the criminal investigation of the Watergate break-in, for abusing the power of the presidency by using federal agencies to deprive citizens of their rights, and for ignoring the committee's subpoena for the tapes. Before the full House could vote on the articles of impeachment and send them to the Senate for trial, Nixon delivered the tapes. One of

The Watergate story captured national attention in 1973 and 1974. Here, Senator Sam Ervin (with his back to the camera) swears in White House aide John Dean III. Dean's decision to testify about his role in the Watergate coverup helped break the story open.

them contained the "smoking gun," direct evidence that Nixon had participated in the coverup on June 23, 1972, and had been lying ever since. On August 8 he announced his resignation, effective the next day.

Watergate was two separate but related stories. On one level, it was about individuals who deceived or manipulated the American people. Nixon and his cronies wanted to win too badly to play by the rules and repeatedly broke the law. Nixon paid for his overreaching ambition with the end of his political career; more than twenty others paid with jail terms.

On another level, the crisis was a lesson about the Constitution. The separation of powers allowed Congress and the courts to rein in a president who had spun out of control. The Ervin Committee hearings in 1973 and the House Judiciary Committee proceedings in 1974 were rituals to assure Americans that the system still worked. Nevertheless, the sequence of political events from 1968 to 1974 disillusioned many citizens.

The Ford Footnote

Gerald Ford was the first president who had been elected neither president nor vice president. Ford was Nixon's appointee to replace Spiro Agnew, who resigned and pleaded no contest to charges of bribery and income tax evasion in 1973 as Watergate was gathering steam. Ford was competent but unimaginative. His first major act was his most controversial. On September 8, he pardoned Richard Nixon for "any and all crimes" committed while president. Because Nixon had not yet been indicted, the pardon saved him from future prosecution. To many Americans, it looked like a payoff. Ford insisted that the purpose was to clear the decks so that the nation could think about the future rather than the past. He also offered clemency to thousands of draft resisters.

In 1975, South Vietnam collapsed. Only the American presence had kept its political, ethnic, and religious factions together. For the first two years after the Paris agreement, North Vietnam quietly rebuilt its military capacity. In the spring of 1975, it opened an offensive, and South Vietnamese morale evaporated. Resistance crumbled so rapidly that the United States had to evacuate its embassy in Saigon by helicopter while frantic Vietnamese tried to join the flight.

Elsewhere in the world, *détente* continued. American diplomats joined the Soviet Union and thirty other European nations in the capital of Finland to sign the **Helsinki Accords**. The agreements called for increased commerce between the Eastern and Western blocs and human rights guarantees. They also legitimized the national boundaries that had been set in eastern Europe in 1945.

At home, the federal government did little new during Ford's two and a half years in office. The economy slid into recession; unemployment climbed above 10 percent; inflation diminished the value of savings and wages. Ford beat back Ronald Reagan for the Republican presidential nomination, but he was clearly vulnerable.

His Democratic opponent was a political enigma. James Earl Carter, Jr., had been a navy officer, a farmer, and governor of Georgia. He was one of several new-style politicians who transformed southern politics in the 1970s. Carter and the others left race-baiting behind to talk like modern New Dealers, emphasizing that white and black Americans all needed better schools and economic growth. He appealed to Democrats as someone who could reassemble LBJ's political coalition and return the South to the Democratic party. In his successful campaign, Carter presented himself as an alternative to party hacks and Washington insiders (see Map 31-3).

Map 31-3　The Election of 1976

Georgian Jimmy Carter ran in 1976 as an outsider to Washington politics. He capitalized on a reputation as a progressive governor and on the Watergate scandal, which had damaged the Republican party.

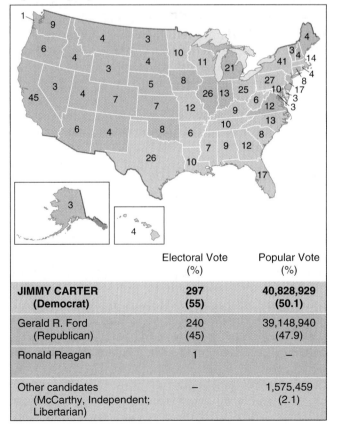

	Electoral Vote (%)	Popular Vote (%)
JIMMY CARTER (Democrat)	**297 (55)**	**40,828,929 (50.1)**
Gerald R. Ford (Republican)	240 (45)	39,148,940 (47.9)
Ronald Reagan	1	–
Other candidates (McCarthy, Independent; Libertarian)	–	1,575,459 (2.1)

Jimmy Carter: Idealism and Frustration in the White House

Johnson and Nixon had both thought of themselves as outsiders even after nearly thirty years in national politics. Carter was the real thing, a stranger to the national policy establishment that revolves around Washington think tanks and New York law firms. As an outsider, Carter had one great advantage: freedom from the narrow mind-set of experts who talk only to each other. However, he lacked both the knowledge of key political players and the experience to resolve legislative gridlock.

The new president's personal background compounded his problems. Intellectuals found this devout Baptist hard to fathom. Labor leaders and political bosses didn't know what to make of a deep Southerner. The national press was baffled. It was only after his presidency, when Americans took a clear look at Carter's moral character, that they decided they liked what they saw.

Even had he been the most skilled of politicians, however, Carter took office with little room to maneuver. Watergate bequeathed him a powerful and self-satisfied Congress and a combative press. OPEC oil producers, Islamic fundamentalists, and Soviet generals followed their own agendas. The American people themselves were fractionalized and quarrelsome, uneasy with the new advocacy of equality for women, uncertain as a nation whether they shared the same values and goals. Carter's attempt to govern like a preacher, with appeals to moral principles, did more to reveal divisions than establish common ground.

Carter, Energy, and the Economy

Carter was refreshingly low-key. After his inauguration, he walked from the Capitol to the White House as Jefferson had. He preferred sweaters to tuxedos and signed official documents "Jimmy." He tended to tell the public what he thought rather than what pollsters said the people wanted to hear.

Carter's approach to politics reflected his training as an engineer. He was analytical, logical, and given to breaking a problem into its component parts. He was better at working with details than at defining broad goals. He filled his cabinet with experts rather than political operators. He failed to understand the importance of personalities and was uncomfortable with compromise. Carter even found it hard to deal with the Democrats who ran Congress. He didn't seem to understand the basic rules of Washington politics. For example, he and his cabinet officers developed policies and made appointments without consulting key congressional committee chairs.

Carter got into political trouble in his first month in office. Federal water and land policy in the West had long subsidized big agricultural businesses. Carter's team decided to kill a long list of wasteful water projects. Westerners in Congress were astonished when the proposal arrived without warning, for it attacked powerful interests. Carter eventually managed to get half of what he wanted, but the battle soured relations between the White House and Capitol Hill.

The biggest domestic problem remained the economy, which slid into another recession in 1978. Another jump in petroleum prices helped make 1979 and 1980 the worst years for inflation in the postwar era. Interest rates surged past 20 percent as the Federal Reserve tried to reduce inflation by squeezing business and consumer credit. Carter himself was a fiscal conservative whose impulse was to cut federal spending. This worsened unemployment and alienated liberal Democrats, who wanted to revive the Great Society.

Carter simultaneously proposed a comprehensive energy policy. He asked Americans to make energy conservation the moral equivalent of war—to accept individual sacrifices for the common good. Congress created the Department of Energy but refused to raise taxes on oil and natural gas to reduce consumption. However, the Energy Policy and Conservation Act (1978) did encourage alternative energy sources to replace foreign petroleum. Big oil companies poured billions of dollars into western Colorado to squeeze a petroleum substitute from shale. Solar energy research prospered. Breezy western hillsides sprouted "wind farms" to wring electricity out of the air.

However, antinuclear activism blocked one obvious alternative to fossil fuels. The antinuclear movement had started with concern about the ability of the Atomic Energy Commission to monitor the safety of nuclear power plants and about the disposal of spent fuel rods. In the late 1970s, activists staged sit-ins at the construction sites of nuclear plants. A near-meltdown at the Three Mile Island nuclear plant in Pennsylvania in March 1979 stalemated efforts to expand nuclear power capacity. Utilities were soon worrying about the costs of shutting down and dismantling their old nuclear plants rather than trying to build new ones.

When the OPEC price hikes undermined the inflation-fighting effort in the summer of 1979,

Carter told the nation that a "moral and spiritual crisis" demanded a rebirth of the American spirit. He also proposed new steps to solve the energy crisis. The public did not know whether he had preached a sermon or given them marching orders. A cabinet reshuffle a few days later was supposed to show that he was firmly in charge. Instead, the media painted the president as inconsistent and incompetent.

Carter's problems were both personal and structural. In effect, opinion leaders by 1979 had decided that he was not capable of leading the nation and then interpreted every action as confirming that belief. There was also the practical problem of trying to hold the loyalty of Democratic liberals while attracting middle-of-the-road voters.

Building a Cooperative World

Despite troubles on the home front, Carter's first two years brought foreign policy success that reflected a new vision of a multilateral world. As a relative newcomer to international politics, Carter was willing to try to work with African, Asian, and Latin American nations on a basis of mutual respect. He appointed Andrew Young—a fellow Georgian with long experience in the civil rights movement—as ambassador to the United Nations, where he worked effectively to build bridges to third-world nations.

Carter's moral convictions were responsible for a new concern with human rights around the globe. He criticized the Soviet Union for preventing free speech and denying its citizens the right to emigrate, angering Soviet leaders, who didn't expect the human rights clauses of the Helsinki Accords to be taken seriously. Carter was also willing to criticize some (but not all) American allies. He withheld economic aid from South Africa, Guatemala, Chile, and Nicaragua, which had long records of human rights abuses. In Nicaragua, the change in policy helped left-wing Sandinista rebels topple the Somoza dictatorship.

The triumph of the new foreign policy was the **Camp David Agreement** between Egypt and Israel. Carter risked his reputation and credibility in September 1978 to bring Egyptian President Anwar el-Sadat and Israeli Prime Minister Menachem Begin together at Camp David, the presidential retreat. He refused to admit failure and dissuaded the two leaders from walking out. A formal treaty was signed in Washington on March 26, 1979. The pact normalized relations between Israel and its most powerful neighbor and led to Israeli withdrawal from the Sinai Peninsula. It was a vital prelude to further progress toward Arab-Israeli peace in the mid 1990s.

Return of the Cold War

The Cold War was a noxious weed that détente trimmed but did not uproot. In the last two years of Carter's administration, it sprang back to life around the globe and smothered the promise of a new foreign policy. The Soviets ignored the human rights provisions of the Helsinki Accords. Soviet advisers or Cuban troops intervened in African civil wars. At home, Cold Warriors who had never accepted *détente* found it easier to attack Carter than Nixon.

Carter inherited negotiations for SALT II—a strategic arms limitation treaty that would have reduced both the American and Soviet nuclear arsenals—from the Ford administration. SALT II met stiff resistance in the Senate. Opponents claimed it would create a "window of vulnerability" in the 1980s that would invite the Soviets to launch a nuclear first strike. Carter tried to counter criticism by stepping up defense spending, starting a buildup that would accelerate under Ronald Reagan.

Hopes for SALT II vanished on January 3, 1980, when Soviet troops entered Afghanistan, a neutral Muslim nation on the southern border of the USSR. Muslim tribespeople unhappy with modernization had attacked Afghanistan's procommunist government, which invited Soviet intervention. The situation resembled the American involvement in South Vietnam. Similar too was the inability of Soviet forces to suppress the Afghan guerrillas, with their American weapons and control of the mountains. In the end, it took the Soviets a decade to find a way out.

The final blow to Carter's foreign policy came in Iran. Since 1953, the United States had strongly backed Iran's monarch, the Shah. The Shah modernized Iran's economy but jailed political opponents. U.S. aid and oil revenues helped him build a vast army, but the Iranian middle class despised his authoritarianism, and Muslim fundamentalists opposed modernization. Revolution toppled the Shah at the start of 1979.

The upheaval installed a nominally democratic government, but the Ayatollah Ruhollah Khomeini, a Muslim cleric who hated the United States, exercised real power. Throughout 1979, Iran grew increasingly anti-American. After the United States allowed the exiled Shah to seek medical treatment in New York, a mob stormed the U.S. embassy in Tehran on November 4, 1979, and took more than sixty Americans hostage. They demanded that Carter surrender the Shah.

Television brought pictures of blindfolded hostages and anti-American mobs burning effigies of Uncle Sam and wrapping American flags around garbage. Americans returned the hate. The administration tried economic pressure and diplomacy, but Khomeini had no desire for accommodation. When Iran announced in April 1980 that the hostages would remain in the hands of the militants rather than be transferred to the government, Carter ordered an airborne rescue. Even a perfectly managed effort would have been difficult. The hostages were held in the heart of a city of 4 million hostile Iranians, hundreds of miles from the nearest aircraft carrier and thousands of miles from U.S. bases. The attempt misfired when three of eight helicopters malfunctioned and one crashed in the Iranian desert. The fiasco added to the national embarrassment. The United States and Iran finally reached agreement on the eve of the 1980 election. The hostages gained their freedom after 444 days at the moment Ronald Reagan took office as the new president.

The hostage crisis consumed Jimmy Carter the way that Vietnam had consumed Lyndon Johnson. It gripped the public and stalemated other issues. For weeks, Carter limited public appearances to statements in the White House Rose Garden. The public blamed him for problems literally beyond his control, for failing to use military force, and then for using it and failing. Carter's tragedy was that "his" Iranian crisis was the fruit of policies hatched by the Eisenhower administration and pursued by every president since then, all of whom overlooked the Shah's despotic government because of his firm anticommunism.

After thirty years in which the United States had viewed the entire world as a Cold War battlefield, Carter was willing to accept the developing world on its own terms. His human rights efforts showed that evangelical religious convictions could be tied to progressive aims. He wanted to prevent overreliance on oppressive regimes, but the past was too burdensome. Iranian rage at past policies of the sort Carter hoped to change destroyed his ability to direct a new course.

The Iran hostage crisis reflected intense anti-American feelings in Iran and provoked an equally bitter anti-Iranian reaction in the United States. Fifty-two of the more than sixty U.S. embassy employees first seized were held for 444 days, giving the United States a painful lesson about the limits on its ability to influence events around the world.

Conclusion

In the mid-1970s, Americans encountered real limits to national capacity. From 1945 to 1973, they had enjoyed remarkable prosperity. That ended in 1974. Long lines at gas stations suggested that prosperity was fragile. Cities and regions began to feel the costs of obsolete industries. Environmental damage caused many Americans to reconsider the goal of economic expansion.

The nation also had to recognize that it could not run the world. American withdrawal from Vietnam in 1973 and the collapse of the South Vietnamese government in 1975 were defeats; the United States ended up with little to show for a long and painful war. SALT I stabilized the arms race, but it also recognized that the Soviet Union was an equal. The American nuclear arsenal might help deter a third world war, but it could not prevent the seizure of hostages in Iran.

These challenges came amid profound social and economic revolutions in the United States. Renewed immigration was changing the mix of the American population. The ways that Americans made their livings, built their families, ran their personal lives, and sought spiritual reassurance were in flux. The nation finished the 1970s more egalitarian than it had been in the early 1960s but also more divided. More citizens had the opportunity to advance economically and to seek political power, but there were deepening fissures between social liberals and cultural conservatives, old and new views about roles for women, rich and poor, white and black. In 1961, John Kennedy had called on his fellow citizens to "bear any burden, pay any price" to defend freedom. By 1980, the nation had neither the economic capacity to pay any price nor the unity to agree on what burdens it should bear.

Review Questions

1. Why did the United States fail to achieve its objectives in Vietnam? What factors limited President Johnson's freedom of action there? How did the Tet Offensive affect U.S. policy? How did antiwar protests in the United States influence national policy?

2. How did racial relations change between 1965 and 1970? What were the relationships between the civil rights movement and minority separatism? What were the similarities and differences among African-American, Latino, and Native American activism?

3. In what ways was 1968 a pivotal year for American politics and society?

4. What were the implications of *détente?* Why did the Cold War reappear in the late 1970s? How and why did U.S. influence over the rest of the world change during the 1970s?

5. How did Richard Nixon's political strategy respond to the growth of the South and West? How did it respond to the shift of population from central cities to suburbs?

6. How did the backgrounds of Presidents Johnson, Nixon, and Carter shape their successes and failures as national leaders?

7. What political and constitutional issues were at stake in the Watergate scandal? How did it change American politics?

Recommended Reading

Tom Bates, *Rads: The 1970 Bombing of the Army Math Research Center at the University of Wisconsin and Its Aftermath* (1992). Uses a specific episode to understand the collapse of the New Left.

John Morton Blum, *Years of Discord: American Politics and Society, 1961–1974* (1991). Shares with McQuaid (below) a disillusionment with America's development since the hope of the 1960s.

David Caute, *Year of the Barricades* (1988). Tours the events of 1968 on both sides of the Atlantic.

Gloria Emerson, *Winners and Losers* (1976). The impact of the war in Vietnam on American society, told through the stories of individuals changed by the war.

David Farber, *The Age of Great Dreams: America in the 1960s* (1994). A positive assessment of the legacy of the 1960s.

David Farber, *Chicago '68* (1988). Contrasts the perspectives and language of city officials and protesters.

David Halberstam, *October 1964* (1994). Uses the baseball season of 1964 and the World Series between the St. Louis Cardinals and New York Yankees to encapsulate the impacts of changing racial relations on American society.

Stanley Karnow, *Vietnam: A History* (1983). A comprehensive history of American involvement in Vietnam that details the collapse of French rule and early U.S. relations with Vietnam.

Kim McQuaid, *The Anxious Years: America in the Vietnam-Watergate Era* (1989). Tries to understand how the United States turned aside from the promise of the early 1960s.

Haskell Wexler, director, *Medium Cool* (1969). A film that captures the tension of Chicago in the hot summer of 1968 through the eyes of a reporter.

Additional Sources

War in Vietnam

Christian Appy, *Working-Class War: American Combat Soldiers and Vietnam* (1993).

Albert Auster and Leonard Quart, *How the War Was Remembered: Hollywood and Vietnam* (1988).

Robert Buzzanco, *Masters of War* (1996).

Francis Fitzgerald, *Fire on the Lake* (1972).

George Herring, *America's Longest War* (1986).

David W. Levy, *The Debate over Vietnam* (1991).

Robert Schulzinger, *A Time for War. The United States and Vietnam, 1941–1975* (1997).

William Shawcross, *Sideshow: Kissinger, Nixon, and the Destruction of Cambodia* (1979).

Neil Sheehan, *A Bright Shining Lie: John Paul Vann and America in Vietnam* (1988).

Brian Van De Mark, *Into the Quagmire: Johnson and the Escalation of the Vietnam War* (1991).

Lynda Van Devanter, *Home before Morning* (1984).

Tom Wells, *The War Within: America's Battle over Vietnam* (1994).

Marilyn Young, *The Vietnam Wars, 1945–1990* (1991).

The Revolt of the Young

Terry Anderson, *The Movement and the Sixties* (1995).

Wini Breines, *Community and Organization in the New Left, 1962–1968* (1982).

Sara Evans, *Personal Politics: The Roots of Women's Liberation in the Civil Rights Movement and the New Left* (1979).

Todd Gitlin, *The Sixties: Years of Hope, Days of Rage* (1987).

Kenneth Heineman, *Campus Wars: The Peace Movement at American State Universities in the Vietnam Era* (1993).

Marty Jezer, *Abbie Hoffman: American Rebel* (1992).

James Miller, *"Democracy Is in the Streets": From Port Huron to the Siege of Chicago* (1987).

Charles Perry, *The Haight-Ashbury* (1985).

William Rorabaugh, *Berkeley at War* (1989).

Kirkpatrick Sale, *SDS* (1973).

Minority Rights and Minority Separatism

Paula Giddings and Cornel West, *Regarding Malcolm X* (1994).

Peter Mathiesson, *In the Spirit of Crazy Horse* (1983).

Russell Means, *Where White Men Fear to Tread* (1995).

Felix Padilla, *Puerto Rican Chicago* (1987).

Donald Parman, *Indians and the American West in the Twentieth Century* (1994).

Piri Thomas, *Down These Mean Streets* (1967).

William L. Van Deburg, *New Day in Babylon: The Black Power Movement and American Culture, 1965–1975* (1993).

Foreign Policy in the 1970s

James A. Bill, *The Eagle and the Lion: The Tragedy of American-Iranian Relations* (1988).

Raymond Garthoff, *Détente and Confrontation* (1985).

Walter Isaacson, *Kissinger: A Biography* (1992).

Walter Le Feber, *The Panama Canal: The Crisis in Historical Perspective* (1978).

Robert Litwak, *Détente and the Nixon Doctrine* (1984).

Keith Nelson, *The Making of Détente* (1995).

William B. Quando, *Camp David: Peacemaking and Politics* (1986).

Robert Schulzinger, *Henry Kissinger: Doctor of Diplomacy* (1989).

Gaddis Smith, *Morality, Reason, and Power* (1986).

Strobe Talbot, *Endgame: The Inside Story of SALT II* (1979).

Watergate and Politics in the Nixon Years

Stephen E. Ambrose, *Nixon: Ruin and Recovery, 1973–1990* (1991).

Dan T. Carter, *The Politics of Rage: George Wallace, the Origins of the New Conservatism, and the Transformation of American Politics* (1996).

John Robert Greene, *The Limits of Power: The Nixon and Ford Administrations* (1992).

Stanley Kutler, *The Wars of Watergate* (1990).

Michael Schudson, *Watergate in American Memory: How We Remember, Forget, and Reconstruct the Past* (1992).

Jimmy Carter and His Presidency

Jimmy Carter, *Keeping Faith: Memoirs of a President* (1982).

Betty Glad, *Jimmy Carter, In Search of the Great White House* (1980).

Erwin C. Hargrove, *Jimmy Carter as President: Leadership and the Politics of the Public Good* (1988).

Charles O. Jones, *The Trusteeship Presidency: Jimmy Carter and the United States Congress* (1988).

Burton I. Kaufman, *The Presidency of James Earl Carter, Jr.* (1993).

William Lee Miller, *Yankee from Georgia: The Emergence of Jimmy Carter* (1978).

Environmental Politics

Robert Gottlieb, *Forcing the Spring: The Transformation of the American Environmental Movement* (1993).

Samuel Hays, *Beauty, Health, and Permanence: Environmental Politics in the United States, 1955–1985* (1987).

Kirkpatrick Sale, *The Green Revolution: The American Environmental Movement, 1962–1992* (1993).

Where to Learn More

❖ **Lyndon B. Johnson National Historical Park, Johnson City, Texas.** Johnson's ranch, southwest of Austin, gives visitors a feeling for the open landscape in which Johnson spent his early years.

❖ **Vietnam Veterans Memorial, Washington, D.C.** A simple wall engraved with the names of the nation's Vietnam War dead is testimony to one of the nation's most divisive wars.

❖ **Richard Nixon Library and Birthplace, Yorba Linda, California.** Exhibits trace Nixon's political career and related world events with a sympathetic interpretation.

❖ **Titan Missile Museum, Green Valley, Arizona.** The Green Valley complex near Tucson held eighteen Titan missiles. They were deactivated after SALT I, and the complex is now open to visitors.

SHAPING A NEW AMERICA,
SINCE 1965

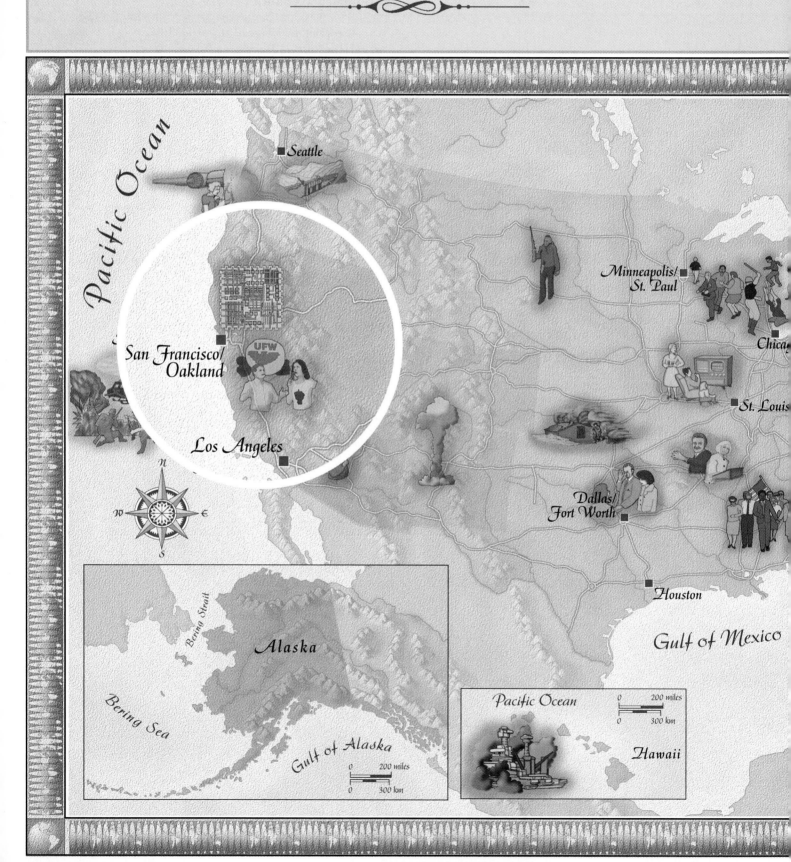

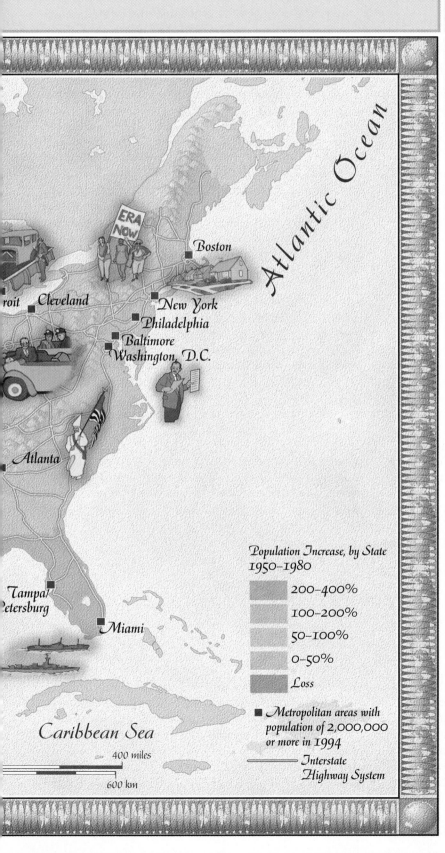

32

Chapter Outline

Key Topics

❖ Changes in immigration policy and the resulting new wave of immigration from Latin America, the Caribbean, and Asia after 1965
❖ The effect of global competition on the U.S. economy
❖ The shift from the Rustbelt to the Sunbelt
❖ The changing role of women
❖ The culture wars

*I*n June 1992, Hiroshi Yamauchi paid $100 million for a controlling interest in the Seattle Mariners baseball team, using a fortune acquired as head of American-based but Japanese-owned Nintendo America. The purchase of the M's demonstrated the growing international dimension of American society. So did other aspects of professional baseball, such as the prominence of players from Latin America, the 1993 World Series victory of Canada's Toronto Blue Jays, and a Baltimore Orioles exhibition game in Havana in 1999, and major league games played in Japan in 2000.

Globalization is not the only way that baseball has responded to changes in the United States. Starting in 1958, when the New York Giants moved to San Francisco and the Brooklyn Dodgers to Los Angeles, the big leagues followed population and business southward and westward, adding teams in cities such as San Diego, Atlanta, and Miami to balance old factory towns like Milwaukee and Detroit. In 1994–1995, a long players' strike mirrored renewed labor–management battles in other industries. Baltimore, Cleveland, San Francisco, and Denver joined the national shift from manufacturing to service employment by leveling old warehouses and factories to build downtown stadiums that could boost tourism and convention business.

Baseball's new look was part of a broad transformation of American society after 1965. After twenty years of relative social and economic stability, seeds of change that were sown in the Eisenhower and Kennedy years began to blossom. Just as the nation entered a decade of political turmoil, Americans reopened basic questions about their personal lives and communities. Who constituted the American people? What were the best ways to earn a living and the preferred places to live? Where could individuals find a sense of reassurance in troubled times? The answers were different by the 1980s and 1990s than they had been in the 1950s; the new voices and ideas were unsettling, but they were also proof of the strength of American democracy.

A globalizing economy was one powerful engine of change. As leader of the Western nations, the United States opened itself to a world developing beyond American control. Immigration reshaped and revitalized cities. Foreign competition accelerated the transition from old industries to new. One effect was to decentralize the United States: Central cities declined relative to their suburbs; the Northeast declined relative to the South and West; mass-production manufacturing declined relative to competitors in Asia and Latin America.

Americans also explored new ways to find their identity as individuals and members of groups. The outcome of such profound questioning was decentering—an erosion of the unspoken assumption that tight, white, middle-class families were the national norm. Growing immigration made the benefits and perils of a multicultural society a topic of concern. As the new economy made it difficult for a single wage earner to support a family, individuals increasingly defined themselves not only as fathers, mothers, and children but also by age group, gender, and sexual orientation. Millions of Americans followed old or new avenues to spiritual assurance and a sense of community, generating conflicts over cultural values that entered the political arena as battles over affirmative action, abortion, or religion in the schools.

A Globalized America

In the years after 1965, the United States reacquainted itself with the world. Nineteenth-century America depended on Europe for immigrants, investment capital, and markets for raw materials, only to turn a cold shoulder to much of the world through high tariffs and immigration restrictions after World War I. Since 1965, however, the United States has built new international connections at every level from the corporate to the personal.

A few examples show the extent of the change. Foreign tourism became big business, exploding from a few hundred thousand annual visitors from outside North America in the 1950s to 20 million a year in the mid-1990s. Thousands of cities

Costumed dancers celebrate during Carnaval Miami along Calle Ocho, or Eighth Street. The two-week celebration of Hispanic culture includes parades and open air performances. The event is typical of the revival of ethnic community culture with the new immigration of the late twentieth century.

and towns now maintain "sister city" exchanges with communities around the globe. Governors and mayors jet off to Seoul and Shanghai on development junkets. Foreign involvement in the U.S. economy benefits New York and San Francisco but also such unexpected places as Greenville and Spartanburg, South Carolina, deeply American communities where the chamber of commerce rolls out the red carpet for German executives and forty thousand residents work for European corporations.

New Americans

Few Americans anticipated the effects of the **Immigration and Nationality Act of 1965**. The new law initiated a change in the composition of the American people by abolishing the national quota system in effect since 1924. Quotas had favored immigrants from western Europe and limited those from other parts of the world. The old law's racial bias contradicted the self-proclaimed role of the United States as a defender of freedom, making immigration reform an episode in the propaganda battles of the Cold War. The new law gave preference to family reunification and welcomed immigrants from all nations equally. The United States also accepted refugees from communism outside the annual limits.

Immigration reform opened the doors to Mediterranean Europe, Latin America, and Asia. Legal migration to the United States surged from 1.1 million in 1960–1964 to nearly 4 million in 1990–1994.

Nonlegal immigrants may have doubled the total number of newcomers in the 1970s and early 1980s. Not since World War I had the United States absorbed so many new residents from other countries. By the early 1990s, legal immigration accounted for 37 percent of all American population growth, compared with 10 percent before 1965. Meanwhile, over 2 million nonlegal immigrants had taken advantage of the **Immigration Reform and Control Act of 1986** to legalize their presence in the United States.

Immigration changed the nation's ethnic mix. Members of officially defined ethnic and racial minorities accounted for one out of every four Americans in 1990. Roughly 20 million Americans had been born in other countries. Asians and Hispanics were the fastest-growing groups. Hispanics are likely to pass African Americans as the largest minority in a decade or two (see Table 32-1).

New immigrant groups did not distribute themselves evenly across American states and regions (see Map 32-1). Most Mexican immigrants moved to the states adjacent to Mexico. The East Coast has meanwhile welcomed migrants from the West Indies and Central America. Many Puerto Ricans, who hold U.S. citizenship, came to Philadelphia and New York in the 1950s and 1960s. The 110th Street subway station in East Harlem marked the center of *El Barrio de Nueva York* for that city's 600,000 Puerto Ricans. Other countries sending large numbers of immigrants include Haiti, the Dominican Republic, Guatemala, Honduras, Nicaragua, El Salvador, and Jamaica. Many immigrants have come as tourists and stayed to live and work in the anonymity of large cities.

In contrast to Puerto Ricans and Mexicans, who can easily travel back and forth between their old and new homes, Cubans have been one-way migrants. Fidel Castro's Cuban revolution pushed 250,000 Cuban businessmen, white-collar workers, and their families to the United States. As many as six planeloads a day touched down in Miami from 1959 to 1962. Another round of "freedom flights" carried 150,000 Cubans to the United States from 1966 to 1973, and a third round added 125,000 in

TABLE 32.1	MAJOR RACIAL AND ETHNIC MINORITIES IN THE UNITED STATES			
	1960 Population (in millions)	Percentage of total	1990 Population (in millions)	Percentage of total
American Indians	.5	0.3	2.0	0.8
Asians and Pacific Islanders	1.1	0.6	7.3	2.9
African Americans	18.9	10.5	30.0	12.1
Hispanics	not available		22.4	9.0

1980. Virtually all Cubans settled in Florida or in major cities, such as New York and Chicago.

Another great immigration has occurred eastward across the Pacific. Chinese, Filipinos, Koreans, Samoans, and other Asians and Pacific Islanders constituted only 6 percent of newcomers to the United States in 1965 but nearly half of all arrivals in 1990.

The numbers of ethnic Chinese in the United States jumped from a quarter of a million in 1965 to 1,645,000 in 1990. Immigrants from Taiwan, Hong Kong, and the People's Republic created new Chinatowns in Houston and San Diego and crowded into the historic Chinatowns of New York and San Francisco. Social and economic divisions appeared between upwardly mobile and assimilating students and professionals, Chinatown businessmen, and isolated immigrant workers in sweatshops and service jobs.

The most publicized Asian immigrants were refugees from Indochina after communist victories in 1975. The first arrivals tended to be highly educated professionals who had worked with the Americans. Another 750,000 Vietnamese, Laotians, and Cambodians arrived after 1976 by way of refugee camps in Thailand. Most settled on the West Coast. The San Francisco Bay area, for example, had more than a dozen Vietnamese-language newspapers, magazines, and cable television programs.

The United States has provided economic opportunity for millions of newcomers. More than half the Cuban households in Miami are homeowners. The 130,000 Vietnamese immigrants of 1975 now have an average adjusted income above the national average. Asians in the early 1980s constituted 20 percent of the students in California's public universities and were moving into the professions. Many black West Indians, Asians, and second-generation Mexicans are now comfortable members of the middle class (see "American Views: Growing Up Mexican American").

The new immigration spread entrepreneurial talent and ambition throughout the country. Like earlier European immigrants, many newcomers have opened groceries, restaurants, and other businesses that serve their own group before expanding into larger markets. Juan Fernandez found it easier to set up a successful car repair shop in Gary, Indiana, than in Guadalajara, Mexico, because his fellow immigrants prefer a Spanish-speaking mechanic. Asian-born business owners have filled retail vacuums in central city neighborhoods abandoned by chain stores. One Korean told a typical story: "A friend of mine came over with his family. He invested a few dollars in a vegetable stand in downtown Manhattan. He and his sons got up early, went to the market early. . . . He took some of his earnings and invested in a candy store. Then he bought two more vegetable and fruit stands. . . . Their kids work hard too and they make a lot of money."

In the World Market

Expanding foreign commerce became a deliberate goal of national policy with the **General Agreement on Tariffs and Trade (GATT)** in 1947. GATT regularized international commerce after World War II and helped ensure that world markets remained open to American industry. The Trade Expansion Act in 1962 authorized President Kennedy to make reciprocal trade agreements to cut tariffs by up to 50 percent to keep American companies competitive in the new European Common Market. Although both measures were aimed at trade with Europe, they also helped expand American commerce across the Pacific.

The value of American imports and exports more than doubled from 7 percent of the gross domestic product in 1965 to 16 percent in 1990—the largest percentage since World War I. Americans in the 1970s began to worry about a "colonial" status in which the United States exported food, lumber, and

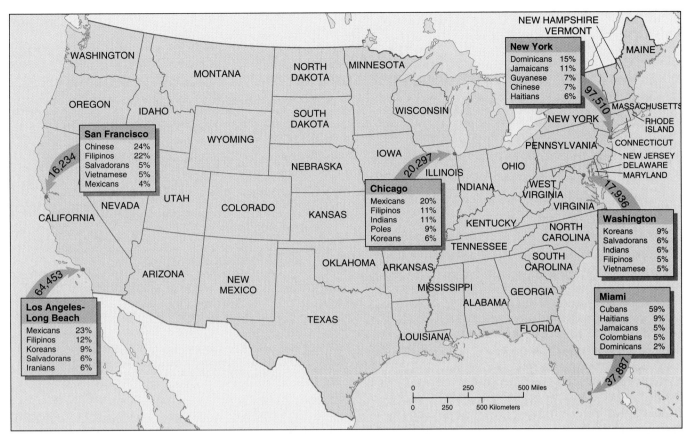

Map 32-1   *Sources of Immigrants to Six Major Metropolitan Areas in 1987*
Immigrants to the United States in the 1980s and 1990s largely settled in large cities. This map shows the sources of immigrants to six major metropolitan areas for a typical year. Immigrants tend to settle in cities that are convenient to their homelands and already have large communities from the same country. Note the contrast between San Francisco's attractiveness for Asian immigrants and Miami's popularity with immigrants from the Caribbean nations.

Data Source: Ruben Rumbaut and Alejandro Portes, Immigrant America, 1990.

minerals and imported automobiles and television sets. By the 1980s, foreign economic competitiveness and trade deficits, especially with Japan, became issues of national concern.

The effects of international competition were more complex than "Japan-bashers" acknowledged. Mass-production industries, such as textiles and aluminum, suffered from cheaper and sometimes higher-quality imports, but many specialized industries and services—such as Houston's oil equipment and exploration firms—thrived. Globalization also created new regional winners and losers. In 1982, the United States began to do more business with Pacific nations than with Europe.

More recent steps to expand the global reach of the American economy were the **North American Free Trade Agreement (NAFTA)** in 1993 and a new worldwide GATT approved in 1994. Negotiated by Republican George Bush and pushed through Congress

in 1993 by Democratic Bill Clinton, NAFTA combined 25 million Canadians, 90 million Mexicans, and 250 million U.S. consumers in a single "common market" similar to that of western Europe. GATT cut tariffs among one hundred nations.

NAFTA revived the old debate between free traders and protectionists. Support was strongest from professional businesses and industries that sought foreign customers, including agriculture and electronics. Opponents included organized labor, communities already hit by industrial shutdowns, and environmentalists worried about lax regulations in Mexico. In contrast to the nineteenth-century arguments for protecting infant industries, new industries now looked to foreign markets, while older and uncompetitive firms hoped for protected domestic markets. Evidence from the early years favored NAFTA supporters, indicating that few manufacturing jobs relocated to Mexico.

CHRONOLOGY

1960 Birth control pill is marketed.

1962 *Baker* v. *Carr* establishes the principle of "one person, one vote" for creating state legislative districts.

1963 Betty Friedan publishes *The Feminine Mystique*.

1964 Beatles make first visit to the United States.

1965 Immigration reform eases immigration for Asians and Latin Americans.

1966 National Organization for Women is founded.

1969 Stonewall Inn riot opens era of gay militancy.

1971 Twenty-Sixth Amendment lowers the voting age to eighteen.

U.S. Supreme Court, in *Swann* v. *Charlotte-Mecklenburg Board of Education*, approves busing for racial integration of public schools.

Walt Disney World opens near Orlando, Florida.

1972 Equal Rights Amendment is sent to the states for ratification.

1973 *Roe* v. *Wade* decision expands abortion rights.

1975 Busing plan is implemented to integrate Boston public schools.

1978 People's Temple adherents commit mass suicide at Jonestown, Guyana.

1981 AIDS is recognized as new disease.

1982 Equal Rights Amendment fails to achieve ratification.

1986 Immigration Reform and Control Act regularizes illegal immigration.

1993 Branch Davidian followers die in flames at Waco, Texas.

North American Free Trade Agreement is ratified.

1996 *Romer* v. *Evans* overturns a Colorado constitutional amendment limiting the legal recourse of homosexuals against discrimination.

Old Gateways and New

The globalization of the United States had its most striking effects in coastal and border cities. New York again became the great mixing bowl of the American population. Between 1965 and 1980, it received a million legally recorded immigrants and between 500,000 and 750,000 illegal newcomers. By 1990, some 28 percent of the population of New York City was foreign-born, compared to 42 percent at the height of European immigration in 1910. Journalist Andy Logan described the new immigrants' impact by the early 1970s: "A third of the children now in the city's public schools are said to be the children of parents who were born in other countries. . . . Whole areas of the city, such as Washington Heights, in Manhattan, and Elmhurst, in Queens, would be half empty without the new arrivals." ZIP code 11373 in North Queens was reportedly the most diverse neighborhood in the world.

Just as important was the transformation of southern and western cities into gateways for immigrants from Latin America and Asia. Los Angeles emerged as "the new Ellis Island." As *Time* magazine put it in 1983, the arrival of more than 2 million immigrants in greater Los Angeles altered "the

collective beat and bop of L.A." In 1960, a mere 1 percent of the Los Angeles County population was Asian and 11 percent was Hispanic. By 1990, the figures for a population of 8.8 million were 11 percent Asian and 37 percent Hispanic. The sprawling neighborhoods of East Los Angeles make up the second-largest Mexican city in the world. New ethnic communities appeared in Los Angeles suburbs—Iranians in Beverly Hills, Chinese in Monterey Park, Japanese in Gardena, Thais in Hollywood, Samoans in Carson, Cambodians in Lakewood. A hundred languages are spoken among students entering Los Angeles schools.

New York and Los Angeles are world cities as well as immigrant destinations. Like London and Tokyo, they are capitals of world trade and finance, with international banks and headquarters of multinational corporations. They have the country's greatest concentrations of international lawyers, accounting firms, and business consultants. The deregulation of international finance and the explosive spread of instant electronic communication in the 1980s confirmed their importance as global decision centers.

Smaller international cities dot the southern border of the United States. Latin American connections have altered the character of Miami, where Hispanics now constitute nearly half of the metropolitan-area population. Cubans by the late 1970s owned about one-third of the area's retail stores and many of its other businesses. Access to the Caribbean and South America make Miami an international banking and commercial center with hundreds of offices for corporations engaged in U.S.–Latin American trade. Two million Latin American tourists and shoppers a year patronized its stores and hotels during the 1980s. Miami is the economic capital of the Caribbean.

Cross-border communities in the Southwest, such as El Paso, Texas, and Juarez, Mexico, or San Diego, California, and Tijuana, Mexico, are "Siamese twins joined at the cash register." Employees with work permits commute from Mexico to the United States. American popular culture flows southward. Bargain hunters and tourists pass in both directions. A shopping center near San Diego makes 60 percent of its sales to Mexicans. In the other direction, most of the signs for roadside attractions for two hours south from Tijuana read in English rather than Spanish.

Both nations have promoted the cross-border economy. The Mexican government in the mid-1960s began to encourage a "platform economy" by allowing companies on the Mexican side of the border to import components and inputs duty-free as long as 80 percent of the items were reexported and 90 percent of the workers were Mexicans. The intent is to encourage American corporations to locate assembly plants south of the border. Such factories can employ lower-wage workers and avoid strict antipollution laws (leading to serious threats to public health on both sides of the border). For Mexico, the so-called *maquila* industries were the second-largest earner of foreign exchange by 1990. From the Gulf of Mexico to the Pacific Ocean, eighteen hundred *maquiladora* plants employed half a million workers. North of the border, U.S. factories supplied components under laws that meshed with the Mexican regulations.

Ethnic Identity and Conflict

Despite its positive economic contributions, the new immigration revived old American racisms and created new racial tensions. It also continued the long-standing process by which immigrants coalesced and identified themselves as members of American ethnic groups.

Some of the deepest conflicts arose between old and new minorities. African Americans have resented special services for political refugees and ambitious immigrants who seem to be shoving their way to the head of the line for economic and political influence. In Miami, Cubans asserted political leverage at the perceived expense of African Americans, who consider Cubans part of the exploitative majority. Black people in every major city have resented Asian immigrant storekeepers who run convenience stores and markets in ghettos, often replacing Jewish retailers as the "middleman minority" between mainstream businesses and African-American and Latino customers. In the Los Angeles riots of 1992, angry black people targeted Korean and Vietnamese shops as symbols of economic discrimination.

White people in the 1980s expressed their own discomfort with the new immigration by moving. In the 1950s, they had fled the growing African-American populations of large cities for segregated suburbs. A generation later, they seemed to be fleeing concentrations of Asians and Hispanics by moving across state borders. Between 1985 and 1990, a net of 1 million white people left the high-immigrant states of New York, Illinois, and Texas. Hundreds of thousands of others left California for "whiter" states, such as Utah, Oregon, and Nevada. These moves may create a new regional pattern in which the ethnically diverse northeast, southeast, and southwest corners of the United States are out of sync with a racially homogeneous heartland.

A second reaction against the new immigration has been discrimination against Latinos. The Immigration Reform and Control Act requires employers to verify the citizenship or immigration status of their workers. Some employers stopped hiring anyone who looked or sounded Hispanic as a way to avoid illegal immigrants. The Immigration and Naturalization Service (INS) under the Reagan and Bush administrations (1981–1993) treated refugees from civil war in El Salvador and murderous dictatorships in Guatemala and Haiti as economic rather than political immigrants; they were denied political asylum and deported. Officials were more likely to grant legal entry to similarly motivated white immigrants from the Soviet Union.

The INS acted while Americans were arguing over the economic impact of illegal immigration. Advocates of tight borders assert that illegal immigrants take jobs away from legal residents and eat up public assistance. Many studies, however, find that illegal immigrants fill jobs that nobody else wants. Over the long run, high employment levels among immigrants mean that their tax contributions through sales taxes and Social Security taxes

American Views
GROWING UP MEXICAN AMERICAN

Three Americans of Mexican heritage—Richard Rodriguez, Dolores Huerta, and Ana Caballero—recall experiences during their school years that have shaped their identification with American culture and their sense of ethnic identity. Rodriguez grew up in Sacramento, the son of immigrants from Mexico who had found steady jobs. He entered school with limited English; his family spoke Spanish at home. He would become a professional writer and scholar. Huerta's family has lived in the United States for many generations. She grew up in Stockton, California, in the 1950s, became a Chicano activist in college, and served as vice president of the United Farm Workers. Here she recalls two formative experiences from her teens. Caballero's grandparents moved to El Paso in 1958; her father, César, became a successful professional as a library director at the University of Texas–El Paso. She was sixteen when the family was interviewed in the late 1980s.

❖ **How do the psychological pressures on new immigrants differ from those that affect Mexican-American families long established in the United States?**

❖ **Do differences between the stories of Dolores Huerta in the 1950s and Ana Caballero in the 1980s result from their different economic positions or from changes in American society?**

❖ **How does the ability to speak a second language, either English or Spanish, affect each person's sense of identity?**

❖ **What does "being Mexican" mean to each individual?**

Richard Rodriguez

When I first entered a classroom, [I was] able to understand some fifty stray English words. . . . Half a year passed. Unsmiling, ever watchful, my teachers noted my silence. They began to connect my behavior with the difficult progress my older brother and sister were having. Until one Saturday morning three nuns arrived at the house to talk to our parents. Stiffly, they sat on the blue living room sofa. . . . I overheard one voice gently wondering, "Do your children speak only Spanish at home, Mrs. Rodriguez? . . . Is it possible for you and your husband to encourage your children to practice their English when they are home?" Of course my parents complied. What would they not do for their children's well-being?

Again and again in the days following, increasingly angry, I was obliged to hear my mother and father: "Speak to us en ingles" . . . Only then did I determine to learn classroom English. Weeks after, it happened: One day in school I raised my

---

and payroll deductions more than pay for their use of welfare, food stamps, and unemployment benefits (which illegal immigrants are often afraid to claim for fear of calling attention to themselves). Nevertheless, high immigration can strain local government budgets even if it benefits the nation as a whole. Partly for this reason, 60 percent of California voters approved Proposition 187 in 1994, cutting off access to state-funded public education and health care for illegal immigrants. The mostly white

supporters of the measure said it was about following the rules; Hispanic opponents saw it as racism.

In struggling for their place in American society, immigrants have added new panethnic identities to their national identities. In the nineteenth century, English-speaking Americans looked at European immigrants from widely separated regions and backgrounds and saw "Italians" or "Jews." In turn, newcomers found economic and political strength by making common cause across their differences, molding identities as

hand to volunteer an answer. I spoke out in a loud voice. And I did not think it remarkable when the entire class understood. . . . At last, seven years old, I came to believe what had been technically true since my birth: I was an American citizen.

Dolores Huerta

When I got to high school, then it was really segregated. There was the real rich and the real poor. We were poor too, and I got hit with a lot of racial discrimination. . . . I got straight A's in all of my compositions. . . . But the teacher told me at the end of the year she couldn't give me an A because she knew that somebody else was writing my papers for me. That really discouraged me, because I used to stay up all night and think, and try to make every paper different, and try to put words in there that I thought were nice. Well, it just kind of crushed me. . . .

I was the only Chicano at Stockton Junior College. . . . I was frustrated . . . because I seemed to be out of step with everybody and everything. You're trying to go to school and yet you see all of these injustices. . . .

Then my mother took me to Mexico City when I was about seventeen. She had never been there either. It was our first trip. But that opened my eyes to the fact that there was nothing wrong with Chicanos.

Ana Caballero and her father, César

Ana: Most of the kids in my high school are Anglo. I'm the only Mexican-American girl on my cheerleading team. I'm the only cheerleader with black hair. . . . There's a lot of competition within the school, but other kids accept me for who I am rather than for my background or nationality.

César: Busing had a lot to do with that. Ana was involved in one of the last phases of court-ordered integration of the schools. . . . There was some tension. But as time moved on, busing has worked really well. . . .

Ana: When I moved to this neighborhood, I felt strange getting started. My first day in fifth grade in the new school, it seemed so different. Not only because they were new kids, but the way they talked. There were so many blondes! Then, when I began to get used to everyone, I was bused to a new school. There were a lot of blondes there, too. But they were the children of doctors and the rich. The way they looked down on certain styles was very upsetting for me. After seventh grade, I started to fit in with them. I became more relaxed. There are a few kids who come from Mexico, so I get to speak some Spanish. . . . I don't speak Spanish as fluently as I should. I'm studying Spanish in school now, because I don't write it well. I was born here, but I'll always feel part Mexican. . . . I think I'll always have a little of both cultures.

ethnic groups within the U.S. context. Along with Native Americans, newer immigrants have gone through a parallel process. Hispanic activists revived the term *Chicano* to bridge the gap between recent Mexican immigrants and Latinos whose families had settled in the Southwest before American conquest in 1848. Great gaps of experience and culture separate Chinese, Koreans, Filipinos, and Vietnamese, but they gain political recognition and influence if they deal with other Americans as "Asians."

Making a Living

The American economy after 1965 told two stories. Fast-growing "sunrise industries" shouldered aside declining industries making obsolete products. Booming southern and western states stood next to shell-shocked industrial states full of padlocked factories and double-digit unemployment (see Figure 32-1). Yuppies with MBAs steered their BMWs along the fast lane to success while displaced mill

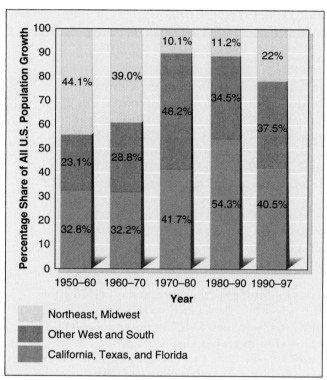

Figure 32-1   Regional Patterns in American Growth
The regional balance of American growth shifted substantially from the 1950s to the 1980s. The figures reflect the national "tilt" toward the South and West as a result of immigration, defense spending, and new industries such as electronics.

hands drove battered pickups along potholed roads to nowhere.

Communities divided between white-collar and working-class worlds. Teenagers in Hamilton, Ohio, recognized the social chasm. On one side were kids with new cars and cashmere sweaters, on the other the girls who planned to be beauticians and the boys who expected to work in the plant. One young woman described the country club set: "The girls act like they don't know you if you're not one of them. You don't have their clothes, you're not in their college prep classes, and you better not go out with their brothers. . . . Not one of my ten best friends is going to college."

The winners and losers among industries and the class division between workers and managers were tied to the U.S. role in the world. The need to project an American military presence around the world fueled a prosperous defense economy. Foreign competitors undercut established industries, but markets abroad helped high-end service industries, such as engineering and professional consulting.

The Defense Economy

The Vietnam buildup and reinvestment in the military during the Carter (1977–1981) and Reagan (1981–1989) administrations made the defense budget one of the most direct paths to prosperity. Over the forty years from the Korean conflict to the **Persian Gulf War**, the United States made itself the mightiest military power ever known. Military bases and defense contractors remolded the economic landscape, as mild winters and clear skies for training and operations helped the South and West attract more than 75 percent of military payrolls (see Map 32-2).

Defense dependents included big cities and small. Southern California thrived on 500,000 jobs in the aircraft industry (the 1967 figure). Lockheed's huge Burbank plant drew thousands of families to the San Fernando Valley; McDonnell-Douglas shaped the area around Los Angeles International Airport. Twelve thousand smaller firms and a third of the area's jobs depended on defense spending. Visitors to Colorado Springs could drive past sprawling Fort Carson and visit the new Air Force Academy, opened in 1958. Sunk deep from view was the North American Air Defense command post beneath Cheyenne Mountain. Malmstrom Air Force Base transformed Great Falls, Montana, into a coordinating center for Minuteman missiles targeted at Moscow and Beijing. Dark blue Air Force vans carried crews from Great Falls to missile sites dotted over a swath of rolling plains as vast as Maryland.

Besides the men and women in uniform, defense employed 4 million civilians through federal agencies and military contractors by the late 1960s. The aggregate impact on metropolitan areas can be calculated by subtracting the taxes that go for defense from the amount spent in each area for military payrolls and supplies. Approximately two-thirds of American metropolitan areas came up losers and one-third winners in the late 1970s. The ten biggest gainers included only two in the old industrial belt, compared to eight in the South and West.

Defense spending underwrote the expansion of American science and technology. Nearly one-third of all engineers worked on military projects. Large universities, such as MIT, Michigan, Cal Tech, and Stanford, were leading defense contractors. The modern electronics business started in Boston and the San Francisco Bay Area with research and development for military uses, such as guided-missile controls. The space component of the aerospace industry was equally reliant on the defense economy, with NASA spending justified by competition with the USSR. NASA's centers of gravity were scattered across

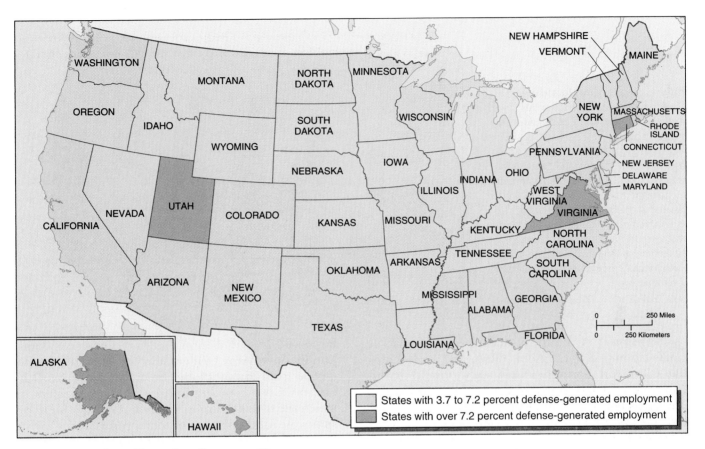

Map 32-2 *Defense Dependent States, 1968*
The federal defense budget benefited primarily the states of the South and West, helping to fuel the sunbelt boom. This map shows the twenty-one states (and Washington, D.C.) where defense-generated employment exceeded the national average of 3.6 percent of the civilian work force.

Data Source: Statistical Abstract of the United States, 1970.

the South—launch facilities at Cape Canaveral, Florida, research labs at Huntsville, Alabama; and Houston's Manned Spacecraft Center, itself the product of an alliance among Texas politicians, Rice University, and Houston corporations.

Deindustrialization

Here's how novelist John Updike described the fictional city of Brewer, Pennsylvania, at the start of the 1970s:

> Railroads and coal made Brewer. Everywhere in this city, once the fourth largest in Pennsylvania but now slipped to seventh, structures speak of expended energy. Great shapely stacks that have not issued smoke for half a century. . . . The old textile plants given over to discount clothing outlets teeming with a gimcrack cheer of banners FACTORY FAIR and slogans Where a Dollar Is Still a Dollar. . . . All this had been cast up in the last century by what now seem giants, in an explosion of iron and brick

still preserved intact in this city where the sole new buildings are funeral parlors and government offices.

Updike's Brewer is like dozens of specialized industrial cities that fell behind a changing economic world in the 1960s and 1970s. Industrial decay stalked "gritty cities" like Allentown, Pennsylvania; Trenton, New Jersey; and Gary, Indiana. Communities whose businesses and workers had made products in high volume for mass markets found that technological revolutions made them obsolete. When radial tires replaced bias-ply tires, Akron rubber workers paid the price. Merchants who replaced mechanical cash registers with electronic models left Dayton with block after block of outmoded factories. Asian steelmakers undercut the aging mills of Pittsburgh and Birmingham. Two dozen metropolitan areas lost population during the 1970s. Critics renamed the old manufacturing region of the Northeast and Middle West the **Rustbelt** in honor of its abandoned factories (see Figure 32-2).

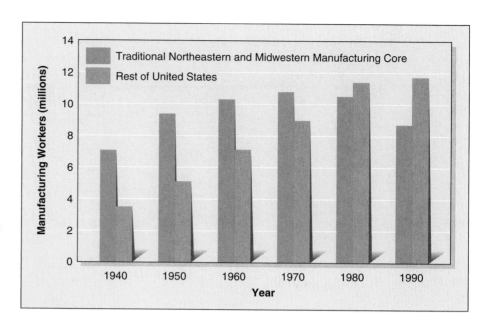

Figure 32-2   Manufacturing Employment in the Industrial Core and the Rest of the United States, 1940–1990
In 1940, the traditional manufacturing core of Northeastern and Midwestern states accounted for two-thirds of manufacturing workers; by 1990 it accounted for just over 40 percent. Although the majority of major corporate headquarters remained in New York and Chicago, cities such as Atlanta, Dallas, and Los Angeles had emerged as new centers of economic power.
Data Source: U.S. Bureau of the Census.

Stories of industrial decline were similar in small cities like Springfield, Ohio, and large cities like Cleveland. Springfield lost ten thousand manufacturing jobs and four thousand people during the 1970s, suffered unemployment of 17 percent, and needed $30 million in public subsidies to keep its largest factory going in 1982. Cleveland had built a century of prosperity on oil refining, steel, and metalworking; the metropolitan area had grown from 1.3 million in 1940 to 2.1 million in 1970. In the 1970s, however, it lost 165,000 people. As high-paying jobs in unionized industries disappeared, sagging income undermined small businesses and neighborhoods. Falling tax revenue brought the city to the verge of bankruptcy in 1978; bankers forced public service cuts and tax increases, which meant further job losses.

Plant closures were only one facet of nationwide efforts to increase productivity by substituting machinery for employees. Between 1947 and 1977, American steelmakers doubled output while cutting their work force from 600,000 to 400,000. Lumber companies used economic recession in the early 1980s to automate mills and rehired only a fraction of their workers when the economy picked up. White-collar industries like insurance computerized operations and farmed out routine work to part-time employees. In the late 1980s and early 1990s, corporations continued to downsize by firing managers who now had fewer workers to supervise.

Parallel to the decline of heavy industry was the continuing transformation of American agriculture from small, family enterprises to corporate "agribusinesses" (see Figure 32-3). The number of farms slid from 4 million in 1960 to just over 2 million in 1998. Many farmers sold out willingly, glad to escape from drudgery and financial insecurity. Others could not compete in an agricultural system in which the 600,000 largest farms and ranches were responsible for 94 percent of total production.

Fewer than 2 percent of all American workers now make their living from farming, down from 8 percent in 1960. Farmers in the Midwest suffered from a roller-coaster economy. Many overinvested in land and equipment when commodity prices climbed in the 1970s, only to be haunted with unpayable debts when prices slumped in the 1980s. Farm bankruptcies in Iowa reached levels unseen since the 1930s. Some family farmers found that they had to farm more acreage to stay competitive; individually owned wheat farms in the western states might total thousands of acres. Other farmers kept their land by working full time in factories and raising crops and livestock on the side.

Corporate farming substituted capital investment for labor in the time-tested manner of industrial maturity. Big farms were also the greatest beneficiaries of federal farm subsidy programs. The downside of corporate investment was excessive irrigation and massive use of pesticides and fertilizers. Wildlife was destroyed, groundwater was contaminated, underground water supplies were exhausted, and flowing streams, such as the lower Colorado River, were polluted with chemical-laden agricultural runoff.

Despite the despairing headlines, some older industries and their workers did find new roles in the sink-or-swim environment of technological and international competition. Buffalo, New York, lost much of its steel industry but retained smaller and more flexible factories making diverse products. The auto industry went through a similar cycle of crisis and response. Prosperity in the 1950s had led automobile executives to believe that they knew how to manipulate U.S. consumers. Booming imports of well-made Toyotas and Hondas and customer demand for smaller cars destroyed that complacency in the fuel-short 1970s. In response, Ford, Chrysler, and finally General Motors remade themselves on the Japanese model as lean and flexible manufacturers. They cast off old plants, workers, and executives, started over, often in new locations, and forced Japanese companies to shift production to U.S. localities and workers.

Sunrise Industries and Service Jobs

Concealed within the story of economic decline was a more complex narrative of changes in the demand for goods and services and adaptation to new markets and technologies. With its fierce competition, the capitalist economy involves what is sometimes called "creative destruction," in which new enterprises push aside inefficient and outmoded industries. After 1965, the pressures for change included both foreign competition and technological breakthroughs that opened new opportunities even while they undermined old industries.

The epitome of the "sunrise" economy was electronics. Employment in computer manufacturing rose in the mid-1960s. California's **Silicon Valley**, north of San Jose, took off with corporate spinoffs and civilian applications of military

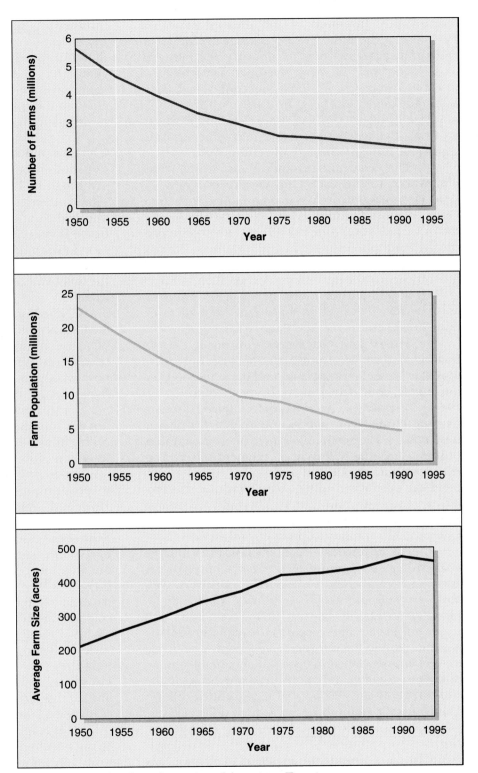

Figure 32-3   *The Transformation of American Farming*
Since 1950, American agriculture has been producing more and more food with fewer and fewer workers. As farm population and the number of farms have dropped, the average farm size has more than doubled. Large-scale agriculture has vastly increased the efficiency of farming at the expense of small family farms.

Data Source: Statistical Abstract of the United States, 1995.

technologies. Invention of the microprocessor in 1971 kicked the industry into high gear. The farmlands of Santa Clara County, California, became a "silicon landscape" of neat one-story factories and research campuses. In 1950, the county had eight hundred factory workers. In 1980, it had 264,000 manufacturing workers and three thousand electronics firms. Related hardware and microchip factories spread the industry through the entire West.

The electronic revolution was an important contributor to the rise of the service economy. As fewer Americans drove tractors and toiled on assembly lines, more became service workers. The service sector includes everyone not directly involved in producing and processing physical products. Service workers range from lawyers to hairstylists, from police officers to theater employees. In 1965, services already accounted for more than half of American jobs. By the 1990s, their share had risen to more than 70 percent.

Service jobs varied greatly in quality. At the bottom of the scale were minimum-wage jobs held mostly by women, immigrants, and the young—cleaning people, child care workers, hospital orderlies, and fast-food workers. These positions offered little in terms of advancement, job security, or benefits. In contrast, many of the best new jobs were in information industries. Teaching, research, government, advertising, mass communications, and professional consulting depend on producing and manipulating information. All of these fields have grown. They add to national wealth by creating and applying new ideas rather than by supplying standardized products and services.

The information economy flourishes in large cities with libraries, universities, research hospitals, advertising agencies, and corporate headquarters. New York's bankers and stockbrokers made Manhattan an island of prosperity in the 1980s. Pittsburgh, with major universities and corporate headquarters, made the transition to the information economy even while its steel industry failed. A good benchmark of a brain-powered economy is if more than a quarter of the adults (people aged 25 or over) have finished college. The District of Columbia, with its high-priced lawyers and lobbyists, ranked first in 1990 with 35 percent. Next was Massachusetts (28 percent), followed closely by California, Colorado, Connecticut, Maryland, New Jersey, Vermont, and Virginia.

The rise of the service economy had political consequences. Rapid expansion of jobs in state and local government triggered popular revolts against state taxes that started in 1978 with passage of California's Proposition 13, which limited property taxes, and continued into the 1990s. Another growth industry was health care. Spending on medical and health services amounted to 12 percent of the gross domestic product in 1990, up from 5 percent in 1960. The need to share this huge expense fairly was the motivation for Medicare and Medicaid in the 1960s and the search for a national health insurance program in the 1990s.

Crisis for Organized Labor

Organized labor counted a million fewer members in 1989 than in 1964, even though the number of employed Americans had nearly doubled. Many unions that had been the mainstays of the labor movement in the Roosevelt and Truman years found themselves in trouble, saddled with leaders who were unable to cope with change. The rank and file in unions like the Steel Workers and Mine Workers had to fight entrenched and unimaginative leadership. Ed Sadlowski, who lost a bid for the presidency of the United Steelworkers in 1976, thought he knew the problem: "The unions missed the boat by not taking unionism beyond the gates and into the community. . . . The pork choppers wanted to become 'part of' rather than 'change' the whole political and social system."

Meanwhile, corporations seized the opportunity for "union busting." They often demanded wage rollbacks and concessions on working conditions as trade-offs for continued employment, squeezing workers in one plant and then using the settlement to pressure another. Hanging over workers in the 1970s and 1980s was the threat that employers might move a factory to a new site elsewhere in the United States or overseas. Or a company might sell out to a new owner, who could close a plant and reopen without a union contract. The wave of corporate consolidations and mergers in the 1980s had especially damaging effects on the workplace. One sixteen-year-old described the changes in the grocery chain where her father worked for twenty-six years: "They're letting people go with no feelings for how long they've worked there, just lay 'em off. It's sad. He should be getting benefits after all these years and all the sacrifices he's made. Now they're almost ready to lay him off without a word."

Immigration, both legal and illegal, added to the numbers of nonunion workers. In the Southwest, for example, low-paid immigrants filled the workforces of the electronics and garment industries. People in Silicon Valley knew the electronics company Hewlett-Packard as "Little Vietnam" in the mid-1980s and Advanced Micro Devices as "Little Manila." By one estimate, two-thirds of the workers in the Los Angeles garment trade were undocumented immigrants. Most worked for small, nonunion firms in basements and storefronts, without health insurance or pensions.

Another cause for shrinking union membership was the overall decline of blue-collar jobs—from 36 percent of the American work force in 1960 to 25 percent in 1997. Unionization of white-collar workers made up only part of the loss from manufacturing. Unions were most successful recruiting government workers, such as police officers, teachers, and bus drivers. By the late 1980s, the American Federation of State, County, and Municipal Employees had twice the membership of the United Steel Workers. In the private sector, however, many white-collar jobs were in small firms and offices that were difficult to organize. In the 1990s, microcomputers and electronic communication allowed companies to create even greater barriers to unionization by turning many of their employees into part-timers or home-based workers paid by output rather than hours.

The union effort that best recaptured the crusading spirit of earlier generations and partly renewed the labor movement was the United Farm Workers, led by César Chávez. Committed to nonviolent action for social justice and to the labor movement, Chávez organized the UFW among Mexican-American farm workers in California in 1965. Their demands included better wages and safer working conditions, such as less exposure to pesticides. UFW Vice President Dolores Huerta spoke for the special needs of women who labored in the fields. Because farm workers were not covered by the National Labor Relations Act of 1935, the issue was whether farm owners would recognize the union as a bargaining agent and sign a contract. Chávez supplemented work stoppages with national boycotts against table grapes, lettuce, and certain brands of wine, making *la huelga* ("the strike") into *la causa* for urban liberals. Rival organizing by the Teamsters Union and the short attention span of the national public gradually undermined the UFW's initial success. Nevertheless, Chávez's dogged toughness and self-sacrifice gave both Chicanos and the country a new hero.

The Rise of the Sunbelt

The rise of the American Sunbelt in the 1970s and 1980s reflected the new economy. In contrast to troubled industrial cities in the Northeast and Midwest, journalists and scholars found headlong prosperity in cities like Orlando, Charlotte, Atlanta, Dallas, and Phoenix (see Map 32-3). Another example was Houston. Its sprawling and unplanned growth, business spinoffs from NASA, and purring air conditioners epitomized the booming metropolitan areas of the South and West. It was, said one reporter in 1976, "the place that scholars flock to for the purpose of seeing what modern civilization has wrought."

The westward and southward tilt dated to the mobilization for World War II, but it caught popular attention with the publication of Kevin Phillips's analysis *The Emerging Republican Majority* in 1969. Phillips described a region of conservative voting habits where Republicans might solidify their status as a majority party (a process that continued in the 1990s). National publications deluged the public with discussions of the Sunbelt's economic and demographic patterns, environmental problems, and impact on the national balance of power.

The Sunbelt benefited from each of the leading economic trends of the years since 1965: Asian and Latin American immigration, defense

Dolores Huerta and César Chávez confer at the 1973 convention of the United Farm Workers. Chávez and Huerta tried to build a union that welcomed workers of all ethnic backgrounds, but the UFW leaders were largely Hispanic, and the union took much of its symbolism from the Mexican heritage shared by most of its membership.

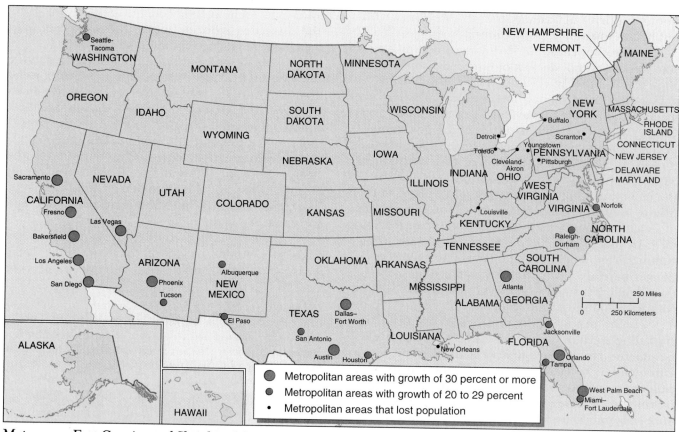

Map 32-3   *Fast-Growing and Shrinking Metropolitan Areas, 1980–1990*
In the 1980s, boom cities were found in the Southeast, Southwest, and on the West Coast. In contrast, seven of the nine large metropolitan areas that lost population were located on or near the Great Lakes, the region hit hardest by the decline of employment in established manufacturing industries.

spending, high-tech industries, and recreation and retirement spending that supported service employment. The South and Southwest also gained from industrial flight from the Northeast. Corporations that wanted to escape union contracts liked the business climate of the Sunbelt, which promised weak unions and low taxes. New factories dotted the southern landscape, often in smaller towns rather than cities. General Motors closed factories in Flint, Michigan, but invested in a new Saturn plant in Spring Hill, Tennessee.

California, Texas, and Florida anchored the Sunbelt. The common definition sets the regional boundary at the line of state borders that runs along the northern edges of North Carolina, Tennessee, Arkansas, Oklahoma, New Mexico, and Arizona with an extension to include greater Los Angeles. However, at least three other areas have shared the underlying patterns of economic change and metropolitan growth: the Pacific coast from Monterey, California, north to Seattle; the central Rocky Mountains of Colorado and Utah; and the Chesa-

peake Bay region. These areas enjoy at least two of the three big S's—sun, sea, and skiing.

However, economic shadows cooled parts of the Sunbelt in the 1980s and 1990s. Oil-producing Texas, Oklahoma, and the Rocky Mountain states felt severe recession from declining oil prices in the 1980s. California suffered from defense cutbacks before recovering in the 1990s. Despite the prosperity and global connections of cities like Atlanta, poverty in the rural South remained as bad as in northern slums. Despite the massive shifts of regional activity, in short, the United States remained a society of economic haves and have-nots, of fast-track cities and industries and places left by the wayside.

It was also increasingly decentered and decentralized. Driven in part by new industries, Pacific trade, and non-Atlantic migrations, the rise of the Sunbelt helped open an insular nation to a wider world and to broaden the cultural range subsumed by the word American. Sections of the South and West, historically controlled from the northeastern industrial core, developed as independent centers of

Seattle in the 1980s and 1990s prospered from the globalizing economy and the rise of the information industries. Only oldtimers noticed the disappearance of fish canneries and lumber mills. Taking their place were Boeing, which fueled an international travel revolution; Microsoft, which made Seattle a high-tech capital; and the many foreign companies that used Seattle's port for access to the U.S. market.

economic change. Income per capita in the South neared the national average in the mid-1990s, ending several generations when it was the poor cousin among American regions. In the 1990s, the region's economic power would be reflected in a conservative tone in both the Republican and Democratic parties and in the prominence of southern political leaders.

Cities and Suburbs

Between 1965 and 1990, the proportion of Americans living in metropolitan areas (large cities and their suburbs) rose from 66 percent to just under 80 percent. Despite social problems and racial riots, urban areas remained the centers of commerce and job creation in the fast-changing economy. New businesses benefit from cities' specialized manufacturers and wholesalers. Corporate executives, bankers, and attorneys depend on easy access to each other's expertise. The diverse urban labor force, including millions of immigrants, meet the employment needs of new and old businesses.

Urban growth itself stimulated the economy. As city officials rebuilt urban centers and new suburbs sprawled over surrounding farmland, the United States had to provide freeways, schools, shopping centers, and housing for 66 million new metropolitan residents. It was the equivalent of building an entire new Paris every three and a half years, a new Singapore every thirteen months.

This immense growth also meant decentralization of metropolitan areas that paralleled the re-

gional decentralization of the Sunbelt. Most of the new development pushed the suburban frontier further into open countryside, spreading people and their daily environments more and more thinly over the landscape. Like the Rustbelt in competition with the South and West, the old central cities had to fight to remain viable against the suburban tide.

Urban Crisis

In the confident years after World War II, big cities had an upbeat image. The typical movie with a New York setting opened with a shot of the towering Manhattan skyline and plunged into the bustling business or theater districts. By the 1970s, slums and squalid back streets dominated popular imagery. *The French Connection* (1971) followed a drug dealer from Fifth Avenue to empty and menacing warehouses. *Klute* (1971) and *Taxi Driver* (1976) took moviegoers through the twilight world of prostitution. *Blade Runner* (1982) showed a Los Angeles driven mad by corporate violence and social isolation. Television cop shows like *Hill Street Blues* (1981–1987) and *Miami Vice* (1984–1990) repeated the message that cities were places of random and frequent violence.

Popular entertainment reflected Americans' growing discomfort with their cities. The nation entered the 1960s with the assumption that urban problems were growing pains. Exploding metropolitan areas needed money for streets, schools, and sewers. Politicians viewed the difficulties of central cities as by-products of exuberant suburban growth, which left outmoded downtowns in need of physical redevelopment. In middecade, however, TV networks and newsmagazines began to run stories of the "Battlefield,

The movie Taxi Driver (1976), in which Jodie Foster played a young prostitute, showed a New York in which isolated individuals lived out desperate lives within failing communities. It reflected the pessimism with which many Americans regarded not only their cities but their larger society in the 1970s.

USA" and "Crisis in the Cities" type. The public heard that American cities were sinking under racial violence, crime, and unemployment.

Central cities had the double responsibility of helping immigrants adjust to a new country and caring for the domestic poor. Baltimore had 27 percent of the Maryland population in 1970 but 66 percent of the state's welfare recipients. Boston had 14 percent of the Massachusetts population but 32 percent of the welfare clients. Impoverished and often fragmented families needed schools that would serve as social work agencies as well as educational institutions. Poor people with no other access to health care treated city hospital emergency rooms as the family doctor.

Many urban problems were associated with the "second ghettos" created by the migration of 2.5 million African Americans from southern farms to northern and western cities in the 1950s and 1960s. At the start of World War II, black Americans had been much more rural than white Americans. By 1970, they were more urban. Fully one-third of all African Americans lived in the twelve largest cities, crowding into ghetto neighborhoods dating from World War I.

Postwar black migrants found systems of race relations that limited their access to decent housing, to the best schools, and to many unionized jobs. Many families also arrived just in time to face the consequences of industrial layoffs and plant closures in the 1970s and 1980s. Already unneeded in the South because of the mechanization of agriculture, the migrants found themselves equally unwanted in the industrial North, caught in decaying neighborhoods and victimized by crime.

The residential ghetto trapped African-American families who tried to follow the expectations of mainstream society. Because ghettos grew block by block, middle-class families had to pioneer as intruders into white neighborhoods and then see ghetto problems crowd in behind them. Their children faced the seductions of the street, which became increasingly violent with the spread of handguns and trade in illegal drugs. Successful African-American families began to flee to suburbs when fair housing laws slowly opened the real estate market, leaving ghettos with fewer middle-class leaders.

Central cities faced additional financial problems unrelated to poverty and race. Many of their roads, bridges, fire stations, and water mains were fifty to one hundred years old. By the 1960s and 1970s, they were wearing out. Closure of the elevated West Side Highway along the Hudson River in Manhattan after huge chunks fell out of the roadway symbolized a spreading urban problem. Decay of the urban infrastructure of utility and transportation systems was a by-product of market forces and public policy. Private developers often borrowed money saved through northeastern bank accounts, insurance policies, and pension funds to finance new construction in the Sunbelt. The defense budget pumped tax dollars from the old industrial cities into the South and West.

High local taxes in older cities were one result, for the American system of local government demands that cities—and the poor—help themselves. By the early 1970s, the average resident of a central city paid roughly twice the state and local taxes per $1,000 of income as the average suburbanite. As Mayor Moon Landrieu of New Orleans commented, "We've taxed everything that moves and everything that stands still; and if anything moves again, we tax that, too."

In part because of their need to increase the value of the real estate on which they collected property taxes, big-city leaders fought back by emphasizing the renewal of downtowns. Office construction booms in the late 1970s and again in the mid-1980s filled skylines with the tracery of steel skeletons and twenty-story cranes. An example of the strategy was Boston. From 1930 to 1960, the city's historic core had attracted virtually no private investment. One banker stated in 1957 that "no one can buy land within the city of Boston, put up an office building, and make money." In the 1960s, the city used urban renewal to level run-down blocks for a new city hall and office buildings. In the 1970s, redevelopment extended to the waterfront, where investors converted nineteenth-century wharves and huge granite warehouses into condominiums and restaurants. The historic Faneuil Hall market reopened in 1976 as an upscale "festival market" for tourists and suburbanites. A private building boom doubled downtown office space. Downtown Boston by 1980 was cramped, crowded, and confusing; it was also a diverse and lively mixture of old and new buildings, districts, and people.

Revitalized cities had clear winners and losers. Obvious beneficiaries were downtown property owners, retailers, metropolitan newspapers, and utilities with huge investments in facilities serving older parts of city. Revitalization also favored managers and professionals who could enjoy the attractions and convenience of strong downtowns. The same benefits largely bypassed men and women who lacked the education the information economy demanded. With fewer unskilled and semiskilled jobs available in manufacturing and construction, undereducated city people either tended the wants of the elite or did nothing. At its worst, the redeveloped city was a community of dangerous extremes, where enormous wealth contrasted with hopeless poverty. In New York, the real incomes of people on the lower third of the economic ladder declined during the 1980s, while those of the top 10 percent rose by 40 percent. Novelist Tom Wolfe fictionalized the cold statistics in his bestselling novel *The Bonfire of the Vanities* (1987), depicting a New York where the art dealers and stockbrokers of glitzy Manhattan meet the poor of the devastated South Bronx only through an automobile accident—to their mutual incomprehension and ruin.

Suburban America

Downtown revitalization ran against the tide of metropolitan sprawl. In the mid-1960s, the United States became a suburban nation. The 1970 census found more people living in the suburban counties of metropolitan areas (37 percent) than in central cities (31 percent) or in small towns and rural areas (31 percent). Just after World War II, most new suburbs had been bedroom communities that depended on the jobs, services, and shopping of central cities. By the late 1960s, suburbs were evolving into "outer cities" whose inhabitants had little need for the old central city. The *New York Times* in 1978 found that 40 percent of the residents of New York's Long Island and New Jersey suburbs visited the city fewer than three times a year, and most denied that they were part of the New York area.

One key to the changing character of the suburbs was a shift in their sources of population. In the first decades after the war, "white flight" described the hundreds of thousands of young families who left old walk-up apartments and row houses for bright new tract houses, distancing themselves from minority and racially changing neighborhoods. After the mid-1960s, however, new residents in a suburban ring typically moved from other suburbs and felt no personal connection to or responsibility for old city neighborhoods. For them, suburban malls and shopping strips were the new American Main Street and suburban communities the new Middle America.

Suburbs captured most new jobs. In the fifteen largest metropolitan areas, the number of central city jobs fell by 800,000 in the 1960s, while the number of suburban jobs rose by 3.2 million. The shift from rail to air for business travel accentuated suburban job growth. Sales representatives and executives could arrive at airports on the edge of town rather than railroad stations at the center and transact business without ever going downtown. The trend was first obvious at Chicago's O'Hare Airport in the 1960s; by the 1970s, every major airport had a fringe of hotels, office parks, and corporate offices.

Suburban rings gained a growing share of public facilities intended to serve the entire metropolitan area. As pioneered in California, community colleges served the suburban children of the baby boom. Many of the new four-year schools that state university systems added in the 1960s and early 1970s were also built for suburbanites, from George Mason University and the University of Maryland–Baltimore County in the Washington-Baltimore area to California State University campuses at Northridge and Fullerton. New sports complexes in the 1980s were as likely to be suburban as urban. The California Angels in baseball and New York Islanders in hockey gave suburban regions exclusive claims to their own major league sports franchises.

In the 1980s and 1990s, suburban retailing, employment, and services fused into so-called **edge cities**. Examples are the Galleria–Post Oak district in Houston and the Tysons Corner area in northern Virginia. Huge complexes of shopping malls, high-rise hotels, and glass-sided office buildings have far more space than old business districts in cities like Fort Wayne or Wichita. Even in edge cities, however, population remained more scattered than in older city neighborhoods. "I live in Garden Grove," one southern Californian reported, "work in Irvine, shop in Santa Ana, go to the dentist in Anaheim, . . . and used to be president of the League of Women Voters in Fullerton."

Suburbs and Politics

Suburban political power grew along with economic clout. In 1962, the Supreme Court handed down a landmark decision in the case of **Baker v. Carr**. Overturning laws that treated counties or other political subdivisions as the units to be represented in state legislatures, Baker required that legislative seats be apportioned on the basis of population. This principle of "one person, one vote" broke the stranglehold of rural counties on state governments, but the big beneficiaries were not older cities but fast-growing suburbs.

School integration controversies in the 1970s reinforced a tendency for suburbanites to separate themselves from city problems. In **Swann v. Charlotte-Mecklenburg Board of Education** (1971), the U.S. Supreme Court held that crosstown busing was an acceptable solution to de facto segregation that resulted from residential patterns within a single school district. When school officials around the country failed to achieve racial balance, federal judges ordered their own busing plans. Although integration through busing occurred peacefully in dozens of cities, many white people resented it. Working-class students who depended on public schools found themselves on the front lines of integration, while many middle-class families switched to private education. For many Americans, the image of busing for racial integration was fixed in 1975 when white citizens in Boston reacted with violence against black students who were bused to largely white high schools in the South Boston and Charlestown neighborhoods. The goal of equal opportunity clashed with equally strong values of neighborhood, community, and ethnic solidarity.

Because the Supreme Court also ruled that busing programs normally stopped at school district boundaries, suburbs with independent districts escaped school integration. One result was to make busing self-defeating, for it caused white families to move out of the integrating school district or to place their children in private academies, as happened frequently in the South. Busing also caused suburbanites to defend their political independence fiercely. In Denver, for example, a bitter debate lasted from 1969 until court-ordered busing in 1974. By-products included incorporation or expansion of several large

suburbs and a state constitutional amendment that blocked further expansion of the city boundaries (and thus of the Denver school district).

Zoning was another powerful tool of suburban self-defense. Restrictive building codes, requirements for large lots, and expensive subdivision fees could price all but the rich out of the local housing market. Many suburbs refused to allow apartments. The various limitations added up to snob zoning. As one Connecticut suburbanite put it, for a moderate-income family to hope to move into one of the state's most exclusive suburbs was "like going into Tiffany and demanding a ring for $12.50. Tiffany doesn't have any rings for $12.50. Well, Greenwich is like Tiffany."

Few suburbs, however, were so privileged. As continued decentralization pushed the suburban share of the U.S. population toward 50 percent in the 1990s, suburban areas displayed the full range of American society. Older suburbs struggled with the same economic problems as central cities, and their minority populations grew. Sprawling new suburbs imposed "urban" costs of traffic congestion and pollution on their residents. As these problems grew, it increasingly appeared that national politics was becoming suburban politics.

New Meanings for American Families

The political and social changes of the 1960s altered the patterns and meaning of family life. Americans began to rethink ideas about families and to emphasize personal identities in addition to traditional family roles. Women redefined themselves as individuals and workers as well as wives and mothers. Gays and lesbians asserted that their sexual orientations were not aberrations from "normal" family patterns but were valid in their own right. As average life spans lengthened, older Americans found personal satisfaction and political influence as members of their own communities and interest groups.

If one result of changing family patterns was new political groupings and new policies, another was deep confusion. In 1992, Vice President Dan Quayle earned headlines, and some derision, by criticizing the television comedy *Murphy Brown* for a positive and unrealistic portrayal of its lead character as a single mother. In the same year, however, opinion pollsters found strong disagreement about what counts as a family. A married couple living with their children was easy; 98 percent of Americans agreed that the label "family" was appropriate in that case. Less reassuring to Quayle was the 81 percent who also applied "family" to the *Murphy Brown* scenario of an unwed mother living with her child. More than a quarter were comfortable using "family" for two lesbian women or two gay men living together and raising children.

The Feminist Critique

The growing dissatisfaction of many women with the domestic role expected of them in the 1950s helped set the stage for a revived feminism. Important steps in this revival included the Presidential Commission on the status of women in 1961; the addition of gender was one of the categories protected by the Civil Rights Act of 1964 (see Chapter 30); and creation of the **National Organization for Women (NOW)** in 1966.

Mainstream feminism targeted unequal opportunity in the job market. Newspapers in the early 1960s segregated help-wanted ads by sex, listing "Girl Friday" jobs in one column and professional work in another. College-educated baby boomers encountered "glass ceilings" and job discrimination in which companies hired less qualified men who "needed the job" rather than more qualified women who supposedly did not. Throughout the 1970s, activists battled to open one job category after another to women who proved that they could indeed use tools, run computers, or pick stocks on Wall Street. They also battled for equal pay for everyone with equal qualifications and responsibilities.

Changes in sexual behavior paralleled efforts to equalize treatment in the workplace. More reliable methods of contraception, especially birth control pills introduced in the early 1960s, gave women greater control over childbearing. In some ways a replay of ideas from the 1920s, a new sexual revolution eroded the double standard that expected chastity of women but tolerated promiscuity among men. Starting in the 1960s, women began to catch up to men by acting as if marriage was not necessary to sanction sexual relations. One consequence was a singles culture that accepted sexual activity between unmarried men and women.

More radical versions of the feminist message came from women who had joined the civil rights and antiwar movements only to find themselves working the copy machine and coffee maker while men plotted strategy. Radicals caught the attention of the national media with a demonstration against the 1968 Miss America pageant. Protesters crowned a sheep as Miss America and encouraged women to make a statement by tossing their bras and makeup in the trash.

Women's liberation took off as a social and political movement in 1970 and 1971. Theoretical works that probed the roots of gender inequality commanded the attention of national reviewers. Women shared their stories and ideas in small "consciousness-raising sessions." *Ms.* magazine gave the movement a national voice in 1972. Within a few years, millions of women had recognized events and patterns in their lives as discrimination based on gender.

Women's Rights and Public Policy

Congress wrote key goals of the feminist movement into law in the early 1970s. Title IX of the Educational Amendments (1972) to the Civil Rights Act prohibited discrimination by sex in any educational program receiving federal aid. The most visible result was the expansion of athletic opportunities for women; another was a slow equalization in the balance of women and men in faculty positions. In the same year, Congress sent the **Equal Rights Amendment (ERA)** to the states for ratification. The amendment read, "Equal rights under the law shall not be denied or abridged by the United States or by any state on account of sex." More than twenty states ratified quickly in the first few months and another dozen after increasingly tough battles in state legislatures. The ERA then stalled, three states short, until the time limit for ratification expired in 1982.

In January 1973, the U.S. Supreme Court expanded the debate about women's rights with the case of *Roe v. Wade*. Voting 7 to 2, the Court struck down state laws forbidding abortion in the first three months of pregnancy and set guidelines for abortion during the remaining months. Drawing on the earlier decision of *Griswold* v. *Connecticut*, which dealt with access to information about birth control, the justices held that the Fourteenth Amendment includes a right to privacy that blocks states from interfering with a woman's right to terminate a pregnancy. In later decisions, the court upheld congressional limitations on the use of federal funds for abortion in *Webster* v. *Reproductive Health Services* (1989) and allowed some state restrictions in *Planned Parenthood* v. *Casey* (1992). Nevertheless, the Roe decision remained in place.

The feminist movement and specific policy measures related to it put equal rights and the fight against sexism (a word no one knew before 1965) on the national agenda and gradually changed how Americans thought about the relationships between men and women. Feminists focused attention on rape as a crime of violence, calling attention to the burdens the legal system placed on rape victims. In the 1980s and 1990s, they also challenged sexual harassment in the workplace, gradually refining the boundaries between acceptable and unacceptable behavior.

These changes came in the context of increasingly sharp conflict over the feminist agenda. Both the ERA and *Roe* stirred impassioned support and equally

Ms. magazine published its first issue in 1972. Edited by Gloria Steinem, the magazine attempted to bring a radical feminist message to a wide audience. Ms. emphasized the need for women to have equal access with men to education, health care, and employment and tried to help Americans rethink traditional gender roles.

passionate opposition. Opponents of the ERA worried about unisex restrooms (not a problem on commercial airliners) and women in the military (not a problem in the Persian Gulf War). Behind the rhetoric were male fears of increased job competition during a time of economic contraction and concern about changing families. Also fueling the debate was a deep split between the mainstream feminist view of women as fully equal individuals and the contrary belief that women had a special role as anchors of families, an updating of the nineteenth-century idea of separate spheres. The debate about abortion drew on the same issue of women's relationship to families but also tapped such deep emotion that the two sides could not even agree on a common language, juxtaposing a right to life against rights to privacy and freedom of choice.

Women in the Labor Force, Women in Poverty

The most sweeping change in the lives of American women did not come from federal legislation or court cases but from the growing likelihood that a woman would work outside the home. In 1960, some 32 percent of married women were in the labor force; thirty-five years later, 62 percent were working or looking for work (along with 67 percent of single women) Federal and state governments slowly responded to the changing demands of work and family with new policies such as a federal child care tax credit.

One reason for more working women was inflation in the 1970s and declining wages in the 1980s, both of which eroded the ability of families to live comfortable lives on one income. Between 1979 and 1986, fully 80 percent of married households saw the husband's income fall in constant dollars. The result, headlined the *Wall Street Journal* in 1994: "More Women Take Low-Wage Jobs Just So Their Families Can Get By." One young woman juggled community college courses and full-time work as an insurance company clerk, earning more than her husband brought home as a heavy equipment operator. Another worked at the drive-up window of a shopping center bank and cleaned offices on Saturdays to help pay the mortgage on a house purchased before her husband's employer imposed pay cuts.

A second reason for the increase in working women from 29 million in 1970 to 64 million in 1998 was the broad shift from manufacturing to service jobs, reducing demand for factory workers and manual laborers and increasing the need for "women's jobs" like data entry clerks, reservation agents, and nurses. Indeed, the American economy still divides job categories by sex. There was some movement toward gender-neutral hiring in the 1970s because of legal changes and the pressures of the women's movement. Women's share of lawyers more than quadrupled, of economists more than tripled, and of police detectives more than doubled. Nevertheless, job types were more segregated by sex than by race in the early 1990s.

Nor could most women, even those working full time, expect to earn as much as men. In the 1960s and 1970s, the average workingwoman earned just 60 percent of the earnings of the average man (see Figure 32-4). Only part of the wage gap could be explained by measurable factors, such as education or experience. The gap narrowed in the 1980s, with women's earnings rising to 73 percent of men's by 1998. About half of the change was the result of bad news, namely, a decline of earnings among men as high-wage factory jobs disappeared. The other half was the positive result of better-educated younger women finding better jobs. Indeed, women took 57 percent of the four-year college degrees awarded in 1995 (up from 38 percent in 1960) and 41 percent of first professional degrees (up from 3 percent).

Despite gains at the top, the low earning capacity of women with limited educations meant that

FROM THEN TO NOW

Women and Work in American Offices

At the end of the twentieth century, women filled the majority of America's office-based jobs. More women than men worked as office managers, receptionists, library administrators, bank tellers, travel agents, administrative assistants, insurance agents, bookkeepers, and other desk-and-computer occupations.

In 1997, women made up 46 percent of the American labor force. Seven out of ten of these women worked in professional, managerial, technical, administrative support, and sales positions. They ranged from corporate CEOs and college professors to clerks in state motor vehicle offices and the voices that take your orders and reservations when you dial 800.

This employment pattern, which most Americans now take for granted, is the product of 140 years of gradual change that began with, and was triggered by, the Civil War. Before the Civil War, American women found employment as domestic servants, sometimes as mill operatives, and increasingly as schoolteachers, but not as office workers. Clerks were men—sometimes settled into lower-status white-collar careers and sometimes learning a business from the inside before rising into management. Their jobs consisted of copying letters and documents by hand, tracing orders and correspondence, and keeping financial records.

The Civil War, however, sharply increased the flow of government paperwork while diverting young men into military service. The U.S. Treasury Department in Washington responded in 1862 by hiring women to sort and package federal bonds and currency. Treasury officials fretted about the moral implications of mixing men and women in offices but overcame these concerns when they found that women were both cheap and reliable workers. By 1870, several hundred women worked in Washington's federal offices, enough for a character in a novel about the Hayes administration (1877–1881) to comment that he could learn from a glance to "single out the young woman who supported her family upon her salary, and the young woman who bought her ribbons with it; the widow who fed half-a-dozen children."

As the national economy grew in the late nineteenth century, it generated ever-increasing flows of information. New technologies such as telephones and typewriters routinized clerical work. These trends increased the need for desk workers, a need largely filled by middle-class women, whose literacy was often guaranteed by the high school diplomas that went disproportionately to women in the later nineteenth century. As women workers filled new downtown skyscrapers, the central districts of large cities lost some of their rough edges and grew more respectable as centers of shopping and entertainment.

By 1900, the division of labor that would characterize the first half of the twentieth century was in place. Women comprised 76 percent of the nation's stenographers and typists and 29 percent of its cashiers, bookkeepers, and accountants. For the most part, however, they occupied the lower echelons of the office hierarchy. It was men who determined what was to be said; women who transcribed, transmitted, recorded, and filed their messages. Only in recent decades have women begun successfully to challenge that established order.

Women clerks at the U.S. Treasury Department sort through used greenbacks and check for counterfeit bills. When this picture was taken around 1890, four thousand women worked in federal offices in Washington, leading the way for the shift of most office work from men to women.

women were far more likely than men to be poor. Women constituted nearly two-thirds of poor adults at the end of the 1980s. Only 6 percent of married-couple households were below poverty level, but 32 percent of households headed by a woman without a husband present were poor. The feminization of poverty and American reliance on private support for child rearing also meant that children had a higher chance of living in poverty than adults and that poor American children were worse off than their peers in other advanced nations.

Coming Out

New militancy among gay men and lesbians drew on several of the social changes of the late 1960s. Willingness to talk about nonstandard sexual behavior was part of a change in public values. Tactics of political pressure came from the antiwar and civil rights movements. The timing, with a series of key events from 1969 to 1974, coincided with that of women's liberation.

Gay activism spread from the biggest cities to smaller communities, from the coasts to Middle America. New York police had long harassed gay bars and their customers. When police raided Manhattan's Stonewall Inn in June 1969, however, patrons fought back in a weekend of disorder. The "Stonewall rebel-

Figure 32-4   Median Salary of Women and Men, 1960–1998

Since the 1960s, the gap between the earnings of women and men working full time and year round has narrowed. One reason is better pay for jobs traditionally considered "women's work," but another has been the declining earning power of men without college educations. Nevertheless, the gender gap in earning power remains an important economic problem.

Data Source: Institute for Women's Policy Research.

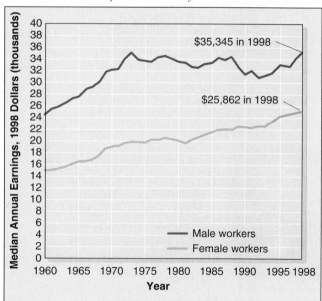

lion" was a catalyst for homosexuals to assert themselves as a political force. San Francisco also became a center of gay life. Its large homosexual community dated to World War II, when gays discharged from the armed forces in the Pacific theater were processed out through San Francisco. Openly gay poets and artists were prominent in the city's avant-garde circles. By the late 1970s, the city had more than three hundred business and social gathering places identified as gay and lesbian.

With New Yorkers and San Franciscans as examples, more and more gay men and lesbians "came out," or went public about their sexual orientation. They published newspapers, organized churches, and lobbied politicians. They staged "gay pride" days and marches. In 1974, the American Psychiatric Association eliminated homosexuality from its official list of mental disorders.

The character of life in gay communities took an abrupt turn in the 1980s when the worldwide **AIDS** epidemic began to have an impact on the United States. Scientists first identified a new disease pattern, acquired immune deficiency syndrome, in 1981. The name described the symptoms resulting from the human immunodeficiency virus (HIV), which destroys the body's ability to resist disease. HIV is transferred through blood and semen. In the 1980s, the most frequent American victims were gay men or intravenous drug users. By the end of 1998, AIDS had been responsible for 411,000 deaths in the United States, and transmission to heterosexual women was increasing. The U.S. Centers for Disease Control and Prevention estimated forty thousand new cases of HIV infection in 1995, bringing the total close to 1 million. HIV infection had spread to every American community.

AIDS triggered many of the same intense emotions as polio. It struck people in their prime and gradually wasted their strength; by the early 1990s, it had become the leading cause of death for men aged 25 to 44. Because many gay men were estranged from their families, death from AIDS was often preceded by social isolation. The spread of the epidemic gave new ammunition to people opposed to homosexuality, who called the plague God's punishment. It inspired intense anger among gays who believed that straight society and government agencies were indifferent to their plight and had failed to fund sufficient research on vaccines and treatment, although spending rose substantially in the late 1980s and 1990s. The public health establishment stressed that the most effective preventive measures were changes in personal behavior.

The Graying of America

Between 1965 and 1990, the number of Americans aged sixty-five and over jumped from 18.2 million to 31.3 million. For the first time, most Americans could

The AIDS Quilt, displayed in Washington in October 1992, combined individual memorials to AIDS victims into a powerful community statement. The quilt project reminded Americans that AIDS had penetrated every American community.

expect to survive into old age. The "young old" are people in their sixties and early seventies who remain sharp, vigorous, and financially secure because of better private pensions, Social Security, and Medicare. The "old old" are people in their eighties and nineties who often require daily assistance. Their increasing numbers—9 million in 1998—have made older and retired Americans both a problem for American society and a force to reckon with.

Older Americans have become a powerful voice in public affairs. They tend to vote against local taxes but fight efforts to slow the growth of Social Security, even though growing numbers of the elderly are being supported by a relatively smaller proportion of working men and women. By the 1990s, observers noted increasing resentment among younger Americans, who fear that public policy is biased against the needs of men and women in their productive years. In turn, the elderly fiercely defend the programs of the 1960s and 1970s that have kept many of them from

poverty. Protecting Medicare and Social Security was one of the Democrats' best campaign issues in 1996 after Republicans suggested cuts in spending growth.

Retired Americans changed the social geography of the United States, moving steadily to attractive Sunbelt communities. Much growth in the South and Southwest has been financed by money earned in the Northeast and Midwest and transferred by retirees. Florida in the 1980s absorbed nearly 1 million new residents aged sixty or older. California, Arizona, Texas, the Carolinas, and the Ozark Mountains of Missouri and Arkansas have all attracted retirees.

Sunbelt developers invented age-segregated new towns in the 1960s as full-service environments for people aged fifty or older. The first Sun City opened south of Tampa and another near Phoenix in 1960. Close behind were several Leisure World communities in California. Sun City's physical characteristics and national advertising helped define retirement as a distinct stage of life offering "an unending treasure of perfect days, filled with interesting activities." Attractions included golf, clean air, low-maintenance housing, and an escape from urban minorities. On a smaller scale, thousands of small retirement developments, many church sponsored, offer apartments, assisted living, and health care.

Large or small, these unprecedented developments substitute organized services and voluntary association with other older people for traditional reliance on care within families. The result changed the balance of responsibility for elder care between families and the broader public. In 1968, more than two-middle aged children (aged forty to fifty-five) were available to care for every elderly person; twenty years later, there was fewer than one middle-aged child for each elderly person. With too many elders and not enough adult family members, the elderly increasingly rely on specially designed institutions and communities.

The Search for Spiritual Grounding

Americans picture mining frontiers as rip-roaring places where a handful of women hold the fort while the men work hard, drink deep, and carry on. Modern Grand Junction, Colorado, however, is far less exciting. Between 1980 and 1984, efforts to develop the oil shale resources of western Colorado pushed the population of Grand Junction from sixty thousand to eighty thousand. Hopes were high and money was easy, but there was also a boom in religion. Newcomers to

Grand Junction, a fast-changing city within a rapidly evolving society, searched for family stability and a sense of community by joining established congregations and organizing new churches. The telephone book in 1985 listed twenty-eight mainstream Protestant and Catholic churches, twenty-four Baptist churches (reflecting the Oklahoma and Texas roots of many oil workers), five more liberal churches (such as Unitarians and Bahais), and more than fifty Pentecostal, Bible, and Evangelical churches. Nearly a dozen Christian schools supplemented the public schools.

Grand Junction's religious bent is typical of the contemporary United States, where religion is prominent in daily lives, institutions, and public policy debates. Americans take their search for spiritual grounding much more seriously than citizens of other industrial nations. Roughly half of privately organized social activity (such as charity work) is church related. In the mid-1970s, 56 percent of Americans said that religion was "very important" to them, compared to only 27 percent of Europeans.

Spiritual searches have followed both the well-marked routes of established denominations and new paths through avant-garde philosophies and feel-good therapies. One pathway has led individuals to isolate themselves from the larger society in communities of fellow believers. Another route, strong among many evangelical Protestants, emphasizes the personal search for salvation and individual relationships with God. A third path leads believers to seek to remold American society in accord with their understanding of divine intention.

Communes and Cults

Self-isolating communes and cults represent a long heritage of American utopian communities. Out of the half-secular, half-spiritual vision of the counterculture came people who not only dropped out of mainstream institutions but also tried to drop into miniature societies built on new principles. Thousands of Americans in the late 1960s and 1970s formed "intentional communities" or "communes." Their members usually tried to combine individual freedom and spontaneity with cooperative living. Upper New England and the Southwest were commune country. The northern California coast and the Pacific Northwest were attractive because of their fine climate for growing marijuana. Rural communes usually located on marginal land too poor to support commercial farming; members pored over *The Whole Earth Catalog* (1968) to figure out how to live on the land.

A few communes followed coherent social theories, but most were free form. It is easy to make fun of them in retrospect, with their tepees, log cabins, and eccentric architecture. Children ended up with off-the-tent names like Catnip, Psyche Joy, and Hummingbird. Adults practiced odd combinations of vegetarianism, Asian religion, and campfire sing-alongs. Journalist Sara Davidson described one California commune in 1970:

> Women in long skirts and shawls, men in lace-up boots, coveralls, and patched jeans tied with pieces of rope, sitting on the grass playing banjos, guitars, lyres, wood flutes, dulcimers, and an accordion. . . . Nine-year-old Michelle is prancing around in a pink shawl and a floppy hat warbling "It's time for the feast." Nancy says, "The pickin's are sort of spare, because tomorrow is welfare day and everybody's broke." She carries from the outdoor wood stove pots of brown rice.

As the description implies, communes were artificial families, financed by inheritances, food stamps, and handicraft sales and suffered from the same inequality between men and women that was fueling the feminist revolt. Like natural families, they were emotional hothouses; most collapsed because their members had incompatible goals.

Similar to communes but far more organized were exotic religious communities. Following an American tradition, they have offered tightly knit group membership and absolute answers to basic questions of human life. One of the most successful has been the Holy Spirit Association for the Unification of World Christianity (Unification Church), which Sun Myung Moon brought from Korea to the United States in 1973. Converts ("Moonies") have never numbered more than a few tens of thousands, but Moon amassed a huge fortune and dabbled in conservative politics.

Americans usually hear about cults only if they clash with authorities or end in disaster. Most tragic was the case of Jim Jones, who founded the People's Temple in California on a program of social justice but became increasingly dictatorial and abusive. He moved nearly a thousand followers to Guyana in South America and violently resisted authorities' efforts to penetrate his walls of secrecy. A congressional investigation of abuses within the colony led to the murder of Congressman Leo Ryan and mass suicide by nine hundred of Jones's followers, who drank cyanide-laced punch on November 18, 1978. On a smaller scale was the 1993 siege and shootout at the Branch Davidian compound near Waco, Texas, when a raid and a seige by federal agents triggered a fire that killed dozens of cult members.

Personal Religion

"The sixties" opened Americans to new spiritual experiences. Many young people in their twenties and thirties had left conventional Christian churches but had not

OVERVIEW

RELIGION AND POLITICS

Americans in the 1980s and 1990s battled over abortion, the teaching of evolution, limits to artistic expression, and other social values. Much of the conflict in social expectations and political goals stems from opposing tendencies in religious belief: the traditional impulse versus the progressive impulse.

	The Traditional Impulse	**The Progressive Impulse**
Religious basis	Orthodox theology that relies on unchanging truths and moral traditions	Theology that reconciles belief with findings of science and respects multiple ways to know the divine
Subscribers	Evangelical and fundamentalist Protestants, Orthodox Jews, conservative Roman Catholics	Mainline and liberal Protestants, Conservative and Reform Jews, Roman Catholics influenced by changes introduced by the Second Vatican Council
Social assumption	Traditional family as the basic social unit	Acceptance of diverse groups and treatment of individuals as equal before God as basis for a just society
Moral imperative	Responsibility to order one's personal life in accord with religious teaching	Responsibility to heed scriptural calls to end inequality and social injustice
Political goals	Protection of opportunities for religious expression (such as prayer in schools), protection of rights of individual economic initiative, support for nuclear families	Strict separation of church and state, protection of individual freedom of expression and belief, assistance for the poor at home and abroad
Political technique	Grassroots organizing and campaigning	Legislative lobbying

lost their spiritual hunger. Some turned to Sufis, Zen Buddhists, Hare Khrishnas, and others who adapted Asian religious traditions for modern Americans. The counterculture softened and blended into human potential movements of the 1970s and **New Age** movements of the 1980s. The secular-minded could pursue a quest for fuller lives through vigorously marketed spiritual therapies like est and encounter groups. For understanding American culture, the particular answers are less important than the strength of the search for greater self-realization and spiritual meaning.

One important change in national religious life has been the continuing "Americanization" of the Roman Catholic church following the **Second Vatican Council** in 1965, in which church leaders sought to respond to postwar industrial society. In the United States, Roman Catholicism moved toward the center of American life, helped by the popularity

of John Kennedy and by worldly success that made Catholics the economic peers of Protestants. The tight connection between Catholicism and membership in particular immigrant communities gradually faded. Church practice lost some of its distinctiveness; celebrating Mass in English rather than Latin was symbolic of numerous changes that split the church between reformers and traditionalists.

The mainline Protestant denominations that traditionally defined the center of American belief struggled after 1960. The United Methodist Church, the Presbyterian Church U.S.A., the United Church of Christ, and the Episcopal Church battled internally over the morality of U.S. foreign policy, the role of women in the ministry, and the reception of gay and lesbian members. They were strengthened by the ecumenical impulse, which united denominational branches that had been divided by ethnicity or regionalism. However, they gradually lost their position among American churches, perhaps because ecumenism diluted the certainty of their message. Liberal Protestantism has also historically been strongest in the slow-growing Northeast and Midwest.

In contrast, evangelical churches have benefited from the direct appeal of their message and from strong roots in the booming Sunbelt. Members of evangelical churches (25 percent of white Americans) now outnumber the members of mainline Protestant churches (20 percent). Major evangelical denominations include Baptists, the Church of the Nazarene, and the Assemblies of God. Fundamentalists, defined by a belief in the literal truth of the Bible, are a subset of evangelicals. So are 8 to 10 million Pentecostals and charismatics, who accept "gifts of the spirit," such as healing by faith and speaking in tongues.

Outsiders know evangelical Christianity through "televangelists." Spending on religious television programming rose from $50 to $600 million in the 1970s. The "electronic church" built on the radio preaching and professional revivalism of the 1950s. By the 1970s, it reached 20 percent of American households. Americans everywhere recognized the Big Four. Oral Roberts had a television show and Oral Roberts University in Oklahoma. Pat Robertson had the 700 Club and the Christian Broadcasting Network in Virginia. Jerry Falwell claimed leadership of the Moral Majority. Jim and Tammy Faye Bakker had grand plans for real estate development before their schemes collapsed in fraud.

Behind the glitz and hype of the television pulpit, evangelical churches emphasized religion as an individual experience focused on personal salvation. Unlike many of the secular and psychological avenues to fulfillment, however, they also offered communities of faith that might stabilize fragmented lives. The conservative nature of their theology and social teaching in a changing society offered certainty that was especially attractive to many younger families.

Values in Conflict

In the 1950s and 1960s, Americans argued most often over foreign policy, racial justice, and the economy. Since the mid-1970s, they have also quarreled over beliefs and values. Religious belief has reentered politics as individuals and groups try to shape America around their particular, and often conflicting, ideas of the godly society. One expert talks about a division between cultural liberals and conservatives, another about "culture wars" between progressivism and orthodoxy. Americans who are undogmatic in religion are often liberal in politics as well, hoping to lessen economic inequities and

Evangelist and politician Pat Robertson works delegates at the 1988 Republican convention. In the late 1980s and 1990s, evangelical Christians became a major constituency of the Republican party.

strengthen individual social freedom. Religious and political conservatism also tend to go together. To some degree, this cultural division runs all the way through American society, dividing liberal North from conservative South, cities from small towns, and college professors from Kiwanis Club members (see the overview table, "Religion and Politics").

The division on social issues is related to theological differences within Protestantism. The "conservative" emphasis on personal salvation and the literal truth of the Bible also expresses itself in a desire to restore "traditional" social patterns. Conservatives worry that social disorder occurs when people follow personal impulses and pleasures. In contrast, the "liberal" or "modern" emphasis on the universality of the Christian message restates the Social Gospel with its call to build the Kingdom of God through social justice and may recognize divergent pathways toward truth. Liberals worry that rampaging greed in the unregulated marketplace creates disorder and injustice.

The cultural conflict transcends the historic three-way division of Americans among Protestants, Catholics, and Jews. Instead, the conservative–liberal division now cuts through each group. For example, conservative Catholics, fundamentalist Protestants, and Orthodox Jews may find themselves in agreement on issues of cultural values despite theologies that are worlds apart. The same may be true of Catholic reformers, liberal Protestants, and Reform Jews.

Conservatives have initiated the culture wars, trying to stabilize what they fear is an American society spinning out of control because of personal sexual indulgence. In fact, the evidence on the sexual revolution is mixed. Growing numbers of teenagers reported being sexually active in the 1970s, but the rate of increase tapered off in the 1980s. The divorce rate began to drop after 1980; births

The Reverend Jesse Jackson used his religious training and convictions to good effect in trying to build a "Rainbow Coalition" of politically progressive voters from all ethnic backgrounds.

to teenagers dropped after 1990, and the number of two-parent families increased. Most adults remained staid and monogamous, according to a survey published in 1994, but sexual self-help and advice books proliferated. Perhaps the logical extension of reading about sex in the 1970s was an astonishing eagerness to talk about sex in the 1990s, a decade whose soap opera story lines and talk shows covered everything from family violence to exotic sexual tastes.

The explosion of explicit attention to sexual behavior set the stage for religiously rooted battles over two sets of issues. One cluster revolves around so-called "family values," questioning the morality of access to abortion, the acceptability of homosexuality, and the roles and rights of women. The debates are a response to changing personal behaviors and family patterns, such as the large increase in the number of children living with a never-married parent, from 2 million in 1980 to 6.3 million in 1993, although the rate of births outside marriage leveled off in the 1990s. A second set of concerns has focused on the supposed role of public schools in undermining morality through sex education, unrestricted reading matter, nonbiblical science, and the absence of prayer. Opinion polls show clear differences among religious denominations on issues such as censorship of library books, acceptability of racially segregated neighborhoods, freedom of choice in terminating pregnancy, and homosexuality.

Not all issues of the culture wars carry the same weight. Censorship of art exhibits and library collections has mostly been an issue for political grandstand-

ing. U.S. senators grabbed headlines beginning in 1989 by attacking the National Endowment for the Arts for funding "obscene" art, but a local jury in Cincinnati proved tolerant of sexually explicit images in a photographic exhibition. Efforts to restrict legal access to abortion mobilized thousands of "right to life" advocates in the late 1980s and early 1990s, but illegal acts remained the work of a radical fringe. A culturally conservative issue with great popular appeal in the early 1990s was an effort to prevent states and localities from protecting homosexuals against discrimination. Using the slogan "No special rights," antigay measures passed in Cincinnati, Colorado, and communities in Oregon in 1993 and 1994, only to have the Supreme Court overturn the Colorado law in ***Romer* v. *Evans*** (1996).

On the national level, President Ronald Reagan gave respectability to what critics called a "politics of nostalgia," but the movement's strength came from outside the political establishment. For example, Jerry Falwell was an outsider to politics before he founded the Moral Majority in 1979 and influenced the 1980 election. Television appeals and direct-mail fund-raising became powerful tools for both sides in the 1980s—for the liberal People for the American Way and the American Civil Liberties Union as well as for the Moral Majority.

A good occasion for observing the full spectrum of religiously based politics came in 1988, when two different preachers sought a presidential nomination. Pat Robertson's campaign for the Republican nomination tapped deep discontent with social change. He used the mailing list from his 700 Club program to mobilize evangelical and charismatic Christians and pushed the Republican party further to the right on family and social issues. Jesse Jackson's grassroots campaign had the opposite goal of moving the Democratic party to the left on social and economic policy. With roots in the black civil rights movement, he assembled a "Rainbow Coalition" that included militant labor unionists, feminists, gay activists, and others whom Robertson's followers feared. Both Jackson and Robertson used their powerful personalities and religious convictions to inspire support from local churches and churchgoers, but the sharp divergence of their goals is a reminder about the continuing variety of American religious beliefs.

Conclusion

After twenty years of consensus, Americans since the mid-1960s have revisited basic questions about our character as a nation and people: Who is an American? How can we earn our livelihoods? Where do we want to live? What values and principles should guide our lives?

Both Pat Robertson and Jesse Jackson are reminders that the countertrend to decentralization and decentering was a search for community and connection. In the face of economic and cultural dislocation, some Americans moved to self-contained suburbs or constructed entirely new communities. Others turned to a wide range of religious organizations. Groups as different as feminists, gays, and evangelicals forged grassroots political movements to place their own concerns on the national agenda.

Even as Americans rallied around conflicting visions of the good society, the clamor of new voices and new concerns demonstrated the strength of American democracy. What remained to be tested was the continuing viability of the political process—the nation's capacity to recognize the values of diverse groups while enlisting them around a common vision of the public good.

Review Questions

1. Describe how the United States has become more international since 1965. What policy changes have promoted globalization? How have increased foreign trade and immigration affected American cities and states? What political conflicts stem from the nation's growing international connections?

2. How did the changing economy affect the various regions of the United State? How does an economy based on information and services differ from the earlier manufacturing economy? Have recent economic changes helped or hurt organized labor?

3. Why did Americans in the 1960s come to believe that larger cities were in crisis? What have been the major trends in suburban growth since the 1960s? How has this growth affected prominent political issues and the balance of political power?

4. Describe key changes in American family patterns since the 1960s. To what extent are these changes the result of economic forces? Of changing social values? How is an aging population likely to affect national politics in the twenty-first century?

5. Describe the variety of ways in which recent Americans have searched for spiritual connection and community. How does the social and political role of religion in the United States differ from that in other industrialized nations? What key issues have brought religious groups into the political arena? What positions do different groups take on these issues?

Recommended Reading

Elijah Anderson, *Streetwise: Race, Class, and Change in an Urban Community* (1990). A deeply troubling portrait of the culture of the streets in the Philadelphia ghetto.

Stephanie Coontz, *The Way We Never Were* (1992) and *The Way We Really Are* (1997). Two books that place modern family patterns in accurate historical context, puncturing a series of myths and preconceptions about family decline.

Peter Davis, *Hometown: A Contemporary American Chronicle* (1982). Profiles the small city of Hamilton, Ohio, in the late 1970s.

Francis Fitzgerald, *Cities on a Hill* (1986). Incisive portraits of new American communities in the 1980s, including retirees' Sun City, Florida; gay San Francisco; and the religious commune of Rajneeshpuram.

Joel Garreau, *Edge City: Life on the New Frontier* (1991). Argues that suburban rings are developing their own "downtowns."

Milton Rogovin and Michael Frisch, *Portraits in Steel* (1993). The transformation of an American industrial city (Buffalo), told through photographs and interviews.

Wade Clark Roof, *A Generation of Seekers: The Spiritual Journeys of the Baby Boom Generation* (1993). Examines the range of religious and spiritual experiences of contemporary Americans.

Additional Sources

Globalization and Economic Change

Barry Bluestone and Bennett Harrison, *The Deindustrialization of America* (1982).

David Calleo, *The Imperious Economy* (1982).

Barbara Ehrenreich, *Fear of Falling: The Inner Life of the Middle Class* (1989).

Thomas Kessner and Betty Boyd Caroli, *Today's Immigrants: Their Stories* (1981).

Tracy Kidder, *The Soul of a New Machine* (1981).

Frank Levy, *Dollars and Dreams: The Changing American Income Distribution* (1987).

Ann Markusen, Scott Campbell, Peter Hall, and Sabina Dietrich, *The Rise of the Gunbelt: The Military Remapping of Industrial America* (1991).

Everett Rogers, *Silicon Valley Fever* (1984).

Hobart Rowen, *Self-Inflicted Wounds: From LBJ's Guns and Butter to Reagan's Voodoo Economics* (1994).

Ruben Rumbaut and Alejandro Portes, *Immigrant America* (1990).

Saskia Sassen, *The Global City* (1991).

William Serrin, *Homestead: The Glory and Tragedy of an American Steel Town* (1992).

Studs Terkel, *Working* (1972).

Urban Growth

Carl Abbott, *The Metropolitan Frontier: Cities in the Modern American West* (1993).

Mike Davis, *City of Quartz: Excavating the Future in Los Angeles* (1992).

John Findlay, *Magic Lands: Western Cityscapes and American Culture since 1940* (1992).

Bernard Frieden and Lynn Sagalyn, *Downtown, Inc.: How America Rebuilds Its Cities* (1989).

Myron Orfield, *Metropolitics: A Regional Agenda for Community and Stability* (1997).

Neal Peirce and Robert Guskind, *Breakthrough: Re-Creating the American City* (1993).

Jon Teaford, *The Rough Road to Renaissance: Urban Revitalization in America, 1940–1985* (1990).

Cities as Places of Ethnic Contact and Conflict

Ronald Formisano, *Boston against Busing: Race, Class, and Political Action* (1991).

Paul Jargowsky, *Poverty and Place: Ghettos, Barrios, and the American City* (1997).

Peter Kwong, *The New Chinatown* (1987).

Nicholas Lemann, *The Promised Land: The Great Black Migration and How It Changed America* (1991).

J. Anthony Lukas, *Common Ground: A Turbulent Decade in the Lives of Three American Families* (1985).

Douglas Massey and Nancy Denton, *American Apartheid: Segregation and the Making of the Underclass* (1993).

Alejandro Portes and Alec Stepick, *City on the Edge* (1992).

Brett Williams, *Upscaling Downtown* (1988).

William Julius Wilson, *The Truly Disadvantaged* (1987).

Women's Rights and Family Change

Sara Evans, *Personal Politics: The Women's Liberation in the Civil Rights Movement and the New Left* (1980).

Jo Freeman, *The Politics of Women's Liberation* (1979).

Blanche Linden-Ward and Carol Hurd Green, *American Women in the 1960s* (1993).

Arlene Skolnick, *Embattled Paradise: The American Family in an Age of Uncertainty* (1991).

The Experience of Sexual Minorities

Margaret Cruikshank, *The Gay and Lesbian Liberation Movement* (1992).

Eric Marcus, *Making History: The Struggle for Gay and Lesbian Equal Rights, 1945–1990, An Oral History* (1992).

Randy Shilts, *And the Band Played On: Politics, People, and the AIDS Epidemic* (1987).

Religion and Public Life

Robert Bellah, Richard Madsen, William Sullivan, and Steven Tipton, *Habits of the Heart: Individualism and Commitment in American Life* (1985).

Paul Boyer, *When Time Shall Be No More: Prophecy Belief and Modern American Culture* (1992).

Allen D. Hertzke, *Echoes of Discontent: Jesse Jackson, Pat Robertson, and the Resurgence of Populism* (1993).

James Davison Hunter, *Culture Wars: The Struggle to Define America* (1991).

Wade Clark Roof and William McKinney, *American Mainline Religion: Its Changing Shape and Future* (1987).

John Woodridge, *The Evangelicals* (1975).

Robert Wuthnow, *The Restructuring of American Religion: Society and Faith since World War II* (1988).

Where to Learn More

❖ **Museum of Broadcast Communication, Chicago, Illinois.**   Exhibits on the rise of broadcasting plus a library of television and radio programs and commercials offer a window into American popular culture.

❖ **Downtown Baltimore, Maryland.**   A visit to the Harborplace festival market, the revitalized waterfront, the old Lexington Market food market, and the new Camden Yards baseball stadium is a quick way to see the sort of "new downtown" that cities tried to build after 1975.

❖ **Youngstown Historical Center of Industry and Labor, Youngstown, Ohio.**   A permanent exhibit, "Forging the Steel Valley," focuses on the daily lives of steelworkers and the decline of the industry.

SEARCHING FOR STABILITY IN A CHANGING WORLD, SINCE 1980

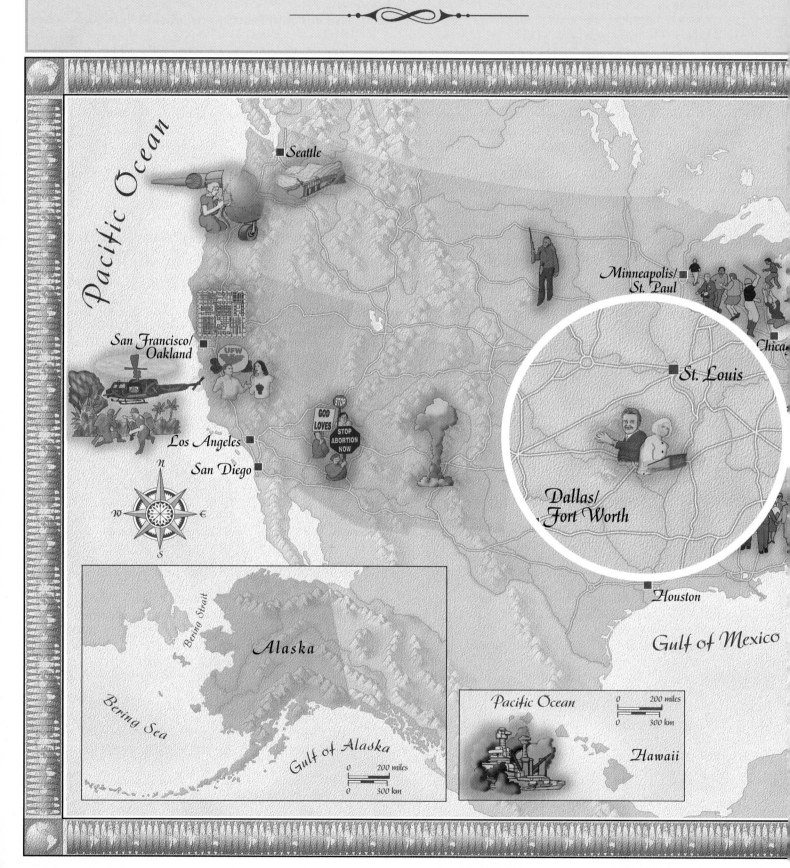

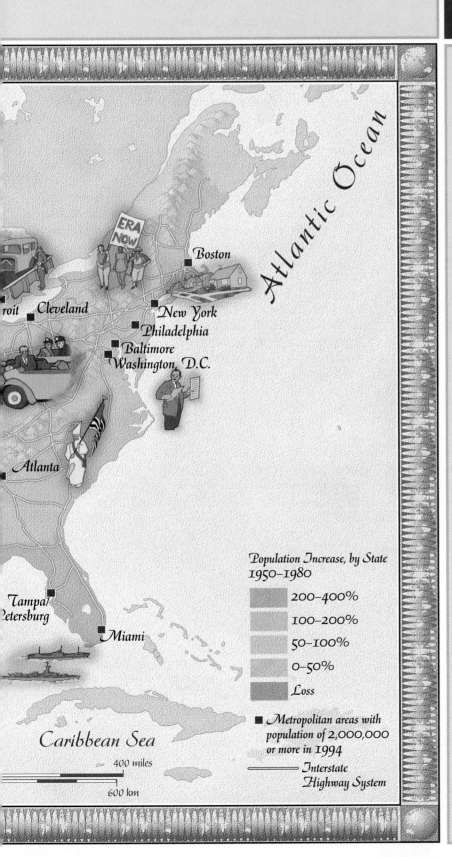

Atlantic Ocean

Boston
New York
Philadelphia
Baltimore
Washington, D.C.

Cleveland
roit
Atlanta

Tampa/
Petersburg
Miami

Caribbean Sea

400 miles
600 km

Population Increase, by State
1950–1980

200–400%
100–200%
50–100%
0–50%
Loss

■ Metropolitan areas with
population of 2,000,000
or more in 1994

—— Interstate
Highway System

33

Chapter Outline

Key Topics

❖ Economic and social change during
  the Reagan Revolution
❖ The collapse of the USSR and the end
  of the Cold War
❖ Concern for the economy, the desire
  for stability, and the election and reelection of Bill Clinton

On June 1, 1980, CNN—Cable News Network—gave television viewers their first chance to watch news coverage twenty-four hours a day. Newscasters Bernard Shaw and Mary Alice Williams brought instant information to an initial audience of 1.7 million subscribers; a decade later, CNN had hundreds of millions of viewers in more than seventy-five countries. Business executives in Zurich, college students in Nairobi, and farmers in Omaha all tuned in to the version of world events pulled together in CNN's Atlanta headquarters.

Fourteen months after CNN came another new cable channel with immediate impact—MTV: Music Television. By the time it reached the key New York and Los Angeles markets in January 1983, MTV's round-the-clock programming of music videos had created a new form of popular art and advertising. With its own programming aimed at viewers aged eighteen to thirty-four, MTV inspired Nickelodeon for kids and VH-1 for baby boomers.

CNN, MTV, and the rest of cable television reflected both the pace of change and the fragmentation of American society in the 1980s and 1990s. As late as 1980, ordinary Americans had few choices for learning about their nation and world—virtually identical newscasts on NBC, CBS, and ABC and similar stories in *Time* and *Newsweek*. Fifteen years later, they had learned to surf through dozens of cable channels in search of specialized programs and were beginning to explore the Internet. Hundreds of magazines for niche markets had replaced the general-circulation periodicals of the postwar generation. Vast quantities of information were more easily available, but much of it was packaged for a subdivided marketplace of specialized consumers.

The new cable channels are also reminders of the powerful connections between the United States and the rest of the world. MTV by 1990 had spawned MTV Europe, MTV Australia, MTV Japan, and MTV Latin America. CNN made a global reputation with live reporting on the student revolt in Beijing in 1989. People in many developing nations prefer CNN news to their local government-controlled stations. When American bombs began to fall on Baghdad in January 1991, White House officials watched CNN to find out how their war was going.

Broadcasting was not the only field where the rules changed. From the mid-1940s to the mid-1970s, politics had followed a well-thumbed script. Lessons about full employment or the communist menace that were learned in 1948 were still applicable in 1968 or 1972. By the end of Ronald Reagan's presidency, however, new rules governed foreign affairs and the national economy. Even as the world grew safer with the breakup of the Soviet Union, it also grew more complicated. Americans had to learn new principles for understanding diplomatic relations when nations no longer had to choose sides in the Cold War. At home, Americans decided to reverse the growth of federal government responsibilities that had marked both Republican and Democratic administrations since the 1930s. By the later 1990s, the center of U.S. politics had shifted substantially to the right, with conservative Republicans recycling arguments from generations earlier and "liberal" Democrat Bill Clinton sounding like an Eisenhower Republican.

The Reagan Revolution

Political change began in 1980, when Ronald Reagan rode the tide of American discontent to a narrow but decisively important victory in the presidential election (see Map 33-1). Building on a conservative critique of American policies and on issues that Jimmy Carter had placed on the national agenda, he presided over revolutionary changes in American government and policies. Reagan was a "Teflon president" who managed to take credit for successes but avoid blame for problems and rolled to a landslide reelection in 1984. The consequences of his two terms were startling. They included an altered role for government, powerful but selective economic growth, and a shift of domestic politics away from bread-and-butter issues toward moral or lifestyle concerns.

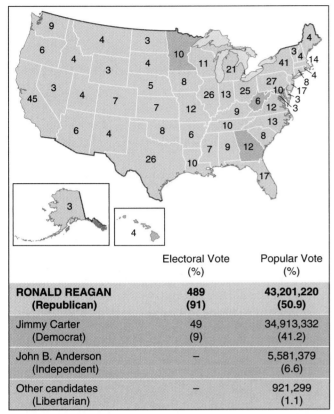

	Electoral Vote (%)	Popular Vote (%)
RONALD REAGAN (Republican)	**489 (91)**	**43,201,220 (50.9)**
Jimmy Carter (Democrat)	49 (9)	34,913,332 (41.2)
John B. Anderson (Independent)	–	5,581,379 (6.6)
Other candidates (Libertarian)	–	921,299 (1.1)

Map 33-1   Election of 1980
Ronald Reagan won in a landslide in 1980. Independent candidate John Anderson took more votes from Jimmy Carter than from Reagan, but Reagan's personal magnetism was a powerful political force. His victory confirmed the shift of the South to the Republican party.

Reagan's Majority

Reagan won in 1980 because many Americans felt buffeted by forces beyond their control. They worried about inflation at home and declining power abroad. A CBS News–*New York Times* poll found that only 11 percent of Reagan's supporters voted for him because of his conservative platform. Fully 38 percent pulled the Reagan lever simply because he was not Jimmy Carter. Reagan's majority was a tenuous alliance of groups with little in common except dissatisfaction with the status quo.

Some of Reagan's most articulate support came from anticommunist conservatives of both parties who feared that the United States was losing influence in the world. Despite Carter's tough actions in 1979 and 1980 and increases in defense spending, such conservatives didn't trust him to do enough. The inability to free the hostages in Iran grated. The Panama Canal and SALT II treaties seemed to give away American power. The Soviet military buildup, charged the critics, was creating a "window of vulner-

ability"—a dangerous period when the Soviet Union might threaten the United States with a first strike by nuclear weapons.

Other Reagan voters directed their anger at government bureaucracies. Christian conservatives worried that social activists were using the federal courts to alter traditional values to the detriment of American society. One young woman from Houston perceived "a parallel [between] the amount of government taking religion out and also America's debt getting worse, crime getting greater." Wealthy entrepreneurs from the Sunbelt states believed that Nixon-era federal offices like the Environmental Protection Agency and the Occupational Safety and Health Administration were choking their businesses in red tape. Many of these critics had amassed fortunes in oil, real estate, retailing, and electronics and hated the taxes that funded social programs. In many ways, the two groups were mismatched. Christian moralists as individuals had little in common with the high-rolling hedonists and Hollywood tycoons with whom Reagan rubbed shoulders. But they shared a deep distrust of the federal establishment.

Foreign policy activists and antiestablishment crusaders would have been unable to elect Reagan without disaffected blue collar and middle-class voters who deserted the Democrats. Reagan's campaign hammered on the question: "Are you better off than you were four years ago?" Many white working-class voters believed that minorities were getting an unfair edge in hiring and social services. The same voters worried about inflation, which had halted growth in the average family's spending

Ronald Reagan and his wife Nancy celebrate Reagan's inauguration as President.

CHRONOLOGY

1980 Ronald Reagan is elected president.

CNN begins cable broadcasting.

1981 Reagan breaks strike by air traffic controllers.

1982 Nuclear freeze movement peaks.

United States begins to finance Contra rebels against the Sandinista government in Nicaragua.

1983 241 Marines are killed by a terrorist bomb in Beirut, Lebanon.

1984 Reagan wins reelection.

1985 Mikhail Gorbachev initiates reforms in the USSR.

1986 Economic Recovery Tax Act is adopted.

1987 Congress holds hearings on the Iran-Contra scandal.

Reagan and Gorbachev sign the Intermediate Nuclear Force treaty.

1988 George Bush is elected president.

1989 Communist regimes in eastern Europe collapse; Germans tear down Berlin Wall.

Financial crisis forces federal bailout of many savings and loans.

United States invades Panama to capture General Manuel Noriega.

1990 Iraq invades Kuwait; and United States sends forces to the Persian Gulf.

West Germany and East Germany reunite.

1991 Operation Desert Storm drives the Iraqis from Kuwait.

Soviet Union dissolves into independent nations.

Strategic Arms Reduction Treaty (START) is signed.

Clarence Thomas is seated on the Supreme Court.

1992 Acquital of officers accused of beating Rodney King triggers Los Angeles riots.

Bill Clinton defeats George Bush for the presidency.

1993 Congress approves the North American Free Trade Agreement.

1994 Independent Counsel Kenneth Starr begins investigation of Bill and Hilary Clinton.

Paula Jones files sexual harassment lawsuit against Bill Clinton.

Republicans sweep to control of Congress.

Federal government temporarily shuts down for lack of money.

1995 United States sends troops to Bosnia.

1996 Clinton wins a second term as president.

1998 Paula Jones lawsuit dismissed.

House of Representatives impeaches Clinton.

1999 Senate acquits Clinton of impeachment charges.

United States leads NATO intervention in Kosovo.

---

power since 1973, and blamed their difficulties on runaway government spending.

These political responses gained in influence as conservative intellectuals offered a coherent critique of the New Deal–New Frontier approach to American government. Edward Banfield's radical ideas about the failures of the Great Society set the tone of the **neoconservative** analysis. In *The Unheavenly City* (1968), he questioned the basic idea of public solutions for social problems. He argued that liberal programs failed because inequality is based on human character and rooted in the basic structure of society; government action can solve only the problems that require better engineering, such as pollution control, better highways, or the delivery of explosives to military targets.

By the late 1970s and early 1980s, other conservatives were elaborating the Banfield thesis. Some were academics, such as Irving Kristol, editor of the magazine *The Public Interest*. Others were journalists, such as Charles Murray, who attacked the welfare system in the book *Losing Ground*. Still others were political activists, such as Reagan's secretary of education, William Bennett. They found support in new conservative think tanks and political lobbying organizations. The *Wall Street Journal* evolved from a narrow business newspaper into a national conservative forum by devoting its editorial page to strident versions of neoconservatism.

The common themes were simple: Free markets work better than government programs; government intervention does more harm than good; government assistance may be acceptable for property owners, but it saps the initiative of the poor. In 1964, three-quarters of Americans had trusted Washington "to do what is right." By 1980, three-quarters were convinced that the federal government wasted tax money. The neoconservatives agreed and offered the details to support Reagan's own summary: "Government is not the solution to our problems; government is the problem."

The president's Hollywood background made it easy for him to use films to make his points. He once threatened to veto unwanted legislation by challenging Congress with Clint Eastwood's "Make my day." Many blockbuster movies reinforced two of Reagan's messages. One was the importance of direct confrontation with the bad guys: communists (*Rambo*), global terrorists (*Die Hard*), drug dealers (*Lethal Weapon*). The second was the incompetence or dishonesty of government bureaucracies from the CIA to local police, whose elitist mistakes could only be set right by average but tough individuals like "Dirty Harry Callahan" and "John Rambo."

Taxes, Deficits, and Deregulation

The heart of the 1980s revolution was the **Economic Recovery and Tax Act of 1981 (ERTA)**, which reduced personal income tax rates by 25 percent over three years. The explicit goal was to stimulate business activity by lowering taxes overall and slashing rates for the rich. Cutting the government's total income by $747 billion over five years, ERTA meant less money for federal programs and more money in the hands of consumers and investors to stimulate economic growth. Most Americans recognized the strategy's unequal impacts on the poor and still thought the benefits were worth the price.

Reagan's first budget director, David Stockman, later revealed a second goal. ERTA would lock in deficits by "pulling the revenue plug." Because defense spending and Social Security were politically untouchable, Congress would find it impossible to create and fund new programs without cutting old ones. The first year's tax reductions were accompanied by cuts of $40 billion in federal aid to mass transit, school lunches, and similar programs. If Americans still wanted social programs, they could enact them at the local or state level, but Washington would no longer pay the tab.

The second part of the economic agenda was to free capitalists from government regulations to increase business initiative, innovation, and efficiency. The **deregulation** revolution built on a head start from the 1970s. A federal antitrust case had split the unified Bell System of AT&T and its subsidiaries into seven regional telephone companies and opened long-distance service to competition. Congress also deregulated air travel in 1978. During the first forty years of commercial air service, the Federal Aviation Administration (FAA) had matched airlines and routes (treating air service like a public utility). Deregulation now allowed air carriers to start and stop service at will. The result has been cheaper and more frequent air service for major hubs and poorer and more expensive service for small cities. Economists tend to be satisfied that the net gains have outweighed the costs. The transformation of telecommunications similarly meant more choices for sophisticated consumers but higher prices for basic phone service.

As the movie character John Rambo, actor Sylvester Stallone in the early 1980s gave voice to American frustrations with the country's place in the world. The "Rambo" movies clearly distinguished the good guys from the bad guys and suggested that stronger determination could have brought victory in Vietnam.

Corporate America used the Reagan administration to attack environmental legislation as "strangulation by regulation." Reagan's new budgets sliced funding for the Council on Environmental Quality and the Environmental Protection Agency. Vice President George Bush headed the White House Task Force on Regulatory Relief, which delayed or blocked regulations on hazardous wastes, automobile emissions, and exposure of workers to chemicals on the job.

Most attention, however, went to the instantly controversial appointment of Colorado lawyer James Watt as Secretary of the Interior. Watt had long worked to open up federal lands in the West to more intensive development. He was sympathetic to a western movement known as the **Sagebrush Rebellion**, which wanted the vast federal land holdings in the West transferred to the states for more rapid economic use. The sagebrush rebels faded in the early 1980s, in part because western resource industries found Watt so sympathetic. He blamed air pollution on natural emissions from trees and compared environmentalists to both Nazis and Bolsheviks. Federal resource agencies sold trees to timber companies at a loss to the Treasury, expanded offshore oil drilling, and expedited exploration for minerals.

The early 1980s also transformed American financial markets. **Individual Retirement Accounts (IRAs)**, a creation of the 1981 tax act, made millions of households into new investors. A new generation of Americans learned to play the stock market through mutual funds and direct stock purchases. Dollars poured from savings accounts into higher-paying money market funds. Savings and loans had traditionally been conservative financial institutions that funneled individual savings into safe home mortgages. Under new rules, they began to compete for deposits by offering high interest rates and reinvested the money in much riskier commercial real estate. By 1990, the result would be a financial crisis in which bad loans destroyed hundreds of S&Ls, especially in the Southwest. American taxpayers were left to bail out depositors to the tune of hundreds of billions of dollars to prevent a collapse of the nation's financial and credit system.

Wide-open financial markets were made to order for corporate consolidations and mergers. Corporate raiders snapped up "cash cows," profitable and cash-rich companies that could be milked of profits and assets. Dealmakers, such as Ivan Boesky and Michael Milken, brought together often mismatched companies into huge conglomerates. They raised money with "junk bonds," high-interest, high-risk securities that could be paid off only in favorable conditions. The merger mania channeled capital into paper transactions rather than investments in new equipment and products. Another effect was to damage the economies of small and middle-sized communities by transferring control of local companies to outside managers.

The flip side of corporate consolidation was another round in the Republican offensive against labor unions. President Reagan set the tone when he fired more than eleven thousand members of PATCO—the Professional Air Traffic Controllers Organization—for violating a no-strike clause in their hiring agreements with the FAA. Reagan claimed to be enforcing the letter of the law, but the message to organized labor was clear. Over the next eight years, the National Labor Relations Board and other federal agencies weakened the power of collective bargaining. The administration's policies reinforced the vigorous effort by American corporations to cut costs by relocating operations to nonunion plants and shifting to part-time workers.

The Election of 1984

An unresolved question is whether Ronald Reagan planned these economic changes as parts of a single strategy. Did he direct an economic revolution, or did he simply preside over changes initiated by others? Most memoirs by White House insiders suggest the latter; so do journalists who titled books about the Reagan administration *Sleepwalking through History, The Acting President,* and *The Role of a Lifetime.* Even if Reagan was acting out a role that was scripted by others, however, he was a hit at the polling place. If Americans had voted against Carter in 1980, they voted for Reagan in 1984.

A sharp recession in 1981–1982 had helped the Democrats slow the progress of Reagan's initiatives in Congress, but the national Democratic party continued to have a problem. National political parties in the United States are coalitions. They bring together people from different regions and ethnic backgrounds, with different social values and ways of making a living. The Democrats' problem was to hold key voting groups, such as labor unions and African Americans, without being labeled the party of "special interests." Indeed, conservatives in the 1980s had trashed the word *liberal* and convinced Americans that oil tycoons, defense contractors, and other members of Reagan's coalition were not special interests.

Democrats faced a special dilemma with the deepening tension between working-class white voters and black voters. Democrats needed both groups to win but found white blue-collar voters deeply alienated by affirmative action and busing for school integration. In one set of focused interviews, pollsters read white Detroiters a statement from Robert Kennedy that called on Americans to recognize special obligations to black citizens who had endured racial discrimination. The responses were vehement: "I can't go along with that." "That's bull!" "No wonder they killed him."

A further Democratic challenge was Ronald Reagan's personal popularity. The president won over many Americans by surviving a 1981 assassination attempt in fine spirits. Reagan's popularity compounded the Democrats' inability to excite younger voters. Polls in the mid-1980s consistently showed that roughly two-thirds of people in their twenties and early thirties were choosing the Republicans as the party of energy and new ideas, leaving the Democrats to the middle-aged and elderly.

Democrats sealed their fate in 1984 by nominating Walter Mondale, who had been vice president under Carter. Mondale was earnest, honest, and dull. He assumed that Americans cared enough about the exploding federal deficit to accept an across-the-board tax increase. With the economy growing and inflation in check, most voters didn't want Mondale to remind them of long-range financial realities. Reagan took 59 percent of the popular vote and 98 percent of the electoral votes.

Progress and Poverty

The national economy boomed in the mid-1980s. Deregulated credit and massive deficit spending fueled exuberant growth. The decade as a whole brought nearly 20 million new jobs. Inflation dipped to 3 percent per year. The stock market mirrored the overall prosperity; the Dow Jones average of blue-chip industrial stock prices more than tripled from August 1982 to August 1987.

However, federal tax and budget changes had different effects on rich and poor (see Figure 33-1). The 1981 tax cuts came with sharp increases in the Social Security tax, which hit lower-income workers the hardest. The tax changes meant that the average annual income of households in the bottom 40 percent declined and that many actually paid higher taxes. In contrast, Americans at the upper end of the economic scale increased their share of after-tax income at the expense of everyone else. The 2.5 million Americans at the very top of the heap (the richest 1 percent) saw their share of all privately held wealth grow from 31 percent to 37 percent.

The new income fueled lavish living by the upper crust and a fascination with the "lifestyles of the rich and famous." With a few exceptions, the "middle class" in television sitcoms enjoyed lives available only to the top 20 percent of Americans. The national media discovered "yuppies"—the "young urban professionals" who supposedly defined themselves by elitist consumerism. Consumers wanted imported beer and ice cream with made-up foreign names. Middle-line retailers like Sears had clothed Americans for decades and furnished their homes. Now consumers who could flocked to upscale retailers like Nieman-Marcus, Bloomingdale's, and Nordstrom. *GQ* and *Metropolitan Home* advised readers on stylish consumption. Dispatches from the consump-

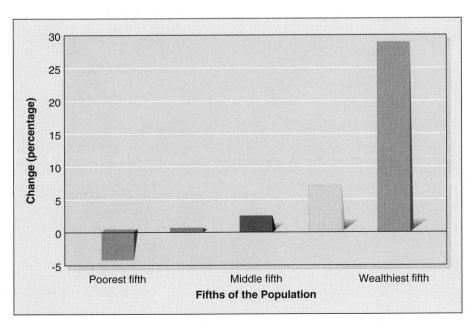

Figure 33-1 Changes in Real Family Income, 1980–1990
In the 1980s, the poor got poorer, the middle class made slight gains, and the most affluent 20 percent of the American people did very well. Tax changes that helped well-off households were one factor. Another factor was the erosion of "family-wage jobs" in manufacturing.

tion capitals of Manhattan and Beverly Hills reported that cocaine was now the intoxicant of choice.

The budget changes that fueled conspicuous consumption put pressure on American cities. Cities and their residents absorbed approximately two-thirds of the cuts in the 1981–1982 federal budget. Provisions for accelerated depreciation (tax write-offs) of factories and equipment in the 1981 tax act encouraged the abandonment of center-city factories in favor of new facilities in the suburbs. Meanwhile, federal aid recognized both the economic independence and political power of America's suburbs. By 1975, suburbanites held the largest block of seats in the House of Representatives—131 suburban districts, 130 rural, 102 central-city, and 72 mixed. Reapportionment in 1982, based on the 1980 census, produced a House that was even more heavily suburban. For a trip to the U.S. Senate, most politicians in earlier generations had needed rural roots or a big-city power base. By the 1980s, however, the Senate included residents of suburbs like Mill Valley, California; Aurora, Colorado; and Island Park, New York.

Federal tax and spending policies made life even harder for middle-class families who were caught by industrial restructuring. The squeeze put pressure on traditional family patterns and pushed into the workforce women who might otherwise have stayed home. By 1992, more than half of younger married women, aged 18 to 33, contributed between 30 and 70 percent of total household income. Even with two incomes, many families found it hard to buy a house because of skyrocketing prices in urban markets and sky-high interest rates. The national home ownership rate actually fell for the first time in almost fifty years, from 66 to 64 percent of American households. Many Americans no longer expected to surpass their parents' standard of living.

An affluent family pedals by a group of homeless people in Santa Barbara, California. In the 1980s a combination of rising housing prices and the closure of most mental hospitals pushed increasing numbers of Americans onto the streets. Estimates of the number of homeless Americans in the late 1980s ranged from 300,000 to 3 million, depending on the definition of homelessness and the political goals of the estimator.

OVERVIEW

WHY ARE 35 MILLION AMERICANS POOR?

	Culture of Poverty Theory	Malfunctioning Economy Theory
Explanation of poverty	Poverty is the result of learned behaviors that are transmitted through families and communities. Individuals learn to scorn education and saving, expect instant gratification, and fall into laziness.	The economy is not structured to generate decent-paying jobs for all Americans who want to work. Economic and social changes have repeatedly yanked opportunity away from African-American families.
Focus of Attention	Individual behavior, poor neighborhoods	Location and availability of family wage jobs, effects of discrimination on employment chances
Political Bias	Conservative	Progressive
Policy Suggestions	Reduce welfare, food stamps, and other public assistance to encourage individuals to behave responsibly.	Ensure equal access to the job market; make the tax system more family-friendly; adequately fund public education and job training.
Buzzwords	"welfare queen," "underclass"	"blaming the victim," "housing-jobs mismatch"

At the lower end of the economic ladder, the proportion of Americans living in poverty increased. After declining steadily from 1960 to a low of 11.1 percent in 1973, the poverty rate climbed back to the 13 to 15 percent range. Conservative critics began to talk about an "underclass" of Americans permanently outside the mainstream economy because of poor education, drug abuse, or sheer laziness. In fact, most of the nation's millions of poor people lived in households with employed adults. In 1992, fully 18 percent of all full-time jobs did not pay enough ($13,091 in 1992 dollars) to lift a family of four out of poverty, a jump of 50 percent over the proportion of underpaid jobs in 1981 (see the overview table, "Why Are 35 Million Americans Poor?").

Falling below even the working poor were growing numbers of homeless Americans. Large cities have always had derelict alcoholics and the voluntarily homeless—tramps, hobos, and transient laborers. In the 1980s, several factors made homelessness more visible and pressing. A new approach to the treatment of the mentally ill reduced the population of mental hospitals from 540,000 in 1960 to only 140,000 in 1980. Deinstitutionalized patients were supposed to receive community-based treatment, but many ended up on the streets and in overnight shelters. New forms of self-destructive drug abuse, such as crack addiction, joined alcoholism. A boom in downtown real estate destroyed old skid row districts with their bars, employment offices, missions, and dollar-a-night hotels.

These factors tripled the number of permanently homeless people during the early and middle 1980s, from 200,000 to somewhere between 500,000 to 700,000. Twice or three times that many may have been homeless for part of a given year. For every person in a shelter on a given night, two people were sleeping on sidewalks, in parks, in cars, and in abandoned buildings. Because homeless people made middle-class Americans uncomfortable, it was reassuring to assume they were outsiders attracted by local conditions, such as tolerant attitudes (as some claimed in Seattle) or mild climate (as some claimed in Phoenix). In fact, few among the down-and-out have the resources to move from town to town. Bag ladies, panhandlers, working people, and yuppies were all parts of the same communities, neighbors in the broadest sense.

The Second (Short) Cold War

Ronald Reagan entered office determined not to lose the Cold War. He considered the Soviet Union not a coequal nation with legitimate world interests but an "evil empire," like something from the *Star Wars* movies. After the era of détente, global tensions had started to mount in the late 1970s. They were soon higher than they had been since the 1960s.

Confronting the USSR

Who renewed the Cold War after Nixon's diplomacy of détente and Carter's early efforts at negotiation? The Soviets had pursued military expansion in the 1970s, triggering the fear that they might stage a nuclear Pearl Harbor. The USSR in 1980 was supporting Marxist regimes in civil wars in Angola, Ethiopia, Nicaragua, and especially Afghanistan. Were these actions parts of a careful plan? Or did they result from the Cold War inertia of a rudderless nation that reacted to situations one at a time? Given the aging Soviet leadership and the economic weaknesses revealed in the late 1980s, it makes more sense to see the Soviets as muddling along rather than executing a well-planned global strategy.

On the American side, Reagan's readiness to confront "the focus of evil in the modern world" reflected the views of many conservative supporters that the USSR was a monolithic and ideologically motivated foe bent on world conquest. In hindsight, some Reaganites claim that the administration's policies were part of a deliberate and coordinated scheme to check a Soviet offensive and bankrupt the USSR by pushing it into a new arms race. Compared with spending patterns in effect in 1980, the Reagan administration shifted $70 billion per year from domestic to military programs (see Map 33-2). It is just as likely, however, that the administration's defense and foreign policy initiatives were a set of discrete but effective decisions.

The new administration reemphasized central Europe as the focus of superpower rivalry. To counter improved Soviet armaments, the United States began to place cruise missiles and midrange Pershing II missiles in Europe in 1983. NATO governments approved the action, but it frightened millions of their citizens. By the mid-1980s, many Europeans saw the United States as the dangerous and aggressive force in world affairs and the Soviet Union as the voice of moderation.

The controversy over the new missile systems was part of new thinking about nuclear weaponry. Multiple warheads on U.S. missiles already allowed Washington to target 25,000 separate places in the Soviet Union. National Security Directive D-13 (1981) stated that a nuclear war might be winnable, despite its enormous costs. A reactivated civil defense program also suggested that the United States was serious about nuclear war. All Americans needed for survival, said one administration official, were "enough shovels" to dig fallout shelters.

Escalation of the nuclear arms race reinvigorated the antiwar and antinuclear movement in the United States as well as Europe. Drawing on the experience of the antiwar movement, the **nuclear freeze** campaign caught the imagination of many

Map 33-2   *Intercontinental Ballistic Missile Sites, 1983*
In the early 1980s, the United States aimed hundreds of ballistic missiles with nuclear warheads at the Soviet Union. The hardened underground silos that housed the missiles were distributed across sparsely populated sections of the middle states between the Rocky Mountains and the Mississippi River.

Intercontinental Ballistic Missile Complexes, 1983

Americans in 1981 and 1982. It sought to halt the manufacture and deployment of new atomic weapons by the great powers. The movement gained urgency when distinguished scientists argued that the smoke and dust thrown up by an atomic war would devastate the ecology of the entire globe by triggering "nuclear winter." Nearly a million people turned out for a nuclear freeze rally in New York in 1982. Voters in several states approved the idea. Hundreds of local communities endorsed the freeze or took the symbolic step of declaring themselves "nuclear-free zones."

In response, Reagan announced the **Strategic Defense Initiative (SDI)** or "Star Wars" program in 1983. SDI was to deploy new defenses that could intercept and destroy ballistic missiles as they rose from the ground and arced through space. Ideas included superlasers, killer satellites, and clouds of projectiles to rip missiles to shreds before they neared their targets. All of the technologies were untested; some existed only in the imagination. Few scientists thought that SDI could work. Many arms control experts thought that defensive systems were dangerous and destabilizing, because strong defenses suggested that a nation might be willing to risk a nuclear exchange. Nevertheless, President Reagan found SDI appealing, for it offered a way around the balance of terror that he hated.

Risky Business: Foreign Policy Adventures

The same administration that sometimes seemed reckless in its grand strategy also took risks to assert U.S. influence in global trouble spots. Nevertheless, Reagan kept the United States out of a major war and backed off in the face of serious trouble. Foreign interventions were designed to achieve symbolic victories rather than change the global balance of power. The exception was the Caribbean and Central America, the "backyard" where the United States had always claimed an overriding interest and where left-wing action infuriated Reagan's conservative supporters.

Lebanon was the model for Reagan's small-scale military interventions. Israel invaded Lebanon in 1982 to clear Palestinian guerrillas from its borders and set up a friendly Lebanese government. In fact, Lebanon was divided between Christian Arabs and Muslims and influenced by Israel's enemies Syria and the Palestine Liberation Organization (PLO). The Israeli army bogged down in a civil war. Reagan sent U.S. Marines to preserve the semblance of a Lebanese state and provide a face-saving exit for Israel. Although the Marines arrived in Beirut to interpose themselves between Israeli tanks and the

Lebanese, they remained on an ill-defined "presence mission" that angered Arabs. In October 1983, a car bomb killed 241 Marines. The remainder were soon gone, confirming the Syrian observation that Americans were "short of breath" when it came to Middle East politics.

The administration had already found an easier target. On October 25, 1983, only days after the disaster in Beirut, U.S. troops invaded the small independent Caribbean island of Grenada. A left-leaning government had invited Cuban help in building an airfield, which the United States feared would turn into a Cuban military base. Two thousand American troops overcame Cuban soldiers who were thinly disguised as construction workers, "rescued" American medical students, and put a more sympathetic and locally popular government in power.

The Caribbean was also the focus of a secret foreign policy operated by the CIA and then by National Security Council staff. They engaged not just in espionage but in attempts to implement policy. The target was Nicaragua, the Central American country where leftist Sandinista rebels had overthrown the Somoza dictatorship in 1979. Reagan and his people were determined to prevent Nicaragua from becoming "another Cuba," especially when Sandinistas helped left-wing insurgents in neighboring El Salvador. The CIA organized perhaps ten thousand "Contras" from remnants of Somoza's national guard. From bases in Honduras, they harassed the Sandinistas with sabotage and raids. Reagan called the Contras "freedom fighters," listened to stories of their exploits, and hunched over maps to follow their operations in detail. Meanwhile, other Americans aided refugees from the war zones of Central America through the church-based sanctuary movement ("sanctuary" could imply both legal economic assistance and direct defiance of efforts to deport refugees).

Constitutional trouble started when an unsympathetic Congress blocked U.S. funding for the Contras. Under the direction of CIA director William Casey, Lieutenant Colonel Oliver North flouted the law by organizing aid from private donors while serving on the staff of the National Security Council. The arms pipeline operated until a supply plane was shot down in 1986.

Even shadier were the administration's arms-for-hostages negotiations with Iran. Using questionable Middle Eastern arms dealers as go-betweens, the United States in 1985 joined Israel in selling five hundred antitank missiles to Iran. The deal followed stern public pronouncements that the United States would never negotiate with terrorists, and it violated this nation's official trade embargo against Iran. In

May 1986, National Security adviser Robert McFarlane flew to Iran to negotiate a second deal, carrying a chocolate cake and a Bible autographed by Reagan to present to the Ayatollah Khomeini. The tit-for-tat was Iran's help in securing the release of several Americans held hostage in Lebanon by pro-Iranian radicals; they were released, but other hostages were soon taken. Just as startling was the revelation that Colonel North funneled proceeds from the arms sales to the Contras, in a double evasion of the law.

As had been true with Watergate, the Iran-Contra affair was a two-sided scandal. First was the blatant misjudgment of operating a secret and bumbling foreign policy that depended on international arms dealers and ousted Nicaraguan military officers. Second was a concerted effort to cover up the actions. North shredded relevant documents and lied to Congress. In his final report in 1994, Special Prosecutor Lawrence Walsh found that President Reagan and Vice President Bush were aware of much that went on and participated in efforts to withhold information and mislead Congress.

American policy in Asia was a refreshing contrast with Central America and the Middle East. In the Philippines, American diplomats helped push corrupt President Ferdinand Marcos out and opened the way for a popular uprising to put Corazon Aquino in office. Secretary of State George Shultz made sure that the United States supported popular democracy while reassuring the Philippine military. In South Korea, the United States similarly helped ease out an unpopular dictator by firmly supporting democratic elections that brought in a more popular but still pro-U.S. government.

Embracing *Perestroika*

Thaw in the Cold War started in Moscow. Mikhail Gorbachev became general secretary of the Communist party in 1985. Gorbachev was the picture of vigor compared to his three sick or elderly predecessors, Leonid Brezhnev, Yuri Andropov, and Constantin Chernenko. He was a master of public relations who charmed western Europe's leaders and public. He was also a modernizer in a long Russian tradition that stretched back to Tsar Peter the Great in the eighteenth century. Gorbachev startled Soviet citizens by urging **glasnost**, or political openness and free discussion of issues. He followed by setting the goal of **perestroika,** or restructuring of the painfully bureaucratic Soviet economy.

Gorbachev decided that he needed to reduce the crushing burden of Soviet defense spending if the USSR was to have any chance of modernizing. In turn, such reductions required basic changes in superpower relations. During Reagan's second term, the Soviets offered one concession after another in a relentless drive for arms control. They agreed to cut the number of land-based strategic weapons in half. They gave up their demand for a stop to SDI research. In negotiations on conventional forces in Europe, they accepted bigger cuts for the Warsaw Pact nations than for NATO. They even agreed to on-site inspections to control chemical weapons.

Reagan had the vision (or audacity) to embrace the new Soviet position. He cast off decades of belief in the dangers of Soviet communism and took Gorbachev seriously. One of his reasons for SDI had been his personal belief that the abolition of nuclear weapons was better than fine-tuning the balance of terror. Now he was willing to forget his own rhetoric and abandon many of his most fervent supporters. He frightened his own staff when he met Gorbachev in Iceland in the summer of 1986 and accepted the principle of deep cuts in strategic forces. A new attitude was clear. Reagan explained that when he railed against the "evil empire," he had been talking about Brezhnev and the bad old days; Gorbachev and *glasnost* were different.

In the end, Reagan negotiated the Intermediate Nuclear Force (INF) agreement over the strong objections of the CIA and the Defense Department but with the support of Secretary of State Shultz. INF was the first true nuclear disarmament treaty (see the overview table, "Controlling Nuclear Weapons: Four Decades of Progress"). Previous treaties had only slowed the growth of nuclear weapons; they were "speed limits" for the arms race. The new pact matched Soviet SS-20s with American cruise missiles as an entire class of weapons that would be destroyed, with on-site inspections for verification.

Mikhail Gorbachev and Ronald Reagan sign the Intermediate Nuclear Forces treaty at the White House in 1987. The treaty marked a radical transformation in Reagan's approach to relations with the Soviet Union and lessened the military tension between NATO and the Soviet bloc in Europe.

OVERVIEW

CONTROLLING NUCLEAR WEAPONS: FOUR DECADES OF PROGRESS

Limiting the Testing of Nuclear Weapons	Limited Test Ban Treaty (1963)	Banned nuclear testing in the atmosphere, ocean, and outer space.
	Comprehensive Test Ban Treaty (1996)	Bans all nuclear tests, including underground tests. Rejected by U.S. Senate in 1999.
Halting the Spread of Nuclear Weapons	Nuclear Non-Proliferation Treaty (1968)	Pledged five recognized nuclear nations (United States, USSR, Britain, France, China) to pursue disarmament in good faith, and 140 other nations not to acquire nuclear weapons.
	Strategic Arms Limitation Treaty (SALT I, 1972)	Limited the number of nuclear-armed missiles and bombers maintained by the United States and USSR. Closely associated with United States–USSR agreement to limit deployment of antiballistic missile systems to one site each.
	Strategic Arms Limitation Treaty (SALT II, 1979)	Further limited the number of nuclear-armed missiles and bombers. Not ratified but followed by Carter and Reagan administrations.
Reducing the Number of Nuclear Weapons	Intermediate Nuclear Force Agreement (1987)	Required the United States to eliminate 846 nuclear armed cruise missiles, and the Soviet Union to eliminate 1846 SS-20 missiles.
	Strategic Arms Reduction Treaty (START I, 1991)	By July 1999, led to reductions of approximately 2750 nuclear warheads by the United States and 3725 warheads by the nations of the former USSR.
	Strategic Arms Reduction Treaty (START II, 1993)	Set further cuts in nuclear arsenals. Ratified by Russia in April 2000.

Data Source: Warhead data from Arms Control Association.

Government by Gestures

George Bush, Reagan's vice president and successor as president, loved to run the world by Rolodex. When someone's name came up at a formal dinner, he was likely to grab a phone and ring the person up. He upgraded the hot line to Moscow from a teletype machine to a modern communications system. When Congress was heading in the wrong direction, he started dialing senators and representatives. When a crisis threatened world peace, he had the same reaction—pick up the phone and start chatting with presidents and prime ministers. He viewed diplomacy as a series of conversations and friend-ships among leaders, not the reconciliation of differing national interests.

This view of national and world politics reflected a background in which personal connections counted. He was raised as part of the New England elite, built his own oil business in Texas, and then held a series of high-level federal appointments that produced a résumé with little impact on American politics. As someone who had survived twenty years of bureaucratic infighting, his watchword was prudence. Using a comparison from baseball, he described himself as the sort of guy who'd play the averages and "bunt 'em over" rather than go for the big inning. The result was a caretaker administration at home and abroad until forced to act by the pressure of events in the Soviet Union and the Middle East.

George Bush, Willie Horton, and Manuel Noriega

Michael Dukakis, the Democratic nominee in 1988, was a dry by-the-numbers manager who offered the American people "competence." The Bush campaign painted him as a liberal ideologue. Campaign Director Lee Atwater looked for "hot button" issues that could fit onto a three-by-five card. He found that Dukakis as governor of Massachusetts had delayed cleanup of Massachusetts Bay, favored gun control, and had vetoed a bill requiring schoolchildren to recite the Pledge of Allegiance (arguing correctly that it would be overturned in the courts). Even more damaging was that Massachusetts officials had allowed a murderer named Willie Horton a weekend furlough from prison, during which he had committed a brutal rape.

The Republican campaign exploited all of these issues. The goal was to hold the blue-collar and independent suburban voters who had gone with Reagan. Pro-Bush advertisements tapped real worries among the voters—fear of crime, racial tension (Willie Horton was black), worry about eroding social values. George Bush, despite his background in prep schools and country clubs, came out looking tough as nails while the Democrats looked like effete snobs.

The ads also locked Bush into a rhetorical war on crime and drugs that was his major domestic policy. Americans had good cause to be worried about public safety, but most were generally unaware that the victimization rate—the likelihood of becoming the target of a violent crime—had leveled off and would continue to fall in the 1990s and that crime was far worse in minority communities than elsewhere, in part due to gang- and drug-related activities.

The Bush administration stepped up the fight against illegal drugs. In his first televised speech from the White House, the president showed a bag of crack purchased just across the street from the White House. He failed to mention that the Drug Enforcement Agency had decoyed a dealer so that the president would have a prop. The federal drug control budget tripled. In the early 1980s, a quarter of federal prison inmates were in jail for drug offenses. Longer sentences, mandatory jail time, and tougher parole terms for drug crimes pushed the proportion over 50 percent by 1990. The United States tried to stop the flow of cocaine by blockading its borders with airplanes, sea patrols, and sniffer dogs at airport customs lines. Casual and middle-class use of cocaine and marijuana began to decline in the mid-1980s.

Drug use and drug sales were increasingly a problem of poor and minority neighborhoods.

The drug war strained relations with Latin America. The United States pressured South American nations like Colombia and Peru to uproot coca plants grown by poor farmers. Bush also parlayed the war on drugs into war on Panama. General Manuel Noriega, the Panamanian strongman, had once been on the CIA payroll. He had since turned to international drug sales in defiance of United States antismuggling efforts. On December 20, 1989, American troops invaded Panama, hunted down Noriega, and brought him back to stand trial in the United States on drug-trafficking charges. A handful of Americans and thousands of Panamanians died, many of them civilians caught in cross fire.

Otherwise, George Bush had little domestic policy, believing that Americans wanted government to leave them alone. He ignored a flood of new ideas from entrepreneurial conservatives, such as HUD Secretary Jack Kemp and "drug tsar" William Bennett. He surrounded himself with advisers who valued short-term political advantage over long-term strategies. He used dozens of vetoes to court favor with special interests, such as antiabortionists and big business.

Major legislation from the Bush years featured two environmental laws and one civil rights measure. Congress reauthorized and strengthened the **Clean Air Act**, passed a transportation bill that shifted federal priorities from highway building toward mass transit, and wrote the **Americans with Disabilities Act** (1990) to prevent discrimination against people with physical handicaps. In the areas of crime and health care, however, Bush's lack of leadership left festering problems.

The administration expected private individuals to take up the slack. Bush's often ridiculed but sincere vision was of a "kinder and gentler America" in which personal acts of social responsibility would shine like a "thousand points of light." If individuals failed to respond, however, Bush did not think that government should step in. He vetoed an extension of unemployment benefits in October 1991 and expressed his concern for "families in America that are having difficulty making ends meet" just before he teed off for Sunday afternoon golf at a suburban country club. George Bush saw little that was wrong with an America that had been so good to him and his friends.

The same attitude produced weak economic policies. The national debt had amounted to 50 percent of personal savings in 1980 but swelled to 125 percent by 1990. The massive budget deficits of the 1980s combined with growing trade deficits to turn the United States from an international creditor to a debtor nation. When Reagan took office, foreigners owed the United States and its citizens the equivalent of $2,500 for every American family. When Bush took office, the United States had used up its foreign assets and become the world's biggest debtor, with liabilities that averaged $7,000 per family. Yet the Bush administration was uninterested in dealing with either the national debt or inequitable taxes. After pledging "no new taxes" in his campaign, Bush backed into a tax increase in 1990. Voters found it hard to forget not the taxes themselves, which a strong leader might have justified to the nation, but the president's waffling and trying to downplay the importance of his decision. Thereafter, Bush ducked the political dangers of a balanced budget and tried not to rock the boat.

Crisis and Democracy in Eastern Europe

As a believer in personal diplomacy, George Bush based much of his foreign policy on his changing attitudes toward Mikhail Gorbachev. He started lukewarm, talking tough to please the Republican right wing. Bush feared that Gorbachev was being imprudent. Before 1989 was over, however, the president had decided that Gorbachev was OK. For the next two years, the United States pushed reform in Europe while being careful not to gloat in public or damage Gorbachev's position at home.

The people of eastern Europe overcame both American and Soviet caution. Gorbachev had urged his eastern European allies to emulate *perestroika* and proclaimed what his foreign ministry called the "Sinatra doctrine," alluding to the ballad "My Way," popularized by Frank Sinatra. Each communist nation could "do it their way" without fearing the Soviet tanks that had crushed change in Hungary in 1956 and Czechoslovakia in 1968. Instead of controlled reform, the War-

saw Pact system collapsed. Poland and Hungary were the first satellite nations to eject their communist leadership in favor of democracy in mid-1989. When East Germans began to flee westward through Hungary, the East German regime bowed to mounting pressure and opened the Berlin Wall on November 9. By the end of 1989, there were new governments in Czechoslovakia, Romania, Bulgaria, and East Germany.

The wall that divided East from West Berlin from 1962 to 1989 was a hated symbol of the Cold War. When the communist government of East Germany collapsed in November 1989, jubilant Berliners celebrated the opening of the wall and the reuniting of the divided city.

These largely peaceful revolutions destroyed the military and economic agreements that had harnessed the satellites to the Soviet economy. The USSR swallowed hard, accepted the loss of its satellites, and slowly withdrew its army from eastern Europe.

Events in Europe left German reunification as a point of possible conflict. Soviet policy since 1945 had sought to prevent the reemergence of a strong united Germany. West German Chancellor Helmut Kohl removed one obstacle when he reassured Poland and Russia that Germany would seek no changes in the boundaries drawn after World War II. By July 1990, the United States and USSR had agreed that a reunited Germany would belong to NATO. The decision satisfied France and Britain that a stronger Germany would still be under the influence of the Western allies. In October, the two Germanies completed their political unification, although it would be years before their mismatched economies functioned as one. Reunification was the final step in the diplomatic legacy of World War II.

Throughout these events, the Bush administration proceeded cautiously. The president wondered if a moderate communist might not be better for Poland than radical reformer Lech Walesa of the Solidarity labor movement; an abrupt change to Walesa might be "more than the market will bear." Asked whether the United States had a new foe after the end of the Cold War, Bush answered without hesitation: "The enemy is unpredictability. The enemy is instability." He tried not to push the Soviet Union too hard and infuriate Russian hard-liners. "I don't want to do something that would inadvertently set back the progress," Bush said.

The same desire not to create "big problems" affected U.S. policy as the Soviet Union itself began to break up. The USSR had absorbed the small Baltic republics of Estonia, Lithuania, and Latvia during World War II. In 1990, they reasserted their independence. When Gorbachev refused to recognize the action, Bush said little. In August 1991, Bush visited the USSR and disappointed an independence-minded crowd in the Ukrainian capital of Kiev by warning against "suicidal nationalism based on ethnic hatred." Critics quickly labeled it the "Chicken Kiev" speech. The administration's desire to work with a known leader also caused the United States to favor Gorbachev over his challenger Boris Yeltsin, who spoke for the Russian Republic rather than the larger USSR.

The Persian Gulf War

On August 2, 1990, President Saddam Hussein of Iraq seized the small neighboring country of Kuwait. The conquest gave Iraq control of 20 percent of the world's oil production and reserves. Bush demanded unconditional withdrawal, enlisted European and Arab allies in an anti-Iraq coalition, and persuaded Saudi Arabia to accept substantial U.S. forces for its protection against Iraqi invasion. Within weeks, the Saudis were host to tens of thousands of U.S. soldiers and hundreds of aircraft.

The background for Iraq's invasion was a simmering dispute over border oil fields and islands in the Persian Gulf. Iraq was a dictatorship that had just emerged from an immensely costly eight-year war with Iran. Saddam Hussein had depended on help from the United States and Arab nations in this war, but Iraq was now economically exhausted. Kuwait itself was a small, rich nation whose ruling dynasty enjoyed few friends but plenty of oil royalties. The U.S. State Department had signaled earlier in 1990 that it might support some concessions by Kuwait in the disputes. Saddam Hussein read the signal as an open invitation to do what he wanted; having been favored in the past by the United States, he probably expected denunciations but no military response.

The Iraqis gave George Bush a golden opportunity to assert America's world influence. The importance of Middle Eastern oil helped enlist France and Britain as military allies and secure billions of dollars from Germany and Japan. A short-term oil glut also meant that the industrial nations could boycott Iraqi production. Iraq itself had antagonized nearly all its neighbors. The collapse of Soviet power and Gorbachev's interest in cooperating with the United States meant that the Soviets would not interfere with U.S. plans.

Bush and his advisers offered a series of justifications for American actions. First and most basic were the desire to punish armed aggression and the presumed need to protect Iraq's other neighbors. In fact, there was scant evidence of Iraqi preparations against Saudi Arabia. The buildup of American air power plus the effective economic sanctions would have accomplished both protection and punishment. Sanctions and diplomatic pressure might also have brought withdrawal from most or all of Kuwait. However, additional American objectives—to destroy Iraq's capacity to create atomic weapons and to topple Saddam's regime—would require direct military action.

The Persian Gulf itself offered an equally golden opportunity to the American and allied armed forces. Here were no tangled jungles, invisible guerrillas, or civilians caught in a civil war. The terrain was open and nearly uninhabited. The enemy had committed regular forces to traditional battle, where the superiority of American equipment and training would be telling. Indeed, the United States

George Bush visits American troops in Saudi Arabia on Thanksgiving Day, 1990. The United States had countered Iraq's seizure of Kuwait in August by rushing forces to protect Saudi Arabia's vital oil fields. The buildup lasted until January, when U.S. planes began a systematic air assault on Iraq.

could try out the tactics of armored maneuver and close land–air cooperation that the Pentagon had devised to protect Germany against Soviet invasion.

Bush probably decided on war in October, eventually increasing the number of American troops in Saudi Arabia to 580,000. The United States stepped up diplomatic pressure by securing a series of increasingly tough United Nations resolutions that culminated in November 1990 with Security Council Resolution 678, authorizing "all necessary means" to liberate Kuwait. The president convinced Congress to agree to military action under the umbrella of the UN. The United States also ignored compromise plans floated by France and last-minute concessions from Iraq.

War began one day after the UN's January 15 deadline for Iraqi withdrawal from Kuwait. **Desert Storm** opened with massive air attacks on command centers, transportation facilities, and Iraqi forward positions. The air war destroyed 40 to 50 percent of Iraqi tanks and artillery by late February. The attacks also seriously hurt Iraqi civilians by disrupting utilities and food supplies.

Americans found the new war fascinating. They bought millions of Middle East maps to follow the conflict. They watched CNN's live transmission of Baghdad under bombardment and stared in fascination at pictures of Patriot missiles presumably intercepting Iraqi Scud missiles. They read about Stealth fighter bombers that were invisible to radar and precision-guided missiles that could home in on specified targets (although most of the damage came from traditional bombing and low-tech A-10 antitank aircraft).

The forty-day rain of bombs was the prelude to a ground attack (see Map 33-3). Despite Saddam Hussein's threats that the coalition faced the "mother of all battles," the Iraqi military made the land war easy. They concentrated their forces near

Map 33-3   Persian Gulf War
Ground operations against Iraq in the Persian Gulf War followed six weeks of aerial bombardment. The ground attack, which met quick success, was a multinational effort by the United States, Britain, France, Saudi Arabia, and other Arab nations threatened by an aggressive Iraq. The war freed Kuwait from Iraqi occupation but stopped before forcing a change in Iraq's government.

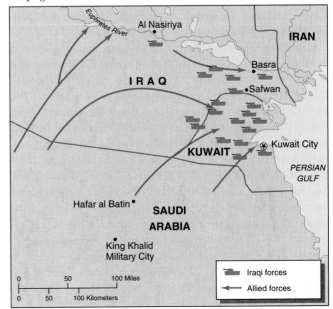

the Persian Gulf in Kuwait itself because they expected an amphibious landing near Kuwait City and a direct strike north along the coast. Instead, the allies moved 235,000 U.S., French, and British soldiers far into the interior. On February 24, 1991, these forces swept into Iraq in a great arc. Americans, Saudis, Syrians, and Egyptians advanced directly to liberate Kuwait. A cease-fire came one hundred hours after the start of the ground war. The Iraqis had been driven out of Kuwait, but the relatively slow advance of the left wing failed to prevent many of the Iraqi troops from escaping. Allied forces suffered only 240 deaths in action, compared to perhaps 100,000 for the Iraqis.

Bush directed Desert Storm with the "Vietnam syndrome" in mind, believing that Americans were willing to accept war only if it involved overwhelming U.S. force and ended quickly. The desire for a quick war, however, posed a problem. The United States hoped to replace Saddam Hussein without disrupting Iraqi society. Instead, the hundred-hour war incited armed rebellions against Saddam by Shi'ite Muslims in southern Iraq and by ethnically distinct Kurds in the north. Because Bush and his advisers were unwilling to get embroiled in a civil war, they stood by while Saddam crushed the uprisings. In one sense, the United States won the war but not the peace. Saddam Hussein became a hero to many in the Islamic world simply by remaining in power. In another sense, Bush had accomplished exactly what he wanted—the restoration of the status quo.

A New World Order?

There was no such status quo in the Soviet Union. The final act in the transformation of the USSR began with an attempted coup against Mikhail Gorbachev in August, 1991. The trigger was a planned vote on a new constitution that would decrease the power of the central Soviet government. Old-line communist bureaucrats arrested Gorbachev in his vacation house and tried to take over the government apparatus in Moscow. They turned out to be bumblers and drunks who hadn't secured military support and even failed to take over radio and television stations. Boris Yeltsin, president of the Russian Republic, organized the resistance. The United States cautiously deplored the coup as "extraconstitutional," then gradually hardened its line as Muscovites flocked to support Yeltsin and defied tank crews in front of the Russian parliament building. Within three days, the plotters themselves were under arrest.

The coup hastened the fragmentation of the Soviet Union. Before the month was out, the Soviet parliament banned the Communist party. By December, Gorbachev had resigned, and all of the fifteen component republics of the Soviet Union had declared their independence. The superpower Union of Soviet Socialist Republics ceased to exist. Russia remained the largest and strongest of the new states, followed by Ukraine and Kazakhstan.

The end of the Cold War leaves the historical assessment of the last half-century of U.S. foreign policy open to debate. Analysts agree that the relentless pressure of American defense spending helped bankrupt and undermine the USSR. It is an open question whether this same American defense spending also weakened the United States' economy and its ability to compete in the world marketplace. Some scholars see the demise of the Soviet empire as ultimate justification for forty years of Cold War. Dissenters argue the opposite—that the collapse of European communism shows that American leaders had magnified its threat. Before we can choose among differing views, we will need to wait for scholars to explore Russian archives and Soviet Cold War policy to place alongside our understanding of U.S. policy.

The end of the Cold War created a multisided world system. Since the 1940s, diplomats and politicians had judged every choice in terms of the great standoff between the United States and the USSR. Now they had to understand the complex interactions of new centers of power—not only the United States and Russia but also Japan, the European Union, and rising economies like China, Brazil, and Mexico.

What role would the United States find? President Bush saw a new world order in which the United States would be a global police force. The problem was no longer the global balance of power but rather disciplining renegade nations like Iraq. In his 1991 State of the Union speech, Bush talked about the necessity for the United States to "bear a major share of leadership" in keeping the world orderly, for only the United States had "both the moral standing and the means" to do so. He seemed to be calling for something like the Pax Britannica of the nineteenth century, when the British navy enforced a British-dominated peace on small nations around the globe.

The debate about foreign policy influenced another debate about the future of American armed forces. In the 1990s, the Pentagon closed dozens of military bases and facilities, disrupting local economies and reducing the military establishment. Military and civilian employment directly related to defense dropped from 7.2 million in 1987 to 4.5 million in 1997. In this context, it is important to remember that the Persian Gulf War cured the "Vietnam syndrome" but not the "Vietnam problem." Public excitement about the successful campaign made future military action more feasible. But Desert Storm did not solve the problem of how to intervene and retain the initiative in civil wars. The "doctrine of invincible force" is not so easy to apply in peacekeeping situations or civil war quagmires. In the mid-1990s, conflict in Somalia, Bosnia, Rwanda, Haiti, and Kosovo presented the United States with far harder choices than Saddam Hussein had offered George Bush. Bill Clinton faced a legacy of expectations about an activist foreign policy but little guidance about how to meet those expectations.

Searching for the Center

In Bill Clinton's race for president in 1992, the "war room" was the decision center where Clinton and his staff planned tactics and countered Republican attacks. On the wall was a sign with a simple message: "It's the economy, stupid." The short sentence was a reminder that victory lay in emphasizing everyday problems that George Bush neglected.

The message also revealed an insight into the character of the United States in the 1990s. What mattered most were down-to-earth issues, not the distant problems of foreign policy. As voters worried about the changing economy and its social consequences, they were eager for leaders who promised practical responses to problems that spanned the left and right. The mid-1990s brought erratic swings between the two major parties, but the most reliable position was the center. As had happened time and again, the nation's two-party system punished extremes and rewarded leaders who claimed the middle of the road with issues such as economic growth.

Political Generations

Every fifteen to twenty years, a new group of voters and leaders comes to power, driven by the desire to fix the mess that the previous generation left behind. The agenda for the Reagan and Bush years arose from the disillusion and crises of the late 1960s and 1970s. The leaders who dominated the 1980s believed that the answer was to turn the nation's social and economic problems over to the market while asserting America's influence and power around the world.

The mid-1990s brought another generation into the political arena. The members of "Generation X" came of voting age with deep worries about the foreclosing of opportunities. They worried that previous administrations had neglected social problems and let the competitive position of the United States deteriorate. The range of suggested solutions differed widely—individual moral reform, a stronger labor movement, leaner competition in world markets—but the generational concern was clear.

This turmoil of generational change made 1992 one of the most volatile national elections in decades. Young and successful but not widely known as governor of Arkansas, Democrat Bill Clinton decided that George Bush was vulnerable. His campaign for the nomination overcame minimal name recognition, accusations of womanizing, and his use of a student deferment to avoid military service in Vietnam. Clinton made sure that the Democrats fielded a full baby boomer (and southern) ticket by choosing the equally youthful Tennessean Albert Gore, Jr., as his running mate.

Bush won renomination by beating back archconservative Patrick Buchanan, who claimed that the last twelve years had been a long betrayal of true conservatism. The Republican National Convention in Houston showed how important cultural issues had become to the Republican party. The party platform conformed to the beliefs of the Christian right. Pat Buchanan called for right-thinking Americans to crusade against unbelievers. Buchanan's startling speech was a reminder of the multiple ways that religious belief was reshaping American politics (see "American Views: The Religious Imperative in Politics").

The wild card was Texas billionaire Ross Perot, whose independent campaign started with an appearance on a television talk show. Perot loved flip charts, distanced himself from professional politicians, and claimed to talk sense to the American people. He also tried to occupy the political center, appealing to the middle of the middle-class—to small business owners, middle managers, and professionals who had approved of Reagan's antigovernment rhetoric but distrusted his corporate cronies. In May, Perot outscored both Bush and Clinton in opinion polls, but his behavior became increasingly erratic. He withdrew from the race and then reentered after floating stories that he was the target of dark conspiracies.

American Views
THE RELIGIOUS IMPERATIVE IN POLITICS

The strong religious faith of many Americans frequently drives them to different stands on political issues. The first of these two documents, a letter by Jerry Falwell to potential supporters of the Moral Majority, reflects the politically conservative outlook of many evangelical Christians. Falwell is pastor of the Thomas Road Baptist Church in Lynchburg, Virginia. He founded the Moral Majority, a conservative religious lobbying and educational organization, in 1979 and served as its president until 1987, the year he wrote the letter reprinted here. The second document, from an open letter issued by the Southside United Presbyterian Church in Tucson in 1982, expresses the conviction of other believers that God may sometimes require civil disobedience to oppose oppressive government actions. The letter explains the church's reasons for violating immigration law to offer sanctuary to refugees from repressive Central American regimes supported by the United States.

❖ **How do Falwell and the Southside Presbyterian Church define the problems that demand a religious response?**

❖ **Are there any points of agreement?**

❖ **How does each statement balance the claims of God and government?**

From the Reverend Jerry Falwell

I believe that the overwhelming majority of Americans are sick and tired of the way that amoral liberals are trying to corrupt our nation from its commitment to freedom, democracy, traditional morality, and the free enterprise system.

And I believe that the majority of Americans agree on the basic moral values which this nation was founded upon over 200 years ago.

Today we face four burning crises as we continue in this Decade of Destiny—the 1980s—loss of our freedom by giving in to the Communists; the destruction of the family unit; the deterioration of the free enterprise system; and the crumbling of basic moral principles which has resulted in the legalizing of abortion, wide-spread pornography, and a drug problem of epidemic proportions.

That is why I went to Washington, D.C., in June of 1979, and started a new organization—The Moral Majority

Right now you may be wondering: "But I thought Jerry Falwell was the preacher on the Old-Time Gospel Hour television program?"

Bush campaigned as a foreign policy expert. He expected voters to reward him for the end of the Cold War, but he ignored anxieties about the nation's direction at home. In fact, voters in November ranked the economy first as an issue, the deficit second, health care third, and foreign policy eighth. Clinton hammered away at economic concerns and the need for change from the Reagan-Bush years, appealing to swing voters, such as suburban independents and blue-collar Reagan Democrats. He presented himself as the leader of new, pragmatic, and livelier Democrats. He put on sunglasses and played the saxophone on a late-night talk show. He answered questions from viewers on MTV. His campaign theme song came from Fleetwood Mac, one of the favorite rock groups of thirty-something Americans: "Don't stop thinking about tomorrow. . . . Yesterday's gone. Yesterday's gone."

Election day gave the Clinton-Gore ticket 43 percent of the popular vote, Bush 38 percent, and Perot 19 percent (see Map 33-4). Clinton held the Democratic core of northern and midwestern industrial states

You are right. For over twenty-four years I have been calling the nation back to God from the pulpit on radio and television.

But in recent months I have been led to do more than just preach—I have been compelled to take action.

I have made the commitment to go right into the halls of Congress and fight for laws that will save America. . . .

I will still be preaching every Sunday on the Old-Time Gospel Hour—and I still must be a husband and father to my precious family in Lynchburg, Virginia.

But as God gives me the strength, I must do more. I must go into the halls of Congress and fight for laws that will protect the grand old flag . . . for the sake of our children and grandchildren.

From Southside United Presbyterian Church

We are writing to inform you that Southside Presbyterian Church will publicly violate the Immigration and Nationality Act, Section 274 (A). . . .

We take this action because we believe the current policy and practice of the United States Government with regard to Central American refugees is illegal and immoral. We believe our government is in violation of the 1980 Refugee Act and international law by continuing to arrest, detain, and forcibly return refugees to the terror, persecution, and murder in El Salvador and Guatemala.

We believe that justice and mercy require the people of conscience actively assert our God-given right to aid anyone fleeing from persecution and murder. . . .

We beg of you, in the name of God, to do justice and love mercy in the administration of your office. We ask that "extended voluntary departure" be granted to refugees from Central America and that current deportation proceedings against these victims be stopped.

Until such time, we will not cease to extend the sanctuary of the church. . . . Obedience to God requires this of us all.

Sources: Gary E. McCuen, ed., *The Religious Right* (*G. E. McCuen Publishers, 1989*); Ann Crittenden, *Sanctuary* (*Weidenfeld and Nicolson, 1988*).

and loosened the Republican hold on the South and West. Millions who voted for Perot were casting a protest vote for "none of the above" and against "politics as usual" rather than hoping for an actual Perot victory. Clinton ran best among voters over 65, who remembered FDR and Harry Truman, and voters under 30.

Minorities at the Ballot Box

Beyond the highly publicized realm of presidential elections, the 1990s saw the continued emergence of new participants in American government. Clinton's first cabinet, in which three women and four minority men balanced seven white men, marked the maturing of minorities and women as distinct political constituencies. In both cases, their new prominence in the national government followed years of growing success in cities and states.

After the racial violence of the 1960s, many black people had turned to local politics to gain control of their own communities. The first black mayor of a major twentieth-century city was Carl Stokes in Cleveland in 1967, followed closely by

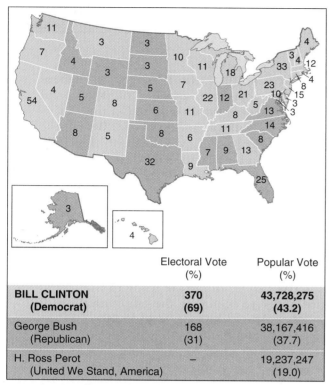

	Electoral Vote (%)	Popular Vote (%)
BILL CLINTON (Democrat)	**370 (69)**	**43,728,275 (43.2)**
George Bush (Republican)	168 (31)	38,167,416 (37.7)
H. Ross Perot (United We Stand, America)	–	19,237,247 (19.0)

Map 33-4   Election of 1992
Bill Clinton defeated George Bush in 1992 by reviving the Democratic party in the industrial Northeast and enlisting new Democratic voters in the western states, where he appealed both to Hispanic immigrants and to people associated with fast-growing high tech industries. He won reelection in 1996 with the same pattern of support. However, the coalition is an unstable combination of "Old Democrats" associated with older industries and labor unions and "New Democrats" favoring economic change, free trade, and globalization.

Richard Hatcher in Gary, Indiana. The 1973 election brought victories for Tom Bradley in Los Angeles, Maynard Jackson in Atlanta, and Coleman Young in Detroit. By 1983, three of the nation's four largest cities had black mayors (Harold Washington in Chicago, Wilson Goode in Philadelphia, and Bradley in Los Angeles). In 1989, Virginia made Douglas Wilder the first black governor in any of the United States since Reconstruction.

The election of a minority mayor was sometimes more important for its symbolism than for the transfer of real power. Efforts to restructure the basis of city council elections, however, struck directly at the balance of power. Most midsized cities had stopped electing city councils by wards or districts during the first half of the twentieth century. Voting at large shifted power away from geographically concentrated ethnic groups. It favored business interests who claimed to speak for the city as a whole but who

could assign most of the costs of economic growth to older and poorer neighborhoods.

In the 1970s, minority leaders and community activists realized that a return to district voting could convert neighborhood segregation from a liability to a political resource. As amended in 1975, the federal Voting Rights Act allowed minorities to use the federal courts to challenge at-large voting systems that diluted the impact of their votes. Blacks and Mexican Americans used the act to reestablish city council districts in the late 1970s and early 1980s in city after city across the South and Southwest. By the 1980s and 1990s, younger Latino and African-American mayors, such as Henry Cisneros in San Antonio, Andrew Young in Atlanta, and Dennis Archer in Detroit, won election on positive platforms of growth and equity; they mended fences with local business leaders and promised newly empowered minorities a fair share of an expanding economic pie.

At the national level, minorities gradually increased their representation in Congress. Ben Nighthorse Campbell of Colorado, a Cheyenne, brought a Native American voice to the U.S. Senate in 1992. The number of African Americans in the House of Representatives topped forty after 1992 with the help of districts drawn to concentrate black voters. Even after a series of Supreme Court cases invalidated districts drawn with race as the "predominant factor," however, African Americans and Latinos held their gains in 1996 and 1998 (see Figure 33-2).

Women from the Grassroots to Congress

A second quiet political change was the increasing prominence of women and family issues in national politics. The period opened with two actions that were both symbolic and substantive. In 1981, President Reagan appointed Arizona judge Sandra Day O'Connor to be the first woman on the United States Supreme Court. In 1984, Walter Mondale chose New York Congresswoman Geraldine Ferraro as his vice presidential candidate.

As with Latinos and African Americans, political gains for women at the national level reflected their growing importance in grassroots politics. The spreading suburbs of postwar America were "frontiers" that required concerted action to solve immediate needs like adequate schools and decent parks. Because pursuit of such community services has often been viewed as "woman's work" (in contrast to the "man's work" of economic development), postwar metropolitan areas offered numerous opportunities for women to engage in volunteer civic work, learn political skills, and run

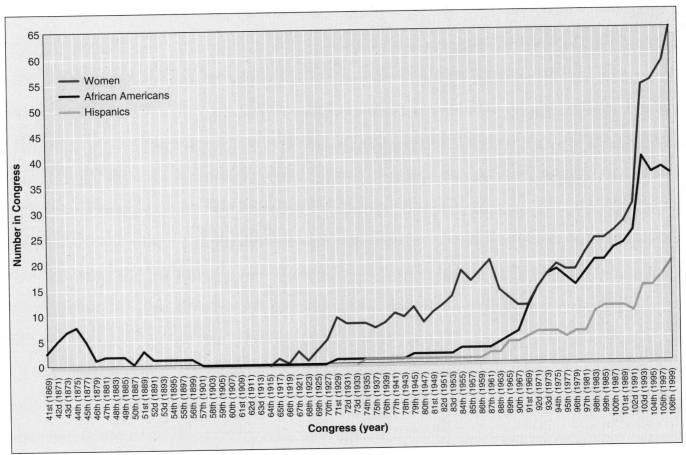

Figure 33-2   *Minorities and Women in Congress, 1869–1999*
The number of African Americans, Hispanics, and women serving in the House of Representatives and Senate increased rapidly in the 1980s and early 1990s and more slowly in the middle 1990s. The increases reflected changing attitudes, the impact of the Voting Rights Act, and decades of political activism at the grassroots.

for local office. Moreover, new cities and suburbs had fewer established political institutions, such as political machines and strong parties; their politics were open to energetic women.

The entry of more women into politics was a bipartisan affair. Important support and training grounds were the League of Women Voters, which did nonpartisan studies of basic issues, and the **National Women's Political Caucus**, designed to support women candidates of both parties. Most women in contemporary politics have been more liberal than men, a difference that political scientists attribute to women's interest in the practical problems of schools, neighborhoods, and two-earner families. But women's grassroots mobilization, especially through evangelical churches, has also strengthened groups committed to conservative social values.

Regional differences have affected women's political gains. The West has long been the part of the country most open to women in state and local government and in business (see Map 33-5). Several western states granted voting rights to women before the adoption of the Nineteenth Amendment. Westerners have been more willing than voters in the East or South to choose women as mayors of major cities and as members of state legislatures.

In 1991, the nomination of Judge Clarence Thomas to the U.S. Supreme Court ensured that everyone knew that the terms of American politics were changing. Thomas, an African American, was controversial because of his conservative positions on social and civil rights issues. Controversy deepened when law professor Anita Hill accused Thomas of harassing her sexually while she had served on his staff at the U.S. Civil Rights Commission. The accusations led to riveting hearings before a U.S. Senate committee. Critics tried to discredit Hill with vicious attacks on her character but failed to shake her story. Thomas presented himself as the victim of false accusations and a media lynching. The public was left with Hill's

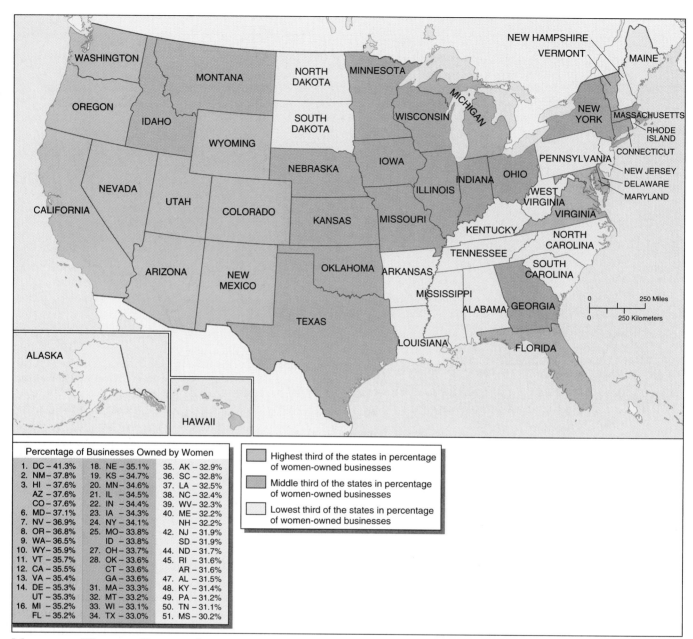

Percentage of Businesses Owned by Women		
1. DC – 41.3%	18. NE – 35.1%	35. AK – 32.9%
2. NM– 37.8%	19. KS – 34.7%	36. SC – 32.8%
3. HI – 37.6%	20. MN– 34.6%	37. LA – 32.5%
AZ – 37.6%	21. IL – 34.5%	38. NC – 32.4%
CO– 37.6%	22. IN – 34.4%	39. WV– 32.3%
6. MD– 37.1%	23. IA – 34.3%	40. ME– 32.2%
7. NV – 36.9%	24. NY – 34.1%	NH – 32.2%
8. OR– 36.8%	25. MO– 33.8%	42. NJ – 31.9%
9. WA– 36.5%	ID – 33.8%	SD – 31.9%
10. WY– 35.9%	27. OH– 33.7%	44. ND – 31.7%
11. VT – 35.7%	28. OK– 33.6%	45. RI – 31.6%
12. CA – 35.5%	CT – 33.6%	AR – 31.6%
13. VA – 35.4%	GA – 33.6%	47. AL – 31.5%
14. DE – 35.3%	31. MA– 33.3%	48. KY – 31.4%
UT – 35.3%	32. MT – 33.2%	49. PA – 31.2%
16. MI – 35.2%	33. WI – 33.1%	50. TN – 31.1%
FL – 35.2%	34. TX – 33.0%	51. MS – 30.2%

Highest third of the states in percentage of women-owned businesses

Middle third of the states in percentage of women-owned businesses

Lowest third of the states in percentage of women-owned businesses

Map 33-5   *Women as Business Owners, 1992*
Some parts of the nation are more inviting to woman-owned businesses than are others. The western and Great Lakes states, with reputations for innovative politics and flexible social environments, stand out as supportive of business opportunities for women.

Data Source: Institute for Women's Policy Research.

plausible but unproved allegations and Thomas's equally vigorous but unproved denials. The Senate confirmed Thomas to the Supreme Court. Partisans on each side continued to believe the version that best suited their preconceptions and agendas.

Whatever the merits of her charges, Hill's badgering by skeptical senators angered millions of women. In the shadow of the hearings, women made impressive gains in the 1992 election, when

the number of women in the U.S. Senate jumped from two to six (and grew further to six Democrats and three Republicans after November 1996). Successful candidates ranged from savvy and experienced politicians like California's Barbara Boxer and Dianne Feinstein to Washington's Patty Murray, who ran as a "mom in tennis shoes." The 1992 election pushed women's share of seats in the fifty state legislatures above 20 percent (it was 22 percent in

Law professor Anita Hill became a national symbol when she accused Clarence Thomas, a nominee to the Supreme Court, of sexual harassment. Her testimony at Thomas's Senate confirmation hearing failed to prevent the Senate from approving him. After confirmation, Thomas became one of the Court's most conservative members.

1999). Bill Clinton appointed women to 37 percent of the five hundred or so high-level jobs in the White House and federal departments (see Figure 33-3). That is far higher than Jimmy Carter's 15 percent or Lyndon Johnson's 4 percent.

Women have influenced national politics as voters as well as candidates and cabinet members. Since the 1980s, voting patterns have shown a widening gender gap. Women in the 1990s identified with the Democratic party and voted for its candidates at a markedly higher rate than men. The reasons include concerns about the effects of government spending cuts and interest in measures to support families rather than conservative rhetoric. This gender gap has helped keep Democrats competitive and dampened the nation's conservative swing.

Clinton as President

Bill Clinton's first term and his reelection in 1996 show the attraction of the political center. The middle and later 1990s also suggest that national politics may be stabilizing around a relatively even balance between political parties and partisan agendas, somewhat like the years from 1876 to 1896. In his first inaugural address in January 1993, Clinton pledged "an end to the era of deadlock and drift—and a new season of American renewal." What he found in his first four years in office was an equilibrium that resulted in narrow, bipartisan victories and defeats. In 1996, voters showed that they liked the nation's break from an activist government by keeping the balance of a Democratic White House and Republican Congress, although they whittled away Republican strength in 1998.

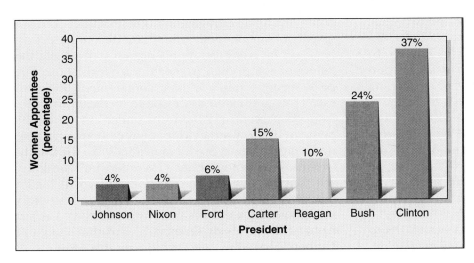

Figure 33-3 Women as a Percentage of Initial High-Level Presidential Appointments: Johnson to Clinton

By the 1990s, Americans were willing to accept women in positions that would have been reserved for "men only" in earlier decades, such as Attorney General and Secretary of State.

Data Source: Portland Oregonian, 28 September 1993.

In foreign affairs, Clinton inherited Bush's New World Order and the expectation that the United States could keep the world on an even keel and counter ethnic hatred. During the administration's first years, U.S. diplomats helped broker an Israel–PLO accord that gave Palestinians self-government in Gaza and the West Bank, only to watch extremists on both sides undermine the accords, which remained fragile but alive in 2000. The United States in 1994 used firm diplomatic pressure to persuade North Korea to stop building nuclear weapons, calming a potentially explosive trouble spot. The world also benefited from a gradual reduction of nuclear arsenals and from a 1996 treaty to ban the testing of nuclear weapons.

Elsewhere in the world, Clinton used American military power with caution. Given the national distaste for overseas entanglements, he responded far more effectively than critics expected. He inherited a U.S. military presence in Somalia (in northeastern Africa) because of a postelection decision by Bush; he withdrew American forces when their humanitarian mission of guarding food relief to starving Somalis was overshadowed by the need to take sides in civil war. Clinton intervened decisively in Haiti to restore an elected president. He reluctantly committed the United States to a multinational effort to end bloody civil war in ethnically and religiously divided Bosnia (in southeastern Europe), where U.S. troops monitored a brittle peace agreement.

The American military revisited the same part of Europe in 1999, when the United States and Britain led NATO's intervention in Kosovo. The majority of people in this Yugoslav province are ethnic Albanians who have chafed under the control of the Serb-controlled Yugoslav government since the breakup of the rest of Yugoslavia. When a Kosovar independence movement began a rebellion, the Yugoslav government responded with brutal repression that threatened to drive over one million ethnic Albanians out of the province. To protect the Kosovars, NATO began a bombing campaign that targeted Yugoslav military bases and Serb forces in Kosovo. In June, Yugoslavia agreed to withdraw its troops and make way for a multinational NATO peacekeeping force, marking a measured success for U.S. policy.

In Washington, Clinton's first four years divided into two parts. In 1993–1994, he worked with a Democratic majority in Congress to modernize the American economy. In 1995 and 1996, however, he faced solid Republican majorities, the result of an unanticipated Republican tide in the November 1994 elections.

The heart of Clinton's agenda was efforts to make the United States economy more equitable domestically and more competitive internationally; these goals marked Clinton as a **neoliberal** who envisioned a partnership between a leaner government and a dynamic private sector. Efforts to "reinvent" government cut federal employment below Reagan administration levels. A new tax bill reversed some of the inequities of the 1980s by increasing taxes on the well-off who had benefited from Reagan's policies (the top 1.2 percent of households). At the other end of the income scale was expansion of the Earned Income Tax Credit, a Nixon-era program that helps lift working Americans out of poverty. An improved college student aid program spread benefits to more students by allowing direct federal loans. The National and Community Service Trust Act created a pilot program for a domestic Peace Corps, although it was hampered by its small size (twenty thousand participants in 1994–1995) and limits on types of work.

The administration's most important victory was the approval of the treaty creating a North American Free Trade Agreement (NAFTA) (see Chapter 32). To overcome Democratic reluctance, Clinton lobbied reluctant Representatives. Al Gore took a political risk and convincingly defended NAFTA against treaty opponent Ross Perot in a debate on CNN. In November 1993, NAFTA finally passed as a measure of the political center with roughly equal numbers from each party outvoting Republican isolationists and Democratic protectionists.

The administration's record in pursuing a broad set of liberal civil rights goals was mixed in its first two years. The Department of Energy began to make public the record of Cold War tests and experiments that had subjected unknowing citizens to nuclear radiation, opening the possibility of medical treatment or compensation. The administration lifted a ban on abortion counseling in federally assisted family planning clinics. It backpedaled on the issue of gays in the military, but Congress and the Pentagon accepted a policy that made engaging in homosexual acts, but not sexual orientation itself, grounds for discharge.

The administration's biggest setback was the failure of comprehensive health care legislation. The goals seemed simple at first: containment of health care costs and extension of basic medical insurance from 83 percent of Americans under age 65 to 100 percent. In the abstract, voters agreed that something needed to be done. So did individuals like the twenty-five-year-old photographer's assistant who found herself facing cancer surgery without savings or health insurance: "I work full-time, and because it's a very small business, we don't get any benefits. . . . It just devastated everybody financially. And that shouldn't happen. That's the American dream that's lost."

Unfortunately, the plan that emerged from the White House ran to 1,342 pages of complex regulations with something for everyone to dislike. Senior citizens worried about limits on Medicare spending. Insurance companies didn't want more regulations. Businesses didn't want the costs of insuring their workers. Taxpayers liked the idea of wider medical insurance coverage but not the idea of paying for it through higher taxes or rationing of medical services.

If Reagan avoided blame for mistakes, Clinton in his first two years in office seemed to avoid credit for successes. Despite his legislative accomplishments, the press emphasized his difficulty in reaching decisions. Perhaps because he sometimes started with absolute statements and positions, what might look in another leader like a willingness to compromise looked like waffling in Clinton. Both the president and his wife attracted extreme and bitter hatred from the far right, of a sort previously reserved for Franklin and Eleanor Roosevelt and the Kennedy family. Indeed, Hillary Rodham Clinton became a symbol of discomfiting changes in American families.

Personal animosity was part of the setting for an extraordinary off-year election in 1994, in which voters defeated dozens of incumbents and gave Republicans control of both House and Senate. For most of 1995, the new speaker of the House, Newt Gingrich of Georgia, dominated political headlines as he pushed the **Contract with America**, the official Republican campaign platform for the 1994 elections, which called for a revolutionary reduction of federal responsibilities.

Clinton took a page from *B'rer Rabbit*. He laid low and let the new Congress attack environmental protections, propose cuts in federal benefits for the elderly, and push a cut in the capital gains tax to help the rich. As Congress and president battled over the budget, congressional Republicans refused to authorize interim spending and forced the federal government to shut down for more than three weeks between November 1995 and January 1996. Gingrich was the clear loser in public opinion, both for the shutdowns and his ideas. Democrats painted Gingrich and his congressional allies as a radical fringe who wanted to gut Medicare and Medicaid, undermine education, punish legal immigrants, and sell off the national parks—core values and programs that most Americans wanted to protect. Democrats, of course, proclaimed themselves the defenders of national values.

After the budget confrontations, 1996 brought a series of measures to reward work—a centrist position acceptable to most Americans. The minimum wage increased. Congress made pension programs easier for employers to create and made health insurance portable when workers changed jobs. After tough negotiations and two Clinton vetos, a welfare reform bill that emphasized work as a condition for public assistance shifted responsibilities to the states. The number of welfare recipients has fallen dramatically, but there are doubts that many of the former recipients have found jobs adequate to support their families.

Bill Clinton significantly expanded the number of women appointed to cabinet offices and other high positions in the federal government. Madeleine K. Albright took office in 1997 as the nation's first woman Secretary of State and the nation's highest-ranking woman official. She appears here with the president and British Prime Minister Tony Blair during NATO's fiftieth anniversary summit.

Underlying politics were continued efforts to cope with a globalizing economy and technological change in a world shaped by CNN and MTV, the unification of Europe, and the rise of East Asian nations. Both the Clinton-Gore team and Gingrich were eager to take on the task. Clinton pushed for free trade and deregulation of the telecommunications industry, Gore promoted wide access to the Internet, and Gingrich preached a new frontier of entrepreneurial energy.

Clinton's reelection in 1996 was a virtual replay of 1992. His opponent, Robert Dole, represented an earlier political generation. Dole's Republican party was uncertain whether to stress free markets or morality. The party tried to paper over its uneasy mix of traditional country club Republicans (probusiness and socially moderate), radical proponents of unregulated markets, and religious conservatives affiliated with the Christian Coalition. Evangelicals dominated state parties from Minnesota to Texas, but they made many traditional party regulars uncomfortable and carried few statewide elections. The Republicans thus displayed many of the internal fractures that characterized American society as a whole.

Because the nation was prosperous and at peace, and because Clinton had claimed the political center (allowing him to sound like Dwight Eisenhower), the results were never in doubt. The Clinton-Gore ticket took 70 percent of the electoral votes and 49 percent of the popular vote (versus 41 percent for Dole and 9 percent for a recycled Ross Perot). Clinton easily won the Northeast, the industrial Midwest, and the Far West; Hispanic voters alienated by anti-immigrant rhetoric from the Republicans helped Clinton also take usually Republican states, such as Florida and Arizona.

A New Prosperity?

In 2000, Americans entered a tenth year of continuous economic expansion. Unemployment dropped from 7.2 percent in 1992 to 4.0 percent at the start of 2000 as American businesses created more than 12 million new jobs. Key states like California rebounded from economic recession with new growth driven by high-tech industries, entertainment, and foreign trade. The stock market soared during the nineties; rising demand for shares in established blue-chip companies and new Internet firms swelled the value of individual portfolios, IRA accounts, and pension funds. The rate of homeownership rose after declining for fifteen years. The proportion of Americans in poverty dropped to 13 percent, and the gap between rich and poor began to narrow (slightly) for the first time in two decades.

The economic boom was good news for the federal budget. Tight spending and rising personal income turned perennial deficits into surpluses for 1998 and 1999. Reduced borrowing by the U.S. Treasury resulted in low interest rates, which further fueled corporate expansion and consumer spending. Both political parties anticipated a growing surplus for the next decade and debated whether to offer massive tax cuts, to buy down the national debt, or to shore up Social Security and Medicare.

Behind the statistics were substantial gains in the efficiency of the American economy. International rivals—especially Japan—experienced severe economic slumps in the mid-1990s. In the United States, in contrast, by the end of the decade the productivity of manufacturing workers was increasing more than 4 percent per year. Part of the gain was the payoff from the painful business restructuring and downsizing of the 1970s and 1980s. Another cause was improvements in efficiency from the full incorporation of personal computers and electronic communication into everyday life and business practice.

It remains to be seen whether the growth of the 1990s marked the beginning of a new wave of sustained economic expansion like earlier waves triggered by technological innovation. In the past, such waves have followed fifty-year cycles that begin with a thirty-year period of rapid expansion followed by two decades of consolidation and slow growth. From 1945 to 1974, for example, the automobile and aerospace industries helped Europe, Japan, and the United States enjoy an era of sustained growth that was followed by two decades of painful economic readjustment and problems. In the later 1990s, fast-growing information-based industries such as electronic communications, software, biotechnology, and medicine may have jump-started another era of prosperity.

Morality and Partisanship

If the economy was the fundamental news of the later 1990s, Bill Clinton's personal life was the hot news. In 1998 and 1999, the United States was riveted by revelations about the president's busy sex life, doubts about his integrity, and debates about his fitness for high office. Years of rumors, innuendoes, and law suits culminated in 1999 in the nation's second presidential impeachment trial.

Clinton's problems began in 1994 with the appointment of a special prosecutor to investigate possible fraud in the Whitewater development, an Arkansas land promotion in which Bill and Hillary Clinton had invested in the 1980s. The probe by Kenneth Starr, the Independent Counsel, however, expanded beyond Whitewater into a wide-ranging

FROM THEN TO NOW

Impeachment

Bill Clinton was the third president to be enmeshed in a serious impeachment process. He was the second to have been formally impeached by the House of Representatives, tried by the Senate, and acquitted of the impeachment charges.

The framers of the Constitution designed impeachment as one of its many checks and balances. Impeachment was to be a method for holding the judicial and executive branches accountable and particularly to assure that the presidency could not turn into a kingship. The Constitution thus included a procedure for charging the president with treason or bribery and removing him from office if the charges held. The makers of the Constitution added "high crimes and misdemeanors" to the list of impeachable offenses based on five hundred years of experience in Britain; the phrase meant actions that undermined the integrity or stability of the government.

As legal historian Stanley Kutler has pointed out, a successful and legitimate impeachment process needs to be bipartisan rather than blatantly political. It also must be a response to a genuine threat to the integrity of the political and governmental process.

The impeachment and trial of Andrew Johnson in 1868 clearly failed the first of these tests, for the affair was driven by a faction of the Republican Party and was defeated by the defection of moderate Republicans. The case did revolve around a basic constitutional issue—Johnson's refusal to accept the Tenure of Office Act—but it also nonetheless failed the second test because the law in question actually altered the political balance in favor of Congress rather than the president.

The impeachment of Bill Clinton also failed both tests. Partisanship in the House Judiciary Committee drove the passage of two articles of impeachment, and the votes of moderate Republicans, as in 1868, provided the margin for acquittal. The Clinton impeachment was flawed as well by the nature of the charges, which had only the faintest relationship to the conduct of government. Clinton was certainly dishonest in shading and withholding the truth before a grand jury, but his actions undermined only his personal reputation, not the stability of the nation.

In comparison, the near impeachment of Richard Nixon more closely meets the two standards. First, the House Judiciary Committee hearings in 1974 were careful and bipartisan, as were its recommendations of impeachment to the full House. Members worked quietly for eight months before they were satisfied that impeachment was the only option. It was conservative Republicans such as Barry Goldwater who told Nixon that resignation was the only alternative to conviction and removal from office. Second, Nixon's active efforts to conceal political cheating did carry a serious threat to the political system. His lies did not just reflect on his character, they also undermined the integrity of national elections.

William Rehnquist, Chief Justice of the Supreme Court, is sworn in as the presiding judge for the impeachment trial of Bill Clinton.

investigation that encompassed the firing of the White House travel office staff, the suicide of White House aide Vincent Foster, and the sexual behavior of the president. Meanwhile, Paula Jones had brought a lawsuit claiming sexual harassment by then-governor Clinton while she was a state worker in Arkansas. The investigation of Whitewater brought convictions of several friends and former associates of the Clintons, but no evidence pointing directly at either Bill or Hilary Clinton themselves.

The legal landscape changed in January 1998 when allegations surfaced about an affair between the president and Monica Lewinsky, a former White House intern. Lewinsky admitted to the relationship privately and then to Starr's staff after the president had denied it in a sworn deposition for the Paula Jones case. This opened him to charges of perjury and obstruction of justice. Although a federal judge dismissed Jones's suit in April, the continued unfolding of the Lewinsky affair treated the nation to a barrage of personal details about Bill Clinton and to semantic debates over what exactly constituted a "sexual relationship." The affair certainly revealed deep flaws in Clinton's character and showed his willingness to shade the truth. Newspaper editorials, radio talk shows, and politicians debated whether such flaws were relevant to his ability to perform his Constitutional duties.

In the fall of 1998, the Republican leaders who controlled Congress decided that Clinton's statements and misstatements justified the Constitutional process of impeachment. In December, the Republican majority on the House Judiciary Committee recommended four articles of impeachment, or specific charges against the president, to the House of Representatives. By a partisan vote, the full House approved two of the charges and forwarded them to the Senate. The formal trial of the charges by the Senate began in January 1999 and ended on February 12. Moderate Republicans joined Democrats to assure that the Senate would fall far short of the two-thirds majority required for conviction and removal from office. Article 1, charging that the president had perjured himself, failed by a vote of 45 to 55. Article 2, charging that he had obstructed justice, failed by a vote of 50 to 50.

Why did Congressional Republicans pursue impeachment to the bitter end? It was clear by the end of 1998 that a majority of Americans strongly disapproved of Clinton's conduct but did not think that his personal behavior merited removal from office. The 1998 election, which reduced the Republican majority in the House and resulted in the resignation of Newt Gingrich, confirmed the opinion polls.

At the same time, 25 to 30 percent of Americans remained convinced that Clinton was a disgrace whose presence in the White House demeaned the nation. It was not so much that they disliked his policies, which were often quite conservative, but that they felt that his personal flaws and sins made him unfit to lead and represent the nation. In other words, although impeachment was certainly motivated by politics (anti-Clinton people are a powerful force within the Republican Party), it was also another battle in America's continuing culture wars.

Conclusion

Americans entered the 1980s searching for stability. The 1970s had brought unexpected and uncomfortable change. Soviet actions in Asia and Africa seemed to be destabilizing the world. The memory of defeat in Vietnam left a bitter taste, and hostages in Tehran seemed to signal the end to America's global postwar dominance. Energy crises, inflation, and boarded-up factories eroded purchasing power and undermined confidence in the future. Traditional values seemed under siege. Ronald Reagan's presidential campaign played to these insecurities by promising to revitalize the older ways of life and restore the United States to its former influence.

Instead of time out from change, the 1980s brought new uncertainties and new efforts to articulate the nation's core values. The political liberalization and then the astonishing collapse of the Soviet Union ended forty years of Cold War. New political leadership in Washington reversed the fifty-year expansion of federal government programs to deal with economic and social inequities. Prosperity alternated with recessions that shifted the balance between regions. The stock market rode a roller coaster, familiar corporate names vanished, and the national media made temporary heroes of business tycoons. Middle-class Latinos and African Americans made substantial gains while many other minority Americans sank deeper into poverty. The outbreak of violence in Los Angeles in 1992, after the acquittal of police officers accused of beating Rodney King, showed that race relations were as tense as they had been in the 1960s.

In the 1990s, the United States found itself with uncontested political and military influence in the world. Despite its growing dependence on foreign goods, it remained a nation of rich resources. It had one of the world's most broadly educated populations and the greatest concentration of scientific and technical capacity. After struggling in the 1980s, its highly flexible economy was outperforming most rivals.

Politics rewarded the pragmatic center rather than extreme positions. Voters were cautious about the radical free-market advocates on the extreme right, showing little interest in having Republicans actually put the Contract with America into practice. They were equally unimpressed by liberal advocates of extensive entitlements on the European model. What voters wanted was to continue the reduction of the federal role in domestic affairs that began in the 1980s without damaging social insurance programs. Successful new initiatives included such middle-of-the-road measures as NAFTA and welfare reform.

Left unsolved were two challenges to basic American values. One was the challenge of equality. The American system distributed the benefits of prosperity less equally than other major industrial nations. Americans also struggled to reconcile their belief in equal opportunity with the realities of long-term poverty and racial discrimination. Insecurity among working families prompted calls in the mid-1990s to restrict immigration and end affirmative action as "reverse discrimination." While most Americans believed in giving everyone a fair chance, they disagreed about how to define and assure that chance.

The second task was to strengthen the nation's civic life. Here, too, Americans disagreed. Was the solution to social problems for individuals to be more upright or for communities to take more responsibility for common needs? Many Americans in the mid-1990s distrusted government but were still willing to attack problems through grassroots organizations. The job for citizens and leaders was to revive faith in public institutions and in the belief that Americans of all backgrounds could work together to achieve common national goals.

Review Questions

1. Is it accurate to talk about a Reagan Revolution in American politics? Did Reagan's presidency change the economic environment for workers and business corporations? How did economic changes in the 1980s affect the prospects of the richest and poorest Americans?

2. What caused the breakup of the Soviet Union and the end of the Cold War? Did U.S. foreign policy under Reagan and Bush contribute significantly to the withdrawal of Soviet power from eastern Europe? Did the collapse of the USSR show the strength of the United States and its allies or the weakness of Soviet communism?

3. Was the American political system more polarized and divided in 1996 than in 1980? How did religiously conservative Americans understand issues of foreign relations and economic policy? How did religiously liberal Americans understand these same issues? What was the gender gap in national politics in the 1990s? Why were Republicans unable to appeal to most black and Hispanic voters in 1992 and 1996?

4. What were Bill Clinton's major policy accomplishments? Do these represent "liberal," "moderate," or "conservative" positions? What was the Contract with America? What are other examples of a conservative political trend in the 1990s?

Recommended Reading

Michael Beschloss and Strobe Talbott, *At the Highest Levels* (1993). A dramatic narrative of the last years of the Cold War, based on detailed interviews with American and Soviet participants.

Susan Bibler Coutin, *The Culture of Protest: Religious Activism and the U.S. Sanctuary Movement* (1993). Examining foreign policy from the grassroots, sympathetically portrays the meanings that participants in the sanctuary movement gave their actions.

Thomas Byrne Edsall and Mary D. Edsall, *Chain Reaction: The Impact of Race, Rights, and Taxes on American Politics* (1991). Argues that the Democratic party has systematically alienated its working-class supporters.

Sara Lawrence-Lightfoot, *I've Known Rivers: Lives of Loss and Liberation* (1994). Conveys the experiences of black women in the changing postwar world.

Elliot Liebow, *Tell Them Who I Am: The Lives of Homeless Women* (1993). A sensitive depiction of "street people" and "bag ladies" as complex individuals coping with personal problems and economic crisis.

Kevin Phillips, *Boiling Point: Democrats, Republicans, and the Decline of Middle-Class Prosperity* (1992). Expresses the belief that the economic policies of the Reagan and Bush administrations systematically damaged working- and middle-class families.

Lillian Rubin, *Families on the Fault Line: American's Working Class Speaks about the Family, the Economy, Race, and Ethnicity* (1994). Interviews with American families about their efforts to cope with economic and social change.

Garry Wills, *Reagan's America: Innocents at Home* (1987). A biography critical of Reagan's ideas but insightful about his personality.

Additional Sources

Economic Change: Opportunity and Inequality

William Bowen and Derek Bok, *The Shape of the River: The Long-Term Consequences of Considering Race in College and University Admissions* (1998).

Michael Lee Cohen, *The Twenty-Something American Dream* (1993).

Andrew Hacker, *Two Nations: Black and White, Separate, Hostile, Unequal* (1992).

William Robbins, *Hard Times in Paradise* (1988).

Daphne Spain and Suzanne Bianchi, *Balancing Act: Motherhood, Marriage and Employment among American Women* (1996).

Ida Susser, *Norman Street: Poverty and Politics in an Urban Neighborhood* (1982).

Sharon Zukin, *Loft Living: Culture and Capital in Urban Change* (1982).

African-American Experiences

Pierre Clavel and Wim Wiewel, eds., *Harold Washington and the Neighborhoods* (1991).

Daniel Coyle, *Hardball: A Season in the Projects* (1993).

Mitchell Duneier, *Slim's Table: Race, Respectability and Masculinity* (1992).

Steven F. Lawson, *In Pursuit of Power: Southern Blacks and Electoral Politics* (1985).

William Julius Wilson, *The Truly Disadvantaged* (1987).

The New Conservatism

William Bennett, *The De-Valuing of America: The Fight for Our Culture and Our Children* (1992).

Lee Edwards, *The Conservative Revolution* (1999).

John Ehrman, *The Rise of Neo-Conservative Intellectuals and Foreign Affairs, 1945-1994* (1995).

J. David Hoeveler, Jr., *Watch on the Right: Conservative Intellectuals in the Reagan Era* (1991).

Linda Kintz, *Between Jesus and the Market: The Emotions That Matter in Right-Wing America* (1997).

Irving Kristol, *Neoconservatism: The Autobiography of an Idea* (1995).

Theodore J. Lowi, *The End of the Republican Era* (1995).

Charles Murray, *Losing Ground: American Social Policy, 1950–1980* (1984).

Politics, Society, and the Mass Media

R. Serge Denisoff, *Inside MTV* (1988).

Don Flournoy, *CNN World Report: Ted Turner's International News Coup* (1992).

Todd Gitlin, *Watching Television* (1987).

Andrew Goodwin, *Dancing in the Distraction Factory: Music Television and Popular Culture* (1992).

Military and Foreign Policy

Dana H. Allin, *Cold War Illusions: America, Europe, and Soviet Power, 1969–1989* (1998).

David Cortright, *Peace Works: The Citizen's Role in Ending the Cold War* (1993).

Theodore Draper, *A Very Thin Line* (1991).

Lawrence Freedman and Efraim Karsh, *The Gulf Conflict, 1990–1991: Diplomacy and the New World Order* (1993).

John L. Gaddis, *Now We Know: Rethinking Cold War History* (1997).

Stephen Graubard, *Mr. Bush's War* (1992).

Michael J. Hogan, ed., *The End of the Cold War: Its Meaning and Implications* (1992).

Christian Smith, *Resisting Reagan: The U.S. Central American Peace Movement* (1997).

Robert W. Tucker and David C. Hendrickson, *The Imperial Temptation: The New World Order and America's Purposes* (1992).

Daniel Wirls, *Buildup: The Politics of Defense in the Reagan Era* (1992).

Politics and Politicians in the 1980s

Martin Anderson, *Revolution* (1989).

William Berman, *America's Right Turn: From Nixon to Bush* (1994).

Michael Duffy and Dan Goodgame, *Marching in Place: The Status Quo Presidency of George Bush* (1992).

Steven M. Gillon, *The Democrats' Dilemma: Walter F. Mondale and the Liberal Legacy* (1992).

Haynes Johnson, *Sleepwalking through History: America in the Reagan Years* (1991).

William Pemberton, *Exit with Honor: The Life and Presidency of Ronald Reagan* (1997).

Peggy Noonan, *What I Saw at the Revolution: A Political Life in the Reagan Era* (1990).

Michael Schaller, *Reckoning with Reagan: American and Its President in the 1980s* (1992).

John W. Sloan, *The Reagan Effect: Economics and Presidential Leadership* (1999).

David Stockman, *The Triumph of Politics: How the Reagan Revolution Failed* (1986).

Politics in the 1990s

Dan Balz and Ronald Brownstein, *Storming the Gates: Protest Politics and the Republican Revival* (1996).

E. J. Dionne, Jr., *Why Americans Hate Politics* (1991).

Mark Rozell and Clyde Wilcox, *Second Coming: The New Christian Right in Virginia Politics* (1996).

Where to Learn More

❖ **Ronald Reagan Boyhood Home, Dixon, Illinois.** The home where Reagan lived from 1920 to 1923 tells relatively little about Reagan himself but a great deal about the small-town context that shaped his ideas.

❖ **State Humanities Councils.** Every state has a council or committee for the humanities that is affiliated with the National Endowment for the Humanities. They sponsor a wide variety of events and publications that often link historical perspectives to current social issues of importance in each state.

❖ **C-SPAN.** The Cable Satellite Public Affairs Network allows cable television viewers to observe the public workings of the national government in ways previously available only to Washington insiders.

APPENDIX

The Declaration of Independence

When in the course of human events it becomes necessary for one people to dissolve the political bands which have connected them with another and to assume, among the powers of the earth, the separate and equal station to which the laws of nature and of nature's God entitle them, a decent respect to the opinions of mankind requires that they should declare the causes which impel them to the separation.

We hold these truths to be self-evident, that all men are created equal; that they are endowed by their Creator with certain unalienable rights; that among these are life, liberty, and the pursuit of happiness. That, to secure these rights, governments are instituted among men, deriving their just powers from the consent of the governed; that, whenever any form of government becomes destructive of these ends, it is the right of the people to alter or to abolish it, and to institute a new government, laying its foundation on such principles, and organizing its powers in such form, as to them shall seem most likely to effect their safety and happiness. Prudence, indeed, will dictate that governments long established should not be changed for light and transient causes; and, accordingly, all experience hath shown that mankind are more disposed to suffer, while evils are sufferable, than to right themselves by abolishing the forms to which they are accustomed. But when a long train of abuses and usurpations, pursuing invariably the same object, evinces a design to reduce them under absolute despotism, it is their right, it is their duty, to throw off such government and to provide new guards for their future security. Such has been the patient sufferance of these colonies, and such is now the necessity which constrains them to alter their former systems of government. The history of the present King of Great Britain is a history of repeated injuries and usurpations, all having, in direct object, the establishment of an absolute tyranny over these States. To prove this, let facts be submitted to a candid world:

He has refused his assent to laws the most wholesome and necessary for the public good.

He has forbidden his governors to pass laws of immediate and pressing importance, unless suspended in their operation till his assent should be obtained; and, when so suspended, he has utterly neglected to attend to them.

He has refused to pass other laws for the accommodation of large districts of people, unless those people would relinquish the right of representation in the legislature, a right inestimable to them and formidable to tyrants only.

He has called together legislative bodies at places unusual, uncomfortable, and distant from the depository of their public records, for the sole purpose of fatiguing them into compliance with his measures.

He has dissolved representative houses, repeatedly for opposing, with manly firmness, his invasions on the rights of the people.

He has refused, for a long time after such dissolutions, to cause others to be elected; whereby the legislative powers, incapable of annihilation, have returned to the people at large for their exercise; the state remaining, in the meantime, exposed to all the danger of invasion from without and convulsions within.

He has endeavored to prevent the population of these States; for that purpose, obstructing the laws for naturalization of foreigners, refusing to pass others to encourage their migration hither, and raising the conditions of new appropriations of lands.

He has obstructed the administration of justice by refusing his assent to laws for establishing judiciary powers.

He has made judges dependent on his will alone for the tenure of their offices and the amount and payment of their salaries.

He has erected a multitude of new offices and sent hither swarms of officers to harass our people and eat out their substance.

He has kept among us, in time of peace, standing armies, without the consent of our legislatures.

He has affected to render the military independent of, and superior to, the civil power.

He has combined with others to subject us to a jurisdiction foreign to our Constitution and unacknowledged by our laws, giving his assent to their acts of pretended legislation—

For quartering large bodies of armed troops among us;

For protecting them by a mock trail from punishment for any murders which they should commit on the inhabitants of these States;

For cutting off our trade with all parts of the world;

For imposing taxes on us without our consent;

For depriving us, in many cases, of the benefit of trial by jury;

For transporting us beyond seas to be tried for pretended offences;

For abolishing the free system of English laws in a neighboring province, establishing therein an arbitrary government, and enlarging its boundaries, so as to render it at once an example and fit instrument for introducing the same absolute rule into these colonies;

For taking away our charters, abolishing our most valuable laws, and altering, fundamentally, the powers of our governments.

For suspending our own legislatures and declaring themselves invested with power to legislate for us in all cases whatsoever.

He has abdicated government here by declaring us out of his protection and waging war against us.

He has plundered our seas, ravaged our coasts, burnt our towns, and destroyed the lives of our people.

He is, at this time, transporting large armies of foreign mercenaries to complete the works of death, desolation, and tyranny already begun with circumstances of cruelty and perfidy scarcely paralleled in the most barbarous ages, and totally unworthy the head of a civilized nation.

He has constrained our fellow citizens, taken captive on the high seas, to bear arms against their country, to become the executioners of their friends and brethren, or to fall themselves by their hands.

He has excited domestic insurrections amongst us and has endeavored to bring on the inhabitants of our frontiers, the merciless Indian savages, whose known rule of warfare is an undistinguished destruction of all ages, sexes, and conditions.

In every stage of these oppressions, we have petitioned for redress in the most humble terms; our repeated petitions have been answered only by repeated injury. A prince whose character is thus marked by every act which may define a tyrant is unfit to be the ruler of a free people.

Nor have we been wanting in attention to our British brethren. We have warned them, from time to time, of attempts made by their legislature to extend an unwarrantable jurisdiction over us. We have reminded them of the circumstances of our emigration and settlement here. We have appealed to their native justice and magnanimity, and we have conjured them, by the ties of our common kindred, to disavow these usurpations, which would inevitably interrupt our connections and correspondence. They, too, have been deaf to the voice of justice and consanguinity. We must, therefore, acquiesce in the necessity which denounces our separation, and hold them, as we hold the rest of mankind, enemies in war, in peace, friends.

We, therefore, the representatives of the United States of America, in general Congress assembled, appealing to the Supreme Judge of the world for the rectitude of our intentions, do, in the name and by the authority of the good people of these colonies, solemnly publish and declare, that these united colonies are, and of right ought to be, free and independent states: that they are absolved from all allegiance to the British Crown, and that all political connection between them and the state of Great Britain is, and ought to be, totally dissolved; and that, as free and independent states, they have full power to levy war, conclude peace, contract alliances, establish commerce, and to do all other acts and things which independent states may of right do. And, for the support of this declaration, with a firm reliance on the protection of Divine Providence, we mutually pledge to each other our lives, our fortunes, and our sacred honor.

The Articles of Confederation and Perpetual Union*

Between the states of New Hampshire, Massachusetts-bay Rhode Island and Providence Plantations, Connecticut, New York, New Jersey, Pennsylvania, Delaware, Maryland, Virginia, North Carolina, South Carolina, and Georgia.

Article I
The Stile of this Confederacy shall be "The United States of America."

Article 2
Each state retains its sovereignty, freedom, and independence, and every power, jurisdiction, and right, which is not by this Confederation expressly delegated to the United States, in Congress assembled.

Article 3
The said States hereby severally enter into a firm league of friendship with each other, for their common defense, the security of their liberties, and their mutual and general welfare, binding themselves to assist each other, against all force offered to, or attacks made upon them, or any of them, on account of religion, sovereignty, trade, or any other pretense whatever.

Article 4
The better to secure and perpetuate mutual friendship and intercourse among the people of the different States in this Union, the free inhabitants of each of these States, paupers, vagabonds, and fugitives from justice excepted, shall be entitled to all privileges and immunities of free citizens in the several States; and the people of each State shall have free ingress and regress to and from any other State, and shall enjoy therein all the privileges of trade and commerce, subject to the same duties, impositions, and restrictions as the inhabitants thereof respectively, provided that such restrictions shall not extend so far as to prevent the removal of property imported into any State, to any other State of which the owner is an inhabitant; provided also that no imposition, du-

---

*Agreed to in Congress November 15, 1777; ratified March 1781.

ties or restriction shall be laid by any State, on the property of the United States, or either of them.

If any person guilty of, or charged with, treason, felony, or other high misdemeanor in any State, shall flee from justice, and be found in any of the United States, he shall, upon demand of the Governor or executive power of the State from which he fled, be delivered up and removed to the State having jurisdiction of his offense.

Full faith and credit shall be given in each of these States to the records, acts, and judicial proceedings of the courts and magistrates of every other State.

Article 5

For the more convenient management of the general interests of the United States, delegates shall be annually appointed in such manner as the legislatures of each State shall direct, to meet in Congress on the first Monday in November, in every year, with a power reserved to each State to recall its delegates, or any of them, at any time within the year, and to send others in their stead for the remainder of the year.

No State shall be represented in Congress by less than two, nor by more than seven members; and no person shall be capable of being a delegate for more than three years in any term of six years; nor shall any person, being a delegate, be capable of holding any office under the United States, for which he, or another for his benefit, receives any salary, fees or emolument of any kind.

Each State shall maintain its own delegates in a meeting of the States, and while they act as members of the committee of the States.

In determining questions in the United States in Congress assembled, each State shall have one vote.

Freedom of speech and debate in Congress shall not be impeached or questioned in any court or place out of Congress, and the members of Congress shall be protected in their persons from arrests or imprisonments, during the time of their going to and from, and attendence on Congress, except for treason, felony, or breach of the peace.

Article 6

No State, without the consent of the United States in Congress assembled, shall send any embassy to, or receive any embassy from, or enter into any conference, agreement, alliance or treaty with any King, Prince or State; nor shall any person holding any office of profit or trust under the United States, or any of them, accept any present, emolument, office or title of any kind whatever from any King, Prince or foreign State; nor shall the United States in Congress assembled, or any of them, grant any title of nobility.

No two or more States shall enter into any treaty, confederation or alliance whatever between them, without the consent of the United States in Congress assembled, specifying accurately the purposes for which the same is to be entered into, and how long it shall continue.

No State shall lay any imposts or duties, which may interfere with any stipulations in treaties, entered into by the United States in Congress assembled, with any King, Prince or State, in pursuance of any treaties already proposed by Congress, to the courts of France and Spain.

No vessel of war shall be kept up in time of peace by any State, except such number only, as shall be deemed necessary by the United States in Congress assembled, for the defense of such State, or its trade; nor shall any body of forces be kept up by any State in time of peace, except such number only, as in the judgement of the United States in Congress assembled, shall be deemed requisite to garrison the forts necessary for the defense of such State; but every State shall always keep up a well-regulated and disciplined militia, sufficiently armed and accoutered, and shall provide and constantly have ready for use, in public stores, a due number of filed pieces and tents, and a proper quantity of arms, ammunition and camp equipage.

No State shall engage in any war without the consent of the United States in Congress assembled, unless such State be actually invaded by enemies, or shall have received certain advice of a resolution being formed by some nation of Indians to invade such State, and the danger is so imminent as not to admit of a delay, till the United States in Congress assembled can be consulted; nor shall any State grant commissions to any ships or vessels of war, nor letters of marque or reprisal, except it be after a declaration of war by the United States in Congress assembled, and then only against the Kingdom or State and the subjects thereof, against which war has been so declared, and under such regulations as shall be established by the United States in Congress assembled, unless such State be infested by pirates, in which case vessels of war may be fitted out for that occasion, and kept so long as the danger shall continue, or until the United States in Congress assembled shall determine otherwise.

Article 7

When land forces are raised by any State for the common defense, all officers of or under the rank of colonel, shall be appointed by the legislature of each State respectively, by whom such forces shall be raised, or in such manner as such State shall direct, and all vacancies shall be filled up by the State which first made the appointment.

Article 8

All charges of war, and all other expenses that shall be incurred for the common defense or general welfare, and allowed by the United States in Congress assembled, shall be defrayed out of a common treasury, which shall be supplied by the several States in proportion to the value of all land within each State, granted to or surveyed for any person, as such land and the buildings and improvements thereon shall be estimated according to such mode as the United States in Congress assembled, shall from time to time direct and appoint.

The taxes for paying that proportion shall be laid and levied by the authority and direction of the legislatures of the several States within the time agreed upon by the United States in Congress assembled.

Article 9

The United States in Congress assembled, shall have the sole and exclusive right and power of determining on peace and war, except in the cases mentioned in the sixth article; of sending and receiving ambassadors; entering into treaties and alliances, provided that no treaty of commerce shall be made whereby the legislative power of the respective States shall be restrained from imposing such imposts and duties on foreigners, as their own people are subjected to, or from prohibiting the exportation or importation of any species of goods or commodities whatsoever; of establishing rules for deciding in all cases, what captures on land or water shall be legal, and in what manner prizes taken by land or naval forces in the service of the United States shall be divided or appropriated; of granting letters of marque and reprisal in times of peace; appointing courts for the trial of piracies and felonies committed on the high seas and establishing courts for receiving and determining finally appeals in all cases of captures, provided that no member of Congress shall be appointed a judge of any of the said courts.

The United States in Congress assembled shall also be the last resort on appeal in all disputes and differences now subsisting or that hereafter may arise between two or more States concerning boundary, jurisdiction or any other causes whatever; which authority shall always be exercised in the manner following. Whenever the legislative or executive authority or lawful agent of any State in controversy with another shall present a petition to Congress stating the matter in question and praying for a hearing, notice thereof shall be given by order of Congress to the legislative or executive authority of the other State in controversy, and a day assigned for the appearance of the parties by their lawful agents, who shall then be directed to appoint by joint consent, commissioners or judges to constitute a court for hearing and determining the matter in question: but if they cannot agree, Congress shall name three persons out of each of the United States, and from the list of such persons each party shall alternately strike out one, the petitioners beginning, until the number shall be reduced to thirteen; and from that number not less than seven, nor more than nine names as Congress shall direct, shall in the presence of Congress be drawn out by lot, and the persons whose names shall be so drawn or any five of them, shall be commissioners or judges, to hear and finally determine the controversy, so always as a major part of the judges who shall hear the cause shall agree in the determination: and if either party shall neglect to attend at the day appointed, without showing reasons, which Congress shall judge sufficient, or being present shall refuse to strike, the Congress shall proceed to nominate three persons out of each State, and the secretary of Congress shall strike in behalf of such party absent or refusing; and the judgement and sentence of the court to be appointed, in the manner before prescribed, shall be final and conclusive; and if any of the parties shall refuse to submit to the authority of such court, or to appear or defend their claim or cause, the court shall nevertheless proceed to pronounce sentence, or judgement, which shall in like manner be final and decisive, the judgement or sentence and other proceedings being in either case transmitted to Congress, and lodged among the acts of Congress for the security of the parties concerned: provided that every commissioner, before he sits in judgment, shall take an oath to be administered by one of the judges of the supreme or superior court of the State, where the cause shall be tried, "well and truly to hear and determine the matter in question, according to the best of his judgement, without favor, affection

or hope of reward:" provided also, that no State shall be deprived of territory for the benefit of the United States.

All controversies concerning the private right of soil claimed under different grants of two or more States, whose jurisdictions as they may respect such lands, and the States which passed such grants are adjusted, the said grants or either of them being at the same time claimed to have originated antecedent to such settlement of jurisdiction, shall on the petition of either party to the Congress of the United States, be finally determined as near as may be in the same manner as is before prescribed for deciding disputes respecting territorial jurisdiction between different States.

The United States in Congress assembled shall also have the sole and exclusive right and power of regulating the alloy and value of coin struck by their own authority, or by that of the respective States; fixing the standards of weights and measures throughout the United States; regulating the trade and managing all affairs with the Indians not members of any of the States; provided that the legislative right of any State within its own limits be not infringed or violated; establishing or regulating post offices from one State to another, throughout all the United States, and exacting such postage on the papers passing through the same as may be requisite to defray the expenses of the said office; appointing all officers of the land forces in the service of the United States, excepting regimental officers; appointing all the officers of the naval forces, and commissioning all officers whatever in the service of the United States; making rules for the government and regulation of the said land and naval forces, and directing their operations.

The United States in Congress assembled shall have authority to appoint a committee, to sit in the recess of Congress, to be denominated "A Committee of the States," and to consist of one delegate from each State; and to appoint such other committees and civil officers as may be necessary for managing the general affairs of the United States under their direction; to appoint one of their members to preside, provided that no person be allowed to serve in the office of president more than one year in any term of three years; to ascertain the necessary sums of money to be raised for the service of the United States, and to appropriate and apply the same for defraying the public expenses; to borrow money, or emit bills on the credit of the United States, transmitting every half year to the respective States an account of the sums of money so borrowed or emitted; to build and equip a navy; to agree upon the number of land forces, and to make requisitions from each State for its quota, in proportion to the number of white inhabitants in such State; which requisition shall be binding, and thereupon the legislature of each State shall appoint the regimental officers, raise the men and cloath, arm and equip them in a soldier-like manner, at the expense of the United States; and the officers and men so cloathed, armed and equipped shall march to the place appointed, and within the time agreed on by the United States in Congress assembled; but if the United States in Congress assembled shall, on consideration of circumstances judge proper that any State should not raise men, or should raise a smaller number of men than the quota thereof, such extra number shall be raised, officered, cloathed, armed and equipped in the same manner as the quota of such State, unless the legislature of such State shall judge that such extra number cannot be safely spared out in the same, in which case they shall raise, officer, cloath, arm and equip as many of such extra number as they judge can be safely spared. And the officers and men so cloathed, armed, and equipped, shall march to the place appointed, and within the time agreed on by the United States in Congress assembled.

The United States in Congress assembled shall never engage in a war, nor grant letters of marque or reprisal in time of peace, nor enter into any treaties or alliances, nor coin money, nor regulate the value thereof, nor ascertain the sums and expenses necessary for the defense and welfare of the United States, or any of them, nor emit bills, nor borrow money on the credit of the United States, nor appropriate money, nor agree upon the number of vessels of war, to be built or purchased, or the number of land or sea forces to be raised, nor appoint a commander in chief of the army or navy, unless nine States assent to the same: nor shall a question on any other point, except for adjourning from day to day be determined, unless by the votes of the majority of the United States in Congress assembled.

The Congress of the United States shall have power to adjourn to any time within the year, and to any place within the United States, so that no period of adjournment be for a longer duration than the space of six months, and shall publish the journal of their proceedings monthly, except such parts thereof relating to treaties, alliances or military operations, as in their judgment require secrecy; and the yeas and nays of the delegates of each State on any question shall be entered on the journal, when it is desired by any delegates of a State, or any of them, at his or their request shall be furnished with a transcript of the said journal, except such parts as are above excepted, to lay before the legislatures of the several States.

Article 10

The Committee of the States, or any nine of them, shall be authorized to execute, in the recess of Congress, such of the powers of Congress as the United States in Congress assembled, by the consent of the nine States, shall from time to time think expedient to vest them with; provided that no power be delegated to the said Committee, for the exercise of which, by the Articles of Confederation, the voice of nine States in the Congress of the United States assembled is requisite.

Article 11

Canada acceding to this confederation, and adjoining in the measures of the United States, shall be admitted into, and entitled to all the advantages of this Union; but no other colony shall be admitted into the same, unless such admission be agreed to by nine States.

Article 12

All bills of credit emitted, monies borrowed, and debts contracted by, or under the authority of Congress, before the assembling of the United States, in pursuance of the present confederation, shall be deemed and considered as a charge against the United States, for payment and satisfaction whereof the said United States, and the public faith are hereby solemnly pledged.

Article 13

Every State shall abide by the determination of the United States in Congress assembled, on all questions which by this confederation are submitted to them. And the Articles of this Confederation shall be inviolably observed by every State, and the Union shall be perpetual; nor shall any alteration at any time hereafter be made in any of them; unless such alteration be agreed to in a Congress of the United States, and be afterwards confirmed by the legislatures of every State.

These articles shall be proposed to the legislatures of all the United States, to be considered, and if approved of by them, they are advised to authorize their delegates to ratify the same in the Congress of the United States; which being done, the same shall become conclusive

The Constitution of the United States of America

We the people of the United States, in order to form a more perfect union, establish justice, insure domestic tranquillity, provide for the common defense, promote the general welfare, and secure the blessings of liberty to ourselves and our posterity, do ordain and establish this Constitution for the United States of America.

Article I

SECTION 1. All legislative powers herein granted shall be vested in a Congress of the United States, which shall consist of a Senate and House of Representatives.

SECTION 2. 1. The House of Representatives shall be composed of members chosen every second year by the people of the several States, and the electors in each State shall have the qualifications requisite for electors of the most numerous branch of the State legislature.

2. No person shall be a representative who shall not have attained to the age of twenty-five years, and been seven years a citizen of the United States, and who shall not, when elected, be an inhabitant of that State in which he shall be chosen.

3. Representatives and direct taxes[1] shall be apportioned

[1]See the Sixteenth Amendment.

among the several States which may be included within this Union, according to their respective numbers, which shall be determined by adding to the whole number of free persons, including those bound to service for a term of years, and excluding Indians not taxed, three fifths of all other persons.[2] The actual enumeration shall be made within three years after the first meeting of the Congress of the United States, and within every subsequent term of ten years, in such manner as they shall by law direct. The number of representatives shall not exceed one for every thirty thousand, but each State shall have at least one representative; and until such enumeration shall be made, the State of New Hampshire shall be entitled to choose three, Massachusetts eight, Rhode Island and Providence Plantations one, Connecticut five, New York six, New Jersey four, Pennsylvania eight, Delaware one, Maryland six, Virginia ten, North Carolina five, South Carolina five, and Georgia three.

4. When vacancies happen in the representation from any State, the executive authority thereof shall issue writs of election to fill such vacancies.

5. The House of Representatives shall choose their speaker and other officers; and shall have the sole power of impeachment.

SECTION 3. 1. The Senate of the United States shall be composed of two senators from each State, chosen by the legislature thereof,[3] for six years; and each senator shall have one vote.

2. Immediately after they shall be assembled in consequence of the first election, they shall be divided as equally as may be into three classes. The seats of the senators of the first class shall be vacated at the expiration of the second year, of the second class at the expiration of the fourth year, and of the third class at the expiration of the sixth year, so that one third may be chosen every second year; and if vacancies happen by resignation, or otherwise, during the recess of the legislature of any State, the executive thereof may make temporary appointments until the next meeting of the legislature, which shall then fill such vacancies.[4]

3. No person shall be a senator who shall not have attained to the age of thirty years, and been nine years a citizen of the United States, and who shall not, when elected, be an inhabitant of that State for which he shall be chosen.

4. The Vice President of the United States shall be President of the Senate, but shall have no vote, unless they be equally divided.

5. The Senate shall choose their other officers, and also a president pro tempore, in the absence of the Vice President, or when he shall exercise the office of the President of the United States.

6. The Senate shall have the sole power to try all impeachments. When sitting for that purpose, they shall be on oath or affirmation. When the President of the United States is tried, the chief justice shall preside: and no person shall be convicted without the concurrence of two thirds of the members present.

7. Judgment in cases of impeachment shall not extend further than to removal from office, and disqualification to hold and enjoy any office of honor, trust or profit under the United States: but the party convicted shall nevertheless be liable and subject to indictment, trial, judgment and punishment, according to law.

SECTION 4. 1. The times, places, and manner of holding elections for senators and representatives, shall be prescribed in each State by the legislature thereof; but the Congress may at any time by law make or alter such regulations, except as to the places of choosing senators.

2. The Congress shall assemble at least once in every year, and such meeting shall be on the first Monday in December, unless they shall by law appoint a different day.

SECTION 5. 1. Each House shall be the judge of the elections, returns and qualifications of its own members, and a majority of each shall constitute a quorum to do business; but a smaller number may adjourn from day to day, and may be authorized to compel the attendance of absent members, in such manner, and under such penalties as each House may provide.

2. Each House may determine the rules of its proceedings, punish its members for disorderly behavior, and, with the concurrence of two thirds, expel a member.

3. Each House shall keep a journal of its proceedings, and from time to time publish the same, excepting such parts as may in their judgment require secrecy; and the yeas and nays of the members of either House on any question shall, at the desire of one fifth of those present, be entered on the journal.

4. Neither House, during the session of Congress, shall, without the consent of the other, adjourn for more than three days, nor to any other place than that in which the two Houses shall be sitting.

SECTION 6. 1. The senators and representatives shall receive a compensation for their services, to be ascertained by law, and paid out of the Treasury of the United States. They shall in all cases, except treason, felony, and breach of the peace, be privileged from arrest during their attendance at the session of their respective Houses, and in going to and returning from the same; and for any speech or debate in either House, they shall not be questioned in any other place.

2. No senator or representative shall, during the time for which he was elected, be appointed to any civil office under the authority of the United States, which shall have been created, or the emoluments whereof shall have been increased, during such time; and no person holding any office under the United States shall be a member of either House during his continuance in office.

SECTION 7. 1. All bills for raising revenue shall originate in the House of Representatives; but the Senate may propose or concur with amendments as on other bills.

2. Every bill which shall have passed the House of Representatives and the Senate, shall, before it become a law, be presented to the President of the United States; If he approves he shall sign it, but if not he shall return it, with his objections, to that House in which it shall have originated, who shall enter the objections at large on their journal, and proceed to reconsider it. If after such reconsideration two thirds

---

[2]See the Fourteenth Amendment.
[3]See the Seventeenth Amendment.
[4]See the Seventeenth Amendment.

of that House shall agree to pass the bill, it shall be sent, together with the objections, to the other House, by which it shall likewise be reconsidered, and if approved by two thirds of that House, it shall become a law. But in all such cases the votes of both Houses shall be determined by yeas and nays, and the names of the persons voting for and against the bill shall be entered on the journal of each House respectively. If any bill shall not be returned by the President within ten days (Sundays excepted) after it shall have been presented to him, the same shall be a law, in like manner as if he had signed it, unless the Congress by their adjournment prevent its return, in which case it shall not be a law.

3. Every order, resolution, or vote to which the concurrence of the Senate and the House of Representatives may be necessary (except on a question of adjournment) shall be presented to the President of the United States; and before the same shall take effect, shall be approved by him, or being disapproved by him, shall be repassed by two thirds of the Senate and House of Representatives, according to the rules and limitations prescribed in the case of a bill.

SECTION 8. 1. The Congress shall have the power

1. To lay and collect taxes, duties, imposts, and excises, to pay the debts and provide for the common defense and general welfare of the United States; but all duties, imposts, and excises shall be uniform throughout the United States.

2. To borrow money on the credit of the United States;

3. To regulate commerce with foreign nations, and among the several States, and with the Indian tribes;

4. To establish a uniform rule of naturalization, and uniform laws on the subject of bankruptcies throughout the United States;

5. To coin money, regulate the value thereof, and of foreign coin, and fix the standard of weights and measures;

6. To provide for the punishment of counterfeiting the securities and current coin of the United States;

7. To establish post offices and post roads;

8. To promote the progress of science and useful arts, by securing for limited times to authors and inventors the exclusive right to their respective writings and discoveries;

9. To constitute tribunals inferior to the Supreme Court;

10. To define and punish piracies and felonies committed on the high seas, and offenses against the law of nations;

11. To declare war, grant letters of marque and reprisal, and make rules concerning captures on land and water;

12. To raise and support armies, but no appropriation of money to that use shall be for a longer term than two years;

13. To provide and maintain a navy;

14. To make rules for the government and regulation of the land and naval forces;

15. To provide for calling forth the militia to execute the laws of the Union, suppress insurrections and repel invasions;

16. To provide for organizing, arming, and disciplining the militia, and for governing such part of them as may be employed in the service of the United States, reserving to the States respectively, the appointment of the officers, and the authority of training the militia according to the discipline prescribed by Congress;

17. To exercise exclusive legislation in all cases whatsoever, over such district (not exceeding ten miles square) as may, by cession of particular States, and the acceptance of Congress, become the seat of the government of the United States, and to exercise like authority over all places purchased by the consent of the legislature of the State in which the same shall be, for the erection of forts, magazines, arsenals, dockyards, and other needful buildings; and

18. To make all laws which shall be necessary and proper for carrying into execution the foregoing powers, and all other powers vested by this Constitution in the government of the United States, or any department or officer thereof.

SECTION 9. 1. The migration or importation of such persons as any of the States now existing shall think proper to admit, shall not be prohibited by the Congress prior to the year one thousand eight hundred and eight, but a tax or duty may be imposed on such importation, not exceeding ten dollars for each person.

2. The privilege of the writ of habeas corpus shall not be suspended, unless when in cases of rebellion or invasion the public safety may require it.

3. No bill of attainder or ex post facto law shall be passed.

4. No capitation, or other direct, tax shall be laid, unless in proportion to the census or enumeration herein-before directed to be taken.[5]

5. No tax or duty shall be laid on articles exported from any State.

6. No preference shall be given by any regulation of commerce or revenue to the ports of one State over those of another: nor shall vessels bound to, or from, one State be obliged to enter, clear, or pay duties in another.

7. No money shall be drawn from the treasury, but in consequence of appropriations made by law; and a regular statement and account of the receipts and expenditures of all public money shall be published from time to time.

8. No title of nobility shall be granted by the United States: and no person holding any office of profit or trust under them, shall, without the consent of the Congress, accept of any present, emolument, office, or title, of any kind whatever, from any king, price, or foreign State.

SECTION 10. 1. No State shall enter into any treaty, alliance, or confederation; grant letters of marque and reprisal; coin money; emit bills of credit; make any thing but gold and silver coin a tender in payment of debts; pass any bill of attainder, ex post facto law, or law impairing the obligation of contracts, or grant, any title of nobility.

2. No State shall, without the consent of the Congress, lay any imposts or duties on imports or exports, except what may be absolutely necessary for executing its inspection laws: and the net produce of all duties and imposts laid by any State on imports or exports, shall be for the use of the treasury of the United States; and all such laws shall be subject to the revision and control of the Congress.

3. No State shall, without the consent of the Congress, lay any duty of tonnage, keep troops, or ships of war in time of peace, enter into any agreement or compact with another State, or with a foreign power, or engage in war, unless actually invaded, or in such imminent danger as will not admit of delay.

---

[5]See the Sixteenth Amendment.

Article II

Section 1. 1. The executive power shall be vested in a President of the United States of America. He shall hold his office during the term of four years, and, together with the Vice President, chosen for the same term, be elected, as follows:

2. Each State shall appoint, in such manner as the legislature thereof may direct, a number of electors, equal to the whole number of senators and representatives to which the State may be entitled in the Congress: but no senator or representative, or person holding any office of trust or profit under the United States, shall be appointed an elector.

The electors shall meet in their respective States, and vote by ballot for two persons, of whom one at least shall not be an inhabitant of the same State with themselves. And they shall make a list of all the persons voted for, and of the number of votes for each; which list they shall sign and certify, and transmit sealed to the seat of the government of the United States, directed to the president of the Senate. The president of the Senate shall, in the presence of the Senate and House of Representatives, open all the certificates, and the votes shall then be counted. The person having the greatest number of votes shall be the President, if such number be a majority of the whole number of electors appointed; and if there be more than one who have such majority, and have an equal number of votes, then the House of Representatives shall immediately choose by ballot one of them for President; and if no person have a majority, then from the five highest on the list the said House shall in like manner choose the President. But in choosing the President, the votes shall be taken by States, the representation from each State having one vote; a quorum for this purpose shall consist of a member or members from two thirds of the States, and a majority of all the States shall be necessary to a choice. In every case after the choice of the President, the person having the greatest number of votes of the electors shall be the Vice President. But if there should remain two or more who have equal votes, the Senate shall chose from them by ballot the Vice President.[6]

3. The Congress may determine the time of choosing the electors, and the day on which they shall give their votes; which day shall be the same throughout the United States.

4. No person except a natural born citizen, or a citizen of the United States, at the time of the adoption of this Constitution, shall be eligible to the office of President; neither shall any person be eligible to the office who shall not have attained to the age of thirty-five years, and been fourteen years a resident within the United States.

5. In case of the removal of the President from office, or of his death, resignation, or inability to discharge the powers and duties of the said office, the same shall devolve on the Vice President, and the congress may by law provide for the case of removal, death, resignation or inability, both of the President and Vice President, declaring what officer shall then act as President, and such officer shall act accordingly until the disability be removed, or a President shall be elected.

6. The President shall, at stated times, receive for his services a compensation which shall neither be increased nor di-

minished during the period for which he shall have been elected, and he shall not receive within that period any other emolument from the United States, or any of them.

7. Before he enter on the execution of his office, he shall take the following oath or affirmation:—"I do solemnly swear (or affirm) that I will faithfully execute the office of President of the United States, and will to the best of my ability, preserve, protect and defend the Constitution of the United States."

SECTION 2. 1. The President shall be commander in chief of the army and navy of the United States, and of the militia of the several States, when called into the actual service of the United States; he may require the opinion in writing, of the principal officer in each of the executive departments, upon any subject relating to the duties of their respective offices, and he shall have power to grant reprieves and pardons for offenses against the United States, except in cases of impeachment.

2. He shall have power, by and with the advice and consent of the Senate, to make treaties, provided two thirds of the senators present concur; and he shall nominate, and by and with the advice and consent of the Senate, shall appoint ambassadors, other public ministers and consuls, judges of the Supreme Court, and all other officers of the United States, whose appointments are not herein otherwise provided for, and which shall be established by law; but the Congress may by law vest the appointment of such inferior officers, as they think proper, in the President alone, in the courts of laws, or in the heads of departments.

3. The President shall have power to fill up all vacancies that may happen during the recess of the Senate, by granting commissions which shall expire at the end of their next session.

SECTION 3. He shall from time to time give to the Congress information of the state of the Union, and recommend to their consideration such measures as he shall judge necessary and expedient; he may, on extraordinary occasions, convene both Houses, or either of them, and in case of disagreement between them with respect to the time of adjournment, he may adjourn them to such time as he shall think proper; he shall receive ambassadors and other public ministers; he shall take care that the laws be faithfully executed, and shall commission all the officers of the United States.

SECTION 4. The President, Vice President, and all civil officers of the United States, shall be removed from office on impeachment for, and conviction of, treason, bribery, or other high crimes and misdemeanors.

Article III

SECTION 1. The judicial power of the United States shall be vested in one Supreme Court, and in such inferior courts as the Congress may from time to time ordain and establish. The judges, both of the Supreme and inferior courts, shall hold their offices during good behavior, and shall, at stated times, receive for their services, a compensation, which shall not be diminished during their continuance in office.

SECTION 2. 2. The judicial power shall extend to all cases, in law and equity, arising under this Constitution, the laws of the United States, and treaties made, or which shall be made,

[6]Superseded by the Twelfth Amendment.

under their authority;—to all cases of admiralty and maritime jurisdiction;—to controversies to which the United States shall be a party;[7]—to controversies between two or more States;—between a State and citizens of another State;—between citizens of different States;—between citizens of the same State claiming lands under grants of different States, and between a State, or the citizens thereof, and foreign States, citizens or subjects.

2. In all cases affecting ambassadors, other public ministers and consuls, and those in which a State shall be party, the Supreme Court shall have original jurisdiction. In all the other cases before mentioned, the Supreme Court shall have appellate jurisdiction, both as to law and fact, with such exceptions, and under such regulations as the Congress shall make.

3. The trial of all crimes, except in cases of impeachment, shall be by jury; and such trial shall be held in the State where the said crimes shall have been committed; but when not committed within any State, the trial shall be such place or places as the congress may by law have directed.

SECTION 3. 1. Treason against the United States shall consist only in levying war against them, or in adhering to their enemies, giving them aid and comfort. No person shall be convicted of treason unless on the testimony of two witnesses to the same overt act, or on confession in open court.

2. The Congress shall have power to declare the punishment of treason, but no attainder of treason shall work corruption of blood, or forfeiture except during the life of the person attained.

Article IV

SECTION 1. Full faith and credit shall be given in each State to the public acts, records, and judicial proceedings of every other State. And the Congress may by general laws prescribe the manner in which such acts, records and proceedings shall be proved, and the effect thereof.

SECTION 2. 1. The citizens of each State shall be entitled to all privileges and immunities of citizens in the several States.[8]

2. A person charged in any State with treason, felony, or other crime, who shall flee from justice, and be found in another State, shall on demand of the executive authority of the State from which he fled, be delivered up to be removed to the State having jurisdiction of the crime.

3. No person held to service or labor in one State under the laws thereof, escaping into another, shall, in consequence of any law or regulation therein, be discharged from such service or labor, but shall be delivered up on claim of the party to whom such service or labor may be due.[9]

SECTION 3. 1. New States may be admitted by the Congress into this Union; but no new State shall be formed or erected within the jurisdiction of any other State, nor any State be formed by the junction of two or more States, or parts of States, without the consent of the legislatures of the States concerned as well as of the Congress.

2. The Congress shall have power to dispose of and make all needful rules and regulations respecting the territory or other property belonging to the United States; and nothing in this Constitution shall be so construed as to prejudice any claims of the United States, or of any particular State.

SECTION 4. The United States shall guarantee to every State in this Union a republican form of government, and shall protect each of them against invasion; and on application of the legislature, or of the executive (when the legislature cannot be convened) against domestic violence.

Article V

The Congress, whenever two thirds of both Houses shall deem it necessary, shall propose amendments to this Constitution, or, on the application of the legislatures of two thirds of the several States, shall call a convention for proposing amendments, which in either case shall be valid to all intents and purposes, as part of this Constitution, when ratified by the legislatures of three fourths of the several States, or by conventions in three fourths thereof, as the one or the other mode of ratification may be proposed by the Congress; Provided that no amendment which may be made prior to the year one thousand eight hundred and eight shall in any manner affect the first and fourth clauses in the ninth section of the first article; and that no State, without its consent, shall be deprived of its equal suffrage in the Senate.

Article VI

1. All debts contracted and engagements entered into, before the adoption of this Constitution, shall be as valid against the United States under this Constitution, as under the Confederation.[10]

2. This Constitution, and the laws of the United States which shall be made in pursuance thereof; and all treaties made, or which shall be made, under the authority of the United States, shall be the supreme law of the land; and the judges in every State shall be bound thereby, any thing in the Constitution or laws of any State to the contrary notwithstanding.

3. The senators and representatives before mentioned, and the members of the several State legislatures, and all executive and judicial officers, both of the United States and of the several States, shall be bound by oath or affirmation to support this Constitution; but no religious test shall ever be required as a qualification to any office or public trust under the United States.

Article VII

The ratification of the conventions of nine States shall be sufficient for the establishment of this Constitution between the States so ratifying the same.

Done in Convention by the unanimous consent of the States present the seventeenth day of September in the year of our Lord one thousand seven hundred and eighty-seven, and of the independence of the United States of America the twelfth. In witness whereof we have hereunto subscribed our names.

[Signatories names omitted]

* * *

---

[7]See the Eleventh Amendment.
[8]See the Fourteenth Amendment, Sec. 1.
[9]See the Thirteenth Amendment.

[10]See the Fourteenth Amendment, Sec. 4.

Articles in addition to, and amendment of, the Constitution of the United States of America, proposed by Congress, and ratified by the legislatures of the several States, pursuant to the fifth article of the original Constitution.

Amendment I

[First ten amendments ratified December 15, 1791]
Congress shall make no law respecting an establishment of religion, or prohibiting the free exercise thereof; or abridging the freedom of speech, or of the press; or the right of the people peaceably to assemble, and to petition the government for a redress of grievances.

Amendment II

A well regulated militia, being necessary to the security of a free State, the right of the people to keep and bear arms, shall not be infringed.

Amendment III

No soldier shall, in time of peace be quartered in any house, without the consent of the owner, nor in time of war, but in a manner to be prescribed by law.

Amendment IV

The right of the people to be secure in their persons, houses, papers, and effects, against unreasonable searches and seizures, shall not be violated, and no warrants shall issue, but upon probable cause, supported by oath or affirmation, and particularly describing the place to be searched, and the persons or things to be seized.

Amendment V

No person shall be held to answer for a capital or otherwise infamous crime, unless on a presentment or indictment of a grand jury, except in cases arising in the land or naval forces, or in the militia, when in actual service in time of war or public danger; nor shall any person be subject for the same offense to be twice put in jeopardy of life or limb; nor shall be compelled in any criminal case to be a witness against himself, nor be deprived of life, liberty, or property, without due process of law; nor shall private property be taken for public use, without just compensation.

Amendment VI

In all criminal prosecutions, the accused shall enjoy the right to a speedy and public trial, by an impartial jury of the State and district wherein the crime shall have been committed, which district shall have been previously ascertained by law, and to be informed of the nature and cause of the accusation; to be confronted with the witnesses against him; to have compulsory process for obtaining witnesses in his favor, and to have the assistance of counsel for his defense.

Amendment VII

In suits at common law, where the value in controversy shall exceed twenty dollars, the right of trial by jury shall be preserved, and no fact tried by a jury shall be otherwise reexamined in any court of the United States, than according to the rules of the common law.

Amendment VIII

Excessive bail shall not be required, nor excessive fines imposed, nor cruel and unusual punishments inflicted.

Amendment IX

The enumeration in the Constitution of certain rights shall not be construed to deny or disparage others retained by the people.

Amendment X

The powers not delegated to the United States by the Constitution, nor prohibited by it to the States, are reserved to the States respectively, or to the people.

Amendment XI [January 8, 1798]

The judicial power of the United States shall not be construed to extend to any suit in law or equity, commended or prosecuted against one of the United States by citizens of another State, or by citizens or subjects of any foreign State.

Amendment XII [September 25, 1804]

The electors shall meet in their respective States, and vote by ballot for President and Vice President, one of whom, at least, shall not be an inhabitant of the same State with themselves; they shall name in their ballots the person voted for as President, and in distinct ballots the person voted for as Vice President, and they shall make distinct lists of all persons voted for as President and of all persons voted for as Vice President, and of the number of votes for each, which lists they shall sign and certify, and transmit sealed to the seat of the government of the United States, directed to the President of the Senate;—The President of the Senate shall, in the presence of the Senate and House of Representatives, open all the certificates and the votes shall then be counted;—The person having the greatest number of votes for President, shall be the President, if such number be a majority of the whole number of electors appointed; and if no person have such majority, then from the persons having the highest numbers not exceeding three on the list of those voted for as President, the House of Representatives shall choose immediately, by ballot, the President. But in choosing the President, the votes shall be taken by States, the representation from each State having one vote; a quorum for this purpose shall consist of a member or members from two thirds of the States, and a majority of all the States shall be necessary to a choice. And if the House of Representatives shall not choose a President whenever the right of choice shall devolve upon them, before the fourth day of March next following, then the Vice President shall act as President, as in the case of the death or other constitutional disability of the President. The person having the greatest number of votes as Vice President shall be the Vice President, if such number be a majority of the whole number of electors appointed, and if no person have a majority, then from the two highest numbers on the list, the Senate shall choose the Vice President; a quorum for the purpose shall consist of two thirds of the whole number of Senators, and a majority of the whole number shall be necessary to a choice. But no person constitutionally ineligible to the office of President shall be eligible to that of Vice President of the United States.

Amendment XIII [December 18, 1865]

SECTION 1. Neither slavery nor involuntary servitude, except as a punishment for crime whereof the party shall have been duly convicted, shall exist within the United States, or any place subject to their jurisdiction.

SECTION 2. Congress shall have power to enforce this article by appropriate legislation.

Amendment XIV [July 28, 1868]

SECTION 1. All persons born or naturalized in the United States, and subject to the jurisdiction thereof, are citizens of the United States and of the State wherein they reside. No State shall make or enforce any law which shall abridge the privileges or immunities of citizens of the United States; nor shall any State deprive any person of life, liberty, or property, without due process of law; nor deny to any person within its jurisdiction the equal protection of the laws.

SECTION 2. Representatives shall be apportioned among the several States according to their respective numbers, counting the whole number of persons in each State, excluding Indians not taxed. But when the right to vote at any election for the choice of electors for President and Vice President of the United States, representatives in Congress, the executive and judicial officers of a State, or the members of the legislature thereof, is denied to any of the male inhabitants of such State, being twenty-one years of age, and citizens of the United States, or in any way abridged, except for participating in rebellion, or other crime, the basis of representation there shall be reduced in the proportion which the number of such male citizens shall bear to the whole number of male citizens twenty-one years of age in such State.

SECTION 3. No person shall be a senator or representative in Congress, or elector of President and Vice President, or hold any office, civil or military, under the United States, or under any State, who having previously taken an oath, as a member of Congress, or as an officer of the United States, or as a member of any State legislature, or as an executive or judicial officer of any State, to support the Constitution of the United States, shall have engaged in insurrection or rebellion against the same, or given aid or comfort to the enemies thereof. But Congress may by a vote of two thirds of each House, remove such disability.

SECTION 4. The validity of the public debt of the United States, authorized by law, including debts incurred for payment of pensions and bounties for services in suppressing insurrection or rebellion; shall not be questioned. But neither the United States nor any State shall assume or pay any debt or obligation incurred in aid of insurrection or rebellion against the United States, or any claim for the loss or emancipation of any slave; but all such debts, obligations, and claims shall be held illegal and void.

SECTION 5. The Congress shall have the power to enforce, by appropriate legislation, the provisions of this article.

Amendment XV [March 30, 1870]

SECTION 1. The right of citizens of the United States to vote shall not be denied or abridged by the United States or by any State on account of race, color, or previous condition of servitude.

SECTION 2. The Congress shall have power to enforce this article by appropriate legislation.

Amendment XVI [February 25, 1913]

The Congress shall have power to lay and collect taxes on incomes, from whatever source derived, without apportionment among the several States, and without regard to any census or enumeration.

Amendment XVII [May 31, 1913]

The Senate of the United States shall be composed of two senators from each State, elected by the people thereof, for six years; and each senator shall have one vote. The electors in each State shall have the qualifications requisite for electors of the most numerous branch of the State legislature.

When vacancies happen in the representation of any State in the Senate, the executive authority of such State shall issue writs of election to fill such vacancies: Provided, That the legislature of any State may empower the executive thereof to make temporary appointments until the people fill the vacancies by election as the legislature may direct.

This amendment shall not be so construed as to affect the election or term of any senator chosen before it becomes valid as part of the Constitution.

Amendment XVIII[11] [January 29, 1919]

After one year from the ratification of this article, the manufacture, sale, or transportation of intoxicating liquors within, the importation thereof into, or the exportation thereof from the United States and all territory subject to the jurisdiction thereof for beverage purposes is thereby prohibited.

The Congress and the several States shall have concurrent power to enforce this article by appropriate legislation.

This article shall be inoperative unless it shall have been ratified as an amendment to the Constitution by the legislatures of the several States, as provided in the constitution, within seven years from the date of the submission hereof to the States by Congress.

Amendment XIX [August 26, 1920]

The right of citizens of the United States to vote shall not be denied or abridged by the United States or by any State on account of sex.

Congress shall have the power to enforce this article by appropriate legislation.

Amendment XX [January 23, 1933]

SECTION 1. The terms of the President and Vice President shall end at noon on the 20th day of January and the terms of Senators and Representatives at noon on the 3d day of January, of the years in which such terms would have ended if this article had not been ratified; and the terms of their successors shall then begin.

SECTION 2. The Congress shall assemble at least once in every year, and such meeting shall begin at noon on the 3d day of January, unless they shall by law appoint a different day.

SECTION 3. If, at the time fixed for the beginning of the term of President, the President-elect shall have died, the

---

[11]Repealed by the Twenty-first Amendment.

Vice President-elect shall become President. If a President shall not have been chosen before the time fixed for the beginning of his term, or if the President-elect shall have failed to qualify, then the Vice President-elect shall act as President until a President shall have qualified; and the Congress may by law provide for the case wherein neither a President-elect nor a Vice President-elect shall have qualified, declaring who shall then act as President, or the manner in which one who is to act shall be selected, and such person shall act accordingly until a President or Vice President shall have qualified.

SECTION 4. The Congress may by law provide for the case of the death of any of the persons from whom, the House of Representatives may choose a President whenever the right of choice shall have devolved upon them, and for the case of the death of any of the persons from whom the Senate may choose a Vice President whenever the right of choice shall have devolved upon them.

SECTION 5. Sections 1 and 2 shall take effect on the 15th day of October following the ratification of this article.

SECTION 6. This article shall be inoperative unless it shall have been ratified as an amendment to the Constitution by the legislatures of three-fourths of the several States within seven years from the date of its submission.

Amendment XXI [December 5, 1933]

SECTION 1. The Eighteenth Article of amendment to the Constitution of the United States is hereby repealed.

SECTION 2. The transportation or importation into any State, Territory, or possession of the United States for delivery or use therein of intoxicating liquors in violation of the laws thereof, is hereby prohibited.

SECTION 3. This article shall be inoperative unless it shall have been ratified as an amendment to the Constitution by conventions in the several States, as provided in the Constitution, within seven years from the date of the submission thereof to the States by the Congress.

Amendment XXII [March 1, 1951]

No person shall be elected to the office of the President more than twice, and no person who has held the office of President, or acted as President, for more than two years of a term to which some other person was elected President shall be elected to the office of the President more than once.

But this article shall not apply to any person holding the office of President when this article was proposed by the Congress, and shall not prevent any person who may be holding the office of President, or acting as President, during the term within which this article becomes operative from holding the office of President or acting as President during the remainder of such term.

This article shall be inoperative unless it shall have been ratified as an amendment to the Constitution by the legislatures of three-fourths of the several States within seven years from the date of its submission to the States by the Congress.

Amendment XXIII [March 29, 1961]

SECTION 1. The District constituting the seat of Government of the United States shall appoint in such manner as the Congress may direct.

A number of electors of President and Vice President equal to the whole number of Senators and Representatives in Congress to which the District would be entitled if it were a State, but in no event more than the least populous State; they shall be in addition to those appointed by the States, but they shall be considered, for the purposes of the election of President and Vice President, to be electors appointed by a State; and they shall meet in the District and perform such duties as provided by the twelfth article of amendment.

SECTION 2. The Congress shall have power to enforce this article by appropriate legislation.

Amendment XXIV [January 23, 1964]

SECTION 1. The right of citizens of the United States to vote in any primary or other election for President or Vice President, for electors for President or Vice President, or for Senator or Representative in Congress, shall not be denied or abridged by the United States or any State by reason of failure to pay any poll tax or other tax.

SECTION 2. The Congress shall have power to enforce this article by appropriate legislation.

Amendment XXV [February 10, 1967]

SECTION 1. In case of the removal of the President from office or of his death or resignation, the Vice President shall become President.

SECTION 2. Whenever there is a vacancy in the office of the Vice president, the President shall nominate a Vice President who shall take office upon confirmation by a majority of both Houses of Congress.

SECTION 3. Whenever the President transmits to the President pro tempore of the Senate and the Speaker of the House of Representatives his written declaration that he is unable to discharge the powers and duties of his office, and until he transmits to them a written declaration to the contrary, such powers and duties shall be discharged by the Vice President as Acting President.

SECTION 4. Whenever the Vice president and a majority of either the principal officers of the executive departments or of such other body as Congress may by law provide, transmit to the President pro tempore of the Senate and the Speaker of the House of Representatives their written declaration that the President is unable to discharge the powers and duties of his office, the Vice President shall immediately assume the powers and duties of the office as Acting President.

Thereafter, when the President transmits to the President pro tempore of the Senate and the Speaker of the House of Representatives his written declaration that no inability exists, he shall resume the powers and duties of his office unless the Vice President and a majority of either the principal officers of the executive departments or of such other body as

Congress may by law provide, transmit within four days to the President pro tempore of the Senate and the Speaker of the House of Representatives their written declaration that the President is unable to discharge the powers and duties of his office. Thereupon Congress shall decide the issue, assembling within forty-eight hours for that purpose if not in session. If the Congress, within twenty-one days after receipt of the latter written declaration, or, if Congress is not in session, within twenty-one days after Congress is required to assemble, determines by two-thirds vote of both Houses that the President is unable to discharge the powers and duties of his office, the Vice President shall continue to discharge the same as Acting President; otherwise, the President shall resume the powers and duties of his office.

Amendment XXVI [June 30, 1971]

SECTION 1. The right of citizens of the United States who are eighteen years of age or older to vote shall not be denied or abridged by the United States or by any State on account of age.

SECTION 2. The Congress shall have power to enforce this article by appropriate legislation.

Amendment XXVII[12] [May 7, 1992]

No law, varying the compensation for services of the Senators and Representatives, shall take effect until an election of Representatives shall have intervened.

---

[12]James Madison proposed this amendment in 1789 together with the ten amendments that were adopted as the Bill of Rights, but it failed to win ratification at the time. Congress, however, had set no deadline for its ratification, and over the years—particularly in the 1980s and 1990s—many states voted to add it to the Constitution. With the ratification of Michigan in 1992 it passed the threshold of 3/4ths of the states required for adoption, but because the process took more than 200 years, its validity remains in doubt.

PRESIDENTIAL ELECTIONS

Year	Number of States	Candidates	Party	Popular Vote*	Electoral Vote†	Percentage of Popular Vote
1789	11	GEORGE WASHINGTON	No party designations		69	
		John Adams			34	
		Other Candidates			35	
1792	15	GEORGE WASHINGTON	No party designations		132	
		John Adams			77	
		George Clinton			50	
		Other Candidates			5	
1796	16	JOHN ADAMS	Federalist		71	
		Thomas Jefferson	Democratic-Republican		68	
		Thomas Pinckney	Federalist		59	
		Aaron Burr	Democratic-Republican		30	
		Other Candidates			48	
1800	16	THOMAS JEFFERSON	Democratic-Republican		73	
		Aaron Burr	Democratic-Republican		73	
		John Adams	Federalist		65	
		Charles C. Pinckney	Federalist		64	
		John Jay	Federalist		1	
1804	17	THOMAS JEFFERSON	Democratic-Republican		162	
		Charles C. Pinckney	Federalist		14	
1808	17	JAMES MADISON	Democratic-Republican		122	
		Charles C. Pinckney	Federalist		47	
		George Clinton	Democratic-Republican		6	
1812	18	JAMES MADISON	Democratic-Republican		128	
		DeWitt Clinton	Federalist		89	
1816	19	JAMES MONROE	Democratic-Republican		183	
		Rufus King	Federalist		34	
1820	24	JAMES MONROE	Democratic-Republican		231	
		John Quincy Adams	Independent Republican		1	
1824	24	JOHN QUINCY ADAMS	Democratic-Republican	108,740	84	30.5
		Andrew Jackson	Democratic-Republican	153,544	99	43.1
		William H. Crawford	Democratic-Republican	46,618	41	13.1
		Henry Clay	Democratic-Republican	47,136	37	13.2
1828	24	ANDREW JACKSON	Democrat	647,286	178	56.0
		John Quincy Adams	National Republican	508,064	83	44.0
1832	24	ANDREW JACKSON	Democrat	687,502	219	55.0
		Henry Clay	National Republican	530,189	49	42.4
		William Wirt	Anti-Masonic	} 33,108	7	2.6
		John Floyd	National Republican		11	

*Percentage of popular vote given for any election year may not total 100 percent because candidates receiving less than 1 percent of the popular vote have been omitted.

†Prior to the passage of the Twelfth Amendment in 1904, the electoral college voted for two presidential candidates; the runner-up became Vice-President. Data from Historical Statistics of the United States, Colonial Times to 1957 (1961), pp. 682–683, and The World Almanac.

PRESIDENTIAL ELECTIONS
(continued)

Year	Number of States	Candidates	Party	Popular Vote	Electoral Vote	Percentage of Popular Vote
1836	26	MARTIN VAN BUREN	Democrat	765,483	170	50.9
		William H. Harrison	Whig		73	
		Hugh L. White	Whig	739,795	26	49.1
		Daniel Webster	Whig		14	
		W. P. Mangum	Whig		11	
1840	26	WILLIAM H. HARRISON	Whig	1,274,624	234	53.1
		Martin Van Buren	Democrat	1,127,781	60	46.9
1844	26	JAMES K. POLK	Democrat	1,338,464	170	49.6
		Henry Clay	Whig	1,300,097	105	48.1
		James G. Birney	Liberty	62,300		2.3
1848	30	ZACHARY TAYLOR	Whig	1,360,967	163	47.4
		Lewis Cass	Democrat	1,222,342	127	42.5
		Martin Van Buren	Free Soil	291,263		10.1
1852	31	FRANKLIN PIERCE	Democrat	1,601,117	254	50.9
		Winfield Scott	Whig	1,385,453	42	44.1
		John P. Hale	Free Soil	155,825		5.0
1856	31	JAMES BUCHANAN	Democrat	1,832,955	174	45.3
		John C. Frémont	Republican	1,339,932	114	33.1
		Millard Fillmore	American ("Know Nothing")	871,731	8	21.6
1860	33	ABRAHAM LINCOLN	Republican	1,865,593	180	39.8
		Stephen A. Douglas	Democrat	1,382,713	12	29.5
		John C. Breckinridge	Democrat	848,356	72	18.1
		John Bell	Constitutional Union	592,906	39	12.6
1864	36	ABRAHAM LINCOLN	Republican	2,206,938	212	55.0
		George B. McClellan	Democrat	1,803,787	21	45.0
1868	37	ULYSSES S. GRANT	Republican	3,013,421	214	52.7
		Horatio Seymour	Democrat	2,706,829	80	47.3
1872	37	ULYSSES S. GRANT	Republican	3,596,745	286	55.6
		Horace Greeley	Democrat	2,843,446	*	43.9
1876	38	RUTHERFORD B. HAYES	Republican	4,036,572	185	48.0
		Samuel J. Tilden	Democrat	4,284,020	184	51.0
1880	38	JAMES A. GARFIELD	Republican	4,453,295	214	48.5
		Winfield S. Hancock	Democrat	4,414,082	155	48.1
		James B. Weaver	Greenback-Labor	308,578		3.4
1884	38	GROVER CLEVELAND	Democrat	4,879,507	219	48.5
		James G. Blaine	Republican	4,850,293	182	48.2
		Benjamin F. Butler	Greenback-Labor	175,370		1.8
		John P. St. John	Prohibition	150,369		1.5
1888	38	BENJAMIN HARRISON	Republican	5,447,129	233	47.9
		Grover Cleveland	Democrat	5,537,857	168	48.6
		Clinton B. Fisk	Prohibition	249,506		2.2
		Anson J. Streeter	Union Labor	146,935		1.3

*Because of the death of Greeley, Democratic electors scattered their votes.

PRESIDENTIAL ELECTIONS
(continued)

Year	Number of States	Candidates	Party	Popular Vote	Electoral Vote	Percentage of Popular Vote
1892	44	GROVER CLEVELAND	Democrat	5,555,426	277	46.1
		Benjamin Harrison	Republican	5,182,690	145	43.0
		James B. Weaver	People's	1,029,846	22	8.5
		John Bidwell	Prohibition	264,133		2.2
1896	45	WILLIAM MCKINLEY	Republican	7,102,246	271	51.1
		William J. Bryan	Democrat	6,492,559	176	47.7
1900	45	WILLIAM MCKINLEY	Republican	7,218,491	292	51.7
		William J. Bryan	Democrat; Populist	6,356,734	155	45.5
		John C. Woolley	Prohibition	208,914		1.5
1904	45	THEODORE ROOSEVELT	Republican	7,628,461	336	57.4
		Alton B. Parker	Democrat	5,084,223	140	37.6
		Eugene V. Debs	Socialist	402,283		3.0
		Silas C. Swallow	Prohibition	258,536		1.9
1908	46	WILLIAM H. TAFT	Republican	7,675,320	321	51.6
		William J. Bryan	Democrat	6,412,294	162	43.1
		Eugene V. Debs	Socialist	420,793		2.8
		Eugene W. Chafin	Prohibition	253,840		1.7
1912	48	WOODROW WILSON	Democrat	6,296,547	435	41.9
		Theodore Roosevelt	Progressive	4,118,571	88	27.4
		William H. Taft	Republican	3,486,720	8	23.2
		Eugene V. Debs	Socialist	900,672		6.0
		Eugene W. Chafin	Prohibition	206,275		1.4
1916	48	WOODROW WILSON	Democrat	9,127,695	277	49.4
		Charles E. Hughes	Republican	8,533,507	254	46.2
		A. L. Benson	Socialist	585,113		3.2
		J. Frank Hanly	Prohibition	220,506		1.2
1920	48	WARREN G. HARDING	Republican	16,143,407	404	60.4
		James M. Cox	Democrat	9,130,328	127	34.2
		Eugene V. Debs	Socialist	919,799		3.4
		P. P. Christensen	Farmer-Labor	265,411		1.0
1924	48	CALVIN COOLIDGE	Republican	15,718,211	382	54.0
		John W. Davis	Democrat	8,385,283	136	28.8
		Robert M. La Follette	Progressive	4,831,289	13	16.6
1928	48	HERBERT C. HOOVER	Republican	21,391,993	444	58.2
		Alfred E. Smith	Democrat	15,016,169	87	40.9
1932	48	FRANKLIN D. ROOSEVELT	Democrat	22,809,638	472	57.4
		Herbert C. Hoover	Republican	15,758,901	59	39.7
		Norman Thomas	Socialist	881,951		2.2
1936	48	FRANKLIN D. ROOSEVELT	Democrat	27,752,869	523	60.8
		Alfred M. Landon	Republican	16,674,665	8	36.5
		William Lemke	Union	882,479		1.9
1940	48	FRANKLIN D. ROOSEVELT	Democrat	27,307,819	449	54.8
		Wendell L. Willkie	Republican	22,321,018	82	44.8
1944	48	FRANKLIN D. ROOSEVELT	Democrat	25,606,585	432	53.5
		Thomas E. Dewey	Republican	22,014,745	99	46.0

PRESIDENTIAL ELECTIONS
(continued)

Year	Number of States	Candidates	Party	Popular Vote	Electoral Vote	Percentage of Popular Vote
1948	48	HARRY S. TRUMAN	Democrat	24,105,812	303	49.5
		Thomas E. Dewey	Republican	21,970,065	189	45.1
		J. Strom Thurmond	States' Rights	1,169,063	39	2.4
		Henry A. Wallace	Progressive	1,157,172		2.4
1952	48	DWIGHT D. EISENHOWER	Republican	33,936,234	442	55.1
		Adlai E. Stevenson	Democrat	27,314,992	89	44.4
1956	48	DWIGHT D. EISENHOWER	Republican	35,590,472	457*	57.6
		Adlai E. Stevenson	Democrat	26,022,752	73	42.1
1960	50	JOHN F. KENNEDY	Democrat	34,227,096	303†	49.9
		Richard M. Nixon	Republican	34,108,546	219	49.6
1964	50	LYNDON B. JOHNSON	Democrat	42,676,220	486	61.3
		Barry M. Goldwater	Republican	26,860,314	52	38.5
1968	50	RICHARD M. NIXON	Republican	31,785,480	301	43.4
		Hubert H. Humphrey	Democrat	31,275,165	191	42.7
		George C. Wallace	American Independent	9,906,473	46	13.5
1972	50	RICHARD M. NIXON ‡	Republican	47,165,234	520	60.6
		George S. McGovern	Democrat	29,168,110	17	37.5
1976	50	JIMMY CARTER	Democrat	40,828,929	297	50.1
		Gerald R. Ford	Republican	39,148,940	240	47.9
		Eugene McCarthy	Independent	739,256		
1980	50	RONALD REAGAN	Republican	43,201,220	489	50.9
		Jimmy Carter	Democrat	34,913,332	49	41.2
		John B. Anderson	Independent	5,581,379		
1984	50	RONALD REAGAN	Republican	53,428,357	525	59.0
		Walter F. Mondale	Democrat	36,930,923	13	41.0
1988	50	GEORGE BUSH	Republican	48,901,046	426	53.4
		Michael Dukakis	Democrat	41,809,030	111	45.6
1992	50	BILL CLINTON	Democrat	43,728,275	370	43.2
		George Bush	Republican	38,167,416	168	37.7
		H. Ross Perot	United We Stand, America	19,237,247		19.0
1996	50	BILL CLINTON	Democrat	45,590,703	379	49.0
		Bob Dole	Republican	37,816,307	159	41.0
		H. Ross Perot	Reform	7,866,284		8.0

Walter B. Jones received 1 electoral vote.

†*Harry F. Byrd received 15 electoral votes.*

‡*Resigned August 9, 1974: Vice President Gerald R. Ford became President.*

PRESIDENTIAL ADMINISTRATIONS

THE WASHINGTON ADMINISTRATION (1789–1797)

Vice President	John Adams	1789–1797
Secretary of State	Thomas Jefferson	1789–1793
	Edmund Randolph	1794–1795
	Timothy Pickering	1795–1797
Secretary of Treasury	Alexander Hamilton	1789–1795
	Oliver Wolcott	1795–1797
Secretary of War	Henry Knox	1789–1794
	Timothy Pickering	1795–1796
	James McHenry	1796–1797
Attorney General	Edmund Randolph	1789–1793
	William Bradford	1794–1795
	Charles Lee	1795–1797
Postmaster General	Samuel Osgood	1789–1791
	Timothy Pickering	1791–1794
	Joseph Habersham	1795–1797

THE JOHN ADAMS ADMINISTRATION (1797–1801)

Vice President	Thomas Jefferson	1797–1801
Secretary of State	Timothy Pickering	1797–1800
	John Marshall	1800–1801
Secretary of Treasury	Oliver Wolcott	1797–1800
	Samuel Dexter	1800–1801
Secretary of War	James McHenry	1797–1800
	Samuel Dexter	1800–1801
Attorney General	Charles Lee	1797–1801
Postmaster General	Joseph Habersham	1797–1801
Secretary of Navy	Benjamin Stoddert	1798–1801

THE JEFFERSON ADMINISTRATION (1801–1809)

Vice President	Aaron Burr	1801–1805
	George Clinton	1805–1809
Secretary of State	James Madison	1801–1809
Secretary of Treasury	Samuel Dexter	1801
	Albert Gallatin	1801–1809
Secretary of War	Henry Dearborn	1801–1809
Attorney General	Levi Lincoln	1801–1805
	Robert Smith	1805
	John Breckinridge	1805–1806
	Caesar Rodney	1807–1809
Postmaster General	Joseph Habersham	1801
	Gideon Granger	1801–1809
Secretary of Navy	Robert Smith	1801–1809

THE MADISON ADMINISTRATION (1809–1817)

Vice President	George Clinton	1809–1813
	Elbridge Gerry	1813–1817
Secretary of State	Robert Smith	1809–1811
	James Monroe	1811–1817
Secretary of Treasury	Albert Gallatin	1809–1813
	George Campbell	1814
	Alexander Dallas	1814–1816
	William Crawford	1816–1817
Secretary of War	William Eustis	1809–1812
	John Armstrong	1813–1814
	James Monroe	1814–1815
	William Crawford	1815–1817
Attorney General	Caesar Rodney	1809–1811
	William Pinkney	1811–1814
	Richard Rush	1814–1817
Postmaster General	Gideon Granger	1809–1814
	Return Meigs	1814–1817
Secretary of Navy	Paul Hamilton	1809–1813
	William Jones	1813–1814
	Benjamin Crowninshield	1814–1817

THE MONROE ADMINISTRATION (1817–1825)

Vice President	Daniel Tompkins	1817–1825
Secretary of State	John Quincy Adams	1817–1825
Secretary of Treasury	William Crawford	1817–1825
Secretary of War	George Graham	1817
	John C. Calhoun	1817–1825
Attorney General	Richard Rush	1817
	William Wirt	1817–1825
Postmaster General	Return Meigs	1817–1823
	John McLean	1823–1825
Secretary of Navy	Benjamin Crowninshield	1817–1818
	Smith Thompson	1818–1823
	Samuel Southard	1823–1825

THE JOHN QUINCY ADAMS ADMINISTRATION (1825–1829)

Vice President	John C. Calhoun	1825–1829
Secretary of State	Henry Clay	1825–1829
Secretary of Treasury	Richard Rush	1825–1829
Secretary of War	James Barbour	1825–1828
	Peter Porter	1828–1829
Attorney General	William Wirt	1825–1829
Postmaster General	John McLean	1825–1829
Secretary of Navy	Samuel Southard	1825–1829

THE JACKSON ADMINISTRATION (1829–1837)

Vice President	John C. Calhoun	1829–1833
	Martin Van Buren	1833–1837
Secretary of State	Martin Van Buren	1829–1831
	Edward Livingston	1831–1833
	Louis McLane	1833–1834
	John Forsyth	1834–1837
Secretary of Treasury	Samuel Ingham	1829–1831
	Louis McLane	1831–1833
	William Duane	1833
	Roger B. Taney	1833–1834
	Levi Woodbury	1834–1837
Secretary of War	John H. Eaton	1829–1831
	Lewis Cass	1831–1837
	Benjamin Butler	1837
Attorney General	John M. Berrien	1829–1831
	Roger B. Taney	1831–1833
	Benjamin Butler	1833–1837
Postmaster General	William Barry	1829–1835
	Amos Kendall	1835–1837

PRESIDENTIAL ADMINISTRATIONS
(continued)

Secretary of Navy	John Branch	1829–1831
	Levi Woodbury	1831–1834
	Mahlon Dickerson	1834–1837

THE VAN BUREN ADMINISTRATION (1837–1841)

Vice President	Richard M. Johnson	1837–1841
Secretary of State	John Forsyth	1837–1841
Secretary of Treasury	Levi Woodbury	1837–1841
Secretary of War	Joel Poinsett	1837–1841
Attorney General	Benjamin Butler	1837–1838
	Felix Grundy	1838–1840
	Henry D. Gilpin	1840–1841
Postmaster General	Amos Kendall	1837–1840
	John M. Niles	1840–1841
Secretary of Navy	Mahlon Dickerson	1837–1838
	James Paulding	1838–1841

THE WILLIAM HARRISON ADMINISTRATION (1841)

Vice President	John Tyler	1841
Secretary of State	Daniel Webster	1841
Secretary of Treasury	Thomas Ewing	1841
Secretary of War	John Bell	1841
Attorney General	John J. Crittenden	1841
Postmaster General	Francis Granger	1841
Secretary of Navy	George Badger	1841

THE TYLER ADMINISTRATION (1841–1845)

Vice President	None	
Secretary of State	Daniel Webster	1841–1843
	Hugh S. Legaré	1843
	Abel P. Upshur	1843–1844
	John C. Calhoun	1844–1845
Secretary of Treasury	Thomas Ewing	1841
	Walter Forward	1841–1843
	John C. Spencer	1843–1844
	George Bibb	1844–1845
Secretary of War	John Bell	1841
	John C. Spencer	184t–1843
	James M. Porter	184–1844
	William Wilkins	1844–1845
Attorney General	John J. Crittenden	1841
	Hugh S. Legaré	1841–1843
	John Nelson	1843–1845
Postmaster General	Francis Granger	1841
	Charles Wickliffe	1841
Secretary of Navy	George Badger	1841
	Abel P. Upshur	1841
	David Henshaw	1843–1844
	Thomas Gilmer	1844
	John Y. Mason	1844–1845

THE POLK ADMINISTRATION (1845–1849)

Vice President	George M. Dallas	1845–1849
Secretary of State	James Buchanan	1845–1849
Secretary of Treasury	Robert J. Walker	1845–1849
Secretary of War	William L. Marcy	1845–1849
Attorney General	John Y. Mason	1845–1846
	Nathan Clifford	1846–1848
	Isaac Toucey	1848–1849
Postmaster General	Cave Johnson	1845–1849
Secretary of Navy	George Bancrocft	1845–1846
	John Y. Mason	1846–1849

THE TAYLOR ADMINISTRATION (1849–1850)

Vice President	Millard Fillmore	1849–1850
Secretary of State	John M. Clayton	1849–1850
Secretary of Treasury	William Meredith	1849–1850
Secretary of War	George Crawford	1849–1850
Attorney General	Reverdy Johnson	1849–1850
Postmaster General	Jacob Collamer	1849–1850
Secretary of Navy	William Preston	1849–1850
Secretary of Interior	Thomas Ewing	1849–1850

THE FILLMORE ADMINISTRATION (1850–1853)

Vice President	None	
Secretary of State	Daniel Webster	1850–1852
	Edward Everett	1852–1853
Secretary of Treasury	Thomas Corwin	1850–1853
Secretary of War	Charles Conrad	1850–1853
Attorney General	John J. Crittenden	1850–1853
Postmaster General	Nathan Hall	1850–1852
	Sam D. Hubbard	1852–1853
Secretary of Navy	William A. Graham	1850–1852
	John P. Kennedy	1852–1853
Secretary of Interior	Thomas McKennan	1850
	Alexander Stuart	1850–1853

THE PIERCE ADMINISTRATION (1853–1857)

Vice President	William R. King	1853–1857
Secretary of State	William L. Marcy	1853–1857
Secretary of Treasury	James Guthrie	1853–1857
Secretary of War	Jefferson Davis	1853–1857
Attorney General	Caleb Cushing	1853–1857
Postmaster General	James Campbell	1853–1857
Secretary of Navy	James C. Dobbin	1853–1857
Secretary of Interior	Robert McClelland	1853–1857

THE BUCHANAN ADMINISTRATION (1857–1861)

Vice President	John C. Breckinridge	1857–1861
Secretary of State	Lewis Cass	1857–1860
	Jeremiah S. Black	1860–1861
Secretary of Treasury	Howell Cobb	1857–1860
	Philip Thomas	1860–1861
	John A. Dix	1861
Secretary of War	John B. Floyd	1857–1861
	Joseph Holt	1861
Attorney General	Jeremiah S. Black	1857–1860
	Edwin M. Stanton	1860–1861
Postmaster General	Aaron V. Brown	1857–1859
	Joseph Holt	1859–1861
	Horatio King	1861

PRESIDENTIAL ADMINISTRATIONS
(continued)

Secretary of Navy	Isaac Toucey	1857–1861
Secretary of Interior	Jacob Thompson	1857–1861

THE LINCOLN ADMINISTRATION (1861–1865)

Vice President	Hannibal Hamlin	1861–1865
	Andrew Jackson	1865
Secretary of State	William H. Seward	1861–1865
Secretary of Treasury	Salmon P. Chase	1861–1864
	William P. Fessenden	1864–1865
	Hugh McCulloch	1865
Secretary of War	Simon Cameron	1861–1862
	Edwin M. Stanton	1862–1865
Attorney General	Edward Bates	1861–1864
	James Speed	1864–1865
Postmaster General	Horatio King	1861
	Montgomery Blair	1861–1864
	William Dennison	1864–1865
Secretary of Navy	Gideon Welles	1861–1865
Secretary of Interior	Caleb B. Smith	1861–1863
	John P. Usher	1863–1865

THE ANDREW JOHNSON ADMINISTRATION (1865–1869)

Vice President	None	
Secretary of State	William H. Seward	1865–1869
Secretary of Treasury	Hugh McCulloch	1865–1869
Secretary of War	Edwin M. Stanton	1865–1867
	Ulysses S. Grant	1867–1868
	Lorenzo Thomas	1868
	John M. Schofield	1868–1869
Attorney General	James Speed	1865–1866
	Henry Stanbery	1866–1868
	William M. Evarts	1868–1869
Postmaster General	William Dennison	1865–1866
	Alexander Randall	1866–1869
Secretary of Navy	Gideon Welles	1865–1869
Secretary of Interior	John P. Usher	1865
	James Harlan	1865–1866
	Orville H. Browning	1866–1869

THE GRANT ADMINISTRATION (1869–1877)

Vice President	Schuyler Colfax	1869–1873
	Henry Wilson	1873–1877
Secretary of State	Elihu B. Washburne	1869
	Hamilton Fish	1869–1877
Secretary of Treasury	George S. Boutwell	1869–1873
	William Richardson	1873–1874
	Benjamin Bristow	1874–1876
	Lot M. Morrill	1876–1877
Secretary of War	John A. Rawlins	1869
	William T. Sherman	1869
	William W. Belknap	1869–1876
	Alphonso Taft	1876
	James D. Cameron	1876–1877
Attorney General	Ebenezer Hoar	1869–1870
	Amos T. Ackerman	1870–1871

	G. H. Williams	1871–1875
	Edwards Pierrepont	1875–1876
	Alphonso Taft	1876–1877
Postmaster General	John A. J. Creswell	1869–1874
	James W. Marshall	1874
	Marshall Jewell	1874–1876
	James N. Tyner	1876–1877
Secretary of Navy	Adolph E. Borie	1869
	George M. Robeson	1869–1877
Secretary of Interior	Jacob D. Cox	1869–1870
	Columbus Delano	1870–1875
	Zachariah Candler	1875–1877

THE HAYES ADMINISTRATION (1877–1881)

Vice President	William A. Wheeler	1877–1881
Secretary of State	William M. Evarts	1877–1881
Secretary of Treasury	John Sherman	1877–1881
Secretary of War	George W. McCrary	1877–1879
	Alex Ramsey	1879–1881
Attorney General	Charles Devens	1877–1881
Postmaster General	David M. Key	1877–1880
	Horace Maynard	1880–1881
Secretary of Navy	Richard W. Thompson	1877–1880
	Nathan Goff, Jr.	1881
Secretary of Interior	Carl Schurz	1877–1881

THE GARFIELD ADMINISTRATION (1881)

Vice President	Chester A. Arthur	1881
Secretary of State	James G. Blaine	1881
Secretary of Treasury	William Windom	1881
Secretary of War	Robert T. Lincoln	1881
Attorney General	Wayne MacVeagh	1881
Postmaster General	Thomas L. James	1881
Secretary of Navy	William H. Hunt	1881
Secretary of Interior	Samuel J. Kirkwood	1881

THE ARTHUR ADMINISTRATION (1881–1885)

Vice President	None	
Secretary of State	F. T. Frelinghuysen	1881–1885
Secretary of Treasury	Charles J. Folger	1881–1884
	Walter Q. Gresham	1884
	Hugh McCulloch	1884–1885
Secretary of War	Robert T. Lincoln	1881–1885
Attorney General	Benjamin H. Brewster	1881–1885
Postmaster General	Timothy O. Howe	1881–1883
	Walter Q. Gresham	1883–1884
	Frank Hatton	1884–1885
Secretary of Navy	William H. Hunt	1881–1882
	William E. Chandler	1882–1885
Secretary of Interior	Samuel J. Kirkwood	1881–1882
	Henry M. Teller	1882–1885

THE CLEVELAND ADMINISTRATION (1885–1889)

Vice President	Thomas A. Hendricks	1885–1889
Secretary of State	Thomas F. Bayard	1885–1889

PRESIDENTIAL ADMINISTRATIONS
(continued)

Secretary of Treasury	Daniel Manning	1885–1887
	Charles S. Fairchild	1887–1889
Secretary of War	William C. Endicott	1885–1889
Attorney General	Augustus H. Garland	1885–1889
Postmaster General	William F. Vilas	1885–1888
	Don M. Dickinson	1888–1889
Secretary of Navy	William C. Whitney	1885–1889
Secretary of Interior	Lucius Q. C. Lamar	1885–1888
	William F. Vilas	1888–1889
Secretary of Agriculture	Norman J. Colman	1889

THE BENJAMIN HARRISON ADMINISTRATION (1889–1893)

Vice President	Levi P. Morton	1889–1893
Secretary of State	James G. Blaine	1889–1892
	John W. Foster	1892–1893
Secretary of Treasury	William Windom	1889–1891
	Charles Foster	1891–1893
Secretary of War	Redfield Proctor	1889–1891
	Stephen B. Elkins	1891–1893
Attorney General	William H. H. Miller	1889–1891
Postmaster General	John Wanamaker	1889–1893
Secretary of Navy	Benjamin F. Tracy	1889–1893
Secretary of Interior	John W. Noble	1889–1893
Secretary of Agriculture	Jeremiah M. Rusk	1889–1893

THE CLEVELAND ADMINISTRATION (1893–1897)

Vice President	Adlai E. Stevenson	1893–1897
Secretary of State	Walter Q. Gresham	1893–1895
	Richard Olney	1895–1897
Secretary of Treasury	John G. Carlisle	1893–1897
Secretary of War	Daniel S. Lamont	1893–1897
Attorney General	Richard Olney	1893–1895
	James Harmon	1895–1897
Postmaster General	Wilson S. Bissell	1893–1895
	William L. Wilson	1895–1897
Secretary of Navy	Hilary A. Herbert	1893–1897
Secretary of Interior	Hoke Smith	1893–1896
	David R. Francis	1896–1897
Secretary of Agriculture	Julius S. Morton	1893–1897

THE MCKINLEY ADMINISTRATION (1897–1901)

Vice President	Garret A. Hobart	1897–1901
	Theodore Roosevelt	1901
Secretary of State	John Serman	1897–1898
	William R. Day	1898
	John Hay	1898–1901
Secretary of Treasury	Lyman J. Gage	1897–1901
Secretary of War	Russell A. Alger	1897–1899
	Elihu Root	1899–1901
Attorney General	Joseph McKenna	1897–1898
	John W. Griggs	1898–1901
	Philander C. Knox	1901

Postmaster General	James A. Gary	1897–1898
	Charles E. Smith	1898–1901
Secretary of Navy	John D. Long	1897–1901
Secretary of Interior	Cornelius N. Bliss	1897–1899
	Ethan A. Hitchcock	1899–1901
Secretary of Agriculture	James Wilson	1897–1901

THE THEODORE ROOSEVELT ADMINISTRATION (1901–1909)

Vice President	Charles Fairbanks	1905–1909
Secretary of State	John Hay	1901–1905
	Elihu Root	1905–1909
	Robert Bacon	1909
Secretary of Treasury	Lyman J. Gage	1901–1902
	Leslie M. Shaw	1902–1907
	George B. Cortelyou	1907–1909
Secretary of War	Elihu Root	1901–1904
	William H. Taft	1904–1908
	Luke E. Wright	1908–1909
Attorney General	Philander C. Knox	1901–1904
	William H. Moody	1904–1906
	Charles J. Bonaparte	1906–1909
Postmaster General	Charles E. Smith	1901–1902
	Henry C. Payne	1902–1904
	Robert J. Wynne	1904–1905
	George B. Cortelyou	1905–1907
	George von L. Meyer	1907–1909
Secretary of Navy	John D. Long	1901–1902
	William H. Moody	1902–1904
	Paul Morton	1904–1905
	Charles J. Bonaparte	1905–1906
	Victor H. Metcalf	1906–1908
	Truman H. Newberry	1908–1909
Secretary of Interior	Ethan A. Hitchcock	1901–1907
	James R. Garfield	1907–1909
Secretary of Agriculture	James Wilson	1901–1909
Secretary of Labor and Commerce	George B. Cortelyou	1903–1904
	Victor H. Metcalf	1904–1906
	Oscar S. Straus	1906–1909
	Charles Nagel	1909

THE TAFT ADMINISTRATION (1909–1913)

Vice President	James S. Sherman	1909–1913
Secretary of State	Philander C. Knox	1909–1913
Secretary of Treasury	Franklin MacVeagh	1909–1913
Secretary of War	Jacob M. Dickinson	1909–1911
	Henry L. Stimson	1911–1913
Attorney General	George W. Wickersham	1909–1913
Postmaster General	Frank H. Hitchcock	1909–1913
Secretary of Navy	George von L. Meyer	1909–1913
Secretary of Interior	Richard A. Ballinger	1909–1911
	Walter L. Fisher	1991–1913
Secretary of Agriculture	James Wilson	1909–1913

PRESIDENTIAL ADMINISTRATIONS
(continued)

Secretary of Labor and Commerce	Charles Nagel	1909–1913

THE WILSON ADMINISTRATION (1913–1921)

Vice President	Thomas R. Marshall	1913–1921
Secretary of State	William J. Bryan	1913–1915
	Robert Lansing	1915–1920
	Bainbridge Colby	1920–1921
Secretary of Treasury	William G. McAdoo	1913–1918
	Carter Glass	1918–1920
	David F. Houston	1920–1921
Secretary of War	Lindley M. Garrison	1913–1916
	Newton D. Baker	1916–1921
Attorney General	James C. McReyolds	1913–1914
	Thomas W. Gregory	1914–1919
	A. Mitchell Palmer	1919–1921
Postmaster General	Albert S. Burleson	1913–1921
Secretary of Navy	Josephus Daniels	1913–1921
Secretary of Interior	Franklin K. Lane	1913–1920
	John B. Payne	1920–1921
Secretary of Agriculture	David F. Houston	1913–1920
	Edwin T. Meredith	1920–1921
Secretary of Commerce	William C. Redfield	1913–1919
	Joshua W. Alexander	1919–1921
Secretary of Labor	William B. Wilson	1913–1921

THE HARDING ADMINISTRATION (1921–1923)

Vice President	Calvin Coolidge	1921–1923
Secretary of State	Charles E. Hughes	1921–1923
Secretary of Treasury	Andrew Mellon	1921–1923
Secretary of War	John W. Weeks	1921–1923
Attorney General	Harry M. Daugherty	1921–1923
Postmaster General	Will H. Hays	1921–1922
	Hubert Work	1922–1923
	Harry S. New	1923
Secretary of Navy	Edwin Denby	1921–1923
Secretary of Interior	Albert B. Fall	1921–1923
	Hubert Work	1923
Secretary of Agriculture	Henry C. Wallace	1921–1923
Secretary of Commerce	Herbert C. Hoover	1921–1923
Secretary of Labor	James J. Davis	1921–1923

THE COOLIDGE ADMINISTRATION (1923–1929)

Vice President	Charles G. Dawes	1925–1929
Secretary of State	Charles E. Hughes	1923–1925
	Frank B. Kellogg	1925–1929
Secretary of Treasury	Andrew Mellon	1923–1929
Secretary of War	John W. Weeks	1923–1925
	Dwight F. Davis	1925–1929
Attorney General	Harry M. Daugherty	1923–1924
	Harlan F. Stone	1924–1925
	John G. Sargent	1925–1929

Postmaster General	Harry S. New	1923–1929
Secretary of Navy	Edwin Derby	1923–1924
	Curtis D. Wilbur	1924–1929
Secretary of Interior	Hubert Work	1923–1928
	Roy O. West	1928–1929
Secretary of Agriculture	Henry C. Wallace	1923–1924
	Howard M. Gore	1924–1925
	William M. Jardine	1925–1929
Secretary of Commerce	Herbert C. Hoover	1923–1928
	William F. Whiting	1928–1929
Secretary of Labor	James J. Davis	1923–1929

THE HOOVER ADMINISTRATION (1929–1933)

Vice President	Charles Curtis	1929–1933
Secretary of State	Henry L. Stimson	1929–1933
Secretary of Treasury	Andrew Mellon	1929–1932
	Ogden L. Mills	1932–1933
Secretary of War	James W. Good	1929
	Patrick J. Hurley	1929–1933
Attorney General	William D. Mitchell	1929–1933
Postmaster General	Walter F. Brown	1929–1933
Secretary of Navy	Charles F. Adams	1929–1933
Secretary of Interior	Ray L. Wilbur	1929–1933
Secretary of Agriculture	Arthur M. Hyde	1929–1933
Secretary of Commerce	Robert P. Lamont	1929–1932
	Roy D. Chapin	1932–1933
Secretary of Labor	James J. Davis	1929–1930
	William N. Doak	1930–1933

THE FRANKLIN D. ROOSEVELT ADMINISTRATION (1933–1945)

Vice President	John Nance Garner	1933–1941
	Henry A. Wallace	1941–1945
	Harry S. Truman	1945
Secretary of State	Cordell Hull	1933–1944
	Edward R. Stettinius, Jr.	1944–1945
Secretary of Treasury	William H. Woodin	1933–1934
	Henry Morgenthau, Jr.	1934–1945
Secretary of War	George H. Dern	1933–1936
	Henry A. Woodring	1936–1940
	Henry L. Stimson	1940–1945
Attorney General	Homer S. Cummings	1933–1939
	Frank Murphy	1939–1940
	Robert H. Jackson	1940–1941
	Francis Biddle	1941–1945
Postmaster General	James A. Farley	1933–1940
	Frank C. Walker	1940–1945
Secretary of Navy	Claude A. Swanson	1933–1940
	Charles Edison	1940
	Frank Knox	1940–1944
	James V. Forrestal	1944–1945
Secretary of Interior	Harold L. Ickes	1933–1945
Secretary of Agriculture	Henry A. Wallace	1933–1940
	Claude R. Wickard	1940–1945

PRESIDENTIAL ADMINISTRATIONS
(continued)

Secretary of Commerce	Daniel C. Roper	1933–1939
	Harry L. Hopkins	1939–1940
	Jesse Jones	1940–1945
	Henry A. Wallace	1945
Secretary of Labor	Frances Perkins	1933–1945

THE TRUMAN ADMINISTRATION (1945–1953)

Vice President	Alben W. Barkley	1949–1953
Secretary of State	Edward R. Stettinius, Jr.	1945
	James F. Byrnes	1945–1947
	George C. Marshall	1947–1949
	Dean G. Acheson	1949–1953
Secretary of Treasury	Fred M. Vinson	1945–1946
	John W. Snyder	1946–1953
Secretary of War	Robert P. Patterson	1945–1947
	Kenneth C. Royall	1947
Attorney General	Tom C. Clark	1945–1949
	J. Howard McGrath	1949–1952
	James P. McGranery	1952–1953
Postmaster General	Frank C. Walker	1945
	Robert E. Hannegan	1945–1947
	Jesse M. Donaldson	1947–1953
Secretary of Navy	James V. Forrestal	1945–1947
Secretary of Interior	Harold L. Ickes	1945–1946
	Julius A. Krug	1946–1949
	Oscar L. Chapman	1949–1953
Secretary of Agriculture	Clinton P. Anderson	1945–1948
	Charles F. Brannan	1948–1953
Secretary of Commerce	Henry A. Wallace	1945–1946
	W. Averell Harriman	1946–1948
	Charles W. Sawyer	1948–1953
Secretary of Labor	Lewis B. Schwellenback	1945–1948
	Maurice J. Tobin	1948–1953
Secretary of Defense	James V. Forrestal	1947–1949
	Louis A. Johnson	1949–1950
	George C. Marshall	1950–1951
	Robert A. Lovett	1951–1953

THE EISENHOWER ADMINISTRATION (1953–1961)

Vice President	Richard M. Nixon	1953–1961
Secretary of State	John Foster Dulles	1953–1959
	Christian A. Herter	1959–1961
Secretary of Treasury	George M. Humphrey	1953–1957
	Robert B. Anderson	1957–1961
Attorney General	Herbert Brownell, Jr.	1953–1958
	William P. Rogers	1958–1961
Postmaster General	Arthur E. Summerfield	1953–1961
Secretary of Interior	Douglas McKay	1953–1956
	Freed A. Seaton	1956–1961
Secretary of Agriculture	Ezra T. Benson	1953–1961
Secretary of Commerce	Sinclair Weeks	1953–1958
	Lewis L. Strauss	1958–1959
	Frederick H. Mueller	1959–1961
Secretary of Labor	Martin P. Durkin	1953
	James P. Mitchell	1953–1961

Secretary of Defense	Charles E. Wilson	1953–1957
	Neil H. McElroy	1957–1959
	Thomas S. Gates Jr.	1959–1961
Secretary of Health, Education, and Welfare	Oveta Culp Hobby	1953–1955
	Marion B. Folsom	1955–1958
	Arthur S. Flemming	1958–1961

THE KENNEDY ADMINISTRATION (1961–1963)

Vice President	Lyndon B. Johnson	1961–1963
Secretary of State	Dean Rusk	1961–1963
Secretary of Treasury	C. Douglas Dillon	1961–1963
Attorney General	Robert F. Kennedy	1961–1963
Postmaster General	J. Edward Day	1961–1963
	John A. Gronouski	1963
Secretary of Interior	Stewart I. Udall	1961–1963
Secretary of Agriculture	Orville L. Freeman	1961–1963
Secretary of Commerce	Luther H. Hodges	1961–1963
Secretary of Labor	Arthur J. Goldberg	1961–1962
	W. Willard Wirtz	1962–1963
Secretary of Defense	Robert S. McNamara	1961–1963
Secretary of Health, Education, and Welfare	Abraham A. Ribicoff	1961–1962
	Anthony J. Celebrezze	1962–1963

THE LYNDON JOHNSON ADMINISTRATION (1963–1969)

Vice President	Hubert H. Humphrey	1965–1969
Secretary of State	Dean Rusk	1963–1969
Secretary of Treasury	C. Douglas Dillon	1963–1965
	Henry H. Fowler	1965–1969
Attorney General	Robert F. Kennedy	1963–1964
	Nicholas Katzenbach	1965–1966
	Ramsey Clark	1967–1969
Postmaster General	John A. Gronouski	1963–1965
	Lawrence F. O'Brien	1965–1968
	Marvin Watson	1968–1969
Secretary of Interior	Stewart L. Udall	1963–1969
Secretary of Agriculture	Orville L. Freeman	1963–1969
Secretary of Commerce	Luther H. Hodges	1963–1964
	John T. Connor	1964–1967
	Alexander B. Trowbridge	1967–1968
	Cyrus R. Smith	1968–1969
Secretary of Labor	W. Willard Wirtz	1963–1969
Secretary of Defense	Robert F. McNamara	1963–1968
	Clark Clifford	1968–1969
Secretary of Health, Education, and Welfare	Anthony J. Celebrezze	1963–1965
	John W. Gardner	1965–1968
	Wilbur J. Cohen	1968–1969
Secretary of Housing and Urban Development	Robert C. Weaver	1966–1969
	Robert C. Wood	1969
Secretary of Transportation	Alan S. Boyd	1967–1969

PRESIDENTIAL ADMINISTRATIONS
(continued)

THE NIXON ADMINISTRATION (1969–1974)

Vice President	Spiro T. Agnew	1969–1973
	Gerald R. Ford	1973–1974
Secretary of State	William P. Rogers	1969–1973
	Henry Kissinger	1973–1974
Secretary of Treasury	David M. Kennedy	1969–1970
	John B. Connally	1972–1974
	George P. Schultz	1972–1974
	William E. Simon	1974
Attorney General	John N. Mitchell	1969–1972
	Richard G. Kleindienst	1972–1973
	Elliot L. Richardson	1973
	William B. Saxbe	1973–1974
Postmaster General	Winton M. Blount	1969–1971
Secretary of Interior	Walter J. Hickel	1969–1970
	Rogers Morton	1971–1974
Secretary of Agriculture	Clifford M. Hardin	1969–1971
	Earl L. Butz	1971–1974
Secretary of Commerce	Maurice H. Stans	1969–1972
	Peter G. Peterson	1972–1973
	Frederick B. Dent	1973–1974
Secretary of Labor	George P. Shultz	1969–1970
	James D. Hodgson	1970–1973
	Peter J. Brennan	1973–1974
Secretary of Defense	Melvin R. Laird	1969–1973
	Eliot L. Richardson	1973
	James R. Schelsinger	1973–1974
Secretary of Health, Education, and Welfare	Robert H. Finch	1969–1970
	Elliot L. Richardson	1970–1973
	Caspar W. Weinberger	1973–1974
Secretary of Housing and Urban Development	George Romney	1969–1973
	James T. Lynn	1973–1974
Secretary of Transportation	John A. Volpe	1969–1973
	Claude S. Brinegar	1973–1974

THE FORD ADMINISTRATION (1974–1977)

Vice President	Nelson A. Rockefeller	1974–1977
Secretary of State	Henry A. Kissinger	1974–1977
Secretary of Treasury	William E. Simon	1974–1977
Attorney General	William Saxbe	1974–1975
	Edward Levi	1975–1977
Secretary of Interior	Rogers Morton	1974–1975
	Stanley K. Hathaway	1975
	Thomas Kleppe	1975–1977
Secretary of Agriculture	Earl I. Butz	1974–1976
	John A. Knebel	1976–1977
Secretary of Commerce	Frederick B. Dent	1974–1975
	Rogers Morton	1975–1976
	Elliot L. Richardson	1976–1977
Secretary of Labor	Peter J. Brennan	1974–1975
	John T. Dunlop	1975–1976
	W. J. Usery	1976–1977
Secretary of Defense	James R. Schlesinger	1974–1975
	Donald Rumsfeld	1975–1977

Secretary of Health, Education, and Welfare	Caspar Weinberger	1974–1975
	Forrest D. Mathews	1975–1977
Secretary of Housing Urban Development	James T. Lynn	1974–1975
	Carla A. Hills	1975–1977
Secretary of Transportation	Claude Brinegar	1974–1975
	William T. Colemn	1975–1977

THE CARTER ADMINISTRATION (1977–1981)

Vice President	Walter F. Mondale	1977–1981
Secretary of State	Cyrus R. Vance	1977–1980
	Edmund Muskie	1980–1981
Secretary of Treasury	W. Michael Blumenthal	1977–1979
	G. William Miller	1979–1981
Attorney General	Griffin Bell	1977–1979
	Benjamin R. Civiletti	1979–1981
Secretary of Interior	Cecil D. Andrus	1977–1981
Secretary of Agriculture	Robert Bergland	1977–1981
Secretary of Commerce	Juanita M. Kreps	1977–1979
	Philip M. Klutznick	1979–1981
Secretary of Labor	F. Ray Marshall	1977–1981
Secretary of Defense	Harold Brown	1977–1981
Secretary of Health, Education, and Welfare	Joseph A. Califano	1977–1979
	Patricia R. Harris	1979
Secretary of Health and Human Services	Patricia R. Harris	1979–1981
Secretary of Education	Shirley M. Hufstedler	1979–1981
Secretary of Housing and Urban Development	Patricia R. Harris	1977–1979
	Moon Landrieu	1979–1981
Secretary of Transportation	Brock Adams	1977–1979
	Neil E. Goldschmidt	1979–1981
Secretary of Energy	James R. Schlesinger	1977–1979
	Charles W. Duncan	1979–1981

THE REAGAN ADMINISTRATION (1981–1989)

Vice President	George Bush	1981–1989
Secretary of State	Alexander M. Haig	1981–1982
	George P. Schultz	1982–1989
Secretary of Treasury	Donald Regan	1981–1985
	James A. Baker III	1985–1988
	Nicholas F. Brady	1988–1989
Attorney General	William F. Smith	1981–1985
	Edwin A. Meese III	1985–1988
	Richard Thornburgh	1988–1989
Secretary of Interior	James Watt	1981–1983
	William P. Clark, Jr.	1983–1985
	Donald P. Hodel	1985–1989
Secretary of Agriculture	John Block	1981–1986
	Richard E. Lyng	1986–1989
Secretary of Commerce	Malcolm Baldridge	1981–1987
	C. William Verity, Jr.	1987–1989
Secretary of Labor	Raymond Donovan	1981–1985
	William Brock	1985–1987
	Ann D. McLaughlin	1987–1989

PRESIDENTIAL ADMINISTRATIONS
(continued)

Secretary of Defense	Caspar Weinberger	1981–1987
	Frank C. Carlucci	1987–1989
Secretary of Health and Human Services	Richard Schweiker	1981–1983
	Margaret Heckler	1983–1985
	Otis R. Bowen	1985–1989
Secretary of Education	Terrel H. Bell	1981–1985
	William J. Bennett	1985–1988
	Laura F. Cavazos	1988–1989
Secretary of Housing and Urban Development	Samuel Pierce	1981–1989
Secretary of Transportation	Drew Lewis	1981–1983
	Elizabeth Dole	1983–1987
	James H. Burnley	1987–1989
Secretary of Energy	James Edwards	1981–1982
	Donald P. Hodel	1982–1985
	John S. Herrington	1984–1989

THE BUSH ADMINISTRATION (1989–1993)

Vice President	J. Danforth Quayle	1989–1993
Secretary of State	James A. Baker III	1989–1992
	Lawrence S. Eagleburger	1992–1993
Secretary of Treasury	Nicholas F. Brady	1989–1993
Attorney General	Richard Thornburgh	1989–1991
	William P. Barr	1991–1993
Secretary of Interior	Manuel Lujan	1989–1993
Secretary of Agriculture	Clayton K. Yeutter	1989–1991
	Edward Madigan	1991–1993
Secretary of Commerce	Robert A. Mosbacher	1989–1992
	Barbara H. Franklin	1992–1993
Secretary of Labor	Elizabeth Dole	1989–1991
	Lynn M. Martin	1991–1993
Secretary of Defense	Richard B. Cheney	1989–1993
Secretary of Health and Human Services	Louis W. Sullivan	1989–1993
Secretary of Education	Laura F. Cavazos	1989–1991
	Lamar Alexander	1991–1993
Secretary of Housing and Urban Development	Jack F. Kemp	1989–1993

Secretary of Transportation	Samuel K. Skinner	1989–1992
	Andrew H. Card	1992–1993
Secretary of Energy	James D. Watkins	1989–1993
Secretary of Veterans Affairs	Edward J. Derwinski	1989–1993

THE CLINTON ADMINISTRATION (1993–)

Vice President	Albert Gore, Jr.	1993–
Secretary of State	Warren M. Christopher	1993–1997
	Madeleine Albright	1997–
Secretary of Treasury	Lloyd M. Bentsen, Jr.	1993–1995
	Robert E. Rubin	1995–1999
	Lawrence H. Summer	1999–
Attorney General	Janet Reno	1993–
Secretary of Interior	Bruce Babbitt	1993–
Secretary of Agriculture	Mike Espy	1993–1995
	Daniel R. Glickman	1995–
Secretary of Commerce	Ronald H. Brown	1993–1996
	William M. Daley	1997–
Secretary of Labor	Robert B. Reich	1993–1997
	Alexis M. Herman	1997–
Secretary of Defense	Les Aspin	1993–1994
	William Perry	1994–1996
	William S. Cohen	1996–
Secretary of Health and Human Services	Donna E. Shalala	1993–
Secretary of Education	Richard W. Riley	1993–
Secretary of Housing and Urban Development	Henry G. Cisneros	1993–1997
	Andrew Cuomo	1997–
Secretary of Energy	Hazel R. O'Leary	1993–1997
	Federico Pena	1997–1998
	Bill Richardson	1998–
Secretary of Transportation	Federico Pena	1993–1997
	Rodney Slater	1997–
Secretary of Veterans Affairs	Jesse Brown	1993–1997
	Togo D. West, Jr.	1998–

SUPREME COURT JUSTICES

Name*	Years on Court	Appointing President
JOHN JAY	1789–1795	Washington
James Wilson	1789–1798	Washington
John Rutledge	1790–1791	Washington
William Cushing	1790–1810	Washington
John Blair	1790–1796	Washington
James Iredell	1790–1799	Washington
Thomas Jefferson	1792–1793	Washington
William Paterson	1793–1806	Washington
JOHN RUTLEDGE†	1795	Washington
Samuel Chase	1796–1811	Washington
OLIVER ELLSWORTH	1796–1800	Washington
Bushrod Washington	1799–1829	J. Adams
Alfred Moore	1800–1804	J. Adams
JOHN MARSHALL	1801–1835	J. Adams
William Johnson	1804–1834	Jefferson
Brockholst Livingston	1807–1823	Jefferson
Thomas Todd	1807–1826	Jefferson
Gabriel Duvall	1811–1835	Madison
Joseph Story	1812–1845	Madison
Smith Thompson	1823–1843	Monroe
Robert Trimble	1826–1828	J. Q. Adams
John McLean	1830–1861	Jackson
Henry Baldwin	1830–1844	Jackson
James M. Wayne	1835–1867	Jackson
ROGER B. TANEY	1836–1864	Jackson
Philip P. Barbour	1836–1841	Jackson
John Cartron	1837–1865	Van Buren
John McKinley	1838–1852	Van Buren
Peter V. Daniel	1842–1860	Van Buren
Samuel Nelson	1845–1872	Tyler
Levi Woodbury	1845–1851	Polk
Robert C. Grier	1846–1870	Polk
Benjamin R. Curtis	1851–1857	Fillmore
John A. Campbell	1853–1861	Pierce
Nathan Clifford	1858–1881	Buchanan
Noah H. Swayne	1862–1881	Lincoln
Samuel F. Miller	1862–1890	Lincoln
David Davis	1862–1877	Lincoln
Stephen J. Field	1863–1897	Lincoln
SALMON P. CHASE	1864–1873	Lincoln
William Strong	1870–1880	Grant
Joseph P. Bradley	1870–1892	Grant
Ward Hunt	1873–1882	Grant
MORRISON R. WAITE	1874–1888	Grant
John M. Harlan	1877–1911	Hayes
William B. Woods	1881–1887	Hayes
Stanley Matthews	1881–1889	Garfield
Horace Gray	1882–1902	Arthur
Samuel Blatchford	1882–1893	Arthur
Lucious Q. C. Lamar	1888–1893	Cleveland
MELVILLE W. FULLER	1888–1910	Cleveland
David J. Brewer	1890–1910	B. Harrison
Henry B. Brown	1891–1906	B. Harrison
George Shiras, Jr.	1892–1903	B. Harrison
Howel E. Jackson	1893–1895	B. Harrison
Edward D. White	1894–1910	Cleveland
Rufus W. Peckman	1896–1909	Cleveland
Joseph McKenna	1898–1925	McKinley

SUPREME COURT JUSTICES
(continued)

Name*	Years on Court	Appointing President
Oliver W. Holmes	1902–1932	T. Roosevelt
William R. Day	1903–1922	T. Roosevelt
William H. Moody	1906–1910	T. Roosevelt
Horace H. Lurton	1910–1914	Taft
Charles E. Hughes	1910–1916	Taft
EDWARD D. WHITE	1910–1921	Taft
Willis Van Devanter	1911–1937	Taft
Joseph R. Lamar	1911–1916	Taft
Mahlon Pitney	1912–1922	Taft
James C. McReynolds	1914–1941	Wilson
Louis D. Brandeis	1916–1939	Wilson
John H. Clarke	1916–1922	Wilson
WILLIAM H. TAFT	1921–1930	Harding
George Sutherland	1922–1938	Harding
Pierce Butler	1923–1939	Harding
Edward T. Sanford	1923–1930	Harding
Harlan F. Stone	1925–1941	Coolidge
CHARLES E. HUGHES	1930–1941	Hoover
Owen J. Roberts	1930–1945	Hoover
Benjamin N. Cardozo	1932–1938	Hoover
Hugo L. Black	1937–1971	F. Roosevelt
Stanley F. Reed	1938–1957	F. Roosevelt
Felix Frankfurter	1939–1962	F. Roosevelt
William O. Douglas	1939–1975	F. Roosevelt
Frank Murphy	1940–1949	F. Roosevelt
HARLAN F. STONE	1941–1946	F. Roosevelt
James F. Brynes	1941–1942	F. Roosevelt
Robert H. Jackson	1941–1954	F. Roosevelt
Wiley B. Rutledge	1943–1949	F. Roosevelt
Harold H. Burton	1945–1958	Truman
FREDERICK M. VINSON	1946–1953	Truman
Tom C. Clark	1949–1967	Truman
Sherman Minton	1949–1956	Truman
EARL WARREN	1953–1969	Eisenhower
John Marshall Harlan	1955–1971	Eisenhower
William J. Brennan, Jr.	1956–1990	Eisenhower
Charles E. Whittaker	1957–1962	Eisenhower
Potter Stewart	1958–1981	Eisenhower
Byron R. White	1962–1993	Kennedy
Arthur J. Goldberg	1962–1965	Kennedy
Abe Fortas	1965–1970	L. Johnson
Thurgood Marshall	1967–1991	L. Johnson
WARREN E. BURGER	1969–1986	Nixon
Harry A. Blackmun	1970–1994	Nixon
Lewis F. Powell, Jr.	1971–1987	Nixon
William H. Rehnquist	1971–1986	Nixon
John Paul Stevens	1975–	Ford
Sandra Day O'Connor	1981–	Reagan
WILLIAM H. REHNQIJIST	1986–	Reagan
Antonin Scalia	1986–	Reagan
Anthony Kennedy	1988–	Reagan
David Souter	1990–	Bush
Clarence Thomas	1991–	Bush
Ruth Bader Ginsburg	1993–	Clinton
Stephen Breyer	1994–	Clinton

*Capital letters designate Chief Justices
†Never confirmed by the Senate as Chief Justice

ADMISSION OF STATES INTO THE UNION

State	Date of Admission	State	Date of Admission
1. Delaware	December 7, 1787	26. Michigan	January 26, 1837
2. Pennsylvania	December 12, 1787	27. Florida	March 3, 1845
3. New Jersey	December 18, 1787	28. Texas	December 29, 1845
4. Georgia	January 2, 1788	29. Iowa	December 28, 1846
5. Connecticut	January 9, 1788	30. Wisconsin	May 29, 1848
6. Massachusetts	February 6, 1788	31. California	September 9, 1850
7. Maryland	April 28, 1788	32. Minnesota	May 11, 1858
8. South Carolina	May 23, 1788	33. Oregon	February 14, 1859
9. New Hampshire	June 21, 1788	34. Kansas	January 29, 1861
10. Virginia	June 25, 1788	35. West Virginia	June 20, 1863
11. New York	July 26, 1788	36. Nevada	October 31, 1864
12. North Carolina	November 21, 1789	37. Nebraska	March 1, 1867
13. Rhode Island	May 29, 1790	38. Colorado	August 1, 1876
14. Vermont	March 4, 1791	39. North Dakota	November 2, 1889
15. Kentucky	June 1, 1792	40. South Dakota	November 2, 1889
16. Tennessee	June 1, 1796	41. Montana	November 8, 1889
17. Ohio	March 1, 1803	42. Washington	November 11, 1889
18. Louisiana	April 30, 1812	43. Idaho	July 3, 1890
19. Indiana	December 11, 1816	44. Wyoming	July 10, 1890
20. Mississippi	December 10, 1817	45. Utah	January 4, 1896
21. Illinois	December 3, 1818	46. Oklahoma	November 16, 1907
22. Alabama	December 14, 1819	47. New Mexico	January 6, 1912
23. Maine	March 15, 1820	48. Arizona	February 14, 1912
24. Missouri	August 10, 1821	49. Alaska	January 3, 1959
25. Arkansas	June 15, 1836	50. Hawaii	August 21, 1959

Demographics of the United States

POPULATION GROWTH

Year	Population	Percent Increase
1630	4,600	
1640	26,600	478.3
1650	50,400	90.8
1660	75,100	49.0
1670	111,900	49.0
1680	151,500	35.4
1690	210,400	38.9
1700	250,900	19.2
1710	331,700	32.2
1720	466,200	40.5
1730	629,400	35.0
1740	905,600	43.9
1750	1,170,800	29.3
1760	1,593,600	36.1
1770	2,148,100	34.8
1780	2,780,400	29.4
1790	3,929,214	41.3
1800	5,308,483	35.1
1810	7,239,881	36.4
1820	9,638,453	33.1
1830	12,866,020	33.5
1840	17,069,453	32.7
1850	23,191,876	35.9
1860	31,443,321	35.6
1870	39,818,449	26.6
1880	50,155,783	26.0
1890	62,947,714	25.5
1900	75,994,575	20.7
1910	91,972,266	21.0
1920	105,710,620	14.9
1930	122,775,046	16.1
1940	131,669,275	7.2
1950	151,325,798	14.5
1960	179,323,175	18.5
1970	203,302,031	13.4
1980	226,542,199	11.4
1990	248,718,301	9.8
1998	270,561,000	8.8

Source: *Historical Statistics of the United States* (1975); *Statistical Abstract by the United States* (1999).
Note: Figures for 1630–1780 include British colonies within limits of present United States only; Native American population included only in 1930 and thereafter.

WORK FORCE

Year	Total Number Workers (1000s)	Farmers as % of Total	Women as % of Total	% Workers in Unions
1810	2,330	84	(NA)	(NA)
1840	5,660	75	(NA)	(NA)
1860	11,110	53	(NA)	(NA)
1870	12,506	53	15	(NA)
1880	17,392	52	15	(NA)
1890	23,318	43	17	(NA)
1900	29,073	40	18	3
1910	38,167	31	21	6
1920	41,614	26	21	12
1930	48,830	22	22	7
1940	53,011	17	24	27
1950	59,643	12	28	25
1960	69,877	8	32	26
1970	82,049	4	37	25
1980	106,940	3	43	23
1990	125,840	3	45	16
1998	137,673	2	46	14

Source: *Historical Statistics of the United States* (1975); *Statistical Abstract of the United States* (1999).

VITAL STATISTICS
(in thousands)

Year	Births	Deaths	Marriages	Divorces
1800	55	(NA)	(NA)	(NA)
1810	54.3	(NA)	(NA)	(NA)
1820	55.2	(NA)	(NA)	(NA)
1830	51.4	(NA)	(NA)	(NA)
1840	51.8	(NA)	(NA)	(NA)
1850	43.3	(NA)	(NA)	(NA)
1860	44.3	(NA)	(NA)	(NA)
1870	38.3	(NA)	9.6 (1867)	0.3 (1867)
1880	39.8	(NA)	9.1 (1875)	0.3 (1875)
1890	31.5	(NA)	9.0	0.5
1900	32.3	17.2	9.3	0.7
1910	30.1	14.7	10.3	0.9
1920	27.7	13.0	12.0	1.6
1930	21.3	11.3	9.2	1.6
1940	19.4	10.8	12.1	2.0
1950	24.1	9.6	11.1	2.6
1960	23.7	9.5	8.5	2.2
1970	18.4	9.5	10.6	3.5
1980	15.9	8.8	10.6	5.2
1990	16.7	8.6	9.8	4.7
1997	14.6	8.6	8.9	4.3

Source: *Historical Statistics of the United States* (1975); *Statistical Abstract of the United States* (1999).

RACIAL COMPOSITION OF THE POPULATION
(in thousands)

Year	White	Black	Indian	Hispanic	Asian
1790	3,172	757	(NA)	(NA)	(NA)
1800	4,306	1,002	(NA)	(NA)	(NA)
1820	7,867	1,772	(NA)	(NA)	(NA)
1840	14,196	2,874	(NA)	(NA)	(NA)
1860	26,923	4,442	(NA)	(NA)	(NA)
1880	43,403	6,581	(NA)	(NA)	(NA)
1900	66,809	8,834	(NA)	(NA)	(NA)
1910	81,732	9,828	(NA)	(NA)	(NA)
1920	94,821	10,463	(NA)	(NA)	(NA)
1930	110,287	11,891	(NA)	(NA)	(NA)
1940	118,215	12,866	(NA)	(NA)	(NA)
1950	134,942	15,042	(NA)	(NA)	(NA)
1960	158,832	18,872	(NA)	(NA)	(NA)
1970	178,098	22,581	(NA)	(NA)	(NA)
1980	194,713	26,683	1,420	14,609	3,729
1990	208,727	30,511	2,065	22,372	2,462
1998	223,001	34,431	2,360	30,250	10,507

Source: U.S. Bureau of the Census, U.S. Census of Population: 1940, vol. II, part 1, and vol. IV, part 1; 1950, vol. II, part 1; 1960, vol. I, part 1; 1970, vol. I, part B; and Current Population Reports, P25-1095 and P25-1104; Statistical Abstract of the United States (1999) and unpublished data.

THE ECONOMY AND FEDERAL SPENDING

Year	Gross National Product (GNP) (in billions)	Foreign Trade (in millions) Exports	Foreign Trade (in millions) Imports	Balance of Trade	Federal Budget (in billions)	Federal Surplus/Deficit (in billions)	Federal Debt (in billions)
1790	(NA)	$ 20	$ 23	$ −3	$ 0.004	$+0.00015	$ 0.076
1800	(NA)	71	91	−20	0.011	+0.0006	0.083
1810	(NA)	67	85	−18	0.008	+0.0012	0.053
1820	(NA)	70	74	−4	0.018	−0.0004	0.091
1830	(NA)	74	71	+3	0.015	+0.100	0.049
1840	(NA)	132	107	+25	0.024	−0.005	0.004
1850	(NA)	152	178	−26	0.040	+0.004	0.064
1860	(NA)	400	362	−38	0.063	−0.01	0.065
1870	$ 7.4	451	462	−11	0.310	+0.10	2.4
1880	11.2	853	761	+92	0.268	+0.07	2.1
1890	13.1	910	823	+87	0.318	+0.09	1.2
1900	18.7	1,499	930	+569	0.521	+0.05	1.2
1910	35.3	1,919	1,646	+273	0.694	−0.02	1.1
1920	91.5	8,664	5,784	+2,880	6.357	+0.3	24.3
1930	90.7	4,013	3,500	+513	3.320	+0.7	16.3
1940	100.0	4,030	7,433	−3,403	9.6	−2.7	43.0
1950	286.5	10,816	9,125	+1,691	43.1	−2.2	257.4
1960	506.5	19,600	15,046	+4,556	92.2	+0.3	286.3
1970	992.7	42,700	40,189	+2,511	195.6	−2.8	371.0
1980	2,631.7	220,783	244,871	+24,088	590.9	−73.8	907.7
1990	5,524.5	394,030	494,042	−101,012	1,251.8	−220.5	3,233.3
1998	8,490.5	933,907	1,098,189	−164,282	1,652.5	+69.2	5,478.7

Source: U.S. Office of Management and Budget, Budget of the United States Government, annual; Statistical Abstract of the United States, 1996; census bureau web site www.gov/foreign-trade/Press-Release/2000pr/01/exh7.txt

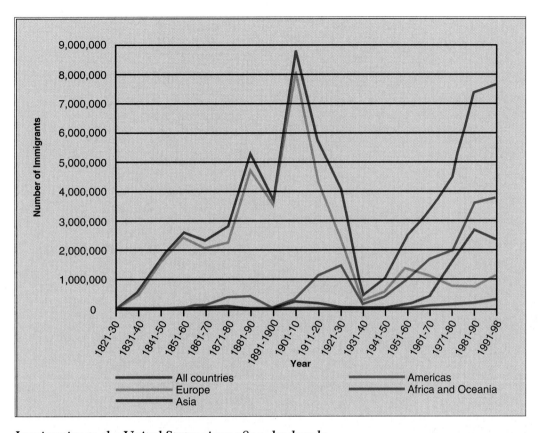

Immigration to the United States since 1820, by decade
Source: *Statistical Yearbook of the Immigration and Naturalization Service, 1997; Annual Report of the Immigration and Naturalization Service: Legal Immigration, Fiscal year 1998.*

GLOSSARY

Acquired immune deficiency syndrome (AIDS) A complex of deadly pathologies resulting from infection with the human immunodeficiency virus (HIV).

African Methodist Episcopal (AME) Church Religious body founded by black people for black people in the North during the early nineteenth century that gained adherents among former slaves in the South after the Civil War.

Agricultural Adjustment Administration (AAA) **New Deal** agency that attempted to regulate agricultural production through farm subsidies.

Agricultural Wheel One of several farmer organizations that emerged in the South during the 1880s. It sought federal legislation to deal with credit and currency issues.

Alliance for Progress Program of economic aid to Latin America during the Kennedy administration.

Allies Britain, France, Russia, Italy, and other belligerent nations fighting against the **Central Powers** in World War I but not including the United States.

America First Committee Officially the Committee to Defend America First, organized in 1940 to promote the policy of building and defending "Fortress America."

American Civil Liberties Union (ACLU) Organization formed in 1920 to guard the constitutional rights of Americans against government infringement.

American Equal Rights Association Formed by women's rights activists in 1866 to advocate universal **suffrage** at the state level after the **Fourteenth Amendment** failed to provide federal guarantees for women's voting rights.

American Expeditionary Force (AEF) The American army that fought with but was independent of the Allied armies in World War I.

American Federation of Labor (AFL) Union formed in 1886 that organized skilled workers along craft lines and emphasized a few workplace issues rather than a broad social program.

American Indian Movement (AIM) Group of Native American political activists who used confrontations with the federal government to publicize their case for Indian rights.

American Liberty League Business group organized to sway popular opinion against the **New Deal**.

American Protective Association (APA) Association formed in 1893 by skilled workers and small businessmen in response to increasing immigration from eastern and southern Europe; sought to limit Catholic civil rights and save jobs for Protestant workers.

American Protective League One of the leading vigilante organizations that suppressed dissent while promoting reactionary causes during World War I.

American Railway Union (ARU) Union led by Eugene V. Debs; supported the **Pullman strike**.

Americans with Disabilities Act Legislation in 1992 that banned discrimination against physically handicapped persons in employment, transportation, and public accommodations.

Anglo-Saxon Broadly, a person of English descent.

Anti-Imperialist League Organization, established in 1898, that opposed the annexation of the Philippines and the ratification of the **Treaty of Paris**.

Atlanta Compromise Booker T. Washington's policy accepting segregation and **disfranchisement** for African Americans in exchange for white assistance in education and job training.

Atlantic, Battle of the A struggle for control of the North Atlantic (1940–1943) between German submarines and British and American naval and air forces.

Atlantic Charter Statement of common principles and war aims developed by President Franklin Roosevelt and British Prime Minister Winston Churchill at a meeting in August 1941.

Atomic Energy Commission (AEC) Civilian agency created in 1946 to develop and control military and civilian uses of atomic energy; its functions were transferred to the Nuclear Regulatory Commission in 1975.

Australian ballot Secret voting and the use of official ballots rather than party tickets.

Axis Powers The opponents of the United States and its allies in World War II. The Rome–Berlin Axis was formed between Germany and Italy in 1936 and included Japan after 1940.

Baker **v.** *Carr* U.S. Supreme Court decision in 1962 that allowed federal courts to review the apportionment of state legislative districts and established the principle that such districts should have roughly equal populations ("one person, one vote").

Banking Act of 1935 Law that strengthened the authority of the Federal Reserve Board over the nation's currency and credit system.

Bay of Pigs Site in Cuba of an unsuccessful landing by fourteen hundred anti-Castro Cuban refugees in April 1961.

Beats Nonconformists in the late 1950s who came together in large cities to reject conventional dress and sexual standards and cultivate poetry, jazz, and folk music; also known as *beatniks*.

Berlin blockade Three-hundred-day Soviet blockade of land access to United States, British, and French occupation zones in Berlin, 1948–1949.

Berlin Wall Wall erected by East Germany in 1961 and torn down in 1989 that isolated West Berlin from the surrounding areas in communist-controlled East Berlin and East Germany.

Black Panthers Political and social movement among black Americans, founded in Oakland, California, in 1966 and emphasizing black economic and political power.

Black Power Philosophy emerging after 1965 that real economic and political gains for African Americans could come only through self-help, **self-determination**, and organizing for direct political influence. Latinos and Native Americans developed their own versions as Brown Power and Red Power, respectively.

Bland-Allison Act An 1878 compromise currency law that provided for limited silver coinage.

Blitzkrieg German war tactic in World War II ("lightning war") involving the concentration of air and armored firepower to punch and exploit holes in opposing defensive lines.

Board of Indian Commissioners A nonpartisan board established in 1869 as an advisory agency to eliminate politics and corruption from the government bureaucracy dealing with Indian affairs.

Bolshevik Member of the communist movement in Russia that established the Soviet government after the 1917 Russian Revolution; hence, by extension, any radical or disruptive person or movement seeking to transform economic and political relationships.

Bonus Army A group of unemployed veterans who demonstrated in Washington for the payment of service bonuses, only to be violently dispersed by the U.S. Army in 1932.

Britain, Battle of Series of air engagements in 1940 during World War II that pitted British interceptor fighter planes against German bombers attacking British cities and industry.

Brown v. Board of Education of Topeka Supreme Court decision in 1954 that declared that "separate but equal" schools for children of different races violated the Constitution.

Bulge, Battle of the German counteroffensive in December 1944 during World War II that slowed the Allied advance on Germany.

Bureau of Indian Affairs Government agency, within the U.S. Department of the Interior, responsible for carrying out official Indian policy.

Bureau of Reclamation Federal agency established in 1902 providing public funds for irrigation projects in arid regions; played a major role in the development of the West by constructing dams, reservoirs, and irrigation systems, especially beginning in the 1930s.

Business unionism The **American Federation of Labor** stance that members should avoid political activism and concentrate on basic workplace issues.

Camp David Agreement Agreement to reduce points of conflict between Israel and Egypt, hammered out in 1977 with the help of President Jimmy Carter.

Carpetbaggers Northerners who came to the post–Civil War South, initially for economic reasons, and then became involved in Republican politics; a disparaging term.

Cattle Kingdom The open-range cattle industry that stretched from Texas into Montana in the 1870s and 1880s.

Centennial Exposition Fair held in Philadelphia in 1876 to celebrate the hundredth anniversary of the United States and to showcase American industry and technology.

Central Intelligence Agency (CIA) Agency that coordinates the gathering and evaluation of military and economic information on other nations, established in 1947.

Central Powers Germany and its World War I allies Austria, Turkey, and Bulgaria.

Chain migration Process common to many immigrant groups whereby one family member brings over other family members, who in turn bring other relatives and friends and occasionally entire villages.

Chicago Defender A major black newspaper that encouraged black migration from the South to the urban North.

Children's Bureau Federal agency established in 1912 to investigate and report on matters pertaining to the welfare of children.

Chinese Consolidated Benevolent Association Umbrella social service organization for Chinese immigrants that pooled their resources to assist in such activities as job hunting, housing, support for the sick or poor, and burial.

Chinese Exclusion Act Law passed by Congress in 1882 prohibiting Chinese immigration to the United States; overturned in 1943.

Chisholm Trail The route followed by Texas cattle raisers driving their herds north to markets at Kansas railheads.

Church of God A religious movement that emerged from the mountains of Tennessee and North Carolina in 1886 as part of the **Holiness movement**. It accepted women, and sometimes black people, on an equal basis with white men.

Civilian Conservation Corps (CCC) Popular **New Deal** program that provided young men with relief jobs working on reforestation, flood control, and other **conservation** projects.

Civil Rights Act of 1866 Law that defined national citizenship and specified the civil rights to which all national citizens were entitled.

Civil Rights Act of 1875 Law that prohibited racial discrimination in jury selection, public transportation, and public accommodations; declared unconstitutional by the U.S. Supreme Court in 1883.

Civil Rights Act of 1964 Federal legislation that outlawed discrimination in public accommodations and employment on the basis of race, skin color, sex, religion, or national origin.

Civil Works Administration (CWA) Government agency under Harry Hopkins that created 4 million relief jobs for the unemployed during the winter of 1933–1934.

Clean Air Act Legislation in 1970 that set federal standards for air quality.

Cold War The political and economic confrontation between the Soviet Union and the United States that dominated world affairs from 1946 to 1989.

Collective bargaining Representatives of a union negotiating with management on behalf of all members.

Colored Farmers' Alliance An organization of southern black farmers formed in Texas in 1886 in response to the **Southern Farmers' Alliance**, which did not accept black people as members.

Comecon The Council for Mutual Economic Assistance, established in 1949 by the Soviet Union and its eastern European satellites.

Committee on Public Information (CPI) Government agency during World War I that sought to shape public opinion in support of the war effort through newspapers, pamphlets, speeches, films, and other media.

Committee to Defend America by Aiding the Allies Group organized to support Franklin Roosevelt's policy of resisting **Nazi** Germany by actively aiding the British war effort.

Community Action Agencies Locally based antipoverty organizations created under federal legislation in 1964 and intended to allow poor people to help plan programs and services.

Compromise of 1877 A deal that settled the contested presidential election of 1876 by installing Republican Rutherford B. Hayes in the White House and returning home rule to the South. It formally ended **Reconstruction** and left the fate of the freedmen in the hands of southern white people.

Concentration camp A prison camp for political dissenters and social undesirables, used extensively in **Nazi** Germany.

Congress of Industrial Organizations An alliance of industrial unions that spurred the 1930s organizational drive among the mass-production industries.

Congress on Racial Equality (CORE) Civil rights group formed in 1942 and committed to nonviolent civil disobedience, such as the 1961 "freedom rides."

Congressional Reconstruction Name given to the period 1867–1870 when the Republican-dominated Congress controlled **Reconstruction** policy. It is sometimes known as Radical Reconstruction, after the radical faction in the **Republican party**.

Conservation The efficient management and use of natural resources, such as forests, grasslands, and rivers, as opposed to **preservation** or uncontrolled exploitation.

Contract with America   Platform on which many Republican candidates ran for Congress in 1994. Associated with House Speaker Newt Gingrich, it proposed a sweeping reduction in the role and activities of the federal government.

Cooperative   An organization that allowed a group of farmers to buy tools, seed, livestock, and other farm-related products at discounted prices in bulk.

Coral Sea, Battle of the   Battle between U.S. and Japanese aircraft carriers that halted the Japanese advance toward Australia in May 1942 during World War II.

Cordon sanitaire   The belt of anticommunist eastern European nations that separated western Europe from the Soviet Union after World War I.

Council of Economic Advisers   Board of three professional economists established in 1946 to advise the president on economic policy.

Council of National Defense   The government body, consisting of cabinet officials and economic leaders, that oversaw the wartime agencies controlling the nation's economy during World War I.

Counterculture   Various alternatives to mainstream values and behaviors that became popular in the 1960s, including experimentation with psychedelic drugs, communal living, a return to the land, Asian religions, and experimental art.

Coxey's Army   A protest march of unemployed workers, led by Populist businessman Jacob Coxey, demanding inflation and a public works program during the depression of the 1890s.

Crop lien   A claim against all or a portion of a farmer's crop as security against a debt.

Crop lien laws   In the **Reconstruction** and post-Reconstruction South, laws that gave merchants the right to sharecroppers' future cotton crop in exchange for credit.

Dawes Act   An 1887 law terminating tribal ownership of land and allotting some parcels of land to individual Indians with the remainder opened for white settlement.

D-Day   June 6, 1944, the day of the first paratroop drops and amphibious landings on the coast of Normandy, France, in the first stage of **Operation OVERLORD** during World War II.

Declaration of London   Statement drafted by an international conference in 1909 to clarify international law and specify the rights of neutral nations.

Deregulation   Reduction or removal of government regulations and encouragement of direct competition in many important industries and economic sectors.

Desert Storm   Code name for the successful offensive against Iraq by the United States and its allies in the Persian Gulf War (1991).

Deskilling   A decline in workforce skills due to discrimination, as for southern black people in the late nineteenth century, or to mechanization, as for white industrial workers in the same period.

Détente   A lessening of tension, applied to improved American relations with the Soviet Union and China in the mid-1970s.

Disfranchisement   The use of legal means to bar individuals or groups from voting.

Dixiecrats   Southern Democrats who broke from the party in 1948 over the issue of civil rights and ran a presidential ticket as the States' Rights Democrats.

Dollar diplomacy   The U.S. policy of using private investment in other nations to promote American diplomatic goals and business interests.

Eastern Front   The area of military operations in World War II located east of Germany in eastern Europe and the Soviet Union.

Economic Recovery and Tax Act of 1981 (ERTA)   A major revision of the federal income tax system.

Edge city   A suburban district that has developed as a center for employment, retailing, and services comparable to a traditional downtown.

El Alamein, Battle of   British victory during World War II that checked the advance of the German army into Egypt in June 1942.

Elementary and Secondary Education Act   Federal legislation in 1965 that provided the first large-scale federal aid for needy public school districts.

Emergency Banking Act of 1933   A law that stabilized the banking system through government aid and supervision.

Emergency Relief Appropriation Act of 1935   Law authorizing a massive program of public work relief projects for the unemployed.

Employment Act of 1946   Federal legislation that committed the United States to the goal of "maximum employment, production and purchasing power."

Enforcement Act of 1870   Largely ineffectual law passed in response to growing political violence in the South, enabling the federal government to appoint supervisors where states failed to protect citizens' voting rights.

Engel* v. *Vitale   Supreme Court decision in 1962 that found that reading a nondenominational prayer in public schools violated the First Amendment to the Constitution.

Environmental Protection Agency (EPA)   Federal agency created in 1970 to oversee environmental monitoring and cleanup programs.

Equal Employment Opportunity Commission (EEOC)   Federal commission established by the **Civil Rights Act of 1964** to monitor and enforce nondiscrimination in employment.

Equal Rights Amendment (ERA)   A proposed but never adopted amendment to the Constitution to prevent abridgement of rights on account of a person's sex.

Espionage Act of 1917   Law whose vague prohibition against obstructing the nation's war effort was used to crush dissent and criticism during World War I.

Executive Order 8802   Presidential order in 1943 that required racial nondiscrimination clauses in war contracts and subcontracts.

Executive Order 9066   Presidential order in February 1942 that authorized the forcible relocation of Japanese Americans from portions of four western states.

Executive Order 9835   Presidential order by President Truman in 1947 implementing a loyalty program for federal employees.

Fair Deal   Program for expanded economic opportunity and civil rights proposed by President Truman in 1949.

Fair Employment Practice Committee (FEPC)   Federal agency established in 1941 to curb racial discrimination in war production jobs and government employment.

Farm Credit Administration   Government agency established in 1933 to refinance farm mortgages, thereby saving farms and protecting banks.

Farmers' Alliance   A broad mass movement in the rural South and West during the late nineteenth century, encompassing several organizations and demanding economic and political reforms; helped create the **Populist party**.

Fascist   Subscribing to a philosophy of governmental dictatorship that merges the interests of the state, armed forces, and big business; associated with the dictatorship of Italian leader Benito Mussolini between 1922 and 1943 and also often applied to **Nazi** Germany.

Federal Communications Commission (FCC)   Government agency established in 1934 with authority to regulate radio and television.

Federal Deposit Insurance Corporation (FDIC) Government agency that guarantees bank deposits, thereby protecting both depositors and banks.

Federal Emergency Relief Administration (FERA) Agency set up to provide direct federal grants to the states for assisting the unemployed in the **Great Depression**.

Federal Highway Act of 1956 Measure that provided federal funding to build a nationwide system of interstate and defense highways.

Federal Reserve Act The 1913 law that revised banking and currency by extending limited government regulation through the creation of the Federal Reserve System.

Federal Trade Commission (FTC) Government agency established in 1914 to provide regulatory oversight of business activity.

Fence laws Legislation that required the penning of animals so that they would not disturb crops.

Field Order No. 15 Order by General William T. Sherman in January 1865 to set aside abandoned land along the southern Atlantic coast for 40-acre grants to freedmen; rescinded by President Andrew Johnson later that year.

Fifteenth Amendment Reconstruction amendment passed by Congress in February 1869 guaranteeing the right of all American male citizens to vote regardless of race.

Fireside chats Speeches broadcast nationally over the radio in which President Franklin Roosevelt explained complex issues and programs in plain language, as though his listeners were gathered around the fireside with him.

Food Administration The agency that sought to increase agricultural production and food conservation to supply the U.S. military and the **Allies** during World War I.

Fourteenth Amendment Constitutional amendment passed by Congress in April 1866 incorporating some of the features of the **Civil Rights Act of 1866**. It prohibited states from violating the civil rights of its citizens and offered states the choice of allowing blacks to vote or losing representation in Congress.

Free silver Philosophy that the government should expand the money supply by purchasing and coining all the silver offered to it.

Free Speech Movement (FSM) Student movement at the University of California, Berkeley, formed in 1964 to protest limitations on political activities on campus.

Freedman's Bureau Agency established by Congress in March 1865 to provide social, educational, and economic services, advice, and protection to former slaves and destitute whites; lasted seven years.

Freedom Summer Voter registration effort in rural Mississippi organized by black and white civil rights workers in 1964.

Fundamentalists Religious conservatives who believe in the literal accuracy and divine inspiration of the Bible; the name derives from an influential series of pamphlets, *The Fundamentals* (1909–1914).

Fusion Political strategy adopted by Populists and Republicans in North Carolina during their successful 1894 election campaign.

General Agreement on Tariffs and Trade (GATT) International agreement aimed at lowering barriers to international trade, first signed in 1947 and updated periodically.

Gentlemen's Agreement A diplomatic agreement in 1907 between Japan and the United States curtailing but not abolishing Japanese immigration.

Ghetto A neighborhood or district in which members of a particular racial or ethnic group are forced to live by law or as a result of economics or social discrimination.

GI World War II slang for a U.S. soldier, derived from the words *government issue* stamped on equipment and supplies.

GI Bill of Rights Legislation in June 1944 that eased the return of veterans into American society by providing educational and employment benefits.

Gilded Age Term applied to late-nineteenth-century America that refers to the shallow display and worship of wealth characteristic of the period.

Glasnost Russian for "openness," applied to Mikhail Gorbachev's encouragement of new ideas and easing of political repression in the Soviet Union.

Glass-Steagall Act of 1933 Law that separated investment from commercial banking to limit speculation by bankers and created the **Federal Deposit Insurance Corporation**.

Gospel of Wealth Thesis that hard work and perseverance lead to wealth, implying that poverty is a character flaw.

Grandfather clause Rule that required potential voters to demonstrate that their grandfathers had been eligible to vote; used in some southern states after 1890 to limit the black electorate, as most black men's grandfathers had been slaves.

Grange The National Grange of the Patrons of Husbandry, a national organization of farm owners formed after the Civil War.

Granger laws State laws enacted in the Midwest in the 1870s that regulated rates charged by railroads, grain elevator operators, and other middlemen.

Great Depression The nation's worst economic crisis, extending throughout the 1930s, producing unprecedented bank failures, unemployment, and industrial and agricultural collapse and prompting an expanded role for the federal government.

Greater East Asia Co-Prosperity Sphere Japanese goal of an East Asian economy controlled by Japan and serving the needs of Japanese industry.

Great Migration The mass movement of African Americans from the rural South to the urban North, spurred especially by new job opportunities during World War I and the 1920s.

Great Society Theme of Lyndon Johnson's administration, focusing on poverty, education, and civil rights.

Great Uprising Unsuccessful railroad strike of 1877 to protest wage cuts and the use of federal troops against strikers; the first nationwide work stoppage in American history.

Greenback party A third party of the 1870s and 1880s that garnered temporary support by advocating currency inflation to expand the economy and assist debtors.

Gulf of Tonkin Resolution Congressional resolution in August 1964 that authorized the president to take all necessary steps to protect South Vietnam, adopted after reports of North Vietnamese attacks on U.S. ships in the Gulf of Tonkin off North Vietnam.

Harlem Renaissance A new African-American cultural awareness that flourished in literature, art, and music in the 1920s.

Harrison Act The 1914 law that prohibited the dispensing and use of narcotics for other than medicinal purposes.

Haymarket Square Location in Chicago where workers gathered in May 1886 to protest the slayings of colleagues who had struck for an eight-hour workday; a bomb exploded, throwing the gathering into chaos and resulting in the arrest and execution of strike leaders and the decline of the **Knights of Labor**.

Head Start Federal program that since 1965 has helped prepare children from disadvantaged backgrounds for success in school.

Helsinki Accords Agreement in 1975 among **NATO** and **Warsaw Pact** members that recognized European national boundaries as set after World War II and included guarantees of human rights.

Higher Education Act   Federal legislation in 1965 that provided federal financial aid for college students.

Hippie   A person who dropped out of mainstream society or adopted some of the styles associated with the **counterculture** of the 1960s and early 1970s.

Holiness movement   Religious movement originating in the antebellum North and revived among Texas farmers in the 1880s that stressed simplicity in lifestyle and appealed especially to the poor.

Holocaust   The systematic murder of millions of European Jews and others deemed undesirable by **Nazi** Germany.

Home mission societies   Organizations founded by white Methodist Church women in the South during the 1870s to promote industrial education among the southern poor and help working-class women become self-sufficient.

Home Owners Loan Corporation   Federal agency that rescued individual homeowners from foreclosure by refinancing mortgage loans.

Homestead strike   A bloody, lengthy, and ultimately unsuccessful strike against Andrew Carnegie's Homestead, Pennsylvania, steelworks in 1892.

Hooverville   Shantytown, sarcastically named after President Hoover, in which unemployed and homeless people lived in makeshift shacks, tents, and boxes. Hoovervilles cropped up in many cities in 1930 and 1931.

Horizontal integration   The merger of competitors in the same industry.

House Committee on Un-American Activities (HUAC)   Congressional committee (1938–1975) that investigated suspected **Nazi** and communist sympathizers.

Hull House   Chicago **settlement house** that became part of a broader neighborhood revitalization project led by Jane Addams.

Immigrant Restriction League (IRL)   New England–based organization formed in 1894 to restrict immigration from southern and eastern Europe by mandating a literacy test for every immigrant.

Immigration and Nationality Act of 1965   Federal legislation that replaced the national quota system for immigration with overall limits of 170,000 immigrants per year from the Eastern Hemisphere and 120,000 per year from the Western Hemisphere.

Immigration Reform and Control Act of 1986   Legislation that granted legal status to 2,650,000 undocumented immigrants and established penalties for employers who knowingly hire illegal immigrants.

Imperialism   The policy and practice of exploiting nations and peoples for the benefit of an imperial power either directly through military occupation and colonial rule or indirectly through economic domination of resources and markets.

Indian Reorganization Act of 1934   Law that reversed previous Indian policy by guaranteeing religious freedom and tribal self-government and providing economic assistance.

Individual Retirement Accounts (IRAs)   Personal saving and investment accounts that allow workers and their spouses to accumulate retirement savings on a tax-deferred basis.

Industrial Workers of the World (IWW)   Militant labor organization founded in 1905 that attracted mostly recent immigrants and espoused a class-conscious program and ideology. Its members were known as **Wobblies**.

Initiative   Procedure by which citizens can introduce a subject for legislation, usually through a petition signed by a specific number of voters.

Intermediate Nuclear Force Agreement (INF)   Disarmament agreement between the United States and the Soviet Union under which an entire class of missiles would be removed and destroyed and on-site inspections would be permitted for verification.

International Monetary Fund (IMF)   International organization established in 1945 to assist nations in maintaining stable currencies.

Interstate Commerce Act   The 1887 law that expanded federal power over business by prohibiting pooling and discriminatory rates by railroads and establishing the first federal regulatory agency, the **Interstate Commerce Commission**.

Interstate Commerce Commission (ICC)   The first federal regulatory agency, established in 1887 to oversee railroad practices.

Irreconcilables   Group of U.S. senators adamantly opposed to ratification of the **Treaty of Versailles** after World War I.

Island hopping   In the Pacific theater during World War II, the strategy in which U.S. land and amphibious forces seized selected Japanese-held islands while bypassing and isolating other islands held by Japan.

Isolationism   The belief that the United States should not involve itself in international (especially European) political and military developments.

Japanese Association of America   Social service organization for Japanese immigrants that stressed assimilation.

Jazz Age   The 1920s, so called for the popular music of the day as a symbol of the many changes taking place in the mass culture.

Jim Crow laws   Segregation laws that became widespread in the South during the 1890s, named for a minstrel show character portrayed satirically by white actors in blackface.

Job Corps   Antipoverty program created in 1964 that has provided job training and public service work for young people aged 16 to 21 in residential centers.

Kasserine Pass   Site of the first large-scale World War II encounter between U.S. and German ground forces, in February 1942 in North Africa.

Kellogg-Briand Pact   International treaty negotiated in 1928 to outlaw war but containing no enforcement provisions.

Knights of Labor   Labor union that included skilled and unskilled workers irrespective of race or gender; founded in 1869, peaked in the 1880s, and declined when its advocacy of the eight-hour workday led to violent strikes in 1886.

Korean War   War between North Korea and South Korea (1950–1953) in which the People's Republic of China fought on the side of North Korea and the United States and other nations fought on the side of South Korea under the auspices of the **United Nations**.

Ku Klux Klan   Perhaps the most prominent of the vigilante groups that terrorized blacks in the South during **Reconstruction**, founded by Confederate veterans in 1866.

Ku Klux Klan Act of 1871   Law that held the perpetrators responsible for denying a citizen's civil rights and allowed the federal government to prosecute and send military assistance if states failed to act.

Kursk Salient   Site of the largest tank battle in World War II (July 1943), when Germans failed to throw back Soviet forces that had pushed a huge bulge or salient into German lines.

Ladies' Memorial Associations   Women's organizations formed in the South after the Civil War to commemorate Confederate soldiers.

Landsmanshaften   Jewish associations that provided social and economic services for their members.

Las Gorras Blancas   Hispanic villagers ("the White Caps") in New Mexico who disguised themselves and employed violent tactics to resist Anglo capitalist disruptions of their traditional life.

League of Nations   International organization created by the **Versailles Treaty** after World War I to ensure world stability.

League of United Latin American Citizens (LULAC)   Organization for Hispanic Americans formed in 1928 to fight segregation and promote equal rights and opportunities.

League of Women Voters   Group formed in 1920 from the **National American Woman Suffrage Association** to encourage informed voting and social reforms.

Levittown   Large post–World War II housing developments built by William Levitt and Sons outside New York and Philadelphia.

Leyte Gulf, Battle of   World War II naval engagement in October 1944 in which the Japanese navy tried to disrupt U.S. landings in the Philippines and suffered a decisive defeat.

Liberal Republicans   Members of a reform movement within the **Republican party** in 1872 that promoted measures to reduce government influence in the economy and restore control of southern governments to local white elites.

Liberty Bonds   Interest-bearing certificates sold by the U.S. government to finance the American World War I effort.

Limited Test Ban Treaty   Agreement in 1963 between the United States, Britain, and the Soviet Union to halt atmospheric and underwater tests of nuclear weapons.

Little Bighorn, Battle of the   Battle in which Colonel George A. Custer and the Seventh Cavalry were defeated by the Sioux and Cheyennes under Sitting Bull and Crazy Horse in Montana in 1876.

Localism   The belief prevalent during much of the nineteenth century that local concerns took precedence over national concerns and that people and institutions should generally resolve issues without the involvement of the national government.

Lost Generation   The intellectuals of the 1920s, disillusioned by the brutality of World War I and alienated by the materialism and conformity of the new mass culture.

Lynching   Execution, usually by a mob, without trial.

Mahanism   The ideas advanced by Alfred Thayer Mahan, stressing U.S. naval, economic, and territorial expansion.

Manhattan Project   The effort, using the code name Manhattan Engineer District, to develop an atomic bomb under the management of the U.S. Army Corps of Engineers during World War II.

Marshall Plan   The European Recovery Program (1949), which provided U.S. economic assistance to European nations; named for Secretary of State George Marshall.

McCarran Committee   The Senate Internal Security Subcommittee, chaired by Senator Pat McCarran and charged to investigate potentially subversive activities.

McCarthyism   Anticommunist attitudes and actions associated with Senator Joe McCarthy in the early 1950s, including smear tactics and innuendo.

McKinley Tariff Act   A Republican enactment of 1890 that sharply raised tariff rates to protect American manufacturers but thereby provoked a political backlash against the GOP.

Medicaid   Supplementary medical insurance for the poor, financed through the federal government; program created in 1965.

Medicare   Basic medical insurance for the elderly, financed through the federal government; program created in 1965.

Memorial Day Massacre   A murderous attack on striking steelworkers and their families by Chicago police in 1937.

Midway, Battle of   Word War II naval and air battle in which the United States turned back a Japanese effort to seize Midway Island in June 1942 and inflicted severe damage on the Japanese navy.

Military Reconstruction Acts   The first major legislation in the period known as **Congressional Reconstruction**. Passed in March 1867 over President Johnson's veto, these laws divided the ten remaining ex-Confederate states into five military districts each headed by a general who was charged to conduct voter registration drives among black people and bar white people who had held office before the Civil War and who had supported the Confederacy. The remaining voters would elect a constitutional convention to write a new state constitution that guaranteed **universal manhood suffrage**. If a majority of voters ratified both the new constitution and the **Fourteenth Amendment**, their state would be readmitted into the Union.

Model Cities Program   Effort to target federal funds to upgrade public services and economic opportunity in specifically defined urban neighborhoods between 1966 and 1974.

Monroe Doctrine   Declaration by President James Monroe in 1823 that the Western Hemisphere was to be closed off to further European colonization and that the United States would not interfere in the internal affairs of European nations.

Muckraking   Journalism exposing economic, social, and political evils, so named by Theodore Roosevelt for its "raking the muck" of American society.

Mugwumps   Elitist and conservative reformers who favored **sound money** and limited government and opposed tariffs and the spoils system.

Muller v. *Oregon*   Supreme Court decision (1908) upholding a maximum-hour law for women workers; opened the way to an expansion of state regulation.

Multinational corporation   Firm with direct investments, branches, factories, and offices in a number of countries.

National Aeronautics and Space Administration (NASA)   Federal agency created in 1958 to manage American space flights and exploration.

National American Woman Suffrage Association   The organization, formed in 1890, that coordinated the ultimately successful campaign to achieve women's right to vote.

National and Community Service Trust Act   Legislation in 1994 creating a pilot program for a domestic Peace Corps for young Americans.

National Association for the Advancement of Colored People (NAACP)   National interracial organization founded in 1910 and dedicated to restoring African-American political and social rights.

National Association of Colored Women   Group founded in 1896 as an umbrella organization for black women's clubs that worked to improve the lives of black women, especially in the rural South.

National Endowment for the Arts   Federal agency created in 1965 to fund research, public programs, and museum exhibits dealing with the performing arts, visual arts, and design arts.

National Endowment for the Humanities   Federal agency created in 1965 to fund research, publications, and museum exhibits dealing with history, literature, and related fields.

National Industrial Recovery Act (NIRA)   A 1933 law that created the National Recovery Administration and, in Section 7a, guaranteed workers the rights to organize unions and bargain collectively.

National Labor Relations Board (NLRB)   Federal board established in 1935 to enforce workers' rights to organize, supervise union elections, and oversee **collective bargaining**.

National Organization for Women (NOW)   Group organized in 1966 to expand civil rights for women.

National Origins Act   A 1924 law sharply restricting immigration on the basis of immigrants' national origins and discriminating against southern and eastern Europeans and Asians.

National Recovery Administration (NRA)   Federal agency established in 1933 to promote economic recovery by promulgating codes to control production, prices, and wages.

National Security Council (NSC)   The formal policymaking body for national defense and foreign relations, created in 1947 and consisting of the president, the secretary of defense, the secretary of state, and others appointed by the president.

National Security Council Paper 68 (NSC-68)   Policy statement that committed the United States to a military approach to the **Cold War**.

National War Labor Board   Government agency that supervised labor relations during World War I, guaranteeing union rights in exchange for industrial stability.

National Women's Party   Political organization formed in 1916 that campaigned aggressively first for **woman suffrage** and thereafter for the **Equal Rights Amendment**.

National Women's Political Caucus   Political organization formed in 1971 to help elect women to local, state, and federal offices.

Nation of Islam   Religious movement among black Americans that emphasizes self-sufficiency, self-help, and separation from white society.

Nativism   Favoring the interests and culture of native-born inhabitants over those of immigrants.

Naturalization Act of 1870   Law passed by Congress in 1870 that limited citizenship to "white persons and persons of African descent."

Nazi   Truncated form of the name of the National Socialist German Workers' Party, led by Adolf Hitler, which ruled Germany from 1933 to 1945.

Neighborhood Union   Organization founded by Lugenia Burns Hope, a middle-class black woman, in Atlanta in 1908 and modeled on similar efforts in the urban North, that provided playgrounds, a health center, and education for young urban black people.

Neighborhood Youth Corps   Antipoverty program that recruited young people from low-income areas for community projects.

Neoconservative   Advocate of or participant in the revitalized conservative politics of the 1980s and 1990s, calling for a strong government role in defense and foreign policy and a limited role in social and economic policy.

Neoliberal   Advocate of or participant in the effort to reshape the Democratic party for the 1990s around a policy emphasizing economic growth and competitiveness in the world economy.

New Age   Term applied to a wide range of ideas and practices that seek to enhance individual potential and spiritual well-being outside the boundaries of traditional religion.

New Deal   The economic and political policies of the Roosevelt administration in the 1930s.

New Federalism   President Richard Nixon's policy to shift responsibilities for government programs from the federal level to the states.

New Freedom   Woodrow Wilson's 1912 program for limited government intervention in the economy to restore competition by curtailing the restrictive influences of trusts and protective tariffs, thereby providing opportunities for individual achievement.

New Frontier   John F. Kennedy's domestic and foreign policy initiatives, designed to reinvigorate a sense of national purpose and energy.

New immigrants   Immigrants from southern and eastern Europe, predominantly Catholic and Jewish and often unskilled and poorly educated, who entered the United States in increasing numbers after the 1880s.

New Nationalism   Theodore Roosevelt's 1912 program calling for a strong national government to foster, regulate, and protect business, industry, workers, and consumers.

New Republicanism   Dwight Eisenhower's vision of the Republicans as a relatively moderate party of the political center.

Niagara Movement   African-American group organized in 1905 to promote racial integration, civil and political rights, and equal access to economic opportunity.

Nineteenth Amendment   Constitutional revision that in 1920 established women citizens' right to vote.

Nisei   U.S. citizens born of immigrant Japanese parents.

Nonpartisan League   A radical farmers' movement in the Great Plains states after 1915 that sought to restrain railroads, banks, elevators, and other major corporations.

North American Free Trade Agreement (NAFTA)   Agreement reached in 1993 by Canada, Mexico, and the United States to substantially reduce barriers to trade.

North Atlantic Treaty Organization (NATO)   Military alliance of the United States, Canada, and western European nations created in 1949 to protect Europe against possible Soviet aggression.

North Carolina Mutual Life Insurance Company   Insurance company founded in Durham, North Carolina, in 1898 that eventually became the largest black-owned business in the nation.

Nuclear freeze   Proposal that the United States and the Soviet Union should stop further production and deployment of nuclear weapons.

Office of Economic Opportunity (OEO)   Federal agency that coordinated many programs of the **War on Poverty** between 1964 and 1975.

Office of Price Administration (OPA)   Federal agency during World War II that fixed price ceilings on all commodities, controlled rents in defense areas, and rationed scare goods such as sugar, fuel, and automobile tires.

Office of Scientific Research and Development   Federal agency established in 1941 to mobilize American science on behalf of national defense.

Old Stock   European ethnic groups prominent in the eighteenth-century United States, especially English, Dutch, German, and Scots-Irish.

Omaha Platform   The 1892 platform of the **Populist party** repudiating laissez-faire and demanding economic and political reforms to aid distressed farmers and workers.

One Hundred Slain, Battle of   An 1866 Sioux defeat of the U.S. Army on the Bozeman Trail that whites call the Fetterman Massacre.

Open Door   American policy of seeking equal trade and investment opportunities in foreign nations or regions.

Open shop   Factory or business employing workers whether or not they are union members; in practice, such a business usually refuses to hire union members and follows antiunion policies.

Operation OVERLORD   U.S. and British invasion of France in June 1944 during World War II.

Operation TORCH   U.S. and British landings in French North Africa in November 1942 during World War II.

Organization of Petroleum Exporting Countries (OPEC)   Cartel of oil-producing nations in Asia, Africa, and Latin America that gained substantial power over the world economy in the mid- to late 1970s by controlling the production and price of oil.

Pan American Union   International organization originally established as the Commercial Bureau of American Republics by Secretary of State James Blaine's first Pan-American Conference in 1889 to promote cooperation among nations of the Western Hemisphere through commercial and diplomatic negotiations.

Paris, Treaty of   The 1898 treaty that ended the **Spanish-American War** and transferred the Spanish colonies of Puerto Rico, Guam, and the Philippines to the United States while recognizing the independence of Cuba.

Patent medicines   Trademarked concoctions, often of little medical value, available for purchase without a physician's prescription.

Pearl Harbor   Site of a United States naval base in Hawaii attacked from Japanese aircraft carriers on December 7, 1941, during World War II.

Pendleton Civil Service Act A law of 1883 that reformed the spoils system by prohibiting government workers from making political contributions and creating the Civil Service Commission to oversee their appointment on the basis of merit rather than politics.

Pentagon Papers Classified Defense Department documents on the history of the United States' involvement in Vietnam, prepared in 1968 and leaked to the press in 1971.

People's party See **Populist party**.

Perestroika Russian for "restructuring," applied to Mikhail Gorbachev's efforts to make the Soviet economic and political systems more modern, flexible, and innovative.

Persian Gulf War War (1991) between Iraq and a U.S. led coalition that followed Iraq's invasion of Kuwait and resulted in the expulsion of Iraqi forces from that country.

Platt Amendment A stipulation the United States had inserted into the Cuban constitution in 1901 restricting Cuban autonomy and authorizing U.S. intervention and naval bases.

Plessy v. *Ferguson* The 1896 case in which the U.S. Supreme Court ruled that providing "separate but equal" facilities for white and black people did not violate the Constitution.

Pogroms Government-directed attacks against Jewish citizens, property, and villages in tsarist Russia beginning in the 1880s; a primary reason for Russian Jewish migration to the United States.

Poll tax A tax imposed on voters as a requirement for voting. Most southern states imposed poll taxes after 1900 as a way to disfranchise black people; the measures also restricted the white vote.

Populist party A major third party of the 1890s, also known as the **People's party**. Formed on the basis of the **Southern Farmers' Alliance** and other reform organizations, it mounted electoral challenges against the Democrats in the South and the Republicans in the West.

Port Huron Statement Founding document of **Students for a Democratic Society**, proclaiming an idealistic vision of grassroots democracy.

Potsdam Declaration Statement issued by the United States during a meeting of U.S. President Harry Truman, British Prime Minister Winston Churchill, and Soviet Premier Joseph Stalin held at Potsdam near Berlin, in July 1945 to plan the defeat of Japan and the future of eastern Europe and Germany. In it, the United States declared its intention to democratize the Japanese political system and reintroduce Japan into the international community and gave Japan an opening for surrender.

Preparedness Military buildup in preparation for possible U.S. participation in World War I.

Preservation Protecting forests, land, and other features of the natural environment from development or destruction, often for aesthetic appreciation.

Progressive Era The period of the twentieth century before World War I when many groups sought to reshape the nation's government and society in response to the pressures of industrialization and urbanization.

Prohibition A ban on the production, sale, and consumption of liquor, achieved temporarily through state laws and the Eighteenth Amendment.

Prohibition party A venerable third party still in existence that has persistently campaigned for the abolition of alcohol but has also introduced many important reform ideas into American politics.

Protective legislation Measures designed to protect women from labor exploitation that also served to narrow their employment opportunities.

Public Utility Holding Company Act of 1935 Law giving the **Securities and Exchange Commission** extensive regulatory powers over public utility companies.

Public Works Administration (PWA) Federal agency under Harold Ickes that provided work relief by building schools, hospitals, roads, and other valuable projects during the 1930s.

Pullman strike Violent 1894 worker protest against wage cuts at the Pullman Palace Sleeping Car Company outside Chicago.

Railroad Administration Federal agency that operated and modernized the nation's railways to improve transportation related to the World War I war effort.

Recall The process of removing an official from office by popular vote, usually after using petitions to call for such a vote.

Reconstruction The era (1865–1877) when the resolution of two major issues—the status of the former slaves and the terms of the Confederate states' readmission into the Union—dominated political debate.

Reconstruction Finance Corporation (RFC) Federal agency established in 1932 to provide funds to financial institutions to save them from bankruptcy.

Red-baiting Accusing a political opponent of sympathizing with or being "soft on" communism.

Redeemers Southern Democrats who wrested control of governments in the former Confederacy, often through electoral fraud and violence, from Republicans beginning in 1870.

Redlining Refusing mortgage loans and insurance to properties in designated inner-city neighborhoods.

Red Scare Post–World War I public hysteria over **Bolshevik** influence in the United States directed against labor activism, radical dissenters, and some ethnic groups.

Referendum Submission of a law, proposed or already in effect, to a direct popular vote for approval or rejection.

Reservationists Group of U.S. senators favoring approval of the **Treaty of Versailles**, the peace agreement after World War I, after amending it to incorporate their reservations.

Resettlement Administration Federal agency established in 1935 to provide financial assistance and social services to displaced tenants and farm workers.

Revenue Act of 1935 Law establishing a more progressive tax system by setting graduated taxes on corporate income and increasing the top tax rates on personal income.

Roe v. *Wade* U.S. Supreme Court decision in 1973 that disallowed state laws prohibiting abortion during the first three months (trimester) of pregnancy and established guidelines for abortion in the second and third trimesters.

Romer v. *Evans* U.S. Supreme Court decision in 1996 that overturned an antigay measure adopted in Colorado.

Roosevelt Corollary President Theodore Roosevelt's policy asserting U.S. authority to intervene in the affairs of Latin American nations; an expansion of the Monroe Doctrine.

Rural Electrification Administration (REA) Federal agency that transformed American rural life by making electricity available in areas that private companies had refused to service.

Rural Free Delivery (RFD) Government delivery of mail directly to farmsteads rather than merely to village post offices to which rural residents would then have to travel to retrieve their mail.

Rustbelt The states of the Midwest and Northeast affected adversely by the decline of manufacturing in the 1970s and 1980s, named for the image of machinery rusting in abandoned factories.

Sagebrush Rebellion   Political movement in the western states in the early 1980s that called for easing of regulations on the economic use of federal lands and the transfer of some or all of those lands to state ownership.

SALT   Strategic Arms Limitation Treaty signed in 1972 by the United States and the Soviet Union to slow the nuclear arms race.

Sand Creek Massacre   The near annihilation in 1864 of Black Kettle's Cheyenne band by Colorado troops under Colonel John Chivington's orders to "kill and scalp all, big and little."

Santa Fe Ring   A group of lawyers and land speculators who dominated New Mexico Territory in the late nineteenth century and amassed great wealth through political corruption and financial chicanery.

Scalawags   Southern whites, mainly small landowning farmers and well-off merchants and planters, who supported the southern **Republican party** for diverse reasons; a disparaging term.

Search and destroy   U.S. military tactic in South Vietnam, using small detachments to locate enemy units and then massive air, artillery, and ground forces to destroy them.

Second New Deal   The policies adopted by the Roosevelt administration from 1935 to 1937 that emphasized social and economic reform.

Second Treaty of Fort Laramie   The treaty acknowledging U.S. defeat in the Great Sioux War in 1868 and supposedly guaranteeing the Sioux perpetual land and hunting rights in South Dakota, Wyoming, and Montana.

Second Vatican Council   A 1965 meeting of the leadership of the Roman Catholic Church that liberalized many church practices.

Securities and Exchange Commission (SEC)   Federal agency with authority to regulate trading practices in stocks and bonds.

Sedition Act of 1918   Broad law restricting criticism of America's involvement in World War I or its government, flag, military, taxes, or officials.

Segregation   A system of racial control that separated the races, initially by custom but increasingly by law during and after **Reconstruction.**

Selective Service Act of 1917   The law establishing the military draft for World War I.

Selective Service System   Federal agency that coordinated military conscription before and during the Vietnam War.

Self-determination   The right of a people or nation to decide on its own political allegiance or form of government without external influence.

Settlement house   A multipurpose structure in a poor neighborhood that offered social welfare, educational, and homemaking services to the poor or immigrants; usually under private auspices and directed by middle-class women.

Seventeenth Amendment   Constitutional change that in 1913 established the direct popular election of U.S. senators.

Sharecropping   Labor system that evolved during and after **Reconstruction** whereby landowners furnished laborers with a house, farm animals, and tools and advanced credit in exchange for a share of the laborer's crop.

Sheppard-Towner Maternity and Infancy Act of 1921   The first federal social welfare law; funded infant and maternity health care programs in local hospitals.

Sherman Antitrust Act   The first federal antitrust measure, passed in 1890; sought to promote economic competition by prohibiting business combinations in restraint of trade or commerce.

Sherman Silver Purchase Act   An 1890 law that required the government to increase silver purchases sharply, but other provisions restricted its inflationary effect; its repeal in 1894 caused a political uproar.

Silicon Valley   The region of California between San Jose and San Francisco that holds the nation's greatest concentration of electronics firms.

Sixteenth Amendment   Constitutional revision that in 1913 authorized a federal income tax.

***Slaughterhouse* cases**   A group of cases resulting in one sweeping decision by the U.S. Supreme Court in 1873 that contradicted the intent of the **Fourteenth Amendment** by decreeing that most citizenship rights remained under state, not federal, control.

Slum   A poor neighborhood with many dwellings in bad repair.

Social Darwinism   The application of Charles Darwin's theory of biological evolution to society, holding that the fittest and the wealthiest survive, the weak and the poor perish, and government action is unable to alter this "natural" and beneficial process.

Social Gospel movement   An effort by leading Protestants to apply religious ethics to industrial conditions and thereby alleviate poverty, **slums**, and labor exploitation.

Socialism   Program calling for government ownership of industry and worker control over corporations as a way to prevent worker exploitation.

Socialist Party of America   Political party formed in 1901 with a strong representation from immigrants; provided a political outlet for worker grievances but fared poorly beyond a few local elections in industrial areas.

Social Security Act   A 1935 law that initiated a federal social insurance system with unemployment compensation, old-age pensions, and aid for dependent mothers and children and the blind.

Soil Conservation Service   A branch of the Department of Agriculture created in 1935 to undertake **conservation** projects on individual farms as well as on a broader national basis.

Solid South   The one-party (Democratic) political system that dominated the South from the 1890s to the 1950s.

Sound money   Misleading slogan that referred to a conservative policy of restricting the money supply and adhering to the gold standard.

Southeast Asia Treaty Organization (SEATO)   Mutual defense alliance signed in 1954 by the United States, Britain, France, Thailand, Pakistan, the Philippines, Australia, and New Zealand.

Southern Christian Leadership Conference (SCLC)   Black civil rights organization founded in 1957 by Martin Luther King, Jr., and other clergy.

Southern Farmers' Alliance   The largest of several organizations that formed in the post-Reconstruction South to advance the interests of beleaguered small farmers.

Southern Homestead Act   Largely unsuccessful law passed in 1866 that gave black people preferential access to public lands in five southern states.

Southern Manifesto   A document signed by 101 members of Congress from southern states in 1956 that argued that the Supreme Court's decision in ***Brown v. Board of Education of Topeka*** itself contradicted the Constitution.

Spanish-American War   Brief 1898 conflict in which the United States defeated Spanish forces in Cuba and the Philippines and forced Spain to relinquish control over Cuba and cede the Philippines, Puerto Rico, and other territories to the United States.

Sphere of influence   A region dominated and controlled by an outside power.

Stagflation   Economic condition of the 1970s in which price inflation accompanied slow economic growth.

Stalingrad, Battle of World War II battle of attrition between German and Soviet armies in Stalingrad, on the Volga River, August 1942–February 1943, ending with the surrender of the encircled German army.

Strategic Arms Reduction Treaty (START) Agreement between the United States and the Soviet Union in 1991 to substantially reduce the number of long-range nuclear weapons held by each side.

Strategic Defense Initiative (SDI) President Reagan's program, announced in 1983, to defend the United States against nuclear missile attack with untested weapons systems and sophisticated technologies; also known as "Star Wars."

Student Nonviolent Coordinating Committee (SNCC) Black civil rights organization founded in 1960 and drawing heavily on younger activists and college students.

Students for a Democratic Society (SDS) The leading student organization of the New Left of the early and mid-1960s.

Subtreasury plan A program promoted by the **Southern Farmers' Alliance** in response to low cotton prices and tight credit. Farmers would store their crop in a warehouse (or "subtreasury") until prices rose, in the meantime borrowing up to 80 percent of the value of the stored crops from the government at a low interest rate.

Sunbelt The states of the American South and Southwest.

Superfund Federal fund devoted to the cleanup of the nation's most severely contaminated industrial and toxic waste sites.

***Sussex* Pledge** Germany's pledge during World War I not to sink merchant ships without warning on the condition that Britain also observe recognized rules of international law.

Swann* v. *Charlotte-Mecklenburg Board of Education U.S. Supreme Court decision in 1971 that upheld cross-city busing to achieve the racial integration of public schools.

Sweatshops Small, poorly ventilated shops or apartments crammed with workers, often family members, who pieced together garments.

Taft-Hartley Act Federal legislation of 1947 that substantially limited the tools available to labor unions in labor-management disputes.

Tammany Hall New York City's **Democratic party** organization, dating from well before the Civil War, that evolved into a powerful political machine after 1860, using **patronage** and bribes to maintain control of the city administration.

Teapot Dome scandal A scandal of the 1920s that sent the secretary of the interior to prison for taking bribes to lease naval oil reserves to private companies.

Teller Amendment A congressional resolution adopted in 1898 renouncing any American intention to annex Cuba.

Tenement Four- to six-story residential dwelling, once common in New York and certain other cities, built on a tiny lot without regard to providing ventilation or light.

Tennessee Valley Authority (TVA) Federal regional planning agency established to promote **conservation**, produce electric power, and encourage economic development in seven southern states.

Ten Percent Plan Plan devised by President Lincoln in 1863 as a method for readmitting the seceding states to the Union; required 10 percent of a state's prewar voters to swear allegiance to the Union and a new state constitution that banned slavery. Many Congressional Republicans considered this standard too thin to support a general reconstruction of the Union and responded with the **Wade-Davis Bill.**

Tenure of Office Act Law Congress passed in 1867 prohibiting the president from removing certain officeholders without the Senate's consent; President Andrew Johnson's defiance of the act led to an **impeachment** trial in the Senate that narrowly failed to remove him from office.

Termination Federal policy of withdrawing official recognition from American Indian tribes and dividing tribal assets among the tribe's members.

Third International International organization of Communist parties created in 1919 under **Bolshevik** control.

Third world Nations that were aligned with neither the communist bloc (the "second world") nor the West (the "first world").

Triangle Shirtwaist Company Clothing manufacturer whose New York factory burned in 1911, prompting outrage over unsafe working conditions and the passage of remedial legislation.

Tripartite Pact An alliance of Germany, Italy, and Japan signed in September 1941 in which each nation agreed to help the others in the event of an attack by the United States.

Truman Doctrine President Harry Truman's statement in 1947 that the United States should assist other nations that were facing external pressure or internal revolution; an important step in the escalation of the **Cold War**.

Tuskegee Institute Educational institution founded by Booker T. Washington in 1881 in rural Alabama to train black people in agricultural and industrial skills.

Underwood-Simmons Tariff Act The 1913 reform law that lowered tariff rates and levied the first regular federal income tax.

Union League A **Republican party** organization in northern cities that became an important organizing device among freedmen in southern cities after 1865.

United Daughters of the Confederacy (UDC) Organization founded in 1892 to preserve southern history and honor its heroes; it reflected the growing role of middle-class white women in public affairs.

United Nations During World War II, the name adopted by the United States, Britain, and their allies against Germany and Italy; after 1945, an international organization joined by nearly all nations.

United States* v. *Cruikshank The 1876 case in which the U.S. Supreme Court nullified the **Enforcement Act of 1870**, overturning the convictions of white people accused of violence against black people in Louisiana and declaring that the **Fifteenth Amendment** did not sanction federal interference in matters that were clearly reserved for the states.

Universal manhood suffrage The right of all male U.S. citizens to vote; a key element of **Radical Republican** policy in the South after 1867.

Universal Negro Improvement Association (UNIA) A black nationalist movement organized by Marcus Garvey to promote black pride, unity, and economic **self-determination**.

Versailles, Treaty of The treaty ending World War I and creating the **League of Nations**.

Vertical integration The consolidation of numerous production functions, from the extraction of the raw materials to the distribution and marketing of the finished products, under the direction of one firm.

Viet Cong Communist rebels in South Vietnam who fought the pro-American government established in South Vietnam in 1954.

VISTA Volunteers in Service to America, the "domestic Peace Corps" of the 1960s that gave individuals an opportunity to work on behalf of low-income communities in the United States.

Volstead Act The 1920 law defining the liquor forbidden under the Eighteenth Amendment and giving enforcement responsibilities to the Prohibition Bureau of the Department of the Treasury.

Voting Rights Act Legislation in 1965 that overturned a variety of practices by which states systematically denied voter registration to minorities.

Wade-Davis Bill Congressional alternative to Lincoln's **Ten Percent Plan**, passed in 1864; required 50 percent of prewar voters to pledge their loyalty and demanded guarantees for black equality. The president exercised a pocket veto, and it never became law.

Wagner National Labor Relations Act   The 1935 law guaranteeing workers' rights to organize unions and establishing the **National Labor Relations Board**.

War Industries Board (WIB)   The federal agency that reorganized industry for maximum efficiency and productivity during World War I.

War Manpower Commission   Federal agency established in 1942 to allocate workers among the armed services, defense industries, and essential civilian industries.

War on Poverty   Set of programs introduced by Lyndon Johnson between 1963 and 1966 designed to break the cycle of poverty by providing funds for job training, community development, nutrition, and supplementary education.

War Production Board   Federal agency established in 1942 to coordinate defense production and allocate scarce resources to serve the war effort.

Warsaw Pact   Military alliance of the Soviet Union and communist nations in eastern Europe from 1955 to 1989.

Watergate   A complex scandal involving attempts to cover up illegal actions taken by administration officials and leading to the resignation of President Richard Nixon in 1974.

Weather Underground   Fringe group of former members of **Students for a Democratic Society**, 1969–1970, who emphasized confrontation and violence.

Welfare capitalism   A paternalistic system of labor relations emphasizing management responsibility for employee well-being. While providing some limited benefits, its function was primarily to forestall the formation of unions or public intervention.

Wesley Houses   Organizations modeled after the **settlement houses** of the North that began appearing in southern cities under the auspices of the Methodist Church in the 1890s to serve working-class neighborhoods.

Western Federation of Miners   A large and radical union of western miners formed in Butte, Montana, in 1893 to coordinate local unions' resistance to corporate threats to workers' wages, working conditions, and health.

White League   One of several military organizations operating openly and in concert with the **Democratic party** in the South to thwart black voting rights during **Reconstruction**.

Wilderness Act   Law, the Wilderness Areas Act, that in 1964 designated certain federal lands as parts of the National Wilderness Preservation System, consisting originally of 9.1 million acres.

Wobblies   Popular name for the members of the **Industrial Workers of the World (IWW)**.

Woman suffrage   The right of women to vote, achieved in the **Nineteenth Amendment**.

Women's Christian Temperance Union (WCTU)   National organization formed after the Civil War dedicated to prohibiting the sale and distribution of alcohol.

Woodstock Generation   Members of the late 1960s **counterculture**, named for a rock festival held in New York State in August 1969.

Works Progress Administration (WPA)   Key **New Deal** agency that provided work relief for the unemployed.

World Bank   Officially the International Bank for Reconstruction and Development, an international organization established in 1945 that assists governments around the world in economic development efforts.

Wounded Knee Massacre   The U.S. Army's brutal winter massacre in 1890 of at least two hundred Sioux men, women, and children as part of the government's assault on the tribe's Ghost Dance religion.

Yalta Conference   Meeting of U.S. President Franklin Roosevelt, British Prime Minister Winston Churchill, and Soviet Premier Joseph Stalin held in February 1945 to plan the final stages of World War II and postwar arrangements.

Yellow-dog contracts   Employment agreements binding workers not to join a union.

Yellow press   A deliberately sensational journalism of scandal and exposure designed to attract an urban mass audience and increase advertising revenues.

Yippies   Fringe group of radical activists, 1968–1972, who emphasized media events.

PHOTO CREDITS

INDEX